Civilization in the West

Civilization

Crane Brinton

*Late McLean Professor of Ancient and Modern History,
Harvard University*

John B. Christopher

University of Rochester

Robert Lee Wolff

*Archibald Cary Coolidge Professor of History,
Harvard University*

in the West

Second Edition

Prentice-Hall, Inc., Englewood Cliffs, New Jersey

CIVILIZATION IN THE WEST, Second Edition

Brinton, Christopher, and Wolff

© Copyright 1964, 1969 by *Prentice-Hall, Inc.*
Englewood Cliffs, New Jersey. All rights reserved.
No part of this book may be reproduced in any form, by mimeograph or any other means, without permission in writing from the publishers.
Library of Congress Catalog Card Number: 69–17534
Printed in the United States of America

Designed by Mark A. Binn

Maps by Vincent Kotschar

PRENTICE-HALL INTERNATIONAL, INC., London
PRENTICE-HALL OF AUSTRALIA, PTY. LTD., Sydney
PRENTICE-HALL OF CANADA, LTD., Toronto
PRENTICE-HALL OF INDIA PRIVATE LTD., New Delhi
PRENTICE-HALL OF JAPAN, INC., Tokyo

13-135004-8

Current printing (last number):

10   9   8   7   6   5   4   3   2

Preface

This new edition of *Civilization in the West,* like its predecessor, is designed in particular for two types of academic courses. It may serve as the chief, perhaps the sole, reading for the rapid survey in a single quarter or semester. For the relatively leisurely survey, extending over two or more quarters or semesters, it may offer the essential narrative briefly enough to permit students wide reading in collateral works.

While basing this revision on our two-volume *A History of Civilization,* third edition (Prentice-Hall, Inc., 1967), we have often reworked and rearranged material from the parent volumes, and we have also made additions to bring the book abreast of events and of present-day scholarship. Those familiar with the original edition will find changes throughout the new volume, especially at the beginning and at the end. The Introduction is new; two chapters (1 and 2) are now devoted to ancient history instead of one; and the chapters (16 and 17) on the contemporary world have been enlarged. The reading suggestions for each chapter have been brought up to date and now include not only paperbacks but also important titles available only in hard covers. The physical aspect of the book has been redesigned to permit greater use of color and tinting and to make the finished product, we hope, more attractive and convenient to read. The page size is larger, though still single-columned; the maps have all been redrawn and printed in color tints; and the illustrations, both in color and otherwise, are almost entirely new.

We wish to record our debt to all those who have contributed directly or indirectly to this revision. We thank the teachers and students who have taken the trouble to send their suggestions for improvements, and the members of the staff at Prentice-Hall, Inc., who have worked so energetically and imaginatively. We express special thanks to the following scholars for their valuable critiques of the original edition: Edward Raymond Barels, Mississippi State College for Women; H. Arnold Barton, University of California, Santa Barbara; C. George Fry, Capital University; Joan Godell, The City College of New York; Ralph L. Lynn, Baylor University; Sol Modell, Los Angeles Valley College; Marshall True, University of Vermont; and Donald L. Wiedner, Temple University.

Our heaviest debt is to our senior co-author, who died when the process of revising was in its final stages and when he had substantially completed his contribution to it. Over the years both of us found him an unfailingly resourceful, stimulating, and agreeable partner. We dedicate this new edition of *Civilization in the West* to the memory of Crane Brinton.

JOHN B. CHRISTOPHER   ROBERT LEE WOLFF

Contents

The Uses of History 3

Man's First Civilizations

I. BEFORE WRITING. *History and Pre-History. The Old Stone Age. The New Stone Age.* II. THE VALLEY PEOPLES. *Mesopotamia. Egypt.* III. PEOPLES OUTSIDE THE VALLEYS. *The Hittites. Hurrians, Canaanites, Philistines, Phoenicians. The Hebrews.* IV. CRETE AND MYCENAE. *Minoans Before Mycenae. Mycenaeans and Minoans. Mycenae, 1400–1100 B.C. The Dark Age; Homer.* 9

1

The Classical World

I. THE GREEKS BEFORE THE PERSIAN WARS. *What the Greeks Were Like. Revival After the Dark Age. The Polis: Sparta. Colonization. Athens.* II. PERSIA AND THE GREEKS, TO 478 B.C. *The Persian Empire. The Ionian Cities; the Threat to Greece; Marathon. The 480's. Xerxes Invades.* III. THE ATHENIAN EMPIRE, 478–404 B.C. *Postwar Reorganization. From Alliance to Empire. The Peloponnesian War.* IV. THE FOURTH CENTURY B.C. AND THE HELLENISTIC AGE. *Spartan Hegemony. Thebes Rises to Hegemony. Macedon. Heirs of Alexander.* V. THE CIVILIZATION OF GREECE. *The Gods. Tragedy. Comedy. History. Science and Philosophy. The Arts.* VI. THE ROMANS. *The Early Republic. Roman Expansion. Crisis of the Republic. Political Generals: Marius, Sulla, Pompey, Caesar. The First Two Centuries of the Roman Empire. The Decline of Rome.* VII. ROMAN CIVILIZATION. *The Romans and Greece. Latin Literature. Law. Engineering and Medicine. Architecture, Sculpture, and Painting. A Final Appraisal.* 43

2

The Making of a New World

To the Year 1000

3   105   I. THE CHRISTIAN REVOLUTION IN THE ROMAN WORLD. *The Spirit of the Times. Christianity. The Triumph of Christianity. Heresy. Literature and Thought in the First Christian Centuries.* II. THE BARBARIAN ONSLAUGHT. *The Barbarians. Franks. Europe and the Northmen. Carolingian Decline. Europe about 1000.* III. FEUDAL EUROPE. *Feudalism: The Rulers. The Civilization of the "Dark Ages" in the West.*

The Medieval World

Western Europe

4   145   I. THE SOCIETY AND ITS ECONOMY. *The Turning-Point of the Eleventh Century. Trade and Town. Town and Countryside.* II. MONARCHY IN THE MEDIEVAL WEST. *France: Hugh Capet through Philip the Fair (987–1314). England: William the Conqueror through Edward I (1066–1307). Germany and the Empire (911–1273).* III. THE CHURCH AND CIVILIZATION. *The Reformers. The Church and Education. Thomas Aquinas. Mysticism. Political Thought. Literature and the Arts.*

The Medieval World

Eastern Europe

5   187   I. LIFE IN BYZANTIUM. *The State. Religion and Civilization.* II. THE FORTUNES OF EMPIRE, 330–1081. *From 330 to 717. The Reorganization of the Seventh and Eighth Centuries. From 717 to 867. From 867 to 1081.* III. ISLAM BEFORE THE CRUSADES. *Mohammed. Expansion. Disunity. Islamic Civilization. Learning, Literature, and the Arts.* IV. THE CRUSADES. *Precedents for the Crusade. The First Crusade. The Later Crusades. The Meeting of East and West.* V. THE FORTUNES OF EMPIRE, 1081–1453. *Byzantine Feudalism. The Fourth Crusade. The Latin Empire. Byzantium after 1261. The Ottoman Advance.* VI. THE OTTOMAN SUCCESSOR-STATE, 1453–1699. *Civilization. The Empire.* VII. MEDIEVAL RUSSIA. *Rus and Byzantium. The Impact of Conversion. Kievan Society and Politics. Politics from 1200 to 1450. The Muscovite State.*

Transition to a New World

Late Middle Ages and Renaissance

6 237

I. THE ECONOMY AND SOCIETY OF THE FOURTEENTH AND FIFTEENTH CENTURIES. *Depression in the West. Commercial Innovation. Capitalism. The New Materialism.* II. THE MAKING OF THE NEW MONARCHIES. *The Hundred Years' War. France: Louis XI. England. Spain.* III. PARTICULARISM. *Germany. Italy.* IV. THE RENAISSANCE: LITERATURE AND LEARNING. *The Meaning of "Renaissance." The Vernacular Tongues. The Humanists. Science and Medicine. Astronomy. Technology.* V. THE RENAISSANCE: THE ARTS. *Main Characteristics of Renaissance Art. Painting. Sculpture. Architecture. Music. The Renaissance Ideal: Castiglione.*

Transition to a New World

Religious Upheaval, Imperial Expansion, Dynastic Conflict

7 277

I. THE PROTESTANT AND CATHOLIC REFORMATIONS. *Luther. Zwingli. Calvin. The English Reformation. The Radical Left: Anabaptists and Unitarians. Protestant Attributes. Protestantism and Progress. The Catholic Reformation. Divided Christendom.* II. THE FIRST OVERSEAS EMPIRES. *The Portuguese. The Spaniards. Competition Begins.* III. THE NEW MONARCHIES AND THE WARS OF THE SIXTEENTH CENTURY. *Spain. France. England.*

The Seventeenth Century

War, Politics, and Empire

8 317

I. THE THIRTY YEARS' WAR. *The Dutch and Spanish Background. The German Background. The Bohemian Period, 1618–1625. The Danish Period, 1625–1629. The Swedish Period, 1630–1635. The Swedish and French Period, 1635–1648. The Peace of Westphalia: Impact of the War.* II. REVOLUTION AND SETTLEMENT IN ENGLAND. *Background: The First Stuarts. The Reign of James I. Charles I and Parliament. Reforms of the Long Parliament. Civil War, 1642–1649. The Commonwealth and Protectorate. The English Revolution in Review. The Restoration. James II and the Glorious Revolution.* III. DIVINE-RIGHT MONARCHY IN FRANCE. *Henry IV, Richelieu, and Mazarin. Louis XIV: Le Grand Monarque. Mercantilism and Colbert. The Wars of Louis XIV. The War of the Spanish Succession.* IV. EUROPE OVERSEAS. *The Thirteen Colonies. New France. The Indies, West and East; Africa. The Balance Sheet of Imperialism. The Beginnings of One World.*

Seventeenth and Eighteenth Centuries

Science, Culture, and the Enlightenment

9   357   I. THE BEGINNINGS OF MODERNIZATION. II. THE GROWTH OF NATURAL SCIENCE. *The Seventeenth Century. The Eighteenth Century. Science, Technology, and Philosophy.* III. THE NEW WORLD-VIEW: NATURE, REASON, AND PROGRESS. *Rationalism. Nature and Natural Law. Deism. Atheism and Toleration. Social Criticism. Utilitarian Ethics. "Natural" Behavior. Formal Philosophy. Political Thought: The Example of England. Libertarian and Authoritarian Remedies. "Juridical Defense" and "Social Contact." Laissez-Faire Economics. The Doctrine of Progress.* IV. CHALLENGES TO THE IDEAS OF THE ENLIGHTENMENT. *Christian Opponents. Intellectual Critics. Pessimism, Conservatism—and Optimism.* V. ARTS AND LETTERS. *Classicism and Romanticism. Prose Literature. Drama and Poetry. Painting. The Other Fine Arts. Music.* VI. CONCLUSION: THE REASONS WHY.

The Eighteenth Century

War, Politics, and Economics

10   395   I. THE EUROPEAN BALANCE. *Eighteenth-Century Warfare. Jenkins' Ear and Silesia. The Seven Years' War. Shifts in the Balance. The Expansion of Europe.* II. POLITICAL AND SOCIAL CHANGES. *The Process of Growth. The State and Society.* III. FRANCE AND BRITAIN. *Unreformed France. Britain: Stable or Revolutionary?* IV. ENLIGHTENED DESPOTISM. *Prussia: Frederick the Great. Austria: Joseph II. Russia: Peter and Catherine. Other Despots.* V. THE AMERICAN REVOLUTION. *The Background. The War and Its Results.* VI. THE GROWTH OF A MODERN ECONOMY. *Administrative and Financial Revolutions. The Agricultural Revolution. The Industrial Revolution.*

The French Revolution and Napoleon

11   435   I. IMPORTANCE OF THE FRENCH REVOLUTION. II. THE CONSTITUTIONAL MONARCHY. *Birth of the National Assembly. The Bastille. The "Great Fear" and Its Effects. The "October Days." The Work of the National Assembly. The Civil Constitution of the Clergy. The Outbreak of War.* III. THE FIRST REPUBLIC. *The Jacobin Clubs. The Tenth of August and the September Massacres. The Convention. Gironde and Mountain. The "Revolutionary Government." The Record of the Revolutionary Government. The Ninth Thermidor. The Directory. The Eighteenth Brumaire.* IV. NAPOLEON. *The Consulate. The Empire Ascendant. The Empire at its Height. The Breakup of Empire. The "Hundred Days." The Place of Napoleon in History.* V. WESTERN CULTURE IN A REVOLUTIONARY AGE. *The Classical and the Romantic. The French Contribution. The German and British Contributions. Political Thought. The Legacy of the French Revolution.*

The Revolutions Renewed
1815-1870

12   471

I. EUROPEAN INTERNATIONAL POLITICS, 1815–1870. *The Congress of Vienna. The Vienna Settlement. Britain and the Postwar Balance of Power. Revolution in Southern and Western Europe, 1820–1830. Revolution in Eastern Europe, 1825–1830. The "Eastern Question." The Crisis of 1848. The Crimean War. Cavour and Italian Unification. Bismarck and German Unification. The New Balance of Power.* II. DOMESTIC POLITICS, 1815–1870: WESTERN EUROPE. *Britain. France. Italy.* III. DOMESTIC POLITICS, 1815–1870: CENTRAL AND EASTERN EUROPE. *Germany. Revolution and Reform in the Habsburg Empire. Russia.* IV. THE EXPANSION OF EUROPE, 1800–1870. *Latin America. The United States. Colonies of Settlement. Colonies of Exploitation.*

Economics, Thought, and Culture in the Nineteenth Century

13   511

I. THE INDUSTRIAL REVOLUTION. *The Timetable of Industrialization. Stages of Economic Growth. Industrial Areas and "Colonial" Areas. Industrialism and the Standard of Living.* II. SCIENCE, RELIGION, AND PHILOSOPHY. *Science. Religion. Philosophy.* III. MAN, THE STATE, AND SOCIETY. *Conservatism. Liberalism. Radicalism. Marxism. Utopian Socialism. Anarchism. Nationalism. Social Darwinism. The Victorian Compromise.* IV. ARTS AND LETTERS. *Romantic Literature. The Novel: Realism and Naturalism. The Fine Arts. Music. The Russian Contribution.* V. THE NINETEENTH CENTURY GROWS INTO THE TWENTIETH. *Hope and Disillusionment. The Arts in Transition.*

Prelude, Theme, and Coda
1870-1919

14   547

I. THE NATIONS OF EUROPE AT HOME, 1870–1914. *Britain. France. Italy and the Smaller Western States. Germany. The Habsburg Monarchy. Russia. The Ottoman Empire.* II. THE WORLD OVERSEAS. *The British Empire. The Other Empires. The United States. The Far East. The Balance Sheet of Imperialism.* III. THE FIRST WORLD WAR. *The Road to War: Triple Alliance and Triple Entente. Crises over Morocco and the Balkans. The Crisis of 1914. Strength of the Belligerents. The Fighting Fronts. The War at Sea and on the Home Fronts. Decision on the Western Front.* IV. THE POSTWAR SETTLEMENTS. *A World in Turmoil. The Fourteen Points—and Other Points of View. The Process of Peacemaking. Territorial Changes. The Punishment of Germany. The Settlement in Retrospect.*

Reprise

1917-1945

15   **585**   I. COMMUNIST RUSSIA, 1917–1941. *The March Revolution and the Provisional Government. Lenin and the November Revolution. Civil War and Foreign Intervention, 1917–1921. The NEP, 1921–1928. Stalin's Rise to Power. Stalin in Power: Collectivization. The Five-Year Plans. Stalin's Dictatorship. Soviet Foreign Policy.* II. FASCISM, 1918–1939. *Italy. Germany. Spain. Eastern Europe.* III. THE DEMOCRACIES BETWEEN THE WARS. *Britain. France. The United States. The Loosening of Imperial Ties. India and the Middle East.* IV. THE SECOND WORLD WAR. *Efforts to Keep the Peace. The Road to War. Early Successes of the Axis. Turning Points. The Allied Victory. Unsolved Problems.*

The Postwar World

Since 1945

16   **633**   I. THE COLD WAR. *A Divided World: Germany and China. The Two Coalitions. The United Nations.* II. THE MAJOR FREE-WORLD STATES. *The United States. Canada. Western Europe.* III. THE COMMUNIST BLOC: THE U.S.S.R. AT HOME. *Stalin's Last Years. The Soviet Succession. The Khrushchev Era and Beyond.* IV. SOVIET FOREIGN POLICY. *The Last Years of Stalin. Stalin's Heirs. U.S.S.R. and U.S. since the Missile Crisis: Czechoslovakia.* V. THE U.S.S.R., CHINA, AND AMERICA IN ASIA. *The Soviet-Chinese Quarrel. Southeast Asia: Vietnam and Loas.* VI. THE EMERGING NATIONS. *The Revolt against Imperialism. The Far East. India and Pakistan. The Middle East. Africa. Latin America. Final Reflections.*

The Temper of Our Times

17   **703**   I. INTRODUCTION: PERSPECTIVES ON A CONFUSED AND CONFUSING AGE. II. MAIN CURRENTS OF THOUGHT. *Psychology. Sociopolitical Thought. Philosophy.* III. SCIENCE AND THE ARTS. *Science and Technology. The Arts.* IV. CONCLUSION: THE DEMOCRATIC DREAM. *The Heritage of the Enlightenment. Optimists and Pessimists. Repudiation or Revision of the Enlightenment.*

Illustrations   735

Index   741

Maps

Man's First Civilizations, 18
Ancient Greece, 55
Alexander's Empire and the Hellenistic World, 67
Growth of Roman Dominions Under the Republic, 85
Growth of Roman Dominions Under the Empire, 94
Spread of Christianity, to the 11th Century, 121
Germanic Kingdoms about 526, 127
Carolingian Empire, 131
Medieval France and England, 155
Medieval Germany and Italy, 166
Byzantine Empire, 199
Moslem Expansion, 203
Crusader States, 211
Ottoman Empire to 1683, 223
Medieval and Early Modern Russia, 229
England and France during the Hundred Years' War, 244
Renaissance Italy about 1494, 263
Expansion of Europe, 1529, 296
Europe in 1555, 306–307
Europe in 1648, 324–325
Europe in 1715, 346–347
Expansion of Europe, 1715, 352

Partitions of Poland, 1772, 1793, 1795, 396
Growth of Prussia, 1740–1795, 400
North America and the Caribbean, 1763, 406
Russian Expansion in Europe, 1689–1796, 422
Napoleonic Europe, 1812, 460–461
Europe after 1815, 474–475
Unification of Italy, 1859–1870, 485
Unification of Germany, 1866–1871, 488
Latin America, 1828, 502
Growth of the United States and Southern Canada, 505
Industrial Europe, 1860, 512
Industrial United States, 1860, 515
Nationalities in Central and Eastern Europe—About 1914, 560
Africa and the Middle East, 1910, 562
Asia and the Pacific, 1910, 565
Europe, 1914–1918, 572
Territorial Settlements in Europe, 1919–1926, 579
Russia in Revolution, 1917–1921, 589
Europe on the Eve, August 1939, 618
European and Mediterranean Theaters, 1939–1945, 622
Asian and Pacific Theaters, 1941–1945, 626
The World, 1969, 650–651
The Soviet Union, 1969, 657
Asia, 1969, 677
The Middle East, 1969, 686
Africa, 1969, 693

Civilization in the West

The Uses of History

The word "history" has two broad general meanings. It can mean everything that has happened, just the past, as contrasted with the present and the future; and it can mean the study of the past and the resulting oral or written record of what has happened in that past. For several thousand years now, the historical record has interested many individuals. But it has never interested everybody. Now that universal education requires nearly everyone to study some history, hundreds of thousands of people are obliged to fill their heads, for a while at least, not merely with the tales and heroes of their nation, but with facts about the Code of Hammurabi, the trade routes of medieval Europe, the influence on American political institutions of the writings of John Locke, and a very great deal more. Since some people dislike the study of history, just as some dislike the study of mathematics, an introduction to the study of history must begin with some justification of that study. In the United States, especially, the historian is confronted with the reluctant student's "Hammurabi—so what?"

Yet the historian ought not to be apologetic, and above all he ought not to yield to the temptation, so natural in modern arguments, to rest his entire case on the practical value of history. Some people love the study of history. Some actually enjoy storing their memories with lists of kings and battles; some are moved by the endless skeins of association the past affords, by the sickle-curve of the beach at Marathon, by the gargoyles of Notre Dame de Paris, by the rude bridge that arches the flood at Concord, by the wheat field at Gettysburg; others are fascinated by the inexhaustible resources the historical record offers for research, for the exercise of the detective instinct. These lovers of Clio, the muse of history, have seemed a bit odd to those who do not share their enthusiasm. They have been called "antiquarians," a term of reproach on the lips of those busied with the practical details of daily life. Yet, in a world where so much human activity is directed toward making others conform, the activity of historians is a refreshing reminder that human beings are not identical, that their interests vary.

There is, however, no sense in maintaining that the study of history ought to be a pleasure for all. Moreover, even those who do find it a pleasure are not above consoling themselves by finding it also useful and edifying. Still, in comparison with the natural sciences, history cannot very readily be shown to be useful in our American common-sense meaning of "useful." For example, the study of history and the practice of politics have not as yet scored over the social disease of race discrimination the kind of victory that the study of biology and the practice of medicine have scored over the physical disease of typhoid fever. And it must be admitted that, in comparison with literature and the arts, history as it is written nowadays—including history as written in this book—does not serve clear aesthetic or moral ends. History in its usual academic form is seldom either a good story or a good sermon. If you want to hold your breath as the blade of the guillotine falls on Marie Antoinette, if you want to laugh or weep, you will have to go to older histories, to fiction, to television or the cinema. Nor will you find in the work of good historians that virtue is always rewarded.

Furthermore, and most important for the many "practical" people who will read this book, the study of history will not produce exact or "correct" answers to problems, answers of the sort that the scientists or engineers or perhaps even the practicing physician expect. Nor, so long as history does not turn into theology, philosophy, or just plain preaching, will it by itself give the kind of answers to questions about man's fate that you would expect from your spiritual guides in Church or State. History, to be specific, will not tell you whether to use steel or aluminum for a given gadget. It will not choose for you between Browning's song of Pippa,

> God's in his heaven—
> All's right with the world

and James Russell Lowell's

> Truth forever on the scaffold,
> Wrong forever on the throne.

In our time there has been a powerful current of thought, commonly called "historicism," which seeks to find in the historical record *and in it alone* the clue to man's fate—in short, to find in history, as the record of how man makes himself and his society, a cosmology, a philosophy, sometimes even a theology, a substitute for revealed religion. This book will record the attempt to make Clio not merely a muse, but a priestess, prophet, even a sole godhead. It will not contribute to the attempt.

What history can do, however, is supply a series of case histories or clinical reports not quite as full as the best medical case histories, but still extensions of human experience, from which certain notions of how to go about handling cases in the present may be obtained. Thus at the very outset of western historical writing the Athenian general Thucydides recounts the struggle between Athens and Sparta, a case history of which the late General George Marshall said, "I doubt seriously whether a man can think with full wisdom and deep convictions regarding certain of the basic international issues today who has not at least reviewed in his mind the period of the Peloponnesian War and the fall of Athens."[*] General Marshall was not repeating the old chestnut that history repeats itself. History is full of repetition and of novelty, of similarities and differences, for history is no more than the imperfect record of the lives of millions of human beings *each like, and each unlike*, the others.

What the individual does with the materials his experience offers him is another matter. Another old chestnut asserts that all we learn from history is that we never learn from history. Certainly there exists in the United States today a tendency to feel that somehow or other we should have learned from the so-called World War I how to avoid World War II, with the panicky addition that apparently we have not learned from the first two how to avoid World War III. To expect, however, to get from the study of history *exact* solutions to problems, neat prescriptions for social ills, is precisely what a true appreciation of historical knowledge can show to be unwise and unprofitable.

History can do more than present a mere random collection of human experiences. It can, though only approximately, show the range of human behavior, with some indication of its extremes and averages. It can, though again by no means perfectly, show how and within what limits human behavior changes. This last is especially important for the social scientist, for the economist, the sociologist, the applied anthropologist. For if these experts studied only the people and institutions existing today, they would have but imperfect notions of the real capacities of human beings. They would be like biologists with no knowledge of the contributions of historical geology and paleontology to their

---

[*] Quoted in *Life*, Jan. 1, 1951, p. 96.

understanding of organic evolution. History, then, provides materials that even the inspiring leader of men into new ways and new worlds—the prophet, the reformer, the columnist, the commentator—will do well to master before he tries to lead us into those new ways.

For it can tell us something—not all—we need to know about the capacities and the limitations of human beings. To use a crude and to some religious temperaments an offensive analogy, history can help us learn what man can stand and what he cannot stand, as the many contributory sciences and technologies involved can tell the engineer what stresses his metals can stand. The historian, incidentally, knows that human beings can stand a lot—much more than any metal.

At the very least, history can give an awareness of the depth of time and space that should check the optimism and the overconfidence of the reformer. Reason can show the inefficiency of many of our ways of doing things—our calendar, for example, or our Anglo-Saxon system of measurements. Millions of man-hours are wasted in the process of teaching children to read English, with its absurd spelling and its over-refined punctuation. Yet the slightest background of history will show that human societies resist changes like the reform of spelling or accept them only in times of revolution, as when the metric system was introduced during the French Revolution, or when the Turkish alphabet was changed from Arabic to Roman by the twentieth-century dictator Atatürk. You may still wish to reform our spelling, even though you know its history; but if you have learned anything at all from history, you will never look at the problem of getting English-speaking peoples to change their spelling as if it were a problem like that of designing a superhighway. You will, or should, however, learn through the study of history something about the differences between *designing* such a highway, an engineer's job, and getting the highway built, a much more complicated job for government experts, economists, businessmen, contractors, workers of many kinds of training, politicians local, state, and national, conservationists and other "pressure groups," and ultimately a problem for you and me as taxpayers and voters.

The historical record is most imperfect, and even the labors of generations of scholars have not filled it out. Notably, historians until quite recently have usually been more interested in the pomp and drama of the lives of the great than in the conditions of life for the masses. They have studied with care political and religious institutions, it is true, and within the last few generations they have studied economic institutions. They have paid less attention to social institutions and to folkways. Since the historians of one generation make the historical record that is handed down to later historians, our record is faulty and cannot always be improved. No one can ever conduct a sort of retrospective Gallup Poll, for instance, to find out just what millions of fifteenth-century Frenchmen thought about Joan of Arc. Yet our ignorance must not be exaggerated either. As you can learn from any manual of historiography—that is, the history of the writing of history—historians have in the last few hundred years built up a technique and a body of verifiable facts that have made history not an exact science, but a useful body of knowledge.

Furthermore, historians have in the last two generations turned increasingly to the study of what the American historian James Harvey Robinson called the "new history"—that is, to social, economic, intellectual, cultural history, to the study of the behavior of the many as well as the behavior of the conspicuous few. History is no longer merely "past politics"—and past wars; it is "past everything." Geographically, it is no longer just the history of Europe and North America; it is the history of the whole world.

Now no sensible person will deny that these newer interpretations have greatly enriched and deepened the study of history. On the other hand, this new history is much more complex, difficult, and unwieldy than was the old. To use a nice old-fashioned figure of speech out of the old "classical" education, adding China, India, the Aztecs, and a lot more in space, adding the centuries back to ancestral sub-humans in time, adding all the innumerable activities of all men to the dramatic activities of a few in politics and war—adding all this is piling Pelion on Ossa indeed. What happens, of course, is that in the ordinary "introduction" to history more ground is now covered, but it is covered less thoroughly. We have what is sometimes wryly called a "gallop through the centuries." Often, the result is sometimes a longer and more arid catalogue of details than the lists of kings, queens, presidents, consuls, generals, popes, and cardinals that used to fill the older histories.

The present book is in part—though only in part—a reaction against the attempt to cover all the past everywhere on earth. We hope to retain the best of the old and add the best of the new. As for space, we shall concentrate on the history of one part of the world, the Europe sometimes scornfully called a "small peninsula of Asia." We shall trace its expansion as Europeans explored, settled, colonized, and traded in all parts of the globe. We shall be concerned with other peoples only as they and their histories impinged on the development of European cultures. In taking this approach we are not motivated by any "self-worship," by any contempt for Asians or Africans, but rather by a desire to get our own record straight. We are not against the study of "world history," but we do hold that it is unwise to begin with world history; we think it wiser to start with the more familiar rather than with the less familiar materials. As for time, after a very brief look at the ages-long prehistoric past of Western man and the beginnings of his history in the Near East, we shall be mostly concerned with the last twenty-five hundred years or so.

Obviously, this is not all a good American citizen of the second half of the twentieth century needs to know about the past of *Homo sapiens*. But it is an essential part of what he needs to know, probably the part he *most* needs to know if he is to face the problems of the jet age and outer space. Finally, though we hope to do justice to the complexity and variety of man's activities, we shall still find the center of our history in his political and military record. A general history must, it seems to us, focus on these activities, for without them "what really happened" cannot be understood. A general history must also give important clues to what are labelled economic history, intellectual history, social history, history of science, history of religions, and so on. We shall do our best to give such clues. But all written history must omit vast amounts of information, facts, "coverage"; indeed, in these days the cluttered modern mind needs the kind of housecleaning a general survey can afford.

READING SUGGESTIONS (asterisk indicates paperbound edition)

G. J. Renier, *History: Its Purpose and Method* (*Torchbooks). Perhaps the most readable of current manuals on historical writing.

J. Barzun and H. F. Graff, *The Modern Researcher* (*Harcourt). An admirable introduction to the study of history, as well as a practical manual for research.

Sherman Kent, *Writing History*, 2nd ed. (*Appleton). A good manual for the novice.

L. R. Gottschalk, ed., *Generalization in the Writing of History* (University of Chicago, 1963). A good collaborative work by practicing historians, investigating the problem of "laws," "uniformities," and "regularities" in the record of the past.

Morton White, *The Foundations of Historical Knowledge* (Harper, 1966). A logician's book, difficult to read but worth the effort because of its balanced defense of the possibility of obtaining working generalizations from the experience of the past.

I. Berlin, *Historical Inevitability* (Oxford, 1955). A fine introduction to the problem of historicism.

A. J. Toynbee, *Civilization on Trial* (*Meridian). Essays introducing the reader to some of the central ideas of this philosopher of history. His views may be found at greater length in his ten-volume *A Study of History* (*Galaxy) and in more summary form in the abridgment of the first six volumes by D. C. Somervell (*Dell).

P. Geyl, *Debates with Historians* (*Meridian). Essays by a historian firmly opposed to Toynbee.

Bruce Mazlish, *The Riddle of History* (Harper, 1966). Admirable survey of modern attempts—from Vico to Freud—to learn from "speculative history."

Marc Bloch, *The Historian's Craft* (*Vintage). A thoughtful essay, at an advanced level, written by a distinguished French historian.

1

Man's First Civilizations

Temple at Idfu, third century B.C.: the best preserved of the Egyptian temples.

I. Before Writing

HISTORY AND PRE-HISTORY

Within the lifetime of men now in their forties and fifties, archeology, with the new tools supplied by other sciences, has revolutionized what human beings know about the remoter past of our earth and the people who live on it. Discoveries continue at a rapid pace. In the 1930's, '40's, and '50's, no writer could have put on paper many of the major statements in this chapter. In the 1980's and '90's, perhaps even sooner, our successors will know enough to dispute or modify or at least greatly add to what we here set forth.

It may at first seem strange that our concepts of the distant past are changing much faster than our concepts of the periods much closer to us in time and much better known. But when we consider the ways in which we know about the past we can quickly see that—far from strange—this is entirely natural. If we want to know about something—almost anything—that happened, let us say, during the American Revolution, we have the letters of George Washington and his contemporaries, the written records of the British government that tried to suppress the American colonists' rebellion, the proceedings of the Continental Congress, the Declaration of Independence, and literally thousands of other *written sources*—diaries, memoirs, documents, newspapers, propaganda leaflets—that bring us instantly into the minds of the men of that time and enable us to work out for ourselves what probably happened. And if we cannot go directly to these written sources for history, we have hundreds of books written since the events of the Revolution by the historians who have been interested in it and who have set down their view of what happened, for us to accept or challenge, but at least to consider. New sources may be discovered and fresh light thrown on some event we thought we understood: we may find out that Paul Revere's teacher at school had been reading radical pamphlets (something that previous students had not known) and that this helped prepare Paul as a youth for his famous ride. But the new sources probably would not force us to reject or even to reconsider everything we had learned before they were discovered.

Most of the sources we would read about the American Revolution would be written in English. But if we wanted to find out about the part played by Lafayette and Rochambeau we would soon find ourselves compelled to read documents in French; if we asked ourselves why a Pole, Taddeusz Kosciuzsko, joined the American side, we might have to learn Polish—and Russian and German—in order to find out. If we were interested in the ideas of Thomas Jefferson, we would have to study several of his favorite classical authors—who wrote in Greek or Latin—and, though we would find translations available, we might feel it important to read them as Jefferson did, in the original. But whatever the problems of learning languages, or of trying to decide which of two contradictory accounts of the same event to follow, or of interpreting what we might find (this is what George III *said;* but what did he *really* think?), we would always be dealing with abundant written sources in languages that modern men know how to read.

For events 2,000 years or more before the American Revolution, or less well known, or taking place in Europe or Asia, we would still usually have written sources, in Persian or Sanskrit, Greek or Latin or Chinese, sometimes fragmentary instead of full, sometimes so biassed as to be unreliable, but written. Where possible we would supplement these with all kinds of other evidence: the coins that rulers struck with pictures or inscriptions on them that might tell us things we could not find out any other way; the statues or paintings or poems or songs of the age that might reflect the attitudes of the artists and their society more surely than a document; indeed, anything that we could find from the period and the place to supplement our written sources.

But suppose our written sources were written in a language we could not read? Or suppose we had no written sources at all? As we move backward in time through human history these problems confront us more and more urgently. The discovery of texts written in both a known and a previously unknown language has over the last couple of centuries enabled scholars to read the language of the Egyptians, and those of the peoples of the ancient Mesopotamian river valleys in the Near East, although uncertainties often remain. Brilliant use of the techniques of cryptography in the 1950's cracked one of the two scripts commonly used in ancient Crete and on the Greek mainland. But the earlier Cretan script remains to be deciphered. Nobody has yet cracked Etruscan, the language—written in Greek letters—of the people that ruled in Italy before the Romans.

And of course there were long, long, *long* centuries and millennia before man had learned to write at all. Only his bones and the bones of his animals and some of the things he made remain to tell us about him: they are our only sources. The recent development of the carbon-14 technique, whereby radioactive carbon is used to enable us to date ancient objects within a couple of centuries, has proved to be a great help in straightening out chronology. Nothing seems surer, however, than that scholars will find many more new objects and new ways of dating them and so will enable our successors to write with more certainty than we about our earliest ancestors.

THE OLD STONE AGE

In the seventeenth century, an Anglican archbishop named Ussher carefully worked out from data given in the Bible the date of the creation of the world by God. It proved to be precisely 4004 B.C.; so if you added the 1,600-odd years since the birth of Christ, you came up with a figure of considerably less than 6,000 years for the age of our earth. We smile now at the generations that accepted Ussher's views—though everybody did so until the nineteenth century—because all of *us* know that the earth is billions of years old; that organic life may go back several billion years; that remains of an animal recognizable as an ancestor of modern man have been recently found in Africa and dated as perhaps two million years old. This creature and his fellows were perhaps the ancestors of both apes and men; he was much older than the remains scientists had previously found and dated. After him, it seems to have taken a mere 1,300,000 years before the first of the true men that scientists have found made his appearance six or seven hundred thousand years ago. A true man has a larger skull, with more brains in it, than an ape, and a true man *makes tools*.

Yet even though we can identify our remote ancestors so many hundreds of thousands of years before Ussher thought the world was made, we know so little about what was happening during all those hundreds of millennia before Ussher's creation date of 4004 B.C. that for the historian—as distinguished from the anthropologist—almost all of that time belongs to "pre-history." We can be certain that during those long, long centuries the advance of the human animal was enormously slow. The first real tools, found in Kenya and dated by radiocarbon at about 600,000 B.C., were stones used to chip other stones into useful instruments. And it was by stone weapons and tools that early man lived for hundreds of thousands of years: lived in a stone age, as the terms that scholars use to describe his life make abundantly clear.

From roughly the beginning to roughly 8000 B.C.—varying by a few thousand years or so according to the region one is describing—man lived in the Old Stone Age—Paleolithic. By about 8000 B.C. in some places—much later in others—he passed into a New Stone Age, Neolithic, marked by certain great changes that we shall consider in a moment. By about 3000 B.C. we are at the beginning of the Bronze Age, and of even greater transitions to new forms of human life and society. And still later came the Iron Age. Wrong though Arch-

Man's First Civilizations

bishop Ussher is about the age of the earth, he is none the less ironically almost right about what a historian can say about the period before 4004 B.C.

Paleolithic man left remains scattered widely in Europe and Asia, and took refuge in Africa from the glaciers that periodically moved south over the northern continents and made life impossible there. Wherever he went, he hunted to eat, and fought and killed his enemies. His skull formation took on different developments in different portions of the world at different times: hence the anthropologist's *Australopithecus* (southern apelike creature), *Pithecanthropus erectus* (the ape-man that stands erect), and many others. Toward the end of the Paleolithic period we find Neanderthal man, named from the valley of the Neander in Germany, who was in fact far less apelike than the frequent modern "restorations" of his features have usually shown him. A recent excavation of a Neanderthal burial has shown that the corpse was buried on a heaping bouquet of flowers, a more delicate attention than one might have expected. Paleolithic man learned how to cook his food, how to take shelter from the cold in caves where there were caves, and eventually how to specialize his tools: he made bone needles with which to sew animal hides into clothes with animal sinews; he made hatchets, spears, arrowheads, awls.

One day in 1940, when two boys in southwest France went hunting rabbits, their pet dog suddenly disappeared down a hole, and did not come back. Following the dog, they literally fell into an underground grotto, hidden for thousands of years. The light of their torches revealed an extraordinary series of paintings on its limestone walls and roofs, of animals portrayed in brilliant colors with astonishing realism and artistry: deer, bison, horses, and others. These were the achievement of Cro-Magnon man, toward the end of the Paleolithic period, perhaps about 12,000 B.C. Lascaux, where they were found, became one of the great tourist centers of Europe. By 1960, despite all the precautions of the authorities, the breath of so many thousands of visitors gazing in awe and wonder began to

Painting of a leaping bison from cave at Altamira, Spain, c. 10,000 B.C.

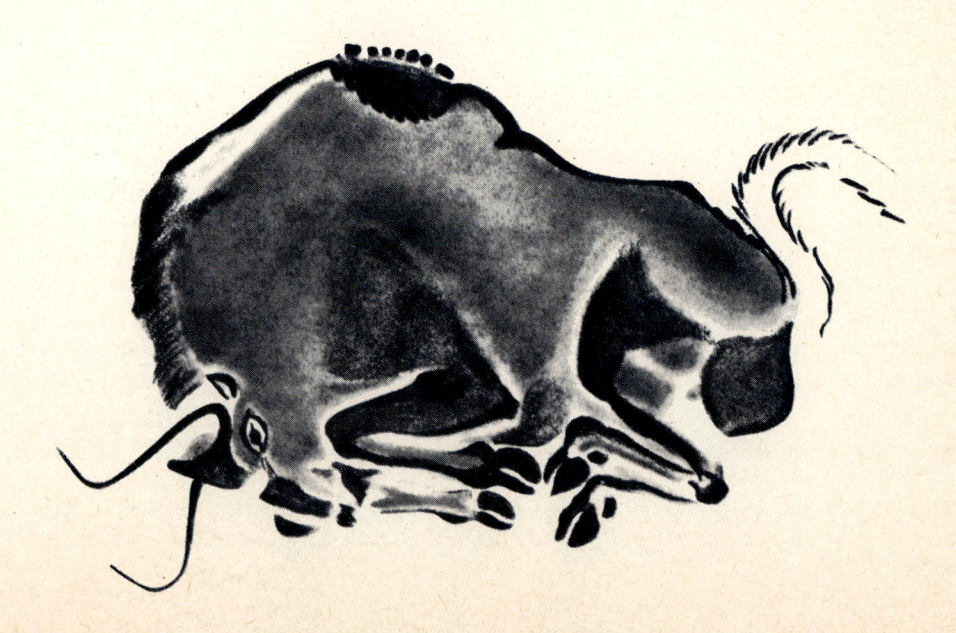

damage the pictures, which had been sealed away from moisture for so many millennia; so the cave has had to be closed to the public. At Altamira, in northern Spain, similar contemporary cave-pictures, not quite so splendid, had long been known, but had suffered somewhat from early souvenir hunters. Long exposed to air and changing temperatures, they are happily immune to moisture, and now remain the most easily visible monument of the great skills of Paleolithic man.

We can only guess but not know for certain why the Paleolithic artist painted the pictures: did he think that by putting animals—in all their realism—on his walls, he could improve his chances in the hunting field? Would their pictures give him power over them, and so ensure his supply of food? Were the different animals also totems of different families or clans? These are probably good guesses. In the paintings so far discovered, no human beings appear—at least none drawn or painted with the same loving attention to form and detail: an occasional little stick-figure is probably a person. Yet the artists of Altamira or Lascaux could have produced human portraits of surpassing beauty had they thought of it or wished to do so. Perhaps that would have been "bad magic" instead of the "good magic" that came from painting animals. Paleolithic man did occasionally produce small female statuettes: crude, often armless, usually grossly overemphasizing the breasts, buttocks, and sexual organs, found widely scattered (and sardonically called "Venuses" by modern archeologists). Were these fertility symbols? or love charms? Quite probably.

Sometimes on the walls of the caves we find paintings of human hands, often with a finger or fingers missing. Were these hands simple testimony of appreciation for one of man's most extraordinary physical gifts: the hand with its apposable thumb (not found in apes), which alone made tool-making possible? or were they efforts to ward off evil spirits by upholding the palm or making a ritual gesture? or were they prayers by hunters and warriors that they should not suffer mutilation of their fingers or that they might retain their strength despite some mutilation they had already suffered? Perhaps. We can say for sure only that, by the end of the Old Stone Age, man was still perhaps a savage, but he was also an artist.

The Venus of Willendorf, a Neolithic statuette found in Austria.

THE NEW STONE AGE

When man first built houses, learned how to bake clay pots, and domesticated animals, he was on his way out of the Old Stone Age. Various terms are used (e.g., Mesolithic) for this period of transition from Paleolithic to Neolithic, which lasted longer in some regions than in others. By common consent, however, the transition is over when men settle down to live in their houses and grow their own food; once this is accomplished man has entered the New Stone Age (Neolithic). Three recent excavations, all in the Near East, have pushed back our previous earliest Neolithic dates; and with the boundaries between periods thus in flux and the terms intended only to be useful and not to confuse, it is probably better here not to try to fix any firm boundaries between late Paleolithic and early Neolithic.

At Jericho in Palestine during the 1950's, archeologists excavated a town of about 7800 B.C. (radiocarbon dating) that extended over about eight acres, and included perhaps 3,000 inhabitants. These people lived in round houses with conical roofs—the oldest permanent houses known—and they had a large, columned building in which were found many mud-modelled figurines of animals and modelled statues of a man, woman, and male child; it was almost surely a temple of some kind. All this dates from a time when people did not yet know how to make pots, which appear only at a later stage. Next oldest, and most recent of the new finds, is Çatalhüyük in southern Turkey, discovered only in 1961, and dating to 6500 B.C. The people who lived there had a wide variety of pottery, grew their own grain, kept sheep, and wove their wool into textiles. A female sculptured in relief, in the posture of giving birth to a child, a bull's head, boars' heads with women's breasts running in rows along the lower jaws, and many small statuettes were all found together in what we can be sure was their shrine. The bull and a double axe painted on a wall seem to look forward to main features of the better-known religion of ancient Crete, as we shall see.

Far to the east, in modern Iraq (ancient Mesopotamia) near the Iranian border, lay Jarmo, to be dated about 4500 B.C., a third Neolithic settlement. A thousand years later than Jarmo, about 3550 B.C., and far to the south, at Uruk on the banks of the Euphrates River, men were using the plow to scratch the soil before sowing their seeds, and were already keeping the accounts of their temple in simple picture-writing. This was the great leap forward that took man out of pre-history and into history. Similar advances are found in Egypt too, at roughly the same time. But archeology seems to show that Mesopotamia took the lead, and indeed that it was from Mesopotamia that major cultural contributions—especially the all-important art of writing—penetrated into Egypt and gave the Egyptians a great push into history.

The Neolithic people of Mesopotamia and of Egypt were not necessarily any more intelligent than those elsewhere. Indeed, Neolithic remains have been found also in many places in the Mediterranean region, and even far to the north. But in those places climate was far less favorable, and even when Neolithic man managed to triumph over his environment—as in the lake settlements of Switzerland, where he built frame houses on piles over the water—the triumph came later (in this case about 2500 B.C.). In Australia and New Guinea and in South America there are people today who still live in the Neolithic Age. It was the inhabitants of the more favored regions who got to the great discoveries first. It was they who learned copper-smelting and the other arts of metallurgy, and who thus led the human race out of the Stone Age—after 597,000 years or so—and into the Bronze Age. And it was they who first lived in cities. Writing, metallurgy, and urban life: these are the marks of civilization. Soon after these phenomena appeared in the Tigris–Euphrates valleys and along the Nile, they appeared also in the valley of the Indus, and along certain Chinese rivers. But it is not to India or China but to Mesopotamia and Egypt that we can trace our own civilization, and it is to these that we must now turn.

II. The Valley Peoples

MESOPOTAMIA

Sumerians. North of the Persian Gulf, in the fertile lower valleys of the two rivers Tigris and Euphrates and in the land between them ("Mesopotamia": the land between the rivers, today southern Iraq), the Sumerians were already well established by the year 3000 B.C., living and writing, in cities. We have known about the Sumerians for only a hundred years. Archeologists working at

Archeologists excavating the walls of Jericho, 1955.

Nineveh in northern Mesopotamia in 1869 found many Babylonian inscribed clay tablets, which they could read because the inscriptions were written in a known Semitic language (Akkadian). But some of the tablets also had writing in another language that was not Semitic, and was previously unknown. Some of these inscriptions made reference to the "king of Sumer and Akkad," and so a scholar suggested that the new language be called Sumerian. But it was not until the 1890's that archeologists digging far to the south of Nineveh found many thousands of tablets inscribed in Sumerian only. Since then, excavations have multiplied; the material has poured in; by working from known Akkadian to previously unknown Sumerian, scholars have pretty well learned how to read the Sumerian language.

We now know that it was the Sumerians who invented writing on clay, using at first a kind of picture-writing, and over the thousand years between 3000 and 2000 B.C. developing a phonetic alphabet. With a reed pen they impressed into the wet clay tablet little wedge-shaped marks, producing a script that we call cuneiform from the Latin *cuneus,* meaning a wedge. The first thousand years of Sumerian history we know from tens of thousands of these tablets that are mostly economic or administrative in their content. It is not until the second thousand years (after 2000 B.C.) that we get purely literary materials, but 5,000 tablets from that period do provide us with them, some short, some very long, many of them not yet transcribed or translated.

In the earliest days, the Sumerians governed themselves through a council of elders, who derived their authority in turn from a general assembly of all the adult free men. This assembly, which decided on such questions as making war and peace, sometimes would grant supreme authority to an individual leader for a limited time. This arrangement—which seems astonishingly "modern" and "democratic" to us—apparently did not last long, and was replaced by one-man rule in each city. But the human ruler acted only as the representative on earth of the god of the city. In this capacity the ruler built temples to the god to keep him appeased, and especially to obtain his divine protection against the floods that often swept torrentially down the river valleys in the springtime with disastrous results for the people in their way. The lives and religion and literature of the peoples of Mesopotamia were pervaded by terror of floods: it is virtually certain that the story of the flood in Genesis echoes the ancient tradition of the Sumerians. The Sumerians devised an elaborate system of canals not only for irrigation but to control the force of the floods, and each city required the blessing of its god on their labors.

A Sumerian dignitary.

Indeed, it took the toil of many centuries for the Sumerians to transform the bleak marshes of the river valleys into fertile and productive farmland, dotted with prosperous cities, each with its own political bureaucracy and its religious institutions; and, as with all human societies, each passing through occasional oppressions, upheavals, and political overturns many of which are recorded by surviving inscriptions. Cities warred with one another, and about 2350 B.C. we find the first inscription recording the ambition of one city ruler to rule the entire region, to be the first universal monarch in history. Moreover, the Sumerians had to fight against infiltrating Semites from the Arabian deserts to the west, and from the hills to the north. In taking the lead against invaders, Gudea, ruler of the city of Lagash, united the Sumerians about 2050 B.C. Soon after he died, Ur replaced Lagash as the capital city, and for a century its rulers played the role of universal monarch. They called themselves already "Kings of Sumer and Akkad," showing the fusion between the non-Semitic Sumerians and the Semitic Akkadians from the north that had already begun to take place. Much of what we know about the Sumerians comes from the recent systematic excavation of Ur. About 1950 B.C. the Semitic desert invaders destroyed Ur too, and with it Sumerian power.

In addition to their city-gods, the Sumerians worshipped a god of the heavens, a god of the region between heaven and earth (the air, hence storms and winds), and a god of earth. Another trinity included gods of the sun and moon, and a goddess of the morning star, who was also associated with fertility. With this female deity was associated a young male god who died and was reborn as a symbol of the seasons.

Here, in the first religion recorded in sources that we can read and therefore interpret surely, we find elements common to all subsequent efforts of men to deal with the supernatural. It was Enki, God of Earth, for instance, who poured the water into the two great fertilizing rivers, Tigris and Euphrates, and stocked them with fish; who created grain, filled the land with cattle, built houses and canals, and set sub-gods over each enterprise.

The Sumerian gods were portrayed in human form, and lived recognizably human lives, with rivalries among themselves. Sumerians also believed in a multitude of demons, mostly bad. Because the temples of the city-god and other gods actually owned most of the land, most of the population worked as serfs of the temple. But the produce of the land was distributed as pay to them. Life was highly diversified: blacksmiths, carpenters, and merchants now appear alongside the hunters, farmers, and shepherds of the older days. Fathers exercised many rights over their children. The society was monogamous, and women held a high position. Punishments seem mild relative to those later found in the Babylonian society that grew out of the Sumerian; in Sumer, they consisted mostly of fines.

In many epic poems, the Sumerians celebrated the brave exploits of Gilgamesh, a mighty hero. He undertakes perilous journeys, fights and overcomes dreadful monsters, and performs great feats of strength. But even Gilgamesh, strong though he was, had to die; and a mournful tone, which scholars recognize as typical of the society, pervades Sumerian literature: hymns, lamentations, prayers, fables, and even schoolboy compositions.

Yet a Sumerian proverb sagely says,

> Praise a young man, and he will do whatever you want;
> Throw a crust to a dog, and he will wag his tail before you.

Obviously these were people who observed each other keenly; they are very recognizably of the same human breed as ourselves. In their literature they often dealt with the seeming injustice of this life, where even righteous men who lead good lives must suffer. We can recognize the type of the future Old Testament Job, and the moral is the same: glorify god, await the end of life, which will set you free from earthly suffering.

Sumerian art was entirely religious, official in intent and impersonal in style. it changed very little for a millennium and more. The Sumerians built their temples of baked brick. In the shrine was an altar against a wall; other rooms and an outer courtyard were later added. The most striking feature of the temple was that the whole structure was set upon a terrace, a first stage toward the multiplication of terraces, each above and smaller than the last, with the sanctuary at the top, reached by stairs from terrace to terrace. This was the *ziggurat,* the typical

Mesopotamian temple, whose construction itself suggests the rigidly hierarchical Sumerian social order. It was a great *ziggurat* that suggested the tower of Babel to the author of Genesis. Sumerian tombs were simple chambers, but were often filled with objects intended for use in the afterlife, which Sumerians envisioned as mournful and dreary. Their statuary consisted of clothed human figures, solemn and stiff, with large, staring eyes: gods were shown as larger than kings, and ordinary human beings as smaller. On monumental slabs (steles), on plaques, and especially on seals the Sumerians showed themselves skillful at carving in relief.

Akkadians: Babylonians and Assyrians. Now that scholars have learned so much about the Sumerians, they have realized the enormous debt to Sumer owed by the people who succeeded them as rulers of Mesopotamia: the Semitic Akkadian-speakers, to whom belonged first the Babylonians and then their successors, the Assyrians, both originally descended from the nomads of the Arabian desert. Power first passed to the Semites with Sargon the Great of Babylon (2350 B.C.), and returned to them after an interlude, about 2000 B.C., with the invasions of the Amorites from the west.

Since 1935 excavations at Mari in the middle Euphrates valley have turned up a palace with more than 260 rooms containing many thousands of tablets throwing much new light on the Amorite kingdom. Mari was one of its main centers, and the documents we have, mostly from the period between 1750 and 1700 B.C., consist of the royal archives, and include the official letters to the king from his own local officials scattered through his territories and from other rulers of local city-states and principalities many of which were previously unknown to scholars. Among the correspondents was an Amorite prince named Hammurabi, who just before 1700 B.C. made his own Babylonian kingdom supreme in Mesopotamia. His descendants were able to maintain their power down to about 1530.

Hammurabi's famous code of law, engraved on an eight-foot pillar, though in part modelled on its Sumerian predecessors, exhibits a much harsher spirit in its punishments. Yet, as its author, the king boasted not of his warlike deeds but of the peace and prosperity he had brought. The code reveals a strongly stratified society: a patrician who put out the eye of a patrician would have his own eye put out; but a patrician who put out the eye of a plebeian only had to pay a fine. Yet perhaps it is most important to note that even the plebeian had rights that, to a degree at least, protected him against violence from his betters. Polygamy and divorce have now made their appearance. The code, in fact, is just about what we would expect: it shows a harmonious grafting of Semitic practice and needs in a changing society upon the original qualities of Sumerian inspiration and orderliness.

New nomads, this time from the east (Iran), the Kassites, shattered Babylonian power about 1530; and gradually supremacy in Mesopotamia passed to the far more warlike Semitic Assyrians, whose power had been rising in Nineveh for several centuries. About 1100 their ruler Tiglath-pileser reached both the Black Sea and the Mediterranean on a conquering expedition north and west, after which he boasted that he had become "lord of the world." Assyrian militarism was harsh, and conquerors regularly transported into captivity entire populations of defeated cities. By the eighth century the Assyrian state was a kind of dual monarchy: Tiglath-pileser III, their ruler, also took the title of ruler of

Man's First Civilizations

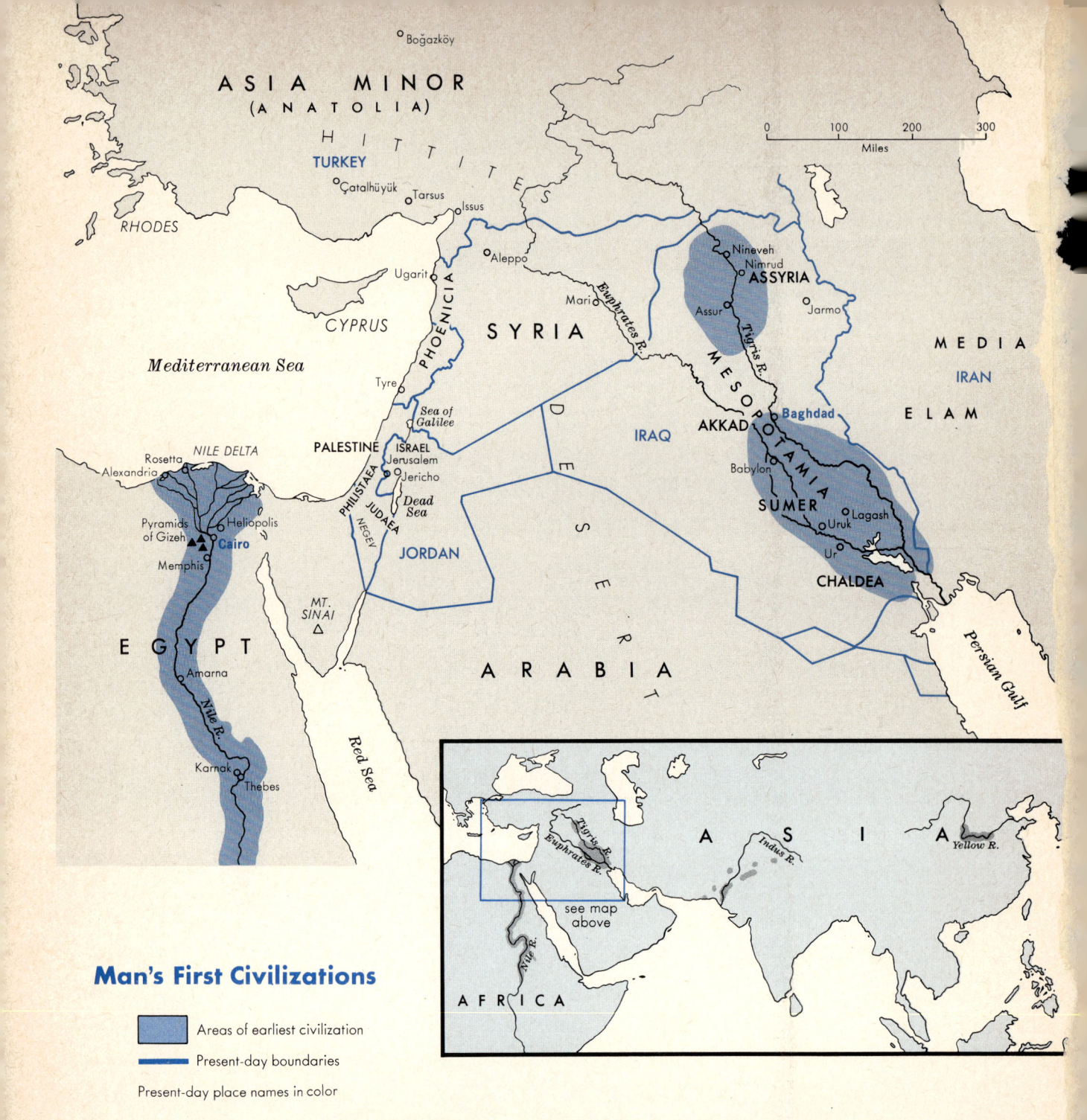

- Areas of earliest civilization
- Present-day boundaries
- Present-day place names in color

Babylonia, thus consciously accepting the Babylonian tradition. During the 670's B.C. the Assyrian king Esarhaddon invaded and conquered Egypt. Then in turn the mighty Assyrian Empire fell to a new power, the Medes (Iranians related to the Persians), who took Nineveh (612 B.C.) with Babylonian help.

For less than a century thereafter (612–538 B.C.) Babylonia experienced a rapid, brilliant revival, during which King Nebuchadnezzar overthrew Jerusalem and took the Hebrews into captivity, and at the end of which the Hebrew prophet Daniel showed King Belshazzar the moving finger on the wall of the banquet-chamber that told him his kingdom was to be given to the Medes and the

Persians. Daniel was right, of course, and Cyrus the Great of Persia took Babylon in 538 B.C., ending the history of the Mesopotamian empires after two and a half millennia at least.

In addition to their cuneiform writing, the Babylonians and Assyrians took much of their religion from the Sumerians. The cosmic gods remained the same, but the local gods of course were different, and under Hammurabi one of them, Marduk, was exalted over all other gods and kept that supremacy thereafter. The religious texts left behind outnumber those of the Sumerians and give us a more detailed picture of Babylonian–Assyrian belief: demons became more numerous and more powerful, and a special class of priests was needed to fight them. Magic practices multiplied; soothsayers consulted the livers of animals in order to predict the future. All external happenings—an encounter with an animal, a sprained wrist, the position and color of the stars at a vital moment—had implications for one's own future that must be discovered. Starting with observation of the stars for such magical purposes, the Babylonians developed substantial knowledge of their movements, and the mathematics to go with it. They even managed to predict eclipses. They could add, subtract, multiply, divide, and extract roots. They could solve equations, and measure both plane areas and solid volumes. But their astronomy and their mathematics remained in the service of astrology and divination.

Like the Sumerians, the Babylonians were a worried and a gloomy people, who feared death and regarded the afterlife as grim and dusty, in the bowels of the earth. Even this depressing fate could be attained only if the living took care to bury the dead and to hold them in memory. Otherwise one had only restlessness and perhaps a career as a demon to look forward to. In Babylonian literature, we find Marduk the center of an epic of the creation; we encounter Gilgamesh again, in a more coherent epic than that of the Sumerians, in which he declines a goddess's offer to make him a god because he knows he is sure to die.

Similarly in art the inspiration remains unchanging, but some variations appear: unlike the Sumerians, the Babylonians in some regions had access to stone, and so now incorporated columns in their buildings; and especially the Assyrians showed greater interest, as one would expect, in scenes of combat. In Assyria too one finds the orthostat, a statue inserted into a wall, and so appearing in high relief; typical Assyrian versions appear as bulls, lions, and fantastic winged beasts. Jewels, gold, and ivory-carving now reached new and extraordinarily beautiful heights, as shown especially in the finds at Nimrud.

EGYPT

Character of the Society. What the Tigris and the Euphrates rivers did for the land between them—Mesopotamia—the Nile River, rising in the hills of Ethiopia and flowing a thousand miles north through Egypt into the Mediterranean, did for the strip of land along its banks on both sides, beyond which, east and west, stretched the dry and inhospitable sands of desert. Nobody can be certain how many millennia had passed in which the people along the Nile had slowly learned to take advantage of the annual summer flood by tilling their fields to receive the silt-laden river waters, and by regulating its flow, but about 3000 B.C., approximately the same time when the Sumerian civilization emerged in Mesopotamia, the Egyptians had reached a comparable stage in their development.

Much better known to us than Mesopotamia—most of us, even as small children, already knew about the pyramids, the sphinx, and King Tut's tomb—Egypt was the other ancient valley civilization that made major contributions to our own.

No sweeping generalizations about peoples and societies are ever wholly acceptable; yet, speaking roughly, scholars who have studied the sources for both Egypt and Mesopotamia and who have compared the two often note that the Egyptians are generally more cheerful and confident than the gloomy and apprehensive Sumerians, Babylonians, and Assyrians; more tolerant and urbane and less harsh and obdurate; more speculative and imaginative and less practical and literal-minded; and—despite the long centuries of apparent sameness—more dynamic and less static in their attitudes and achievements. Life after death the Egyptians regarded as a happy continuation of life on earth with all its fleshly pleasures, not as a dismal eternal sojourn in the dust. When we think of Mesopotamian art we think of temples made of brick and of public monuments; when we think of Egyptian art we think of tombs made of stone and of private monuments. The Mesopotamians have left few statues, the Egyptians many. The Mesopotamian rulers—both the early city-lords and the later kings who aspired to universal monarchy—were agents of the gods on earth; the Egyptian rulers from the beginning were themselves regarded as gods. So, despite the many similarities between the two societies, and the mutual influences which we now know to have passed from each to the other—though chiefly in the direction of Egypt from Mesopotamia—each had its own distinct characteristics.

Because Egyptian territory consisted of the long strip along the banks of the Nile, it always was hard to unify. At the very beginning—3000 B.C.—we can distinguish two rival kingdoms—Lower Egypt: the Nile Delta (so called because it is shaped like the Greek letter of that name)—the wedge-shaped triangle nearest the Mediterranean where the river splits into several streams and flows into the sea; and Upper Egypt: the land along the course of the river for 800 miles between the Delta and the First Cataract. Periodically the two regions were unified in one kingdom, but the ruler, who called himself "King of Upper and Lower Egypt," by his very title recognized that his realms consisted of two somewhat disparate entities, one looking toward the Mediterranean and outward to the other civilizations growing up around its edges, and the other more isolated by its deserts and more self-regarding. The first unifier, perhaps mythical, was a certain Menes, whose reign (about 2850 B.C.) scholars take as the start of the first standard division of Egyptian history, the Old Kingdom (2850–2200).

Old, Middle, and New Kingdoms. When the king is god, his subjects need only listen to his commands to feel sure they are doing the divine will. As each Egyptian king died, his great sepulchral monument in the form of a pyramid told his subjects that he had gone to join his predecessors in the community of gods. The largest of the pyramids took several generations to build, and involved the continual labor of thousands of men, a token that the society accepted and took pride in the divinity of its rulers. A highly centralized bureaucracy carried out the commands of the king. A stratified society worked for him. His forces advanced at times westward into the Libyan desert, and at other times—drawn by the pull that we find exerted on every ruler of Egypt from Menes to President Nasser—east and north into Palestine. The Old Kingdom was first disturbed and eventually shattered by a growing tendency among district governors to pass their offices on to their sons, who in turn tended to strike out on their own or at least to regard their territories as hereditary fiefs and thus to weaken the central authority. At the same time we know the priests of the Sun had also made good their claims to special privileges that helped diminish royal power. After an interim period of disorder lasting perhaps two centuries (2200–2000 B.C.), a new dynasty (eleventh of the thirty in Egyptian history) restored unity in what is known as the Middle Kingdom (2100–1800 B.C.), distinguished for its rulers' land-reclamation policies and its victories abroad.

Brother and sister-in-law of the deceased: relief in tomb of Ramose, Thebes, c. 1375 B.C.

Growing internal weakness combined with a foreign invasion and conquest put an end to the Middle Kingdom about 1800 B.C. The conquerors were called Hyksos, and were Asian nomads of uncertain origin, who imported the war chariot and perhaps the bow. The Egyptians hated their rule, which lasted something over a century, and eventually rallied behind a new dynasty (the seventeenth) to drive out the invaders. By 1600 B.C. the task was accomplished and the New Kingdom (1600–1100 B.C.) well launched. The five centuries of the New Kingdom saw extraordinary advances: in foreign affairs, the Egyptians engaged in a struggle for Syria and Palestine not only with the great powers of Mesopotamia but with the mountain and desert peoples who lived between the two great valley civilizations. The Egyptian ruler (now called Pharaoh) Thutmose I reached the Euphrates on the east, and marched far south into Nubia (what we today call the Sudan). Thutmose III (1501–1447 B.C.) fought seventeen campaigns in the East, and even crossed the Euphrates and beat his Mesopotamian enemies on their own soil. The walls of the great temple of Karnak preserve his own carved account of his military achievements and the enormous tribute paid him by his conquered enemies. It is his obelisk, popularly known as "Cleopatra's Needle," that stands in Central Park in New York. The Egyptians established their own network of local governors throughout the conquered territories, but ruled mildly, and did not, as the Assyrians were soon to do, deport whole masses of the population into captivity.

It was the Pharaoh Amenophis IV (1375–1358 B.C.) who caused a major internal upheaval in the successful New Kingdom by challenging the priests of the sun-god Amon, who had become a powerful privileged class. Amenophis urged the substitution for Amon of the sun-disk, Aten, and, even more dramatic, commanded that Aten alone be worshipped and that all the multitude of other gods, whom we shall shortly discuss, be abandoned. Amenophis changed his name to Akhenaten, "Pleasing to Aten," in honor of his only god. Some have seen in this famous episode a real effort to impose monotheism on Egypt; others doubt that one can be certain. To mark the new policy, Akhenaten and his beautiful wife Nefertiti, whose statue is widely reproduced, ruled from a new capital in Amarna. Amarna gives its name to the "Amarna age" (c. 1417–c. 1358 B.C.). Nearby—beginning in the 1880's—were found the famous "Tell-el-Amarna letters," a collection of about four hundred tablets including the diplomatic correspondence of Akhenaten and his father with the rulers of western Asia, in many languages, an invaluable source for scholars.

Akhenaten's effort to overthrow the entrenched priesthood led to internal dissension and the loss of external strength. His son-in-law, Tut-Ankh-Amen (1361–1352 B.C.), was eventually sent to rule in Thebes, city of the priests of Amon, with whom he compromised: this was "King Tut," the discovery of whose tomb with all its magnificent contents was the archeological sensation of the 1920's. With Akhenaten's death, the new religious experiment collapsed, and the Pharaohs strove to make up for the interval of weakness by restoring their foreign conquests.

About 1300 B.C. we find Rameses II reaching a treaty with a people from Asia Minor, the Hittites. This treaty, of which we have texts both in Egyptian and Hittite, called for a truce in the struggle for Syria and provided for a dynastic marriage between the Pharaoh and a Hittite princess. The interlude was short, however, and soon after 1200 B.C. the New Kingdom in its turn fell to a general invasion of the eastern Mediterranean shores by mixed bands of Sea Peoples, probably including ancestors of the later Greeks and Sicilians, and others.

Now Egypt entered into a period of decline, marked by renewed internal struggles for power between the secular authorities and the priests, and among local and central rulers. Then came the Assyrian conquest of the seventh century, the Persian conquest of 525 B.C., and the conquest by Alexander the Great of Macedonia in 331 B.C.

Religion. Religion was the most powerful force animating Egyptian society, and it was so complicated a religion that modern authorities are hard put to describe it. One of the greatest writes that if one asked an ancient Egyptian "whether the sky was supported by posts or held up by a god, the Egyptian would answer: 'Yes, it is supported by posts or held up by a god—or it rests on walls, or it is a cow, or it is a goddess whose arms and feet touch the earth.'"[*] So the Egyptian was ready to accept multiple and overlapping divinities, and to add new ones whenever it seemed appropriate: if a new area was incorporated into the Egyptian state, its local gods would be added to those already worshipped.

From the beginning, Egyptian cults included animals, totems perhaps: sheep, bulls, gazelles, and cats, still to be found carefully buried in their own cemeteries. As time passed, the figures of Egyptian gods became human, but often retained an animal's head, sometimes an animal's body. Osiris, the Egyptian god best known to most of us, began as a local Nile Delta deity. He taught mankind agriculture; Isis was his wife, and Set (animal-headed) his brother and rival. Set killed Osiris; Isis persuaded the gods to bring him back to life, but thereafter he ruled below (obviously a parallel to the fertility and vegetation-cycle beliefs we have already encountered in Mesopotamia and will encounter in Greece). Naturally enough, Osiris was identified with the life-giving, fertilizing Nile, and Isis with the receptive earth of Egypt.

Horus the sun defeated the evil Set after a long struggle. But Horus was only one kind of sun-god: there was also Re, later joined with Amon, and still later Aten, as we saw. The moon-god was the ibis-headed Thoth. In the great temple-cities like Heliopolis, priests worked out and wrote down hierarchies of divinities. Out in the village, all the forces of nature were deified and worshipped: one local god was part crocodile, part hippopotamus, and part lion, a touching and economical revelation of what simple farmers along the riverbanks had to worry about. However numerous the deities, Egyptian religion itself was unified; unlike a Sumerian temple, however, which was the political center of its city, and for which the population toiled, the Egyptian temple had a more limited religious function.

The Egyptians were preoccupied with life after death. They believed that after death each human being would appear before Osiris and recount all the bad things he had *not* done on earth: "I have not done evil to men. I have not ill-treated animals. I have not blasphemed the gods," and so on, a negative confession, to justify his admission into the kingdom of the blessed. Osiris would then have the man's heart weighed, to test the truth of his self-defense; and he would be admitted or else delivered over to judges for punishment.

Egyptians believed not only in body and soul, but in *ka*, the indestructible vital principle of each human being, which left the body at death but could and

[*] J. A. Wilson, in *The Intellectual Adventure of Ancient Man* (Chicago, 1943), p. 44.

did return at times. That is why the Egyptians preserved the body in their elaborate art of mummification: so that the *ka* in its return would find it not decomposed; and that is why they filled the tombs of the dead with all the objects that the *ka* might need or find delightful on its returns to the body. Otherwise it might come back and haunt the living.

Civilization. We know Egyptian civilization so intimately because of the great number of inscriptions, that give us the historical materials, and of papyri

Relief of cattle fording a stream: from the tomb of Ti, c. 2350 B.C.

(fragments of the ancient material the Egyptians wrote on, made of the pith of a water-plant), that give us the literary materials. Yet what we have represents a smaller percentage of what once existed and of what may yet be found than does our collection of Mesopotamian literature on its carefully copied myriads of clay tablets. The Egyptian language first yielded its secrets only in the 1820's, when the French scholar Champollion first saw on a late obelisk that several Greek personal names were repeated in the Egyptian hieroglyphic (literally, "sacred writing"). With these as a start, Champollion turned to a famous trilingual inscription, the Rosetta Stone, found in the Nile Delta in 1799, that bears the same text in Greek, in hieroglyphic, and in another script used in Egypt after hieroglyphics had gone out of fashion. The Rosetta Stone was soon deciphered, and the lessons learned have been applied to all the texts discovered before and since. Visitors to the British Museum can still see the extraordinary slab that made it possible for men of the nineteenth and twentieth centuries A.D. to understand ancient Egypt.

The famous Egyptian *Book of the Dead* brings together stories of the gods and hymns and prayers, and teaches us much of what we know of Egyptian religion. The Egyptian literature we have includes no epic story of a hero comparable to Gilgamesh, a mortal who cannot quite attain immortality, no doubt because the Egyptians confidently did expect to attain it, whether heroic or not. But it does include love-songs, banquet-songs, and what we would call fiction, both historical and fantastic. "If I kiss her," says an Egyptian lover, "and her lips are open, I am happy even without beer,"* a sentiment that seems irreproachably up-to-date even at the distance of three millennia. "Enjoy thyself as much as thou canst," says a banquet-song, "For a man cannot take his property with him,"† though actually nobody ever tried harder than the Egyptians to do so. The historical romance of Sinuhe tells the story of an Egyptian noble who was forced by intrigue into exile in Asia, was elected chief of a tribe there, won a magnificent single combat against a local champion, and, at the end, full of longing for Egypt, was happily recalled by the Pharaoh and richly dressed, honored, and given a pyramid of his own for his future sepulchre. In another story we hear of the young man who resisted a lady's advances only to find that she was accusing him of having made advances to her: a predicament similar to that of Joseph in Egypt itself as reported by the Old Testament, and to many similar tales in the folklore of other peoples.

We have all seen pictures of Egyptian pyramids and temples, gigantic sculptured pharaohs and divinities, and the rich and ostentatious gold and jewels of a splendid sepulchre like King Tut's. The use of stone in building, the skillful use of great spaces, the skillful portraiture of individuals rather than types, the obelisks and sphinxes, the absence of perspective: these are familiar characteristics of Egyptian art. But less well known are the many scenes of ordinary country or family life that characterize Egyptian painting and that show a characteristic enjoyment and even a sense of humor distinctly not found in Mesopotamia. On the wall of an Egyptian tomb a young man and his wife sit happily playing checkers or listening to music or watching the dancing girls. A thief steals a cow while the herdsman's eyes are elsewhere; a crocodile waits for a baby hippopotamus to be born so that at last he may have his lunch. The people who lived along the Nile all those millennia ago speak to us clearly, and we listen with fascination and recognition.

III. Peoples Outside the Valleys

For well over a thousand years after their first flourishing (3000 B.C.), the peoples of the valley civilizations had held the stage virtually alone. But the Hyksos invasion of Egypt (c. 1800), the Kassite invasion of Mesopotamia, and the Hittite attacks on both have already warned us that the men of the mountains

---

* A. Erman, *Literature of the Ancient Egyptians*, trans. A. M. Blackman (London: Dutton, 1927), p. 244.
† J. H. Breasted, *The Dawn of Conscience* (New York, 1933), pp. 163–164.

and deserts outside the valleys had begun to compete fiercely with the more settled valley societies. The outsiders too had centuries of history behind them, still not well known to scholars, but by 1500 B.C. the Kassites in southern Mesopotamia, the Hurrians with their state of Mitanni in northern Mesopotamia, and the Hittites in Anatolia (Asian Turkey) had all emerged as rivals both to Babylon and to Egypt.

All of them had strong Indo-European ethnic elements: that is, elements of a strain that will become predominant in Iran, and later in the Mediterranean and the West. All of them were ruled by kings, but their kings were neither the Mesopotamian agents of god on earth nor the Egyptian deified monarchs: rather they ruled as the most powerful among a noble class that controlled the instruments of conquest—horses and chariots—and shared the fruits of conquest, dividing new land among themselves. We begin now to find records, not only of war between these newly emerging peoples and the settled valley societies, but also of their diplomatic exchanges and their peace settlements.

For communication everybody used Akkadian, a Semitic tongue often foreign to both parties in a negotiation. The Egyptians, for example, corresponded in it with the peoples who ruled Syria, who did not speak it either. As with the language and the cuneiform letters in which it was written, so with the culture generally: the outside peoples were deeply influenced by Mesopotamian religion and literature and art. Though the outsiders dealt severe blows to the valley societies and sometimes seemed temporarily to have overthrown them, the valley societies—Mesopotamia and Egypt—did not in fact succumb during the centuries from 1500 to 1200 B.C., when the threat was greatest.

THE HITTITES

Until the twentieth century A.D., we knew the Hittites only from a few mentions in other sources—Uriah, whom King David so reprehensibly arranged to have killed in battle in order to keep his wife Bathsheba, was a Hittite, for instance. But the discovery of the Hittite capital, Hattusas, now called Boğazköy, in the high plateau of Anatolia revealed not only monumental inscriptions but also several thousand tablets, largely cuneiform in script and written not only in the Indo-European Hittite language but in many others as well. These finds enable us to date at c. 1700 B.C. the emergence of a strong Hittite kingdom, with its Indo-European ruler and aristocracy in control over the native Anatolian population; to note its great conquests between 1700 and c. 1590, its resumption of successful expansion toward Babylon about 1530, its internal crises and recovery about 1500 with the first of the hereditary monarchs, and its height under Suppiluliumas (1380–1346), contemporary of Akhenaten, who took advantage of Egyptian weakness to assert his own strength.

Surely it was no coincidence that Suppiluliumas began after his intimate contact with the Egypt of Akhenaten to insist that he be addressed as "my Sun" and to use the solar disk as a symbol. Henceforth Hittite sovereigns were deified, but only after death: it is from about this time that the written sources we have begin to speak of a king as "becoming a god" at death. The onslaught of the Sea Peoples that destroyed the Egyptian New Kingdom about 1200 also put an end to the centralized Hittite state, although various smaller "neo-Hittite" petty principalities continued to exist in Asia Minor in the face of Assyrian expansion down to the late eighth century B.C.

To Hittite religion the native Anatolians, the Indo-European Hittite upper crust, the Mesopotamians, and the Egyptians all made contributions: foreign gods were made welcome and domesticated. Once part of Hittite religion, no matter where they had originally come from, they received homage in forms derived from Mesopotamia. But there were differences here too: women played a more prominent role in Hittite religion and society than they did either in Mesopotamia or in Egypt. And alone among the peoples of the ancient Near East, the Hittites cremated their kings.

This has reminded scholars that in Homer's *Iliad* the Trojans cremated their dead prince Hector and that Troy itself stood on the edge of Anatolia and so would have been close to areas of predominant Hittite influence. When to this is added the fact that Hittite sources apparently refer to the Achaeans (the name that Homer gives his Greeks) and to Troy, many have been tempted to see a close historical connection between the Hittites and the tale told by Homer.

That portion of Hittite literature which is preserved is full of Mesopotamian echoes, but it is distinguished by its sober official histories, which—alone up to that time among the literary works of the ancient Near East—sought to determine and record the motives of the rulers for their actions. The treaty, too, as a special literary and diplomatic instrument, was apparently a Hittite invention. Hittite architecture expressed itself in fortresses on peaks, which became the nuclei of cities. Otherwise, the buildings show Mesopotamian influence, as does the sculpture; but the Hittites produced no monumental human statues.

HURRIANS, CANAANITES, PHILISTINES, PHOENICIANS

Far less well known than the Hittites and still posing many unsolved problems are the Hurrians, whose state, called Mitanni, was established about 1500 B.C. in northern Mesopotamia and lasted only about a century and a third. No local archeological finds comparable to Bogazköy for the Hittites have yet turned up; and what we know about the Hurrians comes from Egyptian, Hittite, Amorite, and western Palestinian documents. Like the Hittites, the Hurrians had an Indo-European ruling class, and worshipped some Indo-European deities. Their great importance was to act as intermediaries between the great civilization of Mesopotamia and the less advanced peoples to the north and west, especially the Hittites.

Besides the mountains of Anatolia and northern Mesopotamia, the deserts of Syria (the Old Testament land of Canaan) gave rise to a number of Semitic peoples who from time to time invaded the valley societies. Indeed, the Akkadians themselves, both Babylonians and Assyrians, and the Amorites as well had first emerged into history along this path. But there remained behind, of course, other Semitic peoples who never penetrated into the valleys, and who created societies of their own along the Syrian coast of the Mediterranean and in its hinterland.

At Ugarit on the coast—in the northern portion called Phoenicia—archeologists in 1929 found the royal palace of a Canaanite state that flourished between 1400 and 1200 B.C., complete with tablets in a northwest Semitic tongue—Ugaritic—containing several poems highly important for our knowledge of the religion and culture of the people, and also the archives of official correspondence, including a treaty with the Hittites, written in Akkadian and showing that the Canaanites were under Hittite domination. Though extremely important because of its far-flung relationships with contemporary states, and as a forerunner of the Phoenicians, Ugarit was only one of many Canaanite city-states, and it went down in the general chaos of 1200 B.C. caused by the Sea Peoples' invasion. Among these invading Sea Peoples, we know, were the Indo-European Philistines, who settled to the south of the Canaanites and gave their name to Palestine.

The Canaanites apparently matched their extreme political localism with extreme religious localism, and they seem often not to have taken much trouble to sort out their gods: several gods presided over any given department of life, and gods were sometimes masculine and sometimes feminine, as if nobody was quite sure or cared very much. If this seems primitive, the impression is reinforced by the Canaanite practices of human sacrifice and of religious prostitution. The supreme Canaanite god was El, whose name simply means "god" and who is little known. Baal, on the other hand, whose name means "lord," was a storm god—like the Sumerian god of the air, the region between heaven and earth. Baal and his wife Astarte, like Osiris and Isis in Egypt and parallel figures in Mesopotamia, symbolized the seasons and cyclical fertility.

In the period after 1300 the Phoenecians, still another Semitic people, flourished along the coast south of Ugarit, and carried on a brisk trade with the western Mediterranean, founding Carthage as a colony about 800 B.C. The Phoenicians (whose very name comes from the word for the Tyrian purple dye made from shellfish found along the coast of their capital, Tyre) thus brought their Semitic tongue (Punic) more than halfway to the Straits of Gilbraltar, through which in fact their ships had often sailed. Many Phoenician names, as we shall see, appear among the names the Greeks gave to their gods; and the Phoenician alphabet, a real advanced alphabet, not, like cuneiform, a collection of signs that stood for whole syllables, and perhaps inspired by Ugaritic, became the immediate ancestor of the Greek alphabet.

Land of Canaan, Baal, Philistines: these names have been familiar to us all since childhood. For we have now come into the place and time of the Old Testament, and are prepared to understand some of the regional and cultural background of the Hebrews, who in turn were to pass on so much to the peoples of Europe and America.

THE HEBREWS

History and the Old Testament. With the Hebrews we have reached our first people whose history is recorded in a series of books providing a consecutive story over many centuries. This is of course the Old Testament, which includes much besides the historical accounts in Genesis, Exodus, Joshua, Judges, Samuel, and Kings: genealogy and ritual law (Numbers, Leviticus, and Deuteronomy), tales (Ruth and Job), proverbs (Proverbs, Ecclesiastes), prophetic utterances (Isaiah, Jeremiah, and the rest), and lyric poems (The Psalms, The Song of Solomon). Because for many centuries these books were held by Jew and Christian alike to express the literal and sacred truth, it was not until relatively recently that scholars began to apply to them the same test of authenticity that they apply to ordinary works of history. Nineteenth-century scholars found much material in the Old Testament that they took to be legendary and mythical, and they often questioned its historical accuracy. But most such doubts have tended to be dispelled in our own time, as hard archeological evidence has piled up in support of the general narrative that the Old Testament gives us. It is true that the Old Testament was not written down as the events happened, that many of its earliest portions were compiled long after the event, that the writings were not arranged in their present form until the second century B.C., and that many folklore elements can be easily identified. But the weight of the evidence tends to confirm the biblical story.

Even the biblical account of the mist-shrouded beginnings of the Hebrews now seems authentic: they may well have migrated from Ur "of the Chaldees" sometime after 1950 B.C., when that Sumerian center in southern Mesopotamia was destroyed, northwest to the prosperous center of Harran. Abraham then may well have migrated westward into "Canaan," as Genesis says. The accounts in Genesis of the origins of the universe and the racial origins of the Hebrews, and the stories of Eden, the Flood, and the Tower of Babel all fit into the supposition of a northern Mesopotamian—and no other—place of residence for the Hebrews before about 1500 B.C., when the westward migration took place. Probably a racial mixture including some non-Semitic elements (Hurrian?) from the beginning, the Hebrews may well be the same as a people called Khapiru who appear beginning about 1900 B.C. in the cuneiform tablets and in both Hittite and Egyptian sources as raiders, wanderers, and captives. Historians also are convinced that some of the Hebrews at least did live for several centuries in the Nile Delta during the Hyksos period, before Moses (whose name is Egyptian) became their leader and led them about 1300 B.C. to within sight of the Promised Land. Even the miraculous crossing of the Red Sea in Exodus is not incompatible with the shallow waters, the reedy growth, and the winds of the region.

Outsiders battering their way back into Canaan against the entrenched resistance of those who already lived there, the Hebrew confederation of tribes was held together by the new religion that Moses gave them—the Ten Commandments, the Ark of the Covenant, the many observances that God prescribed. Gradually by ruthless conquest they added to their holdings (Joshua took Jericho about 1230 B.C.), and after the period of the Judges—when many minor leaders directed Hebrew affairs and battles were fought against Canaanites and Philistines—the loose confederation became a monarchy in about 1020 B.C., when the prophet Samuel chose Saul to be the first king. Saul's son-in-law, rival, and successor, David, so well known to us by the virtually contemporary account (1000–960 B.C.) in the Book of Samuel, united the kingdom and strengthened it. His luxury-loving son Solomon brought the Palestinian kingdom of the Jews to new heights of prosperity, but even then it was small in size and resources compared to Sumer, Babylon, Assyria, or Egypt.

But Solomon (960–922 B.C.) lacked the character of David, and in 933 B.C. the kingdom split in two: the northern kingdom of Israel (933–722 B.C.), stronger but lacking the great center of Jerusalem, and the southern kingdom of Judah (933–586 B.C.), which held Jerusalem but had little real strength. The Assyrians destroyed Israel in 722 B.C., and the Babylonians—then, as we have seen, experiencing a brief revival—destroyed Judah in 586 and took the Jews into captivity. When the Persians under Cyrus the Great in turn conquered Babylonia and freed the Jews to return to Palestine after 538, the Jews no longer had a state, but a religious community only. From then on they were held together by religion alone, and depended politically on one empire or another: in succession, the Persian, the Macedonian, the Roman.

Religion. Indeed, had it not been for their extraordinary religion, the Hebrews would seem to us just another people of the ancient Near East, less numerous than most, less talented artistically than any. But of course we would probably not know much about them had it not been for their religion, which gave them and us the books of the Old Testament and an enduring tradition. Many of the most fundamental ideas of Hebrew religion go back to the days when the Hebrews were still nomads, before they had adopted a settled life. Thus God's commandments to Moses on Mount Sinai that "Thou shalt have no other god before me," "Thou shalt not make unto thee a graven image," and "Thou shalt not take the name of the Lord thy God in vain"—which long preceded the settlement in Palestine—determined three fundamental and permanent aspects of Judaism which were new among Near Eastern religions.

The religion of the Hebrews was monotheistic, recognizing only a single god. Despite the experiment of Akhenaten in Egypt and a few Babylonian texts that try to associate all divine power with the chief god, Marduk, alone, the Jews were the first to insist that their god was the only god, and a universal god. Second, the Jews were forbidden to represent him in sculpture or painting—which was an enormous contrast with all other religions of the ancient world. More than that: they were forbidden to make *any* images of living beings, flesh, fish, or fowl, no doubt because their leaders feared that if they did make such images, they would end by worshipping them; and so from these earliest days their art was confined to nonrepresentational subjects. When they deviated from this law, as they sometimes did, it was usually because of the influence upon them of neighbors whose traditions did not forbid animal or human representations in art. Third, the religion of the Hebrews from the beginning would regard the *name* of God—Yahveh or Jehovah, meaning "he causes to be," or "the creator" —as literally not to be spoken, a reverence quite different from any we have found in other ancient Near Eastern religions. From the nomadic period of Hebrew life also come the feast of the Passover, with its offering of a spring lamb and of unleavened bread, celebrating the escape from Egypt; the keeping of the sabbath on the seventh day; the annual day of expiation (Yom Kippur); and other holy days still honored by the Jews in our own times.

The Old Testament swarms with episodes in which the Hebrews proved unable to keep the first commandment, broke away from the worship of the single God, tried to propitiate other gods, and were punished. Yet however often they disobeyed, the first commandment remained the central feature of their religion. With monotheism from the first went morality, as shown in the remaining commandments forbidding murder, adultery, stealing, false witness, and covetousness of one's neighbor's property. Jehovah himself, both merciful and righteous, creator of all things, was human in form, but was not visible to the human eye. Unlike the gods of all the other peoples, he did not lead a human life; he had no family; he dwelt, not in a palace like a human palace only more splendid, but in heaven. When he wished to speak to the leader of his people, he descended onto a mountain top (Mount Sinai) or into a burning bush or into the space left for him by his own direction between the wings of the cherubim to be set atop the sacred box in which the Ten Commandments on their two tablets of stone were to be kept.

This was the Ark of the Covenant, built by artisans to the special orders of God as relayed by Moses. The Covenant was the special pact between God himself and his chosen people, all the tribes of the Hebrews, in tribal confederation, held together by their regard for this most sacred of objects. Kept at first in a very special tent, a portable tabernacle, the ark moved with the Hebrews, first to Shiloh, where the Philistines captured it about 1050 B.C., and then into the temple built for it by Solomon in Jerusalem, a royal chapel, whose decorations included many that violated the commandment about graven images. Solomon's temple was built by a Canaanite architect using Phoenician models, showing the increasing influence of non-Israelite peoples on the cult.

There were prophets (men called by God) among the Jews from the beginning; but they naturally multiplied during the division of the people into the two kingdoms of Israel and Judah. They summoned the people to return to the original purity of the faith and to avoid the paganism that seemed to be threatening if Canaanite influences continued. In ecstasy perhaps brought on by dances, they solemnly warned of fearful punishment to come if the people did not heed them. After the punishment, however, the prophets (notably Isaiah) promised that Israel would rise again, and that a descendant of David would appear as the Messiah to usher in a new golden age. The disaster came, of course, with the Babylonian captivity; and now that the prophecies of evil had been fulfilled, the prophet Ezekiel had a vision of new life being breathed into the dead bones of Israel, and urged the preparation for its restoration. (It was in exile, in the sixth century B.C., that the sacred writings were selected and arranged in a form not unlike the Old Testament we know.) The captivity once over, the priests became the dominant figures in the restored community, with its rebuilt temple but without a state of its own. They strove deliberately to return to what they believed to be the practices of their remote ancestors.

As one would expect, there was much about Hebrew society that recalls what we have already observed about the remaining peoples of the ancient Near East. The father exercised supreme authority within the family; polygamy and divorce were permitted; and, as among the Hittites, a widow married her dead husband's brother. The Hebrews had slaves, but a Hebrew slave could be made to serve no more than six years. A man who had injured his slave was required to set him free. Otherwise the law of an eye for an eye, a tooth for a tooth, held sway. Yet the general prescriptions, such as the Commandments, and even some of the specific regulations—not to wrong strangers, not to exact usurious interest for a loan, to help one's enemies as well as one's friends—strike an ethical note deeper than any found in the earlier Mesopotamian Near East, and presage the Christian principles that would—within another half-millennium—emerge from this Hebrew society.

IV. Crete and Mycenae

MINOANS BEFORE MYCENAE

Among the notable finds in Ugarit was an ivory relief of a bare-breasted goddess, holding wheat ears in each hand and seated between two goats standing on their hind legs. She is like nothing from Mesopotamia or Egypt, but she greatly resembles the goddesses frequently found on the large Mediterranean island of Crete, on the westernmost fringe of the Near East, where there developed beginning about 2600 B.C. the last of the Bronze Age civilizations we shall consider, preceded, like the others, by untold numbers of centuries of gradual Stone Age advance. Cretan civilization is often called Minoan, after Minos, the legendary founder of the local dynasty, whose monarchs were all called Minos after him.

Sir Arthur Evans, the British archeologist whose brilliant work in Crete in the first half of our own century enabled modern scholars to appreciate Minoan society at its true worth, divided the culture into three main periods, Early Minoan (from c. 2600 to about 2000 B.C.), Middle Minoan (from c. 2000 to about 1600 B.C.), and Late Minoan (from c. 1600 to about 1100 B.C.); and each of these three is regularly further subdivided three times to enable easy discussion of the objects found. For all such dating pottery is the key. Different styles found at different levels permit scholars to work out a chronological framework. In Crete such dating is of surpassing importance, partly because we have not yet learned how to read the earliest writing, some of it in hieroglyphics and some of it in a script known as Linear A. The number of Linear A tablets is relatively small compared with the tens of thousands of Mesopotamian writings at our disposal; and no inscription has yet been found written in both Linear A and a known language: Crete has no Rosetta Stone. Since they cannot read the writing, scholars who try to reconstruct Cretan society in its early phases have nothing to go on except the objects uncovered by the archeologist. Of these the greatest are the palace of Minos at Knossos (modern Iráklion), found and partly reconstructed by Evans, and other palaces and tombs in other parts of the island.

The Cretans were—we think—not Indo-Europeans but descendants of Anatolian immigrants to the island. Pottery and seals found on Crete show that the Cretans were in touch both with Egypt and with Mesopotamia. In fact, this was a busy maritime people, whose ships not only plied the Mediterranean but presumably managed to defend the island against invaders, since none of the palaces was fortified. Expanding at the expense of other islanders, the Cretans had garrisons and even colonies abroad, a Bronze Age overseas empire on a small scale exacting tribute from other powers.

The Palace of Minos is a Middle Minoan triumph, resting on earlier foundations, characterized by many rooms, a great staircase, strikingly beautiful wall-frescoes (recovered from the ruins in fragments), massive columns, many six-foot-tall stone storage jars for olive oil or wine, and an elaborate plumbing system with pipes, running water, and ventilation. So complex was the palace that Evans himself believed—probably rightly—that he had discovered that building which had inspired the ancient Greek legend of the Labyrinth, the palace on Crete with a system of rooms and corridors so mazelike that nobody could find his way without a guide or a thread to drop behind him so that he might later retrace his steps.

Minoan craftsmen produced delicate pottery hardly thicker than an egg-shell, decorated with birds, flowers, and marine animals; ivory or pottery statuettes of the bare-breasted goddess, who sometimes holds a snake in each hand; and many paintings of bulls, some showing young athletes—girls and boys—leaping over a bull's back, in what was clearly something like a ritual game. Athenian legend (no doubt a memory of tribute of grain once sent to Crete) said that their ancestors had been forced to send each year young men and maidens to be sacrificed by the Cretans to their half-man, half-bull monster called the Minotaur (a Minos-bull, supposedly the fruit of a union between the Cretan queen Pasiphaë and a bull). This reminiscence too, and the fact that many pairs of bull-horns have been found in Knossos and elsewhere, illustrate the importance of the animal in the Cretan religion, in which a double axe, found in many sizes, from

Ivory and gold snake goddess from Crete, sixteenth century B.C.

full-sized models in bronze to tiny miniatures in gold, also played a role. The word *labyrinth* itself means "place of the double axe" (*labrys*).

Society at Knossos, at least from the Middle Minoan period on, was elegant. Sophisticated court ladies wearing embroidered dresses and gold or silver necklaces enjoyed dances or strolled about viewing the fountains, the carefully laid-out flower beds, and the rock gardens. But Crete had its troubles too, though conjecture must help us in any effort to say just what they were. Was it natural catastrophes (earthquakes, tidal waves, and fires) that destroyed the palace of Minos a little after 1600 B.C., and again about 1500, and a third time about 1400? Or did invading Hyksos, on their way out of Egypt after their occupation, do the damage of 1600? Did mainland Greeks, crossing from the north, cause the destruction of 1500? Nobody can be quite sure about the earlier destructions, which were repaired; but the last disaster may well be attributable to actions of mainland Greeks.

MYCENAEANS AND MINOANS

In Greece too, Bronze Age civilization had taken root. Greece was a largely barren land, mountainous, and divided into small valleys and plains, separated from each other, but none of them far from the sea. From the earliest times the inhabitants took advantage of the rugged coasts and islands, with their many

The bull portico of the Palace of Minos at Knossos.

shelters and good harbors, to sail from place to place, seldom if ever losing sight of land, profiting by the exchange of olive oil and wine for grain and metal and slaves. About 2000 B.C. the village Bronze Age culture of the inhabitants—who were not Indo-Europeans but, like the Cretans, presumably a mixture of Stone Age indigenous peoples and Anatolians who had invaded about 3000 B.C.—was interrupted by the invasion from the North of the first true Greeks: Indo-Europeans, who first destroyed and then settled, no doubt intermarrying with the previous inhabitants. This society had one of its chief centers at Mycenae in the Peloponnesus, suitably situated to control land trade and not far from the sea.

The Mycenaeans were led by warrior chieftains, but they also engaged in commerce with Crete. Minoan objects have been found in the famous royal tombs at Mycenae that perhaps span the century from 1600 to 1500 B.C. In fact, so profound was the Minoan influence at work upon the arts of the mainland that scholars speak now of the Minoanization of mainland Greece. The most celebrated objects are the great gold masks of the warrior princes buried in the tombs and the daggers inlaid with various metals that show hunting scenes of astonishing realism and beauty. When the great German archeologist Heinrich Schliemann found these in the 1870's he was looking for the tomb of the Homeric hero Agamemnon, and thought that he had found it. But, as we shall see, Agamemnon actually lived about three hundred years later. Egypt and Anatolia too shared in the Mycenaean trade, but the chief influences in mainland Greece were Minoan.

Interchange, we now believe, went both ways. Mycenaean Greeks visited Crete as traders or even as tourists; perhaps they observed the absence of physical fortifications that left Knossos vulnerable. Then (it is conjectured) they moved in and seized power, perhaps about 1480, presumably having first built their own fleet. No longer did they need to send to Knossos whatever tribute is remembered in the Minotaur legend. Indeed, they now controlled the very center of the civilization that had already taught them so much. Certain military inno-

The Harvester Vase, c. 1600 B.C., from the villa of Hagia Triada, in southern Crete.

vations now took place in Crete: chariots were introduced and arrows stored for large bodies of troops, but the invaders built no fortifications, presumably because they expected no new invasion. In the palace at Minos the Greeks installed a throne room of the type they were accustomed to build in their own mainland palaces. But, most important, the Minoans showed them how useful it was to keep records; and since Linear A, devised for a non-Indo-European language from Anatolia, would not do, the scribes presumably invented a new script—Linear B— in which to write the language of the conquerors: Greek. On the other hand, Linear B may have been developed gradually out of Linear A.

It is the very existence of this new script, and the conclusive proof worked out only in 1952 by Michael Ventris that in fact it *is* early Greek, that has made possible the foregoing tentative reconstruction of events that are still somewhat uncertain. Of course Evans had found the Linear B tablets in great numbers in his Cretan excavations; but no such tablets were known *from mainland Greece* until 1939, when an American scholar, Carl Blegen, discovered the first of what proved to be a large collection of them in Pylos, where he was excavating a Mycenaean palace, and since then many more have turned up elsewhere in Greece, including some in Mycenae itself. Acting on the assumption that it was probably Greek (since he now knew that Greeks were keeping records in it on the mainland), Ventris used the techniques of cryptography to demonstrate that the signs in the language each represented a syllable (not a single letter), and then cracked the code. The thousands of Linear B tablets have by no means all been read even now, and by no means all readings are certain; but Greek it is. It is too bad in some ways that the tablets are mostly prosaic inventory lists of materials stored in the palaces or of persons in the royal services.

But the disappearance in Crete of Linear A, and the substitution for it about 1460 B.C. of the new Linear B (Greek), points clearly to a Mycenaean occupation of the island that preceded the last great violent destruction of c. 1400 B.C. and lasted almost a century. We cannot be sure to what degree the new Greek rulers of Knossos were independent of direct authority from the mainland: they may have been subordinate Mycenaean princes. The great palace of Knossos and a number of other major Cretan centers were burned down about 1400, apparently after looting. We do not know who did it. Perhaps the Cretans rose against their Greek masters and burned down their own cities; though it has been plausibly suggested that such an act would have invited fierce reprisals and continued occupation after reconstruction. There was no reconstruction. Instead there was permanent disruption. So perhaps it was the Mycenaeans themselves who—in revenge against Cretan rebelliousness which may have made the island ungovernable—decided to cut their losses and destroy the Cretan centers and sail away. Or perhaps it was a volcanic upheaval of the sea-bed. The recent rediscovery (1967) and present active excavation of a Minoan city on the volcanic island of Santorin (Thera) to the north of Crete may furnish us with new evidence and enable us to decide the question one way or another. We do know that after the disaster of 1400 B.C. Crete lost its Mediterranean importance, which passed definitely to the aggressive mainland peoples.

A Mycenaean jar with an inscription in Linear B, now in the museum at Eleusis.

MYCENAE, 1400–1100 B.C.

We still know relatively little about Mycenaean politics and society. We can tell from excavated gold treasures that Mycenae itself was wealthy, which is not surprising considering that it had conquered Crete. But the Mycenaeans seem not to have been overseas empire-builders even in the sense that the Cretans had been; their occupation of Crete may well have been undertaken by an invading captain who retained power for himself in Crete, however much of its revenue he sent back home. The Achaeans (Greeks) of whom the Hittite sources speak may well not have been the Greeks of Mycenae at all but Greeks of Rhodes, another island principality. And there were other settlements in the Peloponnesus itself—

The Lion Gate at Mycenae.

Pylos, Tiryns (the latter very close to Mycenae)—which seem to have been extensive too, and perhaps, under local rulers equally powerful but bound in alliance to the Mycenaeans: a kind of loose confederacy among equals seems to fit best with the evidence. Each of the cities was walled. The walls of Mycenae survive, with their famous Lion Gate showing the two great sculptured beasts who lean forward to face each other, separated by a slender column, over the huge lintel above the gateway.

Tombs from the period before 1400 B.C. are of two sharply distinct types: those carefully built to take the bodies of kings and important noblemen, and simple burial places for the rest of the population. Tombs from the period between 1400 and 1200 show a rise in the general wealth: more chamber-tombs with more gifts to the dead found in them. Similarly at Mycenae itself, Tiryns, Pylos, Athens, and Thebes there arose now great palaces as community centers, with workshops, storage areas, guardrooms, and lesser dwelling-houses attached. Others certainly existed, and more will be found. Good roads with bridges and culverts connected the main towns, and good water-supply systems characterized them. Artisans attached to the palace built and repaired chariots, made jars to hold the wine and oil, tanned leather, wrought bronze in the forge, made bricks, and sewed garments; workmen stored goods for preservation and for sale and exchange. A Mycenaean palace was a businesslike (and noisy) place. The Linear B tablets preserve records of special royal furniture most elaborately inlaid in ivory, glass, and gold: like the Egyptian pharaohs, the Mycenaean rulers obviously valued things most when they took a lot of time and effort to make. Smaller than the great palaces on Crete, those of the Mycenaeans on the mainland nonetheless testify to the vibrant life of an advanced society. One of the richest hoards, containing treasures in gold and jewels and bronze made over a period of five centuries, was found in a private house in Tiryns: it was obviously the stolen booty of a Mycenaean grave-robber, with a fine taste in antiques, who like all men before and since could not take his possessions with him.

Mycenaean religion remains a puzzle. Unlike Crete, where shrines and evidence of worship are everywhere, the Greek mainland furnishes no separate shrines at all, although there are some fragments of an altar in the great room or the courtyard of the palaces, and some portable altars have also been found. The reason is that the Greeks, unlike the Cretans, made burnt and blood offerings to their gods. Gems found in the Mycenaean royal tombs clearly show Cretan deities and religious scenes; so the Cretan goddess was also revered on the mainland. The Linear B tablets from Pylos kept records of offerings made to certain gods—Poseidon, the god of the sea, Ares, the god of war, Artemis, the moon-goddess, and even Zeus and Hera, to later Greeks the ruler of the gods and his consort. But there are other gods who did not survive the Dark Age and who never reappear in classical Greece.

The most famous Mycenaean exploit of the three centuries 1400–1100 was of course the Trojan War, now dated about 1240 B.C., known to every Greek of the classical period from the poems of Homer written down four to five centuries after the event, and known in some measure to all civilized westerners ever since. This was a great expedition led by the King of Mycenae, Agamemnon, in command of a fleet and an army contributed by the other towns and islands of Mycenaean Greece, against Troy, a rich city on the northwest coast of Asia Minor (Anatolia) not far from the mouth of the Dardanelles, the straits that lead from the Aegean into the Sea of Marmora. The Trojans were Indo-Europeans like the

Greeks but not so advanced: they did not write or paint their own pottery; they seem to have had few contacts with their neighbors in the Aegean, the Cretans, or their neighbors in Anatolia, the Hittites. They had a powerfully fortified city, and they traded with mainland Greece (many Mycenaean objects have been found in the ruins of Troy), though what they gave in exchange is not certain: perhaps horses, grain, purple dye, silver, and textiles.

Scholars now dismiss as romance the famous tale of the rape by the Trojan prince Paris of Helen, wife of Menelaus, Mycenaean prince of Sparta, and the war of revenge that followed; and we must believe instead that the Mycenaean expedition was undertaken for plunder of the Trojan citadel. Romantic too—or at least unproven—are the traditions that the siege lasted ten years and that great numbers of ships and men were involved. Agamemnon's force won, and burned Troy. Excavation carried on first by Schliemann and later by other scholars shows that the Troy destroyed by Agamemnon's famous expedition was probably a patched-up reconstruction of a richer Troy that may well have suffered destruction in an earlier Greek attack about 1300.

Soon after the siege of Troy there began the upheaval in the Mediterranean world to which we have already several times referred, the great raiding expeditions of the Sea Peoples that eventually—among other things—shattered the Egyptian New Kingdom and the Hittite state and left the Philistines washed up on the shores of Palestine. Egyptian and Hittite sources show that there were perhaps Greeks among the Sea Peoples, but we cannot tell where these "Achaeans" (or "Argives") and "Danaans" came from. In this period of raiding and migration the general violence did not spare Mycenaean Greece, which began about 1200 to suffer a great wave of destruction.

The great palaces were burned, some perhaps by fellow-Mycenaean Greeks, others perhaps by fragments of other Sea People little better than pirates who landed and conducted hit-and-run raids, and still others perhaps by a new wave of Greek invaders from the North, adding to the general confusion now by entering the Mycenaean society as conquerors. These last were the Dorians, whom scholars can later identify by their special dialect of Greek in inscriptions but who at the beginning were illiterate. It took them a century to obtain mastery in Greece. To them scholars used to attribute most of the destruction that ushered in the Dark Age that began about 1100, but probably much of the destruction preceded their invasion and made it easier.

THE DARK AGE; HOMER

With the destruction of the Mycenaean cities there set in at least three centuries that are called the Dark Age: dark in that we have little conclusive evidence from them to give us a picture of the life, and dark also in that the interlude surely marked a great series of steps backward in Greek civilization. Literacy vanished, for example. It is sometimes argued that Linear B was too clumsy a script ever to have been useful for anything much beyond keeping business records and that in any case only a very small proportion of Mycenaean Greeks (perhaps five per cent) could ever have been able to read and write in it; so that its disappearance now was a positive benefit, for when literacy returned it would be in the new Greek alphabet taken from the Phoenicians. Even this argument would, however, concede the end of progress and the reversion to more primitive conditions, characteristic of the Dorian domination. The political units of the Mycenaean world, already small, gave way to still smaller communities.

There were, we know, migrations of Greeks from Greece itself to the Aegean coasts of Asia Minor: to the central region (later called Ionia) that emerges into daylight again about 800 B.C.; and other Greeks, speaking other dialects into the regions to the north (Aeolic) and south (Doric) of Ionia. In the hinterland behind these regions lived the Anatolian peoples in their own kingdoms: Lydia, Caria, Phrygia. Other Greeks on the mainland were lucky enough to miss the full impact of the Dorian invasion, notably the Athenians, whose later leadership of Greece, once the Dark Age cleared, may perhaps be attributable to a head start gained in this way.

The end of the Dark Age is closely tied in with the writing down of the Homeric poems, the *Iliad* and the *Odyssey*. Did the same person commit both to writing? Was it Homer? Did the *Iliad* precede the *Odyssey*? No certain answer can be given to these questions, but it seems highly likely that at some time between 850 and 750 B.C. (some say even later) both were recorded permanently, and we may as well call the man who did it Homer. Together the two great epics represent only a fraction of the epic material that existed in the Dark Age; there were many other tales of the great deeds of heroes. Minstrels who accompanied themselves on stringed instruments sang the separate songs to audiences around the banquet tables in a princely palace, or to a gathering of villagers in a public square, or to soldiers around a campfire. The songs that together make up the much longer epics that have come down to us were no doubt among the most popular, and the minstrel who put them down was selecting from his repertory the stories that had best stood the test of performance.

The *Iliad* tells the story of a single incident that took place during the siege of Troy: the wrath of the Greek hero Achilles, who stopped fighting and sulked in his tent because the commander Agamemnon had taken from him a Trojan girl captive. Agamemnon had allowed himself to be persuaded to restore to her family his own captive girl, and so made up for his loss by taking Achilles' prize away. While Achilles refused to fight, the great combat continued, and eventually, when Hector the Trojan prince had killed Achilles' best friend and comrade-in-arms, Patroclus, Achilles returned to the battle and in turn slew Hector, whose body at the very end he returned to Hector's sorrowing father, old King Priam. The *Odyssey* tells of the ten-year wanderings of another Greek hero, Odysseus, after the siege of Troy was over; of the extraordinary places and peoples he visited on his way back to his home on the island of Ithaca, where his faithful wife Penelope awaited him despite the attention of many suitors, and whence their son Telemachus had set out in order to find his father.

Put in this summary form, the two stories perhaps seem blunt and commonplace. But a deep humanity pervades both. Despite the continual bloody fighting in the *Iliad*, the modern reader—like all before him—is moved by the terror of Hector's baby son, Astyanax, when he sees his father with his fierce plumed war-helmet on, until Hector takes it off and shows the child who it really is; feels the truth of the passage when the old men of Troy admit that Helen—beautiful as a goddess—was well worth all the fuss; shares the grief and dignity of Priam as he begs Achilles to return Hector's body for decent burial; and appreciates Achilles' courteous generosity to an enemy when he reluctantly agrees. The romantic *Odyssey*, with its lotus-eaters, sirens, men turned to swine by enchantment, and fierce one-eyed giant, provides similar moments of high human drama in the actual homecoming of Odysseus in disguise, and the responses of his favorite dog and his old nurse, or in the sorrow of the beautiful island princess Nausicaa, first seen playing ball on the beach with her maidens, when she finds that Odysseus will not stay and be her lover.

In both poems, the gods—now the standard collection of Greek divinities: Zeus, Hera, Apollo, Artemis, Aphrodite, and the rest—play an intimate part in the affairs of the mortals, intervening in the fighting to give victory to their favorites, supplying Achilles with an extraordinary shield on which are displayed many scenes in cunning metal-work, saving Odysseus from the perils of his voyage. The gods and goddesses on Olympus are only a little more outsize than the heroes; they live thoroughly human lives, quarrelling over the affairs of the mortals and giving way to fits of bad temper. The epics take the reader into the world of a heroic age, like the later and lesser epics that reflected other heroic ages: such as *Beowulf* or *The Song of Roland* (*see* Chapter 4).

We hear at every turn and in great detail about the armor, ships, houses, domestic arrangements, and social behavior of the personages. It has always been a great temptation for scholars to reconstruct Mycenaean society from Homer. But Homer was writing five hundred years after the Trojan War. How far back did even a powerful oral tradition reach? In describing Odysseus' bed was he describing a real Bronze Age Mycenaean bed or the kind of bed that a prince would have slept in in his own day or a little before? Sometimes archeology helps us here; more often it either does not help or adds to the confusion, as when the word that Homer uses for Nestor's drinking cup (*depas*) is found scratched on a Mycenaean storage jar far too big for anyone to drink from. Was Homer sometimes consciously trying to show his readers a world five hundred years earlier than theirs, and if so to what extent and in what passages? How safe are we in using him as a historical source?

To these largely unanswerable questions scholars give varying answers; but most in recent years have preferred to use Homer sparingly if at all. Yet there is the long interpolated Catalogue of the Ships in the *Iliad* that lists the contingents supplied to the Greek armies by the various Greek settlements and names their commanders. Many authorities think it is a genuine Bronze Age document that provides hard, usable evidence with regard to the diverse political organization of Mycenaean society: partly by city, partly by the captain the people follow, partly by tribe. So too the description of Odysseus' household as including more than fifty slaves is taken as an indication of the prevalence of slavery in Mycenaean times, and conclusions are reached from episodes in Homer with regard to the inheritance of royal power and the existence of assemblies of elders. Other scholars would reject such conclusions as dangerous. But whether we use Homer as history or not, the Greeks themselves from his time on certainly did so, and formed their own conception of their ancestral past from the *Iliad* and the *Odyssey*. Together with the Old Testament, some of which was being committed to writing at about the same time, these two poems form the greatest literary and cultural and spiritual legacy of ancient man.

Indeed, certain modern scholars would maintain that both Homeric and Hebrew civilization grew directly from a common eastern Mediterranean background, and they point to many parallels in action and attitude. In many respects archeological evidence serves to suggest that this viewpoint probably deserves a wider acceptance than it has yet won.

READING SUGGESTIONS (asterisk indicates paperbound edition)

Pre-History

J. Pfeiffer, *From Galaxies to Man: A Story of the Beginnings of Things* (Macmillan, 1959). A good popular account of recent evolutionary concepts.

A. L. Kroeber, *Anthropology*, 2 vols. (*Harcourt). A masterly review; the first volume deals with biology and race, and the second with culture patterns and processes.

J. Hawkes, *Prehistory* (*Mentor). A recent and highly respected survey.

L. S. Leakey, *Adam's Ancestors: The Evolution of Man and His Culture* (*Torchbooks). By the expert who discovered remains of man's remote ancestors in Africa.

R. Coulbourn, *The Origins of Civilized Societies* (Princeton University, 1959). A scholarly, readable, and stimulating study.

W. F. Albright, *From the Stone Age to Christianity* (*Anchor). Superb survey of a field much altered by modern scholarship.

The Near East

H. Frankfort, *The Birth of Civilization in the Near East* (*Anchor). A brief and stimulating essay by an expert in the area.

S. Moscati, *The Face of the Ancient Orient: A Panorama of Near Eastern Civilization in Pre-Classical Times* (*Anchor). Good introductory survey.

L. Woolley, *Beginnings of Civilization* (*Mentor). Sequel to survey by Miss Hawkes, above.

G. Bibby, *Four Thousand Years Ago* (Knopf, 1962). A most readable account of the crucial millennium from 2000 to 1000 B.C.

H. Frankfort and others, *Before Philosophy* (*Penguin). Admirable essays in the intellectual history of the ancient Near East.

H. B. Parkes, *Gods and Men: The Origins of Western Culture* (*Vintage). Perceptive survey of early religions.

M. E. L. Mallowan, *Early Mesopotamia and Iran* (*McGraw-Hill). By the archeologist husband of Agatha Christie.

S. N. Kramer, *History Begins at Sumer* (*Anchor). Introduction by an expert.

J. Lassoe, *People of Ancient Assyria* (Barnes & Noble, 1963). An attempt to show the Assyrians as more than mere militarists.

O. R. Gurney, *The Hittites,* 2nd ed. (*Penguin). Survey of a people rescued from almost total oblivion by archeology.

J. A. Wilson, *The Culture of Ancient Egypt* (*Phoenix). The best single-volume study of the subject.

J. H. Breasted, *History of Egypt* (*Bantam). By a celebrated Egyptologist of another generation, and still worth reading.

C. Desroches-Noblecourt, *Egyptian Wall Paintings from Tombs and Temples* (*Mentor). An informative sampler.

H. M. Orlinsky, *The Ancient Jews,* 2nd ed. (*Cornell University). A good introductory manual.

L. Finkelstein, ed., *The Jews: Their History, Culture, and Religion,* 3rd ed., 2 vols. (Harper, 1960). Comprehensive; popular in the best sense.

Cyrus H. Gordon, *Introduction to Old Testament Times* (Ventnor, 1953). See note on Gordon's writing under next heading.

Crete and Early Greece

L. R. Palmer, *Mycenaeans and Minoans* (Knopf, 1962). Controversial reassessment in the light of the Linear B tablets. J. Chadwick, *The Decipherment of Linear B* (*Vintage). By Ventris' collaborator.

C. W. Blegen, *Troy and the Trojans* (Praeger, 1963), and Lord William Taylour, *Mycenaeans* (Praeger, 1964). Clear scholarly introductions.

Emily Vermeule, *Greece in the Bronze Age* (University of Chicago, 1964). Thorough survey of Mycenaean Greece.

Cyrus H. Gordon, *Before the Bible* (Collins, 1962) and *Ugarit and Minoan Crete* (Norton, 1966). Two books that draw highly daring parallels between ancient Near Eastern and Homeric civilization.

2

The Classical World

The Propylaea (entrance gate) and the Temple of Athena Nike, Acropolis, Athens.

I. The Greeks Before the Persian Wars

In the first chapter, seeking to chronicle and understand man's experience from about 3000 B.C. to about 850 B.C.—or in some instances a few centuries later—we have concentrated primarily on the ancient Near East: Mesopotamia, Egypt, the peoples outside the valleys, and the Hebrews; and we have examined as well the Minoan–Mycenaean civilization that grew up on Crete and on the mainland of Greece, peripheral to the Near East but closely connected with it. Sometime about 850, though one would not wish to insist too firmly on any precise date, the focus for chroniclers and interpreters like us shifts away from the Near East to a people that has hitherto been peripheral: the Greeks. Of course, the Near East after 850 continues to engage our attention: indeed we have already noted the military adventures of the Assyrians in the eighth and seventh centuries and the Babylonian captivity of the Hebrews and their release from it by the Persians in the sixth. The Persians we shall soon encounter again. But for fresh ideas, for new contributions to our own heritage, for new attitudes toward the outside world and toward man himself it is the Greeks who move to the center of the stage between the ninth and the third centuries B.C.

WHAT THE GREEKS WERE LIKE

The Greeks were different from the other peoples we have come to know. For one thing, they were more curious: it is still proverbial that a Greek always wants to know some new thing, and that he will ask questions tirelessly of anybody who knows something he does not yet know himself. Where does the stranger come from? how big is his family? how much money does he have? what does it cost to live in his country? The questions may range from such relatively superficial personal matters—the answers to which will only temporarily assuage the questioner's itch for all knowledge—to the most fundamental problems abstract or practical: how do we really know what we *think* we know? what is the universe made of? what causes men to suffer fevers? what are the various possible ways for men to live together and govern themselves? and the myriad other questions to which there may be no real answers but only a multitude of approximations, any one of which will please some Greeks and none of which will please them all; so the argument can continue and the fun rage unchecked.

Then too, the Greeks were less otherworldly than the other peoples. The Mesopotamians and Egyptians—though with differing attitudes—both concentrated their attention upon the life to come; the Greeks were far more interested in life on earth. They did not deny that death was inevitable, and they suffered the fears and anxieties common to the human lot; but they had no feeling of hopelessness with regard to earthly life, and found it delightful to engage in tackling its manifold problems. The Hebrews submitted to the will of an all-powerful single god, who directed not only the footsteps of the entire people but the lives of each of its individual members; the Greeks had no such divinity and no such law, and so man himself, human reason, and human answers to human problems took a central place in their hearts and minds. Gods of course they had, and proper service to the gods they felt it seemly to render; indeed they would often, even usually, attribute human action to the influence of a god; but one gets the feeling that for them this was often only a manner of speaking. They say "Ares strengthened the hero's arm for the deadly spear-thrust" when they seem to mean little more than "the hero summoned up all the resources of his muscular right arm, and let the enemy have it with a spear."

We often hear that the Greeks invented democracy: literally, government by the people. Indeed they did, but they also invented oligarchy: government by the few; and aristocracy: the rule of the best, or noblest or richest; and they also produced many refinements on rule by one man, which they called a tyranny even when it was mild and just and popular. Moreover, although they invented democracy, they had terrible difficulties in making it work. Fierce political infighting between rival groups and rival politicians usually characterized their political life. Rather than absorb a political loss at home, a Greek politician would often intrigue with a foreign enemy.

Modern students have often taken their picture of Greek politics in general from the superb speech that Pericles, the most celebrated of the leaders of Athens, made in 430 B.C. over the Athenian soldiers killed in the first year of a great war against Sparta (*see below,* p. 57), as reported in the history of the war by the historian Thucydides. Praising Athenian democracy, Pericles said that at Athens the law guaranteed equal justice to all, that talent and not wealth was the Athenian qualification for public service, that Athenians expected of everybody a lively interest and participation in public affairs. In fact, his picture corresponded more to an ideal world than to the real Athenian world, where the courts were often markedly prejudiced, where wealth remained an important qualification for office, and where individual political ambition burned as hotly and was often pursued as ruthlessly and unscrupulously as anywhere on earth. In the tough world of Athenian politics one can without much effort see strong parallels to human behavior in other more modern democracies. The Greeks invented democracy but seldom practiced it; when they did, it usually fell far short of their own ideals as expressed by Pericles. We know their politics in great detail—more fully than those of any people we have yet considered.

Then too, the Greeks had far more humor than any of the other peoples, who, as we have seen—except for an occasional bit of playfulness the Egyptians reveal in their art—were by and large a solemn lot. The Greeks enjoyed laughter, whether playful and gentle or raucous and cruel. Moderns who enjoy the American musical comedy *Of Thee I Sing*, which satirizes our powerless Vice-Presidency and our tendency to be sentimental over politics, or who admire the Gilbert and Sullivan operettas that poke fun at the civilian head of Queen Victoria's Nay-vee or lampoon the aesthetic movement of which Oscar Wilde was the symbol, will find comparable topical satire in a light and witty mood in the comedies of Aristophanes (*see below,* p. 72). But Aristophanes is also capable of the violence and vulgarity and indecency typical of such a recent American political satire as, for example, *MacBird*. Touches of Charlie Chaplin and of the Marx Brothers make him instantly understandable and delightful. Brilliant, funny, energetic, inventive, opinionated, arrogant, and immensely quarrelsome, the Greeks are the first people of the ancient world whom we can feel we actually know.

REVIVAL AFTER THE DARK AGE

For the Greeks the Dark Age began to dissipate about 850 B.C., with the renewal of contact between the mainland and the Near East: Phoenicia, whose trade continued brisk, lay close to the Greek island of Cyprus, where Mycenaean culture had continued after the Dorians had ruined it on the mainland. Objects from Phoenicia now appear in mainland Greece; and the earliest traces of the Phoenician alphabet as adapted to the writing of Greek are now dated about 825 B.C. New letters were added for peculiarly Greek sounds. The general disorders of the Dark Age were coming to an end, and orderly life began to resume. New styles of pottery also testify to the renewal of communications. Greece proper now received the Homeric poems, first written down in the Ionian Greek settlements of Asia Minor, and bringing back to the mainland the sense of its glorious and heroic past.

In Greece itself, the poet Hesiod, writing in the language of Homer and in the same meter, in his *Works and Days* (c. 800 B.C.) set down the proper rules of life for the small farmer, and admonished his own brother, who had tried to take more than his fair share of the family estate. Hesiod also wrote a genealogy of the gods (*Theogony*), giving the traditional view of the way the universe had come into being: the gods were the children of earth and heaven, and had themselves created mankind. Preaching justice, human and divine, Hesiod's verse reflected the religious ideas of the Greeks in an early phase, perhaps partly under the influence of the oracle at Delphi, a mountain shrine of the sun-god Apollo in central Greece where a divinely inspired prophetess gave advice to all comers. The invading Dorians had become particular sponsors of the shrine at Delphi. To this earliest period of the revival also belongs the foundation of a famous Greek institution, the Olympic games, held every four years beginning with 776 B.C. at Olympia, shrine of Zeus in the western Peloponnesus. The records of the Olympic victors were preserved in the temple, and together with lists of kings and magistrates formed a source for the first Greek historians.

THE POLIS: SPARTA

The chief social and political form to emerge in reviving Greece was the *polis*, or city-state, which had begun in the Greek settlements of Asia Minor, and consisted of the municipality itself and the territory immediately surrounding it: small in size and in population, often centering on a fortress built on a hill—the high city or Acropolis. It was in the Dorian centers—first Crete, and then especially Sparta on the mainland—that such city-states first emerged. The one at Sparta is of course responsible for the overtones that the word "Spartan" still has in our ordinary language today.

Here, in what the philosopher Aristotle later called "an association of several villages which achieves almost complete self-sufficiency," only the upper five to ten per cent of the population were citizens; descendants of the Dorian conquerors, they were the rulers, hereditary landowners, and soldiers. The overwhelming majority of the people belonged to the *helot* class, farm laborers bound to the soil, servants of the ruling group. In between was a free class called *perioikoi* ("dwellers around"), descendants of the pre-Dorian residents of neighboring areas, who lived in the villages under Spartan control and had personal freedom but no right to participate in politics or to intermarry with the Spartans. The ruling Spartans lived in constant fear of revolution; they kept their secret agents planted among the helots to report subversive talk, and indeed barely managed to put down a helot uprising in the late seventh century.

The constitution, which the Spartans attributed to a divinely inspired lawgiver, Lycurgus, dating perhaps from about 825 B.C., provided that there should be two kings, descendants of two rival Dorian families. Real political power came to reside in five *ephors* (overseers) elected annually by an assembly of all Spartan citizens over 30, excluding, of course, all women, helots, and perioikoi. In addition, there was a kind of council of thirty elders representing the more powerful families.

War dominated Spartan thinking. The males lived under military discipline from the age of seven, when a boy was taken from his parents, and taught reading and music and running and fighting. Weak-looking babies were abandoned to die. So that there might be healthy children, girls too were given strenuous training. Adult males lived in the barracks until they were 30, though they might marry at 20, but they dined in the mess-hall until they were 60. It was a harsh, bleak life, "Spartan" in its merits and in its defects.

The army was excellent and the citizens were patriotic and able to bear misfortune. The need to keep hostile neighbors under control led the Spartans also to introduce clumsy iron bars as money in order to make ordinary commercial pursuits as unattractive and difficult as possible.

Their earliest poets wrote fine, sensitive lyrics, but soon this art vanished, and war-songs first, and then no poetry at all, replaced it. The Spartans were not artists, but fighters. A barracks-state, Sparta reminds twentieth-century students of the fascist states of the 1920's and 1930's.

COLONIZATION

Together with the establishment of city-states there took place a large-scale movement of Greek colonial expansion. The city-states of Asia Minor and of Greece proper sent out naval expeditions of their citizens to plant new settlements in non-Greek areas where there was no power strong enough to prevent it: around the edge of the Black Sea, along the African shore of the Mediterranean in what we now call Libya, in Sicily and along the Italian coasts (which the Romans later called *Magna Graecia*, "Great Greece"), and as far west as the coasts of France and Spain. Each new colony became a new city-state, independent of its mother-city but bound to it by sentimental and economic ties and by similar political and religious practices. It was no doubt overpopulation and internal strife in the settled cities together with the wish for trade and adventure that advanced the colonizing movement. Trebizond in Asia Minor, Panticapaeum in the Crimea, Byzantium (later to be Constantinople and still later Istanbul) at the Black Sea Straits, Syracuse in Sicily, Naples in southern Italy, Marseilles in southern France, and Cadiz beyond the Straits of Gibraltar on the Atlantic southern coast of Spain are among the famous cities that started their lives as Greek colonies.

Such foundations, and many others, combined with the decline of Egypt and the Assyrian conquests in western Asia, set off a whole new period of Mediterranean trade focussing on Greece. First one of the Greek cities and then another would assume prominence in the busy traffic: the Dorian-founded settlements on Crete, Rhodes, Corinth (with its strategic position at the isthmus that attaches the Peloponnesus to northern Greece), Megara: all became powerful and prosperous, as to a lesser extent did many other cities. By the mid-seventh century, coins, invented in the Anatolian kingdom of Lydia, had begun to be struck on the island of Aegina in Greece, where silver was the only precious metal available, and soon this convenient system spread westward. The coins of Aegina had turtles on them, those of Corinth foals, those of Athens from the sixth century onward the owl of Athena, goddess of the city.

ATHENS

Draco and Solon. Athens—which had never undergone a Dorian occupation—did not become a polis as soon as Sparta and Corinth, but lingered as an old-fashioned aristocratic tribal state, dominating the large surrounding hinterland of Attica. It was divided territorially into plains, hills, and coastal land, and politically into four tribes, each of which had three brotherhoods (*phratries*) or territorial subdivisions (*trittyes*). Within each phratry a further distinction was drawn between those who owned and worked their farms (the clans)—which were the earliest category—and those who belonged to a guild of artisans or merchants. The clans included numerous related families or households of varying degrees of nobility. Land descended in the clan and might not be alienated. With it went a deep attachment to the local religious shrines, whose priests were clansmen. Later in creation, the guildsmen were citizens but not aristocrats, and presumably could sell or transfer their property. Each mature male was admitted into a phratry either as a clansman or as a guild-member.

Three *archons* (leaders or principal persons)—one of whom managed religious affairs, one military affairs (the polemarch), and one civil affairs—were joined in the seventh century by a board of six recording archons, making nine in all. Each was elected for a year, at the end of which all nine automatically became members of the Council of the Areopagus (the hill of Ares, god of war, in Athens), the chief judicial and policy-making body. Although a general assembly of all the people directly elected the archons and so the future members of the Areopagus Council, only clansmen—people of birth and wealth, not guildsmen—could be elected.

Already ancient in the seventh century B.C., these political arrangements were challenged in 632 by a young noble's plot to seize power, which led to a scandal when his followers were massacred though they had taken sanctuary at the altar of Athena. The noble family held responsible for the sacrilege was banished, and in 621 a specially appointed official, Draco, published the first Athenian law-code, famous for its severe penalties: hence our term a "Draconian" measure. Harshest of all were the laws on debt: a bankrupt clansman could never sell off or mortgage his land, but was compelled to mortgage the produce of it to the debtor. Thus he would oblige himself and his heirs to work it indefinitely for somebody else, and in effect would lose his own freedom. Bankrupt guildsmen actually became the property of their creditors, as slaves. The growing inequity of this system led to civil strife.

In the 590's the reformer Solon freed both clansmen and guildsmen actually suffering these penalties for debt, cancelled current debts, and abolished the harsh system. He repealed almost all Draco's laws, and published a new code. He tried to improve the general prosperity by emphasizing the need to abandon complete economic dependence on agriculture and to foster a lively new commerce. He even offered citizenship to citizens of other poleis who would come to work in Athens. He opened the most important offices of state to rich guildsmen as well as rich clansmen: money, not birth, now counted chiefly.

He is also said to have founded a new body, the "Council of Four Hundred," consisting of one hundred members from each of the four tribes, all named by Solon himself, to act as a kind of inner circle of the general assembly of the people, preparing the materials for discussion and making recommendations for action: the general assembly now could not act without such a recommendation; but it could vote against it, and it still elected the archons. And Solon also made it a kind of court, by selecting a panel of assembly-members by lot to review the work of the magistrates.

Introducing these democratic innovations but keeping both the older aristocratic election only of the rich to magistracies and the oligarchic power of the few in the Council of Areopagus, Solon's reforms were really a radical set of compromises. In one of his own poems he says of his actions: "I stood holding my stout shield over both parties [the poor and the rich]; I did not allow either party to prevail unjustly." By justice Solon meant more than legal justice; he meant what

Archaic Greek sculpture: statue of a maiden, now in the Acropolis Museum, Athens.

we would call social justice. Though some of his fellow-Athenians jeered at him for not taking advantage of his extraordinary powers to line his own pockets, he answered (again in a poem) that "money flits from man to man, but honor abides forever." Urging the Athenians to abide by his laws for a hundred years, he withdrew from the scene for a decade.

Peisistratus and Cleisthenes. Civil strife at once began again. Athenians seem to have lined up in accordance with both region and class: the plains-people being mostly aristocrats who felt Solon had gone too far, the hill-people mostly poor farmers who felt he had not gone far enough, and the coast-people mostly artisans who thought he was about right. In 561 B.C. their quarrels gave Athens into the hands of a "tyrant," as the Greeks called a dictator, however benevolent: Peisistratus, a noble, who had made himself leader of the hill-people. In and out of office for some years, Peisistratus once managed to get back into power by dressing up a beautiful girl as Athena to show the citizens that the goddess herself wanted him admitted to her sanctuary on the Acropolis. His final return in 546 he owed to vast sums of money that he had made from the silver mines on his estates in the north, and to mercenary troops from Argos whom he hired with his wealth. Peisistratus and his sons dominated Athens until 510 B.C.

Though Solon's constitutional measures had not prevailed, his economic policy made Athens rich, as Athenian pottery became the best and most sought-after in Greece. Peisistratus—who collected ten per cent of all revenues for his personal fortune—pushed commercial success still further, partly by shrewd alliances with other poleis. At home, his was the only party. He exiled those aristocrats who refused to support him; he would often keep the son of a noble family as a hostage to ensure the family's loyalty. Having come to power as leader of the poor, he made them loans, embarked on a lavish program of public works to be sure there were jobs for all, subsidized the arts, and increased the magnificence of state religious celebrations. His sons, who succeeded him on his death in 528 B.C., followed his policies; but of course the noble families whom their father had displaced continued opposition, often from exile. When Hipparchus, one of the sons, was assassinated for personal reasons in 514 B.C., executions multiplied, government grew more tyrannical, and the exiled nobles came back in 510 B.C. By 508 Cleisthenes, one of the exiles, who appealed for the support of the guildsmen—already so much favored by Peisistratus—succeeded in his turn in coming to power by promises of constitutional reform.

These he fulfilled by striking at the political influence of the clans in elections, and giving the guildsmen equal weight. Using as the basic new political unit an old territorial division called a *deme*, a small area something like a ward in a modern city, Cleisthenes ordered all citizens registered as voters within their demes, irrespective of their origins, thus giving the guildsmen equal franchise with the clansmen. Whoever was a member of a given deme in the year 508–507 B.C. remained so permanently, and so did his descendants even if they moved away.

Cleisthenes also rezoned Attica into three new regions that did not coincide with the former coast, hill, and plain. He regrouped the demes into **trittyes** which, unlike the twelve older trittyes (*see above*, p. 47), were in general not arranged compactly and next to each other, but chosen from all three territorial subgroupings. Finally, by drawing lots he put every three trittyes together into a political "tribe." Instead of the four old racial (or genuinely tribal) tribes, there were ten of these new political tribes whose membership cut across the old family and regional and class lines. Each of these new, nontribal, artificial tribes had members from each of the three new territorial divisions, and the former influence of the noble families had been effectively cut down. Cleisthenes had invented a fundamental tool of democracy: the gerrymander.

Each deme annually elected a number of its members (proportionate to its population) as its representatives, and from them the new ten tribes selected by lot fifty each to be members of the new Council of Five Hundred, replacing Solon's Council of Four Hundred. Solon had given Athenians equality before the law; Cleisthenes gave them equality at the ballot box. The four old racial or tribal tribes, the old brotherhoods, the clans, continued to play a major part in religious and social life, but their political role was over.

Of course, the system was clumsy. The archons continued to administer, except that now (501) the whole Assembly of the People elected ten generals a year to serve as operational commanders under the polemarch. The Council of the Areopagus (ex-archons) retained its powers and its aristocratic complexion. Archons and generals continued to be aristocrats, and though they were often able, experienced, and patriotic, they struggled with each other for power and prestige, and tended to become the chiefs of rival factions. These rivalries would lead individuals to take different positions at different times in their careers. Cleisthenes himself had fluctuated between supporting and opposing the family of Peisistratus, had worked with and against both Spartans and Persians, and had at one time appealed to the nobles, at another to the people. These switches in loyalty were normal in Athenian politics but naturally increased its instability.

The ten groups of fifty tribal members of which the Council of Five Hundred was made up each governed in continual session for a tenth of the year (roughly 36 days), and the chairman of the committee of fifty that was sitting at any given time was selected afresh by lot every day. During each continual 36-day session the committee members (*prytaneis*) lived in a special state building and were fed at public expense. They could summon the remaining 450 councillors to a full session whenever they wished. No citizen between the ages of 30 and 60 could be a member of the council more than twice or chairman of a day's session more than once. Thus, with swiftly changing large groups of citizens receiving responsibilities for short times, almost any citizen could hope to enjoy the experience at some time during his life. Fortified by their new constitution—giving all citizens a stake in the community—the Athenians were prepared for their famous historic confrontation with the Persian Empire.

II. Persia and the Greeks, to 478 B.C.

THE PERSIAN EMPIRE

We have already encountered the Medes, an Indo-European people of the Near East, who in 612 B.C. cooperated with the briefly recovering Babylonians to destroy Nineveh and bring down the hated empire of the brutal Assyrians. We have also seen the Medes' southern relatives, the Persians, destroy Babylon (538) and allow the captive Hebrews to return to Jerusalem. It was Cyrus, the Persian ruler (557–529 B.C.) of the southern province, the captor of Babylon and liberator of the Jews, who attacked his northern kinsmen the Medes and took their capital (Ecbatana, south of the Caspian Sea), and so began a meteoric rise toward universal empire, the last and greatest to come out of the ancient Near East.

Uniting his territory with that of the Medes and bypassing Babylon, Cyrus moved westward into Anatolia, absorbed the Lydian kingdom of the rich King Croesus, and then attacked and conquered the Greek cities of Ionia along the Aegean coast. Next he moved east all the way to the borders of India, conquering and annexing as he went, but imposing no such tyranny as the Assyrian. Instead of deporting whole populations, Cyrus allowed them to worship as they pleased, honored their gods and their customs, and allowed them to keep on governing themselves in their own way under his representatives. The fall of Babylon led to the Persian conquest of Syria. Cyrus' son Cambyses (529–522 B.C.) invaded and conquered Egypt, and died on his way home to put down a revolution, which his brother-in-law and successor Darius (512–486 B.C.) succeeded in quelling.

It was Darius who subdivided the Empire into twenty provinces (satrapies), each with its political governor, its military governor, and its tax-collector, but otherwise running its own affairs. Royal agents crossed and crisscrossed the vast area from the Aegean to the Indus, collecting intelligence for the king. Darius took from the Lydians the practice of coining money and introduced it into all his dominions. The highway system was a marvel, a great network whose largest thread was the royal road that ran more than 1,600 miles from Susa, Darius' capital, to Sardis, the chief city of Lydia. It is likely that Darius himself introduced Zoroastrianism, the religion of Zarathustra, who had died only a generation earlier. In any case, Darius himself accepted the religion, and paid honors to its great god Ahuramazda without repudiating other gods.

Zoroastrianism began as a monotheistic faith, proclaiming the one god Ahuramazda, whose chief quality was his wisdom. He is the only intellectual deity we have so far encountered, and the other divinities around him were not gods and goddesses but abstract qualities such as Justice and Integrity, which he had created. It was the existence of evil in the universe that led Zarathustra to imagine that life was a constant struggle between a good spirit and an evil spirit, *both* subordinate to Ahuramazda. A wise man will ponder and then choose the good way; a foolish man will choose the evil way; and the supreme spirit will reward the wise and punish the foolish.

Intellectual and abstract, lacking ritual and priesthood, early Zoroastrianism was perhaps too impersonal and rarefied for a popular faith, and was modified after its founder's death. By identifying Ahuramazda with the good spirit, the next generations in effect demoted the supreme god, who was now no longer the ruler over the evil spirit (Ahriman) but only a contender with him. From a monotheism the religion became dualistic (giving comparable power to good and evil) and also revived elements of earlier polytheism, as old deities and ceremonies reappeared and a powerful priesthood asserted itself. At the moment of Darius' reign, however, the religion was still in its earliest phase.

THE IONIAN CITIES; THE THREAT TO GREECE; MARATHON

Though tolerant with regard to religion and local custom, as we have seen, the new Persian rulers would not allow their subjects political freedom, which was precisely what the now captive Ionian Greek cities most valued. Their prosperity also declined, as the Persians drew toward Asia the wealth of the trade routes that had formerly enriched the Aegean towns. By 513, the Persians had crossed the Bosphorus on a pontoon bridge, sailed up the Danube, and moved north across modern Rumania into the Ukraine in a campaign against the nomadic people called Scythians. Though indecisive, the new advance into Europe alarmed the Greeks, who were now receiving overtures for an alliance from the Scythians: it looked as if Darius would move south against European Greece from his new base in the northern Balkans.

Some of the Greek poleis—Sparta and her allies—were hostile to the Persians; but there were others that had pro-Persian rulers. One of Peisistratus' sons, Hippias, had taken refuge with the Persians, who were backing his return to Athens, but about 505 B.C. the Athenians refused to accept him, and soon afterwards decided to give help to the captive Ionian cities in their resistance to Persian rule. The Ionians then rebelled; with Athenian help they burned down Sardis, the former Lydian capital and now headquarters for the Persians in Asia Minor (499 B.C.). Encouraged, many other Greek cities joined the rebellion.

But the Persians struck back, and by 495 B.C. had defeated the ships of the Greek cities in the Aegean; they burned the most important Ionian city—Miletus—massacred many of its men, and deported its women and children. By 493 B.C. the Ionian revolt was over, and in the next two years the Persians extended their authority along the northern coasts of Greece proper, directly threatening Athens. It was probably Hippias who advised the Persian commanders whom he was accompanying to land at Marathon, in a region once loyal to his father Peisistratus, only about 25 miles north of Athens. There a far smaller Athenian force decisively led by Miltiades defeated the Persians and put an end for ten years to the Persian threat to Greece. Because the Spartans had been celebrating a religious festival during which military operations were taboo, they had been unable to participate in the fighting; only the much smaller polis of Plataea had sent 1,000 troops to join the 10,000 Athenians. The credit for driving off the Persians therefore went primarily to Athens. Darius now planned a much greater invasion, but first an Egyptian uprising and then his death (486) delayed it. His successor Xerxes (486–465), having subdued the Egyptians in 485, resumed the elaborate preparations.

THE 480'S

By the time Xerxes was ready to try again, the Athenians had removed their hero Miltiades from an active role in their affairs. Like other Athenian leaders he had had the usual varied career: at one time pro-Peisistratus, at another anti-, at one time pro-Persian, at another the hero of Marathon. A leader of the nobles, he was eventually brought down by a rival faction.

It was probably now (488 B.C.) that some leader first invented the famous practice known as ostracism. The word comes from *ostrakon,* a fragment of a clay pot on which the individual citizens scribbled the name of any politician they wished to exile from the city for a period of ten years. Apparently a majority of a meeting of 6,000 citizens (i.e., 3,001 votes) was needed to ostracize. The 480's—the decade of preparation for Xerxes' expected attacks—was the decade of ostracism *par excellence:* many hundreds of the original clay potsherds still exist with the names of prominent politicians written on them, a sort of negative ballot. We know that by and large the citizens ostracized the leaders of the Peisistratid party and many other politicians. By 480 they had been eliminated, and Themistocles had emerged as the popular choice to lead the resistance to the new Persian invasion.

The 480's also saw a reform in the method of choosing the nine archons, who after 487 were no longer elected by the people but selected by lot from a preliminary list, drawn up by the demes, of five hundred candidates, who still had to be among the richer citizens. Each deme could put down on the list a number of its own men in proportion to its population. This reform further reduced the influence of the aristocratic clans. Moreover, it gradually reduced the influence of the Council of the Areopagus (made up of ex-archons), since more and more its members became men chosen in the new way. Because the generals were still elected, the old political rivalry for the archonship now shifted to the office of general, and factional struggle continued.

New supplies of silver were discovered in the nick of time, and Themistocles persuaded the Athenians to use the money to build a new fleet instead of passing it out among the citizens, a decision that probably determined the outcome of the Persians' new effort, and that incidentally suited the poor, who built the ships and rowed them and whose fortunes were associated with the navy. As the leading military power of Greece, with many allies including Athens, Sparta took over the leadership of the anti-Persian Greek poleis, which together formed an anti-Persian League with a congress of delegates from the individual cities and a unified command. Knowing that its forces would be greatly outnumbered (perhaps 110,000 against 500,000 Persians), the League did not try to defend the northern cities, where the Persian cavalry could operate freely, but instead abandoned them.

XERXES INVADES

The events of the year 480 B.C. are deservedly celebrated: Xerxes' huge army, its supply-lines greatly overextended and its speed slowed down by its very numbers, crossed into Europe and swung south into Greece, while a fleet, possibly of 3,000 ships of various sizes, sailed along the coast. At the pass of Thermopylae in central Greece a Greek traitor showed the Persians how to outflank the defenders, but a small army of Spartans—only 300 strong—defended the pass to the last man, taking a terrible toll of the Persian infantry. A storm, a battle, and a second storm cut the Persian fleet in half. The Delphic oracle had mysteriously prophesied that Athens would be destroyed but had advised the Athenians to put their trust in their "wooden walls." Themistocles succeeded in persuading the Athenians that the message meant they should abandon the city and rely upon their fleet—their wooden ships—for their defense.

Athens was accordingly evacuated, except for the defenders of the Acropolis, who were killed. Xerxes' men plundered the city. But the fleet in the narrow waters of the harbor of Salamis off Athens awaited the Persian attack, despite fierce debate and disagreement among the Greeks. Themistocles eventually sent a misleading message to the Persians pretending that he would betray the Greeks, and so persuaded them that it was safe to attack. The Greek fleet—helped by deserters from the Persians who revealed Xerxes' battle-plans—won a smashing victory, which Xerxes himself watched from a great throne set up on shore. Xerxes had to withdraw from Greece, for autumn was setting in. In the next year

(479) at Plataea the united Greek forces numbering more than 100,000 men defeated the Persian troops once again, after Attica had again been invaded and devastated. This time they massacred the enemy.

The maintenance of Greek unity was most impressive: in spite of the thousands of personal and municipal rivalries among the Greeks, all members of the League had kept the oath "I shall fight to the death, I shall put freedom before life, I shall not desert colonel or captain alive or dead, I shall carry out the generals' commands, and I shall bury my comrades-in-arms where they fall and leave none unburied." A wildly individualistic people had shown that they could put the general interest ahead of all else. Soon afterwards at Mycale (478 B.C.) the Greeks scored another victory on land and sea. The Persians, as it turned out, had been stopped forever, although peace was not formally made until 448, and at many times during those three decades the threat of renewed invasion hung over the heads of the Greeks.

III. The Athenian Empire, 478–404 B.C.

POSTWAR REORGANIZATION

When the Athenians began to rebuild and refortify Athens, the Spartans asked them to stop, maintaining that the new walls might be useful to the Persians if they ever again invaded Greece; but Themistocles, as ambassador to Sparta, trickily played for time until the walls had already been built. The episode shows Themistocles once again as able and somewhat unscrupulous; it serves as a symbol of Athens' unwillingness to let Sparta, as the strongest military power, take the lead in planning for the future defense against Persia. It was indeed Athens, from 478 on the strongest naval power, that organized the new Greek alliance, designed to liberate the Ionian cities still subject to Persia and to maintain the defenses. Athens contributed most of the ships, but the other cities were assessed contributions in both ships and money. The treasury of the alliance was on the island of Delos; therefore the alliance is sometimes called the Delian League. It scored a major victory over the Persians in Asia Minor about 467 B.C.

Domestic Athenian politics continued savage: Themistocles was ostracized about 472; while in exile, he was charged with corruption; he fled to the Persians, was given rich revenues, and died in the service of Xerxes' son and successor. Immensely able, Themistocles somehow seemed not quite trustworthy. He accurately foresaw both the successes and the great danger that lay ahead for Athens: the long-range threat from Sparta. Like Miltiades, he lost the confidence of the Athenians after he had done them invaluable service.

In 462 a new reform further democratized Athenian government: the Areopagus Council was shorn of its powers and left a mere figurehead, while the Council of Five Hundred and the Assembly were the beneficiaries. Though put through largely by Ephialtes, the reform was partly inspired by a brilliant young aristocratic politician named Pericles (a grandson of Cleisthenes). By about 457 the patriotic and incorruptible Pericles had become the leading Athenian politician, responsible for the many military and naval operations conducted simultaneously against the Persians (chiefly in Egypt: an expensive failure), the Spartans, and certain members of the Athenian alliance itself who resented the dictatorial ways of Athens.

Ancient Greece

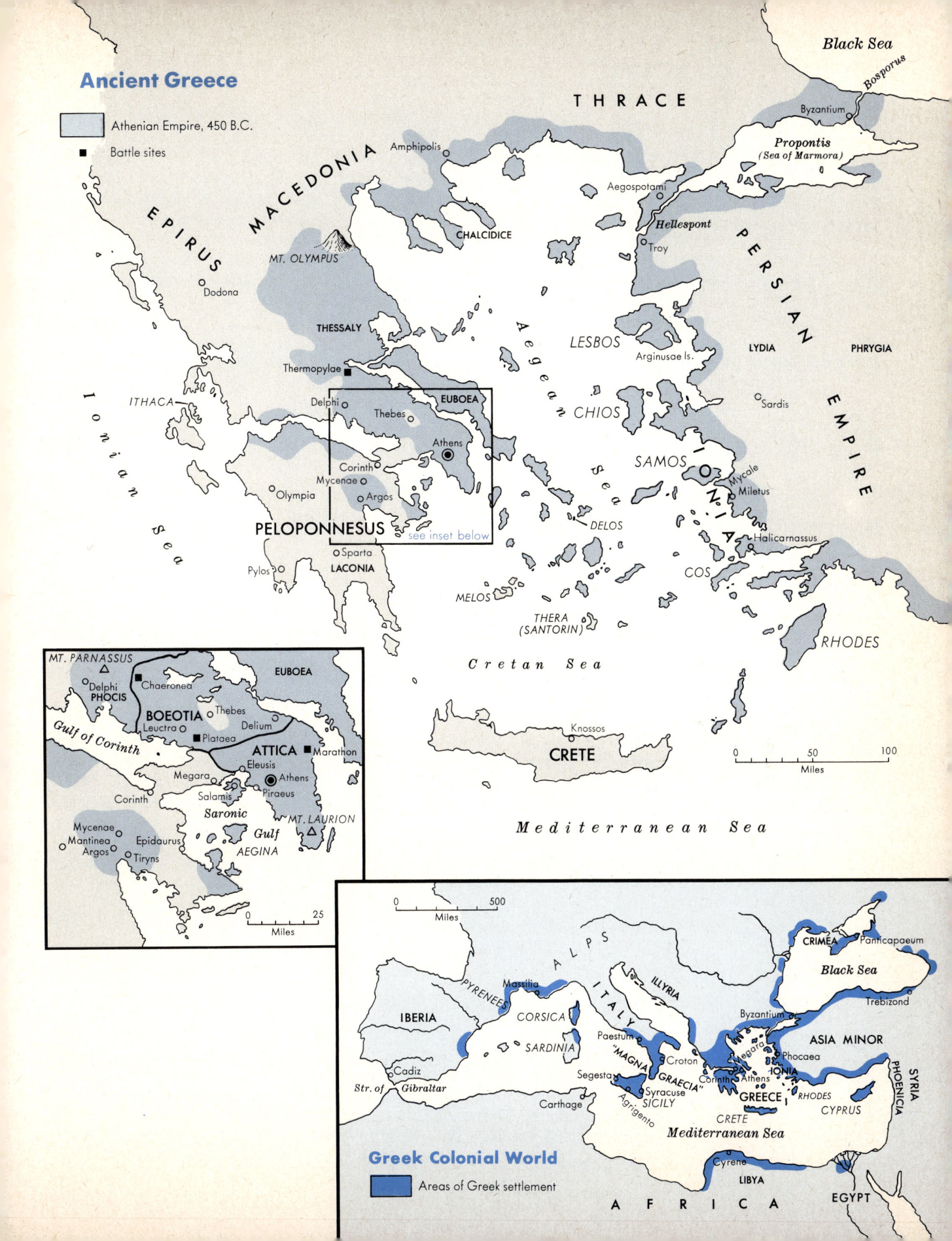

- Athenian Empire, 450 B.C.
- ■ Battle sites

Greek Colonial World
- Areas of Greek settlement

At home Pericles pushed democracy, inaugurating a system of state pay, first for the jurymen (drawn from a panel 6,000 strong, 600 from each tribe) and later for those rendering other services to the state. State service was thus transformed from an activity that the poor could not afford to one that they welcomed. In order to limit the number of those eligible for such payment, Pericles also now limited Athenian citizenship to those both of whose parents were Athenian. The money to pay all these people could come only from the allies.

FROM ALLIANCE TO EMPIRE

In fact, Pericles was in the process of turning the Athenian alliance into an empire, with the subject members providing the money for Athens, which in turn would defend them all, and would be able to challenge Sparta. In 454 the treasury of the alliance was moved from Delos to Athens, and became in effect a major Athenian resource. Since 470, no ally had been allowed to secede. During a truce with the Spartans (451–446 B.C.), the Athenians, operating in the Aegean, increased the number of their allies (about 170 cities at the peak), and in 448 made a peace with Persia that liberated the Ionian cities and bound the Persians not to come within three days' journey of the coast.

Athenian settlements were founded on the territories of some allied states, and Athenian coinage was standard. Resentment against Athens was naturally widespread among the allies. But in 446–445 a new thirty years' treaty with Sparta provided that neither side would commit aggression against the other. Both had lost the good will of the other Greek poleis: Athens was now ruling an empire by force and its services against the Persians seemed less magnanimous; Sparta had suffered defeats and its reputation was dimmed.

The thirty years' truce, as it turned out, lasted only for fifteen (446–431). It was a prosperous period, during which Pericles continued to dominate the affairs of state, but he was elected general democratically every year. He had at his disposal the large surpluses in the imperial treasury, which mounted in these years of peace, and which with Athens' other revenues were much more than enough to pay the 10,000 rowers of the warships, the 700 officials, the 500 councillors, the 6,000 jurors, and many others. Pericles embarked upon a great program of public works, of which the two most famous buildings were the temple of Athena Parthenos (the virgin), the celebrated Parthenon, and the Propylaea (monumental gateway), both on the Acropolis. After one had mounted the steps that led up to the Propylaea, and passed through it, there at the top of the hill was the giant bronze statue of Athena sculptured by Phidias, a personal friend of Pericles, and behind it and to the right was the entrance portico of the magnificent new temple. Inside was another statue of Athena, this one in gold and ivory, also by Phidias.

There were plenty of jobs available in the building program, and slaves as well as freemen participated and were well paid. There was money and opportunity for everybody: for the 30,000 resident aliens ("metics"), who had to pay a special tax, and were not allowed to own land or participate in politics, but contributed to the city's and their own good fortune in a variety of ways, chiefly commercial; for the 200,000 slaves, whose lot was easier than it was elsewhere, and who were often set free; and most of all for the 168,000 Athenian citizens (4,000 upper class, 100,000 middle class, and 64,000 lower class).*

* All such statistics are mere approximations. No exact figures can be given.

THE PELOPONNESIAN WAR

The First Fifteen Years, 431–416 B.C. The splendid civilization of Athens in the fifth century depended upon the continued exercise of complete control over the subject poleis in the empire. A growing number of incidents in which the Athenians ruthlessly asserted their power alarmed the Spartans: if they did not fight soon, they feared, they might not be able to win. They tried to force the Athenians to make concessions, but Pericles, with the support of the Assembly, said only that Athens would consent to have all disputed questions arbitrated.

In 431 began the ruinous Peloponnesian War (431–404 B.C.). The Spartans invaded Attica in order to force a military decision. Pericles countered by withdrawing the entire population within the city walls, which had been extended to include the suburbs and to give access to the sea. He intended to avoid pitched battles with the superior Spartan troops on land, and to match his defensive policy on land by an offensive policy at sea, launching seaborne raids against enemy territory and inviting naval battles.

These tactics worked well in the first year of the war; but in 430 a terrible plague broke out in Athens, where the whole population of Attica was cooped up with no sanitation. In 429 Pericles himself died of it, leaving Athens without the trusted leader who could make even unpopular policies acceptable. The plague raged until the end of 426, and cost Athens about a third of its population, including its best troops. It did not deter the Athenians from continuing the war, with general though costly success at sea and even, contrary to Pericles' policies, on land.

By 424, Athens could probably have ended the war on favorable terms, and the upper and the middle classes that had suffered most from it were eager to do so: it was their lands in Attica which the Spartans ravaged, and their members who made up most of the land-forces that did the heavy fighting. But the lower classes, identified with the fleet, which was still in fine condition, hoped for even greater gains, and wanted to continue the war, and since they now dominated the city's politics, the war continued.

Not until 421 could the peace party conclude the Peace of Nicias (so called after its leader), which provided that each side restore captured places and prisoners, and remain at peace with the other for fifty years. This was soon supplemented by an actual Spartan–Athenian alliance, also concluded for fifty years, but intended chiefly to give each power a chance to put its own alliance in order while secure from an attack by the other. The war had been marked by numerous acts of brutality on both sides: brutality not only by our modern standards (which offer little cause for boasting in any case) but by Greek standards: prisoners were slaughtered and enslaved, and agreements broken in a way that contemporaries felt to be blameworthy.

Alcibiades and Failure. The peace lasted five years, 421–416 B.C., which saw the gradual rise to eminence in Athenian politics of Pericles' nephew, Alcibiades, a brilliant, ambitious, dissolute, and unstable youth, who succeeded the demagogic Cleon as leader of the lower-class war party against the restrained and unglamorous Nicias. Athenian efforts to support Argos against Sparta only ended in the defeat of Argos and Athens and the strengthening of Spartan prestige. By killing all the adult males of the island of Melos and enslaving the women and children as a punishment for Melos' insistence on staying neutral in the war (415), Athens underlined its own ruthlessness. By deciding, against Nicias' prudent counsel, to send off a large naval expedition to Sicily to attack the great Greek city of Syracuse (which had opposed Athens in the past, and was the ally of Selinus, a town engaged in a war with Segesta, an ally of Athens), the Athenian assembly once again followed Alcibiades' lead—he said there would be great glory in it, and that all Sicily and then Greece would become subject to Athens.

Yet the project bore no real relationship to Athenian interests: it was irrelevant to the politics of mainland Greece, and the Athenians had little sound military intelligence about Sicily. Just before the expedition sailed, a scandal broke out in Athens: the statues of Hermes that stood before the doors of temples and houses were mutilated in the night (the sexual organ was broken off), and Alcibiades—who was known to have committed similar sacrilege before when in a wild and dissipated mood—was suspected. But he went off to Sicily, as co-commander with his opponent, the unwilling Nicias, of the greatest naval expedition ever sent out by a Greek polis. Before the fleet reached Syracuse, Alcibiades was recalled to stand trial for the mutilation of the Hermae; but he escaped to Sparta.

The siege of Syracuse was long drawn out (414–413), enormously expensive in ships, money, and men (200 ships, more than 40,000 seamen, at least 10,000 troops), and a total failure: Nicias and other leaders were captured and killed. While it was going on, Sparta, now advised by Alcibiades (who also seduced the wife of the Spartan king, Agis), renewed the war at home, and sent troops to help the Syracusans. The Spartans also stirred up the Ionian cities to revolt against Athens. The Persian satraps in Asia Minor, hoping to regain sea-coast towns lost so long before, joined with the Spartans. Alcibiades, who had worn out his welcome in Sparta, now joined the Persians.

Ironically enough the balance of power between the two great Greek poleis that in 490 and 480–479 had so gloriously expelled the Persians from Greece was now, in 412, held by the very same Persians. Alcibiades tried to blackmail the Athenians by telling them that if they would install an oligarchic government, he would return and exercise his influence with the Persians on their behalf; while the Spartans promised the Persians that in exchange for paying for their fleet, they would permit the cities of Ionia to fall into Persian hands once more.

Civil strife accompanied by assassinations of those who opposed a change in the constitution created a turbulent atmosphere in Athens. A group of conspirators first prevailed on the Assembly to appoint a team to draft a new oligarchic constitution, and then persuaded a rump session to accept the recommendation that the existing officials be dismissed. A group consisting of five presidents appointed a hundred associates, who in turn co-opted three hundred more, and this now became the new Council of State, which ousted the former Council of Five Hundred by an armed but bloodless *coup d'état*. The new 400 could summon at will a new 5,000, ostensibly to replace the traditional assembly of all the citizens. The democratic forces still controlled the fleet.

The leading oligarchs would now have liked to proceed at once to peace with Sparta, and probably intended that the 5,000 should never be summoned. From exile, Alcibiades, however, did not back their aims, but indicated his preference for the summoning of the 5,000. After a naval defeat, the citizens actually deposed the oligarchic 400 and elected the 5,000—all upper class—which gov-

Ten-drachma silver coin from Syracuse (fifth century B.C.) showing a charioteer.

erned the city from 411 to 410 B.C., when, after some Athenian successes at sea, democracy was restored.

Alcibiades continued to command Athenian naval forces at sea without returning home until 407, when he came to Athens and was absolved for the mutilation of the Hermae; but the Spartan fleet defeated him in 406, and he went into retirement on his estates along the Dardanelles, where he was murdered three years later by Spartan and Persian agents. His career vividly illustrates the vulnerability of the Athenian democracy to a plausible, charming, talented scoundrel. Another weakness—the temptation to yield to impulse—was displayed soon afterwards, when the Athenians had defeated the Spartan fleet (at Arginusae) but had suffered heavy casualties, and the Council was intimidated by the mourning families of the drowned soldiers into ordering the collective executions of six generals, on the charge of not rescuing the troops in the water. The Council paid no attention to the fact that one of the generals had himself been swimming for safety at the time. The people later regretted their act, but the generals were dead.

In the final naval action of the war, the Spartans captured most of the Athenian fleet empty on a beach in the Dardanelles while the sailors were hunting food on shore (Aegospotami, 405), and the Spartan infantry rounded up thousands of Athenian prisoners, of whom 3,000 were executed as direct reprisal for recent Athenian atrocities. Starving, blockaded by land and sea, its alliance in ruins as the allies had defected or joined the Spartans, Athens had to surrender. Some of the Spartan allies wanted to punish the Athenians as the Athenians had punished the Melians, but the Spartans refused. The Athenians had to demolish their long walls, abandon their empire, surrender their fleet, and undertake to follow the Spartan lead in foreign policy. But they were not massacred.

IV. The Fourth Century B.C. and the Hellenistic Age

SPARTAN HEGEMONY

As the victors, the Spartans found themselves dominant in a Greece where polis hated polis and, within each polis, faction hated faction. From Ionia, which the Spartans had sold back to Persia as the price of victory, the Persians loomed once more as a threat to the whole Greek world. By mid-century the new state of Macedonia in the north menaced the Greeks. Perhaps wiser or more vigorous leaders would have been able to create some sort of federation among the individual poleis that could have withstood the Persians and the Macedonians, and, still later, the Romans. But since this did not happen, it seems more likely that the polis as an institution was no longer the appropriate way for the Greek world to be organized. Perhaps it was too small, too provincial, too old-fashioned to keep the peace and give men room for economic advancement and intellectual growth.

Sparta proved as unable as Athens to manage Greece. The Spartan government, suitable for a state that had no job but war, was largely in the hands of the elders, too conservative to meet new challenges. Gold and silver had found their way into the simple agricultural economy whose founders had preferred to use bars of iron as exchange. Many Spartans for the first time found themselves disfranchised for debt, and so relegated to the status of "inferiors." They joined the helots and perioikoi as part of a discontented majority, at precisely the moment when Sparta needed more "equals"—full, enfranchised fighting citizens. Away from home the Spartans could neither relinquish the cities of the former Athenian Empire in which they had installed governments of their own oligarchic type, nor occupy them satisfactorily.

At Athens, for example, an oligarchy of thirty (the thirty tyrants) instituted a reign of terror (instigated by the extremist Critias) not only against democrats associated with past regimes but also against moderate oligarchs. In 403 an invading force of exiled democrats killed Critias, and touched off a brief civil war. At Athens they restored democracy, but the thirty tyrants and their sympathizers were set up as a Spartan puppet state nearby at Eleusis. Nobody was allowed to move between the two separate Athenian states. In 401 the Athenians treacherously killed the generals of the Eleusis armies, and the two states were reunited. It was the government of this insecurely re-established Athens that tried and condemned the philosopher Socrates in 399 B.C. (*see below*, p. 76).

The Spartans could not pose as the leaders of Greece and simultaneously keep their bargain with the Persians to sell Ionia back to them; yet if they went back on this bargain, the Persians would start a new war. So in 401 B.C., when the younger brother of Artaxerxes II, King of Persia—Cyrus the Younger, governor of Asia Minor—rebelled against Artaxerxes and asked for Spartan aid, Sparta gave it to him. Cyrus was soon killed in a battle deep in Mesopotamia, and his Greek troops were left high and dry in the heart of Persia. Their disciplined march north to the shores of the Black Sea and the Greek city of Trebizond on its shore forms the substance of a book called the *Anabasis* ("The March Back") by the Athenian Xenophon, one of their officers. The episode left the Spartans at war with Persia.

The Spartans did not unite their land and sea commands, but gave the Persians time to build a fleet, which they put under an Athenian admiral, Conon. The Persians also bribed Thebes, Corinth, Argos, and Athens to stir up so much trouble against Sparta that Spartan troops had to be recalled from Persia to fight a new war in Greece proper. It lasted eight years (to 386); saw the self-assertion of Thebes; seemed to produce the threat of a renewed Athenian Empire; and ended in stalemate, as the Persians and Spartans finally got together and imposed a peace ("The King's Peace," 380 B.C.) by which the Persians resumed control of all Greek states in Asia, and the rest were autonomous.

THEBES RISES TO HEGEMONY

Raising money from their allies, hiring mercenaries to intimidate all resistance, the Spartans systematically disciplined and punished the cities that dared resist, installing an oligarchy at Thebes (382) and in lesser places, breaking their promise to respect the autonomy of all Greek cities. A group of Theban democratic exiles conspired to overthrow the pro-Spartan regime there (379 B.C.), and when the Spartans tried to punish them, a new war broke out, in which Athens participated after 377 as the leading power in a new anti-Spartan league, joined by many Greek cities.

By 371, the Spartans were ready for peace, a guarantee of independence to all Greek states, and disarmament. But the wording of the treaty gave Persia and Athens the leading roles as guarantors, and deliberately limited the Thebans to signing for Thebes only, not for their own league of allies (the Boeotian League). So Epaminondas, the chief Theban delegate, refused to sign, and soon afterward roundly defeated the Spartans at the battle of Leuctra. Cities subject to Sparta began to oust their oligarchic governments and install democracies. Epaminondas followed up his successes by two invasions of the Peloponnesus (369, 368), which destroyed Spartan power in its own homeland. Ugly and tyrannical, Spartan power vanished from Greece unmourned. It was no credit to Athens that in the final stages she helped Sparta out of fear of Thebes.

As head of the Boeotian League, Thebes under Epaminondas not only had a democratic government of its own, but treated its allies rather as equals than as subjects, and so commanded a true federation rather than an empire like the first Athenian Alliance or the Spartan Alliance. Other local leagues of cities followed the Boeotian example and were affiliated with Thebes. Warfare continued despite the effort of the Persians to dictate a general peace (367), as the Athenians reverted to their former imperialist practices and installed colonies of Athenian settlers on the soil of conquered cities. The Thebans fought in the Peloponnesus, in the north, against Athens at sea, and finally in the Peloponnesus again, where an alliance of Sparta and Athens and several other poleis met them in battle at Mantinea (362).

Epaminondas was killed at a moment when his forces were winning, but they stopped fighting when they heard of his death, and their enemies got away. All hope that Thebes could put an end to the interminable fighting among Greeks died with Epaminondas, a leader of extraordinary military talent and political generosity, who preferred leadership to domination, but whose own people, the Boeotians, largely deserved their reputation elsewhere in Greece as country bumpkins, uncultivated and crude, with a strong streak of ruthlessness which even Epaminondas could not always control.

Though a new league of city-states was now formed (362) to end war and to enable the Greeks as a whole to determine their foreign policy, Athens continued to act as the rival of Thebes and to play the traditional political game of alliance-building within the league. Though ineffective, the league was an important effort to create something like a United States of Greece. Without its restraints, Thebes found itself broken in war against the city of Phocis, whose general had seized the shrine of Delphi and used the accumulated funds there to create a large army of mercenaries (354). For its part Athens strove to reconstruct its old Aegean Empire, but in 357 found that many of its most important outposts had rebelled (the "Social War": i.e., war of the allies, 357–355), and was forced to grant them freedom in 355. Athens was exhausted and broke and weak.

Ironically enough, the inability of the Greek cities to give up fighting was almost surely due in part to general prosperity. Whereas during the fifth century only Athens and Sparta had been able to afford large armies and navies, during the fourth many other cities grew rich enough to support such forces. Brisk Mediterranean commerce brought wealth to the distant Greek settlements from the Crimea to Spain; it was not only goods that flowed but also slaves and mercenary troops: it is estimated that shortly after mid-century the Persians alone had 50,000 Greek troops fighting in their armies.

Many of the devices of modern capitalism to make international trade easier now first made their appearance: banking and credit, insurance, trade-treaties, and special privileges. Private wealth grew apace, and was widely distributed. Slaves grew in number; we know of several people who owned more than 1,000 of them; by 338 B.C. there may have been as many as 150,000 in Attica, working in the mines and at other occupations. All this prosperity meant that states quickly recovered from defeats in war and could quickly afford to try again. Patriotism became more and more a matter of cutting up the melon of profits. At the same time, the poor grew poorer; unwilling to declass themselves by engaging in the manual labor that was now the work of slaves, they became vagrants or mercenary soldiers.

MACEDON

North of Thessaly, and extending inland into areas that are today part of Yugoslavia and Albania, lay the kingdom of Macedon, with a considerable coastline along the Aegean. The Macedonians were a mixture of peoples including some of Greek origin; they were organized into tribes, worshipped some of the Greek gods, and spoke a native language which the Greeks could not understand, although it included many words of Greek origin. Their hereditary kings—who were also elected by the people—claimed Greek descent; indeed they believed they were descendants of the hero Herakles, son of Zeus himself.

The king spoke Greek as well as the native language, had title to all land, and ruled absolutely so long as he was not charged with treason (when the people might depose him). He was advised by councillors who were selected from among the nobles of each tribe and felt themselves to be his social equals. Although the Greeks had planted some poleis along the Macedonian shore, and although Greek cultural influence and Greek trade had penetrated deeply into Macedon by the fourth century, Macedon did not copy Greek political institutions, but kept its own, much more nearly like those of Mycenaean Greece in the days of Agamemnon. Traditionally the Macedonians relied on cavalry in war, but in the fourth century they added foot-soldiers in order to fight their neighbors from the west and north, the Illyrians (probable ancestors of the Albanians of today). Both Athens and Sparta interfered and intrigued in internal Macedonian affairs.

The Achievement of Philip. In 359, a prince of the ruling house, Philip, became regent for his infant nephew, the king. Having lived for three years as a hostage in Thebes, where he knew Epaminondas, Philip was well versed in Greek affairs. He applied Theban military principles to his army (emphasizing infantry tactics), led it in person, defeated the Illyrians and various rivals for power within Macedon, was elected king in his own right, and broke the power of Athens in the territory neighboring his own to the east (359–354 B.C.). He exploited the rich gold and silver mines in his kingdom, and struck his own coinage. He scored successes in Thessaly and in Thrace, where he threatened Athenian possessions along the shore of the Dardanelles (354–351).

Athenian politicians viewed Philip's advance with mixed feelings. Some favored him, others opposed. It was not until he had won still more territory and begun to use a fleet successfully that the famous Athenian orator Demosthenes began to warn against the threat from Macedon. But Philip had annexed the peninsula of Chalcidice and detached the big island of Euboea, close to Attica itself, from its Athenian loyalties.

At that point he suggested peace and an alliance with Athens, which was reached with the approval even of Demosthenes (346), though Philip meanwhile had secured control over the Delphic oracle. He was moving south and consolidating his power as he came. By 342, the Athenians had acquired new allies in the Peloponnesus. In retaliation Philip moved into Thrace (modern Bulgaria) to cut off the Athenian grain supplies coming from the Black Sea, and to avert a new Persian–Athenian alliance. Once again Demosthenes pressed for war, and Athens took military action in Euboea (341, 340). Philip declared his intention of punishing her now for unneutral acts. By late 339 he was deep in Greece once again, only two days distant from Attica. Acting under the gun, Demosthenes now arranged an eleventh-hour alliance with Thebes, which however proved unavailing. Protesting at intervals his wishes for peace, Philip totally defeated the Athenian–Theban alliance at Chaeronea in Boeotia (338 B.C.). He occupied Thebes, which had surrendered, but spared Athens a military occupation on condition that the Athenian Alliance be dissolved and an alliance with Macedon adopted. He showed leniency, and proved that in fact he had never intended to destroy Athens, as Demosthenes had maintained.

Philip's victories aroused in many the hope of a unified Greece. In the Peloponnesus all the poleis except Sparta honored him. At Corinth in 337 B.C., all the poleis (again with the exception of Sparta) met and organized a league that called itself "The Greeks," all members of which bound themselves to stop fighting and intervening in each other's affairs. This was a far more closely knit body than the abortive League of 362 (*see above*, p. 61). It immediately allied itself with Macedon, and then joined with Philip in a declaration of war on Persia to revenge the sacrilege of Xerxes' invasion of 143 years earlier. Philip was to command the expedition. By 336 B.C. the advance forces of the army were already liberating the Ionian cities from Persia. But Philip, aged only 46, was now assassinated at his daughter's wedding by a Macedonian noble who was acting for personal rather than political motives.

Philip's accomplishments greatly impressed his contemporaries, who realized that no such powerful consolidated state as his Macedon had ever existed west of Asia. Instead of allowing the resources of Macedon to be dissipated in flashy conquests, he organized the people he conquered, both in the Balkan area from the Adriatic to the Black Sea and in Greece. He kept morale high in the army, and had the various contingents from the various regions competing to see who would do the best job. He differentiated his troops into more specialized units for diverse tasks in war, and he commanded the unit that had the roughest assignment. He could appreciate the strengths of his Greek opponents, and when he had defeated them he utilized their skills and made sure of their loyalty by decent treatment. By his final effort to unify them against their traditional Persian enemy, he associated himself with the ancient patriotic cause that so many of them had so often betrayed but that obviously still had great appeal for them. Though he felt himself to be part of Greek civilization, he reminds many students of the Greece of an earlier age than his own, and is often regarded as a kind of Homeric hero in the flesh almost a thousand years after the siege of Troy.

The Achievement of Alexander. Philip's son Alexander the Great belongs to legend as much as to history. Alexander loved war, politics, athletics, alcohol, poetry, medicine, and science. He was only 20 when he came to the throne. Within a dozen years he led his armies on a series of triumphal marches that won for Macedon the largest empire yet created in the ancient world. He began by crushing a Greek revolt led by Thebes (335 B.C.), whose entire population he sold into slavery (he did not massacre the males, as the Spartans and Athenians often did). Next he crossed the Aegean into Asia Minor to continue the war of the Greek League against Persia, and recapture the Ionian cities. He defeated the Persians at the river Granicus (334 B.C.), and took over Ionia, where he established democracies in the poleis. In territories belonging to the Persians he took title to all land, thus replacing the Persian king, whom he defeated again at Issus (333 B.C.), and so opened up Syria. He reduced Tyre by siege, and refused King Darius' offer of a Persian princess and all territory west of the Euphrates.

Egypt was next, and it fell easily. Here he founded the great port of Alexandria in the Nile Delta (332), a Greek city from the beginning. But he paid his respects to the Egyptian divinities, and allowed himself to be treated as a god, according to the Egyptian way. Then he marched east and defeated the Persians again in Mesopotamia (Gaugamela, near Nineveh, 331 B.C.). The Persian Empire was smashed. Alexander sacrificed to Marduk in Babylon, and ordered his temple restored; the Persians had destroyed it. Vast mopping-up operations continued in Persia proper (330–327), as Alexander's armies seized the chief cities and all the Persian royal treasure—perhaps half a billion dollars in cash. But he treated the Persian royal family with great courtesy, and acted toward his new subjects just as a king of Persia would have done. The Persian nobles came to acknowledge him as King by the grace of Ahuramazda. In fact, Alexander *was* King of Persia, and so called himself, just as he was Pharaoh of Egypt, King of Babylon, King of Macedon, and commander (*hegemon*) of the Greek League.

Far out in Central Asia, Alexander fell in love with and married the daughter of a local chieftain, who joined forces with the conqueror (327 B.C.). This marriage enhanced the new loyalty of the Persians to him, but it helped to strain the loyalty of his own Macedonian noble companions, who also disliked Alexander's own occasional adoption of Persian dress and Persian custom for the benefit of his new subjects, despite the fact that he did not change his own attitude toward or traditional relationships with the Macedonians. In fact, he continued to regard himself as a Greek and as the descendant of Zeus. He had paid his respects to the shade of his ancestor Achilles at Troy before he began his Eastern campaigns, and his favorite reading was the *Iliad*. But Alexander was forced to put to death his own most faithful commander, Parmenio, whose son had plotted against the king: Macedonian law required that all male relatives of a plotter be killed. And in 328 B.C. at Samarkand (now Soviet Central Asia), Alexander in a drunken fury killed one of his own senior companions for having taunted him with his Persian ways.

The tensions of the conquest did not diminish its efficiency: new levies of troops came out from Europe and were raised in Asia; new roads, new money, and new towns sprang up, each named after Alexander. Believing that India was the last region in Asia, that it was small, and that after India one would come upon Ocean, via which one could perhaps return to Europe by sea, Alexander next set out to conquer India (327 B.C.) from a base in what is now Afghanistan. He soon found himself doing battle with the hill tribes and with princes of Kashmir and Punjab (now Pakistan). At first the Indian war elephants terrified Alexander's cavalry and his men, but soon the Macedonians learned how to defeat them, and won many victories. Alexander moved on east; but India was not small, as he had thought, and his troops eventually mutinied. Alexander had to give in, and call off any further advance (326 B.C.). He led his troops on river-boats down the Indus southward toward the Indian Ocean, fighting all the way, and sacrificing a gold cup to Poseidon when he reached the ocean shore. Several new Alexandrias were founded, including the town that is now Karachi (Pakistan), before Alexander led his forces westward again across the southern Persian deserts back to Susa (324).

Here he punished those who had become unruly or corrupt during his long absence, and dramatically pursued his plan to combine the best features of the Macedonian and the Persian nobilities by staging a mass marriage between 80 Macedonian officers and 80 Persian noblewomen. He himself took a new Persian wife, and blessed the unions of 10,000 Macedonian troops with Persian women. Macedonian troops who wished to return home were sent off well rewarded, and those who wished to stay were combined with newly trained Persian recruits. A great double naval expedition from the mouths of the Tigris–Euphrates eastward along the shore of the Persian Gulf to India, and westward around Arabia (never yet circumnavigated) to Egypt, was in preparation at Babylon, where Alexander had great dockyards built. From the Greeks, who had enjoyed a longer period of internal peace than any for over a century, Alexander asked for divine honors: not to be a new god, as has sometimes been thought, but to be recognized as a general benefactor. In 323 B.C., at Babylon, he caught a fever and died, aged 33.

Imagination can hardly conceive of what Alexander might have accomplished had he lived: he might well have made Greece the center of his Empire, and would surely have been able to conquer the two states in the western Mediterranean already looming on the horizon as powers there: Carthage and Rome. He respected all races and religions, and believed in decent politics and a booming economy. Each of the Alexandrias he settled with Greeks and planned as a center for the diffusion of Greek culture. A superb general, a clever governor of subject peoples, a pious believer in the Greek gods, a passionate man who sometimes acted impulsively and bitterly regretted it later, Alexander astonished his contemporaries, and it is little wonder that he became to later generations the hero of a great cycle of romances that circulated in every country, in every language, and among every people, down virtually into our own day.

HEIRS OF ALEXANDER

As soon as the news of Alexander's death was known, his faithful generals began a fierce scramble for portions of his empire. They combined against each other in various shifting alliances, and arranged many intermarriages and murders, in a period of kaleidoscopic political and military change. By about 300 B.C. three dynasties had emerged as supreme, each in a different portion of the Empire: the Ptolemies in Egypt, the Seleucids in Asia, and the Antigonids in Macedon and Greece. In addition, there were various lesser kingdoms, chiefly in Asia Minor. Fighting continued almost without interruption until the rising power of Rome began to challenge them and to destroy and then absorb them one by one.

In Egypt the Ptolemies followed the ancient pattern of government, turning themselves into successors of the Pharaohs. They became gods, they sometimes married their sisters, they exploited the agricultural wealth of the country to the limit. They claimed title to all land, some of which was farmed by peasants directly for their benefit, and some let out to temples or to military settlers or officials. The Ptolemies' own land gave them all its produce except what was needed to feed the farm workers. Land let to others paid the Ptolemies a percentage of the wheat. Oil, flax, and papyrus were royal monopolies. No tree in Egypt could be cut down without royal permission. The Ptolemies governed largely through their Greek officials, who poured into Egypt for several generations after Alexander's death. Even the armies of the first three Ptolemies were made up wholly of Greeks. It was not until 217 B.C. that Egyptian troops participated in the wars of the dynasty, which were directed chiefly against the Seleucids of Asia for the possession of Syria, and against the Antigonids for islands of the Aegean and the Anatolian coasts.

Alexandria, the capital, had two great harbors, broad streets, luxurious palaces, a famous library with 700,000 rolls of papyrus, and a "museum" where scholars, freed from all duties by state subsidies, conducted their researches as they chose ("fat fowls in a coop," a skeptical poet called them). The towering lighthouse 400 feet high was regarded as one of the wonders of the world, and had an elevator that took the attendant from street level to the lamp at the top. This was the biggest city of the ancient world until Rome eventually outstripped it; there were perhaps a million inhabitants of Alexandria in the first century B.C., some of them living in multistoried apartment houses. Alexandria was far too big to be a polis; but its Greek population had its own political organization, as did the Jews and the Egyptians. At Alexandria stood also the Ptolemies' big barn, where all the royal grain was stored after it had come down the Nile.

The Egyptian population lived under its own law, and was judged in its own courts. Those who were discontent with the system that exploited them so thoroughly—and there were many—had no escape except to take sanctuary in a temple; and the government always tried to reduce the number of temples that had the right to provide sanctuary. For a long time the Greek population, with its own language, law-courts, culture, and ways of life, did not mingle with the Egyptians, but remained a large collection of foreigners who were getting rich as fast as they could. By the early second century Greek immigration had tapered off. Greek-Egyptian intermarriages had begun, and the army was more Egyptian and less effective. Rome began to intervene; disorganization set in; and by 118 B.C. Ptolemy VII had to issue a series of decrees calling for reform that show how far the system had begun to disintegrate.

Seleucus I was also one of Alexander's generals, who began as governor of Babylon and eventually won control over all of Alexander's Asian lands except northern and western Asia Minor and the Indian regions in the east, which had to be given up by 303 B.C. Seleucid territorial holdings fluctuated a good deal, however. We know much more about the Ptolemaic kingdom than about the Seleucid because many papyri have survived in the dry climate of Egypt that preserve details of economic and social life; no such source exists for Asia. The Seleucids' Ionian territories centered on the former Lydian capital of Sardis, their Syrian territories on the new city of Antioch-on-Orontes in northern Syria, and their Mesopotamian territories on the new city of Seleucia not far from Babylon. As the heirs of the ancient Near Eastern empires, the Seleucids used the former Assyrian and Persian administrative forms, revived Babylonia, Babylonian religion, and Babylonian literature, still written in cuneiform. Some scholars believe that by deliberately sponsoring a Babylonian religious revival the Seleucids were seeking a counterweight to Zoroastrianism, the Persian faith. It does appear that the Seleucids failed to achieve what Alexander had so well begun: the securing of Persian cooperation in managing the huge Asian territories.

The Seleucids could not count on deification, like the Ptolemies, nor could they create in Asia anything like the extremely centralized Ptolemaic system of exploitation. In Asia, unlike Egypt, there was too vast an area to be governed, there were too many varied traditions of authority, too many local governors to be considered. The Seleucids instead did something the Ptolemies did not do: they founded Greek cities, and sponsored their development. To do this they gave up large areas that were their own royal land, and they also transferred the land of powerful individual landowners to the cities. In such cases the lot of the peasant improved, as he ceased to be private property and gained his freedom. The Greek cities were military colonies, with money and land given by the king, and settlement, housing, financial, and other questions delegated to a military governor. The settlers received land, and were required to serve in the army in exchange.

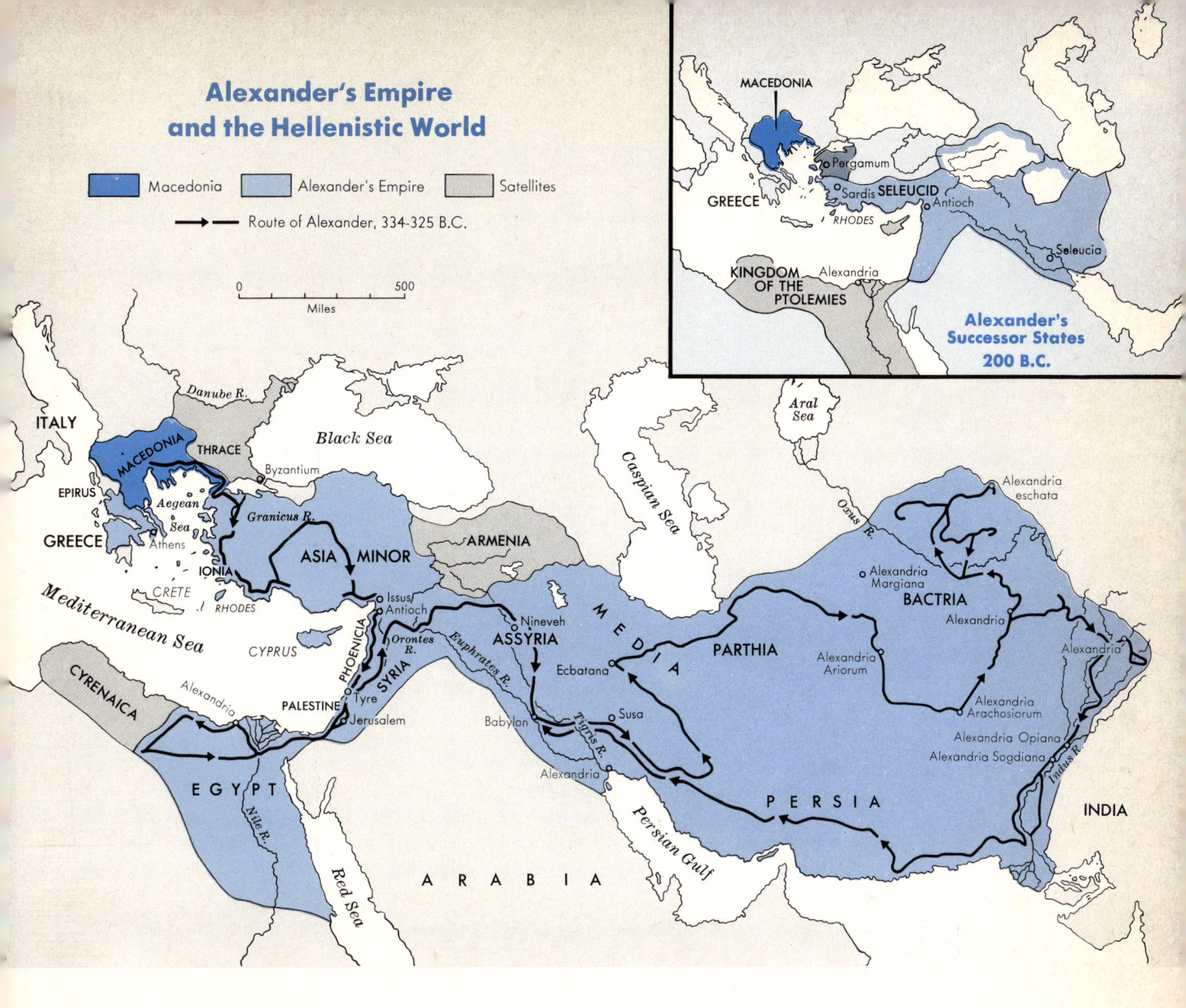

Like Alexander the Seleucid rulers named the cities for themselves; there were many Antiochs named for the Antiochus who had been Seleucus I's father and whose name continued to be given to many of the monarchs of the dynasty; there were also Seleucias, Laodiceas named after Seleucus' mother, and Apameas named after his wife. Some of the earlier Alexandrias now had their names changed to Antioch. The multiple founding of Greek cities all over Asia was a bold attempt to solve the problem of military security, and it failed partly because there were not enough Greeks available to populate the cities and man the armies, partly because the Seleucids did not command the loyalty of the Persian population.

As for Macedon and Greece, the family that won out there were the descendants of Alexander's governor of the western Anatolian province of Phrygia, the Antigonids. It was not until 276 B.C., almost half a century after Alexander's death, that the son of the first Antigonus, known as Antigonus Gonatas, was accepted as king of Macedon; and his success there came because he was such an able general that he had defeated the marauding Gauls. These were Celts (Indo-Europens) from distant western Europe who were now migrating eastward along the Danube, and bursting southward from the wilder and unsettled portion of the Continent on raids into Italy, Greece, and eventually Asia Minor, where they were given a kingdom of their own called Galatia. Having protected Greece from the Gauls (277 B.C.), Antigonus proved a successful ruler in Macedon.

Though the Greek cities were now grouped together into two leagues, the Aetolian and the Achaean, larger in membership and more representative in their joint rule than the Athenian and Spartan alliances of earlier times, they fought against each other and against the Antigonid kings of Macedon with the usual Greek vigor; so that by the 220's, the Greeks were largely independent of Macedon. In these times Athens had become famous largely as a university town, and usually stayed out of the perpetual brawls of the other cities. But Sparta, true to its traditions, tried to take over the Achaean League, and would have succeeded had not the Macedonians been brought back into Greece in 222, to defeat the Spartans finally. By the 220's, however, Rome had begun her interventions in the Greek world, and these were quickly to lead to conquest.

V. The Civilization of Greece

THE GODS

The Olympian gods are already old acquaintances, whom we first learned to know in Homer. The citizens of a polis naturally had special devotion for the divinity who had founded it: Athens for Athena, Sparta for Zeus, but they worshipped the other gods as well. Everybody worshipped the goddess of the hearth, Hestia, the protectress of each individual person's own home and fireside. Births and deaths in a family, solemn political actions in the state, were accompanied by religious rites. Poleis in large numbers grouped together in special devotion to regional shrines: the temple of Apollo at Delphi and of Zeus at Olympia we know; Zeus had another shrine at Dodona. The Olympic games were followed by others held in honor of Apollo at Delphi, of Poseidon the sea-god on the Isthmus of Corinth. At the games religious solemnities accompanied the sports: racing, jumping, throwing the discus, wrestling. The winners were crowned with laurel, as were those who won drinking contests or beauty contests or contests for the best poem or musical composition, including hymns to the god which lovingly

A fifth-century bronze statue, probably Zeus or Poseidon, now in the National Museum, Athens.

and realistically retold the myths that surrounded his birth and life, almost as if he were a human hero.

Two Greek cults of particular importance began outside the ordinary worship of the Olympian gods: that of Demeter at Eleusis near Athens, and that of Dionysus. Demeter (the name means literally "earth-mother") was the goddess of fertility and of the harvests: her daughter (by Zeus), Persephone, was snatched away by the god of the underworld, and had to spend a third of the year with him: the months of barrenness, late autumn and winter. Every spring she returned, and the fields became fertile again. Like the Mesopotamians from Sumer on and like the Egyptians, the Greeks too invented a story to account for the miracle of rebirth every spring. At Eleusis Demeter was worshipped in ceremonies which all initiates swore to keep secret. We know few of the details, but certainly there was a kind of ritual drama in which the initiates acted out the sorrow of the goddess searching for her lost daughter; there was a ritual meal, with communion in bread and water; and there was a sacred purifying bath in the salt waters of the nearby sea. Probably the participants expected that they would enjoy some sort of afterlife.

Dionysus, the god of wine, was not Greek in origin, but a northern foreigner, who also stood for fertility in its more openly sexual aspects: his celebrants originally carried phalluses in his procession, and were themselves often dressed as goats. In its original form the cult inspired its followers with wild frenzy in which they tore up and ate the flesh of living animals, and so acted out the devouring of the god himself. The cult was tamer in Greece, where songs were early written for the god.

TRAGEDY

From these songs there developed at Athens the art of tragedy: the word means "goat-song," and shows the close connection with the god Dionysus. At first largely sung by a chorus and formally religious in tone, the tragedies began to deal with more personal human problems, and individual actors' roles became more and more important. The first competition to choose the best tragedy was sponsored by Peisistratus in 534 B.C., and annual contests were held thereafter. Many hundreds of tragedies were written; comparatively few have survived in full—probably the best—and we have fragments of others. The later Greek philosopher Aristotle believed that it was the purpose of tragedy to arouse pity and terror in the spectators; to purge or purify them by causing them to reflect on the fearful punishments that highly placed men and women brought upon themselves by their own sins, the worst of which was hubris, arrogance.

The first, and some would still say the greatest, of the three chief tragedians whose works survive was Aeschylus (c. 525–456 B.C.), of whose seventy-odd tragedies we have seven. The earliest in time was *The Persians* (472 B.C.), in which Aeschylus explained the defeat of the Persians as the result of Xerxes' efforts to upset the international order established by the gods, and of the arrogance by which he offended Zeus. The audience could ponder recent history (it was only seven years since the Persians had been defeated) and consider the moral reasons for their own victories: such a play would tend to sober up any fire-eater who thought one Greek could lick ten Persians.

In *Prometheus Bound,* Aeschylus dealt with the punishment meted out by Zeus to Prometheus the Titan, who had stolen fire as a gift to mankind and who now lay chained to a rock while a vulture pecked at his liver. Zeus himself behaved tyrannically—he was new to the job of being king of the gods when Prometheus committed his offense—and only gradually learned to temper his wrath with mercy. Just as Xerxes had offended against the proper order of things by trying to impose Persian rule on Greece, so Prometheus had, even out of good will, offended by trying to get mankind the great gift of fire too soon. In the trilogy *The Oresteia,* all three plays of which survive, Aeschylus dealt with the ghastly tragedies in the family of Agamemnon, who sacrificed his daughter Iphigenia to get a favorable wind to go to Troy, was murdered by his unfaithful wife Clytemnestra on his return, and was avenged by his son Orestes, who killed

Attic drinking cup (sixth century B.C.) depicting Dionysus in a boat.

his mother on orders of Apollo. Orestes suffered torments by the Furies, and was acquitted by a court presided over by Athena; but only Zeus succeeded in transforming the Furies into more kindly creatures. Crime and punishment, remorse and release, a benevolent god over all: these Aeschylus portrayed in lofty, moving verse.

Sophocles, the second of the three greatest tragedians (496–406 B.C.), wrote many tragedies, of which only ten survive. He believed deeply in Athenian institutions and in the religion of his fellow-Greeks, and took an active part in the public life of Periclean Athens. In his *Antigone*, the niece of Creon, tyrant of Thebes, defied her uncle's harsh decision that the body of her brother, killed while leading a rebellion, must be exposed to be devoured by beasts of prey. Proclaiming that divine law required decent burial, she disobeyed Creon, and caused the proper ceremonial earth to be sprinkled on the body. She knew she would die for her defiance, but she acted in obedience to her conscience and resisted the dictator. The *Antigone* has carried its message of the sanctity of the individual conscience down the centuries, proclaiming the superiority of what is eternally right and decent to any mere dictator's brutal whim.

Living to be ninety, Sophocles saw the ruin brought by the Peloponnesian War, and his last tragedy, *Oedipus at Colonus*, produced after his death, dealt with the old age of the famous Theban king who in ignorance had killed his father and married his mother, and had torn out his own eyes in horror when he discovered what he had done. A blind beggar, outcast, Oedipus now knew that he could not have avoided the pollution of his unwitting crimes, and that his self-mutilation too was justified. Tempered by years of suffering, he sought sanctuary to die, and received it from Theseus, King of Athens: Oedipus' tomb would forever protect the Athenians against Thebes. Reflecting upon the terrible story of Oedipus and on the trials of all human life, Sophocles' chorus sang that for

The theater at Epidaurus.

mankind the best thing is never to be born, and the next best to die as soon as possible after birth: the passions of youth, the blows dealt one in middle life, and the anguish of old age are not worth it.

Nineteen plays remain of the many written by the third and last of the Attic tragedians, Euripides (c. 485–406 B.C.), who focussed rather more upon human psychology, with far less emphasis on divine majesty. More realistic in their introduction of children, slaves, and other characters upon the scene, his plays were also more romantic in their exploration of the far reaches of the human mind. The *Hippolytus* showed the uncontrollable sexual passion of a decent woman—Phaedra—for her ascetic stepson Hippolytus, who rejected it as he would all passion. She was ashamed of her lust but, as in the case of Potiphar's wife and Joseph, accused Hippolytus of having attacked her; he was executed, she committed suicide. The *Medea* showed a woman so far gone in agony brought about by rejection of her love that she killed her children in a fit of madness. The *Alcestis* showed a husband so selfish that he gladly accepted the offer of his devoted wife to die for him so that she might prolong his life; and then suffered agonies of remorse at his folly, when he had lost her.

The Trojan Women presented the sufferings of the women of Troy at the hands of the Greeks. It was staged in the same year as the Athenian atrocity at Melos, and must have caused the audience many uncomfortable moments of self-questioning. *The Bacchae* explored the excesses of religious ecstasy: in a frenzy a queen tore her own son to bits, thinking he was a lion. Was Euripides saying that men under the impulse of strong emotion were beasts, or that the old religion had too much that was savage in it, or only that the young king had defied the god and his hubris had brought him a fate that he well deserved?

COMEDY

Comedy, like tragedy, also began at the festivals of Dionysus. Aristophanes (c. 450–c. 385 B.C.) (*see above*, p. 45) has left eleven complete plays and parts of a twelfth. Besides making his audience laugh, he hoped to teach them a lesson through laughter. A thoroughgoing conservative, Aristophanes was suspicious of all innovation. In *The Frogs,* for instance, he brought onto the stage actors playing the parts of the two tragedians Aeschylus (then dead) and Euripides (still alive). The god Dionysus himself solemnly weighed verses from their plays on a giant pair of scales. Every time, the rather solemn, didactic, and old-fashioned Aeschylus outweighed the innovating, skeptical, febrile, modern Euripides: a tragedian's duty, Aristophanes thought, was to teach.

In *The Clouds* Aristophanes ridiculed the philosopher Socrates, whom he showed in his "think-shop" dangling from the ceiling in a basket so that he could voyage in air and contemplate the sun. Aristophanes meant to call attention to the dangers offered to Athenian youth by the so-called Sophists (*see below*, p. 75). His identification of Socrates with them was somewhat unfair; but, like the others, Socrates taught young men to question the existing order, and he was therefore fair game.

Aristophanes opposed the Peloponnesian War not because he was a pacifist, but because he thought it unnecessary. In *Lysistrata* the women denied themselves to their husbands until the men made peace, and in other plays Aristophanes denounced the Athenian politicians, including Pericles himself, for going to war. In *The Birds* the leading characters set off to found a Birdville (Cloud-cuckoo-land) to get away from war. In one of his later plays, of which we have only two, the women took over the state and proposed to share all the men among them, putting prostitutes out of business; in the other, Poverty and Wealth appeared in person and argued their cases.

These later plays provided a transition to the "New Comedy" of the fourth century, gentler and more domestic. We have several New Comedies by Menander, including one published for the first time only in the late 1950's. The drama was of course only one form that Greek poetic genius took. From the earliest days, the Greeks were the masters of lyric poetry as well (we have quoted one or two of Solon's own poems above, p. 48): among the most celebrated are poems of love by the poetess Sappho, of war by Spartan poets in the very early days, and of triumph in the games by Pindar.

HISTORY

A large proportion of what we know about the Greeks before and during the Persian Wars we owe to the industry and intelligence of Herodotus (c. 484–420 B.C.), who began to write his history as an account of the origins and course of the struggle between Greeks and Persians, and expanded it into an inquiry into the peoples of the whole world known to the Greeks. Born in Halicarnassus on the Ionian coast of Asia Minor, Herodotus was a great traveller, who visited Egypt, Italy, Mesopotamia, and the lands around the Black Sea, collecting information and listening to whatever stories people would tell him about their own past and about their present customs. He recorded what he learned, much of it of course tinged with myth, and he loved a good story; but he was both experienced and sensible, and he often put his reader on his guard against a story that he himself did not believe but set down in order to fill out the record.

Some have tended to scoff a little, especially at Herodotus' tales of a past that was remote even when he was doing his research; but, like those who have rashly questioned some of the history of the Old Testament, these doubters have often been silenced by recent archeological finds. Herodotus, for instance, said that the founder of Thebes, the semi-mythical Cadmus, was a Phoenician who had brought Phoenician letters with him from Phoenicia to Greece, where he founded Thebes about 1350 B.C., or about 900 years before Herodotus' own day. Herodotus added that Cadmus' dynasty was ousted about 1200 B.C. This was often disbelieved. But in 1964 A.D. archeologists at Thebes found in the palace of Cadmus a large collection of fine cuneiform seals, one of which was datable to 1367–1346 B.C. These instantly demonstrated the high probability of Herodotus' account of Cadmus' origin, date of arrival, and bringing of letters. Even the date of the ouster was verified, since the seals were in a layer of material that had been burned about 1200 B.C. and had survived because they were already baked clay. Herodotus wrote so well and so beguilingly that we would read him with delight even if he were not so reliable. Nor was he a mere collector and organizer of material. Though he wandered far, he never lost sight of his main theme: the conflict between east and west, which he interpreted as a conflict between despotism and freedom.

Always coupled with Herodotus we find the equally intelligent but very different historian Thucydides (c. 460–c. 400 B.C.), who wrote the account of the origins and course of the Peloponnesian War. The difference between the two arose partly from their subject matter: Herodotus was dealing largely with events that had happened before his own time, and he had to accept traditions, and often hearsay accounts. Thucydides was dealing largely with events in which he himself had been a participant: he was an unsuccessful general on the Athenian side in the war, and had been punished for his defeat; but he remained impersonal, scientific, and serious, collecting and weighing his information with the greatest care. Though he followed Herodotus' custom of putting into the mouths of his leading characters words—sometimes long speeches—which represented what they might have said rather than what they actually said, he notified his readers that they must realize what he was doing: the actual words were not available, but the arguments on both sides of any issue could be revived and written up in the form of speeches. Pericles' funeral oration of 430 B.C. with its praise of Athenian democracy is perhaps the most famous; but Thucydides also put into the mouths of the Melians, about to suffer the terrible slaughter and enslavement at Athenian hands, the moving arguments appropriate to those who were about to be massacred.

As deep a student of human psychology as any of the tragedians, Thucydides found in men and nations the cause of war; he knew as much about war and human behavior as anybody since has been able to learn. He wrote as a loser, but not as a mere loser in a sporting event, where time, and perhaps a return match, will assuage the hurt: Thucydides had seen his own Athens, so admirable in its best qualities, brought down by the Spartan militarists. He hoped that human intelligence would in the future realize how risky war was and what damage it did to the highest human values, but he knew that human nature would always respond to certain challenges by force, and that the lessons of the past were hard to learn. He wrote in pain and in iron detachment. His narrative of the great military events, such as the siege of Syracuse, Alcibiades' ill-conceived project, moves with great speed and well-concealed artistry. The much less talented and more pedestrian Xenophon, author of the *Anabasis* (*see above*, p. 60), wrote—in the *Hellenica*—a continuation of Thucydides' work down to the year 362 B.C. And the still less talented Arrian, writing very late but basing his work largely on the now lost account by Ptolemy I himself, has left us an account of Alexander's campaigns.

But for the century or so that followed the death of Alexander we have no historical work comparable with the histories of Herodotus, Thucydides, Xenophon, or Arrian. Therefore, we know the period less intimately than any since the Dark Age. It is only with the decade of the 220's that we once again encounter a narrative history, and then its author and his purpose themselves symbolize the change that has taken place. He was Polybius, a Greek who wrote in Greek but who had spent much time in Rome, where he had become an admirer and agent of the Romans, and the subject of his book was the rise to power of Rome. That he began his account with the year 221 B.C. clearly suggests that by that date the focus of world affairs had begun the shift from Greece to Rome.

SCIENCE AND PHILOSOPHY

Possessed of inquiring, speculative minds, the Greeks showed a deep interest in science. Stimulated by their acquaintance with Egyptian science, the Ionians and later the European Greeks, though they lacked instruments to check and refine their results, correctly attributed to natural rather than supernatural causes a good many phenomena. They knew that the Nile flooded because annual spring freshets took place at its source in Ethiopia. They decided that the straits between Sicily and Italy and Africa and Spain had been caused by earthquakes. They understood what caused eclipses, and knew that the moon shone by light reflected from the sun. Hippocrates of Cos (c. 460–377) founded a school of medicine, from which there survive the Hippocratic oath, with its high concept of medical ethics, and detailed clinical accounts of the symptoms and progress of diseases so accurate that modern doctors have been able to identify cases of diphtheria, epilepsy, and typhoid fever.

The mathematician Pythagoras (c. 580–500) seems to have begun as a musician interested in the mathematical differences among lyre-strings needed to produce various notes. The theorem that in a right-angled triangle the square of the hypotenuse is equal to the sum of the squares of the other two sides we owe to the followers of Pythagoras. They made the concept of numbers into a guide to the problems of life, elevating mathematics almost to a religious cult, perhaps the earliest effort to explain the universe in abstract mathematical language. Pythagoras is said to have been the first to use the word *cosmos*—harmonious and beautiful order—for the universe. Earlier Greeks had found the key to the universe in some single primal substance: water, fire, or air; and Democritus (460–370) decided that all matter consisted of minute, invisible atoms.

Much later, the Hellenistic astronomer Aristarchus, in the mid-third century, concluded that the earth revolves around the sun, a concept not generally accepted till almost 2,000 years later, while his younger contemporary, Eratosthenes, believed that the earth was round, and estimated its circumference quite accurately. Euclid, the great geometrical systematizer, had his own school at Alexandria in the third century B.C., and his pupil Archimedes won a lasting reputation in both theoretical and applied physics, devising machines for removing water from mines and irrigation ditches ("Archimedes' screw," a hand-cranked device, is still in use in Egypt), and demonstrating the power of pulleys and levers by singlehandedly drawing ashore a heavily laden ship. Hence his celebrated boast: "Give me a lever long enough and a place to stand on, and I will move the world."

The Greek scholars of the fifth and fourth centuries B.C. were not specialists like those in a modern university. The same man would study and write books on physics, mathematics, astronomy, music, logic, and rhetoric. Rhetoric became an increasingly important subject, as the Greeks reflected on their own language and developed high standards of self-expression and style. The subject really began with political oratory, as politicians wished to make more and more effective speeches—particularly essential in wartime, when the population was excited anyhow, and each leader strove to be more eloquent than the last. These multipurpose scholars who taught people how to talk and write and think on all subjects were called Sophists: wisdom-men. Sophists generally tended to be highly skeptical of accepted standards of behavior and morality, questioning the traditional ways of doing things.

How could anybody really be sure of anything?, they would ask, and some would answer that we cannot know anything we cannot experience through one or more of our five senses. How could you be sure that the gods existed if you could not see, hear, smell, taste, or touch them? Perhaps you could not know, perhaps they did not exist after all. If there were no gods and therefore no divine laws, how should we behave? Should we trust laws made by other men like us? And what sort of men were making laws and in whose interest? Maybe all existing laws were simply a trick invented by powerful people—members of the establishment—to protect their position. Maybe the general belief in the gods was simply a "put-on," invented by clever people to whose interest it was to have the general public docile. Not all Sophists went this far, of course; but in Athens during the Peloponnesian War, many young people, already troubled by the war or by the sufferings of the plague, were ready to listen to suggestions that the state should not make such severe demands upon them. Such young people would have burned their draft cards if they had had any, and their troubled parents, god-fearing and law-abiding, greatly feared the Sophists as the corrupters of the youth.

It is only against this background that we can understand the career and the eventual fate of Socrates (469–399 B.C.), whose method was that of the Sophists—to question everything, all the current assumptions about religion, politics, and behavior—but who retained unwavering to the end his own deep inner loyalties to Athens and to God. Socrates wrote no books, and held no professorial chair; but we know him well from contemporary reports, chiefly those of his pupil, Plato. Socrates was a stonemason who spent his life talking and arguing in the Assembly, in public places, and in the homes of his friends in Athens. He thought of himself as a "gadfly," challenging everything anybody said to him, and urging people not to take their preconceptions and prejudices as truths. Only a never-ending debate, a process of question and answer—the celebrated "Socratic method"—could lead human beings to truth. Reasoning led Socrates to conclude that man was more than an animal, that he had a mind, and, above all, that he had a true self, a kind of soul or spirit. Man's proper business on earth was to fulfill this true soul and cultivate the virtues that were proper to it—temperance, justice, courage, nobility, truth. Socrates himself listened to the voice of God that spoke within him.

We have already seen Socrates in his basket in mid-air in Aristophanes' *Clouds*. Of course he irritated and alarmed those who were worried about the youth of the day, and who thought of him as just another Sophist and one of the most vocal and dangerous. So when he was about 70 years old he was brought to trial on charges of disrespect to the gods and corrupting the youth of Athens. He argued that he had followed the prescribed religious observances and that he wanted only to make men better citizens; and he defended his gadfly tactics as necessary to stir a sluggish state into life. But a court of 501 jurors voted the death penalty by a narrow margin. Socrates could have gotten off by suggesting that he be punished in some other way. Instead he ironically asked for a tiny fine, and forced the court to choose between that and death. It condemned him again. Socrates drank the poison cup of hemlock, and waited for death serenely optimistic: he was "of good cheer about his soul." Many contemporaries and most men since have recognized that he was the victim of hysteria following a dreadful war.

Thereafter, it was Plato (c. 429–347 B.C.) who carried on his work. Plato founded a school in Athens, the Academy, and wrote a large number of celebrated dialogues: earnest intellectual conversations, in which Socrates and others discuss problems of man and the human spirit. Much influenced by the Pythagoreans, Plato retained a deep reverence for mathematics, but he found cosmic reality in Ideas rather than in numbers. As man has a "true self" (soul) within and superior to his body, so the world we experience with our bodily senses has within and superior to itself a "true world," an invisible universe or cosmos. In the celebrated dialogue *The Republic,* Plato has Socrates compare the relationship between the world of the senses and the world of Ideas with that between the shadows of persons and objects as they would be cast by firelight on the wall of a cave, and the same real persons and objects as they would appear when seen in the direct light of day. So man sees the objects—chairs, tables, trees—of the world as real, whereas they are only reflections of the true realities—the universals—the Idea of the perfect chair, table, or tree. So man's virtues are reflections of ideal virtues, of which the highest is the Idea of the Good. Man can and should strive to know the ultimate Ideas, especially the Idea of the Good.

This theory of Ideas has proved to be one of the great wellsprings of Western thought and has formed the starting point for much later philosophical discussion. Moreover, in teaching that the Idea of the Good was the supreme excellence and the final goal of life, Plato was advancing a kind of monotheism and laying a foundation on which pagan and Christian theologians both would build.

Politically, Athenian democracy did much to disillusion Plato: he had seen its courts condemn his master Socrates. On his travels he had formed a high opinion of the tyrants ruling the cities of Magna Graecia. So when Plato came to sketch the ideal state in *The Republic,* his system resembled that of the Spartans. He recommended that power be entrusted to the Guardians, a small intellectual élite, specially bred and trained to understand Ideas, governing under the wisest man of all, the Philosopher-King. The masses would simply do their jobs as workers or soldiers, and obey their superiors.

Plato's most celebrated pupil was Aristotle (c. 384–322 B.C.), called the "master of those who know." Son of a physician at the court of Philip of Macedon, and tutor to Alexander the Great, Aristotle was interested in everything. He wrote on biology, logic, literary criticism, political theory, ethics. His work survives largely in the form of notes on his lectures taken by his students; despite their lack of polish, these writings have had a prodigious later influence. He wrote 158 studies of the constitutions of Greek cities. Only the study of Athens survives.

Aristotle concerned himself chiefly with things as they are. The first to use scientific methods, he classified living things into groups much as modern biologists do, and extended the system to other fields—government, for example. He maintained that governments were of three forms: by one man, by a few men, or by many men; and that there were good and bad types of each, respectively monarchy and tyranny, aristocracy and oligarchy, polity and democracy (mob rule). Everywhere—in his *Logic, Poetics, Politics*—he laid the foundation for later inquiry. Though he believed that men should strive and aspire, he did not push them on to Socrates' goal of self-knowledge or to Plato's lofty ascent to the Idea of the Good. He urged instead the cultivation of the golden mean, the avoidance of excess on either side: courage, not foolhardiness or cowardice; temperance, not overindulgence or abstinence; liberality in giving, not prodigality or meanness.

Later, in the period after Alexander, two new schools of philosophy developed, the Epicurean and the Stoic. Epicurus (341–270 B.C.) counselled temperance and common sense, carrying further the principle of the golden mean. Though he defined pleasure as the key to happiness, he ranked spiritual joys above those of the body, which he recommended should be satisfied in moderation. The Stoics, founded by Zeno, got their name from the columned porch (*Stoa*) in Athens where he first taught. They preferred to repress the physical desires altogether. Since only the inward man counted, the Stoics preached total disregard for social, physical, or economic differences among men. They became the champions of slaves and other social outcasts, anticipating to some degree one of the moral teachings of Christianity.

THE ARTS

The incalculably rich legacy left by the Greeks in literature was well matched by their achievements in the plastic arts. In architecture, their characteristic public building was a rectangle, with roof supported by fluted columns. Over the centuries, the Greeks developed three principal types or orders of columns, still used today in "classical" buildings: the Doric column, terminating in a simple, unadorned square flat capital; the Ionic, slenderer and with simple curlicues (volutes) at the four corners of the capital; and the Corinthian, where acanthus leaves rise at the base of the volutes. Fluting gives an impression of greater height than the simple cylindrical Egyptian columns.

No matter what the "order" of the columns, a Greek temple strikes the beholder as dignified and simple. On the Acropolis of Athens, the Parthenon, greatest of all Doric temples, rose between 447 and 432 B.C. as the crowning achievement of Pericles' rebuilding program. By means of subtle devices—slightly inclining the columns inward so that they look more stable, giving each column a slight bulge in the center of the shaft so that it does not look concave—the building gives the illusion of perfection. In the triangular gable-ends that crowned its front and back colonnades (the pediments) and on the marble slabs between the beam ends above the columns (the metopes) stood a splendid series of sculptured battle-scenes, whose remains are now in the British Museum (the Elgin Marbles). Originally, the Parthenon and its statues were brightly painted. The building survived almost undamaged until 1697, when a Venetian shell exploded a Turkish powder magazine inside.

The achievement of Phidias and the other sculptors of the Periclean Age (*see above*, p. 56) had gradually developed from the "archaic" statues created a century or more earlier, usually of young men rather rigidly posed, with their arms hanging at their sides and a curiously uniform serene smile on their lips. Probably influenced by Egyptian models, these statues have great charm for moderns, who sometimes find the realism of the finished classical work rather tiresome. Phidias' great gold and ivory statues of Athena and the Olympian Zeus long ago fell to looters. So did most of the Greeks' sculpture in bronze; but every so often a great bronze statue is fished out of the sea or (as happened in 1959) is found under the pavement of a street being excavated for a sewer.

Though Greek painting as such has almost disappeared, we know from written texts that public buildings were adorned with paintings of Greek victories and portraits of political and military leaders. Moreover, the thousands of pottery vases, plates, cups, and bowls that have been discovered preserve on their surfaces—in black on red or in red on black—paintings of extraordinary beauty and of great variety. They show mythological scenes, illustrations to the *Iliad* and *Odyssey*, and the daily round of human activity: an athlete, a fisherman, a shoemaker, a miner, even a drunk vomiting while a sympathetic girl holds his head.

In the Hellenistic age sculpture became more emotional and theatrical: compare the Laocoön group, with its writhing serpents crushing their victims, to a statue of the Periclean period. The Venus de Milo and the Winged Victory of

Samothrace are two of the most successful Hellenistic works of art; but there are a good many imitative and exaggerated efforts which are regarded as comparative failures. In literature, too, beginning with Menander's New Comedy, vigor and originality ebbed, while sophistication and a certain self-consciousness took over.

Such a summary account of the splendors of Greek civilization runs the risk of creating the impression that the Greeks were supermen living in a paradise of physical and cultural triumphs. In fact, of course, few Greeks could understand or follow the ideas of a Plato or an Aristotle, or could afford to spend a great deal of time at the games, at the theater, or arguing with Socrates. Most Greeks worked hard, and their standard of living would seem extremely low today. In all of Athens at its height we know of only one establishment that employed over a hundred workmen. Even wealthy Athenians resided in small, plain houses of stucco or sun-dried brick: nobody until the Hellenistic period lived pretentiously. Athens was a huddle of mean little streets; there was little or no drainage; lighting was by inadequate, ill-smelling oil lamps. Inside a smithy or a pottery, it was so hot that the smith or potter often worked naked, as we know from vase-paintings. But relaxation was at hand: a musician might play in the smithy; and the climate made outdoor living agreeable much of the year.

On the one hand, the Greeks discovered or invented democracy, drama, philosophy. But on the other, they clung to their old-fashioned religious rituals and could not make themselves give up civil war between their city-states. The freedom-loving Athenians executed Socrates. Though they formulated the wisdom of "Know Thyself" and the golden mean, created a beautifully balanced and proportioned architecture, and organized an education that trained the whole man, intellectual and physical, they too often exhibited hubris, the unbridled arrogance that they felt to be the most dangerous of mortal vices. And, as it did in the tragedies of the stage, so in their own lives, their hubris brought nemesis upon them. Their achievements, however, have lived after them, inspiring most of the values that Western man holds dearest.

VI. The Romans

THE EARLY REPUBLIC

The Romans cherished the legend that after the fall of Troy, Aeneas, a Trojan prince, half-divine, led his fugitive followers to Italy and founded Rome on the banks of the Tiber. The poet Vergil (70–19 B.C.) immortalized the story in his *Aeneid,* written as Roman imperial glory approached its zenith. And as Vergil borrowed from Homer, so Rome borrowed extensively from the older Greek and Near Eastern civilizations. The tale of the mythical Aeneas symbolizes the flow into Italy of Greeks and Near-Easterners as well as Rome's debt to the Greco-Oriental world. Yet Rome did not achieve greatness on borrowed capital alone. The practical Romans were builders, generals, administrators, lawgivers.

Compared geographically with Greece, Italy enjoys certain natural advantages: the plains are larger and more fertile, the mountains less of a barrier to communications. The plain of Latium, south of the site of Rome, could be farmed intensively after drainage and irrigation ditches had been dug; the nearby hills provided timber and good pasturage. The city of Rome lay only fifteen miles from the sea and could share in the trade of the Mediterranean; its seven hills overlooking the Tiber could be easily fortified and defended.

To the south, as we know, by the year 600 B.C. Greek colonies dotted the shores of Italy and Sicily: this was Magna Graecia. To the north, the dominant power was held by the Etruscans, a mysterious people, surely foreigners in Italy, perhaps from Asia Minor (and so the source of the Aeneas legend) who had invaded the peninsula and conquered the region north of Latium by 700 B.C. They extended their power southward, surrounding Rome, and then seized it soon after 600. Although we have rich Etruscan remains—pottery, weapons, sculpture, painting, mostly found in tombs—nobody has yet altogether deciphered the language: the Etruscans wrote in Greek letters, but it is not Indo-European at all. No key like the Rosetta Stone has turned up, and so far no expert

Etruscan art: part of a fresco from the "Tomb of the Bulls," Cormeto, Italy.

like Ventris has turned up either. But most of the 10,000 existing inscriptions are very short: even if one could read them, one might not learn very much. The Etruscans were expert farmers and miners, they built huge stone walls around their settlements, and they practiced divination, foretelling the future from observing flocks of birds in flight or from examining the entrails of an animal slain as a sacrifice. Their tomb-decoration seems to show that, like the Egyptians, they believed the afterlife was similar to this one, and that they accorded their women a more nearly equal status with men than was usual in ancient society. They also enjoyed gladitorial combat as a spectacle, a taste which the Romans borrowed from them.

When the Etruscans moved into Latium and took over Rome, the people they conquered were apparently Latin tribesmen, descendants of the prehistoric inhabitants of the peninsula. Under its Etruscan kings, Rome prospered during the sixth century. The Etruscans built new stone structures and drained and paved what became the Forum. But the native population resented foreign rule, and joined with other Latin tribes in a large-scale rebellion. The traditional date for the expulsion from Rome of the last Etruscan king, Tarquin the Proud, is 509 B.C. What he left behind was an independent Latin city-state, still including some Etruscan notables, much smaller than Athens or Sparta, sharing Latium with other city-states. Yet in less than 250 years Rome would dominate the entire Italian peninsula.

We can understand this success only if we examine Roman institutions. Once they had ousted Tarquin, the dominant aristocratic forces at Rome set up a republic. Only the well-established land-owning families, the *patricians* (Latin *pater*, "father")—perhaps not more than 10 per cent of the population—held full citizenship. The remaining 90 per cent were *plebeians* (Latin *plebs*, "the multitude"), who included those engaged in trade or labor, the smallest farmers, and all those who were debtors as the result of the economic upheaval after the expulsion of the Etruscans. The plebeians had no right to hold office; they could amass as much money as they pleased, however, and wealthy plebeians would eventually lead the campaign to gain political emancipation for their class. Fifth-century Rome, then, was not unlike sixth-century Athens before the reforms of Cleisthenes.

The patrician class supplied the two consuls, the executive chiefs of state who governed jointly for a term of a year, enjoying full *imperium*, supreme political power. Each had the right of veto over the other; so that both had to support a measure before it could be put through. Ordinarily they were commanders of the army, but in wartime this power was often wielded, for a period not longer than six months, by an elected *dictator*. (Despite the modern meaning of the term, in the Roman republic it meant a commander who had obtained his authority constitutionally and had to give it up when his term was over.) The consuls usually followed the policies decided on by the Senate, a body consisting of about 300 members, mostly patricians and all ex-officials like the members of the Athenian Council of Aeropagus, and wielding such prestige that it comes first in the famous Roman political device: S.P.Q.R.—*Senatus Populusque Romanus* (The Senate and the People of Rome). The reigning consuls were themselves senators, and appointed new senators. The Romans had another deliberative body, the Centuriate Assembly, based on the century, the smallest unit (a hundred men) of the army. Although some plebeians were surely present, the patricians dominated the deliberations of this body also. It enjoyed a higher legal prerogative but less actual power than the Senate, although it elected the consuls and other officials, and approved or rejected laws submitted to it by consuls and Senate.

Before a man could be chosen consul, he had to pass through an apprenticeship in other posts. The job that led directly to the consulate was that of praetor (*prae-itor*, the one who goes in front), who served as a judge, often had an army command, and later a provincial governorship. He was elected by the Centuriate Assembly, and served for a year. At first there was only one praetor; later the number rose to eight. Men seeking election as praetor or consul wore a special robe whitened with chalk, the *toga candida*, whence our word "candidate." From among the ex-consuls, the Assembly elected two censors, for an eighteen-month term, who took a census to determine which of the population was qualified for army service. They also secured the right to pass on the moral qualifications of men nominated for the Senate, barring those they thought corrupt or too luxury-loving, whence the connotation of our words "censor" and "censorship."

This regime was well-designed to carry on the chief business of the Roman state: war. The Roman army at first had as its basic unit the phalanx, about 80 centuries of foot soldiers, armed with helmet and shield, lance and sword. But experience led to the substitution of the far more maneuverable legion, consisting of 3,600 men, composed of 60- or 120-man bodies called "maniples" or handfuls, armed with the additional weapon of the iron-tipped javelin, which was hurled at the enemy from a distance. Almost all citizens of Rome had to serve. Iron discipline prevailed; punishment for offences was summary and brutal, but the officers also understood the importance of generous recognition and reward of bravery as an incentive.

The plebeians naturally resented their exclusion from political authority. As early as the 490's, they threatened to withdraw from Rome and to found nearby a new city-state of their own, and when this tactic won them a concession, they continued to use it with great effect on and off during the next two hundred years. First (494) they got the right to have officials of their own, the Tribunes of the People, to protect them from unduly harsh application of the laws. By 457 there were ten of these. The plebeians also (471) gained their own assembly, the Tribal Assembly (so named because of the subdivision of the plebeian population into tribes), which chose the Tribunes and had the right, like the Centuriate Assembly, to pass on new laws. Next they complained that the patrician judges could manipulate the law for their own purposes because it had never been written down. So the consuls ordered the (extremely severe) laws engraved on wooden tablets (451 B.C.)—the Twelve Tables, beginning the epochal history of Roman law.

In the early days of the Republic, debt meant that a plebeian farmer would lose his farm and be forced into slavery. Property therefore accumulated in the hands of the patrician landowners. The plebeians obtained legislation limiting the size of an estate that any one man might accumulate, abolishing the penalty of slavery for debt, and opening newly acquired lands to settlement by landless farmers. The farmer–debtor problem, though eased, remained to plague the Romans to the end. During the fifth and fourth centuries, the plebeians won the right to hold all the offices of the state, even that of consul (366 B.C.). They also forced the abrogation of the laws that forbade their intermarriage with patricians. The fusion of wealthy plebeians and patricians formed a new class, the *nobiles*, who were to dominate the later Republic as the patricians had the earlier.

ROMAN EXPANSION

In a long series of wars the Romans made good their supremacy over the other Latin towns, the Etruscan cities, and the half-civilized tribes of the central Apennines (the mountain backbone of the peninsula). Early in the third century B.C. they conquered the Greek cities of southern Italy. Meanwhile, in the north, a Celtic people, the Gauls (*see above*, p. 68), had crossed the Alps and settled in the Lombard plain; their expansion was halted at the little river Rubicon, which formed the northern frontier of Roman dominion. In conquered areas the Romans sometimes planted a colony of their own land-hungry plebeians. Usually they did not try to force the resident population into absolute subjection, but accepted them as allies, and respected their institutions. The cities of Magna Graecia continued to enjoy home rule. Some of the nearest neighbors of Rome became full citizens of the republic, but more often they enjoyed the protection of Roman law as part-citizens who could not participate in the Roman Assemblies. So the expansion of Rome in Italy demonstrated imaginative statesmanship as well as military superiority.

The conquest of Magna Graecia made Rome a near neighbor of the Carthaginian state. Carthage—modern Tunis—was originally a Phoenician colony, but had long since liberated itself from its motherland, and expanded along the African and Spanish shores of the Mediterranean and into the western parts of Sicily. Ruled by a commercial oligarchy, Carthage held a virtual monopoly of western Mediterranean trade. When the Carthaginians began to seize the Greek cities in eastern Sicily also, the Sicilian Greeks appealed to Rome. So the Romans launched the First Punic (from the Latin word for Phoenician) War, 264–241 B.C.

The Romans won by building their first major fleet and defeating the Carthaginians at sea. They forced Carthage to give up all claim to eastern Sicily and to cede western Sicily as well, thus obtaining their first province outside the Italian mainland. Seeking revenge, the Carthaginians used Spain as the base for an overland invasion of Italy in the Second Punic War (218–201 B.C.). Their commander Hannibal led his forces across southern Gaul and then over the Alps into Italy, losing in the snow many of the elephants he used as pack-animals. In northern Italy he recruited many Gauls, and won a string of victories as he marched southward, notably at Cannae (216 B.C.). But gradually the Roman general Fabius *Cunctator* (the delayer) exhausted the Carthaginians. His "Fabian" strategy refrained from an all-out battle while eating away at the Carthaginians by attacking their supplies and patrols.

In 202 B.C., Hannibal was summoned back to defend Carthage itself against

Scene from a Roman battle: relief on the Column of Trajan, Rome.

a Roman invading force under Scipio. Scipio won the battle and the title "Africanus" as a reward. The Romans forced the Carthaginians to surrender Spain, pay a large sum of money, and promise to follow Rome's lead in foreign policy. Hannibal fled to the court of the Seleucid King Antiochus III. Although Carthaginian power had been broken, the speedy recovery of the city's prosperity alarmed a war party at Rome, which agitated for its complete destruction. Cato the censor and senator would end each of his speeches with the words *"Delenda est Carthago"* ("Carthage must be destroyed"). In the Third Punic War (149–146 B.C.) the Romans levelled Carthage to the ground, sprinkled salt on the earth, and took over all its remaining territory.

While the Punic Wars were still going on, Rome had become embroiled in the Balkans and in Greece, sending fleets to put down the Illyrian pirates who were operating in the Adriatic from bases in what is now Albania. By 219, the Greeks, who had been suffering as much as anybody from the Illyrian raids, were so grateful to Rome for intervening that they admitted Romans to the Eleusinian mysteries and the Isthmian Games (*see above,* pp. 68, 70). But Philip V (221–178 B.C.), Antigonid King of Macedon, viewed with great suspicion Roman operations on his side of the Adriatic. He tried to help Hannibal during the Second Punic War, but a Roman fleet prevented him from crossing to Italy, and many of the Greek cities, opponents of Philip but not yet of Rome, helped the Romans in the First Macedonian War (215–205 B.C.).

But, in 202, several powers—Athens, Ptolemy V of Egypt, his ally Attalus, King of the powerful independent kingdom of Pergamum in Asia Minor, and Rhodes, head of a new naval league—appealed to Rome to intervene again against Philip V. In the Second Macedonian War (200–197 B.C.) Rome defeated Philip's armies on their own soil (Cynoscephalae, 197), and forced him to withdraw from Greece altogether and to become an ally of Rome. At the Isthmian Games of 196, a solemn Roman proclamation declared that the Greeks were free. Two years later, after more fighting (chiefly against Sparta), the Roman armies left Greece and a largely disillusioned population. Antiochus III (223–187 B.C.), Seleucid king in Asia, profited by the defeat of Macedon to take over the Greek cities on the Aegean coast of Asia Minor and to cross into Europe and campaign there. Hoping to keep Greece as a buffer against him, and worried at his advance, the Romans, who had their hands full with wars in Spain, kept on negotiating with him. But Antiochus, who had with him the refugee Hannibal, challenged the Romans in Greece, hoping but failing to win wide native support. At Thermopylae in 191 B.C. the Romans defeated Antiochus, and then invaded Asia, forcing Antiochus in 188 to surrender all the Seleucid holdings in Asia Minor. Hannibal made good his escape, but poisoned himself in 183 as he was about to be surrendered to Rome. Rome had become the predominant power in the Greek world.

For the next forty years, the Romans found themselves obliged to arbitrate the constantly recurring quarrels among the Greek states. Rebellions forced repeated armed intervention. Philip V's son and successor, Perseus (179–168 B.C.), seemed to threaten to unite Greece against the Romans, and in the Third Macedonian War (171–168 B.C.) he was eventually captured and his forces were routed at the decisive battle of Pydna (168 B.C.). Rome imposed a ruthless settlement, breaking Macedon up into four republics and exiling from Greece many who had sympathized with Perseus. Twenty years later, after intervening against a leader called Andriscus who pretended he was a son of Perseus, the Romans annexed Macedon (148 B.C.), their first province east of the Adriatic; and two years after that (146 B.C.) they defeated a desperate uprising of the Achaean League, and marked their victory by a particularly brutal sack of Corinth: all the men were killed, the women and children were sold as slaves, and the city was levelled to the ground. It was the same year as the total destruction of Carthage. The Romans henceforth governed Greece from Macedon, but did not yet annex it as a province. Internal fighting in Greece came to an end; there was a religious and economic revival. Rome's prestige was now so great that in 133 the King of Pergamum, whose family had been helpful allies of the Romans—and much hated elsewhere for that reason—left his flourishing Asia Minor state to Rome in his will.

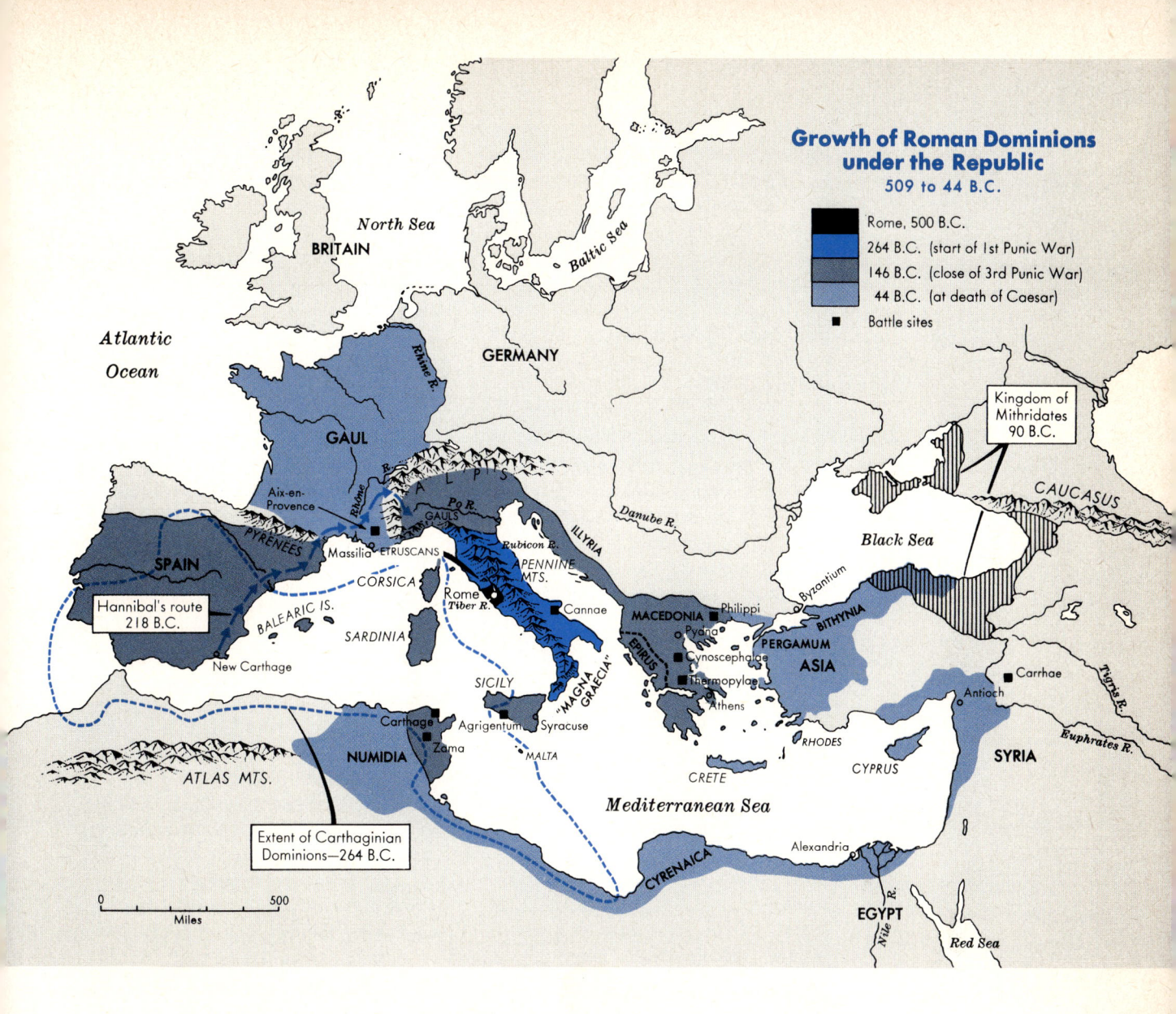

CRISIS OF THE REPUBLIC

As Roman territory increased, signs of trouble multiplied. The Republic allowed a few overseas cities to retain some self-government, but usually organized its new territories as provinces under governors appointed by the Senate.

Some of the governors proved oppressive and lined their own pockets, but as long as they raised recruits for the army and collected taxes, they had a free hand. In Italy, pressure mounted from Rome's allies, who demanded full citizenship and a share in the new wealth flowing into the capital. With the gradual exhaustion of Italian soil, grain had to be imported from Africa; former Italian grainfields were transformed into mixed farms or large cattle-ranches run by slaves, whom only big landowners could afford. While veterans of overseas fighting and retired governors accumulated money and slaves as the spoils of conquest, more and more small farmers lost their land and became penniless and resentful refugees in the city of Rome.

The proprietors of *latifundia* (big estates), the successful generals and governors, and certain merchants and contractors who had built roads for the state or furnished supplies to the army combined to form a new class of very rich men, called *equites* (knights) because they could afford to equip themselves for service in the cavalry, the most expensive branch of the army. Yet the *nobiles* dominated the Senate, increasingly influential because it had managed the Punic Wars successfully. Social tensions became acute: an old fashioned conservative *nobilis* like Cato, for instance, hated the rich men's taste for the luxurious new ways of life, imported from Greece and the East. The political machinery of a small city-state could not cope with the problems of empire, of social tension, and of economic distress.

Two brothers named Gracchus, grandsons of Scipio, hero of the First Punic War, and themselves nobles, emerged during the late 130's and the 120's as the champions of the dispossessed. Tiberius Gracchus, who served as Tribune of the People in 133 B.C., and Gaius, who held the post from 123 to 121, sought to increase the role of the tribunes and the Tribal Assembly at the expense of the Senate. The wild beasts, said Tiberius, have their dens, but the Roman soldiers have not a clod of earth to call their own. The brothers wanted to limit the size of estates that could be owned by one family, to resettle landless farmers either abroad or on state-owned lands in Italy that had been leased to capitalist farmers, and to give the city poor of Rome relief by allowing them to buy grain from the state at cost. Politically, they wanted to give certain judicial posts to the *equites*, to extend Roman citizenship to all Latins, and to raise other Italians to Latin status.

The efforts of the Gracchi to speed democracy failed. Of their economic program only the proposal to sell the Roman people cheap grain was adopted. In the succeeding centuries the state had to lower the price until the poor were getting their bread free. This in itself reveals the failure of the resettlement program: had the dispossessed farmers actually received new allotments, the number in the city needing cheap bread would have fallen off sharply. The agrarian capitalists, after being forced by the Gracchi to give up some of the land they rented from the state, were soon expanding their holdings once more. The *latifundia* had come to stay. Moreover, on the political side, the Senate resented the extension of rights to the *equites*, and balked at granting citizenship to other Italian cities (eventually, after an uprising in 91–88 B.C., this had to be done).

Meantime, politics turned unconstitutional and violent. Tiberius Gracchus ousted a tribune of the people who was blocking his program; both brothers defied precedent and ran for re-election as tribunes. The Senators themselves resorted to murder to stop the Gracchi and assassinated Tiberius in 133; in 121

Gaius killed himself to avoid a similar fate. Were the Gracchi high-minded "New Dealers" blocked by the vested interests of the Senators, or unstable radicals whose high-handed methods only added to the discord? Probably both; at any rate the deadlock between Gracchan reformism and senatorial conservatism moved Rome toward autocracy.

After the Gracchan interlude, political leadership passed to generals who cared less for principle than for power. In the provinces the misrule of the governors provoked uprisings. Along the frontiers, at the end of the second century B.C., Germanic tribes were threatening. In 88 B.C. in Asia Minor, Mithridates, the King of Pontus (along the shores of the Black Sea), attacked the Romans, at least 80,000 of whom were massacred.

A general victorious in the chronic provincial warfare would celebrate in Rome with a great "triumph," a parade of his successful troops and of their prisoners and booty that would dazzle the public. And the troops, properly rewarded by their commanders, became loyal to them rather than to the state. The prescription for political success at Rome was to make a record as a successful general.

POLITICAL GENERALS: MARIUS, SULLA, POMPEY, CAESAR

The first of the generals to reach power was Marius, leader of the *populares*, who had won victories against the Numidians in North Africa—in what is now eastern Algeria (111–105 B.C.)—and against a group of Celtic and Germanic peoples called the Cimbri and Teutones, who had caused a great deal of trouble before he beat them at what is now Aix-en-Provence in southern France (102 B.C.). Violating the custom that a consul had to wait ten years before serving a second term, Marius had himself elected five times between 108 and 103 B.C. He began a major reorganization of the army by abolishing the old requirement that a Roman citizen must pay for his own equipment. This rule had automatically excluded the poor, who could not pay. Now that the state furnished the equipment, the professional soldier gradually replaced the former citizen-soldiers, who in the past had gone back to their normal peacetime occupations once the fighting was over. The nullification by the Senate of a law extending Roman citizenship to all of the Italian cities led to a major "social war," which threatened Rome with the loss of her Italian power. The rebellious secessionists were mostly pacified by the year 89, but only by the extension of citizenship to all of Italy.

When Rome went to war against Mithridates in 88 B.C., Marius emerged from retirement and demanded the command. But the Senate chose Sulla, a younger general who was an optimate, and a bloody civil war broke out between the supporters of the two. Marius died in 86, and Sulla defeated Mithridates in 84, and then returned to assume the office of dictator. On the way to and from the east, his forces plundered Zeus's treasury at Olympia and Apollo's at Delphi, and sacked Athens for having sympathized with Mithridates. The Romans brought back Greek sculpture, painting, books, and other loot.

Back in Rome, Sulla curtailed the powers of the tribunes of the people and the Tribal Assembly, in an effort to move the Senate back into its ancient position as the chief force in political life. He put through a great many laws designed to curb the rise of new younger politicians, and in general tried to turn back the clock. But he was hardly restoring the "good old days": contrary to his promises he exterminated the followers of Marius, and himself broke all precedent by prolonging his tenure as dictator beyond the prescribed six months. He did retire in 80 B.C., but the Senate proved unable to govern.

Within ten years, Pompey, a ruthless and arrogant young veteran of Sulla's campaigns who had won victories first in Spain and then at home against a slave rebellion led by Spartacus (73–71 B.C.), forced the Senate to restore the tribunes and the Tribal Assembly to their old power. In 70 B.C. Pompey became consul before he had reached the minimum legal age. He became grand admiral of Roman naval forces against the troublesome pirates of the Mediterranean. After promptly defeating them (67 B.C.), he took command of a new war against Mithridates, who had attacked Rome again in order to prevent the Romans from picking up a neighboring kingdom (Bithynia) in Asia Minor that had been left them in the will of the king. By 65 B.C. Pompey had driven Mithridates into exile at the court of his son-in-law, Tigranes, King of Armenia, who had also begun to acquire portions of Asia Minor. Mithridates committed suicide in 63 B.C., and Pompey reorganized Asia Minor into Roman provinces and subject kingdoms. Syria too, where the last effective Seleucid had died in 129 B.C., had largely fallen to Tigranes by 83, and Pompey now made it a Roman province (64 B.C.). He even took Jerusalem in that year. The western fringe of Asia was now virtually Roman.

While Pompey had been away, there had taken place a celebrated conspiracy at Rome, led by Catiline, leader of a group of discontented and dispossessed nobles who had been the victims of Sulla's purges, and who now planned a revolution and a comeback. The plot may have had the support of two other leading generals with political ambitions: Crassus, a millionaire who, like Pompey, had played a major part in subduing the earlier slave revolt of Spartacus; and Julius Caesar, nephew by marriage of the *popularis* Marius, but a noble by birth. If they were implicated in Catiline's conspiracy, both Caesar and Crassus pulled out in time, before the consul and famous lawyer Cicero discovered the plot and arrested the plotters, some of whom he illegally had executed. His speeches in the Senate against the ringleader, Catiline, have given much instruction and some pain to generations of schoolboys.

Having returned to Rome as a private citizen, Pompey joined with Crassus and Caesar in a triumvirate, or team of three men. With Caesar as consul in 59 B.C., Pompey married Caesar's daughter, Pompey's soldiers received large land-grants to the south, near Naples, and the eastern Mediterranean settlement was confirmed. Caesar took as his own province for a period of five years the southern strip of Gaul (modern France) which Rome had annexed some sixty years earlier, and other lands rich in revenue. It was, however, Gaul, where his governorship was renewed for another five years in 56 B.C., that gave Caesar his next great opportunity. Between 58 and 50 B.C. he conquered the area in Gaul corresponding to most of modern France and Belgium, and even crossed the English Channel to punish the Celtic Britons for helping their fellow-Celts in Gaul, though he did not try to conquer Britain permanently. His successes meant that, like Italy and Spain, the future France would have a civilization firmly based on Rome and a language based on Latin. In order to give his achievements maximum publicity in Rome, he now wrote his *Commentaries on the Gallic Wars* (a lot easier reading than Cicero).

While Caesar was busy in Gaul, Crassus became governor of Syria, where he became involved in war against the Parthians, a dynasty that had risen in Persia to replace the Seleucids. At Carrhae in Mesopotamia in 53 B.C. the Parthians defeated and killed Crassus. The triumvirate had begun to fall apart even before that, as Pompey's wife, Caesar's daughter Julia, died in 54 B.C. Pompey became sole consul in 52 B.C., and his private thugs killed the chief of Caesar's faction in Rome. This was Clodius, who had been acting to protect Caesar's interests in his absence, and had once succeeded in getting Cicero exiled for a period. A revolution in Gaul kept Caesar busy in 52 and 51 B.C.; when it was over, Caesar faced Pompey for supremacy.

In 49 B.C. Caesar defied an order from the Senate to stay in Gaul, and led his loyal troops south across the Rubicon river boundary. Within a few weeks, he was master of Italy. He then won another war in Spain, and in 48 B.C. defeated Pompey's troops at Pharsalus in Greece, to which most of the Senate had fled with Pompey. Pompey was later murdered in Egypt by troops of Ptolemy XII. Caesar now travelled to the East and to his famous love affair with Ptolemy's sister, Cleopatra. After new victories over former troops of Pompey's in Asia Minor, North Africa, and Spain, he returned to Rome in triumph in 45 B.C. Less than a year later, on the Ides of March, 44 B.C., he lay stabbed to death on the floor of the Senate at the foot of Pompey's statue. His assassins included patriots troubled at his assumption of supreme power and his destruction of the Roman constitution, and others who were merely disloyal or jealous.

But during his brief period of dominance Caesar had carried further the subversion of the institutions of the Republic that Marius and Sulla and Pompey had begun. As dictator, he arrogated to himself many of the powers that usually belonged to the consuls, the tribunes, and the high priest (*pontifex maximus*). He had packed the Senate with his own supporters. His opponents said he was planning to be crowned as king and worshipped as a god, and they may have been right. He did show a deep interest in the social and economic problems of Rome: he gave his veterans grants of land in outlying provinces; he tried to check the importation of slaves into Rome because they took work from free men; he made gifts to the citizens from his own private fortune, and then sharply curtailed the dole of grain that the Gracchi had instituted, forcing the creation of new jobs. At the moment of his death he was projecting a great public-works program: Tiber valley flood-control, a trans-Appennine highway, and a canal through the Isthmus of Corinth in Greece. The rank and file of the Romans seem to have regarded him as a benefactor, the restorer of order and prosperity.

After Caesar's death, his young and shrewd grandnephew and heir, Octavian, and his most trusted lieutenant, Octavian's brother-in-law Mark Antony, who had seized Caesar's private papers, formed a new triumvirate with a third general, Lepidus, to combat the forces of the Senate, led by Brutus, one of Caesar's assassins. Cicero bitterly attacked Antony, who had him murdered along with many other political opponents. After the defeat of Brutus at Philippi in 42 B.C., rivalry broke out between Octavian and Mark Antony. Antony withdrew to Egypt, where he also had an affair with Cleopatra, still beautiful and ambitious. But Antony's forces deserted to Octavian, and in 30 B.C., a few months after a naval defeat at Actium off the western coast of northern Greece (31 B.C.), Antony and Cleopatra committed suicide. Thus Rome acquired Egypt, last of the major Hellenistic states to disappear, and Octavian became sole master of Rome. The Republic had come to an end.

THE FIRST TWO CENTURIES OF THE ROMAN EMPIRE

Octavian sought to preserve republican forms but at the same time to remake the government along the lines suggested by Caesar, so that Rome would have the authority to manage the enormous empire it had acquired. He called himself "restorer of the Roman Republic," avoided all ostentation in his own personal life, and always said his favorite title was *princeps* (first citizen). But history knows Octavian as Augustus ("revered one"), a title bestowed on him by the Senate in 27 B.C., and refers to him and his successors as emperors, from *imperator*, "commander-in-chief." Though Augustus allowed the Senate to retain all its old prestige and its patronage in filling high offices, he packed it with his supporters, and deprived it of control over the army and the collection of taxes. He himself assumed most of the powers formerly held by consuls and tribunes of the people, and these posts became more and more ornamental, as did the roles of the Centuriate and Tribal Assemblies. Once the thorough purges of his enemies had stopped, Augustus abandoned terror, but enjoyed overawing his subjects. He consciously modelled himself on Alexander and even tried to look like him.

One secret of Augustus' power was his money. He had at his personal disposal all the accumulated wealth of Egypt. He was the richest man in Rome, so rich that at first he paid for the soldiers' pensions and dole of bread out of his own pocket. He paid for the repair of the water supply, and for the construction of great new public buildings: "I found Rome a city of brick," he boasted, "and have left it a city of marble."

He asserted himself as undisputed commander-in-chief of the army. No longer did the government have to rush troops to the provinces every time a new threat arose; Augustus stationed legions permanently in the provinces. He permitted no general to raise his own armies and thus to become a threat to political stability. He made tax-collecting the business of the state, instead of selling the privilege, as the republic had done, to private persons who recouped their investment by oppression. He himself personally controlled some of the provinces. He founded an effective civil service for the government of the foreign provinces, minimizing the corruption, extortion, and brutality that had too often characterized Roman rule.

All his policies were popular among the Romans. Tired of turmoil, they made no objection to the sacrifice of their republican institutions in exchange for order and safety. Civil war had come to an end. Public games and spectacles were provided for them in abundance. Even in the provinces, only a few incidents along the frontier broke the period of peace, notably the defeat of the legions in the Teutoburger forest of northwest Germany at the hands of the local tribesmen under Hermann (or Arminius) in A.D. 9. The *Pax Romana* (Roman Peace), interrupted only by such episodes, was to last two hundred years (27 B.C.–A.D. 180).

So solidly had Augustus built that even the unworthiness of his immediate successors could not shake his edifice. The best was Claudius (A.D. 41–54), who conquered Britain in 43. The worst was Nero (54–68), whose mother poisoned Claudius to secure his accession. Nero murdered her anyhow, as well as both his wives and his brother, but delighted the people by participating in musical contests and theatrical performances. He did not start the famous fire that burned much of Rome (A.D. 64), but he did blame the new sect of Christians, and persecuted them to take attention away from himself. His misrule provoked an army revolt that led to his suicide (68). The problem of succession was finally solved by the shrewd lawyer Nerva (96–98), who adopted as his heir a man of proven talent and loyalty; and the new emperor repeated the process when he came to the throne. Over eighty-two years and four successive reigns, this practice worked well. Trajan (98–117), Hadrian (117–138), Antoninus Pius (138–161), and Marcus Aurelius (161–180) proved that ability was a better standard than heredity.

In the machinery of government, the most noteworthy innovation was emperor-worship, which came in gradually. In the Eastern provinces, where the god-ruler was traditional, Augustus and his successors were worshipped while they

A contemporary bronze equestrian statue of Marcus Aurelius (121–180).

were still alive. And by the second century A.D. at Rome itself, the ceremonial the easterners lavished on a god-ruler had begun to surround the living emperor. Worship of the emperor, for westerners at least, held more political than religious significance: it was a solemn political act, not unlike the modern pledge of allegiance to the flag.

Augustus and his successors continued to add to the vast territories of the Roman Empire, which reached its greatest extent in the second century A.D. In western Europe, Britain was conquered as far north as a great wall built by Hadrian and Antoninus Pius across the island to protect the border from raids by the hostile Scots. Across the Channel, Gaul included all of present-day France, Belgium, Luxembourg, and parts of the Netherlands, Germany, and Switzerland. Rome also ruled parts of Austria and Bavaria, the whole of Spain and Portugal, and all of southeast Europe south of the Danube, plus Dacia (part of modern Rumania) north of the river, added by Trajan. Except for the Dacian salient, the Rhine–Danube line formed the boundary between the Romans and the barbarians in Europe. In Africa, the whole northern coast and its hinterland—present-day Morocco, Algeria, Tunisia, Libya—were Roman, as was Egypt. In the Near East Rome ruled Asia Minor, Syria, Palestine, and the Sinai peninsula (called "Arabia"), and had provinces in Armenia and Mesopotamia as well.

No single pattern of government would have suited the diverse populations of this area, ranging from the civilized Egyptians or Greeks to the Britons, some of whom still painted themselves blue. Along the European borderlands, especially in Britain or on the Rhine–Danube line, military government was necessary to guard against invasions and uprisings. The camps of the settled legions often became permanent towns: two of the many that have outlived the Roman Empire are Cologne and Vienna. To the Western provinces such as Gaul and Spain the Romans exported their own city-state machinery for local government, subdividing the province into small units which enjoyed a good deal of autonomy—the *civitates* (plural of *civitas*, city-state)—each with its own senate and assemblies, and with its executive power in the hands of a council (*curia*) of the large local landowners. Seville, Bordeaux, and Trier, now in Spain, France, and West Germany respectively, are only three of the dozens of western European cities that began as Roman *civitates*.

In the East, on the other hand, where powerful local administrative traditions existed, the Romans followed them. The Roman provincial governors in Egypt and the Near East were autocrats of the sort that the population understood. In Greece the Romans continued to allow the city-states some local autonomy. In North Africa the city-states, some of them going back to Phoenician times, enjoyed similar privileges, but much of the area consisted of huge estates owned by the Emperor himself or by Roman capitalists. Only in Palestine did Roman provincial administration fail. There the Jews stubbornly resisted efforts to maintain a satellite kingdom, and repeatedly rebelled against Roman intervention in Jewish life. In A.D. 70, after a four-year siege, the Romans sacked Jerusalem and destroyed the temple. For two generations, the religion of the Jews suffered persecution, and the Jews were gradually dispersed abroad, especially after 130, when Hadrian forbade them to go to the rebuilt temple except on a single day in the year.

Generally, however, the imperial civil service, the common practice of emperor-worship, the common coinage, and the two common languages (Latin in the West and Greek in the East) held the Empire together. Most important of all was the respect for the benefits of the Roman Law and the Roman Peace. In 212, as the culmination of a long process, the Emperor Caracalla bestowed Roman citizenship on all provincials except the lowest social classes. Caracalla's motive was greed: he needed more taxpayers to get the money for increases in soldiers' pay and an ostentatious building program. But none the less it is true that from Britain to the Euphrates the truth of the simple affirmation *Civis Romanus sum* ("I am a Roman citizen") uttered by men of the most diverse origins and circumstances testified to their pride of membership in the Roman system.

THE DECLINE OF ROME

The Stoic philosopher–emperor Marcus Aurelius (161–180) installed as emperor his own son, Commodus (180–193), who cared for nothing but chariot-racing and combats in the arena, and was eventually assassinated. Not only did later emperors fail to return to the practice of adoption but they came to rely on their troops for support. Generals competed with each other in pampering their soldiers in order to secure armed support for an eventual bid to take over the throne. Between 235 and 284 more than two dozen emperors succeeded each other rapidly, as provincial governors or local commanders put rival political armies in the field. Only one of these rulers died a natural death. On the Rhine–Danube frontier, defenses sagged under increasing pressure; Dacia had to be abandoned; Germans raided into Gaul, Britain, and Spain. Rome itself had to be fortified anew. In the East a revival took place in Persia as the vigorous dynasty of the Sassanians came to the throne. In 259 the Persian King Shapur took the Roman Emperor Valerian prisoner, and had his skin tanned for display in a temple.

Total collapse seemed not far off, when the Emperor Diocletian (284–305) and his successors Galerius (305–311) and Constantine (306–337) undertook a series of drastic reforms that eventually completed the transformation of the Empire into a centralized autocracy of the Near Eastern type. To prevent the continued misuse of military power by provincial governors, Diocletian deprived them of all but civil authority and instituted a wholly separate military administration. He also reduced the provinces in size, and so more than doubled their number, regrouping them into larger units called dioceses each under a *vicarius* (vicar), deputy of the emperor.

Believing that the Empire had grown too unwieldy for one-man government, Diocletian invented a new imperial structure. Remaining the senior Augustus himself, he appointed a co-Emperor, who also became Augustus (Maximian). Then each Augustus appointed a Caesar, to be his adopted son and deputy and designated successor. The system of two *augusti* and two *caesares* is called a *tetrarchy*, the Greek for a government by four rulers. Each of the four took responsibility for a major portion of the Empire, called a prefecture, and consisting of a collection of dioceses with their subject provinces. Diocletian took the prefecture of the East, the Asian territories plus Egypt, with his capital at Nicomedia, in northwest Asia Minor; his Caesar took Illyricum, roughly speaking Greece and the Balkans minus most of the Adriatic coast, with its capital at Sirmium in modern Yugoslavia. Maximian took Italy, which included much of the central European regions to the north and east of Italy (Switzerland, Austria, Hungary, the Adriatic) and had its capital at Milan; and his Caesar took Gaul, which included France, Spain, and Britain. A line running through the Adriatic

Sea divided the two Eastern prefectures from the two Western ones, and roughly marked the boundary between Greek-speakers and Latin-speakers. Though abolished by Constantine, this line later reappeared and became permanent in 395. It marked a division between civilizations as well as administrations.

To revitalize the army, Diocletian speeded up a practice already under way and recruited large numbers of barbarian mercenaries, chiefly Germans. Military service became a hereditary obligation, and an enlisted man could rise to the top. To refurbish the prestige of the emperor himself, Diocletian borrowed from Oriental tradition: he sprinkled his hair with gold dust, gilded his nails, wore blue and gold robes to signalize his identity with the sun in the sky, and required slavish obeisances on his every appearance. To halt inflation, which had been

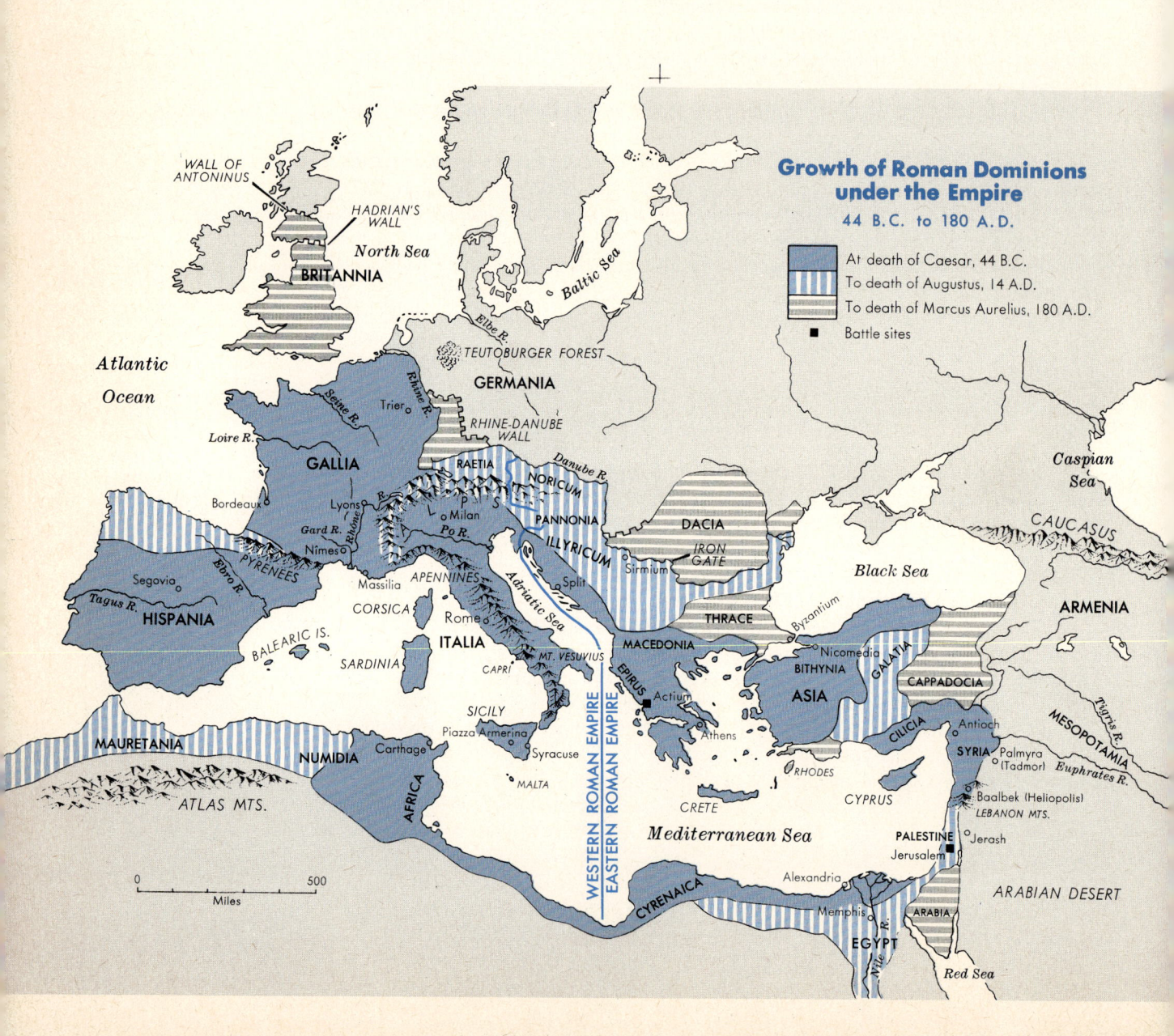

Growth of Roman Dominions under the Empire
44 B.C. to 180 A.D.

- At death of Caesar, 44 B.C.
- To death of Augustus, 14 A.D.
- To death of Marcus Aurelius, 180 A.D.
- ■ Battle sites

speeded by his predecessors' practice of debasing the gold coinage, Diocletian in 301 tried to fix all wages and prices, in a famous edict that went into minute detail and imposed the death-penalty for violations. Riots and black-marketing rendered the edict ineffectual.

In his effort to raise money, Diocletian assigned each *civitas* a quota to be met; if the amount fell short, the members of the local council, the *curiales*, had to make up the deficit out of their own pockets. The *curiales* tried to resign in droves from what had been an honor but was now an intolerable burden. But Diocletian and his successors forced them to keep their jobs, and made the jobs hereditary. Many other social groups experienced the same fate. Because there was a manpower shortage on the land, the government made the status of tenant farmer (*colonus*) hereditary and fixed him to the land he cultivated: he had become a serf. Bakers, aqueduct-workers, merchants, all became frozen in their occupations, and their sons had to succeed them. Roman society became stratified into a rigid caste system.

Diocletian retired in 305 and left his half of the Empire to his Caesar; and he forced his fellow-Augustus, Maximian, to do the same. Each of the new *augusti* in turn named a *caesar;* but the system now broke down, as the four top officials began to struggle against each other for supreme power. By 324, Constantine, who had begun as the son of the Western Caesar, boss of Gaul, emerged as sole Augustus, and the Empire was reunited. Though the tetrarchy did not survive, the other reforms of Diocletian and his immediate successors certainly helped to stave off collapse. But, of course, they did not prevent it.

Few subjects have been more debated than the reasons for the decline of the Roman Empire. The celebrated eighteenth-century historian Edward Gibbon blamed Christianity, charging that it destroyed the civic spirit of the Roman by turning his attention to the afterlife and away from his duties to the state. Michael Rostovtzeff, a learned Russian scholar writing in the 1920's and 1930's, attributed the decline in part to the constant pressure of the underprivileged masses of the Empire to share in the wealth of their rulers, of which there was not enough to go around anyhow. Gibbon and Rostovtzeff each reflected his own time and experience, Gibbon the anticlerical rationalism of the eighteenth century, Rostovtzeff the bitter lesson of the Bolshevik Revolution in his native Russia. Others have emphasized the influx of Greeks and Orientals into Roman society, and intimated that the original "pure" Roman racial virtues were thus diluted, a view shared by few reliable historians. Still others have talked of climatic change, but with little evidence.

Certainly, in the political realm, the abandonment of the adoptive succession helped to create trouble. Economically, losses in population caused by plagues and civil war crippled agriculture, already hampered by backward methods. The growing concentration of land in large estates and the absorption of free farmers into the status of *coloni* diluted Roman prosperity, already suffering from feeble purchasing power and inflation. Psychologically, the masses became alienated from their rulers: the substitution of the mercenary for the old citizen-soldier testified to the decline of the old Roman patriotism. Yet even with all these factors, it would be hard to imagine Roman decline without the terrific pressure of outside forces: the third and fourth centuries were the time when the barbarian world began to move, and it was the barbarian threat that eventually brought about the collapse of the Roman structure in the West while permitting its survival in the East in a modified form.

VII. Roman Civilization

THE ROMANS AND GREECE

Since the end of World War II, when American military power emerged as the decisive force in European affairs, many Europeans have unkindly compared the Americans to the Romans and themselves to the Greeks. Here, they felt, were the Americans, uncultivated boors without much of a civilization of their own but with a great deal of impressive military hardware, trying to tell newly weakened peoples with old and proud military and political traditions how to run their affairs, and at the same time goggling admiringly at the surviving monuments of European culture. It is of course true that American civilization is newer, and that if Americans wish to see ancient temples, medieval castles, and cathedrals, they must go to Europe to do so.

But the parallel breaks down in many places. America did not attack and conquer Europe or attempt to govern it. Rome did these things to Greece. America was founded by Europeans, and inherited its civilization from them; so that Homer, Dante, and Shakespeare are as much a part of our tradition as of theirs. Rome was not founded by Greeks. And if many Americans regarded Europe as a museum for their entertainment and instruction, was it not because they recognized themselves as part of the same tradition rather than because they had found something new and different?

However faulty the modern part of the parallel may be, the ancient generalization still holds true: Greece, though conquered, took her conqueror captive. In literature and the arts, the Romans took virtually everything from the Greeks. It was only in fields where they had talent and originality, such as the law and engineering, that they made a contribution of their own. The Greece the Romans gradually conquered was not the Greece of Homer or Pericles; so that the Romans, for example, did not imitate the Greek tragedians of the fifth century B.C.: there was no Roman Aeschylus, Sophocles, or Euripides. This was the Greece of the decades after the death of Alexander, of the New Comedy of Menander, not the Old Comedy of Aristophanes (*see above*, p. 73), when literature—much of it produced in Alexandria—was more artificial, more purely charming and graceful, often trivial, less grand, less concerned with the central themes of human existence. The surviving Alexandrian epic, Apollonius Rhodius' *Argonautica*, which tells of the adventures of the mythical hero Jason on his way to find the golden fleece, was a scholar's careful (and not very successful) effort to be Homeric long after the heroic age was over. When the Romans first began to imitate the Greeks, the greatest Greek works, though deeply respected, were no longer being written: it was a lesser age.

Before the first contacts with the Greeks, of course, the Romans, in their central Italian provincial agricultural city-state, had already evolved their own simple religion, the worship of the household spirits, the *lares* and *penates* that governed their everyday affairs, along with those that inhabited the local woods and springs and fields. Like the Greek Hestia (*see above*, p. 68), the Roman Vesta presided over the individual hearth, and had in her service the specially trained Vestal Virgins. From the Etruscans the Romans took the belief, which they never abandoned, in divination: they too foretold the future through observing the flight of birds (the auspicies) and examining the entrails of animals (the auguries). From Greece there came the entire Olympic collection of gods and goddesses, some of them merging their identities in existing divinities, and most of them changing their names. Zeus became Jupiter, Hera Juno, Poseidon Neptune, and so on, though Apollo remained Apollo. But the Romans had nothing like the Greek Olympic games or the festivals of Dionysus that had led to the writing of Athenian tragedy and comedy.

LATIN LITERATURE

The chief Roman writers down to the end of the Republic include the comedians Plautus and Terence, the first of the late third, the second of the early second century B.C. Plautus was a knockabout writer of farce in the tradition of the Greek New Comedy: it was he who wrote the play about the two sets of twins, masters and servants, who are always being mixed up, that Shakespeare eventually imitated in *A Comedy of Errors*. Terence was gentler and more romantic. Catullus and Lucretius, both of the first century B.C., wrote splendid verse, Catullus passionate love lyrics to an unworthy mistress, and Lucretius an epic, *On the Nature of Things*. Lucretius wrote under the influence of the Alexandrian philosopher Epicurus, and expounded a hard-headed, unreligious view of the material nature of men and their souls, which are a mere collection of atoms, so that death brings dissolution and sleep instead of immortality.

To the Stoics, following the influence of a rival Alexandrian philosophical school, the human soul was indeed a divine gift, and one of which men should strive to be worthy. Cicero, the orator and politician whom we have already encountered, was a dedicated Stoic, and in philosophical essays, largely based on Greek models, he defended and introduced to generations of readers in the West the concepts of natural law, existing independent of man's efforts, and a law of nations, which should regulate the conduct of peoples to each other. His later influence, especially on the Founding Fathers of the American republic, was incalculable. Other Stoics included the tragedian Seneca, of the first century A.D., who was tutor to the Emperor Nero, and the Emperor Marcus Aurelius of the second century A.D., who wrote his own highly stoical *Meditations* in Greek.

It was the poets of the age of Augustus, the first Emperor, who by common consent gave Rome its literary golden age. Vergil (70–19 B.C.) followed Greek pastoral models in his *Georgics* and *Eclogues*, which praise and describe the pleasures and satisfactions of rural life, and which assisted Augustus' program of propaganda on behalf of farming. In the *Aeneid*, the poet's predictions of the glories that would come to Rome, the city that Aeneas founded, were of course designed to please the Emperor. But they have a ring of sincerity and deep patriotism: self-conscious though it is, the *Aeneid* often achieves almost Homeric qualities. Horace (65–8 B.C.) had more humor than Vergil, and expressed a greater variety of feelings in a greater number of metres; in shorter poems on more limited subjects he also praises the joys of rural life and the virtues of moderation. Much less concerned with virtue, Ovid (43 B.C.–A.D. 17) sang of the mythical transformations into birds or animals or plants that Greek myth reported of the various divinities, and gave worldly and cynical advice on the art of love. He died in exile because of his involvement in a scandal affecting the granddaughter of Augustus.

A few years after Augustus' death, literature was already reflecting discontent and disillusionment with the cynicism of Roman life and politics. **Tacitus** (c. A.D. 55–117) the greatest of the Roman historians, felt so keenly that his countrymen had degenerated that he wrote in his *Germania* an essay ostensibly reporting on the rugged and primitive way of life of the German barbarians, but actually commenting acidly on the Romans' loss of the old virtues. His *Annals*—indeed everything he wrote—were history with the purpose of reminding his readers how effete and ineffectual they were as compared with their ancestors.

LAW

The legal code published on the Twelve Tables in the fifth century B.C. reflected the needs of a small city-state, not those of a huge empire. As Rome became a world capital, thousands of foreigners flocked to live there to pursue their businesses, and of course they often got into disagreements with each other or with a Roman. But Roman law developed the flexibility to adjust to changing conditions: the enactments of the Senate and Assemblies, the decrees of each new emperor, and the decisions of the judges who were often called in as advisers contributed to a great body of legal materials.

It was the praetors, the chief legal officers, who heard both sides in every case, and determined the facts before turning over the matter to the *judex,* a referee, for decision. The judices had to develop a body of rules for deciding cases that were not covered by existing law. As they dealt with many different breeds of foreigner, they worked out a body of legal custom common to all of them, *the law of the peoples* (*jus gentium*) that would be acceptable to all comers. As each new praetor took office for a year, he would announce the laws by which he intended to be bound, usually following his predecessors, and adding to the body of law as necessary. Romans too gradually acquired the benefits of the law of the peoples.

The expert advisers (jurisconsults) to both praetor and judex felt an almost religious concern for equity: it was the spirit rather than the letter of the law that counted. This humane view found support in the philosophical writings of the Stoics, who believed as we saw that above all man-made law stood a higher "natural" law, divinely inspired, and applying to all men everywhere. In practice, of course, judges were often ill-trained, the emperors brutal or arbitrary; Roman law could be used to exalt the authority of the state over the individual. Yet the law recognized the rights of the citizen, afforded legal redress even to slaves, and gave wide scope to local legal practices. Its superiority made it a victor over other legal systems; the law of much of western Europe today goes back to its provisions.

ENGINEERING AND MEDICINE

The Romans devised a formula for making concrete from sand, lime, silica, stone, and water. They combined this concrete with large stones in building roads and bridges so well designed and so long-lasting that even today a few are still in use. The network of roads spread throughout the Empire, making travel overland swift and easy. The Romans went to great trouble and expense to provide their cities with pure and abundant water. A dozen aqueducts served Rome itself, and from Constantinople to Segovia aqueducts form the most spectacular Roman ruins. The concern for water reflected a real interest in bathing and in hygiene: the Romans had the highest sanitary standards known in Europe until the nineteenth century.

Roman surgeons made a variety of ingenious instruments for special operations, including the Caesarean operation—supposed (probably wrongly) to have been first performed at the birth of Julius Caesar—to deliver babies unable to be born normally. The Romans invented the first hospitals, military and civilian. Much superstition survived in Roman medicine, and it was the Greeks, notably Galen (A.D. 131–201), who continued to make the chief theoretical contributions, compiling medical encyclopedias, and diffusing learning. What Galen did for medicine, his contemporary Ptolemy of Alexandria did for ancient geography; both remained the chief authorities on their subjects down to the sixteenth century. Some learned Romans followed the Alexandrian Eratosthenes in believing

Gladiators: detail of a mosaic pavement, c. 300 A.D.

that the earth was round. Pliny the Elder in the first century A.D. made observations of ships approaching the shore to support this view: it was the tip of the mast that appeared first to an observer on shore and the hull last, a proof, Pliny felt, that the surface of the earth was curved.

ARCHITECTURE, SCULPTURE, AND PAINTING

Roman architecture borrowed the Greek column, usually Corinthian, but made wide use also of the round arch, originated by the Etruscans, and from this developed the barrel vault, a continuous series of arches like the roof of a tunnel which could be used to roof over rather large areas. The Romans introduced the dome, and a splendid one surmounts the Pantheon at Rome, built to honor the divine ancestors of Augustus. Roman structures went in for bigness: the Colosseum seated 45,000 spectators; the Baths of the Emperor Caracalla accommodated thousands of bathers at a time (its ruins are still used for grand opera); Diocletian's palace at Split in modern Yugoslavia contains most of the modern city *inside* its walls. All over the Middle East and North Africa, as well as western Europe, one finds amphitheaters, temples, villas, and other monumental remains of the Roman domination.

Roman statues, though derived from Greek and Hellenistic models, often had a realism all their own, as in the cases of imperial portrait busts. Of Roman painting we have chiefly the pretty—sometimes obscene—wall decorations of the villas at Pompeii (the resort town near Naples that was literally buried in 79 B.C. by the sudden eruption of Vesuvius that covered it in a rain of hot ash), and the mosaic floors of public and private buildings, where a favorite subject was a hunting scene in the landscape of the Nile, with crocodiles and hippopotamuses among the papyrus plants. The recently discovered imperial villa at Piazza Armerina in Sicily has a superb series of these floors, including one scene showing a group of bathing girls in bikinis, tossing a beach ball from hand to hand.

A FINAL APPRAISAL

Tacitus was certainly right in thinking that Rome had lost some of its traditional virtues with its conquest of huge territories, its accumulation of wealth, and its assumption of imperial responsibilities. Nevertheless, the first two centuries of the Empire mark the most stable and prosperous era that had yet occurred in human history. No doubt, the profits of flourishing commercial life were unevenly distributed, and there were glaring contrasts between riches and poverty. But many of the harshest aspects of ancient society elsewhere were softened at Rome: slaves could obtain their freedom more easily; women had more rights and commanded more respect (we have much evidence of harmonious family life, though there were more divorces perhaps than at any time until our own day); physical comforts were abundant for those who could afford them.

In Rome itself, however, great areas were slums: six- and seven-story wooden tenements that burned down repeatedly and were rebuilt despite building codes and fire departments. Worst of all was the chronic urban unemployment: At the height of the *Pax Romana,* perhaps half the population of the capital was on the bread dole. The inhabitants also were given free circuses, in the form of chariot races and gladiatorial combats, and the poor squandered their pennies on betting. Bloodshed exerted a morbid fascination: criminals were crucified and even burned alive on the stage as part of spectacles to entertain the populace, and in the last century of Roman life, these shows had become so popular that they had superseded the circus, despite the protests of the occasional horrified citizens, pagan or Christian.

Though the structure of the Roman state would disappear in the West by the end of the fifth century A.D., Roman influence has given a permanent shape to western Europe. Italian, French, Spanish, Portuguese are all languages derived from Latin, and our own English tongue is a hybrid with almost as many Latin as Germanic words. Roman legal concepts provided the foundations of respectability for many a squalid barbarian society. Rome itself, finally, would become the capital of Christianity and its administrative organization a model for the structure of the Church.

READING SUGGESTIONS (asterisk indicates paperbound edition)

Greece: General Accounts

M. I. Finley, *The Ancient Greeks* (*Compass). Compact and perceptive introduction to Greek life and thought.

C. E. Robinson, *Hellas: A Short History of Ancient Greece* (*Beacon). By a good scholar.

M. I. Rostovtzeff, *Greece* (*Galaxy). A famous older account, now somewhat outdated.

J. B. Bury, *A History of Greece to the Death of Alexander the Great*, 3rd ed. rev. (Macmillan, 1951). Another celebrated older account, stressing war and politics.

N. G. L. Hammond, *A History of Greece to 322 B.C.*, 2nd ed. (Oxford University, 1967). A good up-to-date survey.

R. M. Cook, *The Greeks till Alexander* (Praeger, 1962). Well-illustrated survey, stressing material accomplishments.

The Greek Polis

V. Ehrenberg, *The Greek State* (*Norton). Solid, scholarly introduction.

A. Andrewes, *The Greek Tyrants* (*Torchbooks). Informative comparative survey of emerging constitutions.

A. H. M. Jones, *Athenian Democracy* (Praeger, 1957). An up-to-date interpretation.

A. E. Zimmern, *The Greek Commonwealth* (*Galaxy). A celebrated and sympathetic older account, stressing especially Athens.

H. Michell, *Sparta* (*Cambridge University). A comprehensive and sympathetic survey.

Kathleen Freeman, *Greek City-States* (*Norton). Excellent overview, focussing on states other than Athens and Sparta.

A. G. Woodhead, *The Greeks in the West* (Praeger, 1962), and J. M. Cook, *The Greeks in Ionia and the East* (Praeger, 1963), Two volumes in the series titled "Ancient Peoples and Places," also reminding us that the Greek world was not limited to Athens and Sparta.

Greek Civilization

W. Jaeger, *Paideia,* 3 vols. (Oxford University, 1939–1944). An advanced study of Greek culture and ideals (*Vol. I, Galaxy).

C. M. Bowra, *The Greek Experience* (*Mentor). As seen by a literary scholar.

A. Bonnard, *Greek Civilization*, 3 vols. (Macmillan, 1957–1961). Stimulating chapters on a wide range of topics.

W. K. C. Guthrie, *The Greeks and Their Gods* (*Beacon). Detailed but engrossing study of the origins and nature of Greek religion.

F. M. Cornford, *Before and After Socrates* (*Cambridge University). A first-rate short introduction to science and philosophy in Greece.

J. B. Bury, *The Greek Historians* (*Dover). Appraisals by a celebrated English historian.

Rhys Carpenter, *The Esthetic Basis of Greek Art* (*Indiana University). Analysis by an expert.

The Hellenistic World

W. W. Tarn, *Alexander the Great* (*Beacon). Hero-worship that protests too much.

W. W. Tarn and G. T. Griffith, *Hellenistic Civilization*, 3rd ed. (St. Martins, 1952). A comprehensive survey.

M. Rostovtzeff, *The Social and Economic History of the Hellenistic World* (Clarendon, 1941). Detailed study by a great historian.

Rome: General Accounts

M. Rostovtzeff, *Rome* (*Galaxy). Excellent scholarly survey, though a little outdated.

A. E. R. Boak, *A History of Rome to 565*, 5th ed. (Macmillan, 1965). A standard textbook.

C. E. Robinson, *Apollo History of Rome* (*Apollo). A clear introduction.

T. Mommsen, *The History of Rome* (*Philosophical Library). Detailed study by a great nineteenth-century scholar; still worth reading.

M. Grant, *The World of Rome* (World, 1960). Handsomely illustrated introduction to imperial Rome.

R. H. Barrow, *The Romans* (*Penguin). Sound popular survey.

The Etruscan Background and the Roman Republic

O. W. von Vacano, *The Etruscans in the Ancient World* (*Indiana University). Careful study of the archeological evidence.

R. Bloch, *The Etruscans* (Praeger, 1958). Briefer and well-illustrated volume in the series "Ancient Peoples and Places."

———, *The Origins of Rome* (Praeger, 1960). Another volume in the series, taking the story to the early fifth century B.C.

H. H. Scullard, *Roman Politics, 220–150 B.C.* (Clarendon, 1951). Detailed study of the era when Rome began to dominate the Mediterranean world.

———, *From the Gracchi to Nero* (*Barnes & Noble). Up-to-date, clear, and balanced history of the later Republic and early Empire.

R. E. Smith, *The Failure of the Roman Republic* (Cambridge University, 1955). A provocative essay that is critical of the Gracchi.

The Roman Empire

R. Syme, *The Roman Revolution* (*Galaxy). The transformation of state and society under Caesar and Augustus.

H. T. Rowell, *Rome in the Augustan Age* (Oklahoma University, 1962). Sympathetic appraisal of Augustus and his work.

T. W. Africa, *Rome of the Caesars* (*Wiley). The first two centuries of the Empire interpreted through biographies of its leaders.

M. P. Charlesworth, *The Roman Empire* (*Galaxy). Informative sketch.

S. Dill, *Roman Society from Nero to Marcus Aurelius* (*Meridian). A classic of social history.

Roman Civilization and Decline

M. Clarke, *The Roman Mind* (Cohen & West, 1956). Studies in the history of thought from Cicero to Marcus Aurelius.

M. Wheeler, *Roman Art and Architecture* (*Penguin). Clear and well illustrated.

H. Mattingly, *Roman Imperial Civilization* (*Anchor). As illustrated by a study of coins.

E. Gibbon, *A History of the Decline and Fall of the Roman Empire* (*many editions, usually abridged). The earliest chapters of this famous classic relate to the third and fourth centuries.

M. Rostovtzeff, *The Social and Economic History of the Roman Empire*, 2nd ed. (Clarendon, 1957). Magnificently illustrated detailed study, with speculations on the reasons for Roman decline.

R. M. Haywood, *The Myth of Rome's Fall* (*Apollo). Scholarly survey of the centuries of decline, addressed to the general reader.

A Sampling of Sources and Historical Fiction

W. H. Auden, ed., *The Portable Greek Reader* (*Viking).

The Iliad, R. Lattimore, trans. (*Phoenix).

W. J. Oates and E. O'Neill, Jr., eds., *The Complete Greek Drama*, 2 vols. (Random House, 1938). A selection may be found in *Seven Greek Plays* (*Vintage).

The Dialogues of Plato, B. Jowett, trans. (Clarendon, 1953).

The Works of Aristotle, W. D. Ross, ed. (Clarendon, 1908–1931).

Thucydides, *History of the Peloponnesian War*, B. Jowett, trans. (*Bantam).

Mary Renault, *The King Must Die* (*Pocket Books). A novel set in Mycenae and in Minoan Crete.

———, *The Last of the Wine* (*Pocket Books). A novel set in Athens at the time of the Peloponnesian War.

B. Davenport, ed., *The Portable Roman Reader* (*Viking).

N. Lewis and M. Reinhold, *Roman Civilization*, 2 vols. (*Torchbooks). Including both selections from the sources and enlightening comments on them.

Vergil, *The Aeneid*, R. Humphries, trans. (*Scribner's).

Marcus Aurelius, *Meditations* (*several editions).

Bryher, *The Coin of Carthage* (*Harcourt). Novel set against the Second Punic War.

———, *The Roman Wall* (*Vintage). Novel set on the Alpine frontier in the era of decline.

Bernard Shaw, *Caesar and Cleopatra* (*Penguin). Drama depicting Caesar as wise and very talkative.

Shakespeare, *Julius Caesar*.

———, *Antony and Cleopatra* (with a devastating portrait of the ambitious youth who later became Augustus).

———, *Coriolanus*. A thoroughly disenchanted view of republican Roman politicians.

3

The Making of a New World

To the Year 1000

Anglo-Saxon whalebone casket (c. 700) with Runic inscriptions. The panel on the right shows the adoration of the Magi.

I. The Christian Revolution in the Roman World

THE SPIRIT OF THE TIMES

Greek scientific theory and Roman technical skills had brought the ancient world to the threshold of an industrial age. A century before Christ, Hero of Alexandria had even discovered the engineering usefulness of steam pressure in a boiler, and conceived a model of a fire engine, including the piston. It would have been only a short step to the building of steam devices. Why did more than 1700 years pass before man took that step?

The answer must lie in the attitudes of the ruling groups in Roman times. Science formed no part of their education, and scattered statements show that they scorned what we would call research. They feared new inventions that might put still more people out of work: the Emperor Tiberius once executed a man who had invented a process for making unbreakable glass. Although the earlier advance of science in the Greek and Hellenistic world had given rise to small groups of rationalists who believed in improving their lives by using their reasoning powers, even these minorities seem virtually to have disappeared. Everywhere in Rome the student can observe mounting pessimism and a lack of faith in man's ability to work out his own future.

The old gods seemed powerless to intervene; life appeared to be a matter of luck. And so, beginning as early as the third century B.C. and gathering increasing momentum later on, the cult of the goddess Fortune became immensely popular in the Mediterranean world: chance governed everything; today's prosperity might vanish tomorrow; the best thing to do was to enjoy luck while it lasted. Closely related was the belief in Fate: what happened was inevitable, because it had been fated from the beginning; when you were born, the moment of your death was already fixed. Some, like Cicero, protested that men could contribute to their own fate and so take advantage of fortune; Vergil attributed both fate and fortune to the will of the divine providence; but most Romans, like Tacitus, seem to have felt helpless to change their own fates or to influence events.

Astrology. To escape this feeling, most Romans came to believe that the movements of the heavenly bodies influenced the fortunes and the fate of men and governed the decisions they made. Thus the science of astronomy became lost in the false speculation of astrology. If you could do nothing to change your destiny, you could at least try to find out what it might be by consulting an expert astrologer. He would study the seven planets (Saturn, Jupiter, Mars, the Sun, Venus, Mercury, the Moon), each of which had its own will, character, sex, plants, numbers, and animals, and each of which was lord of a sphere. Seven transparent but impenetrable concentric spheres, with Earth at the center, cut man off from heaven. Each planet had its own day: hence the seven-day week. Seven itself became a mystic number: there were seven ages of man, seven wonders of the world. Then too there were the twelve Houses of the Sun, constellations of stars through which the sun passed on his path around the earth: the signs of the Zodiac.

From the position of the heavenly bodies and the signs of the Zodiac at the moment of your conception or birth, astrologers would draw up a horoscope foretelling your fate. The Roman Emperors, like most of their subjects, profoundly believed in astrology. And of course some people have continued to believe, even to our own day. Especially valuable for the art of prophecy were unnatural events: the appearance of a comet, the birth of a monster. Similarly, men believed in all sorts of magic, and tried by its power to force the heavenly bodies to grant their wishes.

New Cults: Cybele, Isis, Mithra. The state religion of the Olympian gods and of the deified Emperor still commanded the loyalty of many Romans, who regarded the proper observance of its rites as the equivalent of patriotism. But the old faith no longer allayed the fears of the millions of people believing in blind fate and inevitable fortune. More and more men sought for a religion that would hold out the hope for an afterlife better than the grim life here on earth. So, along with astrology and magic, a large number of mystery religions began to appear in Rome.

All the new faiths taught that a human being could save his soul by uniting it with the soul of a saviour, who in many cases had himself experienced death and resurrection. Union with the saviour was accomplished by a long initiation, with purifications, ritual banquets, and other ceremonies. The candidate gradually cast aside human unworthiness, the god would enter him, and so after death he would be saved. The initiate sought a mystical guarantee that he would not perish but would survive hereafter. It was perfectly possible to join as many of these cults as one liked and yet at the same time continue to practice the state religion.

The Greeks had had such cults, in the rites of Demeter at Eleusis and in the mysteries of Dionysus. The rites of Dionysus, now called Bacchus, became popular at Rome, celebrating as they did the animal side of human nature and the abandonment of all restraint. On hundreds of Roman sarcophagi can be seen the Bacchic procession, celebrating the joys of drink and sex. But the cult of Bacchus was too materialistic to satisfy all Romans.

One of its major competitors was the cult of the great mother-goddess Cybele, transplanted from Asia Minor. Her young husband, Attis, died and was

The taurobolium (sacrifice of a bull in Mithraism): Roman relief.

reborn annually (like Demeter's daughter, Persephone). Attis was thus a symbol of renewed fertility. The rites of Cybele included fasting, frenzied processions, and the self-flagellation and even self-mutilation of the priests. The first temple to Cybele at Rome dated from 204 B.C., but the zenith of the cult came in the second century A.D. and later, when it spread to the West. By that time the rites included the slaughter of a bull above a pit into which the initiate had descended in order to be bathed by the blood.

Even more popular—especially among women—was the cult of the Egyptian Isis, whose consort, Osiris, also died and was reborn each year. All feminine elements, both lascivious and chaste, were concentrated in an elaborate ritual of worship for Isis, the loving mother-goddess, who promised her adherents personal immortality.

From Persia via Asia Minor came the cult of the god Mithra, allied to the supreme powers of good and light and so connected with the Sun. The male initiates passed in succession through seven grades of initiation (corresponding to the seven planets and named after animals), qualifying for each by severe tests. Baptism and communion were also part of the ritual. Unconquered, physically tough, and self-denying, Mithra became a model for the Roman soldier, to whom he held out the hope of salvation. Mithraism had no priests and welcomed the gods of other cults; it tended to absorb the other sun-worshipping cults, including that of Apollo, into one new cult, often heartily supported by the Emperor. From London to Alexandria and from the Rhine to the Euphrates, temples of Mithra, with altars and statues, have been found.

CHRISTIANITY

But no single one of the mystery religions appealed to men and women of all classes at Rome. Mithraism, which perhaps had the most adherents, excluded women and lacked love and tenderness. Christianity competed with these cults in the Roman world for more than three centuries after the death of its founder, with no assurance that it would triumph. Sharing some things in common with them, it also possessed qualities they lacked. While it is not possible to present an account of Christianity equally acceptable to everyone in the modern world, we take the "historical" approach and hope to exclude partisan distortion.

The Historical Jesus. Jesus was born in Palestine sometime between the years we call 8 and 4 B.C., and was crucified probably in 29, or 30, or 33 A.D. There are no sources absolutely contemporary with his life, but St. Paul's Epistle to the Corinthians was written about 55 A.D., Acts about 60–62, the Gospel according to Mark about 65, Matthew and Luke about 80–85, and John about 100. Late in the second or early in the third century these texts were revised in Alexandria. We have no canonical Christian text written down before this revision. Before the year 60 A.D. a collection of the sayings of Jesus himself existed, written in Aramaic, the Semitic language that he spoke; this is lost. In addition, many other texts existed that were not regarded as canonical. Among them we may note the so-called *Gospel of Thomas*, of which fragments were found in Egypt in 1945 and 1946, consisting of 114 sayings attributed to Jesus, and dating from the early second century.

Thus, because we have no precise, contemporary accounts, the exact details of the preachings of Jesus during his own lifetime cannot always be determined.

But the general nature of his message is clear enough. Although he appealed to the poor, the unlearned, and the weak, he was no simple social revolutionary, no revivalist, no ascetic. He preached the enjoyment of the good things of this world, an enjoyment freed from rivalry, ostentation, and vulgarity. He was kind but stern: good intentions are not enough; "he that heareth and doeth not is like a man that without a foundation built a house upon the earth. . . ." Above all Christ preached gentleness and love: humility, honesty, toleration, charity; but he warned that "wide is the gate, and broad is the way, that leadeth to destruction." Though he preached that men should turn the other cheek, he also said at another time that he came not to bring peace, but a sword.

Christian Ideas. From Jesus' preaching there emerged theological conclusions of great importance: he spoke of his Father in heaven, referred to himself as the Son of Man, and taught that God the Father had sent him to redeem mankind from sin. Those who hearkened and led decent lives on earth would gain eternal bliss in heaven; those who turned a deaf ear and continued in their evil courses would be eternally damned in hell. The Gospels add that Christ (the word means "the anointed one") had died on the cross as the supreme act of redemption, that he had risen from the dead on the third day, and that he would soon return, during the lifetime of some of his hearers, to end this world in a final Day of Judgment. So the earliest Christians expected the second coming of Christ momentarily, and thought little of their earthly lives. Soon the literal expectation of Christ was transformed into a more mystical expectation of "the Comforter."

Christ was miraculously born of a virgin mother. He was baptized in the waters of the Jordan, and his followers too were baptized by their priests. He himself had given bread and wine to his followers, and told them that it was his body and his blood. The virgin mother, the purifying bath, and the mysterious sacrificial meal of communion recall elements that were present in the various mystery cults, as of course does the promise of eternal life. But the Christians held in contempt the excesses of the cult of Cybele, for example, and regarded Mithraic baptism and sacred communion as fiendish parodies of their own practices. Moreover, Jesus' sacrifice of his life for mankind and the intimacy with God promised during the future eternal life gave Christianity an immediacy and an appeal that no mystery religion could duplicate. Christ's message of love—for man, woman, and child, for the weak and lowly—supplied the tenderness so lacking in the world of every day.

By the third century the ritual act of communion—the sacrament of the Eucharist or Mass—had become the central symbol of Christianity. It was the action that made the individual Christian actually partake of his God and feel the wonder of salvation, just as by his baptism he had been figuratively washed clean of the sin that has at birth stained all men since Adam chose to disobey God. Baptism made one a Christian; the Eucharist, if taken reverently, kept one a Christian, provided one's behavior was also suitable. Because Christ by his crucifixion had atoned for the sin of Adam, the individual Christian might now also be saved.

Besides baptism and the Eucharist, five other ritual acts eventually came to be regarded as sacraments. These were confirmation, by which a child was brought into the Church when he had reached the age at which he could understand Christian doctrine; penance, by which the repentant sinner was given a temporal punishment by the priest and was granted absolution (but the performance of the penance could not guarantee salvation, since it might not have satisfied God's justice); extreme unction, the last rites for the dying; matrimony; and, for the priest, ordination.

Judean Backgrounds. Christianity was born in the Kingdom of Judea, ruled over by a Hellenized Jewish dynasty loyal to Rome. Jesus was himself a Jew, and his followers inherited with his own teaching the uncompromising monotheism of the Old Testament, the Jewish tradition of regular education of the faithful, the belief that they formed a chosen people, the acceptance of authority, and the constant indoctrination of the faithful with a code of behavior. The Gospels of Matthew and Luke in particular refer to Christ as the Teacher of Righteousness.

New light on these specifically Palestinian traditions in Christianity may be provided by the so-called Dead Sea Scrolls, which were discovered in caves in Palestine beginning in 1947. The scrolls, dating from 200 to 70 B.C., contain fragments of the teachings of a heretical Jewish sect, the Essenes, who lived in an isolated community and shared their property; their buildings were destroyed by the Romans in 68 A.D. The Dead Sea Scrolls make repeated reference to a Teacher of Righteousness, a Suffering Just One, in whom some see a forerunner of Christ. Although after the Teacher's death, probably a violent one, his followers did not claim that he had been the Messiah awaited by the Jews, there is one passage in which the Teacher spoke of himself as producing a man-child who would have all his own powers. The New Testament makes no reference at all to the Essenes, and Jesus may have had no contact with them or with their tradition, yet the scrolls reveal a reforming movement within Judaism that had much in common with later Christianity. In Christ's own time, the Pharisees, the more adventurous-minded of the two warring sects of Jews, had already developed a belief in a Messiah and in an afterlife.

Paul and the Apostles. To the entrenched Jews of Palestine and to the occupying Roman power, Jesus seemed subversive because he did not accept the existing order of things. Amid circumstances the details of which are still debated, he met his martyrdom. After his crucifixion, the small band of his immediate followers began enthusiastically to spread the good news (Evangel) of his teachings and his future second coming. Palestine and Syria were ready to receive their message. Saul of Tarsus, a Jew converted to Christianity by a vision beheld on the road to Damascus, was renamed Paul, and took the lead in giving the new faith its first organization: the earliest Christian church.

Jesus had proclaimed that he had not come to change the Law of the Jews. Non-Jews, though attracted by the appeal of Christianity, did not wish to comply with the details of the Old Testament prescriptions: for example, they did not want to be circumcised or to abstain from pork. Paul said that Greeks and Syrians need not follow the Law in these and other prescriptions. "The letter killeth," said Paul, "but the Spirit giveth Life." It was not the letter of the Law of the Jews that would save the Christian, but the spirit of the faith in a single God as interpreted by his son. Paul was at once a mystic, who would transcend the world and the flesh, and a practical human being, who knew how to advise ordinary men and women about the problems of their daily lives. He never preached denial of this world, yet he urged that man be constantly aware of the next. He expressed this as the mystic union of Christ and the Christian, "Always bearing about in the body the dying of the Lord Jesus, that the life also of Jesus might be made manifest in our body" (II Corinthians 4:10). Not mere animals, not mere men, Christians are children of God both mortal and immortal. While on earth they must live in the constant imperfections of the flesh; after death, if they have been true Christians, they are destined to eternal bliss.

Paul, of course, was not one of the twelve apostles, the actual companions of Christ, who, according to tradition, separated after the crucifixion to preach the faith in the four quarters of the earth. Peter, it was believed, eventually went to Rome itself, and was martyred there. Since Paul too had the same fate, the Church of Rome had both Peter and Paul as its founders. By the year 100, the new faith had penetrated into many of the eastern territories of Rome and was beginning to find a niche in the West. But it was still a small, obscure, poor sect, and only a visionary could have predicted its triumphant future.

Persecutions. Why were Peter and Paul and others martyred? If Rome could tolerate such a multitude of other sects, why not the Christians? Because, alone among the many sects, they would not sacrifice before the statue of the Emperor and thus fulfill their patriotic duty as Romans. The Emperor was not *their* god, and they were ready to incur the punishment of death for not worshipping him. Had they consented to perform this act, which violated the consciences of no other sect, the Christians could have carried on their own ceremonies undisturbed. But they would not, and therefore they had to conduct their services in secret. The Roman authorities suspected them of great vices: incest, murder, infanticide.

So it was natural for the Emperor Nero, in A.D. 64, to punish the Christians by terrible cruelties and, as Tacitus says, to seek a scapegoat for the fire. According to tradition, Peter and Paul perished at that time. After Nero, persecutions took place only sporadically. When Pliny the Younger, a special representative of Trajan (reigned 98–117) in Asia Minor, asked what to do about Christians, Trajan replied that Pliny should make no effort to hunt them out, but that when he was denounced a Christian should be punished unless he denied his religion and supported his denial by worshipping the gods. Christian willingness to undergo martyrdom rather than worship the gods was regarded by most pagan Romans, including the Stoic Emperor Marcus Aurelius (reigned 161–180), as a kind of exhibitionism. Marcus Aurelius persecuted the Christians both in Asia Minor and in Gaul. In the third century, as the Roman world seemed to be coming apart at the seams, persecutions became more frequent and more severe; Diocletian (reigned 284–305) was especially harsh.

THE TRIUMPH OF CHRISTIANITY

But the church throve on repeated martyrdoms. And by 313, Licinius and Constantine, the successors of Diocletian, agreed that the Christians would be let alone. In 312 Constantine himself had a religious experience akin to Paul's on the Damascus road: just before going into battle, the Emperor saw in the heavens the sign of a cross against the sun and the words "conquer in this." He put the sign on the battle-standards of his army, won the battle, and attributed the victory to the god of the Christians. Though the story has often been challenged, there is little evidence for the counterargument that Constantine acted because he simply foresaw the eventual triumph of Christianity. He continued to appease the sun-god as well as the god of the Christians, but he regarded himself a Christian. Soon he found that, as the first Christian Emperor, he must try to settle the severe quarrels that had broken out among Christians. A little more than half a century after Constantine's death in 337, and in spite of the celebrated attempt of the pagan Emperor Julian (reigned 361–363) to turn back the clock, Christianity became the sole tolerated religion in the Roman Empire.

Why did Christianity triumph? It was at the beginning a despised sect of simple enthusiasts in a rich, well-organized, sophisticated society. Yet it took over the society. In general, we may postulate the need for a religion of love in the savage world of Rome; and in particular we have noted some of the advantages that Jesus' teachings gave Christianity over the mystery cults, which often seem to have degenerated into mere mumbo-jumbo. The cult of Isis lacked a missionary priesthood, that of Mithra any priesthood at all. Isis was chiefly for women, Mithra altogether for men. The Evangel was really "good news," with its promise of personal immortality, its admonition to behave with kindness and with love to one's fellow human beings, its lofty moral code. The Church provided a consoling and beautiful and dramatic ritual, and the opportunity to become a part of the exciting, dangerous, and thoroughly masculine task of spreading the gospel. The would-be convert could find in it ideas and rites closely related to those of Egyptians, Greeks, and Jews. It was at Ephesus, the shrine of the peculiar virgin mother-goddess known as Diana of the Ephesians, that the quarrelsome Christian theologians of the fifth century would proclaim the Virgin Mary the mother of God.

Men will continue to debate, as they do with all major turning points in history, the causes for the triumph of Christianity and will argue over whether the primary cause was its oldness, its newness, its concept of love, or its capacity for adaptation. But scholars agree that in addition to all of these, Christianity greatly benefitted from the organization that the early Christians desired for their church.

Organization of the Church. To maintain order, the Christian community clearly needed some authority to discipline, or even oust, misbehaving individuals. It had to organize in order to survive in the midst of an empire committed in principle to its suppression. Prophets, or teachers, appeared in the very first churches, the informal groups of Christians organized by the missionaries, and soon elders, overseers, and presidents followed.

More and more, the "overseer" (Greek *episkopos*) appeared in authority over a compact administrative area, his "see." This was the bishop, who became the key figure in church administration. Each see claimed to have been founded by one of the original apostles; and its bishop thus held office through "apostolic succession." Since it had been Christ himself who had chosen the apostles, every bishop, in effect, became a direct spiritual heir of Christ. Groups of bishoprics or episcopal sees often were gathered together into larger units, owing obedience to an archbishop, a head-overseer (*archiepiskopos*). Just as the bishop often had his headquarters in a Roman *civitas,* or city-state unit, and exercised authority over the churches in the countryside roundabout, so the archbishop governed the *civitates* from a mother-city, a *metropolis,* usually the capital of a Roman province, and his "see" was called a province.

At the top of the hierarchy stood the bishop of the imperial capital, Rome itself, the father of them all, *Papa* or Pope, who claimed supreme authority. The prestige of Rome contributed powerfully to his claim. So did the association of

Peter and Paul with Rome. Christ had said to Peter, "Thou art Peter and upon this rock I will build my church," a celebrated Greek pun, since the word for Peter is *Petros* and that for rock *petra*. Because Peter had been martyred in Rome, the bishops of that city could claim that Christ himself had picked Rome as the rock upon which to build: a claim that was embodied in their "Petrine theory." The bishops of the great cities of the eastern Mediterranean, Alexandria and Antioch, however, claimed to exercise a paternal rule equal in authority to that of the Pope. They called themselves Patriarch (fatherly governor). Still later, after Constantinople had been made the imperial capital (330 A.D.), its bishop, also a Patriarch, would oppose papal claims to supremacy.

With the departure of imperial government from Rome, the popes gradually made themselves more and more responsible for the government of the great city. And as the barbarians began to pour in and Rome itself came under attack, the Pope became the symbol of the old Roman regularities and certainties, a rock indeed. A succession of outstanding men became Bishop of Rome, notably Leo the Great (reigned 440–461), a theologian, a splendid administrator, and a brave man, who saved the city from the Hun, Attila. By the time of the break-up of the Roman Empire, in the fifth century, nobody in the West would have disputed the claim of papal supremacy; the papacy had emerged as the firmest institution in a new and terrible world.

The government of the Church thus exhibited important characteristics. First, it had arisen gradually, in response to need. Second, the Church strengthened its organization by utilizing the existing political machinery of the Roman Empire, placing its major officials in centers which were already administrative capitals. Third, the bishops and archbishops, meeting in councils, determined which religious ideas or practices would be accepted and which rejected, which writings were truly Christian and which false. In this way the Church selected from other writings the 27 canonical books of the New Testament, written in Greek, and the Old Testament writings as preserved in a Greek translation from the Hebrew. In the Greek Church today, these versions are still in use; in the Roman Church, the Latin version called the Vulgate, made by St. Jerome in the fourth century, is used. Many of the writings that the Church rejected have survived. Though not canonical, they have much interest for the modern historian and theologian.

Each individual bishop presided over several churches. Each church was under the care of a priest (Greek *presbyteros*, elder), who had been qualified by special training and by the ceremony of ordination. The area served by each church and its priest came to be known as the parish. In the early church the office of deacon, often held by a man who had other occupations besides the service of the church, had much importance. In some of the early churches, the congregation itself elected its officers, and the church was governed by boards of elders (presbyteries); but the system of appointment from above prevailed over that of election, although the congregation was often consulted. Before long, then, the distinction between those who were merely faithful worshippers (the laity) and those who conducted the worship and administered the affairs of the church (the clergy) became well defined. Despite frequent rumbles of protest during the two thousand years of Christianity, and despite differences of degree in the Christian churches, the distinction between laity and clergy is maintained in all.

From the time of the conversion of Constantine, the election of bishops became a matter of particular concern to the state. In order to retain the initiative, the officials of the church worked to put the election of each new bishop into the hands of the clergy of the cathedral (episcopal church) of his see. Practice remained uneven, however. Sometimes the citizens simply gave assent to an accomplished fact by approving elections; and at other times they had real power, as when Roman mobs under the sway of rival political leaders controlled the choices to the papal throne. Since bishops often exercised actual governing power and had their own law courts, lay rulers often insisted on approving or even selecting them. The problem of the degree to which laymen could participate in the choice of the bishops remained acute down into the eleventh century, as the popes strove to have the ultimate say.

This struggle, as we shall see, raged only in western Europe. In the East, for more than a thousand years, the successor of the Roman Emperors at Constantinople actually wielded supreme authority over both church and state, and had the final say in the appointment of bishops.

Monasticism. Deacons, priests, bishops, archbishops, all serve the laity of this world, and are called *secular* clergy (Latin *saeculum*, world). Early in the history of the Church, however, another kind of devotee to Christianity appeared in Syria and Egypt—the monk, a man who felt that he must deny the urges of his own flesh and become an ascetic. Monks would leave civilization behind and go into the desert to live in solitude, meditation, and prayer, subsisting on the minimum of food and drink. By the third century, there were a good many of these hermits, who enjoyed reputations for extreme holiness and often competed with each other in torturing themselves or in self-denial; some lived in trees or in holes in the ground, others on the tops of columns.

To keep the extremists from using the cloak of holiness to cover un-Christian self-assertion, certain leaders, such as St. Anthony, early collected groups of monks around themselves and formed communities, living by a rule. The Greek St. Basil (329–379) wrote the most famous of these rules, which became standard in the Greek Church and still regulates Greek monasticism today. Basil prescribed celibacy and poverty but combatted the dangers of extreme asceticism by requiring that the monks work in the fields or elsewhere to make their communities as self-supporting as possible. Because, after Basil, monks lived by a rule, they are known as the regular clergy (Latin *regula*, a rule), as contrasted with the secular clergy.

Similarly, in the West the problem was met by the rule of St. Benedict, who founded the great abbey at Monte Cassino in southern Italy about 520. His Latin rule, like Basil's Greek rule, prescribed hard work for all and urged the monks to try to be tolerant of each other's interests and infirmities. In the West particularly, the monks broke new ground around their monasteries, acted as pioneers in opening up the wilderness, performed missionary service among the still unconverted heathen tribes, and did much charitable and medical work among the poor and the sick. In both East and West scholarship early became one of the recognized occupations for monks, and the monastic scribe, who copied the works of the ancients and built up the library of his foundation, helped preserve the literature of the past.

Tensions often arose between secular and regular clergy, each feeling that its own work was more valuable to Christianity as a whole. Constant care and strict government were needed to maintain the high ideals of the monasteries and of the convents for women which soon appeared. This continuing need prompted the successive monastic reform movements which played a major role in Christian history. The abbots of the greater monasteries often participated, along with the bishops, in the councils of the Church that helped form Christian doctrine and frame the rules of Church observance and discipline.

HERESY

The early centuries of Christianity saw a series of struggles to define the accepted doctrines of the religion—orthodoxy—and to protect them against the challenge of rival doctrinal ideas—heresy. The modern student must make a major effort of the imagination to understand how such seemingly trivial issues generated such heat. Men believed that their future salvation depended upon the proper definition and defense of religious belief and practice. In addition, bitter political, economic, and national issues often underlay disputes that took a theological form.

Gnostics and Manichaeans. Men have always had difficulty in understanding and explaining how evil can exist (as it obviously does) in a physical world created by a good God. The Gnostics affirmed that only the world of the spirit is real (and good); the physical world is evil, or an evil illusion. Thus they could not accept the Old Testament, whose God created this world; they regarded him as a fiend or decided that this world had been created by Satan. Nor could they accept Jesus' human life and work in this world, an essential part of Christian belief. The sharp distinction that the Gnostics drew between the evil present world and the good world of the spirit is often called dualist. Clearly heretical, the Gnostics focussed on Christ's miracle-working and on other sorts of magic. Among them there arose a sharp distinction between an elite, whose members led especially pure lives, and the ordinary flock, less able to bear self-denial or the mysteries of the faith, who usually worked hard to support the elite.

Closely related to Gnosticism were the ideas of Mani, a third-century Mesopotamian prophet who also echoed the dualistic views of the Persians and preached that the God of light and goodness and his emanations were in constant conflict with the god of darkness, evil, and matter and his emanations. These Manichaean views became immensely popular, especially along the North African shores of the Mediterranean during the third and fourth centuries. The Christians combatted them, and throughout the Middle Ages tended to label all doctrinal opposition with the term "Manichaean." Yet the dualist ideas persisted, more or less underground, and cropped up every few decades for a thousand years and more.

Donatists and Arians. Within Christianity itself heresy sometimes involved very practical problems. The Emperor Constantine faced the so-called Donatist movement in North Africa. The movement arose because, during the Roman persecutions of the Christians, a number of priests had lacked the courage to court martyrdom and had instead handed over to the Roman authorities the sacred books. After the persecutions had come to an end, these "handers-over" (*traditores*) had resumed their role as priests. Donatus, Bishop of Carthage, and his followers maintained that the sacraments administered by such a *traditor* were invalid. While one can understand Donatus' wish to punish weakling or collaborationist priests, one can also see that, once a believer suspected the validity of the sacraments as received from one priest, he might suspect it as received from any other. Amidst much bitterness and violence Constantine finally ruled that, once a priest had been properly ordained, the sacraments administered at his hands had validity even if the priest had himself acted badly.

Heresy also arose over essentially philosophical issues. Such was Arianism, named after Arius, a priest of Alexandria who early in the fourth century put forth the view that if God the Father had begotten God the Son (through God the Holy Ghost), then God the Son, as begotten, could not have exactly the same nature as God the Father but must be somehow inferior to, or dependent upon, or at least later in time than his begetter. It is difficult to refute this position on the basis of logical argument alone. But Arius' view threatened to belittle the divinity of Christ as God the Son and to separate Christ from the Trinity. Arius'

Colossal head of the Emperor Constantine.

bitter opponent, Athanasius, Bishop of Alexandria, fought him passionately, disdaining logic and emphasizing mystery. Athanasius and his followers maintained that Christians simply had to take it as a matter of faith that Father and Son are identical in nature and that the Son is equal to, independent of, and contemporaneous with the Father; even though the Father begat the Son, it is heresy to say that there was ever a time when the Son did not exist. In the Greek East especially, this abstract philosophical argument was fought out not only among churchmen and thinkers but in the barbershops and among the longshoremen. The fact that most people did not understand what they were talking about did not prevent their rioting against their opponents.

After trying hard to stay out of the quarrel and urging the bishops to stop discussing it, Constantine realized that it would have to be settled. He himself summoned in 325 the first council of the whole Church, a council called ecumenical (from the Greek *oikoumene*, the inhabited world), at Nicaea, across the straits from Constantinople. A large majority of the bishops decided in favor of the Athanasian view, which was then embodied in the famous Nicene Creed, issued with all the force of an imperial decree by Constantine himself. The Emperor had presided over the council, and against his will found himself assuming the role of head of the church, giving legal sanction to a purely doctrinal decision and so playing the role both of Caesar and of Pope. This "Caesaropapism," in fact, became the tradition of Empire and Church in the East.

But the decree of Nicaea did not dispose of Arianism. Arians disobeyed; Constantine himself wavered; and his immediate successors on the imperial throne were Arians. Between 325 and 381, there were 13 more councils that discussed the problem, deciding first one way, then another. One pagan historian sardonically commented that one could no longer travel on the roads because they were so cluttered up with throngs of bishops riding off to one council or another. Traces of Arianism remained in the Empire for several centuries after Nicaea, and, because the missionary Ulfilas preached the Arian form of Christianity to the Barbarian Goths beyond the frontiers of the Empire, the heresy was spread among many Germanic peoples.

The Two Natures of Christ. Long before Arianism disappeared, a new and related controversy had shaken the eastern portion of the Empire to its foundations. Exactly what was the relationship of Christ the God and Christ the Man? He was both man and God, but just exactly how was this possible? And was the Virgin Mary—a human woman—perhaps the mother only of his human aspect; or if not, how could a human being be the mother of God? The extreme positions were that of the dyophysites (two-nature-ites), who separated the human nature of Christ from the divine and so refused to regard the human virgin as the mother of God, and that of the monophysites (one-nature-ites), who argued that the human and divine natures were merged, but carried their thesis so far that they almost forgot Christ's human attributes and tended to make him a god only. Again the dispute flared up in physical violence in the East; again the decision hung in the balance; again the Emperor (Marcian, reigned 450–457) called an ecumenical council at Chalcedon, near Constantinople, in 451. Supported by the Pope, the council condemned monophysitism and, like the Council of Nicaea, took a mystical rather than a rational decision: the true believer must believe in the two natures of Christ, human and divine, coexisting yet not distinct from each other; the Virgin is properly called the mother of God.

But like the decision at Nicaea, the decision at Chalcedon did not completely or definitively dispose of the opposition. Monophysites were concentrated in the provinces of Egypt and Syria and expressed the deep resentment of the ancient Mediterranean cities of Alexandria and Antioch against the new domination by the upstart Constantinople. So, partly because it was identified with what we would call nationalism, monophysitism did not die out, and the Emperors strove to deal with it by one compromise or another. But, since there were no monophysites in the West, the Roman Church regarded the issue as closed; every time an emperor at Constantinople tried to appease his Egyptian and Syrian monophysite subjects, he would be condemned by the Pope for heresy. The problem remained unsolved.

The disaffection of the monophysite provinces of Syria and Egypt was to facilitate their conquest in the seventh century by the new religion of Islam. To this day there are still monophysite Christians in Egypt and Syria. The continuing quarrel illustrates the lasting political impact that theological disagreement sometimes provides.

LITERATURE AND THOUGHT IN THE FIRST CHRISTIAN CENTURIES

Though a good deal of dislike and mutual misunderstanding had always characterized the attitudes of Greeks and Romans toward each other, Roman admiration for Greek literature and art had given its stamp to the works of Roman writers and artists. The triumph of Christianity tended to contribute, as we have seen, new sources of misunderstanding and tension to the relationships between Easterners and Westerners. The political division imposed by Diocletian and repeated by many of his successors expressed the undoubted geographic distinction between eastern and western provinces. As the barbarian inroads began increasingly to disrupt communications and threaten all the established institutions in the West, the opportunities for Westerners to know Greek and embrace the great classical tradition were fewer. In the eastern provinces few except soldiers and professional administrators had ever spoken or read Latin, though it remained the official language of legislation at Constantinople down through the fifth century. Despite the growing division, however, the literature and art of the late Roman and early Christian world may be treated as a single whole.

In this period letters declined and almost disappeared in the pagan West. In the East a few passionate devotees of the old gods and opponents of Christianity still made their voices heard, notably the teachers of the nephew of Constantine, the young Julian, who became Emperor in 361. In a brief reign of two years, Julian, embued with classical philosophy in its more mystical forms, tried to restore the old beliefs, reviving the sacrifices in the temples, forbidding Christians to teach, threatening new persecutions, even trying to construct a kind of hierarchy to give to the pagan faiths the efficiency of the Christian Church. Julian himself wrote satirical and moralistic essays and orations on behalf of his program, which was doomed to failure, but which has always interested poets and novelists as well as scholars.

Christian letters began to take the center of the stage. In the East, many of the best writers devoted much energy to polemical writings on the burning doctrinal questions and disputes of the day. In both East and West the best minds among Christians faced the problem of how to treat the classical heritage.

A few thinkers, mostly in the West and especially at first, advised against the reading of anything but Scripture, for fear of pagan error. They later came to acknowledge that one had to read the great pagans of the past in order to be able to refute pagan philosophical ideas. Still, there was always the danger that in the pleasure of reading a delightful classical author one might forget that the prime concern was to expose his errors and refute his arguments. The Greek Christians worried far less about this problem, and in the fourth century the three great Cappadocian fathers (so called from the province of Asia Minor where they were born)—Basil, author of the monastic rule; his brother, Gregory of Nyssa; and their friend, Gregory of Nazianzos—all had an excellent classical education and used the techniques of the pagan philosophers in discussing religious ideas.

Jerome, who studied with Gregory of Nazianzos, produced the Latin Bible,

Wall of the nave, S. Apollinare Nuovo, a fifth-century church in Ravenna, Italy.

the Vulgate, as the climax of a life of devoted scholarship that had made him the master of Hebrew and Greek as well as Latin. Ambrose (c. 340–397), a Roman civil servant who became Bishop of Milan, wrote many theological works and commentaries, Christianizing much that he found in the classics, particularly in Cicero; he transformed Cicero's Stoic concept of duty to the state into a Christian concept of duty to God. Ambrose put his own preaching into practice when he publicly humiliated the Emperor Theodosius I (reigned 379–395) and forced him to do penance for savagely punishing some rioters. The act symbolizes the Western Church's insistence that, in matters of morals and of faith, the Church would be supreme, an attitude that ran exactly counter to the practice already growing up in the East.

Augustine (354–430), the greatest of the Western church fathers and a native of North Africa, himself had been a Stoic, a Manichaean, and a Neo-Platonist before he studied under Ambrose and was converted to Christianity. He then became Bishop of the North African city of Hippo, and engaged in energetic controversy with heretics. He was the author of *Confessions,* a vivid and mystical autobiography, and of *The City of God,* which he wrote to refute the pagan argument that Christianity had led to the decline and the misfortunes of Rome. He easily showed that pagan empires innocent of Christianity had often fallen in the past, and he then moved far beyond the specific controversy to outline a complete Christian philosophy of history.

Augustine maintained that God's plan for humanity involved a continuing struggle between the community of those who will be saved, God's community or city, *civitas Dei,* and the community of those who reject God, the earthly community, *civitas terrena.* Ultimately, of course, the triumph of the city of God is assured; its members will be saved, while those of the earthly city will be damned. Since human history is all a preparation for the last judgment, the individual should turn his will toward God, and with the help of divine grace may so order his earthly life by decency, tolerance, trust, and discipline that he may deserve and receive heavenly citizenship hereafter. The help of the divine grace, Augustine taught, was necessary to fortify human wills (even those that had already chosen God) because original sin (inherited from Adam) had turned man away from God, and God's grace must help him to return. At times Augustine's argument led him to minimize the value of good works, or even of the sacraments, for the achieving of salvation: he came near to a belief in predestination: the belief that God has chosen in advance an elect company of men for salvation. The later Church fathers did not follow Augustine, but insisted that both good works and grace were essential to salvation.

So to the Christian, although the heavenly city is the goal, his conduct and attitudes in the earthly city have the utmost importance. He must curb his pride and ambition, control his natural appetites, and avoid yielding too exclusively to the pull of family ties. This does not mean the annihilation of self in extreme asceticism, but rather the combination of control of self with love and kindness for others: all others, high and low. The Christian must love even the sinner, though not the sin. Nor may he, out of softness, attribute sin to environment or temporary influences; sin is *there,* and will be permanent in the earthly city. Nor may a Christian trust too fully the experiences of his senses alone, and try to explain all phenomena by reason and by naturalistic arguments. He must have faith, "the substance of things hoped for, the evidence of things unseen." He must not try to put himself in the place of God, who alone can "understand" the

Spread of Christianity, to 11th Century

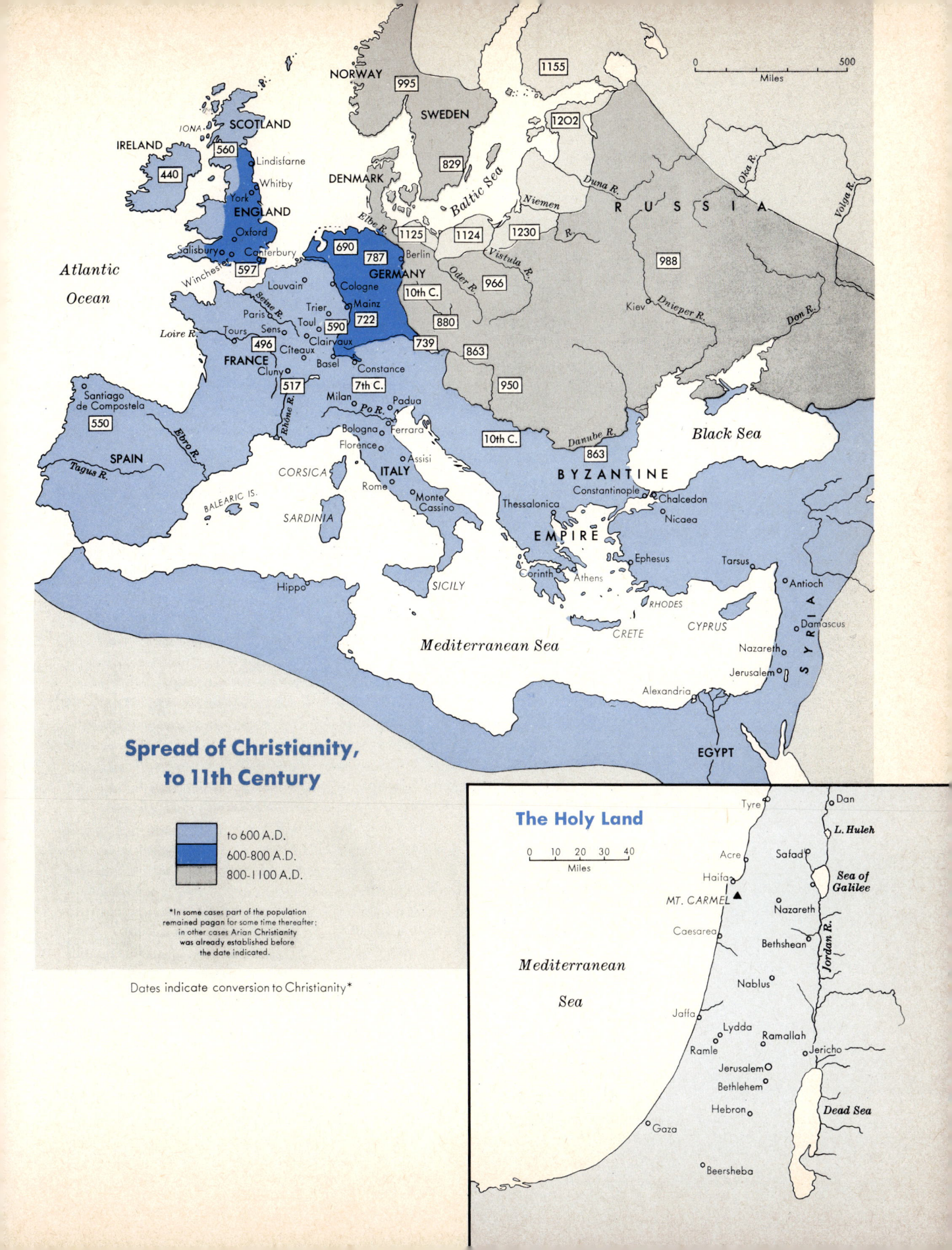

Legend:
- to 600 A.D.
- 600–800 A.D.
- 800–1100 A.D.

*In some cases part of the population remained pagan for some time thereafter; in other cases Arian Christianity was already established before the date indicated.

Dates indicate conversion to Christianity*

The Holy Land

universe. Instead he must believe in God, for then he can feel that the universe is not the puzzling or hostile place it seems to men who do nothing but reason. Yet he must also strive to improve the world around him and the other human beings who live in it, in order to make the earthly city as nearly as possible resemble the city of God.

II. The Barbarian Onslaught

THE BARBARIANS

Even the centuries of the *Pax Romana* were filled with combat against the barbarians on the far side of the Rhine–Danube line. Tacitus lectured his fellow-Romans on the instructive contrast between their own soft degeneracy and what he regarded as the simple toughness and harshness of the Germans. His account of them, partisan though it may be, is the fullest report we have on their simple tribal life before their first major breakthrough to the Roman side of the frontier, which did not take place until the fourth century. In spite of Tacitus' fears, it was apparently not so much Roman decline that opened the way to the Germans as sheer pressure on the Germans from other tribes that drove them in panic to try to cross the Roman borders, by force if necessary.

Indo-European in language, like the Greeks, the Romans, and the Celts, the Germans seem to have dwelled originally along the shores of the Baltic, both on the Continent and in Scandinavia. Very early in ancient times they migrated southward. When the Romans first began to write about them, they were already divided into tribes, but had no over-all political unity. One group of Germanic tribes, the Goths, had settled in what we now call Rumania, on the north side of the Danube boundary, and in the adjacent plains of what is now southern Russia, the Ukraine. In the fourth century, conditions in central Asia about which we still know almost nothing precipitated a fierce Asian people known as the Huns into the territory of the Goths. Living on horseback for days, traveling swiftly, and reveling in cruelty, the Huns started a panic among the Goths and other tribes. The shock waves, beginning in the last half of the fourth century, continued throughout the fifth and into the sixth. They shattered the Roman structure in the West and left its fragments in barbarian hands. The eastern territories suffered much less, and the imperial tradition continued uninterrupted in Constantinople.

In addition to barbarian military raids, penetrations, and conquests, there were slower and more peaceful infiltrations lasting over long periods. Moreover, before, during, and after the invasions, individual barbarians joined the Roman side, often rising to high positions defending the old Empire against their fellow-barbarians. The Romanized barbarian became as familiar a figure as the barbarized Roman.

Visigoths, Vandals, Anglo-Saxons. When the Hunnic push against them began, one tribe of Goths, the Visigoths, or West Goths, petitioned to be allowed to cross the Danube and settle in Roman territory, on the south bank, in what we would call Bulgaria. The Roman border guards took cruel advantage of their fear and hunger; and soon there were many desperate Goths milling around only a few miles from Constantinople. In the year 378, at Adrianople, the mounted

Goths defeated the Roman legions of the eastern Emperor Valens, who was killed in battle. More and more Goths now freely entered the Empire. Unable to take Constantinople or other fortified towns, they proceeded south into the Balkans, ravaged Greece, including Athens, and then marched north again around the head of the Adriatic and south into Italy. In 410, their chieftain Alaric sacked Rome itself, and died soon afterward. His successors led the Visigoths north across the Alps into Gaul, and then south again across the Pyrenees into Spain.

Here, in the westernmost reaches of the continental Roman Empire, after their long wanderings, the Visigoths founded a Spanish kingdom that would last

Relief of a German warrior, c. 700.

until the Moslem invasions of the seventh century. In southern Gaul they had a large area (Aquitaine) given them by the western Roman Emperor Honorius (reigned 395–423), into whose family their king married; but this area they would lose in less than a century to a rival German tribe, the Franks. Since the Visigoths were Arians, they had some difficulty in ruling the orthodox Christians among their subjects.

Almost simultaneously with the Visigothic migration, another Germanic people, the Vandals, crossed the Rhine westward into Gaul and moved southward into southern Spain, where they settled in 411. The Roman governor of

North Africa made the mistake of inviting them across the straits to help him in a struggle against his Roman masters. The Vandals came in 429, but soon seized North Africa for themselves. They moved eastward across modern Morocco and Algeria and established their capital at Carthage. Here they built a fleet and raided the shores of Sicily and Italy, finally sacking Rome (455) in a raid that has made vandalism synonymous to this day with the worst forms of violence. Like the Visigoths, the Vandals were Arian, and they, too, often persecuted the orthodox.

Under pressure on the Continent, the Romans early in the fifth century began to withdraw their legions from Britain. Into the gap thus made began to filter Germanic tribes from across the North Sea in what we would now call north Germany and Denmark. Angles, Saxons, and Jutes, coming from an area that had undergone little Roman influence, were still heathen. In England they established their authority over the Celtic Britons and soon founded seven Anglo-Saxon kingdoms, of which Northumbria and Mercia successively became the most important. Scotland and Wales remained Celtic, as of course did Ireland, which was in large measure converted to Christianity in the fifty century by Catholic missionaries from Gaul.

Ireland escaped the first great wave of barbarian invasions, and its Celtic church promoted learning, poetry, and the illumination of manuscripts such as the famous *Book of Kells*, one of the wonders of the era. By the end of the sixth century Catholic Christianity was moving into England from two directions at once: Celtic Ireland and Rome. The differences between the two were mostly matters of practice, such as the determination of the date of Easter, and, though hotly debated, these questions were eventually settled.

Huns, Ostrogoths. Not only the Germanic peoples but the Asian Huns themselves participated in the onslaught on Roman territories. Emerging into Europe from the East early in the fifth century, the Huns soon conquered what we would call Rumania, Hungary, and parts of Yugoslavia, Poland, and Czechoslovakia. Under their domination lived a large collection of German and other tribes, and the Hunnic rulers extracted tribute-money from the Roman Emperors at Constantinople. Under Attila, in the middle of the fifth century, this savage horde pressed westward, crossed the Rhine, and met with defeat in Gaul in 451 at the hands of a Roman general in a battle usually called Châlons. Pope Leo the Great persuaded Attila to withdraw from Italy without attacking Rome.

Like many nomad empires, that of the Huns fell apart after the death of the conquering founder (452). A plague decimated their ranks, and many withdrew into Asia once more. But other related Asian peoples, nomads and pagans like the Huns, and Mongol in appearance, entered Europe before the age of the barbarian invasions was over: Avars in the sixth century, Bulgars in the sixth and seventh, and Magyars or Hungarians in the ninth, for example. The Magyars eventually set up a lasting state in the Danubian plain, and their Europeanized descendants still inhabit modern Hungary. As the first Asian invaders, the Huns had not only begun the movement of the Germanic tribes but had helped to smash Roman domination in central Europe.

Among the German tribes liberated by the collapse of the Hunnic Empire, the first to make a major impact were the Ostrogoths (East Goths). They moved into the general disorder left in Italy after the last of the western Emperors,

Romulus Augustulus (the little Augustus), had been dethroned by his barbarian protector Odovacar in 476, the date often chosen for the end of the Roman Empire in the West. Actually, like his immediate predecessors, Romulus Augustulus had been an ineffectual tool of the nearest barbarian general who could command loyal troops. Roman imperial power, however, continued uninterruptedly in the East; in fact, the Emperor Zeno in Constantinople had hired the Ostrogoths to intervene in Italy on his behalf against Odovacar.

The leader of the Ostrogoths, Theodoric, had been educated in Constantinople, and admired both Greek civilization and the Roman Empire as an institution. For most of his long rule in Italy (489–526) he was content to serve as nominal subordinate to Zeno and his successors in the East, as a kind of governor of Italy. He was also king of his own Gothic people, and established his capital at Ravenna. Like many other Christianized German tribes, the Ostrogoths were Arian. In the eyes of the popes and of the Italians, they were heretics as well as German foreigners. Although Theodoric hoped to impose upon his subjects the civilization of the Empire, he did not have enough time to bring about any real assimilation. Moreover, toward the end of his reign, Theodoric, who had made dynastic marriages with the Vandal and other Germanic ruling houses, became suspicious of the Empire and planned to go to war against Constantinople.

Many other barbarian peoples participated in the break-up of Roman territory and power in the West during the fifth and sixth centuries, but failed to found any lasting state. They remain mere tribal names: Sciri, Suevi, Alamanni—the German forests seem to have had an inexhaustible supply of them. There were two other German tribes, however, whose achievements we still remember: the Burgundians, who moved into the valleys of the Rhone and Saône rivers in modern France in the 440's and gave their name to a succession of "Burgundies," varying in territory and government, and the Franks, from whom modern France itself derives its name.

FRANKS

Destined to found the most lasting political entity of any of the Germanic tribes, the Franks appeared first as dwellers along the lower Rhine. They engaged in no long migrations, but simply expanded gradually from their native seacoast and river valleys until eventually they were to create an empire that would include most of western Europe except for the Iberian peninsula and the British Isles. Clovis (reigned 481–511), descendant of the house of Merwig or Merovech, called Merovingian, was the founder of Frankish power. He defeated successively a Roman army (486), the Alamanni (496), and the Visigoths of Aquitaine at the battle of Vouillé, in 507. Much of modern France and northwest Germany and the Low Countries thus became Frankish.

The most important factor in Clovis' success, aside from his skill as a general, was his conversion to Christianity, not as an Arian heretic but as an orthodox Catholic. This gave him the instant support of the clergy of Gaul, especially of the powerful bishops of Aquitaine, who welcomed the Franks as a relief from the Arian Visigoths. Probably the greatest liability of the Franks was their habit of dividing up the kingdom between the king's sons in every generation. This meant not only a constant parcelling out of territory into petty kingdoms and lordships but constant secret intrigues and bloody rivalries among brothers and cousins and other relatives who strove to reunite the lands. Merovingian history forms one of the most sordid and savage chapters in the whole record of Western society.

By the end of the seventh century, the Merovingian kings themselves became so degenerate that they are known as *rois fainéants* (do-nothing kings). Real powers had been delegated to their chief officials, the "mayors of the palace," a title showing the close connection between household service of the monarch and actual government. By the eighth century one particular family had made this office hereditary from father to son—the Carolingians (from *Carolus*, Latin for Charles). One of the mayors, Charles (reigned 714–741), called "Martel," the hammer, organized the Frankish nobles into a dependable cavalry and in 732 near Tours defeated a roving band of Moslems that had been raiding northward from Spain. There was no real danger that the Moslems would absorb the Franks, yet since Tours was the farthest north in Europe that the Moslems ever came, the battle is a landmark in Western history. Charles Martel's son, Pepin the Short (reigned 741–768), assumed the title of King of the Franks and consolidated the kingdom once again. Pepin's adventurous policy with regard to Italy initiated a whole new chapter in Western history.

Italy from Theodoric to Pepin. Soon after the death of Theodoric, the great Emperor Justinian launched from Constantinople an ambitious effort to reconquer the major areas of the West that had been lost to the barbarians. The imperial forces overthrew the Vandals first, and then, before consolidating the reconquest of North Africa, invaded Italy from Carthage, via Sicily. For almost twenty years (535–554) increasingly savage and destructive warfare ravaged the peninsula, as Justinian's troops fought the Ostrogoths. The towns and countryside of Italy were left depopulated, and the survivors reduced to misery. Justinian's proclamation of an imperial restoration (554) was hollow. In the same year, imperial forces took a portion of southern Spain from the Visigoths.

Only three years after Justinian's death, a new Germanic tribe, the Arian Lombards, entered Italy (568) from the north. They easily conquered the north Italian plain that still bears their name (Lombardy), and established a kingdom with its capital at Pavia. Further to the south, they set up two duchies (Benevento and Spoleto). Italy lay once again in fragments. Still under imperial domination were the capital of Ravenna and territory surrounding it, the island settlement of Venice, Rome, Naples, and the toe and heel of the peninsula, as well as Sicily. The Emperor at Constantinople appointed a governor called the exarch who had headquarters at Ravenna and was particularly charged with organizing the defense of Italy.

But Constantinople was far away; dangers threatened the emperors from the East, and they often could not afford to pay much attention to Italy's needs or send money and troops to help the exarchs fight the Lombards. In this situation, the Church emerged more and more as the protector of the Catholic population, the bishops often receiving privileges from the Arian Lombard conquerors that conferred upon them virtual governing rights in the towns. Among the bishops, the Pope of course took the lead, and, among the popes, the most remarkable in every way was Gregory I, the Great (reigned 590–604).

Child of a rich and aristocratic Roman family, Gregory abandoned worldly things and became a monk and founder of monasteries. His administrative talents were extraordinary: he served as papal ambassador to the court at Constantinople

Merovingian tombstone, seventh century.

before becoming Pope, against his will, in 590. Besides his religious duties, he had to take virtually full responsibility for maintaining the fortifications of Rome, for feeding its population, for managing the great financial resources of the Church and its lands in Italy, for conducting diplomatic negotiations with exarchate and Lombards, and even for directing military operations. It was he who sent the mission to Britain (596) that began the conversion of the Anglo-Saxons. Gregory had an exalted conception of papal power, and stoutly defended its supremacy over the Church in his letters to the Emperor and to the Patriarch at Constantinople.

During the seventh and early eighth centuries the alienation between the Empire in the East and the papacy was greatly increased by religious disagreements and a related political and economic dispute. And simultaneously, the Lombards gradually consolidated and expanded their power, taking Ravenna in 751 and putting an end to the exarchate. Menaced by the Lombards and unable to count on help from Constantinople, Pope Stephen II in 753 paid a visit to King Pepin of the Franks.

In exchange for papal approval of his title of king, Pepin attacked the Lombards and forced them to abandon Ravenna and other recent conquests. Then he gave these lands to the Pope, as the celebrated "Donation of Pepin." Of course the lands did not belong to Pepin but to the Emperor at Constantinople, but this did not prevent Pepin's disposing of them. Together with Rome itself and the lands immediately around it, the Donation of Pepin formed the territory over which the Pope ruled as temporal sovereign down to the nineteenth century. These were the Papal States, and Vatican City is their present-day remnant. Pepin's son, Charles the Great (Charlemagne), finished off the Lombard kingdom in 774 and assumed the Iron Crown of Lombardy.

From the papal point of view, the new alliance with the Franks marked the end of dependence upon the Empire and the beginning of the papacy as a temporal power. The Franks, too busy to take over these Italian lands themselves and no doubt also aware of the pious responsibilities that they had acquired when they became the protectors of the Church, did not try to dominate the popes. Soon after Pepin's donation, the clerks of the papal chancery forged "proof" that Pepin had only been confirming a gift of lands to the Church made long ago by the Emperor Constantine. The forgery stated, in addition, that Constantine directly declared that the papal power, as divine, was superior to his own imperial power, which was only earthly; that the see of Peter should rule over the other sees (including Antioch, Alexandria, Constantinople); and that the Pope alone should rule in questions of faith. For about seven hundred years, until the Italian Renaissance scholar Lorenzo Valla (*see* Chapter V) proved it a forgery, men believed that this extraordinary document was genuine.

Charlemagne and His Successors. Pepin's son, Charlemagne (771–814)—so his contemporary biographer tells us—was a vigorous, lusty, intelligent man who loved hunting, women, and war. All his life he wore Frankish costume and thought of himself as a Frankish chieftain. Although he kept pen and ink under his pillow, he could never teach himself how to write. He spoke Latin, however, and understood some Greek. He sought to iron out the conflicts between two codes of law that governed his people but had to leave this project unfinished. A great conqueror, Charlemagne turned his armies east and crossed the Rhine. In campaigns lasting more than 30 years, he conquered the heathen Saxons, living south of Denmark, and converted them at sword's point to Christianity. Monks and priests followed his armies.

Charlemagne made the first successful invasion of Germany. This spawning-ground of the barbarians who had shattered Roman society in the West then began the long, slow process of assimilation to Western civilization. In addition to the lands of the Saxons, Charlemagne added to his domain the western areas of modern Czechoslovakia (Bohemia), much of Austria, and portions of Hungary and Yugoslavia; the eastern boundaries of his realm reached the Elbe River in the North, and the Danube, where it turns sharply south below Vienna. Along these wild eastern frontiers he established provinces (marks or marches). His advance into eastern Europe brought him victories also over the Asian Avars, successors to the Huns along the lower Danube. Far to the west, Charlemagne challenged Moslem power in Spain and set up a Spanish march in what is today Catalonia. A defeat of his rear guard at the pass of Roncesvalles in the Pyrenees Mountains in 778 formed the theme of the heroic epic *The Song of Roland* (*Chanson de Roland*), which was composed several centuries later.

By the end of the eighth century, Charlemagne had reunited under Frankish rule all of the western Roman provinces except for Britain, most of Spain, south Italy, Sicily, and North Africa, and had added to his domains central and eastern European areas which the Romans had never possessed. On Christmas Day, 800, the Pope himself, Leo III, crowned Charlemagne Emperor in Rome. So mighty was the tradition of Roman Empire and so great its hold on the minds of men that, more than three centuries after the disappearance of Romulus Augustulus, last of the western Emperors, the chief bishop of the Christian Church, seeking to honor and recognize his mighty Frankish patron, automatically crowned him Emperor of Rome. Even before the coronation a poet in Charlemagne's own circle had hailed him as "Augustus."

It is quite possible that Charlemagne himself was surprised and not altogether pleased by the coronation; he probably relished his title, but he almost surely disliked the role played by the Pope and the implication that the Pope had the right to choose and crown Emperors. The true successors of Augustus, the Roman Emperors at Constantinople, were horrified at the insolence of the barbarian Charlemagne in assuming the sacred title.

Within his territories Charlemagne was, by virtue of his consecration, a sacred ruler, with spiritual rights and duties as well as temporal ones. His lofty concept of his office and his personal power enabled him to govern the Church—even in matters of doctrine—more like Constantine or other eastern Emperors than any other western monarch. He himself named Louis the Pious, by then his only living son, his successor in 813; the Pope had no part in the ceremonies.

Charlemagne's government was very simple: It was only the accidental deaths of his other sons that prevented a standard Frankish division of the heritage. The king's personal household staff were also the government officials: the chamberlain, the count of the stable (constable), and so on. On major decisions the Emperor conferred with great nobles of state and church, but he told them what he (and they) were going to do rather than asking them for advice and permission. Since the Franks, like other Germans, believed that law *existed* and could not be made by men, even Charlemagne could not in theory legislate. But he did issue instructions to his subjects, divided into subheadings or chapters and therefore called *capitularies*, which usually dealt with special administrative problems. It was a highly personal rule.

Charlemagne's territories included about 300 counties, each governed by a count, those in former Roman territory corresponding to the lands of a *civitas*. The count had to maintain order, render justice, and recruit and command soldiers. Alongside the count, the bishop of the diocese and the various local magnates might have considerable powers of their own on their own lands. Only a powerful king could keep the local authorities from arrogating too much power to themselves. Charlemagne required his counts to appoint teams of judges, called *scabini*, whose appointment he would then ratify, and who would actually take over much of the count's role in rendering justice. He also sent out from his own central administrative staff pairs of royal emissaries (the *missi dominici*), usually a layman and a cleric, to investigate local conditions and correct abuses. As representatives of the Emperor, they could overrule the count.

The Carolingian Empire depended too much upon Charlemagne personally; he had assembled more territory than could be effectively governed, in view of the degeneration of administrative machinery and of communication since Roman days. Under his less talented successors, the old Frankish habit of dividing up lands and authority among the heirs to the throne reasserted itself. Quarrels over the allotment of territory raged among brothers and cousins. The title of emperor descended to a single heir in each generation, but as early as the middle of the ninth century it had become an empty honor.

One episode in the struggle among Charlemagne's grandsons deserves special notice: the Strasbourg Oaths of 842. Two of the grandsons, Charles the Bald and Louis the German, swore an alliance against their brother, the Emperor Lothair. Each swore in the language of the other's troops: Louis in a Latin-like language on its way to becoming French, which scholars call "Romance," and Charles in Germanic. Of course this does not mean that there was a France or a Germany in 842: only that the western and eastern Frankish lands spoke divergent tongues. But the symbolism is a striking sign of things to come in European history. Charles and Louis could hardly have chosen a more appropriate place than Strasbourg—center of Alsace, a bone of contention between modern France and Germany—to swear their bilingual oath. In the ninth century, however, there were as yet no national states in Europe. Indeed, instead of coalescing into large national units, the Frankish dominions were even then in the process of breaking up into much smaller ones. As the power of the central Frankish state was frittered away in family squabbles, smaller entities, duchies or counties, emerged as virtually autonomous units of government, many with names we still recognize as belonging to provinces of modern France or Germany: Champagne, Brittany, Saxony, Bavaria.

EUROPE AND THE NORTHMEN

Charlemagne's conquests in Germany had for the first time brought into the area of Western civilization the breeding-ground of many of the barbarians. Still outside lay Scandinavia, from whose shores there began in the ninth century a new wave of barbarian invasions that hit Britain and the western parts of the Frankish lands with savage force. The Northmen conducted their raids from small ships that could easily sail up the Thames, the Seine, or the Loire. Their appetite for booty grew with their successes, and soon they organized fleets of several hundred ships, ventured further abroad, and often wintered along a conquered coast. They ranged as far south as Spain, penetrated into the Mediterranean through the Straits of Gibraltar, and raided Italy. To the west they proceeded far beyond Ireland, and reached Iceland and Greenland. Some possibly reached as far as Canada or New England, although scholars still debate the validity of the scanty evidence we have of this.

The longing for booty may not by itself account for the Norse invasions. Polygamy was common among the upper classes of the pagan Scandinavians (the lower ones could not afford it), and it is probable that the younger sons of these Viking chiefs either had to leave home or stop living in the style to which they

Carolingian Empire

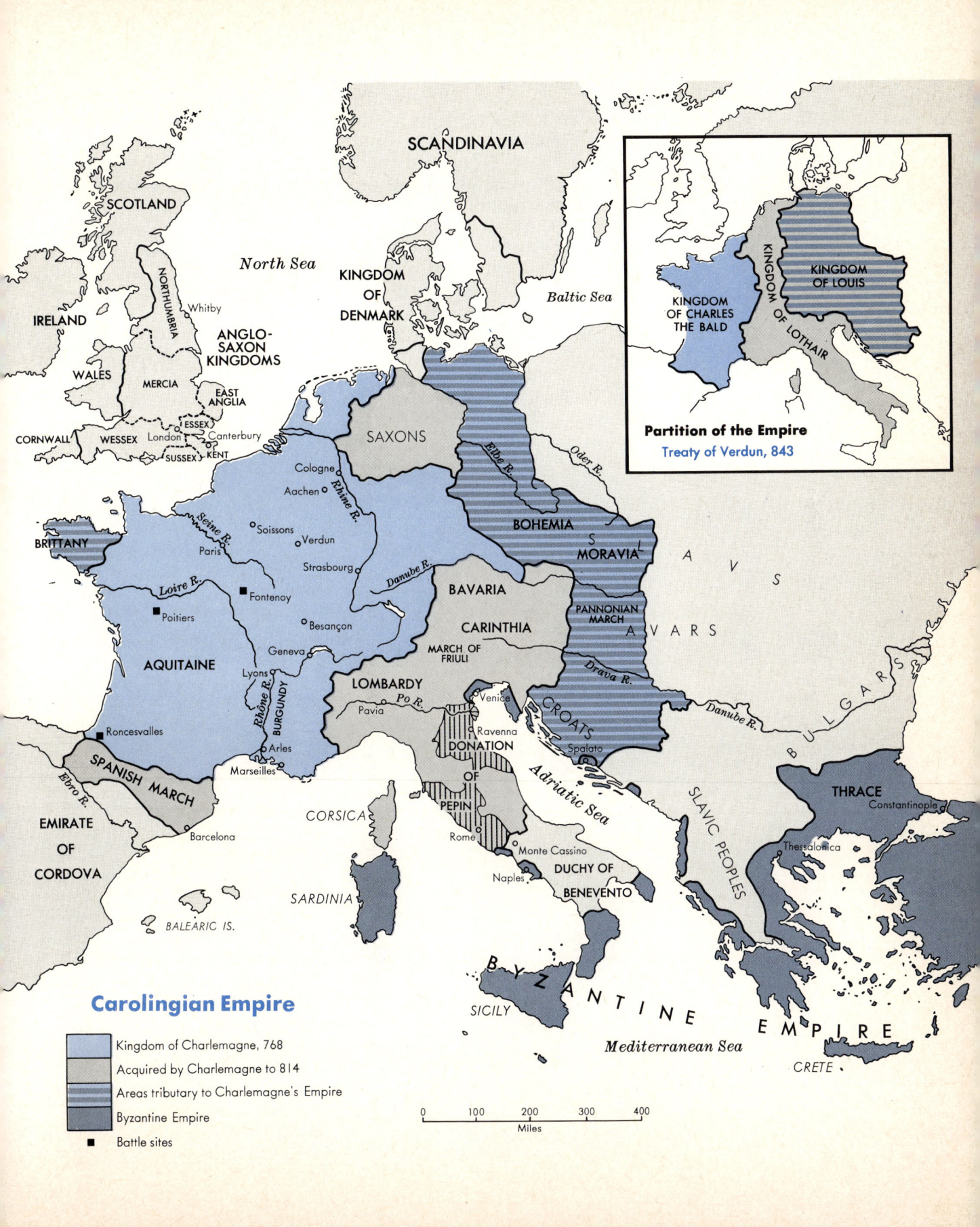

Partition of the Empire
Treaty of Verdun, 843

- Kingdom of Charles the Bald
- Kingdom of Lothair
- Kingdom of Louis

Legend:
- Kingdom of Charlemagne, 768
- Acquired by Charlemagne to 814
- Areas tributary to Charlemagne's Empire
- Byzantine Empire
- ■ Battle sites

had grown accustomed. This possible cause for the Norse expansion is suggested by the fact that even after the Vikings had conquered their first European base of settlement, the younger sons continued to go abroad to plunder and to settle.

Their first captured base was the region along the lower Seine River, which is still called Normandy after these Northmen. In 911, the Frankish king was forced to grant the Norse leader Rolf (or Rollo) a permanent right of settlement. The Normans became an efficient and powerful ruling class—in fact, the best administrators of the new "feudal" age. From Normandy soon after the year 1000 younger sons went off to found a flourishing state in the south Italian and Sicilian territories that still belonged to the East Roman Empire. From Normandy in 1066 Duke William and his followers conquered England.

Bronze Irish crucifix, c. 750.

Kinsmen of these Norsemen who had settled in Normandy also did great deeds. In the 860's the first wave of Viking invaders crossed the Baltic Sea to the territory that is now Russia, and penetrated deep inland to the south along the river valleys. They conquered the indigenous Slavic tribes, and, at Kiev on the middle Dnieper, consolidated the first Russian state.

While the Normans were raiding and developing Normandy, the Danes were almost paralleling their achievements in the British Isles. They seized the Irish ports and coasts; the Celtic inhabitants fought back fiercely and eventually assimilated the Danes, but the brilliance of Irish culture had suffered a fatal interruption. In England, too, the savage Danish attacks on the northern and eastern shores soon led to settlement. The chief organizer of defense against the Danes was the Anglo-Saxon kingdom of Wessex under Alfred the Great (871–899). Although Alfred finally defeated the Danes, he was not strong enough to expel them, and had to concede the whole northeast of England to them, a region thereafter called the Danelaw.

Far more advanced at this stage than the Danes, the Anglo-Saxon kingdom was governed through the royal household and clerical staff. The king's great council, the *witenagemot*, made up of important landholders, churchmen, and officials, advised him when he asked for advice, acted as a court, and elected and deposed kings. The king could count on revenue from his own estates, and also from a special tax imposed for defense against the Danes, called the Danegeld. He also received two-thirds of all the fines imposed by local courts. His army was still the old Germanic host (*fyrd*), in which every landholder was obliged to serve, but he also had additional household troops. Anglo-Saxon institutions in the tenth century were not very different from those of the Franks before Charlemagne or those of any settled Germanic tribe.

Soon after the turn of the eleventh century, new waves of Danes scored important successes under the command of Canute (Knut), the King of Denmark. In 1017 Canute was chosen King of England by the Anglo-Saxon witenagemot. Able ruler of a kind of northern Empire (he was also King of Norway), Canute allied himself with the Roman Church, and brought Scandinavia into the Christian community. His early death (1035) without competent heirs led to the break-up of his holdings, and England reverted to a king of the house of Alfred (Edward the Confessor). The work of Canute in England, though it did not last, belongs with that of the Normans and, in Russia, of the Norsemen, as an example of the political and administrative ability so widely demonstrated by the Scandinavians once they had settled down.

CAROLINGIAN DECLINE

By the end of the ninth century, the power of the Carolingians in their German territories had frittered away in the face of domestic challenge by ambitious local magnates and foreign threats from Norsemen, Slavs, and the Asian Magyars, who poured into the Hungarian plain in the mid-890's. When the last nominal Carolingian ruler, Louis the Child, died in 911, the German magnates elected the Duke of Franconia as King Conrad I (reigned 911–918). The most important units in Germany became the duchies—Franconia, Saxony, Swabia, and Bavaria—each under its autonomous ruler. Conrad I failed to control either the other dukes or the Magyars and finally nominated his strongest enemy, Henry, Duke of Saxony, to succeed him. Henry's son, Otto I (936–973), both checked the rival dukes and, at the battle of the Lechfeld, 955, defeated the Magyars.

Master of his German territories, Otto next sought to revive the title of Emperor, which had passed from one shadowy Carolingian prince to another until it lapsed in 924. Deep in decline after the reign of the great Pope Nicholas I (858–867), the papacy had fallen into the hands of rival Roman noble families, corrupt, wicked, and ineffectual. Without strong central administration and under attack from Moslems and Magyars, Italy had become anarchic. Yet Rome, even at its lowest depths in the mid-tenth century, continued to act as an irresistible magnet for those seeking supreme power. Like Charlemagne almost two hundred years before him, Otto went to Italy. He had himself crowned by the degenerate and dissipated Pope John XII (962), then had John deposed for murder and installed his own candidate on the papal throne. He forced the Roman aristocracy to promise that imperial consent would hereafter be necessary to papal elections, and renewed the Donation of Pepin and the subsequent grants of the Carolingians to the papacy. Though the papacy for the next hundred years was hardly more than an instrument manipulated by Otto's German successors, Otto's action eventually ensured the continuity of the papacy as an independent institution; it also tightly linked the political fortunes of Germany and Italy for centuries to come.

In the western Frankish lands, which we may now call France, Carolingian partitioning, strife, and feebleness led to the fragmentation of both territory and power among ambitious landowners. As early as 887 one faction of these magnates chose a non-Carolingian, Odo, Count of Paris, as king, and civil war between him and the Carolingian claimant added to the chaos. For the next century the families of the two rivals alternated in power. Finally, in 987 the magnates elected as king a descendant of the early Count of Paris, Hugh Capet, who founded the dynasty that would last almost to our own time. (When Louis XVI went to the guillotine in 1793, his executioners called him "Citizen Capet.") In 987, however, several of the nobles who chose Hugh were actually more powerful than he.

EUROPE ABOUT 1000

About the year 1000, then, England was a centralized monarchy; France was nominally ruled by an elected king who was feebler than his great supporters; Germany was divided into duchies, one of which had asserted its supremacy and claimed the old imperial title; and Italy still remained anarchic, but a revived papacy had begun to emerge. Out of the debris of the Roman Empire, buffeted by two waves of barbarian invasions and held together only by their common Christian faith, these major fragments had begun to take on, even as early as this, certain features that we can still recognize today. Elsewhere, the Scandinavian kingdoms had imposed order on the turbulent peoples who had made the Viking expansion, and the little Christian kingdoms in the north of Spain were only beginning their struggle with the Moslem tide that had engulfed the peninsula.

In the East, the Empire, with its direct descent from Rome and its Greco-Oriental character, still stood firm at Constantinople after many shocks. It had started its work of Christianizing those Slavic peoples nearest to it—the Bulgarians, the Russians, the Serbs. The western Slavs—Czechs, Poles, Croats, and others—and the Magyars, lying between the Germans and the influences radiating from Constantinople, had received the attention of Roman missionaries. By the year 1000 there was already visible a fateful line of demarcation between the Western Catholic world and the Eastern Orthodox world, with its different alphabet and its different outlook.

III. Feudal Europe

Historians have long referred to the centuries between the fifth and the fifteenth as the Middle Ages (or medieval)—that portion of man's history in the West that lies between ancient and modern. The half-millennium we have begun reviewing—roughly between 500 and 1000, the early Middle Ages—is often called the Dark Ages. Scholars no longer maintain, as they once did, that the period represents the debasement of high human values and thus spiritual darkness, but it is true that our sources are so scanty that we remain at least partly in the dark as to what happened and how we are to interpret it. Yet we can discern in the Dark Ages elements in human institutions surviving from Roman times, together with innovations introduced by the barbarians and changes linked with conversion to Christianity. The settled inhabitants of western Europe and the invaders underwent a long period of slow mutual adjustment, as new and old ways of regulating human affairs competed and often combined with each other.

FEUDALISM: THE RULERS

To these widely varied social and political combinations scholars give the name *feudalism*. Feudal institutions were the arrangements—personal, territorial, and governmental—between persons that made survival possible under the conditions that obtained in western Europe during the Dark Ages. The arrangements were made between important people who were concerned with maintaining order; feudal institutions involved the governors—the upper classes, both laymen and clerics—not the masses of the population. Because central authority was no longer able to maintain itself locally, local authority had to be improvised to replace it. But because the processes and their results were anything but systematic, we do not use or recommend the outmoded term "feudal system."

One of the most influential arrangements between persons was the warband of the early Germans, the *comitatus*, as Tacitus called it in Latin—the leader commanded the loyalty of his followers, who banded together for fighting and winning of booty. All the Germanic barbarians appear to have had this institution; the Anglo-Saxon word for its chieftain, *hlaford*, is the origin of our word *lord*. In the Roman provinces, too, local landowners had often built their own private armies, while in Rome itself the magnates had their groups of *clients*, to whom they acted as *patron* and gave legal protection. When a humble man wanted to enter the client relationship, he asked for the *patrocinium* of the great man and secured it by performing the act of commendation, commending or entrusting himself to the patron. He remained free, but obtained food and clothing in exchange for his services, whatever they might be. If the man was of the upper classes, he was called *fidelis*. By the Carolingian period, the term *vassus*, originally denoting a man of menial status, had come to mean a man who rendered military service to his patron, or lord. Vassalage meant no disgrace; it was the status gained by the act of commendation. So a combination of old Germanic and old Roman practices contributed to new relationships described in new terms.

With regard to land, a Roman patron sometimes had retained the title to a piece of property but granted a client the temporary use of it, together with the profits to be derived from it so long as he held it, often for life. The Romans used the term *precarium* for this kind of tenure, and the Carolingian rulers commonly adopted the old practice—sometimes using the old Roman term, sometimes the newer *beneficium*, benefice, to describe the land temporarily held by the vassal in exchange for service. By the year 1000 the act of becoming a vassal usually meant that a man got a benefice; indeed he might refuse faithful service or loyalty unless he were satisfied with the land he received. The feeble later Carolingians and their rivals outbid each other in giving benefices to their supporters in order to obtain armed support and service. This was one of the practices that depleted the royal estates.

In the later Carolingian period, the benefice came to be called *feudum*, a fief, the term that has given us the words *feudal* and *feudalism*. As it became a fief, the benefice also became hereditary: though title to it remained with the lord who granted it, the fief itself passed, on the death of a vassal, to the vassal's heir, as did the vassal's obligations to serve the lord and his heirs.

The man who received a fief often got with it certain governmental rights over the farmers who lived and worked on the lands that made it up. This practice too had its precedents: in late Roman times, the Emperors often granted an *immunity* to their own estates, an understanding that the people who lived on these lands would not be visited by imperial tax-collectors or other law-enforcing officials. Because the immunity exempted the inhabitants from onerous duties, it was hoped that the farmers would enjoy their privileged status and therefore stay put and supply the Emperor with needed produce. The Frankish kings adopted this practice, sometimes extending it to lands of the Church and even to those of private proprietors. By the tenth century the immunity meant that the king undertook to keep his officials off the privileged lands, and that the holder of the lands would perform such governmental functions as collecting taxes, establishing police arrangements, and setting up a court, of which he might keep the profits.

From late Roman times, too, came the local offices of duke and count; originally military commanders, they took over increasing civil authority as the power of the central government relaxed. In Frankish times they might be very powerful rulers, kings in all but name. In the disorders of the Carolingian decline, these offices gradually became hereditary; at the same time, the dukes and counts became the vassals of the Carolingians. So the title and office, the duties of the vassal, and the fief (or territory of the office) all became hereditary.

Vassals and Lords. Feudalism and feudal practice did not extend uniformly over all of Europe. Northern France and the Low Countries were the most thoroughly feudalized areas, Germany perhaps the least. Everywhere some pieces of land never became fiefs, but remained the fully owned private property of the owners; these were called *allods*. Feudal practices varied from place to place, and they developed and altered with the passage of time. But certain general conceptions were held pretty much everywhere.

One of the most significant was that of contract: the lord—or *suzerain*, as he was often called—owed something to the vassal just as the vassal owed something to the lord. When they entered upon their relationship the vassal rendered homage to his lord and promised him aid and counsel. That is, he would appear, fully armed, and participate as a knight in the lord's wars (subject perhaps to limits on the number of days' service owed in any one year); and he would join with his fellow-vassals—his "peers," or social equals, to form the lord's court that alone could pass judgment on any one of them. He might also be required at his own expense to entertain his lord for a visit of specific length, and to give him money payments on special occasions—the marriage of the lord's eldest daughter, the knighting of his eldest son, or his departure on a crusade. The vassal also swore fealty (fidelity) to his lord. The lord was understood to owe, in his turn, protection and justice to his vassal.

If the vassal broke this contract, the lord would have to get the approval of the court made up of the vassal's peers before he could proceed to punishments such as forfeiture, depriving the vassal of his fief. If the lord broke the contract, the vassal was expected to withdraw his homage and fealty in a public act of defiance before proceeding to open rebellion. Sometimes the contract was written, sometimes it was oral. Sometimes the ceremony included a formal investiture by the lord: he would give his kneeling vassal a symbol of the fief that was being transferred to him, a twig or a bit of earth. When lord or vassal died, the contract had to be renewed with his successor. The son of a vassal, upon succeeding to his father's fief, often had to pay relief, a special, and often heavy, cash payment like a modern inheritance tax. If the vassal died without heirs, the fief would escheat, or revert to the lord, who could bestow it on another vassal or not as he saw fit. If the heir was still a minor, the lord exercised the right of wardship or guardianship until he came of age; this meant that the lord received the revenues from the fief, and if he was unscrupulous he could milk it dry.

Within a feudal kingdom, the king occupied the top position in a theoretical pyramid of society. Immediately below him would be his vassals, men who held fiefs directly from the king, called tenants-in-chief. But they in turn would be feudal lords: that is, they would have given out various parts of their own property as fiefs to their own vassals. These men, the king's vassals' vassals, would be the king's "rear vassals," and so at the next lower level of the theoretical pyramid. But they too would often have vassals, and so on, for many more levels—a process called "subinfeudation."

Practice was more complicated still. A tenant-in-chief might hold only a very small fief from the king and not be a very important person at all, while a vassal's vassal's vassal might be rich and powerful. The Dukes of Normandy, who were vassals to the King of France, were for some centuries much stronger than their overlord. An individual might receive fiefs from more than one lord, and so would be vassal to more than one lord, owing homage and fealty to both. What was he to do if one of his lords quarreled with another and went to war? To which one would he owe priority? This kind of thing happened very often: one Bavarian count had 20 different fiefs held of 20 different lords. Gradually, there arose a new concept, that of a *liege* lord, the one to whom a vassal owed service ahead of any other; but in practice the difficulties often persisted. Even though feudal law became more and more subtle and complex, this was an era when armed might counted for more than legality.

Manorialism. All the complicated arrangements we have been discussing directly involved only the governing persons who fought on horseback as mounted knights and whose fiefs consisted of landed property known as manors or estates. Even if we include their dependents, the total would hardly reach 10 per cent of the population of Europe. Most of the other 90 per cent of the people worked the land. In late Roman times, the large estate, owned by a magnate and worked by tenant-farmers, was called a *latifundium.* The tenant-farmers or *coloni* were often descendants of small landowners who had turned over their holdings to the magnate in exchange for a guarantee of protection and a percentage of the crop. While the *coloni* were personally free, not slaves, they could not leave the ground they cultivated, nor could their children.

If the *coloni* lived in groups of houses close together, the *latifundium* could be described as a *villa.* Though conditions varied widely, we shall not be far wrong if we think of the late Roman *latifundium* becoming the medieval manor, the late Roman villa becoming the medieval village, and the late Roman *coloni* becoming the medieval serfs. As we shall see, the early German village community also contributed to the new social structure. While the Roman landed estate had often produced its food for sale at a profit in the town and city, the long centuries of disorder beginning with the barbarian invasions led to a decline of commerce, of cities, and of agriculture for profit. The medieval manor usually produced only what was needed to feed its own population.

The oldest method of cultivation was the two-field system, alternating crops and fallow so that fertility could be recovered. Later, especially in grain-producing areas, a three-field system was devised—one field for spring planting, one for autumn planting, and the third lying fallow. Originally, oxen pulled the plow, but the invention of the horse-collar (so that the horse would not strangle on the old-fashioned strap around his neck) and the use of horseshoes (which allowed the horse to plow stony soil that hurt the oxen's feet) helped make it possible to substitute horses for oxen. So did the increasing use of tandem harnessing, enabling the horses to work in single file instead of side by side. A heavy-wheeled plow made its appearance in advanced areas.

The pattern of agricultural settlement varied from region to region. But so far as a "typical" manor existed, each of its peasant families had holdings, usually in the form of scattered long strips, in the big open fields. In theory this gave each family a bit of good arable land, a bit of the less good land, a bit of woodland, and so on. The strips might be separated from each other by narrow, unplowed *balks,* but there were no fences, walls, or hedges. The lord of the manor had his own strips, his *demesne* (perhaps a quarter to a third of the land), reserved for the production of the food that he and his household needed. The peasants had to work this land for the lord, often three days a week throughout the year, except perhaps in harvest time, when the lord could command their services until his crops were safely in the barns.

In exchange for permission to pasture their beasts in the lord's meadows, the peasants performed other duties. They paid to have their grain ground at the lord's mill and their bread baked in his oven. They often had to dig ditches or maintain the roads. They could not marry or allow their daughters to marry outside the manor without the lord's permission and usually the payment of a fine. They were bound to the soil, a hereditary caste of farm-laborers, serfs. But they were not slaves; the lord could not sell them; they and their children de-

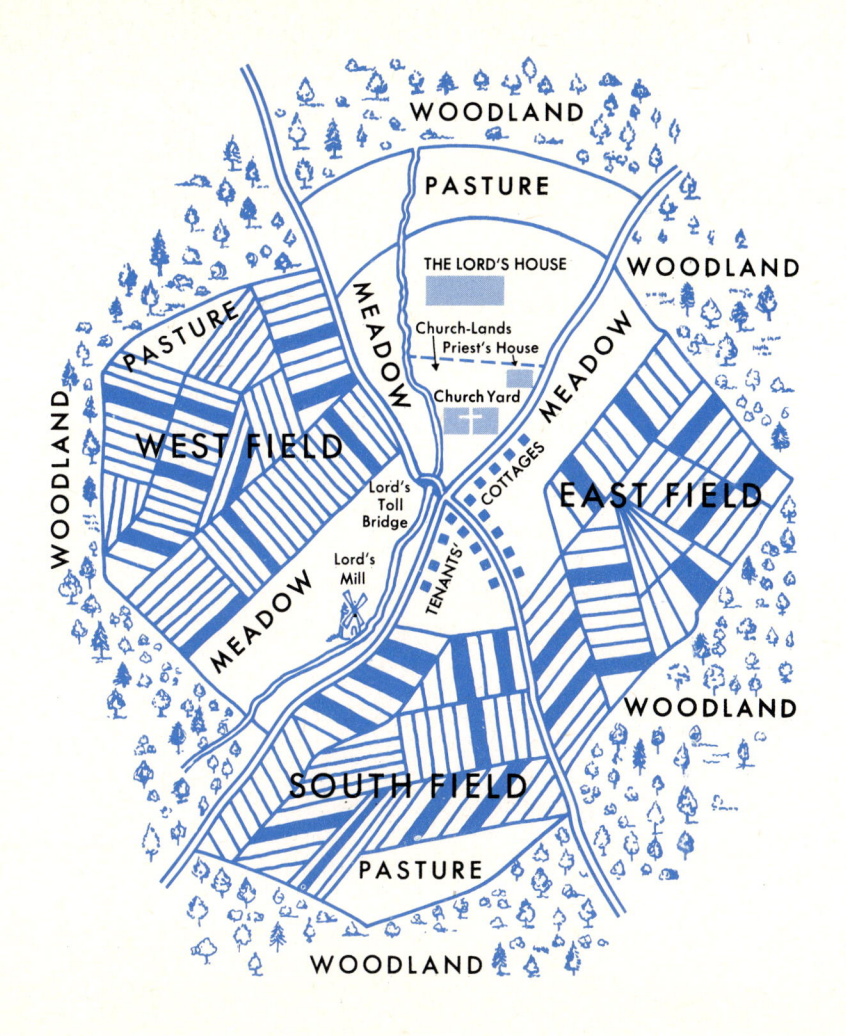

Plan of a medieval manor; the solid strips are the lord's demesne.

scended with the land to the lord's heirs. On such a manor the peasants would live in a cluster of houses close together. A big manor might have several such villages, with perhaps isolated farmsteads in addition. On the other hand, a single village might lie partly in one manor and partly in another belonging to a different lord.

The organization of the countryside by manors was earliest developed in eastern France and in parts of Italy and Germany. Even at its height, it did not include some parts of these and other European countries. But in the large areas where manorialism did prevail, the old Roman landlord's economic power over his tenants had fused with the traditional Germanic village chief's political power, and, by the eleventh century, with the governing rights that the lord received with his fief. The deep respect for custom tended to prevent the lord's extorting from his peasants more work or more food than they traditionally owed him; but they had no rights, and nowhere to appeal in cases where the lord was oppressive. Custom prevailed in the lord's court, when he or his steward sat in judgment on the tenants, enforcing the traditional rules of the village community. Custom regulated the bargaining agreements reached among the peasants for the use in common of plows and plowteams. Custom no doubt retarded inventiveness and stifled initiative, but it was the only thing that gave a serf the sense that he was protected against exactions and cruelties.

THE CIVILIZATION OF THE "DARK AGES" IN THE WEST

The achievements of the West in letters and the arts during the centuries of the barbarian onslaught were feeble indeed by comparison with those of Greek, Hellenistic, or Roman civilizations, or indeed with those of the contemporary eastern Mediterranean world, Christian and Moslem. This is exactly what one would expect in a new world where the masters usually did not have the taste or the judgment to patronize writers or artists, and where life was too turbulent to give men much leisure for the exercise of creativity. Communications became far more precarious than in the Greco-Roman world, as roads and the postal system deteriorated and sea transport became more uncertain. Cities—centers of culture and of the commerce that made culture possible—subsided into ruined shells of their former splendor. Technical skills were lost—the art of sculpture, for example, as the celebrated realism of the ancients gave way to something so crude in the representation of the human body that one finds it hard to believe that men deliberately carved in that style because they wanted to be symbolic. Lost too was the command over language: nobody spoke good Latin any more, and few could write it, and the slowly developing vernacular tongues—the Romance-French or the proto-German—were not yet used in a literary way.

Yet the barbarians loved and admired the Roman world they were destroying. The Christian faith that they took over from it gave them a firmer link both with the city of Empire and with its traditions than they could otherwise have had. Even at moments of low ebb during the Dark Ages, there were exceptions to the decline, signs that a revival and transformation of letters and art were slowly in the making. Under Theodoric in Italy, for example, two men fought against the rot that had already eaten deeply into cultural life: Boethius and Cassiodorus.

Boethius (c. 480–524), surprisingly for someone of his day, knew Greek as well as Latin, and hoped to make Latin translations of Plato and Aristotle; he also made the first effort to use Aristotle's logical methods in dealing with Christian theology, writing works of his own on the art of argument. He was an orthodox Christian, with a mind strong enough to realize the importance of the ancients' methods for Christian thought. If he had survived to complete his work, western Europe perhaps would not have been denied these materials for another five centuries, and men's intellectual processes might well have been greatly improved. Unfortunately Boethius was imprisoned by Theodoric on a charge of plotting against him. For a year before his execution for treason, he wrote *The*

Page from Alcuin's edition of the Vulgate, ninth century.

Consolation of Philosophy, a dialogue between himself and the personification of Philosophy; the work was full of nobility but it was not especially profound or original.

Cassiodorus lived much longer (c. 490–580), and managed to stay in Theodoric's good graces, acting as his secretary of state and collecting his official correspondence. Cassiodorus hoped to found a Christian academy in Rome. Thwarted by the disorders of Justinian's reconquest of Italy, he eventually founded a monastery in southern Italy, and prescribed the study of the classics as a means to strengthen and advance Christian education.

Far more typical of the period were the views of Pope Gregory the Great (reigned 590–604), who had no use for the classics despite his good education. Gregory's own style was crude and vigorous, and everything he wrote had its practical purpose. His commentary on the Book of Job was designed to make people behave better; his *Dialogues*, which included a life of St. Benedict, were written to make the monastic life popular.

The Merovingian period, as one would expect, produced little literature, but the Latin hymns of Fortunatus are moving, and the somewhat childlike history by Gregory (538–594), Bishop of Tours and chronicler of the savage crimes of the Frankish ruling house, provides flashes of insight into the Merovingian mind. In Spain, Isidore (c. 570–636), Archbishop of Seville, wrote a kind of encyclopedia, *The Etymologies,* which became the standard reference book for several hundred years. It reflects both Isidore's learning, which was extraordinary for his time, and his superstition and ignorance, which were more typical.

For a different spirit one must turn to Ireland and England, where the seventh century—elsewhere in Europe the low point of intellectual activity—saw a genuine revival. The monasteries provided a refuge for booklovers and a shelter for their books; and the combined influence of the Celtic and the Roman traditions brought fruitful results.

Of a large number of cultivated men, the greatest was Bede (c. 672–735), who could read Greek, knew the works of the Church Fathers, and produced the remarkable *Ecclesiastical History of the English People,* covering the period 597–731; this is an invaluable source for the student, written in a Latin of astonishing vigor and purity. Churchmen from this separate cultural world of Britain made possible a revival on the Continent under Charlemagne, who supplied the necessary interest and patronage.

Alcuin of York (d. 804), who had studied under a pupil of Bede, came to the court of Charlemagne in 782 and helped transform the palace school into a serious and practical educational institution where men studied the seven liberal arts as then understood—grammar, rhetoric, and dialectic; arithmetic, geometry, astronomy, and music. Alcuin wrote much himself, and also took the lead in biblical scholarship and in improving the handwriting of the scribes in monasteries, thus ensuring a regular and increasing supply of legible books. The survival of much of Latin literature we owe directly to the efforts of Carolingian scribes. Many other poets, scholars, and historians joined Alcuin in making the palace school a center not only for learning but for agreeable and interesting conversation, in which Charlemagne enjoyed taking part. The foundations laid by these men permitted their successors in the next two generations to write personal letters, history, poetry, and even ambitious works on theological and ethical questions.

3

READING SUGGESTIONS (asterisk indicates paperbound edition)

Christianity

F. Cumont, *The Oriental Religions in Roman Paganism* (*Dover). An introduction to the general religious climate in which Christianity took root.

A. Schweitzer, *The Quest of the Historical Jesus,* new ed. (Macmillan, 1948). Fascinating examination of the question of the historicity of Jesus by the celebrated medical missionary.

M. Burrows, *The Dead Sea Scrolls* (Viking, 1955). Of the many books on the subject this is perhaps the most useful for the student of history.

B. H. Streeter, *The Four Gospels* (Macmillan, 1930). A good middle-of-the-road study by a Protestant cleric.

A. D. Nock, *St. Paul* (Oxford, 1955). A classic treatment.

S. J. Case, *The Social Origins of Christianity* (University of Chicago, 1923). Emphasizing the interrelation of environment and ideas.

E. R. Goodenough, *The Church in the Roman Empire* (Holt, 1931). Brief, balanced account directed to the beginning student.

R. Bultmann, *Primitive Christianity in Its Contemporary Setting* (*Meridian). Good scholarly treatment.

A. H. M. Jones, *Constantine and the Conversion of Rome* (*Collier). A short and impartial account by a scholar who has also written more detailed studies on the social history of the declining Roman Empire.

W. H. C. Frend, *Martyrdom and Persecution in the Early Church* (*Anchor). Scholarly and readable study.

C. N. Cochrane, *Christianity and Classical Culture* (*Galaxy). Stimulating survey.

K. S. Latourette, *Christianity through the Ages* (*Harper College Paperbacks). Overview by a sympathetic historian.

C. Dawson, *Religion and the Rise of Western Culture* (*Image). Excellent survey to the thirteenth century from the Catholic point of view.

A. McGiffert, *A History of Christian Thought* (*Scribner's). Good account from the Protestant standpoint.

H. B. Parkes, *Gods and Men: The Origins of Western Culture* (*Vintage). Clear and sympathetic.

R. M. Pope, *The Church and Its Culture* (Bethany, 1965). A brief and sympathetic account, with a full, up-to-date bibliography.

The Barbarian Onslaught

J. M. Wallace-Hadrill, *The Barbarian West: The Early Middle Ages,* A.D. 400–1000 (*Torchbooks). Up-to-date brief account.

J. B. Bury, *The Invasion of Europe by the Barbarians* (*Norton). An older and very good short account.

E. A. Thompson, *The Early Germans* (Oxford, 1965). Up-to-date survey.

F. Lot, *The End of the Ancient World and the Beginnings of the Middle Ages* (*Torchbooks). Balanced assessment by a French historian writing more than a generation ago.

C. Dawson, *The Making of Europe* (*Meridian). Scholarly review by a Catholic historian.

S. Dill, *Roman Society in the Last Century of the Empire* (Macmillan, 1898) and *Roman Society in Gaul in the Merovingian Age* (Macmillan, 1926). Still very much worth reading.

J. Boussard, *Civilization of Charlemagne* (*McGraw-Hill). Brings together materials usually difficult to obtain in English.

R. Winston, *Charlemagne: From the Hammer to the Cross* (*Vintage). The best biography in English.

H. Fichtenau, *The Carolingian Empire: The Age of Charlemagne* (*Torchbooks). A competent study.

H. Pirenne, *Mohammed and Charlemagne* (Norton, 1939). Defense of the highly controversial thesis that the Arab conquest of the Mediterranean harmed western Europe more than the German invasions had done.

F. M. Stenton, *Anglo-Saxon England,* 2nd

ed. (Clarendon, 1950). The authoritative treatment.

P. H. Blair, *Roman Britain and Early England, 55 B.C.–871 A.D.* (*Norton) and *Introduction to Anglo-Saxon England* (*Cambridge). More recent scholarly studies of early medieval England.

J. Bronsted, *The Vikings*, rev. ed. (*Pelican). Up-to-date assessment of the Norse invaders.

M. L. W. Laistner, *Thought and Letters in Western Europe, A.D. 500 to 900* (*Cornell). A good scholarly study.

Feudalism

C. Stephenson, *Medieval Feudalism* (*Cornell). Simple introductory manual.

F. L. Ganshof, *Feudalism* (*Torchbooks). More advanced introduction.

M. Bloch, *Feudal Society*, 2 vols. (*Phoenix). The masterpiece of a great French scholar.

J. Clapham and E. Power, eds., *The Cambridge Economic History*, Vol. I (Cambridge University, 1941). A scholarly study of medieval agrarian life.

A. Dopsch, *The Economic and Social Foundations of European Civilization* (Harcourt, 1937). An important work revising notions of the breakdown that occurred after the "fall" of Rome.

L. J. Daly, *Benedictine Monasticism: Its Formation and Development through the Twelfth Century* (Sheed & Ward, 1965). A valuable history of a major monastic order.

C. Brooke, *Europe in the Central Middle Ages, 962–1154* (Holt, 1964). Good recent scholarly review.

Sources and Fiction

The student may want to sample various translations of the New Testament: the King James (or Authorized version) (*Meridian); the Revised Standard version (*Meridian), which appeared in 1952 and met a hostile reception from literary reviewers and fundamentalists; the Douay version accepted by Catholics (Catholic Book Publishing, 1950); and the American Protestant version by Smith and Goodspeed (Chicago, 1939).

H. S. Bettenson, *Documents of the Christian Church* (*Oxford). Admirably edited collection.

St. Augustine, *Confessions* (Sheed & Ward, 1947), and the more difficult *City of God*, a scholarly edition in seven volumes, of which six have appeared (Harvard University, 1947–   ).

Bryher, *The Roman Wall* (Pantheon, 1954). Novel of the Roman Alpine frontier under German pressure.

———, *Ruan* (Pantheon, 1960). Druids, Celts, and Anglo-Saxons in very early medieval Britain.

4

The Medieval World

Western Europe

Portion of the Bayeux Tapestry (c. 1078), which depicts the Norman conquest of England: Harold, the Saxon King, is killed, and his army collapses.

I. The Society and Its Economy

THE TURNING-POINT OF THE ELEVENTH CENTURY

The eleventh century proved to be a major turning-point in the social and economic life of the West, although nobody alive at the time could have been fully conscious of what was happening. As the raids of the Northmen tapered off, most of western Europe found itself secure against outside attack. By the end of the century, western Europe was able to take the offensive and invade the lands of Islam in the crusades (*see* Chapter 5). During the eleventh century, the population grew rapidly. Although scholars cannot really account for this, it may have reflected the greater security of the individual and his increased expectancy of life. By modern standards, of course, human beings were still exposed to dangers that seem fantastic.

The larger population needed more food and more land. Pioneers felled trees, drained swamps, opened up new areas for farming. When forests or marsh lay within a manor, a lord would often offer special inducements to his serfs to get them to undertake the extra heavy labor of clearing and farming it. Sometimes a group of peasants would move into a new region that had lain empty before, and would clear it and farm it by introducing the usual strip system. If such uninhabited land belonged to a lord, he might invite peasants to colonize it and would offer them freedom from serfdom and the chance to pay a money rent instead of the usual services. This would bring profit to the lord and great advantages to the emancipated serf.

New technology helped to improve the farmer's life. Farmers adopted some devices that had been known earlier, such as the heavy wheeled plow, and the use of horses to draw it. Windmills made their first appearance on the European landscape, especially in flat areas like the Low Countries where there was no falling water to run a watermill. Slowly the anonymous inventors of the Middle Ages perfected systems of gears that would turn the millstones faster and produce more meal in less time.

TRADE AND TOWN

During the eleventh century also, and as part of the same general development, trade began slowly to revive. Medieval farmers were helpless in the face of a bad harvest year, and plenty or scarcity varied widely from region to region. It was the natural thing to bring surpluses into areas of famine and sell them at high prices to the hungry. The first new commercial centers arose in places such as Venice and the Low Countries, where the local farms could not feed the increasing population. Even in the Dark Ages, such trade had never disappeared altogether, but now the incentives to increase its scale were pressing.

When the proprietor of a manor found that year after year he could make large sums by selling a certain crop, he began to plant more and more of that crop and to use the money gained by its sale to buy the things he was no longer raising. Once he had more money than he needed for necessities, he began to think of how to spend it on something extra, a luxury. Such a demand quickly creates its supply: what was once a luxury comes to seem a necessity. Thus, for example, the people of Flanders, living in an area that was poor for growing grain but good for raising sheep, sold their raw wool, developed a woolen-manufacturing industry, and imported the food they needed.

The recovery of commerce and the beginnings of industries stimulated the growth of towns. Old Roman towns like London and Marseilles revived. New towns grew around a castle (*bourg* in France, *burgh* in England, *burg* in Germany), especially if it was strategically located for trade as well as for defense. And so the resident *bourgeois, burgesses,* or *burghers* enter the language as castle-dwellers, but soon become recognizable as residents of towns, engaged in commerce. Protected by the lord of the castle, or sometimes by the abbot of a local monastery, the townsmen built walls and pursued their trade. They would band together into gilds to protect themselves from brigands on the roads, and to bargain with the lord of the next castle, who might be showing unpleasant signs of confiscating their goods or charging indecently high tolls whenever they crossed his land. Grouped in a gild, merchants could often win concessions: if the lord they were bargaining with seemed unreasonable, they might threaten to take a route across the lands of some less rapacious lord and pay a more moderate toll.

Mutual advantage soon led proprietors, including kings as well as lesser lords, to grant privileges to the townsmen by issuing a charter. Although the contents of such documents vary, most of them guaranteed free status to the townsmen; even an escaped serf within the town would acquire freedom if he could avoid capture for a year. The charter might also grant the townsmen the right to hold a perpetual market, to transfer property within the town walls, and

Drapers' hall, Ghent, begun in the fifteenth century.

to have their lawsuits tried in a town court by town custom, which slowly developed into a whole new kind of law, the "law merchant."

Industry followed commerce into the town. The merchant, with his experience of distant markets, learned how to buy raw material, to have workmen do the manufacturing wherever it was cheapest, and to sell the finished products wherever he could get the best price. The workmen also soon began to organize themselves into craft gilds, which provided medical care and burial for the members, and often fixed minimum wages, the standards of quality of the product, and even the prices that were to be asked.

Enterprise was neither free nor private. It was highly regulated, not only as an effort to reduce outside competition but also as a reflection of the ideas of the age. Men believed that a "just price" for a pair of shoes included the cost of the leather and the thread, the amount needed to sustain the shoemaker at his usual standard of life while he made the shoes, and a small addition to pay the seller for his time and trouble. To "make money" in the modern sense of charging all that the traffic would bear was in theory to cheat the customer. No doubt many medieval customers were in fact cheated in this sense, but the ethics of the time condemned the action. Finance capitalism—the use of money to make money, the investment of funds at interest—was condemned as usury.

TOWN AND COUNTRYSIDE

In their turn, the towns greatly affected the overwhelming mass of the population who remained in the countryside, who now had a place to sell their surplus and so an incentive to produce it. Some peasants saved enough cash to buy their freedom; some fled to the town in the hope of acquiring freedom, or at least in the hope that their children might acquire it. The very word "cash" suggests a most important development, the flourishing of a money economy instead of the economy of barter. Barter still continued, but as the magnates came to want more and more manufactured or imported or luxury items, they wanted cash rather than services: a serf's labors would produce more grain, but not the money to buy a piece of armor. So the lord would let the peasant pay him cash, and would forgive (commute) the serf's obligation to work on the lord's land. More demand for money led to more money in circulation, and to a slowly inflationary rise in wages and prices.

With the increase in demand for goods, large-scale fairs became a regular feature of medieval life. Some of them brought together merchants and products from a relatively narrow region, but others attracted men and goods from all over the European world. In Champagne, in northeastern France, for example, there were several great annual fairs each year. The Count of Champagne collected a fee from the towns for the privilege of holding the fair as well as the revenues from a special court set up to try cases that arose during the fair. As large-scale transactions became more frequent, it became less practical for merchants to carry around large amounts of cash, and during the thirteenth century merchants came to use a written promise to pay instead. Acceptance of these bills of exchange, a kind of primitive check, often made it unnecessary to transport money at all, since a Parisian creditor of a London merchant could call upon a Parisian debtor of the same merchant to pay the amount owed.

II. Monarchy in the Medieval West

With the gradual changes in the economy and the society of western Europe went changes also in its political life. As always in politics the central question is: Who has the power? In France, often regarded as the most feudal area of Europe, the monarch successfully asserted his superiority over his vassals. In England, the kings, having made good their superiority, were forced by their vassals to dilute it. In Germany, the nobles in the end became little rulers, each in his miniature realm. We now turn to the histories of these peoples in the centuries between the eleventh and the fourteenth and to their different experiences, which largely determined their future political development and their national character in our own day.

FRANCE: HUGH CAPET THROUGH PHILIP THE FAIR (987–1314)

The Capetians. Chosen King of France by the nobles in 987, Hugh Capet came of a family that for a century had been disputing the throne with the feeble surviving Carolingians (*see* Chapter 3). His own domain was the Ile de France, a compact strip of land including Paris and its environs, and extending south to the Loire at Orléans. It was smaller than the domains of any of the great feudal lords, his vassals, who chose him as king: the Dukes of Normandy or Burgundy or Aquitaine, the Counts of Flanders, Anjou, Champagne, Brittany, or Toulouse. This may have been one of the reasons they could elect him. More powerful than he, they might defy him by withholding the military service, the feudal dues, and the counsel which they owed him.

Yet the Capetians proved to have certain advantages. Hugh's male line continued to inherit the throne for almost 350 years. At first the kings secured the election and coronation of their eldest sons during their own lifetimes, until, by the end of the twelfth century, the hereditary principle was firmly established. The king alone had no suzerain. Moreover, his office gave him a special sanctity: crowned and anointed with holy oil, he seemed to the people partly divine, "the eldest son of the Church." The Church became his partner; he defended it and it assisted him. He nominated bishops to sees near Paris, and the bishops took an oath of fealty to him. Finally, Hugh Capet's domain, though small, was compact and easily governed; he and his successors concentrated their attention on it.

While the Duke of Normandy was conquering England, or relatives of the Duke of Burgundy were making themselves kings of Portugal, Hugh Capet's descendants were doggedly clearing the brigands from the roads in the Ile de France, forcing royal authority upon its inhabitants, and adding territory to it piecemeal. The officers of the royal household became the king's advisory and administrative staff—the *curia regis*, or king's court. By the early twelfth century, the king had prevented these important jobs from becoming hereditary in one family, and had begun to appoint men of his own choice as royal servants. Suger, Abbot of St. Denis, a man of humble birth, faithfully served Louis VI (reigned 1108–1137) and Louis VII (reigned 1137–1180) for several decades. Louis VI introduced royal appointees known as *prévôts* (provosts) to administer justice and taxation in the royal lands. He granted charters to rural pioneers and to new towns, recognizing that the monarchy would gain by new settlements. In these ways the French kings began their long and important alliance with the middle class. By the time of Louis VII, the king had acquired such prestige that far-off vassals in the south of France were appealing to him to settle local disputes.

Then, in the late twelfth century, the monarchy had to face the challenge posed by its Norman vassals. Though Duke William had conquered England in 1066 and thus gained resources that made him much stronger than the King of France, he was still vassal of the Capetians for Normandy. In the early twelfth century an English queen married another great vassal of the King of France, the Count of Anjou; and their son, King Henry II of England (reigned 1154–1190), ruled England, Normandy, Anjou, Maine, and Touraine, in what is sometimes called the "Angevin Empire." Worse still, Henry II married Eleanor of Aquitaine, heiress to all of southwest France, whom Louis VII had divorced in 1152 because she had not borne him a son. Henry II now had more than half of France, and added Brittany and other territories. The survival of the French monarchy was in question.

Philip Augustus and Territorial Expansion. Philip II (reigned 1180–1223), called Philip Augustus, used both cunning and force to win a major first round in the struggle. He supported Henry II's rebellious sons against him and then plotted against Henry's son, Richard the Lionhearted, when he became King of England. He also married a Danish princess in the hope of inheriting the Danish claims to the English throne and utilizing the Danish fleet. In 1200, a year after Richard's brother John became King of England, Philip used feudal law against him: John had foolishly married a girl who was engaged to somebody else; her father complained to Philip, and Philip summoned his vassal John to answer the complaint. When John failed to appear, Philip quite legally declared his fiefs forfeit, and planned to conquer them on behalf of a rival claimant, John's nephew, young Arthur of Brittany. When John murdered Arthur (1203), he lost his sympathizers on the Continent, and played into Philip's hands. In 1204 John had to surrender Normandy, Brittany, Anjou, Maine, and Touraine. Driven out of France north of the Loire, the English retained only Aquitaine. In 1214, at the battle of Bouvines, Philip defeated an army of English and Germans, and made good his territorial gains. The lands John had lost became part of the French royal domain, and the Duchy of Normandy, in royal hands, could serve as a model of administrative efficiency for the rest of France.

The next major conquest took place in the southern territories of Languedoc and Toulouse, whose inhabitants spoke a dialect differing from northern French. Many of them were heretics. This region had become the center of the "Cathari" (Greek, "pure ones"), also called Albigensians, after the town of Albi, one of their strongholds. Albigensian beliefs derived ultimately from those of the Manichaeans (*see* Chapter 3) which had spread, often secretly, from the eastern Mediterranean via the Balkans to northern Italy and southern France. Believing that all matter was created by the forces of evil, the Albigensians held that the earth itself, the body of man, wood, water—anything material—was the work of the devil. So they denied the humanity of Jesus, repudiated the adoration of the cross, and forbade infant baptism, the Mass, and other sacraments. Though strongest among the lower classes, they often had the support of individual nobles.

In 1208 the Pope proclaimed a crusade against the Albigensians, and hundreds of northern French nobles rushed south to kill the heretics and steal their property. Philip Augustus himself did not intervene at first. But by the year of his death (1223), after 15 years of bloody warfare, he saw the chance of annexation and sponsored an expedition under his son Louis VIII (reigned 1223–1226). By the 1240's the royal armies and a special church court, the Inquisition, had driven the heresy underground; in 1249, when the last Count of Toulouse died, his lands went—by marriage—to the brother of the King of France.

The Development of Royal Government. As the royal lands increased, royal government grew in efficiency. Philip Augustus collected detailed information of just exactly what was owing him from the various royal fiefs. He systematically tried to reach over the heads of his own vassals and make *their* vassals dependent on him. He made his vassals promise to perform their feudal duties or else surrender themselves as prisoners. If they did not, the Church would lay an interdict on their lands, depriving the inhabitants of the sacraments and the other comforts of religion; the people feared this punishment more than any other. Philip bought as many estates as he could. He insisted on providing husbands of his own choosing for great heiresses, who in those violent days often survived several husbands and paid the king handsomely each time he married them off.

Philip Augustus supplanted the *prévôts*, whose lands and offices had tended to become hereditary and who were often abusing their powers. The new officials—called *baillis* (bailiffs) in the north and *sénéchaux* (seneschals) in the south—received no fiefs, and their office was not hereditary. They did not reside in their administrative areas, but traveled about enforcing the royal rights, rendering justice on the king's behalf, and collecting money owed to the king. *Baillis* and *sénéchaux* were salaried royal civil servants, removable at the king's will and dependent upon his favor. As a further check upon them, Louis IX (reigned 1226–1270) made it easy for complaints against them to be brought to his attention, and appointed still other new officials to take care of the caretakers. These were the *enquêteurs* (investigators), rather like Charlemagne's *missi dominici*, who had supervisory authority over the *baillis* and *sénéchaux* and toured the country inspecting their work. By this system of royal officials the king could interfere with almost all local and private transactions, exact his just due, and supply royal justice at a price.

New business swamped the old *curia regis*. For the monarchy of Louis IX and his successors to have depended on the household officers, as the immediate successors of Hugh Capet had been able to do, would have been a little like the United States government today trying to get along with no filing system except an old bureau belonging to George Washington. So the old household began to differentiate itself into departments, most of which dealt with the needs of the king and his retainers, clergy, and advisers. When a major policy decision needed to be made or when a major lawsuit needed to be tried, the king could summon all his vassals (lay and clerical) for counsel. When they joined the rest of the *curia regis* and sat in judgment on a lawsuit, the enlarged body was called a *parlement*, a high judicial tribunal.

As law grew more complex, trained lawyers had to handle more and more of the judicial business. At first they explained the law to the vassals sitting in judgment, and then, as time passed, they formed a court and arrived at decisions themselves in the name of the king. By the fourteenth century this court was called the *Parlement de Paris*. When the *curia regis* sat in special session on a financial matter or audited the reports of royal income and expenditure, it was acting as a kind of government accounting bureau. By the fourteenth century this was called the *chambre des comptes*, the chamber of accounts. More and more it, too, needed full-time employees: clerks, auditors, and so on. Though the king got money from his lands, from customs dues and tolls, and from fees of all kinds paid by vassals for justice or for exemption from outmoded feudal services, he could not levy regular taxes on his subjects. The nobles became accustomed to the regular paying of feudal aids, but bitterly objected to anything else, such as two royal efforts (1145 and 1188) to collect special taxes as a penalty from those who stayed home from a crusade.

St. Louis. The medieval French monarchy reached its highest point with Louis IX. Generous and devout, almost monastic in his personal life, he was made a saint by the Church in 1297, less than 30 years after his death. Yet personal piety did not prevent him from defending royal prerogatives against infringements by his own bishops or by the papacy. In 1247 he would not let the Pope assess the churches of France for money and men to fight papal military campaigns. Louis showed the same hardheaded spirit in his dealings with the towns, old allies of the Capetians, where the lower class of tradesmen resented the concentration of authority in the small merchant upper class. The crown intervened, not on behalf of the poor and humble, but for the purpose of ensuring the regular flow of funds to the royal coffers. In 1262 Louis required that the towns present annual accounts. The very form of the decree illustrates Louis' strong assertion of royal prerogative: It was a new kind of enactment, the *ordonnance*, a royal command issued for all of France without the previous assent of the vassals. By *ordonnance* the king also forbade private warfare and declared that royal money was valid everywhere in the realm.

By Louis' day Frenchmen preferred royal justice, and appeals from lower feudal courts flowed in to the *parlement*. The royal court alone could try cases of treason and breaking the peace. To the *parlement* the crown brought in townsmen, the king's *bourgeois*, and so extended royal justice to the towns. Sitting under an oak tree in the forest of Vincennes outside of Paris, St. Louis made himself available to all his subjects and listened to all disputes. Foreigners too came to prize his justice. He settled quarrels in Flanders, Burgundy, Lorraine, and Navarre, and in 1264 was invited to judge a dispute between King Henry III of England and the English nobles. In the conception and enactment of his special God-ordained role as king, St. Louis reached a height attained by no other monarch.

The System Hardens: Philip the Fair. After the death of St. Louis, and especially during the reign of his grandson Philip IV (1285–1314), called "the Fair" because of his good looks, the French royal system experienced a kind of

Carcassonne, a restored medieval walled town in southern France.

hardening—a loss of new forms of expression. This hardening is notable throughout the medieval world during the late thirteenth and early fourteenth centuries. Where St. Louis had been firm and just, Philip the Fair was aggressive and ruthless. The towns, the nobles, the Church all suffered as he and his ubiquitous agents invaded long-standing rights.

Much of this undermining went on in a series of courtroom battles, as the king's lawyers perverted old regal rules in order to push royal claims to the uttermost. The royal agents asserted that if a case was begun in a royal court it had to be completed there, no matter where it legally belonged. They urged plaintiffs to claim on any and all occasions that they had been denied justice in the court of a feudal lord and so to bring their cases before the king's court. They exploited the rule that the loser of a suit could call the judge "wicked and false" and appeal to the next higher court, where the first judge would become the defendant. By using this device in the great lords' courts, the king's men could bring the great lords themselves before the king's court. The system of royal justice was swallowing up the system of feudal justice.

And, as the new cases flowed in, the *parlement* became ever more specialized and professionalized. The *chambre des requêtes* (chamber of petitions) handled all requests that the royal court intervene; the *chambre des enquêtes* (chamber of investigations) would establish the facts in new cases. In the *chambre des plaids* (chamber of pleas) the lawyers actually argued the cases, and judgments were handed down. Members of the *parlement* traveled to the remotest regions of France, bringing royal justice to the king's own domain, and more and more taking over the machinery of justice in the great feudal lordships.

At the same period, the most intimate advisers of the king in the *curia regis*, whom he regularly consulted, became differentiated as the "narrow" or "secret" council, while the larger groups of advisers, consisting of the remaining lords and high clerics, were called the "full council." In 1302, for the first time, representatives of the towns attended a meeting of this large council. At the moment when townsmen first participated, a transition began to a new kind of assembly, later called the "Estates-General." An "estate" is a social class; traditionally, the clergy was the "first estate," the nobility the second, and the townsmen the third. When all three estates were present, an assembly became an Estates-General. Though the clerics and nobles acted as individuals, the townsmen came as chosen delegates from the corporations of their municipalities, and so acted as representatives.

The Struggle for Money. Needing money for his wars, Philip the Fair summoned the Estates to obtain their approval for his preparations to raise it. He usually would not fix an amount because the contributor would have the right to bargain with him. Medieval man felt that no action was proper unless it had always been customary; so that whenever the king wanted to do something new he tried to make it seem like something old. Often a protest that a given effort to raise money constituted "an unheard-of exaction" would suffice to frustrate his efforts. One of Philip's most effective techniques was to demand military service from a man and then let him escape it by paying a specific amount assessed on his property. Philip asked regularly for sums that had in the past been demanded only occasionally. He also took forced loans, debased the coinage, and levied new customs dues and royal taxes on commercial transactions.

Need for money led to a fierce quarrel with the papacy. When Philip claimed the right to tax the clergy for defense, Pope Boniface VIII (reigned 1294-1303) forbade kings to do so without his consent (1296). Philip then forbade the export from France of all precious metals, severely threatening the financial position of the papacy. Boniface backed down in 1297, agreeing that Philip could tax the clergy in an emergency. But in 1300, when Philip's courts tried a French bishop accused of treason, the Pope publicly claimed the right to intervene in the affairs of any land ruled by a wicked king; Philip in reply called the Pope "your fatuousness." Boniface now proclaimed that every human creature, in order to be saved, must be subject to the Pope, and threatened to excommunicate Philip, who had sent a band of thugs to kidnap Boniface. They burst into the Pope's presence (September 7, 1303) and so humiliated the old man, who was over 80, that he died not long afterward from the shock. Philip then obtained the election of a French pope, who never even went to Rome. Thus began the "Babylonian Captivity" of the papacy at Avignon in southern France (1305-1378).

Money also lay at the root of Philip's famous attack on the Knights Templars, originally an order of crusading warriors, who now had a rich banking business. In order to avoid paying the Templars what he owed them, Philip accused them of vicious behavior, brought them to trial, and in 1312 succeeded in having the order abolished. He arrested the Jews of France, stripped them of their property, and expelled them; he also persecuted the agents of the Italian bankers. His agents collected and kept all the debts owing to his victims.

Just before Philip died in 1314, his encroachments led to a kind of taxpayers' strike, in which the towns joined with the local lords in protest against his having raised money for a war and then having made peace instead of fighting. Louis X (reigned 1314–1316) calmed the unrest by returning some of the money and sacrificing some of the unpopular bureaucrats. He also issued a series of charters confirming the rights of his vassals, yet not putting a permanent check on the advance of royal power. Since taxation was still connected with military service, the king's unquestioned feudal right, the king could declare an emergency, summon his vassals to fight, and then allow some of them to commute the service for money. Nor did the French nobles keep a committee (as the English had done) to see to it that the king kept his promises. The French monarch of the early fourteenth century continued to enjoy a position at home more powerful and centralized than that of any other western European ruler.

ENGLAND: WILLIAM THE CONQUEROR THROUGH EDWARD I (1066–1307)

William the Conqueror. William, Duke of Normandy, who crossed the Channel and defeated the Anglo-Saxons at Hastings in 1066, displayed in his new kingdom the full Norman genius for government. As victor, he could retain or modify or add to the Anglo-Saxon institutions that he found: the 34 counties or shires with their sheriffs, the courts of shire and hundred (a subdivision of a shire), the *witenagemot* or royal council, the Danegeld, and the *fyrd* or militia. William assumed the ownership of all the land in England. He kept about one-sixth as royal domain, gave about half as fiefs to his great Norman barons, and returned to the Church the quarter that it had held before. Although many of his barons subinfeudated their lands, their vassals owed military service only to William, and swore primary allegiance to him (in the Salisbury Oath, 1086). The bishops and abbots also owed him feudal services. He permitted no castles to be

Medieval France and England

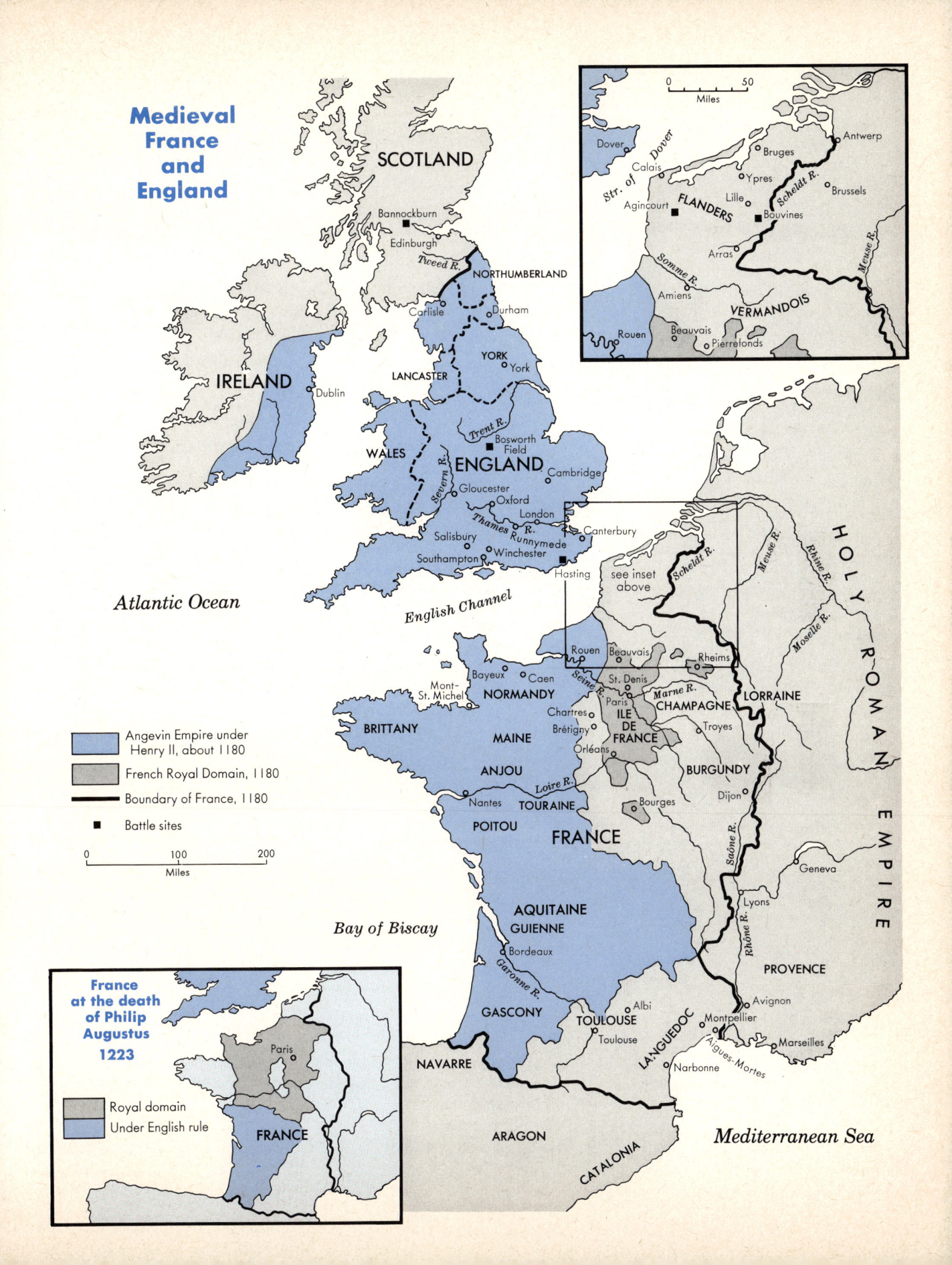

built without a royal license, forbade private war, and allowed only royal coinage. He levied the Danegeld, summoned the *fyrd* as well as the feudal array, and kept the Anglo-Saxon system of courts. He gave the sheriffs authority at the expense of other local officials and bound them closely to the crown.

In sum, the Conqueror respected English custom and law but superimposed the Norman feudal structure; the sheriffs provided continuity between the old and the new. The Norman *curia regis* superseded the Anglo-Saxon *witenagemot;* it gave counsel, tried the cases of the great vassals, and performed duties in the shires. In 1086 William ordered a careful survey of all landed property in England. Its record, the unique Domesday Book, included for each piece of land a full statement of past and present ownership and all resources: forests, fishponds, cattle, so that the king's men might find more revenue if possible. As for the Church, William paid the accustomed dues to Rome, but refused to acquiesce when the Pope asked to be recognized as feudal suzerain of England (none of the Anglo-Saxon kings had ever acknowledged papal sovereignty). William left the English monarchy in 1087 stronger than the French would be for more than two centuries.

William's immediate successors extended the system. More and more they paid their administrators fixed salaries, since payments in land (fiefs) often led the recipient to try to make his office hereditary, and since clerical administrators might feel the rival pull of papal authority. Within the *curia regis*, the king's immediate advisers became a "small council." The royal *chancery* or secretariat grew in size, since the king was also Duke of Normandy and had much business on the Continent. As vassals were allowed to give money payments (*scutage*, "shield money") to commute their military service, and as other forms of revenue became available, the first specialized treasury department came into existence. This was the *exchequer,* so called because the long table on which the clerks rendered the semiannual audit of the royal accounts was covered with a cloth divided into checkerboard squares representing pounds, shillings, and pence. Norman administration was grasping and efficient.

Between 1135 and 1154 civil war raged between rival claimants for the throne, William's granddaughter Matilda, wife of Count Geoffrey of Anjou, and her cousin Stephen. Despite the temporary anarchy, Matilda's son, Henry II (reigned 1154–1189) found the firm foundations for powerful monarchy intact when he succeeded to the throne. He destroyed more than 1100 unlicensed castles that had sprung up during the civil war. Once again money rolled in: from scutage plus special fees for the privilege of paying it, from fines, from aids, from payments by the towns, from a new tax paid by knights who did not want to go on a crusade.

Henry II and the Common Law. Despite the universal feeling that law was what had always existed and that the function of government officials was simply to discover and tell what this was, Henry II was able to make a major contribution to legal institutions by developing new combinations of old instruments. In England the baronial courts, lay and ecclesiastical, often competed for jurisdiction with the Anglo-Saxon hundred and shire courts. Henry's subjects therefore welcomed the chance to obtain uniform royal justice, administered under a law common to all England—hence the common law. Only the king could give Englishmen better ways of settling their quarrels among themselves than the old trial by ordeal or trial by battle, which relied on God's intervention to defend the innocent and punish the guilty.

How did Henry II go about this? First of all, by writs. If somebody seized a subject's property, the victim could buy quite cheaply a royal writ, an order from the king directing a royal official to listen to the plaintiff's case. Then, by juries. The official would assemble a group of 12 neighbors who knew the facts in the case; they were sworn (*juré*), and then they decided whether the plaintiff was the true owner of the property, thus rendering a verdict (*veredictum,* a thing spoken truly). This jury was different from a modern trial jury: its members were people presumed to know the facts already. Similar machinery of writ and jury enabled a man to recover an inheritance or a man falsely held as a serf to win his freedom. The writ and the jury were both old; but their use in combination, and the flexibility permitted by a variety of writs, created new procedure. A decision by a royal judge in effect became law without new legislation in the modern sense. No matter who won, the royal exchequer profited, since the loser paid it a fine.

Henry II extended the system by sending itinerant justices to the shires to try all pending cases. The sheriff brought before the justices a group of sworn men from each hundred and township to report all crimes since the last visit of the justices and to say who they thought was guilty in each case. This was the jury of "presentment" (since it presented the names of suspects), the ancestor of our grand jury today. With all the refinements of old instruments, proof of guilt was still the ordeal by cold water: if the accused, with hands and feet tied, floated in a pool of water blessed by a priest, he was guilty; if he sank, he was innocent.

Henry II failed in his effort to extend royal justice at the expense of the Church. He appointed his friend and chancellor, Thomas à Becket, Archbishop of Canterbury, but Becket at once refused to yield the Church's rights. King and Archbishop quarrelled over which should have the authority to deal with churchmen charged with crimes, "criminous clerks." Henry maintained that clerics should be indicted in the royal courts, and, when convicted in the bishop's court, handed back once more to the royal authorities for punishment. Becket resisted this royal encroachment, and appealed to the Pope for support. The quarrel lasted six years, and the issue was compromised. But Henry, in a fit of temper, asked whether nobody would rid him of Becket, and four of the king's knights then murdered Becket in his own cathedral. Henry had to undergo a humiliating penance and concede that the Church had sole right to punish clerics: "benefit of clergy," the principle was called. Also he had to agree that litigants in church courts could appeal directly to Rome without royal intervention or license. While this was a severe defeat, the King still would not allow the Pope to tax English clerics directly. Only two years after the murder, Becket became a saint, and pilgrimages to his miraculous tomb at Canterbury became a standard part of English life.

Henry's own sons, Richard the Lionhearted (reigned 1189–1199) and John (reigned 1199–1216), made his last years miserable by their attacks on his possessions in France. Yet his work had been so well done that, although Richard spent less than six months of his ten-year reign in England, the royal bureaucracy functioned efficiently in his absence. Its main task was collecting huge sums of money to pay for Richard's crusade, his ransom from captivity, and his wars against Philip Augustus. By the time John came to the throne, Richard had squandered the royal resources and angered the barons. The greedy and tyrannical John also had to face Philip Augustus, and he engaged in a furious new quarrel with the papacy.

John and Magna Carta. Innocent III, greatest of the medieval popes, intervened in a disputed election to the Archbishopric of Canterbury, and when John exiled the members of the cathedral chapter and seized the property of the see, the Pope put all England under an interdict (1208) and excommunicated John (1209). He threatened to depose him, planned to replace him with a Capetian, and encouraged Philip Augustus' project of invading England. Fearing that his own vassals would not stay loyal, John gave in (1213). He accepted the Pope's candidate for the see of Canterbury, and agreed to restore church property and to reinstate banished priests. But he was forced to go much further than this: he recognized England and Ireland as fiefs of the papacy, and did homage to the Pope for them while agreeing to pay an annual tribute to Rome. The Pope had won a startling victory, and from now on supported John in his domestic quarrel with the English barons.

This quarrel became acute after the French had won the battle of Bouvines (1214). "Since I have been reconciled to God, and have submitted to the Roman Church," John exclaimed at the news of Bouvines, "nothing has gone well with me." About a third of the English barons were hostile to him, not only because of his ruthless ways of raising money but because of his habit of punishing vassals without trial. After Bouvines they renounced their homage to him and drew up a list of demands, most of which they made him accept on June 15, 1215, at Runnymede. John promised to send out to all the shires of England under the royal seal a legal document in the form of a grant or conveyance, the Great Charter, Magna Carta, with 63 clauses listing the specific concessions that the barons had extorted from him. John agreed to reform his exactions of scutage, aids, and reliefs; he promised uniform weights and measures (especially important to townsmen), and free elections to bishoprics.

Why do English and American historians and politicians often call this medieval statement of the special interests of the feudal class the foundation-stone of our present liberties? Partly because in later centuries some of its provisions received new and expanded meanings. For instance, the provision "No scutage or aid, save the customary feudal ones, shall be levied *except by the common consent of the realm*" in 1215 meant only that John would have to consult his great council (barons and bishops) before levying extraordinary feudal aids. Yet this could later be expanded into the doctrine that all taxation must be by consent, that taxation without representation was tyranny—which would have astonished everybody at Runnymede. Similarly, the provision "No freeman shall be arrested or imprisoned, or dispossessed or outlawed or banished or in any way molested; nor will we set forth against him, nor send against him, unless by the lawful judgment of his peers and by the law of the land" in 1215 meant only that the barons did not want to be tried by anybody not their social equal, and that they wished to curb the aggressions of royal justice. Yet it was capable of later expansion into the doctrine of "due process of law," that everybody was entitled to a trial "by his peers."

John's medieval successors reissued the charter with modifications some 40 times. Under the Tudor monarchy in the sixteenth century it was ignored, and

Englishmen did not appeal to it until the civil war of 1642–1649 (*see* Chapter 8). Then, some of the enemies of Charles I could interpret it in the same inaccurate modern way that we often do. "This is that which we have fought for," said one of them; another, better informed, found in it "many marks of intolerable bondage." So Magna Carta's lasting importance lies partly in its later misinterpretation. But even when we admit this, we must also recognize that the charter rested upon two underlying general principles that justify our gratitude to its baronial sponsors: the king is subject to the law, and if necessary he can be forced to observe it.

Henry III and the Barons. John instantly tried to break the promises he had made; the Pope supported him, declaring the Charter null and void; John's enemies supported Philip Augustus, and a French army landed and briefly occupied London. But John died in 1216, and the barons rallied to his nine-year-old son Henry III (reigned 1216–1272) and expelled the French from England. Henry appointed many Frenchmen to high administrative posts, and the Pope appointed Italians to the highest posts in the English church. The English barons deeply resented the foreigners, and at times refused Henry money or tried to limit his powers. In the 1250's Henry undertook to conquer Sicily as a kingdom for one of his sons, and to subsidize his brother as a candidate for the Holy Roman Empire, both very expensive undertakings. Bad harvests and new papal demands for money finally precipitated a new armed revolt of the barons in 1258.

They came armed to the session of the great council, and a committee of 24 issued a document called the Provisions of Oxford, which required the king to submit all his requests to a council of 15 barons. The committee took over the high posts in the administration and replaced the great council with a baronial body of 12. They seemed to be founding a baronial tyranny perhaps worse than the king's own. The barons expelled the foreigners but quarreled among themselves; the Pope declared the Provisions of Oxford null and void, and Henry III resumed his personal rule. But in 1263 came civil war, as Simon de Montfort took command of the baronial party, defied an arbitration by St. Louis in favor of the king, captured Henry III himself (1264), and set up a regime of his own, based on the Provisions of Oxford. It came to an end when Henry's heir, Edward, defeated and killed Simon de Montfort in 1265 and restored the king to his throne. For the last seven years of Henry's reign (1265–1272) as well as for his own long reign (1272–1307), Edward I was the real ruler of England.

Parliament. Historians turn to these turbulent years of baronial opposition to Henry III for the earliest signs of the greatest contribution of the English Middle Ages to mankind—Parliament. The word itself is French, and means "a talking," any kind of discussion or conference. We have encountered it as applied to the French *curia regis* acting as a court. In England too, in the thirteenth century, the word seems to have meant a session of the king's large council acting as a court, just as the Anglo-Saxon *witenagemot* had sometimes acted. Feudal law imported by the Normans traditionally reinforced the king's right to get aid and counsel from his vassals. The Norman kings made attendance at the great council compulsory: it was the king's privilege, not his duty, to receive counsel, and it was the vassal's duty, not his privilege, to offer it.

Yet contrary to their own intentions, the kings gave the barons the feeling that they had the right to be consulted, as the scutage and aid provision of Magna Carta shows. Since the kings more and more consulted only the small council of intimate and permanent advisers and called the great council only occasionally, the barons on the great council felt excluded and affronted. The rebels against Henry III in 1258 demanded that the great council should meet three times a year, and they called it a "parliament." When Henry III regained power, he continued to summon the great council, the parliament, as well as his small council.

As England grew more prosperous in the thirteenth century, two new classes began to appear at sessions of the great council, or parliament. These were the "knights of the shire," members of the landed gentry, not direct vassals of the king, and "burgesses" or townsmen. When the king asked for money at the great council and his vassals assented, they would try to raise much of what they owed from *their* vassals; so the subvassals also naturally came to feel that they should

Parliament under Edward I. Note the woolsacks on which the officials are sitting in the center.

assent to the levies. In the early thirteenth century, these knights of the shire had already brought information regularly to itinerant justices, and had otherwise spoken on behalf of their shires. When in 1254 the King summoned two knights from each shire to a great council, or parliament, it can hardly have been felt as a major innovation.

Similarly, burgesses had regularly presented accounts or legal documents on behalf of their towns, and in 1265, when Simon de Montfort summoned an assembly of his supporters, he included burgesses as well as knights of the shire. Scholars no longer think of "Simon de Montfort's parliament" as a representative body in any modern sense, or of Simon himself as a champion of democratic representation. But his parliament did establish precedent: the simultaneous presence of shire and town representatives made it the first true ancestor of the modern House of Commons. Not all later parliaments had shire and town representatives, and not all assemblies attended by them were parliaments. The knights and burgesses had no "right" to come to parliament; no doubt they often felt it a nuisance and an expense to come, rather than a privilege. But gradually, under Edward I and his successors, it became customary for them to attend.

Edward I. Edward I not only accomplished the final conquest of Wales (1283), which had been begun by Henry II, but three times strove to add Scotland to the English crown, dying during his last effort against the rebellious Robert Bruce (1307). In 1314, Bruce defeated Edward's son and heir, Edward II (reigned 1307–1327), at Bannockburn, and Scotland and England remained separate monarchies until 1603, when a Scottish King (James VI) became King of England (James I) as well.

At home Edward I emerged as a great systematizing legislator, causing the laws to evolve in a way that would not have been possible for his custom-shackled predecessors. The experts in the small council now formulated a series of statutes, elaborating and expanding the machinery of government. The Second Statute of Westminster (1285) assured a great landowner that no tenant to whom he had granted an estate could dispose of it except through inheritance. This is what we would call entail. The Statute of Mortmain (French, "dead hand," 1275) prevented the transfer of land to the Church without the consent of the suzerain. Once the Church had a piece of land, it placed a "dead hand" on it and could hold onto it forever; so lay landowners were reluctant to see portions of their holdings transferred to clerics. These statutes reflect an England in which the old feudal relationship was less and less a matter of a vassal giving military aid and more and more a matter of landlord–tenant relationships. Both statutes redounded to the interests of landlords.

Edward also went a long way to assert that all rights held by others derived from the crown. By the writ *quo warranto* (by what authority) he commanded all the barons to explain where they had got their rights to any franchise or privilege—such as a hundred court—that they might possess. Some franchises he revoked, but he was mainly concerned to show that only the king could give them or take them away. As royal justice increased its business, specialized courts made their appearance, all of them the offspring of the *curia regis*. The Court of Common Pleas took cases between subjects, the Court of King's Bench took crown and criminal cases, and the Court of Exchequer took disputes concerning royal finance.

Edward asserted the crown's permanent right to share in export and customs dues, a valuable source of income in this period of flourishing trade. He expelled the Jews from England in 1290; they were not allowed to return until the mid-seventeenth century. He required all freemen to equip themselves appropriately for military service; if you had a certain minimum amount of property you *had* to become a knight (distraint of knighthood), serve on horseback, and so become subject to feudal dues. Baronial opposition naturally arose again, and in 1297 Edward had to confirm Magna Carta and promise not to tax without consent.

Edward's parliament of 1295 included not only the barons, higher clergy, knights of the shire, and burgesses, but representatives of the lower clergy. It is called the "Model Parliament," although the lower clergy did not always attend later parliaments. In the royal summons to its members we find a famous clause, "What touches all should be approved by all," an echo of a provision of Roman law, apparently accepting the principle that consent to taxation was necessary. In 1297 Edward declared that the "good will and assent of the archbishops, bishops, and other prelates, earls, barons, knights, burgesses, and other freemen of our realm" were *essential* to a royal levy. Often in later years this principle would be reasserted, and parliament sometimes made a king confirm it before it would grant him funds.

In England by the early fourteenth century, the monarchs had met with a corporate baronial opposition which had forced consultation upon them, and had begun to create brand-new institutions out of old ones. The regular presence of knights and burgesses at parliaments had gradually made them more and more nearly indispensable to the king's business. The contrast with the French monarchy is a striking one.

GERMANY AND THE EMPIRE (911–1273)

The Saxon Monarchy. As the Carolingian Empire gradually began to disintegrate, the local administrators of five east Frankish areas—Franconia, Saxony, Thuringia, Swabia, and Bavaria—took the title of duke (army commander) and organized their regions as military units. They chose one of their own number, Conrad, Duke of Franconia, as king in 911, on the extinction of the Carolingian line. Each duke made himself a hereditary ruler, took control of the Church in his own duchy, and tried to assert his own domination over the royal administrators —the counts—still active on his lands. After a severe struggle, King Henry I (reigned 919–936) of the house of Saxony and his descendants made good the power of the monarchy, re-established royal control over the counts, and regained the right to appoint bishops.

To govern Germany, the Saxon kings relied largely on the bishops. Churchmen were better educated than laymen, and could not pass on their offices to their sons as the counts tried to do. Even the papacy welcomed the stability of such a system, and recognized the right of the German king to appoint his own bishops. The kings gave special protection to church lands, exempting them from the authority of the counts. Within their own domains, the bishops administered justice and were in fact invested with the powers of counts. Tenants of church lands made up three-quarters of the royal army, while the Church furnished much of the royal revenue. Churchmen shared largely in the *Drang nach Osten,* the German push to the east: the defeat of the Magyars (955) and the advance into Slavic lands along and across the Elbe and Saale rivers. German bishoprics, with Magdeburg as the chief, were established in the new regions, and the Slavs there were christianized.

When King Otto I (reigned 936–973) became Emperor in 962 (*see* Chapter 3), he created for Germany a grave new series of problems. Although the old concept of the Roman Empire as the one true secular power continued uninterruptedly at Constantinople, in the West "emperor" had come to mean a ruler who controlled two or more kingdoms but who did not necessarily claim supremacy over the whole inhabited world. For a German king to call himself emperor meant that he was asserting authority over Italy—weak and divided—and usually Burgundy as well as Germany. If Otto I had not assumed the imperial title, he faced the danger that one of the other German dukes might do so and thus nullify the royal struggle to control them all. Self-defense and consciousness of being the heir to the Carolingians probably motivated Otto I as much as the urge for conquest. In any case, the German monarchs henceforth regularly claimed the imperial title and intervened in Italy.

Otto III (reigned 983–1002), brilliant grandson of Otto I, had a Byzantine mother from whom he probably inherited some of the older conception of empire. His seal read *Renewal of the Roman Empire*. In Rome he tried to restore the Roman imperial palace, titles, and glory, in the hope of winning the support of the old aristocracy. He also installed German officials on Italian church lands, and appointed German bishops to Italian sees in an effort to create in Italy the kind of system he had at home. He did not neglect the affairs of Germany, and his German contemporaries seem to have approved of his Italian involvement. By the early eleventh century it was taken for granted that the German king had the right to be king of Italy and emperor. German intervention ended Italian anarchy and raised the level of the papacy from its tenth-century degeneration. But as the emperors sponsored reforming movements within the Church, they set in motion forces that would make the papacy a world power and bring about their own eventual ruin.

Salian Government. When the Saxon dynasty died out in 1024, the widow of the last Saxon nominated Conrad II (reigned 1024–1039), of the Salian dynasty from Franconia, as his successor. Conrad experimented with ruling through the counts and allowing their offices to become hereditary, in an effort to enlist their support against the pretensions of the great dukes. But the counts felt rather more oppressed by the centralizing tendencies of the crown than by the dukes, and the experiment was a failure. Conrad's successors did maintain another of his innovations: the training of members of the lower classes to serve as administrators, the so-called *ministeriales*. The Church had used such men to run its great estates. Now the kings used them to run the lands of the crown. Though they were rewarded with land, it was often not hereditary and so not a true fief, and they therefore remained dependent directly on the crown, becoming a social group peculiar to Germany. Soon the nobles were complaining that the king listened only to low-born fellows.

Henry III (reigned 1039–1056) chose Goslar in the Harz Mountains as the permanent royal residence. Henry IV (reigned 1056–1106) ordered a survey of crown lands (not *all* of the land of Germany, and so less comprehensive than the Domesday Book) to discover how much money he could count on. By the 1070's the German monarchy was comparable to that of Norman England and more effectively administered than the French monarchy would be for more than a century. Whereas in France the Carolingian counts had become feudal lords in their own counties, the German dukes had no such feudal position. In Germany no free man had to become a vassal of the duke; many small and large estates continued to be owned outright by free men. Allods, as these nonfeudal lands were termed, were more common in Germany than elsewhere in western Europe; and, though the social distinction between rich and poor was great, both were more often free of feudal ties than anywhere else. The German free landowners, without a counterpart in France or England, resisted the policies of the kings.

They were further strengthened by their role as guardians or "advocates" of new monastic foundations, of which perhaps 600 were founded during the eleventh century. The advocate had jurisdiction over the monastic tenants, and also obtained substantial revenues in exchange for protecting the foundations. To keep these new monasteries, sources of wealth and power, out of royal hands, their founders often made them the legal property of the Pope. A nobles' revolt in Saxony, put down by Henry IV in 1075, signalized the nobles' hatred of the royal church, the *ministeriales*, and royal centralizing practices in general.

The Investiture Controversy. The real ruin of the German monarchy came with the Investiture Controversy. This began in 1049, when Henry III installed Pope Leo IX, a close relative, on the papal throne. Leo IX not only was thoroughly committed to an intensive program of monastic reform sponsored by an order of monks active at Cluny in Burgundy, but also, together with his younger assistant, Hildebrand, favored the purging of secular influences from the entire church hierarchy. Ironically, the Emperor was sponsoring reformers whose greatest target would be his own imperial system of government in Germany. When Hildebrand himself became Pope in 1073 as Gregory VII, he determined to secure the canonical (legal) election of all bishops and abbots. This would have meant the end of the German system of royal selection and appointment, and of the subsequent ceremony in which the emperor, a layman, conferred on the prelate his insignia of office (for bishops, a ring and a staff), thus *investing* him. The Pope opposed lay investiture. Yet the Emperor's government in Germany depended on lay investiture, on the sale of church offices, and on many other corrupt practices.

Pope Gregory VII, a statesman of great vigor, shrewdness, and passion, believed that, as wielder of supreme spiritual authority, the Pope had jurisdiction over temporal things as well. Any temporal prince who defied him he condemned as a follower of Antichrist. To many pious men this seemed a new and radical claim. The Emperor's pamphleteers—conservatives—attacked it. The papal pamphleteers—revolutionary innovators—attacked them in turn. In 1059, the papacy had established the College of Cardinals and given it the role of electing new popes. This deprived the emperors of their former role and gave Gregory a real advantage over his opponent. Gregory could also count on the support of the German nobles, always hostile to their ruler, and on an alliance with the new Norman rulers of southern Italy.

In 1075, Gregory forbade lay investiture. Emperor Henry IV and his bishops responded by declaring Gregory's election as Pope null and void. Gregory then excommunicated Henry and declared him deposed, and deprived of office all bishops who supported him. To prevent Gregory from accepting the German nobles' invitation to visit Germany, Henry secretly went to Italy. At the castle of Canossa, Gregory kept him waiting outside for three days, barefoot and in sackcloth, before he let him enter to do penance and receive absolution (1077). Though the drama and symbolism of this famous episode seem to show the power of the Pope, the fact is that Henry had forced Gregory's hand. The Pope had had to absolve him, and once absolved Henry could no longer be deposed.

Though Gregory later deposed Henry again, and supported his rival in a German civil war (1077–1080), Henry triumphed, marched to Rome, which he took in 1084, and installed an anti-Pope who crowned him Emperor. Gregory's Norman allies arrived too late, and the Pope died in defeat in 1085. But Gregory's successor renewed the struggle, supporting civil war in Germany. Henry V (reigned 1106–1125) made peace with his own nobles, conceding them many of the gains they had won in the revolt against his father in the hope that he could then proceed to defeat the Church. But he changed the character of the German monarchy, for, once freed from the restraints imposed by the crown, the nobles indulged in private warfare and the ravaged crown lands could not be reassembled or put into order.

It was the great German nobles who dictated to the Emperor the settlement of the Investiture Controversy reached with the Pope at the Concordat of Worms (1122). Henry V renounced the practice of investing bishops with the clerical symbols of ring and staff, but, with the Pope's permission, continued to bestow the *regalia* (worldly goods pertaining to the bishop's office). The Emperor received an oath of fealty from each new bishop before he was consecrated. Moreover, in Germany the Emperor or his representatives were to be present at episcopal elections, and so continued to exert a strong influence. In Italy and Burgundy, the Emperor had less power: consecration would take place *before* the *regalia* were conferred, and the Emperor could not attend episcopal elections. This compromise ended the overt struggle over investitures.

During the civil war, the German nobles had pretended that there was no king in Germany because the Pope had deposed him. They extended their powers and ran their own affairs without reference to the monarchy. Feudal castles multiplied, free peasants fell into serfdom, lesser nobles had to seek the protection of greater. The feudalizing processes that had gone on in ninth- and tenth-century France were now operating in eleventh- and early twelfth-century Germany. Employing their own *ministeriales*, the great German nobles, or princes, increased the number of their vassals and pyramided their monastic "advocacies." The aftermath of the Investiture Controversy was the beginning of the German territorial principalities and what is known as German *particularism*.

In Italy, the struggle led to the rise in importance of the communes, sworn associations of lesser nobles banded together to resist the local bishops in the towns of the north, where they began to usurp the powers of city government. In Lombardy the Pope supported them, in Tuscany the Emperor. Everywhere they threatened imperial authority.

The Hohenstaufens. In 1138, by choosing a Swabian, Conrad III of Hohenstaufen, as Emperor, the German nobles precipitated a long-lasting feud between Conrad's family, called Waibling (*Ghibelline* in Italy) because of their ancestral castle, and that of a rival claimant, Henry the Proud, Duke of Saxony and Bavaria, of the family of Welf (*Guelf* in Italy). Feudal warfare in Germany resumed. Conrad III's nephew, Frederick I of Hohenstaufen (1152–1190), known as Barbarossa ("redbeard"), strove to rebuild the monarchy. Because the Investiture Controversy had ended the possibility of governing Germany

Medieval Germany and Italy
at death of Frederick II, 1250

Legend:
- Boundary of the Holy Roman Empire
- Kingdom of the Two Sicilies
- Papal States
- Claimed by Papacy
- Venetian possessions
- ■ Battle sites

Labels on map:

North Sea · Mediterranean Sea · Adriatic Sea

PRUSSIA · POMERANIA · POLAND · SILESIA · MORAVIA · BOHEMIA · AUSTRIA · HUNGARY · SERBIA · FRANCE

KINGDOM OF GERMANY
FRIESLAND · SAXONY · BRANDENBURG · THURINGIA · LOWER LORRAINE · UPPER LORRAINE · PALATINATE · FRANCONIA · SWABIA · BAVARIA · STYRIA · CARINTHIA · CARNIOLA · TYROL

KINGDOM OF BURGUNDY (KINGDOM OF ARLES)

KINGDOM OF ITALY
LOMBARDY · TUSCANY · ROMAGNA

PAPAL STATES

KINGDOM OF THE TWO SICILIES (Hohenstaufen, 1194)
APULIA · CALABRIA · SICILY

CORSICA (to Pisa)
SARDINIA (to Pisa and Genoa)

Cities: Danzig, Lübeck, Hamburg, Bremen, Cologne, Aachen, Trier, Mainz, Worms, Frankfurt, Wurzburg, Bamberg, Magdeburg, Goslar, Prague, Ratisbon, Strasbourg, Augsburg, Vienna, Constance, Legnano, Brescia, Milan, Pavia, Roncaglia, Alessandria, Genoa, Canossa, Trieste, Venice, Ferrara, Bologna, Ravenna, Zara, Ragusa, Ancona, Pisa, Florence, Siena, Assisi, Rome, Anagni, Tagliacozzo, Naples, Amalfi, Salerno, Melfi, Bari, Taranto, Palermo, Syracuse, Arles, Avignon

Rivers/Mountains: Meuse R., Weser, Elbe R., Vistula R., Oder R., Saale R., Rhine R., Main R., Danube R., Drava R., Adige R., Po R., Rhône R., Saône R., Harz Mts., ALPS

through the bishops, and Frederick's own royal lands in Germany were not extensive enough to give him the base he needed, he focussed his attention on Italy and Burgundy, marrying the heiress to the latter in 1156, and making Switzerland, with its control over the Alpine passes into Italy, his strategic center.

He tried to turn Swabia into a kind of German Ile de France, at first conciliating his Welf rival, Henry the Lion, who became the leader of a great wave of eastward German expansion against the Slavs and ruled almost independently across the Elbe. Frederick eventually curbed Henry by the same feudal means that Philip Augustus would use against John of England. He received complaints from Henry's vassals, summoned Henry into the royal court to answer the claims, and when Henry did not appear deprived him of his holdings (1180). Frederick was able to break up the great Welf territorial possessions. But he could not add them to the royal domain, as Philip Augustus would hold onto Normandy, because he did not control his vassals so effectively. The Welf lands were parcelled out among the German nobles. In 1180 also, all Frederick's immediate vassals were recognized as Princes of the Empire. The new feudal order had obtained recognition.

Frederick made six trips to Italy. He helped the Pope put down Arnold of Brescia, a rebel against papal rule in Rome (1143) who favored the return of the Church to apostolic poverty and simplicity. In 1155, the Pope crowned Frederick Emperor after a famous argument over whether Frederick would hold the Pope's bridle and stirrup as well as kiss his foot (Frederick lost). Soon afterward (1158) Frederick tried at the Diet of Roncaglia to define the imperial rights (*regalia*) in Italian towns: what role did he have in appointing dukes and counts, in coining money, in collecting taxes? Many of Frederick's claims, though several centuries old, had not been regularly exercised by recent emperors, and Frederick was more interested in asserting his rights in principle than in exercising them in practice. Opposed by the Pope and the Lombard League of communes under Milan, Frederick was forced to fight a long war. Defeated at Legnano in 1176, he finally made the Peace of Constance with the towns in 1183. The towns retained the *regalia* within their own walls, but outside the walls they retained only such rights as they had already bought or might in the future buy from the Emperor: They recognized Frederick as suzerain, and their municipal officials were to take an oath of loyalty to him.

In 1190, Frederick was drowned while on a crusade. He had been so powerful for so long that the legend soon arose that he was not dead but asleep in a cavern with his great red beard flowing over the table on which his arm rested: some day "the old Emperor" would awake and return to bring glory and union to Germany.

Four years before his death, Frederick had married his son Henry VI to the heiress of the flourishing Norman kingdom in Sicily and southern Italy. Here the

The Emperor Frederick Barbarossa portrayed as a crusader, from a Bavarian manuscript of 1188.

descendants of a small band of eleventh-century Norman adventurers had built a rich and powerful realm of mixed Catholic, Orthodox Greek, and Moslem population, tolerating all faiths, and issuing its public documents in Arabic, Greek, and Latin, but governed in the efficient Norman manner. Its kings appointed the members of the *curia regis,* who were not hereditary, and royal officials called justiciars gave justice to the provinces.

By taking over this Norman state together with his German and north Italian lands, Henry VI (reigned 1190–1197), surrounded the papal territories in central Italy. He frustrated an effort by the papacy, the Welfs, and the English to take Sicily away from him, holding Richard the Lionhearted for ransom and securing Sicily by 1194. He was building a fleet to invade the eastern Mediterranean and attack Byzantium when he died suddenly in 1197. To support his grandiose projects and to get the backing of the German princes for the succession of his son, Frederick II, he had to offer the German nobles in their fiefs the same sort of hereditary right he was asking them to recognize. In England or France the problem would not have arisen, because the royal succession was established.

The minority of Frederick II was marked by civil war (1197–1215), in which the great Pope Innocent III (reigned 1198–1216) determined to destroy the German–Sicilian link and to revive the claim of Gregory VII that papal confirmation was needed to legitimize any emperor. Frederick II's uncle, Philip of Swabia, maintained by contrast that an emperor elected by the princes was legitimate by virtue of his election alone. Richard the Lionhearted and Innocent backed a Welf, Otto, against Philip. Philip Augustus of France backed Philip of Swabia, who was assassinated in 1208. Once on the imperial throne, however, Otto undertook to conquer Sicily, a conquest which the Pope was most anxious to prevent. Innocent therefore turned to the young Frederick II, whose position was soon consolidated by the victory of his French ally, Philip Augustus, over the Welf and English forces at Bouvines (1214).

Frederick II. Intelligent and cultivated, speaking Arabic and Greek as well as half a dozen other languages, deeply interested in scientific experiment, the extraordinary Frederick II collected wild animals and women, wrote poetry in the Italian vernacular and a textbook on how to hunt with falcons. He was a brilliant and cynical statesman, perhaps the most interesting monarch of medieval history. He preferred his civilized southern kingdom of Sicily, and inherited his father's dream of creating a great Mediterranean empire. To these ambitions he sacrificed the hard-won rights of the crown in Germany. To obtain the consent of the German bishops and abbots to the coronation of his son, Henry, as King of Germany in 1220, Frederick II gave away the royal rights of levying customs dues, coining money, and exercising justice. He promised also to exclude from imperial towns runaway serfs from church lands, and to build no new towns on such lands. In 1231, the secular princes exacted from Frederick a similar privilege in their favor. Germany was then condemned to six centuries of particularism.

In Sicily, however, Frederick imposed his own tightly centralized monarchy on his subjects, carrying further the policies of his Norman predecessors and buttressing his actions by reference to Roman law, with its lofty conception of the imperial position. He founded a university at Naples to train future officials in Roman law. Like William the Conqueror in England, he assumed title to all property. He wiped out feudal custom, forbidding trial by battle as absurd. He organized his army and navy on a paid basis rather than a feudal one, anticipated modern methods of finance, collected tariffs on imports and exports, and—like the emperors at Byzantium—instituted imperial monopolies in certain industries, such as silk.

The Papal Triumph. Against this most unmedieval monarch the papacy, threatened by his holdings, waged steady and eventually successful war beginning in the 1220's. Pope and emperor quarreled over Frederick's slowness in going on a crusade and over his plans to extend imperial administration to all Italy, including Rome. Troops hired by the Pope attacked Frederick's south Italian lands. Both sides circulated violent propaganda pamphlets, the Pope calling Frederick a heretic, Frederick calling the Pope a hypocrite and urging all kings of Europe to resist the Church. On one occasion (1241) Frederick's fleet captured a delegation of more than a hundred prelates on their way to a council called by the Pope to depose him. Eventually he was deposed, but the struggle went on after Frederick's death in 1250. In 1266 the papacy imported into Italy St. Louis' brother, the ruthless and able Charles of Anjou, who defeated and killed Frederick's illegitimate son, Manfred, and established himself as ruler of the south Italian lands. Then, in 1268 Charles defeated the last of Frederick's descendants, his legitimate grandson, Conradino, executing him soon afterwards. Angevin rule over Naples lasted down to 1435, even though the Aragonese took Sicily in 1282.

With the extinction of the Hohenstaufens the papacy had destroyed the Holy Roman Empire begun by Frederick I and given an Italian rather than a German base by Henry VI and Frederick II. But within 40 years Philip the Fair, grandnephew of the papal instrument of vengeance, Charles of Anjou, would puncture the inflated temporal claims of the papacy and take it off to Avignon. In Germany, the imperial throne remained vacant from the death of Conrad IV, the son of Frederick II, in 1254, to 1272. The German princes enjoyed the absence of an emperor, and utilized the interregnum to consolidate their powers and extend their usurpation of former crown rights. The old links with Italy were greatly weakened, and the earlier form of the imperial idea disappeared. An allodial nobility, the Investiture Controversy, and the imperial preoccupation with Italy had ensured that princely particularism would emerge as the ruling force in Germany.

III. The Church and Civilization

Noble and peasant and townsman, in England or on the Continent, all belonged without question to the Christian Church. Only the Jews were apart; they suffered occasional persecutions and such disabilities as having to live in a separate quarter or ghetto. When heresy arose, the temporal powers joined with the Church in attacking it. For the medieval man, religious and political governance were the "two swords" of God, equally indispensable for maintaining human society. Which was the greater? Gregory VII and Innocent III and Boniface VIII said that the spiritual power outshone the temporal as the sun the moon, but often had trouble making good so extreme a claim. Henry II and John in England, the Emperors Henry IV and Frederick II, St. Louis and Philip the Fair all struggled against papal pretensions.

THE REFORMERS

Cluniacs and Cistercians. In the tenth century, as we have seen, the papacy had become a prize for local Roman politicians, while concubinage, simony (the sale of church offices), and other forms of corruption were growing among the clergy. From this decline the Church was rescued by a reforming movement that began at the monastery of Cluny in France (founded 910). At Cluny the monks reverted to the strict Benedictine rule; from Cluny reformers went out to reform the monasteries and to found more than 300 "daughter" houses inspired by the same ideals and all under the attentive rule of the "mother" abbey. Eventually men trained in the Cluniac spirit reached the papal throne itself as nominees of the Emperor Henry III. They established the principle of clerical celibacy, which has preserved Catholic priests from the natural tendency of fathers to provide property for their offspring. The reformers checked, though of course they did not completely root out, simony.

We have seen Gregory VII (Hildebrand) expand the ideas of reform into a generalized effort to root out secular influences from the entire church, which would then move forward under militant papal leadership. The Lateran Synod of 1059 issued the decree establishing the College of Cardinals, a group of certain key clerics (cardinal from *cardo*, a hinge), who were to elect each new pope. The system remains in force today. When it was instituted it did away with imperial interference with papal elections: henceforth the emperor was notified and could approve of the cardinals' choice, but he could no longer impose his own candidate. The Investiture Controversy over German appointment of bishops was a natural sequel.

The Cluniac movement was only the first of several waves of reforming zeal that swept the medieval church. By the early twelfth century the first wave of zeal had spent itself. The Cluniac order had become rich and powerful, and its original concern for asceticism and morality had grown feeble. A similar pattern was repeated by the successors of the Cluniacs as the leaders of reform, the Cistercians. Founded in the late eleventh century, the mother-house at Citeaux (Cistercium) in Burgundy lay in a desolate spot transformed into a garden by the labor of the monks. The great Cistercian leader was St. Bernard (1098–1153), who in 1115 led a small band to Clairvaux, an equally unpromising site, and from there exercised an extraordinary influence over his age. The King of France took his advice; a whole crusade set out at his bidding. In contrast to the Cluniacs, the Cistercians gave daughter-houses their self-rule, but within a century they too had become wealthy and lax.

Franciscans and Dominicans. By then another wave of reform had already begun, with a new emphasis appropriate to a changing society. Unlike the Cluniacs and Cistercians, the friars of the new orders founded by St. Francis (1182–1226) and St. Dominic (1170–1221) did not intend to live apart from the world and reform monasticism from within. Instead, they went to the increasing populations of the new towns and cities, often neglected by the Church, and so often hostile to its rich and worldly clergy. Such anticlerical sentiment sometimes led to movements of protest, some of them heretical, like that of the Waldensians, who in the 1180's taught that laymen could administer the sacraments, and exalted the authority of the Bible alone.

Gentle, charming, and ascetic, St. Francis, son of a merchant family, had undergone religious conversion in his youth. He loved everything that God had created—men, birds, flowers. Francis prescribed for his followers total poverty: they were to have no monastic house but were to go and preach, and were to rely on charity for their food and shelter. Francis called his order "Friars Minor" (little brothers), and their dependence on alms led to the term "mendicant" friars. In 1210, Innocent III approved Francis' foundation, but even before Francis died (1226) the papacy against his wishes permitted a revised rule, and land and buildings and worldly concerns preoccupied some of the friars to the dismay of the rest. Though Francis had repudiated book-learning and books, later Franciscans often studied in the universities and became distinguished scholars.

St. Dominic, a Spaniard, founded his own mendicant order in 1216. From the beginning study was a cardinal duty of his followers, who were to educate the laity of the world by preaching to them. The Dominicans were given the name Order of Preachers. Their monastic houses or priories (for they, too, soon began to acquire property) were governed by monks elected by the members, and the officials of each priory in turn elected the superior officials of the order.

The reforming movements of the eleventh, twelfth, and thirteenth centuries within the Church helped to keep piety constantly renewed, dispelled the threat of mass disaffection, and played a major role in the intellectual as well as the social life of the age. Dominicans and Franciscans served as the staff of the permanent papal tribunal of the Inquisition formed in 1233 to find, interrogate, judge, and punish suspected heretics and to deliver those who persisted in their heresy to the secular authorities to be burned at the stake.

THE CHURCH AND EDUCATION

It was the Church that alone directed and conducted education in medieval Europe. Unless destined for the priesthood, young men of the upper classes had little formal schooling, though the family chaplain often taught them to read and write. Their training was in war and hunting, and sometimes in the problems of managing their property. But even in the Dark Ages the monastic schools educated future monks and priests, and the Cluniac reform, with its increased demand for piety, stimulated study and the copying of manuscripts. Medieval men reckoned that there were seven "liberal arts," divided into the *trivium* (grammar, rhetoric, dialectic) and the *quadrivium* (arithmetic, geometry, astronomy, and music), the first three including much of what we might call humanities today, the last four corresponding to the sciences. Only a few monastic schools in the eleventh century were prepared to offer instruction in all seven, and in general monks thought of their work as the preservation rather than as the advancement of knowledge.

The cathedral schools, on the other hand, whose teachers were often less timid about studying pagan writings from the great classical past, fostered a more inquiring spirit. In France during the eleventh century at the cathedral schools of Paris, Chartres, Rheims, and other towns, distinguished teachers now were often succeeded by men whom they had trained themselves, and distinguished pupils went on to join or found other schools. Scholarship no longer depended on the occasional advent of a single first-class mind. In Italy, where the connection with cathedrals was not so close, the medical school at Salerno had a tradition stretching back into the Dark Ages; at Bologna law became the specialty, beginning as a branch of rhetoric and so within the trivium. Students were attracted to Bologna from other regions of Italy and even from northern Europe, and in the early twelfth century, as education became fashionable for young men ambitious for advancement in the Church or in the royal service, the numbers of students grew rapidly.

Scenes from student life in the Middle Ages, from "Statutenbuch des Collegium Sapentiae."

Universities. The student body at Bologna organized itself into two associations: students from the near side of the Alps and students from the far side, and the two incorporated as the whole body, the *universitas,* or university. As a corporate body, they could protect themselves against being overcharged for food and lodging by threatening to leave town; they had no property, and could readily have moved. If the students did not like a professor, they simply stayed away from his lectures, and he starved or moved on, for he was dependent on tuition fees for his living. Soon the *universitas,* that is to say the students, fixed the price of room and board in town, and fined professors for absence or for lecturing too long. The professors organized too, and admitted to their number only those who had passed an examination, and so won a *license* to teach, remote ancestor of all our academic degrees.

In Paris and elsewhere in the north, the cathedral schools were the immediate forerunners of the universities, and it was the teachers, not the students, who organized first, as a gild of those who taught the seven liberal arts and who got their licenses from the cathedral authorities. By the thirteenth century pious citizens had founded in Paris the first residence halls for poor students, who might eat and sleep free in these "colleges." The practice crossed the Channel to Oxford and Cambridge. As in later times, the authorities of these medieval universities stoutly defended themselves against encroachment by the secular power; there was often friction between "town" and "gown," as irrepressible high spirits among the students led to rioting and disorder.

The Question of Universals. Much of the learning taught and studied in the Middle Ages seems strange to us today, and it requires imagination to understand how exciting the exercise was to men discovering it for the first time. At the turn of the eleventh century, Gerbert of Aurillac, who spent the last four years of his life as Pope Sylvester II (999–1003), stood out as the most learned man of his day; the smattering of mathematics and science that he had been able to pick up caused his contemporaries to suspect him of witchcraft. His own main interest lay in logic, and he turned back to the work of Boethius (*see* Chapter 3). For the first time, across the gulf of the Dark Ages, a probing mind moved into the portions of Aristotle that Boethius had translated, and discovered in logic a means to approach the writings of the ancients and of the church fathers in a systematic way. By the end of the century churchmen could debate whether it was proper to use human reason in considering a particular theological question (for example, was Christ present in the sacramental wafer and wine?), and in all efforts to explain away inconsistencies in the Bible and the Fathers in general. Even those who attacked the use of reason used it themselves in making new definitions that enabled them to argue that bread and wine could indeed, in a certain way, become flesh and blood.

Once the new method became available, the men of the late eleventh and early twelfth centuries employed it largely in a celebrated controversy over the philosophical problem of universals. A universal is a whole category of things; when we say "dog" or "table" or "man," we may mean not any specific individual dog or table or man, but the idea of all dogs, tables, or men: dogdom, tabledom, mankind. The question that exercised the medieval thinkers was whether universal categories have an existence: *is* there such a thing as dogdom, tabledom, or mankind?

If you said no, you were a nominalist; that is, you thought dogdom, tabledom, mankind were merely *nomina, names* that men give to a general category from their experience of individual members of it. We experience dogs, tables, men, and so we infer the existence of dogdom, tabledom, mankind because the individual members of the category have certain points of resemblance; but the category, the universal, has no existence in itself. If you said yes, you were a realist; that is, you thought that the general categories did exist. Many realists took this view a large step further, and said that the individual dog, table, or man was far less real than the generalizing category or universal or even that the individual was a mere reflection of one aspect of the category, and existed by virtue of belonging to the category; a man exists only because he partakes of the nature of mankind, a dog because he partakes of the nature of dogdom.

If one transfers the problem to politics, and thinks of the state and the individual, one can see at once how great its practical importance may be. A nominalist would say that the state is just a name, and exists only by virtue of the fact that the individuals who make it up are real; he would argue that the state must then serve its subjects, since after all it is only the sum of their individualities. A realist would say that the state is the only real thing, that the individual subjects exist only so far as they partake of its general character, and that the state by virtue of its existence properly dominates the individual. In religion, an extreme nominalist, arguing that what one can perceive through one's senses is alone real, might even have trouble believing in the existence of God. An extreme realist would tend to ignore or even to deny the existence of the physical world and its problems. Moderate realists have to start with faith, to believe so that they may know, as St. Anselm put it.

Peter Abelard (1079–1142), a popular lecturer in the University of Paris, tried to compromise the question. He argued that universals were not merely names, as the nominalists held, nor did they have a real existence, as the realists held. They were, he said, concepts in men's minds, and as such had a real existence of a special kind in the mind, which had created them out of its experience of particulars: mankind from men, dogdom from dogs, and so on. Abelard insisted on the importance of understanding for true faith; he put reason first, and thus understood in order that he might believe, instead of the other way around. His most famous work, *Sic et Non* (Yes and No), lists over 150 theological statements and cites authorities both defending and attacking the truth of each. When Scripture and the Fathers were inconsistent, he seems to argue, how could a man make up his mind what to believe unless he used his head? A rationalist and lover of argument, Abelard was none the less a deeply pious believer. The mystical St. Bernard, however, suspicious of reason, believed him heretical, and had his views condemned and denounced repeatedly.

THOMAS AQUINAS

By the time of Abelard's death in the mid-twelfth century, the Greek scientific writings of antiquity—lost all these centuries to the West—were on their way to recovery, often through translations from Arabic into Latin. In civil law, the great Code of the Emperor Justinian became the text commonly used in the law schools. In canon law, the scholar Gratian published at Bologna about 1140 what became the standard collection of decrees, and reconciled by commentary apparently contradictory judgments.

In the second half of the century came the recovery of Aristotle's lost treatises on logic, which dealt with such subjects as how to build a syllogism, how to prove a point, or how to refute false conclusions. Using these instruments, medieval thinkers were for the first time in a position to systematize and summarize their entire philosophical position. Yet the recovery of Aristotle posed certain new problems. For example, the Moslem Averroës, whose comments accompanied the text of Aristotle's *Metaphysics,* stressed Aristotle's own view that the physical world was eternal; since the soul of man—a nonphysical thing—was essentially common to all humanity, no individual human soul could be saved by itself. Obviously this ran counter to fundamental Christian teaching. Some scholars tried to say that both views could be true, Aristotle's in philosophy and the Christian in theology; but this led directly into heresy. Others tried to forbid the study and reading of Aristotle, but without success. It was the Dominican Albertus Magnus (1193–1280), a German, and his pupil Thomas Aquinas (1225–1274), an Italian, who—in massive multivolume works produced over a lifetime—succeeded in reconciling the apparent differences between Aristotle's teachings and those of the Christian tradition. They were the greatest of the Schoolmen, exponents of the philosophy historians call Scholasticism.

Aquinas' best-known writings were the *Summa Theologica* and the *Summa contra Gentiles*. He discussed God, man, and the universe, arranging his material in systematic, topical order in the form of an inquiry into and discussion of each open question. First he cited the evidence on each side, then he gave his own answer, and finally he demonstrated the falsity of the other position. Though Aquinas always cited authority, he also never failed to provide his own logical analysis. For him reason was a most valuable instrument, but only when it recognized its own limitations. When reason unaided could not comprehend an apparent contradiction with faith, it must yield to faith, since reason by itself could not understand the entire universe. Certain fundamentals must be accepted as unprovable axioms of faith, although, once they had been accepted, reason could show that they are probable.

If a man puts a series of arguments together and comes out with a conclusion contrary to what orthodox Christians believe, he is simply guilty of faulty logic, and the use of correct logic can readily show where he erred. Indeed, Aquinas delighted in the game of inventing arguments against accepted beliefs, matching them with a set of even more ingenious arguments, and then reconciling the two with an intellectual skill suggesting the trained athlete's ability in timing and coordination.

Here is a simple example of the mind and method of Aquinas. He is discussing the specific conditions of "man's first state," and comes to the question: What were babies like in the state of innocence before the Fall of Man? Were they born with such perfect strength of body that they had full use of their limbs at birth, or were they like human babies nowadays, helpless little wrigglers? In the Garden of Eden, one might think that any form of helplessness would detract from perfection and that God might well have made the human infant strong and perfect, or might even have had men and women born adult. Aquinas did not think so; even his Eden was as "natural" as he could make it:

> By faith alone do we hold truths which are above nature, and what we believe rests on authority. Wherefore, in making any assertion, we must be guided by the nature of things, except in those things which are above nature, and are made known to us by Divine authority. Now it is clear that it is as natural as it is befitting to the principles of human nature that children should not have sufficient strength for the use of their limbs immediately after birth. Because in proportion to other animals man has naturally a larger brain. Wherefore it is natural, on account of the considerable humidity of the brain in children, that the sinews which are instruments of movement, should not be apt for moving the limbs. On the other hand, no Catholic doubts it possible for a child to have, by Divine power, the use of its limbs immediately after birth.

Now we have it on the authority of Scripture that *God made man* *right* (Eccles. 7:30), which rightness, as Augustine says, consists in the perfect subjection of the body to the soul. As, therefore, in the primitive state it was impossible to find in the human limbs anything repugnant to man's well-ordered will, so was it impossible for those limbs to fail in executing the will's commands. Now the human will is well ordered when it tends to acts which are befitting to man. But the same acts are not befitting to man at every season of life. We must, therefore, conclude that children would not have had sufficient strength for the use of their limbs for the purpose of performing every kind of act; but only for the acts befitting the state of infancy, such as suckling, and the like.*

This apparently trivial passage contains much that is typical of Thomism, as the Scholastic philosophy of Aquinas is termed. It is close to common sense, yet it grants a clear supremacy to "truths which are above nature," which we hold by faith and receive through divine authority. It expresses the belief that God usually prefers to let nature run its course according to its laws, and that there is a "fitness" in human action conforming to these laws of nature. Finally it makes an appeal to authority, in this case the Old Testament and St. Augustine.

MYSTICISM

In all periods there are many human beings who distrust reason and prefer to rely upon the emotions or the instincts. Not only did Aquinas' rationalism arouse considerable hostility in his own day, but the voices of antirationalist mystics were raised on behalf of their own views. St. Bernard of Clairvaux, the mystic in action, as we saw, fought Abelard's apparent exaltation of reason. St. Francis the mystic distrusted books and told his brethren to throw them away, to rely on love, to discipline the mind as well as the body. Aquinas' Franciscan contemporary Bonaventura (John of Fidanza, 1221–1274) preached to his students in Paris that the human mind, as an organ of Adam's sinful and unredeemed descendants, could understand only things of the physical world. Only by divine illumination could men hope to gain cognition of the divine or supernatural. Prayer, not study, love and longing for God, not reason—this was the answer of Bonaventura, as it always is for mystics. Yet Bonaventura was an accomplished philosopher, quite able to deal on even terms with his rationalist opponents. In his *Voyage of the Mind to God* he echoes Augustine and the earlier Platonists: the grace of God helps the mind achieve the degree of love it needs to undergo the ultimate mystical experience of a kind of union with the divine.

POLITICAL THOUGHT

The medieval thinker believed that the perfection of the kingdom of heaven could not possibly exist on earth, where compromise and imperfection are inescapable. Full equality could not exist on earth. The twelfth-century *Policraticus* (*Statesman's Book*) of the English philosopher John of Salisbury (c. 1115–1180) gives us a view of the order of rank in human society. The prince (or king) is the head of the body of the commonwealth; the senate (legislature) is the heart; the judges and governors of provinces are the eyes, ears, and tongue; the officials and

---

* *The "Summa Theologica" of St. Thomas Aquinas,* 2nd ed. (London, 1922), Vol. IV, Pt. I, Quest. XCIX.

soldiers are the hands; the financial officers are the stomach and intestines; and the peasants "correspond to the feet, which always cleave to the soil." This figure of speech, or, in more ambitious terms, this organic theory of society, has remained a great favorite with those who oppose change. For obviously the foot does not try to become the brain, nor is the hand jealous of the eye; the whole body is at its best when each part does what nature meant it to do. The fieldworker, the blacksmith, the merchant, the lawyer, the priest, and the king himself all have been assigned a part of God's work on earth.

Medieval thought thus distinguished among vocations, but it also insisted on the dignity and worth of all vocations, even the humblest. It accepted the Christian doctrine of the equality of all souls before God and held that no man could be a mere instrument of another man. Even the humblest person on this earth could in the next world hope to enjoy a bliss as full and eternal as any king's. Furthermore, medieval political theory by no means opposed all change on earth. If existing conditions were bad, it was a sign that originally good conditions had been perverted; the thing to do was to restore the original good, God's own plan.

A relatively rigid and authoritarian society needs a sovereign authority whose decisions are final. But the medieval West never gave unquestioning acceptance to a single and final authority, although both popes and emperors competed for the position. Both sides enlisted medieval thinkers; in the strife of propaganda the imperialists insulted the papalists and the papalists insulted the imperialists. Each side had to find backing for its claims to authority, and some of the arguments ring familiarly even in modern ears.

Marsiglio of Padua (c. 1275–1343), the author of *Defensor Pacis* (*Defender of the Peace*), an imperialist pamphlet, maintained that the only true source of authority in a commonwealth was the *universitas civium,* the whole body of the citizens. Marsiglio probably did not mean to be so modern as he may seem. He still used medieval terms, and the constitutionalism, the notions of popular sovereignty, that have been attributed to him are a long way from our notion of counting heads to determine political decisions. But Marsiglio did in all earnestness mean what a great many other medieval thinkers meant: no man's place in the order of rank, even if he is at the top of it, is such that those of lower rank must always and unquestioningly accept what he commands. The feudal relation itself was an admirable example of medieval insistence that the order of rank was not one of mere might. Lords and vassals were held together by a contract binding on *both* parties.

LITERATURE AND THE ARTS

Literature for Laymen. The harshness of the Dark Ages and the early feudal world is reflected in the surviving literary works by laymen: for example, the Anglo-Saxon epic *Beowulf,* with its grim battles against monsters and its gloomy scenery. The eleventh century was a turning point in literature, too. The northern French *Chanson de Roland* (*Song of Roland*), though probably not written down in its present form until after 1100, is essentially an eleventh-century poem, telling of the exploits of Roland, a peer of Charlemagne, against the Moslems and in the face of treachery. Human beings replace monsters as the foe, the landscape brightens, Christian piety softens some of the worst horrors; Roland sees to it that his dead comrades receive a Christian blessing, and combines loyalty to his suzerain, Charlemagne, with love for "sweet France." Charlemagne himself, aged, troubled by the manifold problems of Empire, weeping at the death of his loyal vassal, is a truly human figure.

In southern France, things were gentler still; no doubt the sunny climate, the greater leisure, and the proximity to the cultivated Moslems of Spain all played a part. Here lyric poetry flourished, with love its favorite theme, but love with a curious code of its own, *courtoisie,* or courtly love. The lady was always the wife of somebody else; she was worshipped from afar, and the slightest kindness from her was celebrated in ecstasy, while her merest word was a command, and her knight gladly undertook the most arduous mission on her behalf without hope of reward. But a lady who failed to reward him was not playing quite according to the rules of this elaborate and artificial game. The twelfth-century troubadours who sang of their ladies were sometimes half-humorous as they adhered to the conventions of the sport. Eleanor of Aquitaine, wife of Louis VII of France and then of Henry II of England, held "courts of love" patterned on feudal law courts, where the troubadours sang their songs and where petitions from ladies or gentlemen crossed in love received mock-sober attention. Eleanor's grandfather, Duke William IX of Aquitaine, was himself a skillful troubadour, with a light touch. Ill-fated love like that of Lancelot and Guinevere and other Arthurians or of the heroes of Troy supplied favorite themes to the romancers.

So the southern French modified the general feudal attitude toward women as mere breeders of new generations of fighters, and made life more agreeable and sophisticated for all who heard their songs. Their influence travelled far, appearing in Germany in the works of the minnesingers. The code of courtly love formed part of a general code of behavior and manners for the lord and his vassal that we know as chivalry, from *chevalier,* a horseman or knight. Loyalty to the suzerain, like Roland's to Charlemagne, piety like Roland's, vigor and decency: real men as well as the heroes of romances regarded these as true virtues, and strove to live up to them. St. Louis as king, his faithful biographer the Sieur de Joinville (1224–1317) as vassal accompanying his master on the crusade, both practiced the ideals of chivalry with great success. While lesser men might fail of the goal, at least the ideal was before them.

The chivalric code lent itself readily to exaggeration and to mere posture and pretense. The individual knight was always acutely conscious of his honor, of himself as the final arbiter of what suited and what did not suit his dignity. As time passed, everything was apt to become focussed on the point of honor, and the knight sometimes became a hysterically sensitive person quite cut off from the world of prosaic values. It is probably more than a coincidence that the nation whose aristocracy carried the point of honor furthest, the Spanish, also produced in Cervantes' *Don Quixote* (1605) a book that most of the world has taken to be a devastating attack on the ideals of chivalry (*see* Chapter 7).

Chivalric literature was written in the vernacular tongues—French, German, Provençal (the language of southern France, *Provence*). But the larger portion of medieval writing was in Latin: the sermons and lives of the saints, which continued to enjoy great popularity, and the chronicles, which began in the eleventh century to be better written, more accurate, and more detailed. An occasional biography of a living man or even an autobiography made its appearance. In verse, the Latin hymn reached solemn heights in the twelfth and thirteenth centuries, while the dramatic character of the liturgy suggested that putting dialogue into the mouths of different persons would magnify the effect, and led to the writing and acting of the earliest post-classical plays. Even popular literature—and only fragments survive—was mostly still in Latin, and often shows a shrewd earthy admiration for the cunning fellow and a scorn for fine words.

Unique in the period was the verse of the twelfth-century Goliard poets. These poets, usually renegade scholars or clerics, purported to serve Golias, a sort of Satan, who perhaps was derived from Goliath in the Old Testament. Their verses mocked both the form and the values of serious religious poetry, not sparing the clergy or the Bible itself in their satire, and singing the praises of wine, women, and song. Here is how the "Confession of Golias" (c. 1165) defined the highest good:

> My intention is to die
>   In the tavern drinking;
> Wine must be at hand, for I
>   Want it when I'm sinking.
>
> Angels when they come shall cry,
>   At my frailties winking:
> "Spare this drunkard, God, he's high,
>   Absolutely stinking!"*

Architecture: The Cathedral. Admirers of the Middle Ages often claim that the medieval craftsman worked in anonymity, content to carve or paint for the glory of God and the joy of creating beauty, and not for fame or money. Perhaps so, though the reason we do not know the names of many medieval architects and sculptors is simply that the records have been lost. Yet art and artists seem to have been closely tied to the community in the Middle Ages. The greatest of medieval arts, architecture, clearly shows this community stamp. In a medieval town the cathedral, parish churches, town hall, gild halls, and other *public* buildings dominate the scene.

The great medieval cathedrals were places of worship, and their almost universal cruciform (cross-shaped) plan was dictated by the needs of the Catholic service. But they were also centers of community life where people came to stroll, to get out of the rain, to gossip, to do business, even to court. In the quiet side chapels the worshipper could pray in peace while the people thronged the nave. As long as reasonable decorum was observed, no one thought that these activities profaned God's house. Moreover, the statues, the paintings, the stained-glass windows, and the carvings served in effect as an illustrated Bible and as a history of the Church for a population that could not read. The wealth of detail served not only to decorate but also to teach.

The Gothic architecture of the Middle Ages develops according to the pattern common to most civilized art forms. It begins with youthful simplicity, attains a strong but graceful maturity, and trails off into an old age of overelaboration and pedantry. Its immediate source is the style known as Romanesque, which prevailed in the West toward the end of the Dark Ages and which was derived largely from the classical Roman basilica, a great hall roofed with the round arch perfected by the Romans. The Romanesque church is often built in the form of a Latin cross with a short cross-arm. The east end, or choir, usually points in the general direction of the Holy Land, whence Christianity came. It contains the altar, which forms the center of worship, and places for the celebrants of the Mass. Usually the choir terminates in a semicircular *apse*.

The long arm of the cross, which prolongs the choir toward the west, is the nave, where the congregation normally stays. The shorter arms of the cross make

---

* From *The Goliard Poets* by George F. Whicher. Copyright 1949 by George F. Whicher. Reprinted by permission of New Directions Publishing Corporation.

up the transepts, north and south, into which the congregation may overflow. The larger churches have aisles, with lower roofs, which extend outside the arms of the cross and follow its lines. Opening off these aisles there are usually little chapels dedicated to the saints. At the crossing, where the nave and the transepts meet, many great churches have a central tower; and the west end often has a tower at each side, which, as in Notre Dame de Paris, may dominate the exterior.

Since the medieval builder had no structural steel to work with, he had to support the stone ceiling and the heavy roof with masonry. The round arch of the Romanesque produced barrel vaulting, in which the ceiling presses down evenly all along the walls with great weight. To withstand this weight, the walls had to be strong, with a minimum of openings, so that Romanesque buildings, while often having great dignity and solidity, are usually poorly lighted. What freed the medieval Gothic builder to carry his buildings to soaring heights was the pointed arch. By means of this device, the builder could carry the weight of a vaulted ceiling along masonry ribs to fall on four great supports. These supports could be

Interior of Beauvais Cathedral, France, begun in 1247.

pillars rather than walls, thus freeing space for large windows. A subsidiary device, the flying buttress, supporting the walls from outside, gave the builder a chance to provide for even more light and height.

With these devices, the medieval architect could indulge himself to the full in his passion for height. But this passion sometimes got out of hand, as at Beauvais in northern France, where the cathedral was never rebuilt after the ambitious central tower collapsed. What remains of the apse, choir, and transepts today looks like a remarkable defiance of the law of gravity.

Most of these great cathedrals cost so much that they took several centuries to build. Meanwhile architectural style was changing. Since few great churches were built all of a piece, one may find in a single building perhaps a simple, pre-Gothic, round-arched crypt (a sort of basement church with shrines and chapels), an early Gothic choir, a middle-period nave, and decorations in the elaborate late medieval style called *flamboyant* (flamelike). Chartres cathedral has two towers, one early and simple, one late and more ornate. Yet, with all the mixture of primitive simplicity and late ornateness, most of these Gothic churches do give the modern observer a sense of looking at something unified.

Gothic architecture manifested itself also in two other buildings that expressed community need: the great town halls and gild halls of medieval cities, and the castle. The best of the town halls are those of the Low Countries, comparatively late, profusely decorated, usually with splendid towers and with at least one great high room. Many of the massive castles were first of all designed for the purpose of keeping the enemy out. But even these great fortresses often have a chapel and a hall that bear the mark of the Gothic love of light, height, and decoration. The great monastic abbey often combined elements of the cathedral, town hall, and castle into one splendid Gothic complex. One of the best, no longer a religious community, is Mont-St.-Michel on the border of Brittany and Normandy, a rocky islet linked to the mainland only by a narrow causeway, which is at once a fortress, a town, and a monastery.

Sculpture, Painting, and Music. All the fine arts contributed to these great community buildings; indeed, they had hardly any other major outlet. Sculpture was subordinated to architecture. Statues and carvings were fitted into the design of the great churches, in niches on the fronts and porches, or on altars and shrines in the interior. The greatly admired statues on the early west front of Chartres are unnaturally elongated, but they fit all the better into the builder's purpose of framing the entrance arch. Later, the statues—like those at Rheims or Amiens, for example—are more "lifelike." But even this later Gothic sculpture, if only because it is bringing to life God, Christ, angels, saints, and devils—is never simply realistic in the way of the portrait bust, nor independently grand in the way of the equestrian statue. It is always part of the "stone Bible." It almost always tells a story, as in the many representations of the Last Judgment, which is a favorite subject of the medieval sculptor. Both Romanesque and Gothic sculptors loved the grotesque: savage beasts maul each other on the capitals of columns; elephants and monsters grin from the ends of water-spouts (gargoyles); and imps and devils appear even on the seats in stalls. That mystic St. Bernard distrusted sculpture: it turned monks' thoughts away from prayer. Clairvaux was severely plain.

Painting, too, was subordinated to the building. While the medieval church had no place for the canvas designed to be hung for exhibition, mosaics, wall

Gothic sculpture: ancestors of the Virgin, from one of the portals of the Cathedral of Chartres.

painting, and above all stained glass contributed to the total design. Time has dealt harshly with most of the paintings on walls and pillars, which were apparently brightly colored. The stained glass survives as the great medieval achievement in painting. The glass was not really painted of course; each separate bit of the design was stained in the making, and the whole was pieced together as a mosaic held in place by leaden tracery.

The earlier painting itself often seems stiff to us, whether in glass, murals, altar pieces, or in the miniatures that decorate illuminated manuscripts. Design later grows freer, more "naturalistic." Eventually the Italian painter Giotto (c. 1270–1337) and his successors begin to use highlights and the new science of geometrical perspective to suggest in the two dimensions of painting the three dimensions our eyes see in nature (*see* Chapter 6). But by the time of Giotto we are in a sense emerging from the medieval world. Medieval men did not equate God and nature quite as the modern world does; nor did they have the eye of the camera.

Early twelfth-century relief depicting the Last Judgment, from the west tympanum of the Cathedral of St. Lazare, Autun, France.

Wood-carver and stone-carver contributed their share—an important share—to the Gothic cathedral. Nothing is scamped or hasty in these buildings. A minor bit of vaulting, tucked away on the ceiling almost out of sight of the observer on the floor of the nave far below, is almost always finished with loving care and perfection. The capitals of the columns, unlike the Greco-Roman capitals from which they were probably derived, are carved in infinite variety.

Medieval music was essentially church music, which began in the sixth century with Gregorian chant or plainsong. Plainsong was simply a series of musical tones, separated by no set rhythmic interval, sung in unison. It was used in church services as a setting for the psalms and other prose. But apparently there were also hymns in metrical or verse form that could be accommodated to a simple tune. As Europe emerged from the Dark Ages, music, like the other arts, grew more and more complex. Our present method of musical notation—the staff—was invented, or at any rate developed and taught, by an eleventh-century Italian monk, Guido of Arezzo. Church music developed both melody and harmony—the sounding of two or more notes simultaneously—until the peak of balanced form and matter was reached in the thirteenth century. Later medieval church music sometimes resembles an extremely complex musical puzzle.

Conscious secular musical composition begins in the Middle Ages with the minstrels, who often elaborated popular tunes. By the end of the fourteenth century we get something like the modern composer, for example the Italian Landini, who wrote songs, called madrigals, set for two voices. Music, like the other arts, was anonymous, but the cautious historian can say only that this anonymity may be simply a result of the gaps in our historical record.

4

READING SUGGESTIONS   (asterisk indicates paperbound edition)

Social and Economic Foundations

R. S. Lopez, *The Birth of Europe* (Lippincott, 1967). Basic work by a ranking economic historian.

The Cambridge Economic History, Volumes I and II (Cambridge University, 1944, 1952). Detailed survey of the economy of medieval Europe by various experts.

P. Boissonade, *Life and Work in Medieval Europe* (*Torchbooks). A very good introduction, written by a French scholar in the 1920's.

L. White, Jr., *Medieval Technology and Social Change* (*Galaxy). Scholarly, readable, and suggestive study.

H. Pirenne, *Medieval Cities* (*Anchor). Excellent short essay by a Belgian scholar who wrote several other works on the social and economic life of the Middle Ages.

S. Painter, *Medieval Society* (*Cornell). Handy introduction by a very good scholar.

Politics: Works Touching More than One Country

C. Brooke, *Europe in the Central Middle Ages, 962–1154* (Holt, 1964). Excellent up-to-date survey.

S. Painter, *Rise of the Feudal Monarchies* (*Cornell). Good introduction for the beginner.

C. Petit-Dutaillis, *Feudal Monarchy in France and England from the Tenth to the Thirteenth Century* (*Torchbooks). Standard study by a French expert of the early twentieth century.

W. Ullmann, *Principles of Government and Politics in the Middle Ages* (Barnes &

Noble, 1961). Ambitious synthesis, not acceptable to all specialists; by the author of other controversial studies in the field.

C. H. Haskins, *The Normans in European History* (*Norton). By a celebrated historian and teacher of the early twentieth century; still very much worth reading.

Amy Kelly, *Eleanor of Aquitaine and the Four Kings* (*Vintage). Learned and lively book about the ranking feminine personality of twelfth-century France and England.

The French Monarchy

R. Fawtier, *The Capetian Kings of France* (*Papermac). Most up-to-date account

J. Evans, *Life in Medieval France* (Oxford, 1925). Good picture of French society.

A. Luchaire, *Social France at the Time of Philip Augustus* (*Torchbooks). A famous old account, stressing the seamy side of life about 1200.

The English Monarchy

G. O. Sayles, *The Medieval Foundations of England* (*Perpetua). Excellent basic study. With H. G. Richardson, Sayles is co-author of *The Governance of Medieval England from the Conquest to Magna Carta* (Edinburgh, 1963), a brilliant and provocative analysis.

A. L. Poole, *From Domesday Book to Magna Carta, 1087–1216*, and F. M. Powicke, *The Thirteenth Century, 1216–1307* (Clarendon, 1951, 1953). Very useful volumes in the indispensable Oxford History of England.

D. M. Stenton, *English Society in the Early Middle Ages* (*Pelican); A. R. Myers, *England in the Late Middle Ages* (*Pelican); H. M. Cam, *England before Elizabeth* (*Torchbooks). Good brief popular accounts by sound scholars.

D. C. Douglas, *William the Conqueror and the Norman Impact upon England* (*University of California). The last word on 1066 and all that. Frank Barlow, *William I and the Norman Conquest* (*Collier). A shorter and more popular account.

B. Wilkinson, *The Constitutional History of England, 1216–1399*, 3 vols. (Longmans, 1948–1952). Magisterial treatment of a much debated topic.

G. L. Haskins, *Growth of English Representative Government* (*Perpetua). A clear account of a most difcult and vital subject.

G. C. Homans, *English Villagers of the Thirteenth Century* (Russell & Russell, 1960). Interesting sociological study.

The German Monarchy

G. Barraclough, *The Origins of Modern Germany* (*Capricorn). Best general treatment of medieval Germany in English; Barraclough also translated and edited important revisionist essays by German scholars in *Medieval Germany*, 2 vols. (Blackwell, 1938).

J. Bryce, *The Holy Roman Empire* (*Schocken). First written as an undergraduate honors essay more than a century ago, and still worthwhile.

J. W. Thompson, *Feudal Germany* (University of Chicago, 1928). A standard work, now somewhat outdated.

E. Kantorowicz, *Frederick the Second, 1194–1250* (R. R. Smith, 1931). Scholarly and imaginative treatment. The scholarship has won wide respect; the imagination has not.

Civilization

H. O. Taylor, *The Medieval Mind*, new ed. (Harvard University, 1949). A great inclusive work, now somewhat outdated.

Henry Adams, *Mont-Saint-Michel and Chartres* (*several editions). A highly personal introduction to the values of medieval civilization by the famous American intellectual. Many of its conclusions have been challenged by experts; see, for example, E. Mâle, *The Gothic Image: Religious Art in France in the Thirteenth Century* (*Torchbooks).

M. DeWulf, *Philosophy and Civilization in the Middle Ages* (*Dover). Popular lectures by a ranking scholar of an older generation.

D. Knowles, *The Evolution of Medieval Thought* (*Vintage). Stresses the continuity between classical and Scholastic thought.

C. S. Lewis, *The Discarded Image: An Introduction to Medieval and Renaissance Literature* (Cambridge University, 1964). A subtle commentary, revising traditional interpretations.

K. S. Drew and F. S. Lear, *Perspectives in Medieval History* (Chicago, 1963). Five American medievalists sum up their generation's views.

H. Rashdall, *The Universities of Europe*

in the Middle Ages, 3 vols. (Clarendon, 1936). The classic detailed study.

C. H. Haskins, *The Rise of Universities* (*Cornell). Delightful short essays.

———, *The Renaissance of the Twelfth Century* (*Meridian). An important revisionist work, stressing "modern" elements in medieval civilization.

A. C. Crombie, *Medieval and Early Modern Science,* 2 vols. (*Anchor). A standard succinct account.

A. E. Gilson, *Reason and Revelation in the Middle Ages* (*Scribner's). By a distinguished French Catholic scholar, author of many other important works sympathetic to the Middle Ages.

M. D. Chenu, *Toward Understanding St. Thomas* (Regnery, 1964). Standard French work on Aquinas.

H. Daniel-Rops, *Bernard of Clairvaux* (Hawthorne, 1964). Excellent account of a very medieval figure.

Fiction and Biography

Chaucer, *Canterbury Tales* (many editions). Perhaps the best literary introduction to medieval civilization.

Bryher, *The Fourteenth of October* (Pantheon, 1952), and Hope Muntz, *The Golden Warrior* (*Scribner's). Good novels about the Norman conquest of England.

Eileen Power, *Medieval People* (*Anchor). Biographical sketches of a half-dozen individuals from various walks of medieval life.

Helen Waddell, *Peter Abelard* (*Compass). Novel about the famous affair with Héloise.

C. Whitman, *Peter Abelard* (Harvard University, 1965). Interesting narrative poem.

Z. Oldenbourg, *The World Is Not Enough* and *The Cornerstone* (*Ballantine). Realistic novels about French feudal families.

5

The Medieval World

Eastern Europe

Museum of Santa Sophia, Istanbul. The Bosphorus and Asia are to the right, and the Golden Horn to the left.

In this chapter we introduce two other civilizations, that of the Eastern Christian society centering on Byzantium, and that of the Moslems. Once again, the eleventh century provides a turning point, for it was then that the West undertook a prolonged campaign against the Moslem and Orthodox East: a campaign that temporarily destroyed the Byzantine Empire, so weakening it that the Ottoman Turks could complete their conquest in 1453. Yet in the East, the medieval period really extended down to the end of the seventeenth century. We recognize this fundamental continuity here by carrying our discussion well past the end of the western European Middle Ages, dealing with both Ottoman history after the conquest of Byzantium and the Russian society that owed so much to Byzantine civilization.

I. Life in Byzantium

At the far southeastern corner of Europe, on a little tongue of land still defended by a long line of massive walls and towers, stands a splendid city. Istanbul it is called now, a Turkish corruption of three Greek words meaning "to the city." After 330, when the Roman Emperor Constantine, abandoning Rome, decided to make it his capital, it was often called Constantinople, the city of Constantine, but it also retained its earlier name, Byzantium. For more than eleven hundred years thereafter it remained the capital of the Roman Empire, falling to the Turks in 1453.

The waters that surround it on three sides are those of the Sea of Marmora, the Bosphorus, and the city's own sheltered harbor, the Golden Horn. A few miles north, up the narrow swift-flowing Bosphorus, lies the entrance into the Black Sea. To the southwest of the city, the Sea of Marmora narrows into the Dardanelles, the passage into the Aegean and thus the Mediterranean. Together, the Dardanelles, the Sea of Marmora, and the Bosphorus not only connect the Mediterranean with the Black Sea but separate Europe from Asia. These are the "Straits," perhaps the most important strategic waterway in European diplomatic and military history, dominated by "the city." To the Slavs, both of Russia and of the Balkans, who owe to it their religion and their culture, the city has always been "Tsargrad," city of the Emperor. This was the center of a civilization in many ways similar to that of medieval western Europe, yet in other ways startlingly different.

THE STATE

The Emperor. Byzantium called itself "New Rome." Its emperors ruled in direct succession from Augustus, and its population, while predominantly Greek in race, language, and origin, called itself Rhomaean, Roman. Despite pride in this Roman heritage, many non-Roman elements became increasingly important in Byzantine society. After Constantine himself had become a Christian, the emperor was of course no longer considered a god. But he was ordained of God, and his power remained divine. As there could be but one God in heaven, so there could be but one emperor on earth. The Roman pagan tradition of the God-Emperor was modified but not abandoned.

In theory, the will of God manifested itself in the unanimous consent of the people, the senate (established at Constantinople in the Roman pattern by Constantine himself), and the army to the choice of each new emperor. In practice, the reigning emperor usually chose his heir, often his own son, by co-opting him during his own lifetime, as he had done at Rome. Byzantine dynasties sometimes lasted several centuries. But politicians often intervened: they imprisoned and exiled emperors, murdered them, blinded them (which made them ineligible to rule again), and enthroned their own candidates.

Each new emperor was raised aloft on a shield as a sign of army approval, so becoming *imperator*, commander-in-chief. By the mid-fifth century, he was also formally crowned by the Patriarch of Constantinople. He would swear to defend the Christian faith, and in addition to the crown received a purple robe and purple boots. In the seventh century, the emperor began to call himself *Basileus*, King of Kings, in token that he had defeated the Persians. Later still, he added the term *autokrator*, the autocrat. Empresses bore corresponding feminine titles and in general played an important role. Three times in Byzantine history women ruled without a male emperor.

A conspiracy by a rival might overthrow the emperor, but autocracy as such was not challenged. Divinely awarded powers entailed immense earthly responsibilities. An elaborate and rigid code of etiquette governed the emperor's every activity every day of the year; he spoke and commanded through brief established formulas. His subjects ceremoniously fell on their faces as they approached him with a courtier holding them by each arm, and the emperor would be acclaimed with song and silver trumpets whenever he appeared in public.

As agent of God, the emperor ordered the periodic recompiling of the Roman law. Justinian (527–565) had his lawyers codify all the laws since Hadrian (117–138) in the *Code;* even bulkier was the *Digest,* a collection of authoritative legal opinions. The *Institutes,* a handbook, served to introduce students to the larger works. While all these were in Latin, Justinian issued his own new laws (the *Novels*) in Greek. In the eighth century, the emperors issued the *Ekloga,* a new collection, more Christian in its provisions with regard to family matters, somewhat less severe and less Roman than its predecessors. Under Leo VI (886–912) appeared the *Basilics,* last of the major compilations. The emperor was supreme judge, and all other judges had power only as derived from him. Many emperors enjoyed and prided themselves on their willingness to judge ordinary cases brought them by their subjects. The emperor's palace was the center of the state, and the officials of the palace were the state's most

Sixth-century mosaic from the Church of San Vitale, Ravenna, showing the Emperor Justinian and attendants.

important functionaries. Every official had a title giving him a post in the palace hierarchy and a rank among the nobility. Many of the greatest and most influential officials were eunuchs, an Oriental feature disturbing to most Western visitors.

The Enemies. As defenders of the faith, the Byzantine emperors fought one enemy after another for eleven hundred years. Sometimes the invaders were moving north and west from Asia: Persians in the seventh century, Moslem Arabs from the seventh century on, and Turks beginning in the eleventh century. Persians and Arabs successively seized the East Roman provinces of Syria and Egypt, and the Arabs kept them. Though western Europe too experienced Moslem invasions in Sicily and Spain, Charles Martel's victory at Tours in 732 (*see* Chapter 3) was less decisive than that of the Byzantines in 717, when Emperor Leo III thwarted an Arab siege of Constantinople. Had it not been for the Byzantine resistance to the Moslems over the long centuries, we might all be Moslems today.

The Byzantines fought other Asians too: the Huns of the fifth century, the Avars of the sixth and seventh, the Bulgars of the seventh and later, the Magyars of the ninth and later, and the Pechenegs and Cumans of the eleventh, twelfth, and thirteenth centuries. All these were initially Turkic or Finnish or Mongolian nomads, fierce, swift-riding, savage horsemen who invaded imperial territory. Sometimes the enemies were native Europeans, like the Slavs who first appeared in the sixth century and filtered gradually southward into the Balkans and Greece.

In the northeastern Balkans, the Hunnic tribe of the Bulgars conquered the Slavs, who then absorbed their conquerors; by the tenth century the Bulgarians were thoroughly Slavic. The Bulgarians and the Slavic Serbs to the west of them fought long and exhausting wars against Byzantium. So did the Russians, another Slavic people, whose Scandinavian upper crust was gradually absorbed by a Slavic lower class. They floated in canoes down the river Dnieper, and sailed across the Black Sea to assault Byzantium from the water in 860. Beginning in the eleventh century the Byzantines had to fight western Europeans: Normans from south Italy, crusaders from all the Western countries, freebooting commercial adventurers from the new Italian towns. Against all these the Byzantines held their own until the late eleventh century, when Turks and Normans inflicted simultaneous severe defeats. Even then Constantinople held out, and was never taken by an enemy until 1204, when a mixed force of Venetian traders and western European crusaders seized it for the first time.

Army, Navy, Diplomacy. Only a state with phenomenally good armies and navies could have compiled so successful a military record. The Byzantines were adaptable, learning and applying lessons from their successive enemies. Carefully recruited and trained, well armed and equipped, served by medical and ambulance corps, by a signal corps with flashing mirrors, and by intelligence agents behind the enemy lines, often commanded by the emperor himself, the Byzantine land forces were over the centuries the best in Europe. At its height the Byzantine fleet too played a major role, equipped as it was with a real secret weapon: Greek fire, a mysterious chemical compound squirted from siphons mounted on the prows of ships, which set enemy vessels aflame and terrified their sailors. Like other Byzantine institutions, the navy suffered a decline in the eleventh century from which it never recovered, and the Italian city fleets replaced it as the chief Mediterranean naval power.

The Byzantines fought only if they had to, preferring diplomacy, which they raised to a high level of subtlety. First Persia, and then to some extent the Moslem caliphate, were the only states that the Byzantines regarded as comparable to their own in prestige. All others were barbarians: so Byzantium either disputed or scornfully ignored the claim of Charlemagne and his German successors to the title of emperor. There could be but one emperor and he ruled at Byzantium.

Since negotiations with barbarian states were necessary, a kind of "office of barbarian affairs" kept imperial officials supplied with intelligence reports on the internal feudings among each barbarian people, so that a "pro-Byzantine" party might be created among them and every advantage taken of their internal stresses. When the emperor sent arms to the chieftain of a foreign tribe, the act was the equivalent of adoption. The emperor could make the paternal relationship still stronger by inviting the barbarian to Byzantium, standing sponsor for him at his baptism, and bestowing upon him splendid insignia of office in the palace hierarchy. The imperial court, solemn and dazzling, overawed the simple foreigner.

The Economy. Armies, navies, and diplomacy cost money, and Byzantium was enormously rich. It was a center of trade: from the Black Sea coastal lands came furs and hides and slaves; from the Far East, spices and precious stones; from western Europe, especially Italy, merchants eager to buy for gold the goods in Byzantine markets. Silk-manufacture, for long a closely guarded secret of the Persians, came to Byzantium in the sixth century when—as the story goes—two monks brought from Persia silkworms' eggs hidden in a hollow cane. Thereafter, the emperors maintained a monopoly on the manufacture and sale of silk, and of the purple dye and gold embroidery that were needed by dignitaries of church and state in West and East alike.

The emperors forbade the export of gold, and maintained their reserves at a high level. The *nomisma*, the Byzantine gold coin, was standard currency in the whole Mediterranean world and was never debased until the crisis of the eleventh century; it remained stable for eight hundred years. Constantinople's glitter and sophistication made a great contrast to the prevailing rural way of life in the West. Silken garments, palaces and churches aglow with marbles and mosaics, precious stones lavishly used in decoration were the dazzling reflection of a thriving commerce and industry and a substantial revenue.

Money came in from state property in land: farms, gold and silver mines, cattle ranches, quarries. It came from booty seized in war or property confiscated from rich men in disgrace, and from taxation: on land and persons, sales and profits, imports and exports, and inheritances. From Diocletian the Byzantines inherited the concept that land and labor were taxable together: in order to be taxable each unit of land had to have its farmer to work it; in order to be taxable as a person, each farmer had to have his land to work. While this system promoted the binding of the peasant to the soil as a serf, large private landowners flourished because the state leased large tracts of land, leaving the landowner to supply the labor. The treasury assigned marginal land or abandoned farms to the nearest landowner, who became responsible for the taxes on them. Only the proprietor of rich and productive acreage could be expected to take on the responsibility for the less productive. Yet, though the large private estate predominated, the small private freeholder seems never to have disappeared entirely.

The Capital and the Factions. As the capital, Constantinople had its own special administration, under a "prefect of the city," or *eparch*. He was mayor, chief of police, and judge rolled into one, responsible for public order, inspecting the markets, fixing fair prices for food, and supervising the lawyers, notaries, money-changers, and bankers as well as the merchants. Each trade or craft was organized into a gild or corporation with its own governor under the prefect.

From Rome Byzantium inherited rival parties of chariot-racers, each with its own stables, equipment, and colors, the Blues and the Greens. They raced each other regularly in the Hippodrome, a vast stadium attached to the imperial palace. Blues and Greens represented not only rival sporting groups but opposing factions on all the political, religious, social, and economic issues of the day, so that every chariot race was the occasion for a public demonstration. In general the Blues were the party of the aristocracy, strict orthodoxy, and the better neighborhoods, while the Greens represented the lower classes, the less orthodox, and the poorer quarters. The cleavage existed in all the great provincial cities of the Empire, but in Constantinople it took on special virulence. The political demonstrations sometimes became riots, when bands of one faction would invade the quarter of the other and burn down houses. The "Nika" revolt of 532 (so called from the rioters' shout of "victory") almost overturned the Emperor Justinian. It was not until after the mid-seventh century that the emperors managed to control the Blues and Greens.

RELIGION AND CIVILIZATION

In the Byzantine world, religion governed men's lives from birth to death. It pervaded intellectual life; the most serious questions that intellectuals tried to settle were theological, zestfully attacked by powerful and subtle minds. It dominated the arts and literature, and also economic life and politics: the position taken on a theological question often determined adherence to a political faction. What was the relationship of the Father to the Son? (The Arian controversy, *see above*, p. 116.) What was the relationship between the human and divine natures of Christ? (The Monophysite controversy, *see above*, p. 117.) The right answer meant salvation and immortality, the wrong, damnation and eternal punishment. But men lined up on these issues in part according to the city they lived in and according to their social and economic position. In foreign affairs, too, the emperor went to war as champion of the faith, with a sacred picture borne before him, an icon (image) of the Virgin, perhaps one of those which legend said had been painted by St. Luke or perhaps one not made by human hands at all but sent from heaven.

As we have seen, religion played a not dissimilar role in the medieval West. But the relationship between church and state was different in the East. The very abandonment of Rome by the emperor had permitted the local bishops to create the papal monarchy and in effect challenge Western kings and emperors. In Constantinople, however, the emperor remained in residence. Constantine summoned the Council of Nicaea (325), paid the salaries of the bishops, presided over their deliberations, and gave the force of law to their decrees. When he legislated as head of the Christian church in matters of Christian dogma, he was doing what no layman in the West would or could do; he still had some of the attributes of the Roman *pontifex*. In the East the emperor regularly deposed patriarchs and punished clerics. Constantine's successors were often theologians themselves; they enjoyed argument and speculation on theological questions and sometimes even legislated on matters of faith without consulting churchmen.

In short, the Church in the East was a kind of department of state, and the emperor was the effective head of it as he was of the other departments. The situation that prevails when a single authority plays the role of emperor and pope is called Caesaropapism, a term often applied to Byzantium. From time to time, it is true, the patriarch of Constantinople challenged the emperor successfully. Moreover, absolute though they were, none of the emperors could impose new dogma without church support or risk offending the religious susceptibilities of his people. Some scholars therefore prefer not to apply the term Caesaropapism to Byzantium; but the exceptions seem to us less important than the rule.

The Byzantines assumed, to a far greater extent than the western Europeans, that the individual had very little chance of salvation. In the East more than the West, monasticism became *the* Christian life, since to become a monk was to take a direct route to salvation. Worldly men, including many emperors, became monks on their deathbeds. Monks enjoyed enormous popular prestige, and often influenced political decisions; monks staffed the highest ranks of the church hierarchy; rich and powerful laymen, from the emperor down, founded new monasteries as an act of piety. Often immune from taxation, monasteries acquired vast lands and precious objects.

For the laity the sacraments of the Church provided the way to salvation. In the East every religious act took on a sacramental quality. Every image, every relic of a saint, was felt to preserve in itself the essence of the holy person. So God was felt to be actually present in the sanctuary; he could be reached through the proper performance of the ritual. In the East the emphasis fell on mystery, magic, rituals, a personal approach to the heavenly Saviour, more than on the ethical teachings of Christianity. Once a believer has accepted the proper performance of a magical action as the right way to reach God, he cannot contemplate any change in it; if the old way is wrong, one's parents and grandparents are all damned.

The Schism. A slight difference in the wording of the liturgy, it is sometimes argued, caused the schism, or split, between the Eastern and Western churches that took place in 1054. The Greek creed states that the Holy Ghost "proceeds" from the Father, and the Latin adds the word *filioque*, meaning "and from the Son." But this and other differences might never have been noticed and might not have led to schism had it not been for the political issues at stake also.

After the Monophysite provinces of Syria and Egypt had been lost to the Moslems in the seventh century, a new religious controversy raged in Byzantium over the use of sculptured and painted sacred images, and the nature and amount of reverence that a Christian might pay them. Something very like idolatry was widespread in the East, and twice for long periods in the eighth and ninth centuries the emperors adopted the rule that all images must be banned (iconoclasm, that is, image-breaking). The impulse came from the puritanism of the soldiers, country boys from Anatolia and Armenia who took seriously the Old Testament prohibition against worshipping graven images and who were able to install their officers on the imperial throne. The popes, who felt that images were educational and might be venerated (but of course not worshipped), condemned iconoclasm. In the end, the emperors restored the images, but not before an iconoclastic emperor had punished the pope by removing southern Italy with its rich church revenues from papal jurisdiction and placing it under that of the patriarch of Constantinople. Even more decisive than iconoclasm was the papacy's fear that the Byzantine emperor could not defend the pope or Italy against Lombards and Moslems. As we know, Pope Stephen II decided to turn instead to Pepin and Charlemagne (*see above*, p. 128).

Again, in the 860's, competition between papal and Byzantine missionaries to convert the Bulgarians led to a political quarrel. It was only then that the Greeks "discovered" the Roman "error" in adding *filioque* to the creed. When the papacy fell into corruption during the tenth century, the Byzantines became accustomed to going their own way without reference to the bishops of Rome. And when the reforms of Hildebrand re-established a powerful papacy in the eleventh century, the Byzantines found that the Normans were turning over to papal jurisdiction churches and church revenues in the areas they had conquered in Byzantine southern Italy. The ambitious and vigorous popes welcomed the return of both souls and income. The Byzantine Patriarch, unhappy at his losses, revived the *filioque* controversy as a pretext for pushing his more solid grievances. But the Pope sent to Constantinople a most unbending emissary. In 1054 Cardinal and Patriarch mutually excommunicated each other. Despite many efforts, the churches have never been reunited for more than a very brief period since the schism. Only in the mid-1960's has hope revived for a genuine reconciliation.

In general, Greeks and Westerners (who were called "Latins" or "Franks") detested each other. To the visiting western European, no doubt envious of the high Byzantine standard of living, the Greeks seemed soft, effeminate, and treacherous. To the Byzantine, the Latins seemed savage, fickle, and dangerous, barbarians like other barbarians. This antagonism made the schism even harder to heal.

Byzantine Civilization. Like the civilization of the West in the Middle Ages, that of Byzantium was derived from Greece and Rome. Yet in the West long centuries passed during which nobody knew Greek. During all this time the Byzantines preserved ancient Greek works of philosophy, science, and literature, copied and recopied them, and rendered them the homage of constant study. Had it not been for Byzantium, Plato, Aristotle, Homer, and Sophocles would have been lost, to the great impoverishment of our own cultural inheritance.

Byzantine learning, unlike that in the West before the twelfth-century growth of universities, was not confined to monasteries. Secular libraries and schools never disappeared in the East. The teacher occupied an important position in society; many of the emperors were themselves scholars and lovers of literature. Though the pious Justinian closed the university at Athens because of its strong pagan traditions, the imperial university at Constantinople supplied a steady stream of learned and cultivated men to the bureaucracy and the lawcourts. It emphasized secular subjects, while the Patriarch presided over a theological school of his own.

The Byzantines were creative writers, although their literature has remained little known. From the tenth or eleventh century there survives an epic poem about a warrior who had fought the Moslems in Asia Minor two or three hundred years before, Basil Digenes Akritas. Half Greek, half Moslem (*Digenes* means "of two races"), he conquers wild beasts and brigands along the frontier (*Akritas* means "a frontiersman") and engages in single combat with a magnificent Amazon (female) warrior. The author, while no Homer, is fully comparable to the author of *The Song of Roland*. In prose, the most striking Byzantine achievement was that of the historians who set down the record of the Empire over the centuries in a fashion sometimes violently partisan but extraordinarily valuable to the modern student. Nothing in the medieval West corresponds to their work.

Naturally, theological writing loomed large at Byzantium. The hotly debated controversies of the early period produced volumes much too difficult for most people to understand but immensely influential in determining the policies of Byzantine leaders. Theologians drew up the rule for monks, trying to moderate the ascetic zeal of the extremists. Saints' lives, written often for a popular audience, took the place the novel has in our society. The hero undergoes adventures, trials, agony of various sorts, and reaps the ultimate rewards of his own piety and virtue. These saints' lives often supply valuable bits of information about daily life and popular attitudes.

Unique among the saints' lives is a tenth-century tale of an Indian king who tries to prevent his son Ioasaph from learning about Christianity by shutting him away in a remote palace. But a wise monk, Barlaam, penetrates to his retreat and converts him by instructing him in the faith and telling him ten moral tales illustrating the Christian life. A christianized version of the life of Buddha, *Barlaam and Ioasaph* had travelled from India across Asia before it was turned into Christian legend and transmitted by the Byzantines to the West. The stories Barlaam tells are also Indian in origin, and have entered our literature too: one, for example, is the casket story of Shakespeare's *Merchant of Venice*. The very name "Ioasaph" is the same as the Indian word "Boddhisattva," which means a person destined to attain Buddhahood. Prince Ioasaph was canonized as a saint in both the Orthodox and Roman Catholic churches, so that through this legend Buddha himself became and has remained a Christian saint.

In the plastic arts the Byzantine achievement is still visible. The Church of Santa Sophia in Constantinople was designed to be "a church the like of which has never been seen since Adam nor ever will be." The dome, said an early observer, "seems rather to hang by a golden chain from heaven than to be supported by solid masonry," and Justinian (527–565), the emperor who built it, was able to exclaim "I have outdone thee, O Solomon!" The Turks, who seized the city in 1453, ever since have paid Santa Sophia the compliment of imitation; the mosques that throng present-day Istanbul are all more or less copies of it. In plan it is a fusion of the Hellenistic or Roman basilica with a dome taken from Persia, a striking example of the blending of Greek and Oriental elements. In decoration, the use of colored marbles, enamel, gold, silver, and jewels, and the glowing mosaics on the walls and ceilings, reflect the sumptuousness of the Orient.

The tourist of today wishing to see a Byzantine church of Justinian's time need not go all the way to Istanbul. On the Adriatic coast of Italy, south of Venice, at Ravenna (capital of the Byzantine exarchate until 751; *see above*, Chapter 3), there are three smaller churches of the sixth century with superb mosaics still well preserved, including portraits of Justinian himself and of his Empress Theodora. And at Venice, first the client, then the peer, and finally the conqueror of Byzantium, St. Mark's is a true Byzantine church of the later period, whose richness and magnificence epitomize perhaps better than any surviving church in Istanbul itself the splendor of later Byzantine architecture.

Along with the major arts of architecture and mosaics went the so-called minor arts, whose level the Byzantines raised so high that the term "minor arts" seems almost absurd. The silks, the ivories, the work of goldsmiths and silversmiths, the enamel and jeweled bookcovers, the elaborate containers made especially to hold the sacred relics of a saint, the great Hungarian sacred Crown of Saint Stephen, the superb miniatures of the illuminated manuscripts in many European libraries—all testify to the endless variety and fertility of Byzantine inspiration.

II. The Fortunes of Empire, 330–1081

Against this general background, we turn now to examine the course of Byzantine history between 330 and the end of the eleventh century, the year 1081, when the decline of imperial strength could be plainly seen. This long stretch of 751 years may be divided into several shorter periods, beginning with that running from 330 to 717.

FROM 330 TO 717

Constantine's immediate successors were Arian heretics. The first truly orthodox emperor after him, Theodosius the Great (reigned 379–395), proclaimed orthodox Nicene Christianity to be the sole permitted state religion. Although the Empire East and West was united under Theodosius, his sons Arcadius (395–408) and Honorius divided it, with Arcadius ruling at Constantinople. It was never again fully united in fact, although in theory it had never been divided.

Until the accession of Justinian in 527, the eastern portion of the Empire used Germans as troops in its own armies, and at the same time usually managed to deflect the new blows of invaders so that they fell chiefly upon the West. Though the Huns and the Persians presented a challenge, the cities of the East continued prosperous, and government operated undisturbed. The only warning of internal weakness came from the Monophysite controversy, in which the real issue was whether Alexandria would successfully challenge Constantinople for leadership.

With Justinian we encounter an emperor so controversial that his own historian Procopius, in addition to several works praising him to the skies, wrote a *Secret History,* never published in his own day, violently denouncing him. Justinian's armies reconquered North Africa from the Vandals, Italy from the Ostrogoths, and part of southern Spain from the Visigoths—a last desperate effort to reunite all of Rome's Mediterranean lands. Both the long drawn-out campaigns and a vast new system of fortifications proved extremely costly. The focus of imperial attention on the West permitted the Persian danger on the eastern frontier to grow to the point where Justinian's immediate successors could not check it, while in Europe Slavs and Avars were able to dent the Danube line and filter into the Balkans.

Justinian began a process of administrative reorganization that his successors would finish. In the provinces of the Roman Empire he reversed the system of Diocletian and Constantine, and occasionally entrusted both civil and military power to a single officer. After Justinian's death the military emergency caused in Italy by the invasion of the Lombards and in North Africa by the savage native Berbers forced the authorities to create large military districts, the exarchates of Ravenna and Carthage, whose commanders, called exarchs, also served as civil governors.

In the early years of the seventh century, internal bankruptcy and external attacks from the Persians seemed to threaten total destruction, when Heraclius (610–641), son of the Exarch of Africa, sailed from Carthage to Byzantium and seized the throne. He absorbed heavy losses, as the Persians took Antioch, Damascus, and Jerusalem, bearing off the True Cross in triumph. Soon afterwards they entered Alexandria, and Egypt too was gone. After 622 Heraclius began a great counteroffensive, defeating the Persians on their own territory, recapturing all the lost provinces, and returning the True Cross to Jerusalem in 629.

But only a few years later, the new movement of Islam exploded out of Arabia and took away once more the very provinces that Heraclius had recaptured from the Persians. In both the Persian and the Moslem victories over Byzantium the disaffection of Monophysite Syrians and Egyptians played a major part. From Egypt the Moslems pushed on westward and took Carthage in 698, putting an end to the North African exarchate. Moslem ships began to operate from Cyprus and Rhodes. In northern Italy the Lombard kingdom had increased its power, while Lombard duchies threatened in the center and south. Heraclius' work and that of Justinian were seemingly undone.

THE REORGANIZATION OF THE SEVENTH AND EIGHTH CENTURIES

The loss of Syria and Egypt required the transformation of Asia Minor into a reservoir of military manpower and a stronghold of defense. The perpetual raids of Slavs, Avars, and Bulgars into the Balkan provinces made the emergency the more acute. The emperors now extended to their remaining territories in Asia Minor and the Balkans the system of government previously introduced into the two exarchates, dividing them into what we would call army corps areas, with the local military commanders also exercising civil authority.

These new military districts were called *themes,* from a word meaning a permanent garrison. In each theme, many scholars believe, the troops were recruited from the native population; in return for their services, the yeoman farmers were granted land, but they might not dispose of it or evade their duties as soldiers. Their sons inherited the property along with the obligation to fight. Commanding generals of the themes, though in theory responsible to the emperor, often revolted, and in the seventh and eighth centuries many of them seized the throne. The imperial government strove to combat this danger by dividing up the large original themes into smaller ones. From seven big themes at the end of the seventh century, the number mounted to about thirty smaller ones by the year 900. From the start, one of the themes was naval. The emperor also asserted more and more direct supervision over the civil-service departments.

The new system embodied a change in concepts of taxation. Since immigration and settlement had apparently put an end to the labor shortage of earlier centuries, it was possible to begin separating the land tax from the tax on persons. The latter was transformed into a "hearth-tax," which fell on every peasant household without exception. For purposes of the land tax, each peasant village was considered a single unit. Imperial tax-assessors regularly visited each village, calculated its total tax, and assessed the individual inhabitants the portion of the tax that each would owe. The community as a whole was held responsible for the total tax, and often the neighbor of a poor peasant or of one who had abandoned his farm would have to pay the extra amount to make up the total.

Thus, in the period 330–717, the emperors, despite their efforts, failed to reconquer the West and to reconstitute the Roman Empire of Augustus. Worse still, theological controversy, reflecting internal political strain, combined with Persian and Arab aggression, cost the Empire both Syria and Egypt and forced a complete reorganization of the machinery of state, still incomplete in 717.

FROM 717 TO 867

In 717, Leo III defeated the Arabs, who were besieging Constantinople itself. Thereafter the struggle against the Moslems gradually became stabilized along a fixed frontier in Asia Minor. But the Moslem capture of Crete and Sicily opened the way for pirate raids against the shores of imperial lands in Greece and southern Italy. In northern Italy, the Lombards extinguished the Exarchate of Ravenna in 751, and Byzantine rule was interrupted by the alliance between the Franks and the papacy. The Byzantine *dux* (originally, army commander) of Venetia moved his headquarters to the famous island of the Rialto and thus became the forerunner of the *doges* of Venice.

In the Balkans, the Bulgarians had long been engaged in intermittent warfare against Byzantium. In 811, their ruler, Krum, defeated the imperial armies and killed Emperor Nicephorus I (802–811), the first emperor to fall in battle since Valens at Adrianople in 378. Krum had Nicephorus' skull lined with silver, and used it as a drinking-cup. Despite their primitive paganism, the Bulgarians none the less wanted to be converted to Christianity, an essential step for any ambitious ruler or state in the medieval world. Yet the Bulgarian rulers hesitated to accept Byzantine missionaries, for fear of Byzantine political influence.

Simultaneously another Slavic people, the Moravians, living in what is now Czechoslovakia, reached the same stage. But they feared the encroachments of their powerful neighbors, the Germans, and in 862, to avoid German influence, sent to Byzantium for missionaries. The Emperor Michael III sent to Moravia two missionaries, Cyril (or Constantine) and his brother Methodius, who had invented the Slavic alphabet, still in use today, and called Cyrillic. At the same time, Boris, ruler of the Bulgarians, asked for Christianity from the Germans. But the attempts of the two Slavic peoples to avoid being converted by their powerful neighbors failed. The Germans and Roman Catholicism triumphed in Moravia, and Boris had to yield to the Byzantines, though within the fold of the Eastern church he unified his people and consolidated his power.

For Byzantine internal development the years during which iconoclastic emperors held the throne (726–787 and 813–842) were the most critical. Beginning in Anatolia as a puritan reaction against excessive or superstitious adoration of religious pictures and images, iconoclasm later took on a violent anti-monastic aspect, since Byzantine monks were great defenders of the images. The images were twice restored by imperial decree (each time by an empress) as they had twice been banned by imperial decree. As a result of the struggle, the Byzantines drew more careful distinctions between superstitious adoration paid to images and proper reverence. When the controversy ended, it was tacitly understood that no more religious statues would be sculptured in the round, though the religious pictures that we call icons were permitted. Thus, containment of the Arabs, conversion of the Bulgarians, and the convulsions of iconoclasm characterized the period 717–867.

FROM 867 TO 1081

In Byzantium the people developed a deep loyalty to the new ruling house that was established in 867 by the Armenian Basil I (867–886) and called the "Macedonian" dynasty. As political disintegration began to weaken the Moslem world, the Byzantines went over to the counteroffensive in the tenth century. Their fleets and armies recaptured Crete (961), and soon afterward Antioch and much of northern Syria after three centuries of Arab domination. A new Moslem dynasty in Egypt, which took over in Palestine also, stopped the Byzantine advance short of Jerusalem. But, much like the later Crusaders from the West, the Byzantine emperors hoped to liberate Christ's city from the infidel. While pushing

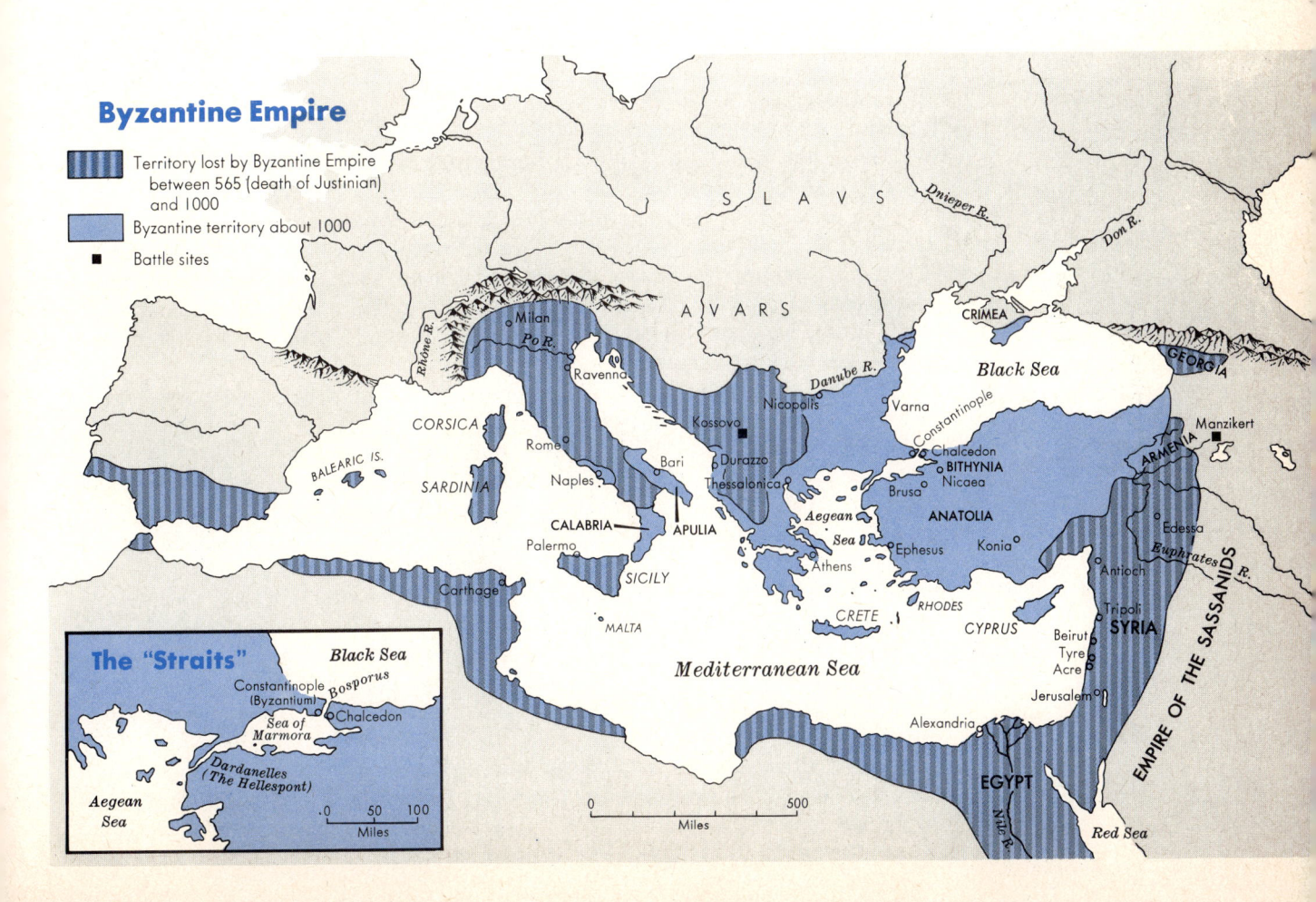

Byzantine Empire

- Territory lost by Byzantine Empire between 565 (death of Justinian) and 1000
- Byzantine territory about 1000
- ■ Battle sites

The "Straits"

back the Moslems, the Byzantines allied themselves with the Armenians, penetrated the state of Armenia, and at the end of the period annexed it. This was an error in judgment: what had been a valuable buffer against the Turks of Central Asia who were beginning to raid into eastern Asia Minor now lay open to attack. In the face of the Moslem threat from Sicily, the Byzantines re-established themselves in southern Italy, and dominated the neighboring Lombard duchies until the early eleventh century, when the Normans gained a foothold in the peninsula.

Meantime, ambitious Bulgarian rulers initiated a bitter hundred-years' war against Byzantium, during which they tried to make themselves emperors by conquering Constantinople. Toward the end of the tenth century, the conflict became more intense under a Bulgarian ruler named Samuel. In 1014 the Emperor Basil II (976–1025) captured fourteen or fifteen thousand Bulgarian prisoners and savagely blinded ninety-nine out of every hundred, allowing the hundredth man to keep the sight of one eye to lead his miserable fellows home. At the ghastly sight of his blinded warriors, Samuel fell dead. Basil II took the appropriate name of "Bulgarslayer," and shortly afterward Byzantium made Bulgaria a conquered province.

The great expenditures of money and manpower of the Bulgarian war weakened Byzantium for the military disasters that were to come. But the Bulgarian decision to accept Christianity from Constantinople, and the subsequent Byzantine military conquest of the country, helped to determine where the line between East and West would be drawn for all future history. The Bulgarians are an Orthodox people to this day, and their architecture, their literature, and their art throughout the Middle Ages directly reflected the overpowering influence of Byzantium. Similarly, more than 300 years later, the western neighbors of the Bulgarians, the Serbs, also took their faith from the Greek East after an initial flirtation with the Latin West.

Under the early emperors of the Macedonian dynasty the large landowners flourished. Nobles with great estates, "the powerful," constantly bought up the holdings of "the poor" and made the peasantry once more dependent upon them. The growing power of "the powerful" threatened the state in two important ways: it was losing its best taxpayers—the free peasants—and its best soldiers—the military settlers.

During the tenth and eleventh centuries, a great struggle developed between the emperors and "the powerful." Repeated imperial laws striving to end the acquisition of land by "the powerful" could not be enforced; in times of bad harvest especially, the small free proprietor was forced to sell out to his rich neighbor. Basil II (976–1025) forced "the powerful" to pay all the tax arrears of the delinquent peasants, thus relieving the village communities of the heavy burden that was so difficult for them to bear, and placing it on the shoulders of the rich. But a few years after Basil died, this law was repealed under the influence of "the powerful." As the landlords got more of the free military peasants as tenants on their estates, they became virtual commanders of private armies. To reduce the landlords' power, the imperial civil servants tried to cut down the expenses of the army, in which the landlords were now playing the leading role.

This strife weakened the imperial defenses. The Normans drove the Byzantines from the Italian peninsula by taking the great southern port of Bari in 1071. In the same year, after three decades of raids across the eastern frontier of Asia Minor, the Seljuk Turks defeated the imperial armies at Manzikert in Armenia and captured the Emperor Romanos IV. Asia Minor, mainstay of the Empire, now lay open to the Turks, who pushed their way almost to the Straits and established their capital in Nicaea. Meanwhile other Turkic tribes, Pechenegs and Magyars, raided southward into the Balkans almost at will. The situation was desperate in 1081, when there came to the throne one of the "powerful" magnates of Asia Minor, Alexius I Comnenus.

Thus between 867 and 1025, the Byzantine Empire reached its height. The emperors went over to the offensive against the Moslems and regained much territory and prestige. They fought the grim Bulgarian struggle to its bloody conclusion and strove to check the power of the great landlords. From 1025 to 1081 came a period of decline, accelerating as the period drew to a close, in which the triumph of the landowners was accompanied by—and related to—external military disaster.

III. Islam Before the Crusades

Islam (the Arabic word means "submission") is the most recently founded of the world's great religions. Its adherents (Moslems, "those who submit") today inhabit the entire North African coast of the Mediterranean, sections of tropical Africa, part of Yugoslavia and Albania, the entire Middle East, Pakistan and parts of India, the Malay Peninsula, Indonesia, and the Philippine Islands, to say nothing of Russian Central Asia and portions of China. From the point of view of Western civilization, relationships with the Moslem world have been of crucial importance ever since Mohammed founded Islam in the early seventh century.

MOHAMMED

The Arabia into which Mohammed was born about the year 570 was inhabited largely by nomad tribes, each under its own chief. They raided each other's flocks and lived on the meat and milk of their animals, and on dates from the palm trees. They were pagans, who worshipped sacred stones and trees. Their chief center was Mecca, 50 miles inland from the coast of the Red Sea. In a sacred building called the Kaaba, or cube, they revered idols, especially a small black stone fallen from heaven, perhaps a meteorite.

Mohammed was born into one of the poorer clans of the Kuraish, a trading tribe that lived by caravan commerce with Syria. Early orphaned, he was brought up by relatives, and as a young man he entered the service of a wealthy widow much older than himself, whom he later married. Mohammed was then free to devote himself to his divine mission, though we do not know exactly how he came to believe that he was the bearer of a new revelation. On his caravan journeys he no doubt observed and talked with Christians and Jews. He spent much time in fasting and vigils, and suffered from nervousness and hysteria. He became convinced that God was revealing the truth to him, having singled him out to be his messenger. The revelations came to him gradually over the rest of his life; he cast them in a rhythmic, sometimes rhyming prose, and included entertaining stories from the Old Testament of the Hebrews and from Arabian folklore.

Some little time later Moslem revelation was put together as the Koran or "book." The chapters were not arranged in order by subject matter, but put together mechanically by length, with the longest first. This makes the Koran difficult to follow, and a large body of Moslem writings explaining it has grown up over the centuries. Mohammed regarded his revelation as the confirmation of Hebrew and Christian scriptures, as a religion designed for all men, the perfection of both Judaism and Christianity, the final revelation and synthesis of God's truth.

Mohammed was a firm monotheist, yet he did not deny that his pagan fellow-Arabs had previous knowledge of God. He declared only that it was idolatry to worship more than one God, and he believed the trinity of the Christians to be three Gods and therefore idolatry. A major innovation for the Arabs was Mohammed's idea of an afterlife, which was to be experienced in the flesh. The delights of paradise for Mohammed are fleshly indeed, and the punishments of hell are torture.

The requirements of Islam are not severe. Five times a day in prayer, facing toward Mecca, the Moslem must bear witness that there is no God but God and that Mohammed is his prophet. During the sacred month of Ramadan—perhaps suggested by Lent—he may not eat or drink between sunrise and sunset. He must give alms to the poor. And, if he can, he should at least once in his lifetime make a pilgrimage to the sacred city of Mecca. This was, and is, all, except for regulation of certain aspects of daily life—for example, the prohibition against strong drink, and other rules about food and its preparation, mostly taken from Jewish practice. The rest is social legislation: polygamy is sanctioned, but four wives are the most a man, save for the Prophet himself, may have; divorce is easy for the husband. The condition of women and of slaves, however, was markedly improved by the new laws.

At first, Mohammed preached this faith only to members of his family, then to the people of Mecca, who repudiated him scornfully. In 622, some pilgrims from a place called Yathrib, two hundred miles north of Mecca, invited Mohammed to come to their oasis. This move from Mecca is the famous *Hegira* from which the Islamic calendar has ever since been dated; 622 is the Moslem year 1. Yathrib, to which he went, had its name changed to al-Medina, *the* city, and became the center of the expanding new faith. God told Mohammed to fight against those who had not been converted. The holy war, or *jihad*, is a concept very like the Christian crusade: those who die in battle against the infidel die in a holy cause. In 630, Mohammed returned to Mecca as a conqueror, cleansed the Kaaba of all the idols except the black stone, and incorporated it into his religion. Two years later, in 632, he died; perhaps one-third of Arabia had by then become Moslem. Only one century later, Charles Martel was battling Mohammed's coreligionists in far-off France; the great Byzantine Empire was locked in a struggle with them for its very existence; and Islam had reached India.

EXPANSION

Scholars used to think that this startling expansion was due to the zeal of converts to the new faith; now they usually contend that overpopulation of the Arabian peninsula set off the explosion of the Arabs. In fact, Arabs had been quietly emigrating for some time before Mohammed, settling in Iraq, Palestine, and Syria. The new faith served to unify them, but, while Islam might now be the battle cry of the emigrants, their motives seem to have been the age-old ones of

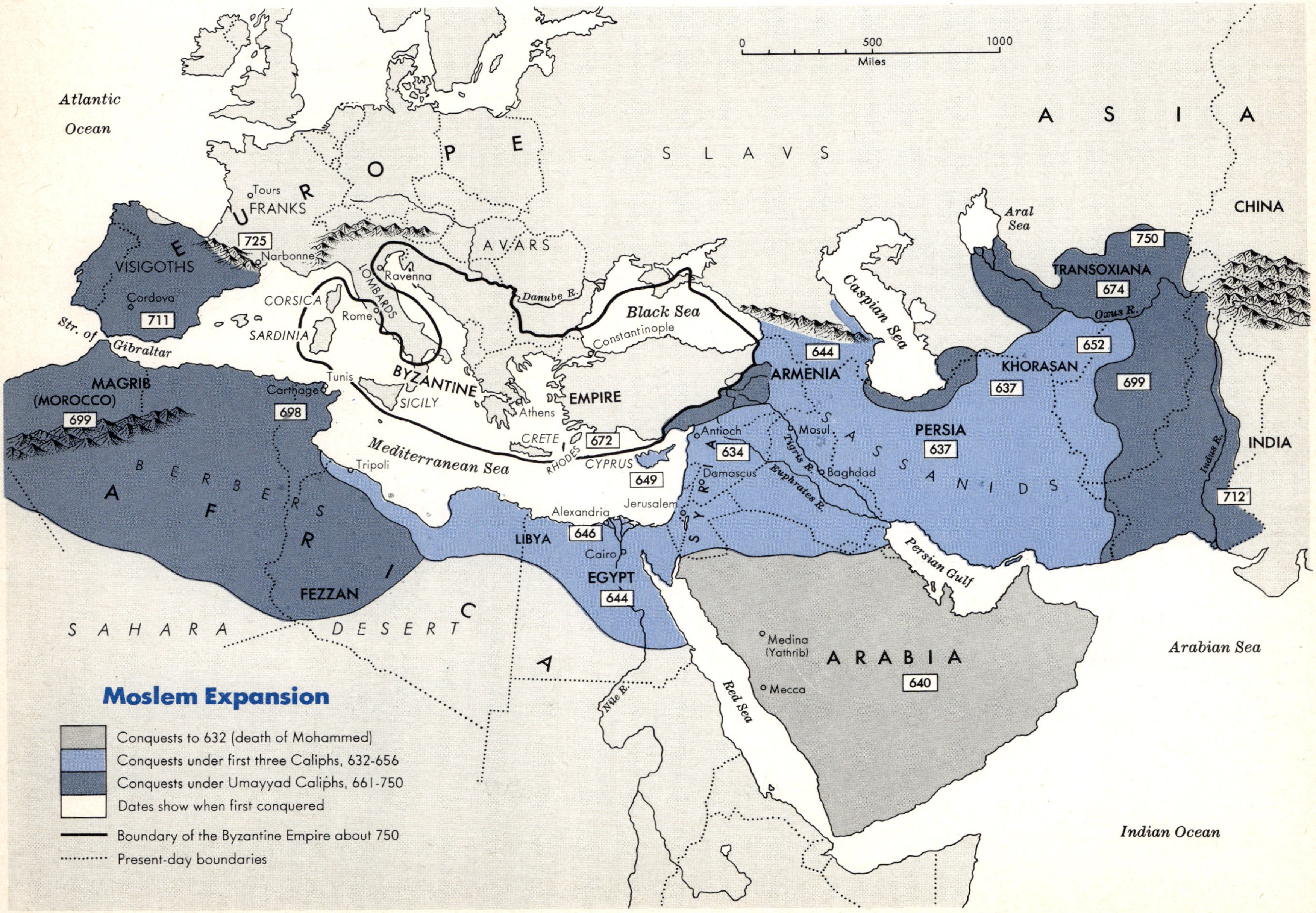
Moslem Expansion
Conquests to 632 (death of Mohammed)
Conquests under first three Caliphs, 632-656
Conquests under Umayyad Caliphs, 661-750
Dates show when first conquered
Boundary of the Byzantine Empire about 750
Present-day boundaries
0
500
1000
Miles
Atlantic Ocean
EUROPE
ASIA
AFRICA
SLAVS
CHINA
INDIA
FRANKS
Tours
Narbonne
725
AVARS
VISIGOTHS
Cordova
711
Str. of Gibraltar
MAGRIB (MOROCCO)
699
BERBERS
Carthage
698
Tunis
FEZZAN
SAHARA DESERT
CORSICA
SARDINIA
Rome
LOMBARDS
Ravenna
BYZANTINE
SICILY
EMPIRE
Danube R.
Black Sea
Constantinople
Athens
CRETE
RHODES
672
CYPRUS
649
Mediterranean Sea
Tripoli
Alexandria
646
LIBYA
Cairo
EGYPT
644
Nile R.
Jerusalem
SYRIA
Antioch
634
Damascus
Mosul
Tigris R.
Euphrates R.
Baghdad
SASSANIDS
ARMENIA
644
Caspian Sea
PERSIA
637
KHORASAN
637
652
Aral Sea
TRANSOXIANA
674
750
Oxus R.
699
Indus R.
712
Persian Gulf
Red Sea
Medina (Yathrib)
Mecca
ARABIA
640
Arabian Sea
Indian Ocean

conquest for living-space and booty. Toward Christians and Jews the Moslems generally were tolerant, regarding both as "peoples of the Book."

Syria and Persia were conquered almost simultaneously during the decade after Mohammed's death. The Syrian province, disaffected from Byzantium by Monophysitism, fell easily. And the Persians, because of their weakness after recent defeats at the hands of Heraclius, failed to put up the resistance that might have been expected. In 639–640, the Arabs took Egypt, the major Byzantine naval base, which was Monophysite in religion and, like Syria, ripe for conquest. Launching ships, they now seized the islands of Cyprus and Rhodes and began attacking southern Italy and Sicily. Moving west across North Africa, they took Carthage in 698. In 711, under the command of Tarik, they launched the invasion of Spain across the Straits of Gibraltar ("Rock of Tarik"). By 725, the first Moslems had crossed the Pyrenees, to meet Charles Martel at Tours seven years later. Meanwhile, they had been spreading east from Persia and in 724 reached the Indus and the western frontiers of China. Simultaneously, they moved south from Egypt and North Africa into the little-known desert regions of Central Africa. Of all this territory only the Mediterranean islands and Spain were ever permanently reconquered by Christians.

DISUNITY

The wide variety in the lands and peoples conquered and the internal dissensions among the conquerors made it impossible for the Arabs to establish a unified state. After Mohammed's death, they disagreed over the succession, finally choosing his eldest companion, Abu Bekr, as Caliph (*khalifa*, the representative of Mohammed). The next two caliphs were also chosen from outside Mohammed's family, to the distress of many Moslems. By 656, when the third caliph was murdered, those who favored choosing only a member of Mohammed's own family had grouped themselves around Ali, son-in-law of the prophet; they were known as Shiites (Sectarians). Opposed to them were the Sunnites (traditionalists), who favored the election to the caliphate of any eligible person and who also advocated supplementing the Koran with commentaries called "traditions," which were disapproved by the Shiites.

In 656, Ali was chosen Caliph; civil war broke out, and Ali was murdered in 661. His opponent Muawiya, of the Umayyad family, leader of the Sunnites, had already proclaimed himself Caliph in Damascus. Thus began the Umayyad caliphate (660–750), which was on the whole a period of good government, brisk trade, and cultural advance under Byzantine influence. (It produced the famous "Dome of the Rock" mosque in Jerusalem.) The civil service was manned by Greeks, and Greek artists worked for the caliph; the Christian population, except for the payment of a poll tax, was better off than it had been under Byzantium.

Shiite opposition to the Umayyads, however, remained strong. The Shiites felt it their duty to curse the first three caliphs, who had ruled before their hero, Ali, and who were deeply revered by the Sunnites. The Shiites were far more intolerant of the unbeliever, conspired in secret against the government, and were given to self-pity and to wild outbursts of grief for Ali's son Husein, who was killed in 680. Southern Iraq was then the center of Shiite strength.

From these eastern regions came the leadership of the plot which in 750 was responsible for the murder of the last of the Umayyad caliphs, together with 90 members of his family. The leader of the conspirators was Abu-'l Abbas, not a

Shiite himself, but the great-grandson of a cousin of Mohammed. The new Abbasid caliphate soon moved east to Baghdad, capital of present-day Iraq, and the days when Islam was primarily an Arab movement under Byzantine influence were over. At Baghdad, the caliphate took on more and more the color of the Persian Empire, in whose former territory it was situated. Its Christian subjects were on the whole, though, well treated.

The rest of the Moslem world slipped away from Abbasid control. One of the few Umayyads to escape death in 750 made his way to Spain and built himself a state centered around the city of Cordova. Rich and strong, his descendants declared themselves caliphs in 929. Separate Moslem states appeared in Morocco, in Tunis, and in Egypt, where still another dynasty, this time Shiite, built Cairo in the tenth century and began to call themselves caliphs. Rival dynasties also appeared in Persia itself, in Syria, and in the other eastern provinces. At Baghdad, though the state took much of its character and culture from Persia, power fell gradually into the hands of Turkish troops. The Seljuk Turks emerged supreme from the struggle for power when they took Baghdad in 1055. Although the caliphate at Baghdad lasted down to 1258, when the Mongols finally ended it, the caliphs were mere puppets in Turkish hands.

ISLAMIC CIVILIZATION

Many of the regions conquered by the Arabs had been parts of the Byzantine or Persian empires, and had an ancient tradition of culture. The new religion and the Arabic language brought to them by the conquerors often stimulated new artistic and literary development. The requirement of pilgrimage to Mecca made Moslems a mobile people and encouraged the exchange of ideas from all quarters of the Islamic world. Everybody who wanted to read the Koran had to learn Arabic: translation of the Book was forbidden. Since Arabic is an extraordinarily flexible and powerful instrument, it became the standard literary language of the whole Islamic world. The Moslems gave poetry the highest rank among the arts.

Like both Roman and Greek Christianity, Islam was convinced of its innate superiority to all other religions and ways of life. Like the Byzantines, the Moslems aspired to dominate the civilized world, which they thought of as divided between those lands already part of Islam and those lands still to be conquered. Like the Byzantine emperor, the caliph was an autocrat, a vicar of God, chosen by a mixture of election and the hereditary principle. The caliph, however, could not add to or change the religious law, although the Byzantine emperor sometimes pronounced on dogmas. Both courts stressed show and ceremony, largely derived from the Persian tradition. Christians and Moslems, however strong their mutual hatred, felt themselves to be worshippers in two religions that were on the same level of intellectual advancement and that held similar views on creation, human history, the last judgment, and the instability of everything mortal. When at peace with the Moslems, the Byzantines thought of them as the successors of the Persians, and as such the only other civilized people.

LEARNING, LITERATURE, AND THE ARTS

The reign of Mamun (813–833) is often said to mark the high point in the civilization of the caliphate. In Baghdad, he built observatories, founded a uni-

The great mosque at Mecca, with the Kaaba in the foreground.

versity, and ordered the great works of ancient Greek and Indian scientists and philosophers translated into Arabic. The Moslems developed medicine beyond the standard works of the Greek masters. They wrote textbooks on diseases of the eye, on smallpox, and on measles, which remained the best authorities until the eighteenth century. Avicenna (980–1037) was famous for his systematization of all known medical science and also for his philosophical and poetic writings.

Moslem scientists adopted Indian numerals, the ones that we use today and call Arabic. The new numerals included the zero, a concept unknown to the Romans, without which it is hard to see how higher mathematical research could be carried on. The Moslems began analytical geometry, and founded plane and spherical trigonometry. They made much progress in algebra, which is itself an Arabic word, as, for example, are alcohol, cipher, alchemy, zenith, and nadir.

In philosophy, the Moslems eagerly studied Plato, Aristotle, and the Neo-Platonists. Like the Byzantines and the western Europeans, they used what they learned to solve theological problems about the nature and the power of God and his relationship to the universe. Efforts to reconcile philosophy and religion occupied the great Spanish Moslem Averroës (c. 1126–1198), whose commentaries on Aristotle, translated from Arabic into Latin, were available to the Christian West well before the original Greek text of Aristotle himself.

Spanish Christians complained that their fellow Christians were irresistibly attracted by Moslem poetry and its portrayal of life in the desert, with its camels and horses, its warfare and hunting, its feasts and drinking-bouts, and its emphasis on love. Arabic love poetry, as developed in Spain, influenced the troubadours across the Pyrenees in France and so indirectly the minnesingers in Germany (see p. 178). Some of the greatest masterpieces of Western love poetry thus find their ancestry in the songs of Spanish Moslems. Besides poetry there is a great deal of interesting autobiography and excellent history in Arabic. The fiction is limited to a few subjects—the adventures of a rogue, the sad misfortunes of a pair of lovers, or exciting incidents of life in the capital, with the caliph participating. These tales were collected in the celebrated *Arabian Nights* together with stories of Indian and Jewish origin, as well as some that derive from the Greek classics and from Hellenistic works.

In the arts, the Moslems adapted Byzantine churches in building mosques, which needed a front courtyard with a fountain where the faithful must wash before entering. All that was necessary inside was a quiet and dignified place to

Interior of the Umayyad Mosque, Damascus. From the eighth century.

pray and rest, with a small niche in the wall showing the direction of Mecca, and a pulpit from which the Koran might be read aloud. Since the muezzin's call to prayer summoned the faithful, slender towers or minarets were built next to the mosque. Beautiful and elaborate geometric patterns, in wood, stone, mosaic, and porcelain tile, characterized the interior decoration, which also utilized the highly ornamental Arabic script, particularly the names of the first four caliphs and passages from the Koran. The great mosques of Damascus, Cairo, Jerusalem, and Cordova are perhaps the finest surviving specimens, but there are thousands of others all over the Moslem world.

The Gothic architecture of the West owes a still largely unexplored and unacknowledged debt to the pointed arches and ribbed vaults, the stone tracery (often called "arabesque"), and the other striking features of these buildings. In the architecture of the Norman period in Sicily we can see direct traces of Moslem influence, as of course we can in Spain, whose entire civilization has been permanently shaped by the Moslems. Through Sicily and Spain came Greco-Roman and Moslem science, philosophy, and art. In music, the "Morris dance," for instance, is simply a "Moorish dance"; lute, tambourine, guitar, and fanfare are all words of Arabic origin. When we consider all the contributions of the Byzantines and the Moslems to medieval Western culture, we are altogether justified in saying that much light came from the East.

IV. The Crusades

PRECEDENTS FOR THE CRUSADE

In the last quarter of the eleventh century, the relationships between Roman Christendom, Greek Christendom, and Islam entered upon a long period of crisis. One striking new development was that the Pope in 1095 proclaimed a Holy War against the Moslems, a war for the Cross, or Crusade, with the recovery of the Holy Sepulchre as its ultimate aim. The idea itself was not new. The Byzantines regarded their wars against the Moslems as sacred campaigns for the faith, and had once almost reconquered Jerusalem. In Spain, Christian had been fighting Moslem ever since the invasion of 711; the small Christian states pushed southward whenever they could. When the Cordovan caliphate weakened just after the year 1000, the abbey of Cluny prodded French nobles to join the Spanish Christians and war on the Moslems. The Pope offered an indulgence for all who would fight for the Cross in Spain. The fighting in Spain continued on into the twelfth century, the Christians recovering a large area of central Spain. Another precedent for the crusades was the warfare of the Normans against the Moslems in Sicily.

Moreover, Christians had been undertaking expeditions of another kind to the Holy Land ever since Constantine had become converted: these were the pilgrimages to the scenes of Christ's life and Passion. Even the Moslem conquest of the seventh century did not interrupt pilgrimages for long. Charlemagne, for example, had excellent relations with Caliph Harun al-Rashid (785–809), who once sent him an elephant as a present and allowed him to endow a hostel at Jerusalem for pilgrims. The belief grew that pilgrimage would bring God's pardon for sin. Cluny fostered pilgrimages, and large organized groups flocked eastward in the tenth and eleventh centuries; one of them was 7000 strong.

Stable conditions in both Moslem and Byzantine dominions were needed for the safety of the pilgrims. Yet the late eleventh century brought civil strife at Byzantium and the catastrophes of Bari and Manzikert (1071) (*see* p. 200). Seljuk Turks flooded Asia Minor; Normans crossed the Adriatic to attack the Dalmatian coast; Pechenegs poured into the Balkans. Amidst intrigue and disorder Alexius I Comnenus (reigned 1081–1118), a general and a big landowner, came to the Byzantine throne. He made an expensive alliance with Venice—giving the Venetians special trade concessions and a quarter of Constantinople to live in—and held off the Normans. But he could do little about conditions in Asia Minor or Syria, where civil wars among the Turks and brigandage on the highways made pilgrimages very dangerous.

Besides their concern for the pilgrims, the vigorous reforming popes of the later eleventh century felt that the schism between Roman and Greek churches was intolerable. In 1073, Gregory VII himself sent an ambassador to Constantinople, who reported that the Byzantine Empire too was anxious for a reconciliation. Gregory planned to send Western armies to help the Byzantines against the Turks, and even intended to take personal command and bring about a reunion of the churches. It was only the quarrel with the German Emperor Henry IV (*see* p. 164) that prevented Gregory's acting on the project. Here, more than 20 years before the First Crusade, we have all the essential elements: a holy war under papal sponsorship to be fought in alliance with the Greeks against the Moslems in Asia.

THE FIRST CRUSADE

In 1095 envoys from Emperor Alexius I Comnenus came to a papal council and asked for help against the Turks, stressing the sufferings of the Christians in the East and arguing that the time was ripe to defeat the weakening Turkish power. Eight months later at the Council of Clermont (1095) Pope Urban II proclaimed the First Crusade. In his sermon to the crowd he emphasized the anguish of the Greek Christians and the hardships faced by pilgrims. He also mentioned the riches that might be gained, and promised that any sinner who might be killed doing this work of God would receive automatic absolution and

Krak des Chevaliers, the great Crusader fortress in western Syria.

could count on salvation. His audience greeted his oration with cries of "God wills it." Thousands of volunteers took a solemn oath, and sewed crosses of cloth onto their clothes.

As it turned out, the expedition that Urban launched was only the first of a series continuing for almost two centuries. Crusaders battled the Moslems, most often in Syria and Palestine, but also in Egypt, North Africa, and Portugal. Under the command, sometimes of kings or emperors, sometimes of lesser nobles, the armies won some successes, but more often they failed. Reinforcements flowed to the East in almost a constant stream. Therefore the practice of calling certain specific expeditions the Second, Third, or Fourth Crusade, and so on up to the Eighth, is really not very accurate, though it is convenient.

After Clermont, an undisciplined mob of ignorant and often starving peasants under a certain Peter the Hermit poured eastward to Constantinople. The Byzantines, who had hoped for the loan of a few hundred well-trained knights, were appalled at this mob. The Crusaders burned houses and stole everything that was not chained down, including the lead from the roofs of the churches. Alexius Comnenus shipped them out of Constantinople and across the Straits as fast as he could. In Asia Minor they were eventually massacred.

Meanwhile, a considerable number of great lords had also enlisted, of whom the most famous were Godfrey of Bouillon (Duke of Lower Lorraine) and his brother Baldwin, Count Raymond of Toulouse, and Bohemond, a Norman prince from southern Italy. Far better equipped and disciplined than Peter the Hermit's forces, the armies led by these lords began to converge on Constantinople by different routes. Alexius was willing to have the Western lords carve out principalities for themselves from the Turkish-occupied territory which they hoped to conquer, but he wanted to recover Byzantine territory and to dominate whatever new states the crusaders might create, so he extracted from each great Western lord an oath of liege homage to him.

Once in Asia Minor, the Crusaders took Nicaea, the Seljuk capital, in 1097, and at Dorylaeum captured the Seljuk Sultan's tent and treasure. Baldwin, brother of Godfrey, marched to Edessa, a splendid ancient imperial city near the Euphrates, and was accepted by its local Armenian rulers as its Count (1098). This was the first Crusader State to be established. Meanwhile the main body of the armies took Antioch after a long siege, and Bohemond now became its Prince and thus the ruler of a second Crusader State. Finally, in July 1099 the Crusaders took Jerusalem itself by assault, and massacred its Moslem and Jewish inhabitants.

The Crusader States. Godfrey of Bouillon would not consent to wear a royal crown in the city where Christ had worn the crown of thorns, and he accepted the title only of "defender of the Holy Sepulchre." But Jerusalem became the third of the Crusader States. Godfrey's brother, Baldwin of Edessa, became first King of Jerusalem in 1100. Venetian, Genoese, and Pisan fleets now assisted in the gradual conquest of the coastal cities, ensuring sea communications with the West. In 1109, the son of Raymond of Toulouse founded the fourth and last of the new states, centering around the seaport of Tripoli. The King of Jerusalem was the suzerain of the other three rulers, but was often unable to enforce his authority. The Byzantine emperors never relinquished their rights.

The holdings of the Westerners lay within a narrow Syrian coastal strip extending from the Euphrates River to the Egyptian borders, more than five

Crusader States

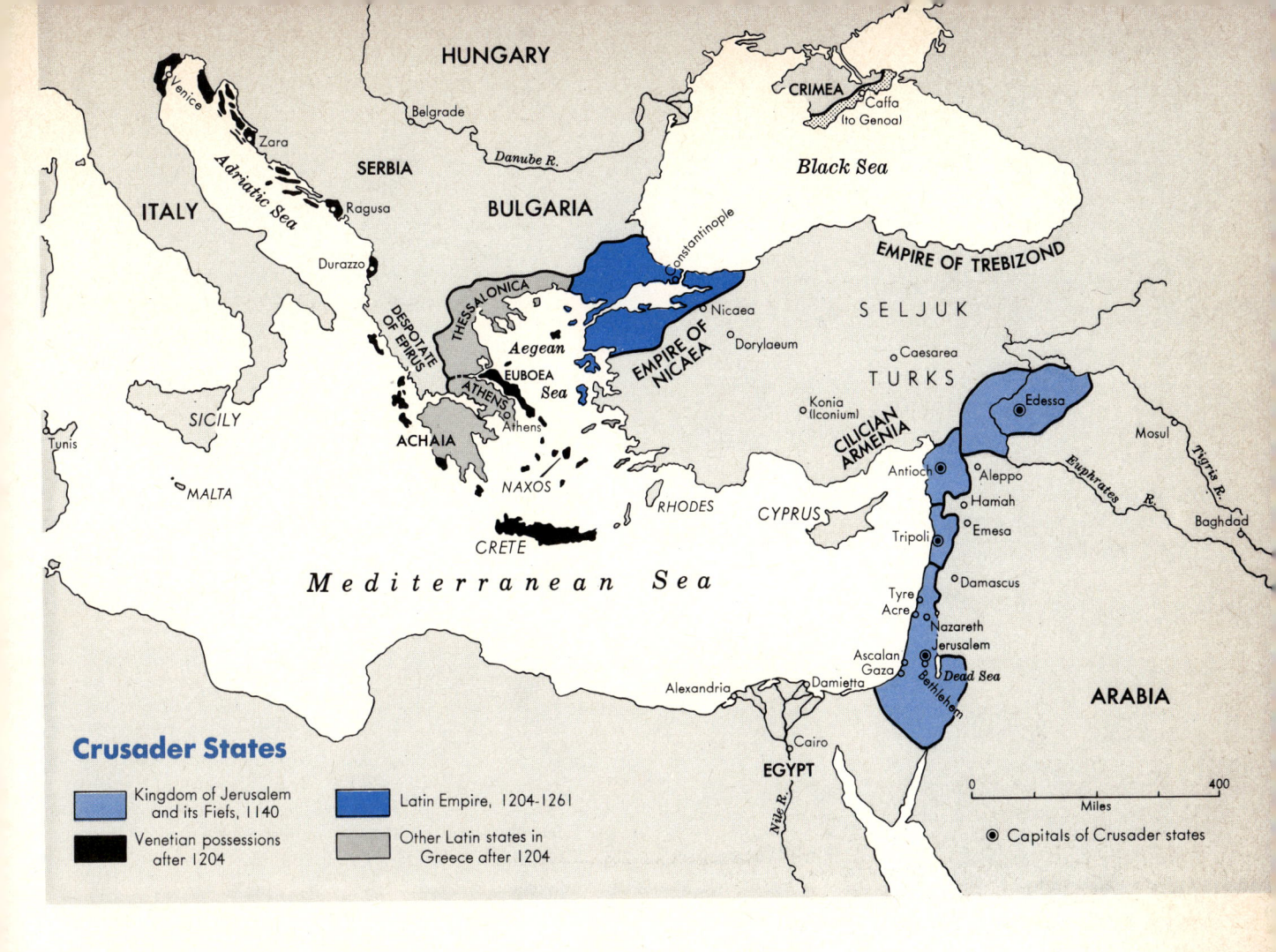

- Kingdom of Jerusalem and its Fiefs, 1140
- Venetian possessions after 1204
- Latin Empire, 1204-1261
- Other Latin states in Greece after 1204
- Capitals of Crusader states

hundred miles long and seldom as much as fifty miles wide. From the Moslem cities of Aleppo, Hamah, Emesa (Homs), and Damascus, all just inland from the strip, and from Egypt, danger constantly threatened. Yet the Crusader lords often ignored the common defense, fighting with one another in alliance with neighboring Moslems. At strategic places they erected superb castles, among the finest ever built.

The Crusaders established a purely feudal government, whose institutions may be studied in the *Assizes of Jerusalem,* written down in the thirteenth century, when the Crusader States were dying. The great officers of the realm were the officers of the king's household: seneschal, constable, marshal. The high court of the barons adjudicated disputes and acted as council of state for the king's business. The Italian commercial cities, as colonial powers, had quarters of their own in the coastal cities, with privileged status. Revenues were raised by carefully collected customs dues, by monopolies, by a poll tax on Moslems and Jews, and by a land tax on the native population. Ecclesiastical organization was complex—the two Latin patriarchs of Jerusalem and Antioch each had a hierarchy of subject Roman Catholic archbishoprics and bishoprics. Greek, Syrian, and Armenian churches continued to exist, each with its own clergy, in addition to the Moslem and Jewish faiths.

The Crusaders created new "military orders" of religious knights: the Templars were founded about 1119 to afford protection to pilgrims on their way to the Holy Places. The knights took the vows of poverty, chastity, and obedience, and were given headquarters near the Temple of Solomon—hence their name. St. Bernard himself (see p. 170) inspired their rule, based on that of his own Cistercians and confirmed by the Pope in 1128. A second order, founded shortly after, was attached to the ancient Hospital of St. John of Jerusalem, and was therefore called the Hospitallers. Made up of knights, chaplains, and serving brothers, under the command of a master, with subordinate provincial commanders both in the East and at home in the West, the two orders put into the field the most effective fighting forces in the Holy Land. A purely German group became the Teutonic Knights.

The orders quickly acquired fortresses and churches and villages of their own; Western monarchs endowed them with lands in Europe. Sometimes allied with Moslems, they quarrelled with the nobility and clergy of the Holy Land, with new arrivals, with the Italian cities, and with one another. Eventually the rich orders forgot their original vows of poverty so far that they engaged in banking. In the early fourteenth century, Philip IV of France destroyed the Templars (see Chapter 4). The Teutonic Knights, most of whose fighting was done along the eastern Baltic shore, were disbanded only in 1525; some of their lands and many of their attitudes passed to the modern state of Prussia. The Hospitallers moved first to Cyprus, then to Rhodes, and were driven to Malta by the Turks in 1522, where they continued until Napoleon's seizure of the island in 1798.

The Moslem Reconquest. The disunion of the Moslems did more than the castles or military orders to keep the Crusader States alive. Beginning in the late 1120's, Zangi, governor of Mosul on the Tigris (the town that gives its name to "muslin"), succeeded in unifying the local Moslem rulers. In 1144, he took Edessa, first of the Crusader cities to fall; it was never to be recaptured. Two years later, Zangi was assassinated, but the Moslem reconquest had begun.

As an answer to the loss of Edessa, St. Bernard himself preached the so-called Second Crusade in Europe. He aroused enormous enthusiasm, and for the first time Western monarchs—King Louis VII of France and King Conrad III of Germany—came to the East. But the armies of the Second Crusade were almost wiped out in Asia Minor. When the remnants reached the Holy Land, they found themselves in conflict with the local Christian lords, who sabotaged the siege of the key Moslem city, Damascus (1149). In 1154 Zangi's son, Nureddin, took Damascus, and Moslem Syria was united against the Latins.

In Egypt, one of Nureddin's generals became vizier (minister). When this general died in 1169, he left his office to his nephew Saladin, the greatest Moslem leader of the crusading era, renowned for his generalship and chivalry. Saladin brought the Moslem cities of Syria and Mesopotamia under his control and distributed them to members of his own family. Internal decay in the Kingdom of Jerusalem and a squabble over the throne gave Saladin his chance, and a violation of a truce by a Crusader lord gave him his excuse. In 1187 Jerusalem fell, and soon there was nothing of the kingdom left to the Christians except the port of Tyre.

THE LATER CRUSADES

These events elicited the Third Crusade (1189–1192). The Holy Roman Emperor, Frederick Barbarossa, led a German force but was drowned in Asia

Minor (1190) before reaching the Holy Land. Some of his troops, however, continued to Palestine. There they were joined by Philip Augustus of France and Richard the Lionhearted of England, deadly rivals in the West (*see* Chapter 4). Each was at least as interested in thwarting the other as he was in furthering what was supposed to be the common cause. The main operation of the Third Crusade was a long siege of the seaport of Acre, which was finally successful in 1191. Jerusalem itself could not be recaptured, but Saladin signed a treaty with Richard allowing Christians to visit it freely. A small strip of seacoast with Acre as its center remained in the hands of the Crusaders as a pitiful remnant of the Kingdom of Jerusalem. The cities of Tripoli and Antioch, their surrounding territories greatly shrunken, were also preserved.

When Saladin died in 1193, his dominions were divided among his relatives, and the Christians obtained a respite. But from the end of the twelfth century, the story of the Crusades and of the Crusader States in Syria is a mere epilogue. Innocent III's great effort at a Fourth Crusade was, as we shall see, diverted away from the Holy Land. The failures in the East were partly balanced by the successes in Spain, where, by the end of the thirteenth century, the Moslems were reduced to the Kingdom of Granada in the southeastern corner of the peninsula. Far to the northeast in the Baltic region, the pagan Lithuanians and Slavs received the attention of the Teutonic Knights.

The zeal that had driven men toward the Holy Land was diluted, perhaps most of all, by the struggle between the papacy and its European opponents—the Albigensian heretics of southern France and the Emperor Frederick II (*see* Chapter 4). Now the Pope was offering to give those who would fight against a purely European and nominally Christian enemy the same indulgence as he offered to those who fought the infidel. This brought disillusionment, especially when combined with the spectacle of repeated military failure and internal Christian dissension in the Holy Land itself.

The high point of tragic futility was the famous Children's Crusade of 1212, when throngs of French and German children went down to the Mediterranean in the expectation that its waters would divide before them and open a path to the Holy Land, along which they could march to a bloodless victory. When this failed to happen, several thousand pushed on to Marseilles and other seaports where many were sold into slavery.

The Fifth Crusade (1219–1221) was a vain attempt at the conquest of Egypt, which had become the center of Moslem strength. The sophisticated Western Emperor Frederick II led the Sixth Crusade. Speaking Arabic and long familiar with the Moslems, Frederick secured more for the Christians by negotiation than any military commander since the First Crusade. In 1229, his treaty with Saladin's nephew restored Jerusalem to the Latins again, except for the site of the Temple, where stood the great mosque of the Dome of the Rock. The Moslems restored Bethlehem and Nazareth and made a ten-year truce.

But because Frederick II was on bad terms with the papacy (*see* Chapter 4), the Christians put Jerusalem under an interdict when he visited it to crown himself king. The ruler of Egypt now took into his service several thousand Turks from Central Asia, displaced by the invasions of Genghiz Khan and his Mongols, then raging through western Asia and eastern Europe. These Turks took Jerusalem in 1244; it remained in Moslem hands until 1917. The Mongols themselves appeared in the neighborhood of Antioch and forced the ruler of the principality to pay tribute.

Now Louis IX of France launched the Seventh Crusade. St. Louis himself was taken prisoner in Egypt (1250) and had to pay a very heavy ransom. In 1250 also, the household troops of the Egyptian sultan, called Mamluks (slaves), took power in Egypt. Soon after, the Mongols, fresh from victories in Asia, where they had extinguished the Abbasid caliphate in Baghdad (1258), invaded Syria and were defeated in 1260 by the Mamluk general Baibars, who then gradually took the Christian fortresses. Antioch fell in 1268. Baibars delayed his advance in fear of a new crusade (the Eighth) of St. Louis in 1270, but resumed it when Louis landed in Tunis and died there. The Mamluks took Tripoli in 1289 and Acre in 1291, massacring 60,000 Christians. The Christian settlements were wiped out, but they were not deeply mourned even in western Europe, from which so much blood and treasure had flowed for their establishment and defense.

THE MEETING OF EAST AND WEST

From the first, Crusaders had had mixed motives: the wish to make a pilgrimage and to win indulgence, the desire for gain and the love of adventure. Some intended to return home, others to stay. A new world neither eastern nor western but compounded of both was growing up in the narrow strip of Crusader territory. As one Crusader put it:

God has poured the West into the East; we who were Westerns are now Easterns. He who was a Roman or a Frank is now a Galilean or Palestinian. He who was from Rheims or Chartres is now a Tyrian or an Antiochene. We have all forgotten our native soil; it has grown strange unto us.*

A Moslem reports an old Crusader knight who

presented an excellent table, with food extraordinarily clean and delicious. Seeing me abstaining from food, he said, "Eat, be of good cheer! I never eat Frankish dishes, but I have Egyptian women cooks and never eat except their cooking. Besides pork never enters my home."†

Once Christians and Moslems had begun to mix, the spirit of tolerance moved both. Each side respected the valor of the other. The Latins were never numerous enough to cultivate the soil of Syria, and needed the labor of the Christian and Moslem peasants. The natives were also most useful in commerce.

As time passed, some Westerners married Easterners, and a race of half-breeds came into existence. Even those who did not intermarry often had their houses, palaces, or churches built by native craftsmen. They wore Oriental clothes, let their beards grow, and ate squatting on carpets, Eastern-style. They enjoyed watching the Moslem dancing girls, hired Moslem physicians, joined Moslems in tournaments and hunts, shared certain shrines, and debated the theology of each other's religions. To pilgrims freshly arrived from the West, these easternized Westerners were suspect, yet the visitors who went back to the

---

* Fulcher of Chartres, quoted by Archer and Kingsford, *The Crusades* (New York, 1895), p. 170.
† *Memoirs of Usamah Ibn-Munqudh*, P. K. Hitti, trans. (Princeton, 1930), p. 170.

West probably had a greater effect on European society than did those who stayed in the East. From Marseilles alone, the ships of the Hospitallers and the Templars carried 6,000 pilgrims a year, so many that the shipowners of the port sued the knightly orders for unfair competition.

Arabic words in Western languages testify to the concepts and products borrowed by the Westerners—in commerce: bazaar, tariff, the French *douane,* the Italian *dogana* (a customs house, from the Arabic *diwan,* the sofa on which the officials sat); in foods: sugar, saffron, rice, lemons, apricots, melons, and pistachios; in manufactured goods: cotton, muslin, damask (from Damascus), and many others. All the new products proved a stimulus to the markets and fairs of the West. Venice and Genoa, the ports from which much of the produce of the East was funnelled into Europe, prospered. So did the cities of Flanders, whose own manufacture of woolen goods was stimulated by the availability of Eastern luxuries for trade. Letters of credit and bills of exchange became more and more necessary as commercial arrangements grew complex. Italian banking houses sprang up with offices in the Holy Land, and the orders of knighthood—especially the Templars—joined in the money trade.

Some historians believe that the Crusades helped to weaken and impoverish the feudal nobility and that the monarchies thereby benefitted. Certainly kings were able to tax directly for the first time, as a result of the need to raise money for the expeditions to the Holy Land. The papacy was no doubt strengthened in its climb to leadership over all Western Christendom by the initiative it took in sponsoring so vast an international movement and by the degree of control it exercised over its course; yet this short-run gain may have been outweighed by a long-run loss. The religious motive was increasingly diluted by worldly considerations. The misuse of the crusading indulgences for purely European papal purposes and the cumulative effect of failure and incompetence in the Holy Land surely contributed to a disillusionment with the papal concept of the Crusades. Moreover, the discovery that all Moslems were not savage beasts, that profit lay in trade with them, and that living together was possible must have led Christians to question statements to the contrary even when issued by Rome.

The influence of the Crusades upon western European art and architecture was slight. It was greater in the writing of history and personal memoirs, especially in the vernacular languages. In the thirteenth century, French, not Latin, was used by Villehardouin in his account of the Fourth Crusade against Constantinople, and Joinville wrote his moving and vivid life of St. Louis, including an account of the Seventh Crusade. Still more important was the great increase in geographical interest and knowledge; our first reliable maps and the beginnings of European journeys to the Far East date from the crusading period.

The fourteenth- and fifteenth-century Europeans who fought against the Ottoman Turks, who explored the West African coasts and rounded the Cape of Good Hope, emerging into the Indian Ocean and fighting Moslems there, who eventually crossed the broad Atlantic with the mistaken idea that they would find at the other side that old hypothetical ally against the Turks, the lord of the Mongols, were the direct descendants of the Crusaders of the earlier period. It is perhaps as a colonizing movement, inspired, like all else in the Middle Ages, largely by the Church, that the Crusades are best considered. The Westerners called the Crusader States in Syria *Outremer,* the "land beyond the sea." The Crusaders were as truly overseas colonists as the followers of Columbus.

V. The Fortunes of Empire, 1081–1453

During its last 372 years, the fate of the Byzantine Empire rested increasingly on the actions of western Europeans. Pisans and Genoese joined the Venetians as privileged residents of Constantinople; the Empire came to depend on them for its merchant marine and navy. The floods of Crusaders rendered the Byzantines first uneasy, then insecure. Popular hatred mounted until it broke out in a series of violent acts, culminating in the capture of Constantinople by the Fourth Crusade in 1204. The Crusaders set up a "Latin Empire" and drove the Byzantine into exile. After the Byzantine leaders returned to power in 1261, they were unable to shake off the economic and military dominance of the Westerners. Twice—in 1274 and 1439—the Byzantine emperors had to conclude a formal "union" with the Church of Rome, only to have it repudiated by the forces of Greek public opinion. Mutual hatred between Christians played a major part in the final downfall of Byzantium.

BYZANTINE FEUDALISM

"The powerful," in the person of Alexius Comnenus, had captured the throne in 1081. Thereafter the accumulation of lands and tenants—who could serve as soldiers in the landlords' private armies—seems to have gone unchecked. As early as the middle of the eleventh century the emperor granted land to be administered by a magnate in exchange for military service. Such a grant was called *pronoia*. Although it was not hereditary, and although no *pronoia* was held except from the emperor directly, there was a fundamental similarity between the *pronoia* and the Western fief. Military service now depended on the holders of *pronoias*.

A form of feudalism thus became the characteristic way of life on Byzantine soil. In the cities, imperial police officials or local garrison commanders often formed petty dynasties of their own, acting as virtually independent potentates. Many individual Western knights entered imperial service. Western concepts of feudalism were apparent as early as the oath exacted by Alexius from the Crusaders (*see* p. 210); and Alexius' successors acted as feudal suzerains of the Latin principality of Antioch.

Along with political feudalism went economic ruin and social misery, which mounted steadily during the twelfth century. Periodic reassessment of the taxes gave assessors unlimited opportunity for graft. They demanded food and lodging, presents and bribes; they would seize cattle on the pretext that they were needed for work on state projects, and then sell them back to the owners. The Aegean coasts and islands became nests of pirates, preying not only on merchant shipping but also upon the population on shore. Bands of wandering monks, at odds with the secular clergy, and without visible means of support, acted like brigands.

Toward the end of the twelfth century, these processes reached a climax. In 1171, the Emperor Manuel I Comnenus (1143–1180) made a desperate effort to rid the capital of Venetian merchants by arresting more than ten thousand. But the Emperor was soon forced to restore Venetian privileges. In 1182, a passionate wave of anti-Latin feeling led to a savage massacre by the Constantinople mob of thousands of Westerners who were resident in the capital. In 1185, the Normans of Sicily avenged this outrage by sacking Thessalonica, second city of the Byzantines. The last of the Comnenian dynasty, Andronicus I (1183–1185), was torn to pieces by the frantic citizens of Constantinople as the Norman forces approached the city walls. The weak dynasty of the Angeloi succeeded. Four years later, in 1189–90, the crusading forces of Frederick Barbarossa nearly opened hostilities against the Greeks; his son, Henry VI (*see* Chapter 4), prepared a fleet to attack Byzantium, but died in 1197 before it could sail.

THE FOURTH CRUSADE

In 1195, Alexius III deposed, blinded, and imprisoned his elder brother, Emperor Isaac Angelus (1185–1195). Three years later Pope Innocent III called for a new crusade. Count Baldwin of Flanders and numbers of other powerful lords took the Cross. The Venetians agreed to furnish transportation at a high price, more than the Crusaders could pay, and also to contribute 50 armed warships, on condition that they would share equally in all future conquest. The shrewd old Doge of Venice agreed to forgive the debt temporarily if the Crusaders would help him reconquer Zara, a town on the Dalmatian side of the Adriatic which had revolted against Venice. So the Fourth Crusade began with the destruction of a Roman Catholic town, in 1202. Angrily, the Pope excommunicated the Crusaders, but worse was to follow.

The son of the blinded Isaac Angelus, known as the young Alexius, had escaped to the West and was trying to recruit assistance to overthrow his uncle, the usurper Alexius III, and to restore Isaac. The brother of the late Henry VI, Philip of Swabia, candidate for the Western imperial throne, had married a daughter of Isaac, and so welcomed his brother-in-law Alexius. Young Alexius offered to pay off the rest of the Crusaders' debt to Venice and to assist their efforts in the Holy Land if they would go first to Constantinople and free his father; this proposal suited the ambitions of both the Venetians and the many sympathizers of Philip of Swabia among the Crusaders.

In July 1203, the Crusaders took Constantinople by assault. Isaac was set free and his son the young Alexius was crowned as Alexius IV. When he failed to pay off his obligations to the Crusaders, they drew up a solemn treaty (March 1204) with their Venetian allies; they agreed to seize the city a second time, to elect a Latin emperor, who was to have a quarter of the Empire, and to divide the other three-quarters evenly between the Venetians and the non-Venetians. Then came a second siege, a second capture, and a dreadful sack of Byzantium. What was destroyed in the libraries we shall never know. Many relics and some notable works of art were sent to the West, among them the famous gilded bronze horses from the Hippodrome still to be seen over the door of St. Mark's in Venice.

THE LATIN EMPIRE

After the sack, the Latins elected Baldwin of Flanders as their first Emperor, and the title continued in his family during the 57 years of Latin occupation. The Venetians chose the first Latin Patriarch and kept a monopoly on that rich office. The territories of the Empire were divided by treaty, with the Venetians claiming the coastal towns and strategic islands. A strange hybrid state was created, in which the emperor's council consisted half of his own barons and half of members of the Venetian merchant colony under the leadership of their governor. Though in theory the Latin emperors were the successors of Constantine and Justinian, and wore the sacred purple boots, in practice they never commanded the loyalty of the Greek population and could not make important decisions without the counsel of their barons.

As neighbors they had hostile Greeks and a new Bulgarian Empire, whose ruler promptly took Baldwin prisoner and had him murdered. Across the Straits, Greek refugees from Constantinople set up an empire at Nicaea. The Latins could not concentrate upon the enemies in Asia because of the threat from Europe. Outnumbered, incompetent as diplomats, slow to learn new military tactics, miserably poor after the treasures of Byzantium had been siphoned away, the Westerners could not maintain their Latin Empire, especially after the popes became involved in the quarrel with the Western Emperor Frederick II (see Chapter 4). The Greeks of Nicaea recaptured Constantinople (1261) and reestablished the Byzantine Empire.

Meanwhile, however, the Latins had fanned out from Constantinople, establishing a series of principalities where the externals of Western feudal society were faithfully copied. Templars, Hospitallers, and Teutonic Knights had lands in Greece. The laws were codified in the *Assizes of Romania*, like the *Assizes of Jerusalem* a valuable source book of feudal custom. As in the Latin states of Syria, intermarriage took place between Latins and Greeks, but the native population never became reconciled to alien domination. Most of the feudal states in Greece were wiped out during the Turkish conquest in the fifteenth century, and none existed after the sixteenth.

BYZANTIUM AFTER 1261

The Greeks of Nicaea, under Michael VIII Palaeologus (reigned 1261–1282), found Byzantium depopulated and badly damaged, while the old territory of the Empire was mostly in Latin hands. He and his successors could reconquer only occasional fragments of continental Greece or the islands. In Asia Minor the frontier remained near Konia, the Seljuk capital. Michael VIII staved off the threat posed to his empire by Charles of Anjou, a younger brother of St. Louis, to whom the popes had given the south Italian kingdom of the Normans and Hohenstaufens. Just as Charles was about to invade from Sicily, Michael helped precipitate the revolt of 1282, known as the "Sicilian Vespers." The Sicilians massacred Charles' French troops, and the Aragonese from Spain took over Sicily.

The incompetent and frivolous successors of Michael VIII added materially to the decline of the Empire, now little more than a small Balkan state. Wars among rival claimants for the throne tore the Empire apart internally. Social unrest appeared, and for a few years in the 1340's Thessalonica was run as a kind of independent proletarian republic. In the 1350's the leader of the Serbian state, the lawgiver King Stephen Dushan, proclaimed himself Emperor of the Serbians and Greeks. In 1355, he was about to seize Constantinople and make it the capital of a new Greco-Slavic state when he suddenly died. The Genoese and the Venetians, usually at war with each other, interfered at every turn in the internal affairs of the Empire.

THE OTTOMAN ADVANCE

The Ottoman Turks gave the Empire its final blow. Ablest and luckiest of the groups to whom the Seljuk Empire in Asia Minor was now passing, the Ottomans in the last quarter of the thirteenth century settled on the borders of the province of Bithynia, across the Straits from Constantinople. The discontented population of this region turned to them in preference to the harsh and ineffectual officials of the Byzantine government. As time went on, many Greeks were converted to Islam in order to avoid the payment of tribute. They taught the

The Anastasis: recently uncovered fourteenth century Byzantine fresco in the Church of the Chora (Turkish mosque of Kariye Camii), Istanbul. Note the locks, bolts, and hinges of the smashed gates of Hell, as Christ raises Adam and Eve from the dead.

nomadic Turkish conquerors some of the arts of a settled agricultural life; the Turks, in turn, adopted Byzantine practices in government.

The corporations of the Akhis, a combination of craft gild, monastic order, and social service agency, built hostels for travellers in the towns of Anatolia. There they staged religious dances and read the Koran, presenting Islam at its most attractive and thus aiding the conversion of Christians. Within a generation or two it is highly likely that the original Ottoman Turks had become greatly mixed with the native Greeks of Anatolia.

Meantime, the Turks were engaged in warfare with the Byzantines; they built a fleet and began raiding in the Sea of Marmora and the Aegean. They were invited into Europe by one of the rival claimants to the Byzantine throne, who in 1354 allowed them to settle in the Gallipoli peninsula. Soon the Turks occupied much of the neighboring province of Thrace and, in 1363, moved their capital to the European city of Adrianople. Constantinople was now surrounded by Turkish territory, and could be reached from the West only by sea. In order to survive at all, the emperors had to reach humiliating arrangements with the Turkish rulers, in some cases becoming their vassals.

The Byzantine Empire survived down to 1453 largely because the Turks chose to conquer much of the Balkan region first, putting an end to the independent Bulgarian and Serbian states in the 1370's and 1380's. The final defeat of the Serbs at the battle of Kossovo on June 28, 1389, has long been celebrated by the defeated Serbs themselves in poetry and song. June 28, St. Vitus' day, is their national holiday, and the day on which the Archduke Francis Ferdinand was assassinated by the Serb nationalists in 1914.

Turkish conquests were delayed for half a century when a new wave of Mongols under Timur or Tamerlane emerged from Central Asia in 1402 and defeated the Ottoman armies at Ankara, the present-day capital of Turkey. Like most Mongol efforts, this proved a temporary one, and the Ottoman armies and state soon recovered. In 1453 Sultan Mohammed II ordered a great siege of Constantinople. As final defeat seemed inevitable, the Greeks with their Latin auxiliaries took communion together inside Santa Sophia for the last time, and the last emperor, Constantine XI, died bravely defending the walls.

On May 29, 1453, the Turks poured into the city. Mohammed II, the Conqueror, gave thanks to Allah in Santa Sophia itself, and ground the altar of the sanctuary beneath his feet. Thenceforth it was to be a mosque. Shortly thereafter, he installed a new Greek patriarch, and proclaimed himself protector of the Christian Church. During the centuries that followed, the Orthodox Church for the most part accepted the sultans as successors to the Byzantine emperors. But the Empire that traced its origins to Augustus had come to an end.

VI. The Ottoman Successor-State, 1453–1699

The Ottoman sultans ruled over the same territory and the same subjects as the Byzantine emperors. In many ways their state was a successor-state to Byzantium. The Ottoman fondness and capacity for war, their rigid adherence to custom, and their native Turkish language came from their far-distant past in Central Asia. From the Persians and the Byzantines, who themselves had been influenced by Persia, the Ottomans seem to have derived their exaltation of the ruler, their tolerance of religious minorities, and their practice of encouraging such minorities to form independent communities inside their state. From Persia the Turks took much of their literary language, and from Islam they took the sacred law and their approach to legal problems, the Arabic alphabet with which they wrote until the 1930's, and the Arabic vocabulary of religious, philosophical, and other abstract terms. All the wellsprings of their inheritance—Asian, Persian-Byzantine, and Moslem—tended to make them an exceptionally conservative people.

CIVILIZATION

The Slave System. The most unusual feature of Ottoman society was the advancement of slaves to the highest position within the state. Except for the sultan himself, all the major officials of government and of the sultan's household, as well as all the officers of the army and large bodies of picked troops, were slaves, almost always the children of Christians. They were picked in their early youth for their promising appearance and were especially educated for the sultan's service. As slaves, they owed advancement to the sultan, and could be instantly removed from office and punished by death at any moment in their careers. Every four years from the late fourteenth to the early seventeenth century specially trained officers, each with a quota of places to fill, visited the Balkan Christian villages and took away the ablest appearing youths, from ten to twenty years old. Two considerations made this less dreadful than it seems at first: since a married boy was ineligible, marriage was always an escape; moreover, unlimited opportunities were open to the chosen boys. In poverty-stricken villages, being chosen was sometimes regarded as a privilege. We know of cases where Moslem families paid Christian parents to take their sons and pass them off as Christian in the hope that they would be selected. Once taken, all these youths were converted to Islam, and most of them seem to have become good Moslems. No born Moslem could in theory ever be recruited into the system, since the law said that no born Moslem could be a slave.

This ruling class of slaves was carefully educated. Of the seven or eight thousand chosen annually, all got systematic physical and military training. About one-tenth received higher education, and the very cream of the crop became pages in the sultan's own household and attended his palace school, where they were taught languages, Moslem and Turkish law, ethics, and theology, as well as horsemanship and military science. All left school at the age of 25, and the graduates of the picked schools were then given jobs in the administration; the rest became *spahis* or cavalrymen. There was always plenty of room for advancement, since many were killed in war and at the top levels many were demoted, dismissed, or executed for inefficiency or disloyalty. Splendid financial rewards awaited any man lucky enough to rise to one of the top posts.

At the lower level, the less intelligent slaves were often drafted into the janissaries (from the Turkish words *yeni cheri,* new forces). Their training emphasized physical endurance, and they served not only as infantrymen in the army but as shipyard workers, palace gardeners, and the like. They lived in special barracks and had special privileges. A source of strength, they also posed a constant potential danger to the state. At the height of Turkish military successes, the sultans could put into the field formidable armies, sometimes amounting to more than a quarter of a million men.

The sultan's harem was a part of the slave institution since all the women in it were slaves, together with their household staffs. The sultan's consorts, as slaves, gave birth to the heir to the Empire, so that each new sultan was by birth half-slave. The sultan picked his favorite, not necessarily his eldest, son to succeed him, and the custom arose that the heir to the throne must kill all his brothers and half-brothers upon his succession. Every son of a sultan knew as he was growing up that he either must obtain the throne himself or be killed by whichever of his brothers did obtain it. In 1595, for instance, Mohammed III killed no fewer than 19 brothers and half-brothers.

The Four Pillars of Administration. Turkish writers thought of the state as a tent resting on four pillars. The first was the viziers, varying in number, to whom the sultan actually delegated many powers. They presided over the council of state, kept the great seal, and could sometimes make decisions on policy. The second pillar was the financial officers, organized to collect revenues: the poll tax on the Christians, one-tenth of all produce, and many of the old Byzantine taxes on commerce, as well as special levies, including money realized by confiscating the great fortunes of disgraced officials. The third pillar was the chancery, a secretariat that affixed the sultan's signature to documents, and prepared, recorded, and transmitted them.

The fourth pillar, unlike the other three, was not a department of state manned by slaves born as Christians. It was composed of the judges, all of whom were born Moslems. Islam itself had responsibility for all legal matters and for education. One-third of state lands were set aside as religious property. Each tract had its own purpose: the support of mosques, of charitable or educational institutions, and even of inns or public baths. Income from such property supported the entire class of *ulema*, the learned men of Islam.

Among the *ulema* were the *muftis*, or jurists, who answered questions that arose in the course of lawsuits. The grand *mufti* in Istanbul, whom the sultan himself consulted, was known as the *Sheikh-ul-Islam*, the "ancient" of Islam, and outranked everybody but the grand vizier. Since he could speak the final word on the sacred law, it may be said that he exercised a kind of check on the absolute power of the sultan. He alone could proclaim the beginning of war, or denounce a sultan for transgression of the sacred law and summon his subjects to depose him. The opinions of the *muftis* were collected as a body of interpretative law. The general acceptance by all Moslems of the supremacy of the sacred law and the reluctance of the *muftis* to accept change helped to account for the failure of the Ottoman system to develop with the times. There are no full-scale "reformations" in Ottoman history until the twentieth century.

Weaknesses of the System. The effectiveness of the entire structure depended upon the character of the sultan. Harem upbringing and ruthless family antagonisms did not produce wise and statesmanlike sultans. Rather, more and more sultans became weaklings, drunkards, debauchees, and men of little political experience or understanding. Harem intrigue played a great role in the state.

Efficient operation of the administration depended upon maintaining the slave-system by excluding from participation the born Moslem sons of the slave ruling-class. But in practice this rigid exclusion broke down early, and born Moslems, attracted by the possibilities of gain and power, were admitted. Since they could not be regarded as slaves, the chief restraints that kept the machine running thus faded. Insubordinate soldiers also sped the decay of the state, as turbulent janissaries frequently deposed sultans.

Finally, in a society where religion was the only test of nationality, all Orthodox Christians were automatically regarded as Greeks, and lived under the control of the patriarch. As time passed this alienated many Slavs and Rumanians who might otherwise have been loyal subjects.

THE EMPIRE

Expansion, to 1566. The core of the Ottoman state was the same as that around which the Byzantine Empire had been built—Asia Minor and the Balkans. From this core before the death of Mohammed II in 1481, the Turks expanded across the Danube into modern Rumania, seized the Genoese outposts

Ottoman Empire to 1683

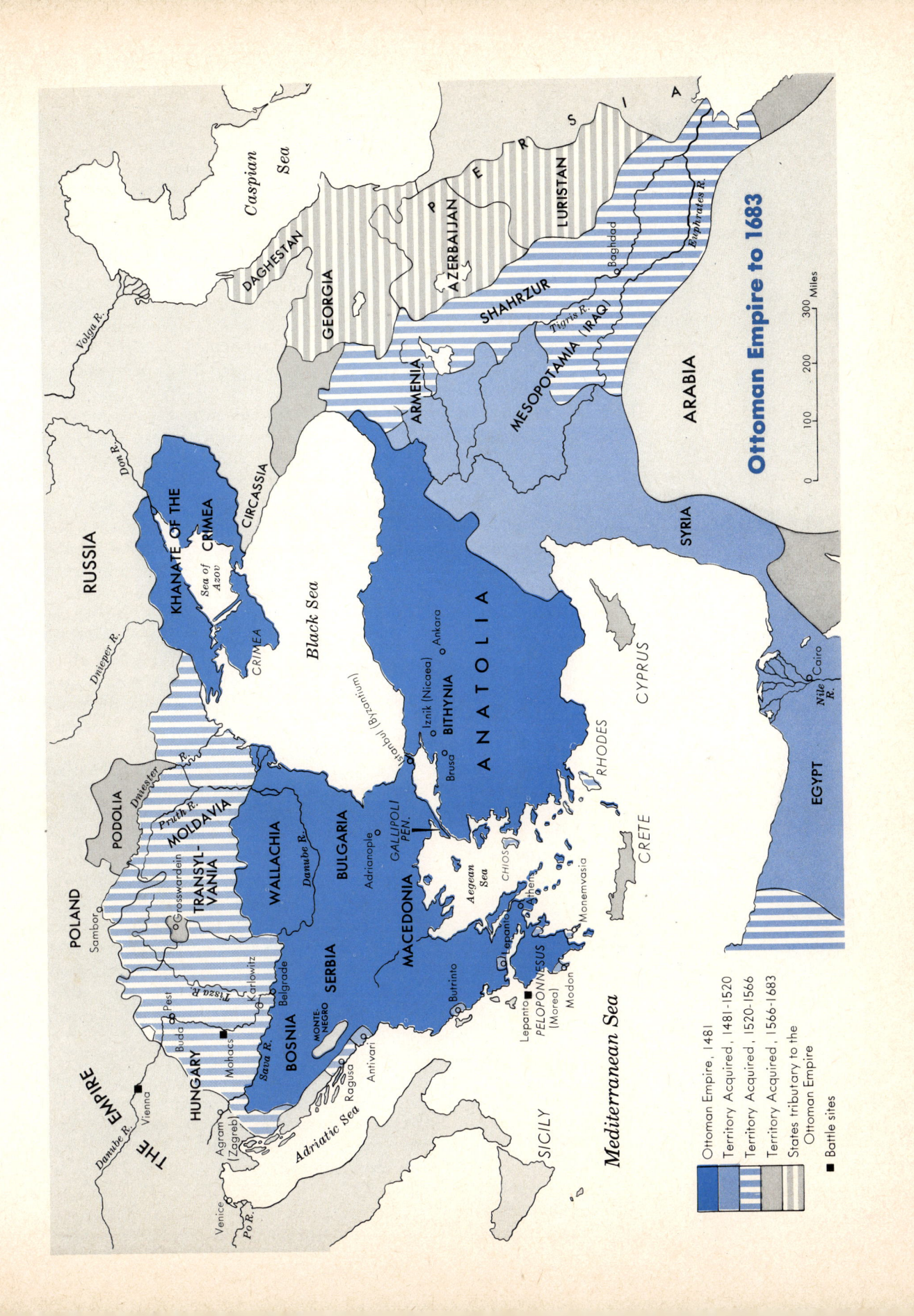

- Ottoman Empire, 1481
- Territory Acquired, 1481–1520
- Territory Acquired, 1520–1566
- Territory Acquired, 1566–1683
- States tributary to the Ottoman Empire
- Battle sites

0 100 200 300 Miles

in the Crimea, and made this southern Russian region a vassal state under its Tartar rulers. But they failed to take either the great Hungarian fortress of Belgrade, key to a further advance into Central Europe, or the island fortress of Rhodes in the Mediterranean, stronghold of the Hospitallers and key to a further naval advance westward.

Sultan Selim I (reigned 1512–1520) nearly doubled the territories of the Empire—in Asia, at the expense of the Persians, and in Africa, where Egypt was annexed in 1517 and the rule of the Mamluks ended. From them the Sultan inherited the duty of protecting Mecca and Medina, and he also assumed the title of caliph. The character of the Ottoman state was substantially altered by these acquisitions, for the overwhelming majority of the population was now Moslem, mostly Arabs, often more fanatical than the Turks.

The advance into Europe was resumed by Suleiman the Magnificent (reigned 1520–1566), who participated in the dynastic wars between the Habsburgs and the French Valois, and even affected the course of the Protestant Reformation by the threat of a military invasion of Germany (see Chapter 7). In 1521, Suleiman took Belgrade, and in 1522, Rhodes, thus removing the two chief obstacles to westward advance. In 1526, at Mohács in Hungary, he defeated the Christian armies, and the Turks entered Buda, the Hungarian capital on the middle Danube. In September 1529, Suleiman besieged Vienna, posing a threat to Christendom greater than any since Leo III and Charles Martel had defeated the Arabs in the early eighth century. But the Turkish lines of communication were greatly overextended, and Suleiman had to abandon the siege after two weeks. He retained control over the south-central portion of Hungary and added other lands north and east of the Danube. In North Africa he acquired Algeria, which remained an Ottoman vassal state in the western Mediterranean until the nineteenth century. In Asia he defeated the Persians, annexed modern Iraq, including Baghdad, and secured an outlet on the Persian Gulf.

In 1536, a formal treaty was concluded between France and the Ottoman Empire, the first of the famous "capitulations," so designated because it was divided into "articles" or "little heads" (Latin, *capitula*), not because it was a surrender. It permitted the French to buy and sell throughout the Turkish dominions on the same basis as any Turk. They could have resident consuls with civil and criminal jurisdiction over Frenchmen in Turkey. In Turkish territory, Frenchmen were to enjoy complete religious liberty and were also granted a protectorate over the Holy Places, the old aim of the Crusades. The Orthodox Church resented the Roman Catholic gains and the dispute would survive to precipitate the Crimean War in the nineteenth century. These "capitulations" gave France a better position in the Ottoman Empire than that of any other European power; their terms paralleled those of earlier Byzantine trade treaties with Venice and Genoa.

Decline, 1566–1699. After Suleiman, the Ottoman system deteriorated, despite occasional periods of Turkish success. The Ottoman capture of Cyprus in 1571 led to the formation of a Western league against the Turk, headed by the pope. In the same year the league won the great naval battle of Lepanto, off the Greek coast, but failed to follow up the victory, thus permitting the Turks to recover.

Within the Ottoman state, the sale of government offices had become a regular practice by the end of the sixteenth century, and the repeated rebellions of janissaries were jeopardizing the sultan's position. Had it not been for the Thirty Years' War (1618–1648), which preoccupied the states of western Europe (*see* Chapter 8), the Ottoman Empire might have suffered even more severely in the first half of the seventeenth century than it did. Several sultans were deposed within a few years; the Persians recaptured Baghdad; rebellion raged in the provinces.

Yet a firm sultan, Murad IV (1623–1640), temporarily restored order through the most brutal means, and what looked like a real revival began with the accession to power of an able family of viziers, the Köprülüs. The first Köprülü ruthlessly executed 36,000 people in a five-year period (1656–1661), hanged the Greek patriarch for predicting that Christianity would defeat Islam, rebuilt the army and navy, and suppressed revolt. Between 1661 and 1676 the second Köprülü led the Ottoman navy to a triumph in Crete, taken from Venice. The Turks temporarily won large areas of the Ukraine from the Russians and Poles, only to lose them again in 1681. In 1683, the Turks again besieged Vienna, with all Europe anxiously awaiting the outcome. For the second time in two centuries, the Turkish wave was broken, and Europe began a great counteroffensive. The Habsburgs drove the Turks out of Hungary, and the Venetians seized the Peloponnesus, while the Russians made their first effective appearance as enemies of the Ottomans. Although the Köprülüs had galvanized the Ottoman armies into a last successful effort, they did not touch the real evils of the Ottoman system.

In 1699 an international congress at Karlovitz on the Danube confirmed Ottoman territorial losses. From then on the European powers could stop worrying about the Ottoman menace, which had preoccupied them ever since the fourteenth century. The importance of Turkey was no longer its military potential, but its diplomatic position as a power in decline over whose possible disintegration and division the states of Europe might squabble and negotiate. With the meeting at Karlovitz, what we call the "Eastern question" began. Forced onto the defensive, the Ottoman Turks had to go outside their slave-family for administrators. Against their will they came to rely for diplomacy upon Christian Greeks, born negotiators, with generations of experience in commerce, who retained the talents of their Byzantine ancestors.

VII. Medieval Russia

Of all the achievements of the Byzantines perhaps the most remarkable was their impact on the Slavic world. As old Rome civilized and eventually christianized large groups of "barbarians" in western Europe, so Constantinople, the new Rome, civilized and christianized the Slavs. Many of the problems that beset the West today in its dealings with the Soviet Union arise from the fact that the Soviet Union is still essentially Russia, a country in the Orthodox and not in the Western tradition, a country that still shows the effects of having experienced its conversion from Byzantium.

RUS AND BYZANTIUM

Into the great plains of European Russia, lying between the Baltic and the Black Sea—where movement is easiest along the north–south courses of the rivers—Scandinavians called "Rus" began to penetrate in the eighth century. We know few details of their conquests of the peoples then living on the steppe, mostly Slavs, but also Lithuanians and Finns. The Old Russian Primary Chronicle, compiled during the eleventh century, reports that during the 850's the struggling tribes of the steppe actually invited the Scandinavians in to keep order, and that Rurik, a Danish warrior, accepted. Moving south along the Dnieper River from the Baltic area and the trading center of Novgorod, the Scandinavians seized the settlement called Kiev and made it the center of a state, at first loosely organized and especially devoted to trade. And in 860, for the first time, a fleet of two hundred of their warships appeared off Constantinople. In this and later clashes, the Byzantines were victorious.

The Primary Chronicle also preserves the texts of the trade treaties between Byzantium and the Russians. While the Byzantines took precautions to protect their lives and property from the wild barbarians, they wanted the furs and timber that the Russians brought them. In the trade treaty of 945, some of the Russians were already Christians, for they swore by the Holy Cross. But the conversion of the Russians as a whole occurred in the 980's in the reign of Vladimir. Like Boris the Bulgarian before him, Vladimir felt that the old worship of forest- and water-spirits and a thunder-god was inadequate. The Primary Chronicle tells how Vladimir surveyed Islam, Judaism, and the Christianity of the Germans (Roman Catholicism) and finally chose the Christianity of Byzantium because of the awe-inspiring beauty of Santa Sophia and the services held there. No doubt Vladimir was also moved by the opportunity to marry a Byzantine princess, and so to acquire some of Byzantium's prestige. In one day he threw down all the idols in Kiev and had the entire population forcibly baptized in the waters of the Dnieper.

THE IMPACT OF CONVERSION

Conversion meant the introduction of priests, a new and important social class. The clergy had jurisdiction over all Christians in cases involving morals, family affairs, or religious questions. Christianity brought with it the advanced concept that crime should be punished by the state rather than avenged by the victim or his family. The Church introduced the first education, and churchmen, using the Cyrillic alphabet, wrote the first literature, chiefly ecclesiastical. Byzantine art-forms were imported and imitated; the great church of Santa Sophia at Kiev is in its way as magnificent as its prototype at Constantinople. Culture was confined to the few cities and to the monasteries, for paganism died slowly in the countryside. In the early period, the archbishops of Kiev were Greeks from Byzantium, but the Russian Church soon asserted its practical independence. From the first it became a large landowner, and monasteries quickly multiplied.

In the West every educated priest, no matter what his native tongue, knew Latin and had access to Latin classics and the Latin Church Fathers. The Russian priests had no such advantage; since Slavic was used in the liturgy, few of them learned Greek. Sermons, saints' lives, some chronicles, and *Basil Digenes Akritas* (*see* p. 195) were translated from Greek and circulated in Slavic, but they were no substitutes for the classics or the Fathers. Indeed, in the nineteenth century an influential group of Russian thinkers argued that the Byzantine faith had fostered stagnation and intellectual sterility; their opponents, however, argued that it had given the Russians spirituality, a willingness to bend to God's will, and other great virtues. It would be hard to deny that conversion from Byzantium cut Russia off from access to the treasure-house of Western culture and was in some measure responsible for Russian "cultural lag."

KIEVAN SOCIETY AND POLITICS

Kievan Russia developed a society rather similar to that in medieval western Europe. The entourage of the prince, which began as a Scandinavian war-band, gradually became a group of councilors appropriate to a settled state. The law-codes reflected social conditions: arson and horse-theft were more heavily punishable than murder. Because the Byzantines paid cash for the Russian forest products, Kiev had more of a money-economy than manorial western Europe.

The Kievan ruling house contracted dynastic marriages with the royal families of Sweden and France, and made alliances with the Holy Roman Emperors. Merchants from the West appeared in the area, especially at Novgorod ("new town") in the north and at Kiev itself. Had the Russians been able to maintain and develop these promising lines of communication, they might have overcome whatever handicap had been imposed by Byzantine Christianity. But they were denied the opportunity.

When a Kievan prince died, his sons divided up the land as if it were their private property—a custom that caused the fragmentation of territory and authority. The mutually hostile petty principalities thus established weakened Kievan society in the face of outside dangers. In the eleventh century, the Turkic tribe of Polovtsy or Cumans appeared on the southern steppes. The warring Russian princes made the tragic mistake of hiring bands of Polovtsy. The sole surviving heroic poem of the Kievan period, the *Song of the Expedition of Igor*, quite comparable with the French *Chanson de Roland* (*see* p. 177), reproves the princes for introducing the infidels and compounding chaos. Shortly after 1200, the Mongol Tartars made their appearance, and the Kievan state as such disappeared. It bequeathed to later Russians the ideal of unity, the common heritage of language, and the Christian faith.

POLITICS FROM 1200 TO 1450

The Western Lands and Novgorod. During the confused 250 years following the collapse of Kiev, Russian national life continued in several centers. The southwestern region, including Kiev itself, became a virtually independent principality, distinguished by an unruly nobility who hampered all efforts of the princes to consolidate their power in the face of pressure from their Polish and Lithuanian neighbors. A parallel development marked the northwest region, centering around the cities of Polotsk and Smolensk. By the early fourteenth century, the Grand Duke of Lithuania held nominal rule over most of these western lands. Still mostly pagan, the Lithuanians in some measure took over the language and attitudes of their more advanced Russian vassals. In 1386, a famous dynastic marriage united Lithuania with Poland, and the influence of the Polish Roman Catholic Church and the Polish nobility now superseded that of the Orthodox Russians.

The western lands comprised feudal Russia, where the local nobles, Russian or Polish, ruled their lands without interference from the Grand Duke of Lithuania. The economic base was manorial like that in the West, and restrictions on the movement of peasants appeared here long before they did elsewhere in Russia. Feudal decentralization and the heavy Polish-Catholic influence meant that the western lands could never become the center around which Russia could reunite.

The northern regions of Russia, between the Baltic shore and Lake Ilmen, and stretching far north and northeast over empty wastes to the Arctic Ocean and Siberia, lay under the dominion of the town commonwealth of Novgorod. Long before Kiev collapsed, Novgorod cherished a tradition of municipal independence; its city council became its most powerful institution. Novgorod traded with the West, especially Germany, exchanging its forest products for cloth and metalwork. Since its soil was infertile, it depended on the area to the southeast, around Moscow, for grain. Novgorod's inability to solve its social and economic problems deprived it of a chance to unify Russia. A few rich merchant families came to control its council and struggled with each other for power; the poor, meantime, might be sold into slavery for debt or turn brigand. In the fifteenth century, when Poland–Lithuania and the principality of Moscow competed, the upper classes supported the Poles and Lithuanians, and the lower classes supported Moscow. In 1478 Moscow conquered Novgorod, wiped out the upper classes, and took away the bell, symbol of town independence.

Moscow and the Tartars. After the collapse of Kiev the principality of Moscow to the northeast was still a newly settled frontier area. Though agriculturally poorer than the fertile southwest, it was richer than the north and could provide food enough for its people; it also had flourishing forest industries. Since neither cities nor a nobility had developed to any marked extent, the pioneers turned to the prince for leadership.

This was also the region most exposed to the Tartars. By the early thirteenth century, Genghis Khan had consolidated a large number of the Mongolian nomads of Central Asia; he then led them into the steppes of southern Russia, defeating Russians and Polovtsy together in 1223. His nephew Baty returned in the 1230's, sacked Moscow in 1237 and Kiev in 1240, and moved on into the western Russian regions and Poland, Hungary, and Bohemia. The success of the Tartars seems to have been due to their excellent military organization and deceptive battle tactics. Though Baty defeated the Poles and the Germans in 1241, political affairs in Asia drew him eastward, and the Tartars never again appeared so far to the west. At Sarai, near the great bend of the Volga, he founded the capital of a new state—the "Golden Horde," which accepted the overlordship of the far-off central government of the Mongols, in Peking.

In Russia the Tartars laid waste to the land while they were conquering it, but after the conquest they shifted their emphasis to levying tribute. It was not to their interest to disturb economic life, so long as their authority was recognized. They drafted some Russian recruits for their armies, but generally made the Russian princes responsible for the deliveries of men and money, and stayed out of Russian territory except to take censuses, survey property, and punish the recalcitrant. The tributary Russian princes, on assuming office, travelled to Sarai to do homage. The expensive burden of tribute and the humiliating sense of subservience fell most heavily upon the region of Moscow.

Toward the end of the fourteenth century, as the Mongol Empire grew feebler, the Russians became bolder. The first Russian victories over the Tartars, scored by a prince of Moscow in 1378 and 1380, were fiercely avenged; yet they served to show that the Tartars could be defeated. When the Golden Horde disintegrated in the early fifteenth century, three Tartar states were formed from its debris: one at Kazan on the middle Volga, which blocked the course of the river to Russian trade for another century and a half; a second at Astrakhan at the mouth of the Volga on the Caspian; and a third in the Crimea, which later became a vassal of the Ottoman sultan.

Though some argue that the Tartar impact was beneficial to Russia because it eventually enabled the prince of Moscow to centralize his power, it seems certain that the conquest also had a very serious negative effect. The Tartars, despite their military efficiency, were bearers of a lower culture than the Russians of the Kievan period had already achieved; when their power was finally shattered in the fifteenth century, Russian civilization was far behind that of the West. To the retarding effect of Byzantine Christianity had been added the tremendous handicap of two centuries of cultural stagnation.

THE MUSCOVITE STATE

During these two centuries, the princes of Moscow assumed leadership. They were shrewd administrators, who married into powerful families and acquired land by inheritance, by purchase, and by foreclosing mortgages. They

Medieval and Early Modern Russia

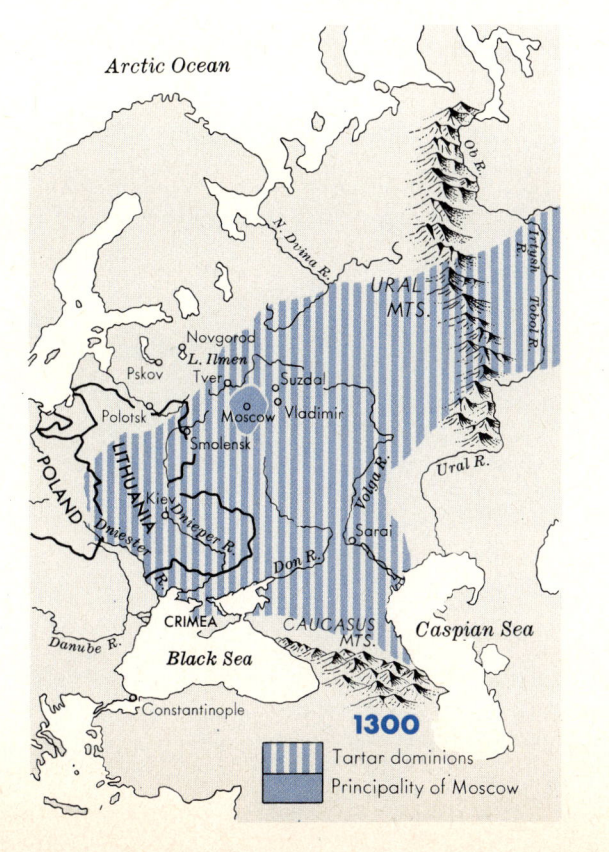

1300
Tartar dominions
Principality of Moscow

1689
At accession of Peter the Great

established the principle of seniority, so that their domain was not divided among their sons and the tragedy of Kiev was not repeated. They developed useful relations with their Tartar overlords, who chose them to collect the tribute from neighboring princes and to deliver it to Sarai. The princes kept a close watch on the Tartars, so that when the moment of Tartar weakness came, they could take advantage of it. They could truthfully claim to be the agents of liberation and champions of Russia.

Finally, and very possibly most important, the princes of Moscow secured the support of the Russian Church. In the early fourteenth century the Metropolitan Archbishop deliberately transferred his see to Moscow, and made it the ecclesiastical capital of Russia. When the effective line of Muscovite princes faltered temporarily, the Metropolitan administered the principality loyally and effectively until the princely house recovered. Ivan III of Moscow (reigned 1462–1503) put himself forward as the heir to the princes of Kiev and declared that he intended to regain the ancient Russian lands that had been lost to Catholic Poles and Moslem Tartars—a national and religious appeal. His wars took on the character of a purely Russian crusade. Many nobles living in the western lands came over to him with their estates and renounced their loyalties to the Lithuanian–Polish state. In 1492, the Prince of Lithuania was forced to recognize Ivan III as sovereign of "all the Russians."

In 1472, Ivan had married the niece of the last Byzantine emperor, Constantine XI. He adopted the Byzantine title of *autocrat,* used the Byzantine double-headed eagle as his seal, and began to behave like a Byzantine emperor. He sometimes used the title tsar (Caesar) and no longer consulted his nobles on matters of state but reached decisions in solitude. Italian architects built him an enormous palace, the Kremlin, a building set apart, like the one at Byzantium.

In short, from the late fifteenth century on, we find the tsars acting like autocrats. Perhaps constant war helped foster autocracy: a national emergency prolonged over centuries naturally led to a kind of national dictatorship. Unlike the nobles of western Europe, those of Muscovy did not unite to fight the rising monarchy for their privileges, but split into various factions, with which the monarch could deal individually. In the West, the Church itself was a part of feudal society, and jealous of its prerogatives; in Russia it became the ally of the monarchy and a department of state. Russian churchmen knew all about Rome's claim to world empire and Constantinople's centuries-long position as "new Rome." With the fall of Constantinople to the Turks, they elaborated a famous theory that Moscow was the successor to the two former world capitals:

> The Church of Old Rome fell because of its heresy; the gates of the Second Rome, Constantinople, have been hewn down by the infidel Turks; but the Church of Moscow, the Church of the New Rome, shines brighter than the Sun in the whole Universe.... Two Romes have fallen, but the Third stands fast; a fourth there cannot be.*

Between the accession of Ivan III in 1462 and the accession of Peter the Great in 1689, the autocracy succeeded in overcoming the opposition of the old nobility. This was done in part by fostering a class of military service gentry who owed everything to the tsar. Their estates, at first granted only for life in exchange for service, eventually became hereditary. The estates of the old nobility, which

---

* Quoted by A. J. Toynbee, in *Civilization on Trial* (New York, 1948), p. 171.

had always been hereditary but for which they had owed no service, became service-estates. Thus, by the end of the period, the two types of noble and the two types of estate had by a gradual process become almost identical. The hereditary nobles often owed service; the military-service nobles often had hereditary land.

This tremendously important social process was accompanied by another, which is really the other side of the coin—the growth of serfdom. Economic factors and political unrest had forced more and more peasants to become dependent on large landowners. The peasants would accept contracts that involved a money loan and that required rent in produce and service on the landlord's lands. By the early seventeenth century it had become customary that the peasant could not leave his plot until he had paid off the loan. Since the debt was often too big for him to repay, he could in practice never leave.

The process was enormously speeded up when the tsars gave estates to the military service gentry, who received help from the government in keeping farmers on the land. Since the peasants paid most of the taxes, it was easier for the government to collect revenues if it kept the peasants where they were. Gradually it was made harder and harder for a tenant to leave his landlord, until by 1649 the avenues of escape were closed and the serf was fixed to the soil. The landlord administered justice, had police rights on the estate, and collected the serfs' taxes. He himself could sell, exchange, or give away his serfs, whose status became hereditary. Together with the absolute autocracy, the institution of serfdom was *the* most characteristic feature of Russian society, and its consequences are still with us today.

Ivan the Terrible and the Time of Troubles. Most of the disorders of sixteenth- and seventeenth-century Russia had their origin in the long reign of Ivan IV, the Terrible (1534–1584). Ivan succeeded to the throne as a small child, suffering helplessly the indignities inflicted on him by rival groups of intriguing nobles. When Ivan was strong enough to assume power, he regulated the rapacity of the provincial administrators who had oppressed the population. He also convoked the first *zemski sobor* (land assembly), a consultative body consisting of nobles, clerics, and town representatives, to assist particularly with important questions of war and peace. Comparable to the various assemblies of the medieval western European world, the *zemski sobor* under Ivan seems to have met only once.

When Ivan became ill in 1553, the nobles refused to swear allegiance to his son. Upon his recovery he created a fantastic new institution: the *oprichnina,* or "separate realm," which was to belong to him personally, while the rest of Russia continued to be administered as before. His new officers (called *oprichniks*), grimly dressed in black, and riding black horses, bore on their saddle-bows a dog's head (for vigilance) and a broom (symbolizing a clean sweep). These forerunners of the secret police waged a relentless war on the nobles, confiscating their estates, exiling them, killing them off. By the time of Ivan's death Russian

Ivan the Terrible, a contemporary portrait now in the National Museum of Denmark.

administration had degenerated to a state approximating chaos. Pathologically cruel, Ivan had seven wives and murdered his own son in a fit of rage. Yet Ivan extended Russian authority to the east against the Tartars, thus opening the whole Volga waterway to Russian commerce and facilitating expansion further east, into Siberia.

The few foreign observers who knew the Russia of Ivan could foresee collapse. And the Tsar himself wrote in his last will: "The body is exhausted, the spirit is ailing, the spiritual and physical wounds multiply, and there is no doctor to cure me."* With the death of his imbecile son Fedor (1598), the Moscow dynasty, descended from the Kievan princes, died out. Fedor's able brother-in-law, Boris Godunov (reigned 1598–1605), could not deal with the legacy of disorder, especially after a famine and plague began in 1601. Brigands roamed the countryside, a pretender under Polish protection claimed to be a son of Ivan the Terrible, and Russia was launched on the "Time of Troubles" (1603–1613).

The Pretender himself ruled briefly as Tsar, but was murdered within a year. New pretenders arose; civil war continued as Poles and Swedes intervened. Polish forces took Moscow, and the King of Poland planned to become Tsar. In answer to an appeal from the Patriarch, a kind of Russian national militia assembled, drawn from the prosperous free farmers of the middle Volga region. Under the combined command of a butcher and a nobleman, the militia drove the Poles from Moscow in 1613. The prospect of foreign Catholic rule had produced an explosion of Russian national sentiment.

The First Romanovs. A *zemski sobor* now elected Michael Romanov Tsar. From the election of Michael in 1613 to the Russian Revolution of 1917, the Romanovs held the throne. Michael succeeded with no limitations placed upon his power by the *zemski sobor*; he was an elected autocrat. For the first ten years of his reign the *zemski sobor* stayed in continuous session to give the new dynasty the semblance of popular support if needed. But the *zemski sobor* never transformed itself into a parliament, and after 1623 it was summoned only to help declare war or make peace, to approve new taxation, and to sanction important new legislation. It endorsed the accession of Michael's son Alexius (1645–1676), and in 1649 it confirmed a new law code. After 1653 Alexius did not summon it again, nor did his son, Fedor (1676–1682). Its last meetings were in 1682.

The early Romanovs were neither distinguished nor talented. The ill-defined departments of the central government often had overlapping areas of competence. Provincial governors milked the long-suffering population, and local efforts at self-government were in practice limited to the choice of officials who collected taxes for the central authorities. Opposition came not from articulate citizens but from the oppressed and hungry peasantry, who burned manor houses and killed landlords or tax-collectors. Such uprisings were almost never directed against the tsar; often indeed the peasant leaders would arouse their followers *in the name* of the tsar, or pretend to be tsars.

During the sixteenth and seventeenth centuries Russian pioneers, in search of furs to sell and new land to settle, led the way in the tremendous physical expansion of the Russian domain. Russian frontiersmen known as Cossacks (a Tartar word meaning "free adventurer") organized themselves for self-defense

---

* Quoted by M. T. Florinsky, *Russia, A History and an Interpretation,* Vol. I (New York, 1953), p. 208.

against the Tartars. Two Cossack republics arose, one on the Dnieper, the other on the Don, living in a kind of primitive democracy relatively independent of Moscow. As time passed, more Cossack groups formed in the Volga, in the Urals, and elsewhere.

The most dramatic expansion rapidly took the Russians eastward into the Urals and across Siberia to the Pacific. Far more slowly, because of Tartar, Turkish, and Polish opposition, the Russians also moved southeast toward the Black Sea. Repeatedly Russians and Poles fought over the old west-Russian territory of the Ukraine, but by 1682 the Poles were beginning to yield. The Swedes still blocked the Baltic exit into the North Sea. On the southern steppes the Russians struggled against the Crimean Tartars. The Turks, overlords of the Tartars, held the key fort of Azov, controlled the Black Sea, participated in the wars over the Ukraine, and now became perennial enemies of the tsars.

The Church and Foreign Influences. The Church remained the partner of the autocracy. The tsar controlled the election of the Metropolitan of Moscow, and after 1589 that of the newly proclaimed Patriarch of Moscow. Tsar Alexius (1645–1676) appointed to the patriarchal throne a cleric named Nikon, whose arrogance aroused protests from both the clergy and the laity. He seriously advanced the theory that, since the spiritual realm was superior to the temporal, the patriarch was actually superior to the tsar. In the West the more powerful popes had maintained this view, but in Byzantium or in Russia few churchmen ever dared. In 1666, a church council deposed Nikon, who died a mere monk, and Peter the Great was to abolish the patriarchate largely because he wished to silence Nikon's claims forever.

By 1500 the Russian monasteries owned more than one-third of the land available for cultivation. Opposition to monastic worldliness arose within the Church itself. But those who favored monastic poverty also wished to enforce the noninterference of the state in monastic affairs. To preserve its rights to control the monasteries in other respects, the government of the tsar therefore opposed the reforming movement that it would otherwise have acclaimed.

The Church, almost alone, inspired the art and literature of the Muscovite period. The icon, inherited from Byzantium, was the type of painting that flourished. Historical chronicles were written by the monks, and theological tracts attacked both Catholics and Protestants, whose doctrines were known in the western regions. This limited literature was written in Old Church Slavonic, the language of the liturgy but not of everyday speech. There was no Russian secular learning, no science, no flowering of vernacular literature, no lively philosophical debate.

Slowly and gradually, during the sixteenth and seventeenth centuries foreigners and foreign ideas penetrated into Russia. The small group of talented

Fourteenth-century icon of St. Nicholas.

Italians who built the Kremlin in the late fifteenth century had little lasting influence. Ivan IV welcomed the English and encouraged them to trade their woolen cloth for Russian timber, rope, pitch, and other naval supplies, which helped build the Elizabethan fleets that defeated the Spanish Armada. The English taught the Russians some industrial techniques and supplied a large number of officers, mostly Scots, for the Tsar's armies. In the mid-seventeenth century the Dutch displaced them as the leading foreign residents, managing their own glass, paper, and textile plants in Russia.

The foreign quarter of Moscow, always called the "German suburb," grew rapidly. German, Dutch, Danish technicians—bronze-founders, textile-weavers, clock-makers—received large salaries from the state. Foreign physicians and druggists became fashionable, though the common people thought they were wizards. Merchants continued to enjoy special privileges much to the disgust of their native competitors. A few nobles began to buy books, assemble libraries, and learn Latin, French, or German; some began to eat salad and take snuff and even to converse politely. Some Russians went abroad to travel, and most of these refused to go home. The lower classes, however, distrusted and hated the foreigners, and jeered at them on the street.

The most dramatic outburst of antiforeign feeling was precipitated by learned clerics from the Ukraine and Greece who recommended to Patriarch Nikon that the Holy Books be corrected in certain places where the texts were unsound. Many Russians were horrified. With their deep regard for the externals, the rite, the magic, they were now told that they were spelling the name of Jesus wrong, and using the wrong number of fingers in crossing themselves. Opponents of change split away from the Church, and some 20,000 of them burned themselves alive, convinced that the end of the world was at hand, since Moscow, the Third Rome, had become heretical, and there would be no fourth. Survivors settled down and became sober, solid citizens, called "Old Believers," many of them merchants and well-to-do farmers. Some later Russian governments persecuted them. The influx of foreigners thus not only introduced the Russians to Western technology well before the advent of Peter the Great, but also profoundly split Russian society and the Russian Church.

5

READING SUGGESTIONS (asterisk indicates paperbound edition)

Byzantium

G. Ostrogorsky, *History of the Byzantine State* (Rutgers, 1957). A brilliant historical synthesis, with rich bibliography.

A. A. Vasiliev, *History of the Byzantine Empire, 324–1453*, 2 vols. (*Wisconsin). A good comprehensive work.

J. M. Hussey, *The Byzantine World* (*Torchbooks). Useful shorter sketch.

The Cambridge Medieval History, IV, Part I (Cambridge University, 1966). Collaborative work by many excellent scholars treating Byzantium and its neighbors.

J. B. Bury, *A History of the Later Roman Empire, 395–802*, 2 vols. (Macmillan, 1889). A celebrated old study; a revision of the first volume (*Dover) is the best work on the period 395–565.

———, *A History of the Eastern Roman Empire, 802–867* (Macmillan, 1912). Distinguished scholarly treatment.

C. Diehl, *Byzantine Portraits* (Knopf, 1927). Excellent essays on personalities.

———, *Byzantium: Greatness and Decline* (*Rutgers). Another thoughtful study.

J. M. Hussey, *Church and Learning in the Byzantine Empire 867–1185* (Oxford, 1937).

An excellent introduction to the subject.

A. Grabar, *Byzantine Painting* (Skira, 1953). Superb reproductions of mosaics and frescoes.

Islam

F. Rahman, *Islam* (Weidenfeld & Nicholson, 1966). Sound comprehensive introduction by a Moslem scholar.

H. A. R. Gibb, *Mohammedanism: An Historical Survey* (°Galaxy). A meaty introduction by a great authority.

———, *Studies in the Civilization of Islam* (°Beacon). A collection of perceptive essays.

B. Lewis, *The Arabs in History* (°Torchbooks). Crisp and suggestive survey.

W. Montgomery Watt, *Muhammad: Prophet and Statesman* (°Oxford). Clear and informative study.

T. Andrae, *Mohammed: The Man and His Faith* (°Torchbooks). A scholarly appreciation and interpretation.

K. Cragg, *Call of the Minaret* (°Galaxy). Analysis by a Protestant missionary.

The Crusades

A History of the Crusades: Vol. I, *The First Hundred Years,* ed. by M. W. Baldwin; Vol. II, *The Later Crusades, 1189–1311,* ed. by R. L. Wolff and H. W. Hazard (University of Pennsylvania, 1955, 1962). Collaborative and authoritative work.

S. Runciman, *A History of the Crusades,* 3 vols. (°Torchbooks). The fullest treatment of the topic by a single scholar.

J. L. LaMonte, *Feudal Monarchy in the Latin Kingdom of Jerusalem* (Medieval Academy, 1932). Important study of Crusader political institutions.

W. Miller, *The Latins in the Levant: A History of Frankish Greece, 1204–1566* (Dutton, 1908), and *Essay on the Latin Orient* (Cambridge, 1921). Two good studies of Westerners in Greece.

The Ottoman Empire

E. S. Creasy, *History of the Ottoman Turks* (Khayats, 1961). New edition of a good general account that was first published in the 1850's.

H. A. R. Gibb and H. Bowen, *Islamic Society and the West,* Vol. I, Parts 1 and 2 (Oxford University, 1950, 1956). Scholarly survey of Ottoman institutions.

E. Pears, *The Destruction of the Greek Empire and the Story of the Capture of Constantinople by the Turks* (Longmans, 1903).

A solid work, not superseded by later studies.

H. A. Gibbons, *The Foundation of the Ottoman Empire* (Century, 1916), and P. Wittek, *The Rise of the Ottoman Empire* (Luzac, 1958). Two perceptive studies of the forces accounting for the rapid development of the Turkish state.

A. H. Lybyer, *The Government of the Ottoman Empire in the Time of Suleiman the Magnificent* (Harvard University, 1913). Lively pioneering study, now outdated.

Medieval Russia

V. O. Kluchevsky, *A History of Russia,* 5 vols. (Dent, 1911–1931). The greatest single work on the subject, poorly translated.

M. Florinsky, *Russia: A History and an Interpretation,* Vol. I (Macmillan, 1953). A good textbook, solid and accurate.

G. Vernadsky, *Kievan Russia* and *The Mongols and Russia* (Yale, 1948, 1953). Vols. II and III of the Yale History of Russia; authoritative and complete.

G. P. Fedotov, *The Russian Religious Mind,* 2 vols. (Harvard, 1946, 1966). A study of the Kievan period from a most unusual point of view.

Sources

Procopius, 7 vols. (Loeb Classical Library, 1914–1940). Writings of a major historian who lived through the events recounted.

Digenes Akritas (Clarendon, 1956). The Byzantine frontier epic.

A. J. Arberry, *The Koran Interpreted* (°Macmillan). The best modern translation.

William, Archbishop of Tyre, *A History of Deeds Done beyond the Sea,* 2 vols. (Columbia University, 1943). The best contemporary account of the Crusades.

Memoirs of the Crusades (°Everyman). Eyewitness accounts of the Fourth Crusade and of the crusade of St. Louis.

Memoirs of Usamah ibn-Munqidh (Columbia, 1929). An Easterner observes the Western invaders.

The Life and Letters of Ogier Ghiselin de Busbecq (C. K. Paul, 1881). By the Habsburg ambassador to Suleiman the Magnificent.

The Russian Primary Chronicle, Laurentian Text (Medieval Academy, 1953). Our oldest source for early Russian history.

The Correspondence between Prince A. M. Kurbsky and Tsar Ivan IV of Russia and *Kurbsky's History of Ivan IV,* both ed. by J. L. I. Fennell (Cambridge, 1955, 1965). Fundamental sources for the political theories of the Tsar and his opponents.

6

Transition to a New World

Late Middle Ages and Renaissance

The Piazza del Campidoglio, Rome, designed by Michelangelo in 1538.

The transition from the medieval to the modern world begins with the fourteenth and fifteen centuries. Everywhere in the West we find the hastening growth of a materialistic spirit. In France and the Low Countries, in Germany, and in England, the prevailing mood (with variations, of course) was one of depression and uncertainty, as old institutions were decaying and people became unsure and pessimistic about the future. By contrast, in Italy—where feudalism and manorialism had never gained so strong a hold—the exuberant life of the city-states produced a spirit very like that of the greatest days of ancient Greece. Here, in spite of the cynicism and brutality of politics, the mood was one of optimism. Italy gave civilization itself a new impetus that would later inspire the regions north of the Alps.

We begin with the economy and with society: depression, plague, and agricultural decline accompanied commercial advances. As the hired mercenary replaced the feudal noble in the battlefield, the rich townsman was gradually inheriting his economic influence. We continue with politics: in France, England, and Spain the centralized new national monarchies triumphed. In Germany, particularism developed still further. In Italy the towns became the centers of the national life. We conclude with the Renaissance, the unparalleled flowering of literature and learning, of painting, sculpture, and the other arts, beginning in Italy but soon spreading northward.

I. The Economy and Society of the Fourteenth and Fifteenth Centuries

DEPRESSION IN THE WEST

Just as the population growth of the eleventh century helped to advance the European economy (*see* Chapter 4), so a population decline in the fourteenth and fifteenth centuries helped to shrink both the supply of labor and the market for products. Large-scale warfare caused most regimes to debase their coinage, leading to inflation and wild price fluctuation. One can sense everywhere except in Italy that the optimism of the thirteenth century shifted to a mood of deepening pessimism in the fourteenth and fifteenth. Nobody really understood what was going on, uneasiness prevailed, and many people strove to deny that any changes were taking place.

More and more, money underlay social relationships as it never had during the earlier period. For the peasant in good times, the gain was great: it was more agreeable to pay cash than owe physical labor. But then in hard times, when there was no cash to pay, his loss was great. The security of serfdom, the inherited right to work and live on certain land and eat its produce, had diminished, sometimes to the vanishing point. Often the peasants would simply move off the land and try to sell their labor in the towns. Since the price of farm products fell off while the prices of other commodities rose, the landowner was caught in a squeeze.

The Black Death (bubonic plague) of 1348–1349 and subsequent plagues speeded these tendencies. Disease wiped out between a fifth to a third of the population, especially in thickly settled regions. Having suddenly become scarce, manpower grew expensive. Peasants found they could force the landlords to commute for cash the services they still owed; the landlords, in turn, strove to hold on to whatever services they could and sought the help of governments in keeping wages down. In France, in England, in Florence, we shall encounter wild outbreaks of social unrest. In towns, it was the same: the gilds refused to admit new members; employers and city governments fought to keep wages down. It was not until the later fifteenth century that things gradually got better. In France and England and in much of western Germany, the services owed by the peasantry were now commuted into cash payments, and serfdom was nearing an end, though in eastern Germany the landlords frequently attempted to enforce their old rights. Still further east, as we have seen (Chapter 5) the bonds of serfdom were actually tightening.

COMMERCIAL INNOVATION

The Hansa, Venice, Genoa. During the long depression and slow recovery, we find much new experimentation in commercial methods and organization. Among the most striking was the Hanseatic League, an association (Hansa) of north German seaport trading towns that began by occasionally consulting among themselves and ended by organizing a real federation in the fourteenth century. The cities of Lübeck, Bremen, Hamburg, and Wisby (on the island of Gotland in the Baltic) joined with the German traders abroad in Novgorod, London, Venice, and Bruges to protect and increase their business. They put down piracy and brigands; tried to secure monopolies in fish, timber, amber, furs, and metals; assessed themselves for common expenses; and fought and won a war (1367–1370) against Denmark, which tried to impose tolls on Hanseatic ships. The Hansa regularly called meetings of its representatives at Lübeck, sent its diplomatic agents abroad to negotiate, and did not hesitate to use force to drive English intruders, for example, out of Norwegian fishing grounds (1406). Of course rivalries between the Hansa's own members did not disappear, and the shift of trade-routes to the Atlantic after 1500 helped dry up Hanseatic prosperity.

Venice, by dint of long and repeated warfare, especially against Genoa, and as a result of earlier colonial conquests, dominated the Mediterranean trade as the Hansa did the Baltic. Venice was the marketplace for the spices, silk, sugar, and cotton of the East, and the woolen cloth of the West. In the huge government-operated shipyard, the Arsenal, shipbuilders improved the traditional long, narrow, oar-propelled galley into a faster and more capacious merchant ship. Four galleys a year in this period sailed to Flanders, four to Beirut in Syria, three to the Black Sea, traditional preserve of the Genoese, and about three dozen others to all the major ports of the Mediterranean. The Flanders service (begun in 1317), calling also in London and Southampton, was the first regular all-water service between Italy and northwestern Europe. The Venetians had their own ambassador resident in London, a step soon to be copied by other states.

Genoa, too, had many enterprising merchants. Benedetto Zaccaria, for example, in the 1340's obtained from the Byzantine emperor concessions of alum, a chemical essential in the manufacture of woolens. He built his own fleet to transport alum to the woolen factories in the Low Countries, established a company town with medical services and a population of 3000 at the alum mines in Asia Minor, and in Italy organized a woolen-manufacturing plant of his own. He then obtained a second monopoly, the mastic plant (a luxury useful in perfume and chewed like chewing-gum) on the island of Chios; he kept mastic prices high by limiting the supply. He became so influential that he married his son into the imperial house at Constantinople, and finally flew his own flag.

CAPITALISM

Bankers and Merchant-Princes. Zaccaria's operations—like those of Hanseatic or Venetian merchants—were clearly capitalistic. These men built up their capital in cash and in goods; they used credit on a large scale; they went in for long-range planning; they took heavy risks; they went all out for profits; they counted their labor as part of their costs. One should not overestimate the "modern" features of their operations any more than one should imagine medieval factories as comparable in technology with those of later centuries. But equally, one should not fail to see that their economic attitudes and methods were often the same as ours.

Credit came then, as now, from bankers, but the risks were larger then, and the profits also. Florentine bankers charged 266 per cent annual interest on a loan they thought to be really risky; in 1420 an effort to cut interest rates to a maximum of 20 per cent proved a failure. All this of course came in a period when the Church regarded the loan of money at interest as the sin of usury. Contrary to widespread belief, the Jews did *not* dominate the field of banking; only in Spain did they play a role, and then not after 1492. The Templars were the leading bankers until they were destroyed by Philip the Fair (*see* Chapter 4). Then came the Italians, called "Lombards" (though many came from Tuscany); their memory is preserved in London's Lombard Street. Florentines handled the papal revenues, seeing to it that income from distant lands flowed safely into Rome. The Bardi and Peruzzi families financed both sides in the Hundred Years' War, and went bankrupt when Edward III of England defaulted on his debts in the 1340's. The Medici, who began in the wool business and then added silk and spices to their interests, had branches of their bank in 16 cities in Italy and abroad. In Genoa, the Bank of St. George (founded 1407) took over much of the Mediterranean business of Spanish Jews. In Barcelona, in London, everywhere in cities, men in the profession of making money breed upon money won wealth, power, and influence.

Jacques Coeur (1395–1456) of Bourges obtained the favor of Charles VII of France when that monarch was only a refugee (*see* p. 245). He ran a fleet of trading vessels to and from the Levant, became the director of the mint and chief fiscal agent of the crown, and financed the last campaigns of the Hundred Years' War. He built up a business empire of textile workshops and mines, bought landed estates from impoverished nobles, loaned money to half the dignitaries of France, and arranged noble marriages for his middle-class relatives. But he had too much power; and too many highly placed people owed him too much money. He was disgraced on a trumped-up charge, and died in papal service on an expedition against the Turks.

Jacques Coeur's slightly later German counterparts were the Fugger family of Augsburg. Beginning as linen-weavers, this mighty financial dynasty in the late 1400's became bankers for the popes and the Habsburgs. Soon they had mining concessions scattered throughout central Europe and made a colossal fortune. It was not until 1607, after the Habsburg ruler Philip II of Spain had defaulted on his debts, that the Fuggers were ruined. The Fuggers had the modern spirit of social service, and built for the deserving poor of Augsburg a charming garden village called the "Fuggerei."

Jacob Fugger with his clerk. Note the filing cabinet with labels for Rome, Nuremberg, Lisbon, Venice (Venedig), Milan (Mayland), and other trading centers.

THE NEW MATERIALISM

The Impact on Feudalism. The business class, the bourgeoisie, began to assume an ever greater role, not only in the economy but in political life. Sometimes its members actually came to power, as in Venice or Florence or the Hanseatic towns; sometimes, like the Bardi or the Fuggers, they financed those who wielded power. Often their talents helped a monarch further his interests: Jacques Coeur helped Charles VII; Charles' successor, Louis XI (reigned 1461–1483), depended on the bourgeoisie; so did Henry VII, the first Tudor monarch of England. Similarly, the middle classes, with their wealth and their interest in letters and the arts, moved into the role of patron hitherto reserved for the Church and a few great princes. Bourgeois materialism also pervaded the Church, and many popes were indistinguishable from the economic and political magnates of the day in their attitudes toward money, power, and the arts.

In the upper levels of the feudal world, the new materialism played havoc with old established attitudes and relationships, though often those affected hardly realized what was happening. Some nobles lost all but the name of noble, as their manors came no longer to support them. Their descendants, finding their pockets empty, their status vanishing, were often altogether declassed. Even those who retained or increased their wealth found that in the new monarchies they had to put their obligations to the monarch ahead of their duties to any other suzerain, and so did their vassals.

Moreover, cash transformed warfare. In the great struggles of the fourteenth and fifteenth centuries it was no longer practical to rely on the feudal levy, which was required to fight for a limited time only, and had only miscellaneous equipment. War now required professional troops, who would fight on indefinitely, and could be properly trained and equipped. Commutation of a vassal's military service for money to pay regular troops became a regular practice. Even if a vassal of the king actually did fight, he now did so on the basis of an indenture, stipulating that he would fight for pay. Not only monarchs offered such inducements to their troops; great lords, especially in times when the monarchy was in difficulties, recruited private forces in the same way.

This military system is sometimes called "bastard feudalism," because, while superficially resembling feudalism, it had become something quite different. Both in France and in England, in the fifteenth century, great rival parties of nobles with private armies fought for the control of the central government. The standards of chivalrous conduct that had softened the harshness of earlier feudal periods became corrupt or disappeared. Lords no longer even had as their ideal the maintenance of the peace or the protection of the poor. New knightly orders were founded in the fourteenth and fifteenth centuries: the Garter in England, the Star in France, the Golden Fleece in Burgundy. But all the protestations that these were devout chivalrous bodies with pious work to do could not conceal the fact that they did little and were simply exclusive clubs that all ambitious nobles yearned to join.

The Impact on the Church. Snatched off to Avignon in 1305, the papacy remained there under seven successive popes down to 1378. Though the charming city on the Rhone, deep inside French territory, thus became a papal enclave, their absence from Rome cut the popes off from the ancient source of their spiritual authority. In their magnificent palace and amidst the ostentation of their court, with its smoothly functioning diplomatic service and bureaucracy dedicated to collecting money from Christendom, they too were deeply affected by the materialism of the time. From 1378 to 1409 there were two lines of popes, one at Rome and one at Avignon, and in 1409 a third was added. In this Great Schism, the rulers of Europe decided which pope they preferred on the basis of their national interest. The French supported the Avignonese; the English, naturally enough, the Roman; the Scots, hostile to England, the Avignonese; and so on.

Against this scandal, the Church rallied in the Conciliar Movement, a series of councils beginning at Pisa in 1409, and continuing at Constance (1414–1417) and at Basel (1431–1449). At Constance the unity of the papacy was restored with the election of Martin V (1417–1431), who returned to Rome. The long crisis had given rise to a school of thinkers who urged that the popes yield their autocratic power within the Church and act as constitutional monarchs, with the general councils serving as a kind of parliament. But the restored popes stoutly refused to yield any of their traditional power; and, though often cultivated and able, the popes of the late fifteenth century were also usually corrupt, cynical, and ruthless—for example, the notorious Alexander VI, the Borgia pope (reigned 1492–1503).

Protests against the wealth of the clergy, frequent throughout the Middle Ages, multiplied in this period of ecclesiastical decline. Echoing the Waldensians (*see* Chapter 4), John Wyclif (d. 1384) in England and John Hus (1369–1415) in Bohemia strove for reform. Hus wanted to rid his fellow Czechs of German clerical domination; he was given a safe-conduct to attend the Council of Constance and answer for his opinions, but once there was tried and executed. His Czech followers went underground. Girolamo Savonarola (1452–1498), a Florentine Dominican, led a puritanical reform movement against the vices of the age, calling Alexander VI a devil and a monster. Though for a brief period (1497–1498) he virtually ruled Florence, in the end he failed and was executed.

II. The Making of the New Monarchies

THE HUNDRED YEARS' WAR

Round I. Ever since 987, the Capetian kings of France had regularly produced sons and heirs who survived to take the throne. In 1328 this streak of luck ran out. Three sons of Philip the Fair (*see* Chapter 4) ruled in succession for the years between 1314 and 1328; then the throne passed to a nephew of Philip the Fair, Philip VI of Valois (reigned 1328–1350). But Philip the Fair's daughter Isabelle had married Edward II (reigned 1307–1327) of England, and this made Edward III (reigned 1327–1377) Philip the Fair's grandson. Did not he have a better claim to the throne of France than a mere nephew? In order to dispose of Edward's claim, French lawyers cited a Frankish law of the sixth century (the "Salic" law) that a woman could not inherit land; therefore, they argued, Isabelle never had any rights in France to pass on to Edward.

Although Edward III took this decision as pretext for war, there were other

A Note on the Color Plates

The plates in full color on the succeeding pages are arranged by groups, each providing samples of the varying or contrasting treatments of an artistic theme in different eras. Five of the groups are focussed on great classical subjects—battles, the nativity, the female nude, the landscape, and farming, with its endless cycle of sowing and harvesting. Four groups deal with somewhat less conventional subject matter—animals, sport and recreation, the fantastic, and calligraphy, that is, the adaptation of writing or lettering to ornamental purposes.

The plates range in time from the work of living artists back to the remarkable cave painting by Paleolithic man 14,000 years ago. They range in place from the West itself (Europe and America) to the cradles of Western civilization in the Middle East and to countries like Japan, China, India, and Persia, whose cultures exerted a significant influence on the later development of Western art. Most of the plates are concerned with painting—on the walls of caves, tombs, or churches, on canvas or scrolls, or on the pages of medieval manuscripts. A few illustrate other media—mosaics, for instance, enamel, or pottery. Sculpture, architecture, and formal portraiture have been omitted, since they lend themselves well to reproduction without full color and may be sampled in the illustrations accompanying the text itself.

The plates, then, do not claim to serve as a capsule guide to the history of art. What we hope to accomplish is to give intimations of the extraordinary variety of human artistic achievement and to suggest that any picture must be judged on its own merits, not simply filed into the pigeonhole of antiquity, Renaissance, or modernity. A recent picture is not necessarily better or worse than an older treatment of the same subject; nor is it necessarily more "modern" in the sense of being more imaginative, unconventional, or experimental. The arts, like many other fields of human endeavor, remind us that history is no simple record of progress from primitive crudeness or of decline from some golden age long ago but a very complex cycle of ebb and flow.

Menena superintends the measuring of a field of standing grain and the recording of the result of the harvest. Tempera copy of a wall painting from the tomb of Menena, Thebes, XVIII Dynasty (c. 1415 B.C.). The Metropolitan Museum of Art.

Farming

Pieter Brueghel the Elder, "The Harvesters," 1565.
The Metropolitan Museum of Art, Rogers Fund, 1919.

The Limbourg Brothers, "March," from *Les Très Riches Heures du Duc de Berry*, 1413-1416.
Musée Condé, Chantilly. European Art Color, Peter Adelberg, N.Y.C.

Edward Hicks (1790-1849), "Farm of the Cornells." Brooklyn Museum. Three Lions.

Vincent Van Gogh (1853-1890), "Sower with Setting Sun." Gemeentemuseum, The Hague. Three Lions.

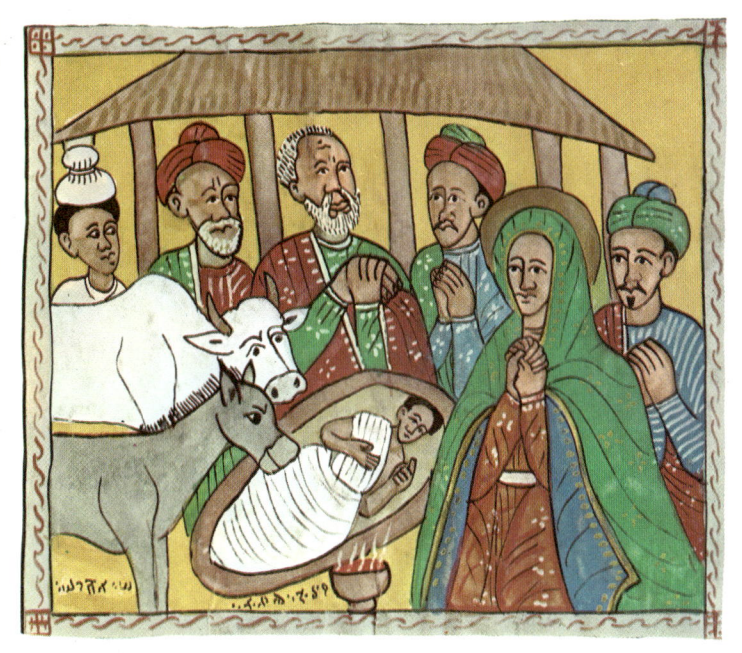

The Nativity

"Adoration of the Shepherds." Coptic, fifth century. Three Lions.

"Adoration of the Magi" (detail). Eighth century mosaic. Sta. Maria in Cosmedin, Rome. Three Lions.

Geertgen van Sint Jans (1465-1493), "Adoration of the Magi."
National Gallery, Prague. Three Lions.

Giovanni Battista Tiepolo (1696-1770), "Adoration of the Kings."
Collection: Prince von Liechtenstein, Vaduz. Three Lions.

Gil de Siloe (fl. 1486/99), "Adoration of the Magi."
Church of Covarrubias, Province of Burgos, Spain. Three Lions.

Emil Nolde (1867-1956), "Adoration of the Magi." Private collection, Germany. Three Lions.

"The Toreador Fresco." Cretan, c. 1500 B.C. Archaeological Museum, Heraklion.

Sport and Recreation

King spearing a lion. Egyptian ostrakon, XIX-XX Dynasty, from Thebes, Valley of the Kings. Painted limestone.

The Metropolitan Museum of Art, The Carnarvon Collection, Gift of Edward S. Harkness, 1926.

Francesco di Giorgio (1439-1502), "The Chess Players."
The Metropolitan Museum of Art, Bequest of Maitland Fuller Griggs, 1943.

Jan Steen (1626-1679), "A Game of Skittles."
Samuel H. Kress Collection, Seattle Art Museum. Three Lions.

Jean-Baptiste Siméon Chardin (1699-1779), "The House of Cards."
National Gallery of Art, Washington, D.C. Three Lions.

Edouard Manet (1832-1883), "Boating."
The Metropolitan Museum of Art. Bequest of Mrs. H. O. Havemeyer, The H. O. Havemeyer Collection. 1929.

Marc Chagall (1877-   ),
"Circus."
National Museum of Fine Arts, Stockholm.
European Art Color, Peter Adelberg, N.Y.C.

Salvador Dali, "Dance with Butterflies," 1951.
Collection: Mrs. Albert D. Lasker.
Three Lions.

Battles

Battle of Alexander the Great against Darius at Issus. Pompeian mosaic.
National Museum, Naples. European Art Color, Peter Adelberg, N.Y.C.

Paolo Uccello (1397-1475), "The Battle of San Romano."
The Louvre, Paris. European Art Color, Peter Adelberg, N.Y.C.

The Earl of Pembroke attacked by the Spanish fleet off La Rochelle, 1372.
Bibliothèque Nationale, Paris. Three Lions.

Francisco de Zurbarán (1598-1664), "The Battle with the Moors at Jerez."

The Metropolitan Museum of Art, Kretschmar Fund, 1920.

good reasons for the French and English to fight. England still possessed the rich French province of Aquitaine, and the French kings constantly encroached there upon the rights of their vassal, the King of England, just as they encroached on other vassals' rights elsewhere. The English wanted to get back all that John had lost to Philip Augustus (*see* Chapter 4). Moreover, in Flanders, where the Count was a vassal of France, the French had been backing the Count and many of the wealthy merchants in a quarrel with other merchants and most of the workers in the woolen industry, backed by the English. Since England exported raw wool to Flanders and bought back manufactured goods, Edward could cut off supplies, thus causing unemployment in Flanders. But since the English crown taxed the wool going and coming, Edward III hurt his own pocketbook too. Jacob van Artevelde, leader of the pro-English party, rose against the French, organized his own government, and recognized Edward III as King of France in exchange for military help and the promise of a steady flow of wool.

In response to Flemish pressure, Edward launched what proved to be the Hundred Years' War (1338–1453). The English won the major battles, and at times controlled most of France. But the French developed a standing army supported by a system of direct taxation, and eventually expelled the English and unified France under a strong national monarchy supported by the middle classes.

After winning command of the Channel (1340), the English invaded France in 1345, and by superior tactics, including the effective use of the longbow, defeated the French at Crécy (1346) and took Calais. After an eight-year truce, marked by the ravages of the Black Death (1348–1349), the English repeated their success at Poitiers (1356), this time taking prisoner King John of France (reigned 1350–1364). John's son, the future Charles V, the Wise (reigned 1364–1380), became regent.

The defeats brought bitter criticism of the French monarchy: the Estates-General (*see* Chapter 4) insisted not only on specifying what sort of taxes might be levied (sales-tax and salt-tax), but also on having their own men collect them. For the first time they scheduled future meetings "to discuss the state of the realm," and they also demanded that the regent Charles dismiss and punish his advisers and substitute a 28-man committee from the Estates. When Charles hesitated, Etienne Marcel, a Parisian bourgeois who was leader of the Estates, led a revolution in the capital, the first of many in French history, and forced Charles to yield in 1357.

Marcel allied himself with a violent peasant uprising, the *Jacquerie* (from the popular name for a peasant, Jacques Bonhomme, "James Goodfellow"), that broke out in 1358. Charles' forces put down the Jacquerie, and Marcel was killed. Although the Estates had dominated France during 1356 and 1357, they had imposed no permanent principle of constitutional limitation upon the king. Nor did the members of the three estates—clergy, nobles, townsmen—trust each other or share the same interests. Even members of a single estate were divided by conflicting regional interests. Thus the Estates-General did not take the road toward becoming the French counterpart of the English parliament.

In 1360, by the Treaty of Brétigny, Edward III renounced his claim to the French throne, but only in exchange for all southwestern France plus Calais. The treaty, however, never really went into effect, since the French did not pay the huge ransom required for King John. John died in captivity (1364), and when the

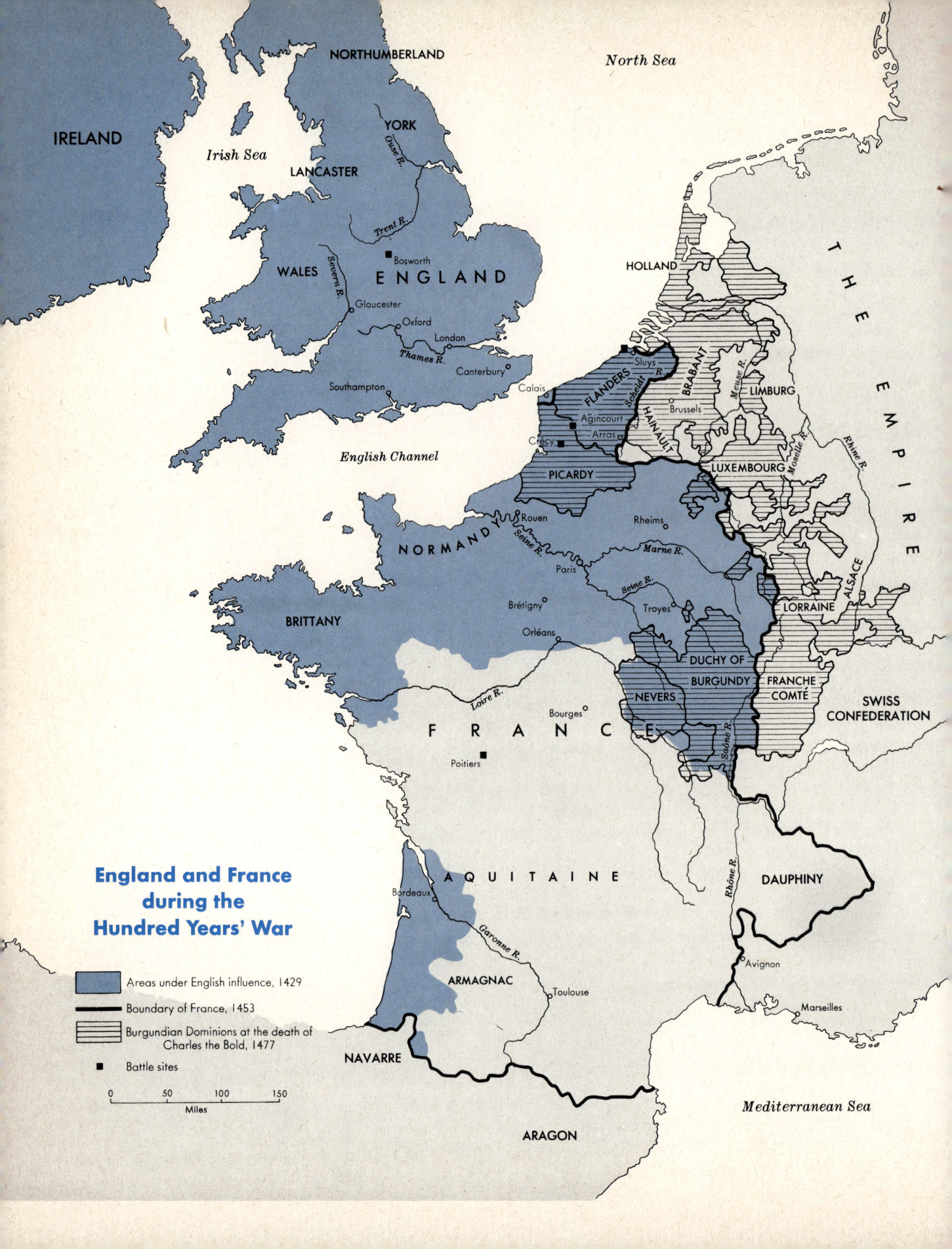

England and France during the Hundred Years' War

- Areas under English influence, 1429
- Boundary of France, 1453
- Burgundian Dominions at the death of Charles the Bold, 1477
- ■ Battle sites

war resumed, the French made substantial gains. By the time Charles V died (1380), they had ejected the English from all except a string of seaports including Bordeaux and Calais. For the first time since 1340 French ships could sail the Channel and raid the English coast. In domestic affairs Charles V was also successful, getting the Estates to agree that the existing taxes would be permanent.

Round II. But Charles VI (reigned 1380–1422) went insane. A struggle broke out between his brother, the Duke of Orléans, and his uncle, the Duke of Burgundy, who had been given this duchy by King John. In 1407, the Burgundians murdered the Duke of Orléans, and Count Bernard of Armagnac, father-in-law of the new Duke, took command of the royal party. Known thereafter as Armagnacs, they commanded the loyalty of Frenchmen in the south and southwest, and of the great nobles; they were anti-English. The Burgundians, who were pro-English, controlled the north and east, and had the support of the upper bourgeoisie in the towns. Furthermore, the Duke of Burgundy had inherited the County of Flanders in 1381, and thus had become very rich.

In alliance with the Burgundians, the English reopened the war. Henry V of England (reigned 1413–1422) won the battle of Agincourt (1415) and reconquered Normandy, thus undoing the work of Philip Augustus and Charles V. In Paris, the Burgundians massacred the Armagnacs, whose partisans fled in disorder to set up a rival regime south of the Loire, with the heir to the throne, the future Charles VII, as its nominal head. The English reached the peak of their success in the Treaty of Troyes (1420), whereby Charles VI cast off his son as illegitimate, and adopted Henry V as his heir and as his regent during his lifetime. Henry married Charles' daughter, and retained all his conquests north of the Loire until he should inherit the whole of France on the death of Charles VI. This fantastic settlement would have ended French national sovereignty.

When Henry V and Charles VI both died in 1422, the regent for Henry's heir, Henry VI, prepared to march against the pitiful Charles VII, the rightful King of France, who ruled at Bourges with Armagnac support. At this juncture, the miracle of Joan of Arc saved France. The visionary peasant girl who reflected the deep patriotism of the French put heart and strength into the demoralized forces of Charles VII. Saints and angels told her she must bring Charles to be crowned at Rheims. Inspired by her presence, French troops drove the English out of Orléans and Charles was crowned. Joan was later captured by the Burgundians, sold to the English, turned over to the French Inquisition, and burned as a witch at Rouen (1431). The papacy itself reversed the verdict against her in 1456 and made her a saint in 1920.

Her cause triumphed despite her own martyrdom. In 1435 Charles VII and the Burgundians concluded a separate peace; without the Burgundian alliance, the English could not win, and Paris fell to the French (1436). France still suffered from the depredations of private companies of soldiers in the countryside and from the unruliness of factions among the nobles. Charles VII, however, was able to win from the Estates (1439) not only the right to have an army but also the *taille,* a tax to be levied directly on individuals and collected by royal agents. He got money also from Jacques Coeur and chose as his closest advisers members of the bourgeoisie. With his new army Charles proceeded to retake Normandy and Aquitaine. When the Hundred Years' War finally ended in 1453, Calais alone of French territory remained in English hands.

FRANCE: LOUIS XI

Charles' son was Louis XI (reigned 1461–1483), plainly dressed, crafty, penny-pinching, hard-working, a constant traveller about his kingdom, inquisitive and cautious, accessible and ruthless. He put the seal on the work that his father's bureaucrats had accomplished. He had reason enough to be impatient with the quarrels of nobles, and so trusted only bourgeois advisers whom he could control. He kept the army in fighting trim, but hated the thought of risking it in war. His great achievement was settling the problems posed by the existence on his eastern and northern borders of the great collection of territories controlled by the Duke of Burgundy—the Duchy of Burgundy itself and the adjacent Free County (Franche Comté), and most of the Low Countries. Though divided by Alsace and Lorraine, this sprawling realm could have been the basis for a "middle kingdom" between France and the Empire.

Philip the Good of Burgundy (reigned 1419–1467), who had inherited most of it, and his heir Charles the Bold (reigned 1467–1477) hoped to use its great wealth for just this purpose. Louis XI subsidized the Swiss, who also were threatened by Charles' expansive plans, and the Swiss forces defeated Charles the

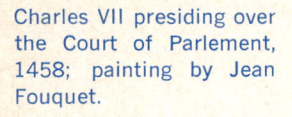

Charles VII presiding over the Court of Parlement, 1458; painting by Jean Fouquet.

Bold and killed him (1477). France took Burgundy and the Franche Comté; Charles' daughter, Mary, inherited the Low Countries, and took them with her as dowry when she married Maximilian of Habsburg, who later became Holy Roman Emperor. Burgundian ambition and hostility to France were now united to the Empire, and in subsequent generations would trouble Louis XI's successors. But Louis himself had consolidated French territory and given it a strong central administration.

ENGLAND

Edward II and Edward III. For England, too, the Hundred Years' War was the major preoccupation of the fourteenth and fifteenth centuries. English internal development moved along different lines from the French. Under the weak and inept Edward II (reigned 1307–1327), dominated by his favorites and his French queen, the barons revolted again (1311) as they had under his grandfather Henry III, and virtually re-enacted the Provisions of Oxford of 1258 (*see* Chapter 4). They established as the real rulers of England 21 Lords Ordainers, who had to assent to all appointments and to any declarations of war. But the barons were as selfish and grasping as the king's bureaucrats had been. Edward's queen, Isabelle, led a revolt against him; he was imprisoned and murdered.

Edward III (reigned 1327–1377) needed a constant supply of money to fight the French; since Parliament voted it without opposition while objecting to all other royal forms of money-raising, he summoned Parliament often. By the middle of the fourteenth century, the knights of the shire and the burgesses regularly met together, apart from the great lords and clergy. Though little is known about the details of the process, this gradual coalescence of knights and burgesses is the origin of the House of Commons. A similar coalescence of higher clergy and earls and barons, lords spiritual and lords temporal, is the origin of the House of Lords. By the end of the fourteenth century, the knights and burgesses chose a chairman to conduct their meeting and report their deliberations to the king: the Speaker of the House of Commons.

Because the king had so often asked them for money, the Commons gradually began to make certain assumptions: that he must do so, that they might withhold the money unless certain conditions were fulfilled, and that they might sometimes say how it should be spent and later check to see if it had been. The British tradition that money bills originate in the Commons had its foundation here. Moreover, the first foreshadowing of the legislative rights of the Commons can be found in the knights' and burgesses' device of drawing up a single petition embodying all their individual petitions. They would send this omnibus document to the Lords, who, if they approved, would forward it to the king for his decision. Finally, the Commons began to impeach royal officials for misconduct, and the Lords would acquit or condemn the accused. Usually such an impeachment meant only that one faction of the powerful Lords had become influential enough to rally a majority of Commons in trying to ruin individual members of an opposing faction.

In Edward III's reign a great economic crisis arose, in part out of the ravages of the Black Death (1348–1349), which killed almost half the population. A terrible shortage of manpower resulted; crops rotted in the fields and good land dropped out of cultivation. The agricultural laborers of England, aware of their suddenly increased bargaining power (and of the wealth gained by their masters from the French war), began to break the bonds of serfdom, or left home and flocked to the towns. In 1351, Parliament passed the Statute of Laborers, an attempt to fix wages and prices as they had been before the plague, to prevent workmen from quitting, and to force the unemployed to accept work at the old rates. It failed, and the labor shortage hastened the end of serfdom and paved the way for the disorders that took place under Edward's successor.

To enforce the Statute of Laborers, Edward III appointed the first justices of the peace, chosen from the gentry in each shire. They received no pay, but served from a sense of duty or a wish for prestige. The old shire and hundred courts disappeared. In later centuries, and down almost to our own times, the justices of the peace dominated English rural life.

Because the Avignonese popes were thought to be instruments of the French, Parliament in 1351 passed a statute restricting the appointment of aliens to church offices in England, and in 1353 checked the appeal of legal cases to the papal courts. Dislike for the papacy, the widespread economic discontent, and a growing sense of national identity can all be seen in England's first real heresy, which appeared at the end of Edward III's reign. John Wyclif, an Oxford scholar, advocated a church without property in the spirit of the early Christians. He wanted to abolish or weaken most of the functions of the priests, so that the individual could have direct access to God. He and his followers—called Lollards (babblers)—also translated the Bible into English, in defiance of the long-established supremacy of Latin. English became the language of the courts (1352), was taught in the schools (1375), and was used to open Parliament (1399). Love for a native language was always and everywhere a fundamental part of quickening national feeling.

Richard II. Under Richard II (reigned 1377–1399), grandson of Edward III, peasant discontent reached an intensity comparable to that of the French Jacquerie. Many landlords were still trying to enforce serfdom. In 1378, 1379, and 1380 the crown imposed a poll-tax (head-tax) on every person over 15; the rich scarcely noticed it, but the poor bitterly resented it. In 1381, the peasants revolted, burned manor records to destroy evidence of their obligations, and marched on London. Their demand for the end of serfdom and the confiscation of clerical wealth reflected the widespread influence of Wyclif's ideas among the lower classes. In the capital, Richard II, who was 15 years old, showed heroism by interviewing the peasants' leaders and promising to fulfill their demands. In the end, however, the revolt was harshly suppressed; had it been economically possible to restore serfdom, the authorities would have done so.

Meantime, the great nobles took advantage of Richard's youth to conspire against each other to seize power. More and more each of them became a commander of his own private hired army. Gradually, the feudal practice of a lord's calling for military assistance on vassals of his own social class gave way to the new practice of simply hiring strong-arm men. These were social inferiors, had no feudal ties, held no fiefs, but were bound by written indenture and a retaining fee. The custom, known as "livery and maintenance," was forbidden by statute in 1390, but continued to flourish. Every time there was an interlude in the Hundred Years' War, these plundering mercenaries came to England from France and continued their disorderly behavior.

One of the noble factions was called Lancastrian, after the Duke of Lancaster, John of Gaunt, one of Edward III's sons and uncle of Richard II. Two other uncles, the Dukes of Gloucester and York, also had their factions. In 1387, Gloucester defeated Richard's forces and in 1388 forced a packed Parliament to condemn the royal ministers for treason. Richard himself made an effort at absolutism in 1397, arresting Gloucester, packing Parliament with his own supporters, pushing through severe antitreason laws, many of them retroactive, and confiscating the estates of Henry, exiled son of John of Gaunt. This royal highhandedness precipitated a revolution. Henry returned to England with troops, gained wide support because of Richard's behavior, defeated and deposed Richard, and became Henry IV, first monarch of the House of Lancaster.

Lancaster and York. Henry IV (reigned 1399–1413), preoccupied with rebellions against him, made no effort to tax or legislate without parliamentary approval. Moreover, he and his successors recognized that they needed parliamentary support; the nobles in turn used Parliament as an instrument to prevent a recurrence of Richard II's tyrannous behavior, and to further their own interests. Henry V (reigned 1413–1422), whose great victories in France were won at the expense of neglecting England, died young, and left as his heir the infant Henry VI (reigned 1422–1461), who proved mentally unstable as he grew up. Disaster followed.

The English defeats in the war with France were accompanied by quarrels at home between Queen Margaret of Anjou and her noble English allies on one hand (the Lancastrians), and Richard, Duke of York, a great-grandson of Edward III who was heir to the throne until Henry VI had a son in 1453. These quarrels led directly to the dreary Wars of the Roses (1455–1485), named for the red rose, badge of the House of Lancaster, and the white rose, badge of the House of York. Without too severe an impact on the daily life of the ordinary man, the nobles and their private liveried armies slaughtered each other in droves for three decades.

Parliament became the tool of one or the other faction. Even the throne repeatedly changed hands: in 1461, the Earl of Warwick, leader of the Yorkist side, put on the throne the son of Richard of York, Edward IV (1461–1483); but quarreled with him and in 1470–1471 staged a revolution that briefly restored Henry VI. Edward IV soon regained control, and Henry VI and Warwick were killed. Edward IV might well have restored stability, but himself died in 1483 while still young. The throne passed momentarily to his son, Edward V, and then to Edward IV's brother, Richard III (1483–1485), last of the Yorkist kings, whose responsibility for the murder of the "little princes of the Tower"—Edward V and his younger brother—is still a matter of controversy. In 1485, on Bosworth Field, Richard III was defeated and killed by Henry Tudor, an illegitimate great-grandson of John of Gaunt, the Lancastrian leader. Henry became King Henry VII (1485–1509), and promptly made his tenuous claim to the crown stronger by marrying the Yorkist princess Elizabeth, daughter of Edward IV.

Henry VII. With Bosworth Field the Wars of the Roses at last ended, and England had a tough, new-style monarch who could not only command but enforce his commands. Henry VII forbade livery and maintenance, and private armies disappeared; he kept the nobles from intimidating litigants in cases before the royal courts. He appointed a special administrative court within the King's Council, the Court of Star Chamber (so-called from the stars painted on the ceiling of the room in which it met), which bypassed the customary procedures of the common law, including trial by jury. Although Henry was striking at local resistance, local abuses, and local privileges, the Star Chamber procedure could easily become tyrannical, trampling on the rights of defendants. Its worst period did not come until the seventeenth century (see Chapter 8), however, and under Henry VII most Englishmen probably found little fault with its activities.

Henry and his self-made middle-class officials, whom he kindly rewarded with lands confiscated from the Yorkists, managed to double the royal revenue. "Morton's Fork," a practice attributed to the Archbishop of Canterbury, an able lawyer, penalized high churchmen when they were summoned to make payments to the king. The richly dressed were told they could obviously afford to pay heavily; the poorly dressed that, since they were economical, they too could make a large contribution. Threatening foreign governments with loss of the valuable trading privileges enjoyed by their merchants. Henry's bureaucrats secured comparable advantages for English traders abroad, especially in Italy. Henry VII had the support of the growing middle classes, and, like Louis XI in France, he restored the prestige of the monarchy and made it the rallying-point of English national feeling. The vigor of the royal policies sometimes obscured Parliament, yet Lords and Commons kept alive the unique English tradition that the monarch could not levy taxes or make laws without consulting Parliament.

SPAIN

Though both France and England had been racked by severe internal troubles, they had long been national states with established and accepted centralized monarchial institutions. By contrast, Spain, as a result of its history, had no national identity until the fifteenth century. The gradual and painful reconquest of the peninsula from the Moslems has often been compared to a Crusade that lasted more than five centuries. The little Christian kingdoms in the north, however, often put more energy into fighting each other. By the middle of the fifteenth century, when the Moslems were confined to the Kingdom of Granada in the south, there were three separate and often mutually hostile Christian kingdoms.

Castile, in the center of the peninsula, had scored some of the major victories over the Moslems. But its kings shared their authority with the *Mesta*, a powerful organization of sheep-ranchers, and the nobles and the towns were also independent-minded. Castile had a counterpart of Parliament or the French Estates-General—the *Cortes*, with all three estates represented. Portugal, to the west, once a Castilian province but independent since 1179, looked out to the Atlantic and to commerce and exploration overseas. Aragon, in the northeast, comprised both backward mountain areas and the vigorous commercial towns of Catalonia, especially Barcelona. Aragon, with a long tradition of trade and conquest in the Mediterranean, had ruled Sicily since 1282 and took Naples in 1435. At home, the Catalans championed autonomy and made trouble for the King of Aragon in his Cortes.

When Ferdinand, heir to Aragon, married Isabella, heiress to Castile (1469), the dynastic alliance made possible union of the two largest states of Spain. Castilians and Aragonese, however, did not even speak the same language (Catalan still today thrives in Catalonia), and royal power was weak in both states. While Ferdinand looked outward to the Mediterranean and was relatively tolerant in his religious attitudes, Isabella focussed her attention on Castile and was fanatically pious. She summoned the Cortes only when she could not avoid it, and appointed her own council, to which she gave large powers. She allied herself with the towns, using their militias as troops rather than relying on feudal levies from the nobles. She met opposition from three large military brotherhoods similar to the crusading orders of knighthood (*see* Chapter 5), founded by nobles to fight the Moslems; Isabella controlled them by having Ferdinand made the commander of all three.

Ferdinand and Isabella made a firm alliance with the Church. Isabella's chief minister, Cardinal Ximenes, Archbishop of Toledo, was instrumental in executing her policies, which included a thoroughgoing reform of the Church itself. From the papacy, the Spanish crown obtained the right to dispose of ecclesiastical appointments and of some church revenues. In 1478, the Inquisition was imported into Spain, where it served as an instrument of Isabella's aims: Spanish unity and universal Catholicism. Jews and Moslems, who had long enjoyed toleration and had become prosperous, were its first targets. In 1492, the Jews were offered the choice between baptism and exile. In the same year Granada fell, and the last Moslem foothold in Spain was eliminated. Ten years later, the remaining Moslem residents of Spain were offered the same choice as the Jews.

To avoid exile, many Jews and Moslems became nominal Christians, conforming outwardly to escape the harsh punishments of the Inquisition, but inwardly loyal to their old faiths. Many others did go into exile, and cost Spain some of its ablest and most productive people. The year 1492, which marks the fall of Granada and the onset of persecution, also marks Columbus' first voyage. The Spanish monarchy and its future colonial empire already bore the stamp of the bigotry that would prove both a strength and a weakness in the generations to come.

III. Particularism

GERMANY

In Germany, no "new" monarch made his appearance. Rudolf of Habsburg (reigned 1273–1291), the first emperor chosen after the Interregnum (1254–1273; *see* Chapter 4), came of a family of lesser nobles whose estates lay most in Switzerland. Rudolf cared nothing for imperial politics but wanted to enlarge the family holdings and to secure a hereditary monarchy for the Habsburgs in Germany. He acquired Austria, and his descendants ruled at Vienna until 1918. Because his own interests lay in the southeastern portions of the Empire, Rudolf made concessions to the French in its western lands, in order to win their support. Thus the French moved into the region east of the Rhone and obtained a foothold in Lorraine. Those who supported this eastern-based, pro-French policy of Rudolf may be called the Habsburg Party. Those who opposed it—chiefly the rich and powerful archbishops of the Rhine valley and other princes in western Germany—were anti-French and anti-Habsburg.

This whole development helped perpetuate particularism: the gravitation of political power to the rulers of the many particular territorial units composing the Empire, at the expense of the central authority. The imperial office sometimes went to a Habsburg, and sometimes to members of other houses: Nassau,

Luxembourg, Bohemia, the Wittelsbach family of Bavaria. During the fourteenth century, the central monarchy became simply another territorial princedom, since the German princes wanted to be emperor chiefly because the title would help them add to their possessions. They won a great victory in 1356, when the Emperor Charles IV issued a "Golden Bull," proclaiming that the imperial dignity was of God, that the emperor was to be elected by the German electoral princes, and that their choices needed no confirmation by the pope. The seven electors thereafter were the Archbishops of Mainz, Trier, and Cologne, the Count Palatine of the Rhine, the Duke of Saxony, the Margrave of Brandenburg, and the King of Bohemia. Each of the electors would have full rights of coinage in his own territory, and there would be no appeal from the decisions of his court: he would be all but sovereign.

Within each of the many German principalities, the prince faced the threat of the nobility, now strengthened by the addition to its numbers of the former *ministeriales* (*see* Chapter 4), who had acquired lands, feudal rights, and titles. Within the state of Brunswick, for example. the duke had to face in miniature the same problem from the knights, towns, and clergy—the "estates"—that the kings of France and England faced. Power shared with the estates meant increasing disorder, as urban–rural antagonism increased, robber barons infested the roads, and local wars became common.

But in the decades after 1400 the princes combatted the estates by adopting the rule of primogeniture and the indivisibility of their princedoms. Increased use of Roman law helped them assert their claims to absolute control over public rights and offices. Gunpowder and artillery, now coming into use, made it impractical for an unruly vassal to defy his prince successfully inside medieval fortifications. By the end of the fifteenth century, the German princes had achieved, inside individual principalities, orderly finance, indivisible hereditary domains, and taxation granted by the estates; cooperation with the estates had replaced hostility. The Empire as such had lost its meaning. Territorially it had lost control not only over the western lands gained by the French but also over Switzerland, where, beginning with a revolt in 1291, a confederation of cantons had taken form with a weak central authority and wide cantonal autonomy. In 1438, the title of Emperor passed permanently to the House of Habsburg. Though the emperors who followed immediately were weak, Maximilian (reigned 1493–1519) not only re-established strong Habsburg rule in Austria and its dependencies, but arranged for his children and grandchildren a stunning series of dynastic marriages that would make his grandson, Charles V, the ruler of half of Europe. Thus German national sentiment could not overcome the particularism of the princes and the dynastic interest of the emperors.

ITALY

In Italy, the struggle between popes and emperors had promoted the growth of communes or city-states, much like those of ancient Greece. In the twelfth and thirteenth centuries, the communes had been mostly oligarchic republics, dominated by nobles and rich businessmen. Within the ruling group, in each town, the pro-papal Guelf faction struggled against the pro-imperial Ghibelline faction, while smaller businessmen and artisans fought their own fight against the ruling oligarchy as a whole. Just as the city-states of Greece went through a phase of government by tyrant, so those of late medieval Italy mostly passed from

A part of the city of Venice, c. 1500; woodcut by Iacopo de Barbari.

oligarchy to despotism. Sometimes a despot seized power; sometimes the struggling factions in the town invited him in. Often he was a *condottiere*, a captain of the mercenary troops hired to fight the city-state's enemies.

The city-state was characteristic of northern Italy. The south comprised the kingdom of the Two Sicilies (the island plus Naples and its large territories on the mainland), which had experienced Byzantine, Moslem, Norman, Hohenstaufen, and Angevin domination during the course of the Middle Ages. Sicily passed to Aragon in 1282, Naples in 1435. Though some of the Aragonese rulers, notably Alfonso the Magnanimous (reigned 1416–1458), were generous patrons of learning, the Two Sicilies never recovered the prosperity or the cultural leadership they had enjoyed in earlier days.

Similarly, central Italy, consisting chiefly of the Papal States, went into eclipse during the "Babylonian Captivity" at Avignon. The government of Rome fell into the hands of the great nobles; twice, in the middle of the fourteenth century, they put down attempts by Cola di Rienzi to establish a kind of republic with himself as tribune of the people. It was another century before Popes Nicholas V (1447–1455) and Pius II (1458–1464) were able to restore Rome to its old position as a center of learning and of power.

Milan, Florence, Venice. The northern city-states emerged in the later Middle Ages as the centers of Italian political life. Milan, strategically located in the fertile Lombard plain, meeting-place of the routes over the Alps from the north, manufactured the best velvets and the best armor in Europe. It had led the opposition to Frederick Barbarossa in the twelfth century, and then pushed its holdings south into Tuscany. In 1277 Milan substituted for its previous republican government a despotism by the rich and high-handed Visconti family. Extending their rule to include Genoa, intermarrying with the royal houses of England and France, the Visconti dukes at the turn of the fifteenth century had most of northern Italy in their hands.

In 1447, the direct Visconti line died out, but Francesco Sforza, husband of the illegitimate daughter of the last Visconti, made himself duke in 1450. His son, Ludovico (reigned 1479–1500), called *il Moro*, "the Moor," was a clever diplomat and great patron of art and learning who made the mistake of becoming embroiled in the Italian projects of the French (*see* p. 304) and ended his days in a French prison.

On the banks of the Arno in Tuscany, midway between Milan and Rome, Florence shared with Milan and Venice the leadership of Italy. The rich merchants and bankers of the town were mainly Guelfs, the older nobility with estates in the environs and great palaces in town mostly Ghibelline. A bloody seesaw struggle raged through most of the thirteenth century, while prosperity grew, and the gold florin (minted first in 1252) replaced the Byzantine gold nomisma (the besant) as standard coinage in Europe. By 1282, the Guelfs had placed political power in the hands of the seven major gilds, including banking and wool-making, and a law of 1293 closed off the last possibility of noble participation in government, as all those not actually practicing their professions were expelled from the gilds. The Guelfs themselves now split, the Black Guelf extremists favoring repeal of the law of 1293, and the White Guelf moderates taking a position approximating that of the Ghibellines. The continuing factional struggle claimed many victims, among them the poet Dante (1265–1321), permanently exiled with many fellow White Guelfs from his beloved Florence.

The politically unprivileged sought to make Florence more democratic. They failed because the lesser gilds, with their lower middle-class membership, could never join with the poor workmen in a joint alliance against the entrenched oligarchy. Bank failures and the Black Death of the 1340's led to revolutions, including a serious uprising of the poorest workers in 1378, but the ruling oligarchy returned to power (1382–1434), buying the towns of Pisa and Leghorn, which gave the Florentines access to the sea. Military reverses brought to power in 1434 Cosimo de' Medici, member of a family with large woolen and banking interests, who was none the less a champion of the poor.

Between 1434 and 1494, the Medici ran Florence, introducing a progressive income tax to lighten the burden of the poor. Though Cosimo was a despot, he ruled quietly by managing to pack the city council, traditionally chosen every two months through random drawing of the names of eligible citizens from leather bags. Cosimo's grandson, Lorenzo de' Medici (reigned 1469–1492), earned his name of "the Magnificent" by his lavish patronage of all the arts, his charm, tolerance, intelligence, and wisdom. In 1474 the Pazzi family, rivals to the Medici, obtained the valuable concession of receivers of papal revenues, as a result of a quarrel between Lorenzo and Pope Sixtus IV, which led to an attempt (1478) to assassinate Lorenzo. The fierce Medici vengeance against the Pazzi precipitated a papal interdict on Florence and the excommunication of Lorenzo. A general upheaval in Italian city-state relationships followed. After Lorenzo's death in

1492, economic decline, the French invasions, and two expulsions and two returns of the Medici family marked the history of Florence, now a petty state despite its transformation into the Grand Duchy of Tuscany.

Third of the great north Italian states, Venice had founded an overseas empire along the eastern Adriatic shore and in Greece and the Aegean (see Chapter 5). This expansion led to fighting with the Genoese during most of the later thirteenth and the fourteenth centuries. Venice was governed by a doge, in the early Middle Ages appointed by the Byzantine Emperor, and later elected. After 1171, he was appointed by an elected assembly of 480 members, which became the Great Council. In 1297, the members of the Council restricted future membership to the descendants of those who had served during the preceding four years, plus certain other families. These names were listed in the Golden Book, and all others were permanently excluded from the government. A rebellion in 1310 led to the creation of an inner Council of Ten, especially charged with maintaining security.

The doge now became chiefly a ceremonial figure, who, for example, annually "married" the Adriatic in a famous ceremony, by throwing a ring into the sea. Despite the tight control of the great families and their ruthlessness, Venice was by no means insensitive to the welfare of its poorer subjects. It enjoyed great stability: no despots overthrew the oligarchy; no factionalism tormented its citizens. Its imposing fleets challenged Turks as well as Genoese. Money poured in, and Venice's wealth, power, and unique location made it a city unlike any other.

The Lessons of Despotism: Machiavelli. In the cynical age of Louis XI of France and Henry VII of England, the Venetian oligarchs and Italian despots like the Sforza, Borgia, and Medici served as models for statesmanship. The Venetian diplomatic service, with its shrewd ambassadors sending detailed and informative reports from abroad, soon had its imitators. The Italian despots' reliance on mercenaries foreshadowed the general use of paid troops and the abandonment of the old feudal levies. The balance of power precariously maintained in the peninsula by the Italians served as a model for the new European monarchies. Italy was in a real sense the "school of Europe" in statesmanship. Yet the very balance among the Italian states made it impossible for them to unite in the face of a foreign threat, and the French invasion of 1494 ushered in a new period of French, Spanish, and Habsburg competition in the disunited peninsula.

Summing up the lessons that long observation of Italian political behavior had taught him, Niccolò Machiavelli (1469–1527), a Florentine diplomat, wrote his celebrated book, *The Prince*. Arguing that men in general were "ungrateful, voluble dissemblers, anxious to avoid danger and covetous of gain," he counsels a prince "not to keep faith when by so doing it would be against his interest," but to be as deceitful and unscrupulous as Ludovico Sforza, Lorenzo the Magnificent, or especially Cesare Borgia, the son of Pope Alexander VI. Was Machiavelli perhaps being satirical and might he mean the opposite of what he said? Some scholars think so, but it seems improbable. His overriding aim was to expel the French, Spanish, and Habsburg intruders and to unify Italy, and he was ready to sanction any means to gain that end.

In a second work, *The Discourses* on the Roman historian Livy, Machiavelli dealt not with the immediate Italian crisis, but with the problem of building a lasting government. In this context, he prescribed not a single all-powerful prince but magistrates elected by the people, whom he regarded as more prudent and stable than a prince. The contradiction between *The Discourses* and *The Prince* is more apparent than real: in *The Discourses* Machiavelli was discussing the ancients with all their republican virtue, in *The Prince* the modern Italians who had, he was convinced, in their despotism lost theirs. For this loss Machiavelli blamed the Church: not only the worldly papacy with all its temporal interest, but Christianity itself, which by exalting humility and a contempt for this world, and by focusing on the City of God, had left men less well prepared than the pagans to fight, work, and die for their country here on earth.

In defending secularism and power politics, Machiavelli was only preaching what others practiced. Louis XI, Henry VII, Ferdinand of Aragon, and the successful German princes and Italian despots were all Machiavellians in action before Machiavelli himself set down the theories. Machiavellianism seemed an essential part of the age, the era of the Renaissance.

IV. The Renaissance: Literature and Learning

THE MEANING OF "RENAISSANCE"

The term *renaissance* means "rebirth." When men have applied it to the extraordinary flowering of letters and the arts begun in fourteenth-century Italy and spreading at varying speeds and with varying intensity to the other countries of Europe, they have wanted it to mean a rebirth of classical culture, a return to the standards of the Greeks and Romans of antiquity, and a repudiation of everything for which the Middle Ages had stood. Not so long ago most people believed that, when Constantinople fell to the Turks in 1453, refugee Greek scholars brought to the West the precious manuscripts of the classics and taught the West to appreciate them. Then suddenly a continent cloaked in darkness and inhabited by barbarians was illuminated by a blaze of light that enabled the ignorant brutes to behold the truth and to transform themselves into cultivated skeptical gentlemen.

We have learned enough now to see that this view is largely wrong. No very large migration of Greeks took place after 1453; many more had migrated earlier. In the twelfth century, the Western rediscovery of the classical heritage was already well under way, and in the thirteenth Aquinas and others had already incorporated Aristotelian philosophy into the Christian scheme. The so-called barbarian Middle Ages had seen a great Christian civilization come to maturity. Some scholars indeed have pointed to earlier "rebirths" and refer to the "Carolingian Renaissance," the "Renaissance of the Twelfth Century," and even to tenth- and eleventh-century renaissances. It is, however, just as misleading to regard the whole medieval period as a series of rebirths culminating in a great rebirth as it is to overestimate the suddenness and originality of the transition.

Transition there certainly was: a period in which the world was growing less medieval and increasingly modern. *Renaissance* is not a bad name for the civilization of the transition period if we understand our terminology: a movement away from devoutness, caste-consciousness, otherworldliness, and credulousness, and toward secularism, individualism, skepticism, and materialism. This does not mean that all scholars or artists of the Renaissance suddenly appear totally devoid of medieval qualities or totally imbued with modern ones. It does mean that most could be found moving away from the older standards, somewhere on the path toward the newer ones. Some men moved fast and far along all these lines; other men far on some lines and not at all on others.

THE VERNACULAR TONGUES

Though Latin remained the language of the Church and the international language of scholars, more and more writers now turned to the vernacular (native or local) languages of Europe. In the Middle Ages, as we have seen, the authors of *The Song of Roland* and the historians Villehardouin and Joinville wrote in French, the dialect of the north: the *langue d'oïl* (where *oïl*, the modern *oui*, meant "yes"). The Provençal troubadours wrote in the dialect of the south, the *langue d'oc* (where the word for "yes" was *oc*), which had given its name to the region of Languedoc; it is somewhat akin to Catalan, the language still spoken on both sides of the Pyrenees. Like Portuguese, Spanish, and Italian, all these languages originally derive from Latin. Germany had its minnesingers, who wrote in Middle High German, ancestor of the modern literary language, while the Anglo-Saxon Low German dialect found literary expression in *Beowulf*. Norman French and Latin influenced Anglo-Saxon (Old English) and transformed it into Middle English. With the growing sense of national identity in all countries, the vernacular came to be used increasingly, above all in Italy. Although there had been experiments in the Italian vernacular at the court of Frederick II in Sicily (*see* p. 168), especially love poems written in what was called the "sweet new style," it was not until the end of the thirteenth century that the vernacular in Italy began to win acceptance.

THE HUMANISTS

The learned men of the new period called themselves humanists (from *humanista*, a new name originating in student slang for teachers of grammar, rhetoric, and the other "humane studies"; the *legista* or the *jurista* taught law). The humanists were scholars of the classics. As we know, medieval scholars had preceded them, but the increased emphasis on the classics was so great that it constituted a real change. Humanists rediscovered texts hitherto lost—the Roman historians Tacitus and Lucretius, for example. At an extraordinary rate they multiplied copies of texts already known, so that knowledge of the texts was diffused far beyond the narrow circle of medieval scholars who previously had had access to them. Most striking was the quickening in Greek studies. Despite the long contacts between Europe and Byzantium, almost nobody in the West before the late fourteenth century knew Greek or cared about Greek literature; the earlier translations of Greek often came from an intermediary Arabic version and consisted almost entirely of medical, scientific, and Aristotelian philosophical works.

With the help of Greek exiles like Manuel Chrysoloras, who lectured in Florence between 1396 and 1400, the Greek visitors, like the scientist and Platonist Gemistos Plethon, who attended the Church Council of Florence in 1437, the humanists now began to teach Greek in the universities, and to translate Homer and the other poets, the orators, the historians, and the philosophers other than Aristotle. In 1462, Cosimo de' Medici founded a "Platonic Academy" in

Florence, where Marsiglio Ficino translated Plato and taught Platonism. One of its outstanding members was the brilliant and short-lived Pico della Mirandola (1463–1494), who knew Hebrew and Arabic, in addition to Greek, and studied Jewish allegory and Arab philosophy. By examining the varied beliefs and ideas of the past he hoped to find a set of keys to man and the universe, the common denominator of faith. Pico's effort was typical of the best in humanist scholarship.

But the humanists were more than scholars: they themselves wrote voluminous letters, speeches, poems, and treatises on grammar and rhetoric, history, politics, education, and religion. They proclaimed an ideal of eloquence; as professional rhetoricians, they were convinced that classical models supplied the best guides. Many of them had contempt for the learning of their medieval predecessors, whose ideas on life and learning they did not share. But many others had a deep regard for medieval scholastic thought, and continued to study it. By the mid-fifteenth century many lawyers and doctors and other professional men were humanists as well. Only a few humanists were what we would term "free-lance" writers; most were either teachers or acted as secretaries to princes or city governments. In any role, however, they prided themselves on writing correct Latin letters and speeches, much as their medieval predecessors had done.

Dante. At the very beginning of both new movements—the use of the vernacular and the practice of humanism—stands the towering figure of Dante Alighieri (1265–1321), in many ways still very much a medieval man, and so a kind of incarnation of the transition we are studying. He wrote sometimes in Latin: his *De monarchia* is a long treatise yearning for the restoration in Italy of the medieval Empire that had forever disappeared. Another treatise, however, *De vulgari eloquentia* (*On the Common Speech*), stoutly defends (in Latin) the use of the vernacular. And for his own very greatest work, *The Divine Comedy*, Dante used the native Italian.

Here he tells of his travels through Hell, Purgatory, and Paradise. Lost in a dark wood, Dante meets the Latin poet Vergil, who acts as his guide throughout Hell and Purgatory, where they encounter the souls of those who have died in past ages. The great classical figures, including Vergil himself, born before the time of Christ, and so never baptized, must spend their hopeless eternity in Limbo, on the edge of Hell, and there Dante sees not only historic figures like Homer, Plato, Socrates, and Caesar but characters in ancient myth or poetry like Hector, Ulysses, and Aeneas. The nine circles of Hell are peopled with the shades of real persons from Judas to Florentines of Dante's own time. In Paradise, Dante's guide is Beatrice, a Florentine girl with whom he had fallen desperately in love in his youth, but whom he had worshipped only at a distance. Accepting and expounding the full philosophy of the devout medieval Christian, Dante yet avoids the abstractions of the medieval allegorist. He makes his ideas on good and evil the more convincing by putting them into the mouths of historic personages well known to his readers.

Petrarch, Boccaccio, Chaucer. The next generation of humanists was headed by Petrarch (Francesco Petrarca, 1304–1374), more steeped in the passion for the classics and more preoccupied with his own posthumous fame. Petrarch collected and copied manuscripts, assembled a great library, discovered some lost letters of Cicero, and even addressed letters of his own to Cicero and other ancient writers. Imitating Vergil, he composed a Latin epic to celebrate Scipio Africanus, conqueror of the Carthaginians. He strove to learn Greek and employed a teacher, but to his sorrow never mastered the language.

Crowned with laurels by the "Senate" (city council) of Rome, Petrarch would have been painfully surprised to discover that posterity remembers best, not the Latin works that he himself valued most, but the Italian sonnets (little songs) he wrote in honor of his beloved Laura. These charming verses gave definitive form to the Italian sonnet: fourteen lines, divided into an octave and a sestet, each with its own rhyme scheme. Petrarch admired the beauties of this world, as most Renaissance men did, but he too remained in many ways a man of the Middle Ages, turning for inspiration as much to St. Augustine's *Confessions* as to Cicero. Yet like many humanists he felt that the scholastic philosophers had missed the forest (the spirit of Christianity) in their concern for the trees (the detail of controversy).

Petrarch's famous pupil, Boccaccio (1313–1375), was also a hard-working humanist, who discovered a lost manuscript of Tacitus, succeeded in learning Greek, and taught at the University of Florence. When the Florentines wanted to find a man who had mastered Dante's *Divine Comedy* and could give public lectures on it, they selected Boccaccio. Having started life as apprentice in his father's banking business, he came to detest the sharp practices he saw, and to scorn the pious professions of the hypocritical rich. Boccaccio is most celebrated for his vernacular work, *The Decameron*, a series of stories told during ten days by a company of ten lively young people fleeing Florence to escape the Black Death of 1348. In these tales we find wronged husbands and clever adulterous wives, cheating merchants and frivolous youths, lustful priests and cynical apprentices, a convincingly sinful cast of characters given to all the human failings, treated with an earthy light-heartedness. Boccaccio of course did not invent all the *Decameron* stories: he took old fabliaux (traveling-salesman jokes that everybody knew) and gave them literary form.

Outside Italy, only one contemporary of these writers deserves to be ranked with them. The Englishman Geoffrey Chaucer (c. 1340–1400) was not a scholarly humanist but an experienced man of affairs, who made several trips to the Continent on business for the King of England and eventually received the important posts of Controller of Customs and Clerk of the King's Works. Chaucer actually met Petrarch in Padua, and knew a good many of Boccaccio's works, although apparently not *The Decameron*. Chaucer's *Canterbury Tales* have a framework not unlike that of *The Decameron:* they are told by a group of pilgrims on their way to the tomb of Becket at Canterbury. But Chaucer's range of inventiveness and characterization is far broader than Boccaccio's. The individual pilgrims—a knight, a squire, a prioress, a clerk, a monk, a friar, a sailor, a miller, and others—come from all walks of late medieval English life except the high nobility. They are brilliantly characterized in the author's prologue to the stories they tell, and emerge more fully as people than do Boccaccio's rather stilted and indistinguishable young ladies and gentlemen. Each of Chaucer's pilgrims tells a story quite consonant with his own personality and experience: the knight, a romance of chivalry (built on a tale of Boccaccio), the miller, a raw fabliau, the clerk, a tale of patient womanhood which Petrarch himself had used, the prioress, a saint's legend, and so on. Chaucer does not hesitate to satirize his churchmen, nor in the England of Wyclif and the Peasants' Revolt is this surprising. The sophistication, delicacy, power, passion, and humor which he commands make him incomparably the best English writer before Shakespeare. France and Germany produced nobody to compare with him or with the great Italian humanists.

Lorenzo Valla, Erasmus. Among many Italian humanists not so versatile as Petrarch or Boccaccio but perhaps even more scholarly, we may single out Lorenzo Valla (c. 1405–1477). Immensely learned and courageous, Valla also was petty and vindictive, and enjoyed the favorite contemporary game of trading insults with his fellow humanists. His great achievement was to prove that the Donation of Constantine (*see* Chapter 3), the basis since the eighth century for sweeping papal claims to temporal power, was a forgery. Valla showed that the Latin of the document could not possibly be as early as the time of Constantine, and pointed to several glaring anachronisms: for instance, the Donation referred to Constantinople as a "patriarchate," when in fact, in 314, the purported date of the document, Valla argued "it was not yet a patriarchate, nor a see, nor a Christian city, nor named Constantinople, nor founded, nor planned. . . ." Valla published his exposure in 1440, as secretary to Alfonso the Magnanimous of Naples, whose claim to Naples was being challenged by the Pope on the basis of the Donation. Not only did the Pope not condemn Valla as a heretic, which one might have expected at any time during the Middle Ages, but he even later commissioned Valla to translate Thucydides.

The "Prince of Humanists" was not an Italian but a Dutchman, Desiderius Erasmus (1466–1536), who studied, taught, and lived at Oxford, Cambridge, and Paris, in Italy, Germany, and Switzerland. Erasmus knew Greek so well that he published a scholarly edition of the Greek New Testament. He carried on a prodigious correspondence in Latin, and compiled a series of *Adages* and *Colloquies* to give students examples of how to write Latin. But he cared for content as well as style, and sneered not only at the "knowledge factories" of the grammarians but at the mutual admiration society of his fellow humanists, who were "scratching each other's itch." Erasmus played no favorites; he satirized any group or class inflated by a sense of its own importance—merchants, churchmen, scientists, philosophers, courtiers, and kings. In appraising human nature, however, Erasmus tempered criticism with geniality, and concluded that we must cherish particularly the few outstanding individuals who have led great and good lives. Christ heads his list of great men; Cicero and Socrates rank very high. Plato's account of the death of Socrates moved Erasmus so deeply that he almost cried out, "Pray for us, Saint Socrates."

Erasmus joined love of the classics with respect for Christian values. Both testy and vain, he had little use for the finespun arguments of Scholasticism and was a tireless advocate of what he called his "philosophy of Christ," the application, in the most humane spirit, of the doctrines of charity and love taught by Jesus. Yet though Erasmus always considered himself a loyal son of the Church, he nevertheless helped to destroy the universality of Catholicism. His edition of the Greek New Testament raised disquieting doubts about the correctness of the Vulgate and therefore of Catholic biblical interpretations. His attacks on the laxity of the clergy implied that the wide gap between the professed ideals and the corrupt practices of the Church could not long endure. A famous sixteenth-century epigram states: "Where Erasmus merely nodded, Luther rushed in; where Erasmus laid eggs, Luther hatched the chicks; where Erasmus merely doubted, Luther laid down the law." Erasmus was still in his prime when Luther "laid down the law" in 1517 and launched the Protestant revolt (*see* Chapter 7).

SCIENCE AND MEDICINE

In the history of science the fourteenth, fifteenth, and sixteenth centuries were a time of preparation for a larger revolution, as scientists absorbed, enlarged, and modified the knowledge handed down to them from the Middle Ages and antiquity. The medieval Schoolmen, with their intellectual discipline and their enthusiasm for Aristotle, were far from antiscientific. In the fourteenth and fifteenth centuries Aristotelian studies continued to be pursued vigorously at Paris and Padua. The humanists for the first time translated Galen, Ptolemy, Archimedes, and other scientists from Greek into Latin.

But the humanists' worship of classical antiquity tended to put old authorities high on a pedestal, beyond the reach of criticism. How could one improve on the medicine taught by Galen during the second century A.D.? Galen, for example, said that the blood moved from one side of the heart to the other by passing through invisible pores in the thick wall of tissue that divides the organ. Galen was wrong, as Harvey was to discover in the seventeenth century: the blood gets from the one side to the other by circulating through the body and lungs. But Galen's theory of invisible pores was enough to keep Leonardo da Vinci (1452–1519) from anticipating Harvey. Leonardo's anatomical studies led him to the brink of discovery; then he backed away, for he was certain that Galen must have been right.

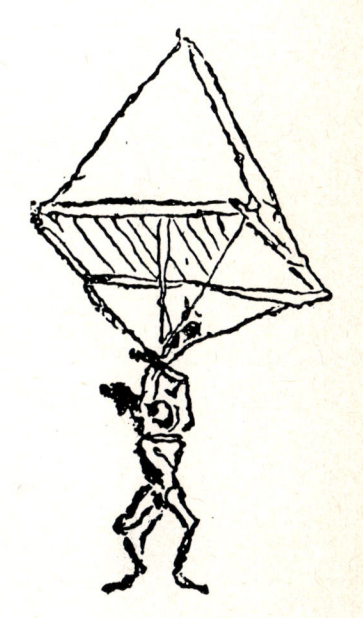

Leonardo, in fact, illustrates both the shortcomings and the achievements of Renaissance science. He took notes in a hit-or-miss fashion, without the modern scientist's concern for the systematic cataloguing of observations and for the publication of findings and speculations. Yet he projected lathes, pumps, war machines, flying machines, and many other contraptions, not all of them workable, to be sure, but all highly imaginative. He did not always bow before established authority, as he did before Galen. His geological studies convinced him that the earth was far older than the men of his time thought it to be; the Po River, he estimated, must have been flowing for about 200,000 years to wash down the sediments forming its alluvial plain.

In medicine, the University of Padua maintained a lively tradition of scientific inquiry that presaged the seventeenth-century triumphs of the experimental method. A young Belgian named Vesalius (1514–1564), who taught at Padua, rejected Galen's notion of invisible pores in the wall of tissue within the heart because he could not find such pores. In 1543, Vesalius published the splendidly illustrated *De humanis corporis fabrica* (*Concerning the Structure of the Human Body*), largely accepting older authorities, but also pointing out some of their shortcomings.

Leonardo da Vinci: sketch for a parachute.

ASTRONOMY

In 1543 Copernicus launched modern astronomical studies with *De revolutionibus orbium coelestium* (*Concerning the Revolutions of Heavenly Bodies*). Born in Poland of German extraction, Copernicus (1473–1543) studied law and medicine at Padua and other Italian universities and spent 30 years as canon of a cathedral near Danzig. His work in mathematics and astronomy led him to attack the generally accepted hypothesis of the *geocentric* (earth-centered) universe derived from Ptolemy and other astronomers of antiquity. He now advanced the revolutionary new hypothesis of the *heliocentric* (sun-centered) universe.

The concept of the geocentric universe included an elaborate system of spheres. Around the stationary earth there revolved some 80 separate circles (crystalline spheres) containing some of the heavenly bodies, each moving on an invisible circular path, each transparent so that we mortals could see the spheres beyond it. This imaginative and symmetrical picture of the universe had been questioned before the time of Copernicus, as scientists had trouble making it agree with the observable behavior of heavenly bodies. Copernicus used both these earlier criticisms and his own computations to arrive at the heliocentric concept.

Once Copernicus had reversed the roles of the sun and the earth, his universe retained many Ptolemaic characteristics. Its heavens were still filled with spheres revolving along their invisible orbits. Only they now moved about a stationary sun, instead of the stationary earth. Though Copernicus dedicated his book to the Pope, Christendom viewed it with dismay and found it hard to accept the disappearance of the earth-centered and man-centered universe. Yet Copernicus only began the revolution in astronomy, which was to be carried much further in the next century by Galileo and Newton (*see* Chapter 9).

TECHNOLOGY

The most important Renaissance contribution to technology was printing. The revolution in book production began in the fourteenth century, when Europeans imported paper from China and found it to be cheaper than the lambskin or sheepskin previously used. The next step came when engravers made woodcuts or copper plates that could produce many copies of the same drawing. Then sentences were added to the cuts or plates. Finally, almost certainly in the German Rhineland, during the 1440's, movable type was devised. Each piece of type was simply a minute bit of engraving; it could be combined with other pieces to form words, sentences, a whole page, and then salvaged to be used again. This crucial invention used to be credited to Gutenberg; some scholars now disagree.

By 1500, Italy alone had 73 presses employing movable type. The most famous of them was the Aldine Press in Venice (founded by Aldus Manutius, 1450–1515), which sold at reasonable prices scholarly editions of the classics printed in a beautiful typeface reportedly based on the handwriting of Petrarch. Everywhere the printing press suddenly made both classical and vernacular literature available to large numbers of people who could never have afforded hand-copied manuscripts. Without the perfection of printing, Erasmus might not have become the arbiter of European letters, and Luther might not have secured the rapid distribution of his antipapal tracts and sped the Reformation on its way.

Another technical innovation was gunpowder, brought from China, and used in the fighting of the early 1400's, notably the later campaigns of the Hundred Years' War. Firearms and artillery doomed both the feudal knight and the feudal castle. At sea, important aids to navigation came into general use, particularly the magnetic compass and more accurate sailing charts. By the close of the

**Renaissance Italy
about 1494**

fifteenth century, Europeans possessed the equipment needed for the oncoming age of world discovery.

V. The Renaissance: The Arts

MAIN CHARACTERISTICS OF RENAISSANCE ART

Exploiting both the humanistic enthusiasm for classical antiquity and the growing secularism of the age, and aided by technical advances, artists of genius now produced an extraordinary number of masterpieces. They released painting and sculpture from their previous subservience to architecture in the West. The individual picture or statue emerged as an independent work of art rather than as a part of a larger whole; the individual painter or sculptor sometimes reveled in an artistic self-assertion that was quite unmedieval. Reflecting the classical revival, the fashion in building changed from the soaring Gothic to adaptations of the ancient Roman temple, emphasizing symmetry and the horizontal line. Reflecting the expanding wealth and materialism of the age, palaces and private residences began to rival cathedrals and churches in magnificence.

The arts as a whole, like society and culture in general, became less Christian and more secular than they had been during the Middle Ages. For patrons, artists turned increasingly to men of state and business; for subjects they chose not only the traditional Virgin, Christ, and saints but also pagan gods and their own patrons. Interest in the things of this world, however, did not exclude concern with the next world; the Renaissance was *both* worldly *and* otherworldly.

The artists of the Renaissance, even more than its writers and thinkers, displayed an extraordinary range of talents and interests. They produced both secular and sacred works; they copied classical models and launched bold experiments in artistic expression; some of the very greatest were also the most versatile. Giotto painted, designed, and ornamented buildings,ced verses, and did handsomely in business. Leonardo was a jack of all trades and a master of many—painter and sculptor, musician and physicist, anatomist and geologist, inventor and city-planner. Michelangelo executed heroic frescoes and heroic statues, and

Giotto. "The Lamentation" (1305–1306). Fresco in the Arena Chapel, Padua.

PAINTING

Giotto and His Successors. Before 1300, Italian painters had generally followed Byzantine models: their work, while often splendid in color and drawing, was also flat and two-dimensional. Giotto (c. 1270–1337), though not entirely forsaking the Byzantine tradition, experimented to make painting more lifelike and less austere. He learned much from the realistic statues of Italian sculptors, who, in turn, had been influenced by the striking sculptures of French Gothic cathedrals. We may take as examples the frescoes Giotto executed for the Arena Chapel at Padua. In the "Return of Joachim to the Sheepfold," the dog greets his returned master with his right forepaw raised to scratch a welcome. In "The Lamentation," the mood of grief is intensified by the angels who are flying above the dead Christ and seem to be beating their wings in a transport of sorrow.

Giotto was no anonymous craftsman, content to work in obscurity, but a many-sided man, hungry for fame, and famous in his own day for his verses and his witty remarks as well as for his artistic accomplishments. His artistic commissions netted him a fortune, which he augmented through lending money, running a debt-collection service, and renting looms (at stiff fees) to poor woolen-weavers. Giotto had many connections with the great and wealthy; he won the patronage of Roman cardinals, the King of Naples, and the gilds and millionaires of Florence.

In the two centuries after Giotto, more and more despots, kings, and merchant princes joined the ranks of patrons. In Florence, the government, the wealthy magnates, and the churches and monasteries all engaged in a campaign for civic beauty. Lorenzo the Magnificent subsidized the great painter Botticelli as well as the humanists of the Platonic Academy. Il Moro, the Sforza despot in Milan, made Leonardo da Vinci in effect his Minister of Fine Arts, Director of Public Works, and Master of the Revels. After the collapse of Il Moro's fortunes, Leonardo found new patrons in Cesare Borgia, the Pope, and the French Kings Louis XII and Francis I. The popes, who employed Leonardo, Botticelli, Michelangelo, and many others, intended to make Rome the artistic capital of the world.

Masaccio, "Expulsion of Adam and Eve from Eden," c. 1425. Fresco in the Brancacci Chapel, Florence.

In subject matter, the sacred and the secular could often be found in the same picture. In a Florentine chapel, for instance, Giotto placed around a religious fresco a border of medallions portraying the sponsors, the banking family of the Peruzzi. Giotto's successors often introduced into a sacred painting a portrait of the person who had commissioned it. Usually the patron assumed a duly reverent posture, but with a hint of the ambition that had won him worldly success and permitted him to afford the luxury of subsidizing a work of art.

In treating pagan and classical themes Renaissance artists often showed great delicacy. There is nothing crude or carnal, for instance, in the *Primavera*, the pagan allegory of Spring painted by the Florentine master Botticelli (1445–1510). Mercury, the Three Graces, a surprisingly wistful Venus, the goddess Flora, bedecked with flowers, and Spring herself, blown in by the west wind, are all youthful, slender, almost, dainty, with the air of otherworldly sweetness for which Botticelli is famous. Botticelli seems to have moved in the circle of Pico della Mirandola, and his paintings often suggest an aspiration to some lofty Platonic realm. Yet he threw some of his own paintings of nudes onto the flames at the demand of the puritanical Savonarola.

Somewhat earlier Masaccio (1401–c. 1428), another Florentine genius, advanced the technique of painting by bold experiments. By varying the brightness of his colors and attempting contrasts in light and shade, called *chiaroscuro* (bright-dark), Masaccio achieved a three-dimensional quality, an illusion of depth. In painting the expulsion from the Garden of Eden, he conveyed the shame of Adam and Eve both by their facial expressions and by the forlorn posture of their bodies. The contrasts of light and shadow on their bodies heightened the dramatic impact. Where Masaccio relied, as it were, on mass to achieve his artistic effects, others turned to line and to color. Botticelli was a superb colorist and such a painstaking draughtsman that a botanist can identify the plants and flowers in his *Primavera*.

Leonardo, Michelangelo, Titian. The major trends that we have been following in patronage, subject matter, and technical proficiency reached a climax with the masters of the High Renaissance. We may take three of them as examples—Leonardo, Michelangelo, and Titian. Leonardo da Vinci completed relatively few pictures. His scientific activities and his innumerable services for his patrons took a large part of his time and energy. Some of his surviving paintings are badly damaged, notably the "Last Supper," a fresco executed on the wall of a monastery in Milan. Fortunately, one may discover Leonardo's superb talent and his extraordinary range of interests in the voluminous collections of his drawings and notebooks. The drawings include every sort of sketch, from preliminary work for paintings through realistic human embryos and fanciful war-machines to mere doodles.

From an intensive study of human anatomy Leonardo drew up rules for indicating the actions of human muscles and for establishing the proportions between the parts of the human body. He combined a zeal for scientific precision with a fondness for the grotesque that recalls the gargoyles of a Gothic cathedral; he did many sketches of the deformed and of people suffering intense strain and anguish. He made the "Last Supper" in part an exercise in artistic geometry, arranging the apostles in four groups of three men each around the central figure of Christ, and keeping the background deliberately simple. Older painters had usually shown the solemn yet peaceful moment of the final communion, and had suggested the coming treachery of Judas by placing him in isolation from the others. Not Leonardo. He chose the tense moment when Jesus announced the coming betrayal, and he placed Judas among the apostles, relying on facial and bodily expression to convey the guilt of the one and the consternation of the others.

Leonardo got on fairly amicably with his patrons. By contrast, Michelangelo Buonarroti (1475–1564) quarrelled repeatedly with the imperious Pope Julius II (reigned 1503–1513); it took all the Pope's cajolery to get Michelangelo to complete a fresco for the ceiling of the Sistine Chapel in the Vatican. The Sistine ceiling is in every respect a prodigious piece of work. The area is approximately 14 by 40 yards, and Michelangelo covered it with 343 separate figures. He executed the whole in the space of four years, working almost single-handed, assisted only by a plasterer and a color-mixer, painting uncomfortably on his back atop a scaffolding, sometimes not bothering to descend for his night's rest.

For this massive undertaking Michelangelo boldly chose the grandest scenes from Genesis—the creation of the sun and moon, God hovering over the waters, the creation of Adam and of Eve, the eating of the forbidden fruit, and the expulsion from Paradise. In this vast gallery of nudes in all types of poses, Michelangelo summed up all that Renaissance art had learned about perspective, anatomy, and motion. The Sistine ceiling also comes close to summarizing man's concepts of God; no medieval artist would have dared to represent the deity so directly. God appears repeatedly, draped in a mantle, an ever changing patriarch. Hovering over the waters, he is benign; giving life to the motionless Adam or directing Eve to arise, he is gently commanding; creating the sun and moon, he is the all-powerful deity, formidable and urgent as a whirlwind.

Both Michelangelo and Leonardo had received their artistic training in Florence. Their contemporary, Titian (1477–1576), who was identified with Venice, for 80 years enjoyed almost unbroken professional success and produced an average of one picture a month. He painted frescoes for the headquarters of the German merchant colony in Venice, portraits of rich merchants, altarpieces and madonnas for churches and monasteries, and a great battle scene for the palace of the Doge. By the middle decades of the sixteenth century, Titian was receiving offers from half the despots of Italy and the crowned heads of Europe. Titian transferred to paint much of the flamboyance and pageantry of Venice, using rich, intense colors, particularly reds and purples. A gallery of his portraits, at once elegant and revealing of character, would make a splendid introduction to the high politics—and politicians—of the sixteenth century.

Northern European Painting. The fame and influence of the Italians helped to stimulate the flowering of northern European painting in the sixteenth century. This northern Renaissance, however, also grew out of native traditions of Gothic art passed down from the Middle Ages. It centered in southern Germany and in the Low Countries. Its leading artists were Albrecht Dürer (1471–1528) and Hans Holbein (c. 1497–1543), Germans both, and Pieter Breughel the Elder (c. 1520–1569), who was born near Brussels. Dürer received commissions from the Emperor Maximilian. Armed with an introduction from Erasmus, Holbein moved to England, where he won the custom of humanists, aristocrats, and the court of King Henry VIII. Breughel had the support of businessmen in Antwerp and Brussels.

Michelangelo, David, 1501–1504. Academy, Florence.

Dürer was in many ways the Leonardo of Germany. His realistic yet compassionate portrait of his aged and homely mother might almost have come from da Vinci's sketchbook. He collected monkeys and other tropical specimens, painted the Virgin in the unusual pose of a "Madonna with Many Animals," and wrote treatises on perspective and human proportions. By sensitive use of line and shading Dürer revolutionized the hitherto primitive techniques of copper engraving and woodcuts. These innovations permitted the reproduction of drawings in many copies, enabling an artist to illustrate a whole edition prepared by the new process of printing. They brought Dürer closer than any Italian painter to the rapidly expanding public of readers; they made him in effect the first artist in history to become a "best seller."

Breughel delighted in scenes of peasant life—weddings, dances, festivals, skating parties—and also enjoyed painting a series of landscapes showing the cycle of farming activities during the various seasons. Northern art also retained the old medieval fascination with the monstrous and supernatural. Dürer, in a series of 16 woodcuts, depicted the Four Horsemen and the other grim marvels of the Apocalypse. Breughel's "Tower of Babel" is a nightmarish skyscraper, decayed, hideous, and unclean; and his bizarre "Battle of the Angels and the Demons" is full of "things" whose nearest relatives populate the science fiction and the surrealist art of the twentieth century—coats of arms that actually fight, shellfish that fly, hybrids with insect wings, artichoke bodies, and flower heads. Most of these fantasies were designed to teach a moral lesson; they were sermons in paint or ink. The painting of northern Europe demonstrates once more the medieval aspects of Renaissance men.

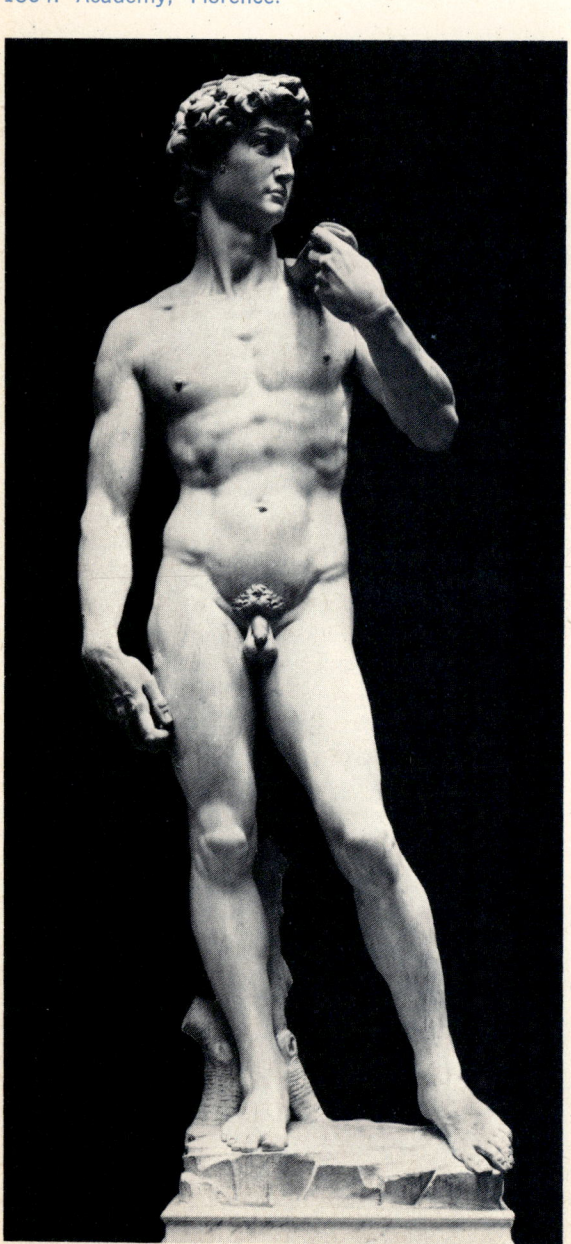

SCULPTURE

Renaissance painting owed its three-dimensional qualities partly to the painters' knowledge of sculpture; indeed Giotto, Leonardo, and Michelangelo were accomplished sculptors as well as painters. Sculptors, too, turned to classical models and secular themes, studied human anatomy, and experimented with new techniques. Donatello (c. 1386–1466), a Florentine, produced an equestrian statue of the *condottiere* Gattamelata in Padua that illustrates these changes: the subject is secular; the treatment is classical (Gattamelata looks like the commander of a Roman legion); and the material is bronze, not the traditional stone. Donatello also created one of the most remarkable religious sculptures of the Renaissance, a statue of Mary Magdalen, called by one critic "an emaciated monster." Emaciated the figure certainly is, all skin and bone, lank hair, and tattered clothing; but Mary Magdalen is a saint who looks the part.

 The genius of Michelangelo brought sculpture to the highest summit it had reached since the Age of Pericles, perhaps the highest in the whole record of the art. Early in his career, when the government of Florence invited him to create something beautiful from an enormous chunk of marble that another artist had seemingly spoiled, Michelangelo produced the renowned colossal statue of David. Late in his career, he met another exacting challenge in carving the figures of Dawn, Day, Dusk, and Night that adorn the tombs of the Medici family in Florence. The figures recline on sloping cornices yet do not seem about to slide

Donatello, detail of head, Mary Magdalen, c. 1454–1455. Baptistery, Florence.

off; they are relaxed but have enormous latent power. In portraying the Virgin grieving over the dead Christ—the *Pietà*—Michelangelo brilliantly solved the difficult technical problem of posing a seated woman with a corpse lying across her lap, and he triumphantly called attention to his feat by executing the work in highly polished marble. The face of Mary is sorrowful yet composed, and younger than that of the dead Christ. She is the eternal Virgin, Michelangelo explained, and so is always youthful and does not grieve in the manner of an earthly mother.

ARCHITECTURE

In 1546, at the age of 70, Michelangelo shouldered one more artistic burden: he agreed to be the chief architect of St. Peter's. He died in 1564 long before the great Roman basilica was finally completed in 1626, and his successors altered many of his details. But the great dome, the key feature of the whole structure, and the basic Greek-cross ground-plan with four equal arms followed his design.

Verrocchio, Equestrian monument of the **condottiere** Bartolommeo Colleoni, erected in Venice, 1485–1488.

Instead of Gothic towers, St. Peter's has Michelangelo's dome, which rises 435 feet above the floor below yet is dwarfed in mass by the immense building underneath. The great windows, pointed arches, and high-flung vaults of medieval churches sometimes create an impression of strain and instability; not so St. Peter's with its round arches, heavier walls, stout columns, and its Renaissance symmetry.

The architects of the Renaissance thus adapted domes, columns, round arches, and many other elements used in the buildings of ancient Rome; they also had some knowledge of humanistic learning, particularly the Greek concepts of perfect ideas and perfect geometric forms. Palladio, the foremost architectural theorist of the age, praised the Greek-cross plan for churches because of its symbolic values. If the apses (at the ends of the four arms) were rounded, and if the spaces between the arms were filled with rounded chapels, then the whole structure became an almost perfect circle. And the circle, according to Palladio, "demonstrates extremely well the unity, the infinite essence, the uniformity, and the justice of God."* Some scholars have detected a shift in religious emphasis in the change from the plan of the Latin cross, shaped like a crucifix, to the circled Greek cross; the medieval stress on the sacrifice of Christ yields to the Renaissance celebration of the perfection of God.

The lavish residences built during the Renaissance celebrated success in business or politics. Moreover, the growth of effective government meant that a man's home could be a showplace and no longer had to be, quite literally, his castle. Elaborately symmetrical villas now ornamented the countryside; in the cities rose the *palazzo* or palace, often not a royal or official structure but a private townhouse, combining business offices and residential apartments. Rome and Florence were dotted with them; in Venice they lined the Grand Canal from one end to the other. The usual palazzo was three-storied and rectangular, with its windows arranged in symmetrical rows.

The fame of Italian builders soon spread throughout Europe, even to distant Moscow, where Italian experts supervised the remodeling of the Kremlin for Ivan III. Most countries did not copy the Italian style outright but grafted it onto older native architecture. The resulting compound produced some very striking buildings, particularly the great sixteenth-century chateaux of central France, which gracefully combine elements taken from the Gothic church, the feudal castle, and the Italian palace.

MUSIC

A musical composition, like a building, has its basic skeleton or form, its over-all line, and its surface decorations and embellishments. Medieval sacred music had achieved very complex and elaborate combinations of form, line, and decoration. The center of Gothic music in the late Middle Ages was northern France and the Low Countries. By the fifteenth century French and Flemish musicians were journeying to Italy, where a process of mutual influence developed. The northerners took up the simple tunes of folk songs and dances; the Italians, in turn, added a strain of Gothic complexity to their austere plainsong. The end-product was the beautiful sacred music of the Italian composer Pales-

---

* Rudolf Wittkower, *The Architectural Principles of the Age of Humanism* (London, 1949), p. 21.

trina (c. 1525–1594), which was at once intricate in the northern manner and devout in the Italian.

Even in music the secularism and individualism of the Renaissance exerted an influence: the Flemings based their Masses on popular tunes. Moreover, Renaissance music was no longer anonymous; the day of the celebrated individual composer like Palestrina was at hand. And, like other artists, composers and performers of music experimented. They developed or imported a variety of new instruments—the violin, double bass, and harpsichord; the organ, with its complement of keyboards, pipes, and stops; the kettledrum, which was adopted from the Polish army; and the lute, which had originally been developed in medieval Persia and reached Italy by way of Moslem Spain.

Music played its role at almost every level of Renaissance society. The retinue of musicians became a fixture of court life, with the Dukes of Burgundy, Philip the Good and Charles the Bold, leading the way. In German towns "mastersingers" organized choral groups; the most famous of them, Hans Sachs, a cobbler in Nuremberg in the 1500's, was later immortalized in Wagner's opera *Die Meistersinger*. But the mastersingers followed directly in the tradition of the thirteenth-century minnesinger, and princely patronage of music went back at least to the twelfth-century court of Eleanor of Aquitaine and its chivalric troubadours. In music, too, the Renaissance built on the legacy it had received from the Middle Ages.

THE RENAISSANCE IDEAL: CASTIGLIONE

It is difficult to summarize an era as complex as the Renaissance. While no one man, nor single masterpiece of art or literature, was fully representative of it, its distinctive values and ideals were presented most sympathetically in a dialogue of manners published in 1528, *The Courtier* by Baldassare di Castiglione. Although Castiglione, like a medieval man, believes the profession of arms is the proper one for a gentleman, he recommends a quite unmedieval moderation and balance, and prescribes a humane and literary education in Latin and Greek. His courtier is to be a "universal man" like Leonardo. Castiglione is both reviving the old classical ideal of the well-rounded individual, "the sound mind in the sound body," and anticipating modern champions of the humanities and a liberal education.

Castiglione sings the praises of beauty: of God's physical world, of man, a little world in himself, and of the world of art. "The world," he says, is praised when one acclaims "the beautiful heaven, beautiful earth, beautiful sea, beautiful river, beautiful woods, trees, gardens, beautiful cities, beautiful churches, houses, armies. . . . And it may be said that good and beautiful be after a sort one self thing. . . ."* A medieval man might also have coupled the good and the beautiful, but he would have stressed the good and the ways in which God led man to righteousness. Medieval man had a vision of God's world. The Renaissance man, for whom Castiglione so eloquently speaks, had a vision not only of God's world but also of nature's world and man's world.

* Baldassare di Castiglione, *The Courtier,* T. Hoby translation, modernized (1907), p. 348.

6

READING SUGGESTIONS (asterisk indicates paperbound edition)

General Accounts

W. K. Ferguson, *Europe in Transition, 1300–1520* (Houghton, 1962). A comprehensive survey by a Canadian scholar.

D. Hay, *Europe in the Fourteenth and Fifteenth Centuries* (*Holt). An up-to-date survey by a British scholar.

E. P. Cheyney, *The Dawn of a New Era, 1250–1453* (*Torchbooks), and M. Gilmore, *The World of Humanism, 1453–1517* (*Torchbooks). Good introductory accounts, with very full bibliographies; the first two volumes in the series The Rise of Modern Europe, edited by W. L. Langer.

J. Huizinga, *The Waning of the Middle Ages* (*Anchor). A remarkable re-creation of the atmosphere of an entire period of European history, with particular stress on France and the Low Countries.

Economics and Society

W. K. Ferguson, *The Renaissance* (*Holt). Excellent short survey, stressing the social and economic background.

Miriam Beard, *A History of Business*, 2 vols. (*Ann Arbor). With good sketches of Renaissance millionaires.

A. W. O. von Martin, *Sociology of the Renaissance* (*Torchbooks). Instructive study of Italian society in the 1300's and 1400's.

F. C. Lane, *Venetian Ships and Shipping of the Renaissance* (Johns Hopkins, 1934). An exceptionally interesting monograph.

R. de Roover, *Rise and Decline of the Medici Bank, 1397–1494* (*Norton). A case history of the profits and pitfalls of Renaissance finance.

R. Ehrenberg, *Capital and Finance in the Age of the Renaissance: A Study of the Fuggers and Their Connections* (Harcourt, 1928). Another instructive case history.

The New Monarchies

G. Mattingly, *Renaissance Diplomacy* (*Penguin). A stimulating study concerning the origins of modern diplomatic techniques.

E. Perroy, *The Hundred Years' War* (*Capricorn). The authoritative book on the war; an excellent introduction to French history during the fourteenth and fifteenth centuries.

A. J. Slavin, ed., *New Monarchies and Representative Assemblies* (*Heath). A wide sample of views on constitutional developments.

May McKisack, *The Fourteenth Century* (Clarendon, 1959), and E. F. Jacob, *The Fifteenth Century* (Clarendon, 1961). Scholarly and detailed volumes in the Oxford History of England.

A. R. Myers, *England in the Late Middle Ages, 1307–1536* (*Penguin). Brief survey.

E. F. Jacob, *Henry V and the Invasion of France* (*Collier). A good popular treatment.

C. W. S. Williams, *Henry VII* (Barker, 1937). A solid study of the first Tudor monarch.

B. Wilkinson, *The Constitutional History of Medieval England, 1216–1485*, 3 vols. (Longmans, 1948–1964). Detailed scholarly treatment.

S. B. Chrimes, *English Constitutional History* (*Oxford). Reliable short survey.

J. H. Elliott, *Imperial Spain, 1469–1716* (*Mentor). An excellent up-to-date survey of Spain.

J. H. Mariéjol, *The Spain of Ferdinand and Isabella* (Rutgers, 1961). Readable study by a French scholar.

Germany and Italy

G. Barraclough, *The Origins of Modern Germany* (*Capricorn). The best general treatment of medieval Germany in English.

D. Hay, *The Italian Renaissance in Its Historical Background* (*Cambridge). An up-to-date introduction.

J. C. L. de Sismondi, *A History of the Italian Republics* (*Anchor). Famous old account from the early Middle Ages to the Renaissance.

J. A. Symonds, *The Age of the Despots* (*Capricorn). Another famous old account, the first volume of an extended study of Renaissance Italy.

H. Baron, *The Crisis of the Early Italian Renaissance* (*Princeton). Monograph affording many insights into Italian politics; fully abreast of modern scholarship.

F. Schevill, *Medieval and Renaissance Florence*, 2 vols. (*Torchbooks) and *The Medici* (*Torchbooks). Clear and useful.

C. M. Ady, *Lorenzo de' Medici and Renaissance Italy* (*Collier). A brief, popular account.

DeL. Jensen, ed., *Machiavelli—Cynic, Patriot, or Political Scientist?* (*Heath). Introduction to the many conflicting interpretations of the author of *The Prince.*

J. R. Hale, *Machiavelli and Renaissance Italy* (*Torchbooks). Good short biography.

Interpretations of the Renaissance

K. H. Dannenfeldt, ed., *Renaissance—Medieval or Modern?* (*Heath). A good sampler.

G. C. Sellery, *The Renaissance: Its Nature and Origins* (*Wisconsin). Clear and helpful survey.

W. K. Ferguson, *The Renaissance in Historical Thought: Five Centuries of Interpretation* (Houghton, 1948). Stimulating.

J. Burckhardt, *The Civilization of the Renaissance in Italy*, 2 vols. (*Torchbooks). The classic defense of the Renaissance as unique and revolutionary.

F. Chabod, *Machiavelli and the Renaissance* (*Torchbooks). With a fruitful chapter, "The Concept of the Renaissance."

L. Olschki, *The Genius of Italy* (Cornell, 1954). Solid essays on many aspects of the Renaissance.

Literature and Learning

P. O. Kristeller, *Renaissance Thought*, 2 vols. (*Torchbooks). Valuable study, emphasizing its diversity.

H. O. Taylor, *The Humanism of Italy* (*Collier). Excerpted from the author's highly regarded *Thought and Expression in the Sixteenth Century.*

R. R. Bolgar, *The Classical Heritage and Its Beneficiaries from the Carolingian Age to the End of the Renaissance* (*Torchbooks). The last third of this scholarly study treats the Renaissance.

G. Highet, *The Classical Tradition: Greek and Roman Influences on Western Literature* (*Galaxy). A lively survey.

J. Huizinga, *Erasmus and the Age of the Reformation* (*Torchbooks). Excellent.

A. Hyma, *The Christian Renaissance* (Shoe String, 1965). Study of an aspect of the era often neglected.

Marie Boas, *The Scientific Renaissance, 1450–1630* (*Torchbooks). Helpful account.

H. Butterfield, *The Origins of Modern Science, 1300–1800* (*Free Press). Controversial study, minimizing the scientific contribution of the Renaissance.

G. Sarton, *Six Wings: Men of Science in the Renaissance* (*Meridian). Appreciations by a famous historian of science.

A. C. Crombie, *Medieval and Early Modern Science*, Vol. II (*Anchor). A good survey.

L. Thorndike, *Science and Thought in the Fifteenth Century* (Columbia, 1929). By a specialist on medieval science.

The Arts

G. Vasari, *Lives of the Artists* (*several editions). Famous biographies of Italian painters, sculptors, and architects.

H. Wölfflin, *The Art of the Italian Renaissance: A Handbook for Students and Travellers* (*Schocken). By a ranking expert of an earlier day.

B. Berenson, *The Italian Painters of the Renaissance* (*Meridian). Essays by a famous collector and enthusiast.

F. Antal, *Florentine Painting and Its Social Background* (Kegan Paul, 1948). An attempt to relate art to economic and social currents.

E. Panofsky, *Studies in Iconology: Humanistic Themes in the Art of the Renaissance* (*Torchbooks). By a distinguished and stimulating scholar.

E. J. Dent, *Music of the Renaissance in Italy* (British Academy, 1935). By a great authority.

Sources

J. Froissart, *Chronicles of England, France, and Spain* (*Dutton). A great narrative source of late medieval history.

The History of Comines, T. Danett, trans. (D. Nutt, 1897). Account of Louis XI and Charles the Bold by a contemporary.

Machiavelli, *The Prince* and *The Discourses* (*Modern Library).

J. B. Ross and M. M. McLaughlin, eds., *The Portable Renaissance Reader* (*Viking). A wide-ranging anthology.

W. L. Gundesheimer, ed., *The Italian Renaissance* (*Spectrum). Selections from eleven representative writers.

Erasmus, *The Praise of Folly* (*Ann Arbor).

P. Taylor, ed., *The Notebooks of Leonardo da Vinci: A New Selection* (*Mentor).

A. H. Popham, ed., *The Drawings of Leonardo da Vinci* (*Harvest).

Fiction

G. B. Shaw, *St. Joan* (*Penguin). Perhaps a more successful drama than history.

Josephine Tey, *The Daughter of Time* (*Dell). Fascinating effort to rehabilitate Richard III of England; by a writer of detective stories.

D. Merezhkovsky, *The Romance of Leonardo da Vinci* (*Signet). The best novel on the Renaissance, romanticized but based on Leonardo's notebooks.

V. Hugo, *Notre Dame de Paris* (*several editions), and W. Scott, *Quentin Durward* (*Signet). Celebrated Romantic novels set in the France of Louis XI.

N. Balchin, *The Borgia Testament* (Houghton, 1949). Autobiography as Cesare might have written it.

7

Transition to a New World

Religious Upheaval,
Imperial Expansion, Dynastic Conflict

The Chateau of Chambord, built by Francis I in the Loire Valley.

I. The Protestant and Catholic Reformations

LUTHER

Though all aspects of the past arouse our emotions to some extent at least, most of us can remain relatively detached until we come to the issues that engage us in this chapter. Here even the terms in common use betray involvement: the Protestant refers to the Protestant *"Reformation,"* the Catholic to the Protestant *"Revolt."* Even the secularist or skeptic can hardly claim to be impartial, for he inevitably feels that Protestantism, if only because it did shatter the unity and conformity of medieval Catholicism, prepared the way for men like him to exist. Old exaggerations, old slanders from the partisan struggle of the times are still bandied about: that Luther led a revolt against the Church so that he, a monk, could marry; that the Catholic clergy sold salvation; that Henry VIII broke with the Pope so that he might marry.

Luther's Revolt. On October 31, 1517, Martin Luther (1483–1546) nailed his 95 Theses to the door of the court church at Wittenberg in Saxony. The action touched off what proved to be a major social, economic, and intellectual revolution. Neither Luther nor other later major leaders like Calvin intended such a revolution. They conceived of themselves not as starting *new* churches but as going back to the true *old* church as reformers. Again and again, as we know, the Catholic Church had faced reform movements like the Cluniac, the Cistercian, the Franciscan, and had absorbed them. In the fourteenth and fifteenth centuries Wyclif and Hus had almost created separate, or schismatic, churches. The Conciliar movement, in the early fifteenth century, had challenged papal authority, though it had failed to subordinate the pope to the views of a general council.

Luther's action, however, led to the organization of a separate church outside the Catholic communion. Within a generation after 1517, dozens of sects or denominations in addition to the Lutheran came into existence: Anglican, Calvinist, Anabaptist, and many others. We take this multiplicity so much for granted today that it is worth emphasizing how great a departure this was in the sixteenth century, what a real revolution from medieval religious unity.

Son of a German peasant who became a miner and eventually a prosperous investor in mining enterprises, Luther studied law in his youth; then in 1505, at the age of 22, he had a shattering experience. Caught in a severe thunderstorm and greatly frightened, he prayed to St. Anne for help, and pledged himself to become a monk. Once in the monastery, however, he underwent a major personal crisis: he was sure he was a lost soul without hope of salvation. Though he submitted to the monastic discipline of his order and made a pilgrimage to Rome in 1510, none of the good works he did could free him from the fear that he could not attain God's grace, and that he must therefore be destined for hell. It was only when his confessor told him to study the Bible that Luther, from his readings in the Epistles of St. Paul and in St. Augustine, found an answer to his anxiety: he must have faith in God, faith in the possibility of his own salvation. The Roman Church had of course always taught this. What was new about Luther was his emphasis on *faith alone, to the exclusion of works.* The promise that faith alone might mean salvation had a particular attraction in an age of doubt and gloom, rather like the era when men had first turned to Christianity.

Luther then began to question practices which in his view were abuses tending to corrupt or weaken faith. He cast his questions in the form of the 95 Theses, written in Latin and in the manner of the medieval Scholastics as a challenge to debate. The specific abuse that he attacked he called the "sale" of indulgences, particularly the activities of Tetzel, a Dominican who, with papal authorization, was conducting a "drive" for contributions to rebuild St. Peter's in Rome.

The theory of indulgences did *not* concern forgiveness for sins: only God could forgive a sin; no indulgence could assure such forgiveness. But repentant sinners had to do penance on earth and suffer punishment after death in purgatory, in order to prepare for heaven. The theory of indulgences *did* concern remission of such punishment. The Church claimed that Christ, the Virgin, and the Saints had performed so many good works that the surplus constituted a

Martin Luther, by Cranach (1525).

Treasury of Merit. A priest could secure for a layman a draft, as it were, on this heavenly treasury. This was an indulgence and could remit penance on earth and part or all of the punishment in purgatory. Such an indulgence was "granted" by the priest; any monetary contribution thereupon made by the recipient was a free-will offering. But Luther said that Tetzel was selling indulgences.

To the man in the street it seemed as though a sinner could obtain *not only* remission of punishment *but also* forgiveness of sin, *if only* he secured enough indulgences, and that this depended on his money-gifts to Tetzel. In the 95 Theses, Luther objected vehemently both to Tetzel's perversion of indulgences and to the whole doctrine behind them. He thus minimized the importance of good works at a moment when many ordinary believers were trying to increase their stock of such works by drawing on the Treasury of Merit. Christian theory usually insists on the need for *both* faith and good works. Luther's emphasis on faith drove his papal opponents into a corresponding extreme emphasis on works, and this in turn drove him, in moments of excitement, to deny the uses of works and to insist on faith alone. Since "works" include all earthly ecclesiastical organization and the priestly way of doing things, Luther before long was denying that priests are necessary. He had enunciated the doctrine of the priesthood of all believers; in popular terms, "every man his own priest."

In 1518, Luther defied a papal emissary, and refused to recant some of his propositions on indulgences. In 1519, at Leipzig, in debate with the learned theologian John Eck, who accused him of disobeying the authority of the popes and church councils, Luther said that popes and councils were not necessarily authoritative. He said he accepted certain views of Hus which the Council of Constance had declared heretical. In 1520, in his *Appeal to the Christian Nobility of the German Nation*, Luther called the term "spiritual estate," as used to describe the clergy, a "lie," and declared that "all Christians are truly of the spiritual estate, and there is no difference among them save of office." When Pope Leo X issued a bull condemning Luther's teaching, Luther burnt it. In 1520 he was excommunicated, and the Emperor Charles V and the imperial diet solemnly declared him an outlaw at Worms. Once again he was asked whether he would recant. His reply contained his most famous words:

> Your Imperial Majesty and Your Lordships demand a simple answer. Here it is, plain and unvarnished. Unless I am convicted of error by the testimony of Scripture or (since I put not trust in the unsupported authority of Pope or of councils, since it is plain that they have often erred and often contradicted themselves) by manifest reasoning I stand convicted by the Scriptures to which I have appealed, and my conscience is taken captive by God's word, I cannot and will not recant anything, for to act against our conscience is neither safe for us, nor open to us.
> *Hier stehe ich. Ich kann nicht anders. Gott helff mir. Amen.* [On this I take my stand. I can do no other. God help me. Amen.]*

The empire and the papacy took their drastic actions in vain, for Luther was already gathering a substantial following and becoming a national hero. He had the protection of the ruler of his own German state, the Elector Frederick the Wise of Saxony, and was soon to secure the backing of other princes. In the next few years he translated the Bible into vigorous and effective German, and re-

* *Documents of the Christian Church,* H. Bettenson, ed. (New York, 1947), p. 285.

modelled the church in Saxony according to his own views. His revolt was a success.

The Reasons for Luther's Success. More than theology was at issue in Luther's revolt. The Catholic Church that Luther attacked was, as many Catholic historians grant, at the time in one of its more worldly periods. Especially in its center at Rome, it had come under the influence of the new wealth of the Renaissance and the new fashions of good living. The papacy, triumphant over the councils, had been drawn into Italian politics, and the Rome Luther visited in his younger days was a shocking spectacle of intrigue, display, and corruption. Some part of Luther's success lay in the fact that he was attacking practices abhorrent to decent men, and reasserting the primacy of the spirit over materialism.

There was a second great reason for his success: in the name of good Germans he was attacking the practices of Italians and Italianate Germans. In the eyes of Luther and his followers, Tetzel was not only performing theologically and morally outrageous acts; he was raising money to enrich Italy:

> For Rome is the greatest thief and robber that had ever appeared on earth, or ever will. . . . Poor Germans that we are—we have been deceived! We were born to be masters, and we have been compelled to bow the head beneath the yoke of our tyrants. . . . It is time the glorious Teutonic people should cease to be the puppet of the Roman pontiff.*

What Luther started, a good many German princes soon took out of his hands. They stood to gain, not only by cutting off the flow of German money to Italy, but by confiscating Catholic property, especially monastic property, which was not needed for the Lutheran Church. Moreover, Luther gave them a new weapon in their eternal struggle against their feudal overlord, the emperor. The princes were also moved by Luther's German patriotism.

Luther's personal energy, courage, and intelligence were of major importance. He wrote the pamphlets that did for this revolution what Tom Paine and the Declaration of Independence did for the American. He wrote his *Appeal to the Christian Nobility of the German Nation* in the vernacular German, not the academic Latin, so that it became a "best seller." Luther's translation made the Bible a part of German life. Its language became one of the bases of modern literary German. Luther's marriage to a former nun and his raising of a large family dramatized the break with Rome. And behind all this was his passionate conviction that he was doing what he had to do: "*Ich kann nicht anders.*"

The forces that opposed Luther were relatively weak. Clerical opposition centered in the top levels of the Catholic bureaucracy: Pope Leo X was only its willing instrument. Many moderate Catholics were anxious to compromise and avert a schism. Had there been at the head of the Catholic Church a pope willing to reform and to make concessions not harmful to the Church as God's chosen instrument on earth, even Luther might perhaps have been reconciled. Yet, as in all the great modern revolutions, the moderates—gifted, numerous, and active though they were—could not hold up against the extremists. Once Leo X had excommunicated Luther in 1520, the way to compromise was probably blocked, for Luther's associates could have been won away from him only by concessions too great for a Catholic to make.

* *Ibid.*, pp. 278–279.

Politically, the Catholic opposition in these critical years found its leader in the young Emperor Charles V (reigned 1519–1556). Grandson on his father's side of the Emperor Maximilian and Mary, daughter of Charles the Bold of Burgundy, and on his mother's side of Ferdinand and Isabella, Charles of Habsburg was the fruit of a series of marriages that gave rise to the epigram "Let other wage wars; thou, happy Austria, marry." Together with the Habsburgs' lands in Austria and elsewhere and their claim to the title of Emperor, Charles V inherited the Low Countries, Spain and the Spanish lands overseas, and parts of Italy. This was geographically the nearest thing to a European superstate since Charlemagne, and Charles V wanted to make it a political reality. The activities of Luther's princely German supporters threatened his hold over Germany; moreover, Charles, though by no means a mere papal instrument, was a devout Catholic. He decided to fight.

War and Rebellion in the 1520's. Charles V entrusted the government of the Germans to his younger brother Ferdinand, who formed alliances with Bavaria and other Catholic German states to oppose the Lutheran states. Thus began a long series of combinations, the fruits of which were the religious wars of the next few generations, and the enduring territorial division of Germany into, roughly, a Protestant north and east and a Catholic south and west. But the imperial Habsburg power also had to fight against the French, and so could not steadily concentrate on defeating the Lutherans in Germany. In 1529 the Lutheran princes protested against the sudden new imperial severity against them.

In Germany, below the level of the princes, the knights espoused Luther's cause. Some of them held castles and small estates direct from the Emperor and were in theory just as "independent" as a greater prince. Others were vassals of some greater lord. Some were younger sons, who were feeling the decline of their status caused by changing economic and social conditions (*see* Chapter 6). Under the leadership of Ulrich von Hutten and Franz von Sickingen, they rose in 1522, in what is called the "Knights' War." Troops of the western German archbishoprics put them down, but their struggle added to the disorder of the period.

Worse still was the Peasants' Rebellion of 1524–1525, not unlike the French Jacquerie of 1358 or the English Peasants' Revolt of 1381: like them directed against the remaining burdens of the manorial system, like them without competent military commanders, and like them ruthlessly suppressed. It centered, not in the eastern German regions where serfdom had been completely enforced, but in the southwest, where the peasants had begun to emancipate themselves and wanted to finish the process. Much as Wyclif and the Lollards had influenced the English peasants, Luther's preaching stirred those in Germany. More than their English counterparts of the fourteenth century, the German peasants had educated leaders with a revolutionary program of their own which they embodied in the "Twelve Articles." Couched in biblical language, the articles seem moderate enough today: each parish should choose its own priest; tithes and taxes should be lowered; the peasants should have the right to take game and firewood from the forests; and so on.

Lutheran Conservatism. Horrified at the peasants' interpretation of the Bible that he had translated into German for them, Luther denounced the rebels in unbridled terms. He intended his church to be respectful of established political authority, and once said, "The princes of the world are gods, the common people are Satan." This conservatism is quite consistent with Luther's fundamental spiritual position. If the visible external world is subordinate to the invisible spiritual world, the best one can hope for here on earth is that good order be maintained. Kings, princes, authority, custom, law: all existing institutions are preferable to discussion and dissension.

The princes of northern Germany and the Scandinavian kingdoms reciprocated. They superintended and hastened the process of converting the willing to Lutheranism and evicting the unwilling. By the mid-sixteenth century Lutheranism had become the state religion of these regions, and, as such, it was often the docile instrument of political rulers.

In organizing his own church, Luther showed the same conservatism. After all, the logical extreme of the priesthood of all believers is no church at all, or as many churches as there are individual human beings; in Saxony, reformers influenced by Luther tried out these anarchical concepts before Luther himself and the moderates intervened. Luther's new church often simply took over the existing church buildings. It did have priests; but they were free to marry, a sign that they had no more sacramental powers than other men. The Lutherans retained two of the sacraments: baptism and the Eucharist, both specifically mentioned in the Bible, but deprived them of their miraculous quality. Veneration of saints and relics, fasts, pilgrimages, monastic orders all vanished. Yet the forms of worship retained much that had been traditional. To Luther this new church was not merely an alternative to the Church of Rome, it was the *one true church,* a return to early Christianity before Rome had corrupted it.

ZWINGLI

Only a year after Luther nailed his theses to the door at Wittenberg, a Swiss priest named Ulrich Zwingli (1484–1531), a humanist trained in the tradition of Erasmus, launched a quieter reform in Zurich. It produced no single organized church, but extended and deepened some of the fundamental theological and moral concepts of Protestantism. Like Luther, Zwingli objected to the idea that priests had miraculous powers not possessed by laymen. But he felt that the social conscience of enlightened people led by good pastors would achieve a common discipline that would promote righteous living. Like Luther, Zwingli opposed priestly celibacy, fasts, monasticism, confession, and indulgences. He thought the appeal to saints and the use of incense, candles, and images were "superstition." He began the process of making the church building an almost undecorated hall, of making the service a sermon and responsive reading, and of abolishing the Catholic liturgy.

Zwingli's chief point of difference with Luther was sacramental. The Catholics believed in transubstantiation: that the bread and wine of the communion miraculously became in *substance* the body and blood of Christ, although their chemical make-up—their accidents—remained unchanged. Luther denied the miracle of the Mass, and believed in consubstantiation: that the body and blood were somehow *present* in the bread and wine. Zwingli believed what has become the usual Protestant doctrine: that the bread and wine merely *symbolized* the body and blood.

Zwingli won over the government of Zurich and most of its citizens; and many of the other German-speaking towns of Switzerland became Protestant. But the Catholic cantons went to war against the Protestants, and Zwingli was killed in 1531. Though the individual Swiss cantons were allowed to choose their form of worship thereafter, Protestant leadership had suffered a severe blow.

CALVIN

It recovered a decade later, when John Calvin (1509–1564) took power in Geneva. French-born and Paris-educated, Calvin was a classicist and lawyer, converted from Catholicism by his reading of Erasmus and Luther. He took refuge in the Swiss town of Basel, and there published his *Institutes of the Christian Religion* (1536), a complete summary of his theological and moral views and a work of great influence in spreading Protestant thought. Both Calvin and Luther rejected good works as a way to salvation. But, where Luther emphasized the view that a man could save himself by faith, Calvin emphasized the awe-inspiring majesty of God and the littleness of man.

In fact, Calvin said, man cannot save himself by faith, or by anything else, since God alone can save. God from the beginning predetermined—predestined—who among men would be saved and who eternally damned. He had chosen very few, his "elect," for salvation; no man could attain it by his own merit. Nor was there any way for a man to know certainly whether he was among the elect. Of course, he *could* be sure, if he led a life contrary to Christian morality, that he was damned. But no matter how moral a life he led he could never be sure that he was saved; he just *might* possibly be among the elect. This was the only crumb of comfort Calvin's system held out.

Calvinist Practice. Stern logic, rigorous morality, an Old Testament conception of God, and emphasis on strict observance of commandments characterized Calvinist views and Calvinist behavior. The French-speaking city of Geneva asked Calvin in 1541 to help in a rebellion against its Catholic Bishop and the Count of Savoy. From 1541 until his death 23 years later, Calvin was the supreme ruler of the city. Geneva became a theocracy, literally a government by God, in practice a system in which the church governed all aspects of the citizen's life. Protestant refugees from other parts of Europe came to learn from Calvin. John Knox (1513–1572) took the system back to Scotland; others took Calvinism to Holland, to France, to England (whence it crossed the Atlantic to Massachusetts), and to Hungary and Poland.

In the Low Countries, Calvinism became in the second half of the sixteenth century the symbol of Dutch nationalism against the Spanish rule of Charles V's heir, Philip II (*see* p. 301). In France, Calvinist ideas led to the foundation of churches called "Huguenot" (perhaps from the German word *Eidgenosse*, "covenanted"), chiefly in the old southwestern strongholds of the Albigensian heresy (*see* Chapter 4). Here,

Classroom sketches of Calvin, by one of his students.

as elsewhere in Europe, the Protestants would have to fight not for toleration but for supremacy. Few men of the time could conceive of subjects of the same ruler peacefully practicing different religions.

Where the Calvinists controlled an area, they censored, interfered, and punished; they were petty tyrants, denying the individual much of his privacy, pleasure, and individualism. They were sure they were God's agents, doing God's work. These firm believers in the inability of human efforts to change anything were the most ardent workers for change in human behavior. The world to them was a serious place, and they were sure that music, dancing, gambling, fine clothes, drinking, and the theater were to Satan's liking. Sexual intercourse, they said, had as its sole purpose the perpetuation of the race, not the pleasure of the participants. This philosophy of life is called Puritanism. Within each man the struggle raged between the temptations of the world and his "Puritan conscience"; in his dealings with others, the Puritan tried not only to coerce but also to convert. We shall encounter Puritanism again in sixteenth- and seventeenth-century England.

THE ENGLISH REFORMATION

Henry VIII. In England, the signal for religious overturn was very different from Luther's 95 Theses. Henry VIII (reigned 1509–1547), the second Tudor king, badly wanted a male heir, and his wife, Catherine of Aragon, aunt of the Emperor Charles V, had not produced one. His legal case for separation was thin: Catherine had been married first to his deceased brother, Arthur, and Henry now discovered after 20 years of marriage that canon law forbade marriage with a deceased brother's widow. Henry, who had published an attack on Lutheran ideas, for which the Pope had declared him Defender of the Faith, tried hard to obtain an annulment from the Pope. But the Pope was unwilling to risk offending Charles V, whose troops were in control of Rome at the time (1527). In 1530, the obliging Archbishop of Canterbury, Thomas Cranmer, pronounced the marriage annulled, and Henry married Anne Boleyn. The Pope excommunicated Henry and declared the annulment invalid. Henry broke relations with the papacy and, by the Act of Supremacy (1534), became "supreme head" of the Church of England.

In these drastic actions, Henry had the support of Parliament, which voted the Act of Supremacy. This is the clearest proof that there was more than the King's private life involved. Had it not been for the substantial body of antipapal opinion among Englishmen, Henry could not have acted as he did. In fact, antipapal and more generalized anticlerical sentiment was nothing new in England. The ideas of Luther and other Protestants had won the sympathies of a good many Englishmen, though many others, including Thomas More (1478–1535), author of *Utopia,* favored reform only within the church. (More lost his head for opposing the Act of Supremacy.)

One target of the English anti-Catholics was the monasteries, many of which were wealthy and corrupt. By closing them and confiscating their property, Henry VIII won the favor of the nobles and gentry to whom he passed on the loot. The confiscation and redistribution of monastic properties virtually amounted to a social and economic revolution, binding the recipients more closely to their benefactor, the King, and greatly increasing their wealth.

Yet all through, Henry considered himself a Catholic, not a Protestant. In his eyes and in those of some of its communicants today, the Church of England remained a Catholic body. Except for the abolition of monasteries and the break with Rome, Henry was determined to make no change. In this way he stimulated two kinds of opposition: from Catholics like More who felt that Henry had gone much too far, and from militant Protestants who felt that Henry had not gone nearly far enough, and who wanted to introduce clerical marriage and the use of English in the ritual, and to abolish auricular confession (i.e., confession spoken into the ear of a priest in private) and the invocation of saints. Partly because so many of its members were now complacent with their new riches, Parliament did

Henry VIII, by Holbein.

what Henry wanted. In 1539 it passed the Six Articles, reaffirming clerical celibacy, confession, and four other important Catholic points of doctrine and ritual, and making their denial heresy. But by this definition there were far too many heretics to be rooted out, and England became the scene of wide religious experiment and variation.

The Later Tudors. When the frail young Edward VI (reigned 1547–1553) succeeded his father Henry VIII, the government for a time turned more strongly Protestant. The Six Articles were repealed in 1547, and in 1549 Parliament passed an Act requiring uniformity of church services, and introduced an official prayer book. Cranmer, still Archbishop of Canterbury, and a convinced Protestant (he had married), published 42 Articles of Religion in 1551. But when Edward VI died, the crown passed to his half-sister, the Catholic Mary Tudor (reigned 1553–1558), daughter of Henry VIII by Catherine of Aragon. A plot to put her cousin, the Protestant Lady Jane Grey, on the throne failed, and Mary as Queen tried to restore Catholicism.

When she announced her intention of marrying the very Catholic Philip II of Spain, who was, however, to be without power in England, a rebellion broke out. Mary suppressed it. Lady Jane Grey was executed, and Mary married Philip. A Catholic became Archbishop of Canterbury, and Cranmer was burned at the stake. Perhaps 300 in all lost their lives in Mary's persecutions, which won her the celebrated sobriquet of "Bloody Mary."

When she died in 1558, her half-sister Elizabeth, daughter of Henry VIII by Anne Boleyn, succeeded her as Queen (reigned 1558–1603). Elizabeth was a Protestant, and soon after her accession all of Mary's Catholic legislation was repealed and all of Henry VIII's laws regarding the Church were re-enacted. In 1563 Parliament adopted the 39 Articles, modified from Cranmer's 42 of 1551. The Articles rejected clerical celibacy, auricular confession, papal supremacy, and the use of Latin. They required that the laity receive communion in both wine and bread, whereas the Catholic Church gave only the bread. Though they rejected Catholic doctrine on the Eucharist, they also rejected Zwinglian symbolism: the members of the Anglican Church would receive the Eucharist as the body and blood of Christ. The Articles avoided the Lutheran doctrines of justification by faith and the priesthood of all believers.

Ever since, the 39 Articles of 1563 and the Elizabethan prayer book have remained the essential documents of the Anglican faith. At the time, however, Elizabeth was faced by Catholic opposition, both within England and abroad, where Spaniards and Scots, in particular, were hostile. Even more serious was the opposition of Protestants who wanted to purify the Church of England of what they considered papist survivals. Some of these Puritans were moderates, who were willing to retain bishops if the ritual were simplified. Some were Presbyterians, who accepted the full Calvinist theology and wanted to abolish bishops and substitute synods of elders (presbyters) as the government of the church. Some were radicals—called Brownists after their leader Robert Browne—who wanted each congregation to be an independent body, and who anticipated the later Congregationalists and Independents. Elizabeth tolerated all but Catholics at one extreme and Brownists at the other.

Indeed, the Church of England has ever since reflected the wide range of religious sentiment in the country. It has always had "High Church" communicants who think of themselves as Catholics, and "Low Church" communicants who are far more Protestant in outlook, as well as those of intermediate opinion. It retains a modified form of the Catholic hierarchy, with archbishops and bishops, though of course it does not recognize papal authority, and its clergy may marry. Moderation—of ritual, hierarchy, discipline—has been its outstanding characteristic. But it has also had many people who emphasize earnest evangelical piety, social service, plain living, and high thinking: Puritans who have not left the church.

THE RADICAL LEFT: ANABAPTISTS AND UNITARIANS

Among those touched by Luther's teachings in Germany were some who took quite literally his doctrine of justification by faith, and fell into the anarchy which he avoided. Since each man was to find in his own conscience God's universal law, all written law was to be rejected: these people were Antinomian (from the Greek "against law"). They did not believe in class distinctions or in the customary forms of private property. Some of them practiced polygamy: if they took several wives, it was clear that God wanted them to, since they wanted to. In 1534–1535 a group of these radicals under the leadership of a Dutch tailor, John of Leyden, took control of the city of Münster in western Germany, where John was crowned as "King David" and kept a kind of harem in attendance. They were put down by force, and John was killed.

These radicals believed that the Catholic sacrament of baptism for infants was invalid, since no infant could "understand" the significance of the act. By "understanding" they did not mean an intellectual process but emotional or instinctive comprehension and participation. Therefore they baptized again anybody who joined them: as an adult, he was now for the first time able to "understand" what he was doing, and this kind of baptism alone had validity. Thus arose the name Anabaptists (from the Greek for "baptizing again"); later generations were not baptized until they came of age, and so the prefix "ana" was dropped. Most of the sixteenth-century Anabaptists were by no means as wild or fanatical as the followers of John of Leyden. They established communities and lived as they thought the early Christians had lived—working, sharing, and praying together.

The wide divergence of beliefs and practices among the sixteenth-century groups loosely called Anabaptist arose in part because many very earnest and ignorant people were for the first time reading the Bible for individual guidance, and—especially in the apocalyptic books of the Old Testament and in the Book of Revelation—were finding just about anything they were looking for. Many Anabaptist groups broke sharply with the old forms of worship; their congregations no longer remained quiet during the services, but shouted or danced. All sang hymns with great fervor. The sermon became very important, and was often highly charged emotionally with hopes of heaven and fears of hell. Some of the sects expected the Second Coming of Christ immediately. Some shared among themselves what little property they had, and so were communists of a sort.

Distrusting the state, refusing to take oaths on grounds of conscience, coming mostly from the poorest classes, occasionally going to such radical extremes as those at Münster, the Anabaptists frightened the conventional and the comfortable in society. They became the objects of vigorous persecution, which made no distinction between the socially dangerous and the brave, quiet, humble

Christians among them. Their high sense of community, their asceticism, their sober, industrious behavior have outlived the excesses of the more eccentric, and can be seen today among Baptists, Quakers, Mennonites, Moravians, and a good many other sects.

Close to the Anabaptists, too, was one other strain of Protestantism: Unitarianism, the denial of the Trinity and of the full divinity of Christ. Its most famous advocate, the Spanish mystic Michael Servetus (1511–1553), stressed the humanity of Christ without depriving him of his divine attributes altogether. He hoped thereby to make it easier for individual human beings to feel a sense of mystic identification with Christ, and thus achieve salvation. Both Catholics and Protestants found these views alarming. Calvin had Servetus burnt at the stake in Geneva in 1553 for heresy. Another Unitarian, however, the Italian Socinus (Sozzini, 1539–1604), preached successfully among Poles and Hungarians. Present-day Unitarians in England and the United States are not the direct heirs of the mystic tradition of Servetus: imbued instead with the rationalism of the eighteenth-century Enlightenment, they believe that Christ was simply a particularly inspired human being, but not divine.

PROTESTANT ATTRIBUTES

From Henry VIII (who almost certainly never thought of himself as a Protestant) through Luther, Zwingli, and Calvin to John of Leyden and Servetus is a broad spectrum indeed. What did these Protestants have in common? All repudiated the claim of the Roman Catholic Church to be supreme. Each was convinced that his own church was the true successor of Christ and the Apostles. Even the Antinomians, who believed that each man carried the truth in his own bosom, went on to say that if one could sweep away the obstacles to truth, each man would find the *same* truth in his own bosom. Some Protestants were prepared to educate humanity in the correctness of their own beliefs, and so convert it; others could not wait: so Calvin, having been persecuted himself, persecuted Servetus. Religious tolerance and the peaceful coexistence of many churches—concepts that we today take for granted—were rare indeed in the sixteenth and seventeenth centuries.

All Protestants reduced the ritual and other external manifestations of belief. The seven sacraments of the Catholic Church were diminished, often to only two, baptism and the Eucharist; the various sects differed widely in their views on the meaning of the sacraments. "Papist" practices like the veneration of saints, the saying of rosaries, and the making of pilgrimages disappeared among all Protestants. The more radical banished music and painting, and greatly simplified church architecture and decoration. All Protestants appealed from an established order to a "higher law," so echoing Luther's appeal from works to faith. All had at least a tinge of individualism, which they bequeathed to the modern world.

PROTESTANTISM AND PROGRESS

Friends of Protestantism often maintain that there was also something fundamentally "modern" and "progressive" about the Reformation that sets it off from the "medieval" and "stagnant" centuries that preceded it. They contrast the predominantly Protestant British Empire and United States, their economic prosperity, their democratic constitutional government, their progress in the sciences, with Catholic nations, which they regard as poorer, less stable, less scientific. And where they find a Catholic nation that has some Protestant qualities, such as France, they attribute this to the presence of a strong anticlerical tradition. Within the Protestant countries themselves men have often believed that they owe their prosperity and success to their Protestantism.

Yet the original sixteenth-century Protestants shared with Catholics most of the basic Christian concepts. Neither Catholic nor Protestant believed that life on earth was improving or should improve. They were not rationalists: Luther threw his ink bottle at the devil, Calvinists killed witches. They were just as intolerant as the Catholics and, like them, believed in rank and status. Lutheranism and Anglicanism were hierarchical and conservative; Calvinism was deeply undemocratic in its view of the small number of the elect, and authoritarian in its theocracy. Only the radicals in the sixteenth century, with their appeal to the Bible, voiced demands for political and social equality, and many of them were less concerned with this world than with the next.

What Protestantism did, however, was to challenge authority and start all sorts of men, many of them in humble circumstances, thinking about fundamental problems. And Protestant moral ideas fitted in with the strengthening of a commercial middle class. Max Weber, a modern German sociologist, has traced the connection between Protestant ethics and the "spirit of capital," the spirit that animated the middle classes who were to lay the foundations of modern Western democracy. Capital accumulation of course means that profits are not spent but "ploughed back" into the business. If ploughing back reduces the costs of production, still more capital accumulates. In its simplest terms this means hard work and no play all along the line, especially at the top.

Much evidence can be advanced to support Weber's thesis. The Calvinists in particular preached that the devil lies in wait for idle hands, and that work keeps a man from temptation to run after women, or play silly games, or drink, or do many other things unpleasing to God; moreover, work in itself is a kind of pleasing tribute to the Lord. Luther, too, glorified work, and affirmed the dignity of the vocation a man is called to, however humble. All this is quite contrary to the feudal, chivalric contempt for the work of the fields and the counting-house. The Calvinists in particular also discouraged the kind of consumption that would interfere with capital accumulation. They frowned upon the fine arts, the theater, expensive clothing, and beautiful and "useless" objects in general. They favored not only "all work" but also "no play," or at least almost none.

The Calvinist countries had a maximum number of working days in the year; they kept the Sabbath most rigorously, but they eliminated the numerous religious holidays, sometimes even Christmas. The Scots, the Dutch, the Swiss, the New England Yankees—all of them with a strong Calvinist background—have long had a popular reputation for thrift, diligence, and driving a hard bargain. Many Protestant theologians rejected the Catholic view that all interest was usury, and the medieval idea of a "just price" (*see* p. 148) in favor of something much closer to our modern notions of free competition in the market, where God would certainly take care of his own.

Finally, the Calvinist focus on the other world as the supreme goal, but one that could never be *certain* for any individual, helped shield the newly rich

Calvinist from the temptation to squander his money and imitate a free-spending, loose-living aristocrat: if he did this, he could be pretty sure he was not of the elect. So the faith itself tended to give cohesion to the middle class. Family fortunes founded on hard work and maintained by reinvestment tended to hold together for several generations.

Not all the evidence, however, supports Weber's thesis. Banking, for example, began before the time of Luther in Catholic countries such as Italy, southern Germany, and Belgium, which Protestants never won over. Nor is there any complete correspondence between Protestantism and capitalism on the one hand and Catholicism and slower industrial development on the other: compare the Catholic Rhineland with its great modern industries to Protestant East Prussia, a rural agricultural region. Resources remain important too: had Italy turned Calvinist this still would not have given Italy coal and iron; had England remained Catholic, it would still have had them. Yet, with all allowances made, it does seem that the "Protestant ethic" gave a little extra push to the economic development of the Protestant regions, and helped to start the West on its modern path.

THE CATHOLIC REFORMATION

At first, the Catholic authorities tried to deal with the Reformation by suppressing it. But the Protestant movement itself had begun within the Church, and many Catholics not dissatisfied enough to leave the Church still wanted reform within it. The sixteenth century saw a revival, notably in Spain but elsewhere as well, of mysticism and popular participation in religion. These diverse forces produced the Catholic Reformation. Protestant historians often call it a "Counter-Reformation," but it was far more than a defensive or negative movement. Though it failed to restore the medieval unity of Christendom, it did preserve and reinvigorate fundamental Catholic beliefs and practice.

Politically speaking, the house of Habsburg, in both its Spanish and German branches, supplied the secular support for the Catholic movement. The French monarchs too helped preserve France as a Catholic country, and in the seventeenth century (*see* Chapter 8) France would witness a great Catholic revival. Other ruling houses too, in Germany, Italy, eastern Europe, gave the Catholic faith their powerful support. And once again, as so often during the Middle Ages, there arose a series of new orders of the regular clergy, a revival of the old monastic ideals of austere simplicity and social service. In the 1520's, while the struggle with Luther was still young, an earnest group at Rome founded the Oratory of Divine Love, dedicated to the deepening of spiritual experience through special services and religious exercises. The Oratory inspired the foundation of the Theatines, an order designed particularly to advance the education of the clergy. In the same decade a new branch of the Franciscans appeared, the Capuchins (hooded friars), to lead the order back to Francis' own ideals.

By far the greatest of the new orders was the Society of Jesus, founded in 1540 by the Spaniard Ignatius Loyola (1491–1556). Loyola, who had been wounded in battle as a soldier, intended the Jesuits to be an army for the church. His *Spiritual Exercises* emphasized absolute obedience to higher authority (the hierarchy of the church), and displayed a realistic middle-of-the-road estimate of what can be expected of ordinary human beings in this world, cautioning against undue emphasis even on the truth of a religious controversy lest a delicate balance be upset.

Always the center of controversy, the Jesuits have been accused by their enemies of devotion to worldly power, and of a willingness to use any tactics to win. This last is indeed a slander, for the Jesuits have never underestimated the hold that moral decency has on human beings. They not only struck shrewd blows for Catholicism in Hungary, Poland, England, and Holland, trying to win back souls lost to the Protestants, but moved with the expanding frontiers of the West to India, to China, to Japan, to North America to win new lands and new converts. They were preachers, teachers, social workers, martyrs, always disciplined, never lapsing into the kind of fleshly worldliness that had been the fate of other monastic orders.

The Church used also an old weapon, the Inquisition, in its struggle with Protestantism. In its papal form, this tribunal goes back to the Albigensian Crusade of the early thirteenth century (*see* Chapter 4), and in its Spanish form to Isabella's efforts in the fifteenth century to make Jews and Moslems conform (*see* Chapter 6). These medieval courts used medieval measures of torture, and perpetrated horrors against former Moslems in Spain and against Protestants in the Low Countries. As weapons against Protestantism, however, the Inquisition in particular and persecution in general were not effective. The Inquisition was most active in Italy, Spain, and Portugal, persecuting heretics in regions where Protestantism was never a threat; while in those areas that the Church eventually won back—Poland, parts of Hungary and Germany—it accomplished its victory chiefly in other ways.

Catholics did not yield to doctrinal pressure from Protestants. The Protestant tendency toward some form of the "priesthood of the believer" hardened Catholic insistence on the unique powers of the ordained priest. The Church did not even change its views on indulgences, but reaffirmed them—not, of course, as a money transaction but as a spiritual return for spiritual efforts. The Council of Trent, called by Pope Paul III in 1545 and meeting on and off for 20 years, gave formal voice to the total refusal to compromise with Protestant doctrine. It reaffirmed all seven sacraments, transubstantiation, the importance of both faith *and* works, and the authority of both the Bible and unwritten tradition; it also forbade individuals to interpret scripture contrary to the teaching of the Church. Though it was intended to provide a chance for reconciliation, certain conservative Protestants, while invited, never came. Liberals, even liberal Catholics, have always felt that the Council was a rubber stamp in the hands of the popes and the Jesuits.

The Council of Trent and the reforming popes of the later sixteenth century did effect in Catholic practice the kind of reform that the Cluniacs had put through five centuries earlier, enforcing priestly celibacy, combatting simony, and improving the training of priests. The Council also founded the *Index,* a continuing list of books that Catholics must not read because of peril to their faith; it included the writings of anticlericals like Machiavelli and Boccaccio, as well as those of heretics and Protestants. Since the civil authorities were enlisted to prevent the publication and circulation of anything contrary to the faith, this amounted to censorship of the press. Under Pius V (reigned 1566–1572) a standard catechism, breviary, and missal were drawn up to embody the work of the Council of Trent for purposes of instruction. The whole Catholic system had been greatly tightened. The papacy had ceased to be the corrupt center against which Luther and others had inveighed, nor did it ever again become so.

DIVIDED CHRISTENDOM

Once the Catholic Reformation had been launched, the Protestants gained little more territory. By the end of the sixteenth century, the territorial division between areas dominantly Catholic and areas dominantly Protestant was much as it is now. England, Scotland, Holland, northern and eastern Germany (with a southern projection in Württemberg and Switzerland), and Scandinavia were predominantly Protestant. Ireland, Belgium, southern Germany and the Rhine valley, the Habsburg lands, Poland, Italy, and the Iberian peninsula were predominantly Catholic. But there were Catholic minorities in England, Scotland, and Holland; there were Protestant minorities in Ireland, France, and some of the Habsburg lands; and the two faiths interpenetrated most confusedly in greatly divided Germany.

To some extent the religious differences contributed to the growth of national patriotism. Where a specific form of religion became identified with a given political unit, religious feeling and patriotic feeling reinforced each other, especially in a struggle for independence. So Protestantism heightened Dutch resistance to the Spaniards; Catholicism, Irish resistance to the English. In states already independent, religion often strengthened patriotism. England since Elizabeth I—despite its Catholic minority—has taken pride in being a Protestant nation, Spain in being Catholic. In the campaign of the Spanish Armada and the other great wars to which we turn later in the chapter, religion and politics were both at issue, together with competition for overseas trade and empire.

II. The First Overseas Empires

In the mid-fifteenth century, Western society began an expansion which within 250 years or so revealed to Europe almost the whole world. It was the first time—except perhaps for a few half-legendary Viking voyages—that Westerners had crossed the oceans. For the first time Europeans traveled far outside the orbits of the only two other societies—the Byzantine and the Moslem—that they had so far encountered, and into touch with a bewildering variety of races, creeds, and cultures, from naked savages to cultivated Chinese.

The Europeans were superior in strength to the peoples they met, and so were able to extend their influence around the world in a quite unprecedented way. They had guns; but non-Europeans could quickly acquire these, and did. More important, European technological superiority was mixed with superior political and military organization in a combination very difficult to imitate. Half a dozen competing Western nations, each eager to destroy the others, shared in the superiority. In the Far East, Portuguese, Spaniards, Dutchmen, Frenchmen, and Englishmen intrigued against each other, and other Western nations later joined. But not until the twentieth century did there arise an Asian nation, Japan, that could compete.

Why did this great movement begin just when it did? There were technological reasons: the magnetic compass that makes navigation possible even when the sun and stars are hidden was known by the early fifteenth century, and by the end of the century had become a regular piece of ship's equipment. Shipbuilders were building vessels longer and narrower than the older types of Mediterranean ship, better adapted to ocean swells. There were economic–political reasons: the Ottoman conquest had to some extent interfered with the trade routes through the Near East, although Venice and Genoa had agreements with the Turks. The very predominance of the Italians in the Levant attracted the rising Western states to try the Atlantic waters.

And there were surely also reasons of another sort. The rise of a scientific investigating spirit impelled men, if for instance they heard about the existence of unicorns, to go and look for some. Columbus deliberately set out across the unknown ocean to prove his theory that because the world is round one can travel from Europe westward and reach Asia. In sum, those who carried out the expansion had motives as mixed as those of the Crusaders (*see* Chapter 5); like the Crusaders, they were, in part, convinced that they were also doing God's work.

THE PORTUGUESE

East by Sea to the Indies. The first of the great pioneers in this modern expansion was Prince Henry of Portugal (1393–1450), known as "the Navigator." Deeply religious, he wanted to convert to Christianity the peoples of Asia, already known in the West through the reports of overland travelers such as Marco Polo the Venetian (c. 1254–c. 1324) and others. Since the thirteenth century many Europeans had believed that most Asians were already Christian, and needed only to be brought into touch with Rome. While there were indeed some Christians in Asia, descendants of refugees from the theological controversies in fifth-century Byzantium (*see* Chapter 3), the medieval legend of Prester (Priest) John, the great Christian ruler somewhere in the distant East, remained only a legend. Henry the Navigator also wanted to promote Portuguese commerce and national power. Carefully he and his fellow-workers planned each successive expedition and equipped it with the best instruments available.

The Portuguese had already discovered the Atlantic islands—the Azores, Madeira, and the Canaries. Creeping southward along the west coast of Africa, they now doubled Cape Verde in 1445, and thought they could circumnavigate Africa by turning east. By 1472 they had reached the end of the west African bulge, and had seen that the coastline turned south once more. In 1488 Bartholomew Diaz was blown far south in a storm and rounded the Cape of Good Hope. In 1497, Vasco da Gama followed him, worked his way north along the east coast of Africa, and came to an area of Arab traders who knew how to sail across the Indian Ocean to India. Ten months and fourteen days out from Lisbon, da Gama reached the Indian coast. The Portuguese had an ocean route to the East.

On the next great voyage toward India in 1500, Pedro Cabral—no longer feeling the need to creep along the west African coast—stayed out in the Atlantic after rounding the western African bulge, and was blown so far west that he made a landing in Brazil. It may be that this was not as accidental as it seems. By 1500, the Spanish were well launched in exploration, and Columbus' voyages were well known. In 1493, after Columbus' first voyage, Pope Alexander VI had granted to Spain all lands south and west of a north–south line drawn in the Atlantic between the Azores and the Cape Verde Islands. In 1494, the Portuguese, by the Treaty of Tordesillas with Spain, succeeded in having this line moved 270 leagues further west. Brazil thus fell into the sphere of the Portuguese, who may have known about it all along and who only announced their landing there after Cabral's voyage. In any case, it was now determined that Brazil alone in Latin America would be Portuguese; everything else lay on the Spanish side of the line.

The main Portuguese push, however, was toward India and the Far East. By the first years of the sixteenth century Portugal owned a string of fortified trading posts along the Indian coast and had won control of navigation on the Indian Ocean from the Moslems. Alfonso de Albuquerque established Goa as the capital of the Portuguese holdings (it was lost by the Portuguese to Nehru's India only in 1962), and began to organize communications with southeastern Asia and China. By 1557, the Portuguese had a base at Macao near Canton, which they still possess. They first landed in Japan in 1542 or 1543, introduced firearms, and opened trade relations. Portugal, then, had assembled a colonial empire.

Africa, India, and China. The Africa the Portuguese had opened up was hot, relatively poor, and thinly populated. The coastal stations they and later European voyagers established carried on a flourishing slave trade, as did the Arabs in northern and northwestern Africa. Central and southern African natives were largely still in a Stone Age culture, so primitive that few Europeans made any effort to understand them. By and large Africa offered little attraction, and was bypassed. India, China, and much of southeast Asia, by contrast, were thickly populated, with great wealth accumulated in a few hands, and with much to offer the Europeans in the way of luxuries like silks and spices. Moreover, here were the seats of very ancient and very advanced civilizations.

India, known only vaguely to the West during the Middle Ages through the intermediary of the Arabs, proved to be the home not of Christians but of people belonging to faiths unknown to the Europeans. This in part no doubt accounted for the contemptuous attitude of the Portuguese and later Europeans, a contempt reinforced by the Westerners' military superiority. India itself was politically disunited. In the north, Mongol invaders, the Moguls, were consolidating their foreign rule. In the south, where the Europeans appeared, the local rulers fought each other in bitter rivalry. There was vast diversity among the populations: some tribesmen in the south were at the Stone Age level; some in the northern highlands were similar to the nomadic warriors of Central Asia. In the Indus and Ganges valleys there was a wealthy Hindu society, in part dominated by Moslem invaders.

Among the Hindus the institution of *caste* prevailed—the determination of status by birth. The Europeans found the Indians divided into more than a thousand separate castes, including at the bottom a group of "untouchables." The two ruling castes at the top were the Brahmins or priests, and the Kshatriya or warriors. Marriage between castes and all social mobility were in theory impossible.

The Brahmins presided over a faith that believed in the evils of fleshly life and the attainment of salvation by mystic transcendence in ascetic denial. A sinful life here on earth brings reincarnation in a lower animal form; a virtuous one in an ever higher, until—some believed—final union with the perfect might be attained. These doctrines were overlaid and contaminated by a popular belief in a multiplicity of gods and by a rigid and complex Brahmin ritual. In the sixth century B.C. a great religious leader, Gautama Buddha, had led a movement against these corruptions. Though Buddhism, one of the great higher religions of the world, accepts the Brahminical concept that the world of the flesh is bad, it finds salvation, the *nirvana* of peaceful release from the chain of earthly birth and rebirth, in a life ascetic but not withdrawn, a life of charity and good works. In India Buddhism died out, but it spread to China, Japan, and southeastern Asia.

Chinese civilization arose in the valleys of the Yellow and Yangtze rivers several thousand years before Christ. Like the Mesopotamian civilization (*see* Chapter 1), it was subject to incursions from the nomads of Asia, against whom the Chinese built the famous Great Wall in the third century B.C. Chinese culture gradually spread southward and eastward to the region of Canton, to Korea, and to Japan. Chinese society was tightly cemented by a communal village organization characterized by strong family ties.

China was always ruled by an emperor, the "Son of Heaven," and by a bureaucracy of intellectuals, the mandarins who were selected by rigorous examinations in classic Chinese literature and philosophy. Though open in theory to anybody with talent, the mandarin class in fact required so expensive a preliminary education that very few poor men's sons managed to rise into it. Worldly and realistic, with little mysticism or interest in an afterlife, the Chinese, it has been said, never had a religion. Confucianism, a code of manners and morals, prescribing temperance, decorum, obedience to the wise and good, governed the behavior of the ruling classes.

The Portuguese Empire. The Portuguese, bursting for the first time into these lands so strange to Europeans, created a trading empire, not an empire of settlement. Along the coasts of Africa, India, and China, they established a series of posts, or "factories," over which they raised the Portuguese flag as a sign that they had annexed these bits of territory for the Portuguese crown. To the natives they offered relatively cheap mass-produced articles: guns, knives, and cloth. In return they got gold and silver when they could, spices, silks and other luxuries, and cotton and slaves. The principles first followed by the Portuguese later became general among the colonizing powers: the mother country produced the manufactured goods, the colonies the raw materials; foreigners were excluded from the trade between the two. These policies were applications of the economic philosophy called mercantilism, which we shall soon examine in more detail.

Relatively few land troops were needed to keep the natives under control and ward off rival European powers. But the Portuguese needed and built a large and powerful navy to protect their vessels from piracy at sea; in the early days of overseas expansion, a power would often unofficially turn pirates loose to prey on the shipping of its rivals. The Portuguese did not settle large numbers of their own people in their colonial outposts or rule the inhabitants directly, but left the old chiefs and ruling groups pretty much as they had found them. Except for a few natives who learned the language, the masses were little affected by the Western goods and ideas brought to their shores.

But, like the other colonial powers later, the Portuguese did try to convert the natives to Christianity. Christian missionaries worked hard and devotedly, often becoming very fond of their charges. Some of the Jesuits in China, the first European intellectuals to live in that very civilized land, seriously believed that a reconciliation between Christianity and Confucianism was just around the corner. Often the missionaries, anxious to protect the natives, conflicted with the traders, eager to exploit them. The missionaries, however, made comparatively few converts in the vast populations of India and China.

In the seventeenth century the Portuguese would lose ground to the French,

Expansion of Europe, 1529

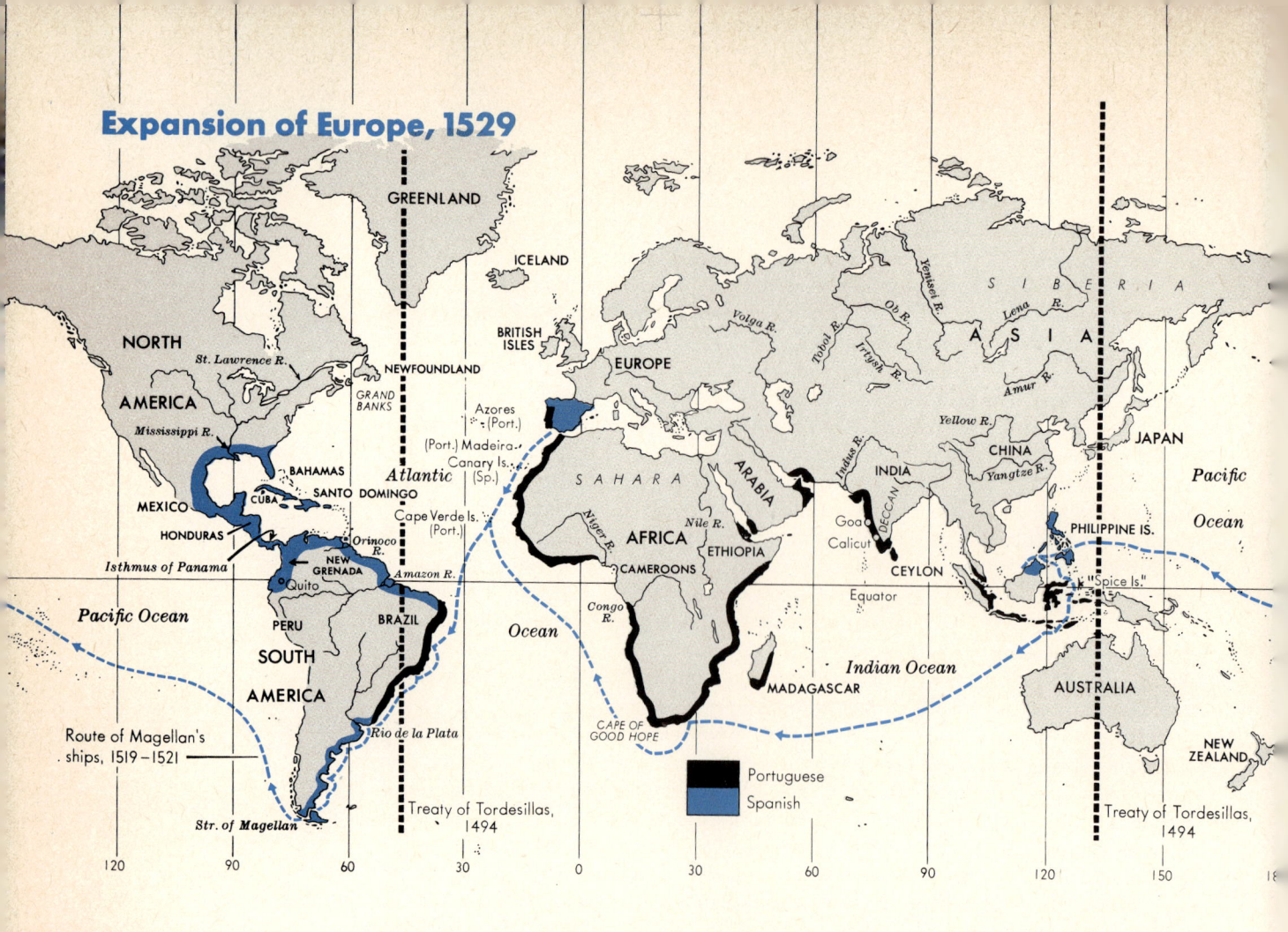

Dutch, and English, more advanced than they in industrial and banking techniques. But they did leave as a lasting monument a superb poem, *The Lusiads* (1572), by Camoens, commemorating their overseas expansion. And they kept their trading stations: Timor in the East Indies, Goa, Macao. In Africa their empire, almost 800,000 square miles—Angola and Portuguese Guinea in the west, Mozambique in the east—has continued to exist down to our own day, past the moment when other empires have been dissolved.

THE SPANIARDS

West by Sea to the Indies. Second to Portugal in exploring and colonizing came Spain. Ferdinand and Isabella commissioned Columbus (1451–1506) largely as a way of catching up with Portugal. Genoese-born, and competently self-educated in navigation and geography, Columbus was not the only man to think that one could reach the Far East by sailing west. Ancient Greek geographers had believed the earth was round, and the belief revived during the Renaissance. Toscanelli had published a map at Florence in 1474, and Behaim one at Nuremberg in 1492 showing the earth as a globe—without the Americas, of course, and with the combined Atlantic and Pacific much narrower than they are in fact. But the ingenuity and persistence with which Columbus promoted the idea of sailing west in order to go east were strikingly novel. He was commissioned not only to reach the Indies but to discover and secure for Spain new islands and territories, a mission that probably reflects old legends about Atlantis or other lost continents and islands beyond the Azores.

Of course Columbus did not reach the Indies, but a New World. On October 12, 1492, after a voyage of a little more than two months with three small ships, he made a landfall on one of the Bahama Islands, and continued on to discover the islands of Cuba and Santo Domingo (Hispaniola). On his second voyage, in 1493, with seventeen ships and fifteen hundred colonists, he explored further in the Caribbean, and laid the foundations of the Spanish Empire in America. On his third voyage, in 1498–1500, he reached the mouth of the Orinoco on the north coast of South America, and was sent home in irons after difficulties with the royal governor. He was released on his return to Spain, and in 1502–1504 made a fourth and final voyage, reaching the mainland of what is now Honduras. He died in Spain in 1506, unaware that he had reached not Asia but a new continent, which received the name of another Italian in Spanish service, Amerigo Vespucci, a far more prolific writer of letters about his own explorations.

During the next few years many other explorers discovered that the new continent was a barrier to the westward voyage. In 1513 Balboa saw the limitless Pacific from the Isthmus of Panama. The new problem was how to get *through* the Americas by sea and into the Pacific, and the promising openings—Chesapeake, Delaware, Hudson, St. Lawrence—all proved to be nothing but rivermouths after all. There was a Northwest Passage waiting to be discovered, but it was usually ice-choked, and it was not actually found until the 1850's by the Englishman Sir John Franklin, who died in the Arctic wastes. The Southwest Passage, around the southernmost tip of South America, however, was found by Ferdinand Magellan, a Portuguese in the service of Spain, on an extraordinary voyage that began in 1519 and lasted until 1522. It took him through the Strait that still bears his name, into and across the Pacific amid dreadful hardship, and

The earliest known European illustration of the natives of South America; German woodcut, about 1505.

to the Philippines, where he was killed. But one of his captains sailed on across the Indian Ocean and home around the Cape of Good Hope to complete the first circumnavigation of the globe. The Philippine landing brought Spain into the Far East.

In the New World, the Spaniards soon explored by land, and annexed great territories. Led by the *conquistadores*, who were explorers, soldiers, and administrators, they conquered the only two civilized regions of the New World. Hernando Cortés took the Aztec empire of Mexico (1519) and Francisco Pizarro the Inca empire of Peru (1531–1533). In dramatic, toilsome, and often bloody adventures, many *conquistadores* opened up other regions of the vast and strange New World for Spain: Quesada in what is now Colombia, Coronado, de Soto, and Cabeza de Vaca in the southwestern portions of the United States, Mendoza in the La Plata region of Argentina and Uruguay, Valdivia in Chile, Alvarado in Guatemala. Although throughout Central and South America millions of people of Indian stock survive today, the structure of the Aztec and Incan civilizations—unlike that of China or India—disintegrated or disappeared before the often brutal conquest of the Spaniards.

The Latin Empires of the New World. Before the end of the sixteenth century the Spaniards and, in Brazil, the Portuguese had completed the foundation of the first colonial empires of settlement. But only in the La Plata region and in central Chile did a European population replace the natives. Elsewhere a crust of Spanish or Portuguese settlers formed at the top of society and made their European language the language of culture. From the union, formal or informal, of Europeans and natives arose a class called *mestizos*, mixed bloods. In many areas the Indians maintained their stock and their old ways of life almost untouched. But in the Caribbean the Indians were exterminated, and in Brazil they proved inadequate as a labor force. In both cases large-scale importation of Negro slaves from Africa added another element to the racial mixture.

Machu Picchu, ancient Incan city in the Andes of Peru. Corn and potatoes were grown on the terraces.

The physical features of South America broke it into separate regions. Between Argentina and Chile the great chain of the Andes, crossed only with great difficulty through high mountain passes, prevented a political union. The Andes and the great tropical rain forests of the Amazon Basin divided the colonies of the La Plata from those of Peru and Colombia (New Granada). Similar mountain formations determined the creation of small states in Central America. Even had Brazil been settled by Spaniards, it would almost surely have remained separate because of the difficulty of communications with the rest of the continent.

The Spaniards put their colonial administration under two viceroys, one of Peru, with his capital at Lima, and the other of "New Spain," with his capital at Mexico City. The viceroy at Lima ruled over all of Spanish South America except Venezuela. The viceroy at Mexico City ruled all the mainland north of Panama, the West Indies, Venezuela—and—far across the Pacific—the Philippines! In each capital, and also in Guatemala, New Granada, Quito, the Philippines, and elsewhere, there were *audiencias,* advisory councils that also operated as courts.

This regime seems highly centralized, but in view of the vast areas and the varied peoples under its control, it could not be absolute in practice. The citizens were consulted in assemblies and before long the colonial bureaucracy was largely managed by colonials—men who had been born overseas and had never seen Spain. It was impossible for the mother country to enforce mercantilist practices completely; not only did domestic industry grow in the colonies, but in time the local officials connived at trade with other Europeans: English, Dutch, and French.

In the sixteenth century, the Spaniards were interested chiefly in mining and exporting to Spain the rich and easily accessible deposits of gold and silver in Mexico and Peru. The Crown got a fifth of all metals mined. Except for jewelry and other crafts, the precious metals were doing the natives no good; but they did the Spaniards little good either, as it turned out, since Spain spent the vast resources to finance a vain bid for European supremacy. By the seventeenth century sugar, tobacco, chocolate, cotton, and hides were flowing to Europe in exchange for manufactured goods. The chief beneficiaries of this trade were the Creoles (Americans born of pure European stock) and the *mestizos,* but not the Indians.

All over Latin America the Indians fell to the bottom of the social system. Especially in the Caribbean, but to a degree everywhere, the initial European policy of using native labor proved disastrous for the natives, who died in droves from diseases to which they had no immunity. Tragedy also marked the installation of the *encomienda,* a semi-manorial system of forced labor, and the efforts to regiment native labor on plantations. Most Spanish colonists were hard-boiled and tough with the natives.

The record of contact between whites and nonwhites everywhere in the world, however, is marked by harshness and brutality. The Spaniards were no worse than other nationalities, and they did make an effort to mitigate the cruelties. In 1542 the enslavement of the natives was forbidden. Other laws, though often flouted, at least were designed to protect the natives, who found a warm champion in the distinguished humanitarian Bishop of Chiapas in Mexico, Bartholomew de las Casas (1474–1566), "Father of the Indians." Everywhere in New Spain missionaries were active; the Indians, unlike the Asian or African masses, were converted to Catholicism. In Paraguay the Jesuits set up among the

Guarani Indians a benevolent despotism, a utopia of good order, good habits, and eternal childhood for the Guarani. On the northern fringes of the Spanish world, where it was to meet the Anglo-Saxons, a long line of missions in California and the American southwest held the frontier.

COMPETITION BEGINS

Portugal and Spain were the only two European countries to found colonial empires during the sixteenth century. France and England were just beginning their explorations, and did not enter the competition in earnest until the seventeenth century. Verrazzano, an Italian in French service, in 1524 explored the North American coast in what is now Canada, and between 1534 and 1541 Jacques Cartier several times sailed into the St. Lawrence River, proceeding as far as the site of Montreal. But the French did not for the moment follow up these efforts by settlement.

Nor were the English any quicker to pursue the opportunities in North America, although their agents, the Italians John and Sebastian Cabot, had in 1497 and 1498 touched on Nova Scotia, Newfoundland, and the American coast as far south as Delaware. Instead, the English began some six decades later to challenge the Spaniards to the south. In the 1560's, John Hawkins, despite opposition, made three voyages into Spanish territory to sell slaves. His nephew Sir Francis Drake attacked Spanish shipping on his celebrated trip around the world (1572–1580)—the first by an Englishman—when he touched on California and claimed it for England under the name of New Albion.

The pace now quickened, as Martin Frobisher explored Labrador and the regions to the north and west, Sir Humphrey Gilbert (1583) claimed Newfoundland for England, and other English explorers began to search for the Northwest Passage, continuing to plunder Spanish commerce. In 1584, Sir Walter Raleigh tried to found a settlement on Roanoke Island (North Carolina), but neither his colonists nor a second group sent out in 1587 survived. All these efforts only faintly foreshadowed the great English seventeenth-century settlements in North America.

III. The New Monarchies and the Wars of the Sixteenth Century

By the end of the fifteenth century, the Spanish, French, and English monarchies dominated Western Europe. The Holy Roman Empire of the Germanies, occupying much of Central Europe, had no comparable internal unity. Yet under the Habsburgs the Germanies, too, entered into competition for supremacy. Italy, with its city-states, attracted outsiders by its riches and its civilization. Between the Habsburg lands and the French lay the zone of fragmentation which the Burgundian dukes of the fifteenth century had almost cemented into a major state (*see* p. 246). Out of this zone have come the modern nations of Holland, Belgium, Luxembourg, and Switzerland. To the east, Muscovite Russia was just coalescing as a state, and the feudalized, Catholic kingdom of Poland occupied vast areas. To the southeast, the Ottoman Turks were already ensconced in the Balkans, threatening Italy and Central Europe. In short, the picture has become a recognizable one, though the unification of Germany and Italy into nations, the entrance of Russia onto the European stage, and the gradual expulsion of the Turks from Europe all still lay far in the future.

In succession, individual states tried to dominate the entire western portion of the continent, and break down what was already becoming a "system" of states. In the sixteenth century, Spain, in the seventeenth and eighteenth and down to 1815, France, in the twentieth, Germany, have tried either to absorb or to control the other states, to limit their sovereignty. Each time, the threatened states sooner or later joined in a coalition, overthrew the threat to stability, and restored the system. Each time, England—not itself a continental power after the Hundred Years' War—intervened to support or lead the coalition against the aggressor. What we have been describing is called the preservation of the "balance of power." Whenever one power has sought to overthrow the balance on the continent of Europe, it has in the end been thwarted.

During the sixteenth century, the "New Monarchies" of Spain, France, and England evolved, each in its own way, toward a more and more centralized regime. All had central foreign offices, paid professional armies, and paid professional diplomats and spies. All had paid professional civilian bureaucrats, a central financial system with some control over taxation, and a central legal system that tried to render uniform justice. In each, the monarch had inherited the throne, and passed it on without question to his nearest heir. Everywhere he claimed the right to make final decisions, and overshadowed the traditional assembly—Spanish Cortes, French Estates-General, English Parliament. The efficiency of absolutism, however, was limited by poor communications and by the continued survival of many medieval local privileges and local ways of life.

SPAIN

Charles V and Philip II. The sixteenth century was the Spanish century, when Spain tried and failed to upset the balance of power—first of all the European nations to do so. For most of the century she was ruled by Charles V (1516–1556—technically, Charles V as Emperor and Charles I as Spanish monarch) and by his son, Philip II (1556–1598). Brought up in the Low Countries, Charles came to Spain a stranger who hardly spoke the language. He brought with him a Flemish entourage who did not conceal their contempt for this old-fashioned, divided, slow-moving land.

Three years after inheriting Spain from his maternal grandfather, Ferdinand of Aragon, Charles inherited the Empire on the death of his paternal grandfather, Maximilian (1519). Soon there was an outburst of indignation at his leaving Spain and spending Spanish money and the lives of Spanish troops for purposes that were not Spanish. In 1520, a group of Spanish cities, led by Toledo, revolted. The rebels, called the *Comuneros*, included many nobles hostile to the King and many members of the lower classes with strong radical aims. They were put down in 1521 (the upper-class rebels had been frightened by the radicalism of the lower), and Charles thereafter simply tried not to antagonize the Spaniards.

Philip II, on the other hand, was profoundly Spanish in character and attitudes. Personally self-denying and extremely hard-working, he was a religious fanatic. He changed the internal administration of Spain, devising a system of consultative councils with a council of state at the top, all manned by nobles. But the decisions were his alone and were put into effect by his personal secretariat and the local authorities, who were not noble. Especially in Castile, Philip diluted the power of the Cortes almost to nothing: nobles and priests no longer could attend, since they paid no taxes, and the delegates from the towns could do little by themselves.

Philip thought he did not need to ask the Cortes for money because of the wealth that came from the tax of one-fifth on the cargoes from the New World, from his own royal estates, from the sale of offices and titles, and even from a royal percentage of the profits of the sale of papal dispensations, not unlike indulgences. He spent it all on foreign wars, and left Spain almost bankrupt in 1598. His vast domains—divided Spain, the Low Countries, lands in Italy, and the overseas empire in America and the Philippines (named after Philip himself)—had no common organs of consultation; the richest of his subjects were tax exempt; there was no accumulated Spanish administrative experience that prevented graft or promoted efficiency.

Spanish Regionalism and Mercantilism. Spanish regionalism (*see* Chapter 6) was so extreme that the separate provinces often levied customs dues on each other's goods, and had no arrangements for extraditing criminals to each other. In the extreme north, the provinces that the Moslems had never conquered retained many jealously guarded privileges, the *fueros*. Aragon had its own chief justice, the *justicia major*, nominated by the Crown, but possessing within the province authority like that of the United States Supreme Court, and holding office for life.

Had Charles V and Philip II devoted themselves and their wealth to uniting and developing Spain, they might have accomplished wonders. Spain had great agricultural potentialities and mineral resources, notably iron. With its head start on overseas imperial development and its flourishing navy and merchant marine, it had a tremendous opportunity. But the monarchs spent their efforts and their gold in trying to dominate Europe and to extirpate Protestantism. The Spanish

The Escorial, the combined palace, monastery, and mausoleum built by Philip II near Madrid.

infantry, the best in Europe, had to be paid everywhere it went, and the drain was never made up. Although expenditure on armed forces can stimulate economic productivity, it did not do so in Spain. The vast sums from the New World, while enabling her to fight her wars, passed out of her hands and into those of foreign bankers and merchants to pay for manufactured goods needed by Spanish colonies.

In accordance with the mercantilist ideas of the time, Spain forbade the colonies to engage in manufacturing. But she did not develop her own industrial production to supply the colonies; instead she bought goods abroad, thus helping the industries of other states and sometimes tempting their citizens to attempt a little smuggling into the Spanish dominions. In Spain, there was little room for individual economic initiative; the government controlled all enterprise, especially the colonial trade, with detailed regulations. The Castilian *Casa de Contratación* (House of Trade) licensed every export and import to and from the colonies. Equally important was the whole attitude of the Spaniards. They retained a medieval contempt for business and preferred war, politics, religion, art, or living like an *hidalgo,* a nobleman (*hijo de algo,* "son of somebody"). Numerous holidays, the siesta, the thronging soldiers, priests, monks, and other economically unproductive persons, combining with monopoly, the heavy hand of bureaucracy, and the lack of encouragement to new enterprise stimulated the exact opposite of Weber's "capitalist spirit" (*see* p. 289), and in the long run disqualified Spain for competition with those nations that had it.

Spanish Literature and Painting. Yet the sixteenth-century man could not see all this. What he saw was the richest of states, with the best of armies and a magnificent literature and art. Spanish culture reflects a spirit strange to those who know the books and paintings of other countries: a serious, darkly passionate, unsmiling spirit, fascinated with death and all the details of death, preoccupied with honor and "face," agonized and pious, intensely proud. Loyola the Jesuit represents this Spanish spirit. So do St. Theresa of Avila (1515–1582), the ascetic and mystical girl who reorganized the Carmelite nunneries and wrote her autobiography, and St. John of the Cross (1542–1581), her disciple. They do not withdraw from the world of the senses like the ascetics of the early Church, but combat and try to transcend the necessity of living in the flesh.

In a very different way, Miguel de Cervantes (1547–1616), whose *Don Quixote* (1605) is one of the few universal books, carries the mark of this Spanish spirit. Cervantes gently satirizes the concepts of chivalric behavior that have addled the pate of his poor old hero: anyone that does a disinterested deed, in these degenerate times, Cervantes seems to say, is a crazy man tilting with windmills. And yet there was something magnificent about self-denial and chivalry and protecting the innocent that we in our superior wisdom have lost. Speaking for earthy common sense is Don Quixote's devoted squire, Sancho Panza, sharing the mad adventures of the Don but protecting him from their worst consequences, never forgetting that man after all must eat.

The Spanish spirit was caught by a painter, El Greco (1541–1614), not a Spaniard at all but a Greek, born Domenico Theotokopouli on the island of Crete and trained both in the Byzantine tradition of the Aegean world and at the school of Titian in Venice. He settled at Toledo in 1575, and lived there the rest of his life. His long, thin figures, with their eyes often turned upward in piety or simulated piety, the greyish flesh tones, often contrasting with the brilliant colors of landscape and dress, suggest the Spanish combination of energy and otherworldliness that created the Inquisition and built and misused the first overseas empire.

FRANCE

The Italian Adventure of Charles VIII and Louis XII. Far more centralized both by geography and history than Spain, France too spent most of the sixteenth century in war: foreign wars against the Habsburgs down to 1559, and religious civil wars from 1562 to 1598. From his father, the canny Louis XI (*see* Chapter 6), Charles VIII (reigned 1483–1498) inherited a well-filled treasury, a good army, and a docile nobility. By marriage in 1491 he added to the crown the province of Brittany. Secure at home, he decided on foreign adventures. He had inherited the claim of the Angevins to the throne of Naples. Italy, with its great material riches and its political instability, was very tempting. In 1494–1495, Charles led his armies triumphantly all the way to Naples, but then a coalition formed against him: the Holy League of the Papacy, the Empire, Spain, Venice, Milan, and England. Charles was forced to withdraw. His cousin Louis XII (reigned 1498–1515), who succeeded him, had a Visconti grandmother, and so a claim to Milan against the Sforzas. In 1499 Louis took Milan, avoided the isolation that had ruined Charles' campaign, and allied himself with Ferdinand of Aragon to share the conquest of Naples. But the allies fell out, and Ferdinand's forces drove Louis out of Naples (1503).

With the greedy French in Milan and the greedy Spaniards in Naples, fresh interventions and new illustrations of the workings of the balance of power were only a matter of time. In 1508 Louis joined with Ferdinand, the Emperor Maximilian, and the Pope in the League of Cambrai to seize the rich possessions of Venice in the Po valley. But the League broke up when the Pope and Ferdinand had what they wanted, and the Pope now formed a Holy League (Ferdinand, Venice, Maximilian, England) *against* France. In 1513, Henry VIII's invading forces defeated the French at home and the Swiss defeated them in Italy. So Louis XII, like Charles VIII before him, had to withdraw, and the Sforzas returned to Milan. The Italian campaigns were the prelude to the great series of Habsburg–Valois wars that began under Charles V of Habsburg and Francis I (reigned 1515–1547), successor of Louis XII as King of France.

Francis I and the Habsburg–Valois Wars. Dashing, self-indulgent, energetic, extravagant, Francis was a Renaissance despot thoroughly at home in the age of Machiavelli. He began his reign with a brilliant victory over the Swiss that brought Milan back to France. In 1520 he held the celebrated ostentatious meeting with Henry VIII near Calais, the "Field of the Cloth of Gold," so-called because of the splendor that surrounded the monarchs. But Francis was soon preoccupied with Charles V, whose enormous territories surrounded France. The struggle that broke out in 1521 was inconclusive until 1525, when the imperial forces defeated Francis at Pavia and took him prisoner. He was held in Madrid until he renounced all claims to Milan, Genoa, and Naples, and ceded Burgundy to Charles (1526). Francis soon repudiated the settlement after allying himself with the Pope, Venice, and the Sforzas in the League of Cognac, and the war resumed. In 1527, Charles' Spanish and German mercenaries, restless at being unpaid, and commanded by a great French noble, the Constable of Bourbon, who had quarreled with Francis I, sacked Rome. The horrors of the sack shocked contemporaries, who said it was worse than anything since the one by Alaric the Visigoth in 410 (*see* Chapter 3). By the treaty of Cambrai (1529) Francis renounced his claims to Italy and other territories and paid a large indemnity; Charles promised to postpone any demand for Burgundy, and set free Francis' sons, whom he was holding as hostages. In 1530, Charles was crowned Emperor by the Pope. Despite the Lutheran disturbances in Germany, and the French threat, Charles was now at the height of his power.

Twice more (1536–1538 and 1542–1544) in the lifetime of Francis I, Habsburg and Valois renewed their struggles. After the death of the Sforza ruler of Milan (1535), Francis revived his claim there, and Charles invaded southern France. Francis, "eldest son of the Church," first allied himself with Suleiman the Magnificent, the Ottoman Sultan, who menaced the imperial forces both in the Mediterranean and on land in Hungary. This was a perfectly Machiavellian action: Francis not only won valuable commercial concessions from the Turks (*see* Chapter 5) but also seriously embarrassed his enemy, Charles.

War broke out again in 1542 over Charles' investment of his son Philip as

Francis I, by Clouet.

Europe in 1555

Inset map (top right)

- London
- Amsterdam
- Leyden
- Utrecht
- Armada sea fight
- Calais
- Boulogne
- Bruges
- Antwerp
- Guinegate
- Cambray
- Cateau-Cambrésis
- FLANDERS
- ARTOIS
- NETHERLANDS
- FRANCE

Scale: 0–100 Miles

Main map

Regions / Polities
- TEUTONIC ORDER
- PRUSSIA
- POLAND
- LITHUANIA
- RUSSIA
- UKRAINE
- KHANATE OF THE CRIMEA
- MOLDAVIA
- TRANSYLVANIA
- WALLACHIA
- MONTENEGRO
- OTTOMAN EMPIRE
- PELOPONNESUS
- CRETE (to Venice)
- RHODES
- CYPRUS (to Venice)
- IONIAN IS. (Venice)

Cities
- Warsaw
- Moscow
- Kiev
- Belgrade
- Constantinople
- Salonika
- Lepanto
- Athens

Rivers / Waters
- W. Dvina R.
- Vistula R.
- Oka R.
- Volga R.
- Don R.
- Dnieper R.
- Dniester R.
- Danube R.
- Ural R.
- Tigris R.
- Euphrates R.
- Caspian Sea
- Black Sea
- Aegean Sea

Scale: 0–500 Miles

Duke of Milan, and the capture and execution by Charles of two French secret agents on their way to Istanbul. The Ottoman fleet used French naval bases, and this time the Catholic Francis I also allied himself with the Protestant Duke of Cleves, one of the German princes in rebellion against the Catholic Emperor. The turmoil inside Germany made it impossible for Charles V ever to count on much German assistance against the French. In this war, Henry VIII joined Charles against Francis, partly in revulsion against the Franco-Turkish alliance, and for a time Paris was threatened. But, obeying the principles of the balance of power, the English did not want Charles too strong, and did not give him all the help they might have; Paris escaped capture.

The Second Round: Augsburg and Cateau-Cambrésis. Once this particular war was over, Charles was temporarily free to concentrate his strength against the German Protestants. Victories over them led in 1552 to another Habsburg–Valois war, as Henry II of France (1547–1559), son of Francis I, continued the Protestant alliance. Henry seized the imperial fortresses of Metz, Toul, and Verdun on the northeastern border of France, and held them against Charles. Unable to knock out the Protestants, Charles allowed in 1555 the religious Peace of Augsburg, which recognized them as established in those regions they had already won. The principle was that called *cuius regio, eius religio*, which may be freely rendered as "Whoever is the ruler of an area may require that it follow his religion." If the Elector of Saxony is Lutheran (as he was), Saxony is Lutheran; if the Duke of Bavaria is Catholic (as he was), Bavaria is Catholic. The peace failed to solve the problem of what should happen to the property of Catholic bishops or abbots who were converted to Protestantism. Also, it made no provision for Calvinism or any religion except Catholicism and Lutheranism.

Charles V abdicated in 1556, and spent the last two years of his life in a monastery. The Austrian territories and the title of emperor passed to his brother, Ferdinand; Spain and the rest of the Habsburg lands went to his son, Philip II. The last of the Habsburg–Valois wars was fought between Philip and Henry II of France between 1556 and 1559. The English, fighting on the side of Spain, lost Calais, their last foothold in France (1558). By the Treaty of Cateau-Cambrésis (1559) the French retained Calais and also Metz, Toul, and Verdun. In the same year Henry II died of a wound received in a tournament; he was followed on the throne by his three sons—Francis II (1559–1560), Charles IX (1560–1574), and Henry III (1574–1589)—who were greatly influenced by their strongly Catholic mother, the Florentine Catherine de' Medici. Under the sons of Henry II the French monarchy underwent its worst crisis since the Hundred Years' War: the Wars of Religion, precipitated by the existence of a powerful French Protestant minority, the Huguenots.

The French Wars of Religion. Protestantism in France made a great appeal to the nobles, almost half of whom were Huguenots at the peak of the movement, and to the middle classes in the towns. It affected the great masses of the peasantry much less. Regionally, it was strong in the south (where it did win many peasants), while it scarcely penetrated Brittany, Normandy, or the region of Paris. Conversion to Protestantism for the nobility was not exclusively a matter of conscience and conviction: the new faith also offered a chance to challenge the centralizing Catholic monarchy and its agents. For the French monarchy, Protestantism offered no temptations, as it had to the German princes.

In France, beginning in 1438, the kings had asserted their rights over the French Church, and by the Concordat of Bologna (1516) Francis I had won from the papacy the right to choose bishops and abbots. Conversion to Protestantism could have brought the kings no more.

Between 1562 and 1589 there were no fewer than eight religious wars. The most savage episode was the St. Bartholomew's Day massacre (1572) when the Protestant leader Coligny and thousands of other Protestants in Paris and the provinces were dragged from their beds and murdered. As the struggle continued, the great noble house of Guise assumed the command of a Catholic League, while a Huguenot prince, Henry of Navarre, the nearest male heir of the childless King Henry III, took command of the Protestants. The prospect of a Protestant succession caused the Catholic League to redouble its efforts. The Catholics negotiated with Spain, the Protestants with England. The monarchy, though Catholic, found itself threatened not only by the Protestants but by the intransigence of the Catholic League and the ambitions of the Guises, who sought to put on the throne the uncle of Henry of Navarre, not only a Catholic but a Cardinal. This prospect horrified public opinion generally.

In the War of the Three Henrys (King Henry III, Henry, Duke of Guise, and Henry of Navarre), an insurrection in Paris (1588) drove Henry III out of the city, which then acclaimed Guise. Henry III arranged the murder of Guise, was forced by the Catholic League to take refuge with Henry of Navarre, and was in turn murdered. Henry of Navarre—still a Protestant—became King Henry IV (reigned 1589–1610), first of the House of Bourbon. He defeated the Catholics, besieged Paris, and was persuaded that if he himself should accept Catholicism he could at least obtain toleration for the Huguenots. In 1593 he did so, although he probably did not make the celebrated remark attributed to him: "Paris is well worth a mass"; in 1594 the city surrendered.

In 1598 Henry IV issued the Edict of Nantes, giving the Huguenots not full freedom of worship by any means but a measure of toleration unequalled in any other Catholic country. Citizens of certain cities and towns, and nobles having the old feudal judicial rights, might exercise their religion freely. Public worship by Huguenots was forbidden in and around Paris and in all archiepiscopal and episcopal cities. Religious concessions alone would probably not have been enough to persuade the Huguenots to lay down their arms. They obtained also certain fortified towns in the southwest, where they were strongest, notably the port and fortress of La Rochelle, and thus won recognition as a political party in arms, entitled to defend itself. The Edict of Nantes brought religious peace to France.

This compromise peace would probably have been impossible had it not been for the long and exhausting wars that had disrupted France for almost 40 years. The men who worked hardest to bring it about were moderates, usually practicing Catholics themselves. Michel de l'Hospital (1505–1573) believed that

Henry IV (Henry of Navarre).

it was un-Christian to try by force to impose religious conformity, although he could not believe that men of different faiths could live peacefully together. He appealed to Protestant and Catholic to submerge their differences in their common Christianity. Jean Bodin (d. 1596) similarly longed for a strong centralized monarchy tempered by the limitations imposed by history and tradition, and thought that the quarrelling factions should submerge their differences in loyalty to the French Crown. These men and many who shared their views were known as *politiques*, political moralists.

The French Renaissance. Despite almost constant warfare, sixteenth-century France experienced a cultural renaissance, which began in large measure under the influence of Italian models. The French humanist François Rabelais (1494–1553), who began life as a monk, studied the classics, practiced and taught medicine, and created two of the greatest comic figures in literary history, the giant Gargantua and his son Pantagruel. Gargantua helped to found a wonderful unmonastic monastery, the Abbey of Theleme, whose motto was "Do What Thou Wilt," and whose happy inmates got up and went to bed when they wished, ate and drank and worked and slept whenever they felt like it, and did anything else they pleased. Exuberant, fleshly, optimistic, Rabelais is often obscene. His language comes pouring out in a torrent of synonyms, full of energy, almost tiring to read. But he recommends more than self-indulgence: Gargantua wants Pantagruel to learn everything—Arabic, Latin, Hebrew, Greek, all the arts and all the sciences, with the true humanist zeal for discovery. Typical of another strain in humanism was the reasonable, self-analytical, and somewhat skeptical Michel de Montaigne (1533–1592), an essayist who was one of the first great stylists of French letters.

Perhaps the single most characteristic monument of the Renaissance in France was the great chateau, in which the grim fortress of medieval days was transformed into a residential palace, often charmingly domesticated, retaining its thick walls and its towers, which now served a decorative rather than a defensive purpose. The Loire valley is the site of many. Two of the most celebrated are Chambord, built by Francis I, and Chenonceaux, built on a bridge over a small river, which Henry II gave to his aging but still beautiful mistress, Diane de Poitiers, and which Catherine de' Medici took from Diane after Henry's death. In sculpture, Jean Goujon returned to the classical nude as the inspiration for his statues—of Diane de Poitiers as well as of anonymous nymphs. In painting, the French, though producing no artists of the stature of the great Italians and Spaniards of the sixteenth century, did enjoy a school of portraitists, including Clouet and Fouquet, that left sensitive and realistic likenesses of the men and women of the Valois court.

For the court Francis remodelled the Louvre, the royal residence in Paris. As a patron of the arts, he employed both Leonardo da Vinci and the famous Florentine sculptor, goldsmith, rake, and autobiographer, Benvenuto Cellini. Catherine de' Medici continued the Italian influence: in behavior as well as in decoration the court echoed Italian originals.

ENGLAND

The Tudor Monarchy of Henry VIII and Elizabeth. Henry VIII (reigned 1509–1547), the instigator of the Anglican Reformation, is perhaps the most familiar figure in sixteenth-century history: fat, lavishly bejeweled, with shrewd little eyes staring out of his broad face fringed with beard, his velvet hat jauntily cocked. Six times married, self-willed and intelligent, personally extravagant, he was yet economical where it counted. While the Spanish royal house squandered its wealth in war, Henry contented himself with much cheaper pleasures. He never risked big English armies on the Continent, but intervened inexpensively to maintain the balance of power when necessary. Rewarding his followers with the proceeds of confiscated monastic properties (*see* p. 284), he created a whole new class of loyal nobles, replacing those exterminated during the Wars of the Roses. He continued the policies of his father, Henry VII, strengthening the central administration and maintaining adequate supervision of the justices of the peace, who continued to be the keystone of English local government (*see* Chapter 6).

Henry's parliaments granted him what he wanted. The Tudor House of Lords had a safe majority of his newly ennobled men, who, together with the bishops of the new church (after 1534), owed their place in the House to him. As for the House of Commons, a small minority of the people chose these knights of the shire and burgesses of the towns. In the countryside, only freeholders voted, not the majority of the residents, who were tenant farmers or agricultural workers; the country gentlemen and squires chose their representatives from among their own number. In the towns, too, the franchise was usually a narrow one.

Yet the very combination of knights of the shire and burgesses meeting together made the Tudor House of Commons unique among contemporary European assemblies, since the third estate on the Continent usually represented townsmen only. In England, too, unlike the Continent, only the eldest sons of noblemen, who actually inherited the title, could sit in the House of Lords, while the younger ones, as gentry, had to seek representation in the Commons. Finally, the English Parliament, unlike Continental assemblies, had during the Middle Ages acquired the right to legislate, especially on money. Why did the Tudor parliaments not quarrel with the monarch, as the Stuart parliaments would do in the seventeenth century? In part because they owed the king so much gratitude, but partly also because the Tudor monarchs, Henry VIII and Elizabeth I particularly, were skillful, dignified, persuasive, and popular, symbolizing in their own glittering persons the national sense of patriotism and of hostility to Spain and the Roman Church.

We have already seen how Elizabeth I (reigned 1558–1603) completed the establishment of the Church of England upon acceding to the throne at the death of her half-sister Mary. But Elizabeth did more: her name has become a synonym for the flowering of English achievement and self-confidence in every field of endeavor. Proud, cool, and remarkably intelligent, she loved flattery but never let it lead her astray when important matters were at stake. She more than held her own among her contemporaries as a Machiavellian statesman. Her people loved her more than did those who knew her best. She never married, and in her early years she played off foreign and domestic suitors against each other with excellent political results. Like her father, she enjoyed getting her successes as cheaply as possible. Under her able ministers Burleigh and Walsingham she maintained and heightened the administrative efficiency of her government.

The Spanish Threat and Mary Queen of Scots. Elizabeth's chief problem was the hostility of Philip II, who had been married to her Catholic half-sister Mary, and who resented both the very existence of a Protestant England and the

Elizabeth I, portrayed on the silver medal commemorating the defeat of the Armada.

beginnings of English penetration into the Spanish New World. Had Philip been able to concentrate on England, especially early in Elizabeth's reign, her position would have been precarious indeed. But at first he hoped to marry Elizabeth; then he hoped to capitalize on her fears that the French would succeed in backing Mary Queen of Scots against her; then he was delayed by a great Dutch revolt.

Mary Stuart, Queen of Scots, was the great-granddaughter of Henry VII. Her grandmother was Henry VIII's sister Margaret, who had married King James IV of Scotland. Her father was James V, who had married a Guise, and who left Mary as his heiress. She was not only a Catholic and half a Guise (and so of the extreme Catholic faction in France), but she lived in France, while her mother acted as regent for her in Scotland. She married the short-lived King Francis II of France (reigned 1559–1560) and took the title of Queen of England as well as Queen of Scots. Since Catholics regarded Elizabeth, daughter of Henry VIII by Anne Boleyn, as illegitimate, Mary might have given Elizabeth a very anxious time if she had been able to combine Scottish with French support.

But in 1555 John Knox returned to Scotland from Geneva, and found the ground ready for Calvinist preaching. The Scots had come to associate Catholicism with the hated French influence; in 1557 Scotch nobles signed the first covenant to defend Protestantism; in 1559 they revolted against Mary's mother, Mary of Guise; and in 1560 Elizabeth helped them oust the French troops. So when Mary Stuart returned to Scotland in 1561, after the death of Francis II, she found a Presbyterian church, the authority of which resided in the elders of each congregation, who could not be easily dominated by a monarch. Mary's reckless love affairs, punctuated with murder and scandal, made her extremely unpopular. In 1568, she was forced by revolution to take refuge in England, where Elizabeth put her into confinement. Mary left behind her infant son, later James I of England (and VI of Scotland). Her very existence was a threat to Elizabeth, who had her executed in 1587 for involvement in an alleged plot.

The Dutch Revolt and the Armada. Meantime, the Dutch had staged a great revolt against Philip II. Charles V had resided in the Low Countries by preference, and had confirmed their traditional privileges. Philip, who was thoroughly Spanish, tried to curb the feudal and municipal liberties of the Netherlands. The more pressure he applied, the more Calvinist his subjects became; the more Protestants there were, the more he sent Spanish garrisons and tried to enforce edicts against heretics. The Dutch were also a seafaring commercial people determined to conduct their trade free from the jealous restrictions of Spanish mercantilism.

So economic considerations joined religious and political ones to precipitate a revolt by a league including nobles, rich townsmen, and members of the lower classes. They proudly called themselves Beggars, a name which had first been applied to them with scorn. In 1567 Philip sent an army under the stupid and ruthless Duke of Alba, who tried but failed to hold down the thoroughly disaffected population by force alone. Alba's punitive Council of Troubles only forced the southern provinces (modern Belgium) to join the northern (Holland) in revolt. The Beggars had the support of virtually the whole population, from William the Silent, Prince of Orange, down.

In 1578 Philip sent the Duke of Parma to effect a compromise, and he did win back the southern provinces by political concessions; they remained basically

Catholic. But the northern Protestant provinces could have been won over only by religious concessions more radical than Philip II was by temperament able to make. In 1581 the Dutch declared themselves independent of Spain. The assassination of William the Silent (1584) gave them a national Protestant martyr and strengthened their determination.

It was at this point that Queen Elizabeth came to the aid of the Dutch. She had always sympathized with them, but had so far hesitated to take on the powerful Spaniards, especially for fear that the French Catholic party and the Spaniards might unite against her. But a series of crude Spanish plots against Elizabeth's life and throne had aroused public opinion. In 1585 Elizabeth sent troops to Holland. After she executed Mary Queen of Scots (1587), Philip declared open war. The great armed fleet (armada) that he sent out in 1588 met its defeat in the English Channel at the hands of a lighter, skillfully maneuvered English fleet; a great storm north of Scotland scattered and destroyed what was left of the Spaniards. The battle marked the fading of Spanish preponderance in Europe, the beginning of English maritime greatness, and the decisive step in achieving Dutch independence. Protestants everywhere took heart and called the great storm that had sent Philip's galleons to the bottom the "Protestant wind." Desultory fighting continued in Holland after Philip's death in 1598 and down to 1609, when a truce established the virtual independence of the Dutch.

Ireland. Elizabeth's last years were marked by a great crisis in Ireland. Henry VIII had put the Irish Parliament completely under English control, and Henry VIII's Act of Supremacy, combined with the decision (1542) that the King of England was also King of Ireland, required the Catholic Irish to acknowledge the English monarch as head of the Church. Ireland was an ancient Celtic feudal land, where most of the Norman and English settlers had been assimilated to Irish ways, spoke the native Irish Gaelic, and remained Catholic. Chieftains regarded themselves as local kings, commanded the loyalty of their followers in war, and were still incited to battle by a professional class of bards. Ireland had only a few Protestant English inhabitants settled near Dublin. Thus the insurrection of 1597 led by "the O'Neill," whom Elizabeth had made Earl of Tyrone, was a serious affair. It was not suppressed until 1601, and the Irish Question in its various phases remained to trouble the English Crown well into the twentieth century.

The English Renaissance. The solid administration, economic prosperity, and steadily growing national feeling of the Elizabethan age was accompanied by a Renaissance that had actually begun under Henry VIII, and was the latest of the European Renaissances. It took its start, as all of them did, with the classics; more than the others, it was chiefly literary. St. Thomas More, Shakespeare, Francis Bacon, Edmund Spenser, Ben Jonson, and others are part of the birthright of English-speaking peoples. They vary greatly among themselves, but Shakespeare by common consent towers not only above all the rest but above everybody else of any age, save perhaps Homer or Dante.

To admirers of order and precision the Elizabethans appear excessive, undisciplined, even uncouth. The plots of Elizabethan tragedies are often bloody, and the dramatists sometimes seem to love words for their own sake. Yet the Elizabethans in their exuberance were bursting with life and with a passionate love of country. Shakespeare sums up the Englishman's patriotic pride, in the famous lines given to John of Gaunt in *Richard II*:

> This royal throne of kings, this scepter'd isle,
> This earth of majesty, this seat of Mars,
> This other Eden, demi-paradise,
> This fortress built by Nature for herself
> Against infection and the hand of war,
> This happy breed of men, this little world,
> This precious stone set in the silver sea,
> Which serves it in the office of a wall
> Or as a moat defensive to a house,
> Against the envy of less happier lands,
> This blessed plot, this earth, this realm, this England.

7

READING SUGGESTIONS (asterisk indicates paperbound edition)

The Reformation

G. R. Elton, ed., *Reformation Europe, 1517–1559* (*Torchbooks). A recent general history, with a selective bibliography.

E. H. Harbison, *The Age of Reformation* (*Cornell). Admirable introduction.

H. J. Grimm, *The Reformation Era, 1500–1650* (Macmillan, 1954). A good American textbook, with a thorough critical bibliography.

H. Holborn, *A History of Modern Germany*, Vol. I: *The Reformation* (Knopf, 1959). Scholarly, readable, and up-to-date.

O. Chadwick, *The Reformation* (*Penguin). A very good popular account.

R. H. Bainton, *The Reformation of the Sixteenth Century* (*Beacon). By a sound Protestant historian, fully abreast of modern research.

———, *Here I Stand: A Life of Martin Luther* (*Apex). Sympathetic, scholarly, and readable.

E. Erikson, *Young Man Luther* (*Norton). An important book by a distinguished psychoanalyst who is also a historian.

J. Courvoisier; *Zwingli: A Reformed Theologian* (*John Knox). Good study of an important and neglected figure.

G. Harkness, *John Calvin: The Man and His Ethics* (*Apex). A good introduction.

J. Mackinnon, *Calvin and the Reformation* (Longmans, 1936). Solid longer study.

E. H. Harbison, *The Christian Scholar in the Age of Reformation* (*Scribner's). Helpful exploration of the connection between intellectual and religious history.

A. G. Dickens, *The English Reformation* (*Schocken), and T. M. Parker, *The English Reformation to 1558* (*Oxford). Good introductions.

F. M. Powicke, *The Reformation in England* (*Oxford). A scholarly study.

G. H. Williams, *The Radical Reformation* (Westminster, 1962). The indispensable book concerning the Anabaptists and other radicals.

H. Daniel-Rops, *The Catholic Reformation*, 2 vols. (*Image). Admirable work by a French Catholic historian.

B. J. Kidd, *The Counter-Reformation* (S.P.C.K., 1933). Modern scholarly account by an Anglican.

L. W. Spitz, ed., *The Reformation: Material or Spiritual?* (*Heath). Brief collection of readings illustrating divergent views, with a useful critical bibliography.

Max Weber, *The Protestant Ethic and the Spirit of Capitalism* (*Scribner's). Celebrated controversial work on the interrelation of religion and economics.

R. H. Tawney, *Religion and the Rise of Capitalism* (*Mentor). Revision of the Weber thesis by an English intellectual associated with the Labour party.

E. Troeltsch, *Protestantism and Progress* (*Beacon). By one of the most important religious philosophers of modern times.

Overseas Empires

J. N. L. Baker, *A History of Geographical Discovery and Exploration,* rev. ed. (Barnes & Noble, 1963). Standard work of reference.

J. H. Parry, *Age of Reconnaissance* (*Mentor) and *Establishment of the European Hegemony, 1415–1715* (*Torchbooks). First-rate works by an expert.

B. Penrose, *Travel and Discovery in the Renaissance* (*Atheneum). Good survey.

S. E. Morison, *Admiral of the Ocean Sea,* 2 vols. (Little, Brown, 1942). The best book on Columbus.

H. H. Hart, *Sea Road to the Indies* (Macmillan, 1950). Treating Da Gama and other Portuguese explorers.

C. McK. Parr, *So Noble a Captain* (Crowell, 1953). A very scholarly treatment of Magellan and his circumnavigation.

J. H. Brebner, *The Explorers of North America, 1492–1806* (*Meridian). A good brief account.

H. R. Trevor-Roper, ed., *The Age of Expansion: Europe and the World, 1559–1660* (Thames & Hudson, 1968). Sumptuously illustrated collaborative volume.

D. F. Lach, *China in the Eyes of Europe: The Sixteenth Century* (*Phoenix). Lach has published companion volumes on India, Japan, and Southeast Asia (*Phoenix).

K. S. Latourette, *China* (*Spectrum). Excellent introduction.

G. B. Sansom, *Japan: A Short Cultural History,* rev. ed. (Appleton, 1962). Stimulating introduction by a distinguished British expert.

A. L. Basham, *The Wonder That Was India* (*Evergreen). A sober and careful analysis of medieval India.

I. R. Bladen, ed., *The Portable Prescott* (*Viking). Excerpts from the accounts of the conquest of Mexico and Peru by a famous American historian.

C. H. Haring, *The Spanish Empire in America* (*Harbinger). The best general study of the subject.

R. E. Poppino, *Brazil: The Land and People* (*Oxford). Recent social and economic study.

Monarchy and Warfare in the Sixteenth Century

G. H. Sabine, *A History of Political Theory,* rev. ed. (Holt, 1950). An admirably lucid survey.

J. W. Allen, *History of Political Thought in the Sixteenth Century,* 3rd ed. (*Barnes & Noble). More detailed treatment.

C. W. C. Oman, *A History of the Art of War in the Sixteenth Century* (Dutton, 1937). Highly interesting study.

S. T. Bindoff, *Tudor England* (*Penguin). Short scholarly introduction.

J. D. Mackie, *The Earlier Tudors, 1485–1558* (Clarendon, 1952), and J. B. Black, *The Reign of Elizabeth* (Clarendon, 1936). Somewhat longer historical accounts.

J. E. Neale, *Queen Elizabeth* (*Anchor). The best volume on the famous queen; by a scholar who has written several specialized works on political life during her reign.

E. Jenkins, *Elizabeth the Great* (*Capricorn). Focussing on the queen as a person.

G. Mattingly, *The Armada* (*Sentry). Topnotch account.

J. Ridley, *Thomas Cranmer* (*Oxford). Biography of Henry VIII's collaborator.

J. Lynch, *Spain under the Habsburgs,* Vol. 1 (Oxford, 1964). Up-to-date scholarly treatment of sixteenth-century Spain.

R. Trevor Davies, *The Golden Century of Spain* (*Torchbooks). Sound popular introduction to the sixteenth century.

K. Brandi, *The Emperor Charles V* (*Humanities). A comprehensive account.

L. Goldscheider, *El Greco* (Phaidon, 1954). Well illustrated study of the artist who expressed so well the Spanish style.

P. Geyl, *The Revolt of the Netherlands, 1555–1609* (*Barnes & Noble). By a celebrated Dutch historian who regretted the separation of the Dutch and the Flemings.

C. V. Wedgwood, *William the Silent* (*Norton). Sympathetic biography.

J. E. Neale, *The Age of Catherine de' Medici* (*Torchbooks). Short and lucid introduction to a complex era.

Q. Hurst, *Henry of Navarre* (Appleton, 1938). Standard biography of Henry IV.

Sources and Fiction

H. S. Bettenson, ed. *Documents of the Christian Church* (*Oxford). An admirable compilation, useful for the Reformation.

R. H. Bainton, *The Age of the Reformation* (*Anvil). Selections from the great men and great books of the era.

Lew Wallace, *The Fair God* (*Popular). Thriller on Aztec Mexico.

C. S. Forester, *To the Indies* (Little, Brown, 1940). Excellent novel on Columbus.

R. Sabatini, *The Sea Hawk* (Houghton, 1923). Good melodramatic novel of life on the main in the late sixteenth century.

S. Putnam, ed., *The Portable Cervantes* (*Viking). Excerpts from a widely acclaimed translation of *Don Quixote.*

8

The Seventeenth Century

War, Politics, and Empire

The Palace of Versailles, begun in 1669.

Ancient Greek mythology tells of Proteus, a sea-divinity on whom it was difficult to keep one's grasp. To avoid capture he would turn into a flapping fish, a wriggling serpent, a bird, a trickle of water, or a ribbon of sand. The problems of the sixteenth and seventeenth centuries seem truly Protean. The internal history of each state is at once the story of the local dynasty and of other dynasties intervening in its affairs, so that domestic issues suddenly become foreign issues. Problems of conscience arise, so that what looks like a political issue proves to be largely religious, or what looks religious proves to be mainly political. Economic and social values are involved with both politics and religion, so that a wealthy bourgeois, excluded from political power by the aristocracy, may be tempted to refuse his nominal ruler financial support, to desert the ruler's religion, to listen to the siren voice of foreign agents, or even to take arms in open rebellion.

In the last chapter we saw that the French nobles who turned to Calvinism did so in part to maintain their traditional privileges against the encroachments of the king. Elizabeth helped the Dutch against the Spaniards partly because the Dutch were fellow-Protestants, but more because of Philip II's threat to herself. The Catholic Reformation failed to win back some areas of Europe because the Habsburg monarchy headed the Catholic cause, and many powerful persons who otherwise would have helped Rome could not bear at the same time to help the Habsburgs. The papacy itself was determined to avoid Habsburg domination. The Peace of Augsburg of 1555, the triumph of Henry IV in France, and the execution of Mary Queen of Scots all contributed to the containment of Habsburg power. Yet none of these interlocking problems was finally resolved when the Habsburg leader of the late sixteenth century, Philip II, died in his colossal monastic palace of the Escorial in the bleak hills near Madrid, in 1598, with an open coffin standing at his order beside his bed, and a skull grinning at him beneath a golden crown.

I. The Thirty Years' War

THE DUTCH AND SPANISH BACKGROUND

The Dutch played a part of outstanding importance in the international affairs of the seventeenth century. In 1609 they concluded their successful revolt against Spain by negotiating a truce for twelve years that made their state virtually independent. The United Provinces, which made up the Dutch republic, were, however, united only in opposition to Spain. Each of the seven provinces preserved its local traditions of government and sent delegates (the *Hooge Moogende,* High Mightinesses) to the Estates-General, which behaved like a diplomatic congress rather than a central legislature. Each province had its own *Stadholder* as executive, though several of them often elected the same man to the office. After the truce of 1609, Maurice, Prince of Orange, son of William the Silent, was chosen Stadholder by five of the seven. Religious differences also divided the Dutch nation. There was a large Catholic minority, and the Protestant majority was badly split between orthodox Calvinists and moderates called Arminians (after Arminius, a Dutch theologian), who believed that what a man did on earth might change God's original intentions about his individual fate: predestination, therefore, was conditional.

The Dutch were the world's best businessmen; by the early seventeenth century they controlled most of the coastwise shipping of Europe. They went into the wine business in France and into the fishing grounds of the Arctic. In 1602 they organized the Dutch East India Company, and soon launched other ventures overseas. The Bank of Amsterdam (1609) minted its own florins, which became standard in Europe; its services to its depositors were so much in demand that Amsterdam became the financial capital of Europe. The Dutch invented life insurance, and made it a big business. Diamond-cutting, shipbuilding, gin-distilling, and tulip-growing all made the Dutch provinces rich and famous. Their opulent middle-class way of life is mirrored in the great paintings of Hals, Vermeer, and Rembrandt.

It was no wonder that Philip II's successors in Spain dreamed of reconquering the United Provinces. Spanish strength was visibly declining in the seventeenth century, as a result of the country's bad administration, its underdeveloped economy, and all the other chronic difficulties discussed in Chapter 7. Nevertheless, Spain could still draw on important resources—the wealth of the Americas, the reserves of military manpower in her north Italian possessions, and the loyalty of her Catholic Belgian provinces. After the Dutch revolt, the Spaniards wanted to stabilize a line of communications between their Italian and Belgian lands, so that men and money could move over the Alps and down the Rhine, which flowed through the lands of some rulers who were friendly and others who were hostile to the Habsburgs. To deny this communication-line to the Spaniards was a great goal both for the Dutch and for the French: the Bourbons did not relish the idea of being surrounded by Habsburg territory any more than the Valois had done.

THE GERMAN BACKGROUND

Thus the key to the situation was Germany—by the early seventeenth century a truly fantastic conglomeration of states. Some of the German principalities had been divided and subdivided until an ostensibly independent princeling might rule over only a village or a few hundred acres of forest. Free cities acknowledged no authority but the emperor; some held huge lands outside their walls, others not. The Church governed certain cities and regions, and these too varied greatly in extent. There were more than 2,000 governing authorities; but since many of the smaller ones combined or reached understandings locally, this number can be reduced to perhaps 300.

Particularly influential in Germany were the seven electors, who chose each new emperor and enjoyed other prerogatives. One elector, the King of Bohemia, was in practice always a Habsburg, so that the imperial family always had at least one vote at election-time. The three Rhineland electors—the Archbishops of Mainz, Trier, and Cologne—were Catholic, and the electors of Saxony and Brandenburg were Lutheran. The Elector of the Palatinate, with his capital at Heidelberg, was a Calvinist; his lands, in a rich vineyard area along the Rhine, constituted a major block to the Habsburg plan of securing communications to the Low Countries. In addition, some princes who were not electors exercised much influence, especially the great Catholic Duke of Bavaria, Maximilian.

Triumphant German particularism paralyzed the central institutions of the Empire. The imperial diet, consisting in theory of all the independent German rulers, always quarrelled when it met; some princes refused to accept its decisions. The emperor was virtually forced to bypass the diet, and attempted to rule by decree and pressure. Altogether, Germany did not possess the machinery to resolve the religious difficulties stemming from the Augsburg settlement of 1555 (*see* p. 308).

The Peace of Augsburg had not recognized Calvinism; yet Calvinism spread rapidly after 1555, horrifying both Lutherans and Catholics. Calvinist princes ignored the provision in the peace against proselytizing, and proved equally vigorous in Lutheran and in Catholic regions. Sudden conversion of a prince meant sudden conversion of his subjects, or else persecution. The consequences were riots and disorder, followed by the formation of the Calvinist Protestant Union (1608) and the Catholic League (1609) under Maximilian of Bavaria. It was not surprising that war broke out in Germany in 1618, three years before the truce between Spain and the Dutch was due to elapse.

THE BOHEMIAN PERIOD, 1618-1625

In 1618 the head of the Protestant Union was the Calvinist Elector of the Palatinate, Frederick, who was married to the daughter of James I of England. Frederick hoped to break the Catholic hold on the Empire upon the death of the Emperor Matthias (reigned 1612-1619), who was old and childless. If there could be four Protestant electors instead of three when Matthias died, the majority could then install a Protestant emperor. Because three electors were Catholic archbishops, the only way to get an additional Protestant was to oust the one lay Catholic elector, the King of Bohemia. The King-elect of Bohemia, Ferdinand, was a strongly Catholic Habsburg prince, already chosen by Matthias to be his heir.

Bohemia presented its own special problems. The native Czechs expressed their national defiance of the Germans in part by following the faith that John Hus had taught them (*see* p. 242), the chief feature of which was "Utraquism," the practice of giving the laity communion in wine as well as in bread. While Lutherans, Calvinists, and Utraquists were tolerated, Catholicism remained the state religion. Though Ferdinand guaranteed freedom of Protestant worship, the prospect of his becoming King of Bohemia and then Emperor alarmed the Protestants. The arrest of some Protestants who had lost two legal cases touched off a revolt, which began with the famous Defenestration of Prague (May 23, 1618), when the angry rebels actually threw two Catholic imperial governors out of a window into a courtyard 70 feet below. They landed on a pile of dung, and escaped with their lives.

The Czech rebels set up their own government and offered the crown of Bohemia to the Elector Frederick of the Palatinate. The inept Frederick went off to Prague, leaving badly defended the Rhineland territories which the Spaniards most wanted and which they occupied in 1620. Meantime, Catholics in Bohemia, Spain, and Flanders rallied against the rebels with money and men. After the Emperor Matthias died in 1619, the Electors chose the Habsburg Ferdinand to be Emperor (Ferdinand II, reigned 1619-1637). Maximilian of Bavaria, head of the Catholic League, joined Ferdinand, in return for a promise of Frederick's electoral post; even the Lutheran Elector of Saxony joined the Catholic Ferdinand, who also secured the neutrality of the Protestant Union. In Bohemia, Maximilian and the Catholic forces won the battle of the White Mountain (November 8, 1620). Frederick, derisively nicknamed "the Winter King," fled, and Ferdinand made the Bohemian throne hereditary in his own family. With the aid of the Jesuits, he enforced Catholicism and abolished toleration for Utraquists and Calvinists, but granted it temporarily to Lutherans because of his obligations to the Elector of Saxony. He executed the Czech leaders of the rebellion and permitted terrible destruction in Bohemia.

The continued presence of Spanish forces in the Palatinate posed a threat to others. The Protestant King Christian IV of Denmark (1588-1648) feared the Habsburgs would move northward to the Baltic; the French faced a new Habsburg encirclement; and the Dutch, menaced by an immediate Spanish attack, were worst off of all. They made an alliance with Christian IV, and another with the fugitive Frederick of the Palatinate, agreeing to subsidize his reconquest of his Rhenish lands. Had Frederick accepted a proposal of the Spanish to return to the Palatinate under their auspices, there might have been no

Thirty Years' War; but he turned it down. When fighting resumed, Frederick was routed again, whereupon Ferdinand transferred the Palatine electorate to Maximilian (1625).

In France, meantime, Cardinal Richelieu, who was emerging as chief minister of Louis XIII (reigned 1610–1643), fully recognized the Habsburg danger. Richelieu was ready to arrange a dynastic marriage between the future Charles I of England and Louis XIII's sister, Henrietta Maria, and to make an alliance with other Protestants—Frederick, the Dutch, Christian IV of Denmark, and also Gustavus Adolphus, the Lutheran King of Sweden. Richelieu could count on the understanding of Pope Urban VIII, who felt that the fulfillment of Habsburg ambitions would be bad for the interests of the Church. By the summer of 1624 the new coalition was in being. But Spanish victories in Holland (1625) and the unwillingness of Gustavus Adolphus to serve under the Danes spoiled the plan. Christian IV now had to fight for the Protestants alone, thus inaugurating the Danish phase of the war.

THE DANISH PERIOD, 1625–1629

In the new phase Catholic military operations fell into the hands of Count Wallenstein, who had recruited a private army, which lived off the land by requisitions and open plunder. Born a Protestant and converted to Catholicism, Wallenstein had bought up one quarter of the lands in Bohemia after Ferdinand's suppression of the Czech rebellion and now dreamed of creating a new-model monarchy in Germany. Together with the forces of Maximilian and the Catholic League under the command of Count Tilly, Wallenstein's armies defeated the Danes and moved northward into Danish territory.

In 1629 the Emperor Ferdinand dramatized his successes by the Edict of Restitution and the Treaty of Lübeck. The edict reaffirmed the religious Peace of Augsburg, still making no provision for Calvinists, and declared that the Catholics were entitled to recover all ecclesiastical property that had passed to the Lutherans since 1551—a vast amount of land and wealth. It meant changing boundaries throughout northern and western Germany, and dispossessing many whose wealth rested on former Church property. In the Treaty of Lübeck Christian IV acknowledged defeat, and undertook not to interfere again in German affairs; he received his lands back. Wallenstein further enriched himself by increasing his own land-holdings. But the Habsburgs had moved into regions hitherto Protestant and only on the periphery of imperial interest, and they had shown that in victory they would revert to religious extremism.

More and more Ferdinand became indebted to his ambitious general Wallenstein, and less and less could he control him. Wallenstein planned to found a new Baltic trading company with the remnants of the Hanseatic League (*see* Chapter 6), and by opening the Baltic to the Spaniards make possible a complete Spanish victory over the Dutch. When Ferdinand asked Wallenstein for troops to use in Italy against the French, Wallenstein, intent on his northern plans, at first refused to send them because Gustavus Adolphus of Sweden had decided to attack the imperial forces in Germany.

Soon Ferdinand dismissed Wallenstein, and so placated Maximilian of Bavaria. The imperial troops defeated the French in Italy, and the Emperor was able to make the French agree not to help the Dutch or the Swedes. If Ferdinand had next revoked the Edict of Restitution and placated the Protestants, peace still might have been possible. But he refused. Maximilian and Tilly were now in command of the imperial armies, and Gustavus Adolphus was invading. The Swedish phase of the war was beginning.

THE SWEDISH PERIOD, 1630–1635

Highly intelligent, physically powerful, competent in every way, Gustavus Adolphus (reigned 1611–1632) had tamed the unruly Swedish nobility, given his

The siege of Magdeburg during the Thirty Years' War, 1631.

country an efficient government and a sound economy, taken lessons from the Dutch in military tactics, and proved himself and his armies against Russians and Poles by establishing a Swedish foothold on the south shores of the Baltic. A Lutheran, tolerant of Calvinists, he brought a large, well-disciplined army of Swedes, Finns, and Lapps, equipped with hymn-books, and added to them all the recruits, even prisoners, that he could induce to join his forces. Sharing their hardships, he usually restrained them from plunder. Richelieu agreed to subsidize his forces, and Gustavus agreed not to fight against Maximilian and to guarantee freedom of worship for Catholics. The Protestant Electors of Saxony and Brandenburg denounced the Edict of Restitution, and mobilized, in part to revive the Protestant cause, but also in part to protect the Germans against the Swedes.

Protestant hesitation ended after the terrible sack of Magdeburg by the Catholic forces of Tilly in May, 1631, accompanied by a fire that left the city in ashes. The Elector of Brandenburg had to ally himself with Gustavus, and so did the Elector of Saxony, threatened by Tilly's starving troops. At Breitenfeld, in September, 1631, Gustavus defeated Tilly; combined with a defeat of the Spaniards off the Dutch coast, this turned the tide against the Habsburgs. Now the Saxons invaded Bohemia and recaptured Prague in the name of Frederick of the Palatinate, while Gustavus invaded the Catholic lands of south central Germany, taking Frankfurt and Mainz, and obtaining the alliance of many princes and free cities. In the crisis, Ferdinand turned back to Wallenstein, who consented to return to his command.

Gustavus had been more successful than Richelieu, his sponsor, had expected; indeed, too successful, since not only the Habsburgs but Maximilian and the Catholic League, still friends of France, were suffering from the Swedes. Gustavus was planning to reorganize all Germany, to unite Lutheran and Calvinist churches, and even to become Emperor—aims opposed by all the German princes, Catholic and Protestant alike. But the strength of Gustavus' position declined: his allies were untrustworthy and his enemies, Maximilian and Wallenstein, drew together. In November, 1632, the Swedes won the battle of Lützen, defeating Wallenstein; Gustavus Adolphus, however, was killed.

Once more a moment had arrived when peace might have been possible, yet the fighting, and the plague, famine, and death accompanying it, continued. The Pope, suspect among the cardinals as hostile to the Catholic cause, wanted peace. Richelieu preferred war, in order to further French aims in the Rhineland; the Swedes needed to protect their heavy investment and come out of the fighting with some territory; the Spaniards hoped that Gustavus' death meant that the Habsburg cause could be saved and the Dutch defeated. Gustavus' chancellor, Oxenstierna, an able diplomat, was recognized by the German Protestants in 1633 as chief of the Protestant cause.

Wallenstein negotiated with the enemies of the Empire (he wanted the French to recognize him as King of Bohemia); his army began to dribble away and he was again dismissed by the Emperor Ferdinand, who suspected him of treachery. On February 24, 1634, an English mercenary in the imperial service murdered Wallenstein and won an imperial reward. At Nordlingen, in September, 1634, the forces of Ferdinand defeated the Protestants, thereby lessening the influence of Sweden and making Cardinal Richelieu the chief strategist for the Protestant cause, which now became the Bourbon cause.

THE SWEDISH AND FRENCH PERIOD, 1635–1648

The remaining years of the Thirty Years' War were years of Habsburg–Bourbon conflict, a sequel to the Habsburg–Valois wars. The Protestant commander had to promise future toleration for Catholicism in Germany, and undertake to keep on fighting indefinitely in exchange for French men and money. More and more the original religious character of the war became transformed into a purely dynastic and political struggle. The armies themselves on both sides were made up of a mixture of men from just about every nationality in Europe; they fought as professional soldiers, changing sides frequently, and taking their women and children with them everywhere.

In 1635 the Emperor Ferdinand at last relinquished the Edict of Restitution and made a compromise peace with the Elector of Saxony. Most of the other Lutheran princes signed also. Alarmed by the imperial gains and by the renewed

Europe in 1648

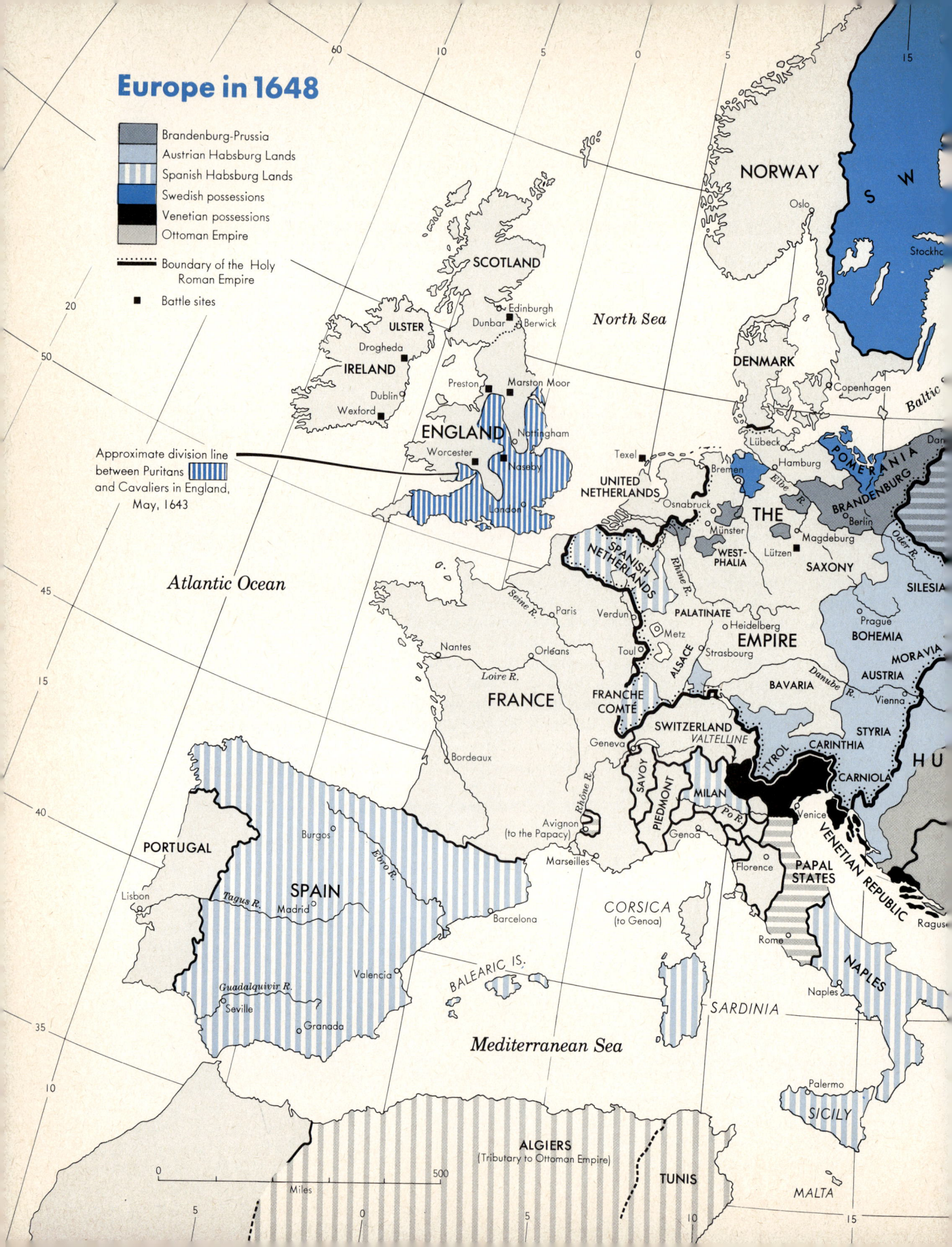

Legend:
- Brandenburg-Prussia
- Austrian Habsburg Lands
- Spanish Habsburg Lands
- Swedish possessions
- Venetian possessions
- Ottoman Empire
- ······ Boundary of the Holy Roman Empire
- ■ Battle sites

Approximate division line between Puritans and Cavaliers in England, May, 1643

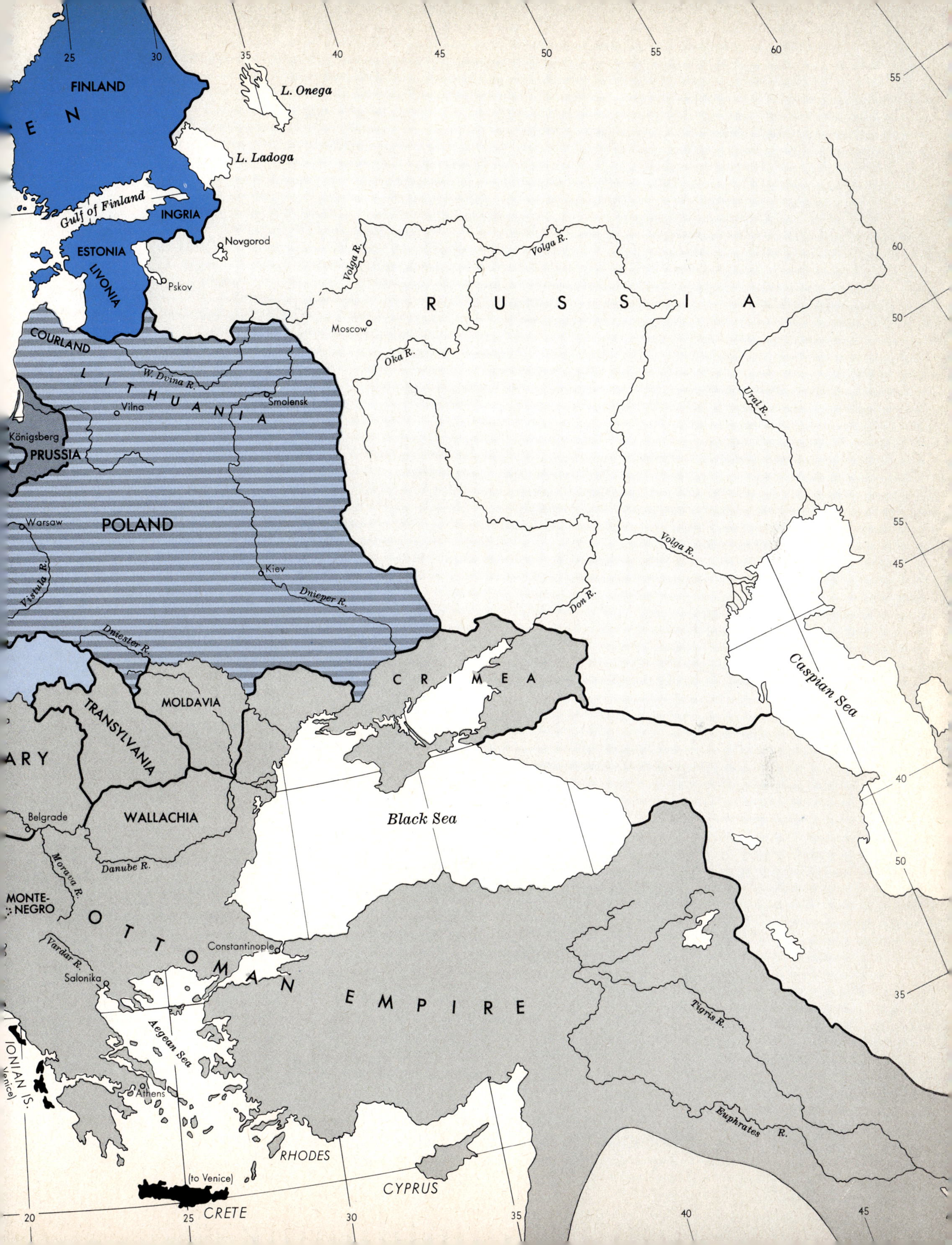

FINLAND
E N
L. Onega
L. Ladoga
Gulf of Finland
INGRIA
Novgorod
ESTONIA
LIVONIA
Pskov
Volga R.
R U S S I A
Moscow
Oka R.
COURLAND
W. Dvina R.
L I T H U A N I A
Smolensk
Vilna
Königsberg
PRUSSIA
Ural R.
Warsaw
POLAND
Kiev
Vistula R.
Dnieper R.
Don R.
Dniester R.
Caspian Sea
C R I M E A
MOLDAVIA
TRANSYLVANIA
ARY
WALLACHIA
Belgrade
Black Sea
Danube R.
Morava R.
MONTE-NEGRO
O T T O M A N E M P I R E
Constantinople
Vardar R.
Salonika
Tigris R.
Aegean Sea
IONIAN IS. (to Venice)
Athens
Euphrates R.
RHODES
(to Venice)
CYPRUS
CRETE

activity of the Spaniards in the Low Countries, Richelieu made new arrangements with Oxenstierna in Germany and a new alliance with the Dutch. No longer confining himself to the role of subsidizer, he declared war on Spain. The war would go on, though the only German allies the French and Swedes still had were a few Calvinist princes.

A great Dutch naval victory over Spain (1639) put an end to the power of the Spanish navy, which had been declining for some years. The power of Spain was further sapped by unrest in Catalonia and by the revolt (1640) of Portugal, which Philip II had annexed in 1580 and which now proceeded to re-establish its independence. The death of Richelieu (1642) and of Louis XIII (1643) did not alter French policy. Within a few days after the death of Louis, the French defeated the Spaniards at Rocroy so thoroughly that Spain was knocked out of the war, and in fact out of the competition for European hegemony. The dreams of Charles V and Philip II ended here.

Two peace conferences now opened: between Habsburgs and Swedes at Osnabrück, and between Habsburgs and French not far away at Münster. At Osnabrück proceedings were delayed by the sudden Swedish invasion of Denmark, where Christian IV had shown his jealousy of rising Swedish power. At Münster, the French refused to treat with a Spanish delegate: they wished to make peace with the Austrian Habsburgs only. The Baltic quarrel petered out when Christina, Gustavus Adolphus' daughter, who greatly wanted peace, became Queen of Sweden in 1644.

The problems for settlement were many and delicate, the negotiations complex; differences between the allies that had been unimportant during open warfare proved critical when it came to a religious settlement. The meetings dragged on for several years while the fighting and destruction continued. The Dutch made a separate peace with the Spaniards, and pulled out of the French alliance after they learned of secret French negotiations with Spain hostile to their interests. French victories forced the wavering Emperor Ferdinand III (reigned 1637–1657) to agree to the terms that had been so painstakingly hammered out, and on October 24, 1648, the Peace of Westphalia put an end to the Thirty Years' War.

THE PEACE OF WESTPHALIA: IMPACT OF THE WAR

The religious terms of the peace extended the *cuius regio eius religio* principles of the Peace of Augsburg to Calvinists as well as Lutherans and Catholics. The year 1624 was designated by compromise as the normal year for establishing the status of Church property; for the Protestants this was a great improvement over the Edict of Restitution. States forcibly converted to Catholicism during the war won the right to revert to Protestantism; the Protestants of the Habsburg lands, however, won no toleration at all.

Territorially, France secured Alsace and sovereignty over Metz, Toul, and Verdun. Sweden received most of Pomerania, along the Baltic shore of Germany, a large cash indemnity with which to pay the huge armies still mobilized, and three votes in the German Diet. As recompense for the loss of Pomerania, Brandenburg received the Archbishopric of Magdeburg and several other bishoprics. The family of Maximilian of Bavaria kept the Electorate of the Palatinate and a part of its territory; the rest was returned to the son of Frederick, who was restored as an elector, thus raising the total number of electors to eight. German particularism gained, as the individual German states secured the right to conduct their own foreign affairs, making treaties among themselves and with foreign powers if these were not directed against the emperor. The Dutch and Swiss republics were recognized as independent.

Despite the peace, the danger was great that fighting would resume. Sweden had 100,000 soldiers in arms in Germany, of whom only a few were Swedes; the rest were professional fighting men, whose whole life was war. A similar problem of demobilization and resettlement faced the imperial authorities. Many soldiers engaged themselves as mercenaries to any ruler who would hire them, and some simply became brigands. Moreover, since the treaty did not provide a means for enforcing the religious property settlement, any attempt to recover lost property might provoke a new fight. The huge amount of money to be paid the Swedes gave rise to such bitterness that this too endangered the peace.

For more than two centuries after 1648, the Thirty Years' War was blamed for everything that later went wrong in Germany. We now know that the figures given in contemporary sources are inflated and unreliable; sometimes the number of villages allegedly destroyed in a given district was larger than the whole number of villages that had ever existed there. Also scholars traditionally failed to note that the economic decline in Germany had begun well before the war opened in 1618. Yet, even when we make allowances for these early exaggerations, we must note that contemporaries everywhere in Germany felt the catastrophe to have been overwhelming. The over-all diminution in population was from about 21 million in 1618 to less than 13½ million in 1648; the suffering of individuals was indeed extreme.

Once the war was over, the nobility sometimes succeeded in forcing the peasants back onto the soil by denying them the right to leave the village or to engage in home industry. In general the war made little change in the social hierarchy of Germany. Politically the main change was probably the shrinking of the power of the Empire: the recognition that individual German states could, in effect, conduct their own foreign policies limited direct Habsburg power to Habsburg lands. Bavaria, Saxony, and especially Brandenburg-Prussia would now be able to emerge as powers in Germany. Non-Austrian Germans harbored bitter resentment against the Habsburgs for having fought a terrible war simply to protect family interests.

All these issues remained to trouble Europe again, to make more fighting. Neither the Pope, who denounced the Peace of Westphalia, nor many Protestants, who felt betrayed by its provisions, were satisfied with it. As a settlement, it raised as many problems as it solved. Its only merit was that it ended the fighting in a war that had become intolerable.

II. Revolution and Settlement in England

BACKGROUND: THE FIRST STUARTS

England's small part in the Thirty Years' War is explained by the domestic crisis which grew under James I (son of Mary Stuart, whom Elizabeth had executed in 1587) and culminated under his son Charles I in a prolonged civil war and the execution of the King. Thereafter, for eleven years, England was a kind of republic, until Charles' son, Charles II, was restored, and the Stuart family got a second chance. How was it that less than half a century after the death of the enormously popular Elizabeth, Englishmen would be executing their king?

Like the Thirty Years' War, the English Civil War is Protean. James I was a Scot and so a foreigner, and far less popular than Elizabeth. He believed that he ruled by divine right. Kings, he said, were God's "vice-gerents° on earth, and so adorned and furnished with some sparkles of the Divinitie." James was an articulate pedant constantly repeating his views in speaking and writing. While his son, Charles I, was personally far more attractive, he understood no more than his father the kind of compromises the Tudor monarchs had made in order to keep their Parliaments contented. The character of the first two Stuarts had a great deal to do with the breakdown of the monarchy.

Politically speaking, the English king, like other contemporary European monarchs, strove to make the royal administration strong. Unlike the Continental rulers, however, James and Charles found themselves infringing on what the gentry in Parliament and in the countryside felt to be their established rights. At the same time the royal effort to force submission to the Church of England alienated those Protestants who could not accept the Church. So political and religious questions were knit together.

Since the English king was obliged to ask Parliament for funds, quarrels over money proved very important. But it was perhaps more important that Charles I lacked a bureaucracy of the kind that ruled France for Richelieu and Louis XIII. The unpaid English justices of the peace rendered justice in the parishes, administered poor relief, and indeed managed the administration in the countryside. From the same class of gentry came the knights of the shires and burgesses who made up the House of Commons, and included so many "Puritans," or English Calvinists. The same important people and their relatives were alienated from the monarch on many issues. Finally, the actual outbreak of civil war was closely connected with foreign policy: Parliament had become suspicious that the King was pro-Spanish and pro-Catholic, and had ceased to trust him on diplomatic issues.

Actually both parties to the quarrel were trying to make revolutionary changes in the traditional system. The Crown was trying to make England more like a Continental divine-right monarchy, in which the king was the earthly representative of God. The idea, as old as the Roman Empire, was strongly revived in the sixteenth and seventeenth centuries; it was quite different from the Tudor compromise of a strong monarch working with and through his Parliament and satisfying the goals of the gentry and commercial classes. The parliamentarians who revolted against the Stuarts were trying to secure for a legislative body final authority in the execution of policy as well as in the making of law. This was something equally new, not only for England but for the Western world as a whole.

THE REIGN OF JAMES I

All the issues that led to the final explosion may be seen in an earlier phase during the reign of James I (1603–1625). About the House of Commons he once

° The word is "gerents," not "regents"; it comes from Latin *gerere*, "to manage" or "to bear."

remarked "I am surprised that my ancestors should ever have permitted such an institution to come into existence. I am a stranger, and found it here when I arrived, so that I am obliged to put up with what I cannot get rid of."* When Commons expressed national grievances against certain legal but outworn rights of the Crown, James acted as though they were personally insulting him. He tried to develop sources of income outside parliamentary control, and Parliament insisted on the principle that it had to approve any new methods of raising revenue. When Parliament did not enact legislation that James wanted, he would try to get the courts to declare that the desired measure was legal.

One case, seemingly on a small point, involved a question of principle: John Bate, a merchant, refused to pay duty on imported currants. The judges ruled that there was no parliamentary authority for James to levy these customs duties, but that none the less he had the right to levy them. In a matter concerning the common good, they ruled, the king had absolute power, and all foreign affairs, including foreign trade, fell within this category. So James's officials joyfully began to levy sales taxes without parliamentary authority, and when Parliament showed alarm at the prospect that James might make himself financially independent, he tried to forbid discussion of the question. Finally, James dissolved his first Parliament, which had sat from 1604 to 1611. Another met briefly and quarrelsomely in 1614, but thereafter none was elected until 1621. In the interim, to raise money, the King relied to some extent on "benevolences," supposedly free gifts granted by the subject to the monarch when he asked for them, but often in fact extracted under pressure.

James behaved as if Parliament had no legitimate concern in foreign affairs, and for years, in the face of the popular hatred for Spain, tried to arrange a Spanish royal marriage for his son Charles. In 1621 when Parliament petitioned James instead to go to war with Spain and marry Charles to a Protestant, he replied angrily that this was none of their business and threatened to punish the "insolent behavior" of anybody who continued to discuss the question in Parliament. The members admitted that the king alone had the right to make war and peace and to arrange for the marriage of his son, but declared that they wished to call his attention to the European situation as they saw it. James answered that this was merely a way of concealing their real intention to usurp royal prerogative.

The House of Commons then presented the Great Protestation (1621), which denied the king's right to imprison its members at will, and asserted their right to discuss and resolve any question touching the state. James dismissed Parliament and imprisoned three of its leaders. In fact James was right in alleging that the Commons were making a new claim, but the unpopularity of his Spanish policy made their protest a popular one. And James himself threw his case away in 1624, when—the Spanish match having fallen through—he summoned Parliament, gave it a complete report on foreign affairs, and asked its advice on just those questions he had been ready to punish them for discussing.

In religion James was determined to enforce conformity to the Church of England. He rejected a moderate appeal presented by Puritans inside the Church: to relax or make optional certain requirements of the ritual. This probably reflected the majority sentiment in the House of Commons, but James told the Puritan leaders (1604) that he would make them conform or harry them out of the land. He summed up his view as "no bishop, no king," stressing his belief that each depended on the other. And if the bishops did depend on the King for

---

* G. Davies, *The Early Stuarts, 1603–1660* (New York, 1937), p. 17.

their continued support against the Puritans, he no less depended on them, for they preached his views of divine right and from the pulpit kept urging obedience to the royal will. One great service was rendered the English-speaking world by James's love of uniformity: between 1604 and 1611 a commission of 47 scholars prepared the King James version of the Bible, a major influence in the shaping of literary English.

CHARLES I AND PARLIAMENT

Charles I (reigned 1625–1649) shared his father's theories of monarchy, though he proved it more in action and less in words. His first Parliament voted him only a fraction of what he asked for and needed for the war against Spain (1625) which it had itself urged on James. Soon Charles found himself fighting the French as well, and the English forces suffered a severe defeat (1627). Charles raised money by forced loans, always unpopular, and arrested some who refused to contribute; the courts upheld the legality of both loans and arrests. In 1628 both houses of Parliament produced the Petition of Right, which listed alleged royal infringements of ancient statutes and asked for a redress of grievances: no royal taxes without the consent of Parliament, no billeting of troops in private houses, no imprisonment without a charge or legal protection. The King assented.

But by his assent, he later said, he had meant only to affirm previously existing rights, not to hand over any new ones. Nor was his assent to the petition a law. Indeed, after Parliament had voted the subsidies he asked for, he went right on collecting customs duties that Parliament had not voted. Parliament protested. Sir John Eliot, leader of the House of Commons, attacked Charles's religious policies, denouncing the bishops as unfit to interpret the 39 Articles (*see* p. 286), thus in effect claiming the right for Parliament to determine the religion of England. Amid protests Charles dissolved Parliament in 1629, and had Eliot and others arrested; Eliot died in prison, the first martyr in the parliamentary cause.

For the next eleven years (1629–1640) Charles governed without a Parliament. He totally failed to sense the rising popular support for the views of Eliot and the Puritans. To him any subject who did not adhere to the Church of England was disloyal; the whole duty of a loyal subject consisted in obeying king and bishop. Like James, he referred questions of legality to the courts, but if the judges did not say what he wanted to hear, they were dismissed and replaced by judges who would.

To save money and postpone indefinitely the recall of Parliament, Charles made peace with France and Spain. He revived obsolete medieval (but perfectly legal) ways to collect money: he forced all those who owned land worth forty pounds a year and who had not been knighted to pay large fines; he said that large areas now in private hands were in fact royal forest, and collected fines from their owners; he enforced feudal wardships. All this aroused the wealthy against him. He also regularly collected from all of England an imposition called ship money, which had been traditionally levied only on coastal towns to pay for defensive ships. John Hampden, a rich gentleman from Buckinghamshire, an inland county, refused to pay it, and lost his case (1637). But the case dramatized the issue, since the judges who found for the king echoed the divine-right theory, saying that the king is *lex loquens,* a speaking law.

Charles's unpopularity grew, as his Archbishop of Canterbury, William

Laud, vigorously enforced conformity: Laud drove the Puritans from their pulpits, censored all but approved books on religious subjects, and aroused a storm of disapproval. The Puritans denounced the established ritual as popish and contrary to the Bible, and gave their resistance the color of martyrdom.

In Scotland, by reannexing in 1625 all the Church and Crown land that had fallen into private hands since 1542, Charles with one stroke aroused the Scotch nobility that had acquired the land in the interim. English and Scotch often disliked each other, the English thinking of the Scots as barbarous and greedy, the Scots of the English as too rich for their own good and inclined to popery. A

King Charles I, by Van Dyke.

plan of James I to create a constitutional union between the kingdoms had failed early in his reign. Unable as usual to gauge public opinion, Charles decided in 1637 to impose a Book of Common Prayer on the Scots, who rose in their wrath, as if "the mass in Latin had been presented."

In March, 1638, the Presbyterians of Scotland banded together in a Solemn League and Covenant (its members were called Covenanters) to defend their faith; in November, a general assembly—despite royal objections—abolished episcopacy, and prescribed a definitive ritual for the Scottish Kirk (Church). The Covenant united almost all Scots, who insisted all along that they were undertaking nothing against Charles as their king. In fact, however, it was impossible simultaneously to uphold Charles as king and to abolish bishops; Charles went to war in Scotland (the first "Bishops' War," 1639), and at once the question of paying for the campaign arose. In 1640 Charles summoned Parliament once more.

REFORMS OF THE LONG PARLIAMENT

The Short Parliament of 1640 would vote no money until the piled-up grievances of almost forty years were settled; Charles refused all compromise, and dissolved it. But a defeat in Scotland forced him to promise to buy off the Scots, and, since he could not find the money, he had to summon another Parliament. This was the Long Parliament, which sat for twenty years, 1640–1660. It began by arresting the most powerful royal favorite, Thomas Wentworth, Earl of Strafford, who was tried for high treason without a verdict being reached and who was eventually sacrificed by Charles to the passions of the public and executed. Archbishop Laud was imprisoned and later executed.

Parliament now passed the Triennial Act, providing machinery for summoning Parliament if the king did not summon it within three years after a dissolution. It also passed a revolutionary act making it illegal for Charles to dissolve the present Parliament without its own consent. It abolished the Court of Star Chamber (see p. 249), reversed the judgment against Hampden in the ship money case, abolished ship money, reverted to the forest boundaries of 1623, and declared it illegal to require anybody to become a knight. All of this Charles assented to, but hated; many suspected that he would bide his time and do away with these laws.

The Long Parliament, however, could not agree on church affairs; the Lords would not accept a bill excluding bishops from their house, largely because they resented the Commons' interference. A "root and branch" bill abolishing bishops altogether had passionate defenders and a good many lukewarm opponents. The Commons favored, but the Lords did not, various regulations of ritual and sabbath-observance. The extreme radicalism of some of the Puritans began to produce a reaction among the milder ones.

The King's position was improving when it was damaged by a terrible Irish Catholic revolt that began in October, 1641, with a massacre of some 30,000 Protestants, who had been settled in Ulster by James I and, ironically enough, had been oppressed by Strafford, acting as governor for Charles I. Parliament, suspecting that Charles had encouraged the Irish rebels, was unwilling to entrust to royal command the army that would put down the revolt, and threatened to take the appointment of officers into its own hands. Finally, Parliament produced a monster list of grievances, the Grand Remonstrance in 204 clauses (December, 1641).

The House of Commons voted to print the Grand Remonstrance and so advertise its anger to the public; it began to discuss the appointment of a "lord general" who would have power to raise and pay troops; it talked of impeaching the Queen (the French princess Henrietta Maria) on suspicion of instigating the Irish rebellion. Charles unwisely tried to arrest five leading members of Commons for treason and for complicity with the Scots. He took the unprecedented step of entering Parliament with a group of armed men, but found that the five had taken refuge in the privileged City of London. They returned to Parliament in triumph (January, 1642). Charles did consent to a bill removing bishops from any temporal position and depriving them of any private law-court. But he refused other parliamentary demands, including the "Nineteen Propositions" of June, 1642, which would have enabled Parliament to veto appointments to the great offices of state, to approve the education and marriages of the royal children, to consent to all appointments of new peers, and to dictate further reform of the Church.

England was now dividing into two camps that would fight a civil war. Leadership of the Commons passed to the Independents, who were Brownists or extreme Calvinists (see p. 286); around Charles there gathered a party loyal to the Church and to him, including members of both houses. Many of the gentry feared a radical revolution by the lower classes. When Parliament announced that the cost of its own military operations would be borne by its opponents, many who had been neutral joined the King. Yet for Charles money continued to be the problem, as he depended on gifts from rich individuals. The north and west of England were largely royalist, the richer and more populous south and east, including London, largely parliamentarian.

CIVIL WAR, 1642–1649

In the civil war the early advantage lay with the King, but his inability to win quickly a decisive victory cost him the war in the end. His peace with the Irish rebels in 1643 and his intention of using Irish forces in England increased the fear of "popery" that all along had driven neutrals toward Parliament, and helped it reach a "Solemn League and Covenant" with the anti-Catholic Scots. This brought Scotch forces into England against Charles, in exchange for a promise to make English and Irish religion as nearly like Scottish Presbyterianism as possible. Parliament won the battle of Marston Moor (1644) largely owing to the specially trained cavalry led by Oliver Cromwell, one of the radical Puritan gentry. Soon after, Cromwell reorganized the parliamentary forces into the "New Model" army. At Naseby (1645) his Roundheads (so termed from their close-cropped hair) decisively defeated the Cavaliers (royalists).

In 1646 Charles surrendered to the Scots, and stalled for time by launching prolonged negotiations with them and with Parliament. Dissension now developed among his opponents, as the army, representing the radical, Independent (congregationalist) wing of Puritanism, quarrelled with the moderate Presbyterian leadership of Parliament that had begun the civil war. The Independent members (about 60) and the speakers of both houses fled London and joined the army, which marched on London, and forcibly restored them to their places. Even more radical than Cromwell and the Independents was one faction in the army called "Levellers," who advocated a universal franchise and relief from social and economic grievances.

In December, 1647, the King secretly agreed with the Scots to establish Presbyterianism in England for three years and to suppress the Independents. Parliament thereupon renounced its allegiance to the King, and a second civil war began. The Presbyterians, who had formerly supported Parliament, now joined the royalists and the Scots against the army; most Englishmen, however, seem to have remained neutral. In August, 1648, Cromwell thoroughly defeated the Scots at Preston Pans, and ended the second civil war. The army took possession of Charles; Colonel Pride, acting on its behalf, excluded 140 Presbyterian members from Parliament in "Pride's Purge," leaving only about 60 Independents as members. The "Rump," as this much abbreviated body was called, created a special court to try the King. In January, 1649, Charles was tried, condemned, and executed. While the killers of the King believed that they were acting as agents of God, the execution created a new wave of sympathy for the King both in Europe and at home.

THE COMMONWEALTH AND PROTECTORATE

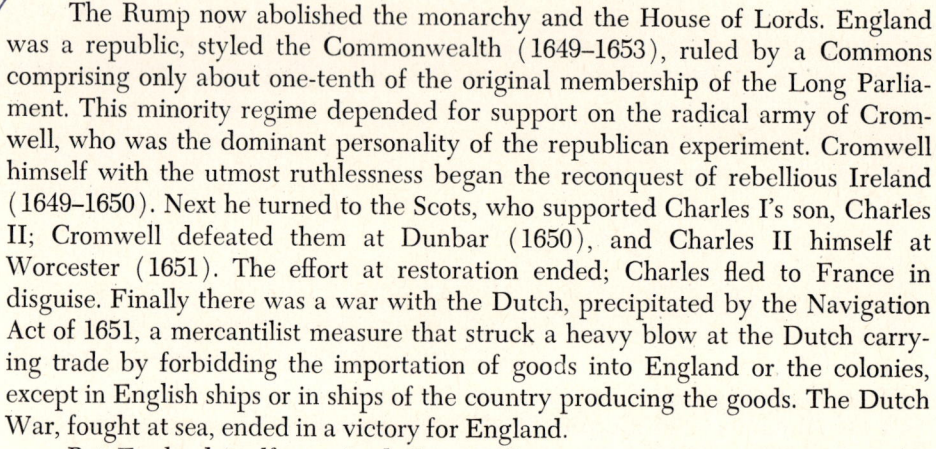

The Rump now abolished the monarchy and the House of Lords. England was a republic, styled the Commonwealth (1649–1653), ruled by a Commons comprising only about one-tenth of the original membership of the Long Parliament. This minority regime depended for support on the radical army of Cromwell, who was the dominant personality of the republican experiment. Cromwell himself with the utmost ruthlessness began the reconquest of rebellious Ireland (1649–1650). Next he turned to the Scots, who supported Charles I's son, Charles II; Cromwell defeated them at Dunbar (1650), and Charles II himself at Worcester (1651). The effort at restoration ended; Charles fled to France in disguise. Finally there was a war with the Dutch, precipitated by the Navigation Act of 1651, a mercantilist measure that struck a heavy blow at the Dutch carrying trade by forbidding the importation of goods into England or the colonies, except in English ships or in ships of the country producing the goods. The Dutch War, fought at sea, ended in a victory for England.

But England itself remained Cromwell's greatest problem. Government by Rump and army aroused much bitter opposition. To grant an amnesty to the royalists and to enact conciliatory reforms seemed to be impossible in the face of parliamentary opposition. Though the Rump under pressure did fix a date for new elections, its members voted to keep their own seats in the new Parliament and to pass on all other representatives who might be chosen. Discarding the last pretensions to be acting legally, Cromwell and his musketeers dissolved the Rump (1653), thus earning the eternal hatred of the extreme republicans. Then the army itself elected a Parliament of members nominated by Congregational ministers in each county, which was called the "nominated" or "Barebone's" Parliament.

After a few months, the members of the new Parliament resigned their powers to Cromwell, who became Lord Protector of England, thus inaugurating the second phase of the republican experiment—the Protectorate (1653–1660). At first he governed under a written constitution, the Instrument of Government, drawn up by some of the army officers. Since the Instrument limited voting to those with an estate worth £200, the new Parliament proved to be an upper-class body. It wanted to amend the Instrument and proved so uncooperative that

The House of Commons, as shown on the Great Seal of England used by the Commonwealth (1651).

Cromwell—who believed that only a military dictatorship could govern England properly—dissolved it in 1654. After a royalist uprising in 1655, Cromwell ordered Catholic priests exiled, forbade Anglicans to preach, and divided England into 11 military districts. The major-general in command of each not only collected the taxes and policed his district but served as censor of public morals. Horse-racing, cock-fighting, and bear-baiting were prohibited (the last, as Macaulay later said, not because it gave pain to the bear but because it gave pleasure to the spectators); alehouses, gambling-dens, brothels were closed or regulated severely; the theater was forbidden.

Englishmen hated this Puritan regime and its attempts to impose Calvinist morality by force. The revulsion of opinion was evident in the parliamentary election of 1656. Even when the army had purged parliamentarians of whom it did not approve, those who were left still produced the "Humble Petition and Advice," revising the Instrument of Government in the direction of traditional English monarchy. It asked Cromwell to become King (he refused), gave the House of Commons the right to exclude any elected member, and created a second house to be nominated by Cromwell. Though Cromwell accepted some of the amendments, he dissolved this Parliament, too (1657).

Cromwell died (September 3, 1658) and was succeeded as Lord Protector by his son, Richard, who proved unable to reorganize the army and weed out the most fanatical extremists. The army forced Richard to recall the Rump, and resign (May, 1659). As tension grew between the army officers and the Rump, royalist activity increased. In October, General Lambert expelled the Rump, and set up a Committee of Safety to govern England. But a popular reaction soon set in against the assumption of such a major political role by the military. General George Monck (or Monk), a leading Cromwellian officer who had always upheld the principles of military obedience to properly constituted civil authority, emerged as the decisive figure in ending the political turbulence. In December, 1659, the army gave in, and restored the Rump for the third time; Monck allowed the members excluded by Pride's Purge to take their old places.

The partially reconstituted Long Parliament prepared to restore the monarchy as the only barrier to chaos. At Monck's suggestion, the exiled Charles II issued the Declaration of Breda, promising a free pardon, confirmation of all land sales during the civil wars, payment of the soldiers' back pay, and liberty of conscience; Charles added, however, that on each point he would be bound by what Parliament wanted. A new Parliament, chosen in free election, summoned the King home in a burst of enthusiasm; Charles II (1660–1685) arrived in London on May 29, 1660.

THE ENGLISH REVOLUTION IN REVIEW

Revolutionary changes had occurred in England since 1642. Divine-right monarchy had been challenged, and a constitutional and representative government set up, based on a legislature backed by politically active private citizens. Though the Stuarts were restored, no English king ever again could hope to rule without a Parliament or reinstate the Court of Star Chamber or take ship money, benevolences, and other controversial taxes. Parliament thenceforward retained that critical weapon: ultimate control of the public purse by periodic grants of taxes.

Moreover, minority groups had gone much further toward political and social democracy. The Levellers put forward a program which was later carried by emigrants to the American colonies, and which favored universal suffrage, progressive taxation, separation of Church and State, and protection of the individual against arbitrary arrest. A more extreme group called the Diggers actually dug up public lands near London and began planting vegetables in a kind of communistic enterprise. They were driven off, but not before they had got their ideas into circulation. The Fifth Monarchy men, the Millennarians, and a dozen other radical sects preached the Second Coming and the achievement of some kind of utopia on earth.

During the English struggles the Puritans urged freedom of speech and of the press, although when they came to power they often failed to practice what they had preached. Another basic liberal idea to emerge from the civil war was religious toleration. Some of the Puritans believed that compulsion should not be exercised to secure conformity, and at least one sect held that religious toleration was a positive good. The Quakers—more properly, the Religious Society of Friends—led by George Fox (1624-1691), were Puritans of the Puritans. They eschewed all worldly show: for example, they regarded the polite form "you" as hypocritical, and so addressed all men as "thou" or "thee." They took so seriously the basic Protestant doctrine of the priesthood of the believer that they did entirely without an ordained ministry, and encouraged any worshipper to testify in a kind of sermon if he felt the spirit move him. The Friends were—and still are today—pacifists, who abstained from the use of force and would have no part in war.

THE RESTORATION

Although many of the ideas advanced during the civil wars were much too revolutionary to win easy acceptance, the Restoration settlement showed a high degree of political tolerance. Except for a few revolutionaries, including surviving judges who had condemned Charles I to death, Parliament pardoned all those who had been involved in the civil war or the republican regimes. It made every effort to injure as few people as possible in settling the claims of royalists and churchmen to their former lands. Parliament appeared to be maintaining its political supremacy, and in the central administration there were the first foreshadowings of what eventually would become the cabinet.

Religion, however, was quite another matter. Though personally rather disposed to toleration, Charles II governed a country where very few people were yet ready to accept it. Not only were bishops restored but Parliament proceeded to enact a long series of repressive acts. The Corporation Act (1661) required all magistrates to take the sacraments according to the Church of England. The Act of Uniformity (1662) required clergymen and teachers to subscribe to the Book of Common Prayer; those who refused were known as "Nonconformists" or "Dissenters." The Conventicle Act (1664) limited to five the number of persons attending a Nonconformist meeting outside a private household, and the Five Mile Act (1665) forbade those who had not accepted the Act of Uniformity to come within five miles of any town unless they swore a special oath.

Much of this was impossible to enforce; it placed the Dissenters under disabilities but did not cause them great suffering. The Test Act of 1673 required that all office-holders take communion in the Church of England and renounce transubstantiation (the Catholic doctrine of the Eucharist). But the practical English found ways around this. One was "occasional conformity," whereby a Dissenter whose conscience was not too strict might take Anglican communion occasionally, while worshipping as a Presbyterian or Congregationalist most of the time. Another way, common after 1689, was to allow Dissenters to hold office, and each year pass a special bill legalizing their acts.

The revulsion against Puritanism carried over into all aspects of the Restoration Period. Where the Commonwealth and Protectorate had forbidden all theatrical performances, the Restoration thoroughly enjoyed them, the more indecent the better. Charles II himself and his court led cheerfully immoral lives. Everywhere in Europe there was a trend back toward Catholicism: in Sweden, for instance, Gustavus Adolphus' own daughter, Christina, had abdicated and become a Catholic (1654). Charles II sympathized with Catholicism, and in 1672 tried but failed to remove disabilities from both Catholics and Dissenters. He greatly admired the flourishing monarchy of Louis XIV across the Channel. Without the knowledge of Parliament, he made a secret treaty with Louis (1670) and promised, in exchange for an annual subsidy, to support the French in their wars and to become a Catholic as soon as he could. His brother James, Duke of York and heir to the throne, openly practiced Catholicism.

English popular suspicion of the Roman Church, however, was still strong. In the late 1670's a series of disclosures about alleged "Popish" plots to murder the King and restore Catholicism aroused great popular excitement. One faction in Parliament wanted to exclude the Catholic and pro-French James from the succession; these "exclusionists" were called *Whigs* (a Scotch variant of "wig"). They included many well-to-do urban merchants and certain very powerful peers, who hoped to enhance their own political influence if the monarchy itself should be weakened. Supporting Charles and the succession of James were the landed gentry, lesser lords and country gentlemen who had been pro-Stuart all along and who suspected the newly rich townsmen. They were called *Tories* (a Gaelic term for "robber").

JAMES II AND THE GLORIOUS REVOLUTION

James II (reigned 1685–1688) alienated even the Tories who had successfully opposed his exclusion. He put down an ineffectual effort of a bastard son of Charles II, the Duke of Monmouth, to invade England (1685), but then sent a savage judge, Jeffreys, to try and punish those suspected of sympathizing with Monmouth. These trials were the "bloody assizes." Disregarding the laws, James appointed Catholics to high office, and judges appointed by him declared that he was acting legally. His Declaration of Liberty of Conscience (1687), extending religious toleration, was issued without parliamentary approval or support; James claimed to be acting on the basis of his right of "dispensation."

When a son was born to James (June, 1688) and the prospect of a Catholic dynasty loomed, seven Whig and Tory leaders decided to act. They offered the throne jointly to James' daughter Mary, who was a Protestant, and to her husband William of Orange, Stadholder since 1673 of six of the seven Dutch provinces, and the most vigorous enemy of Louis XIV. When William landed in

November, 1688, James soon had to flee to France. Elections were held, and the elected body (technically a "convention," not a Parliament, since a royal summons must be issued to elect a Parliament) formally offered the throne to William and Mary. They ruled as William III (1689–1702) and Mary II (1689–1694).

When issuing the invitation, the "Convention Parliament" accompanied it with the Declaration of Rights, summing up what was won in the long struggle with the Stuarts: Parliament alone makes or suspends laws; the king has no power of "dispensation"; he cannot tax without Parliament. Freedom of election, freedom of debate, freedom of petition, frequent elections, no trial without jury, no excessive bail—all these Parliament declared to be the rights of Englishmen, and all William and Mary accepted. Parliament made them into laws as the Bill of Rights (1689), adding that no Catholic could become King of England in the future.

The sum total of the events of 1688–1689, almost bloodless, is called the Glorious Revolution. It was made secure by William's victory in Ireland over James II and an army of Irish Catholic insurgents with French supporters in the battle of the Boyne (1690). It was enhanced by a Toleration Act, allowing Dissenters to practice their religion freely, but still excluding them from office (1689). After the Glorious Revolution three major steps still lay ahead before England could become a full parliamentary democracy. These were: first, the cabinet system, whereby a committee of the majority party would manage affairs of state—the work of the eighteenth and early nineteenth centuries; second, universal suffrage and payment of salaries to members of the Commons—the work of the nineteenth and early twentieth; third, curbs on the power of the Lords to veto legislation—the work of the twentieth.

William and Mary were childless, and Mary's sister Anne, who succeeded as Queen from 1702 to 1714, had no living children. Parliament, fearing that James II's son, the Catholic "James III," would try to seize the throne, settled the succession upon the descendants of Sophia, granddaughter of James I, twelfth child of Frederick of the Palatinate (see p. 320), wife of the Elector of Hanover. When Anne died in 1714, Sophia's son George, Elector of Hanover, became King of England as George I, and his descendants have sat on the throne ever since. By excluding the elder Catholic line of succession, Parliament had shown who really made the kings of England.

There remained the danger that the Scots might prefer a Stuart monarch to a Hanoverian. Under Anne, in 1707, the old problem of Anglo-Scottish union which James I had failed to solve was worked out. Scotland accepted the Protestant succession, would send its own members to both houses of Parliament, and would join its cross of St. Andrew with the English cross of St. George on one flag, the Union Jack—symbol of Great Britain. Protestant fear of Catholic sovereigns made the settlement easy, and, despite occasional outbreaks of Scottish nationalism, the union has worked well. Wider economic and political horizons beckoned the able Scots, who have taken at least their share in governing and increasing the prosperity of the United Kingdom.

Tragedy, by contrast, was the continued lot of the Irish, whose support of the refugee James II led William III to revive the severe Cromwellian policy. Their Catholic worship was hampered by galling "penal laws" and their trade stifled by mercantilist regulation. Their misery was so acute that the Anglican Jonathan Swift made with bitter irony his famous "modest proposal" that they solve their economic problems by selling their babies to be eaten.

III. Divine-Right Monarchy in France

HENRY IV, RICHELIEU, AND MAZARIN

During the first half of the seventeenth century, as we have seen, Europe still feared that a Habsburg combination—Spanish and Austrian—would upset the balance of power. In taking the lead of every attempt to block this danger, the French in later years prepared to make their own bid for European supremacy. At home, France recovered quickly from the wounds of the sixteenth-century religious wars (*see* Chapter 7). Henry IV (reigned 1589–1610), witty, dashing, and popular, took a real interest in the popular welfare. His economic experts reclaimed marshes for farmland, encouraged the luxury crafts of Paris, and planted thousands of mulberry trees to foster the culture and manufacture of silk. They built the canals, roads, and bridges that made the French communications system the best in Europe. Faced with a great deficit on coming to office, Henry IV found an efficient finance minister in Sully (1559–1641), who gradually brought income up and expenditure down until they balanced. Monarch and minister even toyed with an advanced idea for a general European international Christian Republic, including everybody but the Habsburgs. This "grand design" thus had a practical bearing on the ambitions of the French, but it also was an ancestor of future leagues of nations.

Assassinated in 1610 by a madman, Henry IV was succeeded by his nine-year-old son, Louis XIII (reigned 1610–1643). During his minority, things went slack, as his mother Marie de' Medici acted as regent, and her favorites almost undid what Henry IV had accomplished. Finally in 1624 Richelieu became the King's chief minister. We have already seen him subordinating religion to the interests of France during the Thirty Years' War by his alliance with the Protestants. Richelieu made the interests of the state (*raison d'état*) govern his policy everywhere.

Though Richelieu subsidized and helped Lutherans and Calvinists in Germany, he felt that the Edict of Nantes (*see* p. 309) had given too many privileges to the Huguenots of France. The hundred-odd fortified towns in Huguenot hands seemed potential centers of disorder and a threat to his program of increased royal centralization. Foreseeing punitive measures against them, the Huguenots rebelled. It took Richelieu's forces fourteen months to reduce their key port of La Rochelle (1628), largely because there was no French navy to cut its communications. Over the next decade, Richelieu built both an Atlantic and a Mediterranean fleet for France. He also strove to curb the French nobility by ordering some of their chateaux destroyed and by forbidding their favorite pastime of dueling, but he by no means succeeded in taming them completely. He did successfully transfer responsibility for local administration from the nobles to royal officials, the *intendants*, who obtained greatly increased power to assess and collect taxes.

Though historians have disagreed in assessing Richelieu's services to France, all agree that subsequent French greatness under Louis XIV would have been unthinkable without him. His critics feel that he left too little place for government by discussion and for the participation of the middle classes in government, except for a few highly trained professional bureaucrats. His supporters praise the centralization and efficiency on which his successors would build. He himself hand-picked and trained his immediate successor, the Italian-born Cardinal Mazarin.

Succeeding to power after Richelieu's death in 1642, Mazarin soon faced the crisis caused by the death of Louis XIII (1643), whose heir, Louis XIV (1643–1715), was only five years old. Mazarin's foreign birth, his failure to pay obligations on government debts, and the ambitions of rival cliques of nobles led to the complex disturbances known as the Fronde, 1648–1653 (the name refers to a slingshot used by Parisian children to throw mud at passers-by). In the end, Mazarin and his bureaucrats were able to defeat both the old nobles and the newer official nobles of the law-courts, among whom were many disgruntled investors. He maintained himself in power until his death in 1661. By then Louis XIV was 23 and ready for personal rule in the fullest sense of divine-right absolutism.

LOUIS XIV: LE GRAND MONARQUE

It is not James I—despite all his theorizing on the subject—nor even Philip II of Spain whom we think of as *the* divine-right monarch, but Louis XIV, and not merely because he is supposed to have coined the famous summation of the theory: *L'état c'est moi* (I am the State). God had from the beginning destined this descendant of Hugh Capet for the throne of France; to challenge his right to it was to challenge the structure of God's universe. Louis was able to act on these beliefs and be a divine-right monarch in part because of the revival of the concept

Richelieu, by Champaigne.

from Roman law that God directs the affairs of states through his chosen agents. Moreover, the French monarchy had long taken the lead in striving to minimize the deep local loyalties that went so far back in time—to Normandy, Brittany, Burgundy, and so on—and to maximize a new transcendent loyalty to France as such. The subjects of the French Crown spoke several different languages or at least dialects; they had no common educational system, or press, or political life. What they had in common was the king, a symbol of common "Frenchness," who collected taxes and raised armies. Frenchmen had to feel that he had a right to do these things, and was doing it *for* them, not just *to* them.

Though Louis is called absolute, he lacked the physical means for controlling in complete detail all the actions of all of his subjects. Indeed no ruler before the days of twentieth-century dictatorships, with all the totalitarian techniques of propaganda, surveillance, and terror, was ever absolute in this sense. Further limitations were placed on Louis' absolutism by medieval local survivals in language, law, customs, weights and measures—all of which stood in the way of real uniformity. Louis could not ride roughshod over city corporations that appealed to their ancient charters granting them immunities, or over gilds that could show a privileged status which they had "always" possessed. He could not force nobles and clergy to conform completely.

The French Crown, however, shoved the nobles aside, deprived them of their political function, and left them only their social and economic privileges and their military careers. Louis XI had begun to tame them in the fifteenth century. Since they had helped to foment the religious wars, Henry IV's victory was a defeat for their program, and so was Richelieu's increased use of non-nobles as *intendants*, judges, and local officials. The Crown usually granted such commoners titles of nobility which they could pass on to their sons. But they were still *noblesse de robe* (nobles because of the robes or gowns they wore), and lacked the prestige of the older *noblesse d'épée* (nobility of the sword, the traditional fighting nobility).

The French Church, too, had come under the control of the Crown by gradual processes, and under Louis XIV was "Gallican," that is to say national, though of course Catholic. His bishops (like the bishops of Charles I) supported the divine-right monarchy. But the French clergy were not subject to royal taxation; of their own free will in their own assembly they voted gifts of money to the King. Louis abolished the religious toleration that Richelieu had left the Huguenots after taking away their fortresses and political privileges. In 1685 he revoked the Edict of Nantes. As a result, about 50,000 Protestant families fled abroad. In Prussia, some of the exiles found a place in the military services, and their descendants fought against the French in the wars of the nineteenth and twentieth centuries. In Holland, England, North America, and South Africa the talents and skills of these refugees greatly strengthened the lands that received them. Some Huguenots remained in France, where they had to worship secretly.

Mignard's portrait of Louis XIV.

Within the Catholic Church itself, Louis had to contend both with enthusiastic mystics (Madame Guyon and the Quietists) and with the puritanical Jansenists, named after Cornelius Jansen, Bishop of Ypres in the early seventeenth century. The Jansenists, who came close to Calvin's views on predestination, questioned the authority of both pope and king, since both were mere men. Their most distinguished spokesman was the scientist and philosopher Pascal. Though Louis contained the threat that they posed to uniformity, he did not succeed completely in suppressing the Jansenists.

Intent on his own glory, Louis worked hard and in his youth played hard. In middle age, after his Spanish queen's death, he contracted a morganatic marriage with Mme de Maintenon, former governess of his illegitimate children. She was a devout Catholic, and it seems certain that she influenced Louis' decision to revoke the Edict of Nantes. Louis installed the French court at Versailles, where he built a splendid palace on the site of a former hunting lodge. Almost half a mile long, the main buildings at Versailles housed a court of ten thousand nobles and their families, followers, and servants. It was a superb setting for *le grand monarque*.

So completely did Louis make Versailles the center of French social life that everything else in Europe seemed provincial, from the private country houses of the French nobles to the courts of all the other monarchs. The proper standard of sophisticated behavior for all Europe was set here: how to dress, how to speak French, what to read, what sort of story to tell, how far to go in gossip, what games to play, what food to eat at what times of day, what music to listen to, and what dances to dance. At every European court and in every private household with a pretense to gentility the master and mistress would ask what Versailles did before deciding.

Here Louis met with his ministers, the heads of departments of state like those in any modern state: war, finance, foreign policy, interior. They were directly responsible to him and not to any legislative body; indeed, the Estates-General never met at all during Louis' entire reign of 72 years. From the top, the chain of command went down through the *intendants*, in charge of the *généralités*, or large province-sized administrative units, to smaller regional units and then to the towns and villages. Even the indefatigable Louis could hope to do no more than exercise a general supervision over details; but he was helped by the multiplicity of official forms that his subjects filled out; many thousands of them remain today duly filed in the French local archives. As members of the *noblesse de robe,* the *intendants* transmitted their titles and rank to their heirs, and so formed a new kind of privileged corporation, arrogating to themselves more power than the theory of royal absolutism ideally would have allowed, and so asserting provincial initiative against the monarchy.

The judges of the high courts of appeal, too, could not be removed by the king, and so exercised considerable independence. These courts were the *parlements,* of which the Parlement of Paris enjoyed the widest jurisdiction and the most prestige. By their function of registering each royal edict, the *parlements* claimed something like the power of judicial review; that is, they claimed the right to refuse to register an edict if they thought it violated the law of the land. Louis intimidated the Parlement of Paris by summoning the judges before him in a formal session (*lit de justice,* bed of justice) and commanding them to register a royal edict. The claim that the *parlements* might throw out a royal edict, however, remained to plague his successors.

MERCANTILISM AND COLBERT: ECONOMIC POLICY UNDER LOUIS XIV

Just as France under Louis XIV exemplified widely held ideas of divine-right monarchy, so too the economic policies of his regime exemplified the widespread mercantilist theories and practices. Mercantilists held that hard money, gold and silver, was the basic wealth. Therefore the state should try to get as much of it as possible, and to arrange that more should come in than go out. It should maintain this "favorable balance of trade" by encouraging exports (which bring it cash from abroad) perhaps by bounties, and discouraging imports (which cause cash to flow out) perhaps by tariffs. Carried to its extreme, this would be absurd, since gold and silver cannot be much used by the state except as media of exchange.

But the mercantilists were not absurd; they were trying to make their own state as self-sustaining as they could. National production, they held, should provide the necessities of life for the population and the sinews of war for the armed forces. They favored rigorous planning and control, sweeping away the traditional ways of manor and gild and the medieval notion of the "just price" (*see* p. 148), and directing the economy instead by subsidies, grants of monopolies, government participation in industry, encouragement of research, and imposition of tariffs. They viewed the overseas colonies of the mother country as a source of necessary raw materials, possession of which made it unnecessary to import from rival states and encouraged manufacturing at home. For this reason the colonies must be strongly governed and their economies directed as the mother country saw fit.

Louis XIV's great exponent of mercantilism, his finance minister, Jean Baptiste Colbert (1619–1683), exercised more influence over his master than any other royal servant, though he met competition from other royal advisers, for example, Louvois, the War Minister. Colbert supported new inventions, improvements in shipbuilding, technological education, the settlement of foreign experts in France, and the founding of new industries. This was the first major experiment in a modern controlled economy, and the result was prosperity. Might France have done still better had her businessmen been left alone? Those who believe in the anti-mercantilist theory of free trade (*laissez faire*) argue that the mere removal of regulations would have enabled the individual entrepreneur and therefore the whole economy to enrich itself still further. But this rival theory was not practiced anywhere during Colbert's day.

His system gave France the economic leadership of Europe; during the eighteenth century she would lose this lead, partly because England adopted the new methods of power-machinery and large-scale production of inexpensive goods. After Colbert, the French clung to the small-scale production of a large variety of products, chiefly luxuries and consumers' goods. England also had the more easily exploitable resources, like coal, iron, and waterpower, and so got a head start in modern industrialization. Moreover, the expensive wars of Louis XIV built up a burden of debt that depressed the economy in the latter part of his reign and carried on into the eighteenth century.

THE WARS OF LOUIS XIV

As the real victor in the Thirty Years' War, France had achieved the defeat of the Habsburgs and territorial enrichment at comparatively little cost. Prosperous and ambitious, Louis XIV set out to expand; thus France succeeded the Spanish and the Austrian Habsburgs as the threat to the European balance of power. Louis did not envisage an organized world-state in which everyone was his subject. But he did want to push French boundaries east to the Rhine, annexing the Spanish Netherlands and the Franche Comté (Free County of Burgundy); and as time went on, he hoped to secure Spain and the Spanish Empire. He also wanted to assert the predominance of France in every part of the globe and in every area of human life. He had agents in India, in Canada, in Holland, and on the Rhine. He regarded it as natural and proper that French culture, French taste in the arts, French social ways should influence all of Europe; to an astonishing extent they did so. But other European peoples came to feel that France was too threatening, and their rulers united against Louis XIV.

A legal quibble gave Louis the excuse for his first war, the War of Devolution (1667–1668). When he had married the daughter of Philip IV of Spain, his wife had renounced her rights of inheritance; but her dowry had not been paid, and Louis claimed that this voided her renunciation. After the death of Philip IV (1665), the Queen of France, Louis claimed, ought to inherit her father's possessions in the Low Countries by virtue of an old Flemish law of "devolution." The threat to Belgium aroused the Dutch, who made an alliance with England and Sweden against France and thus joined their old enemies, the Spaniards, in supporting the balance of power. Louis made peace at Aix-la-Chapelle in 1668, collecting twelve fortified Flemish towns.

Furious at the Dutch, Louis bought off Charles II by a secret treaty in 1670 (*see* p. 337), and also made a treaty with the Swedes. Then he began his second war, the Dutch War (1672–1678), quickly occupying large areas of southern Holland. Six of the seven Dutch provinces elected William of Orange Stadholder, and decided that the office should be hereditary in his family. William allied himself with Brandenburg and with both Spanish and Austrian Habsburgs, rallying enough forces against Louis to prevent a final and decisive French victory. At the Peace of Nijmegen (Nimwegen), 1678–1679, the Dutch lost no territory but had to promise future neutrality. Spain gave Louis the Franche Comté and some towns in the Spanish Netherlands.

Though the war was technically over, the superb French armed forces really dominated Europe. On the eastern frontiers, special French courts ("chambers of reunion") decreed further annexations of areas that could be shown to have belonged at any time to any of the territories newly acquired by France, and Louis' armies would then proceed to occupy these additional prizes. In this way France "reunited" Strasbourg (1681) and Luxembourg, all of Lorraine (1683), and the Rhineland bishopric of Trier (1684). These French aggressions in time of peace met with no resistance, partly because of the Ottoman siege of Vienna (1683) and its aftermath (*see* Chapter 5).

French pressure eastward continued as Louis now put in a far-fetched claim to the lands of the Palatinate and insisted on pushing his own candidate for the Archbishopric of Cologne (1688). The revocation of the Edict of Nantes (1685) had distressed the Protestants of Europe. Sweden, the Palatinate, Saxony, Bavaria, the Austrian and Spanish Habsburgs, together with William of Orange, who was soon to be King of England, formed the League of Augsburg against Louis XIV. Thus his third war began: the War of the League of Augsburg, 1688–1697. After French occupation of the Palatinate, most of the land operations took place in the Netherlands; in Ireland (at the Boyne) and at sea, the English and Dutch defeated the French. The Treaty of Ryswick (1697) that ended the war deprived the French of much of the land "reunited" since Nijmegen, including Lorraine.

THE WAR OF THE SPANISH SUCCESSION

But within four years Louis embarked on his last and most adventurous war. It had been clear for some time that the death of Louis' brother-in-law, the Habsburg King of Spain, Charles II (1665–1700), who was without an heir, would create a crisis. The powers of Europe had agreed that a Bavarian prince would succeed, but he died first; they then arranged an elaborate partition that would have given Naples, Sicily, and Lorraine to France. But Charles II made a new will, leaving all the vast Spanish possessions in Europe and overseas to his great-nephew, the grandson of Louis XIV, Philip of Anjou. When Charles died in 1700, Louis could not resist the temptation: he proclaimed his grandson Philip V of Spain. At once, England, Holland, the Empire, and the German states formed a grand alliance against the French; they were joined before long by just about all the other states of western Europe.

The War of the Spanish Succession (1701–1713) was fought in Italy and overseas, and especially in the Low Countries. The allies gradually wore down the French. Queen Anne's great general, John Churchill, first Duke of Marlborough and ancestor of Winston Churchill, together with Prince Eugene of Savoy, defeated France four times: at Blenheim (1704), Ramillies (1706), Oudenarde (1708), and Malplaquet (1709). But the defeats were not overwhelming, and Malplaquet alone cost the allies 20,000 casualties, which in those days seemed "butchery" to the people of England. The death of the Emperor Joseph (1711) meant that his brother Charles VI would be the legitimate heir to all the Spanish and Austrian possessions, that the old Empire of Charles V would be recreated, and that the balance of power would be once more upset by the Habsburgs. The English feared this as much as a total French victory. The Tories, who favored peace, came to power in England; Marlborough was removed from command, and negotiations for peace began. They culminated in the Treaty of Utrecht (1713)—like the Treaty of Westphalia (1648) before it and the settlements of Vienna (1815) and Versailles (1919) after it, a landmark in the diplomatic and territorial history of Europe.

By the terms of Utrecht, Philip V was accepted as King of Spain, but Louis promised that the crowns of France and Spain would never be united. He recognized the Protestant succession in England. In America, France gave up Newfoundland, Acadia (Nova Scotia), and the Hudson's Bay territory to England, but retained Quebec and Louisiana. From Spain the English obtained Gibraltar, which they still hold, and the island of Minorca, which they returned later in the century, as well as a contract (the *Asiento*) to supply African Negro slaves to the Spanish colonies. Because the Austrian Habsburgs lost their claim to the Spanish throne, they received the former Spanish Netherlands (Belgium), but the Dutch were allowed to maintain certain garrisons there to help defend themselves against a possible new French attack. The Duke of Savoy was rewarded at first with Sicily, for which Sardinia was substituted in 1720; as Kings of Sardinia, the

Europe in 1715

Legend:
- Brandenburg-Prussia
- Austrian Habsburg Lands
- Swedish possessions
- Venetian possessions
- Ottoman Empire
- ▬ Boundary of the Holy Roman Empire
- ■ Battle sites

Growth of France 1559-1769

- Artois 1659
- Alsace 1648–1681
- Lorraine 1766
- Franche Comté 1678
- 1601
- Roussillon 1659
- Corsica 1768

— Boundary of the Empire, 1559

Dukes of Savoy would later unite the rest of Italy. The Elector of Brandenburg was recognized as "King in Prussia."

Utrecht was on the whole a moderate and sensible peace. Yet it did not end overseas rivalry between the French and English; it did not really protect the Dutch; and it did not really satisfy the Habsburgs, or settle the tangled affairs of Italy. French aggression was halted, but only temporarily, for it would be resumed at the end of the century under the impulse of the great Revolution (*see* Chapter 11). The wars of Louis XIV, however, despite their great cost in human life and in treasure, and despite the popular hatred aroused by the French in their drive into Dutch and German territories, were less savage than the Thirty Years' War or the wars of nationalism and revolution that would follow after 1789. Religion played a minor role, though Louis regarded himself as a Catholic champion, and William of Orange was hailed as a Protestant one. Hundreds of thousands of Catholics were lined up against Louis on the "Protestant" side. Louis' aggressions did not have the passionate quality of religious or political crusades: he was no Napoleon, no Hitler. His wars were in effect measured and "classical," as befitted *le grand monarque*.

IV. Europe Overseas

At Utrecht, Nova Scotia and Newfoundland changed hands as well as Gibraltar. Indeed, the last war of Louis XIV was almost a world war, fought not only to maintain the balance of power in Europe but to gain advantages and resources overseas. The increased concern with the world beyond Europe resulted from the accelerated tempo of colonialism in the seventeenth century, when the English, the French, and the Dutch all joined the ranks of empire builders.

THE THIRTEEN COLONIES

The English got their first two permanent footholds in North America at Jamestown in Virginia (1607), and at Plymouth in Massachusetts (1620). At first similar to Spanish or Portuguese trading posts, these were established by English trading companies which vainly hoped to find gold and silver as the Spaniards had. Both settlements barely managed to survive the early years of hardship. Then the sparse native population was gradually replaced by immigrants of English stock. Tobacco and the resourcefulness of Captain John Smith saved Virginia; furs, codfish, and Calvinist toughness saved Massachusetts. Both gradually built up an agricultural economy and traded with the mother country. While neither received more than a few tens of thousands of immigrants from abroad, natural increase in a country of abundant land added to their numbers.

In 1664 the English defeated the Dutch in another round of the warfare for economic advantage that had broken out under Cromwell a decade earlier. They took over New Amsterdam, founded in 1626, which became New York; its important Dutch families—Stuyvesant, Schuyler, Roosevelt—would supply some leading participants in American development. In 1655 the Dutch had already eliminated the Swedish settlement at Fort Christiana on the Delaware, and here, too, the English ousted the Dutch. Pennsylvania, chartered in 1681 to the wealthy English Quaker William Penn, filled the vacuum left by the expulsion of the Swedes and the Dutch from the Delaware.

By the early eighteenth century, the English settlements formed a continuous string of thirteen colonies from Maine to Georgia. The new settlers came from all strata of English life except from the very top. New England was for the most part settled by Calvinist Independents (Congregationalists), who believed in wide local self-government, and who set up their own Puritan state church, like Calvin's in Geneva or Cromwell's in England. Yet "heresy" appeared from the start, as Baptists, Quakers, and even Anglicans came to New England. The southern colonies, especially tidewater Virginia, were settled for the most part by Anglicans, used to the existence of frank social distinctions and to large landholdings. The Church of England became the established church in Virginia. Yet in the Piedmont section of Virginia and the Carolinas there were small farmers—"Scotch-Irish" Presbyterians, and Germans from Pennsylvania. Geography and climate played their part, making the South the land of one-crop plantations producing tobacco, rice, or indigo, while New England and the Middle Colonies went in for small farming, fishing, and small-scale industry and commerce.

In Maryland, founded partly to give refuge to Catholics; in Rhode Island, founded by Roger Williams and others unwilling to conform to the orthodoxy of Massachusetts; in Pennsylvania, founded by Quakers who believed in the separation of church and state, we find something like the religious freedom that was later to be embodied in the Constitution of the United States. During the eighteenth century, it came to be recognized that people might even be free not to belong to any formal religious organization.

The colonists, as men of the seventeenth century, accepted class distinctions as a matter of course. Yet the seeds of democracy were present. There was no titled colonial nobility, and the egalitarianism of the frontier and the career open to talent in the town balanced the privileged gentry in the coastal cities and in the Hudson Valley. Each colony had some sort of legislative body; government by discussion was firmly planted from the beginning. Though the Crown was represented in most colonies by a royal governor, the English government, torn by revolutionary upheavals, exerted no continuing bureaucratic or absolute rule over the colonies, as the Spaniards and French did over theirs. The English royal governors bickered with the colonial assemblies, and often lost. Local government—in village and town and county—fostered wide popular participation. The English common law which provided for trial by jury and lacked bureaucratic administrative regulation reflected a very different tradition from that of the Spanish or French.

NEW FRANCE

To the north of the thirteen colonies, in the region around the Bay of Fundy and in the St. Lawrence Basin, New France was for a century and a half a serious threat to the English North American colonies. The St. Lawrence and the Great Lakes gave the French easy access to the heart of the continent, whereas the Appalachians stood between the English and the Mississippi. The French were also impelled westward by the fur trade; furs are goods of very great value and comparatively little bulk, easily carried in canoes and small boats. Moreover, led by the Jesuits, the Catholic French gave proof of a far greater missionary zeal than did the Protestant English. The priest, as well as the *coureur des bois* (trapper), led the push westward. Finally, the French in North America were guided in their expansion by a conscious imperial policy directed from the France of the Bourbon monarchs.

The result was that the French, not the English, explored the interior of the continent. The names and accomplishments of the French explorers, missionaries, and traders—Marquette, Joliet, La Salle, Frontenac, Cadillac, Iberville—are a part of our American heritage. By the early eighteenth century, the French had built up a line of isolated trading posts—with miles of empty space between, thinly populated by Indians—which encircled the English colonies on the Atlantic coast. From Quebec, one line of outposts led westward. From Mobile and New Orleans, in a colony founded at the beginning of the eighteenth century and named Louisiana after Louis XIV, lines led northward up the Mississippi to join with those from Canada and Illinois.

Yet, impressive though this French imperial thrust looks on the map, their territory was far too lightly held for them to be equal to the task of containing the English. French loss of Newfoundland, Acadia, and Hudson's Bay to England in the Utrecht settlement was a portent of this weakness. Theirs was a trading empire with military ambitions, and save in Quebec it never became a true colony

View of Delft, by Vermeer, c. 1658.

of settlement. Frenchmen simply did not come over in sufficient numbers, and those who did come spread themselves out over vast distances as traders and adventurers. Frenchmen who might have come, the Huguenots who might have settled as did the Puritans, were excluded by a royal policy bent on maintaining the Catholic faith in New France.

THE INDIES, WEST AND EAST; AFRICA

The French, Dutch, and English intruded upon the pioneer Spanish and Portuguese both in the New World and in the Old. They broke the Spanish hold over the Caribbean and ultimately made that sea of many islands a kaleidoscope of colonial jurisdictions and a center of continuing naval wars and piracy. The West Indies, though today for the most part a seriously depressed area, were in early modern times one of the great prizes of imperialism. Here the cheap Negro slave labor that had replaced the exterminated Indian raised the great staple tropical crops—tobacco, fruits, coffee, and, most basic of all, cane sugar.

In India, the Mogul Empire proved strong enough to confine the Europeans on the whole to the coastal fringes. Gradually, in the course of the seventeenth century both the French and the English established themselves in India on the heels of decaying Portuguese power and wealth. The English defeated a Portuguese fleet in 1612, and immediately thereafter got trading rights at Surat on the western coast. Although the Mogul Emperor, Aurangzeb, tried to revoke their rights in 1685, he soon found their naval and mercantile power too much to withstand. In 1690 the English founded in Bengal in eastern India the city they were to make famous, Calcutta. Meanwhile, the French had got footholds on the south coast near Madras, at a place called Pondichéry, and soon had established other stations. Early in the eighteenth century, the stage was set in India as in North America for the decisive struggle for overseas empire between France and Britain.

Both countries operated in India, as they had initially in North America, by means of chartered trading companies, the English East India Company and the French *Compagnie des Indes Orientales*. The companies were backed up by their governments when it was clear that bits of land around the trading posts had to be held and that the relation with India could not be a purely commercial one. Gradually, in support of their companies, both England and France became involved in Indian politics and wars. But neither country made an effort to found a New England or a New France in the East.

The Dutch, who operated the most profitable of all the East India companies, bypassed India but drove the Portuguese from the nearby island of Ceylon. In the East Indies proper, they built Batavia (from the Latin name for Holland) on the island of Java and founded an empire in Indonesia that lasted almost to our own day. Only after World War II did Batavia become Jakarta. When the Dutch reached Japan in 1609, the Japanese rulers were already suspicious of Christian penetration and irritated at the bickerings between Portuguese Jesuits and Spanish Franciscans. The Japanese gradually expelled all Christians until in 1641 the Dutch alone were left, confined to an island in Nagasaki harbor. Japan had sealed herself off from the West until the mid-nineteenth century.

In Africa, the Dutch took over the Cape of Good Hope from the Portuguese in 1652 and settled there—the ancestors of today's Afrikaners in the Union of South Africa. The French, too, were moving into Africa, first into Senegal on the west coast (1626). In the Indian Ocean, Louis XIV annexed the large island of

Madagascar in 1686, and in 1715 the French took the island of Mauritius from the Dutch, rechristening it the Île de France. The British broke into the competition by securing a foothold at the mouth of the Gambia River in West Africa (1662), and later added other acquisitions at French and Dutch expense. Thus a map of Africa and adjacent waters in the eighteenth century shows a series of coastal stations controlled by various European states, but until the nineteenth century the interior remained untouched, save by the slavers and native traders.

THE BALANCE SHEET OF IMPERIALISM

Seen in terms of economics, the expansion of Europe in early modern times was by no means the pure "exploitation" and "plundering" of anti-imperialist rhetoric. There *was* robbery, just as there was murder or enslavement. In dealing with the natives, the Europeans often gave much too little in exchange for land and goods of great value: the Indians sold the island of Manhattan to the Dutch for $24.00 worth of trinkets. And the almost universally applied mercantilist policy kept money and manufacturing in the hands of the home country. It

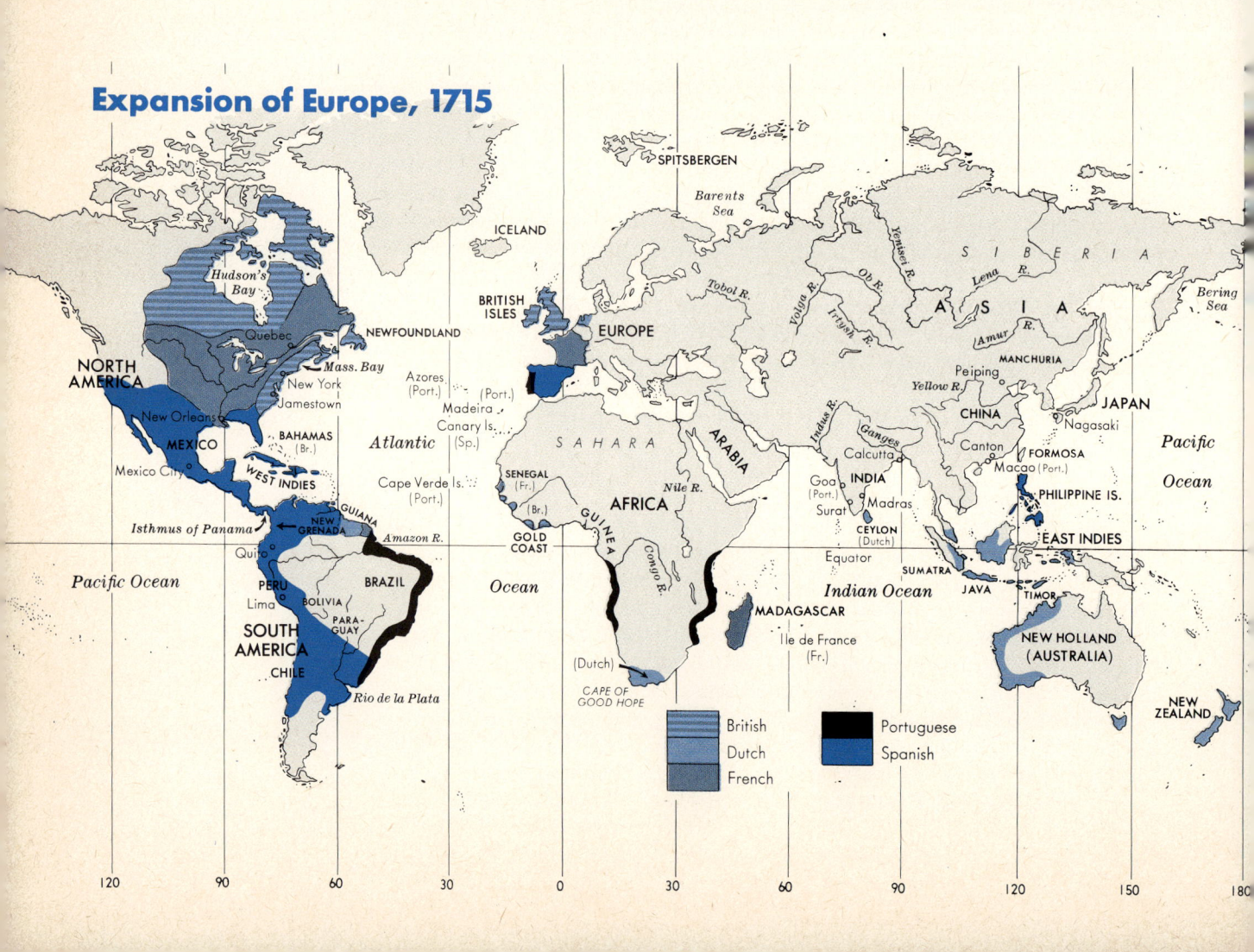

Expansion of Europe, 1715

relegated the colonies to the production of raw materials, a role that tended to keep even colonies of settlement in a relatively primitive and economically dependent condition.

Still, even with all these limitations, the expansion of Europe added to the goods available to non-Europeans. Although few Europeans settled in India or Africa, their wares, and especially their weapons, began gradually the process of Europeanizing, or westernizing, the rest of the world. By the eighteenth century this process was only beginning, and, in particular, few of the improvements in public health and sanitation that Europeans were to bring to the East had yet to come about; nor had any greater public order come to India and Africa. But, in the New World especially, there were signs of the westernization to come.

The West in its turn was greatly affected by the world overseas. The long list of imported items included foodstuffs above all, utensils and gadgets like pipes for smoking, hammocks and pyjamas, and styles of architecture and painting like bungalows and Japanese prints. Some of the novelties caught on more quickly than others. Tobacco, brought into Spain in the mid-sixteenth century as a soothing drug, had established itself by the seventeenth century as essential to the peace of mind of many European males. Potatoes, on the other hand, though highly nourishing and cheaper to grow than the staple breadstuffs, did not immediately catch on in Europe. In France, their consumption had to be popularized in a regular campaign which took generations to be effective.

Among Westerners, knowledge of non-European beliefs and institutions eventually penetrated to the level of popular culture, where it is marked by a host of words—pow wow, kowtow, tabu, totem. At the highest level of cultural interchange, that of religion and ethical ideas, however, the West imported little. The first impression of Westerners, not only when they met the relatively primitive cultures of the New World, but even when they met the old cultures of the East, was that they had nothing to learn from them. In time, some people began to respect the otherworldliness of Hinduism and the high but quite this-worldly ethics of Chinese Confucianism; others came to admire the dignity and simplicity of primitive peoples. But for the most part what struck the Europeans—when they bothered at all to think about anything more than money-making and empire-building—was the poverty, dirt, and superstition they found among the masses in India and China, the low material standards of primitive peoples everywhere, the heathenness of the heathens.

Yet, certainly exposure to these very different cultures acted as a stimulus in the West. One of its first effects was to increase the fund of the marvelous, the incredible. The early accounts of the New World are full of giants and pygmies, El Dorados with gold-paved streets, fountains of eternal youth, wonderful plants and animals. All this was a great stimulus to the literary and artistic imagination, from the island of Shakespeare's *Tempest* to the Xanadu of Coleridge's *Kubla Khan*, two hundred years later. Science, too, was stimulated. A dip into any of the early collections of voyages gives an impression more of the realistic sense and careful observation of travellers than of their credulity and exaggerations. Here is the modern science of geography already well on the way to maturity, and here too are contributions to the modern social sciences of anthropology, comparative government, and economics.

The effects of expansion were harsh and unsettling as well as stimulating. The great new supplies of gold and silver from the Americas set in motion a secular trend toward price rises. This inflation accompanied, perhaps indeed "caused" or at least helped, general economic expansion. In this process, the merchants and financiers, "businessmen" in the broadest sense, gained; those on fixed incomes suffered; and the income of wage-earners, peasants, and the like, while increasing, generally did not rise as fast as prices.

THE BEGINNINGS OF ONE WORLD

By the early part of the eighteenth century, there were still blank spots on the map of the world, especially in the interior of Africa and in our Pacific Northwest. Yet, in spite of this and in spite of the insignificance of the impression made by Europe on China and Japan, it was already clear that only one system of international politics existed in the world. From now on, all general wars tended to be world wars, fought, if only by privateers, on all the seven seas, and, if only by savages and frontiersmen, on all the continents. By the eighteenth century there was One World.

This was certainly not One World of the spirit. No common authority of any kind could reach all men; there were pockets of isolated peoples. And the masses of the world, even at its center in Europe, remained ignorant of, and uninterested in, what really went on in the hearts and heads of men elsewhere. But already Western goods penetrated almost everywhere, led by firearms, then followed by a great many other commodities; not all of them "cheap and nasty," as anticolonialists would claim. Already an educated minority was growing up everywhere, from professional geographers to journalists, diplomatists, and men of business, specialists who had to deal with the problems of the whole world.

READING SUGGESTIONS (asterisk indicates paperbound edition)

Europe in General

C. J. Friedrich, *The Age of the Baroque, 1610–1660;* F. L. Nussbaum, *The Triumph of Science and Reason, 1660–1685;* J. B. Wolf, *The Emergence of the Great Powers, 1685–1715* (*Torchbooks). In the Rise of Modern Europe series, with full, up-to-date bibliographies.

G. N. Clark, *The Seventeenth Century* (*Galaxy), and D. Ogg, *Europe in the Seventeenth Century* (*Collier). Older, briefer, and still useful surveys.

G. Renard and G. Weulersse, *Life and Work in Modern Europe* (Knopf, 1926). For the general economic background.

E. F. Heckscher, *Mercantilism,* 2 vols., rev. ed. (Macmillan, 1955). A famous and controversial work.

A. Vagts, *A History of Militarism* (*Free Press), and E. M. Earle, ed., *Makers of Modern Strategy* (*Atheneum). Both are helpful on seventeenth-century warfare.

F. L. Nussbaum, *A History of Economic Institutions in Modern Europe* (Crofts, 1933). Abridgment of Sombart's work, claiming war is economically creative.

J. U. Nef, *War and Human Progress* (Harvard, 1950). Rebutting Sombart, and arguing that war is economically destructive.

The Thirty Years' War

C. V. Wedgwood, *The Thirty Years' War* (*Anchor). Comprehensive account.

T. K. Rabb, ed., *The Thirty Years' War: Problems of Motive, Extent, and Effect* (*Heath). Good introduction to the main controversies over the war.

H. Holborn, *A History of Modern Germany,* 2 vols. (Knopf, 1959, 1963). Volume 1 of this authoritative study goes to 1648; Volume 2 from 1648 to 1820.

M. Roberts, *Gustavus Adolphus,* 2 vols. (Longmans, 1953, 1958). Sympathetic study of the man and his reign.

England

M. Ashley, *England in the Seventeenth Century* (°Penguin), and C. Hill, *The Century of Revolution, 1603–1714* (°Norton). Two sound surveys by experts.

G. Davies, *The Early Stuarts, 1603–1660*, and G. N. Clark, *The Later Stuarts, 1660–1714*, rev. eds. (Clarendon, 1949). More detailed scholarly treatments, in the Oxford History of England.

W. Notestein, *The English People on the Eve of Colonization, 1603–1660* (°Torchbooks). Admirable social history.

D. H. Willson, *King James Sixth and First* (°Galaxy). Sound fresh study.

C. V. Wedgwood, *The King's Peace, 1637–1641* and *The King's War, 1641–1647* (Macmillan, 1955, 1959). Detailed study of the Great Rebellion by a leading scholar.

M. Ashley, *Oliver Cromwell and the Puritan Revolution* (°Collier). Recent evaluation of a still controversial figure.

A. Bryant, *King Charles II* (Longmans, 1931). Unusually sympathetic in tone.

F. C. Turner, *James II* (Macmillan, 1948). Balanced treatment of a ruler generally subject to partisan interpretation.

J. R. Tanner, *English Constitutional Conflicts of the Seventeenth Century* (°Cambridge University). Full and scholarly.

G. P. Gooch, *English Democratic Ideas in the Seventeenth Century* (°Torchbooks). An older work, still worth reading.

France

J. D. Lough, *An Introduction to Seventeenth Century France* (McKay, 1961). Designed for the student of literature, but useful for anyone interested in the subject.

W. J. Stankiewicz, *Politics and Religion in Seventeenth Century France* (University of California, 1960). Good special study.

J. B. Wolf, *Louis XIV* (°Norton). Recent scholarly political biography.

A. Guérard, *France in the Classical Age: The Life and Death of an Ideal* (°Torchbooks). Stimulating interpretation of early modern France.

W. H. Lewis, *The Splendid Century* (°Anchor). Emphasizing society under Louis XIV.

C. V. Wedgwood, *Richelieu and the French Monarchy* (°Collier), and M. Ashley, *Louis XIV and the Greatness of France* (°Free Press). Good short introductions.

O. Ranum, *Richelieu and the Councillors of Louis XIII* (Oxford, 1963). An important monograph on administration.

C. W. Cole, *Colbert and a Century of French Mercantilism*, 2 vols. (Columbia, 1939). A solid, detailed study.

J. E. King, *Science and Rationalism in the Administration of Louis XIV* (Hopkins, 1949). Monograph showing the relations between intellectual and political history.

W. F. Church, ed., *The Greatness of Louis XIV: Myth or Reality?* (Heath). Samples the wide variety of judgments on the *grand monarque*.

Europe Overseas

Cambridge History of the British Empire, Vol. 1 (Cambridge, 1929). Convenient account of developments up to 1783.

O. T. Black and H. T. Lefler, *Colonial America* (Macmillan, 1958). Good survey.

G. M. Wrong, *The Rise and Fall of New France*, 2 vols. (Macmillan, 1928). French Canada interpreted by a Canadian.

A. P. Newton, *The European Nations in the West Indies, 1493–1688* (Black, 1933). Reviews the days when the islands were prizes of empire.

B. H. M. Vlekke, *Nusantara: A History of Indonesia*, rev. ed. (Lorenz, 1959). Good account of Dutch imperialism.

A. Hyma, *The Dutch in the Far East* (Wahr, 1942). With emphasis on social and economic developments.

Note: see also titles cited in **Chapter 7**.

Sources and Fiction

H. J. C. von Grimmelshausen, *Simplicius Simplicissimus* (°several editions). Picaresque novel of Germany during the Thirty Years' War by a seventeenth-century writer.

Pepys' Diary (°Macmillan). Abridgment of the famous diary by a Londoner.

R. Graves, *Wife to Mr. Milton* (°Noonday). Good novel about Milton, who was Cromwell's secretary.

W. H. Lewis, ed., *Memoirs of the Duc de Saint-Simon* (°Macmillan). Gossipy recollections of a touchy aristocrat.

Willa Cather, *Shadows on the Rock* (Knopf, 1931). Sensitive re-creation of life in New France by a fine American novelist.

A. Dumas, *The Three Musketeers* (°several editions). By the author of other rousing novels on seventeenth-century France.

W. M. Thackeray, *Henry Esmond* (°several editions). Famous novel set in England about 1700.

N. Hawthorne, *The Scarlet Letter* (°several editions). The best introduction to the Puritan spirit through fiction.

9

Seventeenth and Eighteenth Centuries

Science, Culture, and the Enlightenment

Strawberry Hill (1749–1777), home of Horace Walpole.

I. The Beginnings of Modernization

The historian is bound by his profession to hold that all of us today are what we are, behave as we do, in some part because of what happened to our very distant ancestors, even those so distant as the prehistoric men of the first chapter of the book. Yet the impatience of many twentieth-century American students with the study of the distant past, their desire to get at "modern" or even "contemporary" history is by no means wholly unjustified. Our modern world has in the last few centuries undergone vast and in some senses unprecedented changes; it faces problems never faced by men before in quite the form they assume today.

Just when the "modern" begins in the history of our Western society is a problem on which historians are not yet agreed. It used to be generally held that the "medieval" gave way to the "modern" in the Western world at the end of the fifteenth and the beginning of the sixteenth centuries in the period of the Renaissance and Reformation. No sensible person would deny that these years were years of great changes in many fields of human activity, from international relations to all the arts and to philosophy and religion. Yet it will be our contention in this book that, led by the remarkable development of natural science and technology, but by no means in any one-way causal sense, the late seventeenth and the eighteenth centuries, the period usually known as the Age of the Enlightenment, saw the process of modernization firmly established in much of the Western world, and set the stage for our contemporary world.

There is no single simple sign of modernization. Most obvious to all of us is the very great, indeed the amazing increase in human command over material resources. Judged by the engineer's measurements of power, for instance the familiar horsepower, there was no very great increase during all the millennia from the first historical civilizations of Egypt and Mesopotamia on down to the eighteenth century. There were of course in those years important inventions, and many specific advances in human command of the natural environment. But the basic aids to puny human strength—mechanical aid from windmills, water mills, sails and the like, animal aid from horses, other beasts of burden, and, conspicuously, human slaves—had been discovered by 4000 B.C., and they remained substantially unchanged until the great breakthrough marked by the invention and practical applications of steam power in the middle eighteenth century. The two centuries since then have seen a fantastic increase in the sheer horsepower available to even the "underdeveloped" lands of our own day.

Yet it will not do to regard this great development of man's command over his material environment as the "cause" of what we here call modernization. In the following pages we shall attempt to deal with the many phases—philosophic, literary, artistic, ethical, political, and economic—of this great seed-time of our civilization today, the Age of the Enlightenment. And we shall frankly dodge the old and perhaps insoluble problem of whether "material" changes bring about changes of a "spiritual" or "cultural" sort, or whether the reverse is true. For the historian, at least, it should be sufficient to note that in real life the complicated interactions among human beings are not susceptible to such simple analysis as any dualism of "matter" and "spirit." As well ask whether the gasoline or the sparkplug makes our motor cars run. Without both, or the diesel equivalent thereof, and a lot else besides, no car could move.

A motor car is, however, a visible whole. A human culture is immensely more complicated than a motor car, and can hardly be as a whole an object of sense-perception. Yet we are able to grasp something of what our culture means; words do not encompass it all, but they can suggest to our emotions, our feelings, what this "modern," so different from earlier cultures, is like. Basically, perhaps, this new cultural fact can be put as a belief in the possibility of human progress toward a society in which all human beings all over the globe will be able to satisfy completely their needs for food, shelter, sex life, health, and happiness. No such state has as yet been achieved even in the United States, a land in many ways in the vanguard of modernization. But we must insist that *prior to the Age of the Enlightenment* no such general belief could possibly have been formulated and spread to the consciousness of ordinary men and women.

II. The Growth of Natural Science

The most striking aspect of the Enlightenment, as we have noted, is the extraordinary growth and advancement in natural science. Historians of science have brought home to us the fact that the scientific study of the external world goes back as far as written history; they have emphasized that such study has been in a sense continuous, even in the Dark Ages and Middle Ages, which used to be regarded as wholly "unscientific." But again, the Enlightenment embodied the systematization, the extension into wider fields, the actual discovery (perhaps "invention" is a better word) of major laws or uniformities, the beginnings of "popularization" of science, all of which helped to make almost a different thing of science. Consequently, a difference of degree became in these centuries almost a difference in kind.

THE SEVENTEENTH CENTURY

For one thing, science, or "natural philosophy" as it was then usually called, developed into an organized and widespread human activity. Scientific academies were founded, of which the Royal Society for Improving Natural Knowledge (1662) in England and the Académie des Sciences (1666) in France are early examples; these began publishing scientific journals. The American Philosophical Society of Philadelphia (1743), founded in part through the efforts of Benjamin Franklin, was the first of the New World's counterparts to these learned societies. Formally through corresponding secretaries of such academies, informally through private correspondence among friends and acquaintances, an international scientific community arose; members of this body were thus able to be kept informed of experiments and discoveries of other workers and to contribute their own to the general pool. Its first common language was Latin, the language in which Newton's great *Philosophiae naturalis principia mathematica* (*Mathematical Principles of Natural Philosophy,* 1687) was written.

By the early eighteenth century science had become fashionable among the aristocracy, and many a gentleman, and even an occasional lady, dabbled in a private laboratory or observatory. Some indeed, like the chemist Robert Boyle (1627-1691), son of an Irish earl, were very far from being dabblers, achieving real distinction in their fields. From their inception the new advances in science were popularized in books and articles specially written to interest the educated lay public, such as the French writer Fontenelle's *Discourses on the Plurality of Worlds* (1686).

Astronomy and physics, and more particularly mechanics, became the spearheads of early modern science. Some recent historians of science question the established view that Sir Isaac Newton (1642-1727) was a "culture hero" who stamped on the age a mechanical view of the universe as "the Newtonian worldmachine." But there can be no doubt that the cumulative effect of work in astronomy and physics was the greatest single element in widening and deepening the influence of the scientific point of view. Though Copernicus in the sixteenth century had advanced the heliocentric conception of our solar system, it was not until the Italian Galileo, greatly helped by the newly developed telescope, in 1632 published confirmation of Copernicus' work that the much earlier geocentric conception began to be widely discredited among the educated classes. Galileo, in a famous trial before a church court, was forced publicly to recant his theory that the earth moves in orbit around the sun. An unconfirmed tradition holds, however, that as he left the trial, he muttered under his breath "and yet it [the earth] does move." His printed works, which could not be completely suppressed, continued to say what he was not permitted to say out loud.

Working from a discovery made by Galileo, another Italian, Torricelli, invented the barometer. The Frenchman Pascal (1623–1662), using Torricelli's invention, proved by measuring the height of a column of mercury both at the base and at the top of a mountain that what we call air pressure diminishes with altitude; Pascal also showed that a vacuum is possible, in spite of the old adage "Nature abhors a vacuum." Another Frenchman, René Descartes (1596–1650), chiefly known as a philosopher, worked out a system of analytical geometry which makes possible the graph based on "Cartesian coordinates."

Newton built on the work of Galileo, Torricelli, Pascal, and many others, using newly perfected mathematical aids, such as decimals, logarithms, graphs, and above all the infinitesimal calculus, which he and Leibniz (1646–1716) seem to have invented separately at about the same time. He thereby arrived at the great master-generalization we know as the law of gravitation. The sun, the planets, and their satellites are, according to this theory, held in their orbits by the force of mutual attraction. Newton stated the formula that this force is proportional to the product of the masses of two bodies attracted one to another, and inversely proportional to the square of the distance between them. Newton's law still holds today, as modified in the early twentieth century by Einstein, who referred to a gravitational "field" rather than a "force."

What the telescope did for astronomy the microscope achieved for biology. Both instruments rest on the discovery, probably by Dutch glassworkers toward the end of the sixteenth century, that placing two lenses together produced a magnification impossible with merely a single lens. By about 1680 the Dutchman van Leeuwenhoek noticed by using a microscope the existence of tiny creatures—the protozoa—hitherto unknown. Renaissance scientists like Vesalius (see Chapter 6) had cleared up much about human anatomy, but how the heart functioned was a mystery until the Englishman William Harvey (1578–1657) demonstrated that it is a pump, and that blood is forced by the heart along a system of circulation. In 1679 the Italian Borelli showed that the human arm is a lever and that the muscles do mechanical work. The dynamic science of physiology thus developed out of the static science of anatomy.

THE EIGHTEENTH CENTURY

Certainly in the field of science the century of Galileo, Harvey, Descartes, Newton, Leeuwenhoek, and their peers deserved to be called, in the phrase of the distinguished twentieth-century philosopher Alfred North Whitehead, "the century of genius." In comparison with the seventeenth century, in which the seminal discoveries were made, the eighteenth was one of systematization, popularization, and the rounding out of earlier work. The Swedish naturalist Linnaeus (1707–1778) made the classification of plants and animals that is today still the basis for biological taxonomy. Franklin, the first American to figure prominently in the history of science, experimented with electricity and demonstrated its affinity to lightning. The French astronomer and mathematician Laplace wrote a work of synthesis entitled significantly the *Mécanique céleste* (*Heavenly Mechanics*, 1785).

In chemistry, however, the eighteenth century took the great initial steps, the revolutionary breakthrough that achieved for this science what the Copernican–Galilean–Newtonian development achieved for astronomy. The modern science of chemical analysis began with Black and Lavoisier. Joseph Black (1728–1799), a Scottish professor, exploded the old theory that air was composed of a single element and proved the existence of several airlike substances or gases. The French chemist and physicist Lavoisier (1743–1794), building in part on the work of an English contemporary, Joseph Priestley, continued Black's study of gases, invented the name "oxygen," and demonstrated that water was composed of oxygen and hydrogen. He asserted that all substances were composed of a relatively few basic chemical elements, of which he identified 23.

Finally, other natural sciences got a good start in the eighteenth century, though they did not receive quite the synthesizing touches evident in chemistry and physics. Geologists, many of them English or Scottish, by the early nineteenth century had established that the earth was far older than the biblical calculation, and had discovered the natural processes of rock formation and the nature of fossils. They had already set before orthodox Christianity the problem of reconciling the findings of science with the traditional Judaeo-Christian cosmology of the Book of Genesis, and especially with the time-scale of the Bible, which set the whole creation of the universe, with a stationary earth as its center, at about 4000 B.C. A clear sign of how the new sciences were affecting men's view of the world came with the disastrous Lisbon earthquake of 1755. The orthodox—the majority of people—regarded it as a visitation from God, a warning to sinful man. Voltaire used it in *Candide* as a springboard to attack what he held to be silly and unfounded optimism. But others stated that the earthquake had causes quite as "natural" as, say, a rainstorm, that it was, in our language, a seismological event.

Meantime, Englishmen like Locke (1632–1704) and Hartley (1705–1757), Frenchmen like Condillac (1715–1780), Bichat (1771–1802), and Pinel (1745–1826) were laying the foundations for modern psychology. It was a sign of the times that people now began to question the traditional idea that the insane were possessed by real demons and therefore required such harsh treatment as flogging to drive the demons out. Pinel and his fellow-workers at the end of the eighteenth century were pioneers in the now almost universally accepted theory that mental illness is as much a natural form of "disease" as any physical illness and thus has to be treated medically. Indeed, what came to be called the social sciences, though relatively undifferentiated, issue from an eighteenth century matrix of political philosophy, rather uncritical anthropology, linguistics, and of course economics, then called political economy.

SCIENCE, TECHNOLOGY, AND PHILOSOPHY

We may now venture two broad generalizations, first on the relation between science and technology in the seventeenth and eighteenth centuries, and second on the methodology of science and its relation to the intellectual attitudes

—the philosophy—of the age. In these centuries we do not find the close collaboration among "pure" scientists, "applied" scientists, engineers, bankers, private businessmen, and government administrators we find today. Nevertheless, we do find the origins of the socioeconomic channels through which the modern world has achieved its extraordinary material wealth and power. Technologists—craftsmen brought up in a long tradition of manual skills *and inventiveness*—made the achievements of scientists possible. Glassworkers made the lenses without which the advances in astronomy and biology would hardly have been possible; late medieval miners started the long process which led to geology, mineralogy, and the whole train of the "earth sciences"; and they also, through the need to pump water from mines, initiated one of the lines of thought that led to the steam engine; Dutch pioneers in insurance, a characteristic modern business enterprise, began to study life expectancies, and thereby contributed to the science of statistics. Harvey, as the theorist explaining the circulation of the blood, was a pure scientist, but also, as court physician to Charles I of England, was very much an applied scientist. From the beginning modern science has been concerned with getting things made and getting things done; it has always been,

Joseph Wright of Derby, "An Experiment with the Air Pump," 1768.

then, "practical." Even Newton, duly knighted as Sir Isaac, spent his last years as president of the Royal Society and head of the English Mint.

But science has also been "impractical"; or, less crudely and misleadingly put, it has been closely tied up with the kind of intellectual activity we characterize as philosophy. Natural science is a search for truth, but a search conducted by its own rules, which have been several thousand years in the making. In the early seventeenth century the Englishman Francis Bacon, a theorist and publicist of science rather than a working scientist himself, formulated some of these rules in a fashion that gained them wide circulation. To counteract the influence of Aristotle and the Scholastics (*see* Chapter 4) Bacon emphasized the need for "induction," that is, the careful accumulation of data through observation and experimentation, and attacked "deduction," that is, reasoning logically from accepted premises. *Both* induction and deduction are essential to scientific method, but Bacon's emphasis on induction was no doubt a necessary corrective in his time, and it helped give science new impetus.

Men today still argue whether science should try to answer the kinds of questions about the universe and man's place in it that philosophers, theologians, and ordinary people have been asking for centuries. Most scientists would perhaps agree with the English statistician and theorist of science Karl Pearson (1857–1936) that "science may be described as a classified index to the successive pages of sense impression, which enables us readily to find what we want, but it in nowise accounts for the peculiar contents of that strange book of life." But in the eighteenth century science was taken by many enthusiastic believers in the achievements of the Enlightenment to be much more than a useful "index"; it became for them the book of life itself, or, rather, the best support for a relatively new view of the universe. And by casting discredit on the possibility of the miraculous, and indeed on the existence of any God or "force" outside nature and therefore beyond description by science—in short, on the *supernatural*—science gave powerful support to the great eighteenth-century attack on Christianity.

III. The New World-View: Nature, Reason, and Progress

RATIONALISM

Reason, Nature, Progress—these were the key words in the vocabulary of the Enlightenment. This was the age when many believed that human reason could free men of their ills once and for all and lead them infallibly to perpetual peace, utopian government, and a perfect society. *Reason* would discover the *natural laws* regulating existence, and so insure the *progress* of the human race. The prophets of this optimistic creed were known by the French name of *philosophes*, though they were not all French and few of them were philosophers in the formal sense. The *philosophes* were publicists, economists, political scientists, and social reformers. Their basic philosophy may be termed *rationalism*—the view that all human thinking on *any* subject must be, in order to be valid, similar to the kind of thinking the scientist performs in his work.

The methods and achievements of natural science were one, but not the only, source of the attitudes embodied in rationalism. Reason was to the *philo-*

sophes a faculty possessed by all normal persons, by means of which they can learn how to get what they want and, even more important, learn what are the right things to want both for their individual good and for the good of all men. To them reason was exemplified not only by experimental science but by mathematics, logic, and by some philosophies, notably that of the Frenchman René Descartes, whose *Discourse on Method* (1637) is a landmark in the history of ideas, and may be used to mark the beginning of the Age of the Enlightenment rather than the more traditional date of the publication of Newton's *Principia*, half a century later.

Descartes announced that he would begin his "reasoning" by accepting nothing from previous thinking, by doubting everything, including, of course, Christian beliefs; he finally decided that he could have no doubt of one thing—*he was thinking*. Starting with this "I think, therefore I am," and accepting as true only what he thought were clear and certain propositions, like those of mathematics, he built up a whole philosophical system, which included God—or at least the idea of God. Historians have debated whether the dominant influence on the Enlightenment was the stream of thought coming through Bacon, with its emphasis on induction, or through Descartes, with its emphasis on deduction. We incline to believe that the average educated follower of the Enlightenment was *both* a Baconian and a Cartesian, that he thought of reason as working by clear and certain logic on the facts learned through sense-experience.

Reason in this sense could prove very destructive when applied to religious beliefs; such an application was one of the very first the *philosophes* made, for religion, and in particular the Roman Catholic Church, was always a favorite target of their attack. Take any familiar biblical story, that of the collapse of the walls of Jericho (Joshua 6:20) or that of Lazarus rising from the dead (John 11:44): neither inductive nor deductive reasoning finds it easy to confirm belief in the walls of a city falling down because a crowd shouted or in a man coming back to life after death. Indeed, the rationalists, when they did not maintain that such stories were pure fabrications, took to explaining them as distortions of some perfectly natural event. The walls of Jericho, they could say, fell as a result of an earthquake, and Joshua merely took credit in the name of Jehovah; Lazarus did not die, but was merely unconscious, perhaps even hypnotized so Jesus could get credit for a miracle. Beginning with moderate critical skepticism in the hands of writers like Pierre Bayle (1647–1706), strengthened above all by the mordant wit of Voltaire (1694–1778), subtly and philosophically put by the Scotsman David Hume (1711–1776) in his *Essay on Miracles*, these attacks on religion reached a climax in the French Revolution, when in 1793–1794 "dechristianizers" closed the churches and persecuted the faithful. Volney in his once widely read *The Ruins, or Meditation on the Revolutions of Empires* (1791) maintains that all religion is the result of a conspiracy by clever and unscrupulous priests to get power and wealth by preying on their credulous fellowmen.

René Descartes, by Frans Hals.

NATURE AND NATURAL LAW

These same specific examples may illustrate the complex meanings that "Nature," together with "natural" and "natural law," had for the *philosophes* and their followers—indeed, for almost all educated men in the eighteenth century. Nature meant first of all the "external world," this physical world as experienced by our senses and organized by our Reason. Men were aware that their unaided senses could not give them the whole story and might even mislead them—witness a mirage in a desert. But aided by scientific instruments and by right reasoning, men could come to see Nature as it really is. For, second, Nature is seen to be uniform in its operations, following laws which scientists like Newton have discovered; moreover, properly understood Nature is kindly in its intentions, on the whole, toward its favorite child and potential master, man. If men would behave *naturally*, so many of the *philosophes* held, they could all be happy here on earth.

By following out this chain of association we have arrived at a conception of Nature which goes beyond the original view. Nature at the start was held to be the "external world," that which is, a universe of "facts"; but it became that which *ought to be*, a guide, a set of values, a universe of "standards" or "norms." In our first sense Nature means everything that exists, and strictly speaking there can exist nothing not-natural; what is commonly called the "supernatural" or the "miraculous" does not really exist according to this view, although belief in miracles may exist in benighted minds. In the second or normative sense of Nature, belief in miracles for the *philosophes* is deeply unnatural, explicable only by ignorance of natural law. In such a sense the opposite of natural is not the *super*natural but the *un*natural; the unnatural which the *philosophes* usually held to be common enough among human beings in their own time, but which in the future would, they hoped, be rare or nonexistent.

The difficulty in reconciling the concept of Nature as whatever *is* and the concept of the "natural" as something that is not but ought to be did not disturb most believers in the Enlightenment, any more than most Christians are disturbed by the somewhat comparable difficulty of reconciling the existence of actual evil with an all-powerful, all-knowing, and benevolent God. The Enlightened went right ahead applying this devastating tool of Nature-plus-Reason to the institutions and beliefs of the eighteenth-century West. Some of the *philosophes* held that the capacity to use Reason as Nature intended was roughly the same in all men, or at any rate that all possessed a kind of minimum necessary reasoning power, or, as we usually put it, intelligence. But, they went on, ignorance, superstition, poverty had stunted this faculty of Reason in the masses, and wealth and irresponsibility had perverted it in many members of the privileged classes, all with the complicity of the corrupt institutions of Church and State. To restore the natural gift of reasoning correctly in all men the corrupting environment must be radically changed; thus much of the writing of the *philosophes* is taken up with criticism of existing institutions and beliefs. The Enlightenment, then, is first of all a corrosive, a dissolvent.

DEISM

The first attacks of the *philosophes* on Christianity were moderate and made in the name of "natural religion" or "deism." The central position of deism is clear in the very title of one of the earliest of deistic writings, *Christianity not mysterious, showing . . . that no Christian Doctrine can be properly called a Mystery* (1696) by the Englishman John Toland. These moderate critics argued that Christianity has a sound core of "natural religion," the religion in which all men would some day come to believe. This natural religion holds that there is a god who set the universe going (the familiar argument from the necessity of a First Cause) and made the rules by which, as science discovered, the universe really runs; and it believes in the Golden Rule, and all that part of the Christian ethic stemming from common sense. But natural religion rejects the Christian concept of a God who can interfere with the running of the universe by means of miracles; it rejects all theological doctrines, such as those of the Eucharist (Communion), the Trinity, or the Virgin Birth, which depend on mystery and miracle; it does not accept the doctrine of original sin; and it generally rejects that part of the Christian ethic emphasizing ascetic self-denial. On the concept of immortality of the soul and on rewards and punishments in an afterlife, some of the more conservative deists hedged a bit; since deism did retain a belief in a God or at least in a principle not "material," it could hold that men were not merely physico-chemical combinations, but that they possessed souls which *might* be immortal.

While deism may be called the official religion of the Enlightenment, it was never at all widespread among the masses. Even among the Enlightened in the eighteenth century, deistic belief was for the most part an ethical and philosophical position, not a church or denomination with ritual, ministers, or dogmas. Nor was deism quite the simple set of beliefs it might seem in brief analysis. One of the thinkers who did most to establish the basis of deism, the Englishman John Locke (1632–1704), is not fairly labelled a deist at all, but rather a broad-church or liberal Anglican. Locke's temperate rationalism, was, however, at the origin of Enlightened beliefs in philosophy and religion, as indeed in psychology, politics, and education. In his *Essay Concerning Human Understanding* (1683–1689), he denied the existence of innate ideas, and maintained that the human mind is at first like a blank sheet of paper (*tabula rasa*) which comes to be furnished gradually as a result of experience. Wisely planned and administered institutions—that is, controlled environment—can greatly improve the furnishing of the mind. Locke himself was a moderate, and did not believe, as some later thinkers did, that human life can be perfectly happy. But he set the foundations for the typical eighteenth-century belief that environment is all, and that men guided by Reason can shape environment as Nature meant it to be.

Some deists, like Voltaire, took their beliefs lightly. Indeed, Voltaire took his deism so lightly that he could coin the famous—and self-betraying—epigram, "If God did not exist, it would be necessary to invent him." Others, for example Jean-Jacques Rousseau of Swiss Protestant origin, managed somehow to invest this rather chilling world-view with the warmth of sentiment, and even of emotion, as in "The profession of Faith of the Savoyard Vicar," part of Rousseau's famous plea for a "natural" education (*Emile*, 1762). There are numerous examples of deists who prayed, an apparently illogical act, since they believed that God had made the universe much as a clockmaker makes a clock, but that he had wound it up once and for all, leaving it to run on by itself forever without interference by him. By the very fact of their belief in man's ability to guide his actions according to Reason, the deists were disinclined to impose their views by persecution or any other authoritarian methods; they believed in moderation and in toleration. But they were none the less firmly opposed to existing religious beliefs and institutions, and, in particular, Roman Catholicism. Voltaire, using the slogan "*Ecrasez l'infâme*" (Crush the infamous thing), devoted a lifetime to attacking the Church as the major obstacle in the way of Enlightenment.

ATHEISM AND TOLERATION

As the eighteenth century wore on, more daring spirits went further than "natural religion" and its clockmaker god. David Hume adopted a frank skepticism about religion, a suspension of belief in any systematic and evaluating explanation of the universe and man's place in it. By contrast, those who went beyond deism into atheism were not skeptics for the most part but firm believers, indeed dogmatists. They believed in the *reality* of the material world as revealed to them by science and sense-experience, and they believed that scientists would soon understand that world completely. Some of them claimed to be atheists (Greek, "without a god") but in fact they deified Nature and Man as part of Nature. As to the Christian God, they did not *doubt* his existence: they *knew* he did not exist. The *System of Nature* (1770) of the Gallicized German Baron d'Holbach is a good example of the views of these thinkers; a more subtle position is taken by La Mettrie in *Man a Machine* (1748) and in the polished dialogue by Denis Diderot, "Conversation with the Maréchale de ———" (1777).

The tone of these atheists is certainly harsher and more violent than that of the deists, yet there is little in their writings to support the view that they desired complete elimination of Christian religious practices. While they, too, thought that time and Enlightenment were on their side, many of them held that the eighteenth-century masses were much too sunk in ignorance and much too envious of the lot of their betters to be exposed to the new ideas. In the salon of d'Holbach, we are told, atheism was not discussed before the servants. The sanctions of Christian "superstition," these enlightened and privileged people claimed, would be necessary to keep most people on the right moral track. Indeed, among the educated classes all through the century the conviction was widespread that the lower classes needed to believe in Heaven, and more particularly in Hell, or society would disintegrate.

Finally, most followers of the Enlightenment believed in the need for, and usefulness of, toleration in religion. Reason, they held, would inevitably conquer superstition in the open field of discussion. Meanwhile, force and authority were out of place in matters of the spirit. History, they claimed, shows that persecution has been ineffective, if not a positive spur to those persecuted. Reason shows that in all forms of higher religion there is, beneath the variations of ritual and dogma, a common denominator of faith in righteousness. Locke's *Letter Concerning Toleration* (1689) may be taken as a good example of the practical, empirical argument for toleration. The German dramatist Lessing takes a more idealistic stand: his play *Nathan the Wise* (1779), laid at the time of the Crusades, confronts Christian, Moslem, and Jew, and in the famous parable of the ring preaches an effective sermon in defense of mutual toleration.

SOCIAL CRITICISM

In sum, however critical many of the Enlightened were toward Christianity, they were rarely revolutionists who wanted to abolish it immediately. This same gap between the radicalism of critical attacks by the Enlightened and the moderation of their actual sociopolitical programs is observable in other matters. Judged by Nature's simple plan, state and society in the eighteenth-century West were as bad and unnatural as the Church. What could be less natural than the powdered wigs or the clumsy hoop skirts of the upper classes? Or the practice, common among aristocratic and wealthy middle-class ladies, who alone could afford it, of putting newborn babies out to wet-nurse? Rousseau, who installed his own alleged infants, all illegitimate, in a foundling home, preached so eloquently against wet-nursing that some fashionable ladies actually began nursing their babies.

Nor could the distinction between nobles and commoners hold up when tested by its conformity with the intentions of Nature. This was the lesson of Beaumarchais's comedy *The Marriage of Figaro* (1784), which was assured full audiences in Paris after an attempt was made to censor it. The plebeian hero, the barber and valet Figaro, cries, in a much applauded tirade against his master, Count Almaviva:

> Nobility, a fortune, a rank, appointments to office: all this makes a man so proud! What did you do to earn all this? You took the trouble to get born—nothing more.*

Nature, in short, made no distinction between a count and a barber. Nor did Nature make even a king different. Later, in the French Revolution, a popular story for children has the child-hero taken to Versailles where he sees a little boy of his own age playing in the garden, and asks his conventional father who the boy is. "Why," says the father, "that's the Dauphin, who'll be your King some day." The father tries in vain to persuade his son that the Dauphin is not *just* an ordinary little boy: "Does the Dauphin pee?" asks the good philosophic son. When the father has to admit that the Dauphin does, the son then announces that he is sure the Dauphin is just an ordinary little boy like himself.

UTILITARIAN ETHICS

The concepts of Nature and Reason used by the Enlightened to discredit traditions and accepted institutions also had a more positive side. They replaced older concepts, notably pessimistic Christian ones of original sin. The *philosophes* themselves were not in complete agreement about what constituted good natural behavior or good natural standards among men. The main stream was some form of Epicurean or utilitarian ethics (*see* Chapter 2), well represented in France by the *philosophe* Helvetius (1715–1771) and in England by Jeremy Bentham (1748–1832). The famous utilitarian phrase "the greatest good of the greatest number" seems to have been first coined in Italy by Beccaria, whose book on *Crimes and Punishments* (1764) advanced the doctrine that criminals should be punished, not as an act of vengeance by society and certainly not because God

* Act V, scene 3.

wanted them punished, but solely to prevent further crimes harmful to society. If possible, criminals should be reformed; at any rate, their punishment should be just harsh enough to offset the gain from their crime—"Let the punishment fit the crime." Bentham worked out in his *Principles of Morals and Legislation* (1789) an elaborate "felicific calculus" as a guide to human action: if everyone so acted as to maximize his pleasures—true pleasures, not wicked self-indulgence, not selfish acts harmful to others—and minimize his pains, then indeed there would be realized the greatest good of the greatest number. The truly useful is the truly good.

Such a conclusion in *practical* matters is not far from that arrived at by Immanuel Kant (1724–1804), the great German philosopher, though his phraseology is very different and his habit of thought intensely and abstractly "philosophic." It is true that Kant gave to the word "Reason" (in German, *Vernunft*) in some of his writing a transcendental, "idealistic" overtone quite different from the prudential, calculating, common-sense overtone the word had for the *philosophes* in France, Britain, and America. But Kant thought of himself as an Enlightened thinker, and his ethics are eminently Enlightened. Both he and Bentham in their different ways put into elaborate philosophical language the Golden Rule: Do unto others as you would have them do unto you.

In Enlightened thought, then, Nature meant men to act in a socially responsible way and to enjoy happiness thereby. Thus men had a *right* to be happy. We have arrived at one of the great alluring phrases of history, perhaps as good a summary of the goals of "modernization" as can be found: Jefferson's words in the Preamble to the American Declaration of Independence, "that all men are created equal, that they are endowed by their Creator with certain unalienable Rights, that among these are Life, Liberty and the pursuit of Happiness." These deceptively simple, and to Americans rather hackneyed, phrases are still today revolutionary dynamite in Asia and Africa, as they were in eighteenth-century France and America. It is no doubt true that Jefferson and most of his contemporaries meant by "happiness" not merely the pleasurable life for the individual but also the good of the whole society. Where these aims seemed to be in conflict, as for instance when the individual got happiness out of hurting others, the eighteenth-century Enlightened thinkers placed the good of the society above the apparent "happiness" of the individual. But they would go on to point out that the erring individual had been corrupted by a bad upbringing, which in the new society would be corrected. Here is the Earl of Shaftesbury (1671–1713) summing up for his century:

> Thus the wisdom of what rules, and is first and chief in Nature, has made it to be according to the private interest and good of everyone to work towards the general good, which if a creature ceases to promote, he is actually so far wanting to himself, and ceases to promote his own happiness and welfare. He is on this account directly his own enemy, nor can he any otherwise be good or useful to himself than as he continues good to society.*

"NATURAL" BEHAVIOR

The *philosophes* wanted men to behave as good Christians had always wanted them to behave: to be kindly, to refrain from cruelty, to love their fellows,

---

* *Characteristics* (New York, 1900), Vol. I, p. 338.

to subdue their own pride and lusts. Enlightened ethics to a very great extent can be considered a continuation of Christian ethics. But the Enlightened emphasize to a greater degree than Christians the ordinary pleasures of the senses, the prudential virtues, the orderly, efficient conduct they believed they learned from science and from common sense. And they distrusted "enthusiasm," the "holy-rolling" spirit, the mystic's search for wordless ecstasy, the attempt to get beyond the limitations of ordinary reasoning. Indeed, to them these last words were not limitations, but sound "natural" rules like the law of gravity, which only madmen would attempt to contradict. The English poet Alexander Pope (1688–1744) put this distrust of "irrationality" clearly and epigrammatically in his *Essay on Man*:

> Man's superior part
> Uncheck'd may rise, and climb from art to art:
> But when his own great work is but begun,
> What Reason weaves, by Passion is undone.*

Yet, as the eighteenth century wore on, a somewhat different interpretation of good natural behavior came into vogue, exemplified by Jean-Jacques Rousseau. This was the *romantic* sense of Nature, rebelling against the *classical* concept of Nature, which characterized the eighteenth-century Age of Prose and Reason at its height. The romantic view favored releasing the emotions, the sentiments, the simpler appetites of "primitive" or natural" man—that is, man uncorrupted by rationalist philosophy as well as by the accumulated bad traditions and institutions the rationalists had attacked. The ideal now became the *natural* as opposed to the *artificial,* the country man as opposed to the city man, the red Indian as opposed to the white European, the commoner as opposed to the aristocrat, the life of feeling as opposed to the life of reasoning. Here is an extract from the most famous of these books about the delights of the "primitive," Bernardin de Saint-Pierre's *Paul et Virginie* (1789), which deals with two young people lucky enough to grow up in the innocence of a remote island in the Indian Ocean:

> Their lives seemed linked to that of the trees, like those of fauns or dryads. They knew no other historical epochs than those of the lives of their orchards, and no other philosophy than that of doing good, and resigning themselves to the will of Heaven.
> What need, indeed, had these young people of riches or learning such as ours? Even their necessities and their ignorance increased their happiness. No day passed in which they were not of some service to one another, or in which they did not mutually impart some instruction. Yes, instruction; for if errors mingled with it, they were, at least, not of a dangerous character. A pure-minded being has none of that description to fear. Thus grew these children of nature.†

FORMAL PHILOSOPHY

Most of the *philosophes* were too involved with propaganda, agitation, and reform to be called formal philosophers. During the Enlightenment, however, a

---

* Epistle II, ll. 39–42.
† *Paul and Virginia* (London, 1839), pp. 102–103.

famous succession of such philosophers, some of whom we have already discussed, did struggle with the great philosophical problem of epistemology, that is, theory of knowledge. As we have seen, Locke, the empiricist, found the mind a blank sheet on which sense-experience wrote the content. By contrast, George Berkeley (1684–1753), an Irish bishop, made matter depend on mind; he held that "to be is to be perceived," and that all man's ideas are ultimately derived from God's own mind. Hume, the most skeptical of eighteenth-century philosophers, insisted that our minds in organizing sense-experience according to such concepts as causality cannot arrive at effective reality, but only at convenient rules of thinking. Kant, finally, believed he had rescued knowledge from the plight in which Hume had left it. He distinguished between things of our actual experience, *phenomena,* which we can only fit into categories through the work of our minds (much as Hume said) and things-in-themselves, "reality," which Kant called *noumena* and which are in some fashion behind and beyond sense-experience. The mind itself, according to Kant, cannot really grasp *noumena,* yet as moral beings we at least know that *noumena* exist. For Kant "practical reason" thus rescues reality from "pure reason." While simple labels naturally fail to do justice to the ideas of these thinkers, it is not too misleading to think of Locke as an empiricist, Berkeley as a subjectivist, Hume as a skeptic, and Kant as an idealist.

POLITICAL THOUGHT: THE EXAMPLE OF ENGLAND

In political thought, too, the Enlightened appeal to Nature and Reason made evident the inadequacies, the injustices, and the failures of the existing regime. The *philosophes* tended to be especially severe toward the country where most of them lived and worked—France—but they thought even worse of Spain, the Habsburg dominions, and most of the Italian states. The earlier political writers, like the Baron de Montesquieu (1689–1755), admired the English constitution without really understanding it. Indeed, Montesquieu, the Swiss publicist de Lolme, and even Englishmen themselves, like Blackstone in his famous *Commentaries on the Law of England* (1765–1769), believed that English eighteenth-century practice exhibited "separation of powers" and "checks and balances." Crown, Parliament, and the law courts—respectively, the executive, legislative, and judicial powers—were thought of as separate though related fields of action. No one of the three was supreme over the others, and no one power could deprive the individual citizen of his "rights."

We can now see that by the mid-eighteenth century the English government was moving toward the point where the cabinet, a committee of Parliament, would function as part of both the executive and legislative branches and would be in fact supreme or "sovereign" in power. But the widespread misinterpretation of the English constitution had important results, since from it came the principle of checks and balances so fundamental in the American Constitution of 1787. That the twentieth-century United States can sometimes have an executive and a legislature controlled by different parties may be explained in part by the misplaced enthusiasm of eighteenth-century "experts" for the British constitution. In continental Europe, and certainly in France, however, admiration of things British tended to diminish in the second half of the eighteenth century.

LIBERTARIAN AND AUTHORITARIAN REMEDIES

The *philosophes* were by no means agreed as to what new institutions should replace the old regimes in Europe. For purposes of analysis, we may sort them into two contrasting groups, according as they seemed to want an authoritarian state and society or a libertarian state and society. But it must be understood that, being human, the individual thinkers often straddled the line we are trying to draw and were sometimes libertarians, sometimes authoritarians when it came to concrete cases. This is notably true of major figures like Voltaire, Rousseau, and Bentham.

Both libertarians and authoritarians among the *philosophes* start from a position which attributes much, if not all, that is wrong in the human condition to bad environment. But the libertarians take the line that all men, if not absolutely equal in reasoning power, have at least such minimal potential ability to reason that they would behave sensibly if their minds could work as Nature intended them to work. Reason for the libertarians was a seed common to all men but one which could not easily sprout in the stony, waterless soil of Church and State in eighteenth-century Europe. They thought, however, that quite a few such seeds had already begun to sprout in Britain and the United States, and the *philosophes* themselves had, of course, sprouted everywhere in spite of the "bad soil."

The extreme libertarians assumed that elimination of kings, priests, nobles, bewigged judges, stupid professors, and all the rest of the privileged and selfish groups would transform the bad soil into optimum soil, and that all men would then reason perfectly—and there could be no more evil, no more unhappiness. In short, the logical conclusion of the assumption that all men are equally, or at any rate equally enough, gifted with the grace of reason is the doctrine known as philosophical anarchism. The anarchist holds that the whole apparatus of organized society—Church, State, laws, police, any form of compulsion or restraint on the free individual—is bad, and in fact unnecessary. If men are naturally reasonable and impelled by reason to live justly, if the only explanation of their actual wickedness is the corrupting force of institutions, the anarchist solution is certainly logical: do away with the institutions. This extreme doctrine is implicit in much eighteenth-century writing, and quite explicit in a classic of philosophical anarchism, the two-volume *Political Justice* (1793) by the Englishman William Godwin, father-in-law of the poet Shelley. Godwin goes so far as to object to the orchestra leader as an unnecessary and therefore bad wielder of authority; the musicians by themselves, he contends, would make a more perfect, because spontaneous, collaboration.

The opposite pole of thought is occupied by those *philosophes* who did not think that men are naturally reasonable and good enough to be trusted to achieve "spontaneous collaboration." Men, they held, need law, authority, compulsion; but these forms of compulsion ought to be planned and exercised by the right people with the right motives—the *philosophes* and their followers—and not by existing authorities; and these restraints will, of course, be substantially new. In the eighteenth century, this line of thought supported the work of the enlightened despots, as we shall see in the next chapter.

Behind these views lay varying concepts of human nature. The more moderate reformers, like Bentham, held that ordinary men ultimately had the capacity to govern themselves, once enlightened planners had devised and put into practice good institutions, especially utilitarian legal codes and schools. But bad institutions had corrupted people to such an extent that the transition to libertarian government—that is, democracy—had to be carefully managed by wise men, men who could show the people how they had been misled—"brainwashed"—by priests, politicians, and educators. Others, like the utopian socialist Robert Owen, thought that very elaborate institutional bases, at first tried out in small experimental communities, would have to be devised. Under these institutions, men would gradually be molded into the kind of creature the molders—the Enlightened—wanted them to be. Owen put the case for environmentalism as ruthlessly as it has ever been put:

> Any general character, from the best to the worst, from the most ignorant to the most enlightened, may be given to any community, even to the world at large, by the application of proper means; which means are to a great extent at the command and under the control of those who have influence in the affairs of men.*

Still others, notably actual enlightened despots like Frederick the Great of Prussia or Catherine the Great of Russia, seem not to have worried much over the possibility that the masses could be educated for self-government; they seem to have felt that the many must always be sheep, in need of good shepherds to protect them from the wolves.

Very few of the *philosophes* trusted the ability of ordinary men to govern themselves and run a state based on universal suffrage and majority rule. Voltaire, in particular, had the very bright intellectual's impatience with human stupidity and slowness. Yet he was an ardent advocate of reform. As a successful

* Robert Owen, *Essays on the Formation of Human Character* (London, 1840), p. 5. Owen repeats this statement in many of his other works.

Table talk with Voltaire (hand raised); among those present are Diderot and Condorcet.

practical man of business he was indignant at the inefficiencies of the Old Regime, and as a moralist he was indignant at the many obvious injustices in France. Voltaire was the favorite thinker of the enlightened despots and, until a quarrel developed, a close friend of Frederick the Great.

The political writings of the *philosophes*, then, are by no means unambiguously or uniformly egalitarian, libertarian, or democratic, though for the most part they are humanitarian and concerned with the reduction of human suffering. They do, however, consistently attack most existing institutions, and, with few exceptions, they are consistently based on a belief in progress through reform. Most important, these writings, working in men's minds together with the practical demands of the age and also with the inheritance of the recent past, especially that of the English Puritan revolution, brought into existence one of the fundamental institutions of our society—*civil rights*.

"JURIDICAL DEFENSE" AND "SOCIAL CONTACT"

Civil rights are called by the Italian political writer Mosca (1858–1941) rights of "juridical defense," a term which emphasizes their dependence on the law courts. The "right" of an individual or a group to freedom of speech, freedom of assembly, or freedom of worship is in fact the right to appeal from the acts of certain agents of the government (police, censors, even legislators and executives) to other agents (judges) of the same government. In the long history of man "juridical defense" is a remarkable institution, and complex and precarious balances are necessary if a government or a majority of the people are to accept this limitation on their authority. To the historian this is an "unnatural"—that is, a new and unusual—limitation on government, a surprising thing to have emerged from the century that appealed so wholeheartedly to Nature.

Civil rights did not emerge solely as the result of the writings by men like Locke, Montesquieu, Rousseau, and the many others who by the end of the eighteenth century had made "the rights of men" a common phrase. The writers, however, did make possible the successful spread of such doctrines. The process was greatly helped by their use of the concept of a "social contract" which could be invoked to protect juridical defense. This contract for most of these writers was not a specific historical act, signed and delivered at a given time and place in the past; it was rather, in our present terminology, a symbol, a myth, sometimes a more useful way of looking at things than factual history. The concept was used by Locke in *Two Treatises of Government* (1690) to justify actual rebellion by the *governed*, as in the English Glorious Revolution of 1688–1689, if the *government* had violated its contractual obligation to protect the rights of the governed. Locke held that the governed—the "people"—through their elected legislators were the final judges of whether the contract was being fulfilled by the government, the executive. As a moderate, however, Locke did not favor full democratic control of rulers by ruled.

Other writers—Thomas Hobbes in *Leviathan* (1651) and Rousseau in *The Social Contract* (1762)—used this Protean concept of a "social contract" in ways that seem to justify authoritarian rather than libertarian governments. Hobbes, writing amidst the turmoil of the seventeenth-century civil wars in England, claimed that men had found that the complete individual freedom of the "state of nature" made life "solitary, poor, nasty, brutish, and short." Therefore they came together voluntarily in a social contract, by which each man gave up his freedom for the sake of general security. The Leviathan state thus created was to Hobbes wholly sovereign, the individual member wholly without rights against the sovereign—except if the sovereign failed to preserve order and security for members, when the individual thus unprotected might seek other protection.

Rousseau, an intuitive and in our opinion a not wholly consistent thinker, also held that the contract set up a sovereign "general will," against which the individual, if he resisted it, was *morally* wrong. Rousseau's famous phrase, that carrying out this sovereign general will against a recalcitrant individual is *forcing a man to be free,* has provoked endless debate. To us it seems that Rousseau was trying to describe the acceptance of democratically achieved decisions by the good citizen—something like the Quaker "sense of the meeting," that, in short, the concept of the general will is an attempt to understand the psychology of obedience to man-made laws. The difficulty comes when, as often happens, there is no "sense of the meeting," no wholly objective test except the counting of heads to determine majority opinion. But Rousseau definitely says that the general will is not always that of the majority. Clearly no "scientific" test can find the general will.

By the close of the eighteenth century, the right of juridical defense was expressed in something more than philosophical writings. As we shall see in the next chapters, it was embodied in the bills of rights of many American states (especially that of Virginia), in the Bill of Rights added as amendments to the American federal Constitution, and in the French Declaration of the Rights of Man and the Citizen (1789). This basic concept of Western democracy inspired many such constitutional provisions in other countries in the nineteenth and the twentieth centuries. Although juridical defense is not always achieved in the democracies, its existence in law and in aspiration remains a solid distinction between democracy and other forms of state and society in the modern world.

One element that went into the making of juridical defense has perhaps been overemphasized by the cynical but was nevertheless part of the process. The privileged groups who benefitted by the Old Regime—the princes, nobles, higher clergy, holders of all sorts of monopolies and special privileges—made up a major power-complex or "Establishment." The philosophic doctrines of liberty and equality, the emphasis on the individual's rights *against* prescription, against tradition, against the status quo, even against the state, the emphasis in short on *freedom from* controls—all this was part of the complex developed by a rising and prosperous middle class to undermine the Establishment. Cynics and Marxists (by no means the same thing) argue that the middle class used the concepts of individual freedom and equality as a means of attack, not because they believed that the great masses of the lower class were their equals, but because they, the middle class, wanted *freedom from* royal and aristocratic rule. Once more, we observe how much of eighteenth-century philosophical thought was directed against existing arrangements in state and society.

LAISSEZ-FAIRE ECONOMICS

The Enlightenment made classic use of this concept of *freedom from* in the field of economics. French writers known as Physiocrats (Greek, believers in natural rule), and above all Adam Smith in his *Wealth of Nations* (1776), advanced what was essentially an application of the libertarian-anarchist argument to the economic activities of men. From the French came the famous phrase *laissez-faire, laissez-passer* (let be, let pass), which still echoes loudly two centuries later. But while the philosophical anarchist holds that complete individual freedom from any kind of rule is desirable because men are naturally good, the "classical economists," as they are called, had no such optimistic view of human capacity. Indeed, the Scotsman Smith had a characteristically eighteenth-century view of men as being on the whole selfishly covetous of wealth and power.

But, in an equally characteristic eighteenth-century view, Smith maintained that, at least in business matters, if men were allowed to compete freely their selfish attempts to get the most for themselves would result in greater economic production. And, essential to Smith's argument, this competition would actually result in a kind of cancelling out of individual selfishness, and promote a better and more even distribution of wealth, the "greatest good of the greatest number." This "invisible hand," as Smith termed it, of our old eighteenth-century friend, Nature, will do the very best for her favorite child, man, *provided* old cramping institutions and erroneous ideas do not continue to put obstacles (tariffs, monopolies, unwise taxation, licensing, gild restrictions) in the way of such free competition. Adam Smith, however, was no dogmatic extremist: *The Wealth of Nations* recognizes many times that political necessities must often mean government interference with the freedom of the individual, as in national defense.

THE DOCTRINE OF PROGRESS

The men of the eighteenth century felt the need of tearing down, but they also felt the need of rebuilding. The rest of this book is concerned with what has been built on the foundations they left. The process of building has been greatly helped by a new faith, itself the product of the Enlightenment, which sums up and focuses the hopes generated in these centuries of scientific and technological advance. This is the doctrine of Progress.

Most Americans are so used to this doctrine that they do not realize how novel, in the long perspective of history, it is. Presumably, men ever since prehistoric days had been aware of improvements made in their lot, better ways of doing what they wanted to do, indeed of some sort of process or progression in time. But they had no *systematic* idea of what we call progress, above all, no feeling that the masses of men could look forward to a steady improvement in their lot on earth, and in that of their children. They were also aware of bad times succeeding good, of decline, of degeneration. By and large, the Greeks and the Romans saw history as a series of cycles, a Golden Age succeeded by a Silver Age and then by an Iron Age, continuing in unending succession. Orthodox Christianity saw this historical process here on earth as necessarily a decline from the perfection of the Garden of Eden; and if this perfection were ever to come again, it could come not through steady and "rational" human improvement and gradual progress, but only in a Second Coming of Christ. So firmly embedded in men's minds was this concept of the best on earth having been already achieved that even in the Renaissance the humanists looked back to the giants of Greece and Rome as embodiments of a perfection they themselves could not achieve.

Toward the end of the seventeenth century signs appeared that the opposing view was gaining strength: that the present is better than the past, and that the future will be better than the present. These signs in France were the "Quarrel of the Ancients and the Moderns," and in England the "Battle of the Books." The issue in both was whether a "modern," a European of the seventeenth century, could hope to equal, perhaps even to surpass, the achievement of the Greeks and the Romans in art, literature, and philosophy—in short, in their total culture. The quarrel began in 1687 with a poem on "The Century of Louis XIV" read to the Académie Française by Charles Perrault. The distinguished established critic Boileau bitterly attacked Perrault's poem, which he found disparaging to his beloved Greeks and Romans. The quarrel went on for years in France, and crossed the Channel, where the great satirist Jonathan Swift summed it up as pretty much a draw in his *Battle of the Books* (1704).

A tempest in a teapot? On the surface, yes, for most of the participants were literary men concerned with issues of literary taste. Yet the dispute marked a real turning point in men's view of the possibilities of existence on this earth. For, as the eighteenth century wore on, the "moderns" triumphed over the "ancients" all down the line. By the end of the century the French *philosophe* Condorcet wrote his *Sketch of the Progress of the Human Mind* (1794) in which he outlined nine periods of human history, the whole, in spite of a few lapses, indicating a steady upward progress of men toward a fuller, better life. The tenth period, which he believed was being ushered in by the French Revolution of 1789, would mark the final conquest of ignorance, suffering, cruelty, all the train of evil, and the beginnings of a limitless development of human possibilities. Condorcet at least hints at what has been called the doctrine of "natural salvation"—the belief that men may ultimately live as individual organisms forever, in this flesh, on this earth.

Ordinary belief in the doctrine of Progress did not, of course, reach the utopian heights of Condorcet. Even in the eighteenth century there were *philosophes* who had many reservations about the perfectibility of man, many who at least flirted with doctrines of historical decadence. It can be argued that Voltaire was at bottom a historical pessimist, that he thought 1760 showed a decline from 1660. But the central doctrine of the *philosophes* was one of progress, moderate in comparison with Condorcet's, and perhaps best represented by the mathematician d'Alembert's famous introduction to the *Grande Encyclopédie* (1751) or the "Discourse at the Sorbonne" (1750) of Turgot. The multivolumed encyclopedia, edited by Diderot, is a kind of philosophic manifesto, a *summa* of the Enlightenment.

By 1789, then, the average *educated* man in Western Europe and North America had a firm conviction that the course of human history was upward. The obvious cumulative gains of natural science helped him toward this conviction. So, too, did the less obvious but by no means negligible technological improvements of the eighteenth century—better roads, the beginnings of the Industrial Revolution (*see* Chapter 10), geographical discoveries, all nicely recorded in the excellent technical illustrations of the *Grande Encyclopédie*. The average educated man, however, usually found few signs of *moral* progress among mankind, and he was aware that war and disease and poverty and what he called "superstition" were still common. Yet he believed that the steady increase of popular education, the upswing in the arts and sciences, were making inroads on these and other evils. Paradoxically, even the insistence of Rousseau that the progress of the arts and sciences was undermining men's natural innocence and virtue seemed to many of his readers a part of this upswing: men were about to recapture and improve on the original happy state of nature.

What was most significant about these beliefs was the difficulty of reconciling them with the world-view of traditional Christianity. The Enlightened faith in Progress stressed the perfectibility of man *here on earth* in contrast to Christian pessimism about such perfectibility. It questioned, by its reliance on the earth-sciences and on history, the Judaeo-Christian account of creation and much else in the Bible; it questioned the important doctrine of original sin. Together with eighteenth-century beliefs about Nature and Reason, the doctrine of Progress questioned the whole elaborate structure of Christian concepts set up in St. Augustine's *City of God* and in St. Thomas Aquinas's *Summa theologica*. In later chapters we shall see how Christianity endeavored to meet this challenge, and what compromises were made both by Christians and by the Enlightened.

IV. Challenges to the Ideas of the Enlightenment

The ideas of the Enlightenment itself did not go unopposed in the seventeenth and eighteenth centuries. These centuries were "modern," and they displayed that great variety of thought, indeed that existence of contradictory ideologies, still so characteristic of the free West—and nowadays beginning to appear beneath the surface even in the Soviet Union. The intellectual and spiritual range can be sampled if we take some of the leading beliefs and attitudes of the Enlightened on the great questions of man's fate, and set against them examples of different beliefs and attitudes.

CHRISTIAN OPPONENTS

First, there was Christian opposition to Enlightened belief in natural religion, or deism, a rational religion free from mystery and from "enthusiasm." These centuries witnessed the rise in England and in Germany of Protestant sects which had in common an ardent evangelical faith, an emphasis on the emotional and "enthusiastic" phase of Christianity, a dislike for "rational" or "liberal" theology, a fondness for the simple life, and a puritanical distrust of much in human behavior that seemed quite natural to the *philosophes*. In England the Methodists under John Wesley (1703–1791) finally split off from the Church of England; within the relatively conservative Church of England itself these same attitudes were reflected in the "evangelical" group. Both Methodists and evangelical Anglicans worked among the British poor, especially in the new industrial cities. Some historians have gone so far as to maintain that Methodism played a part in halting the spread of French revolutionary ideas in Great Britain after 1789, since good Methodist believers could not accept the atheistic and republican doctrines of the French. In what was to become the United States the eighteenth century saw many Methodist successes, as well as the "great awakening" in New England under the inspiration of Jonathan Edwards (1703–1758) and others.

In Germany, a similar set of beliefs arose among the Pietists, whose name covers a number of groups in rebellion against Lutheran formalism. There were frequent personal interchanges between Methodists and Pietists, and both sent important missionaries and immigrant groups to the thirteen colonies of British North America. Count Zinzendorf (1700-1760) refounded the United Brethren, a sect stemming from John Hus (*see* Chapter 6), and helped many of them to settle in eastern Pennsylvania, where they were often called Moravians. As good Christians, the Pietists and Methodists could hardly be cynical or rigorously pessimistic about ordinary human nature; but they could not accept the worldly materialistic optimism of some *philosophes*, the belief in a coming perfect state of man on earth. Their opposition to the world-view of the Enlightenment was fundamental.

Another very remarkable sect, earlier in origin than the Methodists, may exemplify the complex correlation between Christianity and the Enlightenment. This is the Society of Friends (*see* Chapter 8), generally known as the Quakers because of their trembling when under religious excitement. Their behavior was "enthusiastic," not the calm deportment of the rationalist; moreover, their doctrine of the "inner light" was profoundly mystical. Yet much in the Society of Friends was quite congruous with the Enlightenment and with worldly success. The inner light itself was in some ways like the light of Reason, most of all because of its tenacious roots in moral—and economic—individualism. Like the *philosophes*, the Quakers believed in toleration, in persuasion, in gradualness; like them, the Quakers disliked the artificial, the pretentious, the decorated, the entire hierarchy of rank and status. Both in England and in America, after the first persecutions to which as a radical sect they were subjected—persecutions notably severe in seventeenth-century Massachusetts—the Quakers prospered strikingly in the world of business.

Even in France, the spiritual center of the Enlightenment, the conservative clergy and some court circles opposed the views of the *philosophes*. Moreover, the small but gifted and influential group of Jansenists were far removed from deism. Named after the seventeenth-century Dutch theologian Jansen, they were high-minded, pious puritans, who have been called a bit tritely the Calvinists of the Roman Catholic Church. The Jansenists' mistrust of absolute authority brought them into prolonged conflict with the Crown and with the conservative clergy. Pascal, the great scientist and mathematician, was closely identified with the Jansenists, and defended them—some would say, rather, attacked their opponents, the Jesuits—in a famous pamphlet, the *Provincial Letters* (1657). Pascal's fine, clear style in writing, his respect for a mathematician's logic, and his achievements in science are in basic agreement with the spirit of the Age of Reason; his basic philosophical position, however, was quite opposed to that of the *philosophes*. Here is a celebrated passage from his *Pensées* (*Reflections*):

> We know Truth not only through reason, but also by the heart; it is in this way that we have knowledge of first principles, and it is in vain that Reason, which has no share in them, tries to dispute them . . . it is on the knowledge supplied by the heart and intuition that reason rests, founding thereon all its utterances.

These are surely not the words of a rationalist, yet Pascal did not belittle the intellect, as witness this even more famous quotation from his *Pensées*—"Man is a reed, the feeblest thing in nature; but he is a thinking reed."[*]

---

[*] Pascal, *Pensées*, translated by Martin Turnell (New York, 1962), pp. 161, 221.

INTELLECTUAL CRITICS

Many eighteenth-century intellectuals cannot be labelled "rationalists" in the sense that a major *philosophe* like Bentham can be so labelled. Here are three celebrated examples. Jonathan Swift (1667–1745), the author of the *Battle of the Books,* had a brilliant and inventive mind. Best known for *Gulliver's Travels* (1726), a satire which he would be surprised and perhaps pleased to discover is now edited as a book for children, Swift was a troubled soul, capable of great indignation and deep despondency; he was skeptical of, if not, indeed, hostile to, the natural science of his day (read his attack on the Royal Society as the "Academy of Lagado" in *Gulliver's Travels*), all in all no reasonable eighteenth-century thinker. Denis Diderot (1713–1784), editor of the *Encyclopédie*, spearhead of the French Enlightenment, was a many-sided thinker who by no means thought that Reason is All or that men are perfectible here on earth, and who specifically denied the doctrine that men are wholly the product of their environment. Another man of letters, whom we feel we know intimately through Boswell's famous *Life,* was Samuel Johnson (1709–1784), English Tory, anti-*philosophe,* anti-Scot, anti-American, violently certain of his opinions, a long-lived enjoyer of poor health, and, like Swift, subject to black despair.

The thinkers of the Enlightenment have been charged with considering the processes of human relations as essentially mechanistic, part of the "Newtonian world-machine." Or, to put the matter negatively, they have been accused of not taking sufficient account of organic growth, development, history as *process*. This is true of some thinkers. But the Anglicized Irishman Edmund Burke (1729–1797), opposed to what he held was the *philosophes'* contempt for the past as a "tissue of errors," came to the defense of the past as a living part of the present. Here is Burke's famous passage on the "social contract" in *Reflections on the Revolution in France:*

> Society is, indeed, a contract. Subordinate contracts for objects of mere occasional interest may be dissolved at pleasure; but the state ought not to be considered as nothing better than a partnership agreement in a trade of pepper and coffee, calico or tobacco, or some other such low concern, to be taken up for a little temporary interest, and to be dissolved by the fancy of the parties. It is to be looked on with other reverence; because it is not a partnership in things subservient only to gross animal existence of a temporary and perishable nature. It is a partnership in all science, a partnership in all art, a partnership in every virtue and all perfection. As the ends of such a partnership cannot be obtained in many generations, it becomes a partnership not only between those who are living, but between those who are living, those who are dead, and those who are to be born.*

In the second half of the eighteenth century, especially in Germany, a movement arose which emphasized an organic view of society, insisting on the similarities between a nation and an organism—living, changing, growing—which cannot, like a machine, be planned, put together, and taken apart for repairs. These views were notably expressed in *Ideas for the Philosophy of the History of Mankind* by Herder (1744–1803), who helped to lay the foundations of much of nineteenth-

---

* *Burke's Politics,* edited by R. J. S. Hoffman and Paul Levade (New York, 1959), p. 318.

century thought. Neither Herder nor other great figures of the German Enlightenment like Kant and Lessing fit well into the general frame of the Anglo-French Enlightenment. They were uncertain about the possibilities of rational emancipation for the masses; they disliked mechanistic concepts of society; they were not at all sure that Progress was going to be certain or rapid. At bottom, and in spite of their appeal to *Aufklärung* (Enlightenment), they were romanticists, men of the heart, not of the head.

Thus eighteenth-century thought offers not only the rationalist view of history as a kind of varied if repetitive museum exhibit of human nature, not only the vague notion of history as progress from ignorance to enlightenment, but several other philosophies of history as well. The Italian Vico (1668–1744) in his *Scienza nuova* (*New Science*) anticipated later ideas which combine the notion of historical cycles with that of upward movement in spiral form, and insisted that "to know" in human affairs meant not just passive thinking but "to do" or "to make." In short, the eighteenth century was very far from looking at the past as merely "philosophy teaching by examples," let alone as a "tissue of errors" best buried and forgotten.

PESSIMISM, CONSERVATISM—AND OPTIMISM

Eighteenth-century thought is usually described as optimistic; yet one of the most famous works of the Enlightenment, Voltaire's *Candide* (1759), is a bitterly sarcastic outburst against the philosophic optimism represented by Leibniz (1646–1716), who "proved" by deductive reasoning that all is for the best in this best of all possible worlds. In his tale Voltaire puts his innocent hero Candide through the most horrible experiences of human cruelty and indifference, as well as such "natural" horrors as the Lisbon earthquake of 1755 in which thousands perished. Much of the characteristic writing on human nature and human potential in the Enlightenment takes the form of pessimistic, if not cynical, and even sardonic aphorism. A long line of such witty aphorists runs from the French La Rochefoucauld and La Bruyère through the English Mandeville to the Benjamin Franklin of *Poor Richard,* who was better natured than the others but by no means an idealist.

Nor, finally, was the radical reforming spirit of the *philosophes* without a countervailing current. In Britain, as we have already noted, both Edmund Burke and the Methodists exerted a conservative influence in their differing ways. In the United States, John Adams (1735–1826), though he was one of the leaders of the American Revolution, was certainly a philosophical conservative. And the famous Federalist Papers, written by Hamilton, Madison, and John Jay in defense of the proposed Constitution of 1787, are moderately conservative in outlook. In Europe, as we shall see in the next chapter, some of the enlightened despots, such as the Austrian Joseph II, were rash reformers, but the basic concepts underlying enlightened despotism were quite contrary to the radical democratic trust in the common man which has been one of the major legacies of the Enlightenment.

To sum up: In attitudes toward religion, philosophy, man's essential nature, toward the possibilities of life on this earth, the seventeenth and eighteenth centuries were by no means of one mind. You can find somewhere in these centuries, even if only in primitive form, almost all the problems—and proposed solutions—with which we now live and struggle. Yet there does emerge from the

Watteau, "Embarkation for Cythera," 1717.

Enlightenment something new: a widely—though not universally—held belief that *all men* here on this earth can be, and in a not too distant future should be, well fed, well housed, well clothed, healthy, happy. This belief, we repeat, is a kind of cosmic optimism at variance, at least in its "this-worldliness," with the traditional Judaeo-Christian view of man expressed in Job 5:7: "Man is born unto trouble, as the sparks fly upward"; and at variance too with much traditional lore about human capacities and human behavior. It remains, even today, a revolutionary belief in many parts of the world.

V. Arts and Letters

CLASSICISM AND ROMANTICISM

The art and literature of the "Age of Prose and Reason," as the seventeenth and eighteenth centuries are often labeled, made no more of a single, monolithic block than did its philosophic and religious thought. In these areas, too, the period was one of transition, still best put in the familiar blanket words, from "classicism" to "romanticism." But these isms, if necessary abstractions, are still abstractions; in real life the artists and men of letters, including the *philosophes,* exhibited in their work various mixtures of the classical and the romantic.

There are many attempts to define these old favorites of criticism, usually in contrasting terms. The classical is form, the romantic color; the classical is rational man thinking; the romantic is emotional man feeling; the classical is analytical, didactic, fond of preaching; the romantic is lyrical, mystical, fond of prophesying; the classical is controlled and moderate, the romantic uncontrolled and heaven-storming; the classical sees Nature as orderly, at bottom subject to discernible uniformities in spite of its superficial variety and irregularity; the romantic sees Nature as wild, at bottom somehow escaping into the unpredictable, the miracle, out of the straitjacket of uniformity the scientist tries to impose on it. All these contrasting pairs have some validity. Perhaps the classical and the romantic should each be seen as a "cluster of ideas," to use the term of A. O. Lovejoy, or as "syndromes," to use a word borrowed from medical usage by W. T. Jones, and meaning a set of signs and symptoms (from the Greek, "a running together").*

On the whole, eighteenth-century classicism developed directly from the aristocratic humanism of the Renaissance (*see* Chapter 6). In the arts, and to a degree in literature, the classical tendency was not strikingly turned toward innovation, and most certainly was not turned toward democratic tastes and ways. The romantic tendency remained in these centuries on the whole an undercurrent, appearing in some phases of the realistic novel and in the extremes of baroque art, innovating but not yet revolutionary as it would be in the early nineteenth century. One may risk the broad generalization that both cultural tendencies worked together as *dissolvents* of the old regime in the West, the classical because of its analysis of the irrationalities and inefficiencies of existing institutions, the romantic because of its indignation at the injustices of life under such institutions, sometimes indignation at the very existence of any institutions.

PROSE LITERATURE

Samplings will suggest the variety and many-mindedness of the art and literature of the Enlightenment. First of all, the eighteenth century marked the coming of age of a literary genre that offers a fine field for the study of human behavior in all its range—the novel. By 1800 almost all the familiar forms of the novel existed. The English writer Henry Fielding (1707–1754), in his *Tom Jones* and other novels, is the observer, the moderate but not insistent moralist, in short, the realist. Both Daniel Defoe (1660–1731), in his *Robinson Crusoe* and *Moll Flanders,* and Jonathan Swift, whose *Gulliver's Travels* and *Battle of the Books* we have already noted, were admirable storytellers and remarkably accurate recorders of the little details of life. Samuel Richardson (1689–1761) combined realism and emotionalism in very long and very popular novels, such as *Pamela* and *Clarissa,* composed in the form of letters.

Voltaire used the short novel, or *conte,* for satire, propaganda for the Enlightenment, and, as rather more than a mere by-product, amusement. The long novel *Les Liaisons dangereuses* by Choderlos de Laclos (1741–1803) was clearly in the line of the psychological novel, and more especially in a form of which the French have been very fond, the painstaking, involved, and not very titillating analysis of relations between the sexes. Rousseau wrote a novel, the

---

* Lovejoy, *Essays in the History of Ideas* (Baltimore, 1948); Jones, *The Romantic Syndrome* (The Hague, 1961).

Nouvelle Héloïse, a great success in its day, more a plea for his own sentimental ideas about love and duty than a psychological novel. There was even, in the "Gothic novel" such as Horace Walpole's *The Castle of Otranto* (1764), an anticipation of the nineteenth-century romantic thriller. Toward the end of the century, the Marquis de Sade (1740–1814) anticipated in *Justine* and other novels the twentieth-century novel of sex and violence. Only the historical novel is missing in the list, and this arrived early in the nineteenth century with Sir Walter Scott.

    The English satiric poet Alexander Pope had announced in a famous line that "the proper study of mankind is man," and the eighteenth-century took him at his word. Not only in the novel, but in essays, biography, memoirs, autobiography, and collected correspondence the century was extraordinarily rich in wide-ranging, subtle, and fascinating psychological observations, cast of course in traditional literary terms, not in those of the as yet barely formalized science of psychology. A representative selection might include the *Memoirs* of the Duc de St. Simon (1675–1755), Boswell's *Life of Johnson,* the *Autobiography* of the historian Edward Gibbon (1737–1794), the *Confessions* of Rousseau, the *Autobiography* of Benjamin Franklin, bits of the abundant published correspondence of Voltaire and that of the English dilettante and man of letters Horace Walpole

Rubens, "Lion Hunt," 1616–1621.

(1717–1797), the correspondence, in their old age, between Adams and Jefferson, and some of the writings of the aphorists we have mentioned before. Glancing at even a few of these will vitiate glib generalizations about the undiluted rationalism and optimism of the eighteenth-century view of man.

DRAMA AND POETRY

The Enlightenment was rich also in the literature of the stage. Save for the great classical playwrights of seventeenth-century France, notably Corneille and Racine, this was not a period of great tragic drama. But in comedy the age was at its best. Some of the finest English plays were written in supremely urbane and witty prose by the Restoration dramatists of the second half of the seventeenth century. Wycherly, Congreve, and others, and by Sheridan and Goldsmith in the second half of the eighteenth. Restoration comedy seemed to the nineteenth-century Victorians too indecent to be on the boards, but our own century has staged frequent revivals of *The Country Wife* of Wycherley and Congreve's *Way of the World*, for instance. Sheridan's *School for Scandal* and Goldsmith's *She Stoops to Conquer* have always been popular.

In Molière, contemporary of Corneille and Racine during the age of Louis XIV, French letters possess one of the greatest comic poets in the history of the theater; wit and compassion lend depth and a touch of the tragic to his satire. In a lighter vein the French eighteenth century produced the sophisticated comedies of Marivaux, while the Italian produced those of Goldoni. Forerunners of later romantic mixtures—some would say confusions—of tragedy and comedy were a whole set of what the French sardonically call "tearful comedy" (*comédie larmoyante*). These dramas, or melodramas, deal mostly with middle-class or peasant life, with the trials and tribulations of ordinary, not heroic people; they are of course in prose. Many of them have a touch of soap opera, though some very distinguished men of letters wrote in this genre, notably Diderot himself, whose *The Natural Son* (1757) is a good specimen. So, too, is the English George Lillo's *The London Merchant* (1731), the earliest of this genre. Even the German Lessing, a more capable dramatist than these, and his fellow-countryman Schiller wrote romantic dramas, joining comedy with tragedy.

This Age of Prose was not entirely deficient in great poetry. It had no epic poetry of note save for Milton's *Paradise Lost* (1667), which might be considered the last great work of the Christian humanism of the Renaissance. Voltaire attempted an epic recital of the deeds of Henry IV, the *Henriade*, which, while perhaps mostly responsible for Henry's modern popularity, cannot be considered a great poem. The light verse of the age, however, was excellent, and when concerned with love, as it often was, by no means lacked the lyric touch, though it rarely lost its sense of proportion and swooned. Satiric verse reached its highest point with Boileau in France and Dryden and Pope in England.

In the late eighteenth century, Gray in England with "An Elegy Written in a Country Churchyard," André Chénier in France, and Goethe and Schiller in Germany all composed lyric and dramatic poetry acceptable even to the first generation of nineteenth-century romanticists. Men of this nineteenth-century generation—Wordsworth, Coleridge, Victor Hugo, the German romanticists—in rebellion against their predecessors, fixed on the Enlightenment, and especially on its poets, the reputation of lacking feeling, depth, and passion, of being mere versifiers, not poets at all. But while the Enlightenment produced little profoundly moving poetry, its open-minded concern with understanding human beings as they really are and its ardent reforming zeal made it one of the great ages of Western culture. It by no means deserves the scorn poured on it by Wordsworth, who could refer to Voltaire's *Candide* as "that dull product of a scoffer's pen."

PAINTING

The fine arts during these centuries developed styles set in the Renaissance, in both south and north, and made no radical innovations. As we shall see in Chapter 11, the fine arts remained essentially conservative even during the great political overturn of the French Revolution and Napoleon. In painting, the landscape, incidental in earlier centuries, became a central theme in the luminous and very "classical" work by Claude Lorrain (1600–1682). Gainsborough (1727–1788), better known for his portraits, painted gentle and agreeable landscapes, and laid out some of the foundations for what became a typically nineteenth-century genre. Portraiture was one of the great art forms of the Enlightenment, usually aristocratic, deferential toward its subjects, but not without the touch of realism. The works of Gainsborough and Reynolds in England are among the leading examples. In eighteenth-century France especially, a long line of artists produced graceful and often sensuous paintings for the salons of the rich and the wellborn. Watteau, perhaps the greatest of these, was one of the most delicate and skilled of painters; Boucher and Fragonard continued the tradition. In Italy, the great Venetian line finished in a burst of color and grand architectural forms with Tiepolo, and in the north another line of essentially Renaissance painters in the grand manner runs through Van Dyck and Rubens in the Low Countries, Poussin in France. Poussin, in particular, so sculptures his figures in painting as to deserve the label "neoclassical."

Rembrandt, "Self-Portrait," c. 1660.

But the painting of these centuries was not by any means confined to the "grand manner," with heroic or noble or delicately lascivious subjects, clear and classic lines, clear and classic color. The seventeenth was the great century of painting in the Low Countries and Spain. The Dutch and Flemish—a Vermeer, a Terborch, a Frans Hals—painted with admirable technique both portraits and domestic interiors of their land, which produced the first of the great bourgeois cultures. But the Dutch also had Rembrandt, a supreme painter, always a master draftsman, an admirable realist in his younger days, later a searcher for the mysterious and profound, the light that never was. In Spain, Velásquez, court painter though he was, painted what he saw with an eye that observed more than the surface reality of the camera. At the very end of the eighteenth century Goya also painted what he saw, and with a brush dipped in moral acid as he looked at a decadent court and nobility.

Still another strain in these centuries was the painting with a lesson and a story, mostly concerned with middle-class life and in some ways comparable to the "tearful comedies." In France this school is admirably exemplified by Chardin, with his simple, homely scenes, and by Greuze, though he is at times obvious and even covertly indecent. In England Hogarth did several series, reproduced in comparatively inexpensive prints, such as "The Rake's Progress," "Marriage à la Mode," "Beer Street," and "Gin Lane," which are often entertaining as well as didactic and always technically excellent.

THE OTHER FINE ARTS

In architecture and interior decoration styles moved from a Renaissance base to the baroque of the seventeenth and eighteenth centuries, the rococo of the eighteenth, and, toward the end of the latter, a return to a more direct dependence on the Greco-Roman known as neoclassical. These styles were at their most typical in churches and palaces. Baroque was richly decorated, often both heavy and heaven-storming, predominant in central Europe and at Rome, and also in the Spanish style known as Chirrurgeresque, good examples of which may be seen in many old Mexican churches. Rococo was simply a more delicate outgrowth of baroque, popular above all in France and seen at its best in the furniture style named for Louis XVI. The neoclassical, a frank return to Greek and Roman styles, significantly reached its peak under Napoleon (*see* Chapter 11).

There were, of course, national variants. In England, baroque never quite made itself a home, though in sheer heaviness few palaces exceed Blenheim Palace, given by a grateful nation to the Duke of Marlborough and named for his greatest victory. English architecture generally ran to somewhat simpler and more traditional lines; it culminates in many country houses and urban homes of the wealthy known in England as Georgian and in America as colonial. The public buildings of restored Williamsburg in Virginia are a splendid example of eighteenth-century English architecture.

MUSIC

The crowning artistic glory of the age of Enlightenment was its music. Johann Sebastian Bach (1685–1750) brought to perfection the techniques of seventeenth-century composers, notably the difficult art of the fugue, an intricate musical form in which each voice or instrument begins a theme in turn and adds repetitions and elaborations. Bach composed many works for the organ, the most baroque of instruments, and wrote dramatic choral works on religious themes. His music was thoroughly out of tune with the anticlericalism of the age.

Handel (1685–1759) wrote more than 40 operas, rarely performed today. He used themes from the Bible for *The Messiah, Israel in Egypt,* and other vigorous oratorios directed at a mass audience and arranged for large choruses. These elaborate works differed greatly from the original oratorios of seventeenth-century Italy, written for the tiny prayer chapels called oratories.

Although Bach and Handel composed many instrumental suites and concertos, it was not until the second half of the eighteenth century that orchestral music came to the fore. New instruments then appeared, notably the piano, which greatly extended the limited range and depth of the older keyboard instrument,

Blenheim Palace (begun 1705), home of the Duke of Marlborough.

the harpsichord. New musical forms also appeared, the sonata and the symphony, developed largely by Joseph Haydn (1732–1809). He wrote more than 50 piano pieces in the sonata-allegro form, in which two contrasting themes are stated in turn, developed, interwoven, repeated, and finally resolved in a *coda* (the Italian for "tail").

An operatic landmark of the early century was John Gay's *Beggar's Opera* (1728). This tuneful work caricatured English society and politics in Hogarthian vein. Christoph Gluck (1714–1787) revolutionized the technique of the tragic opera. His operas were well-constructed musical dramas, not merely vehicles for the display of vocal pyrotechnics. Gluck, however, was very "classical" in contrast to later "romantic" musicians. He kept to the established custom of taking heroes and heroines from classical mythology, and he did not try to key music directly to human emotions. It has been said—by a romantic, of course—that the words of the lovely air in which Gluck's Orpheus mourns the loss of Eurydice might just as well read "I have found her" as "I have lost her."

Eighteenth-century opera, symphony, and chamber works all reached a summit with Wolfgang Amadeus Mozart (1756–1791). Unbelievably prolific, he produced the three great symphonies familiar to concert audiences as No. 39 (E flat major), No. 40 (G minor), and No. 41 ("The Jupiter") in two months during the summer of 1788. Three of Mozart's operas were in the comic Italian vein of opera buffa. In *Così fan tutte* (*Thus Do All Women*) he combined amorous farce with enchanting melodic duets. He derived his delightful *Marriage of Figaro* from Beaumarchais's satirical comedy, though some of the satire vanished in the lightness of the opera. Tragic overtones appeared in *Don Giovanni*, depicting the havoc wrought by Don Juan on earth before his eventual punishment in hell. Mozart composed with consummate skill mournfully romantic arias for the Don's victims and elegantly seductive ballads for the Don himself. The lightness of

Mozart's music both underplays and accentuates the essential tragedy of the libretto. In his last opera, *The Magic Flute*, Mozart abandoned the Italian style and tried to create a consciously German work, which apparently sought to vindicate the enlightened ideas of Joseph II and to decry the conservatism of Maria Theresa.

The great composers of the eighteenth century borrowed freely from folktunes and ballads and were rewarded by having their themes whistled in the streets. Mozart's operas, Haydn's symphonies, and the great choral works of Bach and Handel have never lost this popular appeal. They have retained the capacity to engage the listener's emotions. In this sense, music probably came closest to resolving harmoniously the great conflict between reason and emotion, between the abstractions of the Enlightenment and the flesh-and-blood realities of human existence.

VI. Conclusion: The Reasons Why

We must now attempt to answer the question: Why did this great material and spiritual revolution of the Enlightenment take place at the time and in the place it did? The historian is bound to seek the answer in the complex processes of history; he must insist that there is no single factor in the process, but a whole set, some of them already long at work by the eighteenth century, all interacting, all mutually dependent variables. He is dealing with a *syndrome*. He may for convenience distinguish between such material factors as the actual techniques of production and distribution in economic life and such related intellectual factors as belief in Progress, but he will realize that in the real world the material and the spiritual are never separated, always mutually reinforcing. In simplest terms, the "revolution" of modern times meant a vast increase in human ability to create —and distribute—usable material goods and services. But the human desire for more such goods, the feeling, spreading to all classes from the eighteenth century on, that such goods are desirable and attainable, was itself a continuing factor in the revolutionary process. This feeling seems now, in the 1960's, to have spread to peoples all over the globe.

First, and basic to the creation of modern society, was the great leap forward of science and technology. This in turn was made possible by a long cumulative process to which contributed the craft skills of generations of medieval workers, the very real achievements of medieval "pure" science, notably mathematics and logic; also, generations of scholarly monks established a tradition of patience and attention to detail without which there could be no natural science. That all these accumulated skills and intellectual attitudes are not in themselves an adequate explanation of the modern revolution is clear from a simple example: most of these skills and attitudes existed by the third

Bernini's Throne of St. Peter (1657–1666), in the apse of St. Peter's, Rome.

century B.C. in the Hellenistic world without producing any such revolution. As we saw earlier in this book (*see* page 105) the steam engine was known in Alexandria, but only as a curiosity, a toy (compare the invention of gunpowder by the Chinese, who used it in holiday firecrackers, not in engines of war).

One economic difference between the Hellenistic world and that of early modern Europe will give us a second contributing factor. Whereas the former had a large supply of slave labor, the European world, especially in the towns, had only free labor, and perhaps over the years an increasing shortage of such labor. Therefore, the early modern producer had an incentive to encourage invention of better ways of producing goods, the free craftsman of inventive talents had a stimulus lacking to the slave or freedman of the ancient world, and European investors had chances for using their capital not available to the rich financiers of Rome.

To this factor may be added a closely related third, brought out especially in the work of the great German sociologist Max Weber, with whose ideas we have already dealt with at some length. A society with many Calvinists tended to produce much, *to consume solidly but without "waste"* (we are speaking here in terms of economics, not in terms of art or morals). Therefore, under competitive conditions, its business leaders accumulated the kind of surplus we call capital, which they could invest in the methods of production that have so enriched the West. The Weber thesis can be exaggerated; it leaves out the obvious fact that some of the economic foundations of modern Europe were laid in the Mediterranean well before the Protestant revolt took place. But the forces Weber emphasizes did build on these foundations. *Unworldly* or *antiworldly* asceticism such as the retreats to the desert of early Christian times would never have added to our material wealth; but the almost paradoxical *worldly,* even *"materialistic," asceticism* encouraged by the Protestant ethic—and in many parts of Europe such as the Rhineland and the Low Countries by the new Catholic ethic of the Catholic Reformation as well—did contribute to the creation of our productive modern world.

A fourth factor, closely meshed with the moral and intellectual attitude Weber analyzed, was the transformation of the northwest European states into what can be called not unfairly "business" societies, already commercially advanced by the eighteenth century. It is true that some of the trappings of medieval and Renaissance societies survived in these lands even into the nineteenth century; but these trappings were seen by the Enlightened as obstacles, and therefore, to those optimists, as a stimulus to action. With the many changes of the seventeenth and eighteenth centuries, the middle classes had attained great direct economic power and much indirect political power. Sufficient here to cite France, on the surface an unchanged absolutist state up to 1789, in fact a mercantile state from the mid-seventeenth century on, a state in which the business and professional classes, however much they were snubbed and despised by the old nobility, had a very important and even decisive role. The state and the society of Louis XIV were very different from those of Louis XI or Francis I.

A fifth and essential factor in the building of our modern world was the achievement of a degree of ordered and efficient government, without which the new business and industrial enterprise could not flourish. This kind of government emerged first in the city-states of Italy in the late Middle Ages, and, as we have already seen, was developed on a national scale in the "new monarchies" and other states of northern and western Europe in early modern times. Even the best of these states did not achieve perfect order and efficiency; there were various restraints on international trade, and there were intermittent wars. Nonetheless, large political units were well enough run to permit the growth of the new productive methods, and to provide broader markets for the commodities they produced.

Indeed, a sixth and closely related factor may well be the competitive nature of relations among these new states—including their wars. Mercantilism was a new kind of international competition, one that involved deliberate and organized political encouragement of *national productiveness* and not just "glory." Even warfare, in itself economically wasteful, has in the opinion of some historians stimulated inventiveness and productiveness. Note further that the nation-states thus vying with one another in all fields of human action were, in contrast with the petty city-states of ancient Greece, big enough and well organized enough for large-scale production.

A seventh factor was the great discoveries that began in the fifteenth century and were still being extended in the Pacific and in the interior of the New World in the eighteenth. We have noted that in many ways these discoveries seem to have started the modern world on its extraordinary path to wealth. Certainly the new worlds, by providing the raw materials in exchange for the trade goods of the mother country, enabled mercantilism to work as well as it did for so long. And at least as important, these new worlds presented men with new experiences, helped make it possible for them to face innovation without horror, indeed with pleasant anticipation.

This last suggests an eighth factor. Over the ages, most men in most societies have been exceedingly distrustful of innovation of any kind, or have just not innovated. For this attitude the English political writer Bagehot in his *Physics and Politics* (1869) used the suggestive term "cake of custom." For real social change to be effective, that cake of custom must be broken. Our eighth factor, and one that definitely reinforced the others, was the breaking of the cake of medieval culture begun in the late Middle Ages and accepted by most educated persons in the eighteenth century under the name of "Progress." Men were—and are even today—in many little ways more addicted to customary institutions, the old habits, of life than we Americans sometimes think. Yet our culture is now prepared to face change, often very great change, as one of the facts of life; and many of us believe in change as good in itself.

Finally, all these factors had to be summed up in a faith, a philosophy of life, which we have in this chapter sought to explain in some detail. This is the belief that all men have a *right* to expect happiness on this earth, a happiness that must include good food, good shelter, and the satisfaction of certain spiritual as well as material needs; or, negatively, the belief that this earth ought not to be for *any* group or class of men a vale of tears, a place of suffering, a place where men should starve or even be desperately poor—in short, the belief that men should experience no evil, only good. In so utopian and simple a form the Enlightenment never really held this faith. But it none the less became a kind of emotional underpinning for our democratic society, and it remains, despite critical attacks on it which we shall meet later (in Chapter 13), a basic and persistent factor in the present-day world.

9

READING SUGGESTIONS (asterisk indicates paperbound edition)

General Works

P. Smith, *A History of Modern Culture*, 2 vols. (*Collier). An older work, and a mine of information on aspects of culture often neglected in intellectual histories.

C. Brinton, *The Shaping of Modern Thought* (*Spectrum). A survey of intellectual history from the Renaissance on.

F. Manuel, *The Age of Reason* (*Cornell). A brief introduction by a scholar who has also written detailed monographs on the era.

P. Gay, *The Enlightenment: The Rise of Modern Paganism* (Knopf, 1966). An interpretation, with a rich bibliography, by another scholar who has written more detailed works on the period.

C. J. Friedrich, *The Age of the Baroque, 1610–1660*; W. L. Dorn, *Competition for Empire, 1740–1763*; L. Gershoy, *From Despotism to Revolution, 1763–1789* (*Torchbooks). These three volumes in the Rise of Modern Europe series are particularly helpful on questions of intellectual and cultural history; they have full bibliographies.

The New Cambridge Modern History, Vol. V: *The Ascendency of France, 1648–1688*, and Vol. VII: *The Old Regime, 1713–1763* (Cambridge University, 1961, 1957). Contain some useful chapters on topics covered in this chapter.

J. Lively, *The Enlightenment* (*Barnes & Noble). Its meaning and legacy viewed by the *philosophes* themselves and by later interpreters.

Science

H. F. Kearney, *Origins of the Scientific Revolution* (*Barnes & Noble). A many-sided introduction to this controversial topic.

H. Butterfield, *The Origins of Modern Science, 1300–1800* (*Free Press). A lively and controversial survey, minimizing the contribution of scientists before Galileo.

A. N. Whitehead, *Science and the Modern World* (*Free Press). An incisive and influential critique of what modern science really means and implies; rather difficult but well worth the effort.

A. R. Hall, *The Scientific Revolution, 1500–1800* (*Beacon). A solid account, written from the standpoint of the historian.

L. S. Feuer, *The Scientific Intellectual: The Psychological and Sociological Origins of Modern Science* (Basic Books, 1963). A stimulating interpretation from a more controversial point of view.

A. Wolf, *A History of Science, Technology, and Philosophy in the Sixteenth and Seventeenth Centuries* (*Torchbooks). A standard account.

Nature, Reason, Progress

P. Hazard, *The European Mind, 1680–1715* and *European Thought in the Eighteenth Century from Montesquieu to Lessing* (*Meridian). The first of these two studies is especially dramatic, as indicated by its original French title: *La Crise de la conscience européenne*.

C. Becker, *The Heavenly City of the Eighteenth-Century Philosophers* (*Yale). A delightful essay, much influenced by Whitehead's *Science and the Modern World*, and stressing the parallels between the medieval Age of Faith and the Age of Reason. May be coupled with the critiques in R. O. Rockwood, ed., *Carl Becker's Heavenly City Revisited* (Cornell, 1958).

J. B. Bury, *The Idea of Progress* (*Dover). A famous pioneering study of enlightened optimism.

E. Cassirer, *The Philosophy of the Enlightenment* (*Beacon). An important study of basic principles.

G. R. Havens, *The Age of Ideas: From Reaction to Revolution in Eighteenth-Century France* (*Free Press). A most useful volume, full abreast of modern research.

K. Martin, *French Liberal Thought in the Eighteenth Century* (*Torchbooks). A brilliant, comprehensive, and opinionated survey.

L. G. Crocker, *An Age of Crisis: Man and World in Eighteenth Century France*

(Hopkins, 1959). An informative and scholarly study.

N. L. Torrey, *The Spirit of Voltaire* (Columbia, 1938). A thoughtful study.

E. Cassirer, *The Question of Jean-Jacques Rousseau* (°Midland); A. Cobban, *Rousseau and the Modern State* (Allen & Unwin, 1934); J. L. Talmon, *The Origins of Totalitarian Democracy* (°Praeger). Differing judgments on a highly controversial thinker.

Arts and Letters

S. E. Bethell, *The Cultural Revolution of the Seventeenth Century* (Roy, 1951). A literary study with fruitful suggestions for the historian of ideas.

M. R. Bukofzer, *Music in the Baroque Era* (Norton, 1947); H. Leichtentritt, *Music, History, and Ideas* (Harvard, 1938); P. H. Láng, *Music in Western Civilization* (Norton, 1941). Three works helpful for the interpretation of music and history.

Sources

C. Brinton, ed., *The Portable Age of Reason Reader,* and H. Hugo, ed., *The Portable Romantic Reader* (°Viking). Wide-ranging selections, with illuminating introductory comments.

F. Manuel, ed., *The Enlightenment* (°Spectrum), and I. Berlin, ed., *The Age of Enlightenment: The Eighteenth-century Philosophers* (°Mentor). Two other useful anthologies.

B. R. Redman, ed., *The Portable Voltaire* (°Viking). Well-chosen selections, with an informative introduction.

Montesquieu, *The Spirit of the Laws* (°Hafner).

Rousseau, *The First and Second Discourses* (°St. Martin's); *The Social Contract* (°Hafner).

Beccaria, *On Crimes and Punishments* (°Liberal Arts).

10

The Eighteenth Century

War, Politics, and Economics

Battle of Germantown in the American Revolution.

In starting our consideration of the eighteenth century with intellectual history, as we did in the preceding chapter, we violated the modern historian's practice of starting with the "hard facts" of political, economic, institutional, and social history. We did this deliberately, in the conviction that the "ideas" of the *philosophes* are particularly important for understanding the century, that these ideas themselves are "facts." Of course, as we keep insisting, it is only in *analysis* that what men do and what men think, the respective subjects of political and intellectual history, can be separated; in reality they work together in a *process*. Our basic purpose in beginning with the Enlightenment has been to emphasize the radical novelty of Enlightened ideas, the revolutionary character that does not come out so clearly in the "spotted reality" of the confusions of politics, war, and daily living, where the new and the old are mingled, not neatly opposed as in the work of the *philosophes* and their critics.

We shall in this chapter consider the complicated international politics of the eighteenth-century Western world, the social and economic tensions of this troubled yet energetic and hopeful century, the course of domestic politics in the major countries, and finally the financial, agricultural, and industrial changes forming part of the revolutionary process of modernization to which the last chapter introduced us. This eighteenth century in conventional historical periodization is a short one, from the death of the Sun King, Louis XIV, in 1715 to the outbreak of the French Revolution in 1789.

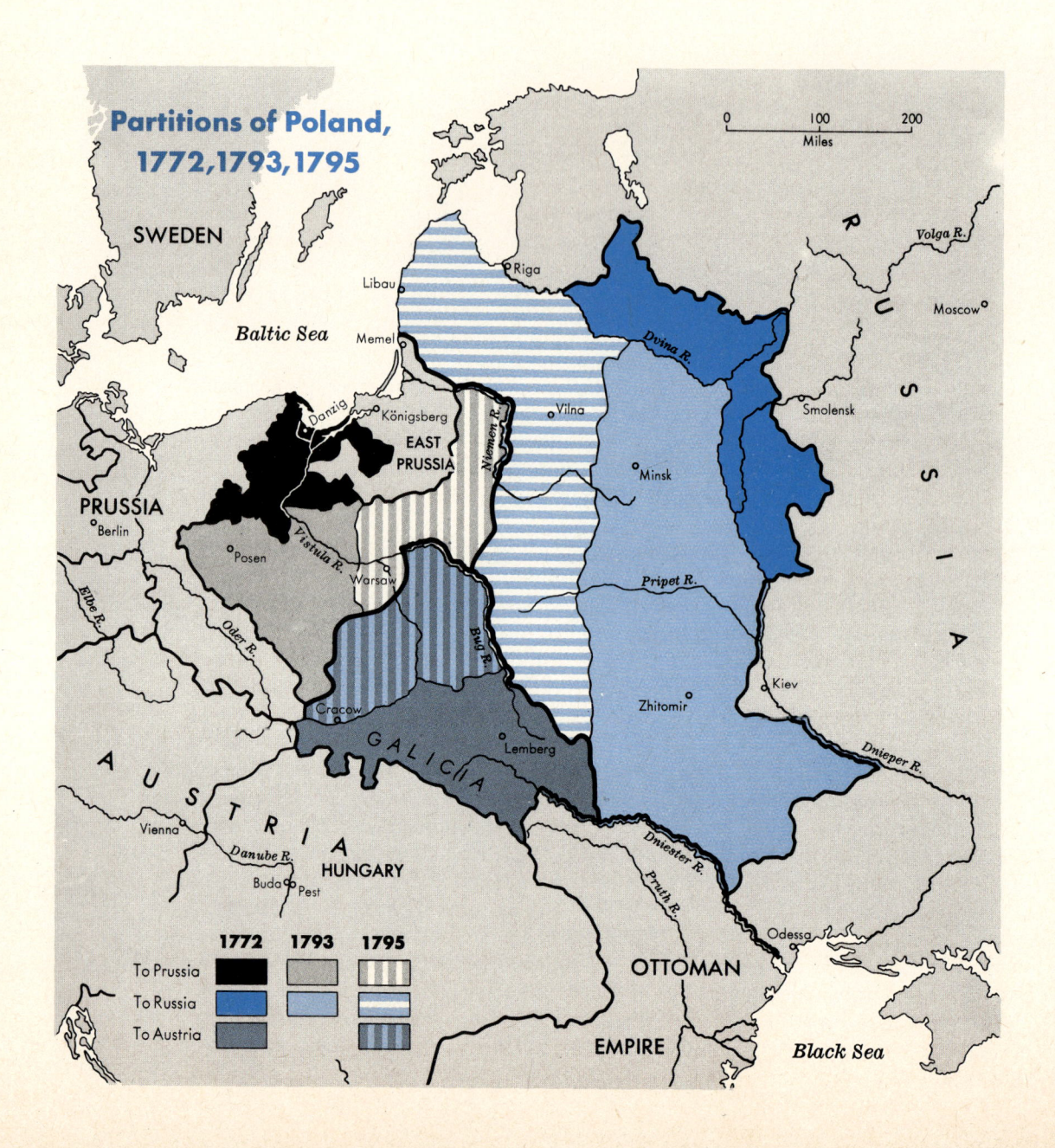

I. The European Balance

The international politics, the wars, the peace conferences, the diplomacy of the eighteenth century are confusing indeed. Many of us will be solaced by the reported confession of the distinguished English writer Lord Morley that he never could remember just who was fighting whom between 1713 and 1740—a period generally considered as comparatively peaceful, but actually full of "little" wars. Nevertheless there are certain generalizations which can help us make sense out of the confusion.

EIGHTEENTH-CENTURY WARFARE

Eighteenth-century wars were classical wars of balance of power, and the peace treaties that concluded them awarded some spoils to the victors, stripped the defeated of bits of territory, but—with the striking exception of wholly partitioned Poland at the end of the century—did not seek to annihilate the defeated state. Soldiers, sailors, and civilians in the way of the fighting were, to be sure, killed by the thousands, but as wars since the invention of gunpowder go, these were not very bloody or destructive. Indeed, until the wars of the French Revolution and Napoleon, no later eighteenth-century war was quite as bloody as Louis XIV's War of the Spanish Succession. "Unconditional surrender" is a phrase not usually to be found in the records of these times.

The common soldiers and sailors were, though ill-paid individually, expensive as a whole to their masters; nor was there anywhere, not even in warlike Prussia, anything like a true mass-army, fired by patriotism, and therefore expendable. Generals were careful of their men, not necessarily out of humane, but at least out of economic motives. Infantry was deployed on the battlefield in serried ranks, but they did not charge in heroic masses as would at times the citizen armies of the French Revolution and Napoleon. The front lines volleyed, but there was little attempt at marksmanship. Indeed, when at Lexington and Concord in 1775 the Yankee farmers took deliberate and effective aim at the Redcoats from behind their stone walls, the British military was deeply shocked by such ungentlemanly guerrilla tactics.

Eighteenth-century wars were serious and bloody games—games in the sense that they were fought under formal rules hallowed by tradition. Though they were fought by professionals for the most part, these mercenaries, unlike those of the Thirty Years' War, were comparatively well-disciplined and did comparatively little looting. The more daring and successful leaders, such as Frederick the Great, often broke some of the rules, but they never were able to make major alterations in the system. So too with diplomacy. International relations were carried on by professionals, usually, though not always, of noble birth, according to rigid rules of protocol. Wars were formally declared, and it is perhaps significant that undeclared wars first broke out in imperial rivalries outside Europe. Britain and France were technically at peace in 1754 and 1755 when there was real fighting between them in the region of Fort Duquesne (later Pittsburgh). Moreover, the rules were derived from a set of general principles, an ethics of a sort, which sought to protect the rulers and ruling classes of great, middling, and little states alike from complete destruction.

In ideal, at least, a ruler who lost something should somehow secure "compensation"—a favorite word—although ultimately someone somewhere had to lose a good deal more than he gained. Still, overseas lands could be swapped around without regard for rights of rulers or peoples, and in Europe itself the extremely subdivided regions of Germany and Italy could always be subdivided some more. As we noted above, Poland in three successive partitions among Russia, Prussia, and Austria (1772, 1792, 1795) was literally wiped off the map; but Poland was an almost anarchical aristocratic republic with an *elected* king, who did not quite belong to the great royal club. Even so, in 1738 when a war of the Polish Succession was finally settled, the losing rival for the throne, Stanislaus Leszczinski, was "compensated" with the Duchy of Lorraine in France.

Later historians, especially in the nineteenth century, were inclined to reproach the eighteenth century as especially cynical and immoral in international relations, and as utterly without regard for any principle of "self-determination of peoples" by nationality. Both reproaches are anachronistic. The beginnings of what we now know so well as nationalism are indeed discernible in the West in the eighteenth century, especially in advanced countries like Great Britain and France, but it is unfair to expect political rulers to be prophets of the future. The reproach of undue cynicism must seem to us, with our fresh memories of undisguised power politics, of "cold," "hot," and "brushfire" wars, equally unfair. After all, these professionals at least had a professional code, not high-minded perhaps, but still more or less well observed, and designed to give the participants in international politics some minimum protection. Above all, the aggressor powers in the eighteenth century knew when to stop; this was true even of Frederick the Great, the most successful of the land-grabbers.

Main Participants and Rivalries. The main lines of this system of limited conflicts are clear enough. There were three Great Powers with a past of several centuries as such—France, Britain, Austria (or the Holy Roman Empire)—and two relatively new, even "upstart" powers—Prussia and Russia. Three powers that had been great or near great in the 1600's were now of declining weight in war and diplomacy—Spain, Sweden, and Holland. Many middling and small "independent" states survived, mostly in the Germanies and in Italy. The papacy, the oldest power of all, was an anomaly, since it was hardly based on territory or an army; it took a relatively inactive, though not entirely negligible, part in eighteenth-century international politics. And on the edges of Europe, not really a part of it, was the Ottoman Empire, already in a decline obvious to alert Western statesmen. Although all during the eighteenth century Russia kept gnawing away with much success at parts of the Turkish Empire around the Black Sea, and Austria nibbled at the Balkan area, the "Eastern Question" did not quite become a major concern until after 1789.

The major rivalries were both very old—that between the French and the English and that between the French and the Germans, or at this particular time, between the French Bourbons and Austrian Habsburgs. Thus France was involved with two different sets of opponents, one led by a great sea power, the other by a great land power—surely one of the reasons why in the course of the next few generations she was beaten, though not annihilated, in contests with both. The Anglo-French contest, which lasted with some fairly long intervals of peace from 1689 to 1815, is sometimes called the Second Hundred Years' War. It may be true that in a profound sense wars decide nothing, but on the common-sense surface this war decided a great deal: among other things, that the North American continent north of the Rio Grande, save for a French enclave in Quebec, should be English,* not French, in language and cultural background. The Franco-German contest in the eighteenth century, though it had some striking ups and downs for both sides, was on the whole something of a stalemate. In the longer run, we can see that the Germans were coming up, but this was hardly evident even by the 1790's.

The sketch above is, of course, a great simplification. Peacetime rivalries and actual wars involved almost all European states, big and little, and were a series of complicated and interwoven agreements, alliances, coalitions. Both in international law, then quite rudimentary, and in actual practice the eighteenth century witnessed the beginnings of what we call "neutrality," notably for the Low Countries and Switzerland. But neutrality has always been a precarious thing in the West, and most European states in the eighteenth century were swept into the great coalitions.

The Quadruple Alliance. Yet attempts were also made to secure general peace and stability and even to transcend the system of balance of power among squabbling "sovereign" states by setting up some kind of political, or at least diplomatic, *structure* (the word is ambiguous, but so is the reality) for regular consultation and decision-making by these states. In fact, at the end of each of the great general or "world" wars of the last few centuries such structures have been set up: after the Peace of Utrecht in 1713, the Concert of Europe and Quadruple Alliance (France, Great Britain, Austria, Holland); after the Treaty of Vienna in 1815, the Congress System and Holy Alliance; after the Treaty of Versailles in 1919, the League of Nations; after the defeat of Germany in 1945, the United Nations Organization. Although none of these structures have been true federal states, they do seem to show a certain progression, for each one has been somewhat closer to a kind of supranational government than the preceding one.

The period of peace and stability that followed the great and exhausting world wars of the end of the reign of Louis XIV of France (*see* Chapter 8) was far from completely peaceful. Though France had been defeated, she had by no means been deprived of the power to try again to dominate Europe; and the Austrian Habsburgs were still dissatisfied with the loss of Spain. The wife of the new Spanish Bourbon king, Elizabeth Farnese, was determined to secure Italian thrones for her own children; and Spaniards were anxious to get back from Britain the great rock of Gibraltar, which they had only reluctantly ceded to the British at Utrecht. The Great Northern War between Russia and Sweden went on until the Peace of Nystadt in 1721, which ended Swedish domination in the Baltic and established Peter's Russia as a major European power. The "Polish Problem" was beginning to get acute, as Russia, Prussia, Austria, and even the Western powers, France and Britain, sought by all sorts of intrigue and bribery to influence the conduct of that chaotic state and society. Yet the wars between 1713 and 1739 were really "little" wars, not worth our listing. After 1718 the Quadruple Alliance among the recent enemies formed a nucleus around which two peace-

---

* Scots, Welsh, and Irish may justifiably complain about this adjective, but there is no *British* language, and perhaps no *British* culture. In ordinary parlance, we have to be forgiving of such ambiguities, just as with the difficulty that we of the United States have in realizing that we are not the only Americans.

loving leaders, Sir Robert Walpole in England and Cardinal Fleury in France, with help from other countries, wove a complicated diplomatic web that held together under many strains for some 20 years.

JENKINS' EAR AND SILESIA

The first serious rift in the web appeared in 1739, when the ironically titled War of Jenkins' Ear broke out between Great Britain and Spain. Britain's commerce and overseas interests grew rapidly in these decades, and she had used the Asiento agreement (*see* p. 345) to do a good deal of illegal trading with the Spanish colonies in America. British trading interests had long been pressing the government to aid them to open up the Latin-American trade. A ship's captain named Jenkins, in the course of what we should now call lobbying, appeared before the House of Commons with a tale of how the Spanish Coast Guard had

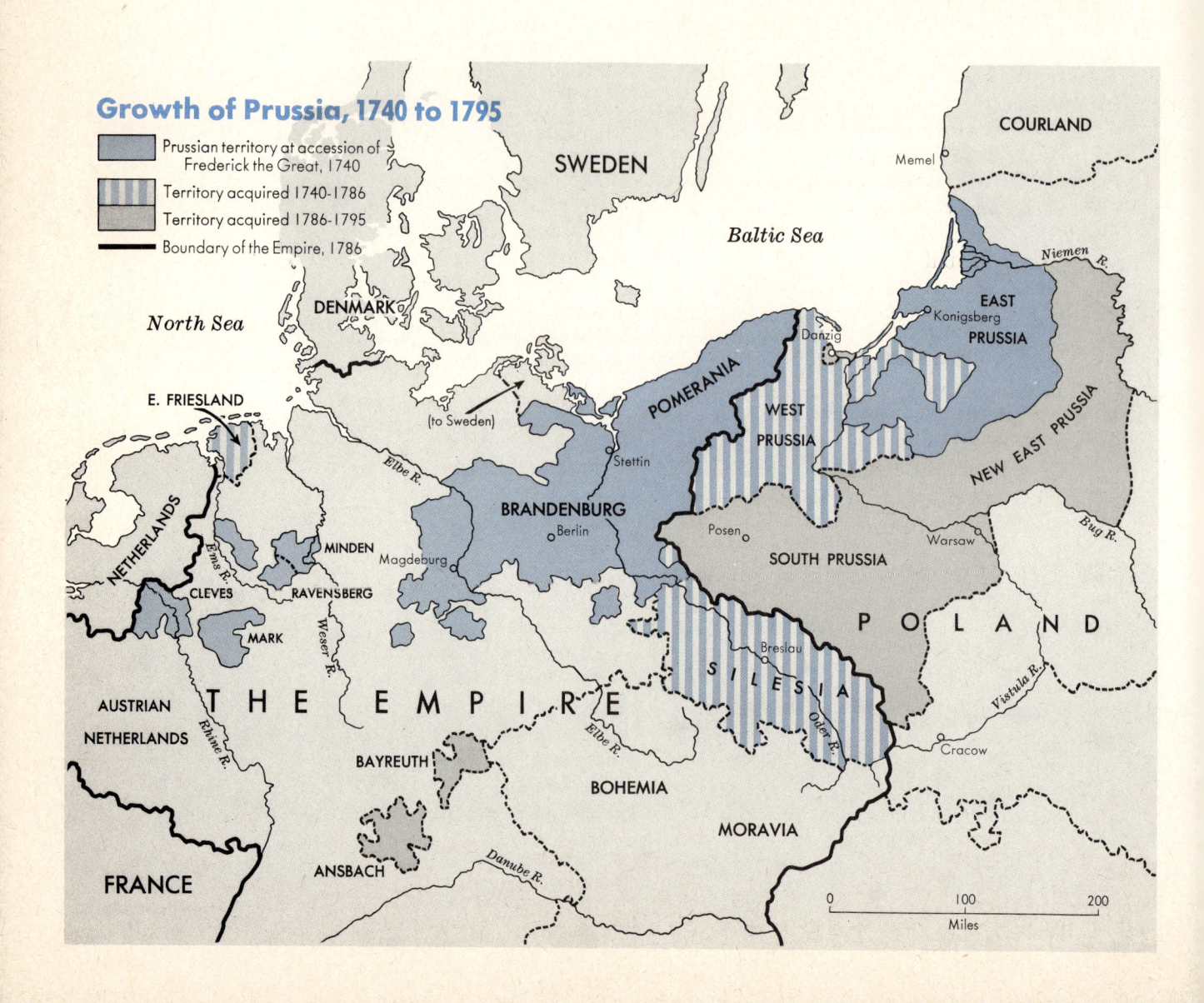

Growth of Prussia, 1740 to 1795

stopped his ship, roughed him up, and indeed cut off his ear, which he exhibited "wrapt in Cotton which he carries about with him in a Box." The incident was trivial, if picturesque; the important point is that here was a deliberately worked-up war crisis and war hysteria quite in the modern manner. George II formally declared war against Spain in October, 1739.

What turned this "little" war into a world or general war, however, was the seizure of Silesia, a part of the Habsburg lands, by the 28-year-old Prussian king, Frederick II, in 1740. Frederick, who was afterward to be called the Great, had antiquarians cook up elaborate "legal" claims to this valuable territory, which in view of the complicated feudal subdivisions of the past was not difficult. Neither then nor since has informed Western opinion regarded this seizure as anything but an ordinary piece of aggression. It is true that no male heir to the Habsburg possessions existed at the death of Charles VI in 1740; but Charles had secured the signature of all European powers including Prussia to the so-called Pragmatic Sanction, by which his daughter Maria Theresa was to inherit his dominions intact. Frederick's invasion of Silesia was a typical act upsetting the balance of power, and a series of general wars, essentially one world war, broke out and lasted with a few intervals of peace until 1763.

At the start, the first Silesian war (1740–1742) was an instance of the policy of ganging up against an apparently weakened power. Austria, with a woman as ruler, and her succession in dispute at that, seemed disabled enough to be beaten. Britain sided with Austria, but British interests were really in the developing war overseas, and help from her could not be immediate, for as usual British land forces were small. France, Bavaria, Spain, Saxony, and Prussia all came in against Austria by 1741, but Frederick, bought off by an alarmed Austria by the cession of part of Silesia, withdrew. Frederick later renewed his attack in alliance with France, and the first phase of these troubles came to an end in Europe with the Treaty of Aix-la-Chapelle in 1748, which confirmed Frederick in his conquest of Silesia, but generally restored the situation described by that great cliché, the status quo (Latin, *status quo ante bellum,* the state existing before the war).

Too much, however, had been stirred up to clear so readily. Notably the two great difficulties remained: Austria and Prussia both wanted Silesia, France and Britain both wanted as much colonial empire as they could get, and in particular both wanted India and North America.

THE SEVEN YEARS' WAR

The last world war of this series, known in its European phase as the Seven Years' War and in its American phase as the French and Indian War, was formally renewed in 1756. By then, a dramatic switch of partners was under way, the "diplomatic revolution" whereby the Austrians lined up with their old enemy France, and the Prussians, enemies of Austria, lined up with Britain. Russia, a comparatively new member of the now discordant concert of Europe, joined the war on the side of Austria and France. The tortuous negotiations which brought about this shift in alignments were held by later historians to be peculiarly characteristic of the old dynastic and aristocratic societies of personal rule, where the hatreds, spites, and ambitions of a few crowned heads could shift the weight of millions of subjects from one alliance to another.

At the start it looked as if, on the European continent at least, the combined forces of Austria, France, and Russia would readily beat Frederick, the more since Britain as usual began the war unprepared, and continued to put her real strength into the overseas struggle. The British helped Frederick in a way they established as a matter of policy, with financial rather than direct military aid with British armies. After early Prussian victories over separate armies, notably over the French at Rossbach in 1757, the tide turned, as Austrians and Russians united their forces and as the government of the new British King, George III (reigned 1760–1820), stopped payment of subsidies to Frederick. But he was saved by another royal accession when in 1762 the Russian Empress Elizabeth, who hated Frederick, died and was succeeded by Peter III, who greatly admired him. Russia withdrew from the conflict, and the stage was set for the Treaty of Hubertusburg (1763), by which Silesia went to Prussia and so remained for nearly two centuries until the defeat of Hitler, when most of it was taken over by the Poles.

The Franco-British duel for colonial supremacy, though it began unfavorably for Britain, ended with her complete victory on land and on sea, where her navy permitted her to supply and support her land forces. Both powers in both parts of the world made free use of "native" auxiliaries, Indians in America, East Indians in Asia. The crucial land battle in North America was the victory of the English over the French, Wolfe over Montcalm, on the Plains of Abraham outside the walls of Quebec City in 1759—a battle in which both commanding generals were killed. In India the crucial battle was the victory of the English under Clive at Plassey in 1757, after the gifted French leader Dupleix had been recalled to France. By the Peace of Paris in 1763 the beaten French relinquished all their interests in India, save for a few minor ports, and ceded to Britain thousands of square miles of the upper Mississippi and St. Lawrence river basins, retaining only the tiny fishing islands of St. Pierre and Miquelon, two "sugar islands," Guadaloupe and Martinique in the Caribbean, and their part of the island of Santo Domingo, a part that later became Haiti. French Louisiana was ceded to Spain by this same treaty.

The treaties of 1763 ended the great general wars of the mid-century; there were to be no more such wars until the outbreak of hostilities against revolutionary France in 1792. To the contemporary European what did indeed turn out to be a major historical event, the American Revolution, was simply another relatively minor European war. France, reassured by the victory of the American colonists over the British at Saratoga in 1777, supported the revolutionaries openly and fought Britain in a successful but materially unprofitable war of revenge for the humiliations suffered in the Seven Years' War. Spain and eventually Holland joined the war against Britain but got little out of it. The Treaty of Paris in 1783 recognized the independence of the thirteen states but gave France only a few small overseas gains. There were a few other jockeyings and lesser wars, such as the War of the Bavarian Succession (1778–1779) between Austrians and Prussians, which ended with minor territorial adjustments. Poland, as we have noted before, was divided among Russia, Austria, and Prussia, with no more than a heroic and unequal struggle in a Polish uprising headed by the patriot Kosciusko in 1794.

SHIFTS IN THE BALANCE

These eighteenth-century wars were critical in the rise of the hitherto minor state of Prussia to greatness, and in the rise of Britain to a position of world supremacy in the nineteenth century, when the sun never set on the British flag. The historian most convinced that broad underlying "forces" and not mere individuals "determine" the course of history has to admit that Frederick the Great was lucky. One of the most interesting "ifs" of history centers on what would have happened if Frederick had been completely beaten, as he well might have been, by a firm and continued Austro-Russian cooperation in 1762. Perhaps the nineteenth-century unification of Germany, actually achieved under the Prussian Bismarck, would have taken place under quite different auspices and with quite different results. Still, it must be admitted that Frederick had an excellent army and an efficient administration. The British victory over the French must be attributed to several factors—to British concentration on their main purpose, defeat of France overseas; to the superiority of Britain in sea power, again in part the product of concentration on it; to the head start which Britain had over France in financial and commercial resources, which enabled her to subsidize Continental allies instead of pouring large armies of her own onto the Continent.

In all forms of contest among men, from games to world wars, the weaknesses and mistakes—or bad luck—of the losers must be taken into account as well as the strengths and wise policies—or good luck—of the winners. Of the great losers in the eighteenth century, France had to pour out her considerable strength against two major enemies, a land enemy in Central Europe (first Austria, then Prussia), and a sea enemy in the British Isles. It is easy to say that she should have concentrated on one foe, fending off the other—and to add that Britain was the antagonist worth beating, for to beat Britain was to inherit the earth. But all her history pushed France to try to expand on the Continent. In spite of her advantage in population over Britain (about three to one) and in some other resources, eighteenth-century France had grave weaknesses. Her government was top-heavy and confused, with conflicting local administrations and with poor leadership, despite occasional gifted statesmen like Fleury or soldiers like Montcalm and Dupleix. Her social structure already showed signs of the tensions between the aristocracy and the middle classes and between the landowners and the peasants which were to snap in 1789. In short, the French state and French society were unable to use their potential of land and people efficiently.

The victory of Prussia over Austria in the duel for control of Central Europe (often called "the Germanies") must also be seen in terms of the assets of the victor and the liabilities of the vanquished. Prussia had a succession of gifted rulers who combined to make her a major power by building up the human and material resources of a state by no means larger or richer or with a better start in competition than other middle-sized German states, say, Saxony or Bavaria. Prussia had a hard-working, conscientious, and self-assured ruling class of nobles and state servants, and a people willing to follow their lead; and at the crisis of the mid-eighteenth century she had in Frederick a lucky military genius.

Austria—or better, the Habsburg complex of lands—presented a contrasting set of weaknesses. Statistically far stronger than Prussia, with five or six times as great a population, Austria was not a true state even by eighteenth-century standards, but a congeries of peoples, administrative areas, legal systems, quite lacking in any common patriotism. Its ruling classes were by no means united, especially since one of the major constituents of the complex, Hungary, had a Magyar ruling class which was by no means Germanized; indeed Hungarian intellectuals and civil servants still used Latin as their *lingua franca*. Austria was badly weakened at a critical moment in 1740 by the disputed succession of Maria Theresa to a post never previously occupied by a woman—her Hungarian subjects, who refused to admit her sex, swore allegiance to *rex noster* (our king) Maria Theresa. Although Maria Theresa proved herself to be in many ways an excellent ruler and certainly a firm one, she had no generals up to the standard of Frederick the Great.

Finally, let us repeat that in these eighteenth-century wars no *major* power, and only Poland among the lesser ones, was crushed, or made to submit to annihilating conditions of peace. Even in the case of France, the empire she lost in 1763 was an empire in potential rather than fact; at home she lost nothing and in mid-century even gained Lorraine and Corsica by diplomatic means. War and diplomacy were still an affair among insiders, professionals, if not gentlemen, and no member in good standing was quite left out.

THE EXPANSION OF EUROPE

The shifts in the colonial balance resulting from the wars of the eighteenth century were the headline events overseas, but there were other noteworthy developments in the history of European expansion. First of all, the eighteenth century saw the exploration and mapping of the Pacific. Such names as those of the Englishman Captain Cook and the Frenchman Bougainville, the Dane Bering (in Russian employ), and many others belong in the great tradition of exploration. Toward the very end of the century the still largely unexplored continent of Australia was first colonized in 1788 when a shipload of British convicts was landed at Botany Bay near the present Sydney to found a penal settlement out of which grew the colony of New South Wales. The last considerable littoral to be explored carefully was the Pacific coast of North America from Alaska south to California. Here at the end of the eighteenth century a fine free-for-all took place, among British, Americans, Spanish, and Russians; it stopped short of war, however, and final decisions as to who was to get just what were delayed until the next century. The English explorer Vancouver, aided by agents of British fur companies, set up solid British claims but failed to discover the mouth of the great river, vaguely known from the Indians, for which everyone was looking. The American Captain Gray out of Boston found and entered its mouth in 1792, and named the river from his ship, the *Columbia*, thus giving the new United States a solid foothold in the Oregon country.

Actual settlement and exploitation of the non-European lands were by no means unimportant in the eighteenth century. Most important for the future was the filling-up of the thirteen English colonies on the Atlantic seaboard. In spite of a high death rate, the natural increase was considerable; white immigration continued, with German, French Huguenot, Welsh, Scotch-Irish, Irish, and a few other strains beginning

Maria Theresa.

the American melting pot; all through the century a lucrative and cruel slave trade brought Negroes from Africa. In Latin America also there was a slow growth in population and in wealth, though the great mass of natives (Indians) continued to be very little westernized save for formal conversion to Roman Catholic Christianity. In the Caribbean, African slaves laid the basis for the great eighteenth-century wealth of the sugar islands, a wealth that went almost wholly to the white planter class.

In Africa no real penetration of the interior occurred during the century. The slave trade alone, of course, insured that the maritime nations would maintain old posts, or "factories," for trading, and seize new ones; but the European traders got their human supplies largely through native chiefs. At the southern tip of the continent the Dutch outpost, originally established at Capetown to permit Dutch vessels to refit on the long voyage from Europe to the Far East, slowly grew into a colony of settlement, relying on black labor; the Cape Dutch were greatly aided by a small but very active group of French Huguenot refugees after the revocation of the Edict of Nantes in 1685. In Asia, too, European establishments, colonies of trade rather than colonies of settlement, grew in wealth. The English, firmly in control in India after 1757, though they hardly westernized the natives, did begin the process of organizing and pacifying that troubled subcontinent. In the process some Englishmen, the "nabobs" so often referred to in eighteenth-century literature, made great fortunes. The famous trial of Warren Hastings, British governor of Bengal at the end of the century, though unfair to Hastings himself, did reveal a condition certainly describable as "exploitation" of India for the benefit of Europeans.

Non-Europeans were exploited all over the world. Some of them were taken into slavery, and in areas like the Caribbean and the seaboard regions of North America the native population was destroyed by actual war and by the white man's diseases and the white man's alcohol. Yet along with all this the process of European expansion had by the end of the eighteenth century laid the foundations for the westernization of the rest of the world.

II. Political and Social Changes

THE PROCESS OF GROWTH

In the eighteenth century, and particularly in western Europe, the complex series of changes from a medieval society to a modern society came to a series of critical turning points. The most dramatic of these turning points, the great French Revolution, so overshadows the others that it is hard to write eighteenth-century history without an eye on what was to happen in 1789. But much else essential to the process that formed the modern world happened during the century. It was a process that went on most unevenly throughout the Western world. By and large it was worked out most fully in Britain and in France, but the American Revolution was an important part of it. And so, in most of Europe, including Russia, was the reform movement, sometimes successful, sometimes abortive, known as "enlightened despotism."

The series of changes may be not unfairly called *growth,* or in good eighteenth-century language, *progress.* In most of the material aspects of civilization which can be statistically measured the figures get larger, the lines of the graphs go upward: production, both agricultural and industrial, trade, gross national product (a term that would not have been readily understood by eighteenth-century economists), population, mechanical inventions, even literacy, all increased. The figures are not so complete and so accurate as those for the contemporary world; and the rate of increase was by no means the same in all countries: for most of the Balkans, in the eighteenth century it was perhaps nil and, in spite of Peter the Great and other subsequent reformers, relatively slight in Russia.

Change, or growth, in a society always injures, or seems to injure, the interests of some individuals and groups in it. Most social psychologists would agree that many individuals even in a highly progressive society dislike and resist even beneficial changes. In the eighteenth-century process of change, the old institutions, old traditions, old ways of doing things, even the old class and personality structures, may be grouped as "medieval" (not necessarily "feudal") and the newer ones as "modern." By and large, the old ways were rooted in local peculiarities, local institutions, and centuries of history. One example, a bit extreme, will make this clear. Baden, one of the smaller German states, a bit larger than Connecticut in area, had 112 separate measures for length, 65 for dry goods, 123 for liquids, and 163 for cereals, not to mention 80 different pound weights! The new ways were marked by a seeking for larger units of administration, more uniform and efficient standards and laws, more willingness to adapt to inventions of all sorts.

Marxist theory sees this century in Europe as the culmination of a struggle between the old aristocratic ruling class, relying on medieval "means of production," and the new bourgeois or middle class of commercial capitalists seeking to seize power from the aristocrats (see Chapter 13). Though Marxist thought often turns this conception into a dogma, greatly oversimplifying the complex course of events, there is a large element of truth in its analysis. Neither class was homogeneous, and in the eighteenth century, before Marxist terminology was invented, social conflicts were not put in the language of outright class struggles. Men talked and wrote about right and wrong, justice and injustice, natural and artificial; many of them still appealed to traditional Christian concepts.

North America and the Caribbean, 1763
Situation after the Seven Years' War

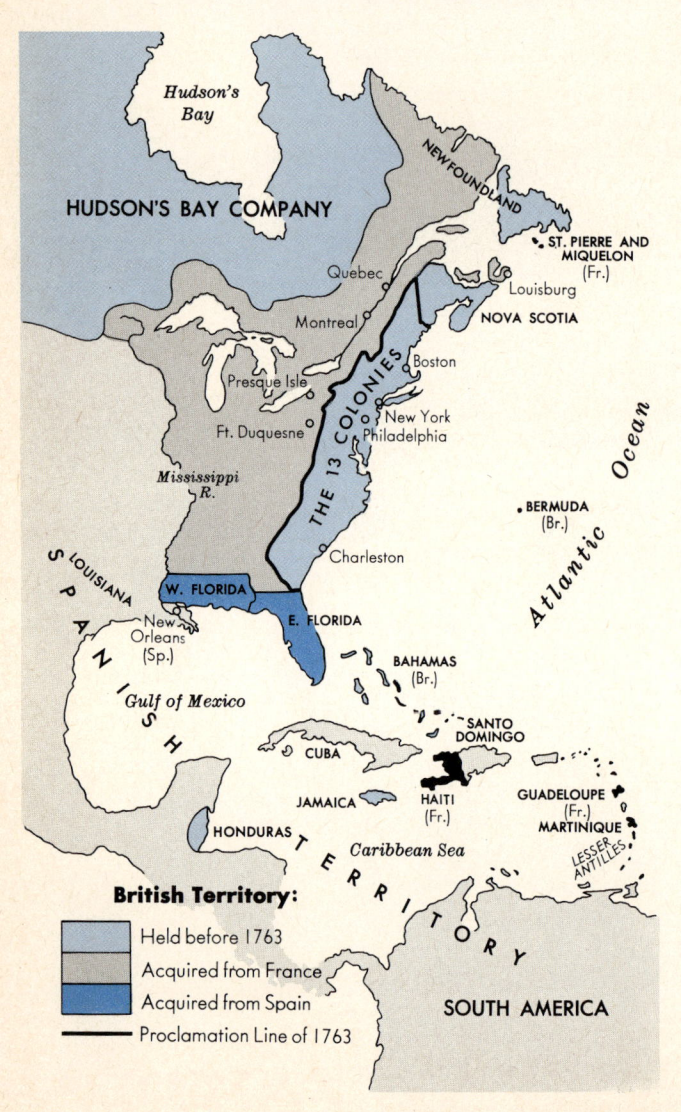

British Territory:
- Held before 1763
- Acquired from France
- Acquired from Spain
- Proclamation Line of 1763

THE STATE AND SOCIETY

The political unit within which these changes took place was the state, the modern dynastic state, in many instances already a nation-state, which we have seen developing out of the feudal nexus of political units. Some of these states, such as England and France, were more advanced administratively and richer than others, such as many of the smaller states of Germany and Italy. Yet in all, even England, the hereditary ruler was still felt to be a real ruler, no mere symbol, and the privileged classes, the aristocracy and gentry, were felt, by most of the people as well as by themselves, to belong by birth in their privileged station. A concrete example: during the Terror in the French Revolution (1794) a servant was arrested and called before the revolutionary authorities in a small town for smuggling in roast chicken to supplement the poor prison fare of his "master," a nobleman imprisoned as a "counter-revolutionary." Interrogated, the servant replied simply. "But M. le Marquis was born to eat chicken." (Chicken, in the United States today a relatively cheap food, was in the past a relatively expensive delicacy.) Even in the few European states not ruled monarchically—Venice, the Swiss cantons, some of the old Hanseatic towns—ruling merchant aristocrats were fully aware of the gap between themselves and the people.

The political situation in the early eighteenth century may be clarified not so much by using positive terms like "absolutism" or "autocracy" but by using a negative description: no eighteenth-century state was a political democracy. Nowhere was there universal suffrage, for female suffrage was unheard of; only in an occasional English constituency, such as Middlesex County just outside London, or in some of the smaller Swiss cantons, was there even an approximation of voting by all adult males. Terms like "rule of the majority," "referendum," "equal rights," and the like were not found in practical politics, though ideas of the sort were beginning to crop up among intellectuals in their modern form. (They had already appeared among religious groups; in a sense and in different terms they have never been wholly absent from Christianity.)

Yet Europe at the beginning of the eighteenth century did not have a rigid, closed aristocracy in complete command, nor did it have a political system in which there were no checks on what the established rulers could do. To clarify this, let us begin with the actual social structure, which varied greatly from state to state. Again in very general terms, the class structure was more rigid—that is to say, it was more difficult for an ambitious individual born into a lower class to rise into a higher one—as one went from the British Isles eastward and southward.

Society in Britain and on the Continent. The subtle and complex gradations of British social life are even today very hard for an outsider to understand. Already by 1700 they were quite definitely modern. The key word is "gentleman," a word to be understood in social connotations, though even in England it came to have ethical ones, as in the favorite Victorian phrase, "nature's gentleman." A gentleman dresses, talks, behaves in quite definite and observable ways. It is better, and certainly easier, to be born a gentleman; but even in the eighteenth century it was possible for adaptable talent to make a man into a gentleman, and even easier for a successful plebeian money-maker to see that his children grew up as gentlemen. This latter process was easiest of all when the plebeian succeeded in marrying the daughter of a gentleman, which for a rich man was not difficult.

"Gentleman" in English is not a synonym for "nobleman." Long before 1700, indeed in the Middle Ages, English law and the custom of rigorous primogeniture among the titled nobility insured that only the eldest son inherited the title, from duke down to baron and baronet; other male children, though gentlemen, were in law commoners, and, if they went into Parliament, went into the House of Commons, not the House of Lords. Occasionally children in a numerous noble family began to sink in the social scale, sometimes producing great-grandchildren who were not even gentlemen (social mobility *downward*).

Most of the family, however, at least kept themselves in the gentry. This last is a term over the exact meaning and limits of which English social historians still dispute. It refers to a kind of lower aristocracy, owning landed estates and usually living on one, having the right to a coat of arms (not always a very old one), and addressed verbally as "sir," and in a letter as "John Smith, Esq." (esquire, originally "shield-bearer"). It is a kind of synopsis of two centuries of English social history since 1750 to note that today almost any neatly dressed person rates both forms of salutation.

Nobility and gentry were originally dependent on income from landed property, either directly or indirectly through pensions from the Crown, for example, or through the revenues of ecclesiastical office. But commercial sources of income had long existed, and by the early eighteenth century there was notably in England and in Holland a financial world, a world of stocks and bonds and big companies—but not, of course, on a General Motors scale. English gentlemen invested in these sources of wealth, married their daughters to nongentlemen who had acquired such wealth; moreover, such nongentlemen could buy country estates and set themselves up as practically members of the gentry, or if very wealthy could be awarded a title, if only a knighthood or a baronetcy (which carried the title "Sir" with a capital "S"). Of course there were social distinctions between "landlords" and "fundlords," and readers of Victorian novels will recall that even in the nineteenth century wives of naval officers, Anglican clergymen, and the like speak scornfully of people "in trade." Still, English society in the early eighteenth century had begun to be a society in which talent of the right sort could lift a man into the upper or the ruling classes—it was a society that already showed much social mobility *upward*.

On the Continent noble status passed to *all* children of a nobleman. Yet, especially in France, the Low Countries, western Germany, and northern Italy, there was real social mobility, and a society on the whole much less different from that of England than historians have usually admitted. True, pride of rank, a sense of being born different from commoners existed among all Continental nobilities, but it was by no means absent from the English aristocracy and gentry. Social mobility downward certainly existed on the Continent. Some French country nobles could hardly be distinguished in appearance and behavior from their peasant neighbors. Everywhere as the eighteenth century went on the poorer nobility tended to be in a bad way in terms of income in comparison with the successful bourgeois. These successful bourgeois could, if they wished, usually manage to find a noble husband for a daughter, or a noble wife for a son. The new bureaucracies at their top levels carried a noble rank (in France, the nobility of the "robe" or "gown") which was thought inferior by the old landed families (the nobility of the "sword"). But in really important matters of wealth and leadership, the gown was by no means inferior to the sword, and even in Prussia military servants of the king and his civil servants were sometimes recruited from the same families.

In short, in western and much of central Europe, the ruling classes, the people who got things done, the successful people, were by no means a fixed, uniform caste. To the forms of the career open to talent which had existed in the Middle Ages—law, the church, which included higher education, war—were now added finance and banking, trade (especially shipping and overseas trade), and journalism, writing, the arts, even the stage. Benjamin Franklin, son of a "tallow chandler and soap boiler," himself a self-made man, printer, journalist, inventor, businessman, diplomatist, in his old age as American Minister the idol of Parisian "society," may seem to be, as a son of free America, quite atypical. But eighteenth-century Europe was filled with self-made men, from charlatans, like the Italian Cagliostro (1743–1795), to noblemen who by unorthodox behavior pulled themselves out of the obscurity most noblemen had to live in, like the Marquis de Lafayette (1757–1834) or the Comte de Mirabeau (1749–1791).

Social Tensions. But this modern, competitive, lively society was divided by all sorts of tensions. As the century wore on, tension between the privileged classes and the commoners, the rich and successful commoners as well as the peasantry and the still not very numerous urban working class, seems to have heightened. At the end of the century the radical young English poet and admirer of the French Revolution, Coleridge, could write the revealing line, "that leprous stain, nobility." The nobles, especially the lesser nobility in the countryside, dependent on relatively fixed incomes from land, suffered from the slow monetary inflation which generally benefitted the business class.

The new world of intellectuals, writers, entertainers, and artists depended for its success, especially in France, on an attitude of critical condemnation of existing ways. Along with the white-collar class in general, it was perhaps overcrowded, subject to too intense a competition, especially in the great cities; even its most successful figures were subject to patronizing or insulting attitudes of their privileged betters. Here the classic instance is the affair between the young Voltaire, of middle-class origins, already for his wit a sought-for guest in the *salons* of Paris, and the Chevalier de Rohan, of an old and exceedingly proud noble family. Rohan, a gentleman and perhaps not a very brave one, refused to duel with the plebeian Voltaire, but did hire thugs to beat him up. When the authorities were apprised of the affair, they automatically considered Voltaire guilty, and he felt obliged to flee to England until the affair blew over.

Americans in particular must guard against the tendency to see these tensions in terms of an oppressed and unaggressive plebeian underdog and a tyrannical and aggressive aristocratic top dog. Indeed, since the underdogs were in the long run to win out decisively, they must have had many sources of strength not merely from force of number. The commoners, the middle classes, were the subversives—or, to put it more generously, they seized the initiative. They did, of course, feel themselves to be mistreated, frustrated, victims of injustice, and very often they were. Especially in late eighteenth-century France, historians have recently emphasized what they call the *réaction nobiliaire,* a definite effort on the part of the privileged classes to press to the limit, even to revive, many of their outworn medieval rights. Naturally, this attempt to bring back the past rubbed its victims, the newer middle classes, the wrong way.

III. France and Britain

UNREFORMED FRANCE

Whereas the social tensions of the eighteenth-century West are still difficult for the historian to analyze, the internal political stresses are more easily discussed. In a nutshell: the institutions that worked adequately for a medieval state, where the basic unit was the feudal manor and where the administration of the central government needed only a small and in a sense amateur personnel, could not work for the new modern state of thousands of square miles, with an elaborate system of production and distribution, and a need for many administrative experts. Yet the thousands of old laws, customs, and offices, the traditions of special local institutions, the network of privileges centuries old—all these "vested interests" stood in the way of reform, especially in the France which produced the great revolution.

Eighteenth-century France was a network of administrative areas, medieval rights, concessions, inherited status, all summed up in the word "privilege." The apparatus of state control from Paris–Versailles was superimposed on the mass of local and provincial ways and institutions. The apparatus was itself the product of centuries of efforts to devise such centralized control by all sorts of means, mostly abandoned or superseded but still "there" in formal offices. In spite of the great efforts of Louis XIV in the previous century, in spite of various efforts to reform from above made in the eighteenth century, in spite of—in an odd way, perhaps because of—the devoted efforts of the intellectuals of the French Enlightenment to make the world better, eighteenth-century France was politically an inefficient and backward state. But France was far from being a backward society; indeed, for many individuals in the world of affairs, it was a society which permitted them to grow rich. Many Frenchmen, however, felt that they deserved a better government, and by 1789 they were ready to try to make one for themselves.

In the eighteenth century a series of attempts were made to reform the French government, and particularly its finances, from above by decree, but the French kings did not give such reforms a firm guiding hand. Louis XV (1715–1774), who was only five years old when he inherited the throne, was intelligent enough, and not without a certain mild good will, but he never grew up to his responsibilities. The real work of government was done by a series of ministers, and one remarkable royal favorite, Madame de Pompadour, who for nearly twenty years (1745–1764) as a mistress of Louis XV had a very great influence, and is usually considered the determining factor in the "diplomatic revolution" of 1756. The private life of Louis XV was as scandalous as any chronicler could desire. His successor in 1774, Louis XVI, was a faithful husband and exemplary father, but a poor king—narrowly loyal to traditional ways, not very bright, and bored by many of the ceremonial duties of his position. In addition, he had the misfortune to have as Queen Marie Antoinette, daughter of the Habsburg Empress Maria Theresa, unpopular as an Austrian, extravagant, tactless, conventional in her loyalties.

Attempts at reform began with the death of the aged Louis XIV in 1715.

Louis had attempted to set up in his will a regency in commission, but the day after his death the Parlement of Paris, a kind of supreme court, upset the will and made his cousin, the Duke of Orleans, sole regent. Orleans had to make concessions to the Parlement as the price of gaining the regency; and to govern he set up a series of councils manned not only by experts of the robe but also by nobles of the sword, such as the Duke of Saint-Simon, whose memoirs rank high in French literature. This government by councils, which the French christened *polysynodie* (Greek, "many councils"), was a reaction against the personal rule of Louis XIV, an attempt to restore the old nobility to the real work of government and in general to widen the basis of politics. It failed dismally: the new councillors quarreled among themselves; Orleans, for all his good intentions, proved to lack a firm hand; the Mississippi Bubble (*see below*, p. 427) brought discredit on the government; the old habits of government by the bureaucrats clung on. Orleans fell from power in 1723, and for the next few decades two able but hardly reforming ministers, Cardinal Dubois and Cardinal Fleury, managed to keep things on a reasonably even keel. But the wars which began in 1740 and lasted until 1763, disastrous enough for French prestige, were even more disastrous for French finances.

Finances. Indeed finance, in particular the taxation system, was the key to much of the troubled political situation which fomented the French Revolution of 1789. France as a society was not poor. But the government of France could not raise enough money by taxation, was increasingly forced to borrow, and finally could not meet interest payments on the debt and at the same time pay its current expenses. There is some truth in the traditional popular notions that large numbers of prosperous privileged persons, many of them nobles, were lightly taxed or not taxed at all; that many commoners with small incomes were heavily taxed; and that large sums of money were spent in pensions to courtiers and other "insiders" in court entertainments, and in "conspicuous consumption" among members of this same privileged class. Certainly the concepts of an extravagant and corrupt privileged class and a hard-working common people ground down supporting it had wide and effective circulation in the France of the late eighteenth century; certainly there were grave injustices in the working of the French government.

Yet the student who has pored over the documents can hardly help feeling that the system was even more strikingly inefficient and chaotic than unjust. Taxation was lighter on the nobility and the clergy no doubt than on the third estate or commoners but many of the *privilégiés* (privileged) were commoners: a tax-roll of the 1780's listed the name of a baker as *privilégié*. Even princes paid some of the direct taxes, like the *capitation* or head-tax. The main direct tax, the *taille*, however, was limited to non-nobles, so that *taillable* (subject to the *taille*) was a synonym for commoner. But this tax was usually in effect a tax on real property, not on persons, and where property was used for commercial purposes, tax was paid on it by the user, even though the title was in the hands of a *privilégié*. On the side of expenditure, though the court was expensive, the whole Versailles community did not come near costing what a military campaign had cost—and continued to cost in terms of services of the national debt. By and large, the trouble with French government finance was that the government had to run a country that required more and more running in the way of civil servants and public services—and also had to pay for past and current wars. The financial and military aid given the rebellious American colonists in the 1770's was for French finances the straw that broke the camel's back.

It is also true, though France was by no means unique in this respect, that the spirit of French society did not promote the full use of potential resources. The great aim of many prosperous Frenchmen was to gain some sort of noble status, usually by purchasing from the Crown an office—a judgeship, a high administrative post—which carried with it membership in the *noblesse de robe*. They preferred to invest in such offices, multiplied by the Crown of course to raise money, rather than put their money into economically productive use. Security and status seemed preferable to the adventures of commerce or industry. A minority of Frenchmen set up the great French effort overseas that was not well supported at home. In short the total taxable wealth of France, great indeed, was proportionately not so great as in England—and the taxation system was notably less efficient.

The *Parlements* and Turgot. A great obstacle to thorough tax and other reforms in France was the system of high courts known as the *parlements*. The *parlementaires* were judges appointed for life, indeed in a sense "owners" of their office. They had had a long record of struggles with the Crown, a record which culminated in their eighteenth-century opposition to specific reforms. Although the judges were themselves *privilégiés*, the mere fact that they resisted the increasingly unpopular central government of the Crown made them popular with the commons. Once the Revolution really got started in 1789, however, popular opinion veered sharply against them.

All through the last years of the reign of Louis XV there was a kind of running fight between the royal ministers and the *parlements*, culminating in 1771 when the Chancellor Maupeou (approximately the equivalent of an American federal attorney general) pushed through a royal edict abolishing the *parlements* and setting up a comparatively streamlined new system of higher courts. The reform was most unpopular, and when three years later the young king Louis XVI came to the throne, he yielded to the temptation to do something pleasing to his people, and restored the old system of *parlementaires*. They promptly repudiated the reservations on their power which had accompanied the decree restoring them, and became a center of opposition to the most complete and—one almost writes "therefore"—least effective of the eighteenth-century attempts at reform.

The reforming minister, Turgot, one of the intellectual leaders of the Enlightenment, put in office in 1774 by the young King, managed to alarm almost all the vested interests by his extensive measures. A sweeping effort to equalize the tax burden offended all sorts of taxpayers; abolition of the old craft gilds offended skilled craftsmen; abolition of all internal restrictions on the grain trade, in those days of poor transportation, stirred up fears of possible local shortages of food; reforms in the system of indirect taxes offended the farmers-general, the rich and powerful financiers who collected them; reductions of pensions, court expenditures, and other leakages in government expenditures offended some very influential persons. Turgot was pushed from power by the organized effort of his many and varied opponents in 1776; none of his major reforms survived.

Turgot's experiment was the chief attempt in France to carry out the radical reforming policies of "enlightened despotism," which were applied with some success in other parts of Europe. His failure presents a very interesting case history in the strategy and tactics of the reformer in an advanced but conflict-filled society. It may be argued that he fell because the society he tried to reform was at once too prosperous and too divided for peaceful and voluntary changes of the necessary scale. But a touch of the spellbinding leader—of which the determined intellectual Turgot had none—might have helped him even in a society not yet politically organized for effective popular agitation.

From 1776 to 1789 the account is a gloomy one. The deficit was the central issue, and a number of ministers, from the Swiss financier Necker to the persuasive courtier Calonne and the ecclesiastic Loménie de Brienne, tried in vain to overcome it. Loans sufficed for a while, but toward the end not even the offer of seven-and-one-half per cent interest brought in subscriptions. In 1788 Louis recalled Necker to arrange for the calling of the Estates-General, the old consultative medieval assembly which had *not* developed as had Britain's Parliament—had, in fact, not met at all since 1614. The Estates-General, called to vote new taxes, voted the Old Regime out of existence, and paved the way for the direct revolutionary action which destroyed the French monarchy and made the First French Republic.

BRITAIN: STABLE OR REVOLUTIONARY?

England—more accurately, after the union with Scotland in 1707, Great Britain—was by no means a stable or politically streamlined modern state in the eighteenth century. Indeed, Britain was regarded by the rest of Europe as France was to be in the nineteenth and twentieth centuries—as liable to riots and attempted revolutions and difficult to govern quietly. And the record is there: Charles I beheaded and James II driven out; two romantic and unsuccessful rebellions to restore the Stuarts, one in 1715 (the "Old Pretender"), another in 1745 (the "Young Pretender"); the troubles of the American Revolution; frequent riots, such as those of 1733 when Walpole attempted to raise new excise taxes, or those in the 1760's over the popular radical John Wilkes, or the Lord George Gordon Riots in 1780 when for several days London was in the hands of a mob stirred up by a fanatical hatred of the papacy.

Yet the record does not, after 1689 and right on down to the present day, include an actual revolution. For nearly three centuries Britain has gone through, without a *political* revolution or even a *coup d'état*, the radical changes that constitute the great, all-inclusive revolution of "modernization." We shall postpone coming to grips with the problems involved here until we come to the nineteenth century, when the pace of change, and particularly material change, was greatest in Britain. But we may note that the eighteenth century in Britain saw the bases for Victorian prosperity and greatness firmly laid, saw also in political life the tensions, the great debates, the freedom to differ in opinion so characteristic of later Britain.

Two distinguished historians, Lecky in Britain and Elie Halévy in France, have attributed the willingness of the British laboring classes to accept the hardships of their lot without revolt to their conversion in large numbers by the Methodists and other evangelical Christian sects. Methodism was a conservative social creed, preaching emotional participation in the hope of a better life in the world to come and rejecting as contrary to God's plan the republican doctrines of the Enlightenment. Like the Weber thesis on the Protestant ethic (*see* Chapter 7), this thesis too is suggestive, and may be accepted as one of the factors in a complex situation. Another decisive factor was the geographical protection afforded, until World War II, by the English Channel, a defense moat that allowed the English to differ among themselves and (save for the civil wars of the 1640's) to compromise in the end rather than resort to the kind of protective centralization adopted by the great military states on the Continent. Another and related factor was that England had been already modernized enough to undergo in the mid-seventeenth century the first of the great "middle-class" revolutions (*see* Chapter 8).

By the beginning of the eighteenth century Britain had a central government that could preserve sufficient order to permit the successful expansion of the British economy and—what would seem to be more decisive—could provide outlets for the energies of the kind of people who in France felt shut out of political life. Britain, like other states, had to wrestle with "medieval" survivals and with newer problems. The legal system was so fearfully complex that due process of law in a given case often took years to get settled. On paper the local government in parish, town, and shire looked at least as irrational and unworkable as that of France, but it did somehow work, even though trained professional local administrators were almost nonexistent. The rural population included, along with increasingly prosperous and efficient capitalist "farmers," a growing class of landless agricultural workers who were in material terms perhaps rather worse off than many Continental peasants. London was already big enough to have incipiently, at least, all the troubles of a modern metropolis—slums, slum dwellers, crimes of violence, even traffic jams—and some troubles the modern metropolis does not have, such as almost complete lack of police and fire protection. (Of juvenile delinquency we do not hear much, partly because it melted indistinguishably into the very considerable adult delinquency, and partly because in those days of universal child labor among the lower classes there were not many idle children.)

Yet Great Britain with not more than eight or ten million inhabitants in the late seventeenth and eighteenth centuries made an extraordinary mark on world history. With Newton, Locke, and many others she was a seminal factor in the Enlightenment, and she was also a leader in new agricultural and industrial techniques. Taking the lead given earlier by the Italians and the Dutch, she developed both governmental and commercial finances to the point where modern capitalist industrial production could be effective. In the eighteenth century she worked out one form of government by discussion (it would be misleading to call it democratic as yet), parliamentary or cabinet government, which has been widely imitated. In these years she also laid the foundations of her great empire, and if in the 1770's she lost the richest potential of that empire in North America, her language and her institutions left a permanent imprint on the United States.

Cabinet Government. "Growth" is a sound term to describe cabinet government in eighteenth-century Britain. This form of government was not planned, not "made," certainly not in the sense that the American government was planned at Philadelphia in 1787, or the French in a dozen constitutions since 1791. The Glorious Revolution of 1688 had insured that Parliament should have a decisive voice in legislation, but it had left administration in the hands of the Crown and its ministers. William III (reigned 1689–1702) did not hesitate to rule, and would have been astounded could he have foreseen the present purely symbolic and ornamental role of the British Crown. His successor, Queen Anne (reigned 1702–

1714), and even more her successor, the German-speaking Hanoverian George I (reigned 1714–1727), were not commanding personalities. One can wonder what a succession of really strongminded and gifted rulers would have done to the burgeoning course of English constitutional development in the early eighteenth century.

Once the Crown weakened, the executive powers which had previously lain in a cabinet of the king's own servants or ministers came gradually under the control of a cabinet which was in fact a committee of the Parliament. Nominally, however, the cabinet was still composed of ministers of the Crown and to this day is formally appointed by the Crown. Today this committee has a chairman, a very powerful one, known as the Prime Minister; its members sit in Parliament and share in its debate. As long as a majority of Parliament support it—that is, vote what we Americans would call "administration bills"—the Prime Minister and his cabinet remain in power. Parliament itself is divided along party lines, and its

Hogarth, "The Polling," from the series "The Election."

great ruling committee, "Her Majesty's Government," the cabinet and its leader, are drawn from the majority party; the minority party or parties make up "Her Majesty's Opposition." In present-day Britain the leader of the *opposition* is himself a paid "servant" of the Crown; in older days outright opposition to the monarch more commonly meant exile or execution.

Of great importance in the growth of cabinet government was the long tenure of power (1721–1742) of Robert Walpole, who deserves the title of the "first Prime Minister" though "revisionist" historians have denied it to him. Walpole was a supremely skillful politician, who was able to hold his cabinet colleagues under firm discipline, and so manage Parliament as not to get beaten in decisive votes. It was not an easy task, for neither internal cabinet unity nor party discipline of a modern kind existed yet; the terms "Whig" and "Tory" referred to informal and shifting interest groups or factions, not to parties in our sense. Only in a very rough sense were these early Tories conservatives, or the early Whigs liberals. More accurately, the Tories reluctantly accepted the Hanoverian succession and were "royalist," for King and Church; the Whigs were for their own aristocratic rule through Parliament. Walpole, a Whig, "manipulated" Parliament in part by distributing government monies, posts, pensions, and other favors, in short, by what we Americans call spoils and graft; but he gave Britain two decades of peace and solid economic development.

The doctrine that an adverse vote of Parliament means either resignation of the Prime Minister or a new general election to Parliament was not yet established. When in 1733 a great popular outcry, reflected in Parliament even in those undemocratic days, arose against a major fiscal reform proposed by Walpole—his Excise Bill—he simply gave up trying to put the bill through. After Walpole's fall in 1742 no great leader arose until the elder Pitt, later made Earl of Chatham, came to office in 1757 at a low point in the Seven Years' War and rallied the nation to victory. Pitt's prestige aided in the growth of the office of Prime Minister; cabinet government, however, now faced a most important test.

George III. In 1760 George III, first Hanoverian king to be thoroughly English, came to the throne after an education in which his mother had kept insisting to him, "George, be king." Twentieth-century specialists in the history of the British eighteenth century have attacked the older view that George III attempted "personal rule," and maintain that this view was foisted on contemporaries and later historians by Whig publicists anxious to defend their policies. Perhaps in this matter the pendulum of "revisionism" has swung too far. True, George was no despot, certainly no "enlightened" despot; true—and this is most important—a radical party or "interest," almost democratic in the modern sense, was growing up in England partly outside parliamentary politics, and was foreshadowing modern parties working directly on public opinion. Still, in the years 1760–1784 a group, christened at the time the "King's friends," and led by Tories like Lords Bute and North, did try to manage Parliament and thus attempt to govern. And they were opposed by varied groups and personalities, all of which at least used the language of the libertarian side of the Enlightenment (*see* Chapter 9). At any rate, the "myth" of an attempt at royal personal rule in the Continental manner, frustrated by Wilkes, the American Revolution, and the Whigs, was firmly held by most Englishmen for well over a century.

John Wilkes, member of Parliament, rake, and journalist, had in 1764 violated custom by attacking in his journal, the *North Briton*, a "speech from the throne" which of course was really a declaration by the cabinet. He was accused of libel, for one did not attack a king in print, and in the course of proceedings a *general* warrant of search was issued without specifically naming any person. A landmark in the history of civil rights was the court's decision that such warrants were illegal, that a search warrant must always name a specific and limited person and place. But the House of Commons agreed that Wilkes's action had been libelous, and he fled to France. In 1768 he returned, was elected to Parliament from the populous constituency of Middlesex County just outside London, and became the focus of a prolonged crisis, centering on whether or not he should be seated. He was twice elected, and twice refused by vote of the Commons. After a third election the House actually seated a Colonel Luttrell, who had been badly beaten in the poll, but who, the House asserted, "ought to have been returned." All this had been punctuated by agitation, indeed rioting, accompanied by the cry "Wilkes and Liberty!" Though denied his seat at this time, Wilkes was returned in 1774 and took his seat amid rejoicing in the streets.

What Wilkes had begun was pretty well completed by Washington and the American Revolution. Tory opinion was generally anti-American, but the Whigs were openly in favor of the colonists from the beginning. Edmund Burke's speeches on the American crisis have become classics, and the American map is strewn with place-names derived from British defenders of American rights—Wilkes-Barre, Burke, Pittsburgh, Chatham. The war was badly handled, and generally unpopular in Britain, and the Tory minister Lord North became more and more discredited. The end of the war in 1783 saw formal recognition of American independence. North, whose ministry had fallen in the previous year, attempted to regain power by a coalition with his bitter Whig opponent, Charles James Fox. To use modern terms, "public opinion" was shocked by so evident a piece of manipulation inside the select circle of parliamentary politicians. The election of 1784 which followed the defeat of Fox's bill reforming the government of India must not be thought of quite in terms of a twentieth-century "appeal to the country," for the House of Commons was still elected by a small minority of the total population. Nevertheless, it was an important step toward modern British democratic government. The younger Pitt (second son of the great Earl of Chatham), who became Prime Minister in 1784 at the age of 24, had a position appreciably nearer that of a modern Prime Minister than that of Walpole 60 years before.

IV. Enlightened Despotism

For most of the rest of Europe, the thread tying together the varied course of internal politics was "enlightened despotism," which by the last quarter of the eighteenth century was an almost universal pattern, much as the divine-right monarchy on the pattern of Louis XIV had been in the seventeenth century and as parliamentary government was at the end of the nineteenth. The term "enlightened despotism" is not altogether a happy one, for to many the adjective swears at the noun, as in a phrase like "clean dirt." Still, we have already seen how the ideas of the Enlightenment provided ammunition for reforming rulers. These rulers were often genuinely desirous of improving the living standards of their subjects, but they were most concerned with achieving what would today be called "efficiency," "economy," "rationalization," even "streamlining." They wanted to eliminate the kind of obstacles that were weakening the Old Regime in France. In a sense Turgot was trying to get Louis XVI to act as enlightened despot of France, a role for which Louis was quite unsuited.

PRUSSIA: FREDERICK THE GREAT

The Prussia of Frederick II (1740–1786), even in his lifetime known as the Great, was the showcase of enlightened despotism, and Frederick himself the darling of the *philosophes*. He owed a great deal, however, to his Hohenzollern predecessors. His great-grandfather, Frederick William, the Great Elector (1640–1688), had built up the Prussian administration, preserved Prussia through the last decade of the Thirty Years' War, and come out fairly well in the Westphalia settlement. Frederick II owed something, if only prestige, to his otherwise undistinguished grandfather, who gained the Habsburg Emperor's consent to the Hohenzollern acquisition of the title of King *in* (though not of) Prussia and reigned as Frederick I. He owed most of all to his father, King Frederick William I (1713–1740), a coarse and tyrannical person—a tyrannical father, too—who nursed as a hobby the excellent Prussian army that his son was to find so useful; further, he left his son a full treasury.

As we have already seen, Frederick II added Silesia and part of Poland to the relatively small domains he had inherited, raising Prussia for the first time to the rank of a Great Power. He did this by ruthless power politics of the kind the *philosophes* normally complained about as quite unenlightened, but most of them forgave him in view of his professed attachment to their principles (especially his skepticism about religion)—and in view of his success. The kingdom he inherited was made up of scattered territories not put completely together until the nineteenth century. But, though they look on a map rather like a crazy quilt, the Hohenzollern lands, save for the last Polish acquisitions, were fairly homogeneous—Protestant, North German, historically not sharply divided by class or other tensions, conditioned to a respect for authority.

Prussia was not particularly rich, and certainly had its full share of medieval institutions, medieval class structure, serfdom, and other stumbling blocks to the unified progressive nation-state. But it had a remarkable bureaucracy (civil service), perhaps the best in Europe, which Frederick maintained and strengthened. It had landed nobility full of pride, yet—in marked contrast to the French nobility—generally loyal to the Crown and willing to serve it faithfully in peace and war. Though it is dangerous to generalize about a national character, it does seem as though the common people of Frederick's dominions were—as compared with either the French or the English—relatively submissive and obedient.

Frederick's role as an enlightened despot was more an intellectual and literary one than one of action. Toward the end of his life he started his experts to work on a great standardized law code, part of which was published in 1782, the rest in the next reign. He undertook a good many "public works" such as canals and draining of marsh lands. But he was rather a good housekeeper than a true innovator and reformer like his younger contemporary, Joseph II of Austria. His wars cost a great deal, and the high taxes, the efficient but expensive administration, and the mercantilist character of his economic policies held back basic

A Norwegian soldier in the army of Frederick William I of Prussia.

Prussian economic growth and perhaps helped to account for the failure of Prussia to stand up to the French in warfare in the next generation (see Chapter 11).

Frederick's reputation as an enlightened man stemmed from his deliberate cultivation of some of the French *philosophes*. With Voltaire, whom he finally persuaded to come and adorn the Prussian court, he had a brief friendship—if two such determined and self-centered great men can be said to have a friendship. Frederick wrote a great deal, always in French, and indeed had a contempt for German as a vehicle for literary expression. He disliked women and seems to have had no need for them. By no means an original thinker, he was also an unbeliever, and merely went through the minimum of Christian ritual necessary to his headship of a Christian people. He welcomed to Prussia the Jesuits, whose order was dissolved by Pope Clement XIV in 1773, but seems to have been essentially motivated by a desire for good publicity among intellectuals. In sum, a very strange "sport," in genetic terms, to come from the solid Germanic Hohenzollern family. We may leave him with a quotation that does neatly sum up the intellectual position of enlightened despotism: "The Enlightenment," he said, "is a light from heaven for those who stand on the heights, and a destructive firebrand for the masses."

AUSTRIA: JOSEPH II

Joseph II, son of Maria Theresa, who had technically shared the throne with his somewhat overshadowing mother since 1765, came into sole power at her death in 1780 and proceeded to decree a series of radical reforms. Joseph's dominions, unlike Frederick's, were contiguous enough (save for the Austrian Netherlands, now Belgium, acquired in 1713), but they were a crazy quilt of diverse peoples, languages, and traditions. Maria Theresa had carried out through her ministers the kind of administrative reforms necessary to hold the Habsburg realm together. She carefully avoided disturbing vested interests wherever possible, however, and in particular those of the Roman Catholic Church, of which the Empress was a very devout member. Joseph, though not the cynical skeptic Frederick was, was determined to cut his dominions "*Los von Rom*" (free from Rome) in all but a formal sense. He was an anticlerical in the original Catholic sense of the word, that is, against priestly control of anything save actual church services. He was in other respects also a good child of his age, a believer in rational reforms, neat systems, and, what is more important, the human ability and desire to accept such reasonable reforms.

Joseph attempted to reform the secular clergy, restoring, he hoped, the purity of primitive Christianity. He straightened out the ecclesiastical map, making the dioceses as equal as possible, organizing new parishes, setting up state-supervised seminaries for the education of candidates for the priesthood, freeing them from Rome—and tying them to Vienna. He abolished by decree in 1781 all monastic societies devoted to the life of contemplation, confiscated their property and turned the capital over to a fund for poor relief, education, and increased stipends for working parish priests—all worthy, humanitarian, and thoroughly "practical" purposes. In the same year, again by edict, he established wide freedom of worship for Protestants and the Greek Orthodox. He even took the very advanced step of granting Jews full freedom, property rights, and relief

Death mask of Frederick the Great.

from the obligation to wear the hated yellow patch. He had earlier begun to set up a rational system of education designed to train good modern citizens in practical ways as well as in the old classical traditions.

Although the papacy opposed many of Joseph's reforms, the power of the Habsburgs was too great, their place in Catholic politics too important—and Pope Pius VI (reigned 1775–1799) too cautious and flexible a diplomatist—for any radical break to take place. But at every level and in every corner of Joseph's dominions there was opposition, the kind of opposition we have seen aroused by Turgot's efforts at radical, wholesale, simultaneous reforms in France. Joseph was an anointed king and emperor, and no mere minister. Even so, just before his death in 1790, the opposition had broken out into violence in Hungary and in the Austrian Netherlands. No one can say what would have happened had Joseph lived to continue his course. His brother Leopold, who succeeded, was a mod-

Emperor Joseph II of Austria working a plow.

erate and tactful ruler who had headed an enlightened administration in Tuscany, and who called a halt to Joseph's root-and-branch policies without wholly abandoning what had been accomplished. He died in 1792, and under his weak successor, Francis II, the Austrian complex became a center of resistance to the new ideas, by then embodied in revolutionary France.

RUSSIA: PETER AND CATHERINE

Russia's contribution to the roster of enlightened despots was Catherine the Great. She was perhaps rather more the despot than the enlightened, and she owed a great deal to her predecessors and in particular to one of the most remarkable men ever born to royalty, Peter the Great (1689–1725). Russia had long been an autocracy, but one without much trace of enlightenment. Peter, at least in his admiration for Western efficiency and, above all, for Western science and technology, deserves to be listed as an early enlightened despot. He was almost seven feet tall, very bright, frantically energetic, completely and barbarously ruthless—indeed, by Western standards, hardly housebroken. With more-than-Renaissance curiosity and fervor, he threw himself into war, reform, science, craftsmanship. At various times he took up carpentry, shoe-making, cooking, clock-making, ivory-carving, etching, and—worst of all for his subjects—dentistry. Born to unchallenged despotism, he simply experimented on the teeth of anyone at hand, whether or not he had a toothache.

He partially remade Russia, not indeed without opposition from the conservative many, whom he exposed to uncomfortable changes, but on the whole with remarkable success. Russian brutality, Russian corruption in high places, Russian barbarism in many ways remained as before; Russian beards, Russian dress, even the Russian calendar, did change. Peter's foundation of the city of St. Petersburg on an arm of the Baltic Sea made Russia geographically part of Europe; his political, economic, and educational reforms began the process of making Russia culturally part of Europe. That acculturation, as we know today, has been incomplete. Notably, Peter helped fix on Russia most of the political and social ways of life we still qualify as "autocracy"; in this sense he was no innovator, no revolutionary, but a most effective agent of a going tradition.

Above all, Peter continued the territorial growth of the "Russia" that had once been merely "Muscovy" (an English derivation from Moscow). Simultaneously with the War of the Spanish Succession (*see* Chapter 8), and lasting for eight years after the Peace of Utrecht, the "Great Northern War" convulsed northern and eastern Europe. The throne of Sweden descended in 1697 to a 15-year-

Peter I striding along the dikes during the building of St. Petersburg; a painting by V. A. Serov.

old monarch, Charles XII. His neighbors, the Danes, together with Peter the Great and Augustus the Strong, King of Poland, thought that the time had come to enrich themselves by attacking the Swedish possessions on the south shore of the Baltic. But the allies underestimated the daring Charles XII, who knocked Denmark out of the war (1699), defeated the Russians (1700), invaded Poland (1701), and spent seven years pursuing Augustus and sponsoring his own candidate for the Polish throne. Only in 1709, deep in the Ukraine at Poltava, did the forces of Peter the Great turn back Charles XII; but the Swedish King escaped and made constant difficulties for the Russians in Turkey and in other European countries for nine years thereafter, until his death in 1718. The Turks, in fact, came into this confusing war in 1710 and actually trapped Peter and his army in what is now Rumania. But Peter bought them off by concessions in south Russia (Azov); much to the anger of Charles XII, he was freed, and peace was made between Turks and Russians.

Even then the Great Northern War was ended only after a Russian landing in Sweden proper (1719) and two long years of negotiations. By the Treaty of Nystadt (1721), Russia received all the former possessions of Sweden along the southeastern coast of the Baltic (parts of the modern Estonia and Latvia). The Baltic was thus opened to Russian sea-borne commerce, and Peter had his famous "window on the west." At the end of the war, also, Peter had made a series of marriage and other alliances with the petty German principalities, for the first time extending Russian diplomacy into the heart of Europe. From a little-known state somewhere behind Poland, Russia had emerged as a major military power, with which the European states would have to reckon. Sweden's bid for Great Power status was ended.

After the death of Peter (1725), a line of weak rulers governed Russia until the accession of Catherine II (reigned 1762–1796). She came to the throne in 1762 after the murder of her husband, Peter III, by one of her lovers (her own role in this is uncertain). Catherine worked essentially in the tradition of Peter the Great, and her basic aim was to set up in Russia an effective service nobility and a faithful bureaucracy rather on the Prussian model. She herself was born into the German nobility and brought up in a petty German court. Like Frederick, she managed very skillfully to sell herself to the *philosophes*. She flattered the aging Voltaire, cultivated, employed, and paid men like Diderot and Grimm, and was rewarded by very good European publicity. Catherine did begin her reign with a grand plan to codify the immense accumulated mass of laws, mostly decrees from local or national administrations over the preceding several centuries; and this was to be done through an assembly representing all classes of the realm. She prefaced her call for this assembly with a preamble or *nakaz* to guide the members, a document done in the best style of Montesquieu, Beccaria, and the other enlightened jurists. The assembly, pretty well rigged as Catherine wanted it, finally met in 1767, debated off and on for a year, but produced nothing. When the first of Catherine's wars with the Turks intervened, the meetings were called off, though committees worked on for some time. Certainly a good deal of information valuable to the administrators who really did, with Catherine's support, get things done came out of this well-publicized move to gain credit in Western eyes—or at least in enlightened Western eyes.

For the rest, Catherine reformed administrative units, and further centralized in practice if not in theory the absolute power of the state. She secured the cooperation of her gentry by allowing them to tighten their hold over their serfs, a step the *philosophes* ought to have held retrogressive. But she also encouraged trade and industry, developing essential waterways and freeing internal trade of many local tolls and other restrictions (which was more than the French government could achieve in France). In spite of her wars, she left Russia at her death in 1796 a more prosperous land than she had found it. Like Frederick, Catherine was a successful aggressor. Through the partitions of Poland she expanded her realm to the west with a minimum of fighting; and she added rich and important lands to the south on the Black Sea by hard fighting with the Turks. Unlike Frederick, she was fond of the opposite sex; but, though she favored her lovers with privileges and high posts, she never allowed them to dupe her. Altogether, Catherine II was a remarkable woman, in many respects well deserving of her title, "the Great."

Catherine the Great.

OTHER DESPOTS

The roster of enlightened despots is a long one. In Sweden, Gustavus III (reigned 1771–1792) achieved absolute authority and used it to abolish judicial torture, proclaim liberty of the press, and encourage economic growth, until he was assassinated because of his own arbitrariness and because of the aristocratic opposition he had aroused. In Germany and Italy rulers followed the new fashion as their grandfathers had followed the fashion of the Sun King at Versailles. Joseph II's younger brother Leopold, Grand Duke of Tuscany (1745–1790), made the old Florentine state a show place of enlightened despotism. Even the impoverished south Italian kingdom of Naples and Sicily under the Bourbon Charles IV (reigned 1735–1759) and his minister Tanucci, who ruled during the youth of Charles's son, enjoyed a brief flowering in music, art, and, with the jurist Filangieri and others, enlightened thought.

On the death of his half-brother Ferdinand I in 1759, Charles IV of Naples became Charles III of Spain, where he reigned until 1788 and presided over administrative and economic reforms that at least lifted that unfortunate kingdom out of the trough it had fallen into under its last Habsburg kings. The other part of the Iberian peninsula, Portugal, provided a minister, the Marquis de Pombal, who can be set beside Joseph II as a thoroughgoing enlightened despot. Unlike Joseph, however, he was by no means a humanitarian by temperament but a rather hard-boiled dictator; like him, he did stir up great opposition, and was eventually exiled in 1782 as the nobles gained influence with the new queen, Maria I. Not the least of Pombal's achievements was the rapid rebuilding of Lisbon in good, rational eighteenth-century style after the horrible earthquake of 1755. He initiated the attack on the Jesuits which resulted in their expulsion from one Catholic state after another and culminated in the abolition of the order by papal decree in 1773. It was restored in 1814.

The eighteenth-century attack on the Society of Jesus exemplifies the intellectual fashion which played so large a part in the Enlightenment. The order was accused of devotion to intrigue, of shocking ethical relativism, and much else. But most of the princes who attacked the order were motivated by a desire to get rid of a powerful group that could not wholly be brought under royal control. Ironically, as educators, especially in secondary schools, the Jesuits were often progressive devotees of the new sciences, and all told a surprising number of the *philosophes* were educated by them.

Charles III, by Goya.

V. The American Revolution

THE BACKGROUND

There is a touch of irony in the fact that the two great rival powers of the twentieth century enter the history of the West during the eighteenth century. Russia came in as a full-fledged despotism sharing in the great struggles for power in Europe and expanding eastward across thinly settled Siberian lands of primitive tribes to the Pacific. The United States made a very different entrance, as a newly emancipated state —hardly yet a "power"—founded on principles dear to the democratic or libertarian side of the Enlightenment. The British North American colonies had attracted little notice from Europeans until their quarrel with the mother country at once focussed the attention of Europe upon them. Hyperbolic and romantic though it is, there is some truth in Emerson's famous line about Concord: "the shot heard round the world."

By 1775 the colonies had a population of some two-and-one-half million including several hundred thousand Negro slaves, and had begun, now that the French had been driven out of the continent, to spill over across the Alleghenies. They had been founded as separate colonies, which in a sense they still were; after independence each could claim to be a "sovereign" state. During the wars with France they had squabbled among themselves and with Britain about their financial and military participation in the campaigns. Yet they had a common language and basically common laws and other institutions, and even the difference between New England and the South fell far short of the sum of the differences between European nation-states such as France and Britain. The thirteen colonies, in spite of their squabbling, had managed to cooperate in conventions and congresses. After the British government tried to tax the colonists more effectively, and otherwise tighten imperial ties, a network of Committees of Correspondence, Sons of Liberty, and the like grew up and showed that Americans could manage something like a common organized movement.

The American Revolution was a nationalist revolution rather than a social revolution. Even before the Congress decided to issue the Declaration of Independence in 1776, the colonists' aim had been for a kind of territorial autonomy, under the Crown but not under Parliament. Yet elements of social revolution were present, as they usually are in any challenge to authority by a group of rebels willing to use force. Marxist or pseudo-Marxist formulas will not fit: bourgeois were not pitted against aristocrats, nor even poor against rich. But a whole series of interest groups—planters in debt to London, Yankee merchants cramped in their business by British mercantilist policies restraining their trade, craftsmen and their workers in towns like Philadelphia, Boston, and New York already imbued with "democratic" ideas, frontiersmen to whom the old seaboard and London were both restrictive authorities on their free new world—combined against British *and* American Tories. These discontented groups were not oppressed and miserable minorities; in fact, neither side can be given a neat sociological or even ideological label. The complexities, perhaps the contradictions, of later American society are already foreshadowed in the Revolution.

THE WAR AND ITS RESULTS

The War of the American Revolution lasted, in a formal sense, from 1775 to 1783. In military operations it was a modest affair, even by eighteenth-century standards, and even after the entry of France in 1778 made it a minor world war. Cornwallis at Yorktown in 1781 surrendered to George Washington with his whole force—seven thousand men. It is tempting to assert that, had Britain used her full potential in men and money, she could have subdued the colonists; yet the area of the thirteen colonies was enormous, and guerrillas would have been hard to put down. The war though fought by few was hard fought, and American national tradition justifiably makes much of names like Concord and Lexington, the Brandywine, Saratoga, Bunker Hill, Valley Forge, the Cowpens. A temporary mastery of the sea by the French navy enabled Washington to isolate Cornwallis at Yorktown. The British, it must be admitted, never put everything into the struggle. Many Englishmen, some in very high position, disapproved of the war entirely; the world wars of 1739–1763 had strained British resources; not even Britain in the eighteenth century had an economy and a policy that could wage the kind of all-out war to which the world is now accustomed.

Already during the war, in 1777, the Congress had agreed upon Articles of Confederation establishing a government of the United States of America. This government lacked many powers, especially in taxation, that the federal government now enjoys. Historians today incline to insist, in opposition to historians writing in the late nineteenth century, that the governmental machinery set up by the Articles of Confederation was not to blame for the grave economic and social difficulties of what used to be called the "critical period," 1781–1789. The new republic was put under difficulties of trade from the mercantilist exclusions practiced by the British and other foreign countries, paper-money experiments ran wild in some states, and there was the usual postwar letdown. At any rate, the new government did get the blame, and alarmed or merely discontented leaders—mostly solid and conservative men—called a convention at Philadelphia in 1787 which produced the Constitution under which, as revised by amendments and even more by time and usage, Americans still live.

The new Constitution had to be ratified in each state, and had to be accepted by nine to be initiated. In June, 1788, New Hampshire became the ninth to ratify. The last of the thirteen, Rhode Island, did not come in until 1790. The contest between those who wanted the new Constitution and those who did not was close and bitterly fought in many states, and prefigured American party politics for many decades ahead. Broadly the Federalists, those in favor of the new more powerful federal government, can be labeled conservatives; the later heirs of their general political position—though not of course of their specific policies and platforms—were the Whigs and then the Republicans. Their opponents, at first called merely antifederalists, then National Republicans, by the early nineteenth century took the name they have kept, Democrats. Yet from the start neither party was a monolithic block; both had regional and other differences within their membership.

The Declaration of Independence, the various state constitutions with their bills of rights, the Constitution of 1787, the Bill of Rights incorporated in the first ten amendments of 1791—these formal documents plus the speeches, pamphlets, books, news reports, travellers' accounts, and personal impressions carried back by Frenchmen like Lafayette make a body of thought of very great interest as political theory, and one that has had a very great influence on Western history. It is by no means national pride that dictates such a statement. What went on in the United States in those years was, at least in European eyes, a kind of experimental testing of the great Enlightenment ideas of Nature and Reason, of Progress and the Rights of Man. Of course there would have been a French Revolution had there been no American Revolution. But "would have been" are rather silly words in this kind of historical situation. The American bills of rights were translated into French, French revolutionists set up busts of Franklin and Washington in their meeting places, Lafayette did become the "Hero of Two Worlds," and the French even christened a variation of whist after those daring revolutionists, *les Bostonnais*.

The American Revolution helped to bring the whole set of "democratic" purposes and values down from the cloudland of theorizing into the arena of practical politics. This statement does not mean that the rest of the Western world set about imitating the American example, nor that it understood correctly the very complicated nature of the great American experiment. It does mean, however, that by the 1780's the very varied groups in Europe discontented with the old regime could hold up the American example as concrete evidence that what they wanted to change could indeed be changed.

VI. The Growth of a Modern Economy

Adding force to the process of change and modernization were the revolutionary developments affecting material life. These may be grouped in three broad categories: the administrative and financial, the agricultural, and the industrial, each of which constitutes in effect a "subrevolution." They are interrelated, and at the same time related to the Enlightenment, for things like the steam engine, the spinning jenny, and systems of credit were ultimately products of the human mind—and human drives.

ADMINISTRATIVE AND FINANCIAL REVOLUTIONS

The modern process of material production is long and unbelievably complex. Compare, for example, the primitive hunter and food-gatherer, consuming at once the game he has stalked or the fruit he has found, at most keeping a small supply for a few days, with your own day's consumption of goods, none of which most probably was produced on the spot, and some of which—for instance, your coffee or tea—came from thousands of miles away and were grown months ago. In this roundabout process a great many people have to be supported by stores of previously produced goods which have been saved rather than consumed while they are producing their "bit" in the process. This saving of goods is the origin of "capital." It consisted originally of such articles as domesticated animals, but the invention of other mediums of exchange, or "money," enabled the development of capital to be greatly extended; and the invention of "credit," by which a promising improvement in production could be financed over a long time, put the final touch on the system. While this process had existed in ancient and medieval times, what the modern period added was a very great refinement in the necessary apparatus of large-scale production and distribution by a series of devices, from double-entry bookkeeping through joint-stock companies to offset printing and electronic computers, without which our contemporary civilization could not possibly exist.

This administrative and financial revolution, sometimes called the commercial revolution, had immediate origins in the later Middle Ages, especially in Italy and the Low Countries. The Dutch had worked out comprehensive improvements in insurance and banking before 1700, and the Bank of Amsterdam had already issued paper notes of stable value. In Britain, the Bank of England (1694) made possible the financing of the War of the Spanish Succession. By the early eighteenth century there was already an international money market, with elements of most of the apparatus of modern finance. In fact, the cycle of expansion and contraction so characteristic of modern capitalist economies was foreshadowed by two great financial crises—the South Sea Bubble in England and the Mississippi Bubble in France. These were not, however, quite the first of such crises: a wild speculation known as "tulipomania" had swept seventeenth-century Holland following the establishment of the tulip-bulb business.

Both "Bubbles" involved trading companies with chartered monopolies. The South Sea Company had the right to exploit the *asiento* agreement of the Treaty of Utrecht (1713) which gave Britain limited trading privileges with Spanish colonies. The Mississippi Company had the right to exploit the French colony of Louisiana (to which the rest of France overseas was later added); it was under the guidance of John Law, a gambler, adventurer, mathematician, and financial "wizard" of Scottish origin. Each company issued stock, which was traded publicly, and also assumed responsibility for the interest on parts of the government debt which they paid for with the cash obtained from sales of stock. Each promoted a speculative boom, which reached a height in 1719–1720. Mississippi stock sold at forty times its par value, and South Seas stock at more than ten times par. Almost everyone took part, from dukes and princes down to the man in the street, and there were the usual scandals involving "insiders," who were "let in on the ground floor." Meantime, dozens of other promoters sprang into action, advertising schemes for wheels of perpetual motion, for making salt water fresh, "for carrying on an undertaking of great advantage, but nobody to know what it is."

In France, Law had combined paper money issues from his bank with the rest of his scheme, and the boom broke when he was forced to suspend specie payments in February, 1720. In England, the shares simply dropped with increasing speed as the public began to unload them, so that those of the South Sea Company fell from £1050 in June, 1720, to £150 in September. Law fled France, and the board of directors of the South Sea Company, having destroyed company records, fled England. There were scandals—more than 100 members of Parliament had borrowed money to buy South Sea stock on the installment plan—recriminations, bitter attacks on the wickedness of modern finance, and appeals to return to the simplicities of the good old days.

But however hard on those caught short, the boom itself helped establish modern large-scale production. Voltaire himself—who was a very successful businessman—later commented that Law's "imaginary system gave birth to a real commerce." The Mississippi Company, reorganized after 1720, consistently made a handsome profit. In England, the South Sea Bubble scarcely affected the strongest institutions. The East India Company went right on paying an annual dividend of 5 to 10 per cent, and the Bank of England, no longer competing with the South Sea Company for government favors, became more than ever the financial mainstay of the realm. In the political shakeup following the Bubble, the Whig statesman Robert Walpole came to power with a program of honoring the debt as a *national* debt. This was a novel concept and a great step forward in fiscal morality in an age when most states still treated their debts as the monarch's personal obligation, to be recognized or repudiated as he saw fit.

By the end of the century, most of the devices of modern business were in existence, at least in their beginnings. There were central banks, the usual apparatus of commercial banking, bank notes, and insurance companies, including the celebrated Lloyd's of London, which began as a marine insurance business early in the century. There were formally organized stock exchanges—and national debts. Above all, there was the limited liability stock company, an institution that would be perfected later, during the early nineteenth century, abbreviated in the United States as "Inc.," in Britain as "Ltd.," and in Germany as "GmbH." The essential here is that the capital of the company is a set of shares, in those days always with an original or "par" value, each one of which must bear its proportionate share of any debts of the company *but no more,* and gets its proportionate share of profits. In

London during the South Sea Bubble. The hunchback is hiring himself out as a desk.

contrast, in a partnership each partner is liable to the full extent of the debts of the whole enterprise. This device of "limited liability" enables capital for enterprises to be gathered in trickles from all sorts of sources—in fact, makes possible the giant companies of today, which could not possibly be managed as partnerships.

THE AGRICULTURAL REVOLUTION

The agricultural revolution, the second of the changes transforming the economy of the modern world, has been based on technological improvements that enabled fewer farmers to produce more crops, often on less land. The application of scientific discoveries to agriculture is an old story, as old as the irrigation ditches of ancient Mesopotamia and the improved plows and horse-collars of the Middle Ages. What was new and revolutionary in the eighteenth century was the tempo: for the first time the advance in farming techniques began to move at a rapid rate. The leaders of the movement were the "improving landlords" of England, notably Jethro Tull and Viscount Townshend.

Jethro Tull (1674–1741) studied the painstaking methods used in French truck-gardens and vineyards, where farmers obtained a heavy yield from small plots by planting seeds individually and by carefully hoeing the soil around each plant and vine. Tull adapted French methods to the much larger grain fields of England. In place of the inefficient custom of scattering seed broadcast, he planted it deeply in regular rows with a horse-drawn "drilling" machine, and he cultivated his crops with a horse-drawn hoe. The outstanding production record of Tull's test farm quickly justified his innovations.

Viscount Townshend (1674–1738), called "Turnip" Townshend, used his Norfolk estate to experiment with two valuable new crops brought in from Holland—turnips and clover. By storing sufficient turnips to feed all the livestock until the arrival of the spring pasturing season, Townshend avoided the customary slaughter of stock at the onset of winter. Clover, by fixing nitrogen in the soil, increased the fertility of the land and curtailed the wasteful practice of letting fields lie fallow every third year. Townshend's four-year rotation—planting the same field to turnips, barley, clover, and wheat in successive years—soon became the standard procedure on many English estates.

Before 1789, the new agricultural techniques gained the support of only the most enterprising landlords. On the Continent, the leaders were to be found in France, Holland, and Prussia, where King Frederick the Great directed his subjects to breed livestock, grow fodder crops, and rotate plantings, all in the advanced English manner. In Britain itself, the new methods appealed chiefly to the holders of large estates, including George III, "Farmer George."

THE INDUSTRIAL REVOLUTION

Latest of the three revolutions, and dependent on both the others, was the great change still called the Industrial Revolution, though many modern historians quarrel with a term they think implies too much suddenness and violence. Here the essence of the change was the machine moved by mechanical, not human or animal, power, steam for the most part; in turn, the large-scale and efficient use of such power-driven machinery required concentration of production in a "factory." (Two curious examples of verbal transference: the capacities of these power-driven machines were measured as h.p.—horsepower; the "factory" was originally a colonial trading station where "factors" or agents of the owners lived.) Machines and factories appeared in Great Britain in the second half of the eighteenth century, and even before 1800 began to spread onto the Continent and to the United States.

Some elements of industrial change had first appeared at the close of the Middle Ages. To take an example from textiles, the making of yarn and cloth had long been organized according to the "domestic system," in which spinners or weavers worked at home on simple wheels or looms. Most of them, however, did not buy their own raw materials or market their finished products; rather, they worked as wage-laborers for a capitalist, an entrepreneur who furnished materials and sold the finished yarn and cloth. In some industries, however, production was organized not under the domestic system but in primitive factories; while these assembled many laborers in a large workshop, they still relied on hand processes rather than on machines. The Industrial Revolution eventually made the domestic system obsolete and transformed the factory system. The power-driven machines, which were often big, complicated, and costly, required larger factories.

By 1789, these revolutionary changes had affected only a few industries; but the industries involved were in key sectors of the economy: mining, metallurgy, munitions, and textiles. Coal-mining already was becoming a big business in the eighteenth century, partly because of the increased demand for coal by iron-smelters. For centuries, the smelters had used charcoal to make iron from the raw ore, and they continued to do so in countries like Sweden that had abundant wood for charcoal. But in England, where almost all the great forests had been cut down, the price of charcoal rose so high that it constituted nearly 80 per cent of the cost of producing iron. Ordinary coal could not replace charcoal as smelter fuel because the chemicals in coal made the iron too brittle. Here necessity

Eighteenth-century grinders at work, as illustrated in the "Encyclopédie."

mothered invention. The Darby family of Coalbrookdale in Shropshire discovered how to remove the chemical impurities from coal by converting it through an oven process into coke, which is almost pure carbon and produces iron of high quality. In England, the Darbys and other private firms were the pioneers in metallurgy; on the Continent, governments took the lead. Warfare required weapons and munitions in unprecedented quantities; France and Prussia met the demand by setting up state-financed and state-operated foundries and arms factories.

The revolution in textiles was focussed on the cheaper production of cotton cloth. The "flying shuttle," a technical device first applied to the hand loom in England (1733), enabled a single weaver to do work that had previously required the services of two. The looms equipped with the flying shuttle used up the supply of hand-spun thread so rapidly that the London Society for the Encouragement of Arts, Manufactures, and Commerce offered a prize for improvement of the spinning process. James Hargreaves won the prize in 1764 with his "spinning jenny," a series of spinning wheels geared together which made eight threads simultaneously. Soon the jenny was adapted to water power, and its output was increased to 100 or more threads at once. The eventual emancipation of industry from dependence on unreliable water power was foreshadowed in the 1760's when James Watt introduced his steam engine.

Although Britain had nearly 150 cotton mills in 1789, woolens and dozens of other basic commodities were still made by hand. The full sweep of industrial development would not appear until the canal and railroad permitted cheap transport of heavy freight, until the shortages of capital and skilled labor were overcome, and until precision tools were made available. A Swedish inventor of the early 1700's designed excellent machines for cutting wheels and files but could not raise the money to put them into operation. And in Britain the difficulty of making precisely fitting parts for Watt's engine held back its production. The eighteenth century had taken many of the initial steps in the Industrial Revolution; it remained for the nineteenth century to apply them on a truly revolutionary scale.

10

READING SUGGESTIONS (asterisk indicates paperbound edition)

General Accounts

P. Roberts, *The Quest for Security, 1715–1740*; W. L. Dorn, *Competition for Empire, 1740–1763*; L. Gershoy, *From Despotism to Revolution, 1763–1789* (*Torchbooks). These three volumes in the Rise of Modern Europe series furnish the best detailed account; full bibliographies.

M. S. Anderson, *Europe in the Eighteenth Century, 1713–1783* (Holt, 1961). Very good introductory volume by a British scholar.

The New Cambridge Modern History, Vols. VII and VIII (Cambridge University, 1957, 1965). Chapters of very uneven quality by many scholars covering the period from 1713 to 1793.

R. R. Palmer, *The Age of the Democratic Revolution*, Vol. 1 (Princeton University, 1959). Major work by an American historian stressing the truly revolutionary character of the uprisings of 1776 and 1789 and the ideas behind them.

The European Balance

L. Déhio, *The Precarious Balance* (*Vintage). Reflections on the shifts in the balance over the centuries; by a German scholar.

A. Sorel, *Europe under the Old Régime* (*Torchbooks). Famous essay on the eighteenth-century balance by a French scholar.

A. M. Wilson, *French Foreign Policy during the Administration of Cardinal Fleury* (Harvard, 1936). A sound monograph on a period often neglected.

France and Britain

A. Cobban, *A History of Modern France*, Vol. 1 (*Penguin). Recent general survey of the period from 1715 to 1799 by a provocative British scholar.

J. Lough, *An Introduction to Eighteenth-Century France* (McKay, 1961). Clear and enlightening discussion, intended primarily for students of literature but useful for all.

G. P. Gooch, *Louis XV* (Longmans, 1956), and N. Mitford, *Madame de Pompadour* (*Pyramid). Old-fashioned but informative biographical studies.

F. Ford, *Robe and Sword* (*Torchbooks). Instructive study of the French aristocracy in the eighteenth century.

B. Williams, *The Whig Supremacy, 1714–1760*, rev. ed. by C. S. Stuart; and J. H. Watson, *The Reign of George III, 1760–1815* (Clarendon, 1962, 1960). These two volumes in the Oxford History of England supply an up-to-date, detailed account.

J. Plumb, *England in the Eighteenth Century* (*Penguin). A good brief account by a scholar who has also written studies of Walpole, the elder Pitt, and the first four Georges.

L. B. Namier, *The Structure of Politics at the Accession of George III* (*St. Martin's) and *England in the Age of the American Revolution* (*St. Martin's). Detailed and controversial studies, revising traditional concepts of eighteenth-century English political institutions.

E. A. Reitan, *George III: Tyrant or Constitutional Monarch?* (*Heath). Sampling of the wide range of judgments passed on the king.

G. Rudé, *Wilkes & Liberty: A Social Study, 1763–1774* (*Oxford). Recent analysis of a tumultuous period in British life.

Enlightened Despotism

S. Andrews, *Enlightened Despotism* (*Barnes & Noble); J. G. Gagliardo, *Enlightened Despotism* (*Crowell); and G. Bruun, *The Enlightened Despots*, 2nd ed. (*Holt). Good introductions.

S. B. Fay, *The Rise of Brandenburg-Prussia to 1786*, rev. by K. Epstein (*Holt). Brief and packed with information.

H. Rosenberg, *Bureaucracy, Aristocracy, Autocracy* (*Beacon). A rather opinionated analysis of Prussian history, 1660–1815.

R. R. Ergang, *The Potsdam Führer* (Columbia University, 1941). Stimulating study of Frederick the Great's father.

G. Ritter, *Frederick the Great* (University of California, 1968). Concise and comprehensive review by a leading German historian.

L. Reniers, *Frederick the Great* (Oswald Wolff, 1960). A critical evaluation.

W. H. Bruford, *Germany in the Eighteenth Century* (*Cambridge University). Enlightening study stressing social and intellectual developments.

C. L. Morris, *Maria Theresa: The Last Conservative* (Knopf, 1937). Sympathetic portrait.

S. K. Padover, *The Revolutionary Emperor* (Ballou, 1934). Warmly favorable account of Joseph II; highly critical of Maria Theresa.

R. Herr, *The Eighteenth-Century Revolution in Spain* (Princeton University, 1958). Important reappraisal of the impact of the Enlightenment on Spain and of the reign of Charles III.

V. Klyuchevsky, *Peter the Great* (*Vintage). Readable new English translation of a famous account by a pre-revolutionary Russian scholar.

E. Schuyler, *Peter the Great*, 2 vols. (Scribner, 1884). Old and still excellent account by an American scholar and diplomat.

B. H. Sumner, *Peter the Great and the Emergence of Russia* (*Collier). Very good pithy introduction.

G. Scott Thomson, *Catherine the Great and the Expansion of Russia* (*Collier). A sound short introduction. Still perhaps the best biography of Catherine is K. Walizewski, *The Romance of an Empress* (Appleton, 1894). More recent ones are by Ian Grey (Lippincott, 1962) and Zoë Oldenbourg (*Bantam).

The American Revolution

E. S. Morgan, *The Birth of the Republic, 1763–1789* (°Phoenix). Very good introductory account.

L. H. Gipson, *The Coming of the Revolution, 1763–1775*, and R. Alden, *The American Revolution, 1775–1783* (°Torchbooks). Fuller and fairly recent accounts.

J. C. Miller, *Origins of the American Revolution* (°Stanford University), and B. Bailyn, *Ideological Origins of the American Revolution* (Harvard, 1967). Analysis of the background.

C. Becker, *The Declaration of Independence* (°Vintage). A close analysis, examining its European background.

The Economic Revolution

J. Carswell, *The South Sea Bubble* (°Stanford, 1960). Excellent monograph on a particularly acute instance of economic growing pains.

P. Mantoux, *The Industrial Revolution in the Eighteenth Century* (°Torchbooks). Scholarly study focussed on England.

T. S. Ashton, *The Industrial Revolution, 1760–1830* (°Galaxy). Admirable brief survey.

M. W. Flinn, *Origins of the Industrial Revolution* (°Barnes & Noble). With stress on the various interpretations of the forces behind Britain's great leap forward, economically.

11

The French Revolution and Napoleon

March of the women to Versailles, October 5, 1789.

I. Importance of the French Revolution

On May 5, 1789, the French Estates-General, the medieval assembly of representatives of the three Estates of the realm, the First or clergy, the Second or nobility, and the Third or commons, which had last been called together in 1614, gathered in accordance with royal decree at Versailles. It had been called as a last resort to vote new taxes to fend off threatened national bankruptcy. When, having changed its name to "National Assembly," it was dissolved—more accurately and most symbolically, when it decreed its own dissolution—on September 30, 1791, it had voted away almost all the institutions of the Old Regime and had given France a written constitution based on the libertarian, but not quite "democratic," political ideas of the Enlightenment. Much of the violence and the drama of the French Revolution was yet to come; but this first Assembly had achieved, on the whole with very little violence, what looked to most Europeans and Americans like the solid beginnings of that better world the leaders of the Enlightenment had dreamed of and fought for. The English poet Wordsworth, looking back later on those years, could write in *The Prelude* of

> France standing on the top of golden hours,
> And human nature seeming born again.

No great revolution in modern times, not even the American, has come about in quite this idyllic atmosphere of the spring of 1789. It is hard for a present-day American, even if he counts himself a liberal, to think of revolution with such a glow of feeling. The revolutions of our twentieth century have not clearly meant the joyful beginnings of a better world for all mankind. They have been born in depression and defeat, as in Hitler's Germany, in wartime breakdown, as in Lenin's Russia, in underdeveloped "colonial" nations overwhelmed by the problems of catching up with the advanced "imperial" powers. But the great French Revolution broke out in one of the most advanced nations of the time, in a period of peace, and in an atmosphere of hope and confidence.

The French Revolution and its aftermath under Napoleon is then the central thread of Western history from 1789 to 1815. What the distinguished American historian R. R. Palmer calls (with a pretty broad definition of "democratic") "The Age of the Democratic Revolution" came to a head in those years, as the commoners of Europe and its colonies of settlement rallied to the "principles of 1776 and 1789." For the French Revolution was a missionary movement, one that was spread as a gospel and made converts, if only minority groups, throughout the Western world. The struggle between those who were against the French Revolution and those who were for it went on everywhere. In the despotic states of Central and Eastern Europe the struggle never got beyond conspiracy; in the youthful United States, it was in the 1790's fought at the polls and in the press amid fine verbal violence.

But the French Revolution has also an importance for the historian or sociologist seeking to establish some kind of laws or uniformities for the understanding of revolutions. Indeed, practical revolutionists ever since, from the Carbonari of the early nineteenth century to Lenin and Trotsky of the early twentieth century to the Algerian Ben Bella and the Vietnamese Ho Chi Minh of our own day, have studied the French Revolution for guidance. Students of revolution of all kinds have found in the French Revolution an almost too neatly typical or classical specimen, with an abundant literature of documents and historical writing, with a reasonably clear beginning and ending, a course, a dynamic, or a growth, that lends itself to description and analysis. It is, compared with our contemporary upheavals, remote in time. But it is not so remote from our own emotions, prejudices, and ideals as many Americans would think. In a sense, the French Revolution is still going on, and therefore cannot be studied with complete detachment.

We have in the last two chapters set the stage for the Revolution of 1789. Many factors contributed to the situation that made it possible for the Estates-General to sponsor a revolution instead of merely reforming the royal tax system. The spark, or the trigger release, was undoubtedly the financial crisis that made the calling of the Estates-General seem necessary. But the explosive character of the total situation in France was the product of decades of history. While the national economy was generally on the upgrade, the government was bankrupt, and its administrative machinery creaked. A rising middle class that felt cramped by medieval survivals faced a privileged class as a whole by no means inclined to give up its privileges, but with many members already won over to the enlightened reformist ideas that most educated people accepted. The intellectual atmosphere made thoroughgoing radical institutional reform seem both easy and necessary. Louis XVI was an ineffective king, often indecisive but at bottom stubborn and conventional; he was further handicapped by his unpopular queen, Marie Antoinette, who almost certainly never made the remark, when told some of her subjects had no bread, "Let them eat cake," *but on whom such a libel could be pinned and made to stick*. Add, finally, the apparent lack of a great leader of any sort—a revolutionary orator made the revealing remark "we live in a time of great events and little men"—and you can perhaps begin to see how the revolutionary movement got started.

II. The Constitutional Monarchy

BIRTH OF THE NATIONAL ASSEMBLY

In 1789 the Estates-General, instead of accepting its traditional role of consultative body divided into the three Estates, clergy, nobility, and Third Estate or commons, each meeting separately and voting their separate *recommendations* (*not* statute laws), managed to turn itself into a true lawmaking National Assembly or legislature, and proceeded to make a new constitution and appropriate institutions for France. But here a curious decisive fact comes in. The King and the popular minister Necker (who had been recalled to office) decided in planning the elections to the Estates-General that, contrary to all precedent, the Third Estate should have doubled representation, actually 600 delegates to 300 each for clergy and nobility. Incidentally, though the representatives of the Third Estate were chosen by election in two stages—local meetings selecting delegates to bigger district meetings which in their turn elected deputies to the national meeting—the basic local elections were on a very wide franchise indeed, almost universal manhood suffrage. But if the Third Estate was only to have one-third voice, no more than each of the others, why the doubling? Did Necker, after all an enlightened Swiss banker, foresee what was to happen? We do not know, but we do know that the decision to double the Third Estate made the first step in revolution easy.

For when each Estate sat, separately as the King had directed them, the Third Estate was soon involved in some rather confused debating and much caucusing and politicking (these people had no previous direct experience of legislative assemblies). Its deputies refused to do anything until they were joined by the delegates of the other two Estates, and were organized into a single body of 1200 members voting *by head*. The King and his advisers tried to insist on separate meetings by the three Estates, and at one point suspended all meetings to prepare for a formal one at which the King would order them all to conform to his will. On June 20, 1789, the Third Estate, finding their regular meeting place closed, adjourned to a nearby indoor tennis court (the *jeu de paume*) and there performed one of the numerous dramatic and symbolic acts of the Revolution, taking a solemn oath not to disband until they had given France a constitution. The King's ceremonial command-meeting three days later did not budge the

Third Estate; slowly a few radical priests and noblemen began coming over to join them; by the end of June the King had given up, consented to the merger, and the National Assembly, which Catherine the Great later liked to call the "Hydra with 1200 heads," was formed. It proved to be indeed much too large for a manageable legislative body.

THE BASTILLE

The next step became *the* great symbolic act of the Revolution, for all French republicans the equivalent of the American Fourth of July. Versailles was only a dozen miles from Paris, a city ardently in agreement with the new climate of reform. Rumors grew that the King and his advisers had yielded to the demand for a single National Assembly only to gain time to gather an army and disperse the Assembly. It was clear that there were troop concentrations going on in the region. Pro-revolutionists then and since have maintained that the King really was about to try to end by force the promising revolution that had begun; royalist defenders then and since have maintained that the King was merely seeking to protect the Assembly from the wild radicals of Paris. We incline to the judgment that, as usual when a good fight is preparing, each side was at least initiating steps against the other. Necker, still popular, was dismissed on July 11. The upshot was a riotous three days in Paris, culminating on July 14, 1789, when the rioters, having somehow got firearms from the royal arsenal at the Invalides, stormed and took the old medieval fortress known as the Bastille.

This shot was heard round the world much more loudly than the shot at Concord bridge. The Bastille, symbol of an outdated tyranny, had fallen to *the people* with very little bloodshed in a spontaneous uprising. In distant Copenhagen the Scandinavian man of letters Steffens told his sons the news with tears of joy, and added that if they were failures in life henceforth they could blame only themselves, for "poverty would vanish, the lowliest would begin the struggles of life on equal terms with the mightiest, with equal arms, on equal ground." No one will dispute the great psychological value of the fall of the Bastille as a symbol around which partisans of the new way of life could rally.

Historians still do dispute, however, just what happened on those three days, and why. The extent to which the uprising was really spontaneous remains in doubt, for there was clearly some planning and organization of demonstrations by Parisian leaders. These men, many of them members of the electoral group that had chosen the city's deputies to the Third Estate, improvised a fairly effective government on the spot, so that public order began to be maintained from July 15 on. There is also debate over the explanation for the lack of firmness on the part of the royal authorities. Although many of the troops were disaffected, it seems likely that foreign mercenaries, many of them Swiss, would have obeyed orders to shoot at the crowds. In modern revolutionary crises the failure to control the insurrectionists by force through police or army is usually crucial; in this particular instance, it looks as though the half-hearted efforts, if not incompetence and weakness, of the constituted authority of the state must be accounted a major factor—and a continuing one. Not until over five years later, in October, 1795, did a government force fire effectively at a Parisian crowd, bunched in a narrow street; when a young officer named Buonaparte in command of the government force did just this at the Rue St. Roch, the crowd turned and ran.

After the fall of the Bastille, a National Guard with Lafayette as commander was organized in Paris, and soon spread throughout the country. The National

Assembly continued at work on the new constitution, though it gradually also took over the position of a governing legislative body, making laws for current use, and maintaining at first a somewhat ambiguous relation with the ministers. Necker was, however, at once recalled, and the ministers began in effect to be "responsible" to the majority in the Assembly.

THE "GREAT FEAR" AND ITS EFFECTS

The third great step in the road to revolution took place in a series of peasant uprisings against medieval survivals, with burning of chateaux, some lynching of nobles and their agents, and much destruction of the old land records on which the payments made by peasants were legally based. The French call this agrarian rioting the "Great Fear," for in many a village what started the rioting was a rumor that "the brigands are coming." Again the question of spontaneity versus planning arises, and again it is impossible, in spite of much good local historical research, to give final answers. Certainly the riots were related to crowd hysteria set off by rumors; whether the rumors were "planted" or not we cannot say. At any rate, what did happen showed clearly the extent and bitterness of peasant discontent. So did the famous *cahiers de doléance* (grievance lists), which were drawn up in the primary electoral assemblies to choose delegates to the secondary assemblies of the Third Estate.

The National Assembly, alarmed by the news of what was happening, on August 4 took the most concrete step yet taken. In the midst of scenes of great emotion, nobles and other *privilégiés* rose and voluntarily gave up their medieval rights and privileges. In broad general decrees, titles of nobility were abolished—the Marquis de Lafayette, for example, becoming legally just Monsieur (later Citizen) Motier—sales of offices forbidden, the gilds abolished; in short, all that Turgot (*see* Chapter 10) had attempted—and much more—was decreed overnight. The Assembly on August 27, 1789, codified these reforms in spirit in its famous and influential Declaration of the Rights of Man and the Citizen, which began, "Men are born and remain free and equal in rights: social distinctions may be based only on general usefulness." Later, as the detailed legislation needed to put all this into effect was worked out, there were qualifications, indeed, in the eyes of the radicals *inconsistencies*, notably a system for the money compensation of owners of many of the abolished rights and privileges. But the first effect of the gesture of August 4 was to satisfy many of the demands of the peasants and the middle classes. The same gesture, coming as it did in response to such rioting, had quite the opposite effect on many nobles. Bastille Day had from their point of view been bad enough, had in fact begun an emigration headed by the King's brother, the Comte d'Artois. From now on there was a series of flights, not solely of nobles but of varied groups alarmed by the direction the revolution was taking.

THE "OCTOBER DAYS"

A fourth, and for a while final, major step on the revolutionary road—the road that was leading to the First French Republic of 1792—came with the "October Days" of 1789. The disorders of the summer, and the mounting troubles of government, had made the provisioning of Paris difficult. There was a scarcity of bread, which for the French lower classes is literally the staff of life. Feelings became more and more bitter on both sides; the freedom of speech and of the press that prevailed with the breakdown of royal government enabled each side to slander and caricature the other. Two trigger releases here: at a banquet in Versailles royalist officers, wine-mellowed, put on the Bourbon white and discarded the new revolutionary *tricolore* of blue, white, and red, toasted the Queen, sang royalist songs; all this was reported at once in Paris. In Paris early in the morning of October 5, a mob, mostly of women crying out for bread, started out for Versailles to appeal to the Assembly. Royalists then and now insist that in fact many of these "women" were male thugs dressed up as women.

As the news spread, the procession increased and, when it got to Versailles, overran the Assembly and swarmed around the palace. Lafayette and the National Guard, after what to royalists looked like a suspicious delay, set out from Paris after the procession, but got to Versailles too late to do much except set a protective line around the palace. In the small hours of October 6, some of the crowd penetrated through this line into the palace, and for a time the lives of the King and Queen seemed endangered. Under this pressure the King agreed to move to Paris; accompanied by the disorderly crowd, he and his family made the trip in the royal coach. The Assembly soon voted to follow him, and took up quarters in Paris near the royal palace of the Tuileries. After more than a century Paris was once more the seat of the government of France.

THE WORK OF THE NATIONAL ASSEMBLY

The next two years were not uneventful. The Assembly kept on at its double task of supervising closely day-to-day government, indeed legislating for it, and also working out the fundamental institutions for the new regime, its constitution. Thus unlike the American Constitutional Convention in Philadelphia, the French National Assembly was constantly distracted by the need for actual governing, and it held all its meetings before crowded galleries into which anyone could come. Very early, pressure groups began to pack the galleries, and no very effective policing of them was ever achieved during the Revolution. Pro-revolutionary pressure groups—shouting groups—soon took over; the anti-revolutionary groups never got a chance. Financial difficulties continued; piecemeal legislation failed to solve many of the most serious problems; the fundamental measures enacted set classes, localities, even families at odds in mounting tension.

While there were "incidents" aplenty, only one of them proved to be a critical step on a par with those already noted. In June, 1791, Louis XVI, his feelings outraged by the new Civil Constitution of the Clergy (discussed below), which the Pope had just condemned, attempted to flee to his northeast border and join an Austrian army there. After careful planning, the royal family escaped from Paris at night, but the coach employed was awkwardly heavy, progress was slow, and at a halt to change horses in an Argonne village Louis was recognized by the postmaster and detained at the next stop, the village of Varennes. He was brought back to Paris under guard, passing through crowded streets in menacing silence. The flight to Varennes proved to all France that their king was willing to disavow the work of the Assembly. There was some demand for his abdication and the declaration of a republic then and there, but the majority of the Assembly were moderate, wanting a constitutional monarchy; they were reluctant to scrap the work of nearly three years. The exceedingly transparent fiction that Louis had been "kidnapped" was officially announced, and the new Constitution went into effect in September, 1791. The Assembly as a last idealistic gesture decreed that none of its members should be eligible for election to the new Legislative Assembly, thus cutting the new body off from a reservoir of political experience it would badly need.

Varennes may well have meant that no amount of political wisdom and experience could have saved the government set up by the Constitution of 1791. The labor of these years was, however, very far from wasted. In purely negative terms, the sweeping away of most of the institutional base of the Old Regime was a remarkable—and, despite some temporary restorations after 1815, permanent—achievement. Feudal remnants were abolished, as it turned out without any substantial compensation to possessors of privileges, for the compensation legislation following the night of August 4 was never enforced. The unfair and inefficient tax system was abolished and soon supplanted by a better one. The incredibly complex network of old and outmoded administrative areas, the confused duplications and consequent rivalries of holders of jurisdiction, all were cleared away.

Positively, much work of the Assembly proved to provide fertile and suggestive first steps and, in a few instances, permanent institutions. The new administrative map of France, in which a neat series of descending areas—*départements*, districts (now called *arrondissements*), cantons, and *communes* (municipalities)—took the place of the old provinces, has been retained ever since. The suffrage for the new elected bodies was made to depend on the possession of a certain amount of property; about four Frenchmen out of seven qualified; yet the Assembly had declared officially that *all* Frenchmen were citizens. Now those who could vote were called "active" citizens, those who for lack of property could not were called "passive" citizens. Needless to say, many "passive" citizens did not feel very passive about this. The new government collapsed in a revolutionary "day" after less than a year. It failed basically because too many, and too well-organized, interest groups attacked its very bases, because some of the institutions set up by the new Constitution provoked such attacks, and because the new government became involved in a European war which at first went very badly, thus strengthening public feeling against the government.

THE CIVIL CONSTITUTION OF THE CLERGY

Certainly the institutional reform that divided Frenchmen most deeply was the Civil Constitution of the Clergy. Its origins go back to the first big attempt of the National Assembly to solve the problem of bankruptcy. After much hesitation and debate, it was decided in November, 1789, to seize what was certainly the largest easily available mass of wealth in the kingdom—the property of the Roman Catholic Church. This property, much of it good agricultural land, was to be sold at public auction. Meantime, it served as security for the issuance of paper money called *assignats*, which in turn were to be used to pay off the government's debts. In theory, the assignats thus paid out to those bond-holders and others to whom the government owed money were to come back eventually to the government in payment for the church property, then be promptly burned, and all would be well. In fact the temptation for the government, always in need of money, not to burn them was too great; their reissue resulted in a steady course of inflation that was not to be solidly arrested until 1796–97. This inflation had a great deal to do with subsequent troubles.

Following the confiscation of church property, the Assembly felt obliged to provide for the continuing cost of church services, support of priests, maintenance of buildings, and the like. Hence the Civil Constitution of the Clergy, hammered out in a special committee, was considered for the most part quite seriously by its makers not to infringe at all on the *religious* side of the Church. Yet the Civil Constitution provided for the *election* of priests and bishops by the same electoral bodies (which might contain Protestants, Jews, and Enlightened freethinkers) that chose the new local and national legislative bodies; it scrapped all the historic dioceses and substituted new ones coinciding with the new *départements;* it standardized the rate of payment of priests; it did not even contain provision for negotiation with the head of the Church—the Pope was merely to be "notified." There was some hesitation at Rome, but, as we have noted, in the spring of 1791 the Pope condemned the Civil Constitution.

This measure split all France, somewhere nearly down the middle in terms of total population, though there were many geographical variations. Those of the clergy who took the oath to support the new Constitution—the "constitutional clergy"—and those who refused—known to their opponents as the "refractory" or nonjuring clergy—seem to have been about evenly divided over the whole country, with perhaps a few more refusing than consenting to take the oath. At first the refractory priests were allowed their freedom, and might even officiate at services, though not on the actual church premises, which now belonged to the state and its constitutional clergy. But very soon the bitterness of quarrels of religion broke out, and in a thousand parishes the "intruding" new priest had trouble with the orthodox faithful—and the orthodox faithful had trouble with the new town government. With the revolutionary government in control, with the Revolution still moving on toward more radical ends, the force of the state was soon enlisted against the nonjuring clergy, and persecution began.

THE OUTBREAK OF WAR

Even though the immediate effect of the work of the National Constituent Assembly was to divide the French into two great groups—one accepting, the other rejecting the Revolution—it is possible that the violent clash of these two groups might have been avoided, or at least softened, had France not been drawn into a European, ultimately a world war. But the war did come, and as usual poses the historian with the difficult task of explaining its origins. Both sides were guilty of its outbreak. The war began with Austria and Prussia, a not very mutually trusting pair in view of their past rivalries, allied against France. The French revolutionists, and some historians sympathetic with them, have insisted that the crowned despots of Europe hated and feared revolutionary ideas, and sought to suppress them in the land where they were being put into effect. Later, it is true, the rulers of the powers at war with republican France showed a semblance of anti-revolutionary crusading spirit. But in the spring of 1792, Louis was still technically king, apparently free and unharmed, and the documents seem to show that the Austrian and Prussian leaders acted from motives very characteristic of eighteenth-century international politics. They believed that a country torn by internal troubles was naturally weakened, and that the moment was opportune to strike at France and perhaps acquire for themselves some of Alsace or Flanders or some other choice bit of French land.

As for France, the active revolutionists were surely beginning to develop a crusading spirit, a desire to spread the new doctrines, embodied later in the slogan "Peace to the cottages, war on the castles." But the decisive move toward war seems to have been the work of an active revolutionary party in the

Assembly, the Girondins. They favored war in part for Machiavellian or realistic motives (which turned out to be not very realistic), hoping that a war would unite popular feeling behind themselves and their program. Concrete difficulties also arose, however, such as Austro-Prussian anger over the revolutionists' seizure of Avignon, a papal enclave in France, and the claims of German nobles with lands in eastern France for special treatment under the legislation abolishing feudal rights.

The actual declaration of war—a necessary formality in those days—was made by the French in April, 1792. The French armies, if only because of the disruption of their officer class, largely noble, by the Revolution, made a very dismal show at first. By early summer the invading armies were well into eastern France, and seemed to be threatening Paris itself. The stage was set for the final series of steps toward the First French Republic.

III. The First Republic

To understand these final steps we must investigate the party politics of the Revolution more thoroughly. The Old Regime had had factions at the top, of course, but no true political parties. Once the National Assembly began to govern, it developed parties within itself, and these very soon began to reach out for a basis in the electorate. But from the very first, modern French party politics were not to follow the developing English and American two-party system. In broad lines one can from 1789 on to the crisis of 1794 make a rough division into two "parties," one for, the other against, the *existing* stage of the Revolution; but each of the two tended to subdivide into special groups. Again broadly, the dividing line moved in these five years from conservative to radical, from Right to Left. It started in May–June, 1789, with only King and court on the Right, and the whole country (hardly an exaggeration) on the Left. But the Left gradually peeled off its Rightist or "moderate" elements in a series of crises until the end, the fall of Robespierre to which we shall later come.

Since this was a major social revolution, the defeated Rightists were not allowed to become legal, peaceful oppositions. They were proscribed, exiled, guillotined, or, if fortunate enough, allowed to retire into obscurity. "The Revolution," said an orator who had had the usual classical education, "like Saturn, devours its children." The first disposed of—luckily for them, by an emigration which saved their lives—were the extreme reactionaries, the King's brothers, a few great nobles and their following in the summer of 1789.

THE JACOBIN CLUBS

A very important agency in advancing this series of shifts to the Left was the network of "Societies of Friends of the Constitution," known as Jacobins from their meeting place in a former Dominican convent of monks whom Parisians called Jacobins. The Jacobins were not quite like an ordinary political party, though some historians hold that they prefigured twentieth-century totalitarian one-party organizations. Their societies were voluntary organizations, political clubs whose members were ardently for the new regime, and who wanted to further its purposes, educate the people to accept it. These clubs spread out from Versailles–Paris with much speed in 1789–1790, and soon had an organized if somewhat impromptu network composed of local clubs in all major towns. Mostly, their membership was middle class and urban or small town in origin.

A parallel to the Jacobin network may be found in the Committees of Correspondence and the Sons of Liberty of the American Revolution or even, for that matter, in the Anti-Saloon League, 1900–1918. Just as these American groups soon went to work gaining control of local and provincial governments for specific purposes, so did the Jacobins. Their methods were electoral campaigning, propaganda of all sorts, lobbying, picketing, right down to beating up opponents. In a major social revolution some such group and not the regular legal government, old or new, is the agency which achieves the revolutionary aims. The Russian revolutionist Trotsky, a keen theorist of revolution, called this process "dual sovereignty." Side by side with the legal government there is an illegal government, sometimes in partial hiding, using guerrilla or hit-and-run methods, sometimes, as the French Jacobins of 1789–1793 or the Russian soviets of 1917, operating openly, as the legal government proves unable or unwilling to suppress its illegal rival.

THE TENTH OF AUGUST AND THE SEPTEMBER MASSACRES

It is not quite true that whoever controls Paris controls France, but such a group certainly has a fine start. The Jacobins, aided by elements of the Parisian populace even more radical than they, got control of Paris and its commune in the summer of 1792. Aided by a real and not unjustified popular fear of the invading armies, they achieved domination of the city council and promoted a series of manifestations which culminated in a storming of the royal palace of the Tuileries on August 10. The King and the royal family took refuge with the nearby Legislative Assembly, which suspended the King from his functions, sent him to prison, and called for elections by universal suffrage of a new assembly to make a new (and republican) constitution. The rioters sacked the palace, and pursued and massacred the loyal Swiss defenders. At the time this Tenth of August figured in the revolutionary calendar as a holy date equal to the Fourteenth of July.

The next few weeks after these events, under a kind of provisional government in which the revolutionary orator Danton played a major part, were tense indeed, as the enemy forces continued their drive on Paris. They were stopped in one of the crucial battles in history, at Valmy, on September 20, 1792. But meantime the fears of the Parisian populace, perhaps also the deliberate policies of some of the Jacobin leaders, culminated during the week of September 2 in the "September Massacres." Mobs invaded the prisons, already full of persons suspected of aiding the enemy, dragged the prisoners out, gave them an improvised trial, and then usually butchered them. Historians still do not agree on explanations for these massacres; their explanations run all the way from "spontaneous" mass hysteria provoked by fear of the invaders to coldly calculated brutality by a few hundred thugs in the pay of Danton and the other Jacobins. Our own interpretation emphasizes a negative factor, the breakdown of central police authority after the Tenth of August; for a few weeks terms like "chaotic" and "anarchic" applied to the state of Paris seem to be more than the mere rhetoric they often are. Tensions were abated somewhat after the French victory at Valmy.

THE CONVENTION

Meantime, elections to the new assembly took place, in theory by universal manhood suffrage, in fact under a Jacobin control that prevented royalists, and in many areas even moderates, from voting. On September 21, 1792, the 749 members of the Convention began their long rule. The Convention, like the National Constituent Assembly elected to produce a new constitution, in fact acted as a governing legislative body until its dissolution in October, 1795. Its first act was to abolish the monarchy and declare France a republic; later in 1793 a decree began a new revolutionary calendar with September 22, 1792, which became in retrospect 1 *Vendémiaire,* Year I.

All this was somewhat more than another shot heard round the world; for many round the world it turned into a shudder of fear and hatred spreading everywhere. The horrors of the storming of the Tuileries and the September Massacres, by no means understated in the world press, turned many who had hitherto welcomed the Revolution into bitter enemies. From then on the Western world was sharply divided into lovers and haters of the Revolution, each blind to the other's arguments and theses. At the end of this chapter we shall consider some of the permanent contributions to political thought that emerged from all this mutual recrimination.

During the first year of the Convention, the Reign of Terror began. In all this, the reader must realize that the progress of the great war was closely interwoven with the course of the Revolution. The great nineteenth-century historian and ardent defender of the Revolution, Aulard, actually maintained that the war explained the Terror, domestic violence coming at times when the French armies were doing badly, comparative quiet coming when the armies were victorious. Such close correlation is rejected by historians today, but the war is certainly one of the many variables that must be considered in any attempt to explain the Terror.

GIRONDE AND MOUNTAIN

In political terms, the Terror was part of the process of moving to the Left and eliminating the defeated Right. The Right in the early days of the Convention were a once quite radical group known as the Girondins, from the *département* of the Gironde (Bordeaux), home of many of their orators and leaders. The Left were shortly known, from their seats high up in the amphitheater where the Convention met, as the "Mountain."* Their composition and leadership were varied, as is usually the case with the revolutionary Left; Danton and Robespierre may serve as examples, the first an earthy man, with a touch of the ward politician, the second a thin, precise doctrinaire. In honesty, however, we may confess that the real personalities of Danton and Robespierre are still the subject of great debate. The historian Aulard thought Danton a hero, a sound realist, Robespierre a vain pedant and "unprincipled idealist"; Aulard's pupil

* The political terms "Left" and "Right" emerge from the French Revolution. They come from the seating position of the delegates relative to that of the presiding officer, who sat on a stage in the middle of the hemicycle, facing them. The radicals sat together to his left, the conservatives to his right, and the moderates or uncommitted members in the middle.

Robespierre, sketched during a meeting of the Convention.

Mathiez thought Danton a corrupt and traitorous politician, Robespierre a wise statesman.

The "parties" of Girondin Right and Mountain Left were perhaps not in ultimate aims very far apart. But personal rivalries, the heat of revolutionary politics, Girondin responsibility for the war, the willingness of the Mountain to support tough measures of central control, and also to woo or at least to placate the Parisian lower classes, suffering from food and other shortages, all contributed to the sharpness of the conflict. Both parties were led and staffed mostly by educated middle-class men. The Girondins were more classbound, believers in individual rights, distrusters of state enterprise, inclined to *laissez faire;* the Mountain was willing to go much further toward centralized rule, suppression of individual rights, rationing, and controls of all sorts. At the very start, the Girondins were reluctant to bring to trial and execute the King; the Mountain was eager to do so. It finally achieved its end, after a formal trial of Louis, on January 21, 1793.

Between Left and Right the great majority of the Convention, as many as two-thirds or even more of the 749, were known as the Plain, the Marsh, and, most scornfully, the Belly. They were mostly moderates elected from quiet constituencies, or merely cautious and indecisive men. They could be, and were, swung by determined minorities backed up by the Jacobin organization, the controlled press, and direct action groups, especially in Paris.

The execution of the King further shocked a Western world in which kings were still for many—perhaps most—touched with divinity. Soon after it took

Left: Marie Antoinette and her children, painted by Le Brun; **right:** Marie on her way to the guillotine, sketched by David.

place, Great Britain joined the first of the fighting coalitions against France, already made up of Austria, Prussia, Spain, and some lesser powers. The French Revolutionists were now faced by a group of enemies which included almost all of Europe except for Russia, where the cautious Catherine contented herself with purely verbal—and quite ineffective—attacks. The war had been going well for the French, who had successfully invaded *and annexed* Belgium. Then in March, 1793, it turned dramatically against them at the battle of Neerwinden. General Dumouriez, a Girondin and the victor at Valmy, went over to the enemy with many of his officers. In France itself, a civil war began in the Vendée as peasants—enemies of the Jacobins—refused to accept compulsory military service.

Under these strains the next step in the Revolution was achieved. In a struggle to the death with the Girondins, the Mountain, collaborating fully with the Commune (city government) of Paris, made use of the now classic maneuver of direct action: it surrounded the hall of the Convention with a living hedge of armed Parisians and forced through the cowed majority in that body the proscription of thirty-one Girondin leaders (June, 1793). Some of the proscribed fled to the country, and in Normandy, Bordeaux, and Lyons raised supporters to resist Jacobin centralized rule in the name of "federalism." The revolts, however, were mastered by the improvised semi-dictatorship which the victorious Mountain called the "revolutionary government."

THE "REVOLUTIONARY GOVERNMENT"

The key institution of the revolutionary government assumed its final form in the summer of 1793. This was the famous "Committee of Public Safety" of twelve members, all deputies to the Convention; it acted as a kind of super-cabinet with almost dictatorial powers and was never upset or really seriously attacked by the Convention until the fall of Robespierre in July, 1794. Danton was eased out of this committee, of which he had been an early leader. Robespierre came to be considered its chief, if not its master, and a dictator, but this is an erroneous view. The best description of these "Twelve Who Ruled" is that theirs was that rare political phenomenon, a "collegial" central executive, even a "dictatorship in commission" which, though not without internal rivalries that were finally to disrupt it, functioned successfully during a year of crises. There was a secondary committee equally free of direct control by the Convention, the Committee of General Security, which managed the special police work that seems always to go with such revolutions.

The Convention itself served this improvised executive as a kind of publicity service, for the debates, or at least the talking, continued tirelessly and were reported in the well-controlled press. It also served as a front disguising the fact that the Committee of Public Safety had absolute power—more absolute than Louis XIV had ever possessed. Moreover, certain trustworthy, and often very competent, deputies of the Convention were used by the Committee as "representatives on mission," sent out to trouble spots and to the provinces generally to rally the Jacobin faithful, to suppress the opposition, to raise supplies for the armies, and for many other purposes.

A few of these "proconsuls" let power go to their heads, and conducted little local Reigns of Terror of their own. Most notorious was that of a certain Carrier at Nantes, who had some of the suspected "traitors" and "aristocrats" put on barges which were scuttled in the river Loire with all on board. But most of these representatives on mission did get things done, did organize the Terror both as a form of national defense and an attempt to consolidate the Jacobin power. Their base was the network of Jacobin clubs, now known as "*sociétés populaires,*" but still recruited mostly from the urban middle classes and the more enterprising workers. The clubs were subjected to purges which left only reliable Jacobins in control. Special local revolutionary committees (*comités de surveillance*) worked with the Committee of General Security to apprehend enemies of the Revolution and bring them before special revolutionary courts capped by the famous Revolutionary Tribunal at Paris. These courts by no means observed due process of law, and at their worst were no more than agents of judicial murder; but they were at least in form courts, and they did not always condemn.

THE RECORD OF THE REVOLUTIONARY GOVERNMENT

In addition to purges of personnel, leaving so far as possible only firm Jacobins in government posts, the revolutionary government undertook a host of significant innovations. Its efforts at price-fixing, wage-fixing, food-rationing, prevention of inflation, and production of war materials made up the first large-scale modern experiment with economic controls in wartime. The "*levée en masse*" of August, 1793, was the first mass conscription of modern times, foreshadowing in its language the "total war" of the twentieth century:

> From this moment until that in which our enemies shall have been driven from the territory of the Republic, all Frenchmen are permanently requisitioned for service in the armies.

The last debris of the Old Regime were cleared away as the provisions for compensation to former *privilégiés* were eliminated; slavery was abolished in the French colonies; and in 1793 a very democratic constitution based on universal manhood suffrage was drawn up, but was suspended during the crisis in favor of the "*gouvernement révolutionnaire.*"

Ardent Jacobins enacted a whole series of measures designed to make revolutionary France an all-sufficing center of human loyalties and devotion—closing down churches, outlawing all forms of organized religion, Catholic, Protestant, Jewish, and substituting the "cult of the fatherland" with all sorts of holy days, civic celebrations, and the like. Typical was the new calendar, the year I beginning with the establishment of the Republic, with twelve months of exactly thirty days each, named for the weather usual in France—Germinal, month of budding, Floréal, month of flowering, Prairial, month of meadows in spring, for instance—each tenth day (*décadi*) a day of rest, with the five extra days (six in leap years) at the end of the year devoted to a series of patriotic festivals. Extreme Marxists have seen in this calendar an evidence of the middle-class capitalist nature of the Revolution: the workingman now got only one day in ten off, instead of one in seven. It is equally sensible to see in it a rationalist obsession with the decimal system. Many committees of the Convention worked on proposals later enacted into law, notably for public education and for the famous metric system of weights and measures. Finally, some legislation aimed at the deliberate transfer of property from the rich to the poor, particularly the decrees of Ventôse, year II (March, 1794), which took property from the "suspects" and gave it to the "deserving indigent."

These last decrees were never really carried out, for within a few months Robespierre fell and the great days of the Jacobin revolution were over. In the reality of French life, all these measures had very varying fates in execution. They were experiments in many fields since then effectively cultivated, and, like most pioneering, with hindsight they look pretty primitive. The economic controls worked badly, because there were all sorts of loopholes, great pockets of resistance, and much black-market activity. The attempt at "de-christianizing" was generally a failure, and the new substitute religions—Robespierre had one based on worship of a Supreme Being—never took solid root.

Still, part of the job got done after a fashion. There was as yet no catastrophic inflation, and food and clothing and other necessities were tolerably well distributed; the new mass armies were raised and outfitted with no worse than routine scandals over war contracts; France was elevated if only briefly to "the height of revolutionary circumstance," to use a phrase of the day. In fact, by the spring of 1794 the troops of the Convention had pretty well begun to get the upper hand of internal opposition and were driving the foreign enemies across the Rhine. On June 26, 1794, at Fleurus in that "cockpit of Europe," Belgium, the French won a victory that opened the way for a great expansion of their power.

The Terror, however much its beginnings can be explained as the hastily devised centralization of power to meet war needs in a modern society, by this time had a momentum of its own. At Paris, at least, the machinery of the Terror had been used to decide struggles for power among groups hardly more clearly defined as to platform and purpose than the various "interest" groups of mid-eighteenth century British politics and, like them, known by names of leaders—*Dantonistes, Hébertistes, Robespierristes*. Some modern specialists complain that the old description of Robespierre in the middle, with a Dantonist group on the Right more conservative, and a Hébertist group on the Left more radical, is oversimplified. But in broad terms it does seem true that Robespierre outmaneuvered his opponents, sending them in admittedly disparate batches before the Revolutionary Tribunal, and thence, almost as a matter of course, to the guillotine (March-April, 1794). It is, however, significant that in the last few months of the Terror there were in Paris groups clearly to the Left of the government (that is, the Committee of Public Safety). These *Enragés*, and a vaguer and larger group known as the *Bras Nus* ("bare arms") or as *sans-culottes* ("without knee-breeches," the garment of the upper and middle classes—but definitely not without the long trousers of the workingman), were vigorously anti-Christian, and recruited their supporters from the working classes. They can be said to foreshadow the proletarians, the "toiling masses" of nineteenth-century socialism and twentieth-century communism. But they seem to have had no well-defined program, no political philosophy, beyond expropriation of the enemies of the Revolution. They clearly were not socialists, collectivists, proto-Marxists. They never attained power, except partially and locally in Paris.

THE NINTH THERMIDOR

The guillotine continued to fall. The trigger release for the last great step in the Revolution proper was a well-organized plot among certain deputies to the Convention who, with good reason, suspected that Robespierre was planning to bring them before the Revolutionary Tribunal. Several of them had during turns in the provinces as "proconsuls" taken bribes and lived (with mistresses and all that) in a way no good Jacobin Puritan should. The plotters decided to attack Robespierre directly, which they did in the Convention on July 26, 1794, after Robespierre had delivered a long, vague, but threatening speech against wicked men who should be purged to deliver the Republic once and for all from its enemies. The Convention in a dramatic session backed the attackers, and Robespierre and his aides appealed to their supporters in Paris. For the first time in the Revolution the people of Paris failed to rise. The Convention summoned courage and sent troops to arrest the now formally outlawed Robespierre, who had taken refuge in the Paris city hall. Still the Parisians did not come out in the street, even though the tocsin rang. Robespierre and his close followers were arrested and summarily guillotined as outlaws on the very next day.

This "day," in the new calendar the Ninth Thermidor, marks the end of the long phase of the Revolution in which power moved ever further to the Left. The plotters showed at first no sign that they had planned an end to the Terror, but for once a whole people took matters in their hands. The Terror was more than a government of national defense: in its last months it had promoted a way of life, a sociopolitical program, touched certainly with idealism, even with puritanism, an attempt to found a "Republic of Virtue." The night life of Paris, already well known, its dance halls, theaters, gambling houses, and brothels had been for the most part closed down. Within a few days or weeks of Ninth Thermidor, hundreds of dance halls opened in Paris. The "Thermidorean reaction"—the return to normal human life, with all its unheroic variety—had begun.

Now occurred a kind of reversal of the process of revolution. Politically, beginning with the survivors of the proscribed Girondins, the old groups came back, until within a few years even the "refractory" or "nonjuring" priests were tolerated, and full services of the Roman Catholic Church unofficially restored. The machinery of the *gouvernement révolutionnaire* was scrapped, the local and departmental administrations now purged of ardent Jacobins, the established civil servants entrusted with the daily work of the government. At the top, the Convention really governed through the two old committees of Public Safety and General Security, to which a Legislative committee was added. The "Three Committees," however, ceased to have the permanence and dictatorial powers of the great committees during the Terror. This new government limped along, finally producing a moderate compromise constitution which set up the next form of government of the Republic, known as the Directory (1795–1799).

THE DIRECTORY

In a compromise between a direct democracy and one of checks and balances, the Constitution of 1795 provided for five executive Directors, to whom ministers were responsible, and a bicameral legislature—a lower Council of 500 elected by a suffrage with a small property qualification, and an upper House of 250, the *Conseil des Anciens* (they had to be over 40, married or widowers, and presumably, therefore, not wild radicals). The Convention in its dying days reversed the error of the first great Assembly in 1791. Instead of *prohibiting* the election of its members to the new legislature as did the National Assembly, the Convention *required* the election of two-thirds of the new one to be made from members of the Convention—who were christened by no means affectionately *les perpétuels*.

In the details of social life the swing of the pendulum away from the Reign of Terror and Virtue was much in evidence. The Directory was one of the most flagrant periods of loose living, of conspicuous consumption, at least among the successful, and of real suffering among the poor. Its atmosphere can be appreciated from the fact that the new social leader, Thérésa de Cabarrus, mistress of Tallien, one of the plotters against Robespierre, was known popularly—and cynically—as Our Lady of Thermidor. The young of the new generation, the *jeunesse dorée* (gilded youth), dressed with affectation, indulged themselves in the usual minor vices, and went about in gangs beating up known Jacobins, called "the tail of Robespierre." As rationing and price fixing were abandoned, the *assignats*, the revolutionary paper money, went into a catastrophic decline, a 1000-franc note in 1796 falling to a value of four old francs. Naturally the Parisian populace suffered, and they rose in two quite abortive and rather pathetic street riots. The days of the fall of the Bastille and the sack of the Tuileries were by then well past.

In foreign affairs the moderate leaders of the last days of the Convention, working through formal diplomatic channels, made peace with Prussia and with Spain at Basel (1795). French armies had already taken care of Belgium and Holland by occupying them, and the Prince of Orange had fled from Holland to England, beginning a long line of royal and aristocratic "displaced persons" from the lands around France. Britain and Austria remained in the war. The Directory attempted negotiations with both, but unsuccessfully, and the way was open for further French expansion.

In 1796 a 27-year-old general who had won his spurs a year earlier by directing artillery against rioters in Paris was given an army command through the influence of one of the Directors, Barras, whose former mistress, Josephine de Beauharnais, he had married. He was assigned to a hitherto quiet front; but he galvanized his French army on the Italian border, and within a year had conquered most of Italy. We shall have to deal much more with General Buonaparte, who soon took the Italianate "u" out of his name, and with the problems of interpretation set the historian by his extraordinary career. The Directory benefitted by his conquests, made peace with Austria at Campoformio (October, 1797), and pursued the policy of setting up all around France proper a set of pro-French satellite republics, endowed with nice classical names—the Batavian (in Holland), the Helvetian (in Switzerland), the Cisalpine (in Lombardy), and the Parthenopean (in Naples).

The years of Thermidor and the Directory, from 1794 to 1799, are far less interesting than the exciting earlier years of the Revolution, and seem to many historians a dull and ineffective interlude before the dramatic events of Napoleon's conquest of Europe. Perhaps some such lull was necessary, for a whole people cannot for long live up to the exhausting tasks of making an ideal republic or conquering the Western world. Moreover, under the Directory the financial trouble which had played so large a part in the beginning and in the whole course of the Revolution was put in the way of solution. New taxes were solidly established, some of the debt incurred was simply repudiated, and the franc was put on a sound specie basis not seriously disturbed again until the 1920's. Under both the Directory and the subsequent regime of Napoleon, requisitions on conquered territories yielded resources that helped France attain financial stability. Progress was also made in education, law, and science. The course of politics under the Directory was by no means smooth. Twice, *coups d'état* effected extralegal changes in the personnel of the Directory; yet these were mere *coups d'état*, not the violent troubles and mass riots of the great "days" of the early Revolution, and may be described as a kind of fumbling toward normal French party politics based on splinter groups and complicated ministerial changes.

THE EIGHTEENTH BRUMAIRE

Still, the Directory did lack glamour. Bonaparte, left by the peace with no European worlds immediately at hand to conquer and with England protected by the Channel, had managed to persuade the Directory to let him try to get at the old and inveterate enemy by way of the road to India. With a strong expeditionary force, he had gone off to Egypt in the footsteps of Alexander the Great. Turkey, nominally in control of Egypt, was thus brought to war against France. Bonaparte had no trouble beating the Egyptians, but the British fleet under Admiral Nelson decisively defeated the French fleet at the Battle of Abukir Bay (August, 1798), cutting his army off from home. Meanwhile the beaten Austrians took heart, and under English urging joined the *second* great coalition against France. In Russia Catherine was dead, and her son, Paul I (1796–1801), romantic and perhaps already insane, joined the coalition. How thoroughly Russia now entered the European system can be seen from the fact that Paul coveted the Ionian Isles and Malta in the Mediterranean. Although Prussia and Spain stayed out, the second coalition was very powerful. The Austrians, joined by the Russians under a gifted general, Suvarov, pressed north and south of the Alps toward France. After defeats on the Rhine and in northern Italy, the French were pushed back almost to their old frontiers. At home the Jacobins started meeting again, and popular discontent with the Directory rose.

At this juncture Bonaparte deserted his army in the Near East, where it was eventually forced to surrender, and sailed home, luckily—for him if not for the Western world—escaping patrol ships of the dominant British navy. Once in Paris, and with help from well-tried politicians, he engineered another *coup d'état* on November 9, 1799, 18 Brumaire of the new calendar. The *coup* involved removing recalcitrant members from the legislature, and in its course Bonaparte came very near disaster. But the army intervened at the critical moment, and actually chased some of the legislators out of their meeting place at the point of the bayonet. This time there was no patching up of the Directory. A provisional government headed by Bonaparte rapidly drew up one more constitution—the fourth since 1789, if we include that of 1793 which never was put into effect.

IV. Napoleon

THE CONSULATE

The new constitution set up as executive a Consulate of three, with Bonaparte, of course, as First Consul; the other two were unimportant, so that, unlike the Directory, this was not an executive in commission. It was, in fact, once more a monarchy, and not very limited. There were four bodies that might be called legislative, including one that debated but did not vote (the Tribunate) and one that voted but did not debate (the Legislative Corps). Technically still a republican form of government, the Consulate began the personal rule of Napoleon I. A plebiscite approved the new constitution in a vote announced as three million to fifteen hundred. Though no full cross section of French opinion—many people did not vote—the result did indicate a widespread desire on the part of Frenchmen for stability, order, and an end to the crises, the "days," the *coups d'état* of the last decade.

Napoleon set about fulfilling this mandate by seeking to establish domestic order and international peace. The Russians had already withdrawn from active participation in the war; but peace feelers did not move the British and the Austrians. Napoleon therefore executed one of his lightning strokes, marching across the Alps by the St. Bernard pass in May, 1800, before the snow had wholly melted, and defeating the Austrians at Marengo in June. He could not do much against Britain, but with all their major Continental allies knocked out or withdrawn from the fight, the British proved ready to negotiate. Peace with Austria at Lunéville, May, 1801, was followed by peace with Britain at Amiens, in March, 1802. For the first time since 1792, there was general peace in Europe.

Though the settlement proved to be very brief, its broad lines were significant. Prussia earlier and secretly had consented to France getting the whole left (western) bank of the Rhine, subject to "compensation" for Prussia elsewhere in the Germanies. Austria had earlier made a brief peace with France which contained a secret provision that Prussia was to get no such compensation. Now the whole German question was to be decided after long negotiations with Napoleon which humiliated German pride. They reached a culmination in 1806 when the Holy Roman Empire of the German People, which we first met so long ago during the Middle Ages (*see* Chapter 4), was dissolved. Three years earlier in 1803 the Chief Decree of the Imperial Delegation (*Reichsdeputationshauptschluss*, a fine German word) had consolidated many of the smallest "independent" German states into the thirty-odd that were to make up nineteenth-century Germany until 1871. The Lunéville settlement of 1801 had confirmed the Habsburg or Austrian Empire, heir of the Holy Roman Empire, in its possession of the wholly Italian territory of the former Venetian Republic. The rest of Italy, save for the territory around Rome itself, which remained under papal sovereignty, continued as a set of "satellite" republics. Prussia was quite definitely frozen out, receiving nothing and losing her lands on the left bank of the Rhine.

With England the peace was essentially a stalemate, the English restoring to France, Spain, and the Dutch all overseas conquests except Trinidad, taken from Spain, and Ceylon, taken from the Dutch. Malta, now in Britain's hands thanks to her fleet, was to be restored to the Order of the Knights Hospitallers. A sign of the times: hardly had the Peace of Amiens been signed when British tourists began pouring into Paris. Many of them were stranded when war between Britain and France was renewed on May 16, 1803, after not quite fourteen months of peace. By order of Napoleon, many of them were interned, a new touch of total "nationalistic" war, for during the eighteenth century travellers from enemy states had circulated with relative freedom in spite of war.

After long negotiations the First Consul made internal peace with the papacy, a step important in

Napoleon, 1798; unfinished portrait by David.

both his domestic and foreign policy of stabilization and respectability. By this Concordat of 1801, the new Pope Pius VII agreed to very strong French state powers over appointment of the clergy and accepted as valid the title deeds of Frenchmen who had bought church property during the Revolution. In return he received confirmation of his sovereignty in the papal lands around Rome, assumption by the French state of the obligation to pay the clergy, and a public statement that the Roman Catholic faith was the faith of the Consuls and of the great majority of Frenchmen. The statement was certainly not true of Napoleon, who was a Christian only in outward conformity. How great the Catholic majority in France was then cannot be stated exactly. Although only a minority of Frenchmen had remained Protestants, a very substantial number of Frenchmen were converted to what we have called Enlightenment, and remained enemies of Catholicism. But it seems clear that in 1801 Napoleon's religious policy did have the backing of most Frenchmen, tired of the last decade of bitter religious conflict.

The domestic settlement was marked by a new form of a very old French institution, the local administrator appointed by and responsible to the central government. The *département*, equivalent to an American county, was placed under the direction of a prefect, an official whose post has since been continued through all forms of government in France. In 1802 another French institution that no regime has dared give up was founded: this is the Legion of Honor, a decoration extensively used for both soldiers and civilians, French and foreign. At the same time Napoleon was declared Consul for life, a step also confirmed by three-and-one-half-million Frenchmen in a plebiscite. The step to imperial rank was easy enough, and on December 2, 1804, following a decree that "the government of the *republic* is entrusted to an *emperor*" (italics ours), Napoleon was crowned Emperor. While the ceremony was consecrated by the presence of Pius VII, Napoleon placed the crown on his own head, in imitation of Charlemagne.

THE EMPIRE ASCENDANT

The British had already renewed the war against France, spurred on by what they took as clear evidence that Napoleon was not going to settle down. He had attempted to revive the French North American empire. Spain had acquired Louisiana from beaten France in 1763 as compensation for ceding Florida to Britain. Napoleon in 1800 got the Spanish to retrocede Louisiana to France, and later sent out an army to reconquer Haiti from the revolting Negroes. In Europe, he was actively intriguing in both Italy and the Germanies, while the English themselves refused to get out of Malta. In America yellow fever destroyed the French army in Haiti, and once Britain with its naval dominance came into the war again the Louisiana venture began to look impossible. In 1803 the whole territory, out of which eventually came, in whole or in part, thirteen states, was sold by Napoleon to the United States for about fifteen million dollars.

Napoleon had established military camps on the English Channel and, in spite of his naval weakness, might have had serious intentions of attempting to invade the British Isles, thus adding William the Conqueror to Alexander the Great and Charlemagne in his list of historical imitations. (It is perhaps significant of Napoleon's basic conservatism that he was unwilling to follow up proposals made by an American named Robert Fulton. Successful steam power would have given him a good chance of beating English Channel winds and tides.) The English now succeeded in forging still another great coalition, the third, with Austria, Russia, and Sweden as allies, Spain, however, allying with France. In another brilliantly rapid march Napoleon swung his troops eastward, and aided by support from the south German states of Bavaria, Württemberg, and Baden, got between an Austrian army and the Habsburg capital at Vienna, forcing the army's surrender at Ulm. Then on December 2, 1805, on the first anniversary of his coronation, he defeated the combined Austro-Russian forces at Austerlitz, perhaps his greatest victory. Austria gave up at once, signing a humiliating treaty on December 26, at Pressburg. Prussia, which had not joined the coalition earlier, was now stung into a war that ended rapidly in her total defeat at Jena on October 14, 1806. (Because of Prussian entrance and Austrian withdrawal, the war from 1806 to its end in 1807 is usually called that of the fourth coalition.) So complete was Prussian collapse that the French cavalry was able to move almost as fast as twentieth-century motorized troops. Napoleon occupied Berlin on October 27.

These campaigns of 1805–1806 illustrate Napoleon's techniques of success very neatly: isolation of his enemies, separating them as far as possible from their allies, both by diplomacy and in the field; the sudden strike, sometimes by forced march, with strong concentration of troops; the calculated risk that the enemy would not strike back at a weakened part of Napoleon's own forces; and—perhaps most important of all—his mass citizen armies, inspired by professional pride as well as by patriotic enthusiasm, and led by officers who owed their position for the most part not to birth or breeding, but to technical military skills. To these factors must be added the failure of his enemies to unite effectively against him. And, no doubt, luck: Napoleon himself gave full credit to his "star."

The Russians had not given up after Austerlitz, but retreated eastward into Poland for regrouping. They came, too late, to help the Prussians, and after a long and hard campaign were beaten badly enough at Friedland in June, 1807, to decide to initiate negotiations. Meeting in July on a raft in the river Niemen, western boundary of Russia, Tsar Alexander I and Napoleon personally negotiated the Treaty of Tilsit. The treaty accepted the numerous changes Napoleon had already made in Germany, set up as the Grand Duchy of Warsaw a partially independent Polish state, and deprived Prussia of almost half her territory.

But French supremacy was not so solidly established as these marvelous victories seemed to make it. Even before Austerlitz, Napoleon had suffered a decisive defeat. Off Cape Trafalgar on the Spanish coast on October 21, 1805, the English Admiral Nelson, mortally wounded in the engagement, defeated the combined French and Spanish fleets. Henceforth the British were in complete command of the seas, challenged only by an occasional French or other hostile privateer, and in a few separate engagements by ships of the American navy, once the United States had entered this world conflict in 1812.

Napoleon and Alexander at Tilsit had made a kind of tacit agreement to share the ascendancy of the West between them. But Britain was still obstinately there, still unsubdued. Napoleon now attempted to get at the British indirectly through their trade. He did not attempt, as the Germans were to attempt in the twentieth century, to *starve* the British out, for while the Industrial Revolution had begun, and with it a great rise in population, Britain could still feed herself from her own farms. What Napoleon hoped to do by his "Continental system," a self-blockade of the coast against British ships, was to close all Europe to British trade, thus bringing about large-scale unemployment in Britain, loss of profits, in short a major economic crisis which would oblige the British government to sue for peace. He could hope to make this Continental blockade work because, on paper, he now controlled the Continent. Let us survey the Napoleonic Empire at its height about 1810.

THE EMPIRE AT ITS HEIGHT

A glance at the map on page 460 shows France proper somewhat expanded to the northeast and east, notably with a French *département* of the Bouches de l'Elbe (mouths of the Elbe), its capital at Hamburg—a wholly German area. Many satellite states were no longer republics but monarchies ruled by members of Napoleon's own family. Brother Joseph was King of Spain. Brother Jerome, divorced from a former Miss Patterson of Baltimore (not sufficiently noble for the Bonapartes) and remarried to a German princess, was King of Westphalia and head of the Confederation of the Rhine, composed of all the Germanies save truncated Prussia and diminished Austria. Brother-in-law Murat was King of Naples, and Napoleon himself King of Italy, with stepson Eugène Beauharnais as Viceroy. Brother Louis was King of Holland until he lost his throne for siding with his Dutch subjects against his brother, who annexed Holland directly to France.

Austria and Prussia, not *directly* under French rule, were none the less after 1807 allies substantially under Napoleon's influence. Russia, independent, was after Tilsit an ally, bound to the "Continental system." There were some curious anomalies. To maintain this system against smuggling, Napoleon had annexed from Austria the Dalmatian coast of what is now Yugoslavia in 1809. The Swedes, with an old and childless king, offered the succession to their Crown to Marshal Bernadotte, one of Napoleon's great generals, who accepted in 1810 and became an adopted son. Austria itself, on land the most consistent enemy of France in these twenty-five years of war, was harnessed to the Corsican clan of Bonaparte by Napoleon's marriage, after he had divorced Josephine, with Marie Louise, daughter of the old Habsburg Emperor Francis II.

If you judge by the map, Napoleon had done better than anyone since Charlemagne to bring Europe by conquest under one head. He did better in fact than his closest competitor in this respect, Adolf Hitler, was to do. But the "order and peace I dreamed of for Europe"—his words in exile later—was never close to reality, and the imposing structure of Napoleonic domination had defective portions from the very start.

THE BREAKUP OF EMPIRE

As early as 1808 there was a clear sign that all was not well with Napoleon's system. The French had occupied Portugal, Britain's "oldest ally" when the Portuguese government refused to enforce the Continental system, and through some very complicated intrigues, the Emperor got the King of Spain and his son to abdicate, and put his brother Joseph on the throne of Spain. To Portugal the British sent a small professional army under Sir Arthur Wellesley, later Duke of Wellington, which began the Peninsular War. They were helped by the long and unsparing guerrilla resistance of the neighboring Spanish people to the hated

French. The heroic rising of the people of Madrid in May, 1808, the tragic *Dos de Mayo*, was something new in the long wars since 1792—civilians moved by patriotic feeling to hurl themselves against the soldiers of the French Revolution, of course in vain.

In 1809 the Tyrolese mountaineers of Austria fought with equal ardor against the French. The Austrian government itself had declared a separate war against France in the spring of 1809, and had actually beaten Napoleon at Aspern and Essling, but no Continental power dared come to the aid of the Austrians, and the British were unable or unwilling to mount another land campaign. Wagram (1809), though a close battle, ended the war as a French victory. In Spain, however, the British army began to advance in 1811, and by the summer of 1812 had forced King Joseph to abandon his capital in Madrid and retreat northward.

1812, of course, marks a blacker event in Napoleon's career than anything that happened in Spain. In June of that year his *Grande Armée* of over 400,000, ultimately, with reinforcements, 600,000—a truly European army of French, Italians, Poles, Dutch, Austrians, Prussians, other Germans—crossed the Niemen and invaded Russia. The two emperors had had increasingly difficult relations, especially over the enforcement of the Continental blockade against Britain, and neither was any longer in the mood to share ascendancy with the other. The *Grande Armée* got as far as Moscow, though not without hard fighting. A great fire, deliberately started, made the city untenable and marked the climax of a "scorched earth" policy that the Russians would again pursue in World War II. With the northern winter already begun, Napoleon on October 19 began a retreat that became a flight, a long and cruel one for his soldiers, no more than 100,000 of

Goya, "The Third of May, 1808"; Spaniards being executed by Napoleon's troops.

whom recrossed the Niemen. Napoleon himself, who had gone ahead to Paris in the comparative comfort of imperial coaches, began to reorganize his forces to face yet another European coalition against him.

The prestige of Napoleon was still so great that the forging of this coalition was no easy task. The Prussians joined Russia and England in February, 1813. In Sweden Bernadotte accepted a subsidy to enlist against his former master and his native country; as a result of this realistic course, his house still reigns in Sweden, the only Napoleonic house to retain its crown. With the Confederation of the Rhine still on his side, Napoleon mustered an army in Germany which in the spring of 1813 won several very expensive victories. In August the Austrians were persuaded to join against him, and the Allies gradually drove the French back into Saxony, whose ruler, with consequences we shall later note, stayed loyal to Napoleon. Here in October, 1813, the Allies won the decisive battle of Leipzig, which the Germans call the *Völkerschlacht* (Battle of the Peoples). From now on Napoleon was battling in retreat, and though in the spring of 1814 he did wonders against superior forces in a campaign on French soil, the odds against him were too great. Moreover, this time his enemies held their fifth coalition together with great firmness; by the Treaties of Chaumont in March, 1814, Great Britain, Prussia, Russia, and Austria swore not to make any separate peace, and to continue their Quadruple Alliance for 20 years. After the Allies had made a triumphant entry into Paris, Napoleon abdicated at Fontainebleau on April 11. He was given "sovereignty" over the 86-square-mile Mediterranean island of Elba off the Tuscan coast and retained the title of Emperor.

THE "HUNDRED DAYS"

The victorious Allies, after much debate, decided to bring about a Bourbon restoration. The brother of the guillotined Louis XVI was brought from his English exile, and took the throne as Louis XVIII, a title he had used privately ever since it became clear that the Dauphin, "Louis XVII," the son of Louis XVI and Marie Antoinette, had died uncrowned in prison, almost certainly on June 8, 1795. (Numerous persons, including Eleazar Williams of Longmeadow, Massachusetts, continued to claim to be the Dauphin, miraculously escaped from prison.) The Allies, anxious to strengthen the Bourbon regime, made a very lenient peace with France which left her the boundaries of 1792, and exacted no indemnity. Yet they could do nothing to spare France the inevitable postwar economic and emotional troubles and particularly the difficulty of adjusting veteran soldiers to civilian life and work. Nor could they seal off Napoleon on his nearby island.

On March 1, 1815, encouraged by reports from France and by the news that the Allies were beginning to quarrel among themselves over the Saxon and Polish territorial settlements, Napoleon landed with a few troops near Cannes on the French Riviera. The restored Bourbon government could not command the loyalty of its own troops, and the way to Paris was easy. There Napoleon started to organize what he claimed would be a "liberal" government, no longer mere personal rule, and one that would not attempt any aggressive expansion. But the Allies refused to trust him, and the Quadruple Alliance held firm. Once more they put armies in the field to fight the revived French armies.

Napoleon's final campaign, which culminated in his defeat at Waterloo on

June 18, 1815, was by no means one-sided. Waterloo itself was finally decided only by the late afternoon arrival of Blücher's fresh Prussian troops on the field where Wellington's Redcoats were still holding out. The Austrians were not engaged, though their army was well on its way; nor were the Russians, also loyal to the Quadruple Alliance. The famous "if"—if Napoleon had won at Waterloo—is of course always debatable. But it looks as if the odds against him were too great, as they had been already in 1814. The Hundred Days, as they are called, fed the Napoleonic Legend, a legend further nourished by Napoleon himself as he talked to his staff on the remote South Atlantic island of St. Helena to which he was sent and where he died in 1821. The second peace with France imposed somewhat harder terms—a seven hundred million franc indemnity, the return of many works of art Napoleon had taken from other countries, and the loss of a few bits of territory on the Rhine and in Savoy. The Rhine loss was not unimportant, for it was the Sarre coal region (in German, Saar), destined to give much trouble in the world wars of the twentieth century.

THE PLACE OF NAPOLEON IN HISTORY

Napoleon has remained a great and controversial historical figure. The Dutch historian Peter Geyl in his *Napoleon: For and Against* makes a remarkable summary of the very varied interpretations of the man and his work. To some historians, Napoleon furthered the work of the French Revolution; to others he destroyed, or at least perverted, the work of the Revolution. To some he is the last—and greatest—of the enlightened despots, essentially an eighteenth-century figure; to others he is the man who put the nineteenth century on its romantic and dynamic course. To some he is a villainous aggressor, to others a great liberator.

Warfare and diplomacy play so major a part in Napoleon's career that domestic affairs are inevitably scanted in any general history. But France is what it is today in considerable part because of what Napoleon and his civilian administrators did. They worked, it is true, on a foundation laid in the days of the first revolutionary assemblies, a foundation already fairly firm under the much-maligned Directory. The Consulate and Empire, however, saw the completion of much that was to last for a long time. The religious settlement of the Concordat, though later bitterly attacked, lasted until the early twentieth century. The Emperor's famous codification of French law, still often known as the *Code Napoléon,* exists today with no more than adjustments made to fit new problems; it has been widely influential in all parts of the world outside the English-speaking countries. His unified system of education, from primary school to university, is still the basic framework of French education. Under Napoleon the great French learned academies, dissolved in the early 1790's in the first access of revolutionary enthusiasm, since they seemed essentially contrary to the spirit of Liberty, Equality, Fraternity, were renewed and consolidated in the *Institut de France.*

The Napoleonic nobility, like the Napoleonic thrones, did not endure, but the Legion of Honor still continues. And the great civil service, begun under the Revolution, has been his most enduring monument. A civil service entirely in the Continental tradition of firm authority, it has been the target of bitter attacks from those who resent the growth of such "bureaucracies" in the modern world; it has been addicted to form-filling and all the rest of what the French call

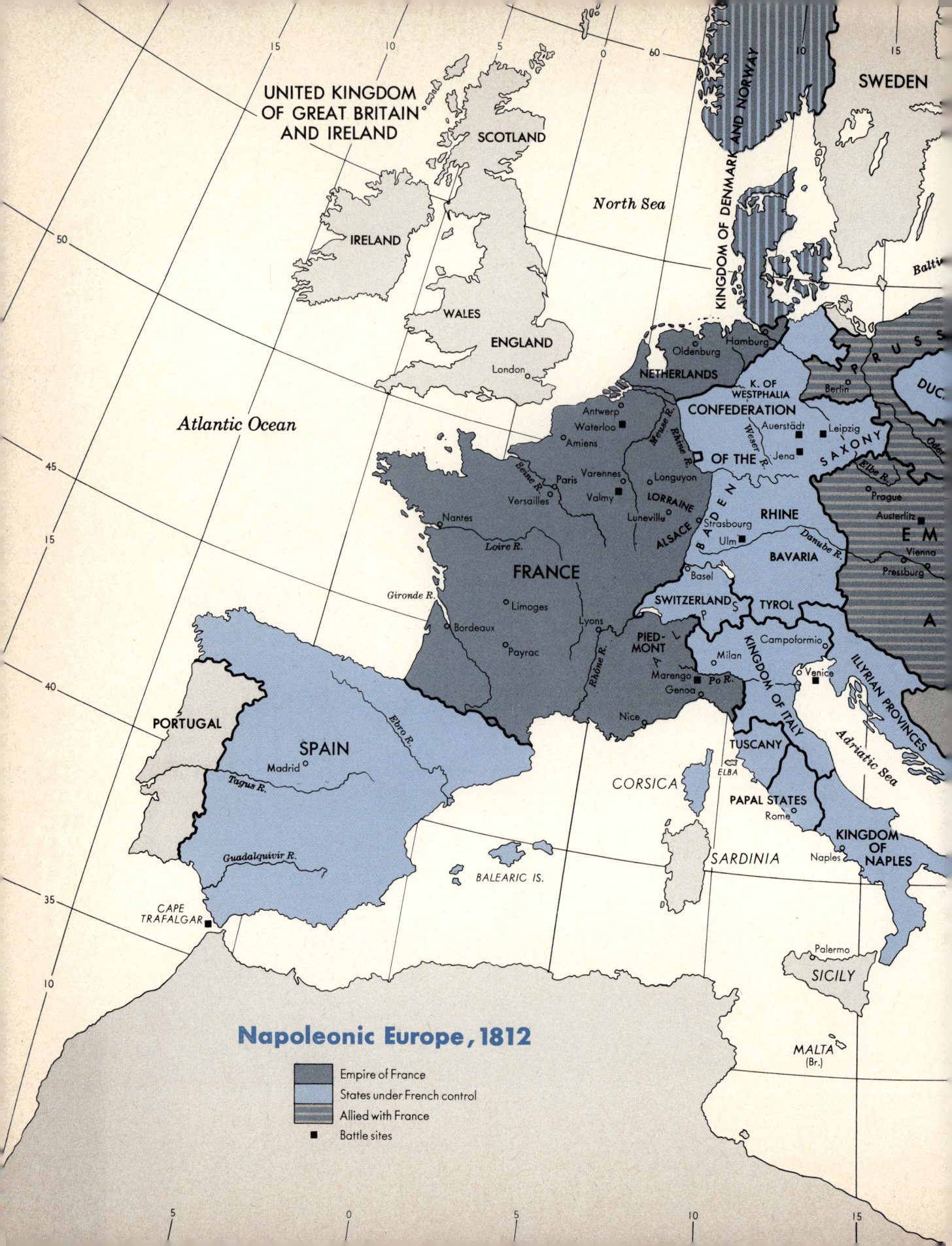

Napoleonic Europe, 1812

- Empire of France
- States under French control
- Allied with France
- ■ Battle sites

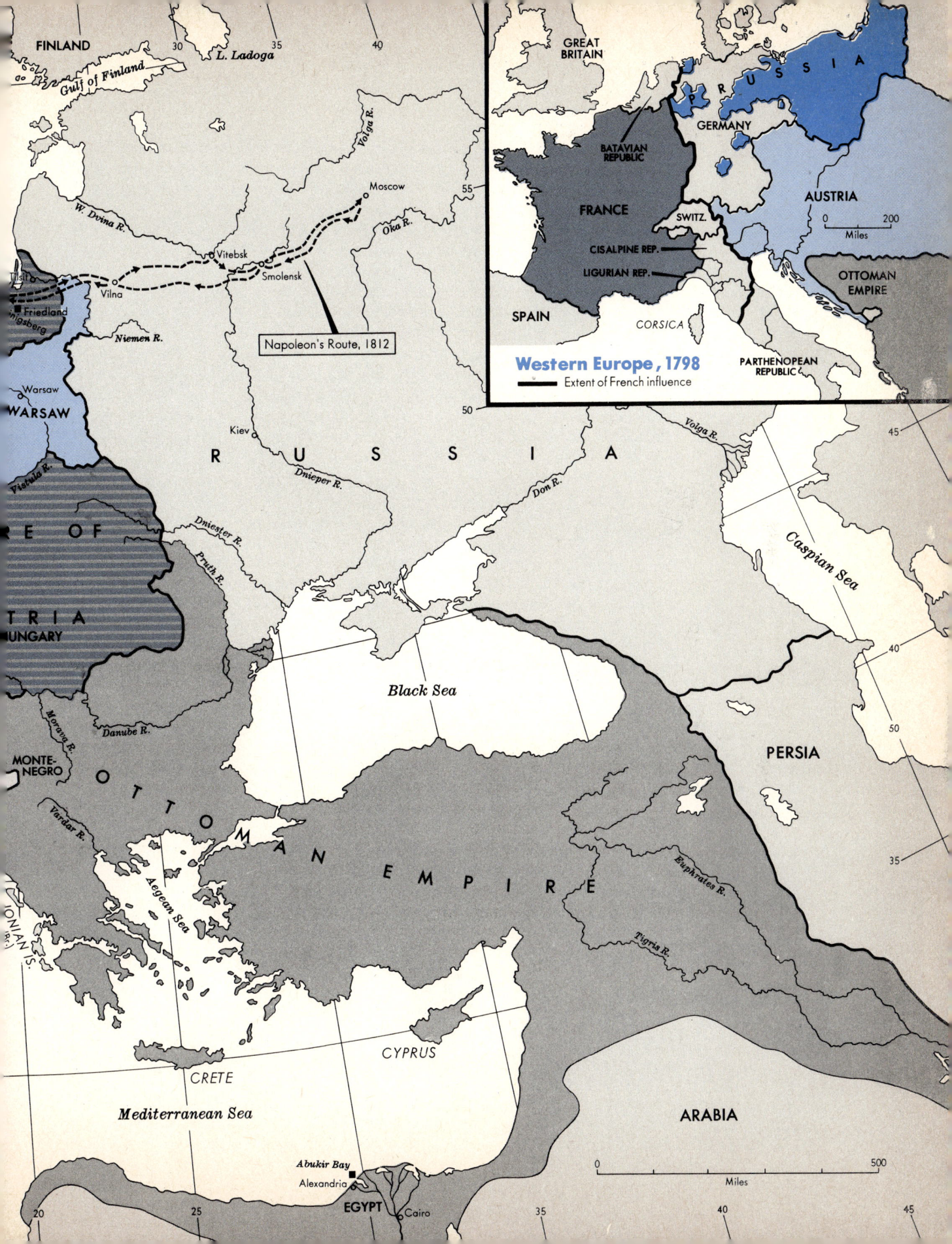

Napoleon's Route, 1812

Western Europe, 1798
Extent of French influence

paperasserie (in English, red tape). But through all the many changes of regime in France since 1800, the bureaucracy has kept the nation fundamentally stable and not nearly so badly governed as foreigners—and even the French themselves—usually think.

The spirit in which these institutions worked in Napoleon's own time, however, was far from libertarian or permissive. Censorship of press and stage was strict; the arts under imperial patronage were conventional and far from daring, for the Emperor, like so many dictators of the twentieth century, had old-fashioned tastes. Education did not encourage exploration and novelty, at least in the humanities and the social studies; science and technology, spurred on by war needs, fared rather better. Yet the straitjacket of the Continental system and the concentration on wars prevented the development of economic initiative. All in all, the authoritarian spirit of the Empire was not favorable to innovation, especially not to the new romanticism of the early nineteenth century. Napoleon disliked such free spirits as Chateaubriand and Madame de Staël, daughter of Necker, both leaders of the romantic movement, and Benjamin Constant, liberal political thinker, and he did his best to quiet them.

Almost everywhere in Europe, and especially in the Iberian peninsula and the Germanies, Napoleon's attempted new system of "order and peace for Europe" stirred up the strong emotional reaction which we call by the cold name of "nationalism." Paradoxically, Napoleon's attempt to found a supranationalist system greatly *helped* produce the nationalism that continues to sweep the world today. France, the Revolution, and Napoleon, however, *did* make friends and converts, mostly among intellectuals and others of the middle classes; they were nevertheless in the minority even in the Rhineland and northern Italy where the Napoleonic experiment was at least partially successful. These converts and their heirs in the next century tended to become liberal opponents of the old or restored "legitimate" or conservative regimes and therefore tended to regard Napoleon as a "liberal." This, aided by Napoleon's own liberal pretensions in the Hundred Days and his declarations at St. Helena, goes far to explain why he is not commonly put down as a *real* (that is, Rightist) dictator. To suggest that in fact he belongs with Hitler and Mussolini is sure to offend many people today.

Yet one can make a good case for so placing him. Napoleon did attempt by force to break down a balance of power among independent states, and the leaders and many of the people of these states regarded him as a disturber who had to be put in his place. He did hold much of his Empire and its satellites by imperialist, that is, authoritarian rule, not by federalist, that is, voluntary rule. In important respects he belongs with Charles V of Austria, Philip II of Spain, Louis XIV of France, and the leaders of Germany in both world wars of the twentieth century. Like them, he led a successful and expanding nation in an attempt to grow territorially at the expense of its neighbors and perhaps to dominate and rule Europe, if not the world. Like them, he failed in the long run. He did, however, come closer than any other to success, surely in part because his enemies did not, until the last campaigns of 1813–1815, hold their coalitions together with any success. Was the failure of the rest of Europe to hold together against the French in those long years from 1792–1813 due to French strength and enterprise or allied weakness and resistance to change? No doubt both were factors, but the historian must emphasize the really striking and prolonged disunity of Europe during these two decades when France was the "perturber."

V. Western Culture in a Revolutionary Age

With the wisdom of hindsight, we can see that the quarter-century covered by this chapter was a struggle between the old and the new in Western philosophical, literary, and artistic culture as well as in war and politics. The two struggles, however, were not perfectly correlated, nor can the participants as individuals be lined up in two neat camps, one solidly for the old in art, letters, philosophy, *and* politics, the other as solidly for the new in all these fields of human thought and action. There were individuals who were revolutionaries in aesthetic and philosophical matters, reactionaries in political matters—and vice versa.

THE CLASSICAL AND THE ROMANTIC

The new in matters aesthetic and philosophical has to be called *romantic,* the old *classical,* or somewhat pejoratively, *neoclassical*. These terms, which we have already attempted to define (*see* Chapter 9), are descriptions of psychological temperament and behavior. No doubt we in the West always have calm, measured, judicious individuals, and temperamental, emotional, heaven-storming individuals. But the classical temperament of the first and the romantic temperament of the second somehow get objectified in writing, painting, architecture, *group* tastes, *group* beliefs, or, to use a lighter term, one of the other of these temperaments becomes a *fashion*. These fashions, however, rarely arrange themselves in neat, simple ranks, but, especially in our modern world, vary with individual and group, and vary also with the cultural field to which they apply.

Let us first give some concrete examples:

> A little learning is a dang'rous thing;
> Drink deep, or taste not the Pierian spring:
> There shallow draughts intoxicate the brain,
> And drinking largely sobers us again.

Thus Alexander Pope, in his "Essay on Criticism," at the height of English classicism in letters in the early eighteenth century, utilizes its characteristic poetic form, the unintoxicating heroic couplet. The first, or the first two lines above are very often quoted; but it is the last and rarely quoted line that rounds out the typical "classical" lesson.

Here is a change:

> Oh lift me from the grass!
> I die! I faint! I fail!
> Let thy love in kisses rain
> On my lips and eyelids pale.
> My cheek is cold and white, alas!
> My heart beats loud and fast:—
> Oh! press it to thine own again,
> Where it will break at last.

Thus Shelley, in his "Indian Serenade," throbbing at one of the high points of English romanticism, sounding most unlike Pope and the heroic couplet. Yet these romantic and the classic opposites are sometimes mixed.

> Enough of science and of art;
> Close up these barren leaves;
> Come forth, and bring with you a heart
> That watches and receives.

Wordsworth's language in "The Tables Turned" is certainly not incongruous with classicism. But his "lesson" is quite romantic, for he maintains that Pope's "Pierian spring" of learning is *better not drunk from at all.*

Or in music, to move beyond the chronological limits of this chapter, compare the aria of Cherubino, "Voi che sapete," from Mozart's *Marriage of Figaro* (1786) with Isolde's "Liebestod" from Wagner's *Tristan and Isolde* (1859). Both are love songs, the first classical, the second romantic.

In the most abstract forms of the art of the word—philosophy—the central line of classicism was rationalist and empirical, with a tendency toward emphasis on the mechanical and the static; the central line of romanticism was intuitive, emotional and transcendental, and with something more than a tendency to emphasis on the organic, the dynamic. This straitjacket, however, does not fit the great philosopher Kant (1724–1804), for instance. Kant certainly had his rationalist side, rejected organized Christianity, and considered himself definitely part of the Enlightenment; yet he was also a transcendentalist, one of the heroes of the nineteenth-century romanticists. Hume (1711–1776) was a rationalist fully aware of the fact that most human beings are not very rational.

The German-language distinction between *Vernunft* and *Verstand*, popularized in England and the United States by the writings of Coleridge (1772–1834), helps to differentiate between the classic and the romantic in philosophy. *Verstand*, translated as "understanding" by Coleridge, is the way the mind of the bookkeeper, the calculator, the pedestrian and practical thinker, perhaps even the routine natural scientist, works; *Vernunft*, translated as "reason" by Coleridge, is the loftier way of using the mind, the way the mind of the true poet, the transcendental philosopher, the *creative* thinker, the scientific genius, perhaps even the player of hunches, operates. If you think this distinction is nonsense, you most likely incline toward the rationalist side, and also toward the run-of-the-mill "classical" of the Enlightenment; if you accept the distinction as valid, you probably incline toward the transcendental, the romantic.

THE FRENCH CONTRIBUTION

In France, the innovating nation in action, the philosophical thought of the revolutionary and Napoleonic eras was far from being new. It was simply more of the eighteenth-century Enlightenment, and not the freshest and the best. Thinkers of the leading school in the 1790's were already known in their own time as the *Idéologues,* a word touched with scorn. Examples are Volney (1757–1820), whose *Ruins of Empire* was once a best seller, and La Harpe (1739–1803), neoclassical critic, the tutor who is supposed to have instilled Tsar Alexander I with liberalism. The Idéologues were rationalists, really very little chastened by the failure of the French Revolutionists to behave rationally. But they were followers, not leaders, and they did not give to the rationalist inheritance of the Enlightenment the new turns nineteenth-century thinkers like Marx, Comte, J. S. Mill were to give it (*see* Chapter 13). Nor did revolutionary and Napoleonic France make great innovations in the arts. Structures like the Church of the Madeleine and Napoleon's triumphal arches in Paris (the Etoile and the Carrousel) were even more imitative of Roman architecture than earlier neoclassical buildings had been. "Gothic" architecture remained, at least in France, a term of reproach. In painting the great master was David (1748–1825), himself active in Jacobin politics during the Revolution and later the court painter to Napoleon. He, too, was almost obsessively classical in his desire to make a two-dimensional painted figure look like a three-dimensional Greek sculptured one. For his famous painting of the Tennis Court Oath he first sketched his main figures in the nude. Napoleon's own taste in furniture and in the decorative arts—conventional and on the heavy and gilded side—is still visible in his palace at Fontainebleau.

In letters, revolutionary and Napoleonic journalists and propagandists produced a mass of undistinguished writing in the eighteenth-century manner. Even in France, however, certain writers did foreshadow the coming triumph of romantic color and sentiment. Madame de Staël (1766–1817) discovered the depths of the German soul, and announced the discovery to the self-centered French in *De L'Allemagne* (*On Germany*, 1813), a most influential book. Chateaubriand (1768–1848) discovered the mysterious spell of the American wilderness—including "crocodiles" in the Mississippi—the romantic character of American Indians, and the beauties of Christian worship, in books published during the neoclassical rule of Napoleon himself.

While the French contributed relatively little in creative art and thought in these years, they made major contributions in science and technology. Among the leaders were the astronomer Laplace (1749–1827), the biologists Cuvier (1769–1832) and Lamarck (1744–1829), and the mathematician Monge (1746–1832), who was also a revolutionary political figure, active in the application of science to war production. Lavoisier (1743–1794), the founder of modern chemistry, was guillotined during the Terror not because he was a scientist and an intellectual, but because of his past role as one of the hated tax-farmers of the Old Regime.

"The Death of Marat," by David, 1793. Marat, one of the leaders of the Revolution, was murdered in his bath by Charlotte Corday.

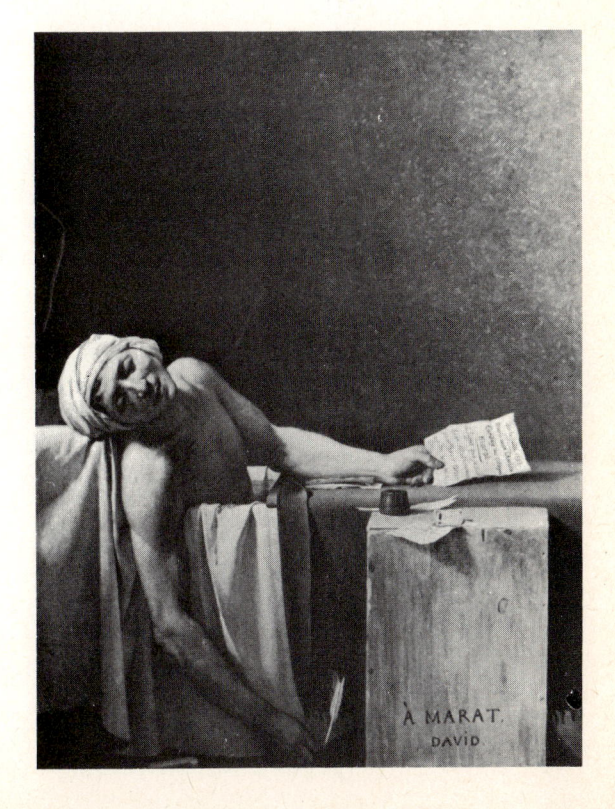

THE GERMAN AND BRITISH CONTRIBUTIONS

The revolutionary quarter-century was a fertile era in German and British thought and letters. The German literary culture-hero, Goethe (1749–1832), published in 1808 the first part of his poetic drama *Faust*. Goethe was a prolific writer, from whom samplings of the most romantic and the most classical can readily be drawn. His youthful epistolary novel, *The Sorrows of Young Werther* (1774), is charged with sentiment; its hero ends his life by suicide, an example which is said to have been responsible for an appreciable number of real suicides among the fashionably sensitive. His epic *Hermann and Dorothea* (1797) is almost neoclassical in its modelling on the antique, as are the poems of the *Roman Elegies*. But *Faust* is one of the great examples of the romantic view of life, and a famous quotation may serve as a distillation of one part of that view:

> Grey, dear friend, is all theory, but the golden tree of life is green.

It is true that these words are uttered by Mephistopheles (the Devil) and may therefore be taken to condemn the sentiment they announce, but this kind of ambivalence is itself one of the earmarks of romanticism. Schiller (1759–1805), who worked closely with Goethe in the little city of Weimar, for a while the intellectual center of Germany, had taken part as a young man in *Sturm und Drang* (Storm and Stress), a very romantic movement indeed. He sobered down in maturity and wrote verse plays in an almost Victorian manner, such as *Wilhelm Tell* (1804). His great work as a "Stormer and Stresser" had been *The Robbers* (1781), a drama of social protest which earned him the award of honorary French citizenship from the Convention. There were many other German romantic writers who in the decade of the 1790's renewed the freshness of the romantic quest for the *die blaue Blume* (the ineffable blue flower) in the face of the satisfied and unduly "established" Weimar group.

In England, two young poets, only barely recovering from their enthusiasm for the French Revolution, Wordsworth and Coleridge, published *Lyrical Ballads* (1798), which broke definitely with the subject matter and form of fashionable eighteenth-century poetry. Coleridge's "Rime of the Ancient Mariner" has remained the best known of these poems:

> Her lips were red, her looks were free,
> Her locks were yellow as gold:
> Her skin was white as leprosy,
> The Night-mare Life-in-Death was she,
> Who thicks man's blood with cold.

Coleridge's poetic vein ran out early, and he turned to philosophy—*German* philosophy. Now, for the first time since Luther, German writers and thinkers using their own native tongue figured prominently in the history of Western culture. Kant's philosophic successors, Fichte, Schleiermacher, and Hegel, all published characteristic and influential work in this quarter-century. The label affixed to their movement is "idealism," a Protean term that we are not rash enough to attempt to define here but that signified the opposite of what the nineteenth century labeled "materialism," "positivism," or "realism." The German idealist philosophers and theologians also laid the foundations on which the New England transcendentalists built during the first half of the nineteenth century.

Above all, the German writers and thinkers of this golden age helped form and strengthen one of the great forces of the nineteenth and twentieth centuries, nationalism—and not only German nationalism. Fichte's best-known work, the *Addresses to the German People* (1808), was an impassioned appeal to assert the profound and world-penetrating collective German personality against the barren and shallow eighteenth-century rationalism of the conquering French. Most of these writers had at least a grain of racism, at least a touch of the notion that the northern peoples are cleaner, morally superior, capable of more profound thought and feeling than the southern European peoples. They also have some mistrust of democracy, and a trace of pessimism about ordinary human nature. Englishmen, too, felt themselves northerners. Southey, a lesser colleague of Wordsworth and Coleridge, wrote that Cintra, a charming town in Portugal, is too lovely for the Portuguese, and should belong to "us Goths," English and German; these "Lake poets" were also agreed that although the English and the Germans had shown *genius*, the best the inferior French could do was to show *talent*. Modern nationalism tends to show these two characteristic faces, love and admiration for one's in-group, hatred or at least scorn for some specific out-group.

POLITICAL THOUGHT

In political thought in this period, Burke's *Reflections on the French Revolution* (1790) and at least one of the replies to it, Thomas Paine's *Rights of Man*, are landmarks. Burke attacked the Revolution in the *Reflections* and a series of sequels, often furiously controversial and unfair in tone. Yet he helped lay the foundations of modern conservative thought in the West. To Burke, the French Jacobins were victims of their own devotion to abstract thinking or "metaphysics," which led them to construct an unreal and impossible utopia and thence to immoral use of force to try to achieve this utopia on earth. On the positive side, Burke argues for gradual reform based on practical experience of what will work and on Christian acceptance of a stratified—that is, non-egalitarian, non-"democratic"—social order consonant with the imperfections of human nature—something much less or much more than any utopia. Paine's reply is a very able defense of the new ideas of liberty, equality, fraternity, one which has always seemed to romantic conservatives to have the shallow unimaginative character they attribute to the eighteenth-century Enlightenment. From this pamphlet war between Burke and Paine, and from the collected newspaper letters of 1788 by Madison, Hamilton, and Jay known as *The Federalist Papers*— all in a sense journalism—there has come a more important contribution to political thinking than is contained in many a heavy treatise of formal political philosophy.

THE LEGACY OF THE FRENCH REVOLUTION

Leaving the Age of the French Revolution and Napoleon, we encounter one more much debated problem of historical interpretation. What is the relationship between the French Revolution and later revolutions, particularly in the Western world? The European and Latin-American revolutions of the early and mid-nineteenth century are commonly seen by historians as influenced by the French Revolution, in a sense sequels to it. In our time, however, the question as to the relation between the French Revolution and the Russian Revolution has been much discussed. Professor R. R. Palmer in his *Age of the Democratic Revolution* finds two tendencies: the "associationist" view sees the Russian Revolution of 1917 as a continuation of, even a final product of, the democratic revolutions of the eighteenth century; twentieth-century communism becomes thus the child or grandchild of Jacobinism. The "dissociationist" view sees the Russian Revolution as basically inspired by authoritarian or totalitarian concepts quite antithetical to the democratic concepts of "juridical defense" and to the other democratic and libertarian "principles of 1776 and 1789."

The simple extreme statement of either view must seem to the historian a distortion. Libertarian and authoritarian ideas and ideals are inextricably mixed in the great literature of the Enlightenment, and, indeed, in all Western history. The ultimate goal of the Jacobins, "Liberty, Equality, Fraternity," can be made to appear identical with the Marxist goal of the "classless society" attained after the "withering away of the state." And the Reigns of Terror in both French and Russian revolutions exhibit behavior in shocking contrast to these professed ideals and hopes. There can be no doubt, however, that in the Western democracies today the living tradition, the "myth," of the eighteenth-century revolutions works to bolster concepts of civil rights in practice as well as in ideal; in the communist states such concepts are not reflected in practice or in ideals, since in the classless society no rights or laws will be necessary. It is surely a good symbolic fact that in the democratic tradition the heroes of the French Revolution are men like the Girondins and Danton, men who resisted the Terror, men who appealed to doctrines of "juridical defense"; in the Communist tradition, the heroes are men like Robespierre and the Parisian *Enragés, Bras Nus,* and *sans-culottes,* men who used and defended the methods of the Terror until they perished by them. In so far as the twentieth-century authoritarians of the Left are descended from the Enlightenment and the French Revolution, they appear to be the heirs of the "enlightened despots," whether royal or plebeian.

11

READING SUGGESTIONS (asterisk indicates paperbound edition)

General Accounts

C. Brinton, *A Decade of Revolution, 1789–1799,* and G. Bruun, *Europe and the French Imperium, 1799–1814* (*Torchbooks). These two volumes in the Rise of Modern Europe series provide comprehensive coverage, with full bibliographies.

G. Lefebvre, *The French Revolution,* 2 vols. (Columbia University, 1962, 1964). Another comprehensive treatment.

R. R. Palmer, *Age of the Democratic Revolution,* 2 vols. (Princeton University, 1959, 1964). Detailed exposition of the thesis that the French Revolution was part of a general movement toward democracy.

P. Amann, ed., *The Eighteenth-Century Revolution: French or Western?* (*Heath). The pros and cons of Palmer's thesis.

L. Gershoy, *The French Revolution and Napoleon* (Appleton, 1964). Lucid and informative textbook account.

The French Revolution

F. A. Kafker and J. M. Laux, eds., *The French Revolution: Conflicting Interpretations* (*Random House). Up-to-date sample.

A. de Tocqueville, *The Old Regime and the Revolution* (*Anchor). A celebrated essay, now more than a century old, stressing the continuities between the old and new regimes.

G. Lefebvre, *The Coming of the French Revolution* (*Vintage). Masterly short study of developments to October, 1789.

A. Mathiez, *The French Revolution* (*Universal). Narrative treatment to 1794 by an eloquent French scholar very sympathetic to the Jacobins.

N. Hampson, *A Social History of the French Revolution* (*University of Toronto). Fine synthesis of recent scholarship.

G. Rudé, *The Crowd in the French Revolution* (*Oxford). Fascinating analysis of the class background of the demonstrators who took part in the great "days" of the Revolution.

A. Soboul, *The Parisian Sans-Culottes and the French Revolution, 1793–1794* (Clarendon, 1964). Enlightening study, based on Paris police records, by a Marxian scholar.

A. Cobban, *The Social Interpretation of the French Revolution* (*Gordian). Critique of attempts to view it as a class struggle.

C. Brinton, *The Jacobins* (Russell, 1962); M. J. Sydenham, *The Girondins* (Oxford, 1961); and R. B. Rose, *The Enragés: Socialists of the French Revolution?* (Australia University Press, 1964). Careful studies greatly revising popular notions of revolutionary factions.

C. H. Tilly, *The Vendée* (*Wiley). Revisionist study, by a very capable sociologist.

R. R. Palmer, *Twelve Who Ruled* (*Atheneum). Very readable collective biography of the Committee of Public Safety.

J. M. Thompson, *Robespierre and the French Revolution* (*Collier); L. R. Gottschalk, *J. P. Marat: A Study in Radicalism* (*Phoenix); G. Bruun, *Saint-Just: Apostle of the Terror* (Houghton, 1932). Enlightening biographies of revolutionary leaders.

C. Brinton, *The Anatomy of Revolution* (*Vintage). Common denominators of the seventeenth-century English, the American, the French, and the Russian revolutions.

Napoleon

P. Geyl, *Napoleon, For and Against* (*Yale). Full survey of judgments passed on Bonaparte by historians.

J. M. Thompson, *Napoleon Bonaparte: His Rise and Fall* (Oxford, 1952), and F. Markham, *Napoleon* (*Mentor). Readable biographies by careful scholars.

H. A. L. Fisher, *Napoleon* (*Oxford), and A. L. Guérard, *Napoleon I* (Knopf, 1956). Good shorter biographies.

R. B. Holtman, *The Napoleonic Revolution* (*Lippincott). Emphasizing institutional changes under Bonaparte.

D. G. Chandler, *The Campaigns of Napoleon* (Macmillan, 1966). Recent scholarly account.

O. Connelly, *Napoleon's Satellite Kingdoms* (Free Press, 1965). Informative studies of Spain, Holland, Westphalia, Italy, and Naples.

F. Markham, *Napoleon and the Awakening of Europe* (*Collier). Brief survey, arguing that European nationalisms, while aroused by French imperialism, were as yet underdeveloped.

Culture

J. B. Halsted, ed., *Romanticism: Problems of Definition, Explanation, Evaluation* (*Heath). Useful introductory sketch.

D. L. Dowd, *Pageant-Master of the Republic: Jacques-Louis David and the French Revolution* (University of Nebraska, 1948). Biography of the neo-classical artist who was the "painter laureate" of the Revolution and Napoleon.

J. Bronowski and B. Mazlish, *The Western Intellectual Tradition from Leonardo to Hegel* (*Torchbooks). Stressing the links between economics, politics, and intellectual history.

Note: See also titles listed for Arts and Letters in the readings for Chapter 13.

Sources and Fiction

J. H. Stewart, *A Documentary Survey of the French Revolution* (Macmillan, 1951). Excellent collection of constitutional texts and other official documents.

A. Young, *Travels in France*, C. Maxwell, ed. Cambridge, 1929). Lively diary by an English farm expert who journeyed throughout France on the eve of the Revolution and during its early months.

E. Burke, *Reflections on the Revolution in France* (*several editions). The celebrated indictment of the destructive character of the Revolution.

J. M. Thompson, ed., *Napoleon's Letters* (Everyman). A fascinating collection, arranged chronologically.

J. C. Herold, ed., *The Mind of Napoleon* (*Columbia University). Another fascinating collection, arranged topically, and including items from his writings and his conversations.

A. de Caulaincourt, *With Napoleon in Russia* (*Universal), and its sequel, *No Peace with Napoleon* (Morrow, 1936). Memoirs of Bonaparte's last campaigns by one of his chief aides.

Anatole France, *The Gods Are Athirst* (Roy). Fine short novel about a Jacobin fanatic.

Tolstoy, *War and Peace* (*several editions, often abridged). The epic novel about 1812.

12

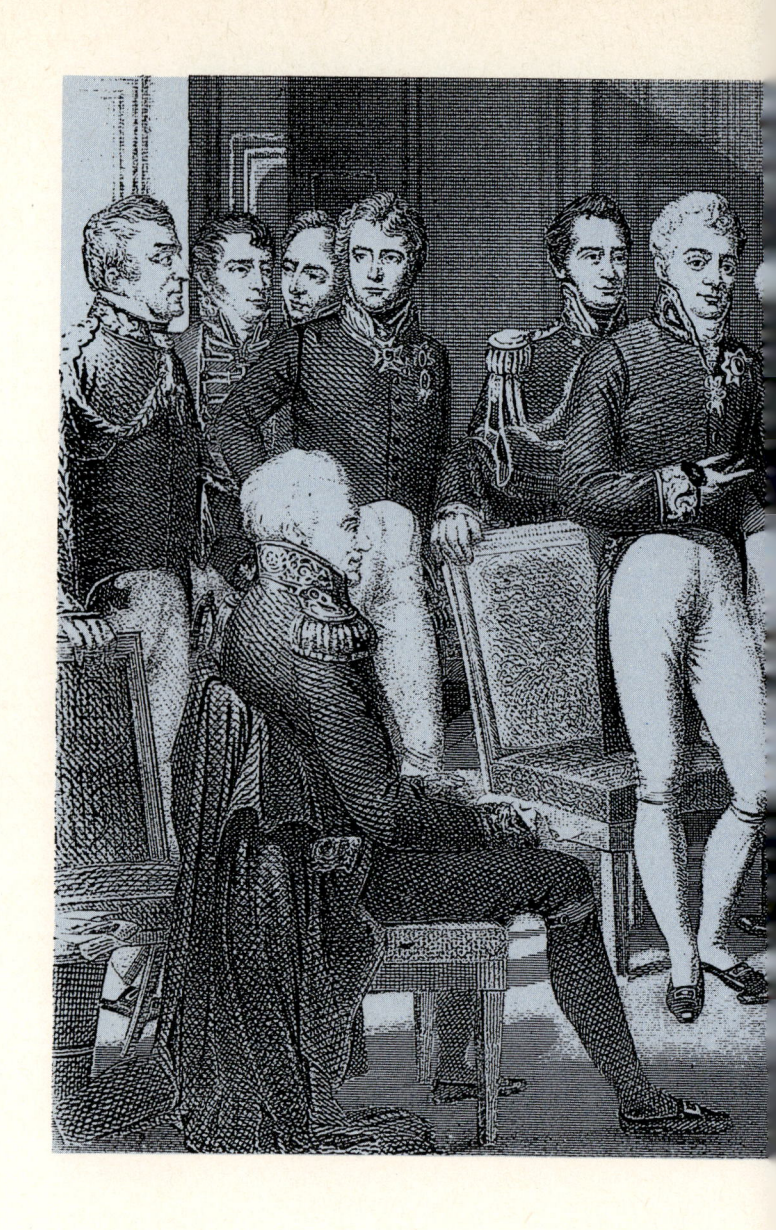

The Revolutions Renewed

1815—1870

The statesmen of Europe at the Congress of Vienna, 1814–1815. Metternich is standing prominently at left front, Wellington at extreme left. Talleyrand is seated at right with his arm resting on the table.

I. European International Politics, 1815–1870

THE CONGRESS OF VIENNA

The Congress of Vienna met in September, 1814, to settle in formal diplomatic negotiations the many problems of a Europe overwhelmed by twenty-five years of war and revolution. Representatives of every state, big or little, gathered in Vienna to work for their causes—and, in generous time off, to play, so that the waggish phrase "The Congress dances but does not march" went round the world. Napoleon's return from Elba frightened the delegates, and they made haste—diplomatists' haste—to gather loose ends together and sign a comprehensive peace settlement on June 8, 1815, ten days before Waterloo. While there were to be wars enough in the next century, no general European or world war broke out again until 1914.

Yet on the whole the work of the Congress of Vienna has not received praise from historians. For one thing, it was based, at least for purposes of publicity, on the principle of Legitimacy, that is, the rule of the princes, privileged classes, and traditions that had prevailed before the "illegitimate" changes made under the influence of the French Revolution and Napoleon. Legitimacy in the abstract denied the validity of much that had been done since 1789, and went against the "trends" or "forces" of liberalism and nationalism that were to be so important—and so upsetting—in the nineteenth century. Yet in practice the Vienna settlement by no means wholly restored the old of 1789 or wholly suppressed the new of 1789–1815. The work of this congress looks the more impressive when it is placed beside the comparative failure of the Conference of Versailles in 1919 and the total failure even to attempt any kind of general peace conference after World War II in 1945.

The powers which had made the Quadruple Alliance of 1813–1814 against France—that is, Austria, Great Britain, Russia, Prussia—were the "Big Four" of the Congress. The small and middling powers were there, vocal enough, and in a few matters not without influence, but the big powers called the tune, as they were to do at Versailles a century later. It soon developed that, in spite of their hard-won unity against Napoleon in 1814, they were now divided, above all about possession of two pieces of territory, Poland and Saxony. Russia wanted almost all of Poland as a satellite kingdom under Tsar Alexander I. Austria wanted no such strengthening of a great rival, preferring the status quo of 1795, after the third partition, which had wiped the Polish state off the map. Prussia wanted all of Saxony, on the ground that its ruler, by remaining too long true to his ally, Napoleon, had forfeited the sacred rights of Legitimacy; Austria, counting on Saxon support in the future against the too successful Prussians, wanted the independence and integrity of Saxony maintained. The split between Austria, supported by Britain, and Prussia, supported by Russia, made it easier for defeated France to gain acceptance as a fifth Great Power, especially since the French delegation was headed by a skilled, unprincipled diplomatist, Talleyrand, who had already served with success under the Old Regime, the Revolution, and Napoleon, and now was serving the legitimate Louis XVIII. France lined up with Britain and Austria in a "secret" treaty well advertised among the insiders, and a compromise on the Saxon-Polish question was achieved.

Prince Talleyrand.

THE VIENNA SETTLEMENT

As far as possible the Vienna settlement brought back the Legitimate rulers of the European states. In Italy and the Iberian peninsula they returned with few constitutional strings attached to their rule. But in France the restored Louis XVIII (reigned 1814–1824) four days before Waterloo issued a "constitutional charter" (the *Charte*) which set up a British-style government, with guarantees of individual civil rights, a Chamber of Peers, and a Chamber of Deputies elected under a suffrage drastically limited by high property qualifications. The Dutch King William I and some of the restored German rulers, as in Baden, Bavaria, and Saxe-Weimar, also set up constitutional regimes.

The Congress did not entirely restore Italy to its status of 1789. Austria, led by one of the outstanding men of the Congress, Prince Metternich, secured the important north Italian territories of Lombardy and Venetia, together with Napoleon's annexations across the Adriatic in Dalmatia. These represented an expansion of Habsburg possessions, not just a restoration. The House of Savoy got back its old lands in northwestern Italy and the island of Sardinia, plus the former republic of Genoa. The other monarchs, including the Pope and the Neapolitan Bourbons, came back to their old states. In Germany, however, the Vienna settlement confirmed the great Napoleonic changes which had reduced the several hundred "sovereign" states of 1789 to thirty-nine. In recognition of the fact that many Germans desired a political entity to replace the defunct Holy Roman Empire, the Congress set up a Germanic Confederation to which both Prussia and Austria, as well as the smaller states, belonged. This Confederation, however, was a very loose and weak union rather than a true federal state. A more significant role in determining the future course of German development was to be taken by the *Zollverein*, a customs union set up under Prussian leadership in 1819, which abolished internal tariffs between member states and levied uniform duties on imports. Twenty-five years later it included almost all the German states except Austria, and its success hinted that Prussia by fostering the economic unification of Germany might promote its political unification as well.

Two other territorial provisions of the Vienna settlement were experiments that proved unsuccessful but were clearly not mere attempts to return to 1789. Holland and Belgium were united, partly to put as strong a power as possible on the northern border of France; the union lasted only until 1830 when the Belgians seceded. Norway was taken from Denmark (which had been pro-Napoleon) and united with Sweden, partly to reward Bernadotte, who in 1818 became Charles XIV of Sweden, for turning against Napoleon, and partly, in good eighteenth-century style, to "compensate" him for the loss of Swedish Pomerania to Prussia. This arrangement lasted until 1905, when it was peacefully dissolved and Norway became an independent kingdom.

The Polish and the Saxon questions were resolved by compromises. Prussia annexed a good part of Saxony, but the remainder continued as a fairly large independent German state. Tsar Alexander got his satellite Kingdom of Poland, that is, most of the Napoleonic Duchy of Warsaw; Prussia got back the western part of her eighteenth-century Polish spoils, and in addition Swedish Pomerania, the last land south of the Baltic of the greater Sweden of the seventeenth century. Alexander had already taken Finland from Sweden in 1808, which Napoleon's permission given at Tilsit.

Vienna was a most unprincipled peace, in spite of all the talk about the principle of Legitimacy; but it was not a vengeful peace. France, while obliged to give up most of her revolutionary and Napoleonic annexations, returned substantially to the frontiers of the Old Regime. Territorially—and it is the disposition of actual pieces of this earth that have usually given the most trouble to peacemakers—most of its dispositions were compromises made in an effort to reward the winners without completely wiping out the losers. The republics of Venice and Genoa, the many political units "mediatized" in Germany by the

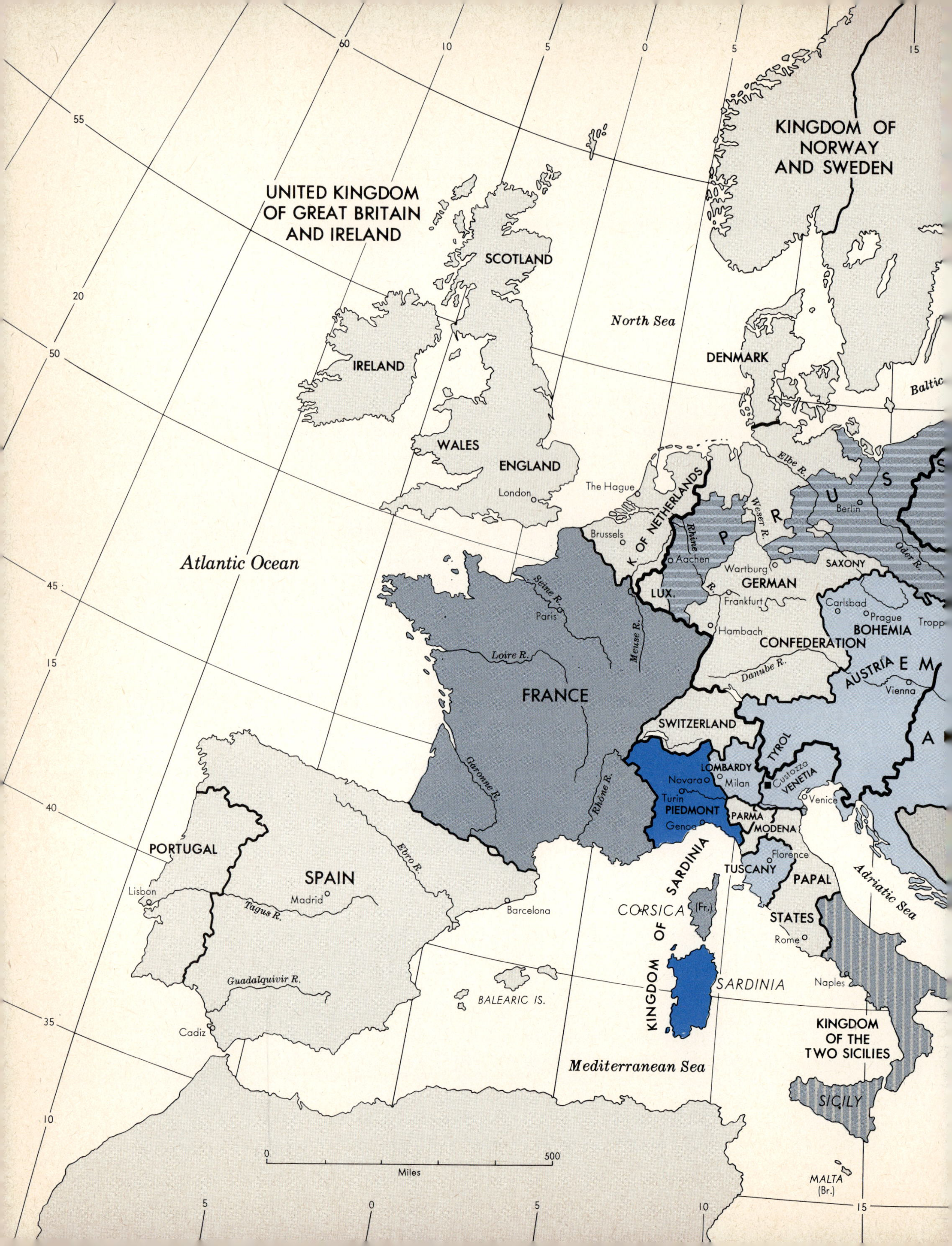

UNITED KINGDOM OF GREAT BRITAIN AND IRELAND
SCOTLAND
IRELAND
WALES
ENGLAND
London
North Sea
KINGDOM OF NORWAY AND SWEDEN
DENMARK
Baltic
The Hague
K. OF NETHERLANDS
Brussels
Aachen
Rhine R.
Elbe R.
Weser R.
Oder R.
P R U S S
Berlin
SAXONY
Wartburg
GERMAN CONFEDERATION
Frankfurt
Hambach
LUX.
Carlsbad
Prague
BOHEMIA
AUSTRIA
Vienna
Danube R.
Atlantic Ocean
Seine R.
Paris
Meuse R.
Loire R.
FRANCE
Garonne R.
Rhône R.
SWITZERLAND
TYROL
LOMBARDY
Milan
Novara
Custozza
VENETIA
Venice
Turin
PIEDMONT
Genoa
PARMA
MODENA
Florence
TUSCANY
PAPAL STATES
Rome
Adriatic Sea
KINGDOM OF SARDINIA
CORSICA
(Fr.)
SARDINIA
Naples
KINGDOM OF THE TWO SICILIES
SICILY
MALTA
(Br.)
Mediterranean Sea
BALEARIC IS.
Barcelona
SPAIN
Madrid
Ebro R.
Tagus R.
Guadalquivir R.
PORTUGAL
Lisbon
Cadiz
0
500
Miles

Europe after 1815

— Boundary of the German Confederation
■ Battle sites

Chief Decree of the Imperial Delegation (1803) (*see* p. 454), could be swallowed up; but even the kings of Saxony and Denmark, too long loyal to Napoleon, had to be kept in the club of legitimate rulers.

BRITAIN AND THE POSTWAR BALANCE OF POWER

A great new fact in the classic balance of European international politics after 1815 was the clear succession of Great Britain to the place of "greatest power" or "dominant nation." Unlike previous holders of this position—France, Spain, the Austria of Charles V—Great Britain made no attempt to expand on the continent of Europe. Anglophiles—and many English too—sometimes treat this British hegemony as an example of a noble, self-denying effort to outlaw war and preserve peace for all. But, as we shall later see, nineteenth-century Britain expanded as fast and as successfully as any earlier aggressor or "perturber" had—but it expanded overseas, not in Europe. Moreover, even though by the end of the century her Conservative leader Lord Salisbury boasted of her "splendid isolation," British policy was firmly set against any European power that threatened to gain a position it might use to break down the rough balance of the European state-system. Since that balance was then, even more than in the two previous centuries, a world balance, Britain also tried to prevent any European power from setting up a major overseas empire. When toward the end of the century the new German Empire seemed to threaten to upset *both* European and world balances, the stage was set for World War I.

The immediate international issues after 1815 arose out of efforts to maintain the peace settlement. The leaders at Vienna—Alexander I, Metternich, Castlereagh, the British foreign secretary—were certainly, as diplomatists go, convinced that their work was valid; but they were all professionals enough to know that it had left many disappointed and disgruntled groups, and that organization of some sort was needed to maintain the settlement. Alexander, under the influence of an enthusiastic and religiously inclined lady, Mme. von Krüdener, was chiefly responsible for what was called—scornfully by liberals—the "Holy Alliance." This document, eventually signed by all European rulers except those of Great Britain, Turkey, and the papacy, was a declaration of noble Christian principles, perhaps meant by Alexander as a preamble to a constitution of something like a League of Nations. The effective organization, however, was the old Quadruple Alliance, plus France, members of which met in three Congresses until 1822, when at the Congress of Verona it was finally apparent that the five major members of the "Congress system" were too divided to make the system work.

This division is usually described as one between the "liberal" powers (Britain and France) and the "conservative" powers (Austria, Russia, Prussia). It was also a division between the powers which sought by common action to enforce the principle of Legitimacy set up at Vienna and the powers which sought to water down the principle, or even revise parts of the settlement of Vienna. The three Eastern monarchies did succeed in maintaining within their own territories the "Metternichian system," though not without opposition and occasional attempts at revolution. The two Western constitutional monarchies were not completely agreed on espousing the cause of nationalism and liberalism in international politics. The first break in the system was in fact the work of Britain and aimed at balking a French effort, backed by the three conservative powers, to rescue Ferdinand VII of Spain from revolutionists. The new British foreign secretary, Canning, refused to back the decision taken at Verona to intervene in Spain.

The tough-minded historian will insist that in this, as in other conflicts with the conservative powers, Canning and his successors in the Foreign Office were not motivated by any ideological sympathy with liberals, let alone revolutionists, but by a desire to further British national interests—usually trade. Thus in the crisis of 1823, Canning feared that successful restoration of full Legitimacy in Spain might lead the Spanish government to try to get back her revolted colonies in America, and thus deprive Britain of lucrative trade with the independent states of Spanish America. A by-product of this crisis, of great importance in United States history, was the enunciation by President Monroe in his annual message to Congress in 1823 of the "Monroe Doctrine." The message warned European powers against any attempts to interfere with the independence achieved by the former Spanish colonies in the Americas. The doctrine was issued in this form to avoid collaboration with Britain, as suggested by Canning; since the United States was still a very young power, however, this unilateral declaration would have been meaningless and ineffective without British naval support at the time.

REVOLUTION IN SOUTHERN AND WESTERN EUROPE, 1820–1830

Revolution and opposition to it were the dominant issue of international politics throughout the post-Napoleonic decades. The changes that revolutionists desired may be roughly classified as aiming at a wider suffrage and other constitutional reforms *in the direction* of democracy or at the achievement of national independence, or at both. The critical revolutionary years were 1820, 1830, and 1848, but much of importance also went on in between.

The first wave of revolutions in 1820 came in Italy and in Spain. They were inspired by memories of the Napoleonic reforms in Italy, and in Spain by those of the very advanced democratic constitution that had been drawn up in 1812 by Spanish patriots in the liberated southern parts of the country. But the middle classes were weak in both peninsulas, and the uprisings of 1820 were conspiracies and attempted *coups d'état* rather than social revolutions. The Great Powers, after meeting in congresses dominated by Metternich, allowed the Austrians to put down the Italians. The French, in their last contribution toward upholding the Metternich system, put down the Spanish revolution in 1823. The Italian revolutions brought to public attention the existence of an international society, the *Carbonari* ("charcoal-burners"), a kind of secret "Jacobin" network. The *Carbonari* were led by professional revolutionists, a new phenomenon in Western history, and they greatly alarmed the conservatives. It is doubtful, however, that they had a decisive influence in producing the next two waves of revolution, the first of which broke in France.

Though France had been treated leniently in the peace settlement even after the folly of the Hundred Days, she had been beaten, and the defeat rankled. The Bourbons had, after all, been put back on the throne by the Allies. In 1824 Charles X, the brother of Louis XVIII, succeeded to the throne. He and his advisers pursued a policy of reviving the medieval trappings of the old monarchy, and managed to offend almost all the politically active elements in the country.

Radical Paris in July, 1830, as in July, 1789, fired the first shot, and began the great nineteenth-century Parisian technique of raising in the streets barricades of paving stones, furniture, and anything else handy.

The provocation for revolution had been a series of ordinances issued from the throne to settle a ministerial crisis by making it clear that royal authority was absolute and that parliamentary government in the British sense did not exist in France. But behind the radical rioters were various more powerful groups—former civil servants and other leaders under Napoleon, middle-class intellectuals and white-collar workers, many of them excluded from the vote by the high suffrage requirements of the *Charte*. These groups, headed by liberal deputies in the Chamber, managed to head off the Republicans, whose nominal leader, the aged Lafayette, was hardly a fire-eater. After Charles X had fled, his cousin—Louis Philippe, Duke of Orleans—accepted the throne as a genuine constitutional monarch, the "Citizen King."

The repercussions of these events on international politics were immediate and important. Britain's defection under Canning had broken up the "Congress system" in 1823; the full defection of France from Legitimacy in 1830, though it by no means made firm allies of Britain and France, did underline the contrast between the liberal West and the reactionary East. The news of events in France triggered a nationalist rising by the Belgians in August, 1830, against what they considered, not without justification, the undue dominance of the Dutch in the enlarged Kingdom of the Netherlands. The two major Belgian parties, Clericals and Liberals, normally bitter opponents in Western countries in the nineteenth century, joined together against the Dutch; workers in Brussels took to the streets and fought Dutch troops. A provisional government dominated by moderates was set up, and began a search for a constitutional monarch. It chose first the Duke of Nemours, second son of Louis Philippe, thus alarming the British, for whom any further French influence in the Low Countries seemed to threaten a repetition of the aggressions of Louis XIV and Napoleon.

Lord Palmerston, then beginning a long and lively career as British Foreign Minister, made known his unyielding opposition to a French king in Belgium. He did this not only through traditional diplomatic channels, but through new channels of publicity in Parliament and press. Faced with hostile British public opinion, Louis Philippe wisely rejected the election for his son, and the Belgians chose a minor German prince, Leopold of Saxe-Coburg, related by marriage to the British royal family. Mounting the throne as Leopold I in 1831, he proved to be a model constitutional monarch and got the new Belgian kingdom off to an excellent start. Since the Dutch King William proved obstinate, it took a French army and a Franco-British fleet to clear the Dutch out of Belgium. In the end, even the three Eastern powers were persuaded to accept this infringement of Legitimacy, and after long negotiations William accepted in 1839 an international treaty signed by all the powers, including Prussia, recognizing Belgium as an "independent and perpetually neutral state." This was the treaty which, violated by Germany (Prussia) in the invasion of 1914, brought Britain into World War I.

REVOLUTION IN EASTERN EUROPE, 1825–1830

In eastern Europe, by contrast, attempts at revolution failed. In Russia the death of Alexander I late in 1825 produced a few days of confusion, since his younger brother Constantine secretly resigned the crown, which passed to a still younger brother, who became Tsar Nicholas I (1825–1855). A few Westernized army officers, aiming at a constitutional regime and organized in two secret societies, took the occasion to attempt a revolution in December, 1825. This pathetic "Decembrist" movement had almost no roots in the country and was readily suppressed; the story has it that the Russian people thought "Constitution" must be Constantine's wife. But Nicholas was alarmed and became fanatically antiliberal.

In 1830 the news from France and Belgium led the Tsar to threaten intervention with the nearest force available to him—the Polish army. The Poles, stirred by his threats and by the example of their French friends, revolted and expelled the Russians from Warsaw. The Poles themselves were divided into quarreling moderates and radicals; even had they been united, however, they could not have held out against Nicholas without aid from abroad. The revolt was put down, and many Poles fled to exile, mainly to France, where they hardly exercised a calming influence.

THE "EASTERN QUESTION"

All had not been quiet in central and southern Europe since the 1820 revolutionary movements, but on the whole the Metternichian system of suppression had worked. There was, however, a danger zone in southeastern Europe. At the beginning of the nineteenth century the Ottoman Empire still included all the lands we call loosely the Balkans. Around Constantinople and in what is now Yugoslavia and Albania were many Moslems, but generally the Balkan peninsula was peopled by Christians who had long been allowed by their Turkish masters a good deal of cultural and religious autonomy. Most of North Africa and the Middle East were technically part of the Ottoman Empire; but the Sultan had no real control over Egypt and the North African coast. It was becoming increasingly evident that Turkey was a declining power, deserving the phrase later applied to it by Tsar Nicholas I, the "Sick Man of Europe."

In the eighteenth century, Catherine of Russia had seized from the already sick man Turkish lands along the Black Sea (*see* Chapter 10). Naturally the Habsburgs wanted their share, and in 1781 at a meeting with Joseph II, Catherine promised Austria the western part of the Turks' possessions in the Balkans for consenting to the establishment of a revived Byzantine Empire with her grandson Constantine as Emperor. This, by no means the last grand scheme for partitioning Turkey, never came near fruition, even though Joseph joined Catherine in 1788 in a war on the Turks. The Austrians gained part of Bosnia after concluding, under Prussian pressure, a separate peace with Turkey.

The mention of Prussia suggests once more the interdependence of Europe. The Eastern or Turkish Question in the nineteenth century involved *all* the Great Powers: Russia and Austria most immediately as neighbors of the Turks, Britain if only because the Sultan's Arab provinces lay athwart her "lifeline of empire," the route to India via the eastern Mediterranean, but also because the British wanted no single European state to acquire too much Turkish land. Prussia, as usual throughout the century, was anxious that neither her Austrian nor her Russian neighbor get much stronger; and France was involved if only because of her material, religious, and sentimental interests in the Levant dating from the

Crusades. But the sharpening of the Eastern Question in the 1820's was due also to quite a new factor, the spread of revolutionary nationalism to the Balkan peoples under Turkish rule. Of these new nationalisms the earliest and most important was the Greek.

Greek Independence. The Greeks of Constantinople, known as Phanariots, had long played a major role in Turkish political and business life. But old Greece had faded into insignificance symbolized by the condition of Athens in 1800, a mere village of huts clustered around and among the ruins of the Acropolis. The revival of Greek self-consciousness owed much to the West and to the continued prestige of classical Greek civilization in Western higher education. The principles of 1776 and 1789 spread to the educated few in the Balkans; the great revolutionary hymn, the *Marseillaise*, was translated into Greek. The now fashionable Western romantics, Lord Byron most conspicuously, took up the Greek cause, and Philhellenic societies sprang up everywhere from Berlin to New York and Boston. Russians, too, patronized the movement, and protected a secret society founded in Odessa in 1814 and joined by Phanariot leaders. The first of the Greek movements was actually unleashed well outside Greece in what is now Rumania, under the wealthy Prince Ypsilanti in March, 1821. Metternich was strong enough to suppress this revolt, but the movement spread to Greece proper, with insurrections in the Peloponnesus (in modern usage, the Morea) and some of the Aegean islands. A merciless revolutionary war broke out, marked by massacres on both sides.

The Turkish Sultan summoned aid from his powerful Egyptian vassal, Mohammed Ali, whose son Ibrahim turned the tide against the rebellious Greeks, already weakened by internal quarrels. The Philhellenes in the West were now frantically appealing to their governments to save the Greeks. These governments, moreover, were already concerned over the threat to the balance of power should the Russians intervene alone in support of the rebels. By the Treaty of London (1827) the improbable combination of Britain, France, and Russia agreed to put pressure on the Sublime Porte (the diplomatists' term for the Turkish government) to grant an armistice to the Greeks. But the Egyptians were now in the adventure on their own, and Ibrahim, angered by renewed Greek attacks, refused to await orders from his father. In a tragicomedy of errors the combined British, French, and Russian fleets in 1827 fired on and sank most of the Egyptian fleet in the harbor of Navarino in the Morea.

The Russians at once went to war with the Turks, while the British and French in uneasy collaboration continued to try to restrain Mohammed Ali and keep some sort of order in the Levant. After taking Adrianople the Russians, afraid of going too far and starting a general war, accepted Prussian mediation with the Porte and in 1829 concluded a peace which gave Greece independence and the Rumanian provinces of Moldavia and Wallachia autonomy (self-government without full sovereignty), but made no other great inroads on Turkish possessions. At a London conference later in 1829 a small independent Greek state was set up by the Powers, and after some search a German prince, Otto of Bavaria, was found willing to accept the throne. An underdeveloped area, torn with factions, ruled by a not very competent monarch, and not yet including large areas ethnically Greek, the Kingdom of Greece found its first years most difficult; but it survived. Another shocking breach of Legitimacy had to be registered.

Egyptian Expansion. In the decade after 1830 the Eastern Question focussed on the Egyptian ruler, Mohammed Ali, and his son Ibrahim, who had shown in the fighting against the revolting Greeks that they were stronger than their suzerain, the Turkish sultan. The Egyptians rebelled against the Sultan, took over Syria, and invaded Anatolia, threatening Istanbul itself. Russia came to the Sultan's rescue but demanded a high price in the Treaty of Unkiar Skelessi (1833—named for a Turkish imperial residence on the Bosphorus), which placed the Ottoman Empire under Russian protection and obliged the Turks to close the Straits (the Dardanelles and Bosphorus) to the warships of all nations. The British under Palmerston took alarm for their lifeline to India, all the more since plans for a railroad or a canal across the Isthmus of Suez were in the air; also Mohammed Ali was too uppish for the British of those days to tolerate.

At this juncture the French backed the Egyptians. Once more, and in spite of the good auguries of the July Revolution, France and England were in open rivalry. Britain, Russia, Prussia, and Austria managed to agree in July, 1840, on the Treaty of London, which laid down strict limits on Egyptian expansion. Mohammed Ali, trusting France to support him, refused to accept these limits. The Turkish Sultan under British urging deposed Mohammed Ali, while the British navy bombarded Beirut, and landed a small British force in Syria.

The crucial role of the British navy in the whole episode was typical of the methods Britain used so successfully throughout the nineteenth century. The French government backed down after a war scare that threw Paris into panic, and Thiers, the minister who had pressed the policy of backing Egypt, was dismissed. Mohammed Ali gave up his Arab conquests but retained Egypt. With the other four Great Powers in 1841, France signed a convention by which the Straits were to be closed to all foreign warships. For the moment there was comparative quiet in the Middle East, but the Eastern Question was far from solved, and remained to plague international politics right down to 1914, when it helped to trigger the First World War.

THE CRISIS OF 1848

The greatest wave of revolution in the nineteenth century, that of the year 1848, had a very grave consequence for international politics: it destroyed the Metternich system. In Austria itself, Metternich was obliged to flee. The question of the unification of Germany, long smoldering and sometimes rather more than smoldering, engaged those old rivals, Austria and Prussia, in still another acute conflict. Italians, long discontented with Austria's possession of the purely Italian territories of Lombardy and Venetia, revolted and put the unification of Italy once more on the active agenda. Milan, Venice, Rome, and smaller states all joined in the effort to expel the hated Austrians; the nationalist movement was led by the House of Savoy, which ruled over the Kingdom of Piedmont–Sardinia in northwestern Italy. A crucial battle at Novara (March 23, 1849) went against the Italians. In Rome, a French expedition besieged the city and drove out republican rebels under Garibaldi. Everywhere the Italian national movement had been suppressed, but only by the forces of foreign powers. In both England and France, liberal public opinion, by now an important factor in international politics, was warmly for the Italians and hostile to the Austrians.

The great wave of revolution had actually begun in France in February,

1848, and produced the Second French Republic. The republic was within three years to give place to the Second Empire under the nephew of the first Napoleon, Prince Louis Napoleon, but for a time it seemed to European diplomatists that the Jacobin expansion of 1794 was about to be renewed as French politicians and journalists—enjoying the broad freedom of speech usual in the first stages of a nineteenth-century popular revolution—announced their support for revolutionists everywhere.

No general war and no French aggression, however, followed this unleashing of all that Metternich had worked so hard to suppress. The Italians were beaten in the field. Russia escaped the revolution entirely, and Tsar Nicholas, alarmed by the successes of revolutionists in Hungary, sent an army to the rescue of Habsburg power. The Hungarians, led by their hero, Kossuth, could not stand up against such odds, and were forced to give up. The Austrian general Haynau took bloody vengeance, executing nine Hungarian generals who thought they had been promised clemency. In Prussia, after an early scare when the revolutionists actually dared raise barricades in Berlin itself, the government was able to resist liberal pressures and issue a constitution which left the ultimate word with the Crown. In Great Britain as in Russia, the government managed to prevent any serious attempt at revolution.

By the end of 1849 it looked as though the old system was restored, at least in central Europe. But a major element in the international situation since 1815, the close collaboration between the rulers of Austria, Russia, and Prussia, had been destroyed, never to be renewed so closely or for so long a time. The cynic

Daumier, "The Uprising, 1848."

may well say that the Austrian rulers never forgave the Russians for helping them in Hungary. Moreover, the effort to achieve unified national statehood in Germany and in Italy, though frustrated, had raised hopes much too vigorously rooted in those countries and in liberal opinion everywhere in the West to be put off for long.

The revolutions of 1848 had been a varied mixture of nationalistic movements and of social movements with liberal, even democratic goals. Both seemed in 1849 to have failed; but by 1870 many goals the revolutionists of 1848 had aimed at had been achieved, the national rather more strikingly than the social. There were "nationalist" difficulties almost everywhere—in the Balkans, in Poland, where another bloody but futile and isolated revolution against Russian rule broke out in 1863, even in old nation-states like Spain, where Catalans and Basques were restive, or like Britain, where Irish nationalism grew in strength throughout the nineteenth century. The gravest nationalist problems centered on divided Germany and divided Italy. In both, the Vienna settlement had consecrated a set of small and middling ruling houses, many of which tended toward political and economic conservatism, and which were independent enough to prevent a fine impressive German or Italian nation-state appearing on maps, in statistical tables of population and wealth—and in diplomatic congresses—on a level with France, Britain, or Russia. In both the Germanies and the Italies an important ruling group had power and interests external to those of the national group; the Habsburgs had Polish, Magyar, South Slavic, and Italian lands and subjects; the Pope, though from Rome he ruled most of central Italy, by his very office had much more than Italian concerns.

THE CRIMEAN WAR

The next great international crisis after 1848 in this far from peaceful century came very close to turning into a world war. Once more, it was bred in the Middle East, where the French under a new Napoleon were renewing their aspirations for a "sphere of influence," this time somewhat paradoxically, in view of past history, in alliance with the British. The tensions that were to culminate in the Crimean War began with a dispute between the French and the Turks, who controlled Palestine, over Christian shrines in the Holy Land. The dispute soon widened as the Russians indicated their support for Greek Orthodox claims to certain shrines, and the French continued to press Roman Catholic claims. But the wider issue was the old one of which powers should profit by the partition of Turkey. It was during a talk with the British ambassador in this crisis in 1853 that Tsar Nicholas christened the Ottoman Empire the "Sick Man of Europe."

Both the diplomacy of the Crimean War and the ensuing military operations were professionally well below par, were in fact botched on both sides. France and England, allied with Turkey, fought an indecisive campaign between September, 1854, and September, 1855, in a corner of the Crimea around the fortified port of Sebastopol. Popular historical memory in the West has saved only two bits from this repressible conflict: a determined Englishwoman of the upper classes, Florence Nightingale, pioneered nursing and, by her example, woman's rights, in the badly supplied, badly managed military hospitals; a British cavalry charge, almost the last in the old picturesque style, failed at Balaclava but inspired Tennyson's poem "The Charge of the Light Brigade," as well as a less heroic but more realistic comment from a French observer, "It's magnificent, but it's not war."

The Austro-Russian rivalry almost turned the Crimean conflict into a general war. In March, 1854, the Russians had begun an invasion of the Turkish Balkan provinces which alarmed the Austrians, who concluded an agreement with Turkey to occupy other parts of the Balkans as a preventive measure. By December, 1855, the Austrians came to the point of sending an ultimatum—the last diplomatic step before a declaration of war—insisting on Russian acceptance of the "Vienna Four Points," earlier agreed on by Austria, Britain, and France. These amounted to a guarantee of Turkish territorial integrity. Russia gave way, and in 1856 the first great pan-European Congress since 1822 was held at Paris to conclude the Crimean crisis.

The Turkish government had previously issued a reform edict which, in principle at least, liberalized the status of Christians and Christian shrines. The Russians accepted this, and the continued closing of the Straits to warships in peacetime, as well as the neutralization of the Black Sea. Although the Powers agreed to respect the integrity of Turkish domains, in fact the full independence of Rumania dates from 1856. Since Greece was already free, and the Serbs had had autonomy since 1829, the settlement at Paris was a long step toward the final break-up of European Turkey.

CAVOUR AND ITALIAN UNIFICATION

A caricature of Camillo di Cavour.

What seemed at the time a minor detail of the Crimean troubles proved in the long run to lead to a major phase in the final wrecking of the Vienna settlement of 1815. Count Cavour, gifted statesman of the small but progressive Italian state of Piedmont, contrived to insinuate himself into the Crimean War as an ally of Britain and France. Piedmontese troops fought, and fought well, in the campaign; Cavour took part in the Congress of Paris; and the prestige of the kingdom was heightened by good publicity in the Western press.

In the years 1858–1871 came the final steps in the long process of revising the Vienna settlement that had begun in 1823 when Canning, with an assist from President Monroe, "called the New World into existence to redress the balance of the Old." In a series of wars fought mostly as duels between two major powers, once more without developing into a general conflict, two new powers emerged from the "mere geographical expressions" left by the Congress of Vienna. The unification of both Germany and Italy was thus achieved to the accompaniment of violence—by "blood and iron," to quote Bismarck, chief architect of German unification. Yet again by standards of real world wars, only the Franco-Prussian duel of 1870–1871 was very bloody, and that was a brief war. The accompanying diplomacy was unprincipled, but for the most part only to the degree conventional in international affairs. Moreover, in neither country could the unification have been achieved, nor could it have endured, had it been based on *merely* "blood and iron." Several generations of intellectual and spiritual preparation, of education and propaganda, which we shall touch on in our next chapter, had helped to form the peoples of the Germanies and Italies into a German and an Italian nation-state. Several generations of economic and technological change had furthered this process of making from many, one.

In Italy, the years which prepared and achieved national unity are known as the *Risorgimento*—literally the "resurgence," with overtones of "resurrection." It is a period of which Italians are rightly very proud, for it brought out many essential national virtues. But neither Italian nor German unification could have been achieved without the complex processes of international politics that we now outline.

The failure of the Italian risings of 1848–1849 had increased the sympathy most educated Europeans felt for Italian nationalists. Austria seemed to most people the villain; France had intervened solely to protect the Pope. Moreover, in the next few years Napoleon III was won over to the Italian side, largely through the skillful diplomacy of the Piedmontese leader, Cavour. At a secret meeting between the Emperor and Cavour in 1858 at Plombières, a French watering place, it was agreed that France would go to war with Austria as soon as such an act could be made to look respectable. Gossip in high quarters spread the news, the Austrians got very annoyed, the French and Italians showed no desire for peace, and in 1859 a war was declared which did not look altogether respectable.

In two close and bloody battles in north Italy, at Magenta and Solferino, the Austrian army, though by no means disastrously beaten, was forced to retreat. (It was a sign of how thoroughly modern the times were becoming that the village where the first of these "glorious" victories took place gave Parisian publicity agents the name for a fashionable new shade of near purple dye, magenta.) Napoleon had agreed to come into the war for the goal of a loose Italian federation, in which, among other rulers, the Pope would remain sovereign in his domains. But as news of Austrian defeats spread there were risings in Tuscany and the Papal States. French Catholics, important supporters of Napoleon's regime, grew alarmed. Prussia threatened France on the Rhine—and in the press. Napoleon hesitated; there is even some evidence that he was sincerely disturbed by the sight of suffering on the battlefields. In the summer of 1859, without consulting his ally, Victor Emmanuel of Piedmont, he concluded an armistice with the Austrians by which Milan and Lombardy were to go to Piedmont, but Austria was to retain Venice and Venetia.

Cavour now resigned in indignation. But after popularly chosen assemblies in Tuscany, in the Romagna (a part of the Papal States), and in the little states of Parma and Modena voted union with Piedmont, he returned to office, and skillfully took advantage of the most romantic of these local revolutions, that in southern Italy. In 1860 Garibaldi, hero of the Roman revolution of 1848–1849, and his Thousand Redshirts landed in Sicily, and with the benevolent connivance of the masters of the sea, the British, crossed the narrow straits of Messina. Their numbers swollen by success, the Redshirts defeated Neapolitan forces and threatened Rome. At this point Cavour ordered Piedmontese forces to invade the Papal States, thus cutting the ground from under the republican Garibaldi. The upshot was the proclamation of the Kingdom of Italy on March 17, 1861, with Victor Emmanuel as King, and a parliamentary government.

Three months later Cavour died at fifty-two, his life's work essentially done. Rome itself and the area around it remained outside the new kingdom, under the somewhat uncertain protection of Napoleon's troops, and Venetia remained for the moment in Austrian hands. As we shall see in a moment, the next two European wars of this belligerent decade, which also saw our bloodiest American war, enabled the Italians to annex Venetia (1866) and Rome (1870). Italy now controlled all lands of Italian speech and culture except for Trent and Trieste, which continued under Austrian rule, and, as *Italia Irredenta* (unredeemed Italy), helped pull Italy into World War I on the side of France and Britain.

BISMARCK AND GERMAN UNIFICATION

The war of 1866 was the last fighting phase of the long rivalry between old Austria and upstart Prussia which had begun with Frederick's seizure of Silesia in 1740. The detailed legal and diplomatic background of the Austro-Prussian War, with its twistings and turnings, can be made a nightmare for the history student. The technical cause of the outbreak was the doubtful status of the north German duchies of Schleswig and Holstein, where the direct male line of succession had failed. Claimed in part by Denmark and by several German princes, the duchies had been an acute problem since 1848. When in 1864 Austria and Prussia went to war as allies against little Denmark, the Danes could offer no effective resistance. The Prussian minister, Bismarck, now making his first great appearance in history, maneuvered Austria into a joint occupation of Schleswig and Holstein, a situation in which it would be easy to provoke "incidents." The basic fact behind the war was, however, simple enough: Prussia sought to dominate some form of strong new German national state, and Austria sought to keep things as they were.

In the war which broke out in June, 1866, between Prussia and Austria, the rulers of most of the other German states sided with Austria. The Italians, who joined the war against the Austrian owners of Venetia, were beaten badly both on land and at sea. But Prussia, revealing an army that had been well built up under leaders like Moltke and Roon, and using the new breech-loading gun, won a great battle at Sadowa in July, 1866, and the "Seven Weeks' War" came to an end in August. Bismarck made a generous peace with the defeated Austrians, asking no more than to be left alone to reconstruct Germany. Italy, though defeated, now acquired Venetia.

Meanwhile, Napoleon III had been watching German difficulties in the hope of picking up something for France. He made the grave mistake of expecting an Austrian victory, or at least a long-drawn-out war which would leave both powers exhausted. After the Prussian victory he tried to save face by intriguing to get the Duchy of Luxembourg from its Dutch suzerain. The attempted deal was exposed, and the German press and German politicians grew indignant; the two powers were clearly spoiling for war. The war itself was quite definitely triggered by Bismarck, who exploited to the full Napoleon's awkward handling of a Hohenzollern candidacy for the vacant throne of Spain, an affair that almost rivalled the Schleswig-Holstein question in complexity. The Hohenzollern involved was a Catholic, south German cousin of the Prussian royal family, and Bismarck maneuvered Napoleon into a position where the French Emperor seemed to be overbearing in insisting that no German prince should ever be considered as a candidate for such a throne. The famous Ems telegram, tampered with by Bismarck in his announcement to the press, made the

Napoleon III.

Unification of Germany, 1866-1871

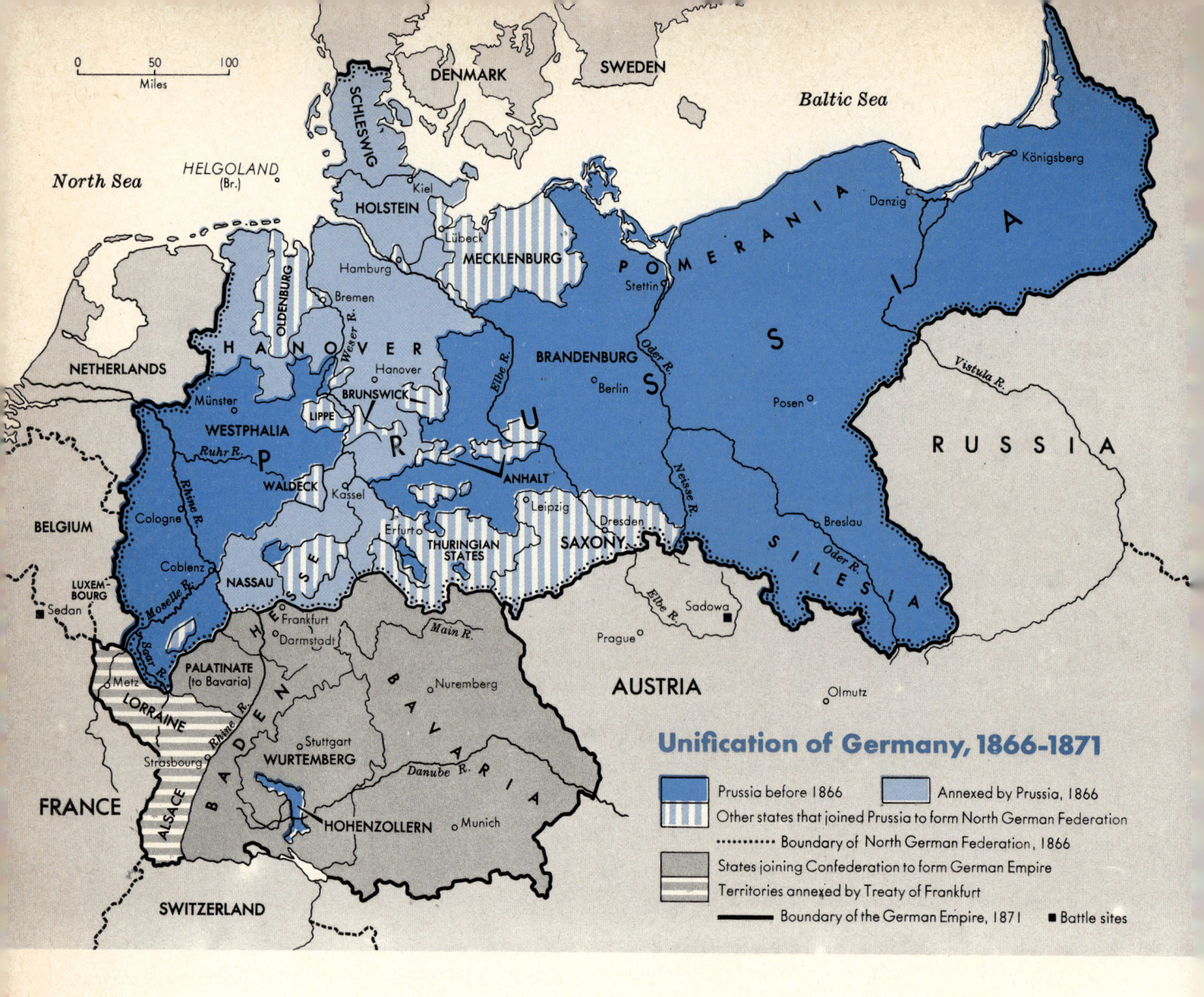

- Prussia before 1866
- Annexed by Prussia, 1866
- Other states that joined Prussia to form North German Federation
- Boundary of North German Federation, 1866
- States joining Confederation to form German Empire
- Territories annexed by Treaty of Frankfurt
- Boundary of the German Empire, 1871
- Battle sites

French ambassador falsely appear to have badgered the old King of Prussia during a conference at Ems, a watering place in the Rhineland. But the Ems telegram was probably a minor factor in the whole situation, since public opinion on both sides was already overheated by a very modern press.

The war broke out on July 19, 1870, amid much excitement, especially in Paris, as the crowds confidently shouted "To Berlin!" Within three months the Prussians laid siege to Paris after crushing French armies in eastern France by taking full advantage of the superior fire-power of their breech-loading needle guns and also taking advantage of French overconfidence, poor preparations, and tactical mistakes. Were history of much use in consolation, Frenchmen might have reflected that they had beaten the Prussians at least as badly and quite as quickly at Jena in 1806. Perhaps the defeat of 1870 was no more than another traumatic experience in France's long history. Yet it bit deep into French minds and was by no means forgotten by 1914.

With France and Austria both beaten, Bismarck could found the united Germany he had so long planned. Under Prussian leadership, not to say domination, the German Empire, with King William of Prussia becoming Kaiser Wilhelm

I, was proclaimed in the Hall of Mirrors at Versailles on January 18, 1871. The peace with France, unlike that with Austria, was far from generous. Alsace and a large part of Lorraine were annexed as imperial territories of the new German Empire, and a billion dollar indemnity imposed on France. The Kingdom of Italy, though not directly engaged in the Franco-Prussian War, obtained the Papal States when French troops were withdrawn from Rome in the crisis of 1870. It thereupon moved its capital from Florence to Rome. Two new Great Powers, Germany and Italy, had been added to the European system; the Treaty of Vienna had vanished into mere history.

THE NEW BALANCE OF POWER

The deep roots of World War I go back to these wars for the unification of Germany and Italy. Now, careless personification of the corporate entities that take part in international politics can be annoying: to say that "France" suffered from wounded pride as a result of her defeat by Prussia, that "France" wanted revenge, is to raise in some minds the question of just who, what personality, had these feelings. While the philosophical problems of the reality of such collections of individuals as the nation-state are beyond the scope of this book, we may make two observations. First, the members of the active ruling or political class, the people who make policy, do at least, to use a current psychological commonplace, *identify* with their country, much as members of a sports team identify with the activities of the group for which they play. Second, in the modern world with universal education, popular newspapers, and all the apparatus of mass communication, the great majority of the people of a nation-state identify with their country; they feel as though they had a personal stake in its successes and its failures.

The achievement of national unification by Germany and Italy in 1870 altered the "standings," the degree of prestige and the kind of competition prevailing in the extraordinarily competitive "league" of European Great Powers. Germany was rocketed to the top place on the European continent, second as a world power only to Great Britain. France fell to third or worse. Italy in spite of the enthusiasms of her Risorgimento was clearly a marginal Great Power, anxious to improve her status. Specific rivalries, specific grievances had grown up or been sharpened since 1815, and especially since 1848. France—and this means Frenchmen of all sorts—was injured by the defeat and the loss of Alsace-Lorraine. Italians were annoyed by the existence of an Italia Irredenta under Austrian rule and anxious to improve their standing as a Great Power. The long-standing rivalry between Austria and Russia for the lion's share in dismembering Turkey in Europe was strengthened by the Crimean War and its indecisive conclusion. The new Germany was already anxious for a "place in the sun," perhaps for first place instead of being second to Great Britain; moreover, comparatively easy though the recent Prussian victories had been, Bismarck was fearful of French desires for revenge. Finally, as we shall shortly see, a new epoch in the expansion of Europe, marked by a grand scramble for lands in Africa and for predominance in China, and for bases and concessions of all sorts over the entire globe, was already being launched. The complex balance of world politics had not broken down completely by 1871, but it was already severely strained.

II. Domestic Politics, 1815–1870: Western Europe

Many good historians today incline to the position that "national" histories, histories of Britain, or France, or Germany, are incomplete and in fact incomprehensible. Only the history of a society or civilization, such as Western civilization or at the very least Europe, makes sense, so much are all nations in constant interrelation in trade, travel, ideas, diplomacy, and war. This position has some justification, but it can be overdone. After all, any group, right down to family or school or fraternity, has a history just because it is a group existing in time. You cannot write a history of England without some concern for the history of France and of all Western civilization, including the Americas; you cannot write of the gradual growth of democracy in nineteenth-century England without acknowledging its relation to similar growth elsewhere. But the fact remains that the growth of English democracy was also in some ways unique, specifically English. In the next few pages we shall attempt to indicate the major developments of domestic affairs in Europe and in America during the years 1815–1870 with an eye on *both* the larger society or civilization *and* the national political units composing it.

The central theme in Western history in these years—in a sense, it is the central theme of all history—is the conflict between men who wanted to keep things as they were and those who wanted to change them. Here we see at once why national histories are still essential, for the interplay of those wanting changes and those resisting changes in the nineteenth century varied greatly in different nations. Of the major states, one can argue that in the United States the *promoters* of change had the easiest time in these years, and that in Russia the *resisters* to change had it easiest.

"Change" is a blanket term, covering a host of specific issues. Those who resisted change in the mid-nineteenth century, though not entirely united, generally approved of Legitimacy, restoration, the Vienna settlement, and the "Metternich system." The advocates of change were less united and often at odds with one another. Some men wanted above all independent statehood or, at a minimum, cultural autonomy for their own nationality; others wanted a wider franchise, a better guarantee of civil rights, something of *political democracy;* still others wanted to eliminate poverty, achieve some kind of rough equality of incomes, *economic democracy.* In good but dangerously simple textbook terms, conservative Legitimacy was attacked by nationalism, liberalism, and socialism. Moreover, everywhere in the West during these years the great transformation of man's command over natural resources—the Industrial Revolution—was going on at increasing rates, even in the most backward and "conservative" Western country.

BRITAIN

The Irish Question and Parliamentary Reform. Within the British Isles there was no serious nationalist problem except in Ireland. The Welsh and the Scots, save for a few eccentric intellectuals, accepted the authority of the essentially centralized United Kingdom established in 1707, soon after the Glorious Revolution. Ireland, "John Bull's other isle," had been made part of this unified state in 1801. By 1870, however, it was quite clear that the bulk of Irishmen did not accept their complete amalgamation with Great Britain. The last major famine in the West, the "potato famine" of the 1840's, the narrow economic selfishness of the British government, and many other factors made "Home Rule"—a degree of autonomy—for Ireland a minimum that might have solved the Irish Question. As we shall see, that minimum was not attained, and in the twentieth century there was to be a full-fledged and successful Irish revolution.

The Irish Question was not, however, an acute one in these early and middle years of nineteenth-century Britain. The important political struggle between those who wanted more political democracy and those who did not *was* acute, and at least in 1832 came close to revolutionary violence. As the revolution of 1789 in France grew more radical, Britain had reacted in domestic policy more decidedly than countries like Russia, which had no trace yet of modern government by discussion. Even in the eighteenth century some British boroughs elected members of Parliament on a wide franchise, and there was an active movement for parliamentary reform. But fear of Jacobinism moved the government of the younger Pitt to strong measures against British reformers. In the great national struggle against Napoleonic France British politics were frozen into conservatism. The long Tory or conservative lease on power continued after 1815. Economic troubles, essentially a postwar depression as an economy geared to war production failed to adapt itself quickly to peacetime conditions, were accompanied by some minor rioting, which evoked official suppression.

But by the 1820's some Tory leaders themselves were at least liberalizing the tariff and taking other measures consonant with middle-class interests. Freedom of agitation was also pretty well restored in the 1820's, as well as the kind of freedom of association that permits trade unions to organize. The essential organ of any democracy, however, the legislature, remained a characteristically British accumulation of historically established inequalities. The House of Lords was of course purely hereditary and noble. The House of Commons in a very few of its constituencies was elected on something close to manhood suffrage; but the overwhelming majority of constituencies had a narrow electorate indeed; some few, known to the reformers as "rotten boroughs," had only a handful of voters, or none at all. Nor was there anything like the electoral districts with equal population of the modern democratic ideal of one man, one vote.

Parliamentary reform, therefore, became the goal of those who wanted political change in a generally democratic direction. Two great steps were in fact achieved in this half-century, without revolution of the Continental type, but not without much verbal violence, written and oratorial, and with full utilization of such paraphernalia of modern democratic politics as pressure groups, lobbying, and meetings of all sorts. At the height of the agitation in 1832, when the ultraconservative House of Lords attempted to block a Reform Bill already passed in the Commons, the reformers threatened to get a run on the Bank of England started, and even planned some sort of street fighting. Serious riots had occurred in the provinces, where a mob had held Bristol for several days. The Reform Bill got through the Lords, however, because King William IV consented to create by royal prerogative enough new peers willing to vote for the bill. The threat of thus "packing" the House of Lords was enough: the Reform Bill went through. The

Whigs had broken the long Tory hold on the government; from 1832 on, the British party struggle was once more real.

The Reform Bills of 1832 and 1867. The Reform Bill of 1832 eliminated many rotten boroughs, added some new constituencies in the growing industrial towns, widened the franchise, and substantially gave political voice to the middle classes. But Britain was still not a political democracy, and the Industrial Revolution was still actively at work, adding to the numbers of the urban laborers and giving them food and shelter enough to make them want something better. A working-class reform movement arose called Chartism, not socialist in its aims, but certainly recruiting much of its strength from what the Marxists term the "proletariat." Some of the Chartist leaders were of humble origin, often self-educated in the ideas of the eighteenth-century Enlightenment. The movement took its name from an effort to secure by petition to Parliament the six points of a "charter" originating in a London Workingman's Association of 1836: (1) manhood suffrage; (2) secret ballot; (3) abolition of property qualification for holding a seat in the Commons; (4) payment of members of the Commons; (5) equal electoral districts; (6) annual elections to Parliament.

Of these, all but the sixth, which seemed unnecessary, with the rapid development of communication and transportation, were to be attained in Britain by 1911. But in the 1840's the Charter alarmed the newly enfranchised middle classes. Serious depressions in both the 1830's and the 1840's, though they added to the sufferings of the working classes, proved at least in Britain to be unfavorable to revolutionary activity. Then the troubles of 1848 on the Continent further alarmed the middle classes. Finally, in the 1850's an economic upturn, aided by the repeal of the Corn Laws (tariffs on imported foodstuffs) in 1846, and the introduction of free trade, did much to raise the standard of living of the laboring classes. The Chartist agitation died a natural death. Under free trade Britain could continue to increase her profitable concentration on manufacturing products and exchanging those products for foodstuffs and raw materials. By 1914 this process had gone on so far that a Britain unable to import any food from abroad would be faced with famine.

The movement for *political* democracy was renewed, and in 1867 a reform in some ways surpassing that of 1832 went through with surprising ease. Disraeli, then head of the Conservatives (as the Tories had rechristened themselves), was engaged in a tight struggle with the Liberals (as the Whigs had rechristened themselves). The Liberals had advanced a program of electoral reform, and Disraeli decided to "steal the Whigs' clothes" by having his own cabinet sponsor a Reform Bill. The reform of 1867 did not quite make Britain a neat political democracy with full manhood suffrage and fully equal electoral districts, but it did further equalize the districts and, most important, it did give the vote to millions of working-class men with settled residences.

Disraeli was motivated by the belief that the bulk of English workingmen were in fact conservative, loyal to the Crown and to old institutions, and would use the vote to keep the Tories in power. His "leap in the dark" did not land him where he hoped, for in the first election after the Reform Bill the Conservatives were beaten and the Liberals, under his rival Gladstone, returned. But "Dizzy" was not wholly wrong in the long run, for the English working class, though it was later to turn to its own Labor Party, has never been a solidly radical, let alone

Marxist, class, but has right up to the 1960's provided some support for the Conservatives.

The titular head of this increasingly democratic state was Victoria, granddaughter of George III, whose long reign lasted from 1837 to 1901, and who has given her name to an era. The term "Victorian Age" can in fact be used loosely for the whole of Western culture during those years when Britain—and the British Empire—were at their height of power and prestige. Not very bright in purely intellectual terms, Queen Victoria was a woman of firm will and great enthusiasms, who survived so long that she became a symbol, and was even loved; but in the traditional sense she was not a ruler. Bagehot, a contemporary, in his *English Constitution* pointed out that the Queen reigned but did not govern. He held that though in her "dignified capacity" she was of incalculable importance, the great decisions—to repeal the Corn Laws, to go to war with Russia, to give the workingmen the vote—were those of her ministers, Peel, Aberdeen, Disraeli, Gladstone, their cabinets and Parliament.

FRANCE

British and French Progress Compared. The half-century or so after 1815 in France may appear very different from the same years in Britain. The French experienced two revolutions—one in 1830 ending the Restoration monarchy and bringing in Louis Philippe, the "Citizen King," symbolized by that most unkingly object he liked to carry, an umbrella; another in 1848, the "February Revolution," when Louis Philippe was overthrown in Paris street riots and France was for the second time made a republic. Then a *coup d'état* in 1851 engineered by Prince Louis Napoleon, who had been elected president of the Second Republic by a landslide popular vote, ushered in the Second Empire. Finally, in September, 1870, at the news of the surrender of Napoleon III and his army to the Prussians at Sedan, came more Paris riots and the flight of Napoleon—the prelude to the establishment of the Third French Republic.

Yet a certain rough parallelism may be discerned in the substantial changes arrived at so differently in the two countries. In both, at the end of the half-century a limited suffrage and a legislative body of definite oligarchic recruitment had given way to a suffrage and legislative body essentially based on wide popular participation. The Revolution of 1830 did for France, and in this case with hardly more violence, what the Reform Bill of 1832 did for Great Britain. It gave political power to the solid middle classes.

In the 1840's both Britain and France, in common with the whole Western world, suffered industrial depression, unemployment, and labor unrest. The British Chartist movement and the French republican drive of the 1840's again had much in common, though in France the Second Republic was very briefly successful in putting through a platform essentially based on that of the Jacobin republic of 1793, and in Britain the Chartists never did attain power. In both countries the decades of the 1850's and the 1860's saw great economic growth through industrialization, greater in Britain than in France, but still substantial in the latter country. Finally, toward the end of the 1860's Napoleon III, under pressure from the political Left, began to move in the direction of what his minister Emile Ollivier called *"l'Empire libéral,"* with wide suffrage and recognition of the responsibility of ministries to the majority of parliament. A plebiscite of 1869 consecrated these liberalizing constitutional changes, and corresponded in a sense with Benjamin Disraeli's leap in the dark of 1867.

But Britain did not undergo the catastrophic defeat France suffered at the hands of Prussia in 1870. Born of this defeat, the Third Republic began under the handicaps of war traumas which deepened the tensions of French national life. We have already noted the series of French blunders and Prussian clever moves by which the war was brought about. The rapidity and completeness of the Prussian victory surprised the world, although it is clear now that the reputation of the French army had been unduly inflated by its marginal successes in the Crimean War and in the Italian campaign of 1859. The Second Empire had been a much looser, more careless and inefficient regime than the world realized. Still, current historical interpretation tends to explain the defeats of 1870 by the ineptness of the top French leaders and by the disciplined ability of the Prussians to fight along lines of their own choosing.

Social Tensions in France. During the early and mid-nineteenth century the rifts and tensions of society were certainly deeper in France than in Britain. More especially, France was torn by a religious quarrel between Catholics and Enlightened "freethinkers," a quarrel heightened by the fact that, unlike Britain and the United States, France was not used to a multiplicity of sects and the consequent practical acceptance of a diversity of belief and opinion in religion. A great deal has been written about the over-intellectual climate of French social and political life, of the tendency of Frenchmen to take ideas and doctrines so seriously that they will not make compromises. The English-speaking peoples generally exaggerate the extent to which the French sacrifice their comfort to their principles, but there is surely something in the commonly held opinion of their political divisions. Even the twistings and turnings of Napoleon III's foreign policy were partly determined by the conflict between his own freethinking inheritance and the Catholic devotion of his wife, the Empress Eugénie.

In the 1840's an additional tension entered French political life with the first major manifestation of what came to be called socialism. We shall see in the next chapter that the intellectual antecedents of Western socialism and communism go back into the Enlightenment of the eighteenth century, but its practical manifestations, save for some partial anticipations during the great French Revolution, begin in the troubled decade of the 1840's. While British Chartism was a genuine working-class movement, its aims were stated in the language of political individualism; somehow, it was believed, a universal rough equality of income and status would ensue once *political* equality was achieved. But in the French Revolution of 1848, under the sponsorship of Louis Blanc, who had already written in defense of this kind of socialism, measures were taken to enlist the powers of government in the direct processes of production and distribution of wealth with the aim of achieving greater *economic* equality.

These measures—National Workshops to help unemployed laborers along the socialist path, and a Luxembourg Commission to bring together employers and workers under government auspices—marked the faint beginnings of the "welfare state." The workshops in their brief course by no means solved even the local problem of unemployment, and proved to be hardly more than make-work efforts worthy of that fine Americanism, "boondoggling." The Commission was soon deserted by the employers, and the government abandoned Louis Blanc. The Parisian workers, under threat of suppression of the workshops, which at their height "employed" 100,000, rose in revolt and were put down by the army in the "June Days" of 1848, perhaps the bloodiest urban fighting in history.

Two obscure agitators, Karl Marx and Friedrich Engels, had exaggerated when they wrote earlier in that year in their *Communist Manifesto* that "a spectre is haunting Europe—the spectre of Communism." But clearly the possessing classes—including the many who possessed little, the "petty bourgeoisie"—did take fright in 1848. In electing the President of the Second Republic, therefore, Frenchmen gave 5,300,000 votes, as against 1,800,000 for all the opposition candidates, to Prince Louis Napoleon, scion of a house that the French peasantry as well as the French bourgeoisie had come to associate not only with national greatness but with internal stability. A prince–president is already halfway to something else. In 1851 Napoleon, carefully selecting December 2nd—lucky day of the dynasty, anniversary of Austerlitz and of his uncle's coronation—staged a *coup d'état* that was marred only by some deaths among Parisian crowds on the boulevards. A plebiscite confirmed the power of the "chief of state," and on December 2, 1852, he became Emperor Napoleon III. (Like Louis XVII, Napoleon II, son of Napoleon I and Marie Louise, never reigned, having died in 1832.)

ITALY

With Italy we come to quite different motivations for revolutionary activity. The Risorgimento certainly was in part a movement for liberal–democratic ends, part of the great nineteenth-century sweep toward government by discussion—and the dominance of middle-class business interests over the old landed aristocracies. But the emotions that drove Italians into revolutionary resistance were essentially those of patriotic hatred for the Austrian interlopers and a patriotic desire for a united Italy capable of taking its place alongside the Great Powers. The actual events of March, 1848, in a great city like Milan look on the surface like the revolutions in Paris in February or in Berlin in March. But the barricades, the street fighting in Milan, were directed against the troops of the Austrian General Radetzky, who was obliged by the sheer force of numbers against him to evacuate the city and retreat to the famous quadrilateral of fortresses—Mantua, Peschiera, Legnano, Verona—the holder of which had for several centuries been able to master northern Italy. There were risings in Venice, headed by a gifted leader, Daniele Manin, and some months later one in Rome itself, from which the Pope was forced to flee to his castle of Gaeta and Neapolitan protection. But the Italian uprisings were not well synchronized, and not at all disciplined. The actual armed intervention of the strongest Italian state, progressive and constitutional Piedmont, proved ineffective because of lack of any active ally abroad. At Custozza in July, 1848, Radetzky defeated the Piedmontese army, which was beaten again in 1849 at Novara. The unfortunate Piedmontese King Charles Albert abdicated in favor of his son Victor Emmanuel II. It looked as if the Italian War of Independence had been fought in vain.

Yet after one decade Victor Emmanuel was crowned Victor Emmanuel I of Italy, and after one more decade he took up his residence in Rome, capital of a united Italy. We have already outlined the complicated diplomacy—and hard fighting—through which this reversal of the failures of 1848–1849 came about. Though the slogan of the Italians after Napoleon III deserted them in 1859—*L'Italia farà da se* (Italy will do it herself)—was exaggerated, very orderly risings all over north and central Italy, together with Garibaldi's not very bloody campaigns in the south, did bring union at last.

The new kingdom started life under heavy handicaps. The Pope, after the withdrawal of French troops supporting him in Rome in 1870, became the "prisoner of the Vatican," refusing to accept the merging of the Papal States with the new Italy or to acknowledge the new kingdom. Catholics were formally forbidden to take part in politics. While actual relations were not so bad as this may suggest, the "Roman Question" sharpened the conflict between Italian Catholics and anticlericals (many of them really anti-Christians). Moreover, Italy had in its backward south, almost wholly agricultural and overpopulated, a very serious problem. The north was on the whole one of the prosperous and progressive parts of Europe. Conflict between the two, based on all sorts of misunderstandings, was inevitable, and has lasted down to our own time. Add to all this a relative lack of experience in parliamentary government, save in Piedmont, and the inevitable desire of the ruling classes to keep up with the Joneses in international competition, and it is not surprising that the new kingdom of Italy was to have hard going.

III. Domestic Politics, 1815–1870: Central and Eastern Europe

GERMANY

The German Revolution of 1848. In central Europe—in the Germanies—the *annus mirabilis* (marvelous year), 1848, was most hectic, complex, and difficult to interpret in terms of the broad sweep of history. There are those who maintain that, although the misbehavior of the Germans in the twentieth century cannot be fully explained unless you go back at least to the defeat of the Romans at the Teutoburger Forest in A.D. 9, the failure of the revolutions of 1848 was crucial. Once German liberalism failed, as it did in 1848, the rest—Bismarck, Wilhelm II, Hitler—all had to come. Few historians would accept this sweeping theory of moral determinism. But most would grant, however, that after 1848 the way was open for the new Germany to develop a more authoritarian government and society than did Britain or France, and an unusually vigorous national sense of its own unique "racial" superiorities.

The February Revolution in Paris surprised no one who kept up with current events; but the news that from March 15 on crowds were raising barricades in Berlin, that faithful and obedient city, astonished the world. There had been earlier risings in various other German states, and soon the movement spread into most of the Habsburg dominions. In Prussia and the smaller German states, and to a degree in Austria proper, the revolutionaries wanted a liberal constitution and some kind of united Germany. But in Hungary, Bohemia (part of contemporary Czechoslovakia), Croatia (part of contemporary Yugoslavia), and in Italy the revolutionaries were non-German, in fact anti-German, nationalists, wanting above all local independence or at least autonomy and only secondarily some kind of constitutional government.

The reader will note that this great wave of revolution in 1848 came from a common center, Paris, and was propagated more rapidly and more extensively than that of 1820 or 1830. No doubt the economic depression of the 1840's had its part in making the universal crisis. So too did the gradual growth of literacy, of the middle classes, and—especially important for speeding the spread of the crisis—the improvement in transportation and communication, which in 1848 was already considerable, with the beginnings of a European railway network and a widespread newspaper press.

In Prussia and many other German states the rulers bowed quickly to the crowds, and promised constitutions and a strong union of all the German states. Frederick William IV of Prussia went so far in his concessions as to tell his "beloved Berliners" that he would head the movement to unite Germany even if Prussia were to be merged in the new state. Politically active commoners showed that the Germans could improvise the kind of institutions for organizing change that the Americans, British, and French had already achieved; a voluntary group of liberals met in Heidelberg and issued a call for something like our Philadelphia Constitutional Convention of 1787, but to be chosen by universal manhood suffrage. This National Assembly of 830 members met at Frankfurt in May, 1848, and began its labors. It was a remarkably talented group, a cross section of the German academic, legal, and official worlds and, to the extent of some 140 deputies, even of the world of business. The Assembly declared the German Confederation set up by the Vienna settlement dissolved and then tried to establish a provisional government with an Austrian archduke as imperial regent. But meanwhile the old state governments kept on governing, and especially in Prussia the old rulers began to get their courage back and to hanker for the good old days.

The Frankfurt parliament had bad luck. At its very start it got itself mired in the desperately complicated Schleswig–Holstein question, as the Danes took steps to absorb Schleswig entire. The ardent patriots of the Frankfurt parliament were not going to let a single German-speaking citizen become a Danish subject. On the crucial question of what form the new German state should take, the parliament split. The Right wing wanted a government in the form of an empire that would leave intact the powers of the old state governments; the Center espoused several varieties of constitutional federalism, and the Left wing wanted a centralized and unified "republic" of Germany. The Frankfurt parliament split further on the issue of a Big Germany, which should *include* Austria in spite of the latter's involvement with non-Germans, versus a Little Germany, which should *exclude* Austria.

By late March, 1849, the Assembly completed its constitution for an imperial Germany with a hereditary emperor and a constitutional federal government having parliamentary responsibility and a bicameral legislature, the lower house of which was to be elected by universal suffrage. The federal government was to have real power over foreign affairs, army, and taxation. Finally, the Assembly offered the imperial crown to Frederick William of Prussia, who turned it down because of his now firmly re-established faith in the divine right of a Hohenzollern to rule without concessions to an un-German liberalism. The Prussians did try to keep face by proposing in 1850 a milder form of German union, but the now fully restored Austrian government stood firm, and the old, feeble German Confederation of 1815 was re-established.

The ground cut out from under it, the Frankfurt parliament died out in a rump session at Stuttgart, which the police dispersed. It has not had good notices from history and has been accused above all of that shocking thing in politics—impractical, wordy idealism. Even at the time the wits made fun of it, as in the famous couplet about its academic members:

> *Hundert fünfzig Professoren!*
> *Lieber Gott, wir sind verloren!*
> (A hundred and fifty professors!
> Good God, we're sunk!)

Yet the Frankfurt Assembly was faced with insoluble difficulties, and it is hard to see how any group, unless continuously supported by the kind of risings that took place in March, 1848, could have stood up against the opposition of the ruling classes of both Prussia and Austria.

The Zollverein and Bismarck. For decades since 1819 a process had been going on that proved in the long run more effective than the work of 1848 and, if not more effective than Bismarck's "blood and iron," certainly an essential supplement to that policy in the final unification of Germany. This was the *Zollverein* (*see above*, p. 473), which expanded gradually in membership and commodities covered until it became an anticipation of a Germany united without Austria. The example of this slow, voluntary breaking down of tariff barriers in preparation for political union still gives heart to the twentieth-century workers in the cause of greater political integration for Europe. In the 1850's the *Zollverein*, coupled with the economic prosperity general throughout Western society and with the renewed confidence of the possessing classes after the failure of the revolutionaries of 1848, started modern Germany on its road to industrial and political ascendancy.

For three decades, down to 1890, that road was dominated by the very gifted conservative and antidemocratic statesman, Otto von Bismarck (1815–1898), whom we have already met in his role as unifier of Germany through skillfully planned wars with Austria and France. Bismarck, called to the head of the Prussian ministry in 1862, fought and won a long struggle with the Liberals of the lower house (*Landtag*) of the legislature, which had been established by the Prussian constitution of 1850 as a gesture toward limited monarchy but had been permitted only a secondary role. The struggle between the Liberals and Bismarck concerned the key point in any attempt to make the legislature a true parliament: Should it have the ultimate power of the purse, the power to grant or refuse to grant taxes? The great expense for a state like Prussia was of course its army. Bismarck defied the *Landtag*, put through the army budget without its consent, and gradually wore down its opposition, which finally vanished in the prestige of his successes in foreign policy. Although the new German Empire of 1871 was in some ways a government by discussion, a society which allowed considerable freedom of thought and assembly, it never became either politically or socially a parliamentary democracy on the full Western model. The shadow of Bismarck's victory over the liberals was a long one.

REVOLUTION AND REFORM IN THE HABSBURG EMPIRE

The first news of 1848 from Austria was electrifying indeed. Alarmed by popular uprisings, mostly of students, in Vienna, Metternich resigned—we almost wrote "abdicated"—and fled the country. For thirty-four years, and in spite of the defection of Britain and France, he had managed to maintain the "Metternich system" in his own country and in eastern Europe generally. Now not only conservative rule, but the whole structure of the Habsburg Empire threatened to collapse—did collapse for some months. The revolts, save in Vienna, were essentially nationalistic, as Hungarians (Magyars), Czechs, and Italians rose against their German rulers. In Prague a "Pan-Slav" congress mostly composed of Czechs met in June, and issued a call to all Slavs to unite; the emotional drive back of the Czechs was hatred of Germans, a hatred strong all through the Habsburg Empire.

Yet somehow the Habsburgs did manage to put their humpty-dumpty empire together again, though as we have seen they soon lost almost all the Italian-speaking parts for good. In the Austrian nucleus the army and the ruling classes held firm. In Bohemia the commander, Windischgrätz, whose wife had been shot during a demonstration at Prague, used his army mercilessly, and soon had Bohemia under control (June, 1848). The Austrian army under Radetzky defeated the Piedmontese at Custozza (July, 1848). Emboldened, the civilian leader Prince Felix Schwarzenberg got the incompetent Emperor Ferdinand to abdicate in favor of his 18-year-old nephew Francis Joseph and drew up plans for a major reform of the patchwork empire. At the news of Schwarzenberg's proposed new unified and centralized state, which would have simply assimilated Hungary, the Magyars under Kossuth set up a Hungarian Republic in April, 1849. This was the point at which Nicholas of Russia decided to come to the rescue of his fellow autocrat of Austria. Between the Russians advancing from the East and the Austrians advancing from the West the Hungarians were crushed in a vise.

Though on the surface the advocates of change had been beaten, and the old guard once more seemed in control, the Habsburg Empire was never again what it had been. The old domination of a German or Germanized ruling class was ended. The Magyars, at least, *had* to be taken into partnership. The constitution of the "Dual Monarchy" was the Compromise (*Ausgleich*) of 1867, worked out after the defeat of Sadowa in 1866 (*see* p. 487). Austria and Hungary became independent monarchies, united in the person of Emperor Franz Joseph (who was King in Hungary), in common ministries of foreign affairs, war, and finanace, and in annual joint meetings of sixty delegates from each of the two parliaments. The ministers in each kingdom were responsible to parliament, and as in Germany, there was substantial freedom of the press and of discussion. The other nationalities, mostly Slavs, remained without rights; the Magyars were to prove at least as harsh and uncompromising masters of *their* Slavs as the Germans had been of theirs. Although Vienna in the second half of the nineteenth century was a city of fecund intellectual life, an artistic, literary, and scientific center at least as productive as any city in Germany proper, the Dual Monarchy was in many ways a relatively backward society, neither as modernized nor as efficient as its neighbor and ally to the

Bismarck in 1859.

north. North Germans habitually expressed toward the Austrians feelings of amused condescension tinged with annoyance.

RUSSIA

Autocracy and the Intelligentsia. Russia seemed to most Westerners the last European refuge of true autocracy. None of the three great waves of nineteenth-century revolution had reached her territories on time. The Decembrist revolution of 1825 had been a pathetic failure, the work of a tiny conspiratorial minority impressed by their exposure in the West to the Jacobin tradition. The Poles did make two desperate attempts to break loose, the first in 1830–1831, the second in 1863–1864. After the repression of the second, an effort was begun to "Russify" the country by requiring Russian in the schools, and assimilating the Polish administration to the Russian. The Russification was unsuccessful, but the part of Poland given Tsar Alexander in 1815 remained a political part of Russia until the end of World War I.

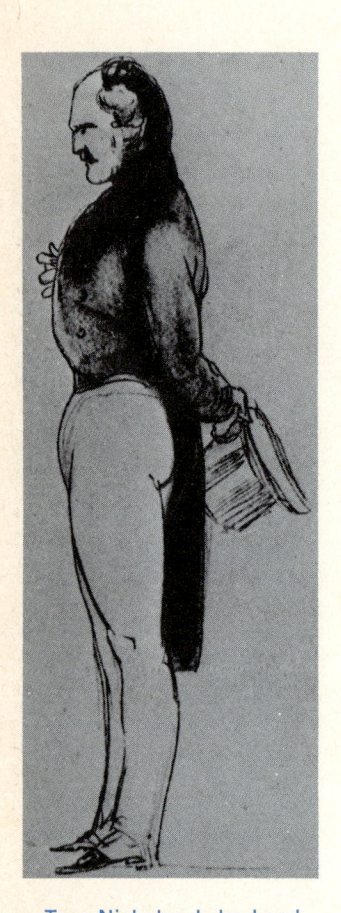

Yet during the half-century from 1815 to 1870 Russia was very far from untouched by the spirit of the age. True, she was no exception to the general rule that measuring in terms of the combined effects of science, technology, and economic progress up to 1870 "modernity" diminished fairly regularly as one moved eastward and southward from England. Poland, just west of Russia, was a bit ahead of her Russian masters in this respect. Yet the absolutism and the ultraconservative behavior of Nicholas I, who reigned from 1825 to 1855, should not blind us to the fact that Russia set up no real barrier to Western ideas and Western ways of life. Alexander II (1855–1881), who succeeded Nicholas, though he permitted the suppression of Polish autonomy, carried out a series of major reforms which marked the beginnings of some limitations on the autocracy and the practice of some government by discussion.

Discussion itself—we mean the flow of ideas through books, magazines, universities, and the talk of that curious and very Russian class they called the *intelligentsia*—had gone on increasing in spite of the efforts of Nicholas, his secret police, his censor, and his other bureaucrats to quarantine Russia from the intellectual life of the West. A central problem for the Russian intelligentsia was whether Russia was and ought to be a part of Western culture, backward perhaps, but due to catch up. The "Westernizers" insisted that it was, whereas the "Slavophils" insisted that Russia was unique, with different origins and different history, and should develop in its own way, defending itself against Western influences. We shall have a few words on this matter in our next chapter, for what has gone on in Russian minds for the last few centuries cannot possibly be omitted in an intellectual history of the West.

Tsar Nicholas I, by Landseer.

Reforms of Alexander II. Alexander's greatest reform was the emancipation of the serfs by imperial edict in 1861. It was, however, no private product of the Tsar, but the result of several generations of study and argument among the educated classes, topped by the work of a special committee of experts. It was clearly a reform for which the time was ripe, since serf labor was not an efficient method of farming, now that Russian agriculture was beginning to compete in the world market. Even the Russian noble landowners, though they hardly understood the causes of their difficulties and would have preferred to retain serfdom, were aware that something had gone wrong somewhere.

A general statute declared that the serfs were now free, laid down the principles of the new administrative organization of the peasantry, and prescribed the rules for the purchase of land. A series of local statutes governed the particular procedures to be followed in the different provinces. All serfs, crown and private, were freed, and each peasant household received its homestead and a certain amount of land, usually the amount the peasant family had cultivated for its own use in the past. The land usually became the property of the village commune, which had the power to redistribute it periodically among the households. The government bought the land from the proprietors, but the peasants had to redeem it by payments extending over a period of forty-nine years. The proprietor retained only the portion of his estate that had been farmed for his own purposes.

This statute, liberating more than 40 million human beings, has been called the greatest single legislative act in history. There can be no doubt that it acted as an immense moral stimulus to peasant self-respect. Yet there were grave difficulties. The peasant had to accept the allotment of land, and since his household became collectively responsible for the taxes and redemption payments, his mobility was not greatly increased. The commune took the place of the proprietor, and differing local conditions caused great difficulty in administering the law. Moreover, the peasants in general got too little land and had to pay too much for it. They did not get important forest and pasture lands. The settlement, however, was on the whole surprisingly liberal, despite the problems it failed to solve and despite the agrarian crises that were to develop later on as a result of its inadequacies.

The end of the landlords' rights of justice and police on their estates made it necessary to reform the entire local administration. By statute, in 1864, provincial and district assemblies, or *zemstvos,* were created. Chosen by an elaborate electoral system that divided the voters into categories by class, the assemblies none the less gave substantial representation to the peasants. They dealt with local finances, education, medical care, scientific agriculture, maintenance of the roads, and similar economic and social questions. Starting from scratch in many cases, the *zemstvos* made great advances in the founding of primary schools and the improvement of public health. They brought together peasant and proprietor to work out local problems. They served as schools of citizenship for all classes, and led tens of thousands of Russians to hope that this progressive step would be crowned by the creation of a central parliament, or *duma.* Despite the pressures on the government, the duma was not granted, partly because after the first attempt on Alexander's life in 1866 the regime swung away from reform toward reaction.

Tsar Alexander II.

But before this happened, other advances had been made. The populations of the cities were given municipal assemblies, with duties much like those of the *zemstvos* in the countryside. The Russian judicial system and legal procedure, which were riddled with inequities, were reformed. For the first time, juries were introduced, cases were argued publicly and orally, all classes were made equal before the law, and the system of courts was completely overhauled. Censorship was relaxed, new schools were encouraged, the universities were freed from the restraints that Nicholas had imposed on them, and the antiquated and often brutal system of military service was modernized and rendered less severe. Altogether, a number of remarkable advances were recorded in Russia in a relatively few years.

IV. The Expansion of Europe, 1800–1870

In analyzing the political evolution of European territories overseas, the distinction between colonies of exploitation and trade and colonies of settlement is most useful. The colonies of settlement, though their European settlers may have spared the lives of many non-European natives, were and are essentially transplanted pieces of Europe, each growing in a different soil, and gradually acquiring a national character of its own. The degree to which the original native stock survived varied enormously: in parts of Latin America, the greater part of the population is still of Indian blood; in the United States east of the Mississippi, there is hardly a trace of the Red Indian left. But even in Peru or Mexico, the dominant culture is European. In colonies of trade or exploitation, on the other hand, the dominant culture, even though much influenced by that of the West, remains native.

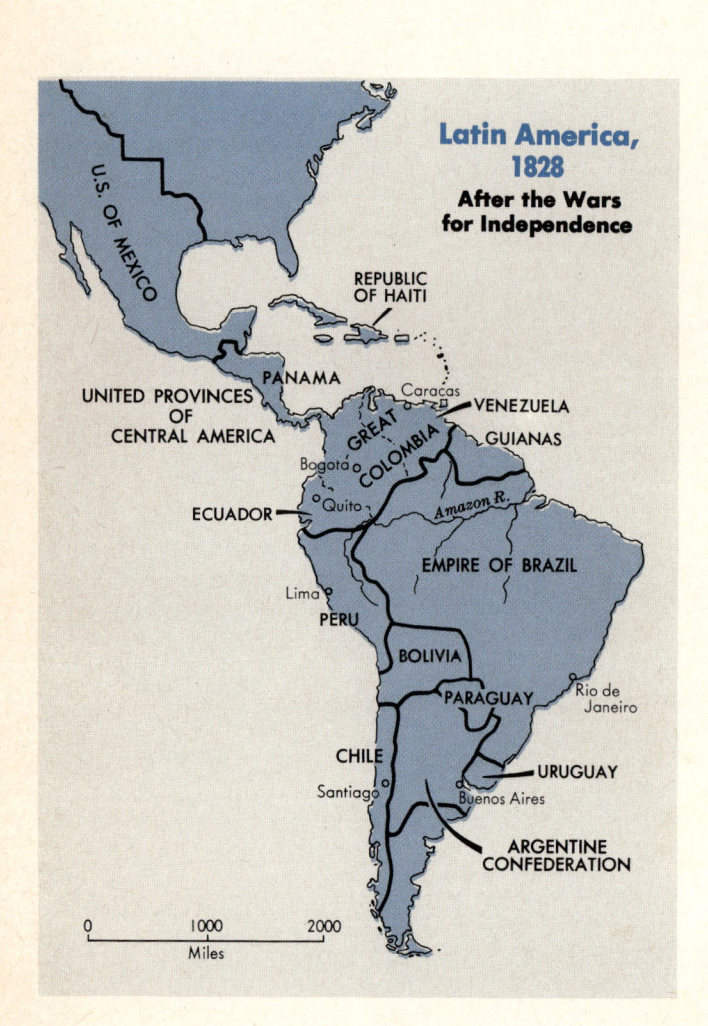

LATIN AMERICA

The Latin-American world experienced in the first decades of the nineteenth century its own series of successful revolutions against the colonial rule of Spain and Portugal. These wars of liberation throughout the regions south of the Rio Grande had much in common. Their occasions were the troubles in the mother countries of the Iberian peninsula, and in particular the seizure of the Spanish throne by Napoleon for his brother Joseph. The American and the French revolutions served as examples, the one for the rising of a colonial people against a mother country from whom they felt alienated, the other for a rising of men much influenced by the ideas of the Enlightenment, to a degree anticlerical, and at least touched with ideas of democracy.

Only in the area of modern Argentina was revolution really successful before 1815. But after the defeat of Napoleon and the return of the Bourbons in Spain, the Mexicans under the conservative leader Iturbide successfully revolted in 1821 at the news of the revolution of 1820 in Spain. In South America two great leaders, Bolívar in the northern regions, San Martín in the Argentine, Chile, and Peru, led a long and difficult series of campaigns which resulted in the establishment of the independent republics we now know. In Brazil in 1821–1822 Prince

Regent Pedro, after his father had returned to Portugal at the end of the Napoleonic wars, himself led the movement for Brazilian independence, and became, without violence, the constitutional Emperor of Brazil. This, the only long-lived monarchy in the New World in the nineteenth century, lasted until 1889; then a republic was set up. European colonies remained in the Guianas (British, Dutch, French) and in the islands of the Caribbean. But, save for the small British Honduras in Central America, the rest of the mainland was free of European control.

The fate of the former Spanish and Portuguese colonies in the New World was strikingly different from that of the former British and French colonies in one very important respect. Instead of two great areas, the United States and Canada, Latin America developed into some 20 independent states, ranging in size from Brazil (bigger in area than the United States less Alaska) to the small republics of Central America and the Caribbean islands. Though both Bolívar and San Martín hoped to unite some of these states into greater ones, the accumulated colonial traditions of local and regional independence, the geographical difficulties frustrating communication, and the comparative backwardness of most of the area made wider union impossible. Latin America was then to enter the twentieth century with many attributes of comparatively advanced culture, especially in the Argentine, Brazil, Chile, and Mexico—big cities, a small but often highly cultivated upper class, and a great tradition inherited from the mother countries. Yet it was, especially in its rural areas, an underdeveloped region, with great extremes of poverty, with sharp class distinctions, and many unassimilated Indians; and its constituent nations were divided by sharp rivalries, some of which produced actual wars. One of these, between Paraguay and a coalition of Brazil, Argentina, and Uruguay (1865–1870), was for the loser, Paraguay, one of the most disastrous in history, almost wiping out its male population.

THE UNITED STATES

The important fact about United States history in the first 70 years of the nineteenth century can be stated in simple figures: population in 1800, 5.3 millions, that of a middling power in terms of international politics; population in 1870, 38.5 millions, approximately equal to that of a European Great Power. These were years when many Americans would have asserted proudly that the United States had no part in international politics and stood in deliberate isolation, above and beyond the squabbling European Powers. Yet from the start the American Department of State concerned itself with diplomatic and trade relations all over the world; our marvelous clipper ships and whalers were everywhere on the seven seas; and by the Monroe Doctrine the United States put up a "No Trespassing" sign against European powers, not only for its own lands but for those of its Latin neighbors in the Western hemisphere.

Only once was there a serious trespass, when in 1861 France, Britain, and Spain intervened in Mexican affairs after Mexico had suspended payments on her foreign debts. Britain and Spain withdrew when it was clear that the ever-adventurous Napoleon III really meant business. French troops, taking advantage of the American Civil War, occupied Mexico City in 1863 and set up an Empire under Maximilian, younger brother of the Habsburg Emperor Francis Joseph, and supported by conservative Mexican interests. With the Civil War concluded, the American government refused to recognize Maximilian and pressed the

French to leave. Napoleon withdrew his forces and in the subsequent fighting with Mexican patriots Maximilian was defeated and executed (1867).

In the early stages of the Civil War there was also some threat that Britain and perhaps France would intervene in behalf of the rebel South. But Lincoln's caution saved the immediate situation in 1861, and as the chances of Northern victory grew stronger in the summer of 1863, the danger of intervention faded.

The Latin Americans and a good many American citizens, too, especially in the North, considered that the United States trespassed against the best intentions of the Monroe Doctrine in 1846 by going to war against Mexico. Americans had peacefully settled in what was undoubtedly Mexican territory in Texas, and had afterwards revolted and won their independence as the Republic of Texas in 1836. The annexation of Texas by joint resolution of the United States Congress in 1845 rankled with Mexicans, and a border dispute allowed President Polk to get Congress to declare war in 1846. The United States won this war easily enough, and in the treaty of Guadalupe Hidalgo in 1848, supplemented by the Gadsden Purchase of 1853, acquired California (just in time for the gold rush), Arizona, New Mexico, and a large part of the mountain states.

Millions of Americans had for years been overflowing from the Atlantic seaboard, and had by 1870 almost filled up the present boundaries of the continental United States. The forward edge of this westward movement has been given the characteristically American name of "frontier," a moving line suggesting not a static European state boundary, but pioneer energies, pioneer freedom, and all the other pioneer virtues—and vices. This westward movement is the great American folk epic, apparently immovably enshrined still as the movie and television "Western." Most historians are nowadays less inclined than they were a generation ago, when the distinguished American historian Frederick Jackson Turner announced his "frontier theory," to accept the westward movement as the all-important determining factor in making Americans what they are today. But it can hardly be denied that the experience of the frontier, with its open competitiveness, its absence of clear-cut lines of status, its freedom from—or distance from—firm legal governing authority, had a lot to do with the "rugged individualism" that has survived as part of the American national character.

Yet the East, the Old South, the Middle West after it ceased to be a frontier about 1840–1850, were by no means stationary in these decades of the mid-nineteenth century. Notably the Industrial Revolution had begun with the first New England textile mills shortly before 1800, and had spread with about the same speed as in western Europe. By 1870 some eight to ten millions of the nearly forty millions of Americans were living in cities, working in factories, or on the railroads, or working in the service industries for weekly wages. These millions were particularly exposed to the penetration of ideas and fashions from Europe. However much the United States may have succeeded in avoiding "entangling alliances" in foreign affairs, it was fully in the current of ideas, tastes, and movements common to the Western world, as we shall see in the next chapter.

The most dramatic event of these years in United States history is the Civil War, 1861–1865. It is still, measured in terms of casualties relative to total population, the deadliest of American wars, more deadly than either world war. Historians still dispute over such big general problems as whether or not this "War between the States" really was an "irrepressible conflict." Now, after a century, the Civil War has become a part of the living emotional history of the United

States. To the liberal-minded, the twentieth-century problem of desegregation may mean that the Civil War was fought in vain, but the fact remains that in the midst of the conflict over desegregation in the 1950's and 1960's no responsible southern politician seriously suggested another attempt at secession. Southern particularism, unlike many European nationalisms, Irish, Polish, Catalan, Flemish, and still others, has not continued to nourish the spirit of secessionist rebellion.

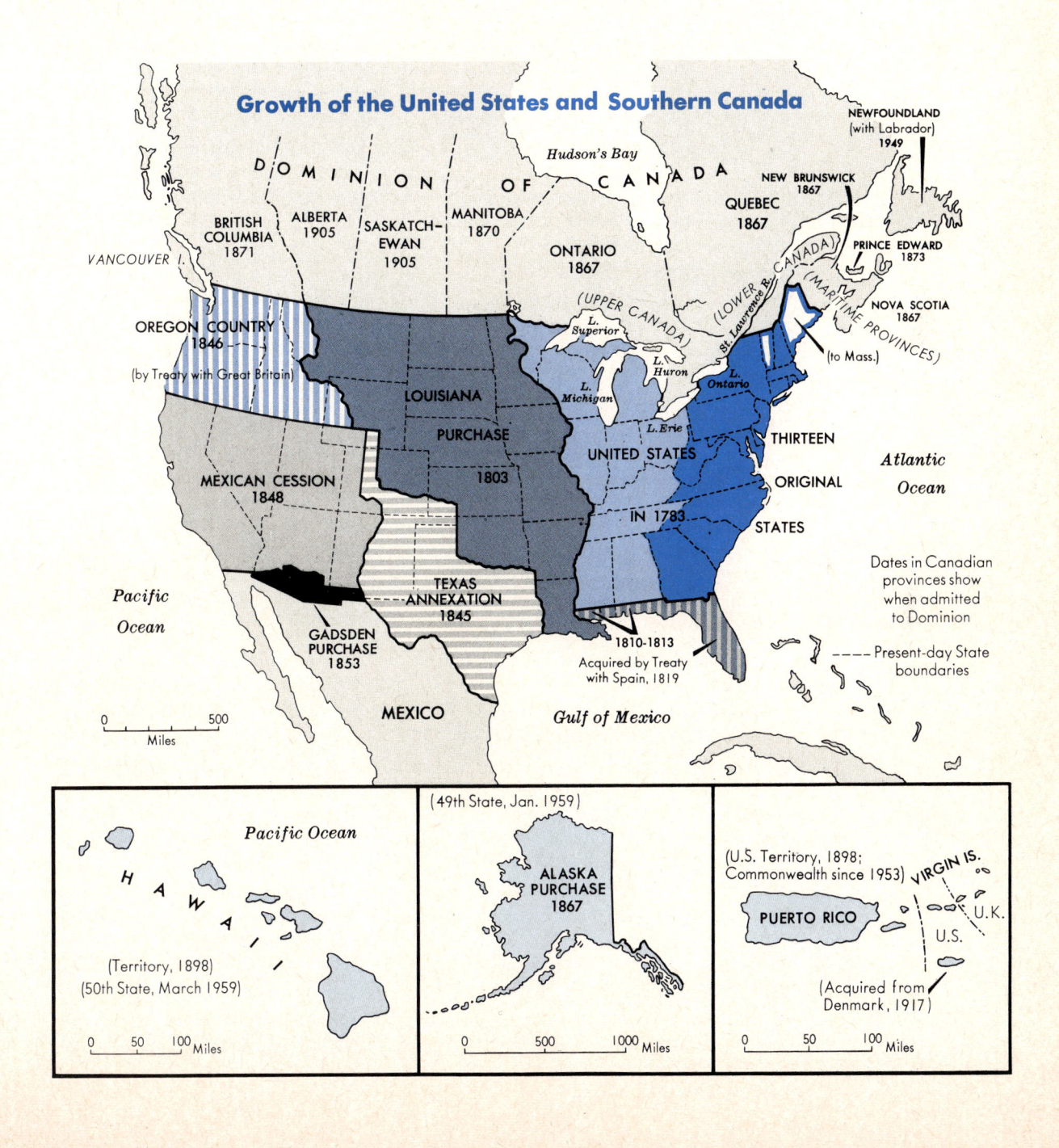

COLONIES OF SETTLEMENT

For the rest of the non-European world, these decades of the nineteenth century up to 1870 were a period of growth and preparation for the culminating period of "colonialism" or "imperialism" to come from about 1870 to the outbreak of World War I in 1914. New colonies of settlement had been founded by Britain in Australia and New Zealand, and increased slowly in population in these years. In Australia, the very primitive natives, the "blackfellows," made no real resistance, and gradually died out almost completely—in Tasmania, wholly so. In New Zealand the native Maoris, Polynesians with an old culture of their own, fought several wars against encroaching settlers, and achieved a kind of survival and acceptance by the whites, who do, however, now considerably outnumber them.

Developments of major importance for Britain in the world occurred during these decades in Canada, which had avoided assimilation by the United States during the American Revolution and the War of 1812. After some disturbances, especially in 1837, the old French region (Lower Canada or Quebec) and the newer English–Scottish region to its West (Upper Canada or Ontario) were united. They were given responsible self-government and what came to be called "dominion status" on the basis of a famous report made in 1839 by Lord Durham, governor-in-chief of all the British North American provinces. By the British North America Act of 1867 the Atlantic provinces of Nova Scotia and New Brunswick (joined by Prince Edward Island in 1873) were united with Quebec and Ontario to form the Dominion of Canada. Like the United States, the Dominion had western lands extending to the Pacific, and these were settled and admitted to the Dominion much as were the western American states to the Union.

Britain had acquired the old Dutch settlement at the Cape of Good Hope during the Napoleonic wars. British colonists commenced to flow in, not in great numbers, but sufficiently to give the region an increasingly English-speaking population. The old Dutch, known in those days as the Boers, nowadays as the Afrikaners—clannish, distrustful of British innovations, annoyed by British antislavery measures—set out in 1835 on their Great Trek, a mass movement into the vast open spaces to the north. There they founded two Boer states, the Transvaal and the Orange Free State, both of which enjoyed a tenuous kind of "sovereignty," confirmed by the Sand River Convention of 1852 between Britain and the Transvaal. Acute native problems existed throughout this South African region, where Negroes always outnumbered whites. Here too, however, the years before 1870 were but a setting of the stage for later crises.

What might be called a colony of semi-settlement was founded by the French in this period. In 1827 the Dey of Algiers, a virtually independent ruler only technically under the suzerainty of the Sultan at Constantinople, annoyed by the demands of the French consul, slapped him in the face with a fly whisk. After prolonged protests, the French invaded in 1830. From this undignified but not untypical incident in the breeding of war (the eighteenth century had had Jenkins' Ear—*see* Chapter 10) sprang the great French acquisition of Algeria. By 1870 French, Spanish, and Italian settlers had moved into Algeria and adjacent Tunis as *colons* (colonists) in significant numbers, which were to increase until they were perhaps one-eighth of the total population, the rest being "natives" of

Berber and Arab stock, Moslems in religion. The *colons* were, as were the whites in South Africa, a ruling class in possession of the greater part of the productive wealth of the regions; but again as in South Africa, they remained numerically a distinct minority of the total population.

COLONIES OF EXPLOITATION

As for colonies of trade or exploitation, the early and mid-nineteenth century saw only the beginnings of the great expansion of Europe that came with the opening up of interior Africa in the last quarter of the century and the increasing rivalry among the Great Powers for "spheres of influence" in the Middle East and in China. While the final blooming of "imperialism" came *after* 1870, the preparations for it commenced much earlier. The British went to war with China in 1839 over the opium trade, a war which put the British in the position of defending a most immoral cause. China, which had had with Europe only the loose trade connections established in the first great wave of Western imperialism in the sixteenth and seventeenth centuries, was from then on disputed among rival Western powers, each of which sought trade concessions, treaty ports, and spheres of influence. Japan, which had closed itself off from the first wave of European expansion in the early seventeenth century, was opened to trade after the visit of the American Commodore Perry with four ships in 1853, and a formal treaty between the United States and Japan in 1854.

In India, the British continued to trade and to administer certain areas through the East India Company directly, the rest through "native princes" subject to a considerable degree of British control. Here in 1857–1858 the Great Mutiny of the native Indian army, officered at the top levels by British, brought an end to an epoch. The British, after severe losses and some trying sieges, mastered the rebellious sepoys, as the native soldiers were called. The anomalous political rule of the East India Company was abolished, and the Crown took over its obligations. When in 1877 Disraeli had his Queen made Empress of India, the great final period of British *raj* in India began. The India thus ruled by a small British minority remained essentially East Indian, a subcontinent for the most part Hindu in culture, yet with an amazing variety of other peoples and religions.

In Africa, the early and mid-nineteenth century was the chief period of exploration of the interior, an undertaking as filled with excitement as that of the great days of Columbus and Magellan. The best known of these dramatic explorations was the successful finding of the lost explorer Livingstone by Stanley ("Dr. Livingstone, I presume?") on Lake Tanganyika in 1871. A significant modern touch: Stanley was sent on his rescuing expedition, not by a Henry the Navigator or a Queen Isabella, but by the New York *Herald!*

Finally, even in the colonies of exploitation, even in areas where the natives seemed relatively untouched by Western influences, the nineteenth century witnessed the beginnings of railways, roads, policing, education, sanitation, modern urban centers, in short, the great material revolution of modern Western culture. Thanks especially to British initiative the early nineteenth century recorded at least one great humanitarian achievement: the abolition of the slave trade. Abolition of slavery itself was decreed throughout the British Empire in 1833. Gradually international agreements enforced the suppression of the trade, and after Lincoln's Emancipation Proclamation of 1863 actual chattel slavery vanished from most of the Western world.

12

READING SUGGESTIONS (asterisk indicates paperbound edition)

General Accounts

F. B. Artz, *Reaction and Revolution, 1814–1832,* and R. C. Binkley, *Realism and Nationalism, 1852–1870* (*Torchbooks). Volumes in the Rise of Modern Europe series, with full bibliographies.

The New Cambridge Modern History, Vols. IX and X (Cambridge University, 1965, 1960). A comprehensive treatment by many hands covering 1793 to 1870.

A. J. May, *The Age of Metternich, 1814–1848,* rev. ed. (*Holt). Brief introduction.

E. J. Hobsbawm, *The Age of Revolution, 1789–1848* (*Mentor). Stimulating analysis, stressing both political and economic developments.

International Affairs

L. C. B. Seaman, *From Vienna to Versailles* (*Colophon). Provocative reinterpretations.

H. A. Kissinger, *A World Restored: The Politics of Conservatism in a Revolutionary Age* (*Universal). Efforts to restore the European balance, 1812–1822.

H. Nicolson, *The Congress of Vienna* (*Compass). Analyzed by an expert on diplomacy.

H. F. Schwarz, ed., *Metternich: The Coachman of Europe—Statesman or Evil Genius?* (*Heath). Good introduction to the divergent appraisals of the man.

P. Viereck, *Conservatism Revisited* (*Free Press). Sympathetic toward Metternich but not so-called German "liberals."

C. Brinton, *The Lives of Talleyrand* (*Norton). Warmly approving biography.

A. J. P. Taylor, *The Struggle for Mastery in Europe, 1848–1918* (Clarendon, 1954). Crisp and provocative review of diplomatic history.

The Revolutions in General

M. Kranzberg, ed., *1848: A Turning Point?* (*Heath). Sampling divergent views on the turning point "where Europe failed to turn."

P. Robertson, *Revolutions of 1848: A Social History* (*Torchbooks). Stressing colorful details.

R. Postgate, *Story of a Year: 1848* (Oxford, 1956). A lively chronicle, well illustrated.

L. B. Namier, *The Revolution of the Intellectuals* (*Anchor). Castigating liberals, especially German liberals, for illiberal attitudes.

Britain, France, Italy

E. Halévy, *A History of the English People in the Nineteenth Century,* 5 vols. (P. Smith, 1949–1951). The classic detailed study, but not covering the entire century. Portions have been published in paperback.

E. L. Woodward, *The Age of Reform,* 2nd. ed. (Clarendon, 1967). A full account.

D. Thomson, *England in the Nineteenth Century* (*Penguin), and A. Wood, *Nineteenth Century Britain* (Longmans, 1960). Excellent surveys.

A. Briggs, *The Making of Modern England, 1784–1867: The Age of Improvement* (*Torchbooks). Lives up to its apt subtitle.

E. Longford, *Queen Victoria* (*Pyramid). Recent and authoritative biography.

G. Wright, *France in Modern Times* (Rand McNally, 1960). The best single volume on the subject, with a good bibliography.

A. Cobban, *A History of Modern France,* Vol. 2 (*Penguin). Survey from 1799 to 1871.

D. W. Brogan, *The French Nation from Napoleon to Pétain, 1814–1940* (*Colophon). Brilliant essay, stressing interpretation.

G. de Bertier de Sauvigny, *The Bourbon Restoration* (University of Pennsylvania, 1967). Sympathetic reappraisal; may be contrasted with F. B. Artz, *France under the Bourbon Restoration, 1814–1830* (Harvard, 1931).

J. M. Thompson, *Louis Napoleon and the Second Empire* (Blackwell, 1954). A useful synthesis of detailed scholarly works.

A. Guérard, *Napoleon III* (Harvard, 1943). Spirited defense of the Emperor as a "Caesarean democrat."

S. M. Osgood, ed., *Napoleon Third: Buffoon, Modern Dictator, or Sphinx?* (*Heath). Wide sampling of differing appraisals of the man.

G. F. Berkeley, *Italy in the Making*, 3 vols. (Cambridge, 1932–1940). Detailed but not very critical study from 1815 through 1848.

A. J. Whyte, *The Evolution of Modern Italy* (*Norton). Sound introduction.

G. Salvemini, *Mazzini* (*Collier). Sympathetic evaluation.

D. Mack Smith, *Italy: A Modern History* (University of Michigan, 1959). Up-to-date and scholarly.

R. Albrecht-Carrié, *Italy from Napoleon to Mussolini* (*Columbia). Introductory survey.

Germany, Austria, Russia

T. S. Hamerow, *Restoration, Revolution, Reaction* (*Princeton). Recent scholarly reappraisal of German developments, 1815–1871.

H. Treitschke, *History of Germany in the Nineteenth Century*, 7 vols. (Humanities Press, 1915–1919). Famous old account, strongly Prussian in tone.

A. J. P. Taylor, *The Course of German History* (*Capricorn). A strongly anti-German antidote to Treitschke.

O. Pflanze, *Bismarck and the Development of Germany* (Princeton, 1963). Recent scholarly treatment to 1871.

E. Eyck, *Bismarck and the German Empire* (*Norton). Condensation of a larger work by a German scholar.

A. J. P. Taylor, *Bismarck: The Man and the Statesman* (*Vintage). An often hostile evaluation.

———, *The Habsburg Monarchy, 1809–1918* (*Torchbooks). Spirited introduction by an always controversial historian.

R. J. Rath, *The Vienna Revolution of 1848* (University of Texas, 1957). Detailed monograph.

A. G. Mazour, *The First Russian Revolution* (*Stanford). Excellent monograph on the Decembrists.

W. E. Mosse, *Alexander II and the Modernization of Russia* (*Collier). Good introduction.

America and the Colonial World

R. Hofstadter, W. Miller, and D. Aaron, *The United States: The History of a Republic*, 2nd. ed. (Prentice-Hall, 1967). A readable up-to-date account.

S. E. Morison, *The Oxford History of the American People*, new ed. (Oxford, 1965). Well-written survey.

D. K. Fieldhouse, *The Colonial Empires: A Comparative Survey from the Eighteenth Century* (Delacorte, 1967). Comprehensive and authoritative.

P. Knaplund, *The British Empire, 1815–1939* (Harper, 1941). Standard treatment.

C. P. de T. Glazebrook, *Canada: A Short History* (Oxford, 1950); M. Barnard, *A History of Australia* (Praeger, 1963); E. A. Walker, *A History of South Africa* (Longmans, 1940). Good accounts of important colonies of settlement.

J. F. Rippy, *Latin America* (*University of Michigan). By a sound historian.

Sources and Fiction

Disraeli, *Coningsby* (*Capricorn). Novel about Tory democracy by the famous politician.

E. Zola, *The Downfall* (Appleton, 1902). Good novel about the Franco-Prussian War by the celebrated naturalistic writer.

J. C. Legge, ed., *Rhyme and Revolution in Germany: A Study in German History, Life, Literature, and Character, 1813–1850* (Constable, 1918). An anthology that fully lives up to the promise of its title.

I. Silone, ed., *The Living Thoughts of Mazzini* (Longmans, 1939). Selected writings of the democratic nationalist.

I. Turgenev, *Fathers and Sons* (sometimes translated as *Fathers and Children*). Superb realistic novel of the "generation gap" in Russia on the eve of Alexander II's reforms.

N. Gogol, *The Inspector General* (*Pitman) and *Dead Souls* (*several editions). A play and a novel about mid-nineteenth-century Russia, both brilliantly satirical.

M. Kantor, *Andersonville* (*Signet). Grimly realistic novel of a Confederate prison during the Civil War.

S. Cloete, *The Turning Wheels* (Houghton, 1937). A novel about Boers trekking northward in nineteenth-century South Africa.

13

Economics, Thought, and Culture
in the Nineteenth Century

The Crystal Palace, home of the Great Exhibition of 1851 in London.

I. The Industrial Revolution

The political history of the West in the nineteenth century cannot be understood without some awareness of its correlation with the dramatic phase of economic growth nurtured by science and technology and called the Industrial Revolution. The previous chapter has furnished striking examples of the hopes and fears focussed on the new industrial working class—Disraeli's bid for the votes of laborers by Tory sponsorship of the Reform Bill of 1867, taking the suffrage a giant step toward democracy; the outbreaks of class warfare in 1848, especially in the June Days in Paris. Nor can the intellectual history of the century be understood without some knowledge of these material, quite nonintellectual factors. One of the major clusters of ideas of the century, Marxist socialism, actually bases its world-view on the assumption that material "events" underlie and in fact explain, in a causal sense, everything in human individual and group behavior. Those who reject the Marxist analysis recognize the great influence exerted on the ideas of the century by the Industrial Revolution and its accompanying increase in wealth and population, in short, on the modernization of the Western world.

THE TIMETABLE OF INDUSTRIALIZATION

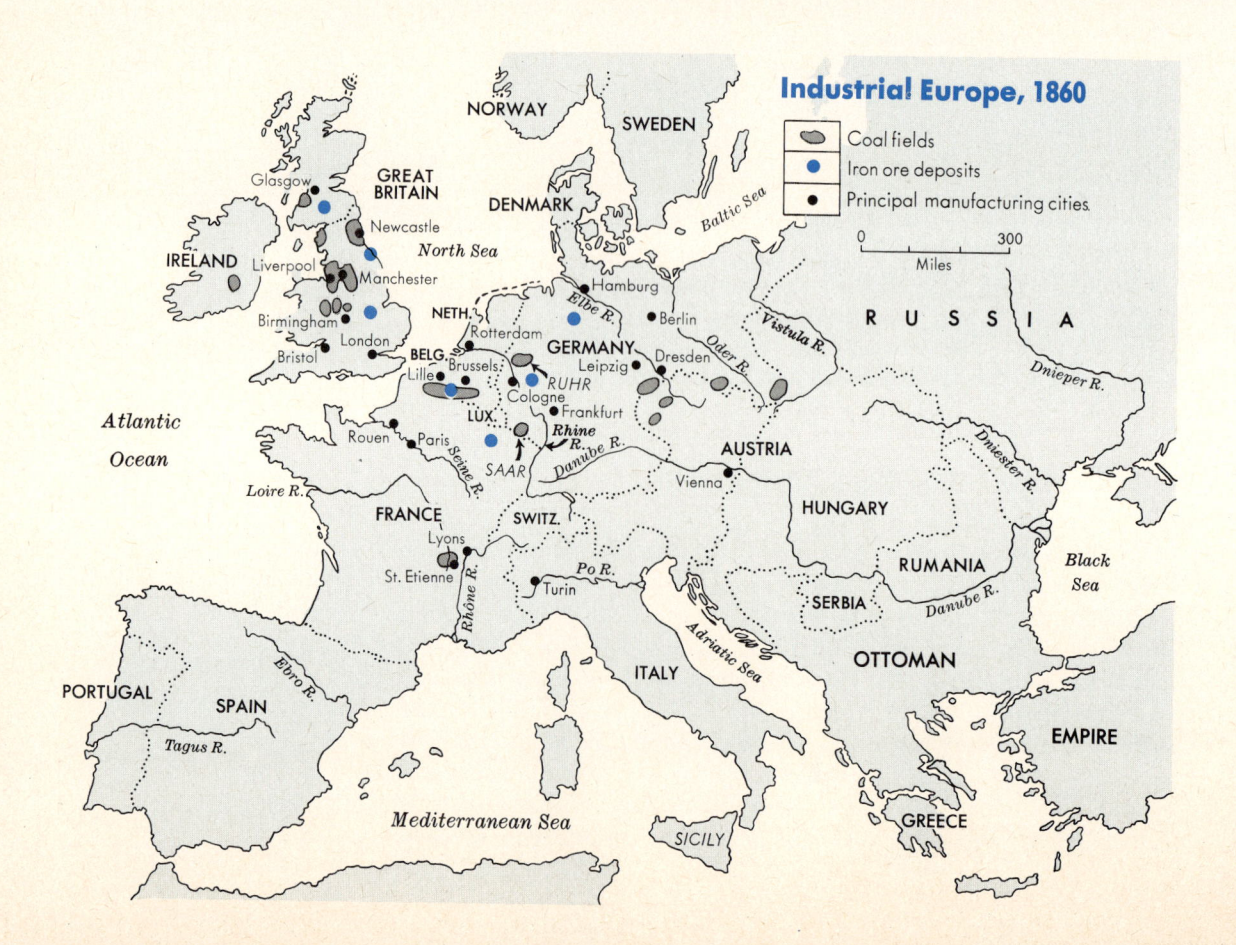

We have already discussed the beginnings and the background of the remarkable increase in human command over natural power and resources that took place in the eighteenth century (see Chapter 9). The Industrial Revolution itself is commonly considered to have begun in England about 1760 with such inventions as the steam engine, the spinning jenny, the power loom, and a host of others which made possible the modern factory with its power-driven machines. Both inventions and factories brought with them large-scale production and distribution, a very wide market, large labor forces, and an elaborate and extensive organization of finances, business, and government administration —this last in spite of a climate of opinion generally hostile to expanded governmental activities. The challenge of the lengthy wars of the French Revolution and Napoleon seems to have accelerated the pace of developments in Britain by stimulating the demand for metal goods, promoting the invention of new machines to speed the outfitting of British warships, and causing the building of great docks along the Thames to serve the mounting activity of the port of London. The English Industrial Revolution attained its majority, so to speak, in the first half of the nineteenth century when Britain led the world in output of coal, in construction of railroads, and in the number of spindles and looms in textile factories. The British economy was to continue to grow after 1850, of course, with the ups and downs of the business cycle, to our own day.

Many factors made Great Britain the pioneer in industrialization. She possessed large and readily available deposits of coal and iron, the basic ingredients of industrial progress, and her geographical compactness made shipments from mine to smelter and from mill to seaport short and cheap. A large reservoir of potential factory labor existed among small farmers driven off the land by the expansion of the estates utilizing the efficient new techniques of the agricultural revolution (*see above*, p. 429) and among emigrants from impoverished, overcrowded Ireland. The financing of new enterprises was facilitated by the early development of British banking, by the rapid growth of Britain's overseas trade in the eighteenth century, and by the willingness of merchants who profited by that trade to invest in new undertakings. The slave traders of Liverpool financed cotton mills in Manchester; the tobacco merchants of Glasgow helped supply the money that made their city, with its shipyards and factories, the industrial hub of Scotland; and the tea importers of London and Bristol aided the ironmasters of South Wales. Political and social institutions were also significant—Britain's relatively stable governmental system after 1689, what was probably a greater degree of social mobility than on the Continent, and greater opportunities for entrepreneurship, again due in part to the relative fluidity or "modernity" of British social structure. A factor of great importance was the security from foreign invasion afforded by the English Channel and the British navy. The navy was a lot less expensive in men and money than the armies *and* navies needed by powers like France; both men and money, and the spirit of enterprise needed to make them effective in economic growth, were used by the British to secure the *comparative* advantage, which is all they ever enjoyed.

For the Industrial Revolution was by no means purely British. In northwestern Continental Europe and in the only European colony of settlement advanced enough for such developments—the United States—factories, machines, capitalism of a modern kind all began to appear by the late eighteenth and early nineteenth centuries. A key invention making possible the cheap large-scale production of cotton textiles, one of the earliest of the great industries, was the cotton gin, invented in 1793 by Eli Whitney in Connecticut. The first American cotton mills—based in part on plans for machines smuggled out of England—were built in New England in the 1790's. One of the essential factors in the most recent phase of the Industrial Revolution, organized collaboration between researchers and producers, had its modest beginnings in revolutionary France; a group of distinguished scientists worked with the Committee of Public Safety to improve steel and iron output and in general to boost war production. The metric system was the work of these same scientists in the French Revolution; standardized and interchangeable parts, forerunners of the assembly line, owed much to Eli Whitney, who made muskets with mutually substitutable parts.

Finally, though the British tried hard to keep their machines and the know-how of running them a monopoly, they could not prevent emigration of skilled workers to America and to France and to the rest of the Continent.

STAGES OF ECONOMIC GROWTH

By 1870 the Industrial Revolution was firmly established in western Europe and the northeastern United States and had begun in much of our Midwest as well; its effects were felt in all parts of the world as a result of steamships, railroads, telegraphs, and the complex apparatus of modern banking and business. The Industrial Revolution may be divided into "periods" according to the main sources of power at the time—water, steam, electric, or atomic; according to economic and technological criteria—simple division of labor, assembly-line methods, automation; or socioeconomic criteria—size of firm, kind of ownership and management, degree of government regulation, and the like. But it is essentially one great and *comparatively* rapid—that is, revolutionary—process.

A very suggestive insight into the process is that of the contemporary American economic historian W. W. Rostow, who suggests that three stages may be discerned in a given country's emergence into the industrial age—preparation, take-off (the figure of speech refers to the airplane), and a final phase when economic growth is self-sustaining and self-renewing, and productivity can be increased much more easily than it could in the pre-industrial age. Great Britain "took off" earliest, followed by the United States after the Civil War and by Germany after the completion of unification in 1871. In the twentieth century Japan, Russia, and others have made their economic take-off successfully, and today almost all the countries of Africa, Asia, and Latin America that we used to call "underdeveloped" and now call "emerging" are seeking to join the club.

INDUSTRIAL AREAS AND "COLONIAL" AREAS

By 1870, the difference between industrial areas and "colonial" areas had become obvious. The industrial areas took the products of agriculture, fishing, and mining (the "extractive" enterprises) and manufactured them into consumer goods as well as into more machines to continue and improve industrial processes. The colonial areas which supplied much of these raw materials were less rich and less "advanced" than the manufacturing areas. (We used the word "areas" rather than "nations" or "countries" because economic boundaries did not necessarily coincide with political ones.) Within the United States in the later nineteenth century, for instance, the West and the South were essentially areas of raw materials and the Northeast and some of the Middle West essentially industrial. Western and Southern publicists did not hesitate to complain about their "colonial" exploitation by the East, and in particular, by "Wall Street." Italy afforded an even more striking contrast, that between the advanced and prosperous North around Milan and Turin and the retarded, poverty-stricken, "colonial" South. The sovereignty of a large independent state might be restricted by the fact that, economically, it remained a colonial area, like Argentina, for example, which depended on Britain as a market for its beef and other agricultural products and as a supplier of its industrial goods.

INDUSTRIALISM AND THE STANDARD OF LIVING

The Industrial Revolution, especially in its early phases, launched a complex series of changes that demanded more adaptability from human beings than they could always provide. It brought with it poorly lighted and ventilated factories, dangerous machines without safety provisions, ugly, unsanitary new housing and long hours of labor at hard or at least dull and repetitive work; above all, it uprooted men and women from traditional village life. Here the effect of the Industrial Revolution on the Western mind was most conspicuous. For all sorts of men reacted vigorously against the ugliness and suffering of the new society, and expressed themselves in an abundant literature of social protest. Karl Marx was in many ways the most typical and most important of these critics, but there were many others, and their criticism, as we shall see, took various forms. Even the defenders of the new society had to base their defense solely on the concrete achievements of the Industrial Revolution. Moreover, the literature and philosophy, the religions, the world-views of the nineteenth century, immensely varied though they were, all had to take economic factors into account.

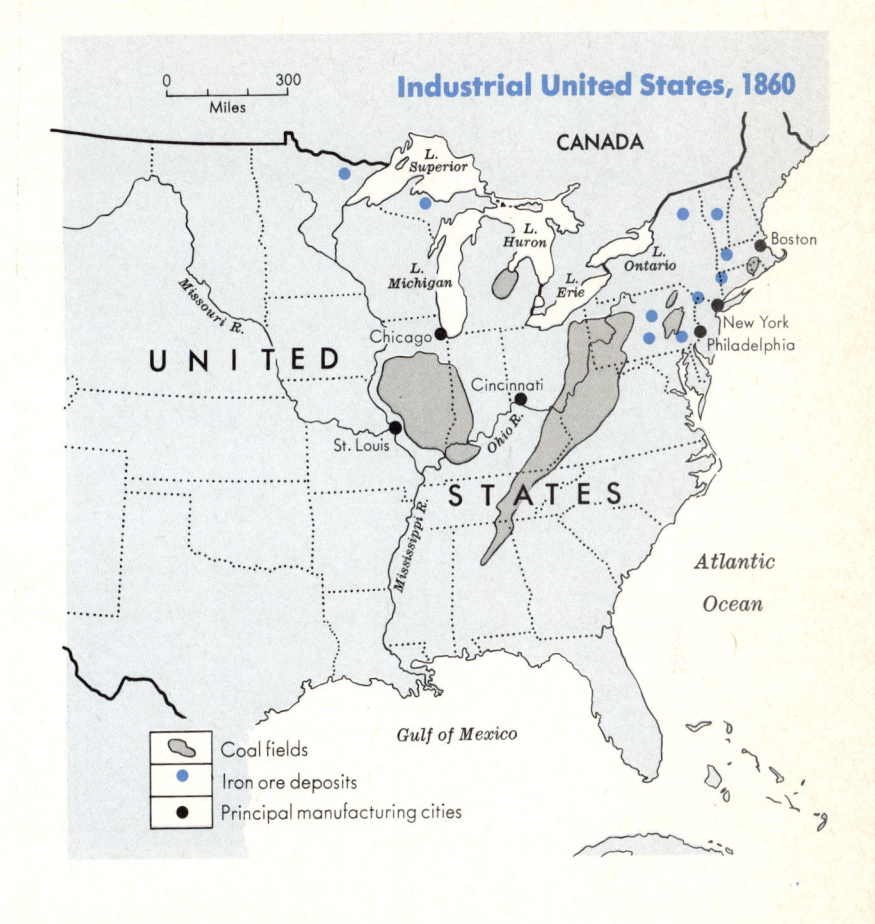

But the historian must examine with care the ugly, oppressive side of the Industrial Revolution: How new, how different from old conditions among the workers, was it? The Marxists and many other radicals argued that the Industrial Revolution made the "condition" (admittedly a vague word) of the lower or working class *worse* than it had been earlier. Nineteenth-century and early twentieth-century historical literature pretty generally painted a dark picture—child labor, new slums, low wages, the constant threat of unemployment in an economy subject to periodic panic and depressions, and much else degrading to the human spirit. Recent Marxist literature in the West has emphasized the "alienation" of the worker from his work, as well as his exploitation by "capitalists." Nevertheless, present-day historians incline to the view that the picture painted by most of their predecessors was too dark. The rhetoric of early Victorian reformers, echoed by some later historians, would if taken literally seem to mean that conditions of living in England in 1840 were not only worse than in 1740 but so bad that men could not physically endure them.

515

Yet the most striking thing about the social and economic history of England in the nineteenth century was the unprecedented growth of population. For England and Wales it went from 9 million in 1800 to 32½ million in 1900, and this not only without significant immigration, but with considerable emigration to the United States and the dominions. The population of towns and cities of over 20,000 increased by more than one million in the decade 1831–1841, and by nearly two million in the next decade. Given the sketchy political and technological resources available in those days, such a growth in population probably set bigger tasks for urban government than those set by the present-day "population explosion." Yet evidently the British people in the nineteenth century, including the working classes, ate enough, had enough shelter and sanitation to bring up more children than ever before. The Industrial Revolution even in its earlier phases did, statistically speaking, raise the standard of living for the working classes of Britain.

The oppression and exploitation visited upon the lower classes by the Industrial Revolution were felt to be ugliness, dreariness, uprooting, and above all injustice. These feelings were expressed by those sympathizers of the poor among the upper and middle classes who did the articulate complaining (Marx himself was middle class). Another basic source of the trouble the Industrial Revolution brought with it in the nineteenth century may be described as *growing pains,* the product of rising standards visible to all, though unequally shared between industrial and colonial areas, between capital and labor. Wherever the Industrial Revolution gets to work, even in our own day, its effects are to raise the standards of living of workers to the point where they can realistically hope for, and plan for, ever-improving standards of living.

Child laborers in a German wallpaper factory, about 1840.

II. Science, Religion, and Philosophy

SCIENCE

Physics. The nineteenth century could well be called the Age of Science. Not only did the improvements in techniques that made industrial take-off possible form part of the history of science; what had been called "natural philosophy" in the eighteenth century became simply science, often capitalized, Science. All of its branches, the separate sciences, developed cumulatively, in spite of conservative resistance, as the teaching of science and scientific research came to take a major place in formal education. The physical sciences—astronomy, physics, chemistry, and their special branches, like mechanics and optics—were so highly developed that technology and engineering became dependent on their initiative, thus reversing the relation that had obtained in early modern science (*see* Chapter 9). By 1900 many well-trained physicists thought their subject was finished, at least in the sense that the basic structure of theory was known, and nothing further would be changed. In fact, however, the early work on radiation by scientists like Becquerel, the Curies, and Roentgen had already begun the twentieth-century "revolution" in physics (*see* Chapter 17).

The major generalization from the physical sciences in the nineteenth century to seep through and influence thought about man's place in the universe was the second law of thermodynamics; it states that though the total amount of energy in the universe remains constant, the amount of energy useful to human beings is being steadily dissipated. Built up in a way thoroughly characteristic of the international character of science, it was the work of many experts, such as the French Carnot, the German Clausius, and the British Lord Kelvin. Transferred to philosophical world-views, the second law of thermodynamics was taken by many laymen to mean that our world was headed toward its end as the sun weakened and the earth grew colder and colder. The old Christian concept of a cataclysmic Day of Judgment was thus given a pseudo-scientific twist, and seems to have obsessed the later years of so firm a non-Christian as the American historian Henry Adams (1838–1918).

Biology: Darwin. But the most important transfer of ideas and theories from natural science to religion, philosophy, and even politics came in the nineteenth century not from physics, as it had in the eighteenth century with Newton and others, but from biology. In 1859 the English naturalist Charles Darwin (1809–1882) published *The Origin of Species,* which was to effect a revolution not only in biology but in men's attitudes toward the question of man's place in nature. Like all important revolutions, the Darwinian was no bolt from the blue. Into Darwin's work had gone long years of preparation, both his and those of his predecessors and colleagues in the scientific study of biology and geology. Already well established by geologists like Sir Charles Lyell and by paleontologists, the record told of the rise, development, and sometimes of the disappearance, over millions of years, of thousands of different forms of plant and animal organisms, or *species*. The Bible in the Book of Genesis described all forms of life as begun in the space of a single week by a Creator about 6,000 years ago and stated explicitly that all existing men and animals were descended from single pairs of each species preserved in Noah's ark during a great universal flood.

Charles Darwin in 1840, by George Richmond.

The men of the Enlightenment had felt compelled by the facts of the record to give up the biblical explanation, and some of them had gone so far as to conceive a very long evolutionary process in which no God, at least no personal, Christian God, had taken a hand, but only the impersonal forces of Nature or the deist's "watchmaker God" (*see* Chapter 9). But they had reached no satisfactory explanation of how Nature had done the job; they had no theory of how organisms had evolved. This Darwin gave the world.

He found one of his clues in the work of the English economist Malthus (1766–1834). In his *Essay on Population,* Malthus had pointed out that organisms tended to multiply to a point where there simply was not food enough for them all; in the intense competition for food, some organisms did not get enough, and died. This was the germ of the conception Darwin phrased as the *struggle for existence*. He next asked himself what determined that certain individuals would survive and that others would die. If they were all identical organisms, the only explanation—apart from the intervention of a supernatural force—would have to be mere chance. But it was clear from observation that variations in individual organisms are present at birth. Thus in a single litter of pigs there may be sturdy piglets and a runt. The runt is likely to get shoved aside in suckling by his more aggressive brothers, and in the wild state would be almost certain to die. In the struggle for existence, the weakling is proved *unfit*.

Here is the second of the key phrases of Darwinism, the *survival of the fittest*. The organism best endowed to get food and shelter lives to procreate young that will tend to inherit these favorable variations. The variations in structure that assist the organism are slight, but they are cumulative after many generations; finally an organism so different from the long-distant ancestor is produced that we can speak of a new species. This new species has *evolved*. It has evolved by the working of *natural selection*. As a plant and animal breeder, man has long made use of this process, and has hastened and guided it by *artificial selection*, by breeding only the best strains—"best," of course, from a human point of view. But man has been doing this for but a tiny period of geological time and with relatively few species. Over the aeons, natural selection has been the working force; *and for man himself*, according to the Darwinian system, natural selection alone has been at work, since man has yet to breed his own kind as he breeds his domestic plants and animals.

Darwin held that the variations in individuals of the same species at birth are accidental, and that they are generally transmitted through inheritance. But orthodox Darwinian biology held that what an organism "learns," what "happens" to it, is not transmitted: it denied the inheritance of "acquired characteristics." A man with an amputated leg will not produce one-legged children; experimenters have docked the tails of generations of laboratory rats, but the rats are still born with long tails.

Today, more than a century after the publication of the *Origin of Species*, Darwin's work as a biologist is still accepted in most of its larger outlines. Later work, however, has found that variations of importance in the ultimate evolution of a *new* species—a process that requires many hundreds of thousands of years—are probably not so much the numerous tiny ones Darwin emphasized, but rather bigger and much rarer ones known as "mutations." Scientists have begun to study the effect of various forms of radiation on such mutations. A still much-disputed geological theory holds that catastrophic movements of the earth's crust in the past have so radically altered environment as to wipe out whole species and speed up the evolution of others. Emphasis on either mutations or on extensive crustal movements tends also to be emphasis on the sudden and catastrophic rather than on the gradual—an attitude perhaps typical of our time, but definitely not of the nineteenth century.

The Other Sciences. So much for Darwin the *biologist;* we shall return later to *Darwinism* as a world-view. After Darwin the most important work in biology was that of the Austrian monk Gregor Mendel (1822–1884), whose experiments with crossbreeding garden peas laid the basis of modern genetics. In terms of important results for daily living, the nineteenth century saw the beginnings, indeed more than the beginnings, of organic chemistry, biochemistry (a twentieth-century term), and pathology. Thanks to scientists from many countries—the French Pasteur, a veritable culture-hero of science whose name has been given the honor of lower-case in "pasteurize," the German Liebig, the English Lister, the German Koch, the American Walter Reed—medicine, surgery, public health, and nutrition had by 1900 reached the "take-off point." Thus in the twentieth century the average life expectancy at birth was increased by 20 to 30 years in the advanced countries of the West, and has been perceptibly increased even in the underdeveloped countries.

Finally during the nineteenth century what are now somewhat hopefully called the "social" or "behavioral" sciences got firmly established in higher education, some of them by 1900 even in such conservative institutions as Oxford and Cambridge. But none of these sciences—economics, sociology, anthropology, social psychology, political science—has even now achieved the standing of the natural sciences in general cultivated opinion. Many (if not most) natural scientists deny them—save for psychological work which is really neurology—the sacred name of science. Yet their supply of facts or data was immensely increased in quantity and improved in quality during the nineteenth century, and their efforts to arrive at laws or uniformities from their data would seem to be at least groping toward the kind of success attained by the natural scientists. At any rate, the prestige of Science was so great that toward the end of the century even professional historians often claimed that the history they wrote was a form of scientific knowledge. They meant, however, that they arrived at their facts as a scientist does, critically and objectively; few of them attempted to derive laws or uniformities with predictive value from their data.

RELIGION

Catholic Thought in an Age of Multanimity. The prestige of Science, coupled with the rising material standards of living made possible by the Industrial Revolution, caused major changes in the religious and intellectual life of the West. In the thirteenth century the West, though sometimes deeply divided in opinions on high matters of philosophy and religion, nevertheless generally accepted Roman Catholic theology. In the eighteenth century there were certainly far more varieties of religious belief than in the thirteenth, yet most of the intellectual classes in the West accepted, if only as a kind of fashion, the aesthetic, moral, and political standards of the Enlightenment. By contrast, the nineteenth century showed such extraordinary variety of beliefs and tastes that it may be called the Age of Multanimity—that is, the age of many views on human existence and destiny, on what is truth and what is beauty.

Among the Christian churches the Roman Catholic increased the number of its communicants, both from the natural growth of population and from converts through missionary work at home and in Asia, Africa, and Latin America. But the Catholic Church was not without its internal differences of opinion. Two often intertwined currents of thought—theological "modernism" and Christian "socialism"—stood out against the central conservative core of Roman Catholic thought, a core that was generally represented by the Holy See itself. The modernists sought to reconcile the scientific attitude of distrust or rejection of the supernatural with the traditional Christian belief in divine planning and intervention. This movement became more important toward the end of the century, and its more prominent leaders were driven to such emphasis on the rationalist side that they broke with the Church; the French priest Loisy (1857-1940), for example, was excommunicated, and the Irish Father Tyrell (1861-1909) was expelled from the Society of Jesus.

Christian democratic movements arose early in the century, and emphasized reconciliation with the political and social side of the democratic way of life more than did the theologically minded modernists. Their "socialism" was by no means of the Marxist kind, but rather a religiously inspired desire to improve the lot of the poor and raise their material as well as their moral standards of life. The Christian democrats sympathized with many aims of the modern welfare state. Some of them, like the French priest Lamennais (1782-1854), finally broke with the Church; most remained within the Church and helped lay the foundations for the important twentieth century Catholic political parties and labor unions, which, on the continent of Europe, have sought to reconcile democratic politics with orthodox Catholic faith.

The papacy, especially during the unusually long pontificate of Pius IX (1846-1878), reacted to these new currents of thought by strengthening its own adherence to tradition. Pius himself was understandably frightened by the violence of the events of 1848 in Italy and especially in Rome, where rather conspicuously anticlerical democrats seized power and obliged him to flee. Pius consistently refused to accept the loss of temporal sovereignty in 1870, when the Kingdom of Italy annexed the last remaining papal territories in Rome and its environs; as compensation, he took steps to strengthen the political influence of the Holy See in other countries. In his pontificate the dogma of the Immaculate Conception was made an article of faith; the encyclical *Quanta Cura* and its appended Syllabus of Errors of 1864 seemed to condemn everything that had sprung from the democratic movements of the previous hundred years. Most important of all, at the Vatican Council of 1870 the dogma of papal infallibility was proclaimed—the doctrine that the Pope, when speaking *ex cathedra*, possesses infallibility in decisions regarding faith and morals.

The next pope, Leo XIII (1878-1903), sought to counteract the extremely reactionary reputation Pius had left behind him. Pope Leo fully recognized the rapid changes being worked by science and technology, which he had observed during service as a papal nuncio in the industrial regions of Belgium, France, and Germany. He also realized that Catholicism was thriving in the supposedly hostile climate of the democratic and Protestant United States. In 1891 his famous encyclical *Rerum Novarum* ("Concerning New Things"), rejecting Marxian doctrines of class warfare, preached the interdependence of capital and labor and sought to impress on employers the need for better wages and better relations with their workers. In the twentieth century the teachings of Leo XIII helped to guide the Catholic labor unions and the Christian Democratic parties in France, Italy, Germany, and other European states.

Protestant Thought. The Protestant churches for the most part increased their membership by missionary activity all over the world. They too were challenged by modernist rejections of the supernatural and by reformist groups seeking to spread some form of "social gospel." The Church of England—in America, the Protestant Episcopal Church—is in itself a fine example of the spectrum of beliefs and attitudes compatible in the nineteenth century with membership in a single religious body. On what may be called its Right wing was the High Church, much strengthened by the Oxford Movement, which began in the 1820's among a small group at Oxford University led by men like J. H. Newman (who in 1845 was converted to the Roman Catholic Church), John Keble, and Edward Pusey. The Oxford Movement emphasized ritual, traditional Christian articles of faith, and hierarchical authority in church government; but it was also deeply imbued with the evangelical and proselytizing spirit. In the Center of the Church of England were conventional Protestants, untouched by any theological fundamentalism, but distrustful of Rome. On the Left wing there were somewhat more disparate groups, such as the Broad Church liberal theologians whose *Essays and Reviews* by 1860 brought on controversy and trials for heresy because of their appeal to the "higher criticism," that is, scholarly historical studies of the Bible as a historical document. Some theologians were so "broad" as to be practically Unitarians, or even deists denying the Trinity; some managed to combine theological conservatism—High Church doctrines—with great political and economic radicalism.

No new Protestant sect as numerous and important as the Methodist or Pietist groups of the eighteenth century (*see* Chapter 9) came out of the nineteenth century. Yet the century did produce two new major sects, both of American origin—the Church of Jesus Christ of Latter-Day Saints founded by Joseph Smith in 1830 and popularly known as the Mormon Church, and the Christian Scientists, founded by Mary Baker Eddy, whose *Science and Health* appeared in 1875. On the fringes of Christian belief, and sometimes quite outside it, there appeared in this many-minded century all sorts of apocalyptic cults, theosophies, spiritualisms, eclectic faiths borrowed from Asian and other sources. In upstate New York, in a region from which came Joseph Smith and which is known as the "burnt-over district" from its historical susceptibility to waves of religious revivalism, the Millerites assembled in 1843 clad in white robes to witness the end of the world.

The overriding fact is, then, that the nineteenth century was for Christianity a century of growth and expansion. In spite of all the attacks the Enlightenment had made on it, and in spite of the brief avowed attempt of the Jacobins at the height of the French Revolution to extirpate it as "superstitious fanaticism," millions of faithful worshippers shared Christian beliefs and consolations. But the "seamless web" of Christianity was not restored, and to outsiders it seemed as though there was no single Christianity but only many Christianities.

The Secularists. These outsiders within the Western world were for the most part adherents of views first spread widely in the eighteenth-century Enlightenment. While many of them denied that they had any kind of religion, they all had views about the place of man in the universe and about how he should behave here on earth. These children of the Enlightenment were at least as divided as the Christians were. Among them were atheists, agnostics, materialists, positivists, secularists, rationalists, deists, ethical culturalists, anticlericals, believers in the "religion of science," Marxists, and "humanists" (this last referring not to Renaissance humanism but to those who hold that "man makes himself" and that there is no God except—perhaps—man).

Closest to formal Christianity no doubt are the Unitarians, who in this country are rather sharply divided as to whether they are or are not Christians. Most obviously a religious "sect," in the somewhat scornful sense of the word, were the Comtean positivists, followers of the Frenchman Auguste Comte (to whom we shall turn in a moment) who worked out an elaborate set of forms of worship, including a calendar of lay saints, in what may be not unfairly described as a secularist parody of Christianity. These Comtean positivists toward the end of the century had numerous "churches" in western Europe and a few in the United States; but they have declined greatly in the twentieth century. Though the faithful Marxists are usually infuriated by the comparison, of all nineteenth-century secularist faiths Marxism has developed most clearly into an organized, dogmatic, intolerant, and proselytizing group of "true believers."

All told, the number of those who rejected Christianity in the West was considerable. As "anticlericals" they were politically active, especially in "Latin" countries like France, Italy, Spain, and some of the Central and South American states. In politics they were generally somewhat Left of center, and as the century wore on, were often, but by no means always, socialists. Even in the English-speaking countries the atheists or agnostics, though they had little influence on politics, were an active and articulate minority, represented by such men as the Englishman Charles Bradlaugh and the American Robert Ingersoll, the latter a very popular orator in the old rotund style.

Most of these freethinkers made full use of what they found in Darwin in their attacks on conventional Christianity. And Christians themselves were very often greatly disturbed by the challenge they found in Darwin's work. The Enlightenment of the eighteenth century had made familiar the work of geologists and paleontologists as well as that of historians who used their newly developed methods of criticism on the "stories" of the Bible; but Darwin's *Origin of Species* cut far deeper than any previous work into the old Christian belief in the separate creation and continued fixity of species. Darwin's later writings not only put the whole story of the flood and Noah's ark in doubt, it suggested man's evolutionary origin in the primate line of the great apes. Especially among the Protestants, there was strong resistance, not all fundamentalist, to the whole concept of man as an animal with an evolutionary background. Only gradually did most Christians arrive at some sort of compromise with theories of organic evolution. Some accepted Darwinian and other theories as scientific hypotheses which have no claim to be *true* in a theological sense; others held to the concept that man's animal nature is fully subject to evolution, while his soul is above and beyond such a process.

PHILOSOPHY

Idealism and Materialism. In formal philosophy the nineteenth century ranged over the full spectrum from "tough-minded" materialism to "tender-minded" idealism. This was the great century for the prestige of German idealism, represented by a long line of thinkers from Kant through Fichte and Schelling on to Hegel (1770–1831), in whom it culminated. Hegel attempted to reconcile philosophic idealism, which traditionally set up an absolute beyond change—change as our senses apprehend it—with the great nineteenth-century belief in historical change, growth, and development. Hegel saw an eternal mind or spirit (*Geist*) as developing throughout the ages by a process called the *dialectic*. Starting as a *thesis*, the despotism of the early Oriental, Mesopotamian, and Egyptian empires, for example, the world-spirit then sets up an *antithesis*, the almost anarchic individual freedom of ancient democratic Athens. Out of the opposition and interplay of these comes finally a *synthesis*, a higher stage which reconciles the two, modern Germanic disciplined freedom. Hegel saw this thesis–antithesis–synthesis everywhere, even in such natural processes as those the mineralogist studies. Since it is essentially mind, an absolute, that moves, Hegel managed to persuade himself that change (development) is the *real* form of permanence.

In the second half of the nineteenth century a school of British philosophers, among them T. H. Green, Bernard Bosanquet, and F. H. Bradley, much influenced by the Germans, asserted the reality of the absolute against the more traditional British empiricism. Bradley in his *Appearance and Reality* (1893) went about as far as any idealist in asserting the reality of permanence and the unreality of what our sense-experience tells us is impermanent. Yet the influence of the school was on the whole toward a simpler *ethical* idealism of high standards of duty. In the United States German idealism inspired the New England transcendentalists and persisted at the end of the century in the Harvard professor Josiah Royce (1855–1916). It has not been a major thread in twentieth-century philosophy, save in that of the Italian Benedetto Croce (1866–1952).

In English-speaking countries, certainly, formal philosophy—metaphysics, epistemology, logic, ethics, and other branches—carried on firmly the tough-minded or empirical tradition. If we lump together the nineteenth-century idealists as asserting that reality is what the mind, understood with overtones of "soul," even "faith," spins out of itself, then with no less unfairness we may lump together nineteenth-century empiricists and materialists as asserting that reality is what the mind, understood with overtones of "scientific reasoning," and "induction," builds out of the varied facts of sense-experience. John Stuart Mill, to whom we return later in this chapter, was so convinced of the reality of what his senses found and his logic organized in this world that he once remarked that even if he had impeccable evidence of the *fact* of spiritualist communication with the dead (or more generally, what we now call "extrasensory perception") he could not bring himself to believe it.

The French philosopher Auguste Comte (1798–1857) produced a science-based triad which in terms of the philosophy of history corresponds with Hegel's triad of thesis–antithesis–synthesis. Starting with primitive cultures which explained phenomena *theologically* in terms of supernatural entities, men, he held, go on to explain phenomena *metaphysically*, in terms of abstract terms like justice, power, and so on, and finally achieve the stage of explaining phenomena *scientifically*, or, in Comte's term, *positively*. Comte found the positivist breakthrough in early modern physics and astronomy, and held that he himself was the first to apply truly positivist methods to the study of human relations, a study for which he invented the term "sociology." But he found even in Western culture regrettable survivals of both earlier stages. Comte's "stadial" theory was also an ordering of the formal sciences according to their coming of age, so to speak, from astronomy and physics, with their origins in the Greco-Roman world and even earlier, through the earth sciences, anthropology, psychology, and finally sociology, which, he held, he himself had begun.

In the English-speaking world the influence of Herbert Spencer (1820–1903) greatly surpassed that of Comte. Spencer was a kind of secular Aquinas who wrote in many volumes what amounted to a nineteenth-century nontheological *Summa*. He referred to God as the Unknowable; only what science arrives at was definitely to him the Knowable.

Voluntarism and Eclecticism. The simple dualism of philosophic idealism and philosophic empiricism or positivism by no means encompasses the full variety of nineteenth-century philosophy. One further important trend was marked by the treatise of the German philosopher Schopenhauer, *The World as Will and Idea* (1818), which advanced the thesis that reality is neither spiritual nor material, but a blind driving force in men and in the universe which he called "will." There were many philosophies of voluntarism basing themselves on will, including such philosophically vague and disreputable ones as racist and imperialist theories. Implicit in many of these philosophies of the will is the concept of "truth" as what works, or as "myth" that consoles, or as the "superman's" transvaluation of values far beyond vulgar common sense and even more vulgar science. This strain of nineteenth-century thought was represented not only by Schopenhauer but also by Nietzsche (1844–1900) and by the strange and isolated figure of the Danish philosopher Sören Kierkegaard (1813–1855). In these men may be found some of the beginnings of such twentieth-century currents of thought as pragmatism, existentialism, and aspects of what is sometimes called anti-intellectualism.

Some nineteenth-century thinkers even attempted to put all possible philosophies together in a grand eclecticism. Of these the most striking example is the Frenchman Victor Cousin (1792–1857), an important figure in the history of French education. Cousin thought there was *some* truth in *all* systems of philosophy, but he hardly succeeded in picking out these pieces of truth and putting them together again.

In summary, there runs through almost all of nineteenth-century religious and philosophical thought a preoccupation with growth and development, in fact with history in the broadest sense. Where the eighteenth century tended to see the universe in Newtonian terms of repetitive and therefore in a sense illusory movement, the nineteenth tended to see the universe in Darwinian terms of evolutionary movement in a specific direction. A striking instance is one of J. H. Newman's major works, the *Development of Christian Doctrine* (1845), written while he was convincing himself of the necessity of becoming a Roman Catholic. In spite of the long Christian tradition that the true Church is above change, Newman insists that at least here on earth the Church *must* change. "In a higher world," he wrote, "it is otherwise, but here below to live is to change, and to be perfect is to have changed often."

III. Man, the State, and Society

Nineteenth-century Western thought on politics in the wide sense of the word was as varied as thought on religion and formal philosophy. It ranged from defense of thoroughly absolute monarchy to defense of philosophical anarchism, and of everything in between; it may be classified from Right to Left into conservative, liberal, radical, and socialist strands. We must, however, note that the meaning of each of these terms has varied not only with nationality but also with the passage of time. "Liberal," for example, implies in the United States today an attitude far more critical of things-as-they-are than in England; and in England itself "liberal" in 1850 implied a distrust of government interference in economic life, yet by 1900 had come to imply acceptance of such activities of the "welfare state" as compulsory social security, the regulation of children's and women's labor, and the hours of labor in general.

CONSERVATISM

The best test for conservatism in the nineteenth century was a dislike for the "principles of 1776 and 1789" or, broadly and loosely put, for *democracy*, a belief in the need for authority from above and obedience from below, that is, in a stratified society in which each stratum was content with its place in the "pecking order," and an adherence to the established sacramental churches, Roman Catholic, Anglican, and Lutheran. Yet nineteenth-century conservatives were far from holding a single set of principles. The central figure among conservative thinkers was no doubt Burke (*see* Chapter 11), who died just before the century began but whose influence lives on even today. Burke had a deep feeling that orderly civil society is a kind of miracle that keeps naturally wild and sinful human beings reasonably well behaved through the workings of tradition, habit, and respect for the existing order of rank and privilege as sanctioned by "legitimacy." But he also had an English distrust of rigid principles in political life, an empiricist's sense of the facts of life. He would therefore accept reform, even in a democratic direction, but only slow change, voted constitutionally and accepted by all classes.

In England, the Burkean tradition was developed by the Young England movement of the 1840's and was well represented by Disraeli, much more than Burke a practical politician but one who indicated a whole political philosophy in two novels, *Coningsby* and *Sybil*. The main point of this very English "Tory democracy" was its insistence that the aristocrats, the men of property, must justify their position and their wealth by using their social and political influence to correct the evils of the Industrial Revolution and see that the working classes get better conditions of life. Much English conservatism therefore in the midcentury backed the welfare state and opposed the laissez-faire principles of the new capitalist manufacturing and business classes.

On the Continent, at least in Catholic countries, the great conservative theorist was Joseph de Maistre (1754–1821), a Savoyard noble and diplomatist exiled by the French Revolution. Maistre and others of his school have been given the derogatory epithet "reactionary." They did indeed "react" against the French Revolution but hardly more vehemently than did Burke. Maistre, like Burke, had the basic conviction that civil society, order, decency are all direct proofs of God's rule in the world, and that those who seek to overturn by violence this divine-natural order are agents of the devil. Maistre's *Concerning the Pope* (1819) is a big treatise in defense of the world's need for an unquestioned authority to settle questions that might lead to division of opinion, quarrels, and rebellions. Among Catholics this book became one of the great supports of the Ultramontane party, which supported papal supremacy and won a great triumph in the 1870 declaration of Papal Infallibility.

In Germany, the influence of Hegel, in his last years, at least, tended to give philosophic support to acceptance of Prussia, an authoritarian and conservative state, as the culminating achievement of a long political process. In England, the general tendency of the High Church Oxford Movement was toward acceptance of hierarchical authority in church and state, and a rejection of optimistic liberalism. Indeed, a passage from Newman (*Apologia pro vita sua*) attacking liberalism is a very neat summary, put negatively though is is, of what the conservative felt about nineteenth-century culture.

By Liberalism I mean false liberty of thought, or the exercise of thought upon matters, in which, from the constitution of the human mind, thought cannot be brought to any successful issue, and therefore is out of place. . . . [Liberalism holds that] no revealed doctrines or precepts may reasonably stand in the way of scientific conclusions. Therefore, *e.g.*, Political Economy may reverse our Lord's declarations about poverty and riches, or a system of Ethics may teach that the highest condition of body is ordinarily essential to the highest state of mind . . . [that] there is a right of Private Judgment: that is, there is no existing authority on earth competent to interfere with the liberty of individuals in reasoning and judging for themselves about the Bible and its contents, as they severally please. Therefore, *e.g.*, religious establishments requiring subscription are Anti-christian. . . . [Liberalism holds that] there is no such thing as a national or state conscience . . . [that] utility and expedience are the measure of political duty . . . [that] the Civil Power may dispose of Church property without sacrilege . . . [that] the people are the legitimate source of power . . . [that] virtue is the child of knowledge, and vice of ignorance. Therefore, *e.g.*, education, periodical literature, railroad travelling, ventilation, drainage, and the arts of life, when fully carried out, serve to make a population moral and happy.

In the United States, at least until the "New Conservatism" of the mid-twentieth century, political thought was rarely out-and-out conservative. There were a good many practical conservatives, but they had to talk the language of the democratic Enlightenment. One of them, Alexander Hamilton, is said to have referred privately to "the people, that great beast"; but it is not certain that he was so indiscreet even in private, and this remark may have been foisted on him by his opponents. There were conservative strains in some of the work of John Adams, and John C. Calhoun was a very able conservative philosopher of states' rights as well as a practical politician.

LIBERALISM

The nineteenth-century liberal may perhaps best be described as somewhat hesitantly, and with many qualifications, accepting the new democratic society of universal suffrage, individual liberties, civil rights, and untrammeled "pursuit of happiness." We may chose two figures, the British John Stuart Mill and the French Alexis de Tocqueville, as samples of the central line of liberalism in the nineteenth century. In the famous essay *On Liberty* (1859—the same year in which Darwin's *Origin of Species* appeared), it is Mill's basic principle that the individual has a *right* to do anything that does not harm any other individual, or, put another way, that does not infringe on any other individual's right to do what *he* wants. A neat formula, but one that gave Mill a great deal of trouble when he tried to distinguish in practice between purely self-regarding acts and acts which affected others. His trouble was increased by the fact that he was a kindly and slightly puritanical soul who did not like the things many of his countrymen did with their liberty. Still, he did his best to live up to his principles; though he disliked strong drink, he opposed governmental prohibition of the liquor trade in the Maine law of 1853, and sadly remarked that there was nothing much to be done about fornication, which he did not like either. Mill's basic intellectual defense of individual liberty was characteristic of the spirit of the age: variation is essential to progress, which of course is itself essential; in society new ideas, which are the essential form of variation in human societies, originate only in *individual* minds; no committee, no formal or informal *group* of men, ever had a new idea; the only way to tell whether a new idea will promote progress is to give its holders a chance to express it and put it to practice; even though most new ideas are unprofitable, no one can know in advance that they will so be; even if only a single idea in thirty is good, we have to try all of them out.

Tocqueville was a nobleman from old but not very rich or distinguished Norman stock. His background and perhaps his temperament inclined him to conservatism, but his mind and his gifts of observation kept him aware that the movement toward democracy in the nineteenth century could not be effectively suppressed. A trip to the United States in the 1830's resulted in the classic two-volume *Democracy in America*. Tocqueville's attitude toward the United States was ambivalent, typical enough of a mid-nineteenth-century liberal. He admired American energies, material strength, and ability to make popular government work; he disliked American brashness, self-assertiveness, and devotion to material success and to the practical. At bottom, he liked what he felt was the American drive toward individual liberty and disliked what he felt was the even stronger drive to equality, conformity, and the "tyranny of the majority." This feeling—it is more than a mere opinion—that democracy is unable to keep in balance the demands of the logically conflicting ideals of liberty and equality, that it must sacrifice individual liberty for the sake of group equality, remains central to nineteenth-century liberal thought. This feeling today tends to earn for those who share it the label "conservative."

RADICALISM

On the Left, the nineteenth-century radicals were heirs of the moderate Jacobins of the French Revolution. Their platform was essentially that of the British Chartists (*see* Chapter 12), an insistence on thoroughgoing political democracy based on equal electoral districts, rotation in office, and universal manhood suffrage (woman suffrage was not an important mid-nineteenth-century demand, though occasional thinkers like John Stuart Mill asserted it). The radicals, however, still distrusted the state and wished to limit its powers over the lives of individual citizens. They tended to believe that full *political* democracy once attained would mean equality of education and opportunity, that in free and open competition great differences of wealth and social prestige would disappear. No great political thinker of the nineteenth century completely represents this radical current, but an extreme example is the English atheist Charles Bradlaugh, and a good moderate example is the parliamentary leader Richard Cobden. With the addition of a strong feeling against trusts and entrenched wealth generally, and an insistence that government step in to limit monopolies and concentrations of wealth, the most characteristic representatives of this political radicalism were the American "populists" of the late nineteenth century. Most of their leaders were working politicians who by no means wrote political philosophy; but one of them, Ignatius Donnelly of Minnesota, wrote a good deal that is still of interest.

MARXISM

Karl Marx (1818–1883), along with his faithful supporter and collaborator Friedrich Engels (1820–1895), produced the fundamental work on which modern socialist and communist movements and societies are based. Much of Marxism is implicit in the brief *Communist Manifesto* issued by Marx and Engels in that revolutionary year, 1848, but the full doctrine depends on the unfinished treatise *Das Kapital* and on more lively controversial writings. We must note that Marxists do not accept as applying to themselves the concept of a faith or religion that we have used above (p. 522), nor will they even settle for philosophical terms; they insist that theirs is the sole "objective" *science* of society; all other forms of political thought they insist are either "subjective" and unreal or deliberate attempts to hold the masses in subjection by drugging them with nice words.

For Marx, Hegel's dialectic of thesis–antithesis–synthesis is a basic fact of history. But Marx's form of this historical determinism is *dialectical materialism*. For the "unreal" spirit (*Geist*) of Hegel's idealist dialectic, Marx substitutes the "real" *means of production*, the material conditions under which men live and work. The means of production determine the class structure of any society. There has always been in all societies a *class struggle*, between a thesis or possessing class and an antithesis or oppressed class. In the nineteenth century this struggle was between the thesis class or *bourgeoisie* (capitalists) and the antithesis class or *proletariat* (workers). Capitalist modes of production determine that members of the proletariat should own nothing and receive as wages only enough to keep them alive; the *surplus value* produced by the proletariat is *expropriated* by the capitalist masters, who plow part of the surplus back into further production to enrich themselves.

Karl Marx.

But since the great mass of laborers is kept poor and cannot buy enough of these produced goods, capitalist society is therefore subject to periodical overproduction and depression. During each depression, the weaker capitalists fail and join the ranks of the proletariat, while the stronger ones recover. The rich thus get richer and fewer, the proletariat poorer and more numerous. In a final economic crisis, the workers in a violent revolution will seize power, and initiate the *dictatorship of the proletariat*. After the necessary adjustments have been made by this dictatorship, notably the *expropriation of the expropriators*, that is, the taking over of the private property of the capitalists by the new government, the *state will wither away* and the *classless society* will be achieved. Since the capitalist–proletariat class struggle is the last of the long series that began in prehistory, the perfect synthesis ends the dialectical process of class conflict—indeed, will apparently end history as it has been, a record of conflict and suffering.

Marxism soon obtained a great hold among many workers and upper-class reformers. Marx could coin phrases of great propaganda value, such as "expropriation of the expropriators" and "surplus value"; he could claim for his system the great prestige of science and link it with the concept of inevitable, historically determined progress. The convert to Marxism had a cause for which to fight, a goal, an explanation of the way things are on this planet, one that carried conviction to many for whom Christianity was inadequate. Finally, Marx himself and his disciples built up an organization for this new cause, a means of bringing the faithful together for thought and action. In 1864 the International Workingmen's Association, usually called the First International, was founded in London. Socialist parties, at first mere splinter parties, began to be founded in western Europe. The years before 1870 were, however, only beginnings, and the story of socialism as a political force will be developed in a later chapter.

UTOPIAN SOCIALISM

Marx and his followers contemptuously referred to other currents of socialist thought in their time as "utopian," meaning impractical, mere "ideas." Among the "utopian" thinkers were the Frenchman Charles Fourier (1772–1837), the Welshman Robert Owen (1772–1858), and a number of others who believed that small experimental societies living according to specific plans for social and economic organization would prove more successful in producing and distributing goods than existing unplanned societies. Such societies, they held, were not really decently and efficiently organized by the free market and Adam Smith's "invisible hand" (*see* Chapter 9). They also believed that these examples would eventually be followed by everybody, thus achieving socialism without violent revolution. Most of their experimental

Robert Owen's vision of an ideal community in New Harmony, Indiana.

"consociate families," however, such as Brook Farm in Massachusetts, New Harmony in Indiana, Icaria in Illinois, and many others failed to hold together.

Yet the Marxist scorn was unfair, the more so in view of the utopian ideals expressed by Marx and Engels in such terms as "withering away of the state" and "classless society." If we add to the thought of Fourier and Owen the program of the French thinker Saint-Simon (1760–1825), who was more a technocrat, a believer in the rule of experts, than a socialist, we find two closely related ideas of great importance for the future. First, there is the concept of planning, organizing economic activity though without necessarily abolishing all forms of private property, and certainly without a violent revolution. And second, there is the concept of the role to be played in such planning by the trained technician, by the manager or, more pretentiously, the "social engineer."

ANARCHISM

Most of the recipes for socialism contained at least a dash of anarchism, the belief that the best government is no government at all; witness the withering-away of the state promised by the Marxists and the utopians' mistrust of big government. Some anarchists, stressing the destruction of existing states by terror, inspired a round of political assassinations at the turn of the century—the French President Carnot in 1894, King Humbert of Italy in 1900, and the American President McKinley in 1901. Meantime, a more positive influence on the proletarian movement was exerted by anarchist personalities and thinkers. The most famous personality was Bakunin (1814–1876), who helped to shape the Russian revolutionary movement (*see* Chapter 14) and achieved international prominence by his flamboyant participation in the First International. Another Russian, Prince Peter Kropotkin (1842–1921), made the most complete statement of anarchist theory in his book *Mutual Aid: A Factor in Evolution* (1902—note the Darwinian overtones of the title).

"Mutualism" was also a central concept in the projects of the French publicist Proudhon (1809–1865). "What is property?" Proudhon asked in a famous pamphlet of 1840; "property is theft." Not all property was theft, however, not the fruits of labor but only the unearned income from investments. Of all the forms of unearned income, the worst, in Proudhon's view, was the "leprosy of interest," and the most evil of capitalists was the money-lender. In his ideal society, therefore, a "People's Bank" would lend to all without charging interest, affording every man the credit to establish his own productive enterprise. Economically, society would become a federation of mutual associations of these individual producers in agriculture and industry, not unlike the producers' farm cooperatives of the present day; politically, it would also take the form of "federalism," replacing the centralized state with institutions resembling those of the loose Swiss confederation of cantons.

Proudhon's doctrines exerted a strong appeal in France, with its devotion to individualism, with its legacy of decentralizing "federalist" teachings from the Girondist current in the great Revolution, and with its tens of thousands of small businessmen who found it difficult to obtain credit from the private bankers denounced by Proudhon and who faced displacement down the social ladder from the lower middle class to the proletariat. Proudhon's attacks

Animals

Egyptian figure of a hippopotamus. XII Dynasty, from Meir, the Tomb of Senbi. Faience.
The Metropolitan Museum of Art, gift of Edward S. Harkness, 1917.

Cave painting from Lascaux, c. 12,000 B.C. Three Lions.

The waters of the Nile. Pompeian mosaic.
National Museum, Naples.
European Art Color,
Peter Adelberg, N.Y.C.

Peacock chasing dove. Decorative detail of a mosaic in San Vitale, Ravenna, sixth century.
Three Lions.

Eucharistic dove. Champlevé enamel, copper-gilt. Thirteenth century.
The Metropolitan Museum of Art, The Cloisters Collection, Purchase, 1947.

Albrecht Dürer (1471-1528), "The Hare."
Albertina Museum, Vienna. Three Lions.

William Baziotes, "Dragon," 1950. The Metropolitan Museum of Art, Arthur H. Hearn Fund, 1950.

"Spring Morning at the Palace of the Han Emperors." Sung Dynasty hand scroll, attributed to Chao Po-Chu (active c. 1130-1160).
The Metropolitan Museum of Art, Fletcher Fund, 1947. The A. W. Bahr Collection.

The Metropolitan Museum of Art. Bequest of Mrs. H. O. Havemeyer, 1929. The H. O. Havemeyer Collection.

Landscapes

El Greco (1541-1614), "View of Toledo."

The Limbourg Brothers, "November," from *Les Très Riches Heures du Duc de Berry*, 1413-1416.

Musée Condé, Chantilly.
European Art Color,
Peter Adelberg, N.Y.C.

John Constable (1776-1837), "Vale of Dedham."
National Gallery of Scotland, Edinburgh. European Art Color, Peter Adelberg, N.Y.C.

Paul Cézanne,
"Mont Sainte Victoire,"
1904-1906.
Philadelphia Museum of Art,
George W. Elkins Collection.

Ivan Rabuzin, "Twin
Villages in Summertime."
Private Collection in Yugoslavia.
Three Lions.

The Fantastic

Hieronymus Bosch, "The Garden of Delights," c. 1500. Detail from right panel.

The Prado, Madrid.
European Art Color,
Peter Adelberg, N.Y.C.

Pieter Brueghel the Elder (1520?-1569), "The Triumph of Death." Detail.
The Prado, Madrid. European Art Color, Peter Adelberg, N.Y.C.

Francisco Goya (1746-1828), "Fantastic Vision."
The Prado, Madrid. European Art Color, Peter Adelberg, N.Y.C.

Salvador Dali (1904-   ), "The Burning Giraffe." Kunstmuseum, Basel. European Art Color, Peter Adelberg, N.Y.C.

Calligraphy

Jacob and his people cross the ford of Jabbok; Jacob receives from a man of God the name 'Israel.' Sixth century Syrian manuscript of the Book of Genesis.
National Library, Vienna. European Art Color, Peter Adelberg, N.Y.C.

Page from the Book of Kells. Ninth century.
Trinity College, Dublin. Three Lions.

"The Poet Taira-no-Kanemori." Kamakura Period (thirteenth century) hanging scroll.
Cleveland Museum of Art, the John L. Severance Fund. European Art Color, Peter Adelberg, N.Y.C.

"The Combat of Sohrab and Rustem." Persian miniature by an unknown artist. From *Shah-nama* by Firdausi, dated 1605-1608.
The Metropolitan Museum of Art.

Wooden vessel with Sanskrit inscription. Eleventh century.
Collection: John G. Powers.
European Art Color,
Peter Adelberg, N.Y.C.

The Nude

Titian (1477-1576), "Venus and the Organ Grinder." Gemäldegalerie, Dahlem, Berlin. Three Lions.

Diego Velázquez (1599-1660), "The Toilet of Venus ('The Rokeby Venus')." National Gallery, London. Three Lions.

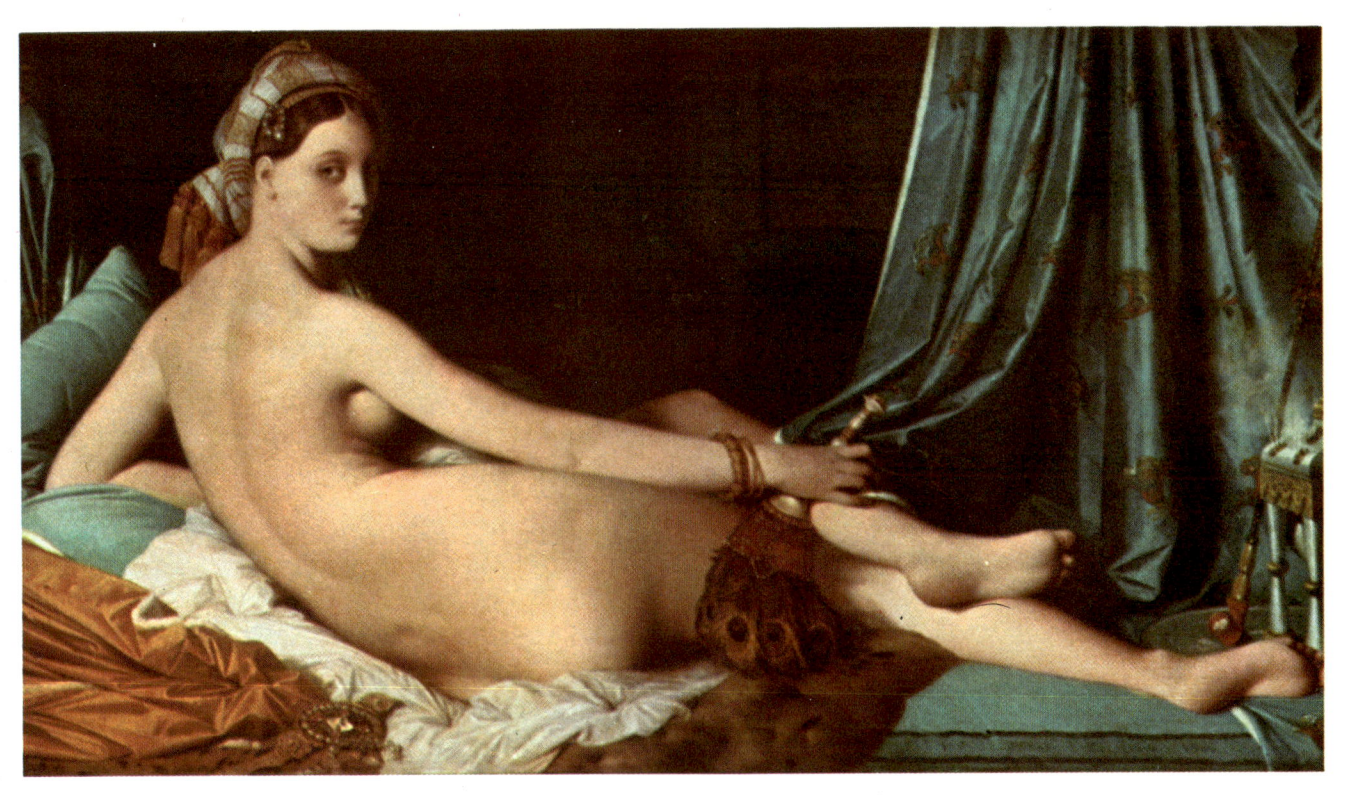

J. A. D. Ingres, "Odalisque," 1814. The Louvre, Paris. European Art Color, Peter Adelberg, N.Y.C.

Henri Matisse (1869-1954), "Reclining Nude."
National Museum of Fine Arts, Stockholm. European Art Color, Peter Adelberg, N.Y.C.

Pablo Picasso, "Nude Woman under a Pine Tree," 1959.
L. Leiris, Paris. Three Lions.

Tom Wesselmann, "Great American Nude #48," 1963. Mixed media, 81 x 106".
Collection: Frederick Weisman, Los Angeles. Photo courtesy Sidney Janis Gallery, N.Y.C.

on the state and his mistrust of politics contributed to the formation of the cluster of ideas known as *anarcho-syndicalism* (from the French word *syndicat*, meaning an economic grouping, particularly a trade union). Rejecting political parties, even Marxist ones, and accepting the terrorist as well as the mutualist strain in anarchism, the anarcho-syndicalists preached direct action by the workers. One fine day a spontaneous general strike would free labor from the yoke of capitalism; workers should prepare for it by forming unions and committing acts of anticapitalist sabotage. These ideas were forcefully expressed in *Reflections on Violence*, published early in the twentieth century by the Frenchman Georges Sorel, and they contributed to the institutions of Italian fascism—or so Mussolini claimed.

NATIONALISM

Cutting across such purely political distinctions as that between Left and Right was a cluster of ideas, or rather two related clusters—nationalism and Social Darwinism. As always in political and social life, both clusters were not mere abstract ideas but part of a larger complex of forces involving human emotions, sentiments, "drives." Nationalism took many forms and adapted itself to many differing material and environmental conditions. It is therefore hard to define neatly, for hardly any simple concrete element is a test of nationality. A common language, for instance, usually identifies a nation; but Switzerland has four, and has long been a well-knit nation. The United States and Britain have one language, in spite of differences of accent, but they are two quite different nations. We may suggest that if enough people think and feel they are a nation, then they *are* a nation. For the historian, the critical question then becomes whether or not a nation wants to be independent, "sovereign." In the nineteenth century the Irish did want independence, the Welsh and the Scots—save for small, almost "lunatic" minorities—did not. In the nineteenth century, divided Germans wanted to be united into an independent nation: by contrast, eleven southern states in America wanted to secede from *their* union.

The many theoretical justifications of nationalism as an ideal may be separated into a pacific, liberal, often democratic group and a more aggressive, potentially at least totalitarian group. The best example of the first is the work of the Italian Mazzini (1805–1872), an active participant in Risorgimento wars and politics. For Mazzini, the "consciousness of kind" that holds people together in a nation is a sort of absolute, and nations have a "right" to be independent just as the individual has a "right" to his liberty. But just as in liberal theory the free individual is free only as he respects the equal freedom of other individuals, so in Mazzini's theory each nation must respect the right of every other nation to its own national independence. He believed, however, that if all national groups in the West gained their independence, a spontaneous supranational society would arise, a kind of voluntary league of nations, and there would be no more war.

The other, or aggressive, group of justifications is more numerous. Jacobin nationalism, from its very first definition in the work of the Convention, though it set up goals not unlike Mazzini's, held that France was the fountainhead of true nationalism; and that any other national group, once free, would in fact be much like France and even would indeed *like* to be part of France.

The mark of the eighteenth-century Enlightenment and its cosmopolitanism of "Reason and Nature" was on this Jacobin nationalism even under Napoleon, when it was frankly aggressive.

Later nineteenth-century nationalism, notably in Germany, justified in a variety of ways this concept that one given nation is the best, the highest, and thus should see that other nations are like it, or properly submissive to it. Racists advanced the concept of a nation as an organic unity, members of which share a common genetic inheritance (supplemented, but only supplemented, by a cultural inheritance) which makes them superior to other "breeds of men." Romantic doctrines of the uniqueness and goodness of this organic growth of a nation—the nation is the oak that was once an acorn, grown, not made, not planned—and idealist doctrines of the soul or spirit also nourished this very German nationalism. Figures as varied as the philosopher Fichte, the composer Wagner, the French aristocratic theorist Gobineau, and the English Germanophile Houston Stewart Chamberlain all contributed to the German self-image of the successful Empire, 1871–1914.

We have singled out Germany here, partly because racist nationalism in the twentieth century was to reach its extreme under Hitler. But no nation was without its prophets of one brand or another of nationalism. The English too justified their "dominion over palm and pine" as the work of a Chosen People, not so much a race as a people forged by history into an efficient yet kindly imperial folk. Rudyard Kipling (1865–1936) was a writer who exemplified this attitude, as Cecil Rhodes (1853–1902), South African premier, exemplified it in practice. The French were never neglectful of their "*mission civilisatrice*" (civilizing misson), and though they inclined to emphasize this as a rational, eighteenth-century thing, they had their prophets who appealed to what they called the Latin genius for law and order contrasting with the wild, romantic, blond barbarians to their north and east. Charles Maurras (1868–1952) may serve as a specimen here. And Americans had their "Manifest Destiny," not crudely aggressive, perhaps, except toward the Red Indians and the Mexicans, but definitely a national gospel, however much many modern American historians may soft-pedal our own "nationalism." The historian George Bancroft was a good exponent of this democratic American gospel, which leaned more to the French than the German. Yet the United States also had its racists, southerners like George Fitzhugh (1806–1881) and, later, men like Madison Grant (1865–1937), who believed the blond races were best.

SOCIAL DARWINISM

Almost all these last nationalists owed something to the second great cluster of ideas, Social Darwinism, which represented not Darwin's own work as biologist, but the adaptation to human affairs of some of his leading ideas and phrases. The biological "struggle for existence" became for the Social Darwinist free competition among individuals in economic, social, and political activity. The "survival of the fittest" became success and leadership in these fields, and, in particular, the economic. These ideas were a fine buttress for the already existing doctrines of laissez faire and the accompanying limitation on governmental action or community planning.

In strict Social Darwinian theory, the man who cannot earn a living in the competitive world is thereby proved unfit; for the sake of "progress," which is just the political and moral equivalent of "evolution," he should be allowed to starve. "Nature," wrote the English philosopher Herbert Spencer, "is often a little cruel that she may be very kind." The true believers in Social Darwinism, the extremists, argued that to try by public or private intervention to keep the incompetent or unfit alive to reproduce their own kind was an unnatural attempt to interfere with the laws of Nature, and if pursued would result in the physical and mental destruction of the human race. This line of thought also had its positive side—the doctrine of planned mating of the fit, or "eugenics." On the negative side, the bark of these Social Darwinists was worse than their bite; Spencer specifically defended charity toward the poor—and therefore presumably unfit—as an evolutionary asset, "if it was not overdone." The poor should not be left to starve, but neither should they be allowed to enjoy life.

Another variant of Social Darwinism, however, treats the units competing in the struggle for life as racial and national units, not individual. *Within* these competing units, the Social Darwinists maintained, the Darwinian struggle for life is rightly abrogated, and mutual help prevails; but *among* all these units, the struggle goes on as evolution intends. The unit that beats another in war and in economic competition is thereby proud to be the fittest and should use individuals of the defeated unit to serve the successful nation or race. Just as Darwin's ideas, transferred to socioeconomic problems, buttressed nineteenth-century laissez-faire individualism, so his ideas, transferred to international relations, justified war and imperial expansion by the dominant nation or race. These ideas were put clearly and in the eyes of our generation most naïvely by the Englishman Benjamin Kidd (1858–1916) in his *Social Evolution* (1894) and *Control of the Tropics* (1898). In this latter book he asserted that some Englishmen and other Europeans will have to sacrifice themselves by living in the tropics and making these areas productive and healthy for the natives, since it is evident that the natives cannot possibly ever do anything of the sort for themselves.

THE VICTORIAN COMPROMISE

Turning now from specific currents of political thought and from individual thinkers and social critics, we attempt the much more treacherous task of describing the attitudes and the assumptions of the multitude, perhaps even of that unknown person, the "average man." The techniques of our own contemporary polling of public opinion, now only a generation old, may be of great value to later historians. For the nineteenth century, however, we have to use much rougher methods, generalizing roughly from disparate materials from novels, plays, letters, biographies, newspapers, and many other sources.

Discernible in the nineteenth-century West is a kind of uncritical center of thought and feeling on matters of politics, morals, and even world-views. While not limited to England, it may still be fairly described as the "Victorian compromise." Basically it is a compromise between the realities of nineteenth-century life and the high hopes and aims for an almost literal heaven on earth cherished by some thinkers of the Enlightenment The ultimate aim, expressed as the doctrine of Progress, is not given up. Indeed, and in spite of much doubt and pessimism expressed by Victorian intellectuals, there is some justification for the phrase F. S. Marvin used to describe the nineteenth century: the Century of Hope. Yet as compared with a Condorcet, a Thomas Paine, a Jeremy Bentham, the comfortable middle-class Victorian accepted a much slower and more uneven rate of progress as inevitable. He did not conclude, as his forefathers did, that "the poor shall never cease out of the land"; but he accepted existing poverty as irremediable, at least for the time being. He hoped that one day men would not make war and would not quarrel over religious or political ideas; but for the moment he patriotically supported his nation in war and adhered more or less firmly to his own political party, his own religious sect, and his own artistic tastes and standards.

Unless he was definitely to the Left or Right in such matters, he believed that political and social democracy, civil rights, and universal education are all part of Progress, arrived at by "evolution, not revolution," gradually, not catastrophically. He placed great hopes on education to prepare the masses for increasing power. He believed in individual liberty *from* state interference save in matters of enforcing contracts and maintaining public order. He still shared a good deal of the Jeffersonian distrust of "government," and accepted the doctrine that "that government governs best which governs least, and least expensively."

This last statement may make Western society in the nineteenth century sound most unstable, not to say anarchic. Yet on the whole it was stable enough to achieve fundamental technological progress. A clue to this stability lies in the Victorian compromise itself. For however much an educated man in the nineteenth century may have believed in freedom of thought, freedom of business enterprise, and freedom of association, he also believed in a strict moral code ("Victorian morality"), in a foundation of social conformity, and above all, in law and order, in gradual change. Revolutions did occur, as we have seen in Chapter 12. But, like the news that makes the headlines, they were exceptional, not typical. It might be argued that the most lawless and most anarchical society in nineteenth-century Western civilization was the United States. But here too there was a solid backlog of unthinking, tradition-bound conformity. The frontier, free land, and a tradition of merely verbal violence not always translated into the physical were no more than balancing forces against the strong American tendency towards conformity and respectability. We too in the United States were a "Victorian" society.

IV. Arts and Letters

ROMANTIC LITERATURE

The two or three decades after 1815 were the heyday of romanticism in all the arts and in literature. Elfin horns rang through the rocky glens, gypsy laughter sounded in the bushes, ghosts haunted the medieval castles, knighthood was in flower again—all at least in words. Alexander Pope ceased to be considered a poet, and it was held that a dearth of true poetry had existed in English from Milton, if not indeed from Shakespeare, on to the *Lyrical Ballads* of Wordsworth and Coleridge in 1798. The "public" of this romantic generation—readers of Scott, Byron, Shelley, and Keats in England, of Victor Hugo and Alfred de Musset in France, of Goethe, Schiller, and Heine in Germany, of Pushkin and Lermontov in Russia, of Leopardi in Italy, of Espronceda in Spain, of Poe in the United States—were about as strongly aware of the gap between "cultural generations" as any generation has ever been. From these romantics comes the judgment on their eighteenth-century predecessors that still has great influence, the notion of the writers of the Enlightenment as dry rationalists unaware of the depths of the human soul. Wordsworth, as we have seen, even dared to call Voltaire dull!

Actually the romantics owed a great deal to such earlier writers as Jean-Jacques Rousseau and to the whole current of eighteenth-century thought that emphasized the importance of feeling, of humanitarian works, and of the "natural" in contrast to the "artificial." But the romantic protest also had very definite tastes and standards to protest against: most strikingly the overconfident eighteenth-century belief in the capacity of human reason to encompass and neatly order all possible human experience. The romantics, on the other hand, believed that at bottom there are more things in heaven and earth than are dreamt of in *anyone's philosophy*. Shakespeare's Hamlet, with whose words we have just tampered, makes a fine prototype of the romantic temperament.

Some of the romantics edge over into what we should now call the neurotic, into excessive concern with their own by no means wholly private troubles. Lord Byron, in the words of Matthew Arnold, carried through Europe "the pageant of his bleeding heart." Byron set the tone for romantic poetry and for the romantic poet in Europe, defiant of convention, passionate, irresistible to women, subject to fits of deep but interesting depression, also capable of heroic action, siding always with the oppressed, a great but not very happy lover. He had many imitators now forgotten. The great romantic poets of other countries were not imitators, but men of genius subject to the same "spirit of the age."

Most romantics loved the past, which they usually found rather more agreeable than the present, and thus made one of their sharpest breaks with the eighteenth-century *philosophes*. Save for the best days of Greece and the Roman republic, and for some phases of the Renaissance, the *philosophes* had thought ill of the past, and in particular the thousand years they called the "Middle Ages," itself a negative term for the "bad" period between the two "good" ones. The romantics on the contrary found the Middle Ages a period of high adventure, true faith, picturesque variety, and natural outpourings of feeling, free from the artificial constraints of their own age—middle-class dullness and respectability and the rationality of the accountant and the cash register. The historical novel came into prominence, with such writers as Sir Walter Scott in England, Victor Hugo in France, James Fenimore Cooper in the United States, and many more.

These novels were often laid in the Middle Ages —Hugo's *Notre Dame de Paris,* for example—and they were full of the trappings of those good old days. Actual historical writing, based on thorough research, was often touched with this romantic feeling for the past; and even more often written history helped bolster national feeling and the consciousness of the

Lord Byron.

uniqueness of a given nation's experience. Here the many-volumed history of France by Jules Michelet (1798–1874) is representative: it is a long paean in praise of the French people, ardently proud of the great revolution just past, but most eloquent and moving in its pages on Joan of Arc. Nationalist history in the hands of the British historian Macaulay (1800–1859) is not so romantic in form, but its ardent and self-centered patriotism equals that of Michelet. The same is true of the somewhat later history of Germany by Treitschke (1834–1896): reasonably prosaic in form, it is in essence a glorification of a Prussia that never quite was.

Yet romanticism was not always antithetical to mundane life, not just "the desire of the moth for the star"; if much romantic writing does seem of this sort, we must note that its readers were sober, steady, unheroic middle-class Victorians. Just as in high matters of philosophy and religion, the Victorian compromise enabled many to have their cake and eat it, combining revolt with conformity, sinning vicariously with Byron while living a virtuous family life.

THE NOVEL: REALISM AND NATURALISM

In some senses, the romantic movement never died and is still alive and active among us, though not in the forefront of innovation as it was in the 1820's. The romantic temperament would seem to depend in part on the make-up of the individual; romanticists are always being born. Yet the full reign of romanticism as a cultural fashion was brief, for toward the middle of the nineteenth century the novel, perhaps the leading literary genre of the century, went over to "realism" and even "naturalism." To some lovers of the classical ideal, such as the late Irving Babbitt, these literary forms are also to be ticketed as "romantic," in the sense that they repudiate the classical standards of morality and decorum, "those rules of old discover'd, not deviz'd," and seem to concentrate on the exceptionally ugly and dismal side of everyday life. Yet novelists like Dickens or Balzac, though they revel in exaggerations, though they write without "classical" restraint, still try to mirror the life of ordinary men and women around them. There were quiet novelists, especially in England, not without sentiment, but never violent or heaven-storming; Anthony Trollope (1815–1882) wrote dozens of novels about Victorian clergymen, politicians, and country gentlemen, never raising his voice or his style. Another example is William Dean Howells (1837–1920), who sought in *The Rise of Silas Lapham* and other novels to apply realism to the American scene.

With the novel of "naturalism" we come toward the end of the nineteenth century, and toward a more contemporary literature of pessimism and protest. Its great representative is the Frenchman Zola (1840–1902), who wrote a long series of novels centering on a fictional French family, the Rougon–Macquart, during the Second Empire. They were a sorry lot, and had a bad time of it. Zola, much under the influence of the Darwinian science of the time, claimed to be doing for human beings the kind of natural history the biologists were doing for simpler organisms. In their own time, the novels of Zola were bitterly attacked as obscene and recording merely the seamy side of life.

THE FINE ARTS

In painting, the romantics went in for exotic themes, such as Arab horsemen and tiger hunts, and for striking colors. The French painter Delacroix (1798–1863) exemplifies this phase of romantic art, which continued on through the century. In a quieter phase, the romantics painted landscapes usually favoring misty delicacy, or, as with some of the Fontainebleau school of the mid-century, simple peasant life or forest scenes of a green "that never was on sea or land." But very characteristic of the century was an essentially conventional and technically often first-rate draftsmanship, with great attention to detail. The English pre-Raphaelites painted flowers, robes, poor Ophelia in *Hamlet* floating as an elegant corpse in the river where she had drowned herself, all with a minute care reminiscent of the Dutch. Even straightforward classicism in the tradition of David survived with Ingres, who lived until 1867. Only toward the end of the century did "modern" painting begin, with its emancipation from academic draftsmanship and the camera eye. Such emancipation was foreshadowed in romantic art, particularly the work of the Spaniard Francisco Goya, who etched unforgettably the horrors of the Spanish uprising of 1808 against Napoleon.

The nineteenth century was not a great period for sculpture. An age that had mastered the industrial arts so well produced monumental statues aplenty. The most famous for Americans is the Statue of Liberty in New York harbor, the work of the French sculptor Bartholdi, a gift from the Third French Republic to the American Republic. But the statues of statesmen and warriors that adorn public places everywhere in the West are so conventional that we hardly look upon them as artistic creations. The civic use of sculpture can be seen at its best—or least bad—in Paris, in the decoration of the Arc de Triomphe, a memorial to the Grand Army of Napoleon I, in the new Opéra, and many other buildings. Toward the end of the century, Frenchmen like Rodin and Maillol began a break with the formal statuary of their time, simplifying and strengthening the contours of their men and women, treating their subjects with less academic convention and more power.

Architecture is almost a caricature of the variety of nineteenth-century tastes and standards—or its *eclecticism*. Somewhere in the West in these years someone built something in almost every style that had ever been used. Western men built Chinese pagodas, Egyptian pyramids, Greek temples, and, especially in England and America, Gothic universities. In the United States buildings were typed for style: banks went back to Greece and Rome, at least for their facades; churches and universities relied on Gothic; public buildings went in for the Renaissance, duly modified by the reigning taste in the Paris Ecole des Beaux-Arts (School of Fine Arts); private citizens went in for anything that pleased them for their own houses, modified perhaps a bit by the traditions of their region. The European "villa" or the American "mansion" of the newly rich was a big, drafty, high-ceilinged house often vaguely "Gothic" in inspiration. Individual architects adapted historic styles for their own purposes. Thus the American Richardson revived the Romanesque, the early medieval predecessor of Gothic, with its round arches and its solidity, achieving certainly a style of his own.

MUSIC

Although music has no such obvious basis in "Nature" as the camera eye gives the representational arts, it is not misleading to take the established "classical" eighteenth-century tonality and forms, from Bach through Haydn and Mozart, as a kind of norm or "law." Nineteenth-century composers revolted against this classicism and sought to go beyond it. Part of their revolt deserves the label "romantic": the composer sought to move his hearers to tears, to rapture, or to ecstasy, by startling novelties, by overpowering orchestral sonorities. Very popular and typical of the age was "programme music," in which music was deliberately associated with parts of human experience and suggested bird songs, waterfalls, the wind in the pines, a thunderstorm—or even, in the *Sinfonia domestica* (1904) of Richard Strauss, the bedlam of child-rearing and household routines. The old forms—sonata, symphony, concerto—were not abandoned; they were, rather, inflated, burst open.

In the late nineteenth century itself, the supreme achievement in music seemed to be the "music dramas" of Richard Wagner (1813–1883). After the usual struggle of the innovating artist to get a hearing, Wagner by the 1870's had become the musical heir of Beethoven. He set out to make opera the supreme synthesis of the arts, with drama, music, and scenery all fused in one great transcendence of this dull world of ordinary living. He gave up the routine recitative—the relatively undramatic passages "explaining" the action—interlarded with arias in which the performers dropped what action there had been to step forward on the stage and launch into song. Instead, he sought to combine music and action in a realistic and dramatic whole by the device of the *leitmotiv,* a recognizable theme associated with a given character or symbolizing an element in the drama. These themes he wove together for both voices and orchestra into a continuous flow of music. He chose epic subjects such as the four operas of the *Ring of the Nibelungen,* in which he drew on the Teutonic myths, by no means without thoughts of contemporary imperial Teutonic greatness.

"How the public feels after listening for an hour to the music of the future by Wagner": a Daumier caricature.

In our own time, Wagner's popularity has suffered because of his Victorian heaviness, his inordinate longwindedness, and the great noise he makes. Moreover, he has suffered—the musical purist often thinks he has suffered unjustly—from the associations of his life and work with German nationalism, racism, and Nazism. (He was Hitler's favorite composer.) Yet Wagner deserves his fame as a composer. His break with the classical past, his orchestration, his chromaticism, his desperate efforts to *transcend* and to express the inexpressible, or at least the extraordinary, are a landmark in the road that leads from Bach's *Well-Tempered Clavier* to the atonality of music today. Even Claude Debussy (1862–1918), who found Wagner too noisy, too unbridled, too *German,* and who sought to capture in his music a French sense of quiet measure, followed Wagner in revolting against classicism and in experimenting with new forms such as the whole-tone scale.

THE RUSSIAN CONTRIBUTION

Nineteenth-century music, while it owed much to the German composers, was international in source and scope. France contributed not only Debussy but Berlioz, a pioneer in applying "programme music" on the grand orchestral scale. Italy, though losing her former leadership, continued to produce successful composers of opera—Verdi, Donizetti, and others. In Russia, Moussorgsky, Borodin, Rimsky-Korsakov, and others utilized tales and folk music from the national past. From the Russians another major national current entered the broad stream of Western culture, for they were for the first time heard abroad in literature and political thought as well as in music.

The Russian novel, in particular, showed a range and a distinction fully equal to that of any other country. In a long life Tolstoy (1828–1910) wrote a vast amount, not only fiction but after his "spiritual awakening" a great deal on religion and ethics. The *War and Peace* of his maturity, a prose epic of the Napoleonic invasion of Russia, is included in every list of the world's greatest novels. Turgenev (1818–1883) is by contrast a quiet, classical, almost Western novelist, with no obvious Slavic "depths." These depths are, however, sounded by Dostoevsky (1821–1881), whose writing is full of psychological disturbers and disturbances, criminals and madmen, who seem almost our own contemporaries.

In political writing, men like Herzen, Bakunin, Kropotkin, and many others attacked the tsarist regime and set up social ideals ranging from a virtuous native Russian autocracy to complete philosophical and presumably republican anarchy. They were read in Russia in spite of censorship. The novelists, too—even Turgenev—added to this chorus of discontent with existing conditions. Though their ideas, their temperaments, and much else were very different from those of the eighteenth-century *philosophes,* these Russian writers and their followers, the intelligentsia, paved the way for the Russian Revolution of 1917 much as the men of the Enlightenment had paved the way for 1789.

V. The Nineteenth Century Grows into the Twentieth

The last decade of the nineteenth century acquired some time after its close the alliterative label "the naughty Nineties." The plays of Oscar Wilde, the posters of Toulouse-Lautrec, the dance called the can-can, Aubrey Beardsley's drawings in the *Yellow Book,* the much publicized "high-life" among the Four Hundred of New York society, the champagne-in-the-slipper touch all seem mild in our four-letter-word days. Yet to many contemporaries such behavior was a sign that the good days of the Victorian compromise were ending, as indeed they were. The two decades before the War of 1914 were clearly, for the historian of culture, years of transition.

HOPE AND DISILLUSIONMENT

In such fields of thought as theology, philosophy, and the whole broad range of the social or behavioral sciences, the transition is clear. The beginnings of what now prevails and will probably stamp the style of our century in the eyes of future historians can be traced back into the nineteenth century and no doubt even further. As we shall see in Chapter 17, the best blanket terms to describe contemporary thought in these fields are relativism, anti-intellectualism, historicism, and a degree of pessimism. Yet as we shall also see, even today there remains a strong current of belief in progress, in reason, in universal standards of right and wrong, and in traditional standards in the arts.

Symptomatic of the strength of these older attitudes early in the twentieth century was the widespread acceptance in 1914–1918 of the notion that the "Great War" really could be, really would be, the last one. Nowadays we read a bit wistfully and perhaps skeptically about "the war to end war" and "the war to make the world safe for democracy"; we cannot quite believe that this was a war in which the bands played and the soldiers sang such songs as George M. Cohan's "Over There." Yet one who remembers those days knows well that the millions were deeply moved by these ideals; doubt and disillusion came after the war. In a sense, the Eighteenth Amendment to the United States Constitution, prohibiting the manufacture and sale of alcoholic beverages, and the Nineteenth, extending the suffrage to women—both in force by 1920—were the last acts of the Victorian age in America. The Eighteenth Amendment it was hoped would end drunkenness; the Nineteenth would by enfranchising the virtuous sex end political corruption.

Disillusionment over the Great War set in early, first among the sensitive intellectuals who in those days of conscripted mass armies had to fight in it. The war poetry of Siegfried Sassoon, the novel *Le Feu* (*Under Fire,* 1916) by the Frenchman Henri Barbusse, and in the 1920's a spate of novels and plays about the war, such as the German Erich Maria Remarque's *All Quiet on the Western Front* (1929), were all marked by an embittered realism about the horrors of trench warfare. American intellectuals shared this feeling, despite the national reputation for optimism; the title alone of the most successful American war play, Maxwell Anderson's *What Price Glory?* (1924), makes its position clear. But the disillusion was by no means limited to the intellectuals, as the great repudiation of Woodrow Wilson's idealistic war aims, notably the League of Nations, shows well enough.

The decade of the 1920's was rather fascinatingly wicked and certainly most un-Victorian. But the social historian can discern well back in the nineteenth century the first signs of the breaking down of the Victorian compromise, that blend of economic laissez-faire and social individualism balanced by strict moral standards and much social conformity. The very coinage of the phrase "the naughty Nineties" is evidence of such a break with the past; nobody would have thought of calling the 1850's, the decade of Darwin's *The Origin of Species,* Mill's *On Liberty,* of major work by Carlyle, Matthew Arnold, and the other great Victorians "the naughty Fifties."

More seriously, well before the shock of war in 1914 there were signs that the "Century of Hope," the nineteenth century, was ending. Many of the key figures of modern culture—Nietzsche, Freud, Pareto, the pioneers of twentieth-century physics—had already done or at least begun their work. And the dissolution of Victorian taboos—or if you prefer, of Victorian morality—had by no means been limited to the upper classes, nor even to the mixed group that rich and successful Americans were to call "café society." By 1920, for example, George Bernard Shaw (1856–1950), that great satirist of "middle-class morality," had already published his successful plays and prefaces attacking Victorian respectabilities and decencies. In the United States H. L. Mencken was about to call the bourgeoisie the "booboisie," and in Russia the Bolsheviks were at work killing off the middle class: the nineteenth century was over at last.

THE ARTS IN TRANSITION

The degree to which the arts and letters of the twenty years or so before 1914 show a transition to our own twentieth-century culture varies somewhat with the specific art. In painting, the "tyranny" of the camera eye and Renaissance perspective began to break down with the romantics early in the nineteenth century and by 1914 had gone a long way toward modernism. The French impres-

"La Gare St. Lazare," by Claude Monet, 1877.

sionist school, best represented by Claude Monet (1840–1926), secured remarkable effects of light by many tiny separate dabs or points of color. Seen from a proper distance, their paintings did achieve a kind of realism by violating the old rules of smooth painting. Edouard Manet (1832–1883) broke completely with Renaissance ideas of perspective: in his famous "Death of Maximilian" he placed his firing squad almost on top of its victim. Somewhat earlier the Englishman Turner (1775–1851) had anticipated these impressionists with his brilliant seascapes and landscapes. The French painted Paul Cézanne (1839–1906), finding impressionism too fuzzy, too obsessed with light, used blocks or chunks of color—anticipating cubism, but still producing a recognizable real landscape or portrait. The first decades of the twentieth century, with cubism, abstractionism, surrealism, dadaism, launch us fully into "modernistic" painting (*see* Chapter 17).

In sculpture and in architecture also the trend of the late nineteenth century was away from the traditions of Greeks, Romans, and their Renaissance and later admirers, and toward what is sometimes called functionalism. Structural steel made the skyscraper possible, and opened the way toward our current glass-and-stainless-steel epoch. The first skyscraper, the Home Insurance Building in Chicago, dates from 1885. The great bridges—the Brooklyn Bridge, the Firth of Forth Bridge—and other engineering works began to be seen as great aesthetic as well as engineering achievements.

In music too the bonds of tradition, notably the rules of harmony classically established in the eighteenth century, already under attack from Wagner, were further loosened as 1914 approached, until the climax was reached in the first performance of a ballet, *The Rite of Spring*, by the Russian composer Igor Stravinsky (1882–   ) in Paris. So shocked were the conservatives in the audience by the dissonances and sheer noise of some of these dances that they provoked a real riot—for the *avant garde* in the audience was all on the side of Stravinsky.

The novel was on the whole an exception to this rule that already in the 1890's "modernistic" art and letters are clearly beginning. Novelists up to 1914, as represented by such figures as William Dean Howells and Stephen Crane in the United States, Galsworthy, Arnold Bennett, and H. G. Wells in Britain, Anatole France and Maurice Barrès in France, Blasco Ibañes in Spain, although some of them do perhaps achieve a tougher and gloomier "realism" than their predecessors, do not innovate in matters of form. The same is true of the drama. Ibsen and Shaw will almost certainly go down as great dramatists, as will perhaps Eugene O'Neill, but they were not great innovators in dramatic form or structure. One has to wait until the Joyces, the Robbe-Grillets, and Pinters, and their peers for the thoroughgoing "modernists" in the novel and the play.

In poetry the transition to the modern is earlier and clearer than in the novel. Already in the nineteenth century the French Parnassians and even more the Symbolists, of whom Stéphane Mallarmé (1842–1898) is best known, were writing difficult, subtle verse far removed from what the ordinary Frenchman understood by poetry. In England the Jesuit Gerard Manley Hopkins (1844–1889) with his "sprung rhythm" and in the United States Emily Dickinson (1830–1886), Imagists and writers of "free verse" like Amy Lowell (1874–1925), and the poets of the "Chicago school"—Edgar Lee Masters (1879–1950) of *Spoon River Anthology* fame and Carl Sandburg (1878–1967)—can all be seen as in some senses forerunners of contemporary poetry. Yet few even of these wrote really esoteric poetry, and between 1890 and 1914 there was a great deal of very popular poetry, readily "understooded of the people," especially in late Victorian and Edwardian England. Rudyard Kipling (1865–1936) was no doubt too popular for the highbrows, who found "Mandalay" and "Gunga Din" on the vulgar side; but even the highbrows then could enjoy poets like A. E. Housman (1859–1936) and Rupert Brooke (1887–1915), nowadays by no means in favor.

To sum up: There is in the last years of the nineteenth and the first of the twentieth century a divide, a watershed, or, to use a current term, a generation gap, between the Victorians and their twentieth-century successors. For the political historian and in a sense for the historian of ideas the outbreak of the "Great War" in 1914 can pinpoint the change. But the historian of our Western culture has to insist that no one event marks a transition from one culture generation to another; such a transition takes at least several decades. And in a culture so complex, pluralistic, multanimous as ours, in which so little seems to disappear entirely, there remains always something of the past. There are Victorians with us still. There are many who still prefer A. E. Housman,

>   Many a rose-lipt maiden
>   And many a lightfoot lad*

to T. S. Eliot,

>   This is the way the world ends
>   Not with a bang but a whimper.†

* *A Shropshire Lad,* liv.
† *The Hollow Men.*

Fifth Avenue, looking north from 65th Street, 1898.

READING SUGGESTIONS (asterisk indicates paperbound edition)

General Accounts

E. J. Hobsbawm, *The Age of Revolution, 1789–1848* (*Mentor). Rapid survey stressing the effects of economic changes.

R. C. Binkley, *Realism and Nationalism, 1851–1871*, and C. J. H. Hayes, *A Generation of Materialism, 1871–1900* (*Torchbooks). Stimulating volumes in the Rise of Modern Europe series, with considerable stress on scientific and intellectual history.

Economics

The Cambridge Economic History of Europe, Vol. VI (Cambridge University, 1965). Recent scholarly analysis of the Industrial Revolution and its impact.

A. Birnie, *Economic History of Europe, 1760–1939* (*Dover). Useful survey.

T. S. Ashton, *The Industrial Revolution, 1760–1830* (*Galaxy). Lucid introduction, centered on Britain.

Phyllis Deane, *The First Industrial Revolution* (*Cambridge). Up-to-date analysis of developments down to 1850.

A. Toynbee, *The Industrial Revolution* (*Beacon). Pioneering study, first published nearly a century ago, and influenced by Christian socialism.

L. Mumford, *Technics and Civilization* (*Harbinger). First published in the 1930's and still very suggestive, though its point of view is outmoded.

W. W. Rostow, *The Process of Economic Growth* (*Norton). Much-cited analysis, responsible for adding the term "take-off stage" to the economic vocabulary.

J. Clapham, *An Economic History of Modern Britain*, 3 vols., rev. ed. (Cambridge University, 1930–1938). Major scholarly study of the nineteenth-century "workshop of the world."

———, *Economic Development of France and Germany, 1815–1914* (*Cambridge). Written almost half a century ago, but still very much worth reading.

W. O. Henderson, *The Industrial Revolution in Europe, 1815–1914* (*Quadrangle). Recent survey, stressing France, Germany, and Russia.

A. L. Dunham, *The Industrial Revolution in France, 1815–1848* (Exposition, 1955). Scholarly monograph.

Science and Thought

C. Brinton, *The Shaping of Modern Thought* (*Spectrum). Brief survey.

F. S. Marvin, *The Century of Hope*, 2nd. ed. (Oxford, 1927). A bird's-eye view of nineteenth-century cultural history, now rather dated.

Morse Peckham, *Beyond Tragic Vision: The Quest for Identity in the Nineteenth Century* (Braziller, 1962). Recent psychological treatment, in sharp contrast with the preceding title.

J. Barzun, *Darwin, Marx, Wagner* (*Anchor). The search for common denominators linking three major figures.

C. Darwin, *The Voyage of H.M.S. "Beagle" round the World* (*Anchor) and *On the Origin of Species by Natural Selection* (*several editions). The two works central to an understanding of Darwin's theories.

C. J. Singer, *A Short History of Scientific Ideas to 1900* (*Oxford). Useful introduction.

A. N. Whitehead, *Science and the Modern World* (*Free Press). An influential critique of the implications of modern science.

P. B. Sears, *Charles Darwin* (Scribner, 1950). Helpful introduction to the man and his thought.

H. Spencer, *The Man versus the State*, A. J. Nock, ed. (Caxton, 1940). Representative work by a thoroughgoing Social Darwinist.

R. Hofstadter, *Social Darwinism in American Thought* (*Beacon). Interesting study of the impact of evolutionary ideas.

G. D. Charlton, *Secular Religions in France, 1815–1870* (Oxford, 1963). A scholarly survey of substitutes for conventional religion.

W. D. Bagehot, *Physics and Politics* (*Beacon). "Biology & Politics" would have been a better title for this early and provocative application of Darwinism to the political realm.

J. Bowle, *Politics and Opinion in the*

Nineteenth Century (*Oxford). An introductory survey of varying ideologies.

C. Brinton, *English Political Thought in the Nineteenth Century* (*Torchbooks). Essays on Bentham, Mill, Owen and others.

E. Halévy, *The Growth of Philosophic Radicalism* (*Beacon). Standard study of Bentham and the Utilitarians.

J. C. Schumpeter, *Capitalism, Socialism, and Democracy* (*Torchbooks). Thoughtful survey extending down to the mid-twentieth century.

E. Wilson, *To the Finland Station* (*Anchor). Sympathetic but not uncritical history of socialism, Utopian and Marxian.

S. Hook, *From Hegel to Marx* (*Ann Arbor). A study of the development of Marxism.

I. Berlin, *Karl Marx: His Life and Environment* (*Galaxy). First-rate brief biography.

G. Lichtheim, *Marxism* (*Praeger). A critical and historical study.

P. Gay, *The Dilemma of Democratic Socialism* (*Collier). Study of efforts to revise Marxism in a democratic direction.

E. H. Carr, *Michael Bakunin* (*Vintage). Biography of the Russian anarchist.

Arts and Letters

S. Giedion, *Mechanization Takes Command* (Oxford, 1948). Assessment of the impact of industrialism on the arts.

G. M. Young, *Victorian England: Portrait of an Age* (*Anchor). A brilliant evocation.

W. L. Burn, *The Age of Equipoise: A Study of the Mid-Victorian Generation* (*Norton). Stimulating study in British intellectual history.

C. Graña, *Modernity and Its Discontents* (*Torchbooks). Interesting study of the bohemian versus the bourgeois in nineteenth-century France.

M. Raynal, *The Nineteenth Century: Goya to Gauguin* (Skira, 1951). Handsomely illustrated survey of painting.

J. C. Sloane, *French Painting between the Past and the Present* (Princeton, 1951). Account of the critical period of transition to modern art, 1848–1870.

K. Clark, *The Gothic Revival* (*Penguin). Entertaining essay, focussed on Britain.

H. R. Hitchcock, *Architecture: Nineteenth and Twentieth Centuries* (Pelican, 1958). Encyclopedic study, covering both Europe and America.

A. Einstein, *Music in the Romantic Era* (Norton, 1947). Helpful survey.

P. H. Láng, *Music in Western Civilization* (Norton, 1941). Massive volume, stressing relations between music and other aspects of civilization.

Sources and Fiction

C. Dickens, *Hard Times* (*several editions). Relatively short novel, with vivid portraits of "Coketown" and its citizens.

E. C. Gaskell, *Mary Barton* (*Norton). Very good mid-nineteenth-century novel of a strike in an English factory; the author, Mrs. Gaskell, was a friend of Dickens.

E. Zola, *Germinal* (*Scribner's). Celebrated naturalistic novel of a strike in a French coal mine.

J. Bowditch and C. Ramsland, *Voices of the Industrial Revolution* (*Ann Arbor). Selections from the laissez-faire economists and their critics.

J. S. Mill, *Autobiography* and *On Liberty* (*several editions). Perhaps the two most interesting works by the great Victorian.

K. Marx and F. Engels, *Basic Writings on Politics and Philosophy* (*Anchor).

G. Flaubert, *Madame Bovary* (*many editions). The classic novel of French realism.

14

Prelude, Theme, and Coda

1870—1919

Wounded soldiers being given first aid along the British front during World War I.

The half-century between 1870 and 1920 saw the Great Powers prepare for and fight the first of the twentieth century's fantastically destructive wars, World War I (1914–1918). But of course it would be a vast oversimplification to regard the entire period between 1870 and 1914 as nothing but the preparation for the explosion. In this chapter we begin with an account of the internal development of Great Britain, France, and the other western European parliamentary states. We turn next to Germany, Austria–Hungary, Russia, and Turkey—the eastern European Empires—and then to the world outside Europe, the colonial empires old and new, the United States, and China and Japan. The largest part of our account is a chronicle of peace and progress, dealing with industrialization, increasing prosperity, improvement in social conditions, the growth of political parties. Yet even domestic developments point to the troubles ahead, as we encounter the political instability and passions of France, the cynical militarism of Germany under Bismarck and especially William II, the incompetence of Russian imperial government, the agitation of minorities in the Habsburg Empire, and the spreading view that national prestige for any power required that it hold large colonial possessions.

I. The Nations of Europe at Home, 1870–1914

BRITAIN

During the last third of the nineteenth century, Britain continued to set an example of steady peaceful progress, with the Liberal party supplying the main impetus for additional reforms in the direction of democratization. William E. Gladstone (1809–1898), four times Prime Minister between 1868 and 1894, personified the Victorian virtues of sobriety, hard work, piety, and moral earnestness. In the early twentieth century, the Welshman David Lloyd George (1863–1945), though he did not serve as Prime Minister until 1916, made his mark as Chancellor of the Exchequer in the Liberal cabinet between 1908 and 1915.

By the Education Bill of 1870, the first Gladstone ministry (1868–1874) accepted the idea that it was the responsibility of government to provide a literate electorate. State aid now went to church-affiliated schools, which were made liable to inspection, and so improved in quality. Local education boards also received help in establishing nonsectarian primary schools open to all. By abolishing the sale of officers' commissions in the army (1871), Gladstone's Secretary for War (Cardwell) defied the vested army interests. The new emphasis on merit helped improve British military efficiency and prepare the way for success in the colonial warfare that lay ahead. By the Third Reform Bill (1884), the second Gladstone ministry (1880–1885) further extended the franchise in rural districts, giving the vote to most adult males and raising the total number of voters from three million to about five. A companion bill (1885) set up single-member parliamentary constituencies nearly uniform in population, and did away with many anachronisms in the historic units of borough and shire.

The latter portion of the nineteenth century saw also the growth of the trade unions, as Parliament lifted restrictions on picketing and other union activities. By 1900 the unions were industry-wide, and included both skilled and unskilled workers. Some workingmen formed a political party of their own, the Labor party, which developed in the early years of the new century. The Laborites favored an evolutionary socialist program, with emphasis on gradual progress toward full economic democracy. Its moderate position reflected the strong religious humanitarian sentiments of its leaders and the influence of the Fabian (from the Roman general Fabius Cunctator, the "delayer") group of intellectuals, including Bernard Shaw, H. G. Wells, and Beatrice and Sidney Webb. Before 1914 Labor never won as many as 10 per cent of the seats in a parliamentary election. But, since the Liberals came to depend on the votes of Labor members, they put through much important legislation in the interest of the working man: the sanctity of trade-union funds, employers' liability to compensate for accidents (both in 1906), and modest state-financed old-age pensions (1908).

The expense of these programs, and still more the costs of a big navy, impelled Lloyd George to present in 1909 a budget increasing income taxes in the higher brackets and raising death-duties (inheritance taxes). The Conservatives, especially in the House of Lords, were opposed, and the Lords rejected the budget. This precipitated a political crisis, since traditionally the Lords had approved all money bills passed by the Commons. When the Liberals won two closely contested elections in 1910, the Commons set out to prevent a recurrence of such action by the Lords. King George V was prevailed upon to use the threat that had allowed the triumph of the Reform Bill of 1832: by threatening to create enough new Liberal Lords to control their House, he forced the Lords to accede to the Parliament Act of 1911. This "Fourth Reform Bill" denied the Lords' right to veto a money bill, and limited their veto to two years over other bills.

Though women still were without the vote, and though some "plural" voters had the right to vote more than once, democracy was far advanced in Britain by 1911. The National Insurance Act (1911) introduced health and unemployment insurance jointly financed by employers, workers, and the state. But the Liberals clung to the traditional doctrines of free trade, advantageous only so long as British industrial development was the most advanced in the world. As American and German industrial competition became severe in the later nineteenth century, the advantage disappeared, and economic stagnation threatened. Agitation for protective tariffs was led by Joseph Chamberlain (1836–1914), a self-made businessman who had served as reforming mayor of the industrial city of Birmingham in the 1870's. He believed in strengthening all of Britain's imperial ties, and so broke with the Liberals in the 1880's, when Gladstone endorsed Home Rule for Ireland. Between 1895 and 1903 Chamberlain served as Colonial Secretary in a Conservative cabinet, and tried to forge the empire into a compact economic unit that would impose tariffs on goods imported from outside, thus assuring the mother country both markets for exports and supplies of raw materials. Though Chamberlain failed and had to resign, his mercantilist scheme would be revived after World War I.

Ireland remained a grievous problem throughout the period. Though the Liberals disestablished the Anglican Church in Ireland, no longer requiring the Catholic majority to support a Protestant state church, and though they tried to protect Irish tenants from extortionate rents imposed by their landlords, who were usually English, what the Irish nationalists wanted was Home Rule. In Parliament, their leader Parnell agitated brilliantly on their behalf in the 1870's and 1880's. In 1886, Gladstone proposed a Home Rule bill that would have given Ireland her own parliament, though leaving control over foreign policy to London. But even this was too much for Joseph Chamberlain, whose followers, calling themselves Unionists, left the Liberals and in effect joined the Conservatives.

The Conservatives now tried to "kill Home Rule by kindness," passing measures that enabled the Irish tenant farmer to buy his own farm on easy terms. But kindness was not enough: Irish nationalism, nourished

Gladstone with Queen Victoria.

by a remarkable literary revival in English and Gaelic that produced Yeats, Synge, and others, demanded full independence. The Liberals passed a new Home Rule bill in 1914, but it could not be enforced because the predominantly Protestant population of Ulster in northern Ireland so feared submersion in a Catholic state that they organized an illegal militia to prevent any loosening of the ties with Britain. As World War I broke out, violence was threatening; Ulstermen who were officers in the British army were planning mutiny, and Irish nationalists were planning to resist them by force.

FRANCE

Bitterness and division characterized French political life in the decades between 1871 and 1914. In 1871 a patriotic minority even wanted to continue the war against the Germans, while the majority in the newly elected National Assembly reluctantly accepted the necessity of signing a peace treaty that ceded Alsace and part of Lorraine to the new German Empire. In March, 1871, the minority revolted, seized control of Paris, and installed the Commune, designed to revive both the name and the patriotic *élan* of the revolutionary city government of 1792. Though Marx hailed the Commune as a true socialist regime, the Communards were rather Jacobins, who lacked a social or economic program but intended to make France a republic and put an end to defeatism. Civil war between the Commune and the Assembly brought new horrors to Paris. Not until May, 1871, was the Commune suppressed, at the cost of 20,000 French lives, about as many as the victims of the Terror.

The Monarchists, who had a majority in the victorious Assembly, were split between the Legitimists, who supported the Count of Chambord, grandson of Charles X, and the Orleanists, who supported the Count of Paris, grandson of Louis Philippe. If the Count of Chambord, who had no son, had agreed to make the Count of Paris his heir, and had accepted the tricolor flag, which Louis Philippe had done in 1830, a compromise would have been possible. But Chambord insisted on the old white flag of the Bourbons with its golden lilies and its symbolism of the Old Regime. Negotiations broke down, and the Orleanists, led by Adolphe Thiers (1797–1877), former Prime Minister under Louis Philippe, decided to settle for a republic. Thiers, who had been appointed provisional chief executive by the Assembly, strongly opposed the Commune, floated a large loan to repay the huge indemnity exacted by the Germans, and was voted "President of the Republic" in August, 1871.

Four years later the Assembly ratified the series of laws known collectively as the Constitution of 1875. France received a two-chamber legislature, with the Senate elected indirectly and the Chamber of Deputies directly by universal male suffrage. Together the two chambers elected the President, who, though chief executive, had to have all his orders countersigned by a member of the council of ministers or cabinet. On May 16, 1877, the President, MacMahon, a Legitimist, precipitated a crisis by forcing the resignation of the cabinet to enable him to put in ministers more to his liking. When the republican Chamber of Deputies would not give the new conservative cabinet a vote of confidence, MacMahon dissolved the chamber and called for new elections. The voters returned a majority of republican deputies, and MacMahon had to accept a cabinet of their choosing. This May 16th affair decided the question for the entire history of the Third Republic, down to 1940: no future president would dissolve the chamber, and his role came to resemble that of an ornamental constitutional monarch. As in Britain, the real executive was a cabinet (or ministry) headed by a prime minister (or premier).

The existence of a dozen or more parties in France enormously complicated political life. A ministry necessarily represented a coalition, working together only temporarily, and subject to collapse at short notice if one or more parties withdrew. Frequent cabinet crises studded the history of the Third Republic; the average life of a ministry was less than a year. Yet many of the crises involved only a few shifts in ministerial personnel, and the professional civil servants continued to run the country while the politicians argued. Government by coalition was truly democratic, for it forced politicians to accustom themselves to avoid extremes, to look for the middle ground, and to compromise incessantly.

The enemies of the republic, however, loathed compromise. The Legitimists yearned for a king. As the republic took a strongly anticlerical turn after the crisis of May 16th and passed laws making divorce possible, curtailing the activities of religious orders, and banning religious instruction from the state school system, some Catholics also became irreconcilable. Royalists and clericals put their hopes in General Georges Boulanger (1837–1891), Minister of War in 1886–1887, who looked good on a horse, and fanned French desires for revenge against Germany. Left-wing malcontents who felt the republic was insufficiently democratic joined the right-wing extremists in supporting Boulanger. In 1889, elected to the Chamber of Deputies, he had a chance to lead a *coup d'état* but turned cowardly at the crucial moment. In the face of a threat that he would be tried for treason, Boulanger ran off to Belgium and committed suicide on his mistress's grave.

In 1894 a more severe crisis began when Alfred Dreyfus, a French army captain of Jewish origin, was accused of passing military information to the Germans. Dreyfus protested innocence, but was convicted and sent to prison on Devil's Island off the coast of French Guiana in South America. Investigation showed that Dreyfus had been convicted on the basis of forged evidence, and that the real traitor was a Major Esterhazy. The French high command tried to hush this up; they did not want to admit their blunder, and it suited them to have a Jew the villain of the piece. In January, 1898, Esterhazy was acquitted by a military court. Two days later, the novelist Emile Zola (*see* Chapter 13) published an open letter accusing the military leaders of sacrificing an innocent man. The forged evidence was publicly exposed, the forger committed suicide, and Dreyfus obtained a new trial, but a military court found him guilty again, "with extenuating circumstances" (1899). This absurd verdict meant only that the army would not admit his innocence. The President of the Republic pardoned him. In 1906, when the excitement had died down, Dreyfus was formally acquitted, restored to the army, and promoted to major.

The *affaire Dreyfus* had ripped French society apart along familiar lines. The heirs of the revolution of 1789—intellectuals, leftists, anticlericals—by and large lined up behind Dreyfus; their opponents—royalists, clericals, the army—lined up against him. There were exceptions: some left-wingers assumed his guilt because he was a rich bourgeois; some Catholics championed him because they were convinced that he was innocent. Anti-Semitism played a major role. When the crisis was over, the army was purged, and new anticlerical laws were passed dissolving Catholic teaching orders and closing some 12,000 Catholic schools. In 1905 Napoleon's Concordat of 1801 (*see* Chapter 11) was abrogated, and the Catholic Church lost its privileged position as a state-supported institution. Since then, the French church has been a private, self-supporting organization, a state of affairs that seems normal enough to Americans but that at first aroused great bitterness among French Catholics.

In social and economic matters, the leaders of the Third Republic before 1914 made fewer concessions to labor's demands for social security and improved conditions than their opposite numbers in England or Germany. Trade unions found the government ready to use force against strikers, and their own members reluctant to pay dues or accept discipline. A Marxist but evolutionary Socialist party gained steadily at the polls, winning one-sixth of the vote in 1914. The French economy was well balanced between farm and factory, although in pace of industrialization France lagged behind England or Germany, and her farmers and businessmen alike practiced extremely conservative methods. Yet neither slow economic growth nor political strains proved to be a severe handicap in the war of 1914–1918. No matter how many Frenchmen hated the republic, they all loved France, and could unite on a program of revenge against the Germans and the recovery of Alsace and Lorraine.

ITALY AND THE SMALLER WESTERN STATES

Like the French, the Italians, too, were divided on religious issues. The clericals supported the popes in their refusal to accept the extinction of papal political authority and the annexation of Rome by the kingdom of Italy. Economically, despite the lack of coal and iron deposits, Italy made significant advances by exploiting hydroelectric power, and after 1890 mass emigration to North and South America relieved the problems of overpopulation and underemployment. The backwardness of the predominantly rural south, however, with its absentee landlords and its differing historic traditions, posed serious economic and political problems that are not fully solved even today. In the period before 1914, the industrial north progressed at the expense of the exploited and neglected south. Parliamentary government had difficulty in functioning because of the lack of a strong democratic tradition and the flourishing of corruption in the illiterate south. In 1912 suffrage was extended to all males of 30, whether or not they could read.

As a result of a war with Turkey in 1911–1912, Italy began to acquire a colonial empire at last, annexing Libya in North Africa and the Dodecanese islands off the Turkish coast. Italians now began to forget some of their chagrin over earlier failures—Tunisia, taken by the French in 1881, and Ethiopia, where a native army defeated the Italians in 1896. The continued Austrian possession of Italia Irredenta (*see* Chapter 12), however, was a chronic source of nationalist frustration.

Elsewhere in western Europe the familiar forces were at work in familiar ways. Belgium, Spain, and Portugal were the scene of strife between clericals and anticlericals. Industrial growth promoted the development of trade unions and socialist parties; among socialists the trend was away from a strict Marxian revolutionary program, because most workers wanted immediate reforms and social gains rather than violence and civil strife. Political trends generally moved toward liberal democracy, and the suffrage was enlarged for the parliaments elected in the Low Countries, Switzerland, and the Scandinavian states. In Italy, Spain, and Portugal, on the other hand, poverty, class antagonism, and regional discontent hampered the advance of liberalism.

GERMANY

Except for the small Balkan states, central and eastern Europe consisted of four empires: the German, the Habsburg, the Russian, and the Ottoman. These were the lands of autocratic monarchies, conservative in social and political traditions, with relatively powerless parliaments appearing relatively late.

The German imperial constitution provided for a federal union of German states under the *Kaiser* (Emperor), who was the King of Prussia. The federal legislature consisted of a lower house, the *Reichstag*, elected by universal male suffrage, and an appointed upper house, the *Bundesrat*, which Prussia dominated. But neither house had much control over the chief minister, the chancellor, who was responsible only to the emperor. In practice, William I, emperor until 1888, left most decisions to Bismarck, chancellor until 1890. Germany was an authoritarian, militaristic, efficient, monarchical regime. During the Bismarckian decades it enjoyed extraordinary industrial development, which brought its coal and steel production up to or past the English levels by 1900. Alsace and Lorraine had brought new resources, unification brought unified railways and a single monetary system, and business and technology cooperated in the new chemical and electrical industries. German efficiency and aggressiveness kept standards high and competition keen; German workers worked longer hours and for lower pay than their English counterparts.

Politically, Bismarck distrusted the patriotism of the Catholics because of their support for the dogma of papal infallibility and their contacts with such potential adversaries of Germany as the French, the Austrians, and the Poles. Moreover, their Center party challenged the ascendancy of the Protestant Prussian aristocracy and middle classes. In the early 1870's Bismarck's *Kulturkampf* (Battle for Civilization) against the Catholics included laws expelling the Jesuits, forbidding clerical criticism of the government, and closing the schools run by religious orders. The Catholics, supported by the papacy, resisted, and by the late 1870's Bismarck had turned his wrath instead against the Socialists, and sought Catholic support against them.

Revisionist and not revolutionary, the German socialists nevertheless alarmed Bismarck by polling 10 per cent of the vote in the election of 1877. In 1878 the Reichstag made the Social Democratic party illegal, banned its meetings, suppressed its newspapers, and made its members liable to expulsion from their homes by the police. Individual Social Democrats, however, were still allowed to run for the Reichstag. Later during the 1880's Bismarck's government put through accident and unemployment insurance and old-age pension laws in order to deprive the socialists of their chief arguments. But in 1912, the last election before the war, the Social Democrats polled one-third of the votes.

William II (reigned 1888–1918), a grandson of William I, impulsive and erratic, was resolved to rule Germany himself. He disagreed with Bismarck's policies of friendship with Russia and opposition to the socialists, and in 1890 secured his resignation. William's own policies were strongly militarist: he nearly doubled the size of the army, until it reached the figure of 900,000 by 1913. In the late 1890's he began to develop a major navy, and thus aroused British alarm. The dangers of his policies were underscored by the interview he gave in 1908 to the London *Daily Telegraph,* in which he protested his friendship for Britain but complained that the British had never shown him proper gratitude for giving

Emperor William II.

them the military advice that had brought them victory in the Boer War (*see* p. 562), a claim as fantastic as it was untrue. The English were disturbed by the interview; there was much protest in Germany, too, but no constitutional change was undertaken that would have limited William II's enormous power.

THE HABSBURG MONARCHY

In the Habsburg Empire, the autocrat was the conscientious but rigid and unimaginative Francis Joseph (reigned 1848–1916). The *Ausgleich* of 1867, which set up the dual monarchy of Austria–Hungary (*see* Chapter 12), eased tensions between Austrians and Magyars, but in each half of the Empire severe minority problems made political life difficult. In Austria, the Czechs of Bohemia wanted rights like those the Magyars had won, and agitated for a triple rather than a dual monarchy; the German minority in Bohemia was, however, bitterly opposed. Though the Czechs were the most advanced of the Slavic peoples culturally and industrially, their thwarted national ambitions sometimes paralyzed the work of the Austrian parliament. The Polish minority, mostly landowners in Galicia, enjoyed a flourishing cultural life, and were better off than the Poles who lived under German or Russian rule. But their peasants, who were mostly Ruthenian (Ukrainian), suffered severe repression. The small minority of Italians wanted union with Italy.

In Hungary, the minority problem was still worse, as the Magyars numbered only a little more than half the population, yet tried to force the rest to use the Magyar language in schools and in all state services. Slovaks, Rumanians, and South Slavs (Serbs and Croats) living in Hungary remained bitterly discontented. The Rumanians of Transylvania wanted to unite with independent Rumania across their borders. Hungary had a still graver problem in the south Slav province of Croatia, where in 1868 a special *Ausgleich* was worked out which failed to satisfy many nationalistic Croatians and only alienated the Serbs. Both within Hungary and in Croatia, Serbs and Croats often agitated for union with independent Serbia.

Conditions were still more explosive in the provinces of Bosnia and Herzegovina, inhabited by Serbs and Croats, which were under Ottoman rule until 1878 and then administered for thirty years from Vienna, though technically remaining part of the Ottoman Empire. Austria–Hungary's annexation of the provinces in 1908 dealt a severe blow to the ambitions of independent Serbia, which had long hoped to take them over. In the years just before the outbreak of World War I Bosnian students began to take pot-shots at the Hungarian governors of Croatia, as the Serbs looked on sympathetically. These were ominous rehearsals for the crime that set off the war itself.

Austrian society was characterized by a high-living and frivolous aristocracy owning large estates, and a peasantry with small holdings and low standards of living and literacy. Between them a relatively small urban middle class included many Jews, who made large contributions to the music and cultivation of the "Viennese" way of life, to medicine and science. Though some Jews were assimilated, many were not, and the influx of poorer Jewish shopkeepers from elsewhere in eastern Europe helped fan serious anti-Semitism among the lower middle classes. On the one hand, this led some Jews to found the Zionist movement for a Jewish state in Palestine, and on the other it produced strongly anti-Semitic politicians.

Emperor Francis Joseph.

Of the Austrian parties, the Christian Socialists, loyal to the monarchy and strongly Catholic, won great support not only among the peasantry but among the small businessmen and eventually among the Catholic clergy. Their leader was the violently anti-Semitic Karl Lueger, perennial Mayor of Vienna (died 1910), who deeply impressed the young Hitler. The Social Democrats, founded in 1888, were gradualist socialists, usually led by intellectuals, many of them Jewish, but winning an increasing number of working-class supporters. They favored democratic federalism as a solution to the minorities problem and wanted to allow each nationality its own schools and free cultural expression.

Socially, Hungary was characterized by a landowning aristocracy with huge estates and by a more numerous group of "gentry" landowners whose holdings were smaller but who exercised great political influence. The towns, traditionally German and Jewish, became steadily more Magyar; in Hungary anti-Semitism was never as important politically as in Austria. Catholicism was the faith only of 60 per cent instead of 90 per cent of the population and a strong Catholic party like the Austrian Christian Socialists never arose. Where Austria had a liberal franchise before 1907 and universal manhood suffrage thereafter, Hungary continued to restrict the vote to about 6 per cent of the population. Hungarian political life thus degenerated into sterile bickerings on petty issues involving the prestige of Hungary within the dual monarchy.

RUSSIA

The reforms of Alexander II of Russia (*see* p. 501), though sweeping, did not have the effect that the tsar hoped for: instead of satisfying the malcontents and silencing the opposition, they stimulated new demands and greater restlessness. A few articulate intellectuals transformed the old debate between Slavophils and Westernizers (*see* Chapter 12) that had raged under the oppressive Nicholas I into something far more serious. As Alexander Herzen (1812–1870) began his career as a Westernizer, and became a revolutionary socialist and Slavophile after witnessing the failure of the Paris revolution of 1848, so others too preferred action to argument. Michael Bakunin (1814–1876) spent much of his career participating in revolutions and in and out of European jails. He expected a great revolution to start in the Slavic world and spread everywhere destroying all institutions. In the 1860's Bakunin and other senior Russian revolutionaries were living in exile in Switzerland. One of them, Lavrov (1823–1900), argued that all Russian intellectuals owed a great historic debt to the peasantry, whose labor had made possible their leisure and education, and that they should pay it by going among the peasants and educating them. Another, Tkachev (1844–1886), felt that the masses were ineffective and that only a tight dedicated élite could touch off a truly revolutionary movement.

Listening to these men and others in Switzerland were many Russian students who had christened themselves *nihilists*, those who believe in nothing, because they liked to think of themselves as hard-boiled and intensely practical, calling only for the useful in art and literature, and for the abolition of old moral values such as marriage and the family tie. In his novel *Fathers and Sons*, Turgenev drew a convincing picture of a nihilist: obstinate, rude, and arrogant. Real people imitated the fictional hero. The nihilist students in Switzerland, prompted by the teachings of Lavrov and the others, returned to Russia in the early 1870's as "populists," determined to "go to the people" and teach them how to improve their lot and prepare themselves for revolution. The movement failed in part because these idealists did not know how to talk to peasants, and were often betrayed to the police. After two great public trials of populists in the 1870's, those who had stayed out of jail formed a determined revolutionary organization, whose more radical wing, called *The People's Will*, turned in 1879 to terrorism.

For two years they hunted Alexander II, shooting at him but missing, mining the track on which his train would travel but blowing up the wrong train, dynamiting the palace dining room but just before he was due for dinner, and eventually killing him with a crude hand grenade (March, 1881) on the very day when he had signed a document that summoned a commission to consider further reforms. His successor, Alexander III (1881–1894), refused to confirm the document, smashed *The People's Will*, and embarked on a period of reaction that would last through the first ten years of the reign of his son, the last tsar, Nicholas II (1894–1917).

During the reaction the government made elections to the *zemstvos* much less democratic: "rural leaders" appointed from the capital replaced the elected justices of the peace in the countryside. The minority peoples—Finns, Poles, Ukrainians, Armenians, and Jews—were subjected to discriminatory "Russifying" policies ranging from suppression of their own institutions in the case of the Finns to outright massacre in the case of the Jews. A peasant bank did make credit easier to obtain, and a few bits of legislation alleviated the lot of the urban workers. This was the quarter-century in which Russian industrialization boomed: the Donets coalfields and the Baku oil wells came into production; steel output soared. A self-made railroad expert, Serge Witte, who served as Minister of Finance from 1892 to 1903, supervised the great expansion of the rail network, which doubled with the building of the Trans-Siberian line. Working conditions in industry were probably the worst in Europe.

Marxism now made its first real impact in Russia, as the younger generation of revolutionaries formed the Social Democratic Party (SD's) in 1898. One of their leaders was a young intellectual from the upper middle class named Vladimir Ilyich Ulyanov (1870–1924), who used the pen-name Lenin, sometimes prefixing the initial "N.," a Russian abbreviation for "nobody," in order to tell his readers that he was using a pseudonym (his first name was *not* Nikolai). Soon the SD's began to quarrel among themselves: Should the party operate under a strongly centralized directorate, or should each local group be free to agitate for its own ends? Following Bakunin and Tkachev, Lenin insisted on the tightly knit directorate, and, at the party congress held in Brussels and London in 1903, the majority of delegates voted with him. Lenin's faction took the name "Bolshevik" (majority), and their opponents called themselves "Menshevik" (minority). In contrast to most of the socialist parties in Europe, there was nothing gradualist or evolutionary about the Bolsheviks.

As Marxists, the SD's were interested chiefly in the urban worker, still a small class numerically in Russia. The direct heirs of the populist tradition, on the other hand, were interested in the peasant as the future revolutionary; these men also organized a political party, the Social Revolutionaries, or SR's, who wanted more land for the peasantry, and who continued the terrorist program of their predecessors. A third political grouping, neither SD nor SR but mostly moderate liberal intellectuals, veterans of the *zemstvos*, also came into being, and called itself Constitutional Democrats, or KD's, or Kadets. They favored a constitution for Russia and the creation of a national parliament or duma. The Tsar's government, however, made no distinction between its violent and its moderate opponents.

The period of reaction culminated with the Russo-Japanese War of 1904–1905, provoked by the rivalry between the two nations in the Chinese province of Manchuria and in Korea, and made possible by the weakness of China. The Russians forced the Chinese to let them build a railroad line across Manchuria which would give them a short-cut to their own Far Eastern province; in 1897 they took the Chinese harbor at Port Arthur, which they had earlier kept out of Japanese hands (1895). Next, adventurous Russians intrigued for concessions in Korea, and Russian politicians who thought war would silence political dissent at home secured the dismissal of the sagacious and cautious Witte. The Japanese began hostilities by a surprise attack on Russian ships in Port Arthur (1904). Though holding their own on land, the Russians suffered a severe defeat when their fleet, which had sailed all the way from the Baltic, was defeated by the Japanese at Tsushima (May, 1905). Both sides accepted President Theodore Roosevelt's offer to mediate; in the subsequent Treaty of Portsmouth (1905), Russia recognized a Japanese protectorate over Korea and ceded Port Arthur and the southern half of Sakhalin Island to Japan, but retained a substantial role as a power in the Far East.

The Revolution of 1905 and the Dumas. Meantime, in Russia itself revolution was breaking out. The SR's fomented peasant riots and assassinated the Minister of the Interior. A police agent of the government, planted in the factories of the capital to combat SD activities among the workers, organized a parade to

Bloody Sunday (January 22, 1905); demonstrators and soldiers in Petersburg.

petition the Tsar for an eight-hour day, the right to strike, and a national assembly. But Nicholas ordered the troops to fire on the peacefully marching workers, and about a thousand of them were killed on "Red Sunday" (January 22, 1905). The massacre infuriated the entire opposition, and moderates joined radicals in demanding concessions; as the timid, vacillating, and unintelligent Tsar hesitated, strikes multiplied, vital services were paralyzed, and the SD's among the printers formed the first "soviet" or workers' council. Witte told Nicholas II that he must either impose a military dictatorship or summon a national legislative assembly, a duma.

By the October Manifesto of 1905, Nicholas promised full civil liberties and the election of a duma by universal manhood suffrage. Not until troops returning from the Far East proved to be loyal to the government, however, could left-wing violence be suppressed after several days of fighting (December, 1905). The Duma was duly elected, but before it could meet Witte secured a French loan, making the government financially independent, and passed a set of "fundamental laws" that the Duma could not change; these left all matters of finance and foreign policy in the hands of the Tsar, and empowered him to dissolve the Duma and to legislate when it was not in session. He did have to set the date for new elections, and any interim law of his own would have to be approved by the Duma. Though a long way from the English Parliament, the Duma was still a major advance over traditional Russian undiluted autocracy.

Rasputin.

The Tsar soon dissolved the first Duma because it demanded radical agrarian reforms that would have given to the peasants lands belonging to the state, the church, and some private owners. The second Duma was also dissolved (1907), and the government illegally altered the election laws, reducing the number of deputies from the peasants and the national minorities, and increasing those from the gentry. Thus the government obtained a majority, and the third Duma (1907–1912) and the fourth (1912–1917) lived out their five-year terms. Unrepresentative and limited in power though these Dumas were, they were still useful forums for the airing of national issues. The initiative in governing, however, rested with the executive.

From 1906 to 1911 the executive was dominated by the intelligent conservative chief minister, Stolypin. Toward revolutionaries Stolypin was ruthless, but toward the peasants he was generous and imaginative, sponsoring a series of laws that enabled them to free themselves from the village commune, to which they had remained attached after the emancipation of 1861 (see Chapter 12). A man wishing to detach his property could demand that he receive a single tract of land rather than the scattered plots previously assigned to him. Stolypin called this program the "wager on the strong and sober"—he was betting on the ability of individual peasants to function on their own as small farmers. The government came close to winning the wager, for between 1906 and 1917, it is estimated, about a quarter of the peasant households in European Russia seceded from the communes. Only war and revolution kept the process from going further and perhaps satisfying the perennial land hunger that made peasants support the SR's and other radicals.

The assassination of Stolypin in 1911 was a disaster for the tsarist regime. The government now inclined toward a purely reactionary policy, spreading a vast web of police spies to trap SD and SR agitators, yet never succeeding in catching them all. Meanwhile, the Tsar and his family drifted into a most perilous situation, as the domineering and fanatically religious Empress fell under the sway of a half-mad, wholly evil, dirty, ignorant, and power-hungry monk from Siberia. Rasputin had the ability, perhaps hypnotic, to stop the dangerous bleeding spells of the Tsar's only son, who suffered from hemophilia. Since the Empress greatly influenced Nicholas II, Rasputin became the real ruler of Russia, much to the horror of loyal supporters of the dynasty, and greatly to the detriment of the rational conduct of affairs in a vast twentieth-century state.

THE OTTOMAN EMPIRE

The last of the Eastern empires also experienced a revolution that never quite came off—the Young Turk uprising of 1908. The Young Turks were the more vigorous heirs of the ineffectual Ottoman reformers of the mid-nineteenth century (*see* Chapter 12). They wanted the modern industrial achievements of the West, they wanted its liberal political apparatus, and they wanted to have Turks respected and feared as members of a modern *nation*. They opposed the ultrareactionary policies of Sultan Abdul Hamid II (1876–1909), and they deplored the chronic debility of the Ottoman Empire, which had already lost large parts of its European possessions. Though it continued to lose its African territories, the Empire still retained an extensive domain in western Asia. While the dominant element in the population was Turkish in nationality and Moslem in religion, there were important minorities—the Christian Greeks and Armenians, and the mainly Moslem Arabs—who wanted a status equalling that of the privileged Turks.

When Young Turk army officers rebelled in 1908, they promised to inaugurate a new era. Abdul Hamid was to become a constitutional monarch, the minorities who had often been promised equality were to secure it now under a new cosmopolitan concept of Ottoman nationality. In general, decrepit Turkish institutions were to be revitalized by the influence of the West. But the promising concept of an Ottoman nationality foundered before the narrow nationalism both of the minorities and of the Young Turks themselves, who increasingly favored an intolerant policy of "Turkification" very like the "Russification" of Tsar Alexander III. Then, from 1911 to 1913 Turkey was involved in disastrous wars with Italy and the Christian states of the Balkans. In this deteriorating situation three Young Turk officers established a dictatorship (1913). Thus the Ottoman Empire, like the Russian and the Habsburg, seemed certain to face critical internal difficulties in the event of a long general war.

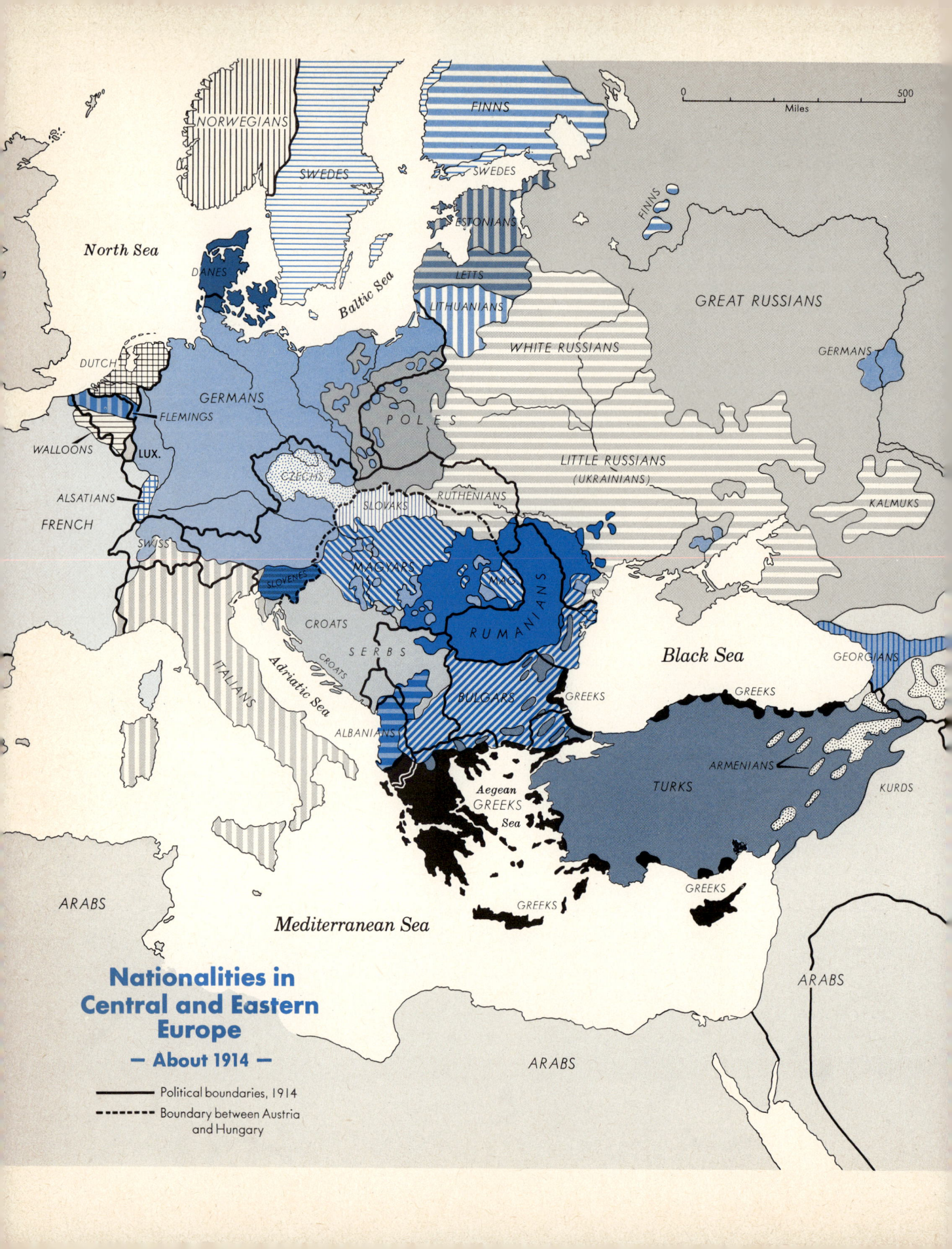

Nationalities in Central and Eastern Europe
— About 1914 —

— Political boundaries, 1914
--- Boundary between Austria and Hungary

II. The World Overseas

In the period between 1870 and 1914, old colonial powers like Britain and France found new lands to conquer, and new powers joined the race for empire: Italy, Germany, Belgium, the United States, and Japan. It was the era in which every government seemed to feel that the possession of colonies was the sign of greatness. This imperialism not only reflected a yearning for national prestige and racist theories about superior and inferior races but often contained an element of sincere religious and humanitarian impulse, the wish to assume "the White Man's burden," as Kipling put it. As free trade gave way to a revived mercantilism, businessmen and politicians also sought colonies to enlarge the market for home manufactures and to provide fresh fields for investment.

THE BRITISH EMPIRE

In Africa the British by 1914 controlled more than one-third of the continent's area and three-fifths of its population; Egypt and South Africa provide instructive and contrasting case histories of imperialism. After the opening of the Suez Canal (1869), built and operated by a French company, Egypt's importance as a way-station to India was greatly enhanced. In 1875, Disraeli bought 178,000 shares of Suez Canal stock, formerly held by the ruler of Egypt, the Khedive Ismaïl, whose extravagant habits led first to his accepting European financial tutelage, and then to his deposition (1879). A nationalist rebellion by Colonel Arabi gave Britain the occasion to send a fleet and troops (1882); thereafter, with a British resident guiding the policies of the Khedive's government, Egypt became a British protectorate. Nationalism grew, for even such improvements as the Aswan Dam, which was opened in 1902 and permitted increased irrigation, were regarded by Egyptians as efforts to perpetuate their country's colonial economic function of supplying raw materials.

In South Africa, the discovery of gold and the growth of the diamond industry in the Boer Republic of the Transvaal brought a new wave of immigration in the 1880's. The new arrivals looked for protection to Britain, especially to Cecil Rhodes, imperialist-minded Prime Minister of the Cape Colony, while the Boers regarded them as intruders. In 1895, a follower of Rhodes, Dr. Jameson, led a raid into the Transvaal. The raid failed, because the immigrants failed to stage a planned uprising, and it prompted Kaiser William II to send a celebrated but tactless telegram congratulating President Kruger of the Transvaal. The tensions following the Jameson raid culminated in the Boer War (1899–1902) between Britain and the republics of Transvaal and the Orange Free State. Britain's prestige suffered, as the stubborn Boers held out for three years; many English Liberals and most foreigners sympathized with them as underdogs. The peace of 1902 brought British rule and the promise of ultimate self-government, fulfilled in 1910, when the Boer republics and the British Cape Colony and Natal were joined in the Union of South Africa. This dominion had a strong central government, with both Afrikaans (the Boer dialect) and English as official languages.

Africa and the Middle East, 1910

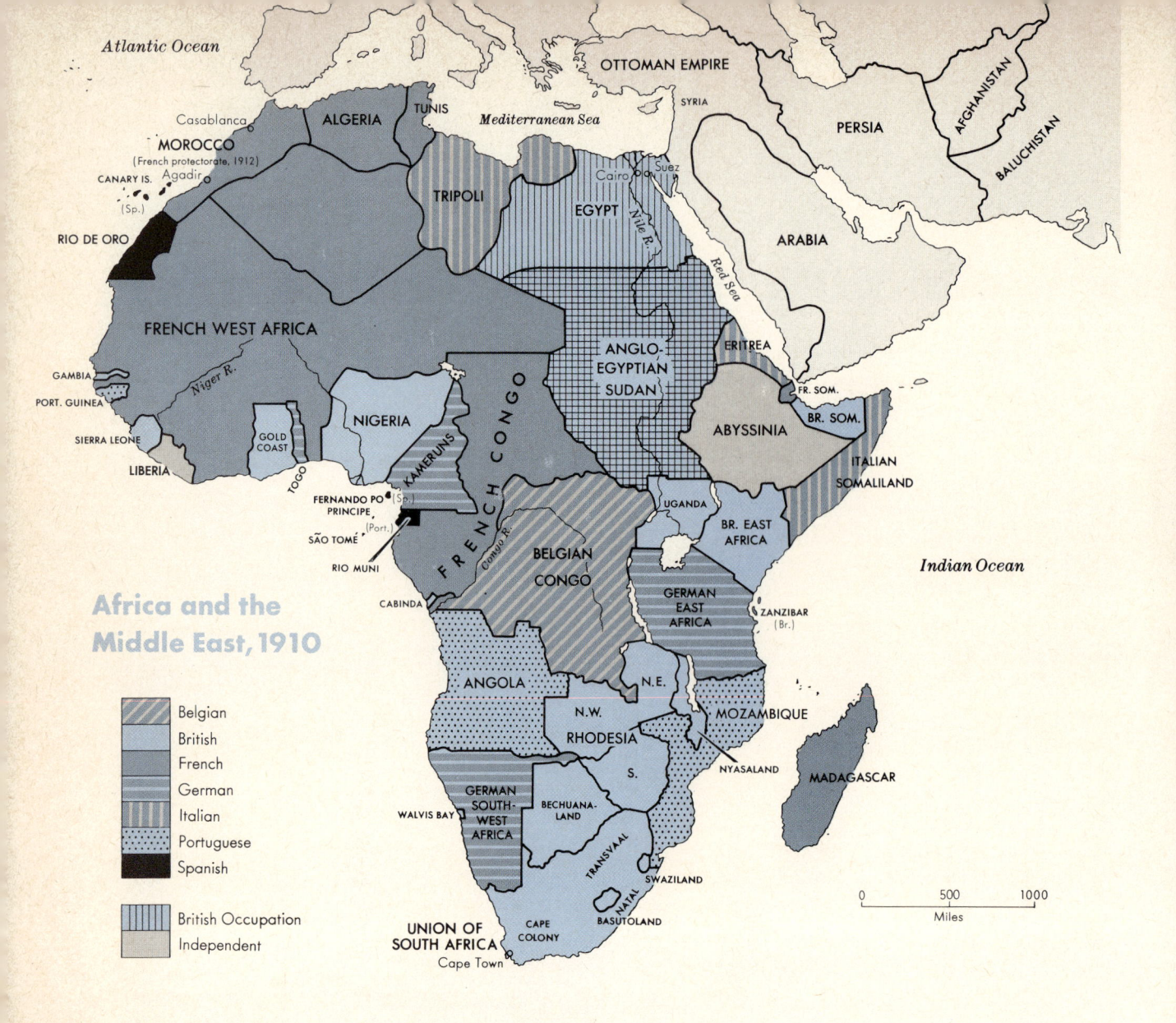

Legend:
- Belgian
- British
- French
- German
- Italian
- Portuguese
- Spanish
- British Occupation
- Independent

But Boer resentment continued to smolder, and both European groups felt deeply uneasy at being outnumbered four to one by the native Africans, the immigrants from India, and the "coloreds," people of mixed blood.

On January 1, 1877, Queen Victoria was proclaimed Empress of India, an act that symbolized the richness and splendor of this vast territory with its mixture of castes, languages, and religions. By 1914 the British had built thousands of miles of railroads and telegraph lines in India, had founded schools and universities, using English as the language of instruction, and had established hospitals and seaports. British capital financed textile and other industries, and Indians were gradually achieving public and private positions of greater and greater responsibility. But the Indian middle class longed for more white-collar jobs, and Indian nationalists were impatient with the slow growth of literacy and disapproved of British toleration for the native princes and their fantastically luxurious style of life side by side with peasant misery. Both the physical and spiritual climate of India were alien to most of the British, who were felt to be overbearing even when they strove not to be.

Elsewhere, the British controlled Malaya and Hong Kong in Asia, some islands in the West Indies, and two small footholds—British Honduras and British Guiana—on the mainland of tropical America. While these were run in traditional colonial style, the self-governing dominions were increasing in number in the early twentieth century as South Africa, Australia, and New Zealand followed the precedent of Canada (*see* Chapter 12). Australia and New Zealand were sparsely populated, partly because they excluded Asians and had to compete with the United States for European immigrants; none the less, they had developed distinctive and contrasting national personalities by 1914: New Zealand, very "English" but egalitarian, somewhat stodgy, Australia individualistic, boisterous, and often anti-English. In Australia the independent-mindedness of the individual states postponed their union in a single commonwealth until 1901. Its constitution provided for an upper legislative body similar to the American Senate, with representatives from the individual states, and for popular representation in a lower house. But no dominion imitated the American presidential system; all followed the British system of prime minister and cabinet controlled by parliament. By 1914 all of them enjoyed full control over their internal affairs, could levy tariffs, even on British goods, and had the beginnings of their own armies. Strategic, economic, cultural, and emotional ties rather than legal subjection, bound the dominions to Britain. The definition of this unique relationship would be worked out in the 1920's and 1930's.

THE OTHER EMPIRES

In 1914 the second largest colonial empire belonged to France. In Asia the French ruthlessly dominated Indo-China, which centered on the rice-growing coastal areas (present-day Vietnam). In Africa, they ruled vast tropical areas: the West African bulge, equatorial Africa to the south of the bulge, and Madagascar, the large island in the Indian Ocean off the east coast. They also held Algeria, French since 1830, and acquired the neighboring lands to the east (Tunisia, which became a French protectorate in 1881) and west (Morocco, which became one some thirty years later). The mild climate of North Africa attracted substantial numbers of European immigrants, the *colons,* Italians and Spaniards as well as Frenchmen. Their presence antagonized the native Moslem Arabs and Berbers, who lost some of their lands to the *colons;* this laid the foundation for future conflict. At the time, however, French colonial administrators hoped to assimilate the native populations of North Africa, and to make Moslem Frenchmen out of them. Though many individual North Africans benefitted by French education and some became assimilated, the masses remained indifferent if not hostile.

Among the newcomers to colonial competition the Germans, led by businessmen seeking new contracts and nationalists seeking new glory, caused a considerable commotion. In Africa by 1914 they had acquired Togoland and the Cameroons on the west coast, South-West Africa, and Tanganyika (then called German East Africa). In the Pacific they had some small islands and part of New Guinea. Poor and primitive, these lands contributed very little to the German economy, but they gave the colonists a chance to be brutal to the natives and helped satisfy the national appetite for prestige. As we have seen, Italy got nothing in the African partition but Libya and two colonies bordering Ethiopia—Eritrea and Somaliland. The Belgian King Leopold II (1865–1909), however, came off with the great area known at first as the Congo Free State. Early grandiose plans for civilizing missions vanished in scandals over slavery, and in 1908 the name, symbolically enough, became simply "Belgian Congo."

THE UNITED STATES

Imperialism also infected the United States in these decades. After the Spanish-American War, touched off by the still mysterious sinking of the battleship *Maine* in Havana harbor (February 15, 1898), the Americans won control of the Spanish colonies of Cuba and Puerto Rico in the Caribbean and of the Philippines near Asia. In addition, the United States annexed the Pacific islands of Hawaii (1898), and in 1903 supported a revolution in Panama, then a part of Colombia, that assured direct American control of the zone of the Panama Canal that would soon be constructed.

The acquisition of an empire delighted some Americans, notably Theodore Roosevelt, president from 1901 to 1909, but aroused others to indignation as a betrayal of democratic principles. By 1914 the United States had become a great industrial nation, with a highly mechanized agriculture and with financial resources so great that, as a banking center, New York was a serious rival to London. Tremendous amounts of manpower were supplied by the influx of European immigrants. Critics of the era then and since have pointed to its crass materialism, its political bossism, and the prevalence of robber barons in its business life. Yet, Americans did cooperate in building and in development, and, despite loud argument, they agreed on political fundamentals. The South completed its difficult "road to reunion," though it remained a problem area, with greater poverty and illiteracy than other regions, and committed to the maintenance of "white supremacy."

Government now began to intervene in economic affairs, setting minimum wages, and limiting child and female labor; the lead was taken by individual states, notably Wisconsin. Crusading journalists called "muckrakers" helped expose questionable practices, and public opinion readied itself to accept federal regulation, a "square deal" for labor (Theodore Roosevelt's term), and the "busting" or at least policing of the trusts that were gaining monopolistic control over important economic areas. The Standard Oil Company was broken up, and, though some of its children grew bigger than the parent, American business was no longer allowed to operate on the principle of "the public be damned!" voiced by the nineteenth-century railroad magnate, **Commodore Vanderbilt**.

THE FAR EAST

When the American Commodore Perry "opened" Japan in 1853 and ended her two centuries of self-imposed isolation, he stimulated the Japanese themselves to move toward modernization. The feudal oligarchy that ruled the country was not only greedy but ineffectual. Urban merchants, craftsmen, and the *samurai*, professional military retainers in the lower ranks of the aristocracy, were the chief beneficiaries of the political revolution that began in 1868. Using the almost forgotten Emperor, and endowing his office with a sacred authority rather like the outmoded Western idea of divine-right monarchy, these ambitious middle-class people moved into the center of power, both economic and political. They easily recruited cheap manpower from the overpopulated countryside for the new industries. The constitution granted by the Emperor in 1889 was far from

Asia and the Pacific, 1910

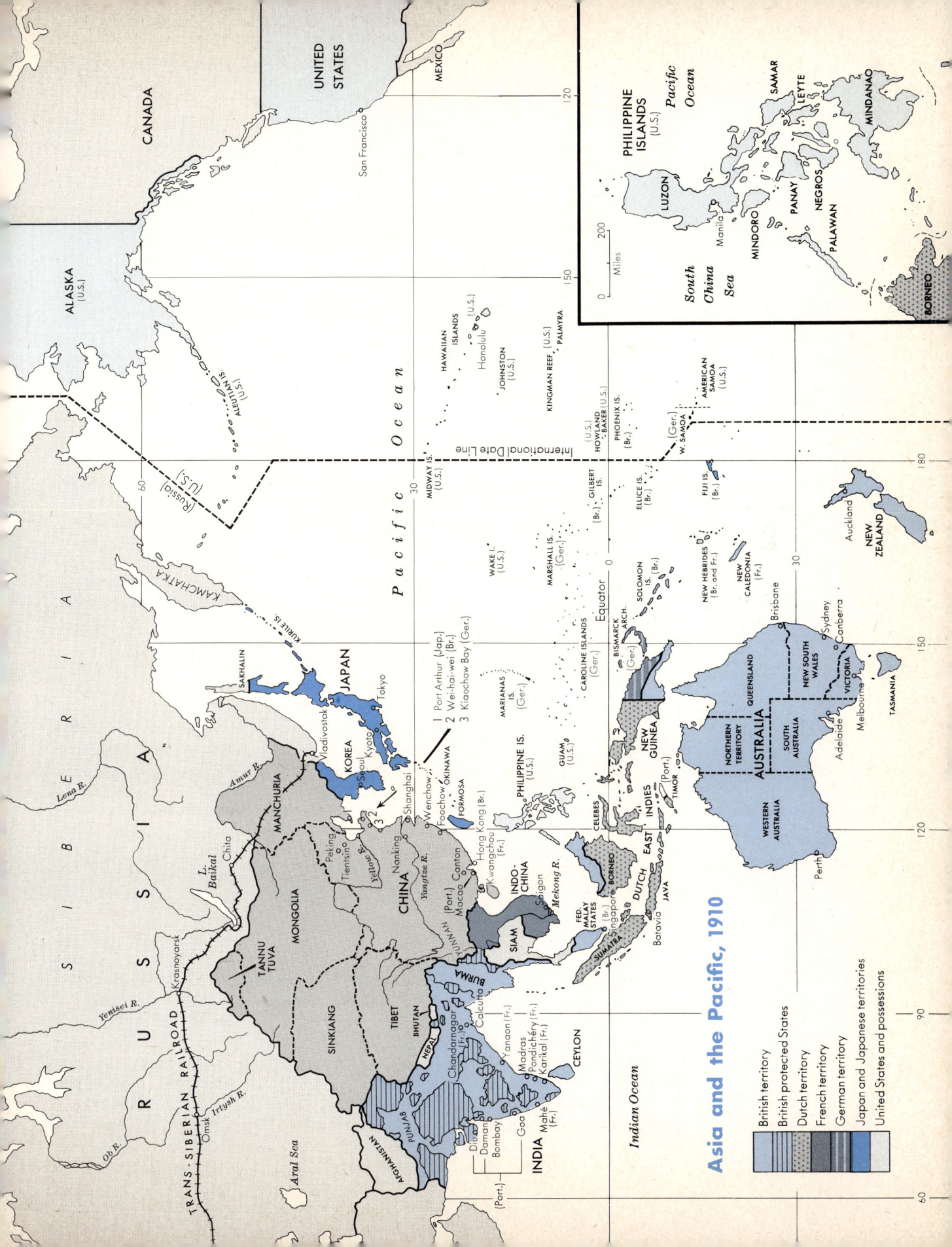

democratic. Though it set up a bicameral diet, neither peasants nor urban workers could vote for representatives, and the cabinet was responsible only to the Emperor and so to the ruling clique.

With modernization came Japanese imperialism, primarily at the expense of China. Ten years later the defeat of Russia gave Japan a free hand in Manchuria and in Korea (annexed in 1910). Japanese imperialists longed to control all of China, but other powers were also scrambling for portions of the prize. In 1899 John Hay, the American Secretary of State, sought to obtain international recognition for the "Open Door" policy, whereby all foreign goods could be marketed in China on even terms. To all this the Chinese responded by forming an antiforeign secret society, the Boxers. The Boxer rebellion in 1900 caused 200 foreign deaths, mostly among missionaries, and led to the despatch of foreign troops, including United States Marines, and to the extraction of a huge indemnity from the Chinese government. In 1911–1912 a new Chinese revolution would break out (*see* Chapter 15) and open a new era in the history of the Far East.

THE BALANCE SHEET OF IMPERIALISM

The Boxers may serve as a symbol of worldwide discontent with imperialist practices. Egyptian and Indian nationalists echoed their arguments and would perhaps have liked to emulate their methods. Western ideas of self-determination and human equality were making converts among these peoples; equality, in particular, threatened the traditional bases of their own cultures at least as much as it did the Western interlopers. Ironically, the introduction of law and order, the extension of communications, the advances in health—all Western contributions—would make resistance to the West easier and more popular.

The imperialist powers found that the colonies were often a well-paying proposition, particularly when they supplied home industry with cheap and abundant raw materials. And, too, the existence of remote and exotic colonies offered ordinary citizens a chance for romantic escape from drab routine. But, always, the seamy side of imperialism gave liberals at home a chance to denounce and advertise its hypocrisies. And the rivalries among the Powers in Africa and Asia certainly added their contribution to the outbreak of World War I.

III. The First World War

THE ROAD TO WAR: TRIPLE ALLIANCE AND TRIPLE ENTENTE

Anglo-German rivalry in trade, empire, and navies; the French wish for revenge; the competition between the Russians and the Austrians to dominate southeastern Europe, exacerbated by the Austrian fear that the Russians would arouse their own Slavic minorities; competing nationalisms: these were the tensions that culminated in war in 1914. Two great alliances—the Triple Entente of France, Britain, and Russia, and the Triple Alliance of Germany, Austria-Hungary, and Italy—stood toe to toe when war broke out; except for the defection of Italy, they fought the war in this alignment.

The road to 1914 began in 1871. After the defeat of France, Bismarck designed a series of alliances for Germany, in the hope of keeping the French isolated. Simultaneously he tried to distract them from any plan for war with Germany by encouraging them in imperial adventures, especially those—like that in Tunisia—where they would annoy another power, in this case, Italy. The German-Austrian alliance of 1879, made possible in the first place by Bismarck's lenient treatment of Austria after the defeat of 1866, lasted down to 1918, and was the cornerstone of the system. In 1882 Italy was brought into the alliance.

Russian-Austrian friction over Ottoman territory in the Balkans gave Bismarck his gravest problem. In 1877 Russia went to war against Turkey in support of the rebellious Christians of Bosnia and Bulgaria, and in 1878 dictated the peace of San Stefano, which, contrary to earlier Russian promises, tried to create a "Big Bulgaria" that the Powers, especially Austria, believed would become a mere Russian satellite. At the Congress of Berlin (1878), Bismarck, acting as "honest broker," presided over a revision of the San Stefano arrangements that reduced the new Bulgaria by two-thirds, awarded Bosnia and Herzegovina to Austria, Cyprus to Britain, and Tunisia to future French domination. Deprived of their chief gains, seeing other powers taking Ottoman territory for which Russia had done the fighting, the Russians grew so resentful that Bismarck feared they might ally themselves with France and "encircle" Germany.

Bismarck strove to prevent this by promoting a secret "Three Emperors' League" of Germany, Austria, and Russia in 1881. When the Russians withdrew, he concluded a secret Reinsurance Treaty (1887) between Germany and Russia alone, but he let the Russians know of his obligations to Austria, to discourage any Russian aggression. Probably even Bismarck could not have kept up these acrobatics indefinitely. And when William II dismissed him (1890), the Kaiser soon afterwards "cut the wire" to Russia by refusing to renew the Reinsurance Treaty, as the Russians requested. Bismarck's nightmare of encirclement now came true: in 1894, France and Russia reached an alliance, despite the mutual dislike of autocratic Tsar and republican politicians.

The next major step came a decade later with Britain's decision to move out of isolation and toward alignment with France and Russia. Although the old colonial rivalry with France flared up in 1898 when French and English forces competed for possession of Fashoda in the disputed Sudan, and although Russia was England's rival for concessions both in the Far and Middle East, these differences proved far less serious than the threat posed to the British by the German naval building program. Traditional British isolation disappeared with the conclusion of the Anglo-Japanese alliance of 1902, designed to check Russia's Far Eastern ambitions. The Russo-Japanese War hastened British negotiations with France, leading to the *Entente Cordiale* of 1904. By the "cordial understanding" England gave France a free hand in Morocco in exchange for a free hand in Egypt and the Sudan, and the two powers began continued collaboration of a sort that amounted to a tight alliance. An Anglo-Russian agreement followed in 1907, never so intimate as that with France, but easing imperial rivalry.

CRISES OVER MOROCCO AND THE BALKANS

In the last decade before 1914, crisis after crisis shook Europe. Two of them arose over Morocco. The first came in 1905, when the Kaiser made a visit to Tangier as a sign that he did not accept French predominance in Morocco; it was settled by the Algeciras conference (1906). In 1911 the Kaiser rashly sent a gunboat to the Moroccan port of Agadir as an anti-French gesture; this second crisis was settled only when France ceded part of the French Congo to Germany in exchange for German recognition of French hegemony in Morocco.

Between the two Moroccan crises came a more important one in the Balkans. The Austrians responded to the Young Turk revolt of 1908 by annexing outright Bosnia and Herzegovina, which they had been administering since 1878. The annexation dealt a crushing blow to the Serbian hope that these provinces would eventually become part of Serbia. It infuriated Russia, not only because of the injury to her Serb protégés, but also because the Austrians went back on a former promise to aid Russian efforts to lift the ban on the use of the Turkish straits by Russian warships (*see* Chapter 12). In 1912 the Balkan states, backed by Russia and encouraged by Italian victories over the Turks, themselves attacked Turkey. Bulgaria, Serbia, and Greece won the first Balkan War (1912–1913). But Austria refused to let the Serbs have the outlet to the Adriatic which they had won, and instead sponsored a new state of Albania; Bulgaria refused to compensate the Serbs for their loss in Macedonia. So Serbia, Greece, Rumania, and the recently defeated Turkey turned on Bulgaria in the second Balkan War (1913).

THE CRISIS OF 1914

Though these crises had been successfully contained, the next could not be. On June 28, 1914, a Serbian student, Gavrilo Princip, assassinated the heir to the Habsburg throne, Archduke Francis Ferdinand, and his wife in the streets of the provincial capital of Bosnia, Sarajevo. Determined to end the Serbian agitations that unsettled their south Slav subjects, and convinced that the Serbian government had had foreknowledge of Princip's plot, the Austrian government consulted the Germans, and received the famous "blank check": a promise that Germany would support any Austrian action against the Serbs. On July 23, Austria sent Serbia a 48-hour ultimatum, deliberately designed to be unacceptable. The Serbs accepted most of its terms, but declined to let Austrian civil or military officials participate in the investigation of Princip's plot. To the world it seemed as though Austria was bullying the Serbs; probably, however, Serbia already had a promise of help from Russia if war should come. Serbian rejection of part of the ultimatum brought an Austrian declaration of war on July 28, 1914.

The Kaiser and his civil advisers, resisting their own generals, now tried to persuade Austria to accept a compromise. William II telegraphed Tsar Nicholas II, and Russia temporarily agreed to substitute a partial mobilization for the full mobilization that had already been ordered. But Russia was a country of long distances and poor communications, and her generals feared that the enemy would get the jump on them; on July 30 they took the fateful decision to resume full mobilization. On August 1, Germany declared war on Russia, and on August 3 against France, Russia's ally. It is possible that Britain would have been brought into the war by the closeness of her ties with France; what made her entry certain was Germany's violation of Belgian neutrality, which both Britain and Prussia had agreed to guarantee in 1839 (*see* Chapter 12). On August 2, Germany notified Belgium that German troops would cross her territory on their way to France; Belgium resisted and appealed to the other guaranteeing powers; on August 4, Britain declared war on Germany. The German chancellor, Bethmann-Hollweg, remarked that Britain had gone to war just for a "scrap of paper." This phrase for the 1839 treaty, seized upon by the press of the world, not only solidified British opinion in favor of the war, but was perhaps more responsible than any other single factor for the charge of war guilt later laid against Germany.

Although we speak of the individual European countries—Germany, England, Russia, France—as single units, in 1914 each was of course only a symbol for millions of human beings with opinions ranging from ultra-militarism to ultra-pacifism. Yet in each country there was a characteristic national opinion. In Germany the Kaiser set the tone: his efforts to prevent war came only in the last hectic week of July, 1914; before that he had been consistently the posturing belligerent leader. German ambition and fear had produced an intense hatred of Britain, mixed with envy and a sense of inferiority, focussing on the English upper classes, perfectly tailored, serene in effortless superiority, the favored

Princip, immediately after the assassination at Sarajevo, June 28, 1914.

children of fortune. The officer's mess in the German navy in the years before the war would drink to *Der Tag*, the day of reckoning against England. This national opinion voiced by many Germans made its own contribution to the later widespread feeling that Germany had been guilty.

Though few Englishmen returned the hate, many of them believed that the ill-mannered Germans should be taught a lesson. The expensive naval race with Germany, the manifest opposition of the Kaiser's government to England in incident after incident, and the growing competition from German industrial goods in world markets all contributed to the feeling. The good liberal internationalists among the British easily identified their cause with righteousness; the nationalists even more easily accepted the necessity of fighting. In France, though many, like the socialists, were committed to pacifism in theory, the characteristic attitude was the embittered patriotism of the losers of 1870–1871. From 1871 onward, the statue representing Strasbourg, capital of Alsace, among the cities of France in the Place de la Concorde in Paris was perpetually draped in black.

Among the other warring powers too, the decision of the governments to fight was not unwelcome to national opinion. Germans and Magyars, if not the minorities in Austria-Hungary, welcomed the chance to punish the troublesome Slavs. Russians believed that God and the right were on their side. In sum, the war could not have been made by the emperors, frock-coated diplomats, and military "brass hats" had not the scores of millions in the competing nations of Europe essentially welcomed this test of strength.

STRENGTH OF THE BELLIGERENTS

From the first, the Central Powers of Germany and Austria–Hungary, later joined by Turkey and Bulgaria, were weaker in manpower and in material resources than the Allies—France, Russia, Britain and the dominions, Serbia, and Belgium, joined in 1915 by Italy and in 1917 by the United States, to name only the most important. Yet it took the Allies four years of hard fighting to win. Why?

The very name "Central Powers" suggests one reason: Germany and Austria were neighbors, spoke the same language, and had interior lines of communications enabling them to make rapid transfers of troops from one front to another. Britain and France, on the other hand, were cut off from Russia, since Germany blocked the Baltic route and Turkey the Black Sea route. Only by the long Arctic journey to Archangel on the White Sea or by the long Pacific journey to Vladivostok could the western Allies reach Russia. Language separated each of the three major allies from the other; they were recent partners and had no long tradition of cooperation. France and Britain were democracies, whose populations, though capable of great sacrifice, found it hard to accept the firm military controls demanded by war. Not until 1918 did they (and the United States) consent to

German soldiers leaving Berlin for the front.

accept the French General Foch as commander-in-chief of all armies on the Western front.

France was slow to mobilize her economic resources; Britain was a naval power, with a small army, and relied on volunteers to man it until reluctantly adopting conscription in 1916. Russian distances, bad communications, and inadequate industrial output hampered the operations of the immense Russian army, whose morale had not recovered from the defeat by Japan. The abortive revolution of 1905 and the increasing corruption and inefficiency of the Tsarist government adversely affected public opinion. Germany, by contrast, was the only belligerent really ready for war in 1914; she had an efficiently organized military machine and an industry readily shifted to a war basis, and further enjoyed the psychological advantage of the offensive.

THE FIGHTING FRONTS

The invasion of Belgium, at the very beginning of the war, was a vital part of the Germans' plan for a quick victory on two fronts: they would first concentrate on the West and win a decision there, before Russia could even complete mobilization and pose a serious threat in the East. The Germans poured into northern France by the Belgian route, but the French rallied and checked their advance short of Paris in the first battle of the Marne River, September, 1914. The Germans' offensive failed partly because they hastily shifted some divisions to the East to counter an unexpected Russian advance there. Later the Germans failed in an attempt to capture the French Channel ports and cut the short cross-Channel communication line to Britain. Now the opposing armies in France dug trenches along a line from the Channel to Switzerland. A prolonged deadlock characterized by bloody trench-warfare set in on the Western front. Here, four years later, the Allies, by then including the Americans, would win the massive test of endurance.

The other fighting fronts, sometimes disparaged as "side-shows," used up German men and resources. On the Eastern front, the Russian advance into East Prussia in August, 1914, was halted at Tannenberg. Thereafter the Germans kept enough troops in the East to help their hard-pressed Austrian ally; they held the Russians at bay, but could not knock them out. The defeat of a major Russian offensive against Austria in 1916 touched off a train of events leading to the Russian revolutions of 1917 (see Chapter 15). The new Bolshevik regime submitted to the punitive Peace of Brest-Litovsk dictated by the Central Powers. The western provinces of Russia—Finland, the Baltic region, eastern Poland, and the Ukraine—passed to German–Austrian domination, and parts of the Caucasus went to Turkey.

A third front—the Italian—was opened in 1915, in the mountains along the Austro-Italian border, after the Allies had won Italy over by the promise of Trent and Trieste, the Dalmatian coast, and other Austrian and Turkish territory (in the Secret Treaty of London, 1915). In the autumn of 1917 the Germans routed the Italians at Caporetto; but the Italians rallied, Britain and France sent reinforcements, and the Austro-German advance was slowed by shortages of supplies.

In southeast Europe the Central Powers gained the adherence of Bulgaria (1915), still smarting from its defeat in the Second Balkan War, and overran Serbia. In an effort to capitalize on Turkish weakness, to strike at the Central Powers through the Balkans, and to open up the Black Sea route to Russia,

Europe, 1914–1918

Legend:
- Allied and Associated Powers
- Central Powers and their Allies
- Neutrals
- —— Political boundaries, 1914
- —·— Boundary between Austria and Hungary
- – – – Greatest advance by Central Powers
- ····· Greatest advance by Allies
- ■ Battle site

Winston Churchill, First Lord of the British Admiralty, sponsored a naval attack on the Gallipoli peninsula, along the European shore of the Dardanelles. Other Allied leaders were skeptical and refused to allot all the men and equipment requested; the landing was bungled, and the Turks resisted fiercely. Though the plan failed in late 1915, Churchill always felt that it had been a good idea. Allied promises of Hungarian territory lured Rumania into the war. In 1916 the Central Powers overran Rumania, left exposed by Russian defeats. Not until the Allies forced Greece into the war on their side (1917) and landed troops who marched northward in the late summer of 1918 did they score successes in the Balkans. Then they knocked Bulgaria out of the war, liberated Serbia, and threatened the complete disintegration of Austria–Hungary.

In the Middle East, the romantic and eccentric English Colonel T. E. Lawrence assisted a "revolt in the desert" against the Turks by discontented Arabs. In 1917 Jerusalem fell, and in 1918 Turkish resistance collapsed. Arab nationalist hopes for a Middle East made up exclusively of Arab states were thwarted by Allied actions and Zionist aspirations. In 1917 the British government, trying to rally Jews throughout the world to the Allied cause, issued the Balfour Declaration (named for the Foreign Secretary) favoring "the establishment in Palestine of a national home for the Jewish people."

THE WAR AT SEA AND ON THE HOME FRONTS

At sea the German fleet of capital ships, whose building had done so much to poison Anglo-German relations before the war, made only one appearance: at the inconclusive battle of Jutland (1916) against part of the British fleet in the North Sea. German losses in tonnage were only half those of the British, but the German fleet never dared put to sea again. The mutiny of its sailors in 1918, when ordered to make a last stand, helped touch off the German revolution that led to the Armistice of 1918.

Much more menacing to the Allies were the German submarines. In May, 1915, one of them torpedoed the British liner *Lusitania*, with the loss of more than a thousand lives, including about a hundred Americans. In the still neutral United States public opinion was outraged. When the Germans declared unrestricted submarine warfare in January, 1917, they were taking a gamble; they knew that the torpedoing of neutral ships carrying nonmilitary cargoes to the Allies might well bring the United States into the war. But they hoped they would sink so many vital cargoes of food and raw materials that Britain would be starved into surrender before America could mobilize.* Indeed, by the time the United States declared war (April 6, 1917), submarine sinkings had reduced British food reserves to barely one month's supply. Counterattack by depth-charges, antisubmarine patrols, and the system of convoying merchant ships with armed escorts—these successful antisubmarine techniques were developed only at the eleventh hour. But soon the Allies turned the weapon of blockade against Germany, so that as time went on the German people suffered increasingly from malnutrition.

On the home front, the governments were slow to organize for war. Eventually all imposed censorship, introduced conscription, set priorities in industry, and rationed scarce commodities, recruiting the necessary armies of bureaucrats for the purpose. Britain began such measures in 1915, when the dynamic Lloyd George became Prime Minister. France achieved tight home-front organization only late in 1917, when Georges Clemenceau became Premier, treating bunglers and defeatists with extreme ruthlessness. Despite the German reputation for technical superiority, the German home front was never properly organized: a better system of rationing would have reduced malnutrition. By 1918 the Allies were putting their potential superiority in resources to work and winning the battle of production; in Germany the home front was ready to collapse under any unusual pressure from the battlefields.

* American public opinion was further aroused by the State Department publication on March 1, 1917, of the "Zimmermann telegram," an intercepted message showing that the German government was encouraging the Mexican government to attack the United States.

DECISION ON THE WESTERN FRONT

The critical pressure came from the Western front, where both sides had long been trying to break the deadlock of trench warfare. They tried airplanes, useful in spotting targets for artillery and also in scouting against submarines, but as yet too flimsy to be effective bombers or fighters. The Germans also experimented with lighter-than-air craft, the Zeppelins, which dropped some bombs on London, but not nearly enough to cause serious damage. On the ground the Germans tried poison gas, only to discover that a shift in the wind might blow the gas back on their own troops, and that the Allies had the protection of gas-masks and could retaliate in kind. The British came nearer to success with the first tanks, a pet project of Winston Churchill; the tanks went into action prematurely in 1916 when they were too few in number and too prone to breakdown to achieve the smashing surprise that more of them might have won later.

The great weapons of trench warfare were the repeating rifle, the machine gun, and the fast-firing artillery pieces. All of them were accurate and deadly, and all of them negated repeated efforts to end the stalemate by frontal assaults of hundreds of thousands of men against enemy fortifications. In 1916 the Germans lost 350,000 men in a vain attempt to capture Verdun, the fortress at the eastern end of the French line, and the French lost the same number in defending it. In

Allied soldiers trying to keep warm, near Ypres in Flanders, 1914.

the same year the British lost over 50,000 men in a single day during another abortive offensive. Men could not indefinitely endure such appalling casualties, and in April and May of 1917 French soldiers mutinied rather than continue an offensive that seemed to achieve nothing except slaughter. The entry of the United States in April, 1917, though of little immediate material assistance, did much to revive the morale of the war-weary Allies, already depressed by the possible withdrawal from the conflict of Russia, now torn by revolution.

The end finally came in the West after a last desperate German offensive had been checked, almost within sight of Paris, in the Second Battle of the Marne during the summer of 1918. The French, British, and Americans counterattacked, laying down a massive artillery barrage as a preliminary to assault, and utilizing tanks to advantage in the actual assualt. The exhausted German soldiers, needing supplies and reinforcements which the demoralized home front could no longer furnish, gave ground steadily. Facing certain defeat in the field and the rapidly mounting threat of revolution at home, the German government requested an armistice; after considerable negotiation, it was signed on November 11, 1918. By then the Kaiser had abdicated, and a republic had been proclaimed; Germany was in the throes of revolution.

IV. The Postwar Settlements

A WORLD IN TURMOIL

The German revolution was but one of many disturbances that kept the world unsettled after the Armistice and deeply influenced the diplomats who assembled at Paris in January, 1919, to make the peace. An acute issue was bolshevism (as communism was then generally termed). The Allies landed detachments at Archangel and Vladivostok to help the anti-Bolsheviks in the civil war raging in Russia (*see* Chapter 15). Meantime, the Bolshevik tide threatened to spread westward; there were communist uprisings in Germany during the winter of 1918–1919, and in Bavaria a Soviet republic was proclaimed in April, 1919. In Hungary a communist dictatorship was established in the spring of 1919 under Bela Kun, who had worked with Lenin in Russia. While all of these proved to be short-lived, the fact that they even existed heightened the tensions of the peacemakers.

In the Middle East, Zionists, Arabs, British, and French were at odds over the future of Palestine and other portions of the defeated Ottoman Empire. The Greeks, dreaming of a restored Byzantium, landed at Izmir (Smyrna) on the coast of Asia Minor, and marched inland, touching off a fierce and eventually successful Turkish resistance. In India, nationalists organized a campaign of disorder to win greater autonomy from Britain. As strikes and riots mounted, a British general at Amritsar ordered his troops to fire on an unarmed mob crowded in a small enclosure; some 1,600 people were killed or wounded (April, 1919). Liberal opinion throughout the world shared the Indian feeling of outrage. As Russia struggled in civil war, Japan saw a chance to renew her aggression against northern China; the American troops sent to Vladivostok went less to oppose the Bolsheviks than to watch the Japanese.

THE FOURTEEN POINTS—AND OTHER POINTS OF VIEW

The world was in turmoil; the peacemakers could obviously not satisfy everyone. Yet idealists everywhere expected that they would do so. Large sections of public opinion regarded the war, just over, as a "war to end war," a "war to make the world safe for democracy." These idealists found their spokesman in President Woodrow Wilson and their program in his celebrated Fourteen Points, advanced in an address to Congress, January 8, 1918.

Some of the Fourteen Points dealt with specific issues: Belgium "must be evacuated and restored" (Point VII), Alsace-Lorraine returned (Point VIII), and the frontiers of Italy readjusted "along clearly recognizable lines of nationality" (Point IX). Wilson repeatedly invoked the principle of national self-determination, promising the minority peoples of Austria-Hungary and the Ottoman Empire "the freest opportunity of autonomous development" (Points X and XII). There was to be an independent Polish state once more, enjoying "free and secure access to the sea" (Point XIII). The Fourteen Points also contained Wilson's diagnosis of the underlying causes of the war and his prescription for dealing with them. Point I, for instance, condemned by implication the secret diplomacy of the Triple Alliance and Triple Entente by demanding:

> Open covenants of peace, openly arrived at, after which there shall be no private international understandings of any kind but diplomacy shall proceed always frankly and in the public view.

Point III urged the "removal, so far as possible, of all economic barriers" among nations, and Point IV recommended that armaments be reduced to the lowest amount "consistent with domestic safety." In Point XIV, finally, Wilson mentioned the project dearest to him, the League of Nations:

> A general association of nations must be formed under specific covenants for the purpose of affording mutual guarantees of political independence and territorial integrity to great and small states alike.*

Wilsonian idealism had to contend with many crosscurrents of emotion: the frenzied nationalism of minorities at last released from alien rule, thirst for glory, vindictiveness against the Germans, selfish opportunism. The Allies had allowed both Arabs and Jews to think that Palestine could be theirs, both Italians and south Slavs to think they could get Dalmatia. Allied propaganda, widely believed by the British and French peoples, had maintained that Germany must be made to suffer for her war guilt and be rendered incapable of future aggression. Above all—and this was a favorite theme of Lloyd George, who led the British delegation to the peace table—Germany must meet the whole cost of the war through payments called reparations. Many Frenchmen—headed by Clemenceau, host to the peacemakers—sought not only reparations but also the restoration of French hegemony in Europe. Many Englishmen longed for a return to Victorian serenity and prosperity, well armored against German economic competition. And many Americans were determined to withdraw from what they saw as the corruption of the Old World and to return to the relative purity and isolation of the New.

---

* Woodrow Wilson, *War and Peace: Presidential Messages, Addresses, and Public Papers*, edited by R. S. Baker and W. E. Dodd (New York, 1927), Vol. I, pp. 159–161.

THE PROCESS OF PEACEMAKING

The peacemakers of 1919 actually convened in the suburbs of Paris—at Versailles to settle with the Germans, at St. Germain to settle with the Austrians, at the Grand Trianon (in the park of Versailles) with the Hungarians, at Neuilly with the Bulgarians, and at Sèvres with the Turks. The separate treaties are usually bracketed together as the Versailles or Paris settlement. Nearly thirty nations sent delegates to the conference, but neither the Russians nor the Central Powers were represented. The principal Allied powers were in no mood to invite the Bolsheviks, and they simply asked the defeated states to sign the finished treaties. The Germans, in particular, resented the refusal of the Allies to negotiate terms with them and were soon referring to the *"Diktat"*—the dictated peace—of Versailles.

Idealists hoped that the enthusiastic welcome given to Wilson in Europe would make possible a peace conference operating according to his principle of "open covenants openly arrived at." They expected a kind of international town meeting that would reach decisions by majority vote after discussion by all the delegates. The conference, however, soon fell into the pattern of traditional diplomacy, very like the Vienna congress of 1815. The "Big Three"—Clemenceau, Lloyd George, and Wilson—did most of the negotiating and deciding, much to the irritation not only of the small and middle-sized nations but also of the technical experts serving the Big Three themselves. Many of these experts in economics, history, political science, and so on were bright young men who sent report after report up to their chiefs with every confidence that their recommendations would be heeded. Their discovery that experts did not make policy and their articulateness in expressing their disillusion did much to discredit the work of the conference, especially among liberal intellectuals everywhere.

The settlement of 1919 represented a series of compromises between the idealistic solutions proposed by Wilson and the material considerations—reparations, security, appetite for territory—advanced by other powers. In resolving territorial issues the peacemakers had to adjust not only the claims of the victors but also the land hunger of the new nations that had sprung up from the disintegrating Habsburg, Russian, and Ottoman empires. And they had to make the adjustment without violating too obviously the Wilsonian principle of national self-determination, which was impossible to apply in any literal sense to the many unassimilated and overlapping minorities of central and eastern Europe. The diplomats made the attempt and thereby created more independent nation-states with new sets of discontented minorities.

TERRITORIAL CHANGES

Austria-Hungary was totally dismembered. The heart of its German-speaking area became the small Republic of Austria, which was forbidden to unite with Germany, and the heart of the Magyar-speaking area became the small Kingdom of Hungary. The Czech lands of Bohemia and Moravia, formerly ruled by Austria, were joined with Slovakia, formerly ruled by Hungary, in the republic of Czechoslovakia, which included a large and potentially troublesome minority of Sudeten Germans, and another of Ruthenians (Ukrainians). The south Slav lands of both Austria and Hungary joined Serbia to become the "Kingdom of the

Serbs, Croats, and Slovenes," later Yugoslavia. Rumania obtained Transylvania, formerly Hungarian, and Bessarabia, a province of tsarist Russia, thereby doubling its territory. The Baltic republics of Estonia, Latvia, and Lithuania were created from Russian lands taken by Germany at Brest-Litovsk.

Wilson's Point XIII was honored by the re-creation of an independent Poland including all the lands that Prussia, Austria, and Russia had grabbed in the eighteenth-century partitions. Access to the sea was secured through the "Polish Corridor," a narrow strip of land separating East Prussia from the rest of Germany and terminating on the Baltic at the wholly German city of Danzig, which the Allies made a Free City. Germans travelling to and from East Prussia had to cross the corridor in sealed trains. The new Poland contained important minorities of non-Polish peoples—Germans, Ukrainians, and Jews.

Italy received Trieste and the Trentino, including sizable Slavic and German-speaking minorities, and eventually in 1924 also got the former Hungarian Adriatic port of Fiume. The Allies, however, reneged on an earlier promise to Italy and gave Dalmatia to the new Yugoslav state, thus poisoning Italo-Yugoslav relations. France recovered Alsace-Lorraine; in addition, Clemenceau hoped to annex the Saar Basin of Germany, rich in coal, to compensate for French coal mines destroyed by the Germans during the war. He also hoped to secure France against possible German aggression by detaching from Germany all lands on the left (west) bank of the Rhine and converting them into a Rhineland republic that might become a French satellite. In both instances the opposition of Lloyd George and Wilson obliged the French to accept only a fraction of what they wanted. The Saar was to be separated from Germany as a ward of the League of Nations for fifteen years, when a plebiscite would determine its future status; meantime, its coal output was to go to France. The Rhineland remained part of Germany, though demilitarized and subject to Allied occupation.

The Treaty of Sèvres gave Greece eastern Thrace, the only European territory remaining to Turkey aside from Istanbul, and it also permitted the Greeks to occupy for at least five years the territories they had invaded around Izmir in western Anatolia. Before the treaty could go into effect, however, a group of army officers led by Mustafa Kemal revolted against the feeble Turkish government in Istanbul and galvanized the Turkish people into a new national life. The rebels drove out the Greek invaders and set up a Turkish republic with its capital not at Istanbul but at Ankara in the heart of Anatolia. With this new government the Allies concluded the Treaty of Lausanne (1923), which permitted the Turks to recover both eastern Thrace and the area of Izmir. Orthodox Christians still living within Turkey's borders were to be exchanged for Moslems living in territory acquired by Greece in the Balkan wars of 1912–1913. More than two million people were involved in this unprecedented exchange which, after many initial hardships, worked out reasonably well.

The Arab lands of the Ottoman Empire and the former German colonies were distributed as mandates. Each mandate was assigned by the League of Nations to a mandatory power which had the duty of preparing the population for self-government and ultimately for independence. In the Middle East Britain obtained the mandates for Palestine, Transjordan, and Iraq (Mesopotamia), while France got those for Syria and Lebanon. German East Africa went to Britain as the mandate called Tanganyika, South-West Africa went to the Union of South Africa, and both Cameroon and Togo were divided between Britain and

France. In the Pacific, Australia got the mandate for the German portions of New Guinea, and Japan that for most of the other German islands. The mandates may look like a device for disguising annexation, and the Japanese so treated theirs, illegally fortifying their new Pacific islands. Yet for the most part the mandatory powers did make at least a show of grooming the populations of their mandates for eventual freedom.

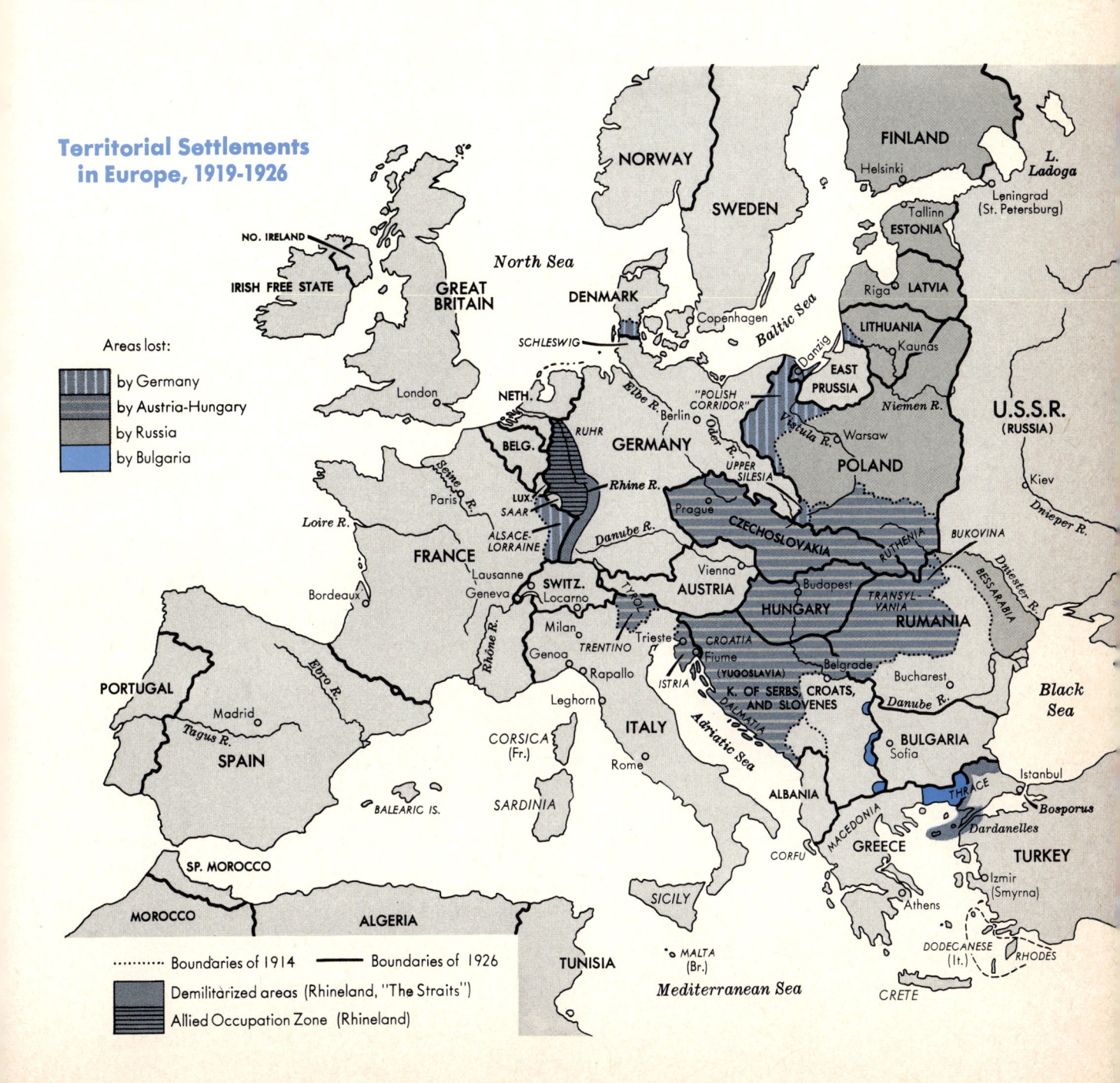

THE PUNISHMENT OF GERMANY

Next to territorial changes the most important business of the peacemakers was the punishment of Germany. The settlement required her to hand over many of her merchant ships to the Allies and to make large deliveries of coal to France, Italy, and Belgium over a ten-year period. By way of reparations the Germans also had to promise payment for all the damage done to Allied civilian property during the war. The annual payment was to be 5 billion dollars—an almost astronomical sum in those days—until a final figure could be agreed upon. This total, it was clear, would be so immense that Germany could pay it only in goods and only if she were prosperous enough to produce these goods, which meant that she could not be the weak and divided Germany desired by Clemenceau.

The Versailles treaty limited the German army to 100,000 men, and the western frontier zone, extending to a line 50 kilometers (about 30 miles) east of the Rhine, was to contain neither fortifications nor soldiers. In addition, the Allies could keep armies of occupation on the left bank of the Rhine for 15 years. Germany was forbidden to have either submarines or military planes and was severely limited with respect to surface warships. Finally, Article 231 of the Treaty of Versailles obliged Germany to admit her "war guilt":

> The Allies and Associated Governments affirm, and Germany accepts, the responsibility of Germany and her allies for causing all the loss and damage to which the Allied and Associated Governments and their nationals have been subjected as a consequence of the war imposed upon them by the aggression of Germany and her allies.

THE SETTLEMENT IN RETROSPECT

The Treaty of Versailles also incorporated Wilson's blueprint for a better world, the covenant of the League of Nations. The capital of the League was to be the Swiss city of Geneva, and its chief organs were the permanent secretariat, the assembly in which each member state had one vote, and the council which had permanent seats for the "Big Five" (Britain, France, Italy, Japan, and the United States) and four seats to be occupied in rotation by lesser powers. The way was left open for Russia and Germany to join, and they later did. The League, however, as we shall see, failed to achieve its main aims of promoting disarmament, preventing and punishing aggression.

To liberals and idealists the whole peace settlement was deeply disappointing. To the Germans it was the *Diktat,* which supplied a chronic national grievance that Hitler would later use effectively. Yet, compared to the German-dictated Treaty of Brest–Litovsk, the Treaty of Versailles was positively generous. And in our world today, with its hot and cold wars and with a permanent settlement of World War II not yet effected, it arouses nostalgia. It was, like the Utrecht and Vienna settlements before it, a compromise, which had both merits and faults. It had the merit of recognizing that the long frustrated nationalities of central and eastern Europe must secure satisfaction, even though this meant the "Balkanization of Europe" by the creation of more small competing political units. And one of its faults, it has been argued persuasively, was its imposition on Germany of "too much insult and too little injury," humiliating her yet permitting her to remain a first-class power, as she was shortly to prove.

It has been argued also that the trouble with the settlement of 1919 lay not with its terms but with the failure of the powers to enforce these terms. To this failure the United States contributed substantially by rejecting the settlement, largely as a result of the antagonism between an impatient Republican congress and an inflexible Democratic president, though isolationist sentiments and postwar disillusionment were also involved. Although the Republicans had won control of both House and Senate in the elections of 1918, Wilson failed to take a bipartisan delegation to Paris with him in 1919, and he rejected modifications in the Versailles treaty that might have met some Republican objections. The Senate refused to ratify the treaty or to authorize American participation in the League of Nations. It also refused to approve the defensive alliance of France, Britain, and the United States, a project into which Wilson had been pushed at Paris as part of the price for France's abandonment of plans to annex the Saar and set up a Rhineland republic.

When Britain also withdrew from the alliance project, France created a system of alliances with the states on the eastern side of Germany: Poland, Czechoslovakia, Yugoslavia, and Rumania. The apparent revival of French hegemony in Europe at first alarmed the British. But in fact the war had so weakened the French that the British need not have worried. Before the 1920's were over, it became apparent that danger to the peace of Europe threatened from quite another quarter. So the world of the peace settlements was not the brave new world for which the idealists had hoped, but one very like the bad old world that had fought the war, a world indeed that faced menaces of a nature and dimension that it did not yet understand.

14

READING SUGGESTIONS (asterisk indicates paperbound edition)

General Accounts

A. J. P. Taylor, *The Struggle for Mastery in Europe, 1848–1918* (Clarendon, 1954). Crisp revisionist survey.

L. C. B. Seaman, *From Vienna to Versailles* (*Colophon). Brief sketch, also stimulating and revisionist.

C. J. H. Hayes, *A Generation of Materialism, 1871–1900* (*Torchbooks). Comprehensive and disenchanted survey.

Barbara Tuchman, *The Proud Tower* (*Bantam). Readable survey of Europe on the eve of World War I.

The Separate European Nations, 1870–1914

R. C. K. Ensor, *England, 1870–1914* (Clarendon, 1936). Comprehensive volume in the Oxford History of England.

E. Halévy, *A History of the English People in the Nineteenth Century*, 2nd. ed. (P. Smith, 1949–1951). Volumes 5 and 6 of this detailed study cover 1895 to 1914.

C. Cross, *The Liberals in Power* (Barrie & Rockliff, 1964); M. Bruce, *The Coming of the Welfare State* (Batsford, 1961); and R. E. Barry, *Nationalisation in British Politics: The Historical Background* (Stanford, 1965). More recent views on British reforms before 1914.

P. Magnus, *Gladstone* (*Dutton); R. Blake, *Disraeli* (*Anchor); R. Jenkins, *Asquith* (Collins, 1964). Good biographies of important leaders.

C. P. Kindleberger, *Economic Growth in France and Britain, 1881–1950* (Harvard, 1964). Stimulating study by an economist.

D. W. Brogan, *The Development of Modern France*, 2 vols. (*Torchbooks). Witty, perceptive, though allusive treatment in detail; the first volume goes from 1870 to 1905, the second from 1905 to 1939.

D. Thomson, *Democracy in France since 1870* (*Oxford). Thoughtful interpretation.

G. Chapman, *The Dreyfus Case: A Reassessment* (Viking, 1956). The most searching treatment in English.

H. Goldberg, *Life of Jean Jaurès* (Wisconsin, 1962), and G. Bruun, *Clemenceau* (Harvard, 1943). Very good biographies of significant leaders.

D. Mack Smith, *Italy: A Modern History* (Michigan, 1959). Sound detailed survey, focussed on the period since 1861.

C. Seton-Watson, *Italy from Liberalism to Fascism, 1870–1925* (Barnes & Noble, 1967). Another useful survey.

B. Croce, *A History of Italy, 1871–1915* (Clarendon, 1929). Thoughtful analysis by the celebrated philosopher.

A. C. Jemolo, *Church and State in Italy, 1850–1950* (Blackwell, 1960). Useful study of a central problem in Italian politics.

S. B. Clough, *The Economic History of Modern Italy* (Columbia, 1964). Authoritative.

E. J. Passant, *A Short History of Germany, 1815–1945* (*Cambridge University); R. Flenley, *Modern German History* (Dutton, 1953); K. S. Pinson, *Modern Germany, Its History and Civilization*, 2nd. ed. (Macmillan, 1966). Good textbook accounts.

A. Rosenberg, *Imperial Germany* (*Beacon). Stressing the deterioration of the regime under William II.

T. Veblen, *Imperial Germany and the Industrial Revolution* (*Ann Arbor). Brilliant analysis by an American sociologist.

A. J. P. Taylor, *The Course of German History* (*Capricorn) and *Bismarck: The Man and the Statesman* (*Vintage). Highly critical evaluations.

F. Meinecke, *The German Catastrophe* (*Beacon). Thoughtful analysis by a great German historian; an antidote to Taylor.

A. J. May, *The Hapsburg Monarchy, 1867–1914* (*Norton). Concise account.

A. J. P. Taylor, *The Habsburg Monarchy, 1809–1918* (*Torchbooks). Spirited brief treatment.

R. A. Kann, *The Multinational Empire*, 2 vols. (Columbia, 1950). Arranged nationality by nationality, with a discussion of Habsburg policy toward each.

H. Seton-Watson, *The Decline of Imperial Russia, 1855–1914* (*Praeger). The best survey in English.

G. T. Robinson, *Rural Russia* (*California). Splendid introduction to the peasant problem.

B. Pares, *The Fall of the Russian Monarchy* (*Vintage). An excellent study of the period, 1905–1917; by an authority who was frequently on the spot.

J. Joll, *The Anarchists* (*Universal). First-rate chapters on Bakunin and Kropotkin.

B. D. Wolfe, *Three Who Made a Revolution* (*Delta). A fine study of Lenin, Trotsky and Stalin, stressing the period before 1914.

The World Overseas

R. Koebner and H. D. Schmidt, *Imperialism: The Story and Significance of a Political Word* (Cambridge University, 1964). Important study, covering the period 1840–1960.

D. K. Fieldhouse, *The Colonial Empires: A Comparative Survey from the Eighteenth Century* (Delacorte, 1967). Indispensable reference work.

W. L. Langer, *The Diplomacy of Imperialism, 1890–1902*, 2nd. ed. (Knopf, 1951). Thorough study of a particularly hectic period of imperial rivalries.

P. Knaplund, *The British Empire, 1815–1939* (Harper, 1941). Authoritative history.

C. F. Carrington, *The British Overseas* (Cambridge, 1950). Detailed study of the "exploits of a nation of shopkeepers."

S. H. Roberts, *History of French Colonial Policy, 1870–1925*, 2 vols. (King, 1929). Excellent detailed account.

H. Brunschwig, *French Colonialism, 1871–1914* (Praeger, 1964). More recent study.

M. E. Townsend, *The Rise and Fall of Germany's Colonial Empire, 1884–1918* (Macmillan, 1930). The attempts to secure "a place in the sun."

J. W. Pratt, *America's Colonial Experiment* (Prentice-Hall, 1950). Valuable survey.

S. N. Fisher, *The Middle East: A History*, 2nd. ed. (Knopf, 1968). A rapid survey, stressing the nineteenth and twentieth centuries.

K. S. Latourette, *China* (*Spectrum). Reliable introduction.

E. O. Reischauer, *Japan Past and Present* (*Knopf). Brief introduction by a great American expert.

G. Sansom, *The Western World and Japan* (Knopf, 1950). Stimulating interpretation by a great British expert.

H. Brown, ed., *The Sahibs* (Hodge, 1948). Illuminating materials on the lives of the British in India.

The First World War

L. Lafore, *The Long Fuse* (°Preceptor). Crisp recent summary of the varying interpretations of the causes of the conflict.

W. L. Langer, *European Alliances and Alignments, 1871–1890* (°Knopf), and S. B. Fay, *Origins of the World War* (°Free Press). Standard older studies, rather sympathetic toward Germany; may be compared with the more Anglophile B. E. Schmitt, *The Coming of the War, 1914*, 2 vols. (Scribner, 1930).

E. R. May, *The World War and American Isolation, 1914–1917* (°Quadrangle). Scholarly study of a controversial problem.

C. R. M. Cruttwell, *History of the Great War*, 2nd ed. (Oxford, 1936); B. H. Liddell Hart, *The Real War, 1914–1918* (°Little, Brown); H. Baldwin, *World War I* (°Grove). Good one-volume histories.

B. Tuchman, *The Guns of August* (°Dell). Dramatic account of the crucial summer of 1914.

A. Moorehead, *Gallipoli* (Harper, 1956), and A. Horne, *The Price of Glory: Verdun, 1916* (°Colophon). Excellent accounts of particular campaigns.

F. P. Chambers, *The War behind the War, 1914–1918* (Harcourt, 1939). Discussion of the home fronts.

H. G. Nicolson, *Peacemaking, 1919* (Constable, 1933). Good account, by a British expert on diplomacy.

P. Birdsall, *Versailles Twenty Years After* (Reynal & Hitchcock, 1939). Dispassionate reappraisal.

J. M. Keynes, *The Economic Consequences of the Peace* (Harcourt, 1920). The famous attack by a bright young expert; thoughtfully reconsidered by E. Mantoux in *The Carthaginian Peace: or the Economic Consequences of Mr. Keynes* (°Pittsburgh).

T. A. Bailey, *Woodrow Wilson and the Great Betrayal* and *Woodrow Wilson and the Lost Peace* (°Quadrangle). Sound studies of America's role.

Fiction

A. Trollope, *The Prime Minister* (Oxford World's Classics). Realistic novel about Victorian politics.

R. Martin du Gard, *Jean Barois* (Viking, 1949). Good novel about the Dreyfus case.

T. Mann, *Buddenbrooks* (°Vintage) and *The Magic Mountain* (°Modern Library). Novels about a family in imperial Germany and about the sickness of European society, respectively.

L. Tolstoy, *Anna Karenina* (°many editions). Celebrated novel set in late nineteenth-century St. Petersburg and the Russian countryside.

The Portable Chekhov (°Viking). Selections from short stories and plays illustrating the malaise of the Russian aristocracy.

H. R. Haggard, *King Solomon's Mines* (°several editions). Rousing novel of imperialist adventure.

E. M. Forster, *A Passage to India* (°Harvest). Superb fictional depiction of the communication gap between Westerners and Easterners.

J. Romains, *Verdun* (Knopf, 1940). Good journalistic novel about the French in the trenches and on the home front, 1914–1916.

E. M. Remarque, *All Quiet on the Western Front* (°Premier), and E. Hemingway, *A Farewell to Arms* (°Scribner). Famous novels, by a German and an American respectively, showing postwar disillusionment.

C. S. Forester, *The General* (°Bantam). Astringent novel about the "brass" in World War I.

15

Reprise

1917—1945

American troops landing in Normandy, June, 1944.

I. Communist Russia, 1917–1941

Why did the first successful Marxist revolution take place in Russia, where conditions according to Marx should have been least favorable, a backward agricultural country almost without an urban proletariat? Marx underestimated the revolutionary force latent in the Russian peasantry and lacked the imagination to conceive such a brilliant, ruthless, and lucky tactician as Lenin. Moreover, the Russian revolution was not wholly Marxist; it temporarily retreated into a kind of capitalism, and then spawned in Stalin a brutal dictator in whose policies nationalism and greed for personal power played as important a role as Marxism. At untold expense in human lives Stalin's programs created an industrial state fed by a collectivized agriculture—a state that with much outside assistance withstood the savage attack that came from Adolf Hitler's Germany in June, 1941.

THE MARCH REVOLUTION AND THE PROVISIONAL GOVERNMENT

World War I took a terrible toll in Russia, almost four million casualties in the first year alone. Munitions manufacture and supply were inefficient. With the Tsar at the front after 1915, and the Duma prorogued, the Empress and her favorite, Rasputin, controlled the government, and adventurers and profiteers speculated in commissions, draft deferments, and commodities. Conservative patriots denounced the scandals, and in December, 1916, murdered Rasputin. Strikes and defeatism spread, while the armies bled to death at the front. The Tsar remained apathetic and refused all appeals to create a responsible ministry to clean up the mess.

The four days between March 8 and 12, 1917, saw a "leaderless, spontaneous, and anonymous revolution" in Petrograd (the new Russian name given to the capital city of St. Petersburg during the war). The troops of the Petrograd garrison refused to fire on workers striking in protest against food shortages and instead joined the strikers. A Soviet (council) of workers and soldiers with a fifteen-man executive committee took over the revolution, installed itself across the hall from the Duma, which remained in session, and asked that the Duma temporarily run the country. In consultation, Duma and Soviet created a "Provisional Government," composed mainly of Kadets (Constitutional Democrats; *see* Chapter 14), headed by a liberal, Prince Lvov, and including a radical labor lawyer and member of both Soviet and Duma, Alexander Kerensky. The Tsar abdicated and was arrested.

Between March and November, 1917, the Provisional Government struggled against enormous difficulties: its members had no experience in government; they felt they had simultaneously to continue the war and democratize the huge, unwieldy Russian Empire. The Soviet had the instruments of power, but would accept no responsibility. The Provisional Government did not have the tools to suppress its opponents, who multiplied especially in the provinces where local peasant-elected Soviets sprang up. The peasants wanted land immediately, but the Provisional Government believed in legality and refused to sanction peasant seizures of land. Virtually all Russians wanted peace, but the Provisional Government felt in honor bound to continue the war. While waiting for a constituent assembly which was to be elected to give Russia a new constitution, the Provisional Government granted complete political liberty.

LENIN AND THE NOVEMBER REVOLUTION

Bolsheviks and other exiles began to return to Russia and to political life. The German general staff thought that the return of Lenin from Switzerland would help disrupt the Russian war effort; so they permitted him to travel across Germany to the Baltic in a sealed railway car (April 16, 1917). Unlike most of his fellow Social Democrats, who believed that a bourgeois parliamentary republic had to precede any eventual socialist revolution, Lenin had long advocated an alliance between workers and peasants to bring about an immediate uprising, from which the Bolsheviks would eventually emerge supreme. Lenin regarded himself as chief of the élite inner group of the Bolshevik party, which in turn would command the working class. The brilliant intellectual Leon Trotsky, who recognized Lenin's implicitly dictatorial tendencies, had long believed that the working class could move to power directly after the bourgeois revolution without waiting for the establishment of a bourgeois republic. In line with these ideas, Lenin returned to Russia, calling for the immediate seizure of power by the Soviets, much to the surprise of all but a very few of his followers. Calling for the immediate confiscation of estates and an immediate end to the war, he suited the popular mood; the army, the police, all government officials must go, and a republic of Soviets must rise. Lenin galvanized the Bolsheviks into a revolutionary group waiting only for the moment to seize power.

When an offensive on the front collapsed in July, and some troops rioted in the capital, the Soviet was too timid to take power. Kerensky became premier, and General Kornilov, commander-in-chief of the army, rallied conservative support, planning a *coup* that would dispossess the Soviet. But railroad and telegraph workers sabotaged his movements, and his troops would not obey him. By September 14, Kornilov had been arrested; the only result of his efforts was increased pro-Bolshevik sentiment. The army mutiny got out of hand and peasant disorders mounted. Late in October, the Bolsheviks seized control of a military revolutionary committee originally chosen to defend the capital against the Germans, and now transformed by Trotsky into a general staff for the revolution. On November 7, with little bloodshed, the Bolsheviks took over Petrograd. Adopting the program of the SR's (Social Revolutionaries; *see* Chapter 14) Lenin abolished landlords' property rights, proposed an immediate peace, and set up a Council of People's Commissars with himself as President. Trotsky was Foreign Commissar; a young Georgian named Joseph Djugashvili, who called himself Stalin, became Commissar of Nationalities. With varying speed, as most provincial garrisons helped them, the Bolsheviks seized power in Moscow and in most of the provinces; Georgia, however, went Menshevik. Kornilov and some Duma politicians took refuge in Rostov-on-Don in southern Russia.

The Russian people were by no means pro-Bolshevik. When Lenin permitted elections for a constituent assembly, the first and last free elections in

Lenin addressing a throng in Moscow's Red Square, 1919.

Russian history, the Bolsheviks polled only about 25 per cent of the vote. The other socialist parties, chiefly the SR's, polled 62 per cent. Lenin permitted the assembly to meet only once (January 18, 1918); he dissolved it the next day by decree, and sent guards with rifles to disperse it. Thus he nullified the popular will. Russia did not have the high literacy rate, the tradition of debate, the respect for individual rights, or the large middle class usually associated with successful constitutional government. But it was Lenin's arbitrary use of force that ended the chance for true parliamentarism in Russia.

CIVIL WAR AND FOREIGN INTERVENTION, 1917–1921

For the next three years, to the end of 1920, civil war raged in Russia, and foreign powers intervened to assist the enemies of the Bolsheviks, who changed their name to Communists and in 1918 shifted the capital to Moscow. The Bolsheviks at first believed that world revolution would soon begin in Germany and then engulf other nations; so they treated foreign affairs casually. By 1920, they completed the nationalization of all banks and all industrial enterprises employing more than ten workers. They requisitioned food from the peasants, mobilized the poorer ones against the richer peasants (*kulak*, meaning "fist," and implying hard-fisted usuriousness), and set up a secret police (the "Cheka," from the initials of the words meaning "extraordinary commission"). Early in 1918, they signed the Treaty of Brest–Litovsk with Germany (*see* Chapter 14) giving away one-third of Russia's population, 80 per cent of its iron, and 90 per cent of its coal (March 3, 1918).

The civil war started when a brigade of Czech soldiers, mostly deserters from the Habsburg armies, originally intended for use against the Germans on the Eastern front, was sent east across Siberia by rail so that they could proceed by ship to the Western front. The Czechs quarreled with Hungarian prisoners on a Siberian railway siding, and when the Soviet regime tried to punish them for killing a Hungarian, they seized some towns in western Siberia. The local SR's were sympathetic to them, and local anti-Bolshevik armies sprang up. It was under threat from one of them in July, 1918, that a local Soviet decided to execute the Tsar and his entire family rather than lose possession of them. All were murdered.

British, French, Japanese, and American forces landed in Vladivostok in August, 1918, after the Czechs had overthrown the local Soviet; British and Americans also landed at Archangel. In Siberia there were three different anti-Communist governments of varying complexions. Trotsky now took the lead in organizing a Red Army, which was to be three million strong by 1920. The Reds moved back into part of the Ukraine, after the Soviet government repudiated Brest–Litovsk following the German collapse in the West. After severe fighting, the Red Army defeated its three main "White" enemies: General Denikin moving north from Rostov and the Caucasus, Admiral Kolchak operating from Omsk in Siberia, and General Yudenich in the Baltic region. Next, in 1920, the Reds fought with the Poles, who drove them from Warsaw with the help of the French chief of staff, General Weygand. At the peace in October, 1920, Poland obtained a large area of the Ukraine and White Russia not inhabited by Poles and far to the east of the ethnic frontier.

The Reds won the civil war in part because the Whites could not unite on a

Russia in Revolution, 1917-1921

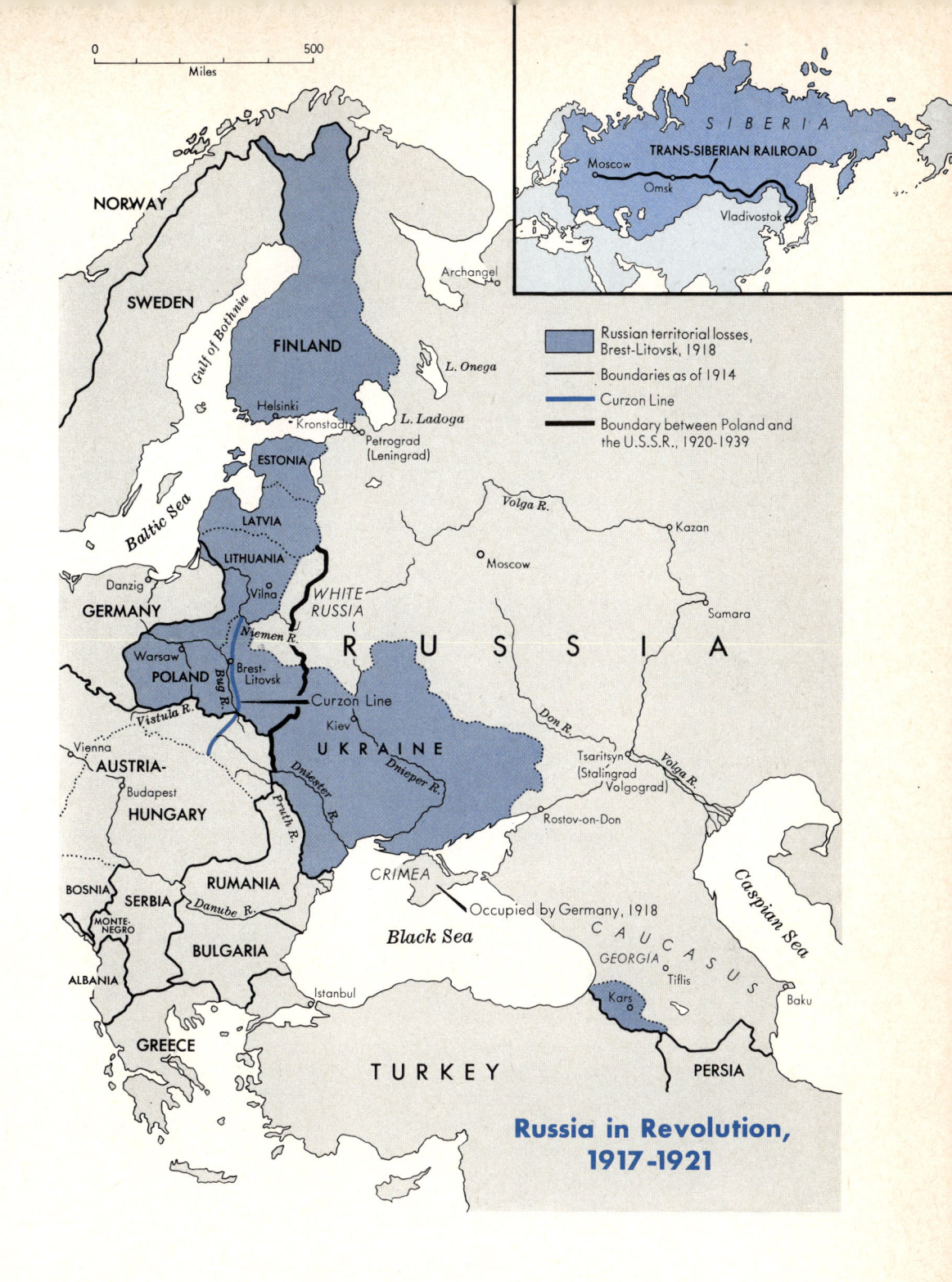

political program beyond the mere overthrow of the Reds. The White forces were located on the outer edge of the huge Russian territory, whereas the Reds had internal lines of communication, greater manpower, and more of the weapons inherited from the tsarist armies. The Whites never gained the support of the peasantry; indeed they often restored the landlords. Allied intervention on the White side was ineffectual and amateurish. It enabled the Reds to pose as defenders of the nation against foreign invaders, but it may at least have prevented the Reds from sponsoring successful revolutions in other countries.

THE NEP, 1921–1928

By the end of the civil war, all vital services had broken down in Russia, and famine was raging; agricultural and industrial output had fallen disastrously. Anarchist revolts broke out, most notably at the naval base of Kronstadt (March, 1921), and were suppressed with much bloodshed; but they frightened Lenin into a change of policy. The "New Economic Policy" (always called NEP), adopted in 1921 and lasting until 1928, marked a temporary retreat from doctrinaire communist programs. Its chief aim was reconstruction, sought by appeasing the peasants and—since there had been no world revolution—by obtaining the resources of capitalist states.

The government now stopped requisitioning the whole of the peasant's crop above the minimum necessary to keep him alive. He paid a very heavy tax in kind, but could sell the rest of his crop to a private purchaser if he wished. Peasant agriculture became capitalist again, and the kulaks grew still richer, while the poor peasants often lost their land and hired out their labor. The state controlled heavy industry, banking, transportation, and foreign trade—what Lenin called the "commanding heights"—but allowed private enterprise in domestic trade and light industry. The partial return to capitalism brought economic recovery by 1926–1927.

Many leading communists hated NEP, and functionaries often subjected enterprising businessmen or farmers to petty persecution. Those who wanted to abolish NEP, liquidate those who profited by it, and push world revolution were called "Left deviationists": they included Trotsky. Those who wanted to push the NEP program still further were the "Right deviationists": their chief spokesman was Nikolai Bukharin. The question agitated the communist leaders, especially as a result of the final illness of Lenin (1922–1924).

STALIN'S RISE TO POWER

The two leading contenders to succeed Lenin were Trotsky and Stalin. Toward the end of his life Lenin was urging that Stalin should be deprived of power, and it was only Lenin's death that saved Stalin's career. To defeat Trotsky, Stalin first allied himself with Bukharin and argued for a kind of gradualism: peasant cooperatives but not collectives, no forced industrialization program, limited cooperation with capitalist states and parties abroad. Having deprived Trotsky of influence, Stalin adopted many of Trotsky's ideas. Finding that agricultural production was not keeping pace with industry, he came out in 1927 for collectivization. He favored rapid industrialization, and realized that this would involve huge investments of capital. Trotsky argued that socialism in a single country could not succeed until world revolution brought communism to the industrial nations, making their skills available to the cause; Stalin, on the other hand, maintained that Russia, while helping communist movements everywhere, could succeed as a "socialist" state by itself. His argument reflected his own Russian nationalism as well as his bid for popularity with the rank and file in Russia.

Stalin's victory, however, had less to do with the merits of the rival theories competing for acceptance in Russia during the 1920's than with his personal power. As Commissar of Nationalities he managed the destiny of almost half the population of the new Russian Soviet Republic and that of all the Asians in the "republics" that he took charge of creating and that preserved and fostered native languages and cultures. In 1922 he sponsored the formation of the USSR (Union of Socialist Soviet Republics), with Moscow firmly controlling war, foreign policy, trade, and transport, coordinating finance, economy, food, and labor, but leaving justice, education, and agriculture in theory to the separate republics. A Council of Nationalities—with equal numbers of delegates from each ethnic group— became a second chamber, the Supreme Soviet being the first. Together they would appoint the administration, the Council of People's Commissars.

As chief of the Workers' and Peasants' Inspectorate, Stalin could send his men anywhere in the government to eliminate inefficiency or corruption. He was also a member of the Politburo, the tight little group of Communist party bosses, where his job was to manage the party: he prepared the agenda for meetings, passed on orders, controlled party patronage, maintained files on individuals' loyalty and achievement. Apparently an unobtrusive bureaucrat, Stalin had in fact got hold of the real reins of power.

Trotsky was much more glamorous: Minister of War, creator of the Red Army, a cultivated intellectual. But Stalin and two Bolshevik collaborators sent Trotsky's supporters to posts abroad, prevented the publication of Lenin's attacks on Stalin, and gradually deprived Trotsky of his positions. In 1927 Stalin had Trotsky expelled from the party and deported to Siberia, the first stage in a long exile that eventually brought him to Mexico, where an emissary from Stalin murdered him with an ice-axe in 1940.

STALIN IN POWER: COLLECTIVIZATION

The same congress that expelled Trotsky in December, 1927, brought NEP to an end, and announced a "new socialist offensive" for 1928. Stalin became supreme, and the years between 1928 and 1941 would see the collectivization of agriculture, forced industrialization, the great political purges, and the building of an authoritarian state apparatus.

In 1929 Stalin declared war on the kulaks and virtually ended individual farming in Russia, proclaiming immediate full-scale collectivization. In exchange for locating and turning over to the state hidden crops belonging to the kulaks, the poorer peasants were promised places in collective farms to be made up of the kulaks' land and equipped with their implements. There were about two million kulak households in Russia, perhaps ten million people in all, who would now not only lose their property but be refused any place in the new collectives. Peasants were gunned into submission, kulaks deported to Siberia or allowed to starve. Rather than join collectives peasants often burned their crops, broke their plows, and killed their cattle. Between one-half and two-thirds of the livestock in Russia were slaughtered. Famine took mil-

The exiled Trotsky and his wife arriving in Mexico, 1937.

lions of human lives. In March, 1930, Stalin blamed local officials who had been "dizzy with success" for the tragedy. In one year 50 per cent of Russian farms had been thrown into collectives. Thereafter the process was more gradual and there were fewer excesses. By 1941 virtually all Russian farms had been collectivized: there were 250,000 collectives, 900,000,000 acres in extent, supporting 19,000,000 families.

The *artel,* or cooperative, in which each family *owned* its homestead, some livestock, and minor implements, soon became the predominant type of collective farm or *kolkhoz.* On the collectively managed land, the peasants labored under brigade-commanders, and were remunerated according to their output, measured by the artificial unit of the "labor day." One day's work in managing a farm might be evaluated as three "labor days," while three days weeding a vegetable patch might be only half a "labor day." Every kolkhoz turned over to the government a fixed amount of produce at fixed rates. The sum total of food collected was supposed to guarantee the feeding of the urban population, especially industrial laborers and members of the army. The kolkhoz also paid taxes for local purposes. Surpluses might be sold by the peasant directly to a consumer, but private resale was punished as speculation. At least two-thirds of the government revenue in the years after 1934 came from resale on the market at a large profit of food acquired cheaply from the kolkhoz; the government profit was called the "turnover tax." By controlling the supply of farm machinery to the kolkhoz through the establishment of Machine Tractor Stations (MTS), the government could maintain surveillance over farm operations and greatly affect the success or failure of any individual kolkhoz manager.

THE FIVE-YEAR PLANS

In industry, 1928 saw the first of the Five-Year Plans, setting ambitious goals for production over the coming five years. Stalin appropriated ever bigger sums for capital investment, and often demanded impossibly high rates of growth. Partly, the motive was to mechanize the new large-scale farms by the rapid production of tractors and by building power stations. Partly, Stalin wanted to create the mass industrial working class that Marxism taught was necessary for socialism. Partly, he was determined to make socialism in Russia secure against outside attack, which he was sure threatened from all directions. Though the goals of the first Five-Year Plan were not attained by 1932, fulfillment was announced, and the second Plan for 1933–1937 went into effect. The third followed in due course, and was interrupted only by German invasion in 1941.

The Five-Year Plans emphasized heavy industry: steel, electric power, cement, coal, oil. Between 1928 and 1940 steel output went up four-and-one-half times, power eight, cement more than two, coal four, and oil almost three, with similar rises in chemical and machine production. Russia did in about twelve years what the rest of Europe had taken three-quarters of a century to do. Enthusiasm was whipped up by publicizing awards to especially productive workers. Yet the hardships were great. Inexperience and inefficiency cost heavily, and housing the workers, moving whole industries, and opening up new resources cost hundreds of thousands of lives. The state managed the economy directly, and *Gosplan* (the state planning commission) drew up the plans and supervised their fulfillment. *Gosbank* regulated capital investment, so that the iron and steel trust, for example, had its own mines, blast-furnaces, and rolling mills. In each plant, as on each kolkhoz, the manager was consulted on setting production targets and was held responsible for meeting the goals.

Russia by 1940 had one-third (instead of 18 per cent) of its people living in cities. Moscow and Leningrad (the former Petrograd and, before that, St. Petersburg) almost doubled in size, and smaller towns grew even faster. The whole social picture had been changed. The pre-revolutionary privileged classes had disappeared; the middle class, temporarily reprieved by NEP, vanished after 1928; most of the old intelligentsia, unable to stomach the dictatorship, emigrated. Those who stayed were forced into line with the new Soviet intellectual movements, and were expected to concentrate their efforts on technological advances. Stalin's new system of incentives rewarded the small minority of skilled laborers, bureaucrats, and kolkhoz bosses, together with writers, artists, and entertainers, who formed the new élite. Although Soviet propaganda predicted the withering away of the state and reasserted that true communism was still the goal, the USSR fostered not Marxist equality but a new caste system.

STALIN'S DICTATORSHIP

Opposition to Stalin's ruthlessness existed, of course, but he imagined it to be everywhere. In 1934 the famous and mysterious purges began. Unlike the Jacobin terror in France, these did not begin until seventeen years after the onset of the revolution; unlike Robespierre, Stalin survived. The murder of the party boss of Leningrad, Sergei Kirov (December 1, 1934), touched off the first purge. Kirov apparently had urged Stalin to relax his pressures, and Stalin probably arranged his murder. At intervals until 1938 a series of trials, some of them secret, and many executions without trial led to the death of every member of Lenin's Politburo except Stalin himself. Most of the Soviet diplomatic corps, 50 of the 71 members of the Communist party's Central Committee, judges, two successive heads of the secret police, and the prime ministers and chief officials of the non-Russian republics of the USSR—all were murdered or disappeared without a trace. It is doubtful whether any of the victims had actually conspired with Hitler, as some were accused of doing, though many of them certainly hated Stalin. Some who confessed publicly probably felt so deep a loyalty to the communist system that they sacrificed themselves for Stalin's Soviet state. Some doubtless hoped to save their families or even themselves; many may have hoped that the confessions were so ridiculous that nobody would believe them. Despite the upheaval, no breakdown in the system took place; new bureaucrats quickly replaced the old.

In 1936, while the purges were going on, Stalin proclaimed a new Soviet Constitution. Though it purported to extend civil liberties, these were nothing but a sham. Only the Communist party organizations had the right to nominate candidates for office. Any citizen might apply for membership in the party to a local branch, which voted on the application after a year of trial. Party organizations existed not only in every territorial subdivision but in every factory, farm, and office; at every level, agitation and propaganda, organization and training were carried on. Government policy was party policy. Stalin was chairman of the Council of People's Commissars (the cabinet, appointed by the Supreme Soviet), chairman of the Politburo (the supreme governing body of the party, appointed by the Central Committee), and General Secretary of the party, as well as Commissar for Defense. Similar overlapping of party and government posts was the regular practice. In 1936 and 1940 new republics were added to the USSR, making the grand total sixteen, each with its government patterned on that of the Soviet Union itself.

The period 1928–1941 also saw a wholesale retreat from many of the ideas of the revolution. In the army traditional ranks were restored. Russia's national past was officially rediscovered and praised. The family, attacked by the old Bolsheviks who had made divorce and abortion easy, was rehabilitated; Stalin stressed the sanctity of marriage, made divorce more difficult to get, and encouraged children to obey their parents. In education, the authority of the teacher over the schoolroom was reaffirmed after a long period of classroom anarchy. But education became indoctrination, as newspapers, books, theaters, movies, music, and art all plugged the party line. Censorship under Stalin outdid censorship under Nicholas I, since it prescribed that all artists constantly praise the system. Even the traditional militant atheism of the Bolsheviks was modified in 1937, as church-going no longer constituted reason for persecution or arrest. All these measures were designed partly to retain popular loyalty during the disruptive purges of the party, and also to prepare for a German attack. Whatever the shift in views, Stalin dictated and managed it.

SOVIET FOREIGN POLICY

After the civil war had ended, the Soviet regime realized that world revolution would not take place immediately; it did not, however, abandon its intention to assist communists everywhere to bring it about. In 1919, Lenin founded the Third International (Comintern) dedicated to the purpose. This operated alongside the Soviet Foreign Office, but sometimes in seeming contradiction to it, giving Soviet foreign policy a peculiar dual nature. The Foreign Office concluded treaties with England and other European countries promising not to stir up revolutions. By the Treaty of Rapallo (1922) with defeated Germany, Russia obtained technical assistance from the Germans while giving them an opportunity to defy the Treaty of Versailles secretly by building arms and aircraft factories in Russia. The Comintern meanwhile tried but failed to install communist regimes in Italy, Bulgaria, Germany, Poland, and China. By 1928, with Stalin in full control, the Comintern was brought into line with the Soviet Foreign Office in order to avoid further foreign-policy conflict.

Stalin himself had contempt for the rest of the world and little real interest in foreign communists. His attack on Social Democrats as the worst enemies of communism helped the triumph of Hitler and the Nazis in Germany. Only the realization that Hitler was proceeding to liquidate German communists and the fear of German attack on Russia led Stalin to join the League of Nations (1934) and to reach pacts with France and Czechoslovakia (1935). Now the Comintern suddenly shifted its line and embraced the Social Democrats it had been attacking, urging the formation of "popular fronts" against fascism. "Popular Front" regimes came to power in France and Spain, and many individuals in the West naïvely sympathized with the communists both inside the Soviet Union and outside, although Stalin's extermination of his own party hierarchy in the purges led to serious doubts about the effectiveness of Russia as an ally.

Hitler, however, repeatedly declared his intention of eventually attacking the Soviet Union. Western appeasement of Hitler and neutrality in the Spanish Civil War, which we treat later in this chapter, convinced Stalin that the western

European nations only intended to turn the full force of Hitler's expansion against Russia. Not until 1939 did the British and French reluctantly conclude that their security demanded a firmer alliance with the USSR, and by then Stalin was negotiating with the Germans. The Soviet–German pact of late August, 1939, freed Hitler to attack first Poland and then the West. It bought Russia less than two years to prepare her defenses, hardly the long period Stalin had hoped for; in June, 1941, came the full-scale German assault on the USSR.

II. Fascism, 1918–1939

By 1939 authoritarian governments of the Right, generally called fascist, were in firm control of Italy, Germany, Spain, and all the countries of eastern Europe except Russia and Czechoslovakia. Fear of revolution from the Left played a large role in bringing them to power; so did economic depression. The fascists expressed a violent—often mystical—nationalism, and usually offered a vaguely radical program to win mass support. All fascist movements had colored shirts, private armies, special salutes and war-cries, mass hypnotism in special ceremonies, and a vast program of eventual conquest. All of them opposed democracy, liberalism, and parliamentary institutions as much as they did communism, with which in fact they shared an abhorrence of constitutional procedure and a disregard for the individual human being. Censorship, political police, concentration camps, the rule of the bludgeon, the end of legal protection—all these characterized both fascism and communism. Yet the circumstances which enabled these movements to take over varied widely from country to country.

ITALY

In Italy, heavy war casualties and a postwar slump bred discontent, intensified by the failure of the Allies to give the Italians promised territories in Dalmatia. Young men released from the army and with no job to go to drifted restlessly, a prey for leaders with glittering promises. Gabriele d'Annunzio, romantic nationalist poet, seized the Adriatic seaport of Fiume with a band of followers clad in black shirts and brandishing daggers, and hysterically threatened to move on Rome and thence conquer the world. Though the Italian government liquidated the Fiume adventure in 1920, Benito Mussolini (1883–1944) imitated d'Annunzio in many ways and to more purpose in building the fascist movement between 1918 and 1922.

Mussolini, who had begun his career as a radical socialist, a pacifist, anti-monarchist, atheist, and anti-nationalist, repudiated all these youthful positions. He subsequently attacked bolshevism, made his peace with crown and church, and became a mystic nationalist and a rabid militarist. He was consistent only in his hatred for parliaments, his love of violence, and his yearning for power. In 1919 he founded the first *fasci di combattimento* ("groups for combat") and began his rise to power by spouting extreme radicalism. He shifted his course when he saw that popular opinion feared the danger of a communist revolution (actually not very probable in Italy), and put himself forward as the protector of Italy against bolshevism. Mussolini's bands went around beating up communists and socialists and indeed anybody in workman's clothes, and obtained army trucks, gasoline, and weapons from a government frightened of revolution. Between 1920 and 1922 perhaps 2,000 people were killed. The fascists entered Parliament and became a political party (1921), gaining highly placed sympathizers in the royal family and among officers and industrialists. In October, 1922, the famous fascist "March on Rome" took place, with Mussolini himself arriving by sleeping-car after the King had invited him to form a government.

Mussolini secured temporary dictatorial powers from Parliament and took over the administration of Italy. A fascist militia owed allegiance to him alone, while the army took an oath of personal loyalty to him. He obtained an amendment to the electoral laws, providing that the political party receiving the largest number of votes, if the total was at least 25 per cent of the vote, should receive two-thirds of the seats in Parliament. By April, 1924, the cabinet was wholly fascist. The murder of a socialist deputy, Matteotti (June, 1924), by members of Mussolini's immediate circle caused a scandal, but Mussolini weathered the storm. Control over the press, arrests of political opponents, a law providing the death penalty for action against Mussolini, the abolition of non-fascist political parties—all strengthened the dictatorship. Like Stalin, Mussolini was both chief of the party (*Duce*) and chief of the government (*Capo di Governo*). His fascist Grand Council of 24 corresponded to the Soviet Politburo.

Mussolini claimed that representation in the government should be based on economic interests organized in "syndicates," a theory advanced before World War I by the French revolutionary syndicalist Georges Sorel. But while Sorel believed in government by syndicates of workers only, and in class warfare, Mussolini believed in producers' syndicates as well as workers' and in capitalism and class collaboration. In April, 1926, the state officially recognized both producers' and workers' syndicates in industry, agriculture, commerce, transportation, and banking, with a separate syndicate of intellectuals. Each of these could bargain and reach contracts, and could assess dues on all those engaged in its own field. Strikes and lockouts were forbidden. Soon afterwards, Mussolini

Mussolini during the fascist "March on Rome," 1922.

became Minister of Corporations, the boss of the syndicate system and the architect of a much publicized "corporative state." In 1928 the law was changed so that parliamentary representation would be by syndicate, although the fascist Grand Council had the veto power over any candidate nominated. Further steps soon pushed the syndicates into greater prominence, until the old Chamber of Deputies "committed suicide" and declared itself replaced by a Chamber of Fasces and Corporations. Whatever the machinery, Mussolini remained firmly in personal control of it, and the fascist bureaucracy continued to run the economic and political life of Italy.

During the 1930's the government strove to make the country self-sufficient in agriculture, to subsidize shipping and air transport, and to protect Italian industry by high tariffs. Public works were undertaken, marshes drained and reclaimed, malaria was attacked, and the hydroelectric system greatly expanded. Despite these modern improvements, however, Italy could not overcome its deficiencies in essential raw materials. Socially, Mussolini made emigration a crime; he encouraged large families in order to swell his armies and bolster his claim that overpopulated Italy must expand abroad. From the age of six, children were drawn into fascist youth movements, while school textbooks, newspapers, books, plays, and movies were all made vehicles of fascist propaganda. The secret police hunted down all those suspected of opposition. Mussolini settled the Roman question (*see* Chapter 14) by recognizing the Vatican City as independent, and Catholicism as the state religion (Lateran Treaty, 1929). Yet friction between government and papacy did not entirely disappear.

In foreign affairs, as we shall see later, Mussolini undertook a policy of adventure that led Italy from aggression to aggression: against Greece (1923), Ethiopia (1935), the Spanish Republic (1936–1939), and Albania (1939). It drove him to ally with his fellow-fascist, Hitler, and to press claims against the French for Corsica, Tunisia, Nice, and Savoy, thus alienating Italy from her natural allies, France and Britain. The German alliance also led to a new domestic policy: anti-Semitism. Italy had only 70,000 Jews, most of them long resident, and thoroughly Italian in sentiment; some of them were fascist. But in 1938 Germany successfully pressed Mussolini to expel Jews from the Fascist party, and to forbid them to teach or attend school, to intermarry with non-Jews, or to obtain licenses to conduct business.

GERMANY

The Early Years of the Weimar Republic. For 15 years before Hitler established his Nazi dictatorship in 1933 Germany conducted an experiment in democratic government. This was the "Weimar Republic," named after the constitution adopted in Weimar in 1919. The immediate postwar years, down through 1923, were very difficult for the young German republic, which faced mounting economic chaos and political threats from both Left and Right.

The defeat in World War I surprised the German people, who had never been given the true news from the battlefields. Seeing their armies come home intact, many Germans simply could not believe they had lost the war. The refusal of the Allies to force the defeated German generals to surrender put the odium of dealing with the victors on the civilian politicians, and the German generals insisted that they had been sold out. So there grew the legend of the "stab in the back": civilians, democrats, liberals, socialists, communists, and Jews had betrayed the armies—or so said the monarchists, agrarians, industrialists, and militarists. The "war-guilt" clause in the Versailles Treaty, which forced Germany to assume full responsibility for the outbreak of the war, made it harder for the Germans to acknowledge defeat; many of them used their energies in denying guilt, hating their enemies, and plotting for a second chance.

The Social Democrats, who proclaimed the Republic two days before the armistice of November 11, 1918, followed a moderate policy. They did not attack large landed estates or attempt to nationalize industry, and they concluded collective bargaining agreements with the industrialists. To their left, communists and fellow-travellers tried to stage a revolution on the Russian model in the winter of 1918–1919, but the Social Democrats used the army to stop it. A Soviet republic did emerge briefly in Bavaria; although it was liquidated in May, 1919, Bavaria became the home of a permanent red-scare. Local Bavarian authorities steadily encouraged right-wing intrigues. Here former soldiers banded together in rabidly antidemocratic "Free Corps" units, which specialized in violence and assassinations; here Hitler got his start.

Parties accepting the Republic were, in addition to the Social Democrats, the Catholic Center, which favored moderate social legislation; the Democrats, a middle-class group; and the People's party, which included the moderate industrialists. On the Right, the anti-republican Nationalists commanded the support of many great industrialists, bureaucrats, and members of the lower middle classes. The parties supporting the Republic won 75 per cent of the seats in the elections for a constituent assembly in 1919. By the Weimar Constitution, the President, though sharing executive authority with the Chancellor and cabinet, had powers that made dictatorship a real possibility: for example, he could temporarily suspend civil liberties and take whatever measures he might deem necessary to restore order. Voting by proportional representation for entire party lists of candidates encouraged small splinter parties to multiply and prevented independent voters from "splitting" the ticket.

The first President, the Social Democrat Friedrich Ebert, overcame a *coup* (*Putsch*) from the Right in 1920 by calling a general strike that paralyzed Germany. A communist uprising in the Ruhr region followed, and when German troops entered the area, demilitarized by the Treaty of Versailles, the French intervened. Extremists were further encouraged by the great bill for reparations (132 billion gold marks) presented by the Allies (April, 1921). Moderate politicians who tried to prove German good will by fulfilling German obligations were murdered: the Catholic Erzberger (1921) and the Jew Rathenau (1922). Amidst the disorders the National Socialist Party of the German Workers, an obscure group founded by an expatriate Austrian and frustrated artist Adolf Hitler (1889–1945), made its appearance.

Drawing on the pseudo-scientific race theories of "Nordic" and "Aryan" supremacy as enunciated by Gobineau (1816–1882) and others, and influenced by Austrian Christian Socialism and Karl Lueger (*see* Chapter 14), Hitler favored the elimination of Jews from all aspects of German life, and a radical economic program including the confiscation of war profits, nationalization of trusts, and land-grants to the peasants. Endowed with hypnotic oratorical gifts, Hitler made himself absolute leader (*Führer:* compare Mussolini's title, *Duce*) of his party. He founded a brown-shirted corps called the SA (*Sturmabteilung,* storm-troops) wearing swastika armbands; like the Italian fascists, the SA had illegal access to government supplies of arms. At first, however, these Nazis (the name comes from the pronunciation of the German word *national*) were merely a minor political force.

Inflation, Fulfillment, and Depression. In 1922 and 1923 Germany suffered from a runaway inflation, resulting in part from the failure of the wartime government to pay the expenses of the war through taxes. Having expected to win and extract the costs from the losers, the Kaiser had simply borrowed from the banks and repaid them with paper money not backed by gold. Prices rose, and wages followed; the inflationary spiral was intensified, though not originally caused, by reparations payments. When the Germans defaulted on their payments, the French occupied the Ruhr area (January, 1923), intending to recoup their loss by the products of this industrial region. The German government ordered the Ruhr workers to quit their jobs.

To finance this passive resistance and support the idle workers the government hastily issued almost incalculable amounts of increasingly worthless currency. The mark, normally worth 4.2 to the dollar, had dropped to 8.4 in 1918; it finally sank to the grotesque extreme of several trillions to the dollar. Lifetime savings were wiped out overnight, real property took on fantastic value, and speculation flourished. While many industrialists took advantage of the inflation to pay off their indebtedness in worthless marks, the workers suffered as the purchasing power of wages vanished. The middle classes suffered too, particu-

Ludendorff (center) and Hitler at their trial for involvement in the beer-hall putsch of 1923.

larly those living on fixed incomes, but in class-conscious Germany they could not make common cause with the working-class parties; instead they turned away from the moderate republican parties to the Nationalists and to Hitler's Nazis.

In the fall of 1923 Gustav Stresemann, leader of the People's party and Chancellor, ordered passive resistance ended and work resumed in the Ruhr. In Munich, the capital of Bavaria, Hitler announced in a beer-hall the beginning of a "national revolution"; troops stopped this premature Nazi effort, and Hitler went to jail. Though sentenced to five years, which was mild enough for high treason, he actually spent only eight months in a comfortable cell writing *Mein Kampf* (My Battle), the famous bible of the Nazis. The episode illustrated the partiality of the courts for conspirators of the Right.

In the last months of 1923 the government granted extraordinary powers to fiscal experts, who stopped printing the old currency and opened a new bank to issue new marks, which were simply assigned the prewar value of 4.2 to the dollar. Not gold but an imaginary "mortgage" on all of Germany's agricultural and industrial wealth backed this currency. One trillion old marks might be exchanged for one new one. These were both psychological and economic measures that restored confidence, but at the cost of further hardships. The government proclaimed rigorous economy and increased taxes; as prices fell, overexpanded businesses collapsed; unemployment rose, wages stayed low, and hours of work remained long. The Allies contributed to ending the crisis by formulating the Dawes Plan (1924); the French were to leave the Ruhr, and a special bank would receive reparations payments; these, in turn, would be financed for the first five years by an international loan. Within Germany, though the Right loudly protested, a moderate coalition accepted the terms.

From late 1924 to late 1929, the Weimar Republic experienced political stability, undertook fulfillment of the Versailles Treaty requirements, and enjoyed seeming economic prosperity. First-rate German equipment, technical skills, and imitation of American industrial methods increased production. "Vertical trusts," like those in the USSR but privately owned, brought together all processes from mining to the finishing of the product. Since heavy industry was emphasized, prosperity depended in part upon a big armaments program. Reparations were paid with no damage to the German economy, as foreign investments, especially American, more than balanced the outflow.

The election of the wartime commander, Marshal von Hindenburg, as President in 1925 created some dismay abroad, but until 1930 Hindenburg conducted himself in accordance with the constitution. Prosperity brought political moderation. Abroad, Germany joined the European system of security, signing the Locarno pact (1925, *see* p. 617), joining the League of Nations (1926), and in 1929 signing the Kellogg–Briand Pact, which outlawed aggressive war. In 1929 the Young Plan reduced the original total of reparations demanded by the Allies and established lower rates of payment. The Allies evacuated the Rhineland in 1930, three years earlier than the date set by the Treaty of Versailles.

But the Great Depression that began in 1929 knocked the props out from under the Weimar Republic. Foreign credit was no longer available; unemployment, hunger, and want reappeared. The middle classes, with no unemployment insurance, were the hardest hit. Hitler, whose fortunes had fallen low in the years of fulfillment, reaped the harvest. The new Chancellor, Bruening of the Center party, appointed in 1930, found himself unable to continue fulfillment or to support republican institutions. Encouraged by a scheming political soldier, von

Schleicher, President Hindenburg longed to rule by decree. In the elections of September, 1930, the Nazis and Communists made great gains; although they fought each other in the streets, they often collaborated in their voting. Depression became acute with the failure of a major Austrian bank in 1931. The Nazis and their SA private army, the armed organization of war veterans known as the Steel Helmets (*Stahlhelm*), and other right-wing groups coalesced and agitated against Bruening. Early in 1932 Hitler won the support of the Ruhr coal and steel magnates at a private meeting. He ran against Hindenburg for President in 1932, and lost, but the 84-year-old President was now himself the tool of the Right.

In May, 1932, Hindenburg dismissed Bruening and installed a government of noblemen under the Right-Centrist von Papen, who succeeded in getting the allies to relieve Germany of all further obligations for reparations. But when the Nazis gained in the elections of July, 1932, Papen resisted the pressure to resign and to let Hitler become Chancellor. Instead, he called new elections, hoping to whittle down the Nazi representation; he succeeded. In November, 1932, the Nazis were slipping, money was drying up, and Hitler was desperate. Schleicher's intrigues, however, prevented Papen's success at this juncture; Schleicher himself, who had no political following, became Chancellor for eight weeks and then gave way to Hitler, whom Papen now supported, and whom the industrialists were ready once again to subsidize. On January 30, 1933, Hitler took office; the Weimar Republic was doomed.

Germany under Hitler, 1933–1939. Hitler's transformation of his chancellorship into a dictatorship was assisted by the famous Reichstag fire (February, 1933), which Hitler may well have ordered set himself but which he blamed on the communists. Applying his emergency powers, President Hindenburg suspended freedom of speech and the press, while the SA used terror freely. In March, 1933, a newly elected Reichstag voted an Enabling Act suspending the constitution; it was renewed in 1937 and 1943. Hitler stripped the state governments of their individual powers, and made Berlin supreme; he assumed the office of President when Hindenburg died (1934), and he dissolved the other political parties. The Nazis followed the lead of the Russian communists and the Italian fascists in their network of party organization and their youth groups. On June 30, 1934, Hitler ruthlessly purged those members of the Nazi party who might embarrass him now he was in power, including many SA leaders and radicals.

Anti-Semitism, long a chief tenet of Hitler, motivated much of his legislation. The Jews of Germany numbered about 600,000 in a country of 60,000,000; they had become leading members of the professions. Most of them were assimilated and patriotic Germans, and many would have followed Hitler in everything but his anti-Semitism. By the Nuremberg Laws (September, 1935) no person with a single Jewish grandparent might be a German citizen, marry a non-Jew, fly the national flag, write or publish, act on stage or screen, teach, work in banks, give concerts, or sell books or antiques; nor might he receive unemployment insurance or charity. The names of Jews who had died for Germany in World War I were erased from war memorials. In November, 1938, a Jewish boy of seventeen, driven to desperation by the persecution of his parents, shot and killed a secretary of the German embassy in Paris. This was the signal for a systematic and organized pillage of Jewish shops in Germany, and for other severe measures, including special costumes and names for Jews. Measures designed to make life impossible for Jews were only the prelude to actual physical extermination in

World War II. Few "civilized" non-Jews in Germany ran the risk of protesting. Meantime, the regime encouraged "Nordic" purity by favoring early marriages and many children, and by introducing sterilization for the racially impure.

Abandoning traditional legal principles, Hitler created a new system of "people's courts" to try all cases of treason. He appointed all the judges. Concentration camps were established for enemies of the regime, and the Gestapo (*Geheime Staatspolizei*, Secret State Police) opened private mail, tapped wires, and spied on the citizenry. In economic life, the Nazis protected large estates, but fixed farm production goals as well as farm prices and wages. As part of preparation for war, Hitler spurred a drive toward agricultural self-sufficiency, which was 83 per cent successful by 1937, except for fats and coffee.

Imitating Stalin, Hitler embarked on industrial planning, with a Four-Year Plan in 1933 and a second one in 1937. The first, by means of labor camps, public works, and armament manufacture, reduced unemployment. The second was designed to render Germany blockade-proof in the event of war. Output of raw materials was increased and their allocation strictly controlled, with war industry getting first priority. New synthetic rubber and motor fuels were produced, and an enormous vertical iron and steel trust was instituted. A Nazi Labor Front replaced all labor unions and employers' organizations. Workers could not change jobs without the state's permission, and all men and women of working age might be conscripted for labor.

In religious affairs, some of the Nazis favored a return to the worship of German pagan gods, but since they ruled a nominally Christian country, they took over the Lutheran national synod and appointed their own bishop. With the Catholics Hitler reached a Concordat in 1933, guaranteeing freedom of worship, and permitting religious instruction in the schools; yet the Nazis broke their promises, often insulting and persecuting individual priests. Millions of Protestants and Catholics alike nonetheless gave complete support to the regime. In the arts, Hitler's own vulgar tastes became standard. In education, Nazi doctrine and the great past achievements of Germany were stressed; the aim of the schools was to develop strong bodies and the military spirit.

The racist doctrines of the Nazis preached that Germany was entitled to incorporate all territories inhabited by Germans: Austria, the western borders of Czechoslovakia, Danzig, the Polish corridor. Also Germans must annex non-German areas that they wanted as living-space (*Lebensraum*), since they were superior to Slavs or other eastern European peoples. To Hitler the medieval German Empire had been the First Reich, Bismarck's Empire had been the Second, his own would be the Third Reich and would last a thousand years. Decadent Britain and France would be chastised and brought into line; lesser states would disappear; Germany would occupy the "heartland" of Eurasia and thus dominate the world. The steps taken to achieve this program brought the world to war.

SPAIN

In the troubled years between the wars, authoritarian governments emerged not only in Germany and Italy but also in the successors of the Habsburg Empire, in other states of eastern Europe, and in Spain. Spanish regionalism and economic backwardness, Spanish Catholicism and the identification of the Church with the propertied classes, and Spanish affection for violent anarchist revolutionary ideas all complicated Spanish politics. Spain had missed not only much of the Enlightenment and the French Revolution, but to a large extent the Reformation and the Renaissance as well; Spanish conservatism is sixteenth century in flavor, rather than eighteenth or nineteenth.

Spain, which had been neutral in World War I, entered the postwar period with Alfonso XIII, the constitutional monarch, ambitious for power. Between 1923 and 1930 a military dictatorship under General Primo de Rivera governed with Alfonso's approval. The dictator could put through no agrarian reform, since he depended on the support of the landlords; he failed to carry through constitutional reform, although he did try to woo the workers from anarchism. After his resignation and death in 1930, the elections of 1931 brought in a large republican majority, and the King left the country. The republican constitution of 1931 provided for a responsible ministry and a single-chamber parliament; from the first, however, the Republic lacked support of army, church, and landowners on the Right or of anarchists on the extreme Left.

Injudicious legislation closing church schools aroused further opposition; repression of an anarchist uprising (1933) cost the Republic support of the socialists. The government swung to the Right and put down a revolt of the coalminers of the Asturias in the north, which was supported by anarchists and socialists (1934). Against them they used Moors from North Africa dispatched by the new Minister of War, General Francisco Franco. Then the Left, united in a "Popular Front," won a victory in the elections of 1936. But some elements of the Left soon deserted the Popular Front, and began to try revolution, the Communist party for the first time emerging as a strong element. On the Right, meanwhile, the *Falange* (Phalanx) made its appearance, a fascist party on the Italian pattern with a program of expansion in Africa and against Portugal, and with its own youth groups and private army.

In July, 1936, General Franco, supported by the Right, led a military *coup* against the government, thus touching off a civil war that lasted until 1939 and cost a million Spanish lives. Decisively aided by Mussolini and Hitler, Franco's forces eventually captured the republican strongholds of Madrid and Barcelona in 1939, and won the war. The government, nominally a Popular Front regime, was powerless to suppress terror in the areas it controlled, when anarchists and communists murdered each other. The Western democracies failed to assist the Republic, while the USSR "helped" mostly by sending agents who fought the Trotskyites and anarchists. The Franco regime, the only fascist government to survive World War II, still depended in the 1960's on the same classes that had supported the Spanish monarchy: the landowners, the army, and the church. Fear of a new civil war, which would renew the horrors of the old, usually prevented overt opposition.

EASTERN EUROPE

In eastern Europe, the lack of a firm parliamentary tradition, combined with a popular fear of Bolshevism and a general failure to solve pressing economic problems, especially after the depression of 1929, brought right-wing governments to power everywhere. Observing the successes of Mussolini and Hitler, little "Führers" put on uniforms and screamed hatred of neighboring states. Especially in the Balkan countries, whose agricultural economy complemented the German industrial economy, German economic pressure after the depression led to German domination of foreign trade and increasing Nazi political influence.

Austria after World War I was a small German state, whose populous capital, Vienna, was cut off from its former economic hinterland by the dismemberment of the Habsburg Monarchy. Union with Germany was forbidden by the Allies. The rival Christian Socialist and Social Democratic parties, almost evenly balanced in Parliament, organized private armies of their own. After 1930 the Christian Socialists became steadily more fascist in outlook, and after a German customs union plan failed in 1931 and the depression caused the collapse of the Vienna *Kredit Anstalt* bank, the first fascist *coup* was attempted. When Hitler came to power in Germany in 1933, many Christian Socialists became openly Nazi. Engelbert Dollfuss, the Christian Socialist Chancellor, resisted the Nazis, but could not join the Social Democrats in a common anti-Nazi coalition. Instead he banned all parties except a new one of his own, raided Social Democratic headquarters, and bombed newly built workers' apartment houses in which the Social Democratic leaders were hiding (February, 1934). Though Dollfuss had become a fascist dictator, the Nazis assassinated him in July, 1934, and only Mussolini's troop concentrations on the frontier prevented Hitler from annexing Austria at that time.

Dollfuss's successor, Schuschnigg, was committed to the same policies, but as Mussolini and Hitler drew closer together Schuschnigg lost ground. His plan to move toward a Habsburg restoration proved impossible because Hitler demanded and obtained privileges for the Nazis in Austria. When Schuschnigg announced that Austria would hold a plebiscite on the question of independence, Hitler simply marched in (March, 1938) and installed a Nazi chancellor. Schuschnigg went to jail, and the Nazis achieved *Anschluss*—that is, the incorporation of Austria into the German Reich—without opposition from Italy.

The other former partner in the Dual Monarchy, Hungary, in 1919 experienced a Bolshevik dictatorship under Lenin's agent, Bela Kun, who put through revolutionary nationalization decrees and slaughtered many peasants. Since the Allies could not tolerate a Bolshevik regime in Hungary, the Rumanians invaded and drove Kun out. Under French protection a counterrevolutionary regime was formed in 1920 under Admiral Horthy, a member of the gentry class, who remained as chief of state through World War II. Horthy presided over a "White Terror" largely directed against Jews, but also against workers and peasants.

The chief political issue in Hungary between the wars was revisionism, that is, the determination of upper-class Magyars to regain the provinces lost by the Treaty of Trianon (1920): Transylvania to Rumania, Slovakia to Czechoslovakia, and Croatia and other south Slav areas to Yugoslavia. Rank and file Hungarians, however, cared as little about revisionism as they had about politics in the past; since there was no land reform, the magnates and gentry retained their traditional dominance. From the first an authoritarian dictatorship operating behind a parliamentary screen, the Hungarian government became more and more

Nazi slap at Austrian Chancellor Dollfuss; Munich, 1934.

fascist in character after the Great Depression, when Nazi-like organizations (the Arrow Cross was the strongest) sprang up. Hitler got what he wanted in Hungary without bringing the Arrow Cross to power until almost the end of World War II. After the annexation of Austria he had Hungary in his pocket; when he broke up Czechoslovakia in March, 1939, Hungary was rewarded with the easternmost portion, Ruthenia. Hungary withdrew from the League of Nations and put through anti-Semitic laws to please Hitler in the hope that he would restore the lost provinces.

The Kingdom of the Serbs, Croats, and Slovenes took the name "Yugoslavia" in 1929; it consisted of the former independent Kingdom of Serbia and the Habsburg south Slav lands. Territorially satisfied, Yugoslavia became a dictatorship because it failed to establish a government satisfying the aspirations of its component nationalities. Many Serbs felt that they should dominate the new state, since it was ruled by their own King and from their own capital of Belgrade. The Croats, especially, with their different tradition, their Latin alphabet, and Catholic religion, wanted a federal state. The mass of the peasant population deeply loved freedom but had little experience with Western parliamentary forms. Corruption and assassination led first to the dictatorship of King Alexander (1929), authoritarian though not fascist. A Croatian fascist extremist, subsidized by Mussolini, assassinated Alexander in 1934. The dictatorship continued, but Croat demands for autonomy were not satisfied until the summer of 1939, on the very eve of a new war. Yugoslav bravery alone in 1941 could not hold Hitler back, and he split the country into its old provinces, turning each over to native fascists or foreign troops.

Elsewhere in eastern Europe, the story varied from country to country, but the outcome was similar. In Poland, Marshal Pilsudski's *coup* (1926) against a democratic government created a military dictatorship that became ever more authoritarian, founded on the support of the landowners and industrialists. In Rumania, corruption, anti-Semitism, and economic dislocation brought fascism; when the leading fascist group, the Iron Guard, began a program of assassination in the 1930's, King Carol, to head off a *coup*, adopted much of its program as his own (1938). In 1940, under pressure of the territorial losses forced by the USSR and Germany, Carol fled, and the government fell into the hands of Hitler's ally Marshal Ion Antonescu. In Bulgaria and Greece, too, fascist regimes made their appearance.

In eastern Europe dictatorship did not rest on the same bases of popular support that it enjoyed in Italy and Germany, but on the police, the bureaucracy, and the army. Yet liberal constitutions on paper and liberal franchises had proved to be inadequate substitutes for liberal parliamentary traditions, especially after the depression. Men turned in the 1930's to extreme doctrines of Left and Right, and the fear of communism, combined with the seductive nationalist propaganda of fascism, brought the victory to the Right.

III. The Democracies Between the Wars

Disappointed in their expectation that the collapse of the tsarist, Habsburg, and German imperial regimes would increase the number of democratic states and strengthen democratic principles, Britain, France, and the United States found themselves the only democracies among the major powers, facing a crisis that grew steadily blacker after the depression and the advent of Hitler. When World War II came in 1939, it was clear that the years since 1919 had been only a truce. Though the dictatorships bore the major responsibility for unleashing the new war, the democracies' relative weakness and their preoccupation with domestic problems gave the dictators the opportunity to consolidate their forces and attempt aggression. In addition to the pressing political and economic problems at home and the increasing menace of the dictators abroad, the democracies faced the developing nationalism of the non-Western peoples still under colonial or semi-colonial rule. This movement did not reach its full height until after World War II, but it already posed severe problems for Britain, France, and the United States.

BRITAIN

Great Britain suffered 750,000 killed and 1,500,000 wounded in World War I, including many of the most promising young men of an entire generation. Its severe economic losses included 40 per cent of the merchant fleet; the national debt had multiplied tenfold, while many British investments abroad had to be liquidated. The system of international trade that had produced a prosperous Britain could not be quickly restored. Moreover, the industrial production of the United States, Canada, and even India had been stimulated by wartime needs, and now competed with that of Britain. By the 1920's the German industrial plant, helped by American investment, was also back in competition. Britain, the pioneer in the Industrial Revolution, had lost its former lead.

British workers, however, were in no mood to accept a lower standard of living, for they had been led to believe that the defeated enemy would pay the costs of the war and give Britain a new start. Yet reparations failed to come through, and by 1921 there were almost one million unemployed, living on the "dole," as payments on unemployment insurance were termed. Britain in the 1920's was by no means a land of ghost towns, though the coal-mining regions of South Wales—facing competition from oil and waterpower abroad, and obsolete machinery and poor methods at home—were deep in economic stagnation. What happened was a gradual slowing up of an economy geared to dynamic growth, and a mounting discontent among a population that knew about prosperity in the United States, and wanted the comforts and luxuries that Americans were enjoying.

One striking political consequence was the virtual disappearance of the Liberal party. The Conservatives by and large commanded the votes of those upper- and middle-class people who believed in traditional methods of problem-solving and a minimum of government intervention. Trade unionists and intellectuals of all classes who wanted more government intervention in the economic problems of the day tended to support the Labor party. The Liberals split between Asquith and the more radical Lloyd George, and in 1922 for the first time Labor polled more votes than the Liberals and became the opposition to the Conservative government in power.

To increase the sales of British goods abroad the Conservatives wanted to make private industry more efficient, but found American tariffs, the uncertainties of trade with Russia, and the drive for industrialization everywhere a block to their goals. So the Conservatives inclined more and more toward the solution once advocated by Joseph Chamberlain (*see* Chapter 14): tariffs and imperial preference agreements, with the dominions and colonies supplying the raw materials and Britain the manufactured goods, both on preferential terms. But such dominions as Canada and Australia wanted their own industries and rejected this neomercantilism.

Labor advocated nationalization of key industries: the government should buy and operate transportation, power, coal, steel, and other industries that required large-scale organization. Some wanted nationalization because they were doctrinaire socialists who believed that private profits meant exploitation of the workers. Others argued that nationalization would give the increased efficiency necessary if Britain was to continue to compete in international markets: wasteful competition and inefficient companies would disappear, while top-heavy managerial and sales forces and unproductive stockholders would have to go to work. Labor also maintained that the British worker would become more productive if he thought of himself as the owner of his industry.

Between the wars Labor twice came to power briefly, in 1924 and in 1929, but its parliamentary position was never strong enough to permit it to nationalize any industry. The Conservatives' program, on the other hand, was blocked by their own internal disagreements and by the ambitions of dominion and colonial countries. As a result, not much changed in Britain between the wars, least of all traditional attitudes and behavior. In a general strike in 1926, when 2.5 million workers briefly tried to tie up all vital services in sympathy with a miners' strike against a wage cut, thousands of men from the middle and upper classes drove trucks or operated locomotives or ran telephone switchboards to keep essential services operating. In Plymouth a soccer team of policemen played a game against a team of strikers. This was a law-abiding land where the parliamentary decencies dominated even the class struggle that the Marxists insisted was going on. Meantime, Britain became more democratic: in 1918 all the old exceptions to universal male suffrage were swept away, and women over 30 were given the vote; in 1928 this remnant of inequality vanished, and women too could vote at 21.

Never having attained full economic recovery, Britain was hard-hit by the depression. The Labor government of Ramsay MacDonald gave way in 1931 to a MacDonald coalition including Conservatives, Liberals, and some right-wing Laborites; it proceeded to cut the dole and social services, abandon the gold standard, and allow the pound to decline in value. Imposition of protective tariffs and cessation of payments on war debts somewhat stemmed the depression. The Conservatives dominated the coalition, and, after the coalition won the election of 1935, their party leader, Stanley Baldwin, became Prime Minister. Unsettled economic and social questions soon began to fade into relative insignificance before the threat of a new war posed by the aggressions of Mussolini and Hitler.

Even during World War I the nagging Irish Question had posed its dangers to Britain. In 1916, with German help, Irish nationalists staged an armed rising in Dublin; in putting down this "Easter rebellion" the British created a new set of martyrs. By the end of the war the old insistence on Home Rule had vanished before the demands for complete independence levelled by the nationalist organization, the Sinn Fein (Gaelic, "ourselves alone"). Between 1919 and 1921 guerrilla warfare raged and revolution was in full swing. A more moderate wing of the Sinn Fein, under Arthur Griffith and Michael Collins, was willing to accept a compromise, giving Catholic southern Ireland dominion status, and leaving

Protestant Ulster under British rule. The more intransigent, under Eamon de Valera, insisted on republican status for the entire island. In 1921 the British accepted the moderates' terms, and southern Ireland became the Irish Free State, with its own parliament, the Dail, and complete self-government under the crown. The De Valera wing moved into civil war against this, but the public was tired of violence, especially after the assassination of Michael Collins, and De Valera himself brought his fellow republicans into the Dail in 1927. In 1933 the oath of loyalty to the crown was abolished; in World War II Ireland was neutral; in 1949 Britain recognized the Republic of Eire. Ulster remained under British rule as part of the United Kingdom of Great Britain and Northern Ireland.

Elsewhere in the far-flung lands under the British crown, increasing constitutional recognition bred increasing loyalty. In the Statute of Westminster of 1931 a long historic process reached its culmination when Britain and the dominions were recognized as "autonomous communities . . . equal in status . . . united by a common allegiance to the crown and freely associated as members of the British Commonwealth of Nations." The statute meant that any dominion that wished to secede from the Commonwealth might do so, and southern Ireland did just that. In 1939 all the others freely decided to enter the war on Britain's side. Only one, the Union of South Africa, where many Afrikaners took a sympathetic view of Hitler's racism, showed signs of remaining neutral; but the pro-British General Smuts finally persuaded the Union to join the war against Germany. Though the two decades between the wars failed to provide solutions for the pressing problems of British domestic policy, and though British statesmanship coped only clumsily with the threat from Hitler, the evolution of the Commonwealth represented a quiet constitutional triumph.

FRANCE

French suffering from World War I was even greater than British: 2,000,000 Frenchmen were killed or incapacitated by the war; 300,000 houses and 20,000 factories were destroyed. As in England, an entire generation of potential leaders in every field had been decimated. The traditional slow methods of building slowed down reconstruction, and the psychological lift given by victory by no means balanced the traumas caused by the horrible four-year struggle.

It was perhaps little wonder that the French should have concentrated on extracting every possible cent in reparations, and at the same time on denying the Germans the means to fight again. Essentially contradictory—in order to pay, Germany needed to recover industrially—these policies encouraged what the French most feared. Their occupation of the Ruhr in 1923 gained them nothing, as German passive resistance rendered the area unproductive. The heavy costs of reconstruction and of maintaining a large army, together with the staggering wartime debt and a low tax policy, led to inflation in the 1920's. Never comparable to the inflation in Germany, the French inflation was stemmed by new taxes, new economies, and the gradual restoration of international trade. None the less, the value of the franc did fall from twenty cents to two cents, and was stabilized at about four in 1928. The decline primarily hit the middle-class bondholders and those living on fixed incomes or dependent on savings; it heightened political and social tensions. So did the depression, which was slow in affecting France, but was in full swing by 1932.

After the war the old conflict between the French anticlerical republican Left and the royalist or authoritarian Right resumed once more. On the Left were the champions of extended social services, the "welfare state," mainly Socialists and Communists, backed by many workers, civil servants, and intellectuals. The Left was weakened by the split between the Communists, who followed the Moscow line, and the Socialists, who did not, and by a similar split within the CGT (*Confédération Générale du Travail*, the General Confederation of Labor), the major union organization. On the Right were the wealthy, many of them monarchist and clerical, indeed opposed to the very existence of the republic. They were supported by conservative peasants and small businessmen who opposed all new "welfare state" measures, in which France lagged behind Britain, Germany, and Scandinavia. In between were the misnamed Radical Socialists, a republican party of the Center, very slow to accept social and economic reforms.

A major political crisis began in December, 1933, when a certain Stavisky, a shady speculator with highly placed connections who had been caught sponsoring a fraudulent bond issue, committed suicide or was murdered. The ensuing scandal rocked France. The royalists, organized as the *Action Française,* had strong-arm squadrons called the *Camelots du Roi* (King's Henchmen); they joined a right-wing fascist-style veterans' organization, the *Croix de Feu* (Cross of Fire), in street fighting against Communists, who retaliated, and in riots against the government (February, 1934). The Left called a general strike in protest, and the immediate crisis was surmounted only by a coalition of all parties except the royalists, Socialists, and Communists. But when the austerity measures taken by the new government to meet a new crisis of the franc proved ineffective, Radical Socialists, Socialists, and Communists, backed by the CGT, formed a Popular Front. The Popular Front won the election of 1936 and came to power under the Socialist Premier Léon Blum.

The Popular Front victory reflected a strong wish for increased social welfare measures, for government spending similar to that of the American New Deal, and for an attack on the Bank of France, citadel and symbol of the conservative financial solution to all social problems, a private institution dominated by the "two hundred families" alleged to control the French economy. Many Frenchmen, too, were alarmed at the unchecked advances of Mussolini and Hitler and at the rearmament of Germany. The USSR seemed to share the apprehension of the West at the increasing power of Hitler, and encouraged Communists to cooperate in such coalitions as the Popular Front. But the bitter political division of France and the reluctance of business and farming classes to pay income taxes to finance the new social services made it a bad time for a French "New Deal." Blum introduced a program for the forty-hour week, partial nationalization of the Bank, the railroads, and the arms industry, and compulsory arbitration of labor disputes. But the Communists were unwilling to let Blum have the credit for making these measures work, and "sit-down" strikes frightened businessmen. The mounting victories of the Right in Spain made French rearmament necessary, but the rich would not subscribe to the huge bond-issues needed unless Blum called a halt, which he did in March, 1937. The Popular Front then collapsed.

The aftermath was an exacerbation of the perennial Right-Left split in French society. The Left resented the abandonment of social welfare measures, and only military control prevented a general strike in 1938. The Right resented the fact that the Blum experiment had been made at all, and had come to advocate a French totalitarian state—"better Hitler than Blum" was the Rightist slogan. Though the Radical Socialist premier, Daladier, kept France aligned with Britain in opposition to Hitler and Mussolini, France in 1939 was psychologically divided, and unprepared both spiritually and materially for the approaching war.

THE UNITED STATES

With a population three times that of France, the United States in World War I lost fewer than one-tenth as many men. In material terms the United States gained from the war: Allied war orders stimulated heavy industry; New York was outstripping London as the financial center of the world; the dollar had begun to dethrone the pound. Some interest on the war debts of the Allies came in until 1933, and the stimulation given American industry as a result of the loans outweighed the losses when the debts were finally repudiated in the early 1930's. Despite American victory and prosperity, however, the national revulsion against the war in 1919 and the years following was as great as that in Europe. In the presidential election of 1920, the Republicans ousted the Democrats, who had been in control since 1913; and the Republican victory was repeated in 1924 and 1928. This was the era of the Republican Presidents Harding (1921–1923), Coolidge (1923–1929), and Hoover (1929–1933).

American public opinion underwent a strong wave of isolationist sentiment: a widespread wish to withdraw from international politics was reflected in the Senate's repudiation of both the Treaty of Versailles and the League of Nations. Yet isolationism was by no means universal, and it may be that a few concessions to the Republicans by President Wilson would have produced the necessary two-thirds majority in the Senate required by the Constitution for treaties; or that a commanding figure on the Republican side might have put through the idea of a bipartisan foreign policy. Many Americans, however, felt that they had done all that was necessary by beating the Germans, and were reluctant to involve American innocence and virtue any further with European sophistication and vice.

Isolationism was reflected in the high tariff policies of the period: the Fordney–McCumber Tariff of 1922 and the Smoot–Hawley Tariff of 1930 set increasingly high duties on foreign goods. These laws, designed to protect American high wage scales against competition from cheaper foreign labor, made it impossible for the European debtor nations to earn dollars in the American markets and so to repay their debts. Although Congress acquiesced in a general scaling-down of the obligations of defeated Germany, it tended to view the complexities of the debts owed us by our Allies in terms of President Coolidge's simple dictum: "They hired the money, didn't they?" Isolationism expressed itself also in a reversal of the traditional American policies of free immigration. In 1924 an annual quota limit was established for all countries as 2 per cent of the number of nationals of that country resident in the United States in 1890. Since the heavy immigration from eastern and southern Europe had come mainly after 1890, the selection of that year was designed to reduce the flow from those areas to a trickle.

But of course isolationism was only relative. In 1928, Frank B. Kellogg, the Secretary of State, submitted to the European powers a proposal for the renunciation of war. Similar proposals came from the French Foreign Minister, Aristide Briand. Together they were incorporated as the Pact of Paris (Kellogg–Briand Pact, August, 1928), eventually signed by twenty-three nations including the United States. The obvious fact that the Pact did not actually prevent World War II should not obscure the deep concern of the United States with the peace of the world. Indeed, American businessmen, American money, and American goods were now everywhere. In the Far East as early as 1922 the United States took the lead in the Nine-Power Treaty, committing them all, including Japan, to respect the sovereignty and integrity of China. Thus, even in the period of isolationism, the United States was committed to certain foreign obligations that it would later honor.

At home, prosperity ruled throughout the Coolidge era of the 1920's. Almost everybody played the stock market and, in those days of prohibition, patronized the speakeasy and the bootlegger. It was the Jazz Age, glimpsed in novels like F. Scott Fitzgerald's *The Great Gatsby*, the age of the short skirt, of the Charleston, and "sex appeal," of a kind of sinfulness that now seems refreshing and naïve. But the high standards of living, in the past limited to the successful few, standards that seemed materialistic and even vulgar to some, were now steadily spreading; America had more human comfort for more human beings than any other society had ever before supplied. Clara Bow, the red-haired "It" girl of the movies, Henry Ford, the enormously successful pioneer in the automobile industry, Al Capone, the gangster who made millions out of prohibition and turned crime into big business, Calvin Coolidge himself, the sober unimaginative business-minded president—each in his way typifies the era.

The crash of 1929 ended it all. Millions of speculators had been buying stocks on margin, paying only a fraction of their cost in cash, and often borrowing even the fraction. Credit had swollen beyond the point of safety in an unregulated economy, and the shrewdest speculators started to sell in the belief that the bubble would burst. Values began to drop disastrously in October, 1929, and continued to fall almost without pause until 1933. Yet the crash was only the immediate cause of the depression. Coolidge prosperity had been distributed unevenly all the time: agriculture, for example, had been in a kind of permanent depression throughout the 1920's. Farmers had expanded their production and borrowed to finance the expansion, in the belief that the great demand and high prices of wartime would continue and increase. But the foreign market dried up, the home market shrank, farm prices fell, and farm mortgages began to be foreclosed. The increased standards of living available to workers were often obtainable only through credit. It was business, especially big business, that had made the greatest gains of the Coolidge era.

The Great Depression was worldwide, but nowhere more serious than in the United States. In the early 1930's 16 million Americans, one-third of the national labor force, were unemployed, and between 1929 and 1933 the value of the gross national product fell amost 50 per cent. Though the agony of the depression turned a few intellectuals to Marxism, it produced no organized movement of revolution. People continued to put their trust in established American institutions; local authorities and private charities helped soften the worst suffering. Although President Hoover established the RFC (Reconstruction Finance Corporation) in 1932 to release frozen assets, he generally clung to the belief that things would take care of themselves. In the election of 1932, very few voted for socialist or communist candidates. Those who wanted a more vigorous government attack on economic problems voted for the Democrats, electing Franklin D. Roosevelt president.

The New Deal. President Roosevelt (1933–1945) took office in the midst of a financial crisis that had closed the banks all over the country. Believing that he had a mandate to marshal the forces of the federal government against depression, he summoned Congress to an emergency session and declared a bank holiday. National morale received a powerful impetus from the government's concern. Gradually the sound banks reopened, and the government enacted a series of measures called the New Deal, aimed in part at immediate problems but also designed to change American society permanently. Often the men who sponsored the measures were not sure in their own minds which motive prevailed or what they were really trying to do. Yet it is clear that the New Deal marked the coming to the United States, under the spur of the Great Depression, of those social welfare measures that we have already encountered in Victorian and Edwardian Britain and in Bismarckian Germany.

By abandoning the gold standard, the New Dealers planned to lower the price of American goods in world markets no longer tied to gold. By a large-scale program of public works they aimed to relieve unemployment. By extending the activities of the RFC and creating new government lending agencies they hoped

FDR on his way to his first inaugural, March 4, 1933.

to thaw out credit. They safeguarded bank deposits and regulated stockmarket speculation through the Federal Deposit Insurance Corporation and the Securities and Exchange Commission. These were immediate measures. The long-term measures of the New Deal included the Social Security Act of 1935, introducing unemployment insurance, old-age pensions, and other benefits of the kind Lloyd George (see Chapter 14) had brought to Britain. Increased federal taxation led to a somewhat more even distribution of the national wealth. Agricultural legislation regulated crops and prices to an unprecedented degree, while a series of new laws dealing with labor relations had the effect of increasing the power of organized labor. In the Tennessee Valley Authority the government created a regional planning board that made over the economic life of a relatively backward area by checking erosion, instituting flood control, and providing cheap electric power generated at government-built dams.

Then and now these measures were hotly debated, for each of them made some Americans protest that the government was interfering with their rights. The New Deal changed American society. Government now tried to prevent the wasteful exploitation of natural resources; it regulated the distribution of wealth to alter if it could the traditional social pyramid—the few rich at the top, the many poor at the bottom. The pyramid was transformed into something resembling a diamond, widest in the middle, with far fewer at the bottom. The gross national product began to mount once more: there was more to be shared, and it was being distributed more evenly.

The New Deal, together with the strength of American institutions and the resilience of the American people, began to pull the United States out of the depression. When war came in Europe, Americans mostly hoped to remain neutral. But they were not tired or skeptical like the French. Although the Republicans often bitterly attacked "that man in the White House" and all his works, they and their Democratic opponents could not be compared with the French Right and Left. Neither side in America ever dreamed of attacking the basic framework of the nation. When the great international crisis came in 1939–1941, Americans were divided but confident, and found little difficulty in closing their ranks for war.

THE LOOSENING OF IMPERIAL TIES

Before World War I, as we have seen in Chapter 14, native nationalist movements occasionally made trouble for a colonial power, in Egypt, the Philippines, Morocco, and China, for example. The war speeded the growth of nationalism. Non-Western peoples had rendered important services to their white masters; the Arabs had raised armies of their own. The Allies had fought the war in the name of self-determination, Wilson himself putting the "interests of the populations" of colonial areas on the same level with the interests of the colonial powers. After the war the Allies did not relinquish their colonies. Instead they added to their territories by the mandate system, but the very terms of the mandates called for gradual emancipation. During the years between the wars, it was in the Far East that old imperial ties were most decisively loosened.

Japan, the only industrialized non-Western nation, was still oligarchical and authoritarian. In the period immediately after World War I, the suffrage was extended to all men; political parties on the Western model came into existence as did labor unions. But European-style parliamentary democratic institutions lost out to a clique of powerful army officers, hostile to civilian government and to business interests. Using the Emperor as spokesman for their views, and systematically assassinating their political enemies, they were erecting a military dictatorship by the 1930's. Elections were held, but their results were disregarded; state Shinto, a cult of emperor-worship designed to win popular support for aggressive foreign policy, was concocted by the military for mass consumption; the "thought police" played the role in Japan of the Gestapo in Hitler's Germany. In foreign policy the Japanese, like the fascists or Nazis claiming to be a have-not nation, strove to increase their already too-large population, and planned a program of aggressive expansion abroad, chiefly at the expense of China.

Defeated by Japan in 1895, China had suffered thereafter the rush of Germans, French, Russians, and British to seize concessions. Though all powers subscribed to John Hay's "Open Door" Treaty, in practice imperialism continued unchecked and stimulated the Boxer Rebellion of 1900 (*see* Chapter 14). In 1911, a revolution, patterned in part on Western ideas and examples, though directed against Westerners and pro-Western Chinese, overthrew the Emperor, Pu-yi. One faction of the revolutionaries, the Nationalists (Kuomintang), led by Sun Yat-sen, wanted a democratic parliamentary republic of China, grafting industrialism onto the old Chinese family and village structure. Their rivals, led by Yuan Shih-k'ai, favored an authoritarian regime that would modernize China by dictation. By 1914, Yuan had won the struggle and became President; yet the defeated Sun has remained the hero of the revolution.

During World War I, after a brief experiment with a revived empire, Yuan died (1916), and authority fell into the hands of rival warlords. Even before, Japan had secretly presented the "twenty-one demands," amounting to a virtual request for a protectorate over China, and the feeble Chinese Republic saved itself only by declaring war on the Central Powers and so winning protection from Britain and France. At the end of the war, the Allies, especially the United States, moved to check the ambitions of Japan, and at the Washington Conference of 1922 Japan signed the Nine-Power Treaty guaranteeing the independence of China. Frustrated in their Chinese ambitions, the Japanese warlords developed a hostility toward the United States that was to culminate with the attack on Pearl Harbor in 1941.

In the years between the wars, the Kuomintang came under the leadership of Chiang Kai-shek, an army officer trained in Japan, and the brother-in-law of Sun Yat-sen. He strove unsuccessfully to combat the warlords and to establish an effective central government. Meanwhile the Communists competed with the Kuomintang for the loyalty of almost 500 million Chinese, mostly illiterate peasants. The Japanese waited for their opportunity to intervene and conquer. In September, 1931, they opened their attack in Manchuria in order to obtain its resources of coal and iron; within a year they proclaimed the puppet state of Manchukuo under the nominal rule of the last of the Manchu Emperors, Pu-yi, who had been dethroned as a boy in 1912. The Chinese started to boycott Japanese goods, and the Japanese attacked the great Chinese port of Shanghai; the League of Nations proved unable to give more than verbal support against the aggressor.

Tension continued to grow until the Japanese in July, 1937, launched a full-fledged invasion designed to conquer all of China. They seized the strategic ports of the coastal area and the thickly peopled lower river valleys. Chiang, his government, and his army withdrew to the inland province of Szechwan, where he established a capital at Chungking. When the United States became involved in World War II, it assisted Chiang by road and air from India and Burma, and Chiang's government survived the Japanese defeat in World War II. Unlike earlier foreign invaders who had been accepted by the Chinese and had firmly established themselves in power, the Japanese met with passive nonacceptance from the mass of the Chinese people, who were now strongly nationalist in sentiment.

But Chiang's inability to resist the Japanese effectively and perhaps also the corruption of his government and his officers kept the Kuomintang from winning the loyalty of all the Chinese. The Communists eventually would succeed in China where the Kuomintang had failed. Encouraged from Moscow in the 1920's, the Communists had begun as the left wing of the Kuomintang, accepted at first by Sun Yat-sen and even by Chiang. In 1926, however, Chiang opened a campaign against them, and they were then expelled from the Kuomintang. Deserted by Moscow during the Stalin–Trotsky fight, the Chinese Communists got no help from Stalin, since he believed the time was not yet ripe for a proletarian regime in China. Led by Mao Tse-tung, the Communists managed to withdraw to the province of Yenan, in the distant north, and established a base among the peasantry there. Throughout the Japanese occupation the Communists organized a network of armies and councils in and around the Japanese positions. They were the fish that could live in the water that surrounded them, as Mao himself put it in a famous definition of a guerrilla. By 1945 they were prepared to come to grips with Chiang.

INDIA AND THE MIDDLE EAST

India's contribution to the British war effort together with Allied propaganda in favor of democracy and self-determination contributed to the growing Indian demand for self-government, which was sharpened by the Amritsar massacre of 1919 (*see* Chapter 14), an exception to the generally mild and beneficent British rule. Among Indians, the Moslems and Hindus were hostile to each other. In the west (the Indus basin, the Punjab) and in a part of Bengal in the east the Moslems were a majority; elsewhere Moslems lived scattered among Hindus. The Moslems were primarily peasants; by and large the Hindu community led them in industry and in financial success. But the Moslem loathed the Hindu worship of many gods and the portrayal of divinities in human form, and resented the caste system of the Hindu with its assertions of Brahmin superiority. The Hindu felt just as strongly that Moslem disregard of Hindu feelings of reverence for the cow was not only insulting but somehow filthy. This mutual dislike led to the foundation of two movements to oust the British, the Indian National Congress and the All-India Moslem League.

The former gained vast influence in India and worldwide fame through the leadership of Mahatma Gandhi (1869–1948), a member of the *bania* or shop-keeping caste of Hindus, educated for law at Oxford, and with long experience in politics as a member of the Indian minority in South Africa. His simple and austere personal life, with its fasts and spinning, endeared him to his own people. His invention of "nonviolent noncooperation" as a political technique appealed to

Hindus, who generally disliked force. The boycott and the voluntary hunger-strike were Gandhi's preferred weapons against the British, though many of his followers used agitation and a kind of nonviolence that was scarcely distinguishable from violence. The British gave concession after concession, and the Indians won experience in provincial government jobs as well as in the civil service. When the Second World War broke out, dominion status for India seemed just around the corner, but mutual antagonism between Moslem and Hindu would later lead to the creation of two new dominions instead of one.

In the Middle East, with the collapse of the Ottoman Empire at the end of World War I, the Arab territories were administered as mandates, the French being responsible for Syria and Lebanon, and the British adding those for Palestine, Transjordan, and Iraq to their protectorate over Egypt. Only Saudi Arabia, occupying the bulk of the desert peninsula, was welded into a personal kingdom by a remarkable tribal chief, Ibn Saud (1880–1953). These arrangements left the Arab nationalists dissatisfied, of course, and their hostility to the immigration of Jews into Palestine and to the prospect of a Jewish "national home" united the otherwise disunited Arab leadership. The French met insurrection with force in Syria in 1925 and 1926. The British tried more conciliatory policies: in 1922, for example, Egypt was proclaimed an independent kingdom, although Britain retained the right to station troops there, and resident Westerners enjoyed special privileges. The Anglo-Egyptian agreement of 1936 provided for the eventual termination of these privileges. But the Second World War with its exacerbation of Arab nationalism spoiled the promising British effort to lead the Arabs toward independence and retain their friendship at the same time. Meanwhile, Western companies were developing and exploiting the oilfields in Iran and Iraq and along the Persian Gulf.

The Turkish core of the old Ottoman state was revitalized by the revolutionary impulse of the nationalist leader Mustafa Kemal (1881–1938). He began by expelling the Greek invaders from Anatolia (1922), founded the new Republic of Turkey, and moved its capital from cosmopolitan Istanbul, with all its European connections, to Ankara, high up on the Anatolian plateau. The new Turkey had a Western-style constitution, and Kemal proceeded to a rapid and sometimes ruthless westernization of Turkish life. He abolished the red fez of the men, a traditional symbol of the old regime, and emancipated women, at least in principle. He forced the Turks to write their language in the Latin alphabet rather than the far more difficult Arabic, which meant that for the first time mass literacy in Turkey would be feasible. Kemal strove to turn society away from the conservative influence of Islam, and to do for the Turks what Peter the Great had once done for the Russians. He called himself appropriately "Atatürk," Father of the Turks. Westernization moved more slowly than Kemal would have liked, and many survivals of the old ways remain in our own times; but he did begin to revolutionize Turkey.

Somewhat similar but far less successful was the effort made in Iran (the name officially taken by Persia in 1935), where the Revolution of 1906, attempting to establish a constitutional monarchy, had proved abortive. The small class of wealthy landlords and the millions of poor peasants and restless tribesmen provided no appropriate social base for political westernization. Reza Shah, an able army officer who seized the throne in 1925 after a *coup d'état* several years earlier, tried feverishly but erratically and vainly to modernize Iran. When he began to support the Germans in the Second World War, the old rivals in Persia, England

and Russia, sent troops to force his abdication. Though imperial ties had been loosened in Iran, they had by no means been dissolved. To a greater or lesser extent this held true throughout the dependent world, where the real revolution against imperialism awaited the end of the new war.

IV. The Second World War

In many ways the period we have been considering was hardly more than a twenty-years' truce. The Western democracies, Britain and France, generally (though often ineffectually) supported by the United States, proved unable to prevent the rise of the fascist and communist powers. In the end Germany, allied with two of its enemies in the First World War, Italy and Japan, took the lead in new aggressions. The Nazis claimed that Versailles—with its war-guilt clause, its reparations, its provisions taking Germany's colonies and denying her the right to rearm—had made a new war a necessity. Yet, despite the handicaps imposed by Versailles on the new German Republic, the 1920's had seen an "era of fulfillment," in which the Germans and their former enemies had come together and collaborated for peace.

EFFORTS TO KEEP THE PEACE

In the Locarno Treaty (October, 1925) Germany, France, and Belgium agreed on a mutual guarantee of their frontiers, and Britain and Italy agreed to punish any power that might violate this treaty. The "Locarno spirit," nourished by the prosperity of France and Germany and the statesmanship of their foreign ministers, Briand and Stresemann, led to Germany's admission to the League of Nations (1926) and signing of the Kellogg-Briand Pact (1928); in turn the French withdrew the last of their Rhineland occupation forces (1930) well before they were obliged to do so. The League of Nations itself, which came into operation in 1920, settled disputes between Sweden and Finland (1920) and between Greece and Bulgaria (1925).

Though not a member of the League, the United States took the lead in furthering disarmament. At the Washington conference of 1921–1922, the naval powers agreed not to build any new battleships or heavy cruisers for a period of ten years, and set the ratio of tonnages for such warships at 5 for the United States and Britain, to 3 for Japan, and 1.67 for France and Italy. But a second conference in London in 1930 failed to reach agreement on further naval limitations. Renewed Franco-German distrust, signalized by a German request for equality of armament and a French refusal to grant it, caused the failure of a military disarmament conference sponsored by the League at Geneva in 1932.

Behind the new tensions that ended the era of fulfillment lay the depression, which decreased the confidence and sapped the morale of the democracies, and played a major role in Hitler's success in Germany. Moreover, the international atmosphere was poisoned by the Soviet Union, openly dedicated to the fomenting of communist revolutions abroad by any means, and convinced that "capitalist" democracy was doomed and should be helped to die. The United States' withdrawal into isolationism may have been less important than some of its critics have maintained, but it surely exacerbated French fears and helped make French policy intransigent. French fear of Germany led not only to insistence on the enforcement of every provision of Versailles that sought to keep Germany weak, but also to a new system of French alliances created as a substitute for the old alliance with Russia that was no longer possible with a communist state. Beginning in 1921 France made alliances with Poland and with the "Little Entente" (Czechoslovakia, Yugoslavia, and Rumania), all of whom had a common interest in forestalling any revival of the Habsburg Empire.

Europe on the Eve, August 1939

Neutral countries

The Axis Powers
Areas annexed by Germany, 1935-39
Areas made "protectorates" of Germany, 1939
Annexed by Italy, 1939

To the British, however, French fear looked much like renewed French ambition to dominate the Continent, a thing they had fought against for centuries. The British attitude contained more than a little old-fashioned British isolationism, expressing itself in unwillingness to make firm Continental commitments. The divergence between France and Britain, more than any other one factor, explains the weaknesses of the League of Nations. It led to British rejection of a "Geneva protocol" (1924) that would have bound its signatories to settle their international disputes by arbitration. And it led to the League's powerlessness when Mussolini bombarded and occupied the Greek island of Corfu (1923) after five Italians working for the League marking out the new frontier between Greece and Albania had been assassinated. Had France and Britain not been in disagreement over French policy in the Ruhr, they could have seen to it that the League punished the aggressor.

THE ROAD TO WAR

What eventually made war inevitable was the dictators' policy of aggression, of which the Corfu affair was merely a warning. Step by step during the 1930's, while the League in general proved powerless to stop them, Japan, Italy, and Germany upset the peace of the world. The Japanese seizure of Manchuria in 1931 was the first step. Henry L. Stimson, the American Secretary of State, declared that the United States would recognize no gains made by armed force; but the other democracies failed to follow his lead. The Lytton report to the League of Nations branded the Japanese as aggressors, but no nation seemed interested; Japan withdrew from the League (March, 1933).

In October, 1933, Hitler withdrew Germany from the League, serving notice on the world of his own aggressive intentions. On March 16, 1935, he denounced the Versailles limitations on German armaments and openly began to rebuild the German armies. In April the League condemned this action, but Hitler went on rearming. In May France hastily concluded a treaty of alliance with the USSR against German aggression; Hitler continued rearming. In June the British signed a naval agreement with Germany, limiting the German navy to one-third the size of the British and their submarine force to 60 per cent of the British. Though this may have been realistic, it seemed to the French like British treachery. In March, 1936, Hitler sent German troops into the Rhineland, the zone demilitarized by the Treaty of Versailles. Once again, he met with nothing but verbal protests. It is altogether probable that a united British–French show of force against this violation of Germany's obligations would have ended Hitler's career then and there.

Having witnessed the Japanese and German success through illegal violence, Mussolini took advantage of a frontier incident to demand Ethiopia for Italy (1934). Though the British and the French tried to appease him by offering great economic and political concessions in Ethiopia, they did insist that its nominal independence be preserved, for it was a member of the League. But Mussolini invaded Ethiopia in October, 1935, avenging with planes, tanks, and poison gas the humiliating defeat inflicted on Italy by the Ethiopians in 1896. While the King of Italy became Emperor of Ethiopia, the rightful Emperor, Haile Selassie, denounced the aggression before the League, most of whose members voted to invoke Article 16 of the Covenant to impose economic sanctions against a member that had gone to war in violation of its pledges. But sanctions failed: oil was not included among the forbidden articles, and the

Italians continued to buy it freely. Britain and France did nothing to check the movement of Italian troops and munitions through the Suez Canal. The failure of the sanctions against Italy finished the League as an instrument in international politics. Italy withdrew in 1937. The trained international civil servants that had dealt with the drug traffic, prostitution, and other problems continued to function until the United Nations absorbed them after World War II.

In July, 1936, came the Franco *coup* against the Spanish Republic and the start of the Spanish Civil War, in which Hitler, Mussolini, and Stalin all intervened. The Western democracies failed to follow the usual practice of sending arms to the legal government as sanctioned by international law. The success of the fascists' intervention in Spain increased their appetites as well as their boldness. In October, 1936, Mussolini signed with Hitler the pact formally establishing a Rome–Berlin "Axis." Early in 1938 Hitler began a violent newspaper and radio propaganda campaign against the Austrian government; he summoned Chancellor Schuschnigg to his Bavarian retreat in Berchtesgaden, unloosed a bullying tirade against him, and then moved the German armies into Vienna. The *Anschluss* of Austria to Germany, favored by Pan-Germans and Nazis and opposed by the victors of the First World War, was an accomplished fact.

Hitler's next target was the Czechoslovak republic, the only central or eastern European state where parliamentary democracy had succeeded, thanks to the rich and well-balanced economy and to the enlightened policies of the first President, Thomas Masaryk. But Czechoslovakia also included a minority of 3,400,000 Germans, who felt contempt for the Slavs and tried to sabotage the republic. Hitler supported the agitation of these "Sudeten" Germans and demanded autonomy for them in the spring of 1938. The Czechs counted on their alliance with France to protect them against the dismemberment of their country, but neither the French nor the British were willing to run the risk of a military showdown with Hitler. By September, 1938, Hitler was in full cry against alleged Czech misdeeds, and a full-fledged European crisis had broken out. Twice the British Prime Minister, Neville Chamberlain, personally pleaded with Hitler to moderate his demands. Then, at Munich (September 29, 1938), Hitler and Mussolini met with Chamberlain and the French Premier, Daladier. Though allied with the French, the Soviet Union was not invited to Munich; the rebuff helped persuade Stalin that the Western powers were interested only in turning Hitler's armies east against him, and that he had better make what terms he could.

At Munich, Hitler won the consent of the democracies to the dismemberment of Czechoslovakia; the Czechs were forced to acquiesce when the West let them down. The Germans took over the Sudeten lands along with the mountain defenses of the Czech border, Poland received small border areas, the agricultural area of Slovakia was given autonomy, and Hitler guaranteed the remainder of the state. But, after a six-months' lull, Hitler violated his last agreement with the Czechs and marched his forces into Prague (March, 1939) after bullying the President of Czechoslovakia, Hacha, as he had bullied Schuschnigg. Somehow, this was at last the last straw. Chamberlain seems finally to have been convinced that Hitler could never be counted on to keep his word. The "peace with honor" that Chamberlain had proudly announced he had won at Munich proved to have been neither. The British followed the march into Prague with a guarantee of assistance to Poland (April, 1939), next on Hitler's calendar. And Mussolini, who had been vainly trying to bully France into ceding Nice and Savoy, Corsica, and

Tunisia, found an enemy he could intimidate and attacked the backward little Balkan state of Albania (April, 1939).

We now know that appeasement of Hitler was hopeless from the first; he had all along intended to destroy Czechoslovakia and move against Poland. Contemptuous of the French and British, he was prepared to fight them if he could avoid a two-front war. To this end he opened negotiations with a Stalin already convinced that the Soviet Union could never depend on Britain and France. On August 23, 1939, to the horror of the West, Germany and Russia reached a nonaggression pact; they agreed secretly on a new partition of Poland. When the Germans invaded Poland a week later, the British and French honored their obligations and declared war on Germany. The victorious Allies of the First World War had with extreme reluctance abandoned their defensive position; World War II was under way.

EARLY SUCCESSES OF THE AXIS

Although the French and the Germans had built two confronting lines of fortifications along their common frontier, the Second World War was not to be decided, as the first had been, in this region. Other theaters assumed major importance: Russia, the Pacific, and the Mediterranean. The airplane came into its own as a major weapon in naval and land warfare alike, and aerial bombardment—carried on by German pilotless planes and rockets toward the end of the war—brought the civil populations into the front lines; civilians confounded the experts by standing up to dreadful punishment. The final act of warfare was the dropping

"Rendezvous"; Low cartoon commenting on the Hitler–Stalin pact, August, 1939.

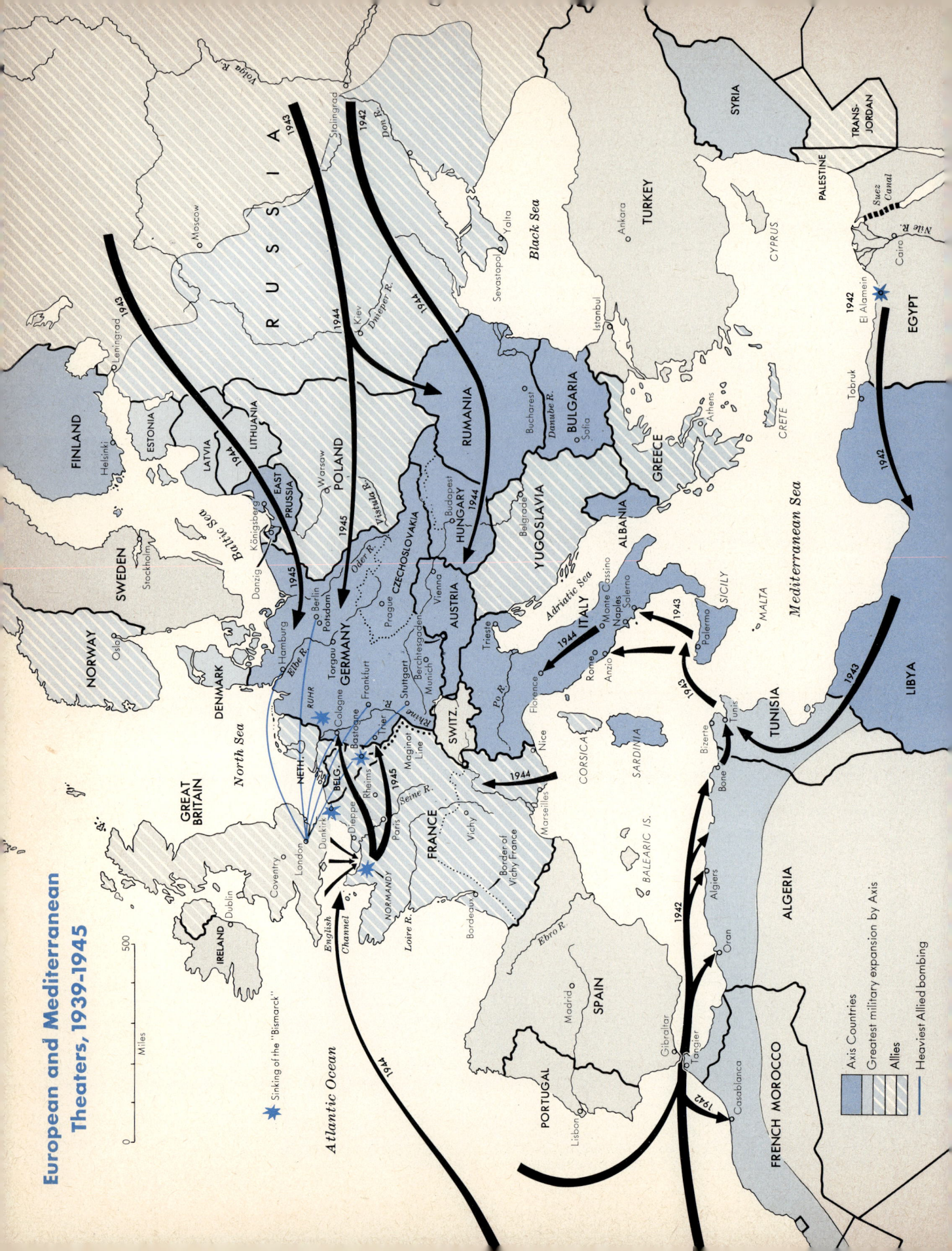

European and Mediterranean Theaters, 1939–1945

by the United States of the first two atomic bombs (August, 1945), which between them killed over 100,000 people in two Japanese cities and opened an era in which the human race had learned how to destroy itself entirely if it could not learn to control its own hostilities.

Hitler began with a speedy and not unexpected conquest of Poland. He permitted Stalin to establish Russian control, as had been agreed, over the eastern areas of Poland and over the Baltic states of Latvia, Estonia, and Lithuania, which were incorporated into the USSR in 1940. In November, 1939, the Russians attacked Finland in order to gain bases on its soil. Though the Finns slowed down the Soviet attack with extraordinary bravery, Stalin had reached his goals by March, 1940; Russian military ineffectiveness, however, made a deep impression on the Germans. Throughout the fall and winter of 1939–1940, Hitler did nothing in the West: a "phony war" of occasional contact between patrols created a false sense of security.

The lull broke in April, 1940, when the Germans suddenly moved into Denmark and Norway, thus securing their northern flanks; Norwegian resistance, helped by token forces from Britain, lasted only a couple of weeks. On May 10, Hitler followed up this victory by a lightning attack on Holland, Belgium, and France, supported by fierce aerial bombardment. Outflanking the French fortifications where they tapered off in the Ardennes region of the Franco-Belgian frontier, the Germans swept to the Channel, separating the British from the French. Neville Chamberlain now fell from office in Britain, and as Prime Minister was replaced by Winston Churchill, the fiery former First Lord of the Admiralty, long an outspoken enemy of appeasement, who rose to heroic stature in the terrible months and years ahead.

The Belgians surrendered. The British managed to evacuate 215,000 of their own and 120,000 French troops from Dunkirk in the last days of May and the first of June, 1940, a withdrawal that might not have been possible if Hitler had determined to destroy the armies. But instead he drove for Paris, which the French evacuated without fighting on June 13. In the hope of persuading Frenchmen to support leaders who would continue the fight either from southern France or from North Africa, Churchill offered France political union with Britain after the war. But French politicians who wished to give in to the Germans installed in office the aged hero of World War I, Marshal Pétain, and the French capitulated on the exact spot where the Germans had signed the Armistice of November, 1918. Too late to affect the outcome, Mussolini too declared war on France, the "stab in the back" that helped further to outrage American opinion, already disturbed by Nazi success.

By the armistice terms, the Germans occupied the northern three-fifths of France, including the Channel and Atlantic coasts, while the rest was governed from Vichy by Pétain and his collaborators. A few of the "men of Vichy" hoped for a German victory; all of them believed it inevitable and were convinced they were making the best terms they could. Their regime was Right-wing: "Labor, Family, Fatherland" replaced "Liberty, Equality, Fraternity" as the slogan of France. Other Frenchmen would not give in. General Charles de Gaulle, with a few followers, flew to London, where with British help he established a "Free French" or "Fighting French" movement. Inside France, underground resistance groups formed to harass the occupiers. Though North Africa was under Vichy control, in the French colonies south of the Sahara there was still a safe base of anti-German activity.

TURNING POINTS

Hitler seems to have expected that the British would make a separate peace, leaving him in control of Europe; he did not understand them. Failing this, he counted on a submarine blockade to starve them out; he overrated its possibilities. He did contemplate landings in England, but had made wholly inadequate preparations; in August, 1940, he decided to try to bomb the British into submission. In the decisive "Battle of Britain" the Royal Air Force, using the new detection apparatus called radar, proved just strong enough to inflict intolerably high losses in planes on the Germans. By late September, 1940, the Germans had been forced to switch from daylight to night bombing, but their raids were unable either to knock out industrial production or to terrorize the British people into submission. By winter, although it was not so clear at the time, Hitler had met his first real defeat.

Itching to get into the act, Mussolini in October, 1940, without German consent, invaded Greece from his bases in Albania, but the Greek army hurled the Italians back and held them on a front stretching across the Albanian mountains. Soon Mussolini needed help. Hitler lined up the Balkan nations of Rumania and Bulgaria, but failed with Yugoslavia, where a Serb-led military *coup* unseated a government that would have allowed the Germans free transit to go to Mussolini's aid. In the spring of 1941, the Germans used time and troops that would later prove precious to invade and dismember Yugoslavia, and to conquer Greece, driving out a British expeditionary force and completing the operation with a spectacular parachute-and-glider conquest of the island of Crete.

In June, 1941, Hitler launched his invasion of Russia; he had always looked upon the fertile and relatively sparsely populated Russian plains, with their wealth of natural resources, as Germany's "living-space." Flushed with a succession of quick triumphs, he felt sure he could knock the USSR out in one campaign and then turn back to Britain. He almost succeeded. Within two months the Germans were besieging Leningrad; by October they had conquered the entire Ukraine and were closing in on Moscow. But winter was also closing in, and the months lost in the Balkans the previous spring could not be regained. The Soviet government had transferred some of its heavy industry far to the east, and American supplies were beginning to reach the Russians. The German armies had not been equipped to withstand a winter of war in Russia; they failed to take advantage of anti-Stalin sentiment in the conquered areas, and Soviet morale continued generally high. Counteroffensives between December, 1941, and May, 1942, pushed the Germans back.

By then Hitler was also at war with the United States. When World War II had begun in 1939, there was a strong body of isolationist sentiment in the United States and a handful of Axis sympathizers. But a more substantial portion of public opinion opposed Hitler from the first; the fall of France and the Battle of Britain strengthened these views. Between June, 1940, and December, 1941, the Roosevelt administration with the consent of Congress took a series of measures "short of war" to aid Britain and then Russia. In exchange for Atlantic naval bases in British colonies, the United States gave the British 50 "over-age" destroyers. It sent arms to Britain and used the American navy to assure delivery. The "Lend-Lease Act" (March, 1941) authorized the President to supply materials to any country whose defense he deemed "vital to the defense of the United States." When the USSR was attacked, American supplies were sent.

Hitler had legal justification for regarding American actions as warlike, but it was his commitments to Japan that eventually involved him in war with the United States. After the fall of France, the Japanese militarists had stepped up their program of expansion in Asia, moving into French Indo-China, and pushing ahead in China itself. The United States maintained its policy of opposition; in the summer and autumn of 1941 the American government froze Japanese credits, strove to shut off Japanese access to raw materials, and pressed the Japanese to withdraw from China and Indo-China.

In the midst of negotiations on these issues, the Japanese without warning struck with carrier-based planes at the American fleet in Pearl Harbor (December 7, 1941). Though the attack did severe damage, it by no means knocked out the American navy, but galvanized American opinion. The United States (with a single Representative in Congress dissenting) declared war on Japan. Thereupon Hitler and Mussolini honored their obligations to Japan and declared war on the United States. At the beginning, the Americans had to limit themselves to increasing lend-lease aid and assisting in the struggle against German submarines. In the Pacific the Japanese overran Guam, Wake Island, and the Philippines; by the spring of 1942, they had also taken Malaya—including Singapore—from the British and Indonesia from the Dutch. In control of Southeast Asia, they seemed poised for an attack on Australia.

Against Japan the first turning point came in the battle of the Coral Sea in May, 1942, when carrier-based American planes dispersed a Japanese fleet aiming at the conquest of Port Moresby, Papua. Against the European Axis, despite Stalin's pressure for a "second front" on the Continent, the United States and Britain landed instead in Morocco and Algeria in November, 1942. Against brief opposition from the Vichy French, the Allies made good their foothold. The plan was to crush the Germans and Italians holding Libya between these Anglo-American forces moving eastward and the British armies in Egypt moving westward. The Vichy regime delivered Tunis to the Germans, and enabled them to reinforce their armies in North Africa. But this only delayed the successful closing of the Allied vise. In May, 1943, the Allies took the last Axis strongholds in Tunisia and accepted the surrender of 300,000 Axis troops. The victory was not decisive, but allied morale soared after the defeat of the German General Rommel, the "desert fox."

More decisive was the successful Russian defense of Stalingrad in the summer and autumn of 1942; it turned into an offensive in November. Hampered by shortages of gasoline and by their enormously extended communications-lines, the Germans never quite made it all the way to the Russian oilfields in the Caucasus. Early in 1943 the Russians were beginning the great push westward that eventually took them

Wreckage of two U.S. destroyers following the Japanese attack on Pearl Harbor, December 7, 1941.

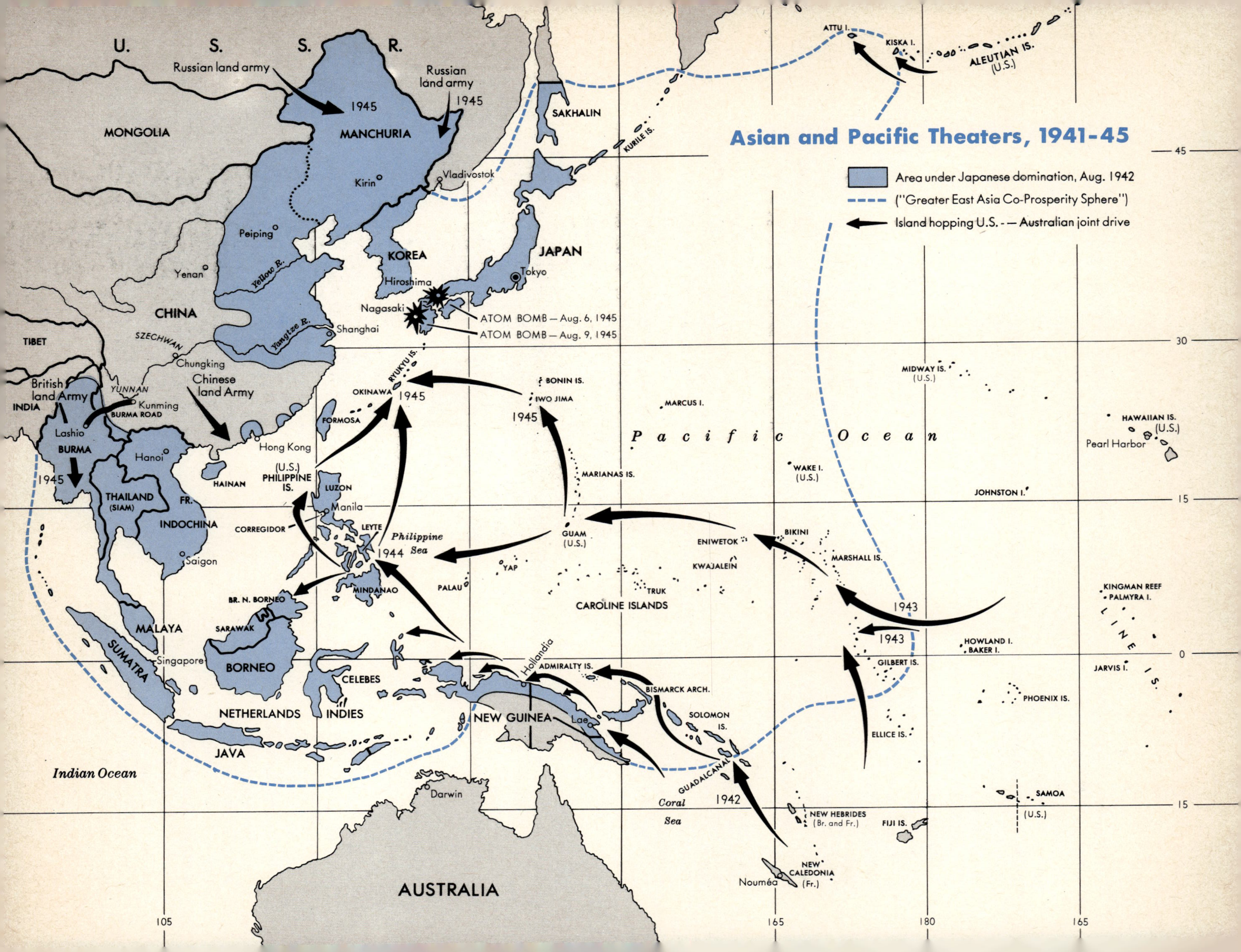

Asian and Pacific Theaters, 1941-45
Area under Japanese domination, Aug. 1942
("Greater East Asia Co-Prosperity Sphere")
Island hopping U.S. - — Australian joint drive
U.
S.
S.
R.
Russian land army
1945
Russian land army
1945
MONGOLIA
MANCHURIA
Kirin
Vladivostok
SAKHALIN
KURILE IS.
ATTU I.
KISKA I.
ALEUTIAN IS.
(U.S.)
Peiping
Yenan
Yellow R.
KOREA
JAPAN
Tokyo
Hiroshima
Nagasaki
ATOM BOMB — Aug. 6, 1945
ATOM BOMB — Aug. 9, 1945
CHINA
TIBET
SZECHWAN
Chungking
Yangtze R.
Shanghai
British land Army
INDIA
YUNNAN
Kunming
BURMA ROAD
Chinese land Army
Lashio
BURMA
1945
Hanoi
Hong Kong
HAINAN
THAILAND
(SIAM)
FR.
INDOCHINA
Saigon
RYUKYU IS.
OKINAWA
1945
FORMOSA
(U.S.)
PHILIPPINE IS.
LUZON
Manila
CORREGIDOR
LEYTE
Philippine Sea
1944
MINDANAO
BR. N. BORNEO
SARAWAK
BORNEO
MALAYA
Singapore
SUMATRA
CELEBES
NETHERLANDS
INDIES
JAVA
Indian Ocean
BONIN IS.
IWO JIMA
1945
MARCUS I.
MARIANAS IS.
GUAM
(U.S.)
YAP
PALAU
Pacific Ocean
MIDWAY IS.
(U.S.)
WAKE I.
(U.S.)
JOHNSTON I.
HAWAIIAN IS.
(U.S.)
Pearl Harbor
BIKINI
ENIWETOK
KWAJALEIN
MARSHALL IS.
TRUK
CAROLINE ISLANDS
1943
1943
HOWLAND I.
BAKER I.
KINGMAN REEF
PALMYRA I.
LINE IS.
JARVIS I.
GILBERT IS.
PHOENIX IS.
ELLICE IS.
SAMOA
(U.S.)
Hollandia
ADMIRALTY IS.
BISMARCK ARCH.
SOLOMON IS.
NEW GUINEA
Lae
GUADALCANAL
1942
Coral Sea
NEW HEBRIDES
(Br. and Fr.)
FIJI IS.
NEW CALEDONIA
(Fr.)
Nouméa
Darwin
AUSTRALIA
45
30
15
0
15
105
165
180
165

to Berlin two years later. Less spectacular, but perhaps most important, was the gradual victory over German submarines in the Atlantic; convoys, plane patrols, and radar slowly cut down the sinkings that in 1942 threatened to keep American supplies from getting to Europe.

THE ALLIED VICTORY

After this series of turning-points, the Allies took the offensive everywhere. Allied air bombardments systematically sought out critical components of enemy war-production: ball-bearing and jet-aircraft plants, oil refineries, locomotives. Planes rained fire on the flimsily built Japanese cities. On land, the Americans and British moved north from Tunis to Sicily (July, 1943) and six weeks later onto the Italian mainland. High Italian officers and dissident fascists organized a *coup* leading to Mussolini's fall and imprisonment and to the beginnings of negotiations between the Allies and a new government under Marshal Badoglio. But a special detachment of German troops rescued Mussolini (September, 1943) and set him up once again as head of a "Fascist Republic" in the north. In 1945 he was caught and executed by partisans. The Allied military campaign moved slowly northward; Rome did not fall until June, 1944, and when the Germans finally collapsed early in 1945, a front still stretched across Italy from a point north of Florence to Rimini.

At a conference in Tehran (December, 1943) Churchill, Roosevelt, and Stalin decided that the main Allied war effort would be in France. The landings under the command of General Eisenhower began on June 6, 1944, in Normandy. Technical innovation—landing-craft, amphibious vehicles, and artificial harbors—combined with superiority in the air, surprise, and a well-organized supply system enabled Eisenhower's men to create and hold, and then break out of, a beachhead. Led by General Patton's Third Army, the Allies then swept the Germans eastward across the Seine, while a second landing was launched in the south of France, and Allied troops moved easily northward. The French resistance assisted the advance, the population generally welcoming the invaders, who included de Gaulle's Free French troops. Paris was liberated before the end of August. Meantime, Hitler survived an attempted assassination (July, 1944) by a group of conservative and military conspirators; retaining his grip on the German state and armies, he continued to fight.

As Patton's forces ran out of gasoline, and German pilotless planes and rockets fell on England and denied to the Allies the use of the key port of Antwerp, the German armies escaped final defeat and withdrew into Germany. From the east, the Russians had driven Hitler's forces out of Russia, and to the south had swept to a junction with the Yugoslav communist resistance forces led by Tito. Not stopping for winter, they had swept through Poland by early 1945, and by March were threatening Berlin. The Western Allies broke the German fortifications in February and entered the heart of Germany. At Yalta (February, 1945), Roosevelt, Churchill, and Stalin coordinated the final plans for the conquest of Hitler; it was necessary to prevent a dangerous race between the Soviet Union and the West for German territory and to outline a scheme for military government. The decision to give the Russians the honor of taking Berlin, and many other decisions reached at Yalta, would later be severely criticized. But at the time it seemed only due recognition for the immense Russian contribution to the German defeat. When the Russians entered a Berlin smashed by Allied bombing, Hitler committed suicide on a Germanic funeral pyre in his underground headquarters. On May 8, 1945, Churchill and Truman (who had succeeded to the presidency after Roosevelt's death in April) proclaimed victory in Europe.

The Allied advance into Germany revealed the full horror of the concentration camps where slave laborers from conquered countries, political opponents, and "inferior" peoples such as Slavs and Jews had been immured. Thousands of living skeletons, piles of emaciated corpses told only part of the story: the gas-ovens systematically had exterminated literally millions of human beings, chiefly Jews. One after another, the concentration camps were liberated—Auschwitz, Belsen, Buchenwald, Dachau, Nordhausen, and others.

Against the Japanese, the American forces began by a concentrated program of "island-hopping," clearing out the bases in the south and central Pacific that blocked the way to the Japanese home islands—from Guadalcanal and the Solomons to New Britain and New Guinea and the Philippines; from Tarawa to Eniwetok to Kwajalein to Iwo Jima; and then from the Philippines and Iwo Jima to Okinawa. Simultaneously in the China–Burma–India theater, the Americans, with the British, supplied Chiang Kai-shek by air and kept Chinese forces in the fight against Japan. Air-raids on Japan proper had done immense damage. But the American government was sure that a major campaign against the Japanese home islands was still necessary to end the war, and President Truman and his advisors decided that only the use of the newly developed atomic bomb could bring a quick decision. The United States had only two bombs; its planes dropped them both, one on Hiroshima, the other on Nagasaki. The great loss of life would have been far greater had they not been used. Two days after the first bomb was dropped on Hiroshima, the Russians declared war on Japan (August 8, 1945) and began a large-scale invasion of Manchuria. On September 2, the Japanese surrendered. American military occupation under General Douglas MacArthur began.

UNSOLVED PROBLEMS

World War II had been an extraordinary effort, much more nearly a world conflict than World War I. The alliance against the Axis during the war had come to call itself the "United Nations." All of Latin America had joined, with Brazilian troops fighting in Italy; governments-in-exile, representing states occupied by Hitler and Mussolini, were active members. But the coalition was of course actually managed by Churchill and Roosevelt and Stalin. Four months before Pearl Harbor Roosevelt and Churchill met off Newfoundland and issued the Atlantic Charter (August 14, 1941) calling for the abandonment of aggression and the restoration of the rights of conquered peoples. Other top-level meetings during the war culminated in Potsdam (July–August, 1945).

The leaders constantly had to make grave decisions. On the military side, the Americans and English avoided some of the tensions that had characterized the First World War by organizing completely intermeshing staffs so that an American in command always had a British second and vice versa. The plan worked well. Anxious not to repeat another mistake of 1918, the Allies insisted that Germany would have to surrender "unconditionally," so that the Germans would be unable to propagate any new myth to the effect that they had not really been defeated but betrayed. During the war and since, many have argued that the words "unconditional surrender" stiffened the German will to resist, and that it might have been a better idea to offer anti-Nazi elements some reward for deserting the Nazi cause.

The British and Americans agreed on unconditional surrender, but they disagreed on how much political purity should be demanded of those who offered to assist the Allies. Churchill was ready to accept help from those tinged with fascism, like Badoglio in Italy, or communism, like Tito in Yugoslavia, so long as they were demonstrably anti-German. Roosevelt opposed the restoration of kings in Italy and Greece, and idealistically hoped for democratic republics everywhere. But in the case of France, neither was consistent: Churchill was far more anti-Vichy and pro-de Gaulle than Roosevelt, who feared de Gaulle as a potential man on horseback.

More complicated was the question of Soviet influence in eastern Europe. At Yalta the USSR promised to allow free elections in Poland, Hungary, Czechoslovakia, and the Balkan countries, and the western Allies accepted the assurance. It is often argued that the West should have realized that by "free" elections the Russians meant only elections that would return a pro-Communist majority; or that it was foolish of the British and Americans to let the Russians advance so far west. At the time, however, the United States and Britain wanted to keep the Russians actively in the war; since nobody knew whether the atomic bomb would work, the arduous prospect of a long war against Japan lay ahead. Even Churchill, who suspected that the Russians would try to communize eastern and southeastern Europe, was ready to run the risk. Moreover, those who picture a democratic eastern Europe betrayed by the West are conveniently forgetting the fact that before World War II all of the eastern European states but Czechoslovakia had moved toward fascist totalitarianism.

Scene in Hiroshima a few hours after the bomb hit, August 6, 1945.

After the victories over the European Axis and Japan, the war ended, but there was no peace. In Asia "colonial" peoples struggled against "imperialism," while in Europe unsolved issues remained far from solution. On both continents, from the Western point of view, Stalin's Russia had succeeded Hitler's Germany as the menace to peace and stability.

15

READING SUGGESTIONS (asterisk indicates paperbound edition)

General Accounts

G. A. Craig, *Europe since 1914* (*Holt); S. Easton, *World since 1918* (*Barnes & Noble). Useful textbook accounts.

A. Cobban, *Dictatorship* (Scribner's, 1939). Pioneering study of its history.

H. Arendt, *Origins of Totalitarianism* (*Meridian). Stressing the role of anti-Semitism and imperialism.

E. Wiskemann, *Europe of the Dictators, 1919–1945* (*Little, Brown). Fine survey.

E. Fischer, *The Passing of the European Age* (Harvard, 1943), and J. R. Western, *The End of European Primacy, 1871–1945* (*Colophon). The titles indicate the point of view.

Communist Russia

E. H. Carr, *A History of Soviet Russia*, 7 vols. (Macmillan, 1950–1964). A detailed history from original sources; the author is a rather uncritical admirer of Lenin.

R. V. Daniels, *The Nature of Communism* (*Vintage). A valuable study by a scholar who has written other works on the Soviet regime.

W. E. Chamberlin, *The Russian Revolution, 1917–1921*, 2 vols. (*Universal). Written over 40 years ago, but still standard.

D. Shub, *Lenin* (*Penguin). The best biography in English.

I. Deutscher, *The Prophet Armed, The Prophet Unarmed, The Prophet Outcast* (*Vintage). Three-volume biography of Trotsky by a great admirer.

———, *Stalin: A Political Biography* (*Galaxy). Fullest study in English.

B. Moore, Jr., *Soviet Politics: The Dilemma of Power* (*Torchbooks). Analyzes the relationship of ideology and practice.

M. Fainsod, *How Russia Is Ruled*, rev. ed. (Harvard, 1963). Good analysis. Fainsod has also written a fascinating case study, *Smolensk under Soviet Rule* (*Vintage).

A. Ulam, *Expansion and Coexistence* (*Praeger, 1968). History of Soviet foreign policy, 1917–1967.

L. Fischer, *The Soviets in World Affairs*, 2nd. ed. (Princeton, 1951), and M. Beloff, *The Foreign Policy of Soviet Russia*, 2 vols. (Oxford, 1947, 1952). Covering the period to 1929 and the period from 1929 to 1941, respectively.

Fascism

E. Nolte, *Three Faces of Fascism* (Holt, 1965). French, Italian and German.

H. Finer, *Mussolini's Italy* (*Universal), and H. A. Steiner, *Government in Fascist Italy* (McGraw-Hill, 1938). Two solid studies by expert political scientists.

G. Salvemini, *Under the Axe of Fascism* (Viking, 1936) and *Prelude to World War II* (Doubleday, 1954). Dissection of Mussolini's internal and foreign policies, respectively.

A. Hitler, *Mein Kampf* (*Sentry). English translation of the Nazi bible.

P. Viereck, *Metapolitics* (*Capricorn), and F. Stern, *Politics of Cultural Despair* (*Anchor). The ideological background of Hitlerism.

S. W. Halperin, *Germany Tried Democracy* (*Norton), and E. Eyck, *History of the Weimar Republic*, 2 vols. (*Science Ed.). Histories of the ill-fated republic.

A. L. C. Bullock, *Hitler* (*Torchbooks). The best biography.

J. Wheeler-Bennett, *Wooden Titan* (Morrow, 1936), and *Nemesis of Power* (Compass). First-rate studies of Hindenburg and of the German army in politics.

F. L. Neumann, *Behemoth: The Structure and Practice of National Socialism* (*Torchbooks). A most illuminating analysis.

H. Thomas, *The Spanish Civil War* (*Colophon). The best treatment.

H. Seton-Watson, *Eastern Europe be-*

tween the Wars, 1918–1941 (*Torchbooks). Useful comprehensive survey.

The Democracies between the Wars

J. K. Galbraith, *The Great Crash, 1929* (*Sentry). By a prominent American economist.

P. Einzig, *The World Economic Crisis, 1929–1932* (Macmillan, 1932); H. V. Hodson, *Slump and Recovery, 1929–1937* (Oxford, 1938); H. W. Arndt, *The Economic Lessons of the 1930's* (Oxford, 1944). Other useful books on the Great Depression.

A. Marwick, *Britain in the Century of Total War* (Little, Brown, 1968). Controversial assessment of the impact of war.

H. Pelling, *Britain, 1885–1955* (*Norton). Stressing the labor movement.

R. Graves and A. Hodge, *The Long Weekend* (*Norton). A lively social history.

G. E. Elton, *The Life of James Ramsay MacDonald* (Collins, 1939); G. M. Young, *Stanley Baldwin* (Hart-Davis, 1952); and K. Feiling, *The Life of Neville Chamberlain* (Macmillan, 1946). Useful biographies.

J. P. Mackintosh, *The British Cabinet* (*Barnes & Noble). Historical appraisal.

D. Brogan, *France under the Republic*, Vol. 2 (*Torchbooks). Detailed and perceptive political survey, 1905–1939.

D. Thomson, *Democracy in France since 1870*, 4th ed. (*Oxford).

A. Werth, *The Twilight of France, 1933–1940* (Harper, 1942). Condensation of several longer studies by an able journalist.

R. Albrecht-Carrié, *France, Europe, and Two World Wars* (Harper, 1961). Admirable account of French difficulties.

A. M. Schlesinger, Jr., *The Age of Roosevelt*, 3 vols. (*Sentry). Sympathetic study of the New Deal and its background.

F. Perkins, *The Roosevelt I Knew* (*Colophon), and R. E. Sherwood, *Roosevelt and Hopkins* (*Universal). By close associates of Franklin Roosevelt.

F. L. Allen, *Only Yesterday* (*Perennial) and *Since Yesterday* (*Bantam). Enlightening social histories of the United States in the 1920's and 1930's, respectively.

K. S. Latourette, *China* (*Spectrum), and E. Reischauer, *Japan Past and Present* (*Knopf). Good introductions.

L. Fischer, *Life of Mahatma Gandhi* (*Collier). Sympathetic biography.

B. Lewis, *The Emergence of Modern Turkey*, 2nd ed. (*Oxford). Thorough study of Atatürk's revolution and its setting.

The Second World War

E. H. Carr, *The Twenty Years' Crisis* (*Torchbooks). Provocative review of interwar diplomacy.

A. J. P. Taylor, *Origins of the Second World War* (*Premier). Also provocative.

A. Wolfers, *Britain and France between Two Wars* (*Norton). Analysis of diplomacy.

J. Wheeler-Bennett, *Munich* (*Compass), and L. B. Namier, *Diplomatic Prelude, 1938–1939* (Macmillan, 1948). Good studies of the final crisis leading to war.

G. Wright, *The Ordeal of Total War* (*Torchbooks). Expert evaluation of Europe's involvement in World War II.

B. Collier, *The Second World War: A Military History* (Morrow, 1967), and J. Creswell, *Sea Warfare, 1939–1945* (Univ. of California, 1967). Reliable accounts.

W. S. Churchill, *The Second World War*, 6 vols. (*Bantam). Magisterial study.

C. Wilmot, *The Struggle for Europe* (*Colophon). Critical of America's role.

R. Wohlstetter, *Pearl Harbor: Warning and Decision* (*Stanford). Fine study.

H. Feis, *Churchill, Roosevelt, Stalin* (*Princeton). Fair-minded review of their war aims and methods.

D. L. Gordon and R. Dangerfield, *The Hidden Weapon* (Harper, 1947). Excellent popular account of economic warfare.

C. de Gaulle, *Complete War Memoirs*, 3 vols. (*Clarion). Most interesting.

16

The Postwar World

Since 1945

Scene in Detroit during the summer riots of 1967.

I. The Cold War

By late 1968 (the time of this writing), more than twenty-three years had elapsed since the end of World War II, two years more than the twenty-one years that separated the end of World War I in 1918 from the beginning of the Second World War in 1939. Already the world had exceeded, if only by a little, the time it allowed itself for peace and reconstruction after the first of its twentieth-century mass wars. It might seem ironical to take comfort in so negative and chilling a reflection, yet there were further ironies: The very existence of the new atomic weapons that would probably kill off much of the human race in another great war had acted as a deterrent. Man's worst fears had not been realized; Armageddon had not yet taken place, and this in itself was indeed a comfort. Nor did

Armageddon in 1968 loom on the horizon, as several times during the tumultuous years since 1945 it had seemed to do. The years after 1945 were full of anxiety, of contention, of fighting in the various parts of the globe, but the worst had not happened, and perhaps it never would happen.

During World War II, most people expected that when the shooting stopped there would be a general peace conference, as there had been after all the major general wars of modern time. But as it turned out, the tensions that arose between the Soviet Union and its Western allies during the war itself made it impossible to plan for, much less convoke, a peace conference. So World War II bequeathed to mankind a legacy of problems to be solved one by one if at all.

The damage done by the war greatly exceeded even that done by World War I: 22 million dead, more than half of them civilians, and more than $2,000 billion in damage. Despite a sharply rising birth rate and vast programs of economic reconstruction, such losses could never be fully repaired. Moreover, new and terrifying problems faced the statesmen of the world. Atomic weapons, hydrogen bombs, the possibility—and soon the development—of guided missiles, made concrete and plausible the threat that a new general war might wipe out the human race or reduce what was left of mankind to something like another Stone Age. At the same time, the United States and the Soviet Union emerged as the only powers capable of initiating or pursuing the new warfare. Given the ideology of the U.S.S.R. and the suspicious and vengeful character of its supreme dictator, Stalin, it was inevitable that the Russians would regard the Americans as their rivals for control of the world, and that the Americans should quickly have been forced to accept the same estimate of the situation. The postwar history of international politics became in large part a history of Soviet–American rivalry: the Cold War.

In 1945 enemy attack and occupation had caused incalculable devastation inside the Russian borders, and left millions of survivors destitute, while Russia's capitalist ally, the United States, had remained intact and had invented and used atomic weapons. Stalin, who liked nothing so much as the destruction of an enemy, and who regarded the whole capitalist world as his enemy, knew that if he had been the sole possessor of the atomic bomb, he would have used it. He attributed to his rival the strategy that he himself would have pursued. It seemed to him that all the technological advance of the Soviet period, undertaken precisely to bring the U.S.S.R. up to the industrialized West, had now been wiped out by the American development of the atomic bomb. It took Stalin four years (1945–1949) to catch up once again, by making his own atomic bomb. No doubt, scientific information given the Russians by agents and spies made some contribution to this achievement, but only the high level of Soviet science and technology and the Soviet capacity to concentrate their investments made it possible at all.

A DIVIDED WORLD: GERMANY AND CHINA

Even before the U.S.S.R. could join the United States as an atomic power in 1949, the two had engaged in a series of tests of will, in Europe and in Asia, that determined where the increasingly clear boundary between a Russian sphere of influence and an American sphere of influence would run. And the confrontation continued after 1949. In Iran, in Greece, in Berlin, in Korea the lines were drawn, tested, and redrawn, sometimes after bloodshed. Though the Soviet Union and its former Western allies were able to reach agreement on peace treaties with Italy and with three of the Axis powers' former European satellites—Hungary, Rumania, and Bulgaria—no such treaty could be concluded with Germany itself or with Japan.

The United States occupied Japan alone. But defeated Germany was divided into four zones—American, British, French, and Russian. The U.S.S.R. obtained the eastern regions of Germany bordering on Poland and extending considerably west of Berlin, which, as the former capital, was also divided into four occupation zones, one for each of the Allies. This arrangement was designed for temporary military occupation, but continued in effect because no treaty could be reached. It proved extremely dangerous, for it left Berlin as an island surrounded by Soviet-dominated territory, yet an island including zones to which the Western allies were entitled to have access. The failure to reach any settlement over Germany left the most serious problem in Europe without a solution.

In 1949, the three Western powers allowed their respective zones to unite in the Federal Republic of Germany, called West Germany, with its capital at Bonn, and the Russians responded by creating the communist German Democratic Republic—East Germany—with its capital at Pankow outside Berlin. Many if not most West Germans were naturally eager for reunion with their fellow-Germans in the Soviet zone. Yet a reunion of Germany under Western capitalist auspices was precisely what the Russians feared most, believing that it would portend a revival of aggression. An all-communist Germany was equally intolerable to the Western powers. Indeed, few Frenchmen or Englishmen looked with enthusiasm upon the idea of any reunified Germany, and if there were more Americans who sympathized with reunion as an ultimate goal, there were no responsible men in high places who failed to understand the dangers of trying to bring it about unilaterally.

In Asia—with Japan under American occupation—the most grievous problem remained that of China. The communists, who had challenged Chiang Kai-shek's ruling Kuomintang (nationalist) party for power (*see above*, Chapter 15), kept their forces in being during the years of Japanese occupation. The United States tried in 1946–47 to bring about an agreement between Chinese nationalists and communists that would end the civil war. The effort failed, and the civil war continued. By 1949, the communists had defeated Chiang Kai-shek, who took refuge on the offshore island of Formosa (Taiwan), where the communists could not follow because they had no fleet. In the last years of the struggle, Chiang had lost his hold over the Chinese people; the morale of his own forces was low, and an ever-mounting inflation ravaged the economy, already ruined by the long Japanese occupation. By 1950, mainland China had gone communist, and formed part of the Soviet bloc. Only Chiang's government in Taiwan remained a part of the American bloc. American foreign policy had suffered a major defeat. Some Americans blamed the failure on a conspiracy by a few evil men, but the magnitude of the change, the huge numbers of Chinese involved, rendered this explanation improbable.

Elsewhere too the Soviet Union pursued its goal of turning the whole world communist through the agencies of individual Communist parties. In virtually every country a Communist party existed, sometimes strong—as in France or Italy—sometimes weak—as in Britain or the United States—often varying in its precise degree of subservience to the Communist party of the Soviet Union (CPSU) and the Soviet government, but almost always prepared to act as the domestic agent for Soviet interests and policies. The United States in most of the world had no such disciplined and reliable supporters.

THE TWO COALITIONS

The Soviet Union thus had a certain advantage in the Cold War, which consisted in part of a competition between the two superpowers for the allegiance and support of the rest of the world. Each became the leader of a great coalition, whose members were attached more or less tightly by bonds of self-interest to the senior partner.

The members of the loose American coalition in 1945 included the Western hemisphere, Great Britain, western Europe, Japan, the Philippines, Australia, and New Zealand. The Soviet coalition included the countries of eastern Europe, and by 1949 China. The border between the two coalitions in Europe—called the "Iron Curtain" by Winston Churchill in 1946—ran along a north–south line extending from Stettin on the Baltic to Trieste on the Adriatic. Yugoslavia lay in the Soviet sphere, and the frontier resumed again with the border between northern Greece and Communist Albania, Yugoslavia, and Bulgaria. Turkey belonged to the Western coalition, and portions of the Middle East and of Southeast Asia were linked to it by a network of pacts. The dividing line between North and South Korea, with the U.S.S.R. occupying the north and the United States the south, represented a kind of Asian extension of the long frontier between the two coalitions. Along the frontier came the aggressive Soviet probing operations that led to crises and in several cases to wars.

Repeatedly the United States sought in vain to ease the relationships between the two coalitions. In 1946, Stalin refused to join in a United Nations atomic energy commission, or to have anything to do with international control of atomic weapons. In 1947, the United States proposed an international plan of massive American economic aid to accelerate European recovery from the ruin of the war, the Marshall Plan, so called for George C. Marshall, then Secretary of State. The Soviet Union refused to accept the aid for itself, and would not let its satellites participate. The Marshall Plan nations subsequently formed the nucleus of the North Atlantic Treaty Organization (NATO: 1949). The Soviet coalition founded the Cominform (Communist Information Bureau) in 1947 as a successor to the former Comintern (see Chapter 15), "abolished" during the war, and created the Warsaw Pact (1955), binding eastern Europe together, as an answer to NATO. The United States and Britain sought in the 1950's and 1960's by a variety of means to prevent the spread of atomic weapons: the chief device was to be a plan for a joint Multilateral (Nuclear) Force in which the Germans would participate. The French rejected MLF, and in 1966 de Gaulle gave notice that at the expiration in 1969 of the treaty establishing NATO he would not renew it in its present form. NATO headquarters were moved from France to Belgium.

In the Near East, the Baghdad Pact and its successor, the Central Treaty Organization (CENTO), proved no more than a series of agreements among the United States, Britain, Turkey, Iran, and Pakistan. With the withdrawal of Iraq from the Baghdad Pact in 1959, no direct alliances linked the Arab world with the West. In the Far East, the Southeast Asia Treaty Organization (SEATO) meant that the United States could count solidly on Australia, New Zealand, the Philippines, and Thailand.

Outside the coalitions remained the neutral nations. Some, like Switzerland or Sweden, were simply maintaining their traditional legal policies of not aligning themselves with any grouping of powers. But most belonged to the new nations that were now emerging as independent, having discarded their former colonial status. Of these India was the most influential, taking from both coalitions much-needed economic assistance. As economic aid became an instrument in the Cold War, neutral nations tried, often with success, to play the Americans off against the Russians, raising the not too subtle threat that if Washington saw fit to deprive them of something they wanted, they might regretfully have to go communist. It was not until the 1960's that the United States learned to regard neutrality as often positively helpful to its interests.

THE UNITED NATIONS

Through the years of cold war, and the occasional outbreaks of something hotter, the United Nations—formed during World War II from among the opponents of the Axis and chartered in 1945 at San Francisco—served as an international organization where members of both coalitions and neutrals alike could meet in peaceful discussion. As direct successor to the League of Nations, it inherited the League's duty of keeping the peace, but like the League it lacked independent sovereignty or authority over its members. To deal with threats to the peace its charter created a Security Council with eleven member states, five of which—the United States, the Soviet Union, Great Britain, France, and China—held permanent memberships. The other six were elected to rotating two-year terms by the General Assembly, to which all member states belonged. The Secretary General, elected by the Security Council, could exert great personal influence in international affairs. But each of the five permanent members of the Security Council had a veto over any substantive question; decisions had to be unanimous before action could go forward. Both the U.S.S.R. and the United States insisted on this provision in the charter. As a result, the Security Council often found itself unable to act because of a veto: of the eighty vetoes cast between 1945 and 1955 the U.S.S.R. cast seventy-seven.

In the mid-Fifties new nations joined the UN: some pro-Western, like Austria and Italy (both former Axis states and so originally excluded), some pro-Soviet, like Rumania, Bulgaria, and the other former Axis satellites in eastern Europe, and some neutral and mostly former colonies, like Ceylon or Libya. Japan joined in 1956. As former colonies obtained their independence during the late Fifties and early Sixties, each joined the United Nations, where the "Afro-Asian bloc" came to command a majority in the General Assembly. Germany remained outside the UN, but both East and West Germany had their observers there. The United States successfully opposed the seating of the Chinese communists, which left the permanent Chinese seat on the Security Council in the possession of Chiang Kai-shek's representative. The three successive Secretaries General were the Norwegian Trygve Lie, the Swedish Dag Hammarskjöld, and the Burmese U Thant.

Though the UN could not "settle" the Cold War, or bring about the international control of atomic weapons, it did repeatedly manage to prevent small wars from becoming big ones. The League of Nations had never been able to put its own forces into the field, but the UN did so repeatedly: in Korea in 1950–1952 (where, because of the absence of the Soviet representative from the Security Council, the Russians failed to veto the Council's decision to intervene, and the

American army fought under the sponsorship of the UN); on the Arab–Israeli frontiers (1956–1967); in the former Belgian Congo; and in Cyprus.

Through its functional councils and special agencies—the Economic and Social Council, the Educational, Scientific, and Cultural Organization (UNESCO), the World Health Organization, the Food and Agricultural Organization, and the World Bank—the UN advanced loans to governments to initiate new development plans, controlled epidemics, and provided experts on modern farming techniques. The UN's international civil servants deserved well of mankind. Occasional critics disliked the organization's striking buildings in New York, and wished that it had never left Switzerland because it might now be mistakenly taken for an instrument of American imperialism. Occasional isolationist Americans demanded that "the U.S. get out of the UN and the UN out of the U.S.," while their opposites could be heard asking that the UN be given more "teeth," and that the nations abandon more of their sovereignty to it. Yet with its successes and its faults the UN reflected both the diversity and the elements of unity in the world of which it was the forum, and perhaps it would have been unreasonable to ask more of it than that.

II. The Major Free-World States

THE UNITED STATES

Instead of reverting to isolationism, as it had in the years after 1918, the United States took the lead in organizing both the United Nations and the network of alliances that constituted its own coalition. Vigorously it put through various programs of economic aid to other countries, beginning with the Marshall Plan and continuing by assisting the newly emerging countries of the former colonial world. Some of the money went for military assistance, most for economic development. Grumblings were many, but both political parties generally espoused these programs, and it was not until the special strains imposed by the Vietnam War in the years after 1965 that the sums appropriated for foreign aid were substantially cut.

The rough agreement between the Republicans and Democrats on foreign policy was actually shared on domestic policies as well, although the statement would be hotly challenged by professional politicians of either side. The stereotyped view continued to prevail that the Democrats were the more liberal and radical of the two parties and the Republicans the more conservative, yet when, in 1952, for the first time in twenty years, the Republicans elected a President, he was not really a politician at all, but General Dwight D. Eisenhower, a popular hero because of his performance as Supreme Allied Commander in World War II.

And during eight years (1952–1960) the Eisenhower administration not only did not repeal the New Deal enactments of the Roosevelt period, which had been continued by Roosevelt's former Vice-President Harry Truman in the years from 1945 to 1952, but left them intact and even extended the system of social security. An occasional Republican politician might darkly threaten to sell the Tennessee Valley Authority to private companies, but no responsible Republican leader ever wasted his time trying to do so. Nor, despite the effort to tag the Democrats as the "war party," did the Republicans shift the bases of foreign policy: Eisenhower's Secretary of State, John Foster Dulles, spoke of "rolling the Russians back" and "liberating" their satellites in eastern Europe, but when he was challenged by Soviet military intervention in Hungary in 1956 (*see below*, p. 666), he did nothing—exactly what the Democrats would have done.

The early 1950's brought—as a kind of domestic response to the Cold War—an extraordinary episode, in which a single senator, Joseph McCarthy of Wisconsin, led an onslaught against American civil servants whom he called communists. The fact that some genuine American communists had actually obtained government posts and had in some cases passed valuable information to the Russians lent some credibility to McCarthy's performances. But he himself never located a single communist in high places, while he did attack many persons on the flimsiest evidence or none at all. Bad as it was, the McCarthy period was no reign of terror: no blood was shed, the prisons were not filled, brave men opposed him, and in 1954 he was condemned by his fellow-senators 67 to 22 for abuse of his powers. The spectacle of McCarthy bullying witnesses on television—then a new device—helped arouse the public against him.

We should also note the American "freeing" of the Philippine Islands, which became a sovereign state in 1946, and the addition of Alaska in 1958 and Hawaii in 1959 to the number of states. Puerto Rico, a colonial dependency until 1952, in that year became a free associated state, or commonwealth, with its own constitution and its own government.

The United States was prosperous and productive during these postwar years, with only occasional recessions and readjustments. So remarkable was the steady growth of the gross national product, and so careful the attention given the economy by experts, that some had come to feel that the Americans had learned how to avoid depressions altogether. The general affluence, which made the United States, despite its very rich men, the most nearly classless country in the world, did not, however, filter down satisfactorily to the poorest members of society. In the presidency of Lyndon Johnson (1963–1969), when a series of programs to assist the poor was proposed, much of the planned effort had to be abandoned because of the heavy expense of the war in Vietnam.

The fact that so many of the poor in the United States were black men exacerbated what was already the gravest American social problem. Though gifted Negroes had won recognition in the arts, in sports, in the fields of entertainment, and often in business and the professions, the race as a whole was none the less handicapped by the failure of the society to provide its members with equal opportunities for education and for jobs. This was true not only in the South, more agricultural than the North, with memories of slavery and the northern victory in the Civil War still fresh, where some whites retained bitter anti-Negro prejudice and refused to permit the black man to advance himself; but also in the cities of the North, where hundreds of thousands of Negroes had flocked to live, and where their lot was often squalid and seemingly hopeless.

In 1954, the Supreme Court unanimously declared that the existence of separate compulsory public schools for Negroes was unconstitutional. This major decision, of course, immediately affected chiefly the South, where "separate but equal" education for the two races had been the theoretical rule, but where the separate Negro schools had usually been markedly inferior. In any case, the Court declared, separate education could not be equal education. The years that followed saw varying degrees of compliance with the new requirement: most parts of the South were determined to disobey the Court by one means or another; or, if they obeyed, to admit only "token" numbers of black students to predominantly white schools. Many efforts were made to speed compliance. By 1968 there were some black students studying with whites in every state of the Union, and in the border states and in some cities of the Deep South, such as Atlanta, the number was large. Southern state universities were also desegregated, after some efforts at resistance. But of course the existence in the northern cities of the black "ghettoes" and the prevalence of neighborhood schools everywhere meant that public education in New York or Boston was often as segregated as it was in Mississippi. Many predominantly white universities were striving to find and admit qualified black students, and institutions previously black had begun to worry about losing their most talented pupils. In 1968 the problem remained a serious one.

The new drive to improve conditions for Negroes extended into other fields. In the late Fifties and early Sixties whites and blacks worked to increase the registration of Negro voters in the South, and to liberalize real-estate practices to enable blacks to buy houses wherever they wished. Both drives made considerable headway. Some blacks, feeling that justice could never be gained by gradual means, turned away from the organizations—such as the National Association for the Advancement of Colored People (NAACP)—which had traditionally preferred to work by persuasion, toward more militant groups. Even the Reverend Martin Luther King, a nonviolent Negro minister from the South who had sponsored the successful Negro boycott of busses in Montgomery, Alabama, and forced the bus-lines to end segregation, lost some of his large following to other groups advocating one form or another of "Black Power."

During the summers of 1965, 1966, and 1967, severe rioting broke out in the Watts district of Los Angeles and in Newark, Detroit, and other Northern cities; Negroes burned large portions of their own neighborhoods, looted shops, and engaged in gunfights with the police. The passage of a federal Civil Rights Bill in 1965 and the outlawing of discrimination in real-estate transactions did not calm the stormy situation. While black violence aroused bitter protest especially among whites who opposed any improvement in the Negro's status, even moderates who favored the Negro advance hated the riots, and grew more and more anxious about public order. This anxiety was a factor in the narrow victory of the Republican Nixon over the Democrat Humphrey in the presidential election of 1968.

Violence in American life derived not only from the civil rights movement and its opponents. John F. Kennedy, the first Roman Catholic to be elected president (1960), was a young man of intelligence, personal elegance, and charm. His successor-movement to the New Deal, which he called the New Frontier, envisioned federal medical care for the aged, tax reform, civil rights, and antipoverty measures. But Kennedy was assassinated in 1963 by a psychopathic killer with a rifle. Televised details of the crime came into every American home, as did the fantastic murder of the assassin by another psychopath.

The deaths and destruction in the summer riots of 1965 through '67, the murder of Martin Luther King himself—also by rifle—in 1968, and the murder by pistol of President Kennedy's brother, Senator Robert F. Kennedy of New York, while he was campaigning to secure the Democratic nomination for the presidency in 1968, all combined with lesser crimes to produce a major public revulsion: but not one powerful enough to persuade the Congress to enact a drastic statute against the easy public procurement of guns.

Lyndon Johnson's administration successfully put through much of the social program that President Kennedy had not been able to achieve. But the gains were outweighed in the public mind by the cost in life and money of the war in Vietnam (*see below,* p. 679) and the rising discontent with a society that could not better distribute its own affluence. Children of the well-to-do, pampered by any standard, were "opting out" of the society in large numbers. Some took drugs—the increasingly fashionable marijuana, or "pot," which they insisted (against much medical evidence) was no more harmful than the alcohol their parents had always indulged in; or more addictive and dangerous drugs, such as heroin, or LSD, or even the deadly "speed." Many of these left home, congregated in special places (San Francisco's Haight–Ashbury district, New York's East Village), living from hand to mouth or handout to handout, eccentrically dressed in American Indian feathers or beads, affecting what they believed to be Buddhist ideas, speaking a special dialect, and protesting their love for everybody, which often looked uncommonly like hate. These were the "hippies." Some young people actively rebelled against the institutions of their immediate world, the university or the draft board. Some strongly supported the candidacy of Senator Eugene McCarthy of Minnesota for the Democratic nomination for President in 1968, and when that failed, were bitterly disappointed. Some took Mao Tse-tung or the Cuban guerrilla leader Che Guevara, killed in Bolivia, as their heroes, and the difficult writings of Herbert Marcuse as their inspiration. By no means exclusively an American phenomenon, the rebellion of the well-to-do children of the rich had not reached its end in 1968. It reminded many observers of the Russian nihilists and anarchists of the nineteenth century (*see* Chapter 14). The Russian "establishment" of the nineteenth century had not understood how to isolate the extremists among the rebels by embracing the moderates. Perhaps twentieth-century Americans would ponder the lesson.

The election of 1968 saw the victory of Richard M. Nixon, the Republican candidate who had served as Eisenhower's Vice-President, over Hubert Humphrey, the Democratic candidate who had served as Lyndon Johnson's Vice-President. The victory, however, was a singularly narrow one: less than one per cent of the popular vote separated Nixon from Humphrey, and the campaign of George Wallace, who won more than ten per cent of the total vote, meant that neither major candidate had a majority. As often before, the two parties seemed to differ in their programs largely in emphasis. With the Congress still Democratic, Nixon would presumably govern by conciliation and compromise, rather than by dramatic departures from Johnson's policies.

CANADA

After 1945, Canada enjoyed an economic growth and prosperity proportionately even greater than that of the United States. American capital poured in, and much was raised at home and in Britain. Though still producing vast amounts of raw materials from farm, mine, and forest, Canada came now to be a great industrial nation, exploiting her remarkable hydroelectric resources and her oil and mineral wealth. In the mid-Fifties Canada took the lead in carrying out a long-discussed plan for a canal from the Great Lakes to the lower St. Lawrence, deep enough to accommodate ocean-going ships, and producing in addition important hydroelectric power. In the United States, vested interests long succeeded in preventing American participation. But when Canada announced her intention of going ahead with the canal entirely on Canadian territory, the United States joined in a collaborative development; work began in 1954, and the canal was opened in 1959. Many Canadians had begun to worry over what they felt was undue cultural and economic dependence on the United States. But the three-thousand-mile frontier without a fort remained wholly peaceful.

Until the late 1950's Canada was politically one of the stablest of Western nations. While other parties at times held power in the provinces, the federal government remained under the control of the Liberals, who depended for their support on an effective collaboration between the English-speaking provinces and the French-speaking province of Quebec. In 1957 the Conservatives won a close victory, and in 1959 a new election gave them a landslide majority. In 1963, the Liberals returned to power, but without a majority, which meant that they had to govern as the principal party in a coalition. Still another election in 1965 failed to give them a solid majority. In addition to Conservatives and Liberals there were minority parties—New Democrats, to the left; Social Credit, favoring unorthodox economic ideas but not socialist; and a French-Canadian variant of this last. It seemed possible that Canada was beginning to develop a splinter-party system like those of many European democracies.

One reason for this was the rise of French–Canadian nationalist feeling in the province of Quebec and French-speaking regions elsewhere. The few thousands of French left in Canada in 1763 had multiplied by the 1960's to some seven million. Since World War II they had for the first time enjoyed a vigorous economic growth and increasingly high standards of living, after lagging for decades, in this respect, behind the rest of Canada. Their unrest was in part a demand for a greater share in the Canadian managerial and financial worlds. It was also a demand for greater cultural participation in dominion life, and especially for true bilingualism after the Swiss pattern. Many people in the rest of Canada resisted their demands. By 1967, the French extremists who actually proposed to secede and set up an independent Quebec were probably no more than a noisy few. A federal commission on biculturalism was set up.

Into this somewhat tense situation the French President de Gaulle—with

Citizens of Quebec greet French President de Gaulle during his state visit in 1967.

typical drama and concern for French *"grandeur"*—intruded in 1967, on a state visit to Canada. By shouting "Long live free Quebec!" (*"Vive le Québec libre!"*) to an enthusiastic crowd he seemed to be sponsoring secession. When the Canadian federal government called his performance inadmissible he ended his visit, but made a strenuous attempt thereafter to open special official cultural and economic relations with Quebec. No doubt the episode reflected in part de Gaulle's eager wish to make trouble for all "Anglo-Saxons," and for all friends of the United States. The Canadians responded by producing a brand new political leader: when Prime Minister Lester Pearson resigned, a previously unknown Liberal, Pierre Elliott Trudeau, emerged as party leader, and won a smashing victory in 1968. Half-French, bilingual, handsome, and intelligent, he had a free hand to cope with separatism as with all other questions that might arise.

WESTERN EUROPE

The nations of western Europe preserved the form of the sovereign state, and many of the sentiments we call nationalism, but after 1945 they made real attempts to organize a "free Europe" on a level above and beyond that of the national state.

The first step was the successful establishment of the European Coal and Steel Community (1952), named for the man who did much to organize it as the "Schuman Plan." (Schuman, appropriately enough, was a Frenchman with a German name.) France, West Germany, and Italy joined Belgium, the Netherlands, and Luxembourg ("Benelux") in creating for their coal and iron industries a free market area of all six nations in which a joint administrative body could make certain final and binding decisions without the participation of any government officials. Each nation had given up some part of its sovereignty, and the plan was a success.

In 1957, these six countries set up, by the Treaty of Rome, the European Economic Community (EEC), better known as the Common Market, or sometimes "the Six." This was the beginning of true economic union under a central administration composed of delegates from each partner nation. Its administration had certain rights independent of any member government. The treaty also provided for increasing powers over trade, production, immigration, and other matters for the Common Market, according to a carefully worked-out schedule. By the 1970's, it was planned, there would be in effect one common trading and producing society, a single market free from internal tariffs, and a population of some 180 million or more, substantially equal to that of the United States and equipped with equal economic skills and experience, and with similar "mixed" economies—free enterprise under government regulation.

The years after 1957 saw substantial progress toward this goal. The tourist by car or rail, remembering pre-war delays at the frontiers of the six countries, was astonished to be able to pass from one country to another almost as easily as he crossed state lines in the United States, and quite as easily as he crossed the Canadian–American frontier. Yet difficulties arose in the orderly carrying out of the schedule. Twice France vetoed Britain's proposed entry into the EEC, and insisted on specific provisions favoring French farmers in the Common Market. The difficulty about a British part in any European supranational arrangement was real, for many of the British regarded themselves as primarily part of the Commonwealth and not as Europeans. The British set up in 1959 the European

Free Trade Association, often called the "Outer Seven," with Britain, Sweden, Norway, Denmark, Austria, Switzerland, and Portugal as members. A much looser arrangement than the Common Market, it allowed each member to set its own external tariffs as it wished, thus protecting British "imperial preference" in favor of Commonwealth countries. The anti-British bias of de Gaulle was also real, however, and seemed unlikely to disappear.

Great Britain. In the United Kingdom of Great Britain and Northern Ireland (all of Ireland except six northern counties had gained complete independence), a general election held in July, 1945, after the war had ended in Europe, ousted Churchill and his Conservative party, and for the first time returned the Labour party with an absolute majority in the House of Commons. The Liberal party was practically extinguished. The new Prime Minister was Clement Attlee, a middle-class social worker.

The new government—with a mandate for social change—proceeded to take over, with due compensation to the owners, the coal industry, the railroads, and some parts of commercial road transportation, and began to nationalize the steel industry. Britain already had a well-developed system of various social insurances; this was now capped by a system of socialized medical care for all who wished it. The educational system was partly reformed in an effort to make it more democratic, and to lengthen the required period of compulsory education. In accordance with Labour party philosophy, some parts of the old Empire were given independence, and others were granted dominion status—that is, national independence within the extraordinary British multinational system.

What emerged was a British economy pushed a little more toward collectivism than before, but still a "mixed" economy. Coal and railroads, nationalized, did not become great state trusts run by bureaucrats on the Russian model, but rather public corporations with a structure not unlike that of great private industries in the West, run by boards not dominated by bureaucrats or politicians. Broad sectors of the economy remained in private hands, under no more than the kind of government regulation common in the United States.

Proof of the essential moderation of this British revolution was afforded by the conduct of the Conservatives, who with Churchill still at their head were returned to power once more in 1951 and remained there for twelve years. The nationalization of steel, which had begun, was indeed stopped; but otherwise the Conservatives kept intact the "socialism" of their opponents, including the national health scheme.

In the postwar years the British were not resilient enough to keep up with the extraordinary pace of technological innovation. The British automobile industry, for example, which immediately after the war gained a big share of the world market, in the 1950's saw the Germans, with their inexpensive, standardized light car, the *Volkswagen*, take the lead. Although British production was behind that of the United States or West Germany, the British were still a great industrial people, suffering from the fact that because they had been the *first* to industrialize in the modern manner their plant tended toward obsolescence and inefficiency. Observers often found Britain's managers lacking in enterprise, unwilling to adopt new ways, and uninterested in research; while the workers were suspicious of any change in methods, regarded management as the perpetual enemy, and were more interested in the tea-break than in the quality of the product.

And, even in apparent prosperity, Britain remained in economic trouble. The pound, a currency still used as standard along with the dollar in the "free world," was always in danger. Its exchange value, already reduced in 1940 from $4.85 to $4.00, had after 1949 been pegged at $2.80. But continued pressure on the pound in the 1960's repeatedly required help from Britain's allies in the form of rather complex financial measures to maintain this value. This weakness of the pound signalled an unfavorable "balance of trade": the British people were buying more from the rest of the world than they could sell to it.

In the Fifties and Sixties, in what came to be called the "brain drain," many of Britain's distinguished scientists and engineers left home to migrate to the United States, Canada, or Australia. Having lost much of her nineteenth-century Empire as well, Britain had to pay relatively more for necessary imports than she did in the nineteenth century while at the same time facing even in her old "colonies" the competition of new and more efficient industries and new tariff barriers.

Political stability prevailed. The Conservatives in the general election of 1964 gave way to the Labour party, which had won only a tiny majority of three in the House of Commons. The new Prime Minister, Harold Wilson, held on until a new election in 1966, when he emerged with a greatly increased majority. Thus strengthened, he proposed new measures to cope with the ever-present danger to the pound: a freeze of wages and prices in an effort to restore the balance between what British workmen—and managers—spent and what they produced. Wilson was asking the British to work harder for less cash return. His proposals threatened to split his own party; radical Labourites insisted that he was playing the capitalists' game, exploiting the poor to support the rich. At the critical Trades Union Congress of September, 1966, he won a precarious victory. Yet in 1967 he had to devalue the pound once more, to $2.40, after heavy foreign pressure—largely French—against it. By 1968 he was personally unpopular and widely mistrusted.

Under both Conservative and Labour party governments, Britain remained a firm, if at times somewhat critical, ally of the United States. Much English public opinion opposed the war in Vietnam, and anti-American sentiment was common among Leftists who regarded us as too rich; among Rightists who regarded us as too pushing; and among "intellectuals" who regarded us as too immature. Behind all this there remained a common realization of common interests.

France. World War II inflicted on the French what psychologists call a trauma—a deep wound in the soul. Defeat by the Germans, brutal German occupation and economic exploitation, the spectacle of much French collaboration with the enemy, all this was succeeded by liberation, which, in spite of the part played in it by the Fighting French and the French Resistance movement, was still clearly the work of American and British and, indirectly, of Russian arms. Nor had France since the early nineteenth century kept pace with the leading industrial nations in production, in finance, above all in population. Only one fact gave cause for optimism: while the "net reproduction rate" for 100 women had in 1942 sunk to 85 (that is, fifteen less than the figure needed to maintain without immigration the existing population), by 1949 it had risen to 133—that is, 33 above mere stability. The rate continued at 124 or higher through 1955. This meant that hundreds of thousands of French men and women deliberately decided to have children, a clear sign of the recovery that lay ahead.

The French government-in-exile, led by General de Gaulle, in 1944 easily reestablished in liberated France the old republican forms of government. Frenchmen called this state the Fourth Republic; but after de Gaulle, disappointed by his failure to attain real power in a state still ruled by unstable parliamentary coalitions of "splinter parties," retired from politics in 1946, the Fourth Republic began to look exactly like the Third. Cabinets lasted on an average only a few months; to the old splinter parties was added a Communist party of renewed strength, openly dedicated to revolutionary change. The problems of the old empire, now known as the French Union, seemed insoluble; its peoples were in ferment. After nine years of war, Indo-China (Vietnam) was lost in 1954 in a great defeat at Dienbienphu. In the same year an active rebellion against the French began in Algeria, which France regarded not as a colony but as an overseas portion of France itself. Morocco and Tunisia were both lost in 1956, and the crisis deepened.

In 1958 General de Gaulle took power again, as financial instability, inflation resulting from the war costs in Indo-China and Algeria, and a rising popular disgust with the "politicians" combined to bring about the fall of the Fourth Republic. A military and Rightist *coup d'état* in Algeria took place on May 13, 1958. De Gaulle then announced that he was willing to come out of retirement. The leaders of the *coup* wrongly assumed that he would carry out their policies for keeping Algeria French.

In France there was very little violence, as a plebiscite confirmed the change. The Constitution of the new Fifth Republic provided for a President of France, to be elected for a seven-year term by direct popular vote. An absolute majority was required, and, if not achieved in a first election, was to be obtained in a run-off between the two candidates with the greatest number of votes. Elected outright in 1958, de Gaulle was re-elected to a second term in 1965 in a run-off. Under the constitution the French president appointed the premier, who could dissolve the legislature and order new elections at any time after the first year. Thus the new constitution gave the executive more power, the legislature much less. Those who disliked the new constitution complained that it made the legislature a mere rubber stamp.

De Gaulle's enemies called him a dictator. Cartoonists enjoyed drawing him as Louis XIV, the *roi soleil*, with wig and silk stockings, the personification of French haughtiness and superiority. He was certainly an obstinate, opinionated man, but though a general and personally authoritarian, he was no Napoleon III or Boulanger or Pétain. Frenchmen still enjoyed freedom of speech, of the press, of public assembly. French journalists could and did say as nasty things about their president as American journalists could and did say about ours. Yet the regime did control radio and television. In the general election of 1965 it yielded to the pressure of public opinion, and consented to give de Gaulle's opposition candidates some time if not quite "equal time" on the air.

The French ruling classes believed that their colonial subjects, especially the Algerians, could be persuaded to want to become real Frenchmen. But most of the Moslem nine-tenths of the Algerian population disagreed. Against the wishes of those who had brought him to power, de Gaulle in 1962 worked out a settlement making Algeria independent, leaving France some "influence" and some rights over Saharan oil. The Right regarded this as treason. Most of the Leftists, on the other hand, never gave him even grudging credit for it.

Starting with the Marshall Plan aid in 1947, a great series of economic and social changes began in France. Unlike the United States and Britain and Germany, France down to that time had preserved much of the small-scale, individualistic methods of production and distribution characteristic of the period before the Industrial Revolution. Now there began full-scale reorientation of the economy in accordance with the usual practices of modern industry. Helped by foreign investment, especially American, France began to experience a real boom. The growth rate in the Sixties was about a steady six per cent per year, ahead even of West Germany; inflation, though a problem, had until 1966 or 1967 been held down to three per cent. Prosperity meant that for the first time Frenchmen by the hundreds of thousands got their first cars, television sets, and hi-fi record players; that they travelled in ever growing numbers; that they enjoyed fearful traffic jams and incredible highway accidents; and that many of those who found the new ways unsettling blamed all the changes, like Coca-Cola, *le drugstore,* and blue jeans, on the Americans.

In foreign policy, de Gaulle was a deeply committed old-fashioned nationalist Frenchman. His memoirs showed how much of a love-affair with France his whole life had been, and how deeply he identified himself personally with his country. He never forgot a slight, and a slight to him was a slight to France, to be repaid in due course. The treatment accorded him by Churchill and Roosevelt during World War II he could never forget; and when he came to power he retained a healthy personal dislike of *"les Anglo-Saxons."* To him, the thought of the supranational bodies that would rob France of her sovereignty even to a small degree (the Common Market, NATO, and others) was uncomfortable, and talk of a United States of Europe, in which France would be submerged, anathema. He spoke instead of a *"Europe des patries,"* a Europe of "fatherlands," that would not stop at the Russian frontiers but would include Russia—at least the European part—with all its historic European associations. And within the *Europe des patries,* of course France would take the lead.

To do this France must have her own atomic weapons. Therefore de Gaulle refused to join the U.S., U.K., and U.S.S.R. in a treaty barring atomic tests (*see below,* p. 671), and France continued, like Red China, to test nuclear weapons in the atmosphere, exploding her first hydrogen bomb in 1968. She must also have her own *force de frappe,* the striking force capable of delivering atomic weapons to their targets, and so of deterring an enemy. Vigorously opposed to communism at home, de Gaulle none the less worked out a rapprochement with Russia. The U.S.S.R., he argued, in the 1960's no longer represented the threat to the general peace that it had represented in the '50's. Now—in balancing the scales against the industrial and military power of the United States and its special friend, Britain—France needed to be friends with Russia. To South America, to Canada, with appeals to French separatists in Quebec (*see above*), to Poland, and to Rumania, de Gaulle took his stately presence, and his message that France would be the leader of Europe.

In the spring of 1968, however, while de Gaulle was presenting his case in Rumania, Paris erupted unexpectedly. The French universities, so overcrowded that there were no classrooms for students to use and no way of their listening to their lecturers, had been disregarded by the regime in a period when the young everywhere were full of resentment against the society their parents had brought them into. Led by anarchists and others, the students occupied their buildings, fought the police, and eventually drew a reluctant Communist party into the fray. In order not to lose the support of the French workers, who had already begun to strike in sympathy with the students, the Communist leadership had to support what looked for a few days as if it just might be the beginning of a new French Revolution. De Gaulle returned to Paris, assured himself of army support, proposed a referendum, which he was obliged to abandon in favor of new elections, and won a great victory at the polls, obtaining a larger majority in the legislature than before.

Thereupon he dropped his Prime Minister, the chief organizer of victory, Pompidou, and embarked on a new phase of his regime. His economic and social program called for *participation* by the workers not only in the profits of industry but in its management. His new Minister of Education, acknowledging the justice of many of the grievances of the students, pushed through the legislature (November, 1968) a major radical reform bill decentralizing the educational system. Having established his strength with the strong support of the Right—as in 1958—de Gaulle now appeared to be preparing at least to appease the Left—again, as in 1958. Perhaps the military and foreign programs would have to be slowed down; but nobody who had studied de Gaulle believed they would be abandoned. Astounded for the hundredth time at the superhuman capacities of de Gaulle—if not altogether admiring him—observers realized once again that, though unique, he was none the less 78, and wondered anxiously what or who might possibly replace him if by any chance he should prove not to be immortal.

West Germany. In 1966 West Germany had a population of 59 million, some three times that of East Germany. The wartime destruction of much of Germany's industrial plant paradoxically soon proved beneficial: the new plant was built with the latest technological equipment. The Allied High Commission, never very severe, gradually abolished controls over German industry, save for atomic energy and a few other military restrictions. It advanced economic aid, and scaled down pre-war German debts. By the early 1950's West Germany had a favorable balance of trade and was achieving industrial growth as high as 10 per cent a year.

Gross national product rose from $23 billion in 1950 to $103 billion in 1964, with no serious monetary inflation. This prosperity was to a large degree spread

Overturned and burned cars used by students to barricade Paris streets in 1968.

through all classes of society. The working man in West Germany had begun to enjoy the kind of affluence that his opposite number in the United States had had for some time. New buildings rose everywhere. The divided superhighways Hitler had built for largely military purposes grew overcrowded, and had to be widened and extended.

Politically, the Allies required "de-Nazification." At the Nuremberg trials in 1946, seventy-four top Nazi leaders were convicted of war crimes. Ten were hanged, after two had committed suicide; one was sentenced to life imprisonment, others to shorter terms; and three were acquitted. To have dismissed all civil servants who had held posts under the Nazi regime would have dismantled German administration altogether. A weeding-out of the most compromised Nazis was achieved, though not sufficiently to satisfy many Western anti-Nazis.

The independent West German state had a constitution that provided for a bicameral legislature, with a lower house representing the people directly and an upper house representing the states (*Länder*), together with a president elected by a special assembly for a five-year term, in practice largely a ceremonial figure. Real executive leadership was vested in the chancellor, a prime minister dependent on a parliamentary majority. The old splinter-party system did not return to plague the new republic. Under the leadership of Konrad Adenauer, the Christian Democrats, distant heirs of the old Centrist party (*see* Chapter 15), held power down to 1961.

A Rhineland Catholic, former Mayor of Cologne, conservative, pro-French, and thoroughly democratic, Adenauer was forced to retire only by age, and continued to wield enough influence to weaken his successor, Ludwig Erhard, a Protestant, who remained in office for five more years. The twenty-year reign of the Centrists was one supported by the voters, not the result of one-party totalitarian politics.

West Germany seemed to be approaching two-party democratic politics, with the Christian Democrats challenged chiefly by the Social Democrats, roughly similar to the British Labour party. The Social Democrats held power in some of the states and cities of the federal union, notably in West Berlin, whose popular mayor, Willy Brandt, ran unsuccessfully for the federal chancellorship against Erhard in 1964. A neo-Nazi minority existed in West Germany, but by 1966 it had achieved no very alarming successes at the polls. Militant organizations of war veterans and of refugees from the "lost" Eastern territories now included in Poland, the U.S.S.R., or Czechoslovakia perhaps posed more of a possible threat to stability.

The major political question remained that of an eventual reunion with Communist-dominated East Germany. Neither recognized the other. After long years during which East Germans, attracted by better West German living conditions, crossed the border by the tens of thousands, the East German government in August, 1961, began building a wall between the two parts of the city (*see* p. 670). In 1968 this wall still stood, though on special holidays families in West Berlin were allowed to cross into East Berlin briefly to visit relatives and friends.

As part of the Cold War, the Americans, British, and French permitted the West Germans to rearm early in the 1950's and to join NATO. Military conscription was introduced in 1957, and by 1968 West Germany had a relatively large and very modern army, navy, and air force. Government and people supported the armed forces as a necessity, but the old Wilhelmine and Nazi militarism did

The World, 1969

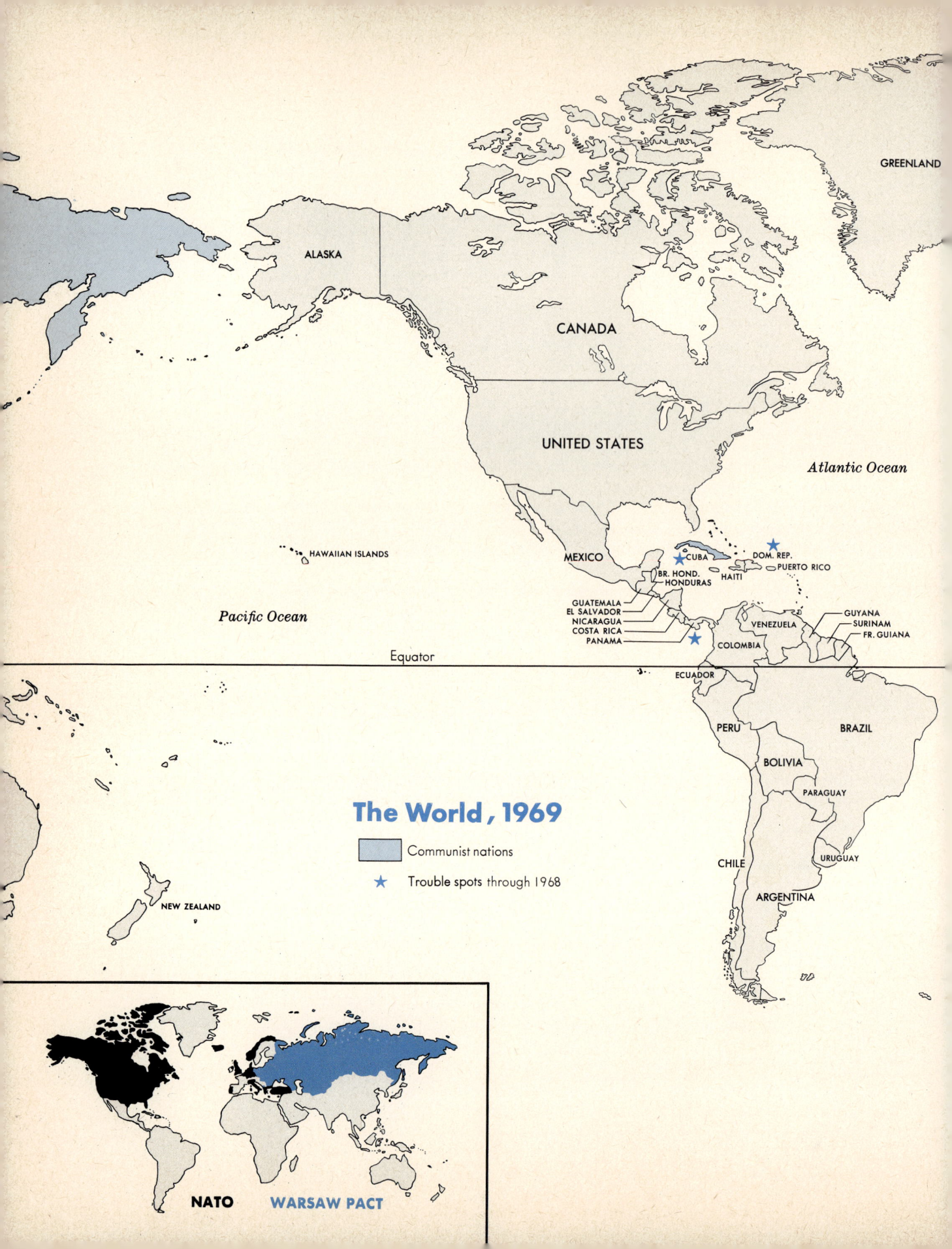

- Communist nations
- ★ Trouble spots through 1968

NATO — **WARSAW PACT**

OAS CENTO
(Incl. U.S.)

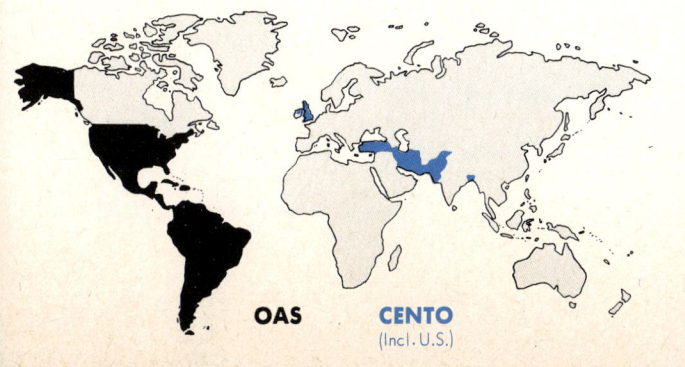

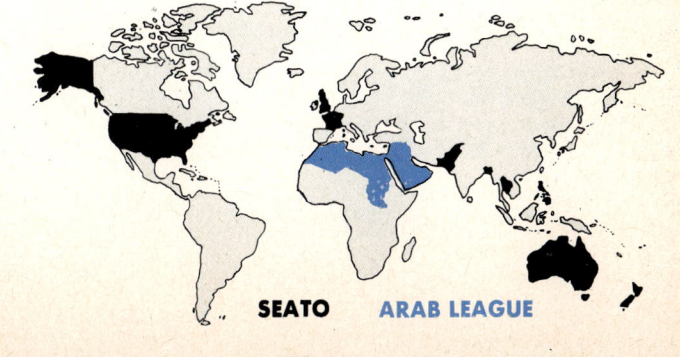

SEATO ARAB LEAGUE

not revive among the people at large. Access to the atom bomb was not included in this rearmament, but German public opinion apparently was not greatly exercised over the exclusion.

In the late autumn of 1966 there arose in West Germany a major political crisis. Neither the Christian Democrats nor the Social Democrats had a secure majority in the Reichstag. Chancellor Erhard was governing in coalition with a small right-wing party, the Free Democrats, basically non-Nazi conservatives opposed to "socialism." There was friction with some of the high command of the armed forces. It was hard to support American policies in Europe and yet not break with France. The slowing down of West German economic growth might, it was feared, presage a real recession. All this contributed to Erhard's downfall. In November, 1966, the Free Democrats refused to support his proposals for higher taxes, and the government fell.

But the Christian Democrats came forward with Kurt Georg Kiesinger, a Catholic, who as Premier succeeded in forming a "grand coalition" with the Social Democrats. Willy Brandt became Vice-Chancellor and Foreign Minister. Though some members of both parties disapproved, and though Kiesinger's past membership in the Nazi party aroused some alarm abroad, the new coalition commanded popular support. It was designed to last until the elections scheduled for 1969. Meanwhile in 1968 provincial elections produced some unprecedented successes for the neo-Nazi group headed by Adolf von Thadden, whose future was not easily predictable. On the Left, meanwhile, uproariously rebellious students demonstrated in Berlin, largely against the newspaper and magazine empire of a rich and powerful publisher, Axel Springer, who began to reduce some of his holdings. A left-wing German refugee even played a considerable role in the French student uprisings.

Prosperous West Germany seemed to have lived down its past as the aggressor that had committed the atrocities of the 1940's. Yet the postwar prosperity might not, in spite of the optimism of many economists, prove to be depression-proof. Anything like the worldwide depression of the 1930's might well destroy the social stability on which West German democracy rested. Moreover, after two decades there were no signs that a United Germany was possible, and loss of much of pre-war Germany to Poland and Russia (*see* Chapter 15) was traumatic for German nationalists. If German nationalism should in the future prove anything like as strong a collective emotion as it clearly had been in the past, the division of Germany might confront the next generation with a grave potential source of that next world war that mankind knows must not be allowed to take place.

The Other Western Countries. In Italy a plebiscite in 1946 showed 54.3 per cent of the voters in favor of a republic, and in spite of the comparative narrowness of the margin, the republic proved a viable state once it was established. There were monarchists who regretted the forced departure of the House of Savoy, and there were even some who regretted the end of the fascist regime. But neither group was able to influence parliamentary politics to any great extent. A strong Christian Democratic party (a Catholic party with a relatively liberal reform program) under a succession of leaders, Alcide de Gasperi, Amintore Fanfani, and Aldo Moro, proved able to hold power thereafter with support from other groups. It took positive measures to break up the large landed estates in the by a very strong Communist party, the largest in the West, with whom the larger faction of the Socialists—that led by Pietro Nenni—was allied. The firmly anti-communist socialist faction led by Giuseppe Saragat participated in the government.

In the Sixties a series of complicated negotiations began a process the Italians called the *"apertura a sinistra,"* the opening to the Left. In this process the Christian Democrats won over some Socialist support. A further weakening of the extreme Left was achieved in 1966, when the Socialists—long split between an anti-communist wing and a wing that often collaborated with the Communists—reunited as one party.

Italy's economic growth between 1953 and 1966 was so remarkable that the Italians themselves refer to it as their *"miracolo economico."* As in France, this was achieved with some government ownership and with much government regulation and planning. Italy was a mixed economy, but a free society. Milan, long a busy and active city, began to look like another Chicago. Rome had perhaps the most desperate traffic problem of any great city in the world. Membership in the Common Market and freedom from the troubles of imperial liquidation gave Italian enterprise opportunities it had never had before.

The grave problems of the *mezzogiorno,* the southern part of the peninsula, and the islands of Sardinia and Sicily, were attacked by programs of investments, by providing jobs in the north or in Germany or Switzerland for the surplus workers of the south, and by old-age pensions. In the Italian balance of payments, an income of about $1 billion annually from tourists provided a useful item on the "export" side.

The smaller states of "free Europe" generally shared the prosperity and problems of their larger brothers. In Belgium, which enjoyed great material well-being, the chronic difficulties between the minority of French-speaking Walloons and the majority of Dutch-speaking Flemings continued to worsen and to threaten the stability of the country. In the Iberian peninsula, which was part of anti-communist Europe without being "free," Spain—still in Franco's control thirty years after the Civil War—had taken major steps toward modernization and a few mild measures to relax political tyranny. Portugal, under the rigidly conservative Salazar, dictator since 1932, lagged well behind Spain. The replacement of Salazar, because of illness, in the autumn of 1968 promised to open a new chapter, though the expenditure of men and money involved in holding onto the Portuguese colonial empire made great changes unlikely.

All the "free world" nations had their troubles, but they remained free.

III. The Communist Bloc: The U.S.S.R. at Home

Alone among the leaders of the "Big Three" of the war years, Stalin remained in power after the war. His remaining years, 1945–1953, marked a continuation and even sharpening of the policies that he had made his own. Some four years of political uncertainty followed his death, but in 1957 Nikita Khrushchev emerged as supreme, and held onto power until 1964. He was succeeded by two co-chiefs, Brezhnev and Kosygin, who remained on top in 1968.

STALIN'S LAST YEARS

Facing the devastation caused by the war, and what he regarded as the immediate threat of American atomic weapons, Stalin felt obliged to decree a continuation of austerity into the postwar years, at just the moment when the Russian people most yearned for new housing and a few creature comforts. The party, still his docile instrument and experiencing regular purges to prevent any relaxation, dominated political life, with the constant assistance of the secret police; while the army, still mobilized at high strength and performing a variety of occupation duties abroad, remained the third Soviet institution with power of its own.

Not long before he died, Stalin in 1952 created a new Presidium, which he planned as a larger body than the Politburo, to include the ten Politburo members and fifteen additional high-ranking Soviet officials. But he did not live to announce the membership of the new body or to summon a meeting of it. After his death, the new "Presidium" simply replaced the old Politburo, with the same ten members. Khrushchev later declared that, in enlarging the membership and changing the name of the Politburo, Stalin had been taking the first step toward the complete purge and liquidation of its ten existing members; so it is perhaps no wonder that, having survived this first step, they declined to take a second.

The fourth Five-Year Plan (1946–50) and its successor the fifth (1951–55) continued to emphasize investment in heavy industry at the expense of consumer goods. Financial measures—the raising of prices, the wiping out of savings by the establishment of a new currency—kept the severest sort of economic pressure on the population. Reparations exacted from Germany and industrial loot from the eastern European countries gave massive stimulus to Soviet reconstruction. The fourth Five-Year Plan saw the first Soviet atomic bomb completed; the fifth saw further advances in armaments and the building of the Volga–Don canal. In agriculture, the regime embarked on a policy of reducing the number and increasing the size of collective farms. In 1951, Nikita Khrushchev, now appearing as a leading party agricultural expert, proposed a plan to create great agricultural cities (*agrogoroda*), in order to concentrate farm labor and abolish rural backwardness.

The cultural policy of the regime was in keeping with the bleak austerity and terror of these years. The cultural boss, Andrei Zhdanov, decreed that literature had to take an active role in the "engineering" of human souls. The official school of "socialist realism" was the only permissible line for a writer to follow. Zhdanov denounced in particular Mikhail Zoshchenko, writer of witty and satirical short stories, whose "Adventures of a Monkey" accidentally set free by a bomb suggested strongly that life in a cage in a zoo was more agreeable than life at large among the Soviet people; and Anna Akhmatova, a sensitive lyric poet, who had had the unpatriotic ill-judgment to lament in verse her feeling of loneliness, which no proper Soviet citizen would do. Both were silenced. Though Zhdanov died suddenly in 1948, his principles continued to reign. Violent anti-Western propaganda filled Soviet books and resounded from the Soviet stage in such a play as *The Unfortunate Haberdasher,* in which President Truman was cast as Hitler.

With the attack on the Western nations went a constant drumbeat of new (and sometimes comic) claims for Soviet, or at least Russian, "firsts" in every field of intellectual and artistic endeavor. No scholar could safely investigate a topic without paying respects to the supreme authorities on everything: Marx, Lenin, and, chiefly, Stalin. Archeologists, historians, students of literature began their work with a compulsory quotation from Stalin, and genuflection before him as the great teacher, the "Choryphaeus of the sciences."

Stalin supported the geneticist Trofim Lysenko, who maintained—contrary to all accepted biological doctrine—that acquired characteristics were hereditary, strongly implying that "new Soviet man" would emerge as a biological phenomenon, and giving support to the political argument that communism would change the human species. In linguistics too, Stalin personally intervened in 1950 to denounce the prevailing theories originated by Nikolai Marr, then sixteen years dead, who had implied that the world's languages corresponded to the degree of social development reached by their speakers. Neither biologist nor linguist, Stalin fearlessly laid down the law for both.

As Stalin grew older, the secrecy, censorship, and conspiratorial miasma at the top of the Soviet state and society all intensified. Catering to ancient prejudices and violating Leninist precepts, Stalin now moved against the Jews. Anti-Semitic propaganda reached its peak with the publicity given an alleged "doctors' plot," in which Jewish doctors were accused of plotting to poison Stalin. When Stalin died, the stage seemed set for a full-scale anti-Semitic drive reminiscent of Hitler. Fear of the West, and detestation of Zionism—many Soviet Jews wanted to live in Israel—did not alone explain Soviet anti-Semitism. Despite their long years of preaching cultural autonomy for nationalities, many Soviet leaders were anti-Semitic, and recognized that the population at large could be expected to welcome anti-Semitism at a moment when there was little else in the government's policies that they could endorse.

THE SOVIET SUCCESSION

By the early 1950's it had become a favorite occupation in the West to speculate on Stalin's succession. Would it be the Communist party, or the secret police, or the army that would emerge supreme? Would it be some combination of two of these against the third? Was this or that member of the Politburo identified with one or another of these three chief agencies? Would the world see a new bitter rivalry comparable to the struggle between Stalin and Trotsky for the succession to Lenin? If so, would the resulting instability go so far as to disrupt the machinery of Soviet government?

When the moment actually came, in March, 1953, Georgi Malenkov, personally close to Stalin, succeeded him as Premier, but surrendered his Communist party secretaryship to Nikita Khrushchev. It was thus clear that nobody would immediately inherit all of Stalin's power. Soon the regime began to denounce the "cult of personality" (i.e., Stalin's former one-man rule), and proclaimed a "collegial" system (i.e., government by committee). The dreaded chief of the secret police, Presidium-member Beria, was executed for treason.

But no free-for-all among the remaining members of the inner circle ensued. Malenkov vanished from the top post of Premier, to be succeeded by the political general Bulganin; but Malenkov was at first simply demoted to a lower cabinet post, and remained in the Presidium. It was noteworthy that when Malenkov confessed error, he took responsibility for the failure of the *agrogoroda,* which were actually Khrushchev's idea. Khrushchev was certainly very powerful, but his fellow-members on the Politburo had great influence, and showed no outward signs of fearing him as all had feared Stalin. On the whole, it appeared that the transfer of power had actually gone quite smoothly.

At a party congress held early in 1956, Khrushchev made a speech in which he denounced Stalin, emotionally detailing the ghastly acts of personal cruelty to which the psychopathically suspicious nature of the late dictator had given rise. Khrushchev thus echoed what Western observers of the U.S.S.R. had been saying for years. As the details of the speech were leaked out to the Soviet public, there was of course some distress at the smashing of the idol they had worshipped so long; but a good many of them no doubt had all along suspected that Stalin was something less than godlike. So the widespread disorders that some observers were predicting failed to materialize.

Abroad, however, the speech led to turmoil in the Soviet satellites in Europe (*see below*, p. 666), and so gave Khrushchev's opponents at home an opportunity to unite against his policies. Within the Presidium they had a majority. But Khrushchev was able to rally to his support the larger body of which the Presidium was the inner core, the Central Committee of the Communist party of the U.S.S.R. A veteran party worker, he had installed his own loyal supporters in all key party posts, repeating Stalin's performance after the death of Lenin (*see* Chapter 15), and emerged from this greatest test with his powers immeasurably enhanced (June, 1957). Now the Soviet press denounced the "anti-party group" of Malenkov, Molotov, and Kaganovich, three of the members of Stalin's own entourage. In Stalin's own day, this would have led them to the execution-block. Khrushchev, however, acted differently. All three were expelled from the Presidium and removed from their high posts, but all three were given minor positions at a safe distance from Moscow. In 1958 Bulganin followed them into the discard: he too had sided against Khrushchev, whose succession to Stalin's position of undisputed power now seemed complete.

THE KHRUSHCHEV ERA AND BEYOND

Bureaucratic Problems. Yet there were certain differences. Already in his sixties, Khrushchev could hardly hope for a quarter-century of dictatorship such as Stalin had had. Moreover, in the very course of making himself supreme he had deprived himself of some of the instruments available to Stalin. After 1953 he had released millions of captives from prisons and slave-labor camps. Almost everybody in Russia had a relative or friend now freed. These men and women now took jobs, some of them even government jobs. Within a year or two Soviet society at every level except at the very top of the bureaucracy had absorbed these sufferers from tyranny. The secret police no longer enjoyed a power almost independent in the state, a power that might challenge the party or the army. Khrushchev himself had emotionally denounced its terror. It was still possible to prosecute and even persecute individuals by terrorist means, but Stalin's mass terror as a system of government had disappeared.

Instead of terror, Khrushchev embarked on a series of bureaucratic changes. He gave the Russian Republic, by far the largest and most populous of the republics, virtually a separate administration, and took complete control of its personnel. In 1963 he took parallel measures for Central Asia and the Transcaucasus. Khrushchev was wrestling with the problems of efficiency, output, and morale. Under Stalin, centralization had reached an intolerable tightness. But how far could one decentralize so huge an operation as the Soviet economy and

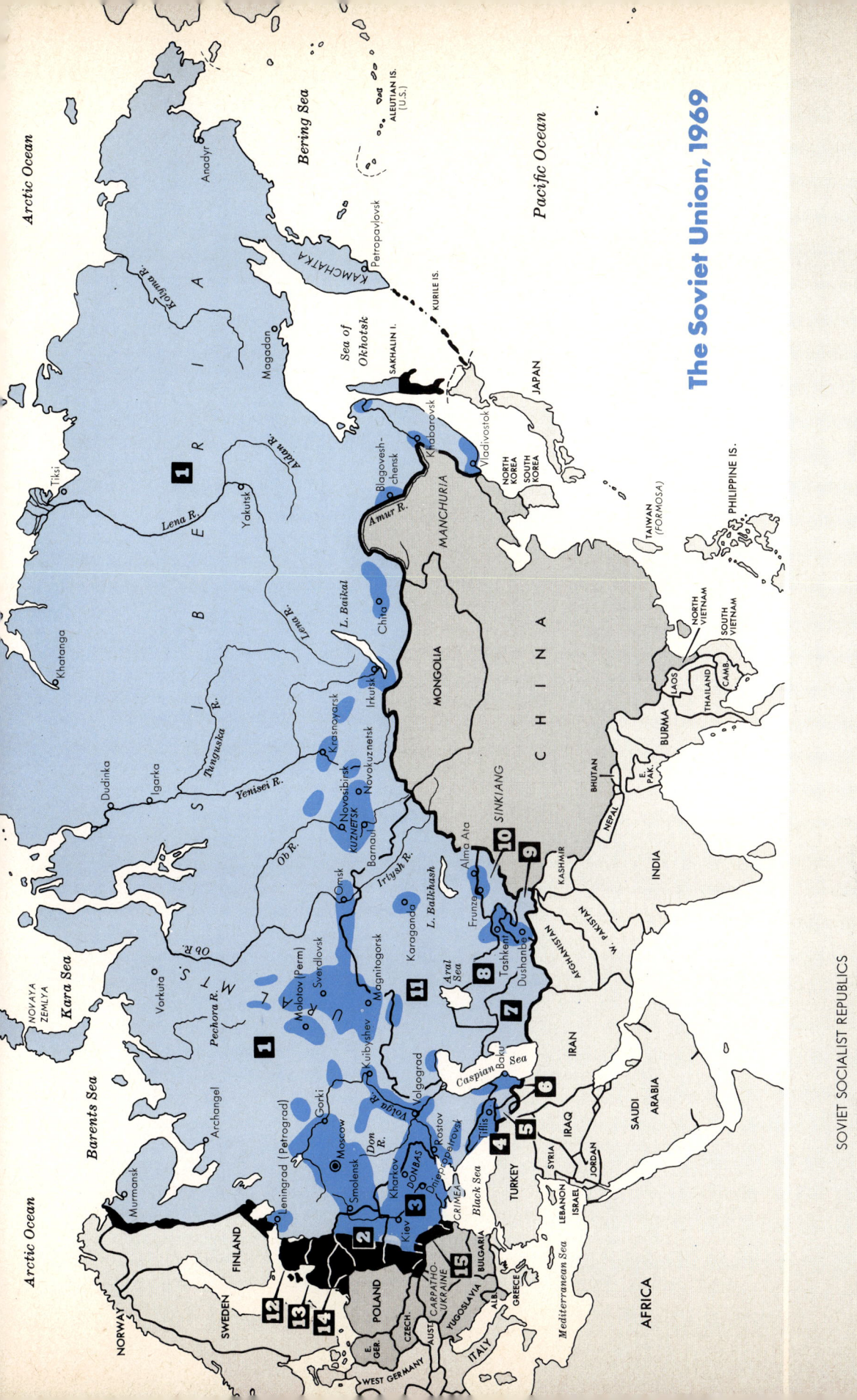

The Soviet Union, 1969

Legend:
- Areas annexed since 1940
- Other Communist countries
- Industrial areas (in U.S.S.R.)

SOVIET SOCIALIST REPUBLICS

1. Russian Soviet Federated Socialist Republic
2. White Russia
3. Ukraine
4. Georgia
5. Armenia
6. Azerbaidjan
7. Turkmenistan
8. Uzbekistan
9. Tadjikistan
10. Kirghiz Republic
11. Kazakh Republic
12. Estonia
13. Latvia
14. Lithuania
15. Moldavia

still retain control over local operations? How far could one centralize and still obtain local cooperation, loyalty, and, especially, production? Between 1953 and 1957, responsibility for many heavy industries was transferred from the ministries of the central government to those of the individual republics. In May, 1957, a decree abolished many central ministries, and transferred their duties to 105 newly created regional economic councils (*sovnarkhoz*), in the hope of giving full play to informed, on-the-spot decisions, of improving the use of local resources, of consolidating overlapping services, and of reassigning experts from the central government to the grass roots. Regionalism—devotion to regional interests as against national ones—replaced what might be called devotion to one industry ahead of others. But patriots for Armenian industry (to the detriment of other regions) were no more helpful to the national economy than patriots for the cement industry (to the detriment of other industries).

By 1960 a process of recentralizing had begun. By the end of 1962, the *sovnarkhozes* were reduced from 105 to about 40, and new state committees appeared to oversee their work. These committees greatly resembled the old ministries, and in fact were before long reorganized as ministries. The pendulum had swung back almost the entire distance. Now all lower levels of the party were divided into agricultural and industrial wings, in an effort to make the political functionaries serve the economy more efficiently.

In mid-October, 1964, the world learned to its astonishment that Khrushchev had been removed from power and succeeded by two members of the Presidium. L. I. Brezhnev replaced him as First Secretary of the Central Committee of the Communist party, and A. N. Kosygin as Premier (Chairman of the U.S.S.R. Council of Ministers). Both were "Khrushchev men": Brezhnev, aged 58, a metallurgist by training, had held posts in the Ukrainian, Moldavian, and Kazakhstan Communist parties, entering the Presidium in 1957; Kosygin, aged 50, an engineer, Commissar of the Textile Industry in 1938, Premier of the Russian Republic throughout World War II, member of the Politburo from 1949 to 1952, and Minister for Light Industry, went into eclipse shortly before Stalin died and re-emerged as a member of the Presidium only in 1957. The published communiqués spoke of Khrushchev's ill health and advanced age, but it was clear that he had not acquiesced in his own removal. How had Brezhnev and Kosygin managed it? And why? And what did they stand for?

Khrushchev did not practice the kind of constant vigilance over his associates that alone could have ensured him security in office. The plotters acted in his absence, and took careful steps to line up the members of the Central Committee in support of their action so that he could not appeal to the Committee over the head of the Presidium as he had done in 1957 (*see* p. 656). Khrushchev continued to live in retirement in Moscow and in his country house. No large-scale purge followed his removal.

Khrushchev was responsible for major agricultural failures at home and much more serious Soviet setbacks abroad, as we shall see. Yet he might have continued in office had it not been for his personal rudeness. The communiqué that announced his replacement referred to his *prozhekterstvo* ("hare-brained scheming"), no doubt in reference to the virgin lands fiasco (*see below,* p. 659), and to "half-baked conclusions and hasty decisions and actions, divorced from reality; bragging and bluster; attraction to rule by fiat [literally, "commandism"]." Caustic and crude, Khrushchev had apparently tried his former supporters too far.

Industry and Agriculture. Khrushchev had faced the same problem that had faced all Soviet leaders: how much emphasis could be put on consumer goods, and how much still must be devoted to heavy industry? Though temperamentally more interested in providing consumer goods than Stalin or Malenkov, Khrushchev made the same choice as they: continued emphasis on the means of production. The sixth Five-Year Plan (1956–1960) set more ambitious goals than ever before, but the huge expenses involved in the Polish and Hungarian outbreaks forced the Soviet government to shelve the plan. By the end of 1958 it announced a new Seven-Year Plan, to run until 1965. Starting from base figures of 500 million tons of coal, 55 million tons of steel, and 113 million tons of oil, output by 1964 had reached 554 million tons of coal, 85 million tons of steel, and 224 million tons of oil. In 1966, the regime returned to the system of Five-Year Plans.

Most spectacular were the successes achieved in the field of rocketry and space. The U.S.S.R. successfully launched the first earth-satellite (Sputnik, 1957) and first reached the moon with a rocket (1959). Heavy payloads soared aloft before American engineers could get their lighter ones off the ground. Spurred to some degree by the Soviet technical advance, the United States itself embarked in the late Fifties on an intensive program of research and development in space. Though the U.S.S.R. got the first man into space, and for some time held the lead in technical achievements, by the mid-Sixties the United States had logged more hours of flight by spaceships with one-man and two-man crews, and had virtually solved the problem of rendezvous in space, while the successful Mars-probe operation of 1965 overshadowed comparable Soviet exploration of the solar system.

Agriculture continued to present the Soviet planners with some of its seemingly most insoluble problems. In 1953 Khrushchev embarked on the "virgin lands" scheme, a crash program to plow under more than 100,000 acres of prairie in the Urals region, Kazakhstan, and Siberia. Drought and poor planning and performance led to a clear failure by 1963. By the following year, the number of collective farms was down to about 40,000 from an original 250,000 and the average size of the new units was far larger, perhaps about 5,000 acres. By 1965, the government recognized that many collectives were now too big.

To increase incentives, the regime in 1958 abolished compulsory deliveries of farm products, the most onerous of the peasants' burdens, and raised agricultural prices. Simultaneously, the government decreed the gradual abolition of the MTS (Machine Tractor Stations; *see* Chapter 15) and the sale of the tractors to the individual collective, which the government undertook to subsidize in part. In 1964, the government for the first time extended its system of old-age and disability pensions to agricultural laborers; it removed the ceilings on the private allotment of land allowed to the individual peasant in a collective and on the number of cattle that he might own privately. Yet yields continued low; animal husbandry caused grave concern, and the regime's agencies thundered against inefficiency and "fascination with administration by fiat."

In the years after Khrushchev's fall from power in 1964, the Soviet authorities engaged in an open debate about the best way to revise the statutes governing the collective farm (*artel*) in view of the immense changes since 1936. The party and the government ordered the collective farms to guarantee the individual farmers a monthly sum in cash for their work, and to pay in addition for the produce actually received. The state bank would advance the farms the credit where necessary. Some economists were arguing for the introduction of a free market economy; others vigorously defended centralized planning (with improvements). Obviously the Soviet authorities were recognizing the importance of "capitalist" incentives in the field of agriculture as in many others.

Education and the Arts. In 1958 Khrushchev introduced an important change in the Soviet educational system: "polytechnization," which emphasized vocational training and on-the-job experience. This represented a retreat from the goal of a ten-year general educational program for all. Khrushchev ordered the universities now to favor applicants who had had practical experience. By the mid-Sixties, almost all children in the U.S.S.R. finished the first four years of school (ages seven to eleven), and illiteracy had virtually disappeared. Almost as many finished the second four years (ages eleven to fifteen), which were now combined with "polytechnization." In 1964, the conventional next course of three years (ages fifteen to eighteen), usually taken by only about 40 per cent of Soviet youth, was reduced to two years. Nationwide talent contests were held to discover the most promising candidates for university study in math and science.

Khrushchev extended to the field of arts and letters the same partial relaxation that accompanied de-Stalinization in other fields. It took Soviet writers some time to accustom themselves to the idea that it might now be possible to voice dissent: too many had vanished forever at Stalin's whim to make the risk an attractive one. Moreover, convinced Stalinists or party hacks who had grown up under Stalinism lay in wait to attack the innovator. Khrushchev was himself opinionated and autocratic, and kept artists and writers in constant uncertainty lest new purges break forth. The dangers of self-expression continued great indeed.

In a few individual books and authors we may find indices of the new policies. Ilya Ehrenburg, veteran propagandist for the regime, in *The Thaw* (1955) hailed the relaxation of coercive measures over artists. Vladimir Dudintsev's novel *Not By Bread Alone* (1956) had as its hero a competent and enthusiastic engineer whose invention of a new pipe-casting machine was thwarted at every turn by the entrenched bureaucrats. Government-controlled writers' agencies denounced Dudintsev, who retracted his views, and for six or seven years was forced to earn his living by translation only. Boris Pasternak's *Dr. Zhivago* (1958) became a *cause célèbre* throughout the world. Pasternak, a brilliant poet who had for years confined himself to translating Shakespeare, took advantage of the "thaw" to offer for publication his novel about a doctor who, through all the agonies of the First World War and the Russian Revolution, affirmed the freedom of the human soul. Accepted for publication in Russia, the novel was also sent to Italy to be published. Then the Soviet censors changed their minds, and forced Pasternak to ask that the manuscript in Italy be returned to him. The Italian publisher refused, and versions in Russian, Italian, English, and other languages appeared abroad, arousing great admiration. In 1958 the Nobel Prize Committee selected Pasternak as the winner of the prize for literature. He accepted. But then the Khrushchev regime reverted to Stalinism: Pasternak's fellow-writers reviled him as a pig and a traitor, and the government threatened him with exile if he accepted the prize. As a patriotic Russian he then declined it.

In the same week that a Soviet physicist accepted the Nobel Prize for physics, the regime called the Nobel Prize for literature a capitalist invention.

And a few years later, Mikhail Sholokhov, author of the famous Cossack trilogy *The Quiet Don* and a personal friend of Khrushchev, accepted the Nobel Prize for literature. Pasternak's persecution revealed the limits of the thaw as of 1958. His Jewish origins, his intellectualism, his proclamation of individualism touched hostile chords in Khrushchev himself and in other Soviet officials and writers, making it impossible to publish *Dr. Zhivago* in the U.S.S.R.

But the spirit of individualism, slow to express itself even when liberated in the older generation, found in the 1960's new and more vigorous expression among the younger poets and novelists who had grown up since the Second World War, and for whom the heroic age of the Revolution and the early Bolshevik struggles were ancient history. The young Ukrainian poet Yevtushenko denounced Soviet anti-Semitism in his *Babi Yar* (the name of the ravine near Kiev in which the Nazis had massacred thousands of Jews), and declared his identity with the murdered human beings. In another poem he begged the government to double and triple the guard over Stalin's tomb,

> So that Stalin may not rise
>   And, with Stalin the past.
>
> . . . the ignoring of the people's welfare
>   The calumnies
>   The arrests of the innocent.

Former supporters of Stalin, he went on,

> Do not like these times
> When the camps are empty
> And the halls where people listen to poetry
> Are crowded.*

When Yevtushenko recited his verse, the halls were indeed always crowded with eager, excited, contentious young people, claiming the right to think for themselves. "We've found out," said another young poet, "what it leads to when

* *Pravda*, October 21, 1962.

Left: Yevgeny Yevtushenko photographed at his home in Moscow; the portrait on the wall is of Boris Pasternak; **right:** Andrei Sinyavsky (foreground) and Yuli Daniel at their trial in Moscow, February, 1966.

somebody else does our thinking for us." Severely disciplined in 1963, Yevtushenko was publicly on the attack again in 1965.

Yevtushenko's mention of "the camps" suggests another new phenomenon in the Soviet writing of the early Sixties, the deep interest in the terrible days of Stalin's labor camps and in the suffering of their inmates, reflected, for example, in the novel by Solzhenitsyn, *A Day in the Life of Ivan Denisovich*. Khrushchev viewed with some apprehension the flood of fiction about the camps that came pouring into the publishing houses, only a little of which was published. Khrushchev tried to remind the younger generation of the glorious revolutionary past through which their elders had triumphantly lived. He declared—as if in answer to their demands for full freedom—that even under full communism it would not be possible to give complete liberty to the individual, who would continue "like a bee in a hive" to make his contribution to society.

After Khrushchev's ouster in 1964, his successors denounced him for interfering in intellectual life, but here, as elsewhere, they did not depart very far from his policies. In September, 1965, two writers, Andrei Sinyavsky and Yuli Daniel, were arrested for writing under pseudonyms and sending abroad anti-Soviet fiction and essays. Writing as Abram Tertz, Sinyavsky, in *The Trial Begins,* had given a candid and revolting picture of the life of the Soviet leaders under Stalin; his novel *Lyubimov* (translated into English as *The Makepeace Experiment*) dealt with a one-man revolt against communism in a small Russian town; and his essay *On Socialist Realism* damned what was still the official literary doctrine of the regime. Writing as Nikolai Arzhak, Daniel, in *Moscow Calling,* produced a fantasy in which the Soviet government set aside one day on which murder was allowed. In 1966, despite the protests of many young people, Sinyavsky and Daniel were tried and condemned to prison.

The defection in 1967 of Stalin's daughter, Svetlana Alliluyeva, to the United States and the publication in this country of her autobiography were treated vituperatively in the Soviet press as part of a vast cultural plot arranged by American spies and agents to spoil the celebrations planned for the fiftieth anniversary of the Revolution of 1917. At the Writers' Congress of 1967 old-line writers reaffirmed the theories of socialist realism, and attacked all who opposed them. Early in 1968 the authorities arrested three young men and one young woman and charged them with treasonable contact with a foreign agent, a spy of Russian origin who had allegedly paid them to circulate anti-Soviet materials from abroad. All were imprisoned after a trial against which some of the young writers protested, thereby bringing down upon themselves vigorous rebukes. At least one of the accused and one of the chief protestors were Jews.

Solzhenitsyn also found himself in trouble in 1968 over manuscripts of his novel *Cancer Ward* that had found their way abroad after the Soviet censors had tried to force him to revise it. It was plain that the regime continued to have severe problems in controlling its "intelligentsia," perhaps 20 per cent of the Soviet working population, and equally plain that freedom of expression would continue to be curbed.

IV. Soviet Foreign Policy

THE LAST YEARS OF STALIN

Europe. When the war ended, the Soviet Union did not immediately terminate all forms of cooperation with its allies. The joint plan for dividing and ruling Germany went through. The four occupying powers together tried the chief surviving Nazi leaders at Nuremberg in 1946. In February, 1947, came the peace treaties with Italy, Rumania, Bulgaria, Hungary, and (for the U.S.S.R.) Finland. These confirmed Soviet territorial gains: from Rumania, Bessarabia and northern Bukovina; from Finland, portions of Karelia and a long lease on the naval base at Porkkala. In addition, the U.S.S.R. annexed part of former East Prussia and the extreme easternmost portion of Czechoslovakia.

In Poland, Rumania, Hungary, and Bulgaria the U.S.S.R., relying on the pressure of the Red Armies, sponsored the creation of new "people's republics" under communist government. In each country, the Russians eliminated all political groups that could be accused of collaboration with the Germans; then formed "progressive" coalitions of parties; next destroyed all non-communist elements in these coalitions, by splitting off from each party a small fragment that would collaborate unquestioningly with the communists; and finally denounced and persecuted the remainder. Elections, despite the promises at Yalta, were accompanied by intimidation and atrocity. Western protest uniformly failed.

Yugoslavia organized its own communist state, and had Albania as its own satellite. Soviet troops occupied about one-third of Germany, roughly between the Elbe and the Oder rivers, where they organized a satellite communist-ruled East Germany. The part of Germany lying east of the line formed by the Oder and Neisse rivers, save for the sections of East Prussia directly annexed to the U.S.S.R., the Russians handed over to their Polish satellite. Here a wholesale transfer of population removed the Germans, and replaced them with Poles. Finland became part of the Russian security system, but retained its pre-war political institutions. The four Allied powers detached Austria from Germany, thus undoing Hitler's *Anschluss* of 1938; and divided it, like Germany, into four occupation zones. The presence of Soviet troops in Hungary and Rumania was specifically guaranteed, in order to "protect" the communication lines between the Soviet Union and its occupying forces in Austria.

In 1948, the communists took over in Czechoslovakia, and ousted the government of Edward Beneš, brave enemy of Hitler in 1938 (*see* Chapter 15), betrayed now for a second time. Within each satellite the communists aped Soviet policies, moving with all speed to collectivize agriculture, impose forced-draft industrialization, control religious and cultural life, and govern by police terror.

As early as 1946 the U.S.S.R. refused to withdraw its forces from northwest Iran, and yielded only to pressure from the United Nations. A more alarming probe of the Soviet perimeter came in Greece, where a communist-dominated guerrilla movement had already during World War II attempted to seize control, and had been thwarted only by British troops. In 1946, the Greek communists tried again, backed this time by the Soviet-dominated governments of Albania,

Yugoslavia, and Bulgaria to the north. Simultaneously, Stalin exerted pressure on the Turks for concessions in the Straits area. In response President Truman proclaimed that countries facing the threat of communist aggression could count on help from the United States. Under this "Truman Doctrine," he sent American military aid to Greece and Turkey. The threat to the Turks evaporated, and by 1949, after severe fighting, the Greeks had put down the communist rebellion with the help of American advisers.

In Germany, the Russians began in 1948 one of the most bitter phases of the Cold War. By shutting off the land routes from the West into Berlin, they attempted to force the Western Allies to turn Berlin wholly over to them. The Allies stood firm, however, and in the next 6 months flew more than 2,300,000 tons of coal, food, and other necessities into West Berlin. Though the Russians gave up and reopened the land routes, Soviet determination to oust the Western powers from Berlin remained unaltered.

The Yugoslav Rebellion. In 1948 the Russians found themselves faced with rebellion from the most loyal of all their newly acquired European satellites, Yugoslavia. Yugoslavia had overthrown a pro-German government in 1941 and remained throughout World War II a theater of intense guerrilla action against the Germans and Italians. There were two main groups of guerrillas, the Chetniks, led by General Mikhailovich, representing the Serb royalist domination over the south Slav kingdom, and the Partisans, led by the Croatian-born communist Joseph Broz, better known by his underground nickname, Tito. As the war continued, the communist-dominated Partisans gained ground against the Chetniks, who preferred to compromise with the German and Italian occupying forces rather than continue a war in alliance with communists. By 1943, Britain and the United States, with their eyes fixed on the paramount need to beat Hitler, decided to support Tito with supplies. When the Russians entered Belgrade in October, 1944, they helped put their fellow-communist Tito in control.

Once in power, Tito installed his own communist government, abolished the Yugoslav monarchy, and for three years adopted all the standard Soviet policies. Yet in June, 1948, the world learned with surprise that the U.S.S.R. had quarrelled with Yugoslavia, and expelled Tito's regime from the Cominform (*see* p. 636). The Soviet satellites broke their economic agreements with Yugoslavia, unloosed great barrages of anti-Tito propaganda, and stirred up border incidents. It was Soviet arrogance and insistence on penetrating the Yugoslav army and security organizations that had aroused Yugoslav national feeling, never very far below the surface. Stalin believed that he could bully the Yugoslavs into submission. "I will shake my little finger," he said, "and there will be no more Tito."

But Tito remained in power, accepting the aid that was quickly offered him by the United States. Washington saw that a communist regime hostile to Stalin was a new phenomenon that could not but embarrass the Russians. Gradually Yugoslav communism evolved a modified ideology of its own, declaring that Stalin was a heretic, and Tito and his followers the only true Leninists. Tito decentralized the economy, beginning in the factories, where workers' committees now began to participate actively in the planning. From the economy, decentralization spread to the local government apparatus, then to the central government, and finally to the Yugoslav Communist party, now rechristened "League of Yugoslav Communists." Though the regime admitted its past outrageous excesses, the police continued to be a powerful force. Tito also gradually abandoned agricultural collectivization, which, as always, was most unpopular with the peasants. Yugoslavia remained communist, however, suspicious of the Western capitalists who were helping it.

In their fear of the spread of the new "national" communism to the other satellites, the Soviets directed the other eastern European regimes in a series of ferocious purges, executing leading communists for "Titoism," and thus terrorizing anyone who might hope to establish any sort of autonomy within the communist bloc. When Stalin died in 1953, his heirs gave high priority to healing the breach with Yugoslavia, and eliminating the weakness it had created in their European position.

Asia. When balked in Europe, tsarist Russian governments had often turned to Asia. After the failures in Greece and Berlin, the Soviet Union similarly embarked on new Asian adventures. Here, communists had tried and failed to win power in Indonesia, Burma, Malaya, and the Philippines, and had succeeded in China. The Korean War, which broke out in June, 1950, was in some measure a Soviet-sponsored operation, although the Russians themselves limited their contribution to support and sympathy, and allowed their Chinese ally to take the military lead.

Korea, a peninsula at the eastern extremity of Asia, bordering on Manchuria and Siberia and close to Japan, had been a target of Russian interest in the late nineteenth and early twentieth centuries, but the Japanese defeat of the Russians in 1905 had led instead to Japanese annexation of the country in 1910. In 1945, at the close of World War II, Russian troops occupied the northern part of Korea, and American troops occupied the southern part. The country was divided in the middle by a line along the 38th parallel of latitude; a communist-inspired People's Democratic Republic of Korea was set up on the north, and an American-inspired Republic of Korea on the south. When all American forces except for a few specialists were withdrawn from South Korea, the North Koreans marched south to unite the nation under communist control.

It is probable that the communists thought the operation was safe, since American pronouncements had stated that Korea was outside the American "defense perimeter." But when the invasion began, the United States—with UN approval, for the vote was taken in the absence of the Russians—at once moved troops into Korea. They halted the North Korean drive, and pushed the enemy back well north of the 38th parallel, almost to the Yalu River, the frontier of China. At this point, Communist China entered the war, and Chinese troops joined the North Koreans in pushing the Americans southward again. By 1951, the line of battle had been stabilized roughly along the old boundary between North and South Korea. After prolonged negotiations, an armistice was finally concluded in July, 1953.

The Korean settlement by no means ended the tension between Communist China and the United States. Serious friction developed over Formosa and the smaller offshore islands, Quemoy and Matsu, now in the hands of Chiang Kai-shek. Nor did the Korean settlement bring closer understanding between the U.S.S.R. and the United States. It was at best a compromise: after all the fighting, the United States had managed to hang on to the devastated southern portion of the country, and the communists had been driven back to the north, which they governed undisturbed. Neither side could call it a victory. By the time it was reached, Stalin had been dead for more than three months.

STALIN'S HEIRS

Eastern Europe. Stalin's heirs realized that any attack that threatened the vital interests of the United States might well touch off the ultimate disaster. A policy of probing to see just which interests the United States considered vital had already led to the Korean War. Continued tension between the two superpowers required the U.S.S.R. to continue to devote its resources to guns rather than to butter. To relax the tension would theoretically have meant more butter, but would in turn raise the danger that the U.S.S.R. would lose its position as leader of the world communist movement. China, with its determination to seize Taiwan and to expand in Asia, might seize the leadership of revolutionary forces at least in Asia, and would represent the Russians as old and tired, no longer true Leninists. In the end it proved to be impossible for Khrushchev to hold all these threats in balance, and the choices he eventually was forced to make led to a major split in the communist world.

In eastern Europe, Khrushchev made a great effort to heal the breach with Tito. In May, 1955, he went in person to Belgrade, and not only publicly apologized for the quarrel, taking the blame upon the U.S.S.R., but openly agreed that "differences in the concrete forms of developing socialism are exclusively matters for the people of the country concerned," which seemed to echo Tito's own views. Relations between Tito and Moscow were temporarily improved, although the Yugoslavs never abandoned their ties to the West. Khrushchev even went so far as to declare that many prominent victims of the "Titoist" purges had been executed wrongly, and he abolished the Cominform, the body that ostensibly had started the quarrel with Tito. But in making these admissions and healing the quarrel Stalin had started, Khrushchev had opened the door to new troubles.

Khrushchev's speech of 1956 denouncing Stalin and admitting so many past injustices proved far too strong a brew for the European satellites. Anticommunist riots by workers in Poznan, Poland, in June, 1956, were followed by severe upheavals in the rest of that country. Though Polish national sentiment was declaring itself, the uprising remained within the grip of one wing of the Communist party, that led by Wladislaw Gomulka, who had been purged for alleged Titoism in 1951. Not even the presence in Warsaw of Khrushchev himself and other members of the Soviet Presidium prevented the rise of Gomulka to power, although at one moment the Russians seem to have contemplated using their army to impose their will by force. Yet because the new government in Poland was, after all, a communist government, they allowed it to remain in power.

In Hungary, however, the movement went farther. Starting, like the Polish uprising, as an anti-Stalinist movement within the Communist party, the Hungarian upheaval at first brought Imre Nagy, a communist like Gomulka, into office as Premier. But popular hatred for communism and for the Russians got out of hand, and young men and women flew to arms in Budapest in the hope of ousting the communists and of taking Hungary altogether out of the Soviet sphere. They even denounced the Warsaw Pact, the Russian alliance of eastern European satellites set up by Moscow to oppose NATO. It was then that Khrushchev ordered full-fledged military action. In November, 1956, Soviet tanks and troops, violating an armistice, swept back into Budapest and put down the revolution in blood and fire. A puppet government led by Janos Kadar was installed. More than 150,000 Hungarian refugees fled to Austria, to be resettled in various Western countries. Despite the Soviet charges that the uprising had been trumped up by the Western "imperialists" and "fascists," the West in fact had played no part at all, not daring to help the Hungarians for fear of starting a world war.

Soviet military intervention in Hungary showed the world how limited was Khrushchev's willingness and ability to permit free choices to other communist states. Tito denounced the Soviet intervention against Nagy, though he was frightened by the wholly anti-communist character that the Hungarian revolt subsequently took on, and he failed to oppose the decisive Soviet operations that put an end to the uprising.

For a second time, relations between Moscow and Tito were strained. They were patched up again in the summer of 1957, but Tito flatly refused to sign a declaration of twelve Communist parties denouncing "revisionism"—as Tito's own views had come to be known. Instead he published his own counter-program declaring that each communist nation should make its own decisions freely. The old quarrel was renewed for the third time. Tito would not re-enter a world communist union led by Russia. Khrushchev's efforts had failed.

Both the harshness of the onslaught against revisionism and Khrushchev's acceptance of defeat in his efforts to win the Yugoslavs by softness reflected Chinese influence. Eager to play a leading role in formulating world communist ideology, the Chinese displayed a strong preference for Stalinist orthodoxy and repression. By the spring of 1958, the Chinese and Khrushchev himself had declared that Stalin's original denunciation of the Yugoslavs back in 1948 had been correct after all. In June, 1958, the Soviet government underlined this decision in

The Hungarian Revolt: head of the statue of Stalin toppled in downtown Budapest, 1956.

grim fashion when it announced the executions of Imre Nagy and other leaders of the Hungarian uprising, in violation of solemn promises of safe-conduct.

All the eastern European satellites were bound together in the Council for Mutual Economic Aid (Comecon) established in 1949, which took measures to standardize machinery and coordinate economic policies, and issued blasts against western European efforts at cooperation like the Common Market. Yugoslavia never was a member, and after 1958 was not invited to send observers. In 1958–1959, Comecon called for a "specialization" plan, in accordance with which the more developed countries would concentrate on heavy industry, and Rumania in particular on the production of raw materials (chiefly food and oil). The Rumanian government, communist though it was, protested, pointing to its already considerable achievements in heavy industry; and in December, 1961, Rumania openly refused to accept the "principles" of the "international socialist division of labor," issued at the twenty-second congress of the CPSU. All through 1962 the disagreement persisted, with Khrushchev trying and failing to force the Rumanians into line.

Thus the Rumanians, like the Yugoslavs, were assuming an independent position within the communist bloc. They increased their trade with the noncommunist world, and they remained neutral in the growing Soviet–Chinese quarrel (see p. 673). In July, 1963, the Russians gave in on the economic question, and sanctioned Rumania's continued efforts to build a steel industry, while postponing the economic integration of the bloc until 1966, by which time Rumania would be entitled to the same status as Czechoslovakia and Poland.

The Soviet-Rumanian disagreement soon widened. Soviet propaganda called for integrating the lower Danube region—which would have meant taking territory from Rumania—and denied that the Rumanians had contributed to the Allied cause in World War II. The Rumanians claimed full credit for their own "liberation from fascism," and—most important—even dared to demand the return to Rumania of the provinces of Bessarabia and northern Bukovina, annexed by the U.S.S.R. in 1940 (see Chapter 15). Yugoslav–Rumanian cooperation became an important part of Rumanian policy.

Elsewhere within the Soviet bloc in eastern Europe, there was a general liberalizing trend in Hungary. Increased tourism, wider trade with the West, better living conditions, even success with agricultural collectivization, a new agreement with the Vatican concerning the Hungarian Church, and improved education, all spoke of relaxed terror. In Poland, however, which had after Gomulka's success for some years enjoyed more freedom of discussion and contact with the West than any other communist country, the trend was reversed. In economic planning, in agriculture, in education, in religious policies, the government tightened the strings, as neo-Stalinist opponents of Gomulka seemed to be moving toward the top. In Czechoslovakia, change began only in the middle Sixties, beginning before Khrushchev's ouster and continuing after it. Economic failure of the communist bureaucracy in a formerly prosperous industrial state and an entrenched and particularly brutal party leadership had aroused great discontent, which was to burst forth dramatically in 1968 (see below, p. 672).

Berlin Again. In East Germany, (D.D.R., *Deutsche Demokratische Republik*) the U.S.S.R. had created its most industrially productive European satellite, now fully geared into the Comecon. Except for a workers' riot in East Berlin in 1953, the German communist puppets had succeeded in repressing the population's aversion to Soviet and communist rule. Moreover, strategically the D.D.R. was of great importance to the U.S.S.R.: control over East Germany enabled the Russians to keep Poland surrounded, helpless to achieve more than a token autonomy. Yet the United States, Britain, and France each retained a zone of occupation in Berlin, deep in the heart of the D.D.R., and accessible by subway from East Berlin. Every year, thousands of East Germans showed how they felt about communism by escaping into West Berlin. The East German population actually declined by 2,000,000 between 1949 and 1961. For those who stayed behind in the D.D.R., West Berlin provided an example of prosperity and free democratic government that acted more effectively on their minds than any mere propaganda.

This situation accounted for Khrushchev's determination to get the Western powers out of Berlin. The method he proposed in 1958 and later years was thoroughly Stalinist: he threatened to sign a peace treaty with the puppet government of East Germany, never recognized by the West; to turn over to it the communications to Berlin; and to support it in any effort it might then make to cut these communications and force the Western powers out. Western refusal to accept this abrogation of agreements concluded during World War II led to a prolonged diplomatic crisis during 1959.

The West could neither permit the U.S.S.R. to recreate the conditions it had fought during the airlift of 1948 nor accept the suggestion that, once Western troops were removed, Berlin would be a "free city." Defenseless and surrounded by communist territory, Berlin and its 2,000,000 "free" citizens, it feared, would soon be swallowed up. Moreover, the negotiations proposed by the U.S.S.R., whereby the D.D.R. would thereafter "confederate" with the West German Federal Republic, aroused the gravest doubts. How could a state that was a full member of the Western system of NATO federate with one that belonged to the Soviet system's Warsaw Pact? How could a state that stood for free capitalist development federate with one completely communized? How could a parliamentary state responsibly governed by a multi-party system with checks and balances federate with a communist totalitarian state? Khrushchev surely did not believe in the possibility of the confederation he was proposing, and hoped instead that any possible union of the Germanies would be discredited, and that the D.D.R., with full control over Berlin, would emerge as a permanent Soviet satellite. But even a Soviet success in Berlin short of this complete victory would have meant that the West had in some measure at least recognized East Germany, which in turn would have severely disturbed West German stability and disrupted NATO.

U-2, the Wall, Testing, Cuba. While the Berlin threat persisted, Vice-President Nixon visited the U.S.S.R., where he and Khrushchev had a famous confrontation in a model kitchen that was part of an American exhibit. President Eisenhower and Khrushchev agreed to exchange visits, and Khrushchev actually made a dramatic tour of the United States. When the leaders of the Great Powers met at the summit in Paris (May, 1960), tensions, however, were once again inflamed by the U-2 incident: a Soviet missile had brought down a light-weight, extremely fast American plane that had been taking high-altitude photographs of Soviet territory, and the Russians had captured the pilot unharmed. After an initial denial, President Eisenhower found himself obliged to acknowledge the truth of the charge; and the incident ended both the summit meeting and the plans for his own visit to the U.S.S.R.

When Eisenhower's successor, John F. Kennedy, met Khrushchev in Vienna (June, 1961), Khrushchev insisted that the U.S.S.R. would sign the treaty with East Germany before the end of the year. Tension mounted, and the number of refugees fleeing East Berlin rose to a thousand a day. On August 13, East German forces cut the communications between East and West Berlin and began to build a barrier—the Berlin Wall—to prevent further departures. Taken by surprise, the United States realized that it could not resort to arms to prevent the closing of the East Germans' own border. The government protested, and sent Vice-President Lyndon Johnson to reassure the West Berliners of America's unshaken resolve. The wall itself became the symbol of a government that had to imprison its own people to keep them at home. Occasional hair-raising escapes and poignant recaptures or shootings continued to take place along the wall's length. But the crisis proved to be over. Khrushchev had backed away from unilateral abrogation of the Berlin treaties.

But Khrushchev announced on August 30, 1961, that the U.S.S.R. would resume atomic testing in the atmosphere, which had been stopped by both powers in 1958. In the two months that followed, the Russians exploded thirty huge bombs, whose total force considerably exceeded all previous American, British, and French explosions. President Kennedy now decided that, unless Khrushchev would agree to a treaty banning all tests, the United States would have to conduct its own new tests. Khrushchev refused, and the American tests began late in April, 1962. All during the months that followed, conversations on disarmament, including of course arrangements for the banning of future tests, continued with the Russians at Geneva.

The Berlin Wall.

It was during the summer of 1962 that Khrushchev moved to place Soviet missiles with nuclear warheads in Cuba, where an American-sponsored landing directed against the pro-communist regime of Fidel Castro (*see below*, p. 698) had failed dismally at the Bay of Pigs the year before. Castro may not have asked for the missiles, but he did accept them. Soviet officers were to retain control over their use. Their installation would effectively have doubled the Soviet capacity to strike directly at the United States, but the chief threat was political: when known, the mere presence of these weapons ninety miles from Florida would shake the confidence of all other nations in the American capacity to protect even the United States. It would enable Khrushchev to blackmail America on the question of Berlin. American military intelligence discovered the sites and photographed them from the air. Khrushchev announced that the Soviet purpose was simply to help the Cubans resist a new invasion from the United States, which he professed to believe threatened.

But Kennedy could not allow the missiles to stay in Cuba. The only course of action at first seemed an air strike, which might well have touched off a new world war. Kennedy found a measure that would prevent the further delivery of missiles—a sea blockade ("quarantine") of the island—and combined it with the demand that the missiles already in Cuba be removed. He thus gave Khrushchev a way to avoid world war, and a chance to save face. After several days of almost unbreakable tension, Khrushchev backed down, and agreed to halt work on the missile sites in Cuba and remove the offensive weapons there, while reaffirming the Soviet wish to continue discussions about disarmament. Soviet ships at sea on their way to Cuba with new missiles turned back to home ports.

U.S.S.R. AND U.S. SINCE THE MISSILE CRISIS; CZECHOSLOVAKIA

President Kennedy did not crow or allow American officials to crow. Khrushchev had moved aggressively in an area close to the United States, where Soviet national security was not threatened. By lying about the missiles, he had destroyed whatever case he might otherwise have had in world opinion. Kennedy did not misread the event by concluding that the U.S.S.R. would have backed down if Soviet vital interests had been affected. He exploited the American victory only to push for a further relaxation in tensions.

Months of often discouraging preparatory interchanges led in July, 1963, to the signing by the United States, the U.S.S.R., and Great Britain of a treaty banning nuclear weapons tests in the atmosphere, in outer space, or under water. Ratified by the Senate in September, the treaty subsequently received the adherence of more than seventy nations, though France and China—a fledgling and a prospective nuclear power—would not sign it. The treaty was hailed as a first step toward reducing the likelihood of a new world war. The installation of the "hot line" communications system between the White House and the Kremlin so that the leaders of the two countries might talk to each other in case of need, and the sale of surplus American wheat to the Russians, marked the final few months of the Kennedy administration.

The administration of President Johnson saw no recurrence of a Soviet–American crisis as acute as that over the missiles. But relations between the two superpowers remained tense and suspicious, despite many American efforts to ease them. The war in Vietnam (*see below*) would alone have made a real relaxation of tension impossible, and the two powers found themselves on opposite sides in the Middle East as well. The visit of Kosygin to the United States in 1967, and the meeting with Johnson at Glassboro, New Jersey, accomplished little, but provided an opportunity for an exchange of views. Progress toward a mutual agreement to curb the increasingly expensive arms race was painfully slow, but the settlement in 1968 on the terms of a nonproliferation treaty, to prevent the spread of atomic arms beyond the nations that already possessed them, represented a step forward. The treaty awaited ratification by the Senate when Soviet intervention in Czechoslovakia in the summer of 1968 at least temporarily made any further rapprochement highly improbable.

Long the most Stalinist of the eastern European governments, the Czech regime aroused much discontent. But a major political upheaval was postponed until 1968, when, after ever-increasing public protest and something of a major literary renaissance, Alexander Dubcek, a Slovak communist trained in the U.S.S.R., took over the Communist party as First Secretary, and ousted the repressive Antonin Novotny. The Dubcek government freed the press from censorship, and the pent-up protests of years now filled its columns. Soviet exploitation and the rigidity of communist dogma had crippled the Czech economy. It now seemed as though the Czechs and Slovaks might even allow opposition political parties to come into existence, and some of their military men apparently favored revision in the Warsaw Pact, which enabled the U.S.S.R. to hold military exercises in the territory of any member state. Both Yugoslavia and Rumania, each of which in its own way had defied the Soviet Union earlier and gotten away with it, encouraged the Czechs in their liberal course they were pursuing, and something very like a revival of the old Little Entente between these three countries seemed to be in the making.

Occupying the westernmost European position in the Soviet sphere, and having long frontiers with both East and West Germany, Czechoslovakia—highly industrialized and with a strong Western cultural tradition—could not put through a radical liberalization without deeply worrying the Russians and the other eastern European communist states. East Germany in particular would be vulnerable to the spread of anti-Stalinist ideas and practices. By spring 1968 the Soviet press was denouncing the Czech leadership. The denunciations grew louder and more violent, and were followed by a summons to the whole Czech leadership to come to Moscow. Dubcek and his colleagues refused, and the entire Soviet Politburo then joined the Czechs for a conference on Czechoslovakian soil, at the border village of Cierna nad Tisou. It appeared that Dubcek had made the required concessions, at least with regard to the Warsaw Pact, and these were confirmed at a conference of all the Warsaw powers at Bratislava. It was expected that the Czechs might have to curb the freedom of the press to some extent, but it did appear as if they too had successfully defied the Russians. Both Yugoslavs and Rumanians joined in the congratulations.

But the U.S.S.R. accused the Czechs of violating the agreements of Cierna and Bratislava. Soviet and satellite tank divisions, more than 500,000 strong, swept into the country, and met no active resistance. Unlike the Soviet attack on Hungary in 1956, that on Czechoslovakia in the summer of 1968 was not directed against a population already in armed rebellion against their communist masters. There was little bloodshed. But there was great shock. Those who had been arguing that the U.S.S.R. had outgrown the Stalinist repressive measures of earlier years—and they included many of the best-informed observers of international affairs—found themselves proved wrong. The French and Italian Communist parties joined the Yugoslav and Rumanian in condemning the invasion. The Soviet government kidnapped the Czech leaders, and sought frantically but vainly for native communists who would govern as puppets, and so lend credence to the Soviet claim that their armies had only acted on an invitation from Czechs and Slovaks who feared "counter-revolution." In the end the Russians restored Dubcek and his colleagues, but apparently after extracting promises from them that the liberalization would be reversed. Soviet occupation of Czechoslovakia continued.

In November, 1968, it was still too soon to analyze fully the Soviet motives for these actions: it was, however, clear enough that the Russians had been so alarmed by the Czech cultural, economic, and political ferment and its military and diplomatic implications that they had been willing to sacrifice much of the international goodwill that they had been able to accumulate. Nor could one yet say whether Dubcek might not sooner or later be replaced with a more docile instrument of Soviet will. Within its eastern European sphere, the U.S.S.R. could obviously do with impunity just about anything it wished. Yugoslavs and Rumanians were understandably alarmed.

V. The U.S.S.R., China, and America in Asia

THE SOVIET–CHINESE QUARREL

During the years between Stalin's death in 1953 and Khrushchev's denunciation of Stalin in 1956, Chinese–Soviet relations were basically amicable, and Chinese influence rose in the communist world. The Russians returned Port Arthur and Dairen to China in 1955. But when Khrushchev denounced Stalin without consulting Mao, the Chinese disapproved. They continued to denounce Tito and the Yugoslavs as "revisionists," and to try to block Khrushchev's reconciliation with them. They also wanted far more economic aid than the U.S.S.R. had been able or willing to provide, especially aid in developing nuclear weapons. In 1957 Mao experimented briefly with a liberated public opinion ("Let one hundred flowers bloom"), but soon returned to, and remained on, a thoroughly Leftist militant course. At home he embarked on forced-draft industrialization, the "great leap forward," with its backyard blast-furnaces and its mass collectivization of the "people's communes," with disastrous results to both industry and agriculture. The Russians disapproved, and the latent disagreement between the two communist giants now began to emerge.

In 1959 Khrushchev told Peking that the U.S.S.R. would not furnish China with atomic weapons, and launched what proved to be an unsuccessful intrigue against Mao. The Chinese bombardment of Quemoy and Matsu (1958), the savage conquest of Tibet, and—as a result—the first invasion of Indian territory in Ladakh (September, 1959) were undertaken without consultation between China and the U.S.S.R.; and the Russians publicly declared themselves to be neutral as between the Chinese and the Indians. In 1960 Khrushchev withdrew all Soviet technicians from China.

The Chinese regularly tried to influence other Communist parties against the Russians, and did succeed in picking up a European satellite: Albania, smallest and poorest of the Balkan countries. The Albanian Communist party, trained and marshalled by emissaries of Tito during World War II into a guerrilla movement, had taken power, and had thrown off Yugoslav domination after Tito's rebellion from Stalin·in 1948. More than anything else the Albanian communists feared a renewed subjection to the Yugoslavs. When Khrushchev made his repeated efforts to conciliate Tito, the Albanians found in the Chinese a counterweight to the U.S.S.R. Albania as a satellite was an economic liability, but the Chinese could rejoice in having subtracted a European communist state from the Russian bloc. As Tito continued to play the role, for the Chinese, of chief traitor to the communist cause, Khrushchev's own relations with Tito grew correspondingly warmer.

In the very midst of the 1962 crisis over Soviet missiles in Cuba, the Chinese chose to attack India, apparently intending chiefly to seize the border regions in Ladakh, including important road communications, which they had long claimed. The Chinese withdrew when they had what they wanted; but the U.S.S.R., though ostensibly neutral, was clearly, like the United States, pro-Indian.

The Chinese built up their own organizations in Africa and Asia, and began to make threatening remarks about their boundary with the U.S.S.R. When the test-ban treaty was signed, the Chinese called the Russians traitors to the international communist movement. Though Khrushchev tried to arrange for a general public excommunication of the Chinese by other Communist parties, he was unable to bring it off. During 1964, Mao not only called for Khrushchev's removal, but accused the Russians of illegally occupying eastern European and Japanese territory.

Implacably hostile to America, the Chinese did not seem to mind having the U.S.S.R. as an enemy at the same time. By the time of Khrushchev's ouster in October, 1964, they had won the support of the North Korean and North Vietnamese Communist parties, and enjoyed a special position of strength in Indonesia and Algeria. In Africa the Chinese had established a predominant influence in two former French colonies, and they took the lead in sponsoring a major rebellion in the tormented former Belgian Congo. In South America they had supported Castroites within the pro-Soviet Latin American parties in the hope of starting active revolutionary movements. In the United States, Chinese propagandists won the support of some American Negroes. They had defeated India. They had exploded an atomic bomb. They were actively supporting, as were the Russians, the communist efforts in South Vietnam.

But 1965 saw major Chinese setbacks. A congress scheduled for Algiers, in which they had expected to condemn the Russians, had been cancelled, in part because the Algerians overthrew their pro-Chinese Premier Ben Bella; the Congo revolt had been put down. An attempted communist *coup* in Indonesia had failed after the assassination of numerous leading army officers. The army had taken power and revenged itself heavily, with the help of the Moslem population, upon the Chinese minority and upon the native communists, of whom perhaps 500,000 were killed.

The Chinese threat to renew the attack on India during the Indian–Pakistani conflict of 1965 evaporated as the United States and the U.S.S.R. tacitly cooperated in the United Nations to force a temporary cease-fire. Early in 1966, Premier Kosygin at Tashkent acted as mediator between India and Pakistan, achieving an agreement to seek a peaceful solution, and thus depriving the Chinese of a pretext for intervention while reasserting Soviet influence in Asia.

Perhaps in part as the result of successive setbacks abroad, the Chinese in 1966 began to behave at home in ways suggesting that the regime was undergoing almost unbearable tensions. Denunciations and removals of important figures at the top of the government and party were accompanied by a new wave of adulation for Chairman Mao. Youngsters in their teens, the "Red Guards," erupted into the streets of the cities of China, beating and sometimes killing older people whose loyalty they professed to suspect, destroying works of art and other memorials of China's pre-communist past, and rioting against foreigners and foreign influences. When in October, 1966, the Chinese successfully fired a guided missile with a nuclear warhead—the third Chinese nuclear explosion in two years—it served notice that the political turmoil was not interfering with progress in military hardware. Yet the turmoil continued, and all of China apparently became embroiled. The Chinese educational system was completely halted, and something like civil war raged in some of its provinces. The disorders had by no means ended in 1968, though the government was trying to curb them.

Behind the series of incidents that revealed the mounting Chinese–Soviet quarrel to the world there lay profound theoretical disagreements about the best way to impose communist control over the peoples of Africa, Asia, and Latin

America. The Chinese favored direct sponsorship of local communist revolutionary movements, the Russians "peaceful" economic competition with the capitalist world for the loyalty and admiration of the emerging peoples. The Russians said the communists would win the competition without world war, while helping along local "wars of national liberation"—i.e., revolutions at least partly under communist control. The Chinese refused to grant that nuclear weapons had changed war or imperialism, and regarded world war as inevitable. "The bourgeoisie," they maintained, "will never step down from the stage of history of its own accord."

The Chinese insisted that communists alone must take charge of all revolutionary movements from the beginning, and claimed that aid to noncommunist countries was a delusion. They particularly objected to Soviet aid to India, their own enemy. They opposed disarmament. They had expected Khrushchev to freeze Soviet living standards at a low level and to invest the savings in helping the Chinese catch up, but of course Khrushchev preferred to let his own people enjoy some of the fruits of their own labors. Remembering their own success as a guerrilla operation that first came to control the countryside and then moved in on the cities, Chinese theoreticians extended this lesson to the whole globe, regarding Asia, Africa, and Latin America—the underdeveloped areas—as the countryside, and Europe and North America as the cities. From the massed peoples of the backward continents the communists would mount an offensive against the peoples of the developed industrial world and conquer them. How seriously even the authors of this startling theory believed what they said we cannot know.

One additional factor, seldom mentioned but extremely important in the Chinese–Russian quarrel, was simply that of race. The Russians—though they would deny the charge—disliked and feared the Chinese, the yellow peril on their borders. The huge masses of Chinese—soon inexorably to number one billion people—who were crowded into territory adjacent to the vast, sparsely populated regions of the U.S.S.R. and already laying claim to some of them,

Red Guardsmen outside the Soviet Embassy in Peking, 1966.

would frighten any reasonable government. Because the threat came, not from fellow whites, but from yellow men, the fear increased. Despite their protestations to the contrary, the Russians were extremely race-conscious, as the experiences of many African students in Moscow testified, and they reserved for the Chinese the deepest dislike of all. The Chinese used race openly as a weapon in their efforts to win support among other Asians, Africans, and Latin Americans, lumping the Soviet Union with the United States as symbols of the evil white intention to continue dominating the world. Convinced of their own superiority to the rest of mankind, the Chinese were racists too.

SOUTHEAST ASIA: VIETNAM AND LAOS

A special problem for the Chinese, Russians, and Americans arose in Southeast Asia as the result of the revolt of the Viet Minh communist forces against France that broke out in French Indo-China with the end of World War II in 1945. During the Korean War, the United States, fearing that the Chinese communists would strike across the border into northern Indo-China, gave substantial assistance to the French. In 1954, with the French defeated after the fall of their stronghold of Dienbienphu, a conference of powers at Geneva gave independence to the Indochinese provinces of Cambodia and Laos.

Vietnam, the third and largest portion of the former French colony, was divided along the 17th parallel. The northern section, with its capital at Hanoi, was governed by the communist Viet Minh party, whose leader was the veteran communist Ho Chi Minh; the southern portion, with its capital at Saigon, was led by a Catholic nationalist leader, Ngo Dinh Diem. The Geneva agreements guaranteed free elections. Though the United States did not sign them, it endorsed their purport, and retained the hope that the area, in which it had already invested more than four billion dollars, might not fall to the communists.

Between 1954 and 1959 Ngo Dinh Diem created the bureaucratic machinery for a new regime, restored order in territory that had long been held by communist guerrillas and was now held by dissident sects, provided for almost a million refugees from the communist north, and resettled in the countryside millions of peasants who had fled to the cities. After the departure of the French in 1956, the Americans assumed the responsibility for assisting in the solution of these problems with financial aid and technical advice.

But Diem failed politically. He cancelled the scheduled elections and, together with his immediate family, governed despotically. In 1958 and 1959, communist-led guerrilla activity broke out again. Now known as the Viet Cong, the guerrillas set up a National Liberation Front. In September, 1960, Ho Chi Minh endorsed the Viet Cong movement, which he was already supplying with arms and training. Using terror in the villages as a weapon, the guerrillas by 1961 were moving almost at will in South Vietnam, overrunning much of the countryside, murdering, looting, and burning.

Neighboring Laos, though strategically important, was nationally a mere collection of unwarlike Buddhist tribes, where only a small clique of families traditionally indulged in politics. In 1953 a communist-oriented political faction, calling itself the Pathet Lao and supported by Ho Chi Minh, seized the northeastern portion of the country. The United States tried with massive financial and military aid to build a national Laotian army and establish a firm regime, but succeeded largely in creating corruption and factionalism. The head of the gov-

Asia, 1969

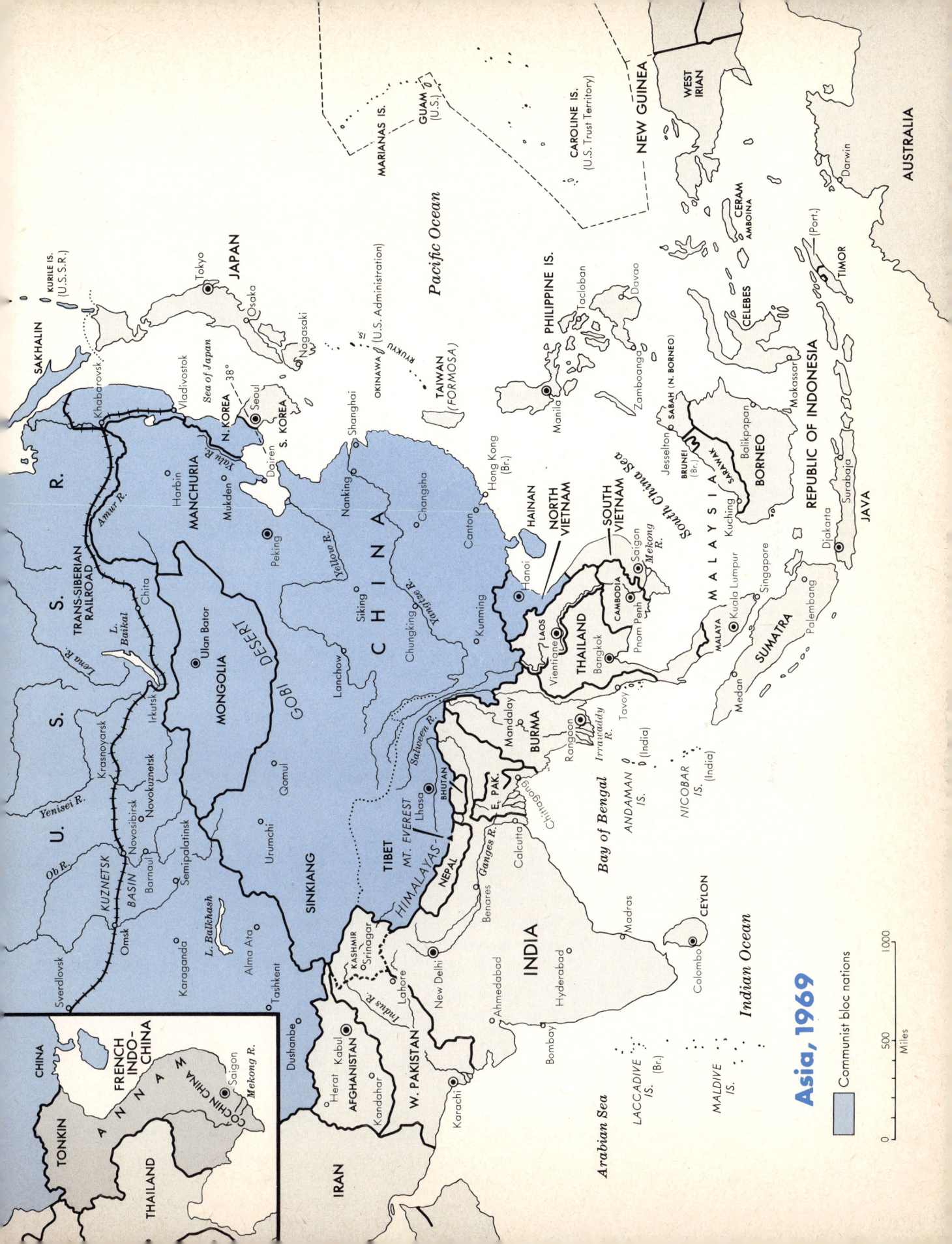

Communist bloc nations

ernment, Souvanna Phouma (who was the brother-in-law of the head of the Pathet Lao), reached agreement with him in 1957 to set up a coalition government and neutralize the country, absorbing the Pathet Lao into the army. This the United States resisted, ousting Souvanna and introducing the right-wing Phoumi Nousavan. By 1960, Souvanna was working with the Russians, and a portion of the army under the neutralist Kong Le (not a communist) was working with the Pathet Lao. Soviet airlifts of supplies to their side enhanced the possibility that the country would fall to the communists, and that Thailand and Burma—to say nothing of South Vietnam—would be endangered also.

President Kennedy sought for ways to neutralize Laos, and to convince the U.S.S.R. that if his efforts failed, American military intervention would follow. In April, 1961, the U.S.S.R. agreed to neutralization, but fighting in Laos itself between Soviet-backed and American-backed forces continued until mid-May, when Khrushchev apparently realized the full implications of American intentions to send marines from Okinawa to Laos. A conference at Geneva followed the cease-fire, but before an agreement was reached in July, 1962, Kennedy had to send marines to Thailand in order to stop the Pathet Lao from continuing to violate the truce. And when the decision to neutralize the country was reached— many years too late—the Pathet Lao, now a strong force armed with Russian weapons and still supported by Ho Chi Minh, withdrew from the coalition and maintained control over its own portion of the country, which bordered on South Vietnam and included the "Ho Chi Minh trail," a road down which came supplies from Hanoi for the Viet Cong guerrillas. But a form of stability had been created in Laos itself. Souvanna and Kong Le, who had all along been neutralist, were now no longer pro-communist but anticommunist, since it now was the Pathet Lao (and not Phoumi—who fled the country—or the United States— which now helped Souvanna) that was keeping Laos divided and in turmoil.

Incomplete and unsatisfactory as the Laos solution was, it far surpassed any arrangement that could be reached for South Vietnam. There guerrilla warfare continued. Effective opposition required political reform, but American efforts to get Ngo Dinh Diem moving politically failed. All that emerged was the "strategic hamlet" plan: a program to create fortified villages and "relocate" peasants in them in the hope that this would provide protection against the guerrillas and make the enemy campaigns first expensive and then impossible. In May, 1963, when Diem's troops fired on a crowd of Buddhists in the city of Hue, protesting against Diem's edict that they might not display flags in honor of Buddha's birthday, riots followed, and several Buddhists soaked themselves in gasoline and set themselves afire. Though the United States tried to persuade Diem to abandon his course, in August he staged a mass arrest of Buddhists, and in November he and his brother were ousted and murdered in a *coup* led by dissident generals.

Between the end of 1963 and the beginning of 1966, the South Vietnamese government changed hands several times, each time by military *coup*. The longest-lived regime, that of General Cao Ky, successfully conducted elections in September, 1966, Ky emerging as Vice-President under President Thieu. But the hamlet program was a failure; insurgency increased; North Vietnamese regular troops appeared in South Vietnam in support of the guerrillas; more than half a million peasant families were made refugees once more by floods and by terrorism.

During 1965 and 1966, the United States stepped up the number of its troops from fewer than a single division to almost 500,000, and initiated a policy of bombing certain selected North Vietnamese installations. Massive American intervention made it impossible for the Viet Cong to conquer the entire country, and assured the United States of certain bases along the coast. Having increased the American commitment to such a level that none could doubt his earnestness, President Johnson then began a thoroughgoing exploration of ways to bring Ho Chi Minh to the conference table. He assured the enemy that the United States had no long-range intention of remaining in the country, and sought no military bases there. In 1966 he suspended the bombing for a time, but got no response. The enemy insisted that there could be no negotiations until all American troops had left the country. And the very act of offering to negotiate with the North aroused uneasiness in the South.

Much articulate public opinion in the United States itself disliked the war or professed not to understand it. Some voices called for American withdrawal. Opposing public opinion urged that it be intensified and "won." Its mounting costs endangered the President's widely hailed domestic programs. On the one hand, continued intensification ("escalation," as it was lamentably called) threatened a land war in Asia of unprecedented difficulty and unpredictable length and severity. On the other hand, withdrawal threatened loss of the aims for which the United States had fought the Asian portion of World War II: the Chinese communists of the 1960's, like the Japanese militarists of the 1940's, would dominate the entire Asian continent in a spirit of intense hostility to the United States.

There could be no doubt of the deep American unrest at the Vietnam War. In 1968, as the time for American elections approached, Senator Eugene McCarthy, Democrat of Minnesota, challenged the administration by announcing his own candidacy for the presidency on an antiwar platform. He scored impressive initial successes in early primaries, and stimulated another opponent of the war, Senator Robert F. Kennedy, Democrat of New York, to enter the race on his own. The visible strength of the antiwar candidates certainly influenced the withdrawal of President Johnson—who had been universally expected to run. Ho Chi Minh, who had always hoped that internal American politics would force the United States out of Vietnam, then consented to open peace talks, which began in Paris, but dragged on for many months. Early in November, 1968, the North Vietnamese apparently consented to permit the South Vietnamese government to join the discussions, and the United States agreed that the Viet Cong might send its representatives. The bombing of North Vietnam was halted. But the South Vietnamese refused to participate, and the deadlock continued.

VI. The Emerging Nations

THE REVOLT AGAINST IMPERIALISM

Laos and Vietnam furnished striking examples of the grave and difficult problems involved in liquidating old colonial empires and endowing newly emerging nations with viable economic and political institutions. The process of liquidation was greatly accelerated and intensified by the Second World War. The use of colonial troops by the Western democracies during the war increased the self-esteem of the peoples providing the troops. Wartime propaganda, designed to show the justice of the Allied cause, had the inevitable effect of fostering native ambitions for the basic democratic rights of self-government and self-determination. Wartime inflation, shortages, conscription of labor, and the enjoyment of war profits by the few rather than the many heightened the ambitions of the colonial populations and added to their sense of grievance.

Moreover, during the war Asians—Japanese—actually seized Western possessions in the Far East, putting an end to the myth of white Western invulnerability. The final defeat of Japan did little to offset the immense damage done to Western prestige. The French and the Dutch, furthermore, were not true victors, and nationalist leaders knew that British power had been seriously weakened, and that the defeat of Conservatives by the Labour party in 1945 promised new colonial policies. The real victors in the war were the United States and the Soviet Union, each in its way anticolonial.

Deeper causes of anticolonialism lay in the 500-year record of Western expansion, and in the Western tradition itself. The West usually laid before educated natives the Bible, the American Declaration of Independence, the French Declaration of the Rights of Man, even the Communist Manifesto. It was hardly possible to keep on insisting that "all men are created equal" really meant "white men are created the superiors of colored men." In terms of ideals and ideology, Western imperialism carried within itself the seeds of its own transfiguration into self-determination for all peoples. The great instrument for the spread of Western ideas was the education provided by the West to non-Western peoples, or rather to a relatively small native minority. Though some non-Europeans turned against this Western education and took refuge in a reaffirmation of the values of their traditional cultures, most of the educated came to feel that independence could be won only by imitating the West, by learning its industrial, technological, and military skills.

These educated natives wanted independence. Many were revolutionaries; some admired the Bolshevik revolution, and a few received training in Moscow. A great many Westerners made the mistake of assuming that these men were not representative of the native populations, and that the great colonial masses asked nothing better than to be ruled by the kindly whites. Instead, the urban masses and then, more gradually, the peasant masses began to share the feelings of nationalism and to demand that the foreigner must go. Often this demand resulted from the social and economic impact of the population explosion, made possible by the dramatically lower death rates resulting from the sanitary engineering, the law and order, and the medical facilities brought by the imperialist powers.

The two decades following World War II saw the liquidation of the British, French, Dutch, and Belgian empires. Portugal alone of the imperial powers in 1968 retained its major possessions overseas—Angola and Mozambique on the west and east coasts of Africa respectively—and this largely because the Portuguese government was a conservative dictatorship that would not yield to native pressures, but only to force.

Britain, to be sure, continued to lead the Commonwealth of Nations, whose membership now included some of the new nonwhite states. Although the Commonwealth continued to have great economic significance as an association of trading partners, its political importance diminished, in part because of the conflicting interests of its Western and non-Western members, and in part because of the further loosening of the ties between the white dominions and the mother country. South Africa severed its bonds with the Commonwealth in 1961 and declared itself a wholly independent republic. Australia and New Zealand looked more and more to the United States as the potential defender of their security.

THE FAR EAST

During the Second World War the Japanese had created a huge empire, the "Greater East Asia Co-Prosperity Sphere." To govern, they had relied chiefly on the time-honored Western device of setting up puppet native governments, and exploiting for their own benefit the economic resources of the conquered lands. Because the Japanese were an Asian people, a colored people, they might well have acted as the emancipators of Asians that their propaganda proclaimed them to be. Instead, their armies looted and committed atrocities; they behaved like a master race. They alienated the people they might have won. Now they were stripped of their overseas possessions.

The occupation of Japan was wholly American. Contrary to a strong current in American opinion, the Emperor was left on his throne, deprived of his divine status, and subjected to the close control of General MacArthur and the forces of occupation. Americans found that, on the surface, at least, the Japanese people did not take the occupation with hostility, but seemed anxious to learn what democracy meant. By the time of the peace treaty in 1952, they had made a promising start on a democracy of the Western type. Their economy—the only well-developed industrial economy in the non-Western world—grew so rapidly in the late 1950's and the 1960's that experts began to predict that it would soon overtake France and West Germany and rank third in the world after the U.S. and the U.S.S.R. Sales of Japanese goods in other quarters of the world continued to mount, and the domestic market underwent a phenomenal expansion.

Signs of change and of affluence multiplied. Programs of birth-control education were successful, and the birth rate dropped, to become one of the lowest in the world. Peasants migrated to the cities, especially to Tokyo, which surpassed London and New York to rank as the most populous city in the world. Tokyo and Osaka, Japan's second city, were linked by a new high-speed rail line, the fastest in the world, while weekend traffic jams resulted from the rush of Tokyo residents to the beaches in the summer and the ski slopes in winter. As of the late 1960's, inflation appeared to be the main threat to Japan's continued prosperity and to her social and economic westernization.

Politically, the democratic parliamentary institutions so carefully fostered by the American occupation forces flourished under successive cabinets of the essentially conservative Liberal Democratic party. The left-wing opposition, including both socialists and communists, objected to the mutual security pact binding Japan and the United States after the official restoration of full Japanese sovereignty in 1952. The opposition staged demonstrations, causing the last-minute cancellation of President Eisenhower's planned visit to Japan in 1960. Anti-Americanism derived from resentment over the continued United States occupation of Okinawa (to the south of the main Japanese islands), from a bitterness left by the atomic blasts over Hiroshima and Nagasaki, and from left-wing mistrust of American policy and aims in Vietnam. In addition, despite the claim of the Japanese to have the highest rate of literacy in the world, the extreme insularity of many Japanese and their ignorance of the world outside their islands combined to make Japan seem at times more nationalist and neutralist than pro-Western.

South Korea also attempted constitutional government in the Western manner but ran into serious difficulties. After the disruptive Korean War of the early 1950's, the government of Syngman Rhee, the perennial South Korean president, came under mounting criticism for its corruption and its arbitrary actions. In 1960, massive protests by students forced the 85-year-old Rhee out of office, and inaugurated a tumultuous period marked first by the political intervention of the army and then by another attempt at constitutional rule. The economy depended heavily on American assistance. The South Koreans sent troops to fight in Vietnam, and in the years after 1965 were deeply alarmed when the communist North Koreans stepped up their military pressure. The threat remained, as part of the pressure used by the communist states in the Vietnam war.

Once the Japanese occupation ended in Southeast Asia, the major Western colonial powers found that they could not revert to the pre-war arrangements. In 1949, the Dutch had to recognize the independence of the Netherlands East Indies as the Republic of Indonesia, with a population of 100,000,000 people. The U.S. gave the Philippines independence in 1946. Britain gave Burma independence outside the Commonwealth (1948) and the Federation of Malaya independence within the Commonwealth (1957); the port of Singapore at the tip of Malaya, with its largely Chinese population, secured a special autonomous status (1958). When Malaya joined with the former British protectorates on the island of Borneo in the Federation of Malaysia (1963), Singapore at first participated, then withdrew (1965).

Like other colonial powers in other places, the Dutch in Indonesia had not prepared the people for independence by education. Nevertheless, the Indonesians attempted to run their government along the lines of a parliamentary democracy. Almost everything went wrong. The economy was crippled by inflation and shortages, by administrative corruption and the black market, and by the expulsion of experienced Dutch businessmen. The Moslems, who made up the bulk of the population, were unable to form coherent, responsible political parties. The outlying islands of the archipelago, resentful of domination by the island of Java, which contained the capital (Djakarta, the former Batavia) and two-thirds of the population, rebelled against the central government. As the high expectations raised by the achievement of independence were disappointed, President Sukarno, the hero of the Indonesian struggle for independence, began to speak of the need for "guided democracy" and for the operation of indigenous rather than borrowed political institutions.

In 1959 and 1960, Sukarno suspended the ineffectual parliamentary regime and vested authority in himself and in the army and an appointive council. But "guided democracy" created still more turmoil. Inflation ran wild, necessities vanished from the market, pretentious new government buildings were left unfinished for lack of funds, and all foreign enterprises were confiscated. In external policy, Sukarno initiated an alternating hot and cold war with the new Federation of Malaysia for control of the island of Borneo, where both states had territory. By threat and intimidation he managed to annex former Dutch New Guinea. When the United Nations recognized Malaysia, Sukarno withdrew Indonesia from membership early in 1965; he also told the United States "to go to hell with their aid" and moved closer and closer to Red China.

As we have already seen (*above*, p. 674), however, a *coup* planned by Indonesian communists misfired at the last moment in the autumn of 1965, and the result was a wholesale slaughter of local communists. The anticommunist forces came to power under military leadership. For a time they allowed President Sukarno to remain in office, but they reduced his authority, brought some of his pro-communist associates to trial, and reversed his policies by reaching a settlement with Malaysia and rejoining the United Nations. By 1968, Sukarno had virtually disappeared, and Indonesia was gradually reviving.

Communist efforts in Southeast Asia were not confined to Indonesia and Vietnam (Indo-China). In the Philippine Republic and Malaya too, the communists launched stubborn guerrilla campaigns, which were not checked finally until the late 1950's.

INDIA AND PAKISTAN

The Labour victory in Britain in 1945 made Indian emancipation a certainty. But the deep-seated tension between Moslems and Hindus now assumed critical importance. When the Hindus' Congress party and the All-India Moslem League faced the need to make a working constitution for India, they found themselves in complete disagreement. The Moslems had long been working for a partition into separate Hindu and Moslem states, and this was in the end reluctantly accepted by the Hindus. In 1947, Hindu India and Moslem Pakistan were set up as self-governing dominions within the British Commonwealth.

Pakistan ("land of the pure," a name coined by Moslem students in Britain in the 1930's) was a state divided into two parts, widely separated by intervening Indian territory—the larger, arid West Pakistan in the northwest, and the smaller more fertile, and more densely populated East Pakistan in East Bengal. The rest of the former British Indian Empire and four-fifths of its inhabitants became the Republic of India by virtue of its constitution of 1950. Pakistan, with its smaller population and its relatively poorly developed industry, was weaker than India, and at first kept closer political ties with the British Commonwealth.

Violence accompanied partition. It was not possible to draw any line that would leave all Hindus in one state and all Moslems in another. Bitter Hindu–Moslem fighting cost hundreds of thousands of lives, as Hindus moved from Pakistani territory into India and Moslems moved from Indian territory into Pakistan. A particular source of trouble was the beautiful mountainous province of Kashmir. Though mainly Moslem in population, it was at the time of partition ruled by a Hindu princely house which turned it over to India. India continued to occupy most of Kashmir, to the great economic disadvantage of Pakistan. The United Nations sought to determine the fate of Kashmir by arranging a plebiscite, but failed to secure the needed approval of both parties.

In domestic politics the two states went through sharply contrasting experiences. The chief architect of Pakistani independence, Mohammed Ali Jinnah (head of the Moslem League), died in 1948. Deprived of its leader, Pakistan floundered in its attempts to make parliamentary government work and to attack pressing economic difficulties. In 1958 the army commander Ayub Khan took full powers, attacked administrative corruption and the black market, and instituted a program of "basic democracies" to train the population in self-government at the local level and thence gradually upward through a pyramid of advisory councils. Ayub's "basic democracies" proved more workable than Sukarno's "guided democracy," and led to the proclamation of a new constitution in 1962, which provided for a national assembly and also for a strengthened president, an office that Ayub continued to fill.

Newly emancipated India suffered a grievous loss when Gandhi was assassinated by an anti-Moslem Hindu fanatic in 1948. But Jawaharlal Nehru, already a seasoned politician, at once assumed leadership. India successfully inaugurated a genuine parliamentary democracy of the Western type, and conducted free and hotly fought elections, based on universal suffrage, among voters who were in the main illiterate and rural. Understandably, Indians have been very proud of their accomplishment. India faced in an acute form the problem of overpopulation: by 1960 there were over 500,000,000 people, with approximately 15,000,000 added annually. The threat of famine and actual death through starvation was always present. In 1950, the government launched the first in a series of Five-Year Plans for economic development, permitting the expansion of private industry but stressing government projects: irrigation and flood control, transport and communications, and especially agricultural education. Low yields could be improved by more fertilizers, by small local irrigation projects to supplement the showy large ones, and by modern tools and equipment. Expert opinion held that India put too much stress on industrial growth and too little on the agricultural sector. The United States helped by furnishing technical experts, money, and the surplus grain need to avert the repeated threat of famine. In the late 1960's a new strain of high-yielding Mexican wheat was planted experimentally; the initial results were promising. Meantime, the government sponsored a campaign for birth control, which was repugnant to many Hindus.

Indeed, Hindu society found it difficult to adopt Western ways. The tradition of Hinduism, an immensely complex and ancient way of life, taught that each living man, indeed each living thing, was a soul alienated by the very fact of living from the ultimate, universal soul which is peace, absence of struggle and desire, ineffable non-being. By turning away entirely from the world, by living without desire, the holiest of men could perhaps attain this non-being in the end. But most human beings—and all animals—were now living out in this world the consequences of a sinful life as another personality in the past. That is why the most orthodox of Hindus would harm no living thing. This specifically included the millions of "sacred" cattle that competed with starving people for food. Proposals for curbing the cattle were anathema, and led to riots as late as 1966.

Hindus believed that man's sins in past incarnations were reflected by his status, his *caste*. The poor and humble *were* poor and humble because their sins had been greater; they could not improve their lot, for they could only slowly in subsequent incarnations redeem their wickedness by living as holy a life as possible. Below and outside the caste system were the "untouchables," so called because even their shadow would corrupt a caste-Hindu. The Indian Constitution of 1950 abolished the outcast status of the untouchables as undemocratic. The legal change, however, penetrated Indian custom only very slowly.

In 1964, when Nehru died, and again early in 1966, when his successor, Shastri, fell victim to a heart attack, India chose a new prime minister by due constitutional process. The choice in 1966 was Nehru's daughter, Mrs. Indira Gandhi. The Congress party, long the spearhead of Hindu nationalism, continued to dominate the parliament, though torn by factionalism.

Political controversy arose over the question of language, for India contained nearly a dozen major linguistic regions, each with its own distinctive tongue. Believing a common language essential to a common sense of national identity, the government supported a new national language, Hindi, to which it gave official status in 1965. It also recognized English as an associate language, though ardent nationalists deplored this as an "ignoble concession" to colonialism. In fact, English was indispensable, both because of its modern scientific and technical vocabulary, which Hindi could not provide, and also because it was the only common language of educated Indians, who could not understand one another's native tongues. The elevation of Hindi to official status aroused especially strong opposition among the speakers of Tamil in the south, who viewed it as an instrument of the central government's hostility to regional or provincial pride in language and political home rule. The government met the problem by making some concessions but without abandoning its aim of promoting national loyalties in every possible way.

Relations with Pakistan also continued to be strained. Sporadic outbreaks of religious warfare took place, especially near the line dividing Bengal between India and East Pakistan. The Kashmir question continued open, since neither side would concede anything. In 1965 war broke out briefly over the issue, until the Soviet Union invited leaders of both countries to confer at Tashkent, where they agreed on a mutual withdrawal of troops from their common frontier but not to a permanent settlement. The Pakistanis, who tended to measure every country by its attitude toward India, remained suspicious of the United States because of American aid to India, despite U.S. eagerness to provide it for Pakistan as well; Pakistan was similarly suspicious of the U.S.S.R., because the Russians also helped the Indians; and so the Pakistanis evolved a curiously unnatural friendship with Red China because it at least was anti-Indian.

THE MIDDLE EAST

In the Near East—especially in Arabia, in the small states along the Persian Gulf, and in Iraq and Iran—lay the greatest oil reserves in the world, a producing area second only to North America. Developed by European and American companies, which paid royalties to the local governments, these oil resources directly and indirectly influenced the policies of all the powers. Dissatisfaction over the amounts of royalties led to upheavals in Iran in 1951–53. Western European dependence on Middle Eastern oil led to general alarm over the closing of the Suez Canal by Egypt in 1956 and 1967. No doubt General de Gaulle's abandonment in 1967 of Israel, an ally of the French in 1956, and his newly adopted pro-Arab position had something to do with oil. But except for Iran no crisis depended upon oil alone; and unquestionably the greatest single issue in the area in the postwar years was that between the Arabs and Israel.

Since the 1890's Zionism had maintained its goal of creating a new Jewish state on the site of the ancient Jewish homeland. It received a great lift from the Balfour Declaration of 1917, after which the British admitted Jewish immigrants into Palestine. Nazi anti-Jewish policies before and during World War II left the remnant of European Jews more determined than ever to go to Palestine. But now Britain wished to protect its interests in the Middle East by cultivating the friendship of the Arabs, who had long been settled in Palestine and felt that this was *their* homeland.

Finding compromise impossible, the British turned the problem over to the General Assembly of the United Nations, which proposed to partition the country

The Middle East, 1969

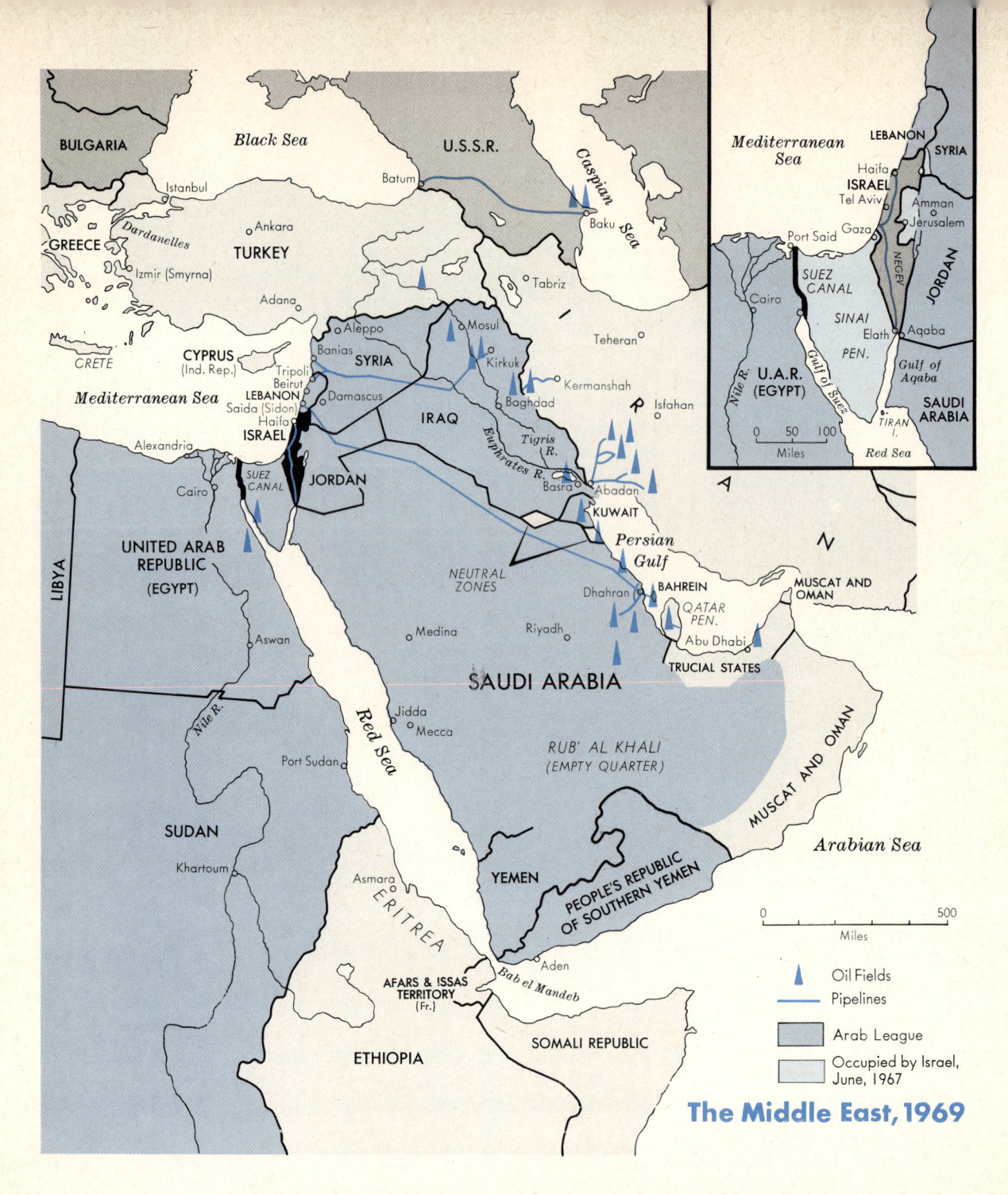

- ▲ Oil Fields
- — Pipelines
- ▨ Arab League
- ▧ Occupied by Israel, June, 1967

into an Arab state and a Jewish state. When the British withdrew their forces from Palestine in 1948, the Jews proclaimed their state of Israel and secured its recognition by the UN. The Arabs declared the proclamation illegal and invaded the new state. Outnumbered but faced by an inefficient enemy, the Israelis won the war. A truce, but not a formal peace, was patched up under the auspices of the United Nations (1949).

Israel secured more of Palestine than the UN had proposed, and took over the western part of Jerusalem, the spiritual capital of Judaism, a city which the UN had proposed to neutralize. The "old city" of Jerusalem, however, including the site of Solomon's temple, the Wailing Wall, together with eastern Palestine, remained in the hands of the Arab state of Jordan. During the war almost 1,000,000 Palestinian Arabs fled from Israel to the surrounding Arab states. The United Nations organized a special agency that built camps and gave relief to the refugees, and tried to arrange for their permanent resettlement. The Arab states, however, did not wish to absorb them, and many refugees regarded resettlement as an abandonment of their belief that the Israelis would soon "be pushed into the sea," and that they themselves would return to their old homes. This acute problem made the truce of 1949 a most uneasy affair, frequently broken in frontier incidents by both sides.

The new state of Israel could not trust its Arab minority, numbering about 200,000. It continued to admit as many Jewish immigrants as possible, some of them from Europe, but others, from North Africa and Yemen, still largely living in the Middle Ages. The welding of these disparate human elements into a single nationality was a formidable task. Much of the country was mountainous, and some of it was desert. The Israelis applied talents and training derived from the West to make the best use of their limited resources, but they depended on outside aid, especially from their many sympathizers in the United States. To most Arabs Israel appeared to be a new outpost of Western imperialism, set up in their midst under the influence of Jewish financiers, Jewish journalists, and Jewish voters. Therefore it was difficult for the United States and other Western nations to retain cordial relations with the Arabs, who were in any case passing through a highly nationalistic phase.

In 1952, less than four years after the Arab defeat in Palestine, revolution broke out in Egypt, where a corrupt royal regime was overthrown by a group of army officers chiefly sparked by Gamal Abdel Nasser. They abolished the monarchy, established a republic, encouraged the emancipation of women, and pared down the role of the conservative courts of religious law. Only one party was tolerated, elections were closely supervised, and press campaigns were orchestrated by the Ministry of National Guidance. As an enemy of the West, which he associated not only with past colonialism but with support for Israel, Nasser turned for aid to the U.S.S.R. Czechoslovak and Russian arms flowed to Egypt, and Russian technicians followed. Nasser was determined to take the lead in uniting the disunited Arab world to destroy Israel.

Nasser's chief showpiece of revolutionary planning was to be a new high dam of the Nile at Aswan. He had expected the United States to contribute largely to its construction, but in June, 1956, Dulles, Eisenhower's Secretary of State, told Nasser that the United States had changed its mind. In retaliation Nasser nationalized the Suez Canal, hitherto operated by a Franco-British Company, and announced that he would use the revenues thus obtained to build the dam. For several months, contrary to expectation, the new Egyptian management kept canal traffic moving smoothly. The French and British governments, however, concealing their intentions from the United States, determined to teach Nasser a lesson, and secretly allied themselves with Israel.

In the fall of 1956, the Israeli forces invaded Egyptian territory, and French and British troops were also landed at Suez. The Israeli operations were skillful and successful; the British and French blundered badly. The Soviet Union threatened to send "volunteers" to defend Egypt, despite the fact that Soviet troops were at the very moment of the Suez crisis engaged in putting down the Hungarian revolution. Nor did the United States, angry at its British and French friends for concealing their plans, give them support. With the United States and the Soviet Union on the same side of the issue, the United Nations condemned the British–French–Israeli attack, and eventually a United Nations force was moved into the Egyptian–Israeli frontier areas, while the Canal, blocked by the Egyptians, was reopened, and finally bought from the company by Nasser. Nasser experienced some disillusion with Russia during the summer of 1958, when revolution broke out in Iraq, where Soviet-sponsored communists were opposing Nasser's own pan-Arab aims. Prompt American intervention in Lebanon and British intervention in Jordan may have temporarily countered the threat of the spread of Soviet influence. The Russians provided the aid that eventually made possible the high dam at Aswan and much armament for the Egyptian armies, but Nasser remained unaligned with either major bloc.

In 1958, Nasser proclaimed the merger of Egypt and Syria into the United Arab Republic. The two components of the U.A.R. were separated by territories of Israel, Lebanon, and Jordan; Nasser was trying to prevent a *coup* by Syrian communists or fellow travellers. When the almost ungovernable Syrians revolted in 1961, Nasser announced that he could never fire on "brother Arabs," and permitted them to regain their independence as the Syrian Arab Republic. Yet Egypt continued to style itself the U.A.R. The Arab League, a loose association of the Arabic-speaking states of the Middle East and North Africa, proved to be little more than a forum for expressing the conflicts of views and personalities that kept the Arab world disunited.

After the Suez crisis, Nasser tried one experiment after another to create a party and other institutions that would gain support for his regime at the grass roots. His economic policy was governed by the grim struggle to support a fast-growing population (the birth rate in Egypt was double that in the United States). He undertook programs to reclaim land from the desert by exploiting underground water, and to limit the size of an individual's landholdings so that the surplus might be redistributed to land-short peasants. To provide more jobs and to bolster national pride he also accelerated the pace of industrialization, often at very high cost. Most foreign enterprises were nationalized.

But the temptations of foreign adventure proved irresistible to Nasser. In far-off Yemen, a primitive kingdom in southern Arabia where republican rebels overthrew the monarchy in 1962, Nasser sent Egyptian forces to assist the revolution. This was a blow to the largest state of Arabia proper, the Saudi kingdom, generally aligned with the United States, since the activities of American oil companies on its soil provided much of its enormous revenues. Not even in tiny Yemen could Nasser's modern forces score a victory, though they freely used poison gas against their fellow-Arabs. By 1967 the Egyptian forces had suffered a defeat, though the Yemeni republican regime continued in power.

Needing a victory, Nasser in 1967 demanded that the United Nations troops which had kept Egyptians

Nasser receiving the plaudits of fellow Egyptians after announcing the nationalization of the Suez Canal, 1956.

and Israelis separated since 1956 be removed. Secretary General U Thant complied, and the Egyptians simultaneously began a severe propaganda barrage against Israel, and also closed the Strait of Tiran at the northeast corner of the Red Sea that provided the only water access to the newly developed Israeli port of Eilath. Expecting an attack at any moment, and with no likelihood that they could recover initiative or territory once it had begun, the Israelis struck the first blow, knocking out the Egyptian air force on the ground, and hitting also at Jordan, Syria, and Iraq. In six days, they overran the Sinai peninsula, all of Palestine west of the Jordan, including the Jordanian portion of Jerusalem, and the heights on their northern frontier with Syria from which the Syrians had been launching dangerous and painful raids for several years. The third Arab–Israel war in nineteen years ended in an all-out Israeli victory.

It was a humiliation not only for Nasser but for the U.S.S.R., which had supplied so much of the equipment he had now lost. The Russians moved vigorously to support the Arab position, arguing their case in the United Nations, moving token naval forces into the Mediterranean, denouncing Israel, and ostentatiously beginning at once the rearmament of Egypt. Israeli armies remained in control of all the territory they had occupied. Had it been possible to begin negotiations soon after the war, much of this territory could perhaps have been recovered. As time passed, the Israeli attitude hardened, and it became difficult to imagine that any Israeli government could ever consent to give up any part of Jerusalem, now reunited in a wave of historic and emotional sentiment, or the Syrian heights, whose possession insured Israeli territory against attack. Sinai, the Gaza strip, perhaps some other areas might be negotiable.

But the Arabs, led by Nasser, steadfastly refused to negotiate directly with the Israelis or to take any step that would admit the existence of the state of Israel. Rearmed and partly retrained by the Russians, the Egyptians repeatedly proclaimed their intention of trying again, while occasionally leaking a suggestion that a new United Nations force might be acceptable. Since the last one had been withdrawn by Nasser's unilateral request, this had little appeal for Israel. Blocked again, the Suez Canal was now being somewhat outmoded by the development of oil tankers that would have been too large to pass through the Canal in any case, and that went around the Cape of Good Hope, transporting oil more cheaply because of their great capacity. Perhaps the most important result of the war of 1967, however, was not the Israeli victory but the fact that the U.S.S.R.—whose ally had lost—had gained naval bases at Alexandria and even in Algeria. The Russians had a firmer position in the Mediterranean area than at any time in history.

Among the other Arab states, Iraq, closely aligned with the British after the war, and using its share of profits from the Western-controlled Iraq Petroleum Company to build public works, in 1958 experienced a nationalist uprising which ousted the monarchy and proclaimed a republic. Pro- and anti-Nasser factions, pro- and anticommunists, thereafter subjected the country to a series of *coups* and abortive *coups,* and the rebellious Kurdish tribes in the northern mountains contributed to the disorder and to the abrupt slackening of economic development after 1958.

In Iran, where the Anglo-Iranian Oil Company had the oil concession, the government demanded that the company follow the example set after the war in Saudi Arabia by the Arabian American Oil Company, which paid fifty per cent to King Saud. Supported by a wave of antiforeign nationalism, the demagogue

Mossadeq in 1951 secured the nationalization of the oil company. But the Iranian economy was badly hurt by an international boycott of the oil, and Mossadeq himself was overthrown in 1953 by a *coup d'état* allegedly masterminded by the American CIA. The government reached an agreement to pay foreign oil companies to assist in exploiting and marketing the oil. A measure of land reform sponsored vigorously by the Shah himself led to greatly improved economic conditions. Iran maintained satisfactory relations with both the United States and the U.S.S.R.

In Turkey, Atatürk's Republican People's party, the only political formation allowed in Atatürk's day, after the war permitted the activities of an opposition, and in the election of 1950 went down to defeat at the hands of the young Democrat party. Western opinion saluted this peaceful shift of power as the coming of age of Turkish parliamentary democracy. The Democrat government of Prime Minister Menderes proceeded to promote both state and private industry, to build roads and schools, and in other ways to bring the spirit of modernization to the villages, which had been neglected in Atatürk's day but contained three-quarters of the population. To propitiate Moslem opinion, some of Atatürk's secularist policies were moderated, religious instruction was restored in the schools, and the call to prayer sounded once more in Arabic from the minarets (sometimes on amplified tape-recordings made in Mecca).

But Menderes' regime became increasingly arbitrary, muzzling the press, persecuting the Republican opposition both in and out of the Grand National Assembly, and restricting more and more the free conduct of elections. In May, 1960, student riots touched off a *coup* by the Turkish army, which overthrew the government, outlawed the Democrat party, and brought Menderes to trial and execution. A new constitution, in 1961, sought to avert a repetition of the experience with Menderes by strengthening the legislature and judiciary against the executive. It was the army, however, that exercised the real power. Moreover, the new Justice party, to which followers of Menderes gravitated, won a majority of the seats in the parliamentary election of 1965. Thus tensions persisted between the urban champions of secularization and westernization, represented by army leaders and by Atatürk's old Republican People's party, and the defenders of the conservative Moslem way of life in Turkish towns and villages, who tended to support the Justice party.

Meantime, low wages and the lack of employment opportunities at home were impelling tens of thousands of Turks to take jobs abroad, especially in West Germany, and the marginal quality of much Anatolian farmland, with its thin soil and scanty rainfall, promoted an even greater exodus from the villages to the towns and cities. Turkey appeared to be suffering a sharp attack of social and economic growing pains. Its hopes for achieving a quick "take-off" were thwarted by the country's meager resources, by its chronic difficulty in paying for needed imports, especially oil, and by the government's slowness in fashioning an effective organization for economic planning. Friendship for the United States, very warm down to the 1960's, and cemented especially by the brave Turkish fighting in the Korean War, dwindled because of the disenchantment of sensitive Turkish nationalists with NATO and with the American refusal to support Turkey wholly against Greece in the Cyprus question. Radical student groups and others had even begun to look to the U.S.S.R.—traditionally the bugbear of all Turks.

AFRICA

The revolution against imperialism reached Africa in the 1950's, although there had long been ominous rumblings, such as an uprising in 1947 on the large French island of Madagascar off the east coast, put down by the French in a bloody massacre. The independent Empire of Ethiopia was taken from its Italian conquerors after the war, and restored to the durable Emperor Haile Selassie, who had been ousted in 1935. He still ruled in 1968. In 1952 he annexed the former Italian colony of Eritrea. He had embarked on various programs of internal modernization—though not liberalization—and he worked hard to assist in the development of African unity.

Among the northern tier of states bordering the Mediterranean, all Moslem and Arabic-speaking, the former Italian colony of Libya achieved independence in 1951, and the French-dominated areas of Morocco and Tunisia in 1956, Morocco as a somewhat autocratic monarchy, Tunisia as a republic under the moderate and intelligent presidency of Habib Bourguiba, a veteran nationalist leader, educated at the Sorbonne. The huge area of Algeria, between Morocco and Tunisia, followed, but only after a debilitating and severe war of independence against the French. Its first ruler after independence, Ahmed Ben Bella, was intimate with the Chinese communists. Colonel Houari Bourmédienne, who ousted Ben Bella in 1965—perhaps in large part because of the slumping economy—seemed to favor the U.S.S.R. Algeria and Libya strongly supported the Arab cause against Israel, distant Morocco more feebly, and Tunisia under Bourguiba not at all. Bourguiba's voice could occasionally be heard calling for a reasonable accommodation between Arabs and Israelis.

South of the Moslem tier lay the colonies of the French, British, and Belgians, inhabited chiefly by blacks. West African climatic conditions had always discouraged large-scale white settlement except in portions of the Belgian Congo; but in East Africa—in the British colonies of Kenya and Uganda especially—whites had settled in the fertile highlands in large numbers, farmed the land, and regarded the country as their own, as of course did the large white population of the Union of South Africa—which seceded from the British Commonwealth in 1961 and became the Republic of South Africa—and the whites of some of the lands in between, such as Rhodesia.

In the areas of small white settlement, the revolution moved swiftly. Often regions whose names were barely familiar in the West took new and totally unfamiliar names as they became independent. The Gold Coast—a West African British colony with a good many well-educated natives and a start on economic development—became the nation of Ghana in 1957. Its leader, the American-educated Kwame Nkrumah, the pioneer of African emancipation, made what seemed like a hopeful start on economic planning within a political democracy. But he grew increasingly dictatorial, jailing and mistreating his political enemies and insisting on being worshipped as a virtual god by his subjects. He also abandoned sound and gradual policies of development in favor of unrealistic and grandiose projects that enriched him and his followers personally. And he became fanatically anti-Western and determined to court Chinese communist favor in an effort to unite Africa into a kind of personal empire. He was ousted in 1966, and his successors—warmly cheered by the population—embarked on a sober program of putting Ghana back on the track once more.

The French colonies—covering huge areas of territory often sparsely populated—achieved independence simultaneously in 1960, except for Guinea, a small West African state that broke away in 1958 under the leadership of a pro-Russian politician, Sekou Touré. With independence, some of the colonies retained close economic ties with France, as members of the "French Community." Guinea did not; all Frenchmen had left in 1958, and the country had virtually come to a stop. The neighboring state of Mali (formerly the French Sudan) and Mauritania also pursued a generally pro-Russian line. By 1968 Touré had begun to regret his economic dependence on the U.S.S.R., and was seeking change. Some of the newly independent French colonies—Upper Volta, Niger, Chad, Gabon—were hardly more than geographical expressions without national traditions or even tribal cohesion. Others proved stable and successful, such as Senegal—governed by Léopold Senghor, a celebrated poet who wrote in French of the beauties of *négritude* (being black); Ivory Coast—whose leader Houphouet-Boigny had long parliamentary experience as a Deputy in Paris; and the Malagasy Republic (formerly Madagascar)—which had a flourishing economy based in large part on vanilla. In at least one case (Gabon), the French intervened with troops to save the government from a military *coup d'état*. In others—Togo, Dahomey, Cameroon, the *coups* took place unimpeded.

In 1960 also, Nigeria, most important of the British colonies, achieved independence. With 60,000,000 people and large and varied economic resources, it represented a great hope for the future. The British had carefully educated and trained many thousands of Nigerians both in England and in excellent schools and universities established in the country itself. A land of many tribes, Nigeria was divided into four regions, each semi-autonomous, to ease mutual tribal tensions, of which perhaps the most severe was that between the Moslem Hausa tribe of the northern region and the Ibo tribe of the eastern region. In the Hausa areas, the well-educated, aggressive, and competent Ibos ran the railroads, power stations, and other modern facilities, and formed an important element in the cities. When army plotters led by an Ibo officer murdered the Moslem Prime Minister of Nigeria, and seized power in 1966, the Hausas rose and massacred the Ibos living in the north, killing many thousands, while others escaped in disorder to their native east. By 1967, the Ibo east had seceded and called itself the Republic of Biafra, and the Nigerian central government embarked on full-scale war to force the Ibos and other eastern tribesmen to return to Nigerian rule. The general who headed the central government and the officer who headed Biafra were both graduates of British institutions. Misery and famine accompanied the operations, and the war still was unsettled in 1968.

In East Africa, the British settlers in Kenya struggled for eight years (1952–1960) against a secret terrorist society formed within the Kikuyu tribe, the Mau Mau, with the aim of driving all white men out of the country. The Mau Mau horribly murdered white settlers and their families, and also Kikuyus and other tribesmen who would not join them. Though the British imprisoned one of its founders, the educated Kikuyu Jomo Kenyatta, and eventually put down the movement, they did give Kenya independence in 1963, against the bitter protests of many white settlers. Kenyatta became the first post-liberation chief of state. By 1962 neighboring Uganda attained independence, and in 1964, under the leadership of Julius Nyerere (educated at Edinburgh), so did Tanganyika—which had been German before World War I, and British since. A violent pro-Chinese communist *coup d'état* had taken place on the offshore spice island of Zanzibar, which merged with Tanganyika as the new country of Tanzania. Nyerere, who had been pro-Western, thereafter became more notably neutralist. In 1964, Nyasaland became Malawi under Dr. Hastings Banda, who had formerly been a dentist in London, and Northern Rhodesia became Zambia under Kenneth Kaunda, a Western-educated moderate.

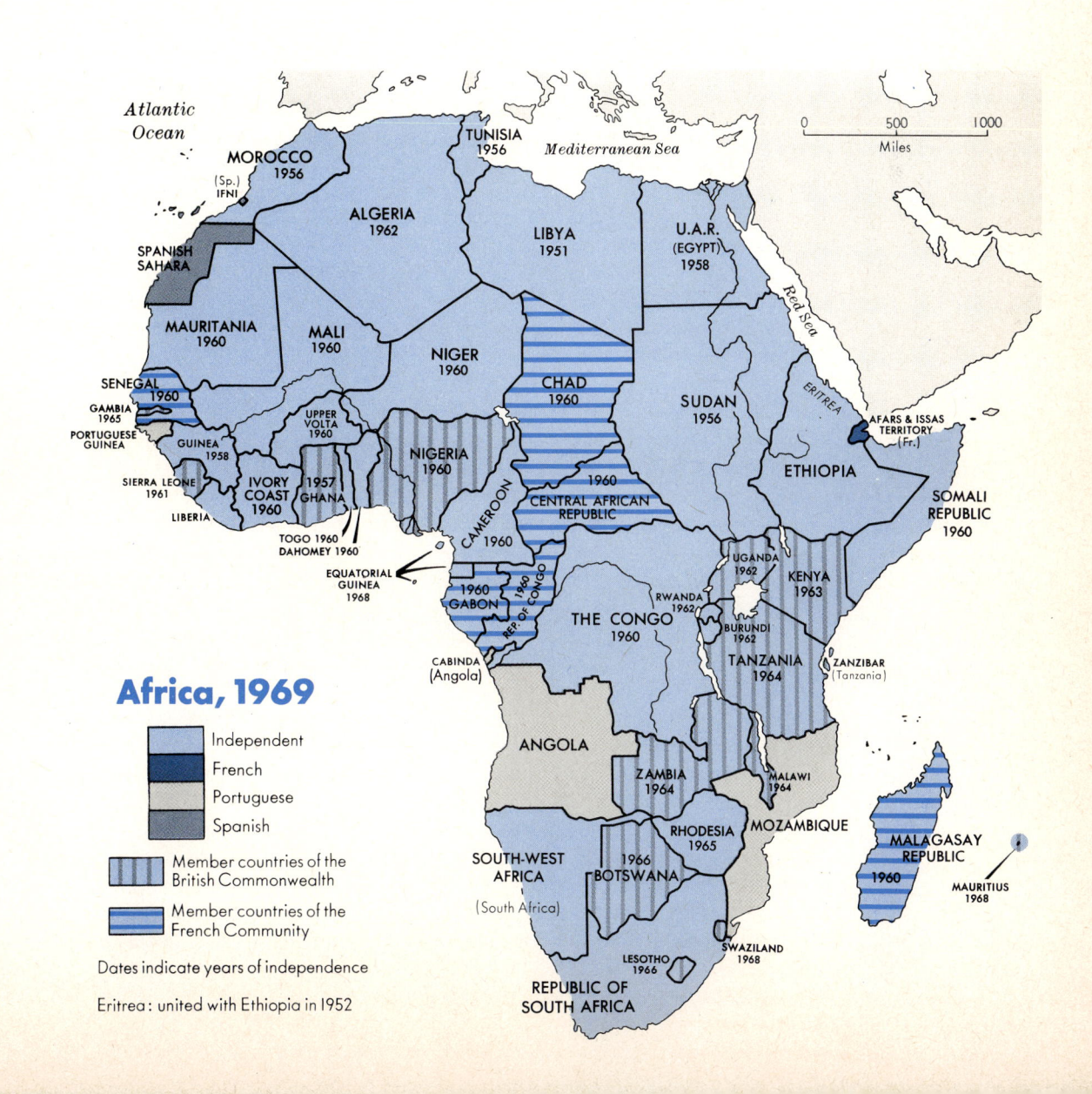

In contrast to the British, who had at least tried to prepare the way for African independence by providing education and administrative experience for Africans, and who could not be held responsible for the troubles in Ghana and Nigeria, the Belgians, who had since the late nineteenth century governed the huge Central African area known as the Congo, made no such effort. When the Belgian rulers suddenly pulled out in 1960, leaving a wholly artificial Western-style parliamentary structure, it was not long before tribal and regional rivalries between native leaders asserted themselves, and virtual chaos prevailed. A leftist leader, Patrice Lumumba, was assassinated (the Russians soon named their "university" for Africans in Moscow after him); the province of Katanga, site of rich copper mines with many European residents, seceded under its local leader, Moise Tshombe, who was strongly pro-Belgian. Other areas revolted. Africans in rebellion murdered whites, or took them prisoner and kept them as hostages; white mercenaries enlisted in the forces of Tshombe and others. The United Nations sent troops to restore order and force the end of the Katangese secession, while the Chinese supported certain rebel factions, and the South Africans and Belgians others. By 1968 (after an improbable interlude in which Tshombe had returned from exile to lead the country briefly, and had eventually wound up in an Algerian jail after the plane he was flying had been hijacked) the military regime of General Joseph Mobuto seemed relatively firmly in control.

The Congolese troubles overflowed the borders of the Congo into Portuguese Angola to the south, where a local rebellion, at first supplied from the Congo, forced Portuguese military intervention. In 1968 Angola, which provided Portugal with much of its oil, together with Mozambique on the east coast and the tiny enclave of Portuguese Guinea on the west, remained firmly under Lisbon's control. Portuguese political theory regarded these countries not as colonies but as overseas extensions of metropolitan Portugal, and it was Portuguese policy to grant the status of an "assimilated" Portuguese to every African who had had a certain minimum education. Nor did the Portuguese draw the color-line as other colonial powers had generally done. Against the overwhelming trend toward setting former colonies "free" the Portuguese held fast.

So—with far more menacing overtones—did the white-dominated Republic of South Africa and its northern neighbor, the state of Rhodesia (formerly Southern Rhodesia), which broke its political ties with Britain in 1965 rather than agree to any African participation in political life. In South Africa, the whites included not only descendants of the Dutch settlers, the "Boers" or farmers who in the nineteenth century had made the great trek northward from the Cape, settled the countryside, and now called themselves Afrikaners, but also a minority of English descent. But altogether the whites were themselves a minority, of about one in five of the population. The non-whites included blacks, "coloreds," as those of mixed European and African blood were called, and Asians, mostly Indians who were usually shopkeepers.

The Afrikaners, who had tried unsuccessfully to keep South Africa from fighting on Britain's side in World War II, and some of whom sympathized with Hitler, emerged after the war as a political majority. Imbued with an extremely narrow and reactionary form of Calvinist religion that taught that God had ordained the inferiority of the blacks, the ruling group moved steadily to impose on the black majority their policies of rigid segregation: *apartheid*. Separate townships to live in, separate facilities of all sorts, no political rights, no opportunity for higher education or advancement beyond manual labor, internment of black leaders including the Zulu Chief Albert Luthulli, winner of the Nobel Peace Prize: these were the conditions that a succession of Afrikaner governments defended and extended. Supported by some of those of English descent, who were fearful that the black upheaval to the north would spread to South Africa, the Afrikaners also introduced emergency laws making it possible to arrest people on suspicion, to keep them incommunicado, and to punish them without trial. Severe censorship prevailed, and dissent was silenced. It was no doubt true that communist agents had been at work among the Africans, but the combination of policies known as apartheid was calculated not to thwart them but to make their message more credible.

The regime sought to disarm criticism by founding in Botswana and Lesotho (1966) two black states on South African territory. Lesotho was the former Basutoland, an enclave entirely surrounded by South African territory, and Botswana the former Bechuanaland, which had also previously had the status of an African reservation. Inhabited solely by blacks, but dominated by whites, these two states were not likely to produce much black enthusiasm. In 1949, defying the UN, South Africa annexed the former German colony and League-mandate of South-West Africa. Here too the policies of apartheid held sway.

White South African writers who opposed apartheid, like Alan Paton or Nadine Gordimer, were heard and appreciated outside South Africa, and vilified and repressed at home. The Rhodesians who defied the British in 1965 rather than allow Africans to participate in politics were many of them originally emigrants from South Africa. Boycotted by the British government and later by the UN, they managed to get supplies from South Africa and from Mozambique. The whites at the southern end of the continent seemed determined to defy what seemed to be the lessons of history elsewhere. Whenever the blacks of the remainder of the continent could put aside their own rivalries long enough to work out some practicable plan of unity—and that would no doubt take a long time—the whites of the south might expect short shrift.

LATIN AMERICA

Although most of the Latin American republics had by 1945 enjoyed political independence for more than a century, they had much in common economically and socially with the emerging nations of Asia and Africa. Like the Asians and Africans, the Latin Americans had traditionally been suppliers of foods and raw materials to the rest of the world. Bananas, coffee, sugar, beef, oil, nitrates, and copper fluctuated widely in price on the world market, and before the Latin Americans could raise their standards of living they would have to build on a more stable economic base. Like the other emerging nations too, most of Latin America had a racially mixed population: some native-born whites (Creoles) or immigrants from Europe (like the Italians in Argentina), some descended from the indigenous Indians, and some blacks (chiefly in Brazil and Haiti). Nominally governed under a democratic system of elected officials and parliaments, they had all too often lived under military dictatorships that shifted whenever a new army officer felt strong enough to challenge the one in power.

Toward the United States, Latin Americans traditionally felt a mixture of envy, dislike, and suspicion. The United States was rich and powerful, the "Colossus of the North." Upper-class Latin Americans educated in Europe believed that North Americans lacked true culture. North Americans generally seemed to know little and care less about Latin America. Whenever the United States ceased to be indifferent and devoted some attention to Latin America, we did it by what seemed like intervention in Latin affairs. Upper-class Latin Americans, aware of the miserable poverty in which the majority of their people lived, often had a bad conscience. Usually they did not care whether the conditions of the poor improved or not: theirs was not the Anglo-American tradition of *richesse oblige*. By and large they cared only for their own comforts and hoped that nothing—least of all a social revolution—would disturb the system. So it made them uneasy to find the United States worrying more about the Bolivian or Peruvian peasant than the Bolivians or Peruvians themselves had ever done. Craving attention and admiration yet at the same time longing to be left alone, the Latin Americans made it very difficult for the United States to develop consistent satisfactory policies toward them. And by and large the Latin complaints about us were true: we *were* indifferent except when crises arose. When crises arose we tended to intervene. We were tactless, we were crude, we did not understand, our motives were often questionable.

President Franklin Roosevelt's "Good Neighbor" policy after 1932 was an attempt to overcome these difficulties. The Pan-American Conference that dated back to 1890 became a Pan-American Union in 1910; both of these were primarily cultural in emphasis. But after World War II the Pan-American Union became the Organization of American States (OAS). Somewhat looser than an alliance, the OAS provided a means for consultation among all the American nations, North, South, and Central, on all important matters of mutual concern. The United States was—quite naturally—accused by its enemies of having forged just another instrument of its imperialistic policies, yet OAS did in fact enable all the American states to reach genuine joint decisions. The Alliance for Progress, launched under President Kennedy's impulse and designed to enable the United States to help the Latin Americans to help themselves, proved a disappointment, in part because it was so difficult to allay Latin American suspicions of our intentions, in part because of the deeply entrenched oligarchies that dominated most Latin American countries.

Broad generalizations are of course subject to challenge: not every Latin American country was oligarchical or backward. Uruguay, for example, a small country with a population largely European in origin, had gone further toward creating an advanced welfare state than any other in the world, even the Scandinavian countries or Britain—so far, indeed, that the Uruguayan economy in 1968 was near collapse, largely because of the payment of state funds to individual citizens for the many types of benefits available. Venezuela, with rapidly developing oil resources, in 1959 ousted the last of its long line of military-oligarchic dictators, and ten years later had apparently made the transition to moderate democratic rule, though still threatened by communists sponsored from outside. Chile, too, though plagued by a continual economic crisis, staunchly maintained democratic government. Colombia experienced a lengthy terrorist campaign in the countryside—virtually a civil war—in which many thousands were killed, and even when this drew to an end was still experiencing extremes of wealth and poverty. Brazil, the enormous Portuguese-speaking land larger than the United States territorially, and with more inhabitants of African origin than any other Latin American country, suffered from recurrent economic crises and military *coups*. Its poverty-stricken northeast, where many thousands lived in virtual peonage on big plantations, contrasted sharply with the luxurious apartment-house and beach life of the big cities; but each of these too had its festering slums.

Alone in Latin America, Mexico had passed through and recovered from a true social revolution. The overthrow of the Emperor Maximilian in 1867 (*see* Chapter 12) was followed only nine years later by the advent of the dictator Porfirio Díaz, who ruled in the interests of foreign investors and large landholders until 1910, when a peasant revolution broke out that lasted with interruptions for thirty years, marked by violence and insurrection, by revolutionary reformers who turned into wealthy dictators, and by radical social and economic experimentation. The Catholic Church, long regarded by many Mexicans as opposed to economic and political reform and indifferent to the welfare of the masses, was the target of extreme anticlerical measures. The foreign oil companies, American and British, suffered expropriation. The revolutionary governments gave labor unions extensive privileges and power, expropriated great estates to emancipate the poor peasant, and began a vigorous program of educating the large and neglected population of native Indians. A remarkable cultural awakening took place, based on native traditions and crafts. Mexican revolutionary painters like Rivera and Orozco won international fame. The Mexican revolution, however, stopped short of installing a socialist system, and by 1945 had lost much of its radical dogmatism. The new leaders were more reconciled to the need for foreign capital, for patience in the long task of raising the standards of the masses.

But the successful Mexican revolution was an exception in Latin America. By contrast, Argentina, peopled almost entirely by European immigrants and their descendants, and dependent on the export of beef and grain to Europe, continued to have a social system that gave power to a small landlord class. The beginnings of industrialization, and especially the growth by 1945 of the capital, Buenos Aires, into a great metropolis of nearly five million, increased the numbers of working-class and middle-class people and deepened popular dissatisfaction with the regime.

Brought to power in the national election of 1946, Colonel Juan Perón became a dictator on the model of Mussolini, Hitler, and Franco. In 1955 he went down before a characteristic Latin American military *coup d'état*. He had begun more and more to appeal to the poorer masses, the *descamisados* ("shirtless ones"), and thus lost much of his following in the conservative upper classes. Moreover he quarrelled with the Roman Catholic Church and put through anticlerical measures that cost him further support. Nor could he solve the grave economic and financial problems arising out of his country's essentially colonial position; indeed, his extravagant spending on public works and welfare projects virtually bankrupted Argentina.

During the eleven years that followed, Perónist sentiment continued strong among workers and some other groups, and twice (1962 and 1966) a weak elected government was overthrown by a military *coup*. The army regime installed in 1966 promised to purge Argentina of corruption but aroused much opposition by its repression of academic freedom. The old problems remained unsolved, almost untackled.

And they remained unsolved as well in Peru, which had a relatively advanced urban life at the time of the latest military *coup* in 1968, and in Ecuador and Paraguay, which were still largely rural. It was, of course, Cuba that in the postwar years provided the new revolution. Beginning in the late 1950's under the leadership of Fidel Castro as a guerrilla movement in the hills of the eastern province (Oriente), it succeeded in ousting the government of Fulgencio Batista in 1959. American attitudes toward Castro had been ambivalent: on the one hand, the Batista regime was singularly corrupt and unsavory; on the other, nobody really knew how deeply Castro was committed to communism or to Soviet domination. After his success, he made a series of increasingly pro-Soviet pronouncements, and quarrelled bitterly with the United States, which boycotted Cuban goods. Since the Cuban economy was dependent upon the export of sugar and tobacco, Castro soon found himself exporting largely to the U.S.S.R. and its associated powers, and obtaining most of his imports from them. In 1961, the Kennedy administration backed an expedition of anti-Castro exiles, who landed at the Bay of Pigs and were thoroughly defeated.

In 1962, as we have seen, Castro opened Cuba to the installation of Soviet missiles, leading to the great crisis of October. Once the crisis was over and the missiles were withdrawn, Castro seemed to grow more and more impatient with what he felt to be the inadequate amount of Soviet assistance, and tried to take advantage of the Soviet–Chinese quarrel to extract more from the U.S.S.R. He also tried strenuously to export his revolution into the rest of Latin America: to Venezuela, where there was a great deal of Castroite violence especially just before the presidential elections of 1963; to Guatemala, where communist terrorists dominated portions of the country and murdered the American ambassador in 1968; and to Bolivia, where a band of guerrillas operating under the Argentine revolutionary theorist Ernesto ("Che") Guevara, formerly a member of Castro's cabinet, was finally wiped out in 1967. Guevara was killed, and his diary captured and sold abroad by the Bolivian Interior Minister, Arguedes, in 1968.

Given this Castroite activity, the United States in 1965 concluded, perhaps prematurely, that a revolution in the Dominican Republic, on the neighboring island to Cuba, was also inspired by Castro. Between 1930 and 1961, the Dominican Republic had been ruled by General Trujillo, a ruthless, corrupt, and bloodthirsty dictator. After his assassination, the first freely elected government in a generation took office under Juan Bosch, but increasing tension between the army and the new reformers led to military *coups* and finally to a civil war in 1965. Fearing that communists might soon take over, President Johnson sent in a division of marines, and then tried to internationalize the intervention by appealing to the Organization of American States. By a narrow margin, the OAS responded, and five of its member states, all with conservative military regimes, sent troops to join the Americans. The Dominican Republic was pacified sufficiently for constitutional elections to be held in 1966; a moderate, Joaquin Balaguer, became President.

It would have been political suicide in 1965 for any President of the United States to allow another Caribbean country to fall into pro-Soviet hands at a time when public opinion in this country had hardly reconciled itself to the Castro regime. But the entire episode aroused much opposition among Americans, despite the fact that the OAS had backed Johnson's actions. And in Latin America, where Mexico, for example, had opposed intervention, the reappearance of American marines served to heighten the suspicion that the United States was still up to its bad old tricks.

Physically located in Latin America, but with a population consisting chiefly of East Indians and Negroes, deeply at odds with each other, British Guiana also had a strong communist movement, led by an Indian, Cheddi Jagan. When it appeared that independence from Britain would be followed by Jagan's assuming power, the British postponed independence until an effective anticommunist coalition of Jagan's opponents was safely in office. The new state of Guyana was created in 1966.

FINAL REFLECTIONS

Not the least important aspect of the Cold War was the competition between the United States and the Soviet Union for the support of the emerging nations. In their programs of foreign aid, both countries made mistakes: as when American aid enabled a Ghanian politician to buy himself a solid gold bed, or when Soviet aid supplied quantities of obsolete and inappropriate agricultural machinery that rusted uselessly on a Guinean dock. In the larger sense, it was a mistake for an American or a Russian to promise that his system would usher in the millennium promptly for those who imitated it. New nations would have to wait for most of the consumer goods they yearned for until they had educated enough of their own people to do the work of modernizing that would earn the money to buy them. Then political stability and economic growth might each contribute to the other. Perhaps the American experiment of the Peace Corps, launched by President Kennedy, provided the most hopeful model: education by example for the hard pull ahead.

As to the Cold War itself, many in the mid-Sixties thought the term was obsolete, that the United States and its partners had won without realizing it, that the U.S.S.R. was undergoing a fundamental change, and that a worldwide relaxation of tensions might be in prospect had America not—by its policies in Vietnam—forfeited such a large measure of international goodwill and weakened its ability to negotiate. These views vanished like a puff of smoke after the Soviet intervention in Czechoslovakia in 1968. The U.S.S.R. would still intervene with force in its own bailiwick; if it showed signs of wanting the Vietnam war to end, this was because such a solution would hurt the Chinese; it would negotiate only when it could further its own immediate interests. American intervention in Vietnam had perhaps helped save us from still worse agonies. The Cold War was still very much with us, and in its next phases would require of us not less than an understanding of its origins and development since 1945.

A Peace Corps volunteer in Bolivia demonstrating efficient methods of sheep shearing.

16

READING SUGGESTIONS (asterisk indicates paperbound edition)

General Accounts

N. A. Graebner, ed., *The Cold War: Ideological Conflict or Power Struggle?* (*Heath). Introduction to divergent interpretations.

D. Donnelly, *Struggle for the World* (St. Martin's, 1965). A history of the Cold War, tracing it back to 1917.

C. Quigley, *The World since 1939*, rev. ed. (*Collier). Thoughtful survey.

P. Calvocoressi, *International Politics since 1945* (*Praeger). Helpful factual survey.

C. E. Black, *Dynamics of Modernization* (*Torchbooks). Illuminating comparative study.

S. Kuznets, *Post-War Economic Growth* (Harvard, 1964). Very good analysis.

S. P. Huntington, *Political Order in Changing Societies* (Yale, 1968); L. L. Snyder, *The New Nationalism* (Cornell, 1968). Wide-ranging and provocative surveys.

The Free World

J. Freymond, *Western Europe since the War* (Praeger, 1964). Good brief manual.

T. H. White, *Fire in the Ashes* (*Apollo). Postwar economic recovery and the role of the Marshall Plan.

M. M. Postan, *An Economic History of Western Europe, 1945–1964* (*Barnes & Noble). Comprehensive and most informative review.

W. O. Henderson, *The Genesis of the Common Market* (F. Cass, 1963); U. W. Kitzinger, *Politics and Economics of European Integration* (*Praeger); L. B. Krause, ed., *The Common Market: Progress and Controversy* (*Spectrum). Useful works on an important economic development.

A. Marwick, *Britain in the Century of Total War* (Little, Brown, 1968). Controversial assessment of the impact of war on society.

A. Sampson, *Anatomy of Britain Today*, rev. ed. (*Colophon). Lively analysis.

F. Boyd, *British Politics in Transition, 1945–1963* (Praeger, 1964). Solid account.

C. Cross, *The Fall of the British Empire, 1918–1968* (Hodder & Stoughton, 1968). Analysis of a central aspect of Britain's altered position.

S. Hoffmann et al., *In Search of France* (*Torchbooks). Essays on economics, politics, and society in twentieth-century France.

D. Pickles, *Fifth French Republic*, 3rd ed. (*Praeger). Good political handbook.

P. Williams, *Crisis and Compromise* (*Anchor). Analyzing the failures of the Fourth Republic.

D. Schoenbrun, *Three Lives of Charles de Gaulle* (*Atheneum). By an informed journalist.

C. Brinton, *The Americans and the French* (Harvard, 1968). Perceptive essay on the French in the postwar world.

H. S. Hughes, *The United States and Italy*, rev. ed. (*Norton). The intelligent American's guide to postwar Italian politics and society.

M. Salvadori, *Italy* (*Spectrum). Handy introduction.

K. P. Tauber, *Beyond Eagle and Swastika*, 2 vols. (Wesleyan, 1967). Detailed study of German nationalism since World War II.

A. Grosser, *The Federal Republic of Germany* (*Praeger). Good concise history.

G. M. Craig, *The United States and Canada* (Harvard, 1968). The intelligent American's guide to the problems of his northern neighbor.

T. H. White, *The Making of the President, 1960* and *The Making of the President, 1964* (*Signet). Highly informative political analyses.

A. M. Schlesinger, Jr., *A Thousand Days* (Houghton, 1965), and T. C. Sorenson, *Kennedy* (*Bantam). Memoirs by aides of President Kennedy, particularly enlightening on foreign policy.

H. Sidey, *A Very Personal Presidency* (*Atheneum). Perceptive study of the Johnson presidency.

The Communist Bloc

C. E. Black, *The Eastern World since 1945* (*Ginn). Instructive scholarly survey.

L. Schapiro, *The Government and Poli-*

tics of the Soviet Union, rev. ed. (*Vintage). Short treatment by a leading authority.

A. G. Meyer, *The Soviet Political System* (Random House, 1965). An interpretation by a capable political scientist.

Z. Brzezinski, *The Soviet Bloc,* rev. ed. (Harvard, 1967). Solid study of the elements of unity and conflict by a leading political scientist.

D. Zagoria, *The Sino-Soviet Conflict, 1956–1961* (*Atheneum); W. E. Griffith, *Albania and the Sino-Soviet Rift* and *The Sino-Soviet Rift* (*MIT). Useful studies of Russo-Chinese antagonism.

R. L. Wolff, *The Balkans in Our Time* (*Norton). Informed survey.

The Emerging Nations

S. C. Easton, *The Rise and Fall of Modern Colonialism* (Praeger, 1962). Sweeping survey.

V. M. Dean, *Nature of the Non-Western World* (*Mentor). Brief overview.

B. Ward, *Interplay of East and West* and *Rich Nations and Poor Nations* (*Norton). General study by an articulate economist.

F. W. Houn, *A Short History of Chinese Communism* (*Spectrum). Useful recent introduction.

J. K. Fairbank, *The United States and China,* rev. ed. (*Compass); E. O. Reischauer, *The United States and Japan,* rev. ed. (*Compass). Authoritative surveys.

D. J. Duncannon, *Government and Revolution in Vietnam* (Oxford, 1968). Authoritative political history.

B. B. Fall, *The Two Viet-Nams,* rev. ed. (Praeger, 1965), and R. Shaplen, *The Lost Revolution: The U.S. in Vietnam, 1946–1966* (*Colophon). Outstanding titles among the flood of works on the subject.

J. D. Legge, *Indonesia* (*Spectrum). Handy introduction.

W. N. Brown, *The United States and India and Pakistan,* rev. ed. (Harvard, 1963); S. Wolpert, *India* (*Spectrum); D. N. Wilber, *Pakistan Yesterday and Today* (*Holt). Useful introductory studies.

R. H. Davison, *Turkey* (*Spectrum); N. Safran, *The United States and Israel* (Harvard, 1963); W. R. Polk, *The United States and the Arab World* (Harvard, 1965); H. B. Sharabi, *Nationalism and Revolution in the Arab World* (*Van Nostrand); T. Prittie, *Israel: Miracle in the Desert,* rev. ed. (*Penguin); M. Harari, *Government and Politics in the Middle East* (*Spectrum);

R. W. Cottam, *Nationalism in Iran* (*Pittsburgh). Recent studies of the Middle East.

J. Hatch, *A History of Postwar Africa* (*Praeger). Clear and helpful guide.

B. Ward, *Africa in the Making* (Norton, 1966). Stimulating general discussion.

L. G. Cowan, *The Dilemmas of African Independence,* rev. ed. (*Walker). A mine of information.

J. F. Gallagher, *The United States and North Africa* (Harvard, 1963); W. Schwarz, *Nigeria* (Praeger, 1968); J. Cope, *South Africa* (Praeger, 1965). Good studies of particularly important areas.

G. M. Carter, ed., *Politics in Africa: Seven Cases* (*Harcourt). Informative studies.

V. Alba, *Nationalists without Nations* (Praeger, 1968). Attack on the ruling oligarchies as barriers to progress in Latin America.

R. J. Alexander, *Today's Latin America,* 2nd ed. (*Anchor); T. Szulc, *Winds of Revolution: Latin America Today and Tomorrow,* rev. ed. (*Praeger). Suggestive introductions.

C. C. Cumberland, *Mexico: The Struggle for Modernity* (*Oxford); A. P. Whitaker, *Argentina* (*Spectrum); A. Marshall, *Brazil* (*Walker); K. Silvert, *Chile Yesterday and Today* (*Holt); J. E. Fagg, *Cuba, Haiti, and the Dominican Republic* (*Spectrum); H. Bernstein, *Venezuela and Colombia* (*Spectrum); M. Rodriguez, *Central America* (*Spectrum). Useful guides to particular areas.

Literature Discussed in the Chapter

I. Ehrenburg, *The Thaw* (Harvil, 1955).

V. Dudinstev, *Not by Bread Alone* (Dutton, 1957).

B. Pasternak, *Dr. Zhivago* (*Signet).

M. Sholokhov, *And Quiet Flows the Don* (*Vintage); *The Don Flows Home to the Sea* (*Vintage); *Harvest on the Don* (*Signet).

A. I. Solzhenitsyn, *A Day in the Life of Ivan Denisovitch* (*several editions).

A. Tertz, pseud., *The Makepeace Experiment* (*Vintage); *Socialist Realism; The Trial Begins* (*Vintage).

Y. Yevtushenko, *A Precocious Autobiography* (*Dutton); *Selected Poetry* (*Penguin); *Bratsk Station and Other New Poems* (*Anchor).

S. Alliluyeva, *Twenty Letters to a Friend* (*Colophon).

17

The Temper of Our Times

The TWA Building at Kennedy International Airport, designed by Eero Saarinen (1960).

I. Introduction: Perspectives on a Confused and Confusing Age

It is quite possible that future historians, say in the twenty-first century, will be able to give our twentieth century some neat and acceptable label of the kind we have used, without too much apology, in this book for earlier centuries—the Century of Genius, the Age of Enlightenment, the Century of Hope. Those suggested for our own times by our contemporary publicists—for example, the Age of Anxiety, the Aspirin Age, the Age of Overkill, the Age of Tranquillizers, the Age of Conformity—suggest that there has been a great and on the whole unpleasant set of changes since Victorian times. In terms of cultural generations, it is certainly difficult to see ourselves as others will see us; it is just possible that we are not quite so badly off, not in quite so deep a cultural trough, as the labels above would suggest.

Yet the twentieth century has been very different from what most publicists of the late nineteenth thought it would be. Herbert Spencer (died 1903), whom we have noticed briefly in Chapter 13, thought that, with England setting the example, the coming industrial society would have no place for wars, that such antiquated institutions as Oxford and Cambridge would abandon the snobbery of Greek and Latin and concentrate on engineering and other practical subjects, that politicians would give up their mistaken efforts to regulate economic life, and, finally, that, although he had to note among them "the still occasional use of cosmetics," women, with Englishwomen in the lead, would gradually rise above their irrational feminine limitations.

The literary device of bringing the long dead back to life is to the historian an illegitimate way of trying to measure the flow of historical change; still, we may hazard the statement that Herbert Spencer, brought back to life and confronted in our day with a single issue of the very respectable *New York Times*, let alone a tabloid newspaper, would just not believe his eyes.

The big events of the twentieth century, the events that the historian has to headline, are clearly not what the Victorians believed, or at least hoped, they would be: two disastrous world wars, in absolute terms the most costly in human lives and in material destruction of all wars hitherto; a worldwide economic crisis that also in absolute terms was the most serious of all such modern "depressions," to use the mild term by which it is commonly described; a continuing, perhaps worsening, series of "revolutionary" or "guerrilla" wars in lands a Victorian like Benjamin Kidd held to be utterly incapable of self-rule (*see* p. 533); a "population explosion," especially in just these "underdeveloped" lands, an explosion that seems to many experts in demography to threaten famine and starvation on a scale hitherto unknown. With all this the reader of our last few chapters is familiar.

Yet even at this level of the big, sweeping developments, there is another side of the picture. In spite of death and destruction, the developed lands of Europe, North America, and Australia have by all statistical standards—gross national product, income per capita, industrial growth rate, and the like—in the last two decades attained both relatively and absolutely a greater material prosperity than ever before; and some of this material prosperity has spread even to the poorer of the "underdeveloped" lands, though this increase in material wealth has in large part been cancelled out by the very great increase in population in just those lands. And even at the political level, bad as international relations have been, the always threatening World War III has as yet not broken out; the United Nations Organization is still in being, having already had a longer life than the League of Nations; and what at the end of World War II seemed a pretty solid bloc of Communist nations is now, with the development of Russo-Chinese rivalry, by no means so solid.

If we turn our attention to cultural history in its broadest sense, the broad view is much the same: elements of what must look to many conventional people like decadence, purposeless revolt, blind alleys of artistic innovation, cultural anarchy; yet also, evidence even in "modernism" in art, literature, philosophy—indeed, above all in these—of continuing human energies, willingness to experiment, in short, signs of *life*.

The old rift between the culture of the few, the "highbrows," and that of the many, the "lowbrows," visible as far back in our Western history as the Athens of Plato and Aristophanes (*see* Chapter 2), we have already noted in Chapter 13 as having increased. It has hardly diminished in the twentieth century, but it has taken on somewhat different forms. For one thing, an intermediate group which the American critic Russell Lynes has called "the middlebrows" has increased in numbers with the spread of secondary and higher education in the United States and in much of Europe. The middlebrows tend towards conventional tastes and conservative morals, tend indeed to like what the highbrows liked a generation or two ago; they are perhaps as much shocked by what the lowbrows like and do as by what the highbrows like and do. But in sociological terms they are definitely not "anti-intellectuals," and on the whole they act as a stabilizing force in our highly experimental age.

The Herbert Spencer we have used above as a yardstick to measure, if only approximately, some of the differences between the nineteenth and the twentieth centuries was not much interested in art and letters. Still, he would see and sense much today for which he would be wholly unprepared. Our hot jazz would not sound to him much like a Viennese waltz, the violent and sexy "whodunits" would not be to him much like Sherlock Holmes stories, the picture magazines would not remind him of Currier and Ives prints, and even in the so-called comic strips the frustrations, the inferiority complexes, "hangups," violence, and horrors would seem worlds apart from the naïve buffoonery of the first strips of about 1900, "Happy Hooligan," for instance, or "Buster Brown" or "The Yellow Kid."

Nor were Spencer to concentrate on the high culture would he be any less struck with the great changes since 1890; perhaps in fact he would be more struck with them. It is true that he would readily see in the *avant garde* writers and artists and in the "anti-intellectual" philosophers of the late nineteenth century (*see* Chapter 13) precursors of twentieth-century philosophical and artistic movements. Yet he would surely be struck by the way the twentieth century has gone beyond its precursors. He would not confuse contemporary abstractionists with Monet or Cézanne, nor atonal music, let alone "concrete" music, with the music of Brahms, nor James Joyce's *Finnegan's Wake* or some modern French "anti-novels" with the novels of Henry James.

We shall slowly return to some of these specific representatives of contemporary high—or simply highbrow—culture. Here let us revert to our hypothetical twenty-first century historian, who, while noting the differences between the highbrow and the popular culture of our time, would not conclude that they were wholly separate and wholly different cultures. He would see that they have much in common, that both have strong elements of contrast with the culture of the nineteenth century. We cannot of course begin to guess how he would feel toward us and our culture, nor with what terms he would try to tell his readers about us. But he would surely call attention to the notes of violence and despair, the unprecedented frankness with which the Anglo-Saxon four-letter words are printed as well as uttered, the repudiation of conventional representational art, the vogue of such fashions as pop art and op art, the preoccupation with such psychological matters as "alienation," "identity crisis," and "commitment," the great premium set upon originality, novelty, youth against age (perhaps a bit radically expressed among the young as "Don't trust anybody over thirty"), the rise of a popular slick urban cynicism, the doubts about even so ingrained a belief, in the United States at least, as the belief in inevitable progress with a capital P. We shall in conclusion consider how far all this is in fact a repudiation of, a resistance to, our democratic inheritance from the eighteenth-century Enlightenment. Meanwhile, we must essay some more specific analysis of the attitudes, the tastes, the "ideas" of our confused and confusing age. We shall not attempt a detailed "coverage," but rather attempt by concentrating on representative figures to illustrate the characteristics of our high culture and how it differs from that of the nineteenth century.

II. Main Currents of Thought

PSYCHOLOGY

Freud. Following leads from the biological sciences, the nineteenth century came to put particular emphasis on *process*, on the dynamics of change in time. The twentieth century, although continuing its predecessor's interest in process, indeed in history, has taken a cue from psychology, has come to put particular emphasis on the role of the unconscious in human thought and action, on the irrationality—or at least nonrationality—of much human behavior. Foremost among thinkers responsible for his emphasis was Sigmund Freud (1856–1939). Freud was a physician, trained in Vienna in the rationalist medical tradition of the late nineteenth century. His interest was early drawn to mental illness, where he soon found cases in which patients exhibited symptoms of very real organic disturbances for which no obvious organic or physiological causes could be found. Under analysis, as Freud's therapeutic treatment came to be called, the patient, relaxed on a couch, is urged to pour out what he can remember of his earliest childhood, or indeed infancy. After many such treatments the analyst can hope to find what is disturbing the patient, and by making him aware of what that is, hope to help him.

Had Freud merely contented himself with this kind of therapy, few of us would have heard of him. But from all this clinical experience he worked out a system of psychology that has had a very great influence, not only on psychiatry and psychology, but on some of our basic conceptions of human relations. Freud starts with the concept of a set of "drives" with which each person is born. These drives, which have their source in the unconscious, he called the id. Freud never tried to locate the id physiologically; he used the term which in Latin means "this [thing]" to avoid the moralistic overtones in words like "desires" or such then unfashionable terms—at least among psychologists—as "instincts."

These drives try to get satisfaction and pleasure, to express themselves in action. The infant, notably, is "uninhibited"—that is, his drives well up into action from the id without restraint from his conscious mind. But by no means without restraint from his parents or nurse—and there's the difficulty. The infant finds himself frustrated. As he grows, as his mind is formed, he comes to be conscious of the fact that some of the things he wants to do are objectionable to those closest to him, and on whom he is so dependent. He himself therefore begins to repress these drives from his id. Note that for Freud sexual drives are a major element in the id, but by no means the whole id.

With his dawning consciousness of the world outside himself, the child has

Freud, as interpreted by Jean Cocteau.

in fact developed another part of his psyche, which Freud at first called the censor, and later divided into two phases which he called the ego and the superego. The ego is the individual's private censor, his awareness that in accordance with what Freudians call the reality principle certain drives from his id simply cannot succeed. The superego, in a way, is what common language calls conscience; it is the individual's response as a trained member of a social system in which certain actions are proper and certain actions improper. Now these drives of the id, and indeed in most of its phases the dictates of the superego, are for Freud a sort of great reservoir of which the individual is not normally aware—that is, they are part of his "unconscious." In a mentally healthy individual, enough of the drives of the id succeed so that he feels contented. But even the healthiest of individuals has had to repress a great deal of his drives from the id. This successful repression the Freudians account for in part at least by a process they call sublimation. They think that the healthy individual somehow finds for a drive suppressed by ego or superego, or by both working together, a new and socially approved outlet or expression. Thus a drive toward sexual relations not approved in one's circle might be sublimated into the writing of poetry or music, into social or religious work, or even into athletics.

With the neurotic person, however, Freud held that drives, having been suppressed, driven back down into the unconscious, find no suitable other outlet or sublimation, and continue, so to speak, festering in the id, trying to find some outlet. They find all sorts of outlets of an abnormal sort, symptoms of illness in great variety. They display themselves in all sorts of neuroses and phobias, which have in common a failure to conform to the reality principle. The neurotic individual is "maladjusted." And if the failure to meet the reality principle is really complete, the individual is insane, "psychotic," and lives in an utterly unreal private world of his own.

Freud's therapy rested on the belief that if the individual neurotic could come to understand why he behaved as he did he could frequently make a proper adjustment and lead a normal life. But here Freud parted company with the rationalist tradition of the eighteenth century. He held that there was no use preaching at the individual, nor even reasoning with him, telling him the error of his ways, pointing out what was unreasonable in his behavior. Reason, logic, could not get directly into the unconscious, where the source of his trouble lay. Only by the long, slow process of psychoanalysis, in which the individual day after day sought in memories of his earliest childhood for concrete details, could the listening analyst pick from this stream of consciousness the significant details that pointed to the hidden repression, the "blocking" that came out in neurotic behavior. Freud gave special importance to the dreams of the patient, which he must patiently describe to the analyst; for in dreams, Freud thought, the unconscious wells up out of control, or but partly controlled, by the ego and the superego. Once the patient, however, got beneath the surface of his conscious life, and became aware of what had gone wrong with his hitherto unconscious life, he might then adjust himself to society.

The Implications of Freudianism. Now it is true that in the second half of the twentieth century Freud's reputation is under attack from several quarters, scientific, artistic, philosophical. Still, what is important for us here in the wider implications of Freud's work is first this concept of the very great role of the unconscious drives—that is, the unthinking, the nonrational, in our lives. Ordinary reflective thinking is for the Freudian a very small part of our existence. We arrive at the metaphor of reason as a flickering candle, or, to use another well-worn metaphor, of reason as simply the small part of the iceberg that shows above the water, while submerged down below is the great mass of the unconscious. Much even of our conscious thinking is, according to the Freudian, what psychologists call rationalization, thinking dictated, not by an awareness of the reality principle, but the drives of our id. One can get a good measure of the difference between eighteenth-century rationalism and Freudian psychology by contrasting the older belief in the innocence and natural goodness of the untrained child, Wordsworth's "mighty prophet, seer blest," with the Freudian view of such a child as a bundle of unsocial or antisocial drives, as in fact a little untamed savage. A useful corrective to the excessively pessimistic Freudian view of the child has been offered by the great Swiss psychologist Jean Piaget (1896–   ), who seeks to explain how children's "reasoning power" grows.

But second, and most important, note that the Freudians do not wish to blow out the candle of human reason. They are moderate, not extreme, antirationalists; they are chastened rationalists. Their whole therapy is based on the concept, which has Christian as well as eighteenth-century roots, that "ye shall know the truth, and the truth shall make you free." Only, for the Freudian, truth is not easily found, cannot be distilled into a few simple rules of conduct which all men, being reasonable and good, can use as guides to individual and collective happiness. Such truth cannot be simply taught by the usual methods of teaching. It is on the contrary very hard to establish, and can be reached only by a long and precarious struggle. Many will not reach it, and will have to put up with all sorts of maladjustments and frustrations. The Freudian is at bottom a pessimist, in that he does not believe in the perfectibility of man as a species. Indeed, there are those who see in the Freudian concept of human nature something like a return to the Christian concept of original sin. They continue the parallel, which many others find absurd or offensive, by maintaining that for the Freudian too there is, though difficult to find, a way out, a form of salvation, in the full self-knowledge that comes from successful psychoanalysis.

Freud, to whom religion was an "illusion," was himself a cult-leader. His faithful disciples still form an orthodox nucleus of strict Freudian psychoanalysts, most numerous, almost certainly, in the United States. Other disciples parted with the master, notably the Swiss Jung (1875–1961), who did believe in religion, and whose great popular phrase was the "collective unconscious," and the Austrian Adler (1870–1937), who rejected the master's emphasis on the sexual, and popularized the familiar phrase "inferiority complex."

Full psychoanalysis remains an extremely expensive process limited to those who can afford it or can receive it through charity. There are, however, modified forms of analytical therapy, such as group therapy and the like, which are much less expensive. The Freudian influence on imaginative writing, indeed on philosophy and the arts generally, was and remains very great indeed, though usually dispersed, vague, indirect, and very hard to summarize. Negatively, the life work of this nineteenth-century-trained scientist went in these "humanistic" fields to reinforce the reaction against nineteenth-century scientific and rationalistic materialism. Positively, Freud's work helped all sorts of modernisms, strengthened the revival of intuition, "hunch," sensibility, and, perhaps paradoxically, a Stoic or existentialist rejection of middle-class optimism.

Behaviorism. It need hardly be said that in this multanimous century of ours that Freudians hold no monopoly of the field of psychology. Indeed, the eighteenth-century tendency to regard human nature, though not by any means as wholly rational, at least as wholly malleable by those who could manipulate the human and nonhuman environment, still had representatives in the mid-twentieth century. Yet at least one of these "behaviorist" tendencies in psychology had its own flareback to reinforce pessimism over the possibilities of immediate reform of the human condition. The Russian psychologist Pavlov (1849–1936), Nobel Prize Winner in 1904, has given us the now familiar term "conditioned reflex." Pavlov's laboratory dogs, after being fed at a given signal, came to water at the mouth at this signal though no food was within sight or smell. The "natural" —that is, inborn—response of watering at the mouth would ordinarily come only when the dog's senses showed him actual food; Pavlov got the same response artificially by a signal that certainly did not smell or look like food to the dog. The upshot was clear evidence that training or conditioning can produce artificially automatic responses in the animal that are consonant with the kind of automatic responses the animal is born with.

Pavlov's experiments had important implications for the social scientist. They confirmed eighteenth-century notions about the power of environment, of training and education, in the sense that environment can be manipulated to produce specific responses from organisms. But—and this is a bitter blow to eighteenth-century optimism—they suggested that once such training has taken hold, the organism has, so to speak, incorporated the results almost as if they had been the product of heredity, not environment, and further change becomes very difficult, in some instances impossible. Pavlov, after having trained some of his dogs, tried mixing his signals, frustrating and confusing the dogs by withholding food at the signal that had always produced food for them. He succeeded in producing symptoms of a kind close to what in human beings would be neurosis.

Still another lead, this time from biologists interested not in the most fashionable "microbiology" but rather in the behavior of individuals (the old-fashioned name for it was "natural history"), came from such scientists as the Austrian Konrad Lorenz (1903–   ) and the Dutchman Nikolaas Tinbergen (1907–   ), founders of what is called ethology. Their key phrase is "species-specific behavior." This behavior does indeed derive from hereditary constitutional features of the organism, but its realization depends on key moments when development of the organism must be triggered by specific normal features of the environment. Thus, for instance, newly hatched goslings normally see first and attach themselves to the mother goose; but if she is removed before they hatch, they will attach themselves to a foster mother, a hen, even a human being. Modern ethology thus *reinforces* the notion that neither heredity nor environment alone, but rather a complex and subtle interaction of the two, "determines" behavior, including human behavior. There is room for accident, and even for "will," if not quite free will.

SOCIOPOLITICAL THOUGHT

We have in the foregoing already edged over naturally enough from psychology to the wider field of man's behavior as a political animal. In what are sometimes optimistically called the social or behavioral sciences, the twentieth century has continued to develop the critique of our eighteenth-century inheritance of belief in the perfectibility of "human nature." In fact, the very term "human nature" seems to some social scientists to be so all-embracing as to make no sense. Once more, let us re-emphasize, first, that this "revolt against reason" is better and more fully to be described as a revolt against reason as exemplified in popular concepts of what science is and does. Second, that many thinkers in this revolt did not attack scientific reason as such in its own fields of established sciences, but simply urged that there are other valuable ways of using the human mind. And third, that though many of these thinkers were antirationalists, and almost always "élitists," fascists, racists, reactionaries hostile to the democratic tradition, others were "chastened rationalists," thinkers who wished to salvage what they could of the eighteenth-century basis of the democratic tradition.

The specific programs, the emotional allegiances, the "values" of twentieth-century thinkers in this broad field we may hesitantly call "sociological" were varied indeed. And yet most of them, certainly the great ones, do have in common a sense of the subtlety, the complexities, the delicacy—and paradoxically the toughness and durability—of the ties that bind human beings together—and hold them apart—in society. Indeed, that last sentence of ours, with its coupling of opposites in tension, is typical of this twentieth-century approach to problems of man in society. Compare an incidental and therefore significant remark tossed off by Arthur Koestler, "for we are moving here through strata that are held together by the cement of contradiction."* Or, as the Swiss writer Denis de Rougemont puts the same kind of challenge to our conventional notions of what makes sense, tensions between two terms that are *"true, contradictory, and essential."*† The distinguished American sociologist Talcott Parsons, in his *The Structure of Social Action* (1937), finds in the work of many different thinkers, such as the German Max Weber, the Frenchman Durkheim, the Englishman Alfred Marshal, the Italian Pareto, and others, a common aim to put the study of man in society on a basis that takes full account of the difficulties of "objectivity" in such study, and gives full place to our contemporary awareness of the place of the subjective and nonrational in human life.

Pareto. We may here speak for a moment about Pareto (1848–1923), not because he was the greatest or the most influential thinker, for he was not, but because the work of this scientifically trained engineer is such a clear example of the difficulties of thinking about men as we think about things. Pareto tried hard to establish a genuine *science* of sociology; but it was a sociology very different from that of his only slightly older contemporary Herbert Spencer. Pareto in his *The Mind and Society* (original Italian edition, 1916) is concerned chiefly with the problem of separating in human actions the rational from the nonrational. What interests Pareto is the kind of action that is expressed in words, rationalizations, ritual, symbolism of some kind. Buying wool socks for cold weather is one such action. If they are bought deliberately to get the best socks at a price the buyer can afford, this is rational action in accord with the doer's interests; it is the kind of action the economist can study statistically. If, however, they are bought because the buyer thinks wool is "natural" (as compared with "synthetic" and therefore to his mind inferior fibers) or because he finds snob value in imported English socks or wants to help the hard-hit British economy or because he wants to help bring sheep-raising back to Vermont, we are in a field less "rational" than

* *The Invisible Writing* (Boston, 1954), p. 349.
† *Man's Western Quest* (New York, 1957), p. 116.

price. The practical economist will still study marketing and consumer demand, but he will have to cope with many complex psychological variables, variables in a sense outside his professional training. It is unlikely that "pure" economics can ever *wholly* explain even economic growth or recessions.

It is these "nonlogical" elements in human sentiments that Pareto studies under the name of "derivations," which are close to what most of us know as rationalizations. These are the explanations and accompanying ritualistic acts associated with our religion, our patriotism, our feelings as members of groups of all kinds, right down to the family. The idea of prayer, for instance, is for Pareto a "derivation"; he was, like so many of this period, a materialist, at bottom hostile to Christianity, though he approved of it as means of social concord, and was fascinated by its hold over men. It is irrational, or nonrational, to pray for rain, because we know as meteorologists that rain has purely material causes quite beyond the reach of prayer. These derivations are indeed a factor in human social life, but they do not really move men to social action.

What does move men in society, and keeps them together in society, says Pareto, are the *residues*. These are expressions of relatively permanent, abiding sentiments in men, expressions that usually have to be separated from the part that is actually a derivation, which may change greatly and even quickly. Pagan Greek sailors sacrificed to Poseidon, god of the sea, before setting out on a voyage; a few centuries later, Christian Greek sailors prayed, lighted candles, and made vows to the Virgin Mary just before sailing. The derivations are the explanations of what Poseidon and the Virgin respectively do. They vary. The believer in the Virgin thinks his pagan predecessor was dead wrong. The residues are the needs to secure divine aid and comfort in a difficult undertaking, and to perform certain ritual acts that give the performer assurance of such aid and comfort. The residues are nearly the same for our two sets of sailors. Both the pagans and the Christians have the same social and psychological needs and satisfy them in much the same ways, though with very different "explanations" of what they are doing.

Two of the major classes of residues Pareto distinguishes stand out, and help form his philosophy of history. These are first the residues of persistent aggregates, the sentiments that mark men who like regular ways, solid discipline, tradition and habit, men like the Spartans, the Prussians, or any rigorously disciplined military class. Second, there are the residues of the instinct for combinations, the sentiments that mark men who like novelty and adventure, who invent new ways of doing things, who like to cut loose from the old and the tried, men not easily shocked, men who hate discipline, men like most intellectuals and inventors—and many entrepreneurs and businessmen. In societies of many individual members, men influenced largely by one or the other of these major residues tend to rise to the top and to characterize that society. Like most philosophers of history, Pareto is far from clear on just how a conservative society where the residues of persistent aggregates predominate changes into another kind of society. But he does have this conception of a pendulum swing, even a struggle of thesis and antithesis.

The nineteenth century in the West was in Pareto's mind a society in which the residues of instinct for combinations played perhaps the greatest role of which they are capable in a human society. That is to say, it was a society with the maximum degree of individual freedom, at least for the successful individuals in it; it was not such a society for the masses. The nineteenth century was a century of competition among individuals full of new ideas, inventions, enterprises, convinced that the old ways were bad, that novelty was the great thing to strive for at the expense of everything else. It was a society notably out of equilibrium. It had to run toward the other kind of residues, toward the persistent aggregates, toward a society with more security and less competition, more discipline and less freedom, more equality and less inequality, more uniformity and less variety. It had to go the way some writers hold that we are going in the twentieth century, toward the welfare state, even toward the totalitarian state.

The Planners and Persuaders. Yet the abiding influence of the newer psychological and sociological approach to the study of man in society has by no means been in the Paretan and conservative direction. Those who want to influence human behavior, all the way from the microcosmic field of personal consumer choices to the macrocosmic field of international relations, have been willing to make use of the new psychological insights. From the latest piece of "motivational research" to show the cigarette manufacturer how to overcome the effects on his customers of recent medical research on the causes of lung cancer to the high-minded efforts of proponents of world government to devise for their projected state some symbol, visual, musical, concrete, that will supplant nationalist symbols, such as patriotic hymns, flags, and the like, hard-working planners are busily engaged in trying, often successfully, to change our habits, even our prejudices. To use Pareto's now little-used terminology, they are seeking, not to change our behavior by appealing to our "reason" in the plain sense of that word; they are trying to "activate" certain of our sentiments, prejudices, emotions, our residues, and "de-activate" others.

In the field of serious political and social thought, this characteristic twentieth-century emphasis on the psychology of motivation has been appealed to not only by conservatives or "reactionaries" like Pareto and others, including both Mussolini and Hitler, who had pretensions to philosophy, but also by many who were democrats, or at least "progressives," at heart. An early example of this latter type of political thinker is Graham Wallas (1858–1932), a British leftist whose *Human Nature in Politics* (1908) was a most influential book. Wallas, campaigning as a Progressive for a seat in the London County Council, discovered by experience that the voters he canvassed were more pleased and influenced by little tricks of baby-kissing, chit-chat, and personal flattery than by appeals to reason or even to self-interest. Something of the same emphasis on the need to go beyond abstractions to practical psychology in politics appears in the earlier writings of the American Walter Lippmann (1889–   ), whose *Preface to Politics* appeared in 1913. It has, of course, always been known to politicians.

There remains, especially among American intellectuals, a strong current of thought–feeling that refuses to descend into Machiavellian strategy, even—indeed most of all—in a righteous cause. It still seems to these good children of the eighteenth-century Enlightenment that reason and high ethical principles must and will prevail together, and that to appeal to the "lower" elements in nature so emphasized by modern psychology is no way to reform the existing society. Such opinions are by no means commonly held, or, at an rate, commonly put into practice by active politicians, and one of the many gaps that seem in our society to widen rather than to narrow in these days is the old gap between the idealistic "theorist" and the "practical man" who wants to get things done.

Yet the intellectual leaders of mid-twentieth-century progressive political thought are increasingly forced to the conclusion that more has to be done in the way of planning. Notably, they urge, we must plan—and carry out our planning primarily by governmental action—in the whole sector of our economy that deals with such essentials as education, social service, housing, hospital care, scientific research, public transportation, and the means of preserving natural resources and curtailing air- and water-pollution. All these are expensive. The planners know, or should know, that in a democracy plans cannot simply be imposed on those planned for, as to a great degree they can in a totalitarian state like Russia. They are paying great attention to the problems, on which modern thinking in the field of the social sciences does throw some light, of how to get the many to want and ask for—and pay for—what the planners think the people really need, and *ought* to want. A representative writer who is concerned with such matters is the persuasive but highly controversial American economist J. K. Galbraith (1908–   ), author of *The Affluent Society*. Yet there is a basic distrust of the expert, above all in matters of politics, that seems built into a modern democracy.

PHILOSOPHY

In the field of formal—which nowadays tends to mean also university-supported—philosophy the twentieth century displays once more its variety. It is safe to say that in the West at least there are today representatives of almost every philosophical system, from extreme idealism to extreme materialism and complete skepticism, that has ever existed; and even in the communist countries, one suspects that there are lurking idealists ready to come out in the open if official Marxist materialist metaphysics are ever relaxed. The currents of voluntarism, pragmatism, and psychologism we noted earlier (*see* Chapter 13) still flow, no doubt a bit diminished.

From such nineteenth-century sources as Nietzsche and the gravely disturbed and disturbing Danish theologian Kierkegaard (1813–1855), there has developed a philosophy known as existentialism. The existentialists can be described as somewhat harried Stoics who find this existing "reality" all there is, and pretty depressing, but are determined to face it as heroically as possible. They are sometimes divided into Christian existentialists, who retain a concept of God, and freethinking or atheistic existentialists. The central theme of existentialism has been stated by the French writer Sartre (1905–   ) as "existence precedes essence." This cryptic pronouncement seems to mean that human awareness of living, of being, of "existing," precedes in time, and is therefore somehow more important than, our thinking, or than our mental ticketing of "reality" by means of words, especially words denoting abstractions, such as most of the key terms of traditional philosophy. Clearly existentialism does at bottom belong in the current of anti-intellectualism of our time.

Yet the existentialists are by no means simple anti-intellectuals who want us to "think with our blood"—or with our hormones; they are sensitive artists and intellectuals who respect the instrument of thought and use it themselves. But they do not quite trust it, and they do not trust its chief representatives in our time, the scientists. Their noblest representative, though not formally one of the existentialist group, the French novelist and philosopher Albert Camus (1913–1960), is perhaps destined to be remembered as a classic of our age.

A generation ago, formal philosophical idealism seemed to be languishing everywhere, except for the Italian Croce and his followers. In recent years it has proved to have considerable vitality, perhaps basically in forms we may call neo-Kantian, as with the late German philosopher Ernst Cassirer (1874–1945), who spent his last years in the United States.

The most original, and in a sense most typical and vital, philosophic movement of our century bears clearly and paradoxically the stamp of the "revolt against reason." It looks to an outsider as if the movement called variously logical analysis, logical positivism, the linguistic philosophy, and, in one of its phases, symbolic logic, accepted most of the strictures the new psychology made on old-fashioned all-around rationalism and then went ahead to insist that, although only a tiny bit of human experience could be brought under rubrics of rational thought, that tiny bit was indeed to be protected and explored very carefully, minutely. This somewhat varied school can be considered as beginning early in the twentieth century in Vienna, the city of Freud. But such distinguished pioneers of the school as Ludwig Wittgenstein (1889–1951) and Rudolf Carnap (1891–   ) emigrated, the first to England, the second to the United States. Logical analysis could hardly flourish in Hitler's Germany or in Stalin's Russia. It is skeptical of too much to flourish in any but a very free and many-minded society.

The American physicist P. W. Bridgman put one of the school's basic positions clearly in various writings. Where, on the pattern of scientific practice, a problem can be answered by the performance of an "operation" and the answer validated by logical and empirical tests or by observations, knowledge can be achieved; where, however, as in such problems as whether democracy is the best form of government, whether a lie is ever justifiable, or whether a given poem is a good one or a bad one—in short, almost all the great questions of philosophy, art, literature, history—no such "operation" is possible, the problem is *for the logician* "meaningless."

Most of these logical positivists would admit that nonlogical or pseudological methods for getting at such moral, political, and aesthetic problems, though they cannot result in the kind of finally accepted answers the scientists expect to get, are none the less for normal human beings useful and indeed necessary. Some of the *popularizers* of this philosophy, however, pretty explicitly held that all mental activity save logical analysis and empirical verification is at best inferior mental activity, or, more likely, nonsense. A distinguished American popularizer, Stuart Chase, in his *Tyranny of Words* (1938) proposed to clarify our thinking by substituting "blah-blah" for terms that have no such good logical or "operational" clearance. Thus the famous French revolutionary slogan would come out simply as "Blah-blah, blah-blah, blah-blah," as would much of Jefferson's Preamble to our Declaration of Independence. Approaching their problems very differently from the way Freud and Pareto did, these logical analysts nevertheless came to a similar conclusion about the reasoning capacity of most human beings. Most human beings, they conclude, are at present incapable of thorough, persistent, successful logical thinking, and they cannot be taught to do this kind of thinking in any foreseeable future. Of course, just as there are radical Freudians who hold that if everybody could be psychoanalyzed all would be well, there are radical positivists, usually labelled "semanticists," who hold that semantics, the study of meaning, if available to everyone would cure all our troubles. The leading expert of this rather naïve semantic therapy was the Polish-American scientist Alfred Korzybski (1879–1950), author of *Science and Sanity* (1933). By a quite different approach, summed up in the phrase "the medium is the message," the Canadian Marshall McLuhan (1911–   ) came to the conclusion that if we all *really understood* communication and the mass media we should all get along together happily.

Once more we encounter the sharp tensions of modern intellectual life. Since these logical analysts seemed to set up the practices of science, as they understood them, as the sole right way of thinking, many of those devoted to the arts and the humanistic studies generally turned in revenge to the denunciation of science as a narrowing, dangerous use of the mind. Anti-scientism is as characteristic of our age as scientism.

Probably the most widespread philosophical movement of our century developed outside of, or on the margin of, formal professional philosophy. This movement may be called historicism, the attempt to find in history an answer to those ultimate questions of the structure of the universe and of man's fate the philosopher has always asked. At bottom, the transfer of Darwinian concepts of organic evolution from biology to this great, sweeping field of philosophical questions contains the essence of twentieth-century historicism. Once the traditional Judaeo-Christian concepts of a single creation in time, a God above nature, and the rest of the traditional world-view were abandoned, men in search of answers to their questions about these ultimates had to fall back on the historical record. Man is not made by God, but by nature, which amounts to saying that *man makes himself* in the course of history. We get our only clues as to man's capacities here on earth, clues as to how he ought to behave, clues as to that future that so concerns him, from the record of the past.

But "clues" is a modest and misleading word here. Many of the thinkers who appealed to history found much more than indications of what *might* be, much more than the always tentative, never dogmatic or absolute "theories" the scientist produces in answer to the less-than-ultimate questions he asks. Many of these philosophers of history, to simplify a bit, found in what they held to be the course of history a substitute for the concepts of God or Providence. They found in the record of the past substantially the equivalent of what Christians found in revelation—the explanation of man's nature and destiny, his *end* in the sense of a teleology or an eschatology. Paradoxically, they found in history something quite outside and beyond history, a substitute for a theology.

Of these historicisms, the most important and the most obviously a substitute for Christianity is of course Marxism. The theological parallels are plain, and have been frequently noted by non-Marxists: for God, absolute and omnipotent, the Marxist substitutes the absolutely determined course of Dialectical Materialism; for the Bible, he substitutes the canonical writings of Marx–Engels, with the addition, for the orthodox of the Soviet Union and its satellites, of those of Lenin; for the Church, the Communist party; for the Christian eschatology of divine judgment and heaven or hell, the revolution and the "classless society."

But Marxism, if the most rigorous, is only one of the historicisms of our time. The German Oswald Spengler (1880–1936), in his *Decline of the West,* just at the end of World War I produced a characteristic specimen. Spengler found from the historical record that societies or civilizations have, like human beings, an average life-span, a thousand years or so for a civilization being the equivalent of seventy years or so for the individual human being. He traced several non-Western civilizations, but in the West he found three main ones, a Hellenic from 1000 B.C. to about the birth of Christ, a Levantine or Middle Eastern from the birth of Christ to about A.D. 1000, and our own modern Western, which began (according to him) about A.D. 1000 and was, therefore, due to end about A.D. 2000. We cannot here analyze his work at length. Spengler had real insights, but his work as a whole, most historians would say, is simply not history—it is metaphysics, or if you like a coined word, meta-history. There are critics who explain Spengler simply; he saw Germany was about to be defeated, and he therefore consoled himself by believing Western civilization was about to end.

Better known nowadays than Spengler's is the work of the English historian Arnold Toynbee (1889–   ), whose many-volumed *Study of History* (1934–1954) has been neatly condensed by D. C. Somervell into two manageable volumes. Toynbee is worth studying as a symptom of the intellectual difficulties of historicism and of our age. He has an evangelical Christian background, a careful training in historical scholarship, and a strong family tradition of social service. World War I marked him with a great hatred for war, and a conviction that nationalism, which he once declared to be the real if unavowed religion of our Western society, is the villain of the piece. His great system is an attempt to trace the causes of the rise and fall of societies in the past, and it owes a good deal to Spengler. But Toynbee is a gentle English Christian humanist, not a German romantic racist brought up on what is no doubt a perversion of Nietzsche. He does, like the majority of contemporary philosophers of history, conclude that our Western society is facing a very serious challenge, that in terms of the cyclical rise and fall of societies he has traced it looks as if we were about to give ourselves the "knockout blow" in World War III. But he refuses to abandon hope. The facts of historical development may, he holds, indicate destruction for us; but we may transcend history, and under the influence of a revived, or new, or Buddhist-influenced Christianity of gentleness and love, pull ourselves out of the hole.

Historicism has, again quite characteristically in our culture, given rise to bitter protests and to its opposite. Almost all professional historians, in the West nowadays mostly conventionally democratic in their values, simply give these philosophers of history the cold shoulder. Independent existentialists like Camus (who did not consider himself an existentialist) are firm in their contention that, though we may not neglect history as a record of human experience, we must find in ourselves something—salvation, perhaps—quite beyond history. And as for the logical positivists, history is far too lacking in precise data to make it a subject worth their while.

III. Science and the Arts

SCIENCE AND TECHNOLOGY

No general history can deal substantively with the history of science and technology in the twentieth century. Each science, each branch of each science, has continued in this century its cumulative course. The cooperation (not without rivalry) among "pure" scientists, applied scientists, engineers, bankers, businessmen, and government officials has produced in all phases of human control over material things the kind of exponential increases that send the lines of our graphs quite off the paper. Man's attained rate of travel is no doubt an extreme example, one not achieved in the same startling degree, for instance, in such fields as those of medicine and genetics. But in 1820 the fastest rate was still 12 to 15 miles an hour; railroads made it 100 miles or so by 1880; piston-engined airplanes made it 300 miles or so by 1940; jet planes broke the sound barrier only yesterday in 1947, making speeds of close to 1,000 miles per hour possible; and by the 1960's rockets had propelled living men in space free of our atmosphere at speeds of thousands of miles an hour.

Each science is of course highly specialized, and the active scientist usually is supreme master of only part of a given science. Indeed, one of the great worries of our numerous contemporary worriers is well expressed in the old tag that has modern specialists knowing more and more about less and less. But the tag really is an old one—and, like most such tags, partly true and worth our attention, yet not quite borne out by any catastrophic break in our culture. For the fact is that at a broad, nonspecialist's level of understanding many educated men in the West have a very good idea of what modern science is trying to do, and how it does it.

The wider implications of modern science as its ways of work and its general concepts affect our world-views is a subject no general history can neglect. In the broadest sense, there can be no doubt that, though many practicing scientists are good Christians, scientific attitudes toward nature and natural laws, and scientific skepticism toward the supernatural, have added powerfully to the modern drive toward rationalism, positivism, materialism. Science continues to promote the world-view we have seen arising in early modern times, and culminating in the Enlightenment of the eighteenth century (*see* Chapter 9). Indeed, many scientists have managed to make the pursuit of scientific knowledge itself a kind of religion.

More particularly, the great event of the twentieth century has been the revolution in physics symbolized for the public in the figure of Albert Einstein (1879–1955). The concepts of relativity, a space–time continuum, and quantum mechanics freed physics from the "Newtonian world-machine" and helped the very great modern innovations in the field, innovations that worked together with the late nineteenth-century discoveries of the phenomena of radiation (X rays, the researches of the Curies, Roentgen, and others) to make possible our contemporary developments in fields like electronics. Einstein's theories on the equivalence of mass and mechanical energy, his concept of time as the fourth dimension, and the representation of gravitation as a field (compare "magnetic field") rather than a force secured wide public attention, if not always comprehension. From all this a few laymen came to the conclusion that since the apparently rigid world of mechanical causation of classic physics had broken down, since there was associated with the name of the distinguished German physicist Werner Heisenberg an "indeterminacy principle" familiar to practicing scientists, the common-sense law of cause-and-effect had in fact been repealed, and the universe was once more a fine free space in which anything could happen. This of course is not true, and the work of Newton has not been so much contradicted by modern physics as supplemented. Heisenberg's principle resulted from close work on the particle called an electron. An *individual* electron observably can jump from one orbit to another without evident and predictable sequence. Yet *statistically* the behavior of many, many electrons together is predictable, as predictable as it was in Newton's day. It is possible that misunderstood doctrines of "relativity" in physics, misapplied to ethics and aesthetics, did have a part in the fashionable doctrines of moral and aesthetic relativism of only yesterday.

The development of astronomy has been largely influenced by that of physics. To the layman, such modern astronomical concepts as that of a finite but expanding universe, of curved space, and perhaps above all the almost inconceivable distances and quantities, light years, galaxies, and the like, have made astronomy the most romantic of sciences. And these distances and quantities *are* almost inconceivable. A light year is the distance traversed by light in one year, or roughly 5,880,000,000,000 miles; our own Milky Way galaxy has some thirty thousand million stars and nebulae, in the form of a disk with a diameter of about 100,000 light years. Recent developments in rocketry have made our moon seem attainable by actual human flight instead of merely by flight of the science-fiction imagination. Chemistry, on the other hand, in spite of the marvels of synthesis it produces, has less attraction for the imagination. Yet in our daily living it is surely the science of chemistry that touches us most closely, in our foods, our medicines, our clothing, almost all the material objects we use.

Chemistry has also aided the very great gains that have been made in the twentieth century in the biological sciences and in their applications to medicine and public health as well. Not only in the United States and the rest of the West, but all over the world, infant mortality, many contagious diseases, even undernourishment, have been so far conquered that the average expectancy of life at birth has gone up as much as twenty years in advanced nations since 1900. In the economically backward areas of the globe, more children are born and more live, so that the population problem has become acute, and is still unsolved. Yet even in this matter of food supply, successful experimentation with high-yielding hybrid corn and Mexican wheat, the development of fertilizers, the use of irrigation, the possibilities of food from the sea opened up by marine biology and other scientific advances promise some considerable alleviation in a foreseeable future. It is significant, however, that the actual extreme limits of the human life span have not yet been significantly affected. It does not seem that an extreme limit of something like 110 to 120 years for human life, historically known to have prevailed for centuries, has yet been exceeded. Tales of Turks, Russians, and others attaining 160 years or so have not been substantiated.

There remains one more major problem which the progress of twentieth-century science has sharpened, a problem closely related to that of specialization in science and learning. There is in some senses a widening gap today between those who pursue what we call "humanistic" studies and those who pursue scientific studies. It is by no means difficult philosophically to reconcile these two pursuits; the poet and the physicist have, as creative human beings, more in common than we others usually can see. But the fact remains that from the point of view of the sociologist the two groups in our cultural life do clash, the scientists finding the humanists fuzzy-minded, sloppy intellectually, and clearly inferior, the humanists finding the scientists limited, pedestrian, cold, inhuman, and quite unable to manage the Frankenstein monster of modern technology they have created. Fortunately, there are good men who are at work mediating between these two sides, men who incline to the belief that the opposition is by no means one rooted in the facts of life and human nature, but merely in present cultural fashion.

In sum, the very great achievements of modern science and technology have raised many problems for our Western democracy: the overriding problem presented by the fact that hydrogen bombs, missiles, and biological warfare have made the destruction of the human race no mere bit of rhetoric, nor a theological doctrine like that of Judgment Day, but a possible situation confronting even common sense; the problem of humanizing science; the problem of overpopulation; the problems of educating scientists and endowing scientific research; and many other problems. Yet the fact remains that science and technology seem to be the deciding factors that have raised the masses in some parts of the world far enough beyond misery and near-starvation to make possible what we Americans call democracy. And perhaps even more important, the continuing very great vitality of Western civilization—a vitality as real in the arts as in the sciences—is at its clearest in the magnificent achievements of modern science. Modern science rightly worries the worriers, but it should also console them, for it shows man still in a light reflected long ago by the Greek Sophocles:

> What a thing is man! Among all wonders
> The wonder of the world is man himself
> . . .
>
> Man the Contriver! Man the Master-mind.*

THE ARTS

In the field of imaginative literature, music, painting, the fine arts, and the arts generally, we invent new styles and attitudes yet by no means wholly destroy what the past has left us. Here, as for all our culture, the contemporary historian has to note the great variety of tastes and standards that have piled up. But he must also note the existence of the wide and deep gap between the art—in the broad sense of "art" to include letters, music, architecture—of the few, or "highbrow" art, and the art of the many, or popular art. Bridges between the two there are, usually built on highbrow initiative from the highbrow side toward the lowbrow side. A good example is the fashion among the cultivated few for some phases, at least, of American popular music, or jazz. For many French intellectuals, as difficult, as refined, as remote from the masses as any intellectuals have ever been, "le jazz hot" is the only cultural achievement of the United States. Every now and then, if only briefly, some contributor to that most popular form of popular art, the American comic strip, gains a following among the highbrows or at least among undergraduates.

Literature. Once more, imaginative writing in the twentieth century makes no striking break with that of the late nineteenth. Poetry and literary criticism remain, as they had begun to be in the 1890's or even earlier (*see* Chapter 13), difficult, cerebral, and addressed to a very small, if fit, audience. An occasional poet like the American Robert Frost breaks from the privacy of the little magazines and the limited editions to wide popularity and a place enshrined in old-fashioned anthologies—and even to participation in a presidential inauguration. But Frost is no more esoteric in form or substance than Wordsworth. More remarkable and more symptomatic, there are signs that T. S. Eliot, born in St. Louis but as an adult wholly Anglicized, an abstruse and allusive poet, an intellectual of intellectuals, is also attaining a wider audience, is on the way to becoming classic, perhaps already there.

The novel remains the most important form of contemporary imaginative

---

* *Antigone,* John Jay Chapman, translation (Boston, 1930), ll. 332–333, 340.

writing. Critics have long bemoaned its exhaustion as an art-form, and the French have even invented what they call the "anti-novel," but the novel does not die. It is quite impossible here for us to give even a thumbnail sketch of the contemporary novel. It is not even wise of us to attempt to indicate writers likely to be read in the twenty-first century. It may be that a middlebrow novelist like the American J. P. Marquand (1893–1960), disliked by the pure highbrow because he wrote best sellers, will survive better than such a favorite of the pure as William Faulkner (1897–1962), who wrote existentialist novels about darkest Mississippi. The late Thomas Mann (1875–1945) seems already enshrined as a classic; but Mann, who began with a traditionally realistic novel of life in his birthplace, the old Hanseatic town of Lübeck, never really belonged to the avant garde. He is typical of the artist in the age of psychology—sensitive, worrying, and class-conscious, his class being no mere Marxian group but that of the artist-intellectual.

More useful for us here, since it illustrates one of the problems of all contemporary art, is the career of the Irishman James Joyce (1882–1941). Joyce began with a subtle, outspoken, but formally conventional series of sketches of life in the Dublin of his youth, *Dubliners* (1914), and the novelist's inevitable, and with Joyce undisguised, autobiography, *Portrait of the Artist as a Young Man* (1916). Then, mostly in exile on the Continent, he wrote what at the moment looks like a classic, the experimental novel *Ulysses* (1922). This novel is an account, rather than a narrative, of twenty-four hours in the life of Leopold Bloom, a Dublin Jew. It is full of difficult allusions, parallels with the *Odyssey* of Homer, puns, rapidly shifting scenes and episodes, and is written without regard for the conventional notions of plot and orderly development. Above all, it makes full use of the then recently developed psychologies of the unconscious as displayed in an individual's "stream of consciousness." The last chapter, printed entirely without punctuation marks, is the record of what went on in the mind of Bloom's Irish wife as she lay in bed waiting for him to come home. What went on in her mind was in large part too shocking for the early century, and *Ulysses*, published in Paris, long had to be smuggled into English-speaking countries. It is now freely available everywhere.

James Joyce.

Joyce's last big work, long known as simply "Work in Progress" but finally published as *Finnegans Wake* (1939), is one of those works of radical experimentation about which, like many modern paintings, the ordinary educated layman simply has to say that it means nothing, or very little, to him. The continuities and conventions of narration and "plain English," not wholly flouted in *Ulysses*, are here quite abandoned. There are words, and even sentences; but *meaning* has to be quarried out by the reader and may when quarried turn out to be quite different from what Joyce intended. But there are keys to *Finnegans Wake*—we cite one in our reading list for this chapter—and the reader who wants to try to get at this interesting experiment in modern art can get his start there. Here is the ending of *Finnegans Wake:*

. . . A gull. Gulls. Far calls. Coming, far! End here. Us then. Finn, again!
Take. Bussoftlhee, mememormee! Till thousendsthee. Lps. The keys to.
Given! A way a lone a last a loved a long the*

Such writing may well be a blind alley, but the traditions of Western invention—
we use that word in a very broad sense—insist that it may not be declared a blind
alley until it has been well explored.

The Fine Arts. It is, however, the fine arts—painting perhaps in first rank,
but with sculpture, architecture, and the minor decorative arts all included—
that confront the ordinary cultivated Westerner with the problem of "modernism"
in its most clear form. The process of getting beyond the camera eye and Renaissance ideas of perspective—in general, "realism"—which we began to trace in
Chapter 13 has gone on right to this day. Indeed, painting done today can be
almost—not quite—sharply divided into two groups: that done traditionally, academically, representational painting of the kind that surprises and puzzles no one
though it still pleases many; and the many kinds of experimental or nonrepresentational, or simply "modern," painting. The variety of these experiments is great
indeed. Most of them have been made by the great figure of contemporary painting, Pablo Picasso (1880–   ).

A native Spaniard, and an adopted Frenchman, Picasso has in his long life
painted in many "styles" or "periods." The paintings of his "blue period," for instance, executed in the first years of our century, exemplify expressionism, the
attempt to express in art such highly subjective emotional states as grief and
despair. These pictures are said to have been influenced by the work of El Greco,
the sixteenth-century master (*see* Chapter 7). Certainly, both artists convey a sense
of concentrated emotion by exaggerating human proportions. Around 1905,
Picasso, stimulated in part by primitive art, turned to more daring innovations,
striving, as Cézanne had striven earlier (*see* Chapter 13), to transfer to the two
dimensions of a picture the three dimensions of the
real world by other than Renaissance methods of
chiaroscuro and the like—their dimensions *in motion*,
so to speak. Sometimes he used the techniques of
abstractionism, the reduction of figures to a kind of
plane geometry, all angles and lines. Sometimes he
used those of cubism, the reduction of figures to a kind
of solid geometry, all cubes, spheres, and cones. Sometimes he even glued onto a picture bits of real objects
—paper or the caning from a chair—in the process
called *collage* ("paste-up"). Later, in his "white period" after World War I, he did many portraits that
were strongly classical in feeling. Yet he has also continued radical experimentation not only on canvas
but also in sculpture, in ceramics, and in "constructions" of wood and other materials that might be
called the sculptor's counterpart of collage. Most disturbing to the ordinary viewer, perhaps, are Picasso's
recurrent efforts, stemming from cubism, to show the
human figure from two or more angles simultaneously

Picasso, "Les Demoiselles d'Avignon."

* (New York, 1959), p. 628.

—whence the apparently misplaced eyes and the anatomical distortions and rearrangements in many of his pictures.

Most remote from this world of sense-experience as organized by common sense and conventional representational painting is the work of various kinds of abstract painters, paintings which are sometimes elaborate patterns of lines and colors, sometimes geometrical, sometimes apparently mere random daubs. It all means something, if only to the painter; but that meaning cannot be seized by the uninitiated.

The conservative worried by modern art can perhaps take some comfort in the fact that the most extreme manifestation of this art is now nearly fifty years past, and has never been quite equalled in its extraordinary defiance of all conventions, all rules, all forms. This extreme manifestation, perhaps more important sociologically than artistically, was the protest made by a very alienated group of intellectuals, the Dadaists, the "angry young men" of World War I and its aftermath. They reacted against a world so much sillier than their Dada that it could slaughter millions in warfare. Here are some characteristic passages from an account of Dada written by a sympathetic observer:

> In the first New York Independents' exhibition, 1917, he [Marcel Duchamp] entered a porcelain urinal with the title *Fontaine* and signed it R. Mutt to test the impartiality of the executive committee of which he himself was a member. By this symbol Duchamp wished to signify his disgust for art and his admiration for ready-made objects. [A Freudian, we feel sure, would find other motives in the choice of a urinal among the vast number of possible ready-made objects.]
>
> . . .
>
> At an exhibition in Paris among the most remarkable entries sent by the poets was a mirror of Soupault's entitled *Portrait of an unknown.* . . . Certain paintings by Duchamp supposed to be in this exhibition were replaced by sheets of paper marked with numbers which corresponded to the Duchamp entries in the catalog. Duchamp, who had been asked to take part in the exhibition, had just cabled from New York: "Nuts."*

It is perfectly possible that in the long run of history the directions taken in the contemporary fine arts by those we now think of as leaders, pioneers, will prove stale and unprofitable. But no one who has not made an effort to understand these arts is justified in condemning them out of hand. And one hostile position the disgruntled conservatives in these fields often take seems quite untenable: this is the labelling of such modern art as "pedantic," "decadent," as a sign of exhaustion, death, lack of creative power. Quite the contrary, this art is alive, inventive, dynamic, an attempt to extend the confines of human experience, an attempt quite as remarkable, though in its results not so readily assessed, as that of modern science and technology. The historian must note that the extreme traditionalists, doing exactly what their forefathers have done, are much more vulnerable to the accusation that their work is a sign of exhaustion and decay.

This remark holds even more strikingly true in architecture. The twentieth century has seen the growth of the first truly original style in architecture since the end of the eighteenth century. "Modern" or "functional" architecture is no revival of a past style, no pastiche of elements of such past styles, no living

---

* Georges Huguet in *Fantastic Art, Dada, Surrealism,* A. H. Barr, Jr., ed. (New York, 1936), pp. 19, 33.

museum of eclectic choice, like most of nineteenth-century architecture. It prides itself on its honest use of modern materials, its adaptation to modern living, its fondness for sunlight, its dislike of waste space and over-display. There is in modern architecture a certain touch of austerity, even puritanism, that should confound those who think that our age is sunk in lush sensuality. In the long run, this architecture will probably seem to have gone rather too far in shunning ornamentation, especially external ornamentation. There are already signs that architects are beginning to tire of vast expanses of plain glass and steel.

Music. "Modern" music, unlike "modern" painting or architecture, has never quite crystallized into a distinctive style. The twentieth century has produced a great many attempts to get beyond classical music and its rules of harmony—by using scales other than the conventional one, by stressing dissonance and discord, by borrowing the insistent rhythms of popular jazz, and, in extreme forms, by abolishing any formal notation and allowing the performer to bang away at will, even on pipes or tin pans. A generation ago, as we have noted, the general public came to identify musical innovation with Stravinsky (*see* Chapter 13). But Stravinsky, unlike the painter Picasso, did not continue to lead the modernists, indeed reverted for a time to eighteenth-century tastes. Many other less well known composers, among them many Americans, have however continued to push the boundaries of music further and further away from Bach's *Well-tempered Clavier*.

The arch in design: Gateway Arch in St. Louis.

The Tastes of the Many and the Tastes of the Few. In sum, almost all contemporary high art is complex and difficult, and as of this moment far from being "understood of the people." The very evident gulf between the tastes of the many and the tastes of the few may be an indication of a dangerous side of our democratic society. Certainly this is a subject on which no one is justified in taking an attitude of "holier than thou." But here the complete prevalence of the popular side, the elimination of the art of the few, seems most unlikely. For it would seem that contrasting sets of standards and tastes, and the consequent great variety of works of art of all kinds, are one of the marks of our democratic society.

It is a fact that the two great attempts to put across a really totalitarian society in this century, that of Stalin in Russia and that of Hitler in Germany, were marked by very successful efforts to suppress highbrow culture, especially in art and in philosophy. Science, and most certainly applied science and technology, as we now know, flourished in Nazi Germany, and continues to flourish in a Russia which banned Boris Pasternak's novel *Dr. Zhivago* and in 1966 sent two other writers, Andrei Sinyavsky and Yuli Daniel, to prison for "literary treason" (*see* Chapter 16). Russia was in most ways the most extreme example. This great socioeconomic experiment banned experiment in the arts and in the whole range of humanistic culture, at least after the accession of Stalin to power. Soviet architecture was even more atrociously monumental than the worst of nineteenth-century commercial architecture. Until Pasternak's novel, sent out of Russia in manuscript for translation into Italian under communist patronage, came in 1958 to widespread attention, no piece of Soviet writing really struck the imagination of the West. This failure cannot justly be laid to Western censorship or banning; it is simply that the crude propaganda literature of Communist Russia did not greatly interest even fellow-travelling Western highbrows. Things got worse under Stalin, when such promising beginnings as Soviet movies—those of Eisenstein, for instance—and the more daring music of Russian composers like Shostakovich came under what one has to call censorship by bourgeois taste. For it is quite clear from the Russian experience that when the proletariat gets power, it wants, and in the arts at least gets, about what the conventional bourgeois of an earlier generation thought desirable and lovely. The Nazis, too, were all against any of the kinds of art and literature we have discussed in this chapter, all in favor of popular art in the taste of a century ago.

Pop art: Marilyn Monroe, by Andy Warhol.

IV. Conclusion: The Democratic Dream

THE HERITAGE OF THE ENLIGHTENMENT

As we have pointed out (*see* Chapters 9 and 13), there arose among Western peoples in the early modern centuries, and there came to full bloom in the eighteenth and nineteenth centuries, a view of man's fate here on earth which was essentially new. This is the view that all men may rightly expect to be happy here on earth. As St. Just, the youthful colleague of Robespierre in the French Revolution, put it, "Happiness is a new idea in Europe"; or as Jefferson, with his gift for phrasing, put it, one of the unalienable rights of man is the "pursuit of happiness." Of course men have presumably always sought happiness here on earth. In historic Christianity, however, the masses did not, could not really expect much happiness, much improvement in their lot here on earth, but, if at all, only in an afterlife; indeed, Christianity had an overtone of belief that happiness in heaven was in part at least a reward for suffering here on earth.

The *philosophes*, the eighteenth-century thinkers who set the broad terms of this modern optimistic world-view, meant by happiness a condition or state in which each man had at any given moment what he wanted, a state in which each man—each woman, and, incredibly, even each baby—was not aware of being thwarted, frustrated. To the inner state of this happiness there would conform an outer state of material plenty in which everyone would have what he wanted to eat, would be well housed, would have a satisfactory sex life, and would of course enjoy good health, both mental and physical. The matter may indeed be put in terms of modern psychology. Man can rightfully expect in this world, certainly before very long, a society in which everyone would have a life of perfect *adjustment,* a life without conflict, aggression, insecurity.

Broadly speaking, the *philosophes* held that such perfect happiness had not yet been attained on earth—an obvious fact—because there had grown up a whole set of institutions, habits, and beliefs that had brought evil into human life. Men in 1750, the *philosophes* believed, were not following the natural laws that would make them happy, but the unnatural laws that made them unhappy. The formulators of the new idea of happiness believed that the unhappy state of the world could be traced to a combination of the privileges unnaturally acquired over the centuries by the few rich and powerful (the leaders in church and state), together with the unnatural ignorance and prejudices these few had imposed on the many. They therefore concluded that the solution lay first in depriving the few of their unnatural privileges and, second, in disclosing to the many by a natural system of education and government the keys to their own happiness. In short, they believed that men are *by nature* potentially good not evil, reasonable not foolish, intelligent not stupid, certainly improvable. Though it is perhaps unfair to say that they believed in the "natural goodness of man" (the antithesis of the Christian doctrine of original sin), at a very minimum most of the philosophers held that men as they are now, but under the rule of "cultural engineers," "engineers of the soul," instead of under their present rulers, could all be happy, certainly again at a minimum, much, much happier. Something close to utopia was to them just around the corner.

OPTIMISTS AND PESSIMISTS

This, then, though put oversimply and neglecting much in eighteenth-century thought that conflicts with these generalizations, is the essence of what may be called the democratic dream of the eighteenth-century *philosophes*, the dream of a heavenly city here on earth. But two hundred years later the dream has not come true. Some men still persist in it, holding that we have not yet conquered the privileged classes, not yet opened men's minds, not yet really tried full democracy or not yet allowed free play to the kindly cultural engineers. We must insist: many are now alive who think and feel about man's destiny in essentially eighteenth-century ways. Marxism, for example, in its simplest outline, is the eighteenth-century formula all over again: the bad institutional environment under which men cannot help being miserable is capitalism; the good institutional environment under which men cannot help being happy is socialism; the utopia, the heaven on this earth, is the "classless society." In fact, it seems that Stalin invented that phrase "engineer of the soul." It is, however, quite unfair to limit these believers in what is essentially eighteenth-century rationalist empiricism to the Marxists. There are many respected and influential Americans—and a few such Europeans—who preserve intact an optimistic belief in the potential rationality of man and in the possibilities of rapid Progress toward the attainment of universal peace and happiness for all. They may concede that some men are irrational, but they hold that *man* is rational.

This optimism has certainly been shaken among the intellectual classes in most of the West, and among young intellectuals, apparently, even in Communist Russia. In the twentieth century two world wars, a great depression, and the failure to achieve peace after the end of the Second World War have made it difficult for most of us to share even the degree of optimism about the possibilities of attaining a vastly better society that still inspired most Victorian intellectuals. Much of serious writing these days has a tone of pessimism, mildly seasoned with the shrug-it-off, laugh-that-we-may-not weep, not very profound cynicism that is a mark of our urban democratic culture. And it surely is also a mark of our age that its most highbrow culture is to an extraordinary degree pessimistic about the present state of man, gloomy and fearsome about the future, though by no means in agreement either on diagnosis of what is wrong with our culture or in prognosis of its development. Here is a dignified and eloquent sample from the late Albert Camus's speech of acceptance of his Nobel Prize in 1958:

> . . . As the heir of a corrupt history that blends blighted revolutions, misguided techniques, dead gods, and worn out ideologies, in which second-rate powers can destroy everything today, but are unable to win anyone over; in which intelligence has stooped to becoming the servant of hatred and oppression, that generation [Camus's own], starting from nothing but its own negations, has had to re-establish both within and without itself a little of what constitutes the dignity of life and death. Faced with a world threatened with disintegration, in which our grand inquisitors may set up once and for all the kingdoms of death, that generation knows that, in a sort of mad race against time, it ought to re-establish among nations a peace not based on slavery, to reconcile labor and culture again, and to reconstruct with all men an Ark of the Covenant. Perhaps it can never accomplish that vast undertaking, but most certainly throughout the world it has already accepted the double challenge of truth and liberty, and, on occasion, has shown that it can lay down its life without hatred. That generation deserves to be acclaimed wherever it happens to be, and especially wherever it is sacrificing itself.*

---

* Reprinted with the permission of Alfred A. Knopf, Inc., from Albert Camus's Speech of Acceptance upon the award of the Nobel Prize for Literature, December 10th, 1957, translated by Justin O'Brien. Copyright © 1958 by Alfred A. Knopf, Inc.

This is not, of course, sheer pessimism, but it is a kind of unhappy faith, a Stoic determination to fight against the way things are.

Let us note that, although from Plato, even from Akhenaten on, our serious literary and artistic culture has always shown a strain of pessimism, our own intellectual leaders are, first, more than usually apprehensive and censorious and, second, more than usually aware of the gulf between their way of living, their standards of value, and those of their fellow citizens. Just one sample—here in a recent work is a well-known American writer complaining that most Americans confuse "normal" with "average," and suggesting that we need a genuine synonym for "average":

> Fortunately, such a genuine and familiar synonym does exist. That which is "average" is also properly described as "mediocre." And if we were accustomed to call the average man, not "the common man" or still less "the normal man," but "the mediocre man" we should not be so easily hypnotized into believing that mediocrity is an ideal to be aimed at.*

This passage is hardly fair to American democratic beliefs; we Americans do not aim at mediocrity as an ideal, but on the contrary admire greatly the record-breaker, the outstanding personality. But, unlike Mr. Krutch, most of us are not indignant over the failure of everybody to measure up to highbrow standards and we do not think "common" a synonym of "mediocre."

Now the historian, in attempting by comparative study of similar phenomena in different times and places to arrive at workable generalizations, has great difficulty with this problem of what is the "normal" or "usual" relation between intellectual classes—the writers, artists, scholars, teachers, preachers, and their followers—and other classes, even within our Western culture. Such study simply isn't well enough developed to permit measurement, graphs, quantitative generalization. Qualitatively, we may risk the assertion that the gravity and extent of the gap between the way American intellectuals, and to a degree Western intellectuals generally, think and feel and the way the rest of Western society thinks and feels—the phenomenon we may call in shorthand "the alienation of the intellectuals" —may well be a grave symptom of weakness in our society.

Yet the degree of alienation of the intellectuals is hard to measure, and we may have exaggerated it in the paragraph above. American intellectuals complain bitterly about the impossibility of the good life in the machine age, but they for the most part use the machines with apparent satisfaction. They find fault with our business civilization, but a great many of them do a very good business in it, and the rank-and-file are not in terms of income as badly off as they think they are. They often regard themselves as a scorned and victimized minority in a hostile society of Babbitts, but a distinguished American sociologist has recently argued that they are in fact well regarded:

"Current," by Bridget Riley: an example of op art, in which the lines are drawn to create the optical illusion of movement.

* J. W. Krutch, *Human Nature and the Human Condition* (New York, 1959), p. 93.

While he [the American intellectual] may feel himself neglected and scorned, his work poorly valued by the community, the community places him fairly high when polled on the relative status of occupations. In one such study of the ranks of ninety-six occupations, conducted in 1947 by the National Opinion Research Center of the University of Chicago, college professors ranked above every non-political position except that of physician; artists, musicians in a symphony orchestra, and authors ranked almost as high. . . . [In another poll in 1950] professors came out fourth among twenty-four categories, and thirty-eight per cent of those polled placed them definitely in the "upper class."*

At any rate, it is clear that the great majority of Americans, and even the great majority of Europeans, are not as cosmically worried, not as pessimistic about man's fate, as are the intellectuals. Indeed, it seems likely that the many, the common people, in Western society still adhere basically to the eighteenth-century belief in progress, moral as well as material. A recent candidate for the American presidency could say in a campaign speech, which by its very nature must be what hearers want to hear, "It is an article of the democratic faith that progress is a basic law of life."† In fact, one of the reproaches the intellectuals make to the many in the West is that the many appear on the whole quite contented with their material prosperity, their gadgets, their amusements, their American-style "classless society," a society where one man can be said to be as good as another, where almost all have a high level of consumption, but where there are real poverty, inequalities, "status seekers," failures, tragedies, not the utopian, theoretical Marxist heaven of an unrealized "classless society"—and certainly no heaven on earth.

Untitled stabile-mobile of painted aluminum, by Alexander Calder.

REPUDIATION OR REVISION OF THE ENLIGHTENMENT

Yet the pessimism of the intellectuals is understandable. The almost-utopia which many of the thinkers of the Enlightenment believed was just around the corner in the eighteenth century is not here yet. Let us, in conclusion, briefly review that eighteenth-century basis of our Western democratic faith, and see what our intellectual guides are making of that faith now, two hundred years later. We may distinguish three broad classifications of the reactions and adjustments made in our present culture to the ideas and ideals of the Enlightenment.

First, there is the reaction of complete repudiation of all the Enlightenment stood for. This reaction takes many forms. One of them, limited largely to some emotional intellectuals, is the sense of doom we have just discussed, the feeling that in trying to make this earth a heaven man has in fact made it a hell. More commonly, this reaction takes the form of

* S. M. Lipset, *Political Man* (New York, 1960).
† Adlai Stevenson, quoted in C. A. Chambers, "Belief in Progress in Twentieth Century America," *Journal of the History of Ideas* (April, 1958), p. 221.

denying all the premises of democracy. It is maintained that most men are wicked or stupid or foolish, or at any rate not up to the burden a democratic society sets on them, that they need to be ruled by their betters, who are always few in number, and that therefore we must return to divine-right monarchy or to the feudal-clerical aristocracy of the Middle Ages, or follow the "new conservatism," or devise some new authoritarianism of the Right or Left. Such views are not commonly held, or at any rate not commonly expressed in the United States. Not even our extreme Rightists quite repudiate the *language* of Jefferson, however much at bottom they really disagree with his democratic ideals.

Second, there is the Christian view that men must return to the basic Christian concept of an unavoidable mixture of good and evil in humanity. In this view, life on earth must always demonstrate the conflict between the divine and the animal in man, a conflict tragic and profound, not mean, vile, and hopeless as the mere pessimist sees it, and, above all, not for the individual a ceaseless "existentialist" conflict, but a conflict that has an end in heaven or hell, and that takes place in a universe dominated by *purpose,* not by *accident* or the *merely natural.* For some of these Christians, the desirable earthly society is indeed rather an aristocracy than a democracy. But many of them, like the American theologian and moralist Reinhold Niebuhr, may be described as moderate democrats. Though they believe that the democratic dream in its radical eighteenth-century form is impious and unrealistic, they none the less hold that a balanced democratic society is the best way of attaining justice on earth, that such a society is the best, or least bad, earthly reflection of man's dual nature.

Third, there are those who accept the aims of the *philosophes* and even in part the eighteenth-century estimate of human nature. But they find that the Enlightenment of the eighteenth century went wrong in its time-sense, wrong in its hope that its claims could be readily attained in a generation or two. These thinkers are essentially chastened children of the Enlightenment. They share the view—or at least the hope—that men are made to be happy, but are convinced by the events of the last two generations that wickedness and unreason are not, as the *philosophes* believed, rooted shallowly in a few bad institutions. On the contrary, they believe that evil, prejudice, and stupidity are deeply rooted in very complex institutions, in tradition, and perhaps even in man as a biological organism. Under Freudian and other influences, they come close to accepting evil as *natural,* though always to be combatted.

These thinkers have been greatly influenced by the emphasis that modern psychology has put on the irrational character of the human personality, on the subconscious and the unconscious, and on the consequent difficulty of the actual task of "enlightenment." They now think the task of making the world better will be long and difficult. But it is a task they believe can and must be continued. And they differ basically from the Christians in that they refuse to accept the Christian tension between this world and the next one, or any other one. They do not subscribe necessarily to naïve scientific "reductionism" which holds that all productive thinking will end up by accepting simple scientific materialism—or in the popular language of the cliché, that "it's all physics and chemistry." But they do hold that man is a product of nature, that the supernatural does not exist, and that individual self-conscious immortality is impossible.

The important thing for us to note at the end of this long historic record is that between the second and the third groups we have been discussing, between the Christians and the chastened children of the Enlightenment, a practical accord is possible, and necessary. It is indeed being worked out in the West. In this accord lies the possibility that the men of the first group, the enemies of democracy, may be defeated, and that democracy may live on to give the lie to the prophets of doom. In such an accord we may preserve the willingness to put up with restraints, with imperfections, with frustration, and with suffering without losing the hope, the dream, that is still alive for us in "liberty, equality, fraternity," in "life, liberty, and the pursuit of happiness," in the "principles of 1776 and 1789." Perhaps, above all, those of us called to intellectual pursuits can relearn the great Christian lesson of humility, can cease in our pride to berate our fellow men as mediocre men. We may thus avoid the illusions and retain the ideals of our historic heritage.

17

READING SUGGESTIONS (asterisk indicates paperbound edition)

Psychology

J. Rickman, ed., *A General Selection from the Works of Sigmund Freud* (*Anchor). A well-chosen anthology.

E. Jones, *The Life and Work of Freud*, 3 vols. (Basic Books, 1953–1957). Detailed study by a great admirer; available also in an abridged version (*Anchor).

R. L. Schoenwald, *Freud: The Man and His Culture* (Knopf, 1956), and P. Rieff, *Freud: The Mind of the Moralist* (*Anchor). Two good studies stressing Freud's place in contemporary culture.

B. F. Skinner, *Science and Human Behavior* (*Free Press). A clear and extreme statement of behavioristic psychology.

Sociopolitical Thought

H. S. Hughes, *Consciousness and Society* (*Vintage). Excellent study treating not only social thought but also other facets of intellectual history, 1870–1930.

V. Pareto, *The Mind and Society*, 4 vols. (Harcourt, 1935). A major work in general sociology. Also available are briefer *Selections* from Pareto's writings (*Crowell).

T. Parsons, *The Structure of Social Action*, 2nd ed. (Free Press, 1949). A landmark in American sociological thinking.

G. Wallas, *Human Nature in Politics* (Constable, 1908) and *The Great Society* (*Bison). Pioneering studies of the psychology of politics.

W. Lippmann, *A Preface to Politics* (*Ann Arbor). Another pioneering study.

J. K. Galbraith, *The Affluent Society* (*Mentor). Lively assessment of recent society by an economist.

Philosophy

M. G. White, ed., *The Age of Analysis: Twentieth-Century Philosophers* (*Mentor). Excerpts and comments, very well chosen.

A. Naess, *Modern Philosophers* (University of Chicago, 1968). Carnap, Wittgenstein, and Sartre are among those discussed.

R. Harper, *Existentialism: A Theory of Man* (Harvard, 1949). A sympathetic introduction.

W. Kaufmann, ed., *Existentialism from Dostoevsky to Sartre* (*Meridian). Instructive selections from existentialist writings, with helpful editorial comments.

A. Camus, *The Stranger* (*Vintage) and *The Plague* (*Modern Library). Moderately existentialist novels by a gifted writer.

E. Cassirer, *An Essay on Man* (*Yale). By a modern idealist philosopher.

P. W. Bridgman, *The Way Things Are* (*Compass). Moderate positivism expressed by a leading physicist.

A. Korzybski, *Science and Society*, 3rd

ed. (Non-Aristotelian Library, 1948). The name of the publisher is indicative of the tone of this work on "general semantics" and "human engineering."

M. McLuhan, *Understanding Media* (*Signet). Controversial appraisal of the significance of communications.

O. Spengler, *The Decline of the West* (Knopf, 1932). By a prophet of doom.

A. J. Toynbee, *A Study of History*, 12 vols. (*Galaxy). This classic of historicism is also available in a faithful abridgement by D. C. Somervell, 2 vols. (*Laurel).

M. F. Ashley-Montagu, *Toynbee and History* (Porter Sargeant, 1956), and I. Berlin, *Historical Inevitability* (Oxford, 1954). Criticisms of Toynbee in particular and historicism in general, respectively.

Science and Technology

I. Asimov, *The Intelligent Man's Guide to the Physical Sciences* and *The Intelligent Man's Guide to the Biological Sciences* (*Pocket). Informative surveys by a prolific popularizer of often difficult material.

C. T. Chase, *The Evolution of Modern Physics* (Van Nostrand, 1947), and L. Barnett, *The Universe and Dr. Einstein*, rev. ed. (*Bantam). Helpful popular accounts of key developments in twentieth-century science.

G. Gamow, *Mister Tompkins in Paperback* (*Cambridge). "Mr. Tompkins" explores the atom and other areas in a scientific wonderland; by an accomplished scientific popularizer.

Literature and the Arts

C. Mauriac, *The New Literature* (Braziller, 1959). Essays translated from the French, and treating mainly French writers.

E. Wilson, *Axel's Castle* (*Scribner's). A study in imaginative literature from 1870 to 1930, extending down to Joyce and Gertrude Stein.

H. Slochower, *Literature and Philosophy between Two World Wars* (*Citadel). Originally called *No Voice Is Wholly Lost;* an informative study of the relations between intellectual and literary history.

F. J. Hoffman, *Freudianism and the Literary Mind*, 2nd ed. (Louisiana State University, 1957). A suggestive exploration.

J. Campbell and H. M. Robinson, *A Skeleton Key to Finnegans Wake* (*Compass), and W. P. Jones, *James Joyce and the Common Reader* (Oklahoma, 1955). Two guides to a baffling writer.

L. Mumford, et al., *The Arts in Renewal* (University of Pennsylvania, 1951), and B. Richman, *The Arts at Mid-Century* (Horizon, 1954). Two wide-ranging collections of essays.

A. H. Barr, Jr., *What Is Modern Painting?* rev. ed. (*New York Graphic Society). Good short introduction.

J. Canaday, *Embattled Critic* (*Noonday). Modern art viewed by the knowledgeable critic of *The New York Times*.

G. Stein, *Picasso* (*Beacon); W. S. Lieberman, ed., *Picasso* (*Abrams); D. D. Duncan, *Picasso's Picassos* (*Ballantine). Three of the many available introductions to the ranking modern master.

M. Compton, *Optical and Kinetic Art* (*Arno), and L. Lippard, *Pop Art* (*Praeger). Guides to new outposts of modern art.

N. Pevsner, *Sources of Modern Architecture and Design* (*Praeger); S. Giedion, *Space, Time and Architecture,* 5th ed. (Harvard, 1967). Modern architecture in its wider setting.

P. Collaer, *A History of Modern Music* (*Universal). A helpful guide.

J. Cage, *Silence: Lectures and Writings* (*MIT). By a great experimenter in extending musical frontiers.

The Intellectuals, Society, and the Future

D. Riesman et al., *The Lonely Crowd,* rev. ed. (*Yale). A very influential sociological evaluation.

F. E. Manuel, ed., *Utopias and Utopian Thought* (Houghton, 1966). An interesting symposium on an eternal human dream.

R. Williams, *Culture and Society, 1780–1950* (*Torchbooks). Indispensable work on the historical background of the alienation of the intellectuals. Among many investigations of the topic, the following may be particularly recommended: L. A. Coser, *Men of Ideals* (Free Press, 1965); G. B. de Huzsar, *The Intellectuals* (Free Press, 1960); J. Benda, *The Treason of the Intellectuals* (*Norton); R. Hofstadter, *Anti-Intellectualism in American Life* (*Vintage).

J. Barzun, *The House of Intellect* (*Torchbooks). An appraisal by a member of the intellectual establishment.

L. Mumford, *The Transformations of Man* (*Collier); C. G. Darwin, *The Next Million Years* (Doubleday, 1953); R. Seidenberg, *Posthistoric Man* (*Beacon); H. Brown, *The Challenge of Man's Future* (*Compass); C. Brinton, *The Fate of Man* (Braziller, 1961). Stimulating forecasts of the human future.

N. O. Brown, *Life against Death* (*Vintage). Examination of the psychoanalytical meaning of history, with rather cheerless conclusions.

C. Frankel, *The Case for Modern Man* (*Beacon) and *Democratic Prospect* (*Colophon). Antidotes to the prophets of gloom.

R. Niebuhr, *The Children of Light and the Children of Darkness* and *The Irony of American History* (*Scribner's). Eloquent defenses of Christian pessimism as a basis for democracy.

Illustrations

Illustrations

Temple at Idfu, *Hirmer Fotoarchiv, Munich,* 8-9
Leaping bison, *courtesy of American Museum of Natural History,* 12
Venus of Willendorf, *courtesy of American Museum of Natural History,* 13
Jericho excavations, *Wide World Photos,* 14
Sumerian dignitary, *The University Museum of Philadelphia,* 15
Brother and sister-in-law of the deceased, *Hirmer Fotoarchiv, Munich,* 21
Cattle fording stream, *Hirmer Fotoarchiv, Munich,* 24
Snake goddess, *Alison Frantz,* 32
Bull portico, Palace of Minos, *Alison Frantz,* 33
The Harvester Vase, *Alison Frantz,* 34
Mycenaean jar, *National Tourist Organization of Greece,* 35
Lion Gate at Mycenae, *Alison Frantz,* 36
The Propylaea, *Alison Frantz,* 42-43
Greek maiden, *Acropolis Museum, Athens,* 48
Silver coin from Syracuse, *Hirmer Fotoarchiv, Munich,* 58
Bronze Poseidon, *Hirmer Fotoarchiv, Munich,* 69
Dionysus in a boat, *Staatliche Antikensammlungen und Glyptothek, Munich,* 70
Theater at Epidaurus, *Ewing Galloway,* 71
Etruscan fresco, 80
Roman battle relief, 83
Marcus Aurelius, *Alinari–Art Reference Bureau,* 91
Gladiators, *Anderson–Art Reference Bureau,* 99
Anglo-Saxon whalebone casket, *The Granger Collection,* 104-105
Taurobolium, *The Granger Collection,* 107
Head of Constantine, 116
Nave Wall, S. Apollinare Nuovo, *Anderson–Art Reference Bureau,* 119
Relief of German Warrior, *The Bettmann Archive,* 123
Merovingian tombstone, 126

Irish Crucifix, *National Museum of Ireland*, 132
Medieval manor plan, 139
Page from Alcuin's Vulgate, *The Granger Collection*, 140
Bayeux Tapestry (detail), *The Granger Collection*, 144-145
Drapers' hall, Ghent, *Marburg–Art Reference Bureau*, 147
Carcassonne, 152
Parliament under Edward I, *The Granger Collection*, 160
Emperor Frederick Barbarossa, *New York Public Library Picture Collection*, 167
Student life in the Middle Ages, *University Library of Freiburg-im-Breisgau*, 172
Interior of Beauvais Cathedral, *Clarence Ward, Oberlin, Ohio*, 180
Ancestors of the Virgin, Chartres Cathedral, *Lauros-Girodon*, 181
The Last Judgment, St. Lazare, *J.-E. Bulloz–Art Reference Bureau*, 182
Santa Sophia, *Turkish Tourism and Information Office*, 186-187
Justinian and Attendants, *Anderson–Art Reference Bureau*, 189
The Great Mosque at Mecca, *Saudi Arabian Public Relations Bureau*, 206
Interior of the Umayyad Mosque, Damascus, *Arab Information Center*, 207
Krak des Chevaliers, *Arab Information Center*, 209
The Anastasis, 219
Ivan the Terrible, *National Museum of Denmark, Copenhagen*, 231
Icon of St. Nicholas, *Sovfoto*, 233
Campidoglio, Rome, *Istituto Italiano de Cultura*, 236-237
Jacob Fugger with his clerk, *The Bettmann Archive*, 240
Charles VII and parlement, *The Bettmann Archive*, 246
View of Venice, *The Bettmann Archive*, 253
DaVinci sketch for a parachute, *The Granger Collection*, 261
Giotto, "The Lamentation," *Arena Chapel, Padua*, 264
Masaccio, "Expulsion of Adam and Eve from Eden," 265
Michelangelo, David, *Alinari–Art Reference Bureau*, 268
Donatello, Mary Magdalen (detail), *Brogi–Art Reference Bureau*, 269
Colleoni monument, *Anderson–Art Reference Bureau*, 270
The Chateau of Chambord, 276-277
Martin Luther, *The Granger Collection*, 278
Sketches of Calvin, *New York Public Library*, 283
Henry VIII, *British Information Service*, 285
South American natives, *The Granger Collection*, 297
Machu Picchu, *Ewing Galloway*, 298
Escorial, *Ewing Galloway*, 302
Francis I, by Clouet, 305
Henry IV, *The Granger Collection*, 309
Elizabeth I, *The Granger Collection*, 311
The Palace of Versailles, *Monkmeyer Press Photo Service*, 316-317
The siege of Magdeburg, *The Granger Collection*, 322
King Charles I, by Van Dyke, 331
House of Commons, *The Granger Collection*, 334
Richelieu, by Champaigne, 340
Louis XIV, by Mignard, *Alinari–Art Reference Bureau*, 341
View of Delft, by Vermeer, *The Royal Picture Gallery, Mauritshuis, the Hague*, 350
Strawberry Hill, *A. F. Kersting, London*, 356-357
Joseph Wright of Derby, "An Experiment with the Air Pump," *Tate Gallery, London*, 362
René Descartes, by Frans Hals, *The Louvre, Paris*, 364
Table talk with Voltaire, *The Granger Collection*, 373
Watteau, "Embarkation for Cythera," *The Louvre, Paris*, 382
Rubens, "Lion Hunt," *The Louvre, Paris*, 384

Rembrandt, "Self-Portrait," © *Greater London Council*, 386
Blenheim Palace, *The Granger Collection*, 388
Bernini's Throne of St. Peter, *Anderson–Art Reference Bureau*, 389
Battle of Germantown, *Library of Congress*, 394-395
Maria Theresa, *Brown Brothers*, 404
Hogarth, "The Polling," *Sir John Soane's Museum, London*, 415
Norwegian soldier, *The Granger Collection*, 418
Death mask of Frederick the Great, *The Bettmann Archive*, 419
Emperor Joseph II, *Austrian Information Service*, 420
Peter I, by Serov, *Sovfoto*, 421
Catherine the Great, *Brown Brothers*, 423
Charles III, by Goya, *The Prado, Madrid*, 424
London during the South Sea Bubble, *The Bettmann Archive*, 428
Eighteenth-century grinders, *The Bettmann Archive*, 430
March of the Women to Versailles, *New York Public Library Prints Division*, 434-435
Robespierre, *The Granger Collection*, 445
Marie Antoinette and her children, *Versailles Museum*, 446
Marie Antoinette on her way to the guillotine, *New York Public Library Picture Collection*, 446
Napoleon, 1798, by David, *The Granger Collection*, 453
Goya, "The Third of May, 1808," *The Prado, Madrid*, 457
David, "The Death of Marat," *Royal Museum of Fine Arts, Brussels*, 465
Congress of Vienna, *The Bettmann Archive*, 470-471
Prince Talleyrand, *The New York Public Library Picture Collection*, 472
Daumier, "The Uprising, 1848," *The Phillips Collection, Washington, D.C.*, 482
Caricature of Camillo di Cavour, *The Bettmann Archive*, 484
Napoleon III, *Brown Brothers*, 487
Bismarck, *The Bettmann Archive*, 499
Tsar Nicholas I, by Landseer, *The Bettmann Archive*, 500
Tsar Alexander II, *The Granger Collection*, 501
The Crystal Palace, *The Bettmann Archive*, 510-511
Child laborers, *The Bettmann Archive*, 516
Charles Darwin, *courtesy of the New York Public Library*, 517
Karl Marx, *The Bettmann Archive*, 528
Robert Owen's vision of an ideal community, *The Bettmann Archive*, 529
Lord Byron, *British Information Service*, 535
Daumier caricature, *The Bettmann Archive*, 538
"La Gare St. Lazare," by Monet, *courtesy The Art Institute of Chicago, Mr. and Mrs. Martin A. Ryerson Collection*, 541
Fifth Avenue in 1898, *The Granger Collection*, 543
U. S. Army troops in France, *U. S. Signal Corps*, 546-547
Gladstone with Queen Victoria, *The Bettmann Archive*, 549
Emperor William II, *The Granger Collection*, 553
Emperor Francis Joseph, *The Granger Collection*, 554
Bloody Sunday, *Soviet Life from Sovfoto*, 557
Rasputin, *The Granger Collection*, 558
Princip, *The Granger Collection*, 569
German soldiers leaving Berlin, *Wide World Photos*, 570
Allied soldiers in Flanders, *Wide World Photos*, 574
American troops landing in Normandy, *Wide World Photos*, 584-585
Lenin addressing a throng in Red Square, *Brown Brothers*, 587
Trotsky and his wife, *Wide World Photos*, 591
Mussolini during fascist "March on Rome," *Brown Brothers*, 596

Ludendorff and Hitler, *The Bettmann Archive*, 599
Nazi slap at Chancellor Dollfuss, *United Press International Photo*, 604
FDR on his way to his First Inaugural, *Franklin D. Roosevelt Library, Hyde Park, New York*, 612
"Rendezvous," Low cartoon, *photo by Low–Evening Standard*, 621
Pearl Harbor wreckage, *United Press International Photo*, 625
Hiroshima, *Wide World Photos*, 629
Detroit riots, *Wide World Photos*, 632-633
President de Gaulle in Quebec, *Wide World Photos*, 642
Paris riots, *Wide World Photos*, 648
Yevgeny Yevtushenko, *Tass from Sovfoto*, 661
Andrei Sinyavsky and Yuli Daniel, *Tass from Sovfoto*, 661
The Hungarian Revolt, *Wide World Photos*, 667
The Berlin Wall, *Wide World Photos*, 670
Red Guardsmen, *Wide World Photos*, 675
Nasser and crowd, *Wide World Photos*, 688
A Peace Corps volunteer in Bolivia, *The Peace Corps*, 699
TWA Building at Kennedy International Airport, *TWA by Ezra Stoller Assoc's.*, 702-703
Freud, by Jean Cocteau, *The Bettmann Archive*, 706
James Joyce, *Monkmeyer Press Photo Service*, 720
Picasso, "Les Demoiselles d'Avignon," *Collection The Museum of Modern Art*, 721
Gateway Arch in St. Louis, © *Arteaga Photos, St. Louis, Mo.*, 723
Marilyn Monroe, by Andy Warhol, *Courtesy Dwan Gallery, N. Y.*, 724
"Current," by Bridget Riley, *Collection The Museum of Modern Art, N. Y.*, 727
Untitled stabile-mobile, by Alexander Calder, *Collection The Museum of Modern Art, N. Y.*, 728

Index

Index

A

Abbasid Caliphate, 205
Abelard, Peter, 174
Achaean League, 68; defeat of, 85
Acre, siege of, 213
Act of Supremacy, 284
Act of Uniformity (1662), 336
Adrianople, battle of, 123
Aegospotami, battle of, 59
Aeneid, 79, 97
Aeschylus, 70-71
Africa: European imperialism in, 351-352; Portuguese exploration of, 293, 294; since 1945, 691-695
Agamemnon, 34, 37, 38, 39
Age of the Democratic Revolution, 467
Agincourt, battle of, 245
Agriculture: 18th century revolution, 429; feudal, 138-140; medieval, 146; prehistoric, 14; Russian, 659-660
Ahriman, 51
Ahuramazda, 51
Aix-la-Chapelle, Peace of (1668), 344
Akhenaten, 22
Akkadian language, 26
Akkadians, 17-19
Alba, Duke of, 312
Albertus Magnus, 175
Albigensians, 150
Alcestis, 72
Alcibiades, 57-59
Alcuin of York, 141
Alexander I (Russia): 455

Alexander II (Russia), 500-501
Alexander III (Russia), 556
Alexander VI, Pope, 242, 293
Alexander the Great, 23, 63-65; heirs of, 65-68
Alexandria, 64, 66; literature of, 96
Alexius, Tsar, 232, 233
Alexius I Comnenus, 201, 209, 216
Alexius III (Angelus), 217
Alexius IV (the Young Alexius), 217
Alfonso XIII (Spain), 603
Alfonso the Magnanimous, 253
Algeria, 506
Ali, 4th Caliph, 204
Alphabet: Cretan, 32; Cyrillic, 226; Greek, 45; Phoenicians and, 28, 45; Sumerian, 15
Altamira paintings, 13
Ambrose, St., 120
Amenophis IV (*see* Akhenaten)
America: English colonies in, 348-349; Seven Years' War and, 402
American Revolution, 424-425
Amon, 23
Amorites, 17
Anabaptists, 287
Anabasis, 60, 74
Anarchism, 530-531
Andriscus, 84
Andronicus I, 217
Anglo-Saxons, 124
Annals, 98
Anne, Queen (England), 338
Anselm, St., 174

Anthony, St., 114
Antigone, 71
Antigonids, 65, 66, 68
Antigonus Gonatas, 68
Antiochus III, 84
Anti-Semitism: Austro-Hungarian Empire and, 554, 555; Dreyfus and, 551; Stalin and, 655
Antony, Mark, 89
Apollonius Rhodius, 96
Appeal to the Christian Nobility of the German Nation, 279
Appearance and Reality, 523
Aqueducts, 98-99
Aquinas, St. Thomas, 174-176
Arabian Nights, 207
Arcadius, 196
Archimedes, 75
Architecture: Byzantine, 195-196; Cretan, 32; 18th century, 387; French Renaissance, 310; Greek, 78; Hittite, 27; Islamic, 207-208; medieval, 179-181; modern, 542; Mycenaean, 37; 19th century, 537; prehistoric, 13-14; Renaissance, 270-271; Roman, 99-100; Sumerian, 16-17; 20th century, 722-723
Archons, 48, 53
Areopagus, Council of the, 48, 50, 53
Arginusae, battle of, 59
Argonautica, 92
Arianism, 116-117
Aristarchus, 75
Aristophanes, 45, 72-73, 76
Aristotle, 46, 70, 77, 174, 175

Armada, Spanish, 312
Armenians, 200
Arminius, 90
Arnold of Brescia, 167
Arrian, 74
Art (*see also* Architecture, Sculpture, etc.): Babylonian, 19; Baroque, 387; Byzantine, 195-196; Enlightenment and, 387; Etruscan, 80, 81; French Renaissance, 310; Greek, 78-79; Hebrew, 30, 31; modern, 541-542; prehistoric, 12-13; Renaissance, 263-272; Rococo, 387; Roman, 99-100; romanticism and, 537; Russian, 233, 660-662; Sumerian, 16, 17; in 20th century, 719-724
Artaxerxes II, 60
Articles of Confederation, 425
Asia: imperialism and, 681-683; Southeast, 676, 678-679
Asiento, 345
Assembly of the People, 50
Assizes of Jerusalem, 211
Assizes of Romania, 218
Assyrians, 17-19
Astarte, 28
Astrology, 19; Romans and, 106
Astronomy: Babylonian, 19; Greek, 75; Renaissance and, 261-262
Atatürk, Kemal, 5, 578, 616
Aten, 23
Atheism, 367
Athens, 47-50; defeat of, 59; empire of, 54-59; Peloponnesian War and, 57-59
Attalus, 84
Attila the Hun, 124
Augsburg, Peace of, 308
Augustine, St., 120
Augustus (Octavian), 89-92
Australia, 563
Australopithecus, 12
Austria: Hitler and, 604; under Joseph II, 419-420
Austro-Hungarian Empire: from *1870-1914*, 554-555; minorities in, 499-500; Versailles Treaty and, 577
Austro-Prussian War, 487
Autokrator, 189
Authoritarianism, 372-374
Avars, 124
Averroës, 174, 206
Avicenna, 206

B

Baal, 28
Babylonia, Seleucid revival of, 66
Babylonian captivity, of Jews, 18
"Babylonian Captivity," of papacy, 154, 241-242
Babylonians, 17-19
Bacchae, The, 72
Bacchus, cult of, 107

Bach, Johann Sebastian, 387
Baibars, 214
Bailiffs, 151
Balboa, Vasco Núñez de, 297
Baldwin I, King of Jerusalem, 210
Baldwin of Flanders, 217, 218
Balfour Declaration, 573
Balkan crises, 568
Balkan Wars (*1912-1913*), 568
Balkans, from *1914* to *1939*, 603-605
Banking, medieval, 240
Bannockburn, battle of, 161
Barbarian invasions of Roman Empire, 122-128
Barebone's Parliament, 334
Barlaam and Ioasaph, 195
Basileus, 189
Basil, St., 114
Basil I (the Macedonian), 199
Basil II (Bulgarslayer), 200
Basil Digenes Akritas, 225
Bastille, fall of, 438
Battle of the Books, 377, 380
Baty (Tartar leader), 228
Bede, Venerable, 141
"Beggars," 312
Behaviorism, 709
Belgium, 653; annexation of, 447; invasion of (*1914*), 571; under Leopold I, 478
Benedict, St., 114
Bentham, Jeremy, 368, 369
Beowulf, 177, 257
Berkeley, George, 371
Bernadotte dynasty, 456
Bernard, St., 170, 174, 176; second crusade and, 212
Bible (*see also* Old and New Testaments): canonical books of, 113; historical accuracy of, 28-29; King James version, 330; Luther's, 280; Vulgate version of, 113; Wyclif's, 248
Birds, The, 72
"Bishops' War," 332
Bismarck, Otto von, 487-488, 489, 553, 566, 567
Black Death, 238, 247, 254
Blackstone, Sir William, 371
Blanc, Louis, 494
Blegen, Carl, 35
Boccaccio, 259
Bodin, Jean, 310
Boeotian League, 61
Boethius, 140-141, 173
Boğazköy, 26
Bohemia, Thirty Years' War and, 320-321
Bohemond I, 210
Boleyn, Anne, 284
Bonaventura, St., 176
Boniface VIII, Pope, 154
Book of Common Prayer, 332, 336
Book of Kells, 124
Book of the Dead, 25
Borgia, Cesare, 255

Boris Godunov, 232
Bosnia and Herzegovina, 554, 568
Botticelli, Sandro, 266
Bouvines, battle of, 158
Boxer Rebellion, 566
Boyne, battle of the (*1690*), 338
Bradley, F. H., 523
Brazil, 502-503; Portugal and, 293-294
Brest-Litovsk, Treaty of, 589
Brétigny, Treaty of, 243
Breughel, Pieter, 267, 268
Britain (*see also* England): barbarian invasion of, 124
British Empire, 562-563
Bruce, Robert, 161
Brutus, 89
Bubonic plague, 238
Buddha, Gautama, 294; as Christian saint, 195
Buddhism, 294-295
Bukharin, Nikolai, 590
Bulgarians, 198, 200; Baldwin of Flanders and, 218
Bulgars, 124
Burgundians, 125, 245
Burke, Edmund, 380; political theory of, 457
Byzantine Empire, 187-201; from *330* to *717*, 196-198; from *717* to *867*, 198-199; from *867* to *1081*, 199-201; from *1081-1453*, 216-220; civilization of, 194-196; enemies of, 190; feudalism and, 216-217; fourth Crusade and, 217; government and, 190-191; Latin Empire and, 217-218
Byzantium (*see also* Constantinople), 188; factions in, 192; sack of during Crusades, 217

C

Cabot, John, 300
Cabot, Sebastian, 300
Cabral, Pedro, 293
Cadmus, 73
Caesar, Julius, 88, 89
California, Drake and, 300
Calvin, John, 283-284
Calvinism, 283-284; capitalism and, 289-290; Knox and, 312; spread of, 319
Cambyses, 51
Camoens, Luís de, 296
Canaanites, 27-28; religion of, 28
Canada: Seven Years' War and, 402; since *1945*, 641-643; union of, 506
Candide, 381
Canning, George, 477, 478
Canterbury Tales, 259
Canute, King, 133
Capet, Hugh, 149

Capetians, 149-150
Capitalism: in Greece, 61; medieval, 239-240; Protestantism and, 289-290
Carbonari, 477
Carbon-14 technique, 11
Carolingian dynasty, 126; decline of, 133-134
Carrhae, battle of, 89
Carthage, 28, 83-84; sack of, 84
Cartier, Jacques, 300
Casa de Contratación, 303
Cassas, Bartholomew de las, 299
Cassiodorus, 141
Castiglione, Baldassare, 272
Castro, Fidel, 670, 697, 698
Cathari, 150
Cathedrals, medieval, 179-181
Catherine II, the Great (Russia), 422-423
Catherine of Aragon, 284
Catholic Reformation, 290-291; Council of Trent and, 291
Catiline, 88
Cato the Censor, 84
Catullus, 97
Cavour, Camillo Benso di, 484-486
Cervantes, Miguel de, 178, 303
Chaeronea, battle of, 63
Chiang Kai-shek, 614, 615, 635
Chalcedon, Council of, 117
Châlons, battle of, 124
Chamberlain, Joseph, 549
Chambre de comptes, 151
Chambre des enquêtes, 153
Chambre des plaids, 153
Chambre des requêtes, 153
Champollion, Jean, 24
Chanson de Roland, 129, 177
Charlemagne, 128-130; Alcuin of York and, 141
Charles I (England), 330-334; Civil War and, 333-334; execution of, 334
Charles II (England), 335, 336-337
Charles III (Spain), 423
Charles V (Emperor), 281, 301, 302
Charles V, the Wise (France), 243, 245
Charles VI (France), 245
Charles VII (France), 245
Charles VIII (France), 304
Charles X (France), 477, 478
Charles XII (Sweden), 422
Charles of Anjou, 169
Charles the Bald, 130
Charles Martel, 126
Charte, 472, 478
Chase, Stuart, 714
Chaucer, Geoffrey, 259-260
Checka, 589
Children's Crusade, 213
China, 614, 615, 635; Boxer Rebellion and, 566; civilization of, 295; Open Door Policy and, 566; Portugal and, 294; Russia and, 673-676; World War II and, 635

Christian IV (Denmark), 320, 321
Christianity (*see also* Jesus Christ, Roman Catholic Church, *etc.*): decline of Roman Empire and, 95; Deism and, 366-367; early history, 108-111; early literature of, 118-122; heresy and, 115-118; organization of, 112-113; persecution and, 111; triumph of, 111-115
Christian Science, 521
Churchill, John, Duke of Marlborough, 345
Churchill, Winston, 572, 574, 623, 644
Church of England, 286-287, 520-521; James I and, 329-330; Oxford Movement and, 520-521
Cicero, 97
Cistercian order, 170
Cities: Alexandria, 64, 66; medieval, 146-148; prehistoric, 13, 14; Roman, 92; Seleucid, 67-68
Civil Constitution of the Clergy, 441-442
Civil rights, Enlightenment and, 374-375
Civil War (England), 333-334
Civil War (Russia), 589-590
Civil War (Spanish), 603
Civil War (United States), 504-505
Civitates, 92
Classicism, 382-383, 463-464
Claudius, Emperor, 90
Cleisthenes, 49
Clemenceau, Georges, 573, 577
Clement XIV, Pope, 419
Cleopatra, 89
Clouds, The, 72, 76
Clovis, 125
Cluniac order, 170
Code of Hammurabi, 17
Code of Justinian, 189
Code Napoléon, 459
Coeur, Jacques, 240, 241, 245
Coinage: Byzantine, 191, 254; florin, 254; Greek, 47; Persian, 51
Colbert, Jean Baptiste, 343
Cold War, 633-638
College of Cardinals, 164, 170
Colonialism, 292-300; Crusades and, 217; Greek, 47; 19th century European, 506-507; Roman, 92; in 17th century, 348-353
Colonus, 95
Columbus, Christopher, 296-297
Comedy, Greek, 72-73
Commentaries on the Gallic Wars, 88
Commentaries on the Law of England, 371
Commerce (*see* Trade)
Commodus, Emperor, 93
Commons, House of, origin of, 247

Commonwealth, of Cromwell, 334-335
Communism, 575; China and, 635; Marxism and, 528-529; in Spain, 603
Compagnie des Indes Orientales, 351
Comte, Auguste, 521, 523
Comtean positivists, 521-522
Comuneros, 301
Concerning the Pope, 525
Conciliar Movement, 242
Concordat of Worms, 165
Condorcet, Marquis de, 377
Condottiere, 253
Confession of Golias, 179
Confucianism, 295
Congress of Berlin (*1878*), 567
Congress of Vienna, 471-473, 476
Conon, 60
Conquistadores, 298
Conrad I (Franconia), 133, 162
Conrad II (Franconia), 163
Conrad III (Swabia), 165
Conservatism, 525-526
Consolation of Philosophy, The, 141
Constance, Peace of, 167
Constantine, Emperor, 93, 95, 111-112; "donation" of, 128
Constantinople (*see also* Byzantium), 126, 188; conquest during fourth Crusade, 216
Control of the Tropics, 533
Convention Parliament, 338
Copernicus, Nicholas, 261-262, 359-360
Corinth, sack of, 85
Corn Laws, 492, 493
Corporation Act (*1661*), 336
Cortes, 302
Cossacks, 232-233
Council, Great, of Venice, 255
Council of the Areopagus, 48, 50, 53
Council of Chalcedon, 117
Council of Five Hundred, 50
Council of Four Hundred, 48
Council of Nicaea, 117, 192
Council of State, Athenian, 58
Council of Ten, 255
Council of Trent, 291
Council of Troubles, 312
Counter-Reformation (*see* Catholic Reformation)
Courtier, The, 272
Court of the Star Chamber (*see* Star Chamber)
Cousin, Victor, 524
Covenanters, 332
Coventicle Act (*1664*), 336
Cranmer, Thomas, 284
Crassus, 88
Crécy, battle of, 243
Crete: civilization of, 31-33; language of, 11
Crimean War, 483-484
Critias, 60
Cro-Magnon man, 12

Index

Cromwell, Oliver, 333, 334-335; Ireland and, 334
Cromwell, Richard, 335
Crusader States, 210-212; Moslem reconquest, 212
Crusades, 208-215; Albigensian, 150; Byzantium and, 199-200; Children's, 213; first, 209-210; later, 212-214; Latin Kingdom of Jerusalem, 210-212; results of, 214-215
Cuba, 697, 698; missile crisis and, 670-671
Cuius regio eius religio, 308, 326
Cults, Roman, 106-108
Cuneiform writing, 15
Curiales, 95
Curia regis, 149, 151, 156, 159, 168
Cybele, cult of, 107-108
Cynoscephalae, battle of, 84
Cyrus the Great, 19, 50-51
Cyrus the Younger, 60
Czechoslovakia, 620, 671-672
Czechs, 554; in Russia, 589; Thirty Years' War and, 320

D

Dadaists, 722
Danes, invasion of Ireland by, 133
Dante Alighieri, 254, 258
Danton, Georges Jacques, 444, 445, 446, 447
Darius the Great, 51
Dark Age, Greek, 38-40, 45
"Dark Ages," medieval, 140-141
Darwin, Charles, 517-518
Darwinism, 518; Social, 532-533
Das Kapital, 528
Dead Sea Scrolls, 110
Decameron, 259
Decembrist revolt, 479
Declaration of Breda, 335
Decline of the West, 715
Defenestration of Prague, 320
Defensor Pacis, 177
De Gaulle, Charles, 646, 647, 648
De humanis corporis fabrica, 261
Deism, 366-367
Delian League, 54
Delphi, oracle of, 46
Deme, 49, 50, 53
Demeter, 69, 70
Democracy: Greece and, 44, 45; parliamentary reform and, 491-492; Solon and, 48; Sumerian, 15
Democracy in America, 527
Democritus, 75
De Monarchia, 258
Demosthenes, 62-63
Denmark, Thirty Years' War and, 321-322
Depression of 1929: Germany and, 600; United States and, 611-613
De revolutionibus orbium coelestium, 261

Descartes, René, 360, 364
Despots, enlightened, 417-424
Development of Christian Doctrine, 524
De vulgari eloquentia, 258
Dictatorship, Greek, 49
Diderot, Denis, 367, 377, 380
Diet of Roncaglia, 167
Diggers, 336
Diocletian, Emperor, 93, 111
Dionysus, 69-70
Diplomacy: balance of power and, 489; Byzantine, 190-191, 225; Congress of Vienna and, 471-473, 476; Hittites and, 27
Discourse on Method, 364
Discourses (Machiavelli), 255, 256
Disraeli, Benjamin, 492
Divine Comedy, 258
Doges, of Venice, 255
Dominican order, 170-171
Dominic, St., 171
Donatello, 268
"Donation of Constantine," 128
"Donation of Pepin," 128
Donatist movement, 115-116
Don Quixote, 178
Dorians, 46
Draco, 48
Drake, Sir Francis, 300
Drama: Greek, 70-73; Enlightenment and, 385
Drang nach Osten, 162
Dreyfus, Alfred, 551
Duma, 558
Dürer, Albrecht, 267, 268
Dutch War (*1672-1678*), 344

E

Eastern Church: Great Schism and, 193-194; Russia and, 226-227, 230, 233-234
"Eastern Question," 479-481
East India Company, 351, 507
East Indies, Dutch in, 351
Ecclesiastical History of the English People, 141
Eck, John, 279
Eclecticism, 524
Eclogues, 97
Economics (*see also* Finance): Byzantine, 191-192; Diocletian and, 94-95; *18th* century, 426-431; laissez-faire, 343, 375-376; Marx and, 528-529; medieval, 148; mercantilism, 343; Spanish colonial, 303
Edict of Nantes, 309; revocation of, 341, 344-345
Edict of Restitution, 321, 323
Education: English reforms of, 548; Jesuits and, 424; medieval, 171-173; Napoleon and, 459; Russian, 680-682
Education Bill of *1870*, 548

Edward I (England), Parliament and, 159-162
Edward II (England), 247
Edward III (England), 242-243, 247-248
Edward IV (England), 249
Edward V (England), 249
Edward VI (England), 286
Edwards, Jonathan, 378
Einstein, Albert, 717
Eisenhower, Dwight D., 638-639
Egypt, 19-25; Alexander the Great and, 64; civilization of, 24-25; expansion under Mohammed Ali, 481; kingdoms of, 20-23; language of, 24, 25; Ptolemies and, 65-67; religion in, 23-24
Elgin Marbles, 78
El Greco, 303
Eliot, John, 330
Elizabeth I (England), 286, 311-313
Emile, 366
Ems telegram, 487, 488
England (*see also* Britain): in *18th* century, 413-417; from *1870-1914*, 548-549; from *1918* to *1939*, 606-608; since *1945*, 644-645; American colonies, 348-349; American Revolution and, 424-425; British Empire and, 562-563; under Charles I, 330-334; under Charles II, 336-337; Civil War, 333-334; Commonwealth period, 334-335; after Congress of Vienna, 476-477; Crimean War and, 483-484; under Cromwell, 334-335; under Edward I, 159-162; under Edward II, 247; under Edward III, 247-248; under Edward VI, 286; under Elizabeth I, 286, 311-313; under George III, 416-417; Gladstone and, 548, 549; Glorious Revolution, 337-338; growth of cabinet government, 414-416; under Henry II, 156-157; under Henry III, 159; under Henry IV, 249-250; under Henry VII, 249-250; under Henry VIII, 284-286, 310-311; Hundred Years' War and, 242-245; Industrial Revolution in, 513; Irish Home Rule and, 490-491, 607-608; under James I, 328-330; under James II, 337-338; under Mary I, 286; Protectorate, 334-335; Protestant Reformation and, 284-287; Reform Bills and, 491-492; Renaissance in, 313; Restoration, 336-337; under Richard II, 248; under Richard III, 249; under Tudors, 284-287; union with Scotland, 338; under Victoria, 493; Wars of the Roses and, 249; under William and Mary, 338; under William the Conqueror, 154, 156; World War I and, 568-581
Enlightenment, 363-378; Christian opposition, 378-379; heritage of, 724-725; repudiation of, 728-730

Enquêteurs, 151
Entente Cordiale (1904), 567
Epaminondas, 61
Eparch, 192
Ephors, 46
Epicurus, 77
Equites, 86
Erasmus, Desiderius, 260-261
Eratosthenes, 75
Esarhaddon, 18
Essay Concerning Human Understanding, 366
Essay on Man, 370
Essay on Miracles, 364
Essay on Population, 517
Estates-General, 153, 243, 413, 435, 437
Etruscans, 80-81; language of, 11
Etymologies, The, 141
Evans, Arthur, 32
Exchequer, 156
Existentialism, 713
Exploration, 292-300; Crusades and, 217; impact on Europe, 354; Renaissance inventions and, 262-263
Euclid, 75
Euripides, 72
Europe (*see also* World War I, World War II): in *18*th century, 397-424; from *1870* to *1914,* 548-559; since *1945,* 643-653; colonialism (*19*th century), 506-507; Congress of Vienna and, 471-473, 476; Eastern, between the Wars, 603-605; Eastern, since *1945,* 666-668; effects of overseas expansion on, 354; expansion of (*18*th century), 404-405; expansion of (*1800-1870*), 502-507; Industrial Revolution and, 511-516; Protestant Reformation and, 277-313; Renaissance and, 256-272; revolutions of *1820-1830,* 477-478; revolutions of *1848* and, 481, 483, 493-498; Seven Years' War and, 401-402; Stalin and, 663-665; Thirty Years' War and, 318-327

F

Fabian Society, 548
Fabius (the Delayer), 83
Fascism, 595-605 (*see also* Hitler, *etc.*)
Federalist Papers, 467
Fedor I, Tsar, 232
Fedor III, Tsar, 232
Ferdinand II (Holy Roman Empire), 320, 321
Ferdinand V (Spain), 250, 251
Frederick the Wise (Saxony), 279
Feudalism (*see also* Manoralism), 135-140; Byzantine, 216-217; rise of capitalism and, 241
Five Hundred, Council of, 50
Five Mile Act (*1665*), 336

Florence, in late Middle Ages, 254-255
Four Hundred, Council of, 48
Fourteen Points, of Wilson, 576
Fox, George, 336
France (*see also* Franks; French Revolution): in *19*th century, 493-495; from *1870* to *1914,* 550-552; from *1918* to *1939,* 608-610; since *1945,* 645-648; American colonies of, 349-351; Calvinism and, 283; Capetian dynasty, 134, 149-150; under Charles VIII, 304; colonial empire of, 563; Commune and, 550; divine-right monarchy and, 339-348; under Francis I, 304-305; Franco-Prussian War and, 487-489; Fronde and, 340; under Henry II, 308; under Henry IV, 339; Hundred Years' War and, 242-245; Joan of Arc and, 245; under Louis VI, 149; under Louis VII, 149-150; under Louis X, 154; under Louis XI, 246-247; under Louis XII, 304; under Louis XIII, 339; under Louis XIV, 340-345, 348; under Louis XV, 410-411; Napoleon Bonaparte and, 451, 452-459, 462; Napoleon III and, 487, 495; National Assembly and, 437-443; Old Regime and, 410-413; under Philip II, 150-151; under Philip the Fair, 152-154; Renaissance in, 310; Revolution of *1830,* 478; Richelieu and, 339; royal government in, 150-151; under St. Louis, 152, 153; Thirty Years' War and, 323, 326; Versailles Treaty and, 578; War of the Spanish Succession and, 345, 348; Wars of Religion and, 308-310; World War I and, 568-581
Francis, St., 171
Francis I (France), 304-305
Francis Ferdinand, assassination of, 568
Francis Joseph (Austria), 499, 554
Franciscan order, 170-171
Franco, Francisco, 603
Franco-Prussian War, 487-489
Franks, 125, 126, 128-130 (*see also* Charlemagne); Merovingian dynasty, 125-126
Frederick II (Frederick the Great), 401, 402, 403, 418-419
Frederick II (Germany), 168-169, 213
Frederick Barbarossa (Frederick I), 165, 167, 212
Frederick of the Palatinate, 320, 321
French Revolution, 434-468; the Convention, 445; the Directory, 450-451; the Eighteenth Brumaire, 452; First Republic and, 443-452; the "Great Fear," 439; importance of, 436; legacy of, 467-468; the "Mountain," 445-447; the Ninth Ther-

French Revolution (*cont.*):
midor, 449-450; the October Days, 439-440; Reign of Terror, 447, 450, 451; the revolutionary government, 447-448; the September Massacres, 444; taxation as a cause of, 411-412; the Tenth of August, 444
Freudianism, 707-708
Freud, Sigmund, 706-707
Frobisher, Martin, 300
Frogs, The, 72
Fronde, The, 340
Fuggers, 240
Fyrd, 154, 156

G

Gadsden Purchase (*1853*), 504
Galatia, 68
Galen, 99, 261
Galerius, Emperor, 93
Galileo, 360
Gallipoli, 572
Gama, Vasco da, 293
Gandhi, Mahatma, 615, 616
Garibaldi, Giuseppe, 486, 496
Gaugamela, battle of, 64
Geneva, Protestant Reformation in, 283, 284
Genghis Khan, 228
Genoa, trade and, 239
Geography: Pliny the Elder and, 99; Romans and, 99
George III (England), 416-417
Georgics, 97
Germania, 98
Germany: from *1870* to *1914,* 553-554; since *1945,* 648-652; Berlin airlift and, 669; Bismarck and, 487-488, 498; colonial empire of, 563; Dawes Plan, 600; Depression of *1929* and, 600; Franco-Prussian War and, 487-489; under Frederick Barbarossa, 165, 167; under Henry III, 163, 164; under Henry IV, 163, 164, 165; under Henry V, 165; under Henry VI, 168; under Hitler to *1939,* 601; Hohenstaufens and, 165, 167, 168; Investiture Controversy and, 164-165; during Middle Ages, 162-169; nationalism and, 532; particularism and, 251-252; Peasants' Revolt and, 281-282; Protestant Reformation and, 278-280; and Revolution of *1848,* 496-498; Thirty Years' War and, 319-323, 326-327; Versailles Treaty and, 577-581; Weimar Republic and, 597-601; World War I and, 568-581; World War II and, 634-635; *Zollverein* and, 473
Gerbert of Aurillac, 173
Gestapo, 602
Geyl, Peter, 459
Ghibellines, 165, 167, 168, 252, 254

Gibbon, Edward, 95
Gilbert, Sir Humphrey, 300
Gilgamesh epic, 16
Giotto, 182, 265-266
Girondins, 445-446
Gladstone, William, 548, 549
Glorious Revolution (England), 337-338
Gluck, Christoph, 388
Gnostics, 115
Godfrey of Bouillon, 210
Godwin, William, 372
Goethe, Johann Wolfgang von, 465-466
"Golden Bull," 252
Golden Horde, 228, 229
Goliard poets, 179
Gospel of Thomas, 108
Gosplan, 592
Government (*see also* Political Theory): Byzantine, 190-191, 221-222; early royal, 150-151; Enlightenment and, 374-375; Napoleon and, 459, 462; Roman, 92-93; Roman republican, 81-82; Russian autocracy, 230-231; Sumerian, 15
Gracchi, reforms of, 86-87
Grande Armée, 457
Grande Encyclopédie, 377
Grand Remonstrance, 332-333
Granicus, battle of, 64
Great Northern War, 421-422
Great Protestation, 329
Great Schism, 193-194
Greco, El, 303-304
Greece (*see also* Athens and Sparta): civilization of, 68-79; democracy and, 44, 45; early civilization in, 33-38; influence on Rome, 96-97; literature of, 70-74; Macedon and, 62-65; Peloponnesian War and, 57-59; Persians and, 50-54, 57-59; religion of, 68-70; War of Independence, 480
Gregorian chants, 183
Gregory VII, Pope, 164-165, 209
Gregory the Great, Pope, 126-127, 141
Grey, Lady Jane, 286
Gudea, of Lagash, 15
Guelfs, 165, 167, 168, 252, 254
Guido of Arezzo, 183
Gunpowder, introduction of, 262
Gustavus Adolphus, 321, 322, 323

H

Habsburgs (*see also* Austria, Holy Roman Empire, Spain), 251, 252, 300, 321, 498-499; Catholic Reformation and, 290; Protestant Reformation and, 281; Valois dynasty and, 304-305, 308
Hampden, John, 330, 332
Handel, George Frederick, 387
Hannibal, 83-84

Hanseatic League, 239
Harun al-Rashid, Caliph, 208
Harvey, William, 261, 360
Hastings, Warren, 405
Hattusas, 26
Hawkins, John, 300
Hay, John, 566
Haydn, Joseph, 388
Hebrews, 28-31; history of, 29; religion of, 30-31
Hegel, Georg W. F., 522-523; influence on Marx, 528
Hegira, 202
Heisenberg, Werner, 717
Hellenica, 74
Helot, 46
Henry II (England), common law and, 156-157
Henry II (France), 308
Henry III (England), 159
Henry III (Germany), 163, 164
Henry IV (England), 249-250
Henry IV (France), 309, 339
Henry IV (Germany), 163, 164, 165
Henry V (England), 245, 249
Henry V (Germany), 165
Henry VI (England), 249
Henry VI (Germany), 168
Henry VII (England), 249-250
Henry VIII (England), 284-286, 310-311; Francis I and, 304
Henry of Navarre, 309
Henry the Navigator, 293
Herder, Johann Gottfried von, 380-381
Heresy, orthodoxy and, 115-118
Hermann (Arminius), 90
Herodotus, 73
Hero of Alexandria, 105
Hesiod, 45, 46
Hidalgo, 303
Hildebrand (*see* Gregory VII, Pope)
Hinduism, 294
Hipparchus, 49
Hippias, 52
Hippocrates, 75
Hippocratic oath, 75
Hippolytus, 72
Historicism, 3-4
History: Greek, 73-74; language and, 10-11; Tacitus and, 98; uses of, 2-6
Hitler, Adolf, 600-602 (*see also* World War II)
Hittites, 26-27; religion of, 26, 27
Hobbes, Thomas, 374, 375
Hohenstaufens, 165, 167, 168
Holbach, Paul, 367
Holbein, Hans, 267
Holland (*see* Netherlands)
Holy Alliance, 476
Holy Roman Empire, 165, 167, 168, 169
Homer, 27, 38-40; historical accuracy of, 40
Horace, 97

Horus, 23
Hospitallers, Knights, 212
House of Commons, 161; James I and, 329
Hsüan-T'ung, Emperor, 614
Huguenots, 283; Louis XIV and, 341; Richelieu and, 339
Humanism, 257-258
Humble Petition and Advice, 335
Hume, David, 354
Hundred Years' War, 242-245
Hungary: revolt of *1956,* 666-667; Turks and, 224
Huns, 124
Hurrians, 27
Hus, John, 242
Hutten, Ulrich von, 281
Hyksos, 22, 33

I

Iconoclasm, 193-194
Idealism, 522-523
Ideas for a Philosophy of the History of Mankind, 380
Ideologues, 464
Iliad, 27, 39, 40
Imperialism (*see also* Colonialism): European, *1800-1870,* 502-507; Italian, 552; Japan and, 566; revolt against, 679-681; Roman, 90-94; in *17*th century, 348-353; United States and, 564
Index librorum prohibitorum, 291
India, 615, 616; Alexander the Great and, 64; British rule in, 507; British rule in *20*th century, 562; caste system and, 294; Clive and, 402; East India Company and, 507; European imperialism in, 351, 683-685; Portuguese and, 294; Sepoy Rebellion, 507
Indians, 502, 503
Industrial Revolution, 429-431, 511-516; in United States, 504
Innocent III, Pope, 168, 171, 213; fourth Crusade and, 217
Inquisition, 171; Catholic Reformation and, 291; Spanish, 251
Institutes of the Christian Religion, 283
Instrument of Government, 334, 335
Intendants, 339, 341, 342
Inventions: early medieval, 138; Greek, 75; prehistoric, 11, 12; printing, 262; Roman, 98-99
Investiture Controversy, 164-165
Iran, 616, 617
Ireland: Catholic revolt (*1641*), 332; early civilization of, 124; Easter Rebellion and, 607-608; Elizabeth I and, 313; Home Rule and, 490-491, 549, 550, 607, 608; invasion by Danes, 133; literary revival in, 550; William III and, 338

Isaac II (Isaac Angelus), 217
Isabella I (Spain), 250-251
Isidore of Seville, 141
Isis, 23; cult of, 108
Islam (*see also* Moslems): before Crusades, 201-208; civilization of, 205-208; disunity in, 204-205; expansion of, 202, 204
Israel (*see also* Palestine): state of, 685-689
Italia Irredenta, 486
Italy (*see also* Papal States, Venice, *etc.*): *Carbonari* and, 477; Cavour and, 484-486; fascism and, 595-597; from *1870-1914*, 552; Mussolini and, 595-597; particularism and, 251-252; revolutions (*1848*), 495-496; since *1945*, 652-653; unification of, 495-496; Versailles Treaty and, 578
Ivan III (the Great), 230
Ivan IV (the Terrible), 231-232

J

Jacobins, 443-444, 448, 452
Jacquerie, 243
James I (England), 328-330
James II (England), 337-338
Jansenists, 342
Japan, 613, 614, 615; imperialism and, 566; invasion of China and, 614-615; modernization of, 564, 566; opening of, 564; Perry and, 564; World War II and, 635
Jenkins' Ear, War of, 400-401
Jerome, St., 113, 119-120
Jerusalem: capture by Turks, 213; Latin Kingdom of, 210-212; Roman sack of, 92
Jesuits, 424; Bismarck and, 553; Catholic Reformation and, 290-291; in China, 295; Frederick the Great and, 419; missionary activities of, 291; in Paraguay, 299-300; Pope Clement XIV and, 419
Jesus Christ: teachings of, 108-109; theological beliefs concerning, 109-111, 115-118
Jews (*see also* Anti-Semitism, Hebrews, Judaism): Austro-Hungarian Empire and, 554-555; Babylonian captivity of, 18; Balfour Declaration and, 573; expulsion from England, 162; Hitler and, 601-602; Joseph II (Austria) and, 419-420; as medieval bankers, 240; Philip the Fair and, 154; Roman Empire and, 92; in Spain, 251; Stalin and, 655
Jihad, 202
Joan of Arc, 245
John I (England), 157-158, 159; Magna Carta and, 158-159
John II, the Good (France), 243
John XII, Pope, 134
John of Leyden, 287
John of Salisbury, 176
John of the Cross, St., 303
Johnson, Lyndon, 640-641
Johnson, Samuel, 380
Joinville, Jean, 215
Joseph II (Austria), 419-420
Judaism (*see also* Jews): Christian origins and, 110
Julian the Apostate, Emperor, 112, 118
Justices of the peace, 248
Justinian, Emperor, 126, 189, 196-197
Jutland, battle of, 573

K

Kassites, 17
Kant, Immanuel, 369, 371
Karachi, 65
Karlovitz, Congress of, 225
Kellogg-Briand Pact, 611
Kemal, Mustafa (*see* Atatürk, Kemal)
Kennedy, John F., 640
Kerensky, Alexander, 586
Khrushchev, Nikita, 652-656, 658-660, 666-670
Kidd, Benjamin, 533
King James Bible, 330
King, Martin Luther, 640
Knights Templars, 154
"Knights War," 281
Knossos, 32, 33
Knox, John, 312
Köprülüs, 225
Koran, 201-202
Korean War, 665
Korzybski, Alfred, 714
Kossovo, battle of, 220
Kremlin, Italian architects of, 234
Kropotkin, Peter, 530
Krum, King of the Bulgarians, 198
Kulaks, 589, 590, 591
Kulturkampf, 553

L

Labour party, in England, 548
Lagash, 15
Laissez-faire theory, 343
Lancaster, house of, 249
Landtag, 498
Languages: Akkadian, 26; Arabic, 205; Catalan, 250, 257; Cretan, 11, 32, 35; Egyptian, 24, 25; Etruscan, 11, 80; German, 257; history and, 10-11; *langue d'oc*, 257; *langue d'oïl*, 257; Latin, 100, 257; Old Church Slavonic, 233; Punic, 28; Romance, 100; Spanish, 250; Sumerian, 15; Ugaritic, 27; vernacular, 257
Laos, 676, 678
Lares, 96
Las Casas, Bartholomew de, 299
Lascaux paintings, 12
Latifundia, 86, 138
Latin America: revolutions of 19th century in, 502-503; since *1945*, 695-698; Spanish empire in, 298-300
Latin Kingdom of Jerusalem, 210-212
Laud, William, 330-331, 332
Law: Babylonian, 17; Blackstone and, 371; civil rights, 374-375; code of Hammurabi, 17; common, 156-157; Draco and, 48; Edward I and, 161-162; first justices of the peace, 248; Frederick II and, 168-169; Greek, 48; Hammurabi's code, 17; Henry II and, 156-157; James II and, 337; juries and, 157; Justinian and, 189; Magna Carta and, 158-159; medieval, 151; Napoleon and, 459; natural law, 365; Roman, 82; Roman contributions to, 98; Russian reforms and, 501; "Salic," 242; Solon and, 48; Sumerian, 16
Law, John, 427-428
Lawrence, T. E., 573
League of Cambrai, 304
League of Nations, 580, 581
Lechfeld, battle of, 134
Leeuwenhoek, Anton van, 360
Legitimists, 550, 551
Legnano, battle of, 167
Leipzig, battle of, 458
Lenin, 556, 586-591
Leo I, Pope (the Great), 113, 124
Leo IX, Pope, 164
Leo X, Pope, 279
Leo XIII, Pope, 520
Leonardo da Vinci, 261, 266-267
Leopold I (Belgium), 478
Lepidus, 89
Lessing, Gotthold E., 367
Letter Concerning Toleration, 367
Leuctra, battle of, 61
Levellers, 333, 336
Leviathan, 374
Lex loquens, 330
L'Hospital, Michel de, 309
Liberalism, 526-527
Liberal party, in England, 548
Libertarianism, 372-374
Libraries, Alexandrian, 66
Linear A script, 32
Linear B script, 35, 38
Linnaeus, Carolus, 360
Literature: Byzantine, 194-195; Christian, 118-122; classicism, 382-383, 463-464; Egyptian, 25; English, 259-260; English Renaissance, 313; Enlightenment and, 383-386; Greek, 38-40, 70-74; Hittite, 27; humanism and, 257-258; Islamic, 206-207; Italian, 257-259; Latin, 97-98; medieval, 177-179; modern, 542-

Literature (*cont.*):
543; naturalism and, 536; realism and, 536; Renaissance, 257-261; romanticism and, 382-383, 463-464, 534-536; Russian, 233, 539; Spanish, 303; Sumerian, 15; in *20*th century, 719-721; vernacular language and, 178

Lloyd George, David, 548, 549, 573, 577
Locke, John, 366, 367, 374
Logical positivism, 714
Lollards, 248
Lombards, 126
"Lombard" bankers, 240
Long Parliament (*1640-1660*), 332-333
Lothair, Emperor, 130
Louis VI (France), 149
Louis VII (France), 149-150
Louis VIII (France), 458
Louis IX, St. Louis (France), 152, 153, 214
Louis X (France), 154
Louis XI (France), 246-247
Louis XII (France), 304
Louis XIII (France), 339
Louis XIV (France), 340-345, 348; wars of, 344-345
Louis XV (France), 410-411
Louis XVI (France), 410, 437-438, 440, 444, 446
Louis XVIII (France), 458
Louis Philippe, King (France), 478
Louis the Child, 133
Louis the German, 130
Low Countries (*see* Belgium, Flanders, Netherlands)
Loyola, Ignatius, 290-291
Lucretius, 97
Lueger, Karl, 555
Lunéville, peace of, 453
Lusitania, 573
Luther, Martin, 260-261, 278-280
Lützen, battle of, 323
Lusiads, The, 296
Lysistrata, 72

M

Macedon, 62-65; Alexander the Great and, 62-65; evaluation of, 62; Philip II and, 62-63; Roman conquest of, 84
Macedonian Wars, 84-85
Machiavelli, Niccolò, 255-256
Magellan, Ferdinand, 297-298
Magic, Babylonian, 19
Magna Carta, 158-159
Magna Graecia, 47, 80, 82, 83
Magyars, 124, 499, 554, 555
Maistre, Joseph de, 525
Malenkov, Georgi, 655

Malthus, Thomas Robert, 517
Mamluks, 214
Man: Cro-Magnon, 12; Neanderthal, 12; origin of, 11; prehistoric, 9-14
Mani, 115
Manichaeans, 115
Manorialism, 138-139
Manuel I Comnenus, 216
Manuscripts, illuminated, 124
Mao Tse-tung, 615
Marathon, battle of, 52
Marcel, Etienne, 243
March Revolution, in Russia, 586
Marcus Aurelius, Emperor, 93, 97, 111
Marduk, 19
Marius, Caius, 87, 88
Marne, second battle of, 575
Marshall, George, 4
Marsiglio of Padua, 177
Marston Moor, battle of, 333
Marx, Karl, 515, 528-529; influence of Hegel on, 528
Marxism, 515, 528-529, 715; as a religion, 522, 715; Russia and, 556
Mary I (England), 286
Mary II (England), 338
Mary Queen of Scots, 312
Masaccio, 266
Mastersingers, 272
Materialism, 523
Mathematics: Babylonian, 19; Descartes and, 360; Greek, 75; Islamic, 206; Newton and, 360
Matilda, Queen (England), 156
Matthias, Emperor, 320
Maximian, Emperor, 93, 95
Maximilian, Emperor of Mexico, 503-504
Maximilian of Bavaria, 320, 321
Mazarin, Cardinal, 340
Mazzini, Giuseppe, 531
McCarthy, Joseph, 639
Medea, 72
Medes, 18
Medieval civilization, East (*see* Byzantine Empire)
Medieval civilization, West, 145-183; education and, 171-173; feudalism, 135-140; late, 237-248; literature, 177-179; manorialism, 138-139; political theory of, 176-177
Medici, Catherine, 308
Medici, Cosimo, 254
Medici, Lorenzo, 254-255
Medicine: bubonic plague and, 238; Enlightenment and, 360; Greek, 75; Islamic, 206; Renaissance and, 261; Roman, 99
Meditations, 97
Menander, 73
Menes, 20
Mercantilism, 343
Merovingian dynasty, 125-126
Mesolithic Age, 13
Mesopotamia, 14-19
Mestizos, 298, 299

Metallurgy, prehistoric, 14
Metaphysics, 174
Methodism, 378, 379, 413
Metternich, Prince Clement, 476-477, 480
Mexican War, 504
Mexico, under Maximilian, 503-504
Michael VIII Paleaologus, 218
Michael Romanov, 232
Michelangelo, 267, 269-271
Middle Ages (*see* Dark Ages, Medieval civilization)
Middle East: imperialism and, 685-690; from *1918* to *1939*, 616-617
Milan, in late Middle Ages, 253-254
Mill, John Stuart, 526, 527
Miltiades, 52
Ministeriales, 163, 164, 165, 252
Minoan civilization, 31-33, 34-35
Minos, palace of, 32
Minotaur, 32
Mirandola, Pico della, 258
Mississippi Company, 427-428
Mithra, cult of, 108
Mithridates VI, 87, 88
Mohács, battle of, 224
Mohammed, the Prophet, 201-202
Mohammed II (the Conqueror), 220
Mohammed Ali (Egypt), 481
Monarchy: abolition of English, 334-335; divine-right, in France, 339-348; Egyptian, 20; in *18*th century, 407-409; Hundred Years' War and, 242-245; medieval, 148-154; Nerva and, 91; restoration of English, 336-337; Roman Empire and, 91-92; in *16*th century, 300-313; Sumerian, 15, 16
Monasticism (*see also* individual orders): Cluniac reform and, 170; early Christian, 114-115; in Eastern Church, 193; Henry VIII and, 284; Russian, 233
Monck, George, 335
Monophysites, 117, 118
Monotheism, 22, 30
Monroe Doctrine, 477, 503, 504
Montaigne, Michel de, 310
Monte Cassino, abbey of, 114
Montfort, Simon de, 159, 161
Moscow: Tartars and, 228-229; as "Third Rome," 230
Moslems (*see also* Islam): Byzantine Empire and, 200-201; crusades and, 208-215; Franks and, 126; in Spain, 250, 251
Moravians, 198
More, Thomas, 284
Mormons, 521
Morocco crises, 567-568
"Morton's Fork," 250
Mozart, Wolfgang Amadeus, 388-389
Murad IV, 225
Muscovite state, 229-231
Music: *18*th century and, 387-389; medieval, 183; modern, 542; *19*th

Music (cont.):
    century, 538; Renaissance and, 271-272; Russian, 539; in 20th century, 723; Wagner and, 538
Mussolini, Benito, 595-597
Mutual Aid: A Factor in Evolution, 530
Mycale, 54
Mycenae, civilization of, 33-38
Mysticism, 176

N

Napoleon Bonaparte, 451, 452-459, 462; the Consulate, 452-454; Empire of, 454-458; the Hundred Days, 458-459; place in history, 459-462; in Russia, 457; wars of, 453-459
Napoleon III (France), 487, 495, 503
Napoleon: For and Against, 459
Naseby, battle of, 333
Nasser, Abdel, 687, 688, 689
Nathan the Wise, 367
Nationalism, 531-532
Natural law, 365
Neanderthal man, 12
Nebuchadnezzar, 18
Necker, Jacques, 413, 437, 438, 439
Neerwinden, battle of, 447
Negroes (*see also* Racism, Slavery): in U.S. since *1945*, 639-640
Neolithic Age (*see* New Stone Age)
NEP (New Economic Policy), 590
Nerva, Emperor, 91
Nero, Emperor, 111
Netherlands: American colonies of, 348-349; Calvinism in, 283; Spain and, 281, 312, 313; Thirty Years' War and, 318-319
New Amsterdam, 348
New Deal, 612-613
New France, 349-351
Newman, John Henry, 521, 524
New Stone Age, 13-14
Newton, Sir Isaac, 359, 360
Nicaea, Council of, 117, 192
Nicephorus I, Emperor, 198
Nicholas I, Pope, 134
Nicholas I (Russia), 479
Nicholas II (Russia), 586, 589
Nicias, Peace of, 57
Nihilists, 555
Nikon, Patriarch, 233, 234
Nineveh, 15; fall of, 18
Nixon, Richard M., 641
Nobiles, 82
Nominalists, 173, 174
Nordlingen, battle of, 323
Northmen, 130, 132-133
November revolution, in Russia, 586-589
Novgorod, 227-228
Nureddin, 212

O

Odovacar, 125
Odyssey, 39, 40
Old Believers, 234
Old Russian Primary Chronicle, 226
Old Stone Age, 11-13
Old Testament, 28-29
Olympic games, 46
O'Neill, Hugh, 313
On Liberty, 526
On the Nature of Things, 97
Open Door Policy, 566
Oprichnina, 231
Oratory of Divine Love, 290
Ordonnance, 152
Oresteia, The, 70-71
Origin of Species, 517, 518, 522
Orleanists, 550
Osiris, 23
Ostrakon, 52
Ostrogoths, 124-125
Otto I, 133-134, 163
Otto III, Emperor, 163
Otto IV, Emperor, 168
Ottoman Empire, 616; Young Turks and, 559
Ottoman Turks, 219-225; decline of, 224-225
Outremer, 215
Ovid, 97
Oxenstierna, Count Axel, 323, 326
Oxford Movement, 520-521
Oxford, Provisions of, 159

P

Paine, Thomas, 467
Painting: cave, 12-13; Enlightenment and, 386-387; Giotto and, 265-266; Greek, 78; medieval, 181-182; modern, 541-542; 19th century, 537; prehistoric, 12-13; Renaissance and, 265-268; Roman, 100; Spain and, 303-304; in 20th century, 721-722
Pakistan, imperialism and, 683-685
Palatinate, Thirty Years' War and, 320
Paleolithic Age (*see* Old Stone Age)
Palestine, Balfour Declaration and, 573
Palladio, Andrea, 271
Palmer, R. R., 467
Palmerston, Lord Henry, 478
Papacy (*see also* names of Popes): "Babylonian Captivity" of, 154, 241-242; Catholic Reformation and, 291; Conciliar Movement and, 242; decline in 10th century, 134; Donation of Constantine and, 128; Donation of Pepin, 128; early history of, 126-127; Henry VIII and, 284; Investiture Controversy and, 164-165; medieval reform of, 169-171;

Papacy (cont.):
    Philip the Fair and, 154; Thirty Years' War and, 323, 327
Papal States, 489, 496; origin of, 128
Papyri, 24
Pareto, Vilfredo, 710-712
Paris, Peace of (*1763*), 402
Parlement, 151, 152, 342, 412-413
Parlement de Paris, 151
Parliament: Barebone's, 334; Charles I and, 330-332; Convention, 338; Edward I and, 159-162; Edward III and, 247; under Henry VIII, 311; Long, 332-333; "model," 162; "Pride's Purge" of, 334; Reform bills and, 491-492; Rump, 334, 335; Short, 332
Parma, Duke of, 312
Parsons, Talcott, 710
Parthenon, 78
Particularism, 165, 168, 169; Germany and, 251-252; Italy and, 252-256
Pascal, Blaise, 342, 360, 379
Patricians, 81
Paul I (Russia), 452
Paul III, Pope, 291
Paul et Virginie, 370
Paul, St., 110-111
Pax Romana, 90
Pazzi family, 254
Peace of Nicias, 57
Peasants' Revolt, 281-282
Peisistratus, 49
Peloponnesian War, 57-59
Penates, 96
Peninsular War, 456-457
Pensées, 379
Pepin the Short, 126; "donation" of, 128
Pergamum, kingdom of, 84, 85
Pericles, 45, 54, 56, 57
Perioikoi, 46
Perón, Juan, 697
Perseus, 84
Persia: Alexander the Great and, 64; Greeks and, 50-54, 57-59; Peloponnesian War and, 57-59
Persians, The, 70
Persian Wars, 60
Peter I, the Great (Russia), 420-422
Peter, St., 111
Peter the Hermit, 210
Petrarch, 258-259
Phidias, 78
Philip II, Augustus (France), 150-151, 213
Philip II (Macedon), 62-63
Philip II (Spain), 301-302, 311-313
Philip IV, the Fair (France), 152-154; finance under, 153-154
Philip V (Macedon), 84
Philip VI (France), 242
Philip of Swabia, 168, 217
Philip, the Good (Burgundy), 246
Philippi, battle of, 89
Philippines, Spain and, 298

Philistines, 28
Philosophes, 363-366, 368, 369, 370, 372, 373, 374, 377, 418, 419, 422, 423, 424, 725, 729
Philosophy (*see also* Hegel, *etc.*): doctrine of progress, 376-378; eclecticism, 524; Enlightenment and, 363-378; Greek, 74-78; idealism, 522-523; Islamic, 206; materialism, 523; medieval, 173-176; natural law, 365; *philosophes* and, 363-366, 368, 369, 370, 372, 373, 374, 377, 418, 419, 422, 423, 424, 725, 729; positivism, 521, 523; rationalism, 363-364; scholasticism, 175; Thomas Aquinas and, 174-176; in 20th century, 713-716; universals, question of, 173-174; utilitarianism, 368-369; voluntarism, 524
Phoenicians, 28; alphabet and, 28
Phratries, 47
Picasso, Pablo, 721
Pindar, 73
Pithecanthropus erectus, 12
Pius V, Pope, 291
Pius IX, Pope, 520
Plague, bubonic, 238
Plataea, battle of, 54
Plato, 76-77
Plautus, 97
Plebeians, 81
Pliny the Elder, 99
Pliny the Younger, 111
Poetry, Enlightenment and, 385-386
Poitiers, battle of, 243
Poland, Versailles Treaty and, 578
Polemarch, 48
Policraticus, 176
Polis, 46
Political Justice, 372
Politiques, 310
Political theory (*see also* Government): 709-713; anarchism, 530-531; conservatism, 525-526; Burke and, 467; Enlightenment and, 371; Greece and, 44, 45; liberalism, 526-527; Marxism, 528-529; medieval, 176-177; nationalism, 531-532; *politiques* and, 310; radicalism, 527
Polybius, 74
Pombal, Marquis de, 423-424
Pompeii, 100
Pompey, the Great, 88, 89
Pope, Alexander, 370
Popular Front, 603
Portugal: empire of, 295-296; overseas expansion of, 293-294
Positivism, 521, 523
Pottery: Athenian, 49; Cretan, 32
Prehistoric man, 9-14; tools and, 11, 12
Presbyterianism, in Scotland, 332
Prester John, 293
Preston Pans, battle of, 334
Prévôts, 149, 151

"Pride's Purge," 334
Prince (Machiavelli), 255-256
Princip, Gavrilo, 568
Principles of Morals and Legislation, 369
Printing, invention of, 262
Progress, doctrine of, 376-378
Prometheus Bound, 70
Protestantism (*see also* Calvinism, *etc.*): attributes of, 288; growth of capitalism and, 289-290; modernism and, 520-521; progress and, 288-290
Protestant Reformation, 277-313 (*see also* Luther, *etc.*); Catholic reaction to, 290-291; in England, 284-287
Proudhon, Pierre Joseph, 530
Provincial Letters, 379
Provisions of Oxford, 159
Prussia, under Frederick the Great, 418-419
Prytaneis, 50
Psychology: behaviorism and, 709; Freud and, 706-708
Ptolemies, 65-67
Ptolemy V, 84
Ptolemy (Claudius Ptolemaeus), 99
Punic language, 28
Punic Wars, 83-84
Puritanism, 284, 329, 330-331, 335-336
Pu-yi, Henry (*see* Hsüan-T'ung)
Pydna, battle of, 84
Pythagoras, 75

Q

Quadrivium, 171
Quadruple Alliance, 399-400, 458, 459, 472, 476
Quakers, 336, 379
Quanta Cura, 520
Quo warranto, 161

R

Rabelais, François, 310
Racism (*see also* Anti-Semitism; Slavery) 532, 533; American, 532, 564, 639; Hitler and, 598, 602; nationalism and, 532-533; South and, 564; Spanish colonial, 299
Radicalism, 527
Raleigh, Sir Walter, 300
Rameses II, 22
Rasputin, Gregory, 559, 586
Rationalism, 363-364
Raymond of Toulouse, 210
Re, 23
Realists, 173, 174
Reflections on the French Revolution, 380, 467

Reflections on Violence, 531
Reformation (*see* Protestant Reformation)
Reform Bills, 491-492, 548, 549
Religion (*see also* Heresy; Protestant Reformation; *specific sects, e.g.* Roman Catholic Church): Babylonian-Assyrian, 19; Canaanite, 28; in colonial America, 349; cults of Rome, 106-108; Egyptian, 23-24; Enlightenment and, 364, 366-367; Greek, 68-70; Hebrews and, 30-31; Hittite, 26, 27; Islam, 205; monotheism, 22, 30; Mycenaean, 37; Roman, 96-97; Sumerian, 15, 16; toleration of, 367; Zoroastrianism, 51
Renaissance, 256-272; architecture and, 270-271; art and, 262-272; astronomy and, 261-262; in England, 313; in France, 310; invention of printing and, 262; literature and, 257-261; medicine and, 261; music and, 271-272; northern Europe and, 267-268; painting and, 265-268; science and, 261-262; sculpture and, 268-270; technology, 262-263
Republic, The, 77
Rerum Novarum, 520
Restoration, in England, 336-337
Revolution: agricultural, 429; of *1825-1830,* 478-479; of *1848,* 481-483, 493-498; European (*1820-1830*), 477-478; French, 434-468; industrial, 429-431, 504, 511-516; March, in Russia, 486; November, in Russia, 586-589; Russian of *1905,* 557-559
Richard the Lionhearted (England), 157, 213
Richard II (England), 248
Richard III (England), 249
Richelieu, Cardinal, 321, 323, 326, 339
Rienzi, Cola di, 253
Rights of Man, 467
Risorgimento, 485, 495
Robert I (Scotland), 161
Robespierre, Maximilien, 445, 446, 447, 449, 450
Robinson, James Harvey, 5
Roman Catholic Church (*see also* Papacy, and names of Popes): Albigensian heresy and, 150; College of Cardinals and, 164, 170; education and, 171-173; Great Schism and, 193-194; Jansenists and, 342, 379; Joseph II and, 419-420; Louis XIV and, 341-342; materialism and, 241-242; medieval reformers of, 169-171; modernism and, 519-520; monastic reforms and, 169-171; Protestant Reformation and, 277-313; reformation within, 290-291

Roman Empire, 90-95; barbarian invasions of, 122-128; decline of, 93-95; expansion of, 92; monarchy and, 91-92; science and, 105-106
Romanos IV, Emperor, 201
Romanov dynasty, establishment of, 232-233
Romanov, Michael, 232
Roman Republic, 79-89; army of, 82; crisis of, 85-87; government of, 81-82
Romanticism, 382-383, 463-464, 534-537
Rome (*see also* Roman Empire, Roman Republic): arts and, 99-100; civilization of, 96-100; contributions of, 100; engineering and, 98-99; Etruscans and, 80-81; Greek influence on, 96-97; law and, 98; literature of, 97-98; medicine and, 99; sack of by Vandals, 124; sack of in *16th* century, 304-305
Romulus Augustulus, Emperor, 125
Roosevelt, Franklin, 612, 613
Roosevelt, Theodore, 564
Rosetta Stone, 24, 25
Rostovtzev, Michael, 95
Rostow, W. W., 514
Rousseau, Jean-Jacques, 366, 374, 375
Rudolf of Habsburg, Emperor, 251
Ruins, The, 364
Rumania, 668
Rump Parliament, 334, 335
Runnymede, 158
Russia (*see also* Stalin, *etc.*): from *1200-1450,* 227-229; from *1870-1914,* 555-559; since *1945,* 653-672; Alexander II and, 500-501; Allied intervention in, 575, 589-590; autocracy and, 230-231; Bismarck and, 567; under Catherine the Great, 422-423; China and, 673-676; Civil War in, 589-590; collectivization and, 591-592; Crimean War and, 483-484; Decembrist revolt and, 479; development of Muscovite state, 229-231; Duma and, 558; early Romanovs, 232-233; Eastern Church and, 230; five-year plans and, 592-593; foreign influences on, 233-234; foreign intervention in, 589-590; foreign policy to *1941,* 594-595; foreign policy since *1945,* 663-665; Genghis Khan and, 228; Ivan the Terrible and, 231-232; Kerensky government of, 586; Kievan society, 227; under Lenin, 586-591; March revolution and, 586; medieval, 225-234; Napoleon and, 457; NEP and, 590; under Nicholas I, 479; Novgorod, 227-228; under Peter I, the Great, 420-422; post-war relations with U.S., 668-671; Provisional government of, 586; Revolution of *1905,* 557-559; Revolution of *1917* and,

Russia (*cont.*):
585-589; Time of Troubles, 232; Western lands of, 227-228; World War I and, 571
Russian Church (*see* Eastern Church)
Russo-Japanese War (*1904-1905*), 557

S

Sachs, Hans, 272
St. Bartholomew's Day, massacre of, 309
St. Louis (Louis IX), 152, 153, 214
Saladin, 212, 213
Salamis, battle of, 53
"Salic" law, 242
Salisbury Oath of *1086,* 154
Samuel, of the Bulgarians, 200
Sappho, 73
Sargon the Great, 17
Savonarola, Girolamo, 242
Schliemann, Heinrich, 34
Scholasticism, 175, 176
Schopenhauer, Arthur, 524
Science (*see also* Inventions, Technology): Greek, 74-77; *19th* century, 516-519; Renaissance and, 261-262; Roman Empire and, 105-106; *20th* century, 716-719
Science and Sanity, 714
Scipio Africanus Major, 84
Scotland: Charles I and, 331-332; union with England, 338
Sculpture: Babylonian, 19; Greek, 56, 78; Hittite, 27; medieval, 181; *19th* century, 537; prehistoric, 13, 14; Renaissance and, 268-270; Roman, 100; Sumerian, 17
Scutage, 156
Sea Peoples, 26, 28, 38
Secret Treaty of Dover, 344
Secularism, 521-522
Seleucid Empire, 65-67
Seleucus I, 66
Selim I (the Grim), 224
Seljuk Turks, 200, 201, 205, 210
Semites, 15, 16, 17-19
Seneca, 97
Seneschals, 151
Sepoy Rebellion, 507
Serbia, 568
Serfdom (*see also* Slavery): Black Death and, 248; bubonic plague and, 238; Russian, 231
Serfs, emancipation of (*1861*), 500-501
Servetus, Michael, 288
Set, 23
Seven Years' War, 401-402
Sforza, Francesco, 254
Sforza, Ludovico, "the Moor," 254
Shakespeare, William, 313
Shapur, King, 93

Shiites, 204
Sic et Non, 174
Sicilian Vespers, 218
Sicilies, Two, 253
Sickingen, Franz von, 281
Silesian war, 401
Simony, Cluniac reform and, 170
Sketch of the Progress of the Human Mind, 377
Slavery (*see also* Racism; Serfdom): abolition of, 507; *Asiento* and, 345; Byzantine Empire and, 220-221; colonial American, 424; *18th* century, 405; England and, 345; Greek, 61-62; Hawkins and, 300; in Latin America, 299; Roman, 82
Slavs, 499
Smith, Adam, 375, 376
Social Contract, The, 374
Social Darwinism, 532-533
Social Evolution, 533
Socialism, 494, 495; Christian, 520; Fabian, 548; utopian, 529-530
Social War, 61
Society of Jesus (*see* Jesuits)
Socrates, 60, 76
Solemn League and Covenant, 332, 333
Solon, 48-49
Song of Roland, The, 129, 177, 257
Song of the Expedition of Igor, 227
Sophists, 75-76
Sophocles, 71-72
Sorel, Georges, 531
South Africa, 506, 507, 562
South America (*see* Latin America)
South Sea Company, 427-428
Spain: Alfonso XIII and, 603; under Charles V, 301, 302; Civil War in, 603; empire of, 296-300; fascism and, 502-503; under Ferdinand and Isabella, 250-251; under Franco, 603; in late middle ages, 250-251; Netherlands and, 281, 312-313; under Philip II, 301-302; in *16th* century, 301-304; Thirty Years' War and, 318-319
Spanish-American War, 564
Spanish Armada, 313
Spanish Inquisition (*see* Inquisition)
Sparta: evaluation of, 46-50, 59-60; Peloponnesian War and, 57-59; Persian Wars and, 60
Spartacus, 88
Spencer, Herbert, 523, 533
Spengler, Oswald, 715
Spiritual Exercises, 290
Stalin, Joseph, 590-595; death of, 653; dictatorship of, 591-595; last years of, 654-655; rise of, 590-591
Star Chamber, 249-250, 332
Statute of Mortmain, 161
Statute of Westminster, 161
Stephen, King (England), 156
Stoics, 77-78
Stolypin, Peter, 558, 559

Strasbourg Oaths of *842*, 130
Structure of Social Action, 710
Study of History, 716
Suger, Abbot of St. Denis, 149
Suleiman I (the Magnificent), 224, 305
Sulla, 87-88
Sumerians, 14-17
Summa contra Gentiles, 175
Summa Theologica, 175
Sunnites, 204
Sun Yat-sen, 614
Suppiluliumas, 26
Sweden: Thirty Years' War and, 322, 323, 326; under Charles XII, 422
Swift, Jonathan, 377, 380
Switzerland, Zwingli and, 282-283
Sylvester II, Pope, 173
Syracuse, siege of, 58
System of Nature, 367

T

Tacitus, 98
Talleyrand, 472
Tamerlane, 220
Tarquin the Proud, 81
Tartars, Moscow and, 228-229
Taxation: American Revolution and, 425; *18*th century French, 411-412; under Richard II, 248
Technology (*see also* Inventions; Science): early Russian, 234; Industrial Revolution and, 429-431; medieval, 146; prehistoric, 14; Renaissance and, 262-263; science and, 361-363; *20*th century, 716-719
Templars, Knights, 211-212
Terence, 97
Test Act of *1673*, 335
Tetrarchy, 93
Tetzel, Johann, 278, 280
Teutonic Knights, 212
Texas, annexation of, 504
Theater, Greek, 70-73
Thebes (Greece), 60-62; defeat of, 63
Themistocles, 53, 54
Theodoric, 125
Theodosius I, Emperor, 120
Theodosius the Great, 196
Theogony, 46
Theresa of Avila, St., 303
Thermopylae, battle of, 53, 84
Third Estate, 437
Thirty Years' War, 318-327; Bohemian period, 320-321; Danish period, 321-322; Dutch and Spanish background, 318-319; German background, 319; results of, 326-327; Swedish and French period, 323, 326
Thomas à Becket, 157

Thomism, 174-176
Thoth, 23
Thucydides, 73-74
Thutmose I, 22
Thutmose III, 22
Tiglath-pilesar I, 17
Tiglath-pilesar III, 17
Tigranes, 88
Tilly, Count Johann, 321-323
Tilsit, Treaty of, 455
"Time of Troubles," 232
Titian, 267
Tito, Marshal, 664
Tocqueville, Alexis de, 527
Toland, John, 366
Toleration Act (*1689*), 338
Tools, prehistoric, 11, 12
Tories, 337
Torricelli, Evangelista, 360
Tours, battle of, 126
Toynbee, Arnold, 716
Trade: Greek, 61; medieval, 146-148; medieval innovations, 239; medieval wool trade, 243; Spanish colonial, 299
Trade Unions, 548; France and, 552
Tragedy, Greek, 70-72
Trajan, Emperor, 111
Treaty: of Brest-Litovsk, 589; of Cambrai, 305; of Cateau-Cambrésis, 308; of Chaumont, 458; of Dover, 344; of Guadalupe Hidalgo, 504; Hittites and, 27; of Hubertsburg, 402; Lateran (*1929*), 597; of Lübeck, 321; of Nystadt (*1721*), 422; of Portsmouth, 557; of Ryswick, 345; of Tilsit, 455; of Tordesillas, 293; of Utrecht, 345, 348; of Versailles, 577-581
Triennial Act, 332
Triple Alliance, World War I and, 566-567
Triple Entente, World War I and, 566-567
Trittyes, 47
Trivium, 171
Trojan War, 37-38
Trojan Women, The, 72
Trotsky, Leon, 587, 589, 590, 591
Troy, 37, 38
Troyes, Treaty of, 245
Tudors, 284-287
Turgot, 412-413
Turkey (*see also* Ottoman Empire): Atatürk and, 578; Eastern question and, 479-481; Greece and, 480; Young Turks and, 559
Turks (*see* Ottoman Turks, Seljuk Turks)
Tut-Ankh-Amen, 22
Twelve Tables, of Roman law, 82
Two Treatises of Government, 374
Tyranny, Greek, 49
Tyranny of Words, 714
Tyre: siege of, 64
Tyrone, Hugh O'Neill, 313

U

Ugarit, 27
Ugaritic language, 27
Ulema, 222
Umayyad Caliphate, 204
Unions (*see* Trade Unions)
Unitarians, 288
United Nations, 637-638
United Kingdom (*see* England)
United States (*see also* America; American Revolution): Civil War, 504-505; Constitution, 426; Depression of *1929* and, 611-613; frontier and, 504; imperialism and, 564; Industrial Revolution in, 504; Mexican War and, 504; New Deal and, 612-613; from *1918* to *1939,* 610-616; during *19*th century, 503-505; Spanish-American War and, 564; World War I and, 575; after World War II, 638-641
Universals, question of, 173-174
Universities, medieval, 172-173
Ur, 15, 16
Urban II, Pope, 209, 210
Ussher, James, 11
Utilitarianism, 368-369
Utopia, 284
Utopian socialism, 529-530
Utraquists, 320

V

Valens, Emperor, 123
Valerian, Emperor, 93
Valla, Lorenzo, 260
Valmy, battle of, 444
Valois dynasty, Habsburgs and, 304-305, 308
Vandals, 123-124
Vassals, feudal, 136-138
Venice: in late Middle Ages, 255; trade and, 239
Ventris, Michael, 35
Verrazzano, Giovanni da, 300
Verdun, battle of, 574
Vergil, 79, 97
Versailles, palace of, 342
Versailles Treaty, 577-581
Vesalius, Andreas, 261
Vespucci, Amerigo, 297
Victorianism, 533-534, 540-541, 543
Victoria, Queen (England), 493
Vienna (*see also* Congress of Vienna): sieges of, 224, 225
Vietnam, 676, 678-679
Vikings, 130, 132-133
Villehardouin, Geoffroi de, 215
Vinci, Leonardo da (*see* Leonardo)
Visconti family, 254
Visigoths, 122-124
Volney, Constantin, 364

Voltaire, 366, 367, 373, 374, 381, 409, 419, 422
Voluntarism, 524
Voyage of the Mind to God, 176
Vulgate, version of Bible, 113

W

Wagner, Richard, 538
Waiblings, 165, 167, 168
Wallenstein, Albrecht von, 321, 323
Walpole, Robert, 416
Wars (*see specific wars, e.g.* Punic Wars)
War of Devolution, 344
War of Jenkins' Ear, 400-401
War of the League of Augsburg, 345
Wars of the Roses, 249
War of the Spanish Succession, 345-348
Warwick, Earl of, 249
Waterloo, battle of, 458-459
Wealth of Nations, 375, 376
Weber, Max, 289-290, 390
Weights and measures, 406
Weimar Republic, 597-601
Welfs, 165, 167, 168
Wesley, John, 378
Westphalia, Peace of, 326-327
Whigs, 337
Whitney, Eli, 513
Wilhelm I (Germany), 488
Wilhelm II (Germany), 553-554
Wilkes, John, 417
William III (England), 338
William the Conqueror (England), 154, 156
William the Silent (Netherlands), 313
Wilson, Woodrow, 576-577, 578, 580, 581
Witenagemot, 133, 154, 159
Witte, Serge, 556, 558
Women, status of: medieval, 178; in Sumer, 16
World as Will and Idea, 524
World War I: armistice and, 575; causes of, 566-569; home fronts and, 573; land warfare and, 571, 573, 574-575; results of, 575-581; sea warfare and, 572, 573; start of, 568-570; Triple Alliance and, 566-567; Triple Entente and, 566-567
World War II, 617-629; Allied victory and, 627-628; causes, 619-621; early Axis success, 621, 623; efforts to avoid, 617-619
Works and Days, 45
Worms, Concordat of, 165
Worms, Diet of, 279
Writing: Cretan, 32; cuneiform, 15; Egyptian, 24; invention of, 14; Sumerian, 15
Wyclif, John, 242, 248

X

Xenophon, 60, 75
Xerxes the Great, 53
Ximenes, Cardinal, 251

Y

York, house of, 249
Yüan Shih-k'ai, 614
Yugoslavia, 664-665

Z

Zaccaria, Benedetto, 239
Zangi, 212
Zarathustra, 51
Zemski sobor, 231, 232
Zemstvos, 501, 556
Zeno, 77
Zeno, Emperor, 125
Ziggurat, 16, 17
Zimmermann telegram, 573n
Zollverein, 473, 498
Zoroastrianism, 51
Zwingli, Ulrich, 282-283